W9-BKW-892

SOUTHERN REGIONS
OF THE UNITED STATES

SOUTHERN REGIONS

OF THE UNITED STATES

By

HOWARD W. ODUM

FOR

THE SOUTHERN REGIONAL COMMITTEE
OF THE
SOCIAL SCIENCE RESEARCH COUNCIL

CHAPEL HILL
THE UNIVERSITY OF NORTH CAROLINA PRESS
1936

FIRST LARGE PRINTING
APRIL, 1936

SECOND LARGE PRINTING
JUNE, 1937

PRINTED IN THE UNITED STATES OF AMERICA BY
THE SEEMAN PRINTERY, INC., DURHAM, N. C.

SOUTHERN REGIONS

OF THE UNITED STATES

THE SOUTHERN REGIONAL COMMITTEE OF THE SOCIAL SCIENCE RESEARCH COUNCIL FROM 1932 TO 1934

BENJAMIN B. KENDRICK, *Chairman*
Woman's College, University of North Carolina

WILSON GEE
University of Virginia

WALTER J. MATHERLY
University of Florida

GEORGE FORT MILTON
Chattanooga News

CHARLES W. PIPKIN
Louisiana State University

GEORGE W. STOCKING
University of Texas

RAYMOND D. THOMAS
Oklahoma A. & M. College

THE SOUTHERN REGIONAL COMMITTEE OF THE SOCIAL SCIENCE RESEARCH COUNCIL FROM 1934 TO 1936

RAYMOND D. THOMAS, *Chairman*
Oklahoma Agricultural and Mechanical College

W. E. GETTYS
University of Texas

SAMUEL D. MYRES
Southern Methodist University

HERMAN C. NIXON
Tulane University

GOODRICH C. WHITE
Emory University

ADVISORY WORK COMMITTEE AT THE UNIVERSITY OF NORTH CAROLINA, CHAPEL HILL

CLARENCE HEER

HARRIET L. HERRING

S. H. HOBBS, JR.

KATHARINE JOCHER

RUPERT B. VANCE

T. J. WOOFTER, JR.

CONTENTS

INTRODUCTORY NOTE

The objectives and framework upon which the Southern Regional Study was projected are set forth on pages 1-5. Special acknowledgments and the conditions under which the inventory was begun for the Southern Regional Committee of the Social Science Research Council in 1932 are given in Part III. These are integral parts of the present work and represent, therefore, more than mere routine explanatory notes.

Throughout the volume certain points of emphasis have been constantly reiterated. One is the regional-national viewpoint as opposed to the earlier local-sectional emphasis. On this assumption the southern regions are inventoried as natural developments of American culture, with special regional conditioning; the promise of the South is envisaged in terms of testing grounds of American regionalism. Regional culture and welfare are inseparable from the national civilization and prospect. A second point of emphasis is found in the redefinition of the South in a more realistic and practical delineation projecting boldly an emerging Southwest clearly differentiated from the old Southeast both as to culture and planning economy. On this assumption there is no longer a regional area or culture which, when analyzed, can be measured in terms of what is currently called "the South." A third is the emphasis upon indices which may be utilized to measure the southern regions in terms of capacity; while a fourth follows in the major conclusion that the regions are characterized by an extraordinary chasm between their potentialities as indicated by resources and actualities as measured by facts. A fifth emphasizes the immaturity and vitality of regional folk capable either of superior achievements or of pathological developments.

Again the facts focus early upon the conclusion that the old general educational and ideological motivation functioning through the upper brackets of leadership must be supplemented powerfully by realistic working plans and procedures in the lower brackets of agriculture and economic reconstruction. Likewise, the premise which has focused upon cultural and historical backgrounds, sound theory, and vital regionalism, is that it is only upon such a basis that permanent and stable practical planning can be achieved. The emphasis has, therefore, been preëminently upon *practical* design and planning so geared to regional reality and national administration as to insure results commensurate with the demands of crisis and change and in harmony with the living principles of American institutions.

The completion of the study and the publication of the volume were postponed for approximately a year for several reasons. It was desired to take into consideration a large number of current factors before determining the final form of publication. It was desired also to check a number of the results through individual conferences, group conferences, and first-hand study and comparative observation in other regions, particularly in the Southwest, the Far West, and the Northwest. It was important, moreover, to check much of the data with a large number of researches projected through the various channels of governmental activities, as well as to compare data with other regional studies and publications which have appeared since this study was begun. It is hoped that the volume in its present form will serve the largest number of purposes. It is, therefore, presented as a relatively comprehensive and enduring index of regional culture which may be variously utilized; as a basis for practical planning and specialized research; as a basis for later comparative studies of the same regions; as a basis for comparative studies of other regions; as hypothetical basis for subsequent regional and subregional classification and analysis; as an introduction to the appraisal of American regional cultures.

The Southern Regional Committees have been generous in their recognition of the difficulty and complexity of the task and in the delegation of the work and arrangements to the director and the local advisory work committee. They are not responsible, therefore, for either the form or the content concerning which they have not always agreed. Both would have benefitted greatly had it been possible to bring them within the logical bounds of their criticism. Of the special work done by members of the Committee, Professor Kendrick's volume has already been published under the title, *The South Looks at Its Past;* Professor Thomas' preliminary inventory of the Southwest, briefly summarized in the present volume, is reserved by him for further use in the Southwest; while Professor Matherly's study of commercial education in the South needs only revising for publication. Special acknowledgment is made also for the generous committee work of Mr. George Fort Milton in the special consideration of the Tennessee Valley area.

In addition to the list of acknowledgments later presented, to page references in the text, and to a large number of typed "work memoranda," very special appreciation must be expressed to the group of scholars who agreed to serve as Advisory Work Committee. To Professor T. J. Woofter, Jr., for much of the data on population and for the special subregional and submarginal classifications; to Professor Clarence Heer for much of the data on fiscal matters; to Professor S. H. Hobbs, Jr., for many of the state rankings and per capita distributions; to Miss Katharine Jocher for many of the regional summaries and rankings; to Miss Harriet L. Herring for data on industries and manufacturing; and to Professor Rupert B. Vance for much of the data on submarginality and agrarian culture.

A most difficult and important task was that of arranging, checking and rechecking tables, graphs, and maps with the additions and revisions demanded. For this coöperative task it is difficult to express adequate appreciation to Dr. Jocher. In addition to secretarial and technical assistance subsequently acknowledged, special mention is due Waller Wynne for the making of most of the maps and graphs, and Miss Belle Mooring, special secretary for the study.

It is desired to give full recognition to the Social Science Research Council, to the officers of the General Education Board who made possible the Council's coöperation, and specifically to Miss Carolyn Allen, Controller, for her special coöperation and many courtesies throughout the period of the Council's participation. Further acknowledgment is made to the Institute for Research in Social Science at the University of North Carolina for its continuing support during the added year of extension.

It must be understood, however, that neither the Council nor any of the committees is in any way responsible for the selected contents of the volume, the nature of its conclusions, or the style of presentation, the final form of which has not passed before them for review.

H. W. O.

Chapel Hill
December, 1935

PART I

CONTENTS OF PART I

CHAPTER 1

THE COMPOSITE PICTURE: A SYLLABUS AND SUMMARY

I. THE OBJECTIVES OF THE SOUTHERN REGIONAL STUDY

1. THE FIRST OBJECTIVE of the Southern Regional Study is to present an adequate picture, partial but representative, of the southern regions of the United States in fair perspective to time-quality, to geographic factors, and to the cultural equipment and behavior of the people.

2. It is desired further to present this picture in such ways as to indicate the place of these regions in the nation and to explain something of the dramatic struggle of a large and powerful segment of the American people for mastery over an environment capable of producing a superior civilization, yet so conditioned by complexity of culture and cumulative handicaps as to make the nature of future development problematical.

3. Over and above any conventional social inventory, it is important to point toward greater realization of the inherent capacities of the southern regions; and to indicate ways and means of bridging the chasm between the superabundance of physical and human resources as potentialities and the actualities of technical deficiencies in their development and waste in their use.

4. It is equally important to point toward a continuously more effective reintegration of the southern regions into the national picture and thereby toward a larger regional contribution to national culture and unity. To this end, it is important to make available and to reinterpret to special groups and to the public in general, within and without the regions, and in as many ways as possible, the facts basic to the understanding of the situation and to the planning of next steps.

5. Partly as purpose and method and partly due to the recognition of the extraordinary difficulty and importance of these tasks, it was desired to project the study upon a theoretical framework which would insure measurable reality in research and attainability in whatever programs might emerge. Such reality was, of course, manifold. It would comprehend not only measurement, but perspective and interpretation; not only the general picture of aggregates and averages, but the specific facts of

distribution and such detailed analysis as would focus upon critical problems toward which continued research might be directed.

6. Basic to such a framework was a clear recognition of the historical and theoretical significance of the region and of the power of the folk-regional society in modern culture, as well as the very practical problem in the United States of what divisions of the nation might meet the largest number of requirements for general regional analysis and planning and what other special regions and subregions might be effective for more specific purposes.

7. More specifically, such a theoretical framework must give reality to the southern picture. This reality, again, is of many kinds. A part is the facing of absolute facts rather than substituting rationalizations which grow out of irrelevant comparisons or defense explanations of how things have come to be as they are. Yet another form of reality must be found in the measurement of conditions in terms of comparison with certain selected standards and with regional and national variations. Yet, still again, a part of the reality must be found in the clear recognition that mere comparisons with national averages or aggregates are valid only within the bounds of their particular limitations and definitions, the problem and methodology of evaluating such comparisons and differentials being a part of the task. Furthermore, the greatest measure of reality can be found in the balanced picture of basic facts rather than, and largely exclusive of, vivid extremes.

8. Again, such a theoretical framework must be practically comprehensive enough to insure a fair picture of the major resources and forces which have determined and will determine the capacity of the southern regions. In terms of "wealth," they are natural wealth, technological wealth, artificial wealth, human wealth, and institutional wealth. In terms of a larger twofold measure, there would be, first, an inventory of natural resources together with the visible ends of technological mastery in human use aspects and in the resulting artificial wealth of the regions; and, second, an appraisal of human resources together with the visualized ends of social achievement in the development of a richer culture and social well-being.

9. One of the special premises of the study is reflected in the past constricting power of sectionalism in contrast to the current motivation of substituting the new regionalism for the old sectionalism in American life. Since sectional conditioning appears more marked in the Southeast than elsewhere, the study was, therefore, projected to feature the regional-national as opposed to the local-sectional emphasis. Such a regional premise manifestly would avoid any hypotheses of a self-contained or self-

sufficing South and would stimulate a greater degree of federal interest and participation on the part of the South.

10. It was understood that many of the dominant forces of the regions, such as tradition, opinion, conflict, arrangements of local stateways and folkways, which constitute a part of the picture, are not measurable in terms of units that can be counted. On this assumption a part of the reality of the picture is inherent in the need and capacity for such authentic interpretation of the South's background as will give "the dignity of cultural history" to its chronological lag, its retarded frontier dominance, its agrarian culture, its youthful and immature population, its lusty vitality, its unevenness of life, and its marginal struggle for survival.

11. The study sought, further, to explore the southern regions as a laboratory for regional research and for experimentation in social planning. Of special importance might be the regional testing field for adjustment between industry and agriculture as the basic economic goal of government, and for the more general objective of reintegrating agrarian culture in the national picture. Again, the study was projected as a regional approach to the new demography which in both method and content may contribute largely to the revitalized study of the people and their institutions. Such a study of contemporary civilization would recognize certain values inherent in logical differentials which abound in the regions. Manifestly, such a theoretical framework must assume a less provincial and a more objective, long-time view of the South than has commonly obtained, and a more generous patience with the realities of societal evolution on the part of all those who seek reform and reconstruction.

12. In view of these objectives, the opportunities for utilizing the results of the study are varied. The present volume is the formal presentation of the main findings in eleven chapters of which this summary and syllabus is one. As a device for presenting a cumulative picture of many elemental factors, some two hundred and fifty maps have been prepared with a view to giving graphic expression to specific combinations which may serve as critical units of analysis. These, together with perhaps as many statistical tables and charts, each complete in itself, supplement the text throughout and strive to give vividness and authenticity to conclusions and interpretation. It must be clear however, that, with such abundance of materials and such inevitable comprehensiveness of approach, the task of selection and arrangement has been a difficult one, and much of the original mass of material cannot be presented.

13. Supplementing the major findings will be other units. Utilization of the study will depend upon developments, needs, resources. Certain of the results appear usable, in addition to the publication of the main

Indices of Measurement for Regional Culture Utilized in the Southern Regional Study

In the attempt to insure measurable reality in research and attainability in emerging programs, more than 700 factors were explored in the Southern Regional Study with varying degrees of completeness with a view to utilizing a larger number of indices than had heretofore been available. The arrangement of such indices on this page follows the general framework of the study; namely, in terms of natural resources and agrarian culture, technological deficiencies and waste, industry and wealth, the southern people, and their institutions and folkways. The present list catalogues only those in which national and regional comparisons are involved and is therefore exclusive of a considerable number in which only the Southeastern States are characterized.

Spec.al limitations of such comparative indices are apparent. In the first place comparisons in terms of census data and other measures are not always in terms of homogeneous figures, in the sense that data gathered by southern enumerators may not be gathered under the same conditions as in some other regions; in the sense that regional estimates of values are often conditioned by other cultural factors and are stated in terms of averages based on unequal quantities and distribution; that various contributing factors to standards, income, wealth, and general culture are often not included; and that many of the cultural factors, such as personality, folkways, motivation, handicaps, are not measureable in terms of our present objective methods. Yet, in spite of these limitations, the picture of the region for the purposes in hand, due to the large number of varying indices susceptible to checking and cross checking, is relatively authentic and complete. More detailed catalogues of these indices appear in the respective chapters and in the maps, tables, and graphs themselves.

Number of Indices	Classification
1–6.	Acres of land, Grades 1-5
7.	Pasture capacity of land
8–11.	Erosion and impoverished land
12–20.	Use of land
21–23.	Farm acreage and regional per cent of total area
24–27.	Ownership of land by class
28–29.	Tenancy ratio and land harvested by tenants
30–40.	Distribution of land by use and production
41–58.	Number and size of farms
59–73.	Number of farms by use
74–80.	Value of chief kinds of livestock
81–99.	Kinds of livestock
100–106.	Increase and decrease of livestock
107–109.	Value farm property, implements, dwellings
110–114.	Value of lands and buildings by ownership
115–116.	Taxes and decreased value of real estate
117–125.	Horse power, vehicles, trucks, tractors, motors, conveniences, per farm
126–138.	Amount and distribution of farm income
139–154.	Production of selected commodities: milk, farm garden vegetables, wheat, corn, livestock, cotton, lumber
155–203.	State and regional production and distribution of chief commodities
204–207.	Farm indebtedness and federal loans and benefits
208–212.	Fertilizer tonnage and distribution
213–216.	Number, value, expenditures, products of nurseries
217–221.	Types of forests and timber
222–223.	Location of waterways
224–227.	Potential water power available
228–239.	Distribution of selected minerals: phosphate, coal, iron, building stone
240–241.	Growing season and precipitation
242–246.	Types of days per year
247–249.	Local, state, and regional taxes
250–253.	Value, investment, and indebtedness of schools
254–255.	Home ownership and owner occupancy
256–257.	Per capita tangible and true wealth
258–263.	Selected measures of wealth: bank resources and deposits, postal receipts, corporation income, life insurance, building and loan
264–266.	Taxable property and ratio of property to taxes
267–268.	Bonded and net state debt
269–270.	Retail and wholesale sales
271–276.	Church wealth, expenditures, and debt
277–286.	Net income and taxable incomes
287–294.	Non-farm income—personal, occupational, property
295.	Average teacher's salary.
296–297.	School revenue and expenditures
298.	Receipts of higher institutions of learning
299–311.	Selected measures of manufacturing: distribution, value of product, earners, wages, horse power, value added
312–313.	Increase per earner, per horse power
314–315.	Cotton spindles—counties and concentration
316–319.	Distribution of developed water power
320–326.	Distribution of completed and projected waterways
327–341.	Distribution of manufacturing establishments by types
342–345.	Distribution of industrial resources: horse power, water power, value of manufactured product, value added by manufacture
346–356.	Production of coal, petroleum, building stone
357–360.	Value of all minerals and per cent of U. S. total
361–366.	Limestone, granite, marble—regional differentials in rank and uses
367–370.	Value increased by manufacture, per earner, per horse power
371–374.	Amount and distribution of wages
375–379.	Distribution of income from sources
380–385.	Apportionment of federal relief
386–391.	Roads and highways
392–398.	Ratio of types of highways and gasoline to population and income
399–404.	Highway funds
405–411.	Illiteracy by race and age groups
412–414.	Population per square mile, local unit, region
415–419.	Population by age, sex, and marital status
420–423.	Reproductive index and increase variations in population
424–437.	Population by residence and race
438–446.	Births and deaths by color and residence
447–452.	Infant mortality and maternal mortality
453–465.	Increase of population—total, by decades, urban, rural
466–483.	Distribution of population: urban, race, and nativity
484–487.	Interregional gain or loss by migration
488–492.	Place of birth and residence of migrants
493–499.	Distribution of wage earners by number and density
500–508.	Age, sex, occupation of wage earners
509–518.	Governmental outlay and state expenditures
519.	Number of local governmental local units
520–525.	Parks, monuments, refuges, sanctuaries
526–534.	Per capita expenditures for general welfare
535–536.	Physicians, hospitals
537–539.	Insanity, suicide
540–548.	Prisoners and offenses
549–550.	Homicides, lynchings
551–557.	Weekly and daily papers and magazines
558–572.	Students by sex and by types of school
573–574.	Increase in graduates and graduates continuing
575.	Extra-regional students
576–597.	Schools by kinds
598–601.	Educational leaders and Who's Who notables
602–605.	Negro schools: teachers, attendance
606–608.	Rural home and farm agents
609–610.	School tax and income
611–620.	Libraries: revenue, readers, circulation, ratio to people, facilities
621.	Distribution of general cultural items
622–624.	Location of dramatics
625–642.	Church members by sects
643–649.	Churches per population and by type of pastor
650.	Church periodicals
651–652.	Highways and airways
653–657.	Types of vehicles
658.	Taxes for roads
659–663.	Political affiliations
664–668.	Selected cultural measurements: radios, stores, automobiles, stills seized
669–685.	Regional classifications of the nation

volume. One volume, *The South Looks at Its Past*, by Kendrick and Arnett, has already appeared. Another by Walter J. Matherly on Commercial Education in the South is about complete. Still other smaller volumes are possible from present data. Other units include a number of articles and brochures, already published or under way; a hundred "work memoranda" making available basic materials; and numerous conferences and discussion groups continuing both theoretical and practical aspects of the regional study.

14. Particularly desirable would seem to be the task of presenting the findings in a small volume popularly written to present the case for *The Promise of the South: A Test of American Regionalism*, and perhaps in a series of syndicated articles featuring a popular picture of the South's capacity and prospects for educational and social development.

15. Of the essence of the whole project is its implication and its framework for continuity of research and effort, a part of which would be an extension of certain of the present units, and a part would comprehend new prospects emerging from the present study. Throughout the study as presented there emerges an extraordinarily clear picture of a fruitful field for research and planning, many units of which are but introduced here.

II. GEOGRAPHIC FACTORS AND PHYSICAL SETTING

16. There is no longer in the United States any single entity which may be designated as "the South." More authentically, there is a Southeast and a Southwest, comparable to four other major regions designated as the Northeast, the Northwest, the Middle States, and the Far West. The old custom of massing together, for aggregate quantitative effects, a large group of "southern" states, including Missouri, Maryland, Delaware, West Virginia, Texas, and the specialized urban District of Columbia is not only inaccurate but detrimental to genuine regional analysis and planning.

17. It is, therefore, neither possible nor desirable to present a single authentic picture of "the South" any more than it is of "the North" or "the East" or "the West," not only because of the magnitude and diversity of the regions but also because of the dynamics of the emerging Southwestern Region, comprising Texas, Oklahoma, New Mexico, and Arizona, which will require separate analysis and interpretation no less critical and comprehensive than that for the Southeast.

18. One of the major contributions of the study is the working hypothesis of the relatively clear-cut differentiation between the older Southeast and the emerging Southwest, a new empire in itself. Inherent also in both content and methodology is the definitive sixfold regional division

The Six Major Regions Basic to the Southern Regional Study

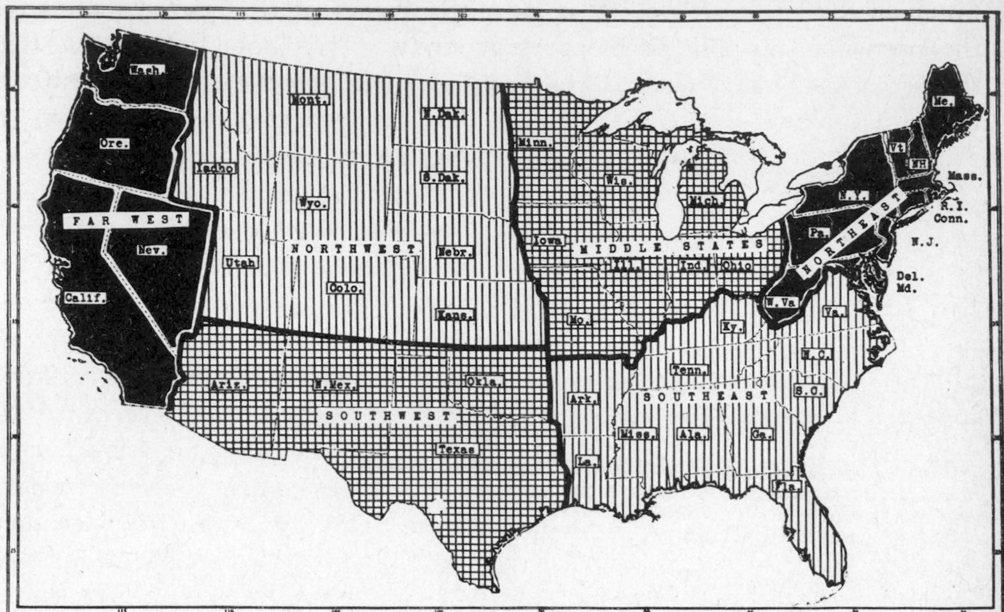

Above: The sixfold regional division of the nation by states, utilized in statistical analysis of the southern regional study, states lines being essential for the use of census materials.

Below: The second map illustrates the same general sixfold division *if state lines could be ignored.* Thus the eastern bounds of the proposed shelter forest belt would mark the western bounds of the Middle States and the Southeast, properly including parts of North Dakota, South Dakota, Nebraska, Kansas in the Middle States, and parts of Oklahoma and Texas in the Southeast. So, too, parts of Ohio and Virginia would be included in the Northeast while the lower parts of Missouri and West Virginia would fall within the Southeast, as would a part of Indiana and Illinois. This is of course only approximate for illustrative purposes. For other similar maps and discussions, see Chapters III and X.

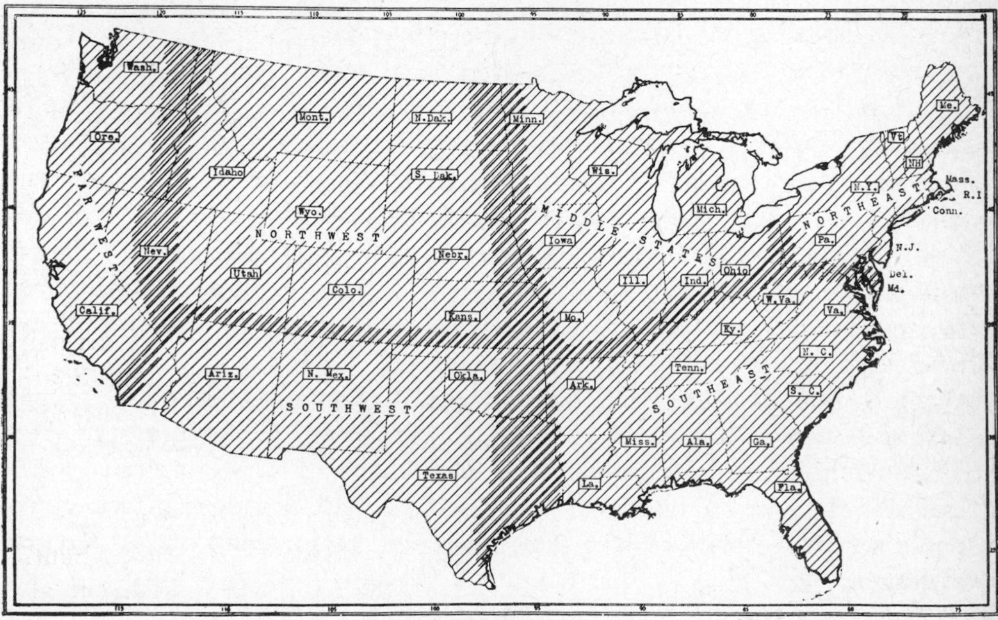

of the United States. A part of the value of this regional division will be found in the effectiveness and comprehensiveness of these six divisions for the particular purpose of the present study. It is hoped, however, that the present arrangement may contribute something toward a more uniform basis for regional study and planning and for experimentation with many subregional divisions for further exploration and planning.

19. The sixfold division basic to the study was evolved from a study of a large number of regional classifications and from many hypothetical groupings tested from various angles. It is, therefore, the most satisfactory arrangement that could be worked out. Allocation of states was made on the basis of the clustering of elemental indices, of which some seven hundred constituted the field of analysis. The basis for this division together with examples of other regional classifications are presented in Chapter III. In addition to the *Southeast* and the new *Southwest*, elsewhere described, the *Northeast*, approximating Frederick Jackson Turner's "Greater New England," includes Maine, New Hampshire, Vermont, Massachusetts, Rhode Island, Connecticut, New York, New Jersey, Delaware, Pennsylvania, Maryland, and West Virginia. The *Middle States*, approximating the earlier "Old Northwest" and the "Middle West," includes Ohio, Indiana, Illinois, Michigan, Wisconsin, Minnesota, Iowa, Missouri. The *Northwest* includes North Dakota, South Dakota, Nebraska, Kansas, Montana, Idaho, Wyoming, Colorado, Utah; and the *Far West* adds Nevada to the Pacific Coast States of Washington, Oregon, and California.

20. It is important to indicate here, however, something of the method by which the Southwest was differentiated from the Southeast and the Southeast redefined to exclude Maryland and Missouri. Basic to any reasonable effort to attain effective regional analysis of "the South" was the first task of delimitation and definition. What were the limits within which valid differentials could be measured and what the limits of desirable homogeneity for the purposes of analysis and planning? The first task within this assignment was to appraise the traditional "South" as a premise for such analysis. This broad grouping generally comprised seventeen or eighteen states including from the Northeast, Maryland, West Virginia, the District of Columbia, and sometimes Delaware; from the Middle States, Missouri; and in the Southwest, Oklahoma and Texas. The first task in the examination of this older and larger regional hypothesis was to seek measures of homogeneity and differentials when compared with the "border" states and adjoining regions and with the national averages.

Maryland and Missouri Are Not Southern States; Maryland Is Not Southeast; Missouri Is Not Southwest or Southeast

The earlier customary characterization of "the South" as comprehending sixteen or seventeen states and the District of Columbia is no longer accurately definitive of either present homogeneity or of changing trends. Nor is it serviceable in the practical delineation of regional differentials which will be realistic enough to conform to factual categories or planning programs.

It is possible, however, within a comprehensive framework of physical, social, and economic measures to arrive at a clearly defined Southeastern Region adequate for purposes of analysis, planning, and administration. Chapter III presents further consideration on regional classifications and also special illustrations. In this page of tabulation and others to follow are samplings of indices through which certain measures of homogeneity are clearly illustrated. Others include pages indicating that Louisiana and Arkansas are Southeast rather than Southwest; Texas and Oklahoma are Southwest rather than Southeast; the Dakotas and Kansas and Nebraska are Northwest rather than Middle States.

Illustrative of a general measure of homogeneity for the Southeast is that of population, gauged by a dozen major indices, such as ethnic composition, urban, rural, age classifications, increase in urban, occupations, wealth, and the like. In none of these major indices do Maryland and Missouri qualify within the Southeastern mode and median.

Still other general cultural indices such as politics, religion, education, folkways, rank these as either clearly marginal states or as clearly qualifying for the Northeast or Middle States. Samplings of the 200 and more indices are given below.

30. Average expenditure per child attending school
31. Per capita cost for each child in daily school attendance
32. Average expenditure per child of school age
33. Expenditure per pupil for purposes other than teachers' salaries
34. Average expenditure per teacher employed
35. Total professional students per 100,000 population
36. Per capita total receipts, exclusive of additions to endowments, universities, colleges and professional schools
37. Enrollment in all colleges per 100,000 population
38. Total graduate students per 100,000 population
39. Per cent of total population attending school
40. Natives in *Men of Science* per 100,000 population
41. Residents in *Men of Science* per 100,000 population
42. Natives in *Who's Who* per 100,000 population
43. Passport applications per 1,000 population
44. Compulsory education in the United States
45. Federal personal income tax payments per capita of total population
46. Per inhabitant estimated true wealth
47. Retail sales per store
48. Per inhabitant retail trade
49. Retail stores per 1,000 population
50. Per capita net income, federal personal and corporation
51. Total personal income
52. Volume of wholesale trade per inhabitant
53. Per capita federal income tax payments
54. Bank resources per inhabitant
55. Per capita savings deposits
56. Per capita postal receipts
57. Per capita assets, building and loan associations
58. Per capita life insurance in force
59. Per cent of total income from agriculture
60. Per cent of income from sources other than agriculture, manufacturing, and mining
61. Per cent of income from all other sources, exclusive of agriculture, manufacturing, mining, construction (wealth)
62. Average value per farm of land and buildings, farms operated by tenants
63. Per capita annual income, eleven-year average, 1920-1930 inclusive
64. Per cent of owner operated farms mortgaged
65. Relative standing of the states in wealth, 26 indices
66. Aggregate net per capita income, 1929
67. Freight rate territory
68. Death rate from pellagra per 1,000 population
69. Deaths from influenza per 1,000 inhabitants
70. Supply of physicians per 10,000 population
71. Hospital beds per 1,000 population
72. Population per dentist
73. Maternal deaths in childbirth per 100,000 population
74. Deaths under one year of age per 1,000 live births
75. Per cent of rural population served by whole-time health units
76. Infant mortality rate per 1,000 live births
77. Sources of migration and population
78. Per cent of total population living on farms
79. Per cent increase or decrease in the rural non-farm population
80. Per cent of population 21 years of age and over native white
81. Per cent of population 21 years of age and over negro
82. Per cent of population 21 years of age and over foreign-born white
83. Per cent of total population 20 to 54 years of age
84. Per cent of total population 55 years of age and over
85. Per cent of total population 19 years of age or less
86. Number of children per 1,000 women
87. Ratio of population 21 and over to those 5-17, inclusive
88. Per cent increase in white population
89. Per cent increase in Negro population
90. Per cent increase or decrease in native whites of mixed parentage
91. Per cent increase in population, native white of foreign or mixed parentage
92. Per cent increase in native white population
93. Per cent increase or decrease in Negro population
94. Per cent increase in urban population
95. Per cent of total population urban
96. Per cent rural farm population is of total population
97. Per cent of total population Negro
98. Per cent native white of total white population
99. Per cent of foreign born in total population
100. Birth rate per 1,000 population
101. Excess of births over deaths
102. Average value per farm of domestic animals
103. Value of land and buildings per acre of farm land
104. Value of all farm property per farm
105. Ratio of charges to debt, mortgaged farms operated by farmers owning no other farm land
106. Average value per acre of land and buildings, full owners reporting mortgage debt
107. Ratio of mortgage debt to value of land and buildings, full owners owning no other farm land
108. Average value of land and buildings, owner operated farms
109. Per cent of owner-operated farms mortgaged
110. Per cent cooperative sales were of cash farm income
111. Total gallons of milk produced per farm
112. Value of farm land and buildings per farm
113. Per cent of farms selling products through cooperatives
114. Average gross income per farm per year
115. Average gross income from livestock per farm per year
116. Per cent of farms having gas engines
117. Per cent of farms having electric motors
118. Per cent of farms having tractors
119. Per capita production of milk
120. Average total acreage per farm
121. Per cent of land area in farms
122. Per cent of farms under 100 acres
123. Decrease of animal units on farms
124. Decrease of swine on farms
125. Decrease of land in harvested crops
126. Decrease in wheat acreage
127. Per cent decrease in farms
128. Per cent fertilizer consumption
129. Per cent farm income spent for fertilizer
130. Farms reporting cows milked
131. Per cent of farms reporting pure-bred cattle
132. Per cent value of hay and forage
133. Per cent farm income from livestock
134. Per cent farm tenancy
135. Number of women employed in agriculture
136. Number of children employed in agriculture
137. Inhabitants per motor car
138. Per cent of farms having telephones
139. Per cent of farms having automobiles
140. Motor cars per 1,000 inhabitants
141. Telephones per 100 inhabitants
142. Inhabitants per residence telephone
143. Motor vehicle registration
144. 1933 gasoline consumption by states
145. Gasoline tax rates by states
146. Distilleries and stills per 100,000 population
147. Homicides per 100,000 population
148. Record of lynchings

21. The second task was to appraise the general historical and cultural factors which might apply to such groupings and to gauge the practicability of encompassing so large a part of the nation in any workable techniques either of study or of planning. Tested by both of these criteria it was clear that so large and traditional a "South" was no longer a reality either in the spirit or the measure of the regions. First of all, Maryland qualified as "South" in no more than a score of a field of nearly 200 indices. And so to attempt to characterize or plan for Maryland as a region of farm tenancy or of Negro-white population or of illiteracy or of agrarian culture or of children per 1,000 women or of wealth and income or bank resources and savings or value of land and buildings or land use and industrial indices, and a hundred other socio-economic factors, basic to needs and planning, was at once to invalidate the scientific validity of regional analysis. On the other hand, to add Maryland's aggregate to the Southeast in the effort to bolster up its claims and ratings would defeat the object of seeking workable differentials upon which to reach accurate diagnosis. Having rejected Maryland as a southern state, Delaware and the District of Columbia, being beyond and to the northeast, were no longer considered hypothetically within the South. Missouri, following much the same process, showed only a score or more indices of homogeneity with the South than Maryland. By the same token, it was overwhelmingly not "southern," except in certain parts of the state and in certain historical, legislative, and institutional affiliations, all of which, however, no longer appear valid as definitive characterizations.

22. Turning next to the western border states, Texas and Oklahoma qualify as "southern" in less than a third of the indices selected. As measured, therefore, both by a predominance of the selected indices and by general geographical, industrial, and cultural conditions, these states do not belong in the "South" of the Southeastern States. Having characterized Texas and Oklahoma as belonging to the Southwestern States, there remained the problem of classifying Louisiana and Arkansas, both west of the Mississippi, and often characterized as Southwest. Tested by the criteria, on the one hand, of the Southeast and, on the other, of Texas and Oklahoma, they qualify overwhelmingly with the Southeast and are differentiated from the emerging greater Southwest in a plurality of indices. In addition to this, they fall within the geographic bounds of practical homogeneity of culture and function. Thus the Southeastern Region of eleven states conforms to a dominance of characteristics which indicate a quite satisfactory general southern homogeneity.

23. The present study, after careful exploratory studies of the Southwest, is therefore limited primarily to the eleven Southeastern States cor-

LOUISIANA AND ARKANSAS ARE SOUTHEAST RATHER THAN SOUTHWEST

In addition to physical factors such as forest area, land use, precipitation, crop area, crops grown and a dozen others

1. Per capita cost for each child in daily school attendance
2. Average number of days attended by each pupil enrolled in school
3. Average length of school term in days
4. Value of school property per pupil enrolled (not Louisiana)
5. Average annual salaries paid public school teachers (not Louisiana)
6. Per capita total expenditures in public day schools
7. Per cent of total enrollment in high school
8. Native white illiterates ten years of age and over
9. Negro illiterates ten years of age and over
10. Students in universities, colleges, and professional schools
11. Volumes per 100 inhabitants in public, society, and school libraries
12. Population per library, public, society, and school
13. Net paid circulation daily newspapers per 1,000 inhabitants
14. Rank of states based on twenty-three cultural tables
15. Composite rank in public education in the states
16. Per cent of school population—17 years of age in daily attendance
17. Average days attended by each child 5-17 years of age
18. Average expenditure per teacher employed (not Louisiana)
19. Per capita cost for each adult, all expenditures
20. Ratio of population 21 years of age and over to those 5-17
21. Per cent boys were to girls in high school
22. Average expenditure per child attending, all expenditures
23. Average expenditure per child of school age
24. Expenditure per pupil for purposes other than teachers' salaries
25. Total professional students per 100,000 population (not Louisiana)
26. Per capital total receipts, exclusive of additions to endowments, universities, colleges, and professional schools
27. Enrollment in all colleges per 100,000 population
28. Total graduate students per 100,000 population
29. Per cent of total population attending school
30. Average number of days schools were in session
31. Expenditure per teacher for salaries
32. State support of colleges and universities for maintenance
33. Students in normal schools and teachers' colleges per 10,000 population
34. Circulation of the *Nation* per 100,000 population
35. Circulation of the *Atlantic Monthly* per 1,000 population
36. Circulation of the *Saturday Evening Post* per 1,000 population
37. Families per radio
38. Inhabitants per magazine
39. Inhabitants per woman's magazine
40. Inhabitants per "class" magazine
41. Inhabitants per literary magazine
42. Inhabitants per daily newspaper
43. Ratio of women's colleges and co-educational institutions
44. Percentage church membership
45. Ratio Protestant churches
46. Ratio of Baptists and Methodists
47. Per cent net income from corporations
48. Per cent of income from manufacture
49. Per cent of income from sources other than agriculture, manufacturing, and mining (not Louisiana)
50. Per cent of income from all other sources, exclusive of agriculture, manufacture, mining, construction (not Louisiana)
51. Per capita cost of state government
51. Federal personal income tax payments per capita
52. Per inhabitant estimated true wealth
53. Retail sales per store
54. Per inhabitant retail trade
55. Retail stores per 1,000 population (not Louisiana)
56. Per capita net income, federal personal and corporation income tax returns
57. Total personal income of those filing federal income tax returns reduced to per capita of total population (not Louisiana)
58. Per capita federal income tax payments
59. Per capita postal receipts
60. Average value of land and buildings, farms operated by tenants
61. Per capita annual income, eleven year average
62. Aggregate net income per capita, 1929
63. Value of mineral products
64. Death rate per 1,000 population
65. Deaths from tuberculosis per 1,000 population
66. Deaths from malaria per 1,000 population
67. Per cent of counties having hospitals
68. Death rate from pellagra per 1,000 population (not Louisiana
69. Deaths from influenza per 1,000 population
70. Maternal deaths in childbirth per 100,000 population
71. Deaths under one year of age per 1,000 live births
72. Per cent of rural population served by whole-time health units
73. Infant mortality rate per 1,000 live births (vital statistics not given for Texas)
74. Per cent Indians in population
75. Per cent Mexicans in population
76. Per cent Negroes in population
77. Per cent increase or decrease in native whites of foreign parentage
78. Per cent of females 15 years of age and over married (not Arkansas)
79. Per cent increase in total population
80. Per cent of females ten years of age and over gainfully employed (not Arkansas)
81. Per cent of total population living on farms (not Louisiana)
82. Per cent of population 21 years of age and over Negro
83. Per cent of population 21 years of age and over foreign-born white (not Louisiana)
84. Per cent of total population 20 to 54 years of age (not Louisiana)
85. Per cent of total population 19 years of age or less
86. Per cent increase in population, native white of foreign or mixed parentage
87. Per cent increase in urban population
88. Per cent of total population urban (not Louisiana)
89. Per cent native white of total white population (not Louisiana)
90. Per cent foreign-born in total population (not Louisiana)
91. Birth rate per 1,000 population
92. Net loss by migration
93. Ratio of mortgaged debt to value, farms operated by full owners
94. Average gross crop income per farm per year
95. Per cent of farms having piped water
96. Per cent of farms having electric lights
97. Per cent of farms having electric motors
98. Average annual cash farm income per farm
99. Per cent of farms having motor trucks
100. Average value per farm of domestic animals
101. Value of all farm property per farm
102. Ratio of mortgaged debt to value of land and buildings, full owners owning no other farm land
103. Average value of land and buildings, owner operated farms
104. Total gallons of milk produced per farm
105. Value of farm land and buildings per farm
106. Average gross income per farm per year
107. Average gross income from livestock per farm per year
108. Per cent of farms having gas engines
109. Per cent of farms having tractors
110. Per capita production of milk
111. Average total acreage per farm
112. Decrease animal units on farms and ranch
113. Sheep and lamb on farms
114. Cattle on farms and ranges
115. Expenditures for fertilizer
116. Value of hay and forage
117. All cattle and calves
118. Railway mileage per 1,000 square miles
119. Railway mileage, square miles of area per mile of line
120. Inhabitants per motor car
121. Per cent of farms having telephones
122. Per cent of farms having automobiles
123. Motor cars per 1,000 inhabitants
124. Inhabitants per residence telephone
125. Federal aid to states
126. Net indebtedness of state governments
127. Prisoners received by federal prisons and reformatories per 100,000 population
128. Homicides per 100,000 population

responding more nearly to the "Old South," beginning with Virginia and comprising also the five pairs of states: North and South Carolina, Kentucky and Tennessee, Georgia and Florida, Alabama and Mississippi, Louisiana and Arkansas. For the purpose of further exploration and comparative study some twenty-five or thirty subdivisions are projected, in addition to the special Tennessee Valley and Appalachian subregions.

24. The Southeastern Region, thus composed, affords not only an excellent laboratory for regional study and planning, but an admirable unit for inventory and work in national reconstruction. In addition to its superabundance of specific natural resources, subsequently catalogued, the Southeast possesses an extraordinary number of those geographic attributes which constitute the optimum setting for economic achievement and cultural adequacy, such as general climate, situation, topography, and more especially, temperature, moisture, surface, soil, growing seasons, sunshine, winds, life zones, and maximum range and variety.

25. Moreover, the geographic factors in the Southeast appear to have exerted a more dominating influence upon the people and their behavior than is often recognized, contributing largely to the special cultural equipment and vicissitudes of the region.

III. CULTURAL EQUIPMENT AND HISTORICAL BACKGROUNDS

26. The cultural equipment of the Southeast is not only powerfully conditioned by its geographic factors but can be understood only through a knowledge of historical backgrounds and regional incidence which have played an extraordinarily dominant rôle in the development of the civilization of the South.

27. The visible ends of this historical influence are manifest in a folk-regional culture of distinctive features, including many special "problems," a long catalogue of crises, handicaps, and deficiencies, and a number of quality characterizations commonly assumed to be superior. The special problems and deficiencies constitute a separate category as do also the cultural distinctions of the past.

28. The "crises" which have faced the region have been almost continuous and more numerous than is commonly understood. Some have been dramatic, some more subtle but not less powerful in their hidden influences upon the culture and economy of the South. These crises have been of several sorts.

29. The most dramatic and tragic group of crises is that centering around secession and war. Following in the wake of the earlier secession crisis, the later secession and war, were the tragedies of reconstruction, of race conflict, of Negro-white and white-Negro domination, of turbulent

STATE AND REGIONAL VARIATIONS IN RATIO OF FARM TENANCY, 1930

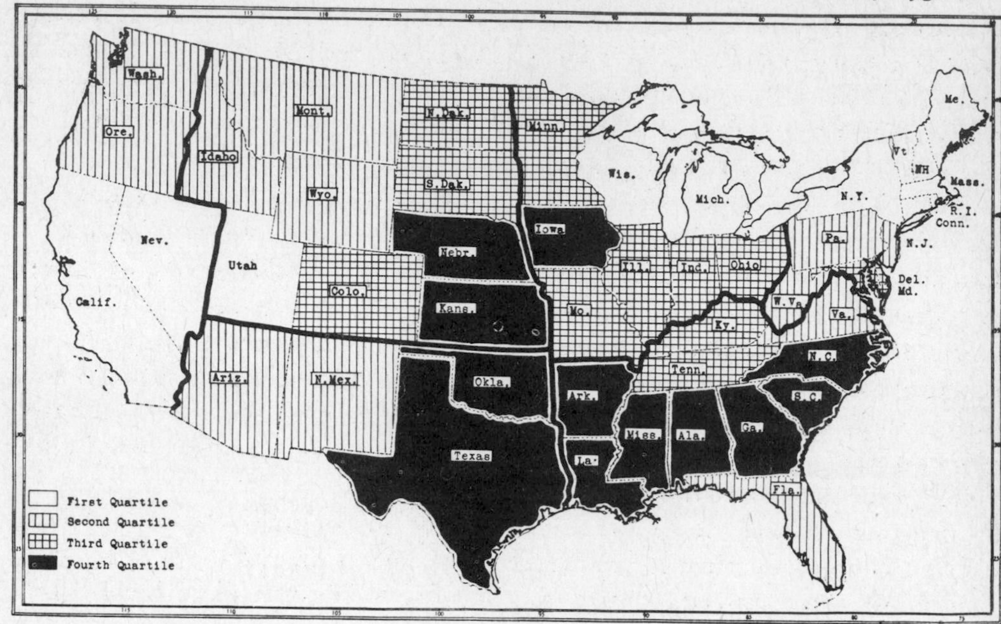

AVERAGE VALUE PER FARM OF LAND AND BUILDING, FARMS OPERATED BY TENANTS, 1930

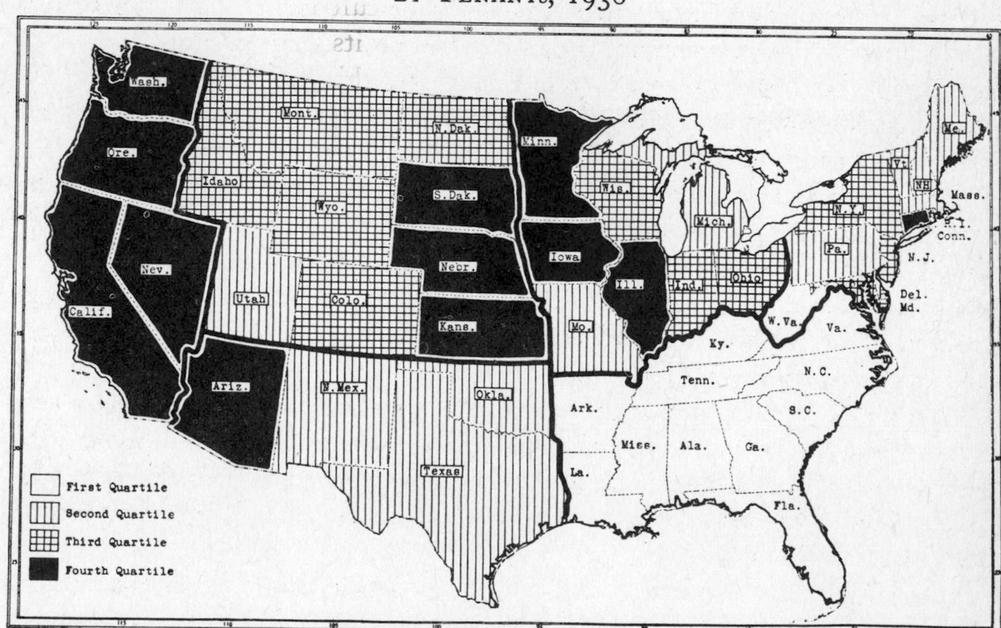

Unless otherwise indicated the maps basic to the regional analyses in the present volume are from Goode's Series of Base Maps by special permission from the University of Chicago Press. Likewise, unless specially noted, data are from the standard sources of the Census and other Federal reports.

politics, and multiple minor crises within the several states and institutions.

30. Sectionalism itself has constituted a continuous major crisis. Powerful in the development of all the nation, it became in the South "America's Tragedy," being the final arbiter of economic and cultural fortunes and conditioning the South to isolation, individualism, ingrowing patriotism, cultural inbreeding, civic immaturity, and social inadequacy.

31. A special group of related crises centered around cotton and its evolving economy. One was the early crisis of the South's expectation that Europe was dependent upon its cotton for industrial adequacy. Earlier, slavery with its economic, philosophical, and political influences was background and motivation for colonial policy, low labor and living standards, the "Negro question," the tenant system, the one-crop economy. Early soil leaching and erosion, waste of land and forests, hard labor of the people, were followed by later and greater soil waste, heavy fertilizer drain of cash value of cotton, the boll weevil, the westward expansion of cotton culture, the cotton crashes of 1914, of 1920, of 1929, the loss of exports and the bankruptcy crises of the early 1930's. Further impending crises may take form from constricting tariffs, from cotton belt competitors in other parts of the world, from economic nationalism, and from the substitution of new materials and processes for cotton.

32. The early emergencies due to the wearing out of lands and the consequent migrations to other and richer lands were not the only crises of physical environment. Rice culture on the coast, indigo and sugar, the prevalence of the cattle tick and "Texas fever," and earlier malarial conditions were dominant influences in shaping and reshaping the southern economy. Deserted lumber towns, the exhaustion of forest and naval stores reserves, the shifting fortunes of fruit grower, Florida freezes and fruit fly, were handicaps alongside crises of Ku Klux and demagoguery, populism and prohibition, lynching and mobs.

33. There was and is the crisis of the agrarian struggle for survival against the overwhelming handicaps of poverty, inefficiency, and the aftermath of the plantation system; and the later rise and sweep of the industrial movement and its creation of new classes and labor relations.

34. Other visible ends of the historical incidence were perhaps less tangible but equally significant. There is the like-mindedness of the region in the politics of the "Solid South," in the protestant religion, in matters of racial culture and conflicts, and in state and sectional patriotism, much of it tending to take the form of loyalties to the past and to outmoded patterns rather than faith in the future and confidence in achievement. There is, therefore, an apparent dominance of a general inferiority complex and defense mechanism alongside widely prevailing inner and

Per Cent of Foreign Born White in the Total Population, 1930

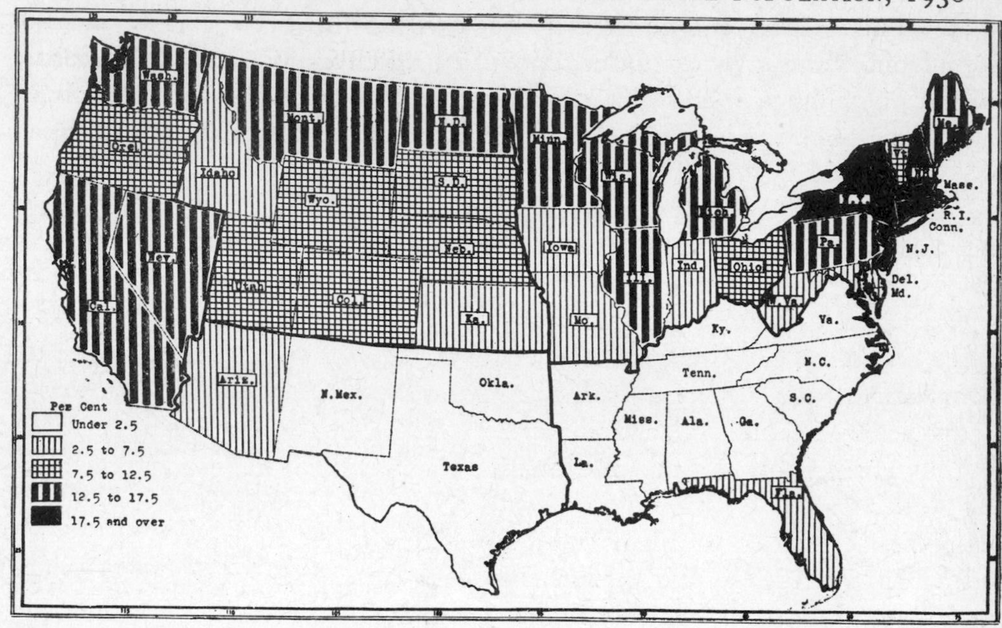

Negro Population, 1930

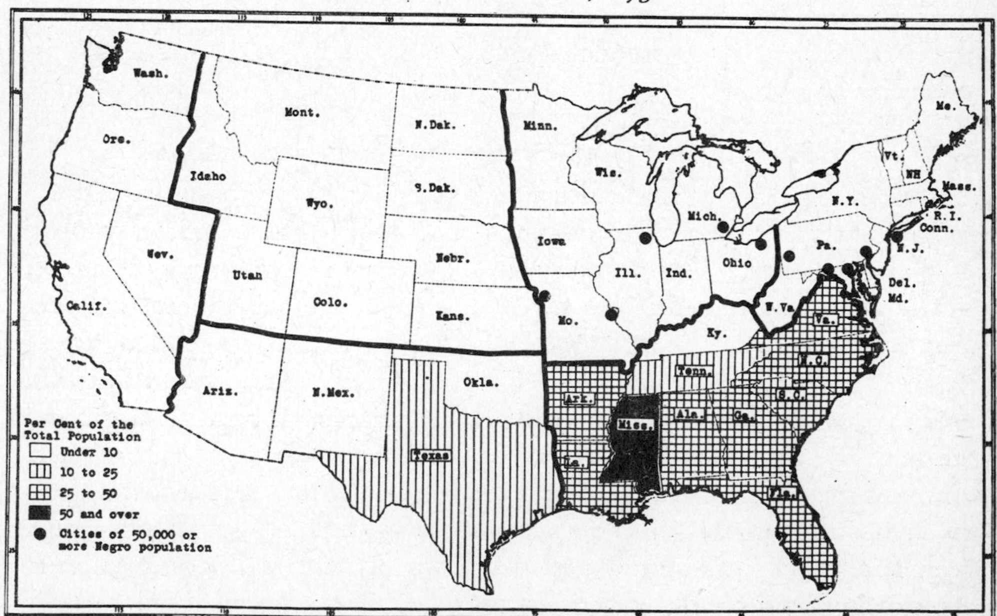

One of the most significant features of recent Negro migration has been the rapid increase in certain cities and industrial communities outside the South, such that the largest Negro population concentrations are in the metropolitan areas of New York, Philadelphia and Chicago. The above map shows cities *outside the South only* with a Negro population of 50,000 or over.

outer conflict forces of race and manners, of intolerance and conservatism, and of pride and work, which constrain and constrict the whole people.

35. This conflict and constraint from within has been greatly accentuated from without by attitudes, criticisms, and actions of other regions. Some of these have reflected unthinking mass assumptions and uncritical judgments; some a prevailing militancy and zeal approximating the missionary spirit and coercive action. Still other parts ignore the ordinary facts of normal societal evolution and local autonomies. Some appear as handicaps, while others appear as helpful stimuli and valuable contributions.

36. Other cumulative regional characteristics are found in the homogeneity of the white people with overwhelming ratios of native born and of prevailing early American stocks alongside certain cultural characteristics of earlier America—frontier patterns, church going, protestant, Sabbath observing, patriarchal folk, taking their honor, their politics, and their liquor hard. And there is always the bi-racial civilization with its ever-present "Negro problem" and dual drain on resources.

37. In anticipation of an authentic cataloguing of "problems," the cumulative product of historical and geographical incidence appears to characterize the region somewhat as follows: as to resources—superabundance; as to science, skills, technology, organization—deficiency; as to general economy—waste; as to culture—richness, with immaturity and multiple handicaps; as to trends—hesitancy and relative retrogression in many aspects of culture.

IV. EMERGING CULTURE "PROBLEMS" AND SITUATIONS

38. Some of the regional culture problems reflect composite products; others indicate more specific developments; and still others appear synonymous with deficiency. For instance, the Southeast is rich in all resources, physical and human, essential to the development of the highest culture. It does not, however, afford adequate facilities—science, invention, management, organization, technology—for the development and utilization of either its physical or human wealth. Moreover, there is a large and unnecessary measure of waste, actual and potential, of both natural and human resources. In reality, therefore, the southern regions are deficiency areas in contrast to their abundance potentialities. This chasm between abundance possibilities and deficiency actualities lies at the heart of the southern problems, and, alongside certain uniform conditions, is in contrast to much of the national picture of actual abundance economy functioning in scarcity of use.

Per Cent Increase in Urban Population, 1920-1930

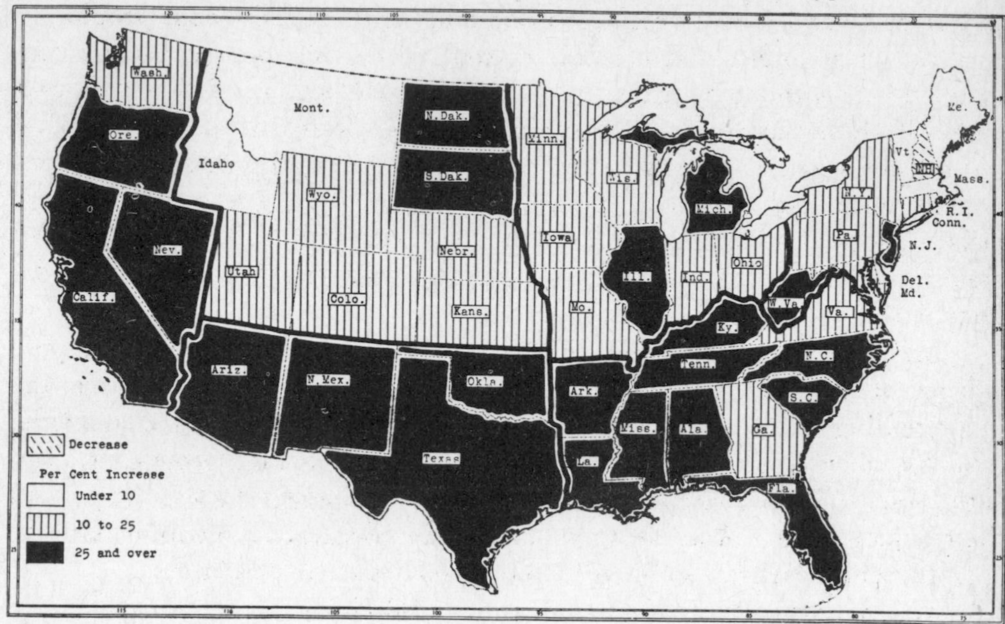

Urban, Metropolitan Village and Metropolitan Unincorporated Population by States, 1930

STATE AND REGION	Census Urban (1)	Metropolitan Village (2)	Metropolitan Unincorporated (3)	New Total Urban Sum of 1, 2 and 3
Southeast	*7,616,831*	*36,489*	*558,228*	*8,211,548*
Alabama	744,273	5,611	72,279	822,163
Arkansas	382,878	2,092	12,064	397,034
Florida	759,778	4,965	42,787	807,530
Georgia	895,492	5,252	94,533	995,277
Kentucky	799,026	14,420	69,452	882,898
Louisiana	833,532	....	22,544	856,076
Mississippi	338,850	....	....	338,850
North Carolina	809,847	....	....	809,847
South Carolina	371,080	....	....	371,080
Tennessee	896,538	4,149	135,307	1,035,994
Virginia	785,537	....	109,262	894,799
Southwest	*3,467,701*	*17,094*	*167,502*	*3,652,297*
Arizona	149,856	....	....	149,856
New Mexico	106,816	....	....	106,816
Oklahoma	821,681	5,088	36,428	836,197
Texas	2,389,348	12,006	131,074	2,532,428
Northeast	*28,296,202*	*369,980*	*2,258,844*	*30,925,026*
Connecticut	1,131,770	8,534	265,381	1,405,685
Delaware	123,146	3,031	32,363	158,540
Maine	321,506	....	....	321,506
Maryland	974,869	1,877	129,965	1,106,711
Massachusetts	3,831,426	....	175,554	4,006,980
New Hampshire	273,079	....	....	273,079
New Jersey	3,339,244	127,336	248,559	3,715,139
New York	10,521,952	55,976	484,801	11,062,729
Pennsylvania	6,533,511	168,628	840,293	7,542,432
Rhode Island	635,429	....	20,939	656,368
Vermont	118,766	....	....	118,766
West Virginia	491,504	4,598	60,989	557,091

STATE AND REGION	Census Urban (1)	Metropolitan Village (2)	Metropolitan Unincorporated (3)	New Total Urban Sum of 1, 2 and 3
Middle States	*20,890,935*	*214,734*	*897,065*	*22,002,734*
Illinois	5,635,727	74,086	116,013	5,825,826
Indiana	1,795,892	19,774	86,022	1,901,688
Iowa	979,292	1,352	19,285	999,929
Michigan	3,302,075	14,353	137,297	3,453,725
Minnesota	1,257,616	12,854	30,750	1,301,220
Missouri	1,859,119	13,061	151,773	2,023,953
Ohio	4,507,371	76,097	294,109	4,877,577
Wisconsin	1,553,843	3,157	61,816	1,618,816
Northwest	*2,626,940*	*15,485*	*98,493*	*2,740,918*
Colorado	519,882	10,789	24,131	554,802
Idaho	129,507	....	....	129,507
Kansas	729,834	....	29,813	759,647
Montana	181,036	....	....	181,036
Nebraska	486,107	809	11,995	498,911
North Dakota	113,306	....	....	113,306
South Dakota	130,907	....	....	130,907
Utah	266,264	3,887	32,554	302,705
Wyoming	70,097	....	....	70,097
Far West	*5,569,345*	*55,485*	*612,954*	*6,237,784*
California	4,160,596	36,888	482,909	4,680,393
Nevada	34,464	....	....	34,464
Oregon	489,746	9,129	45,431	544,306
Washington	884,539	9,468	84,614	978,621
United States*	68,467,954	709,267	4,593,086	73,770,307

*The District of Columbia is omitted here and in many of the tables which feature regional comparisons.

39. The southern deficiency, moreover, includes, besides its marginal and submarginal lands and folks and its deficiencies in technological wealth, and besides its lack of capital and of endowed institutions and its perpetual drain of men and money, a lack of sufficient numbers of matured men and women possessing experience, technical skill, and interregional contacts. It also includes a lack of sufficient matured, experienced leaders from outside the region who have been intelligently conditioned to the understanding of and working with southern regional problems.

40. There are other still more specific and distinctive problems in the Southeast. One is that of planning for the utilization of an unusually large amount of submarginal land and the closely related problem of planning for the readjustment, some in their present habitat and some elsewhere, of displaced or marginal families. Thus it may be estimated that more than half of the eroded land of the nation is in the two southern regions, while millions of farm folk now live below any adequate subsistence farming standard.

41. Experience with the decentralization of industry has given rise to new and distinctive problems of community standards and dependency. These are yet to be fully appraised. Yet more, rather than less, of such industries appear from the evidence to be essential to any sort of regional balance. Some of the background factors pointing to the need for more industry, better planned, include: a surplus of land in use; a surplus of people on the land; of these an unbalanced ratio between owners and tenants, and between good land and poor, with an apparent increase of land area in farms now in process.

42. The rapid rate of urbanization and the extensive migration, especially of Negroes from farms, has resulted in unplanned towns, in low standards of housing, and in inadequate community organization. The South, more than the other regions, fitted by habit and tradition to a life closely attuned to natural processes, finds rapid shift to artificial industrialism beyond its power for quick absorption and effective adaptation.

43. Many of the subregions of the Southeast are characterized by a low standard of consumption of both the principal agricultural commodities and manufactured products. A special problem, therefore, is that of providing for increased basic local consumption of commodities and goods. Increased standards of consumption are essential to both economic and cultural adequacy.

44. There is an extraordinarily large ratio of the people of the region in both urban and rural areas whose standards of living and culture, whose homes and surroundings range from marginal subsistence to submarginal deficiency according to not only the usual mechanical patterns but accord-

Density of Population by States, 1930

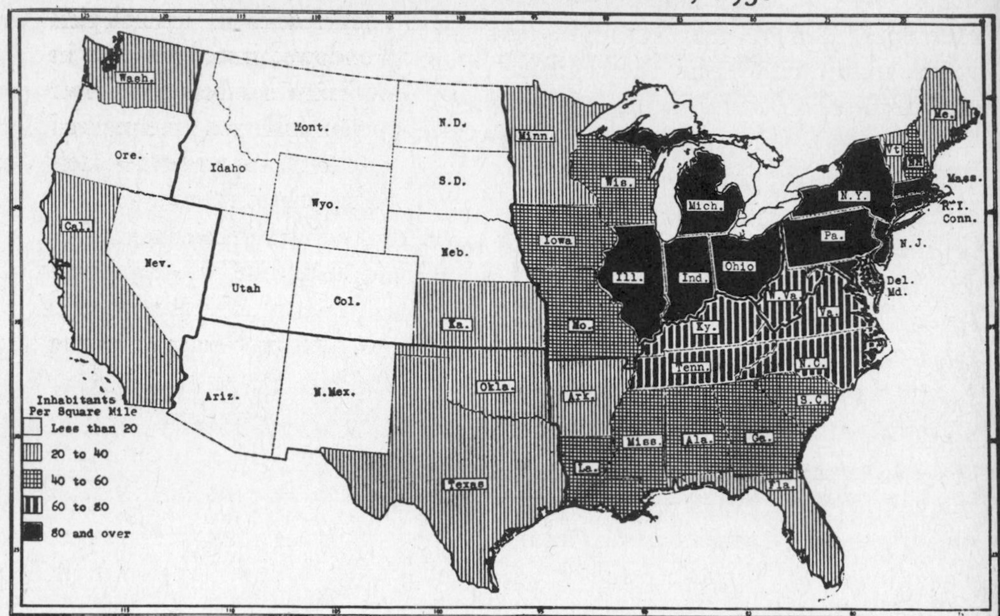

Population per Square Mile of Land Area, Percentages of Urban Population, and Density of Employment in the United States

Adapted from Frederic B. Garver and Others, *The Location of Manufactures in the United States, 1899-1929*. Employment Stabilization Research Institute, Vol. II, No. 6, p. 18.

STATE AND REGION	Population per Square Mile of Land Area, 1930	Percentage of Population that Was Urban, 1930	Density of Employment (Wage Earners per 1000 Population, 1929)	Relative Density of Employment
Southeast				
Virginia	60.2	32.4	49.8	68.5
North Carolina	65.0	25.5	67.1	92.3
South Carolina	57.0	21.3	62.7	86.2
Georgia	49.5	30.8	54.6	75.1
Florida	26.8	51.7	45.3	62.3
Kentucky	65.1	30.6	29.9	41.1
Tennessee	62.8	34.3	49.5	68.1
Alabama	51.6	28.1	45.6	62.7
Mississippi	43.4	16.9	26.1	35.9
Arkansas	35.3	20.6	23.9	32.9
Louisiana	46.3	39.7	42.0	57.8
Southwest				
Oklahoma	34.5	34.3	13.4	18.4
Texas	22.2	41.0	23.4	32.2
New Mexico	3.5	25.2	10.7	14.7
Arizona	3.8	34.4	24.6	33.8
Northeast				
Maine	26.7	40.3	88.2	121.3
New Hampshire	51.5	58.7	141.2	194.2
Vermont	39.4	33.0	76.4	105.1
Massachusetts	528.6	90.2	132.1	181.7
Rhode Island	644.3	92.4	185.1	254.6
Connecticut	333.4	70.4	158.4	217.9
New York	264.2	83.6	89.0	122.4
New Jersey	537.8	82.6	111.2	153.0
Delaware	121.3	51.7	99.4	136.7
Pennsylvania	214.8	67.8	106.0	145.8
Maryland	164.1	59.8	81.0	111.4
West Virginia	72.0	28.4	49.9	68.6
Middle States				
Ohio	163.1	67.8	112.6	154.9
Indiana	89.8	55.5	97.9	134.7
Illinois	136.2	73.9	91.6	126.0
Michigan	84.2	68.2	111.4	153.2
Wisconsin	53.2	52.9	90.8	124.9
Minnesota	31.7	49.0	40.5	55.7
Iowa	44.5	39.6	33.1	45.5
Missouri	52.8	51.2	56.2	77.3
Northwest				
North Dakota	9.7	16.6	5.9	8.1
South Dakota	9.0	18.9	9.5	13.1
Nebraska	17.9	35.3	20.6	28.3
Kansas	23.0	38.8	25.3	34.8
Montana	3.7	33.7	27.6	38.0
Idaho	5.3	29.1	35.2	48.4
Wyoming	2.3	31.1	28.1	38.7
Colorado	10.0	50.2	32.0	44.0
Utah	6.2	52.4	31.0	42.6
Far West				
Nevada	0.8	37.8	24.4	33.6
Washington	23.4	56.6	74.2	102.1
Oregon	10.0	51.3	69.6	95.7
California	36.5	73.3	52.8	72.6
United States	41.3	56.2	72.7	100.0

ing to any composite norm of American life. This includes the remediable elemental deficiencies of the regions as found in the extraordinary part which malnutrition and the regimen of diet and hygiene play in the waste and drain upon work and creative effort.

45. As relates to agricultural economy the southern regions have a special problem in their large ratio of cash crop farming and its related dilemmas. Closely related to this is the special problem of planning new programs of optimum production in the agricultural commodities, of balancing this production with new decentralized industry and self-sufficing farms, and of promoting interregional trade and exchange for the adjustment of interregional optima.

46. Likewise the economy of the southern regions is especially bound up with international relations due to the large exports of cotton and tobacco and of the dominance of these crops in southern agriculture.

47. Special tasks, therefore, are involved in the planning for new industries and new occupations and for the reintegration into a reconstructed economy of tenants and other workers in the South who are being thrown out of employment by the changing incidence of the present cumulative emergency.

48. Of special urgency are the problems of deficiency of institutions and tools of science, education, organization, management. The dual load of dichotomous education for Negroes and for whites, for men and for women, technical and liberal, public and private, and for geographical and denominational representation constitutes a special problem as yet comparatively unexplored.

49. In higher education the region affords no university of the first rank, while nine of the eleven states composing the Southeastern Region have no universities rated by the American Council on Education as capable of giving the Ph.D. degree. No southern university is rated competent to give this degree in civil, chemical, mechanical, electrical, or mining engineering, or in bacteriology, entomology, geography, plant pathology, plant physiology, soil science. There is, therefore, no institution equipped for advanced instruction and training for land study and use or for other highest technical equipment necessary for the development of an agrarian culture. Nor is there anywhere in the South a technical engineering school of the first rank.

50. There are other distinctive tasks straining regional capacity to the breaking point; such as, the economic and educational load of an extraordinarily large ratio of children per thousand women; the largest ratio of any region of children to be educated from the smallest aggregate and per capita wealth; the new tension due to new demands for higher and

Average Gross Income Per Farm Per Year, 1924-1928

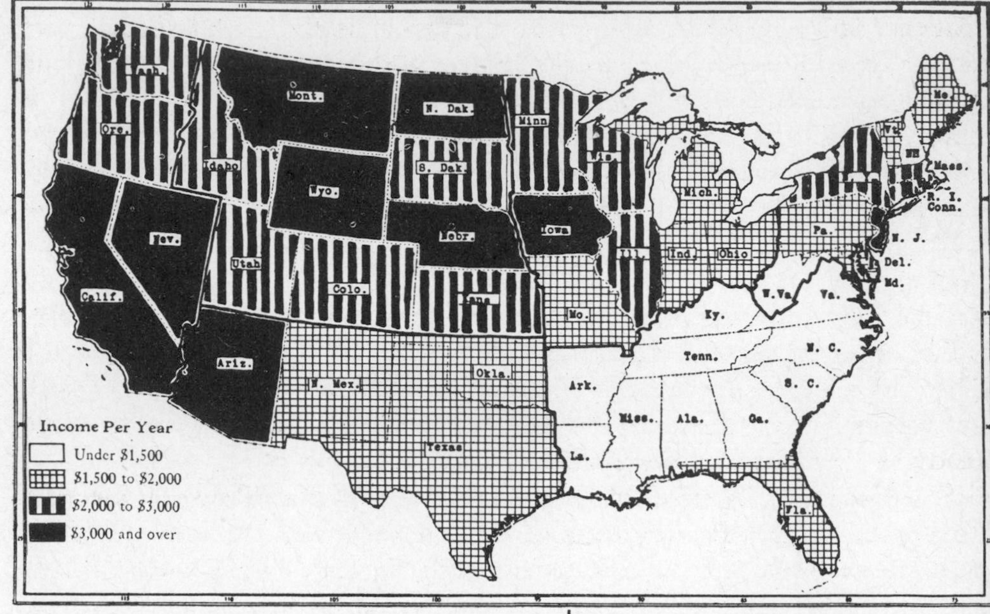

Farm Income, Five and Ten Year Average*

STATE	Rank	Five Year Average Gross Income 1924–1928	Rank	Five Year Average Gross Crop Income 1924–1928	Rank	Ten Year Average** Cash Farm Income 1920–1921 1930–1931
Arizona	1	$5,260	2	$2,825	3	$3,519
Nevada	2	5,130	33	759	2	3,861
California	3	4,360	1	3,035	1	4,235
New Jersey	4	3,550	4	2,038	6	2,814
North Dakota	5	3,420	3	2,319	9	2,492
Wyoming	6	3,310	27	859	7	2,621
Nebraska	7	3,360	17	1,055	5	2,856
Iowa	8	3,310	36	662	4	3,048
Montana	9	3,080	5	1,614	14	2,317
South Dakota	10	2,940	24	955	10	2,486
Idaho	11	2,920	7	1,589	13	2,332
Kansas	12	2,700	11	1,272	12	2,388
Colorado	12	2,700	10	1,326	11	2,424
Illinois	14	2,650	16	1,086	16	2,237
Washington	15	2,560	6	1,590	8	2,511
Connecticut	16	2,530	15	1,123	15	2,289
Rhode Island	17	2,480	25	885	23	1,988
Utah	18	2,430	23	989	24	1,853
Minnesota	19	2,370	34	725	22	2,016
Oregon	20	2,340	14	1,147	17	2,170
Massachusetts	21	2,250	19	1,042	20	2,072
New York	22	2,270	26	877	18	2,077
Wisconsin	23	2,100	48	443	21	2,072
Delaware	24	2,090	12	1,242	26	1,634
Vermont	25	1,980	41	580	19	2,073
Florida	26	1,940	8	1,569	25	1,665
Maryland	27	1,910	18	1,054	27	1,601
Texas	28	1,830	9	1,341	28	1,594
New Mexico	29	1,780	39	628	35	1,368
Oklahoma	29	1,780	13	1,219	36	1,329
Indiana	31	1,740	42	569	30	1,505
Ohio	32	1,700	40	598	32	1,471
Pennsylvania	33	1,670	37	653	31	1,476
Maine	34	1,610	22	990	29	1,588
Missouri	34	1,610	45	486	37	1,292
Michigan	36	1,570	38	644	33	1,405
NewHampshire	37	1,460	43	543	34	1,396
North Carolina	38	1,310	20	1,034	38	994
Louisiana	39	1,270	21	1,025	49	849
Georgia	40	1,140	29	836	44	677
Virginia	41	1,120	35	697	39	871
Arkansas	42	1,090	31	823	42	749
Mississippi	43	1,050	28	841	48	604
South Carolina	44	1,040	30	826	41	784
West Virginia	45	1,030	46	480	45	674
Alabama	45	1,030	32	785	47	629
Tennessee	47	920	44	541	43	710
Kentucky	48	900	47	461	46	664

*Based on crops and Markets, U. S. Department of Agriculture. U. N. C. *News Letter*, Vol. XVI, No. 1.

**Adapted by S. H. Hobbs from *Brookmire's Economic Service*, February, 1931, and U. S. Censuses of Agriculture.

Farm Income, Five Year Average

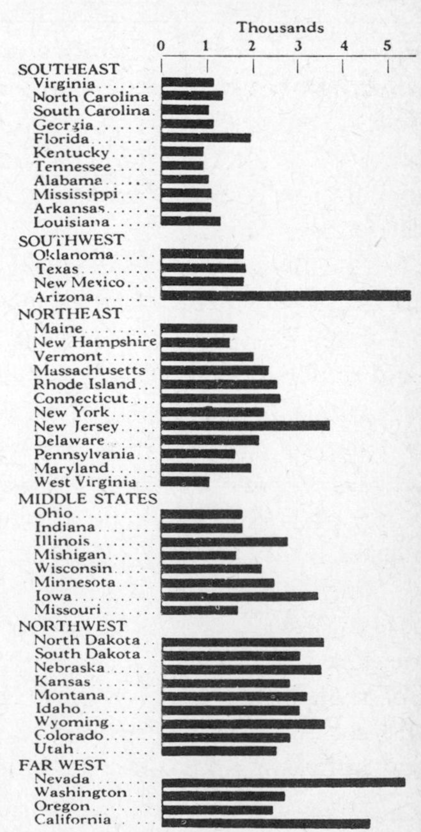

professional education of Negroes and to culture conflicts arising from the impatience and enthusiasm of the younger generation of Negroes.

51. In addition to these illustrations of general situations involving regional differentials, many of the standard problems of taxation, of governmental expenditures and reorganization must be defined in terms of regional basic differentials. For instance, the chief point of departure in the study and planning of public finance is probably the fact that the fiscal problems of the southern regions are derivative in the sense that they grow out of special economic and social conditions. Thus, the problem of submarginal areas and groups, already designated as an elemental factor, is reflected in governmental finance through the absolute certainty that the people do not produce enough to pay for adequate services of any sort. Low values and low incomes necessitate sales taxes to be taken from an already low standard of living in many cases.

52. Again, the special elemental problem of replanning agriculture with a view to optimum programs of production must be closely related to a certain increment of technological and industrial production through new small industries and new occupations. This reflects the present financial dilemma of attempting to make immature and new industry shoulder the cost of nursing a sick agriculture. Further, there are certain industries and problems of national importance, such as rebuilding forest reserves, which may lay legitimate claim to exemption from normal burdens of taxation. Thus are involved not only the planning within the region, but, because of the overwhelming agricultural population, the planning for federal coöperation and subsidy through the mobilization of the resources of the nation.

53. Accordingly, this problem of reconstructing the agricultural economy of the South must feature attainable increase of values: of farm lands, buildings, and property; the increase in permanent producing capacity of land and man; the increase in both cash and total farm income; the increase in the abundance of farm life in a new agrarian culture; increase, in fine, of the attractiveness and profitableness of southern farm life; unless indeed it is expected the present order will continue southern deficiency and national drain in preference to regional abundance and federal income.

54. If the sum of the measures of resources, technology, and culture be expressed in terms of problems and deficiencies as above, the negative measure of prevailing economy may best be expressed in terms of waste. For the southern regions show a very large ratio of waste of both physical and social resources, resulting in an immeasurable drain in land and men and morale. The realities of the situation, therefore, are essentially para-

doxical. No matter what the hidden possibilities may be, the South under the present economy is not capable of attaining the highest economic and cultural development.

V. BASIC FACTORS OF REGIONAL EXCELLENCE

55. The elemental factors in the cultural and natural equipment of the South should be appraised, however, whenever possible, not primarily in terms of dilemma and liability, but as potential favorable factors in the development of a superior civilization. The extraordinary burden of deficiency and waste appears to represent the actualities of the region's particular past cultural and geographic incidence rather than any final measure of its potentiality or promise of the future. For an examination of abundant evidence indicates that every major limitation and deficiency may be explained in terms of logical consequences and may be remediable through normal processes of reintegration and reconstruction, unless indeed the South's indifferent success in meeting many of its crises must be accepted as an index of future capacity.

56. Necessary to such reconstruction and to the attainment of regional excellence will be several essentials. One is to appraise the resources of the region in terms of capacity. Another is so to understand the realities and exceedingly complex nature of the regional culture involved as to insure a working equilibrium between resources and capacities. Another is to sense the immensity and the time quality of cultural reconstruction. Still another is to focus upon the proper number and kind of factors toward which practical study and planning may be directed, such as are listed from the evidence in the present study.

57. This promise of the region, in contrast to its shortcomings, may be illustrated by Walter Lippmann's conclusion about the southern states of the 1920's that "everything that was ever possible for civilized man is possible here." Some of this prospect is indicated in the region's excellence in fundamentals. Thus, of the five major types of resources appraised in this study, the conclusion seems justified that the Southeast excels in the two primary resources; namely, natural wealth and human wealth, while it lags in the secondary resources of technology, artificial wealth, and institutional services. Yet adequate mechanical technology would easily produce from the superabundance of natural resources an abundance of artificial wealth adequate for the social and institutional technology necessary for the development of its superabundance of human wealth.

58. A part of the region's distinctiveness is found in its rural and agrarian culture which may constitute handicap and deficiency or even social pathology; or it may contribute largely to the reintegration of agrarian culture

in America. There is, therefore, the prospect of specialized land planning and utilization which will point to a new and more vital realization of agriculture as a way of rural and village life, such as will constitute fundamental next steps in an American experiment which seeks more of the value-economy of living and less of the money-economy of spending.

59. The region, with its predominance of country life, is poor in capital wealth. While it may abound in great possessions, its chief wealth is characterized by nonliquidity and reserve potentialities. Yet for this reason it ought to be made capable of affording richness and stability of life and a powerful reserve culture for the enrichment not only of its own people but of the national fabric. To this end, there are still many who see the greatest promise in the rebuilding of the agrarian South, not on the old basis but upon a new framework consistent with the equipment and needs of the present changing economy.

60. In addition to the culture complexes inherited from the Old South, there is abiding value in the excellence of its contributions. Just as the measure of the region's ultimate wealth must be found in a working balance between nature's endowment and its use, so the measure of its civilization must be found in the social equilibration achieved through an optimum realization of its total cultural equipment and an abundant enjoyment of the fruits of toil and technology. It is not possible to dismiss with a mere verdict the backgrounds of a dynamic folk whose changing cultures have provided the most dramatic episodes in American history and whose experiences have comprehended all the basic elements in the architecture of modern civilization.

61. Inherent in the glory that was the traditional South were qualities often estimated to be the most distinctive and glamorous in the American picture: a way of living, zestful and colorful; a humanism over and above the basic puritanism of the early fathers; a setting of classical architecture, classical libraries, elegant furnishings, in the midst of groves and gardens and feudal settlements; dignity, polish, respect for form and amenities, pride of family, hospitality with merriment and conviviality abounding.

62. Among the basic factors capable of contributing to excellence, therefore, are certain cumulative composite qualities of the southern people and their culture: a certain heritage abounding in the concepts and experience of good living, strong loyalties, spiritual energy, personal distinctions, and strong individuality; a certain distinctiveness in manners and customs; a certain poignancy and power of cultural tradition, with the promise of considerable distinctive achievement in many avenues of individual and institutional endeavor; evidences of capacity for romantic realism; a certain reserve of social resources as well as of physical wealth;

Trend in Manufacturing, 1914-1929, in Three Regions

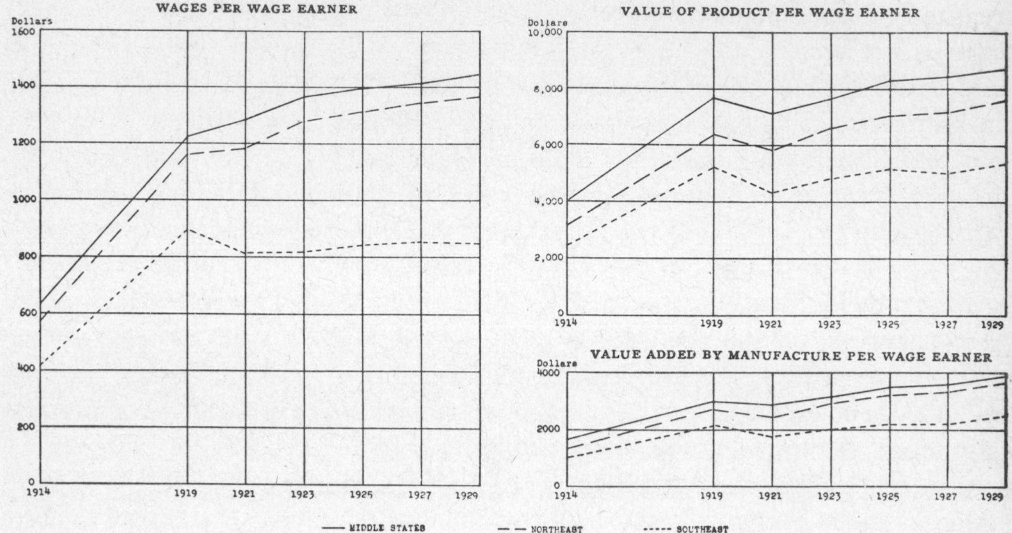

Manufacturing as a Creator and Distributor of Wealth, 1914-1929

	Wages Per Wage Earner	Value of Product Per Wage Earner	Value Added by Manufacture Wage Earner	Value of Product Per Horse Power	Value Added by Manufacture Per Horse Power*
UNITED STATES 1914	$ 580	$3,445	$1,404	$1,075	$438
1919	1,158	6,861	2,752	2,115	848
1921	1,181	6,284	2,636	.....	...
1923	1,254	6,898	2,944	1,829	782
1925	1,279	7,480	3,193	1,753	748
1927	1,299	7,512	3,303	1,615	710
1929	1,323	7,963	3,615	1,638	744
SOUTHEAST 1914	416	2,415	1.012	612	257
1919	890	5,228	2,154	1,362	561
1921	811	4,306	1,750	.....	...
1923	815	4,810	2,016	1,239	520
1925	837	5,177	2,207	1,244	530
1927	848	5,012	2,238	1,146	513
1929	844	5,353	2,481	1,111	516
SOUTHWEST 1914	629	5,212	1,640	1,066	335
1919	1,124	10,179	2,814	2,186	604
1921	1,208	9,810	3,100	.....	...
1923	1,150	10,105	3,299	1,699	554
1925	1,138	12,250	3,752	2,115	648
1927	1,160	10,840	3,258	1,819	547
1929	1,178	11,942	3,760	1,689	532
NORTHEAST 1914	570	3,136	1,322	1,112	469
1919	1,159	6,378	2,742	2,170	933
1921	1,183	5,864	2,644	.....	...
1923	1,276	6,612	2,954	1,875	833
1925	1,313	7,058	3,239	1,744	792
1927	1,343	7,150	3,346	1,617	757
1929	1,364	7,577	3,674	1,661	805
MIDDLE STATES 1914	633	4,015	1,638	1,246	508
1919	1,221	7,653	2,946	2,389	920
1921	1,282	7,114	2,882	.....	...
1923	1,367	7,671	3,193	2,030	851
1925	1,397	8,289	3,493	1,963	827
1927	1,414	8,400	3,635	1,780	772
1929	1,447	8,744	3,881	1,810	803
NORTHWEST 1914	725	6,689	1,798	1,210	325
1919	1,255	11,936	2,890	2,528	612
1921	1,397	10,107	2,919	.....	...
1923	1,328	10,773	3,228	1,877	563
1925	1,320	12,778	3,512	1,983	545
1927	1,348	12,860	3,442	1,785	478
1929	1,420	13,759	4,011	1,966	573
FAR WEST 1914	760	4,532	1,786	960	378
1919	1,336	7,256	2,956	1,791	729
1921	1,372	7,675	3,007	.....	...
1923	1,409	7,714	3,336	1,712	710
1925	1,387	8,324	3,408	1,522	623
1927	1,415	8,528	3,617	1,529	648
1929	1,415	9,184	4,097	1,528	682

*Horse power not asked for on schedule in 1921.

a certain youthful buoyancy and stirring which gives promise of new reaches in economic achievement, creative effort, in the utilization of a certain sort of institutional genius for politics, religion, education, literature, and social science; a certain power arising from the abundance of reserve in human and physical resources, coupled with the first fruits of beginning accomplishments and a growing faith and confidence; a better preparation for larger gains in the future; and a certain drawing power for the rest of the country.

63. Also indicative of the capacity of the region are certain accelerated gains from meagre beginnings to larger undertakings. That is, since 1900 there has been a larger ratio of increase in wealth than in the United States as a whole; a larger increase in certain types of industrial development than in the United States as a whole; a larger increase in the development of roads, water power, and many public utilities; a larger ratio of increase in expenditures and enrollment in public education and in institutions of higher learning, although in the aggregate still far behind; with by and large a remarkable development in all aspects of economic and institutional growth.

64. The two chief basic factors of regional excellence and capacity, however, are found in the oft-emphasized wealth of natural resources and human resources. Of natural resources a geographer has estimated that the South was "one of two regions on this earth and only two which will outdistance all others. . . . Above all the other regions, they are the gardens of the world." With reference to the population, the region affords a human background of unusual wealth in number, in biological prepotency, in the best, as well as poorest, of American stocks, white and black, adequate for the utmost in cultural achievement and continuity of labor supply. Here there are resources, as yet uninventoried, in millions of southern folk to whom no opportunity has ever come to attain more knowledge and to work with and esteem people throughout the rest of the nation.

65. These basic factors of natural and human resources, catalogued in their proper setting, must yet be appraised in relation to their perspective to general regional excellence. All this abundant endowment of natural resources of land and trees, of climate and water, of things that grow and enrich the region, reflect what may be characterized as optimum conditions for the development of vitality in culture and abundance in economy. Thus, of the land and crops there are the rare concurrence of that optimum quartette of temperature, moisture, surface and soil, with variety and abundance of sunshine, winds, and of growing seasons, with also such variety and complexity as to challenge initiative and technology on the part

Motor Cars Per 1,000 Inhabitants, 1929

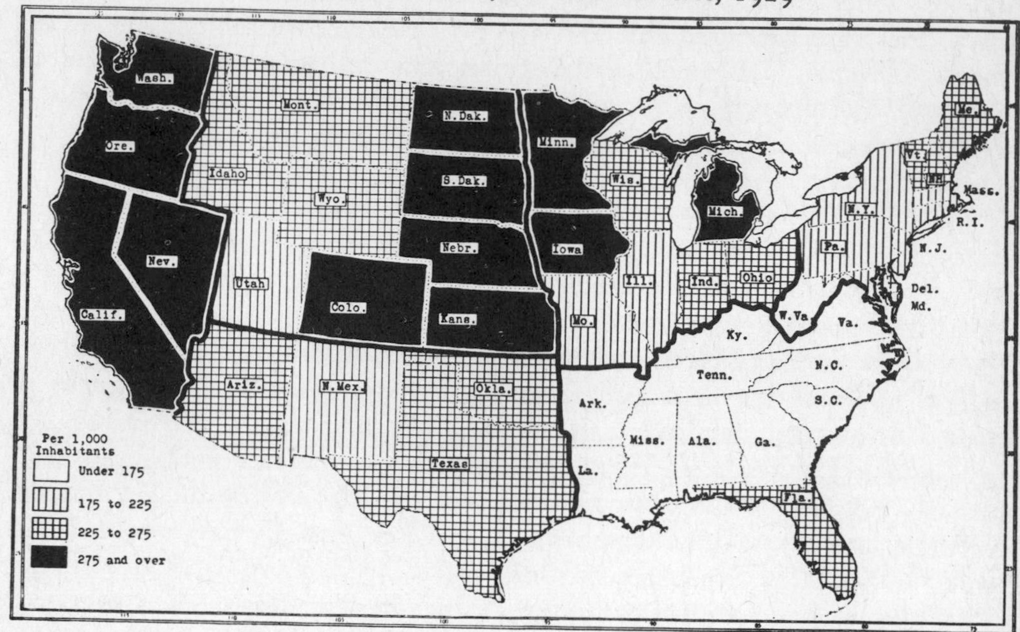

RETAIL AUTOMOTIVE SALES, 1929

STATE	Total Automotive Group (000 Omitted)	Per Cent of U. S. Total	Gasoline Filling Stations (000 Omitted)	Per Cent of U. S. Total
Southeast	*1,167,626*	*12.1*	*236,520*	*13.2*
Virginia	118,669	1.2	23,610	1.3
North Carolina	136,980	1.4	36,522	2.0
South Carolina	62,318	.7	13,907	.7
Georgia	126,536	1.3	23,926	1.3
Florida	111,811	1.2	30,887	1.7
Kentucky	107,721	1.1	16,548	.9
Tennessee	128,857	1.3	18,984	1.1
Alabama	103,838	1.1	18,424	1.0
Mississippi	89,856	.9	17,115	1.0
Arkansas	89,244	.9	17,992	1.0
Louisiana	91,790	1.0	18,597	1.0
Southwest	*789,248*	*8.2*	*161,436*	*9.0*
Oklahoma	215,924	2.3	51,407	2.9
Texas	494,865	5.1	97,031	5.4
New Mexico	28,968	.3	4,812	.3
Arizona	49,490	.5	8,185	.4
Northeast	*2,808,638*	*29.2*	*445,484*	*24.8*
Maine	65,380	.7	6,987	.4
New Hampshire	40,152	.4	5,418	.3
Vermont	36,638	.4	4,388	.2
Massachusetts	344,135	3.6	52,319	2.9
Rhode Island	53,547	.6	8,796	.5
Connecticut	145,897	1.5	26,387	1.5
New York	965,835	10.0	142,791	8.0
New Jersey	325,147	3.4	54,549	3.0
Delaware	20,695	.2	4,254	.2
Pennsylvania	629,958	6.5	102,570	5.7
Maryland	97,480	1.0	17,903	1.0
West Virginia	83,768	.9	19,117	1.1
Middle States	*2,975,258*	*31.0*	*601,006*	*33.5*
Ohio	608,910	6.3	132,796	7.4
Indiana	274,300	2.9	51,214	2.9
Illinois	620,733	6.5	110,482	6.2
Michigan	506,672	5.3	109,068	6.1
Wisconsin	249,884	2.6	48,961	2.7
Minnesota	214,067	2.2	46,720	2.6
Iowa	224,813	2.3	48,341	2.7
Missouri	275,258	2.9	53,419	2.9
Northwest	*759,170*	*7.9*	*150,416*	*8.4*
North Dakota	62,089	.6	10,766	.6
South Dakota	68,502	.7	14,848	.8
Nebraska	138,692	1.4	29,413	1.6
Kansas	199,955	2.1	44,344	2.5
Montana	61,155	.6	10,113	.6
Idaho	43,336	.5	6,268	.4
Wyoming	26,905	.3	4,242	.2
Colorado	112,032	1.2	21,763	1.2
Utah	46,502	.5	8,654	.5
Far West	*1,057,076*	*11.0*	*186,931*	*10.4*
Nevada	12,884	.1	1,350	.1
Washington	168,328	1.8	28,267	1.6
Oregon	105,767	1.1	16,957	.9
California	770,095	8.0	140,356	7.8
United States	9,610,882*	100.0	1,793,149*	100.0

*Includes District of Columbia.

of the people. In the matter of extreme range and variety of climate and life zones and of soil and topography, as well as of other resources listed, there are the intangible and as yet unmeasured combinations which afford the region a superabundance of opportunities for richness of culture, of leisure, and optimum ways of living, such as perhaps obtain in no other region of the nation, provided the component elements of resources, space, time, and cultural equipment can be adequately correlated.

66. Thus, the projection of basic factors of excellence must surely comprehend whatever potential distinctiveness of regional culture the future may have in store. Comparisons are not to be motivated solely for imitation, equalization, or standardization, but often for differentiation. There must surely be room enough in the regional cultures of America for experimentation, for exploration, for a genuine liberalism that seeks a quality civilization in a quantity world. The mechanized perfections of light and heat, moving pictures, and automobiles of the new industrial economy may not rank higher than the vigorous satisfaction of the mountain folk, deep in the living experience of their music and liberty. Folk beauty in the hills may transcend technological pathology. Lyric heritage of the people may be superior to new reaches in technology. Yet progress and capacity in a technological age must somehow be inventoried by means of certain objective measures which neither permit pathological lag nor become mere propaganda standardization. Inherent in a new cultural equilibrium to be worked out is the promise of regional excellence.

67. We have compared the southern regions with other regions to the almost uniform discredit of the South. In seeking effective measures of deficiency or excellence, however, it is important to emphasize again and again the purely relative values of comparative indices. Comparisons are fundamental; they represent visible ways of measuring factors; they help to fix status within accepted frames of changing standards; they stimulate further study and planning; and they challenge original thinking and initiative. Yet like the old fallacies of aggregate figures describing the nation or averages for men and wealth, measures fabricated from arbitrary comparative indices fall short of either scientific accuracy or practical application to living society.

VI. REGIONS OF NATURAL RICHNESS AND ABUNDANCE

68. Inventory of the natural "wealth" of the Southeast, if adequate, must be in terms of enormous aggregates as it relates to range and quantity and in terms of superlatives as it relates to quality and possibilities. There is not only no objection to presenting such a picture in authentic glowing terms but such full appraisal is fundamental to competent regional analysis

Regional Differentials in the Distribution of Acres in Farms, 1930

STATE AND REGION	All Land in Farms	Total Crop Land	Total Pasture Land	Woodland Pasture	Woodland not Used for Pasture	All Other Land in Farms
Southeast	*170,507,839*	*72,417,635*	*44,965,789*	*18,781,958*	*41,429,573*	*11,694,842*
Virginia	16,728,620	5,058,317	5,593,348	1,527,726	5,167,430	909,525
North Carolina	18,055,103	7,012,201	2,845,283	1,423,912	6,902,522	1,295,097
South Carolina	10,393,113	5,036,998	1,792,997	1,051,851	2,850,684	712,434
Georgia	22,078,630	10,446,597	4,651,627	2,880,358	5,492,579	1,487,827
Florida	5,026,617	1,969,234	1,318,585	840,843	1,050,995	687,803
Kentucky	19,927,286	6,926,915	8,119,956	1,402,831	3,393,795	1,486,620
Tennessee	18,003,241	7,665,776	5,167,597	1,528,409	3,884,938	1,284,930
Alabama	17,554,635	8,199,039	4,105,166	2,290,928	4,195,053	1,055,377
Mississippi	17,332,195	7,454,835	5,344,127	2,853,674	3,370,635	1,162,598
Arkansas	16,052,962	7,907,328	3,792,416	2,064,288	3,378,967	974,251
Louisiana	9,355,437	4,740,395	2,234,687	917,138	1,741,975	638,380
Southwest	*199,846,608*	*54,547,222*	*139,757,706*	*20,364,865*	*1,819,237*	*3,722,443*
Oklahoma	33,790,817	17,333,174	14,639,512	3,566,972	492,521	1,325,610
Texas	124,707,130	34,766,166	86,942,437	14,449,011	1,240,472	1,758,055
New Mexico	30,822,034	1,799,190	28,494,225	1,752,177	65,957	462,662
Arizona	10,526,627	648,692	9,681,532	596,705	20,287	176,116
Northeast	*63,407,903*	*25,511,135*	*24,074,492*	*7,822,881*	*10,399,067*	*3,423,209*
Maine	4,639,938	1,401,765	1,637,536	878,810	1,362,100	238,537
New Hampshire	1,960,061	422,182	932,624	576,398	495,599	109,656
Vermont	3,896,097	1,128,017	2,191,671	1,017,750	485,931	90,478
Massachusetts	2,005,461	564,054	753,088	344,719	517,850	170,469
Rhode Island	279,361	68,256	100,432	37,854	83,735	26,938
Connecticut	1,502,279	430,588	651,149	291,405	308,000	112,542
New York	17,979,633	8,154,315	7,300,145	1,949,441	1,684,798	840,375
New Jersey	1,758,027	987,315	339,607	46,576	232,316	198,789
Delaware	900,815	504,259	122,553	16,070	187,628	86,375
Pennsylvania	15,309,485	7,813,826	4,576,192	1,337,773	2,025,542	893,925
Maryland	4,374,398	2,129,264	958,822	205,474	1,007,629	278,683
West Virginia	8,802,348	1,907,294	4,510,673	1,120,611	2,007,939	376,442
Middle States	*209,566,897*	*121,307,367*	*68,368,695*	*23,434,357*	*8,300,445*	*11,590,390*
Ohio	21,514,059	11,269,395	8,037,544	1,853,703	919,926	1,287,194
Indiana	19,688,675	11,722,236	5,956,416	1,833,869	785,611	1,224,412
Illinois	30,695,339	21,139,907	7,607,035	2,009,820	731,936	1,216,461
Michigan	17,118,951	9,094,033	5,891,890	2,410,072	824,666	1,308,362
Wisconsin	21,874,155	10,206,455	8,822,623	4,439,957	1,265,435	1,579,642
Minnesota	30,913,367	19,490,692	8,247,807	3,656,160	1,090,143	2,084,725
Iowa	34,019,332	22,738,377	9,508,644	1,969,134	244,370	1,527,941
Missouri	33,743,019	15,646,272	14,296,736	5,261,642	2,438,358	1,361,653
Northwest	*278,832,755*	*120,118,532*	*146,066,104*	*6,808,048*	*1,219,232*	*11,428,887*
North Dakota	38,657,894	24,528,120	10,758,599	400,056	157,686	3,213,489
South Dakota	36,470,083	19,002,711	15,916,740	394,627	95,930	1,454,702
Nebraska	44,708,565	22,343,612	20,798,031	798,141	143,078	1,423,844
Kansas	46,975,647	26,535,054	18,687,425	781,290	328,216	1,424,952
Montana	44,659,152	11,398,921	31,676,374	1,641,607	178,299	1,405,558
Idaho	9,346,908	4,073,265	4,391,801	736,456	123,452	758,390
Wyoming	23,525,234	2,292,668	20,836,980	468,113	47,530	348,056
Colorado	28,876,171	8,448,684	19,338,377	1,410,744	130,719	958,391
Utah	5,613,101	1,495,497	3,661,777	177,014	14,322	441,505
Far West	*64,605,943*	*19,331,978*	*40,921,200*	*8,109,549*	*1,456,034*	*2,896,731*
Nevada	4,080,906	494,307	3,310,615	56,252	10,121	265,863
Washington	13,533,778	6,275,350	6,240,812	1,487,813	386,427	631,189
Oregon	16,548,678	4,172,519	11,378,824	2,619,478	502,737	494,598
California	30,442,581	8,389,802	19,990,949	3,946,006	556,749	1,505,081
United States	986,767,945	413,233,869	464,153,986	85,321,658	64,623,588	44,756,502
SOUTHEAST	(Per Cent)	42.5	26.4	41.8	24.3	6.8
SOUTHWEST	"	27.3	69.9	14.6	0.9	1.9
NORTHEAST	"	40.2	38.0	32.5	16.4	5.4
MIDDLE STATES	"	57.9	32.6	34.3	4.0	5.5
NORTHWEST	"	43.1	52.4	4.7	0.4	4.1
FAR WEST	"	29.9	63.3	19.8	2.3	4.5
UNITED STATES	"	41.9	47.0	18.4	6.6	4.5

provided the picture is also interpreted in relation to capacity for utilization and actualities of waste and in some comparative relation to other regions.

69. This superabundance of well-nigh limitless sources of natural wealth is measured also by great range and variety: rainfall and rivers; climate and growing seasons; land and forests; minerals and mines, coal and iron and phosphate and hundreds of other minerals from the land undug; sticks and stones of fabulous quality and quantity for the fabrication of great buildings and for the construction of roads and bridges; energy and power, dominant or surging from oil and gas and electricity; sea water minerals and tidal power; iodine and phosphorous and nitrogen wealth; chemical resources from pine and vegetable, cotton and corn; parks and playgrounds, mountain and seashore, summer and winter resorts, play places of a nation; nature reserves and sanctuaries for wild life; flora extraordinary, grasses and cultivated plants to feed man and animal and land; fauna of the woods and fields, millions of game, for commerce and recreation; domesticated animals on farm and grazing lands, race horses and work mules, makers of a culture; and many other tangibles and intangibles of geography's situation, relief, and area.

70. If the enumeration of the superabundance of natural resources begin with oceans and rivers and rainfall, and if to abundant waters be added long, frostless growing seasons and soil of variety and richness, there will be projected boldly the basic vein of natural resources stretching across and throughout this Southeastern Region of eleven states no one of which is outside the range of superior advantage. In the measure of its rainfall, the whole of the Southeast lies within the bounds of that magic area which measures more than forty inches average annual precipitation. Of the 27 per cent of the nation's total land area with a precipitation of forty or more inches, the Southeast's own part is nearly two-thirds. Again, of the 55 per cent of the nation's area in which a frostless growing season of six months or more is available, the Southeast itself has nearly a third, while the Southeast and the Southwest together aggregate more than two-thirds of the total.

71. Yet the first of all American resources is that of land, the source and power of all the Jeffersonian dream of the greater domain and democracy. This has been especially true of the southern agrarian culture. The heart of the southerner has been in his land, the early richness of which, like the prodigality of his rainfall and climate, he has nonchalantly taken for granted. This measure of land resources in the Southeast is reflected in its nearly 325,000,000 acres of the nation's 1,900,000,000; such southern land expanse alone comprehending an area many times greater than all of Jefferson's early America. In other measures of general land

Average Total Acreage Per Farm, 1930

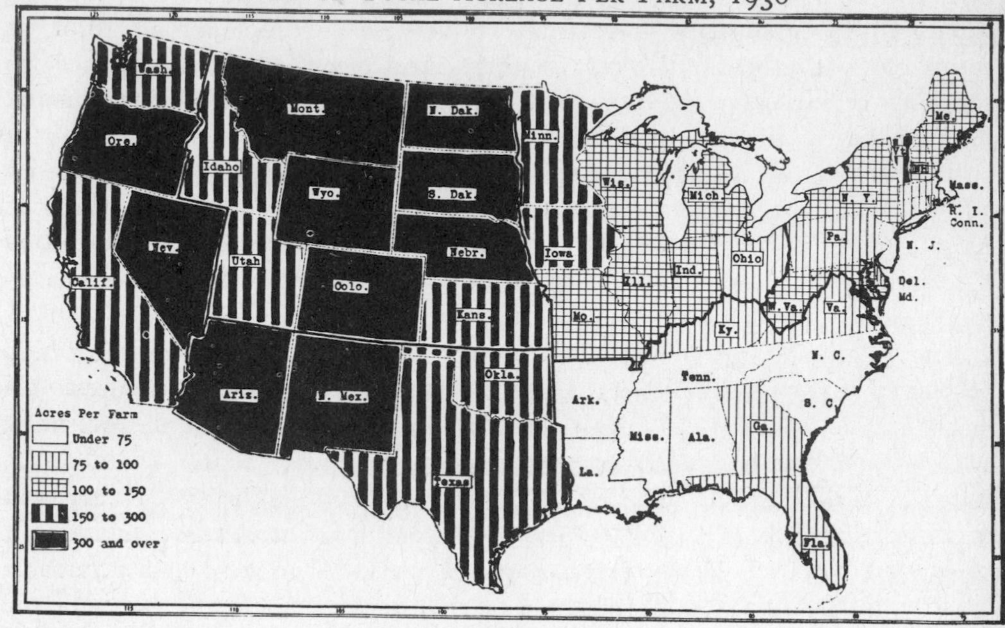

Land in Farms, 1930

STATE AND REGION	Number Farms	Total Acres	Average Acreage	STATE AND REGION	Number Farms	Total Acres	Average Acreage
Southeast	*2,388,806*	*170,507,839*	*71.4*	Pennsylvania	172,419	15,309,485	88.8
Virginia	170,610	16,728,620	98.1	Maryland	43,203	4,374,398	101.3
North Carolina	279,708	18,055,103	64.5	West Virginia	82,641	8,802,348	106.5
South Carolina	157,931	10,393,113	65.8	*Middle States*	*1,622,625*	*209,566,897*	*123.0*
Georgia	255,598	22,078,630	86.4	Ohio	219,296	21,514,059	98.1
Florida	58,966	5,026,617	85.2	Indiana	181,570	19,688,675	108.4
Kentucky	246,499	19,927,286	80.8	Illinois	214,497	30,695,339	143.1
Tennessee	245,657	18,003,241	73.3	Michigan	169,372	17,118,951	101.1
Alabama	257,395	17,554,635	68.2	Wisconsin	181,767	21,874,155	120.3
Mississippi	312,663	17,332,195	53.4	Minnesota	185,255	30,913,367	166.9
Arkansas	242,334	16,052,962	66.2	Iowa	214,928	34,019,332	158.3
Louisiana	161,445	9,355,437	57.9	Missouri	255,940	33,743,019	131.8
Southwest	*744,932*	*199,846,608*	*268.3*	*Northwest*	*648,927*	*278,832,755*	*429.7*
Oklahoma	203,866	33,790,817	165.8	North Dakota	77,975	38,657,894	495.8
Texas	495,489	124,707,130	251.7	South Dakota	83,157	36,470,083	438.6
New Mexico	31,404	30,822,034	981.5	Nebraska	129,458	44,708,565	345.4
Arizona	14,173	10,526,627	742.7	Kansas	166,042	46,975,647	282.9
Northeast	*618,079*	*63,407,903*	*102.6*	Montana	47,495	44,659,152	940.3
Maine	39,006	4,639,938	119.0	Idaho	41,674	9,346,908	224.3
New Hampshire	14,906	1,960,061	131.5	Wyoming	16,011	23,525,234	1,469.3
Vermont	24,898	3,896,097	156.5	Colorado	59,956	28,876,171	481.6
Massachusetts	25,598	2,005,461	78.3	Utah	27,159	5,613,101	206.7
Rhode Island	3,322	279,361	84.1	*Far West*	*265,175*	*64,605,943*	*243.6*
Connecticut	17,195	1,502,279	87.4	Nevada	3,442	4,080,906	1,185.6
New York	159,806	17,979,633	112.5	Washington	70,904	13,533,778	190.9
New Jersey	25,378	1,758,027	69.3	Oregon	55,153	16,548,678	300.1
Delaware	9,707	900,815	92.8	California	135,676	30,442,581	224.4

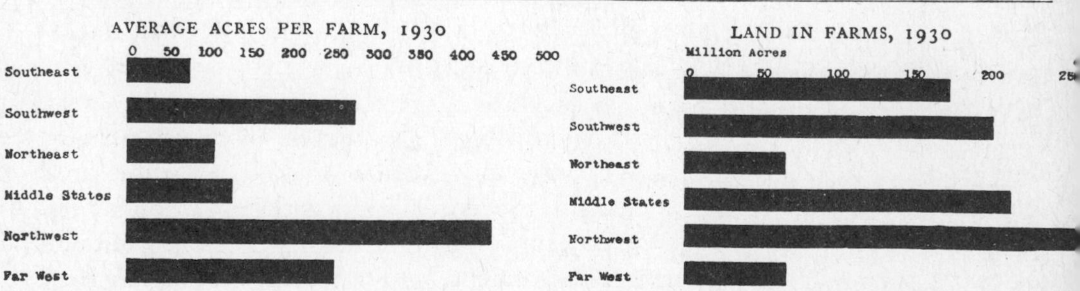

area the Southeast constitutes in itself an empire of more than 500,000 square miles or slightly more than 17 per cent of the nation's total, as compared with the Southwest's slightly more than 19 per cent, the two southern regions aggregating more than a third of America's vast domain. Or, another indication of this superabundance of land resources in the Southeast may be indicated by the fact that this region alone might easily add forty million acres, the commonly quoted post-war surplus of harvested crop lands in the nation, to its present area; or just as easily take out of cultivation that amount and still, through better utilization and management, enrich its agricultural capacity and output.

72. Another way of envisaging the nature and use of the region's land resources is to appraise its farm ratios and classification of land uses. Of the more than 6,250,000 farms in the United States in 1930 the Southeast had a little more than 2,380,000 or nearly 40 per cent. Its acres in farms is of a lesser ratio with 170,507,839 of which the total crop land was a little more than 70,000,000; the total pasture land nearly 45,000,000; woodland not used as pasture 41,000,000; and all other land in farms a little more than 11,500,000 acres. The map picture of the land uses of the Southeast shows practically the entire region classified as featuring the highest multiple land use; namely, "crop land, grazing-hay land, forest."

73. "The richest forest lands in the world," so geographers have described America's heritage, and of this vast area the Southeast has excelled in many ways. "The Southeastern States," wrote A. N. Polk as late as 1932, "represent the most interesting of all regional forestry possibilities. Here are the great areas of long leaf and short leaf pine with a growing season of almost twelve months a year." Of the total commercial forest area, the Southeastern Region contains 198,000,000 acres, or about 40 per cent; and 30 per cent of the saw-timber area and 15 per cent of the old-growth, or virgin, area. At present the Southeastern Region contains 78 billion board feet, or 43 per cent of the hardwood or saw-timber size, and 121 billion, or 8 per cent, of the softwood. Ninety-eight per cent of the 118 billion feet of southern yellow pine is in the Southeast. Practically all of the hardwood saw-timber is in the East, and about 43 per cent of it is in the Southeast. The region has 33 billion feet of old growth hardwood, comprising the only large reserve old growth hardwood timber left in the United States.

74. Like the rest of the nation, the South has begun to reckon its resources in national forests and playgrounds and in the conservation and development of field and stream for the enrichment and recreation of its people. There is an increasing recognition of the new resources in the out-of-doors, a sort of back-to-nature movement, with the emphasis upon rec-

Regional Distribution of Certain Natural Resources Compared With Population, Area, and Wealth, 1930

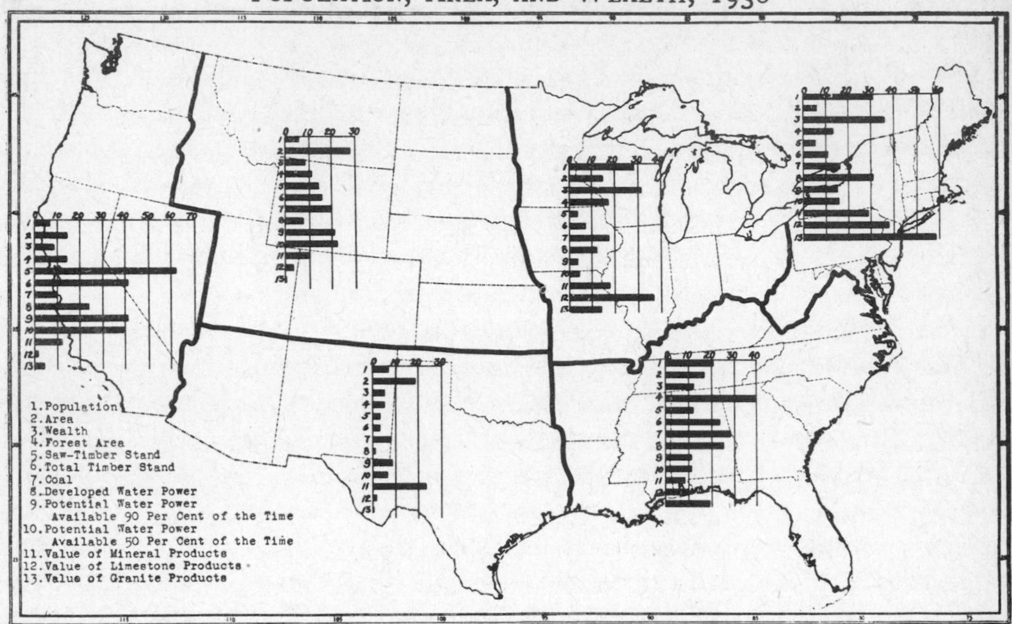

Regional Distribution of Certain Industrial Resources Compared With Population, Area, and Wealth, 1930

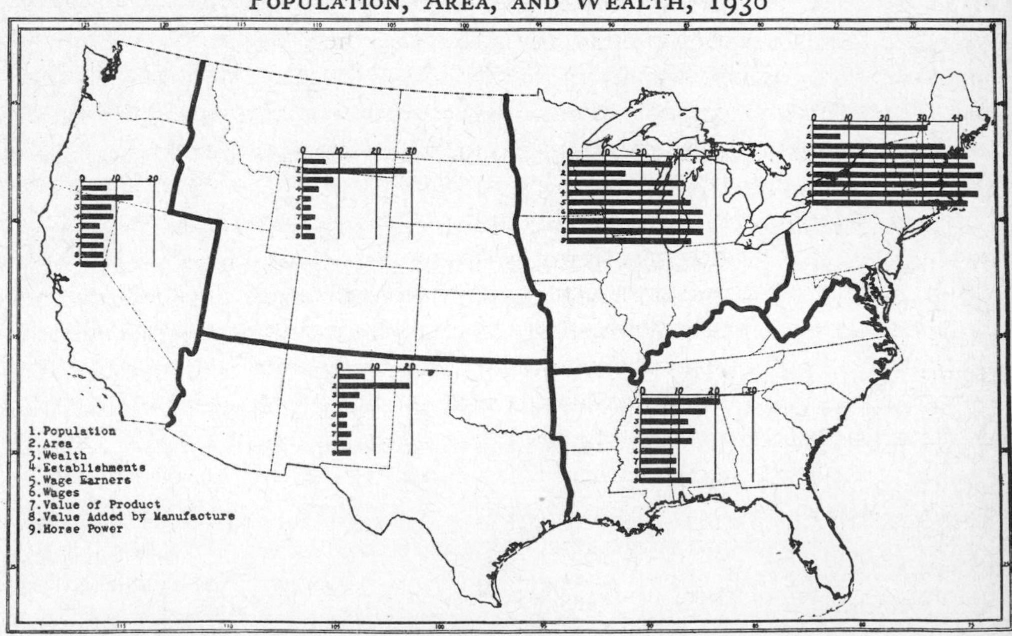

The above mapographs serve to answer certain questions that are often asked concerning the relative position of the different regions within a scale of measurements. They should be rated only for their particular purpose and for certain special comparisons desired, as for instance, to compare the rural Southeast with the rural Northwest in differentials of manufacturing and industrial resources. The measures have certain practical values in matters of administration and business development as well as for purely descriptive purposes. In the above charts, the population is for 1930. Other data are for varying years near 1930.

reation, leisure time, physical reconstruction, picturesque and historical heritage. Parks and playgrounds, national, state, municipal, have multiplied a hundredfold; national forests and bird sanctuaries have become a public interest; and a thousand organizations attend to the promotion and educational features of the new good life. Here is scenic beauty unparalleled, a picture unsurpassed. Yet the southeastern picture is one of potentiality to be realized, although in the wealth of physical resources for summer and winter resorts, the Southeast is coming into its own with its thousands of coast and interior resorts contributing to one of the most colorful of all American pictures.

75. Superabundance and variety again characterize the Southeast in its wealth of game and fish. Millions of dollars in values and potential values illustrated by a single state with an annual output of six million furs from twenty thousand trappers, and a ten million dollar value in southern bobwhites, each being supplemented by an extraordinary expansion of game reserves, large and small, public and private. Extraordinary resources abound again in fishing in the waters of the Atlantic and the Gulf, in sounds and lakes, in rivers and bayous, in mountain streams and flat land marshes. Some of the Carolina Atlantic coast sounds possess resources exceeding any known similar regions, while Florida has, for another example, a clam bed of forty miles in length. Here is abundance in shrimp and shad, oysters and clam, mullet and mackerel, menhaden and sponge, mountain trout and perch, black bass and blue fish, catfish and eel, pickerel and pike, suckers and perch, frogs' legs and turtle. The actual measure of the region's commercial fisheries in terms of 1929 values showed the Southeast with a little more than a fifth of the nation's total.

76. Once again the resources of "nature" are represented in the increasing interest and number of plant nurseries, in the value of their equipment and in the sale of their products, as well as in the southwide sweeping movement of garden clubs. Of the more than seven thousand establishments reporting upon the value of equipment and sale of stocks the Southeast had in 1929 approximately one-fifth. The Southeast's 1,431 in 1929 was an increase from 693 in 1919, or more than 100 per cent as compared with the increase for the whole nation from 4,040 to 7,207. An indication of the basic possibilities may be seen in the case of Florida, which had but 133 nurseries in 1920, yet had more than 530 in 1932. A part of this picture belongs to the inventory of wealth and agriculture, but it is also a part of the natural plant capacity of the region as is further abundantly illustrated in the extraordinary number and variety of fruit trees, nut bearing trees, berries, vegetables, and grasses as yet uninventoried.

The Nation's Supply of Petroleum, Natural Gas, and Natural Gasoline

PLACE OF GULF SOUTHWEST IN PRODUCTION OF PETROLEUM,* 1930

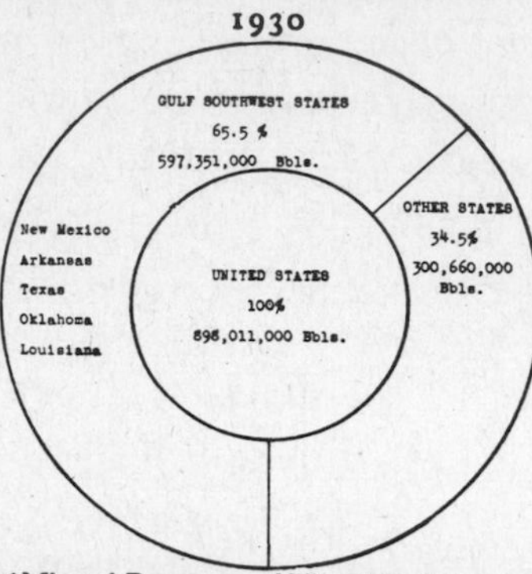

*Mineral Resources of The United States, 1930, Part II, p. 787.

PLACE OF GULF SOUTHWEST IN THE PRODUCTION OF NATURAL GAS*, 1930

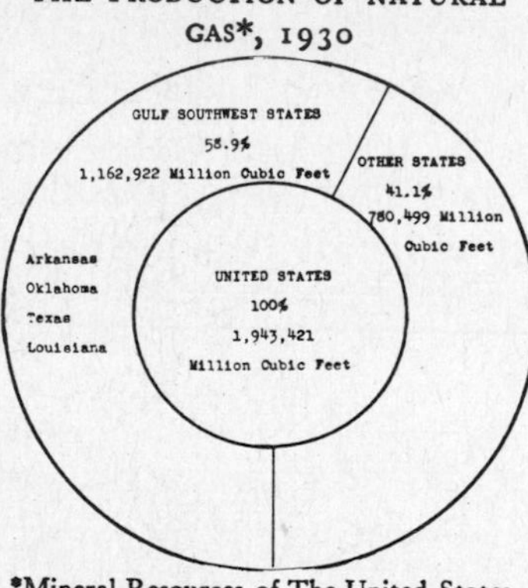

*Mineral Resources of The United States, 1930, Part II, p. 461.

PLACE OF GULF SOUTHWEST IN NATURAL GASOLINE PRODUCTION,* 1930

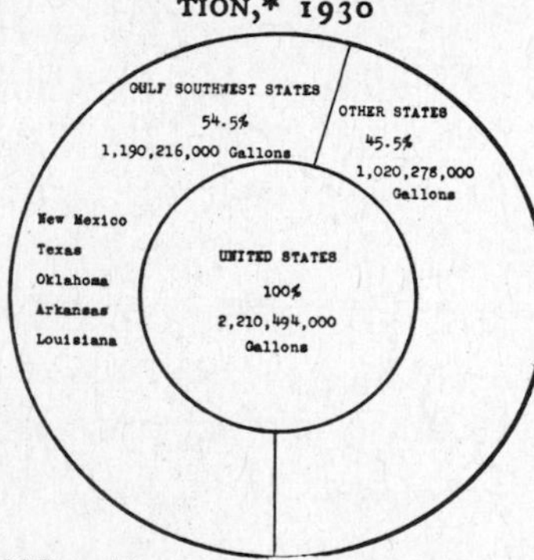

*Mineral Resources of The United States 1930, Part II, p. 437.

PLACE OF GULF SOUTHWEST IN PRODUCTION OF PETROLEUM,* 1906-1930

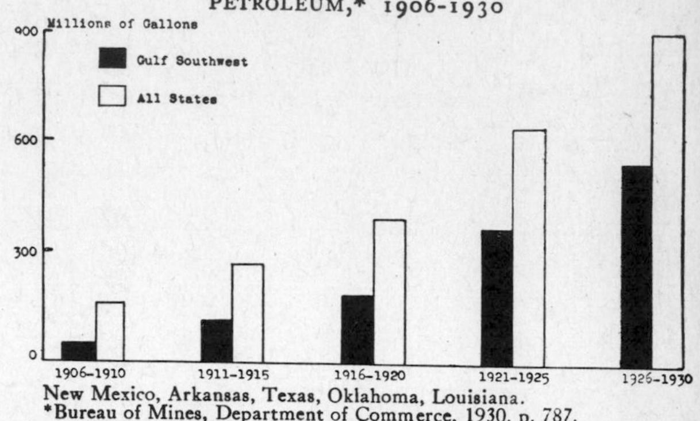

New Mexico, Arkansas, Texas, Oklahoma, Louisiana.
*Bureau of Mines, Department of Commerce, 1930, p. 787.

PLACE OF GULF SOUTHWEST IN THE PRODUCTION OF NATURAL GAS,* 1906-1930

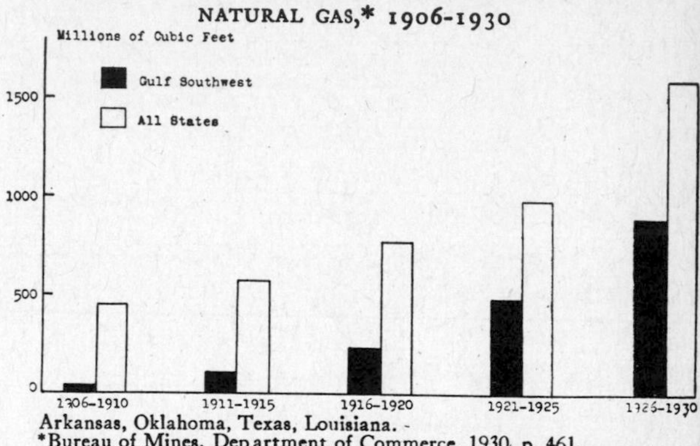

Arkansas, Oklahoma, Texas, Louisiana.
*Bureau of Mines, Department of Commerce, 1930, p. 461.

PLACE OF GULF SOUTHWEST IN NATURAL GASOLINE PRODUCTION,* 1921-1930

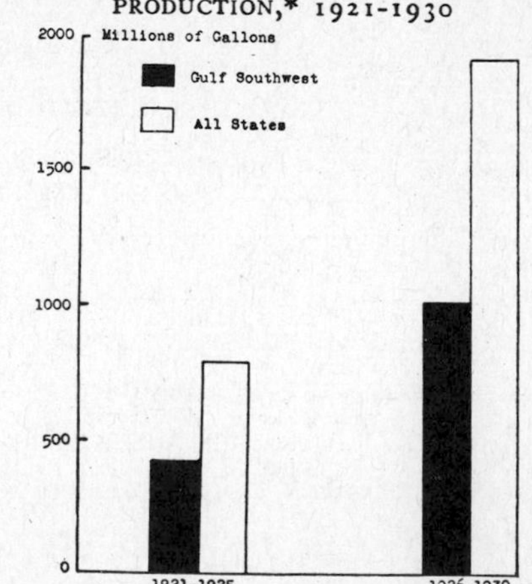

New Mexico, Texas, Oklahoma, Arkansas, Louisiana.
*Mineral Resources of The United States, 1930, Part II. p. 437.

Prepared by Raymond D. Thomas to include the Southeastern States of Arkansas and Louisiana.

77. In the regional picture of natural abundance there must necessarily appear in magnified rôle those other special blocks of resources essential to the flowering of a culture of the first order; namely, minerals and power. Here are minerals of inanimate energy, minerals of fabrication and construction, minerals of life-giving and aesthetic qualities. Here are multiplied varieties of minerals as yet scarcely developed at all; more than three hundred, big and little, important and incidental, catalogue again of extraordinary richness and variety. And with them all, twin resources of fuel and water power of such regional excellence as exists in no other region of the country, thus again combining one group of resources happily with another.

78. Another example of abundant resources available for the strengthening of a regional economy for industrial development, for reconstruction of agriculture, and for the enrichment of agrarian life is that of the water power capacity in the Southeast which appears ample for all purposes without drawing upon outside forces. Abundant evidence indicates, for instance, that the Appalachian subregions of the Southeast are more favored than any other part of the United States in having a topography adapted to the construction of dams and a relatively high rainfall well distributed throughout the year. The result is that both large fall and high stream flow make water-power development particularly attractive. Alongside this is also the abundance of granite and sand suitable to the construction of dams. Moreover, the states of North Carolina, South Carolina, Georgia, and Alabama are among the upper quartile of all states of the nation, ranking third, fourth, sixth, and ninth in developed water power. It seems easily demonstrable that the Southeast alone could provide in plant capacity the full 16,000,000 horse power developed water power which was the whole nation's output around 1930.

79. Turning next to coal, reputed to do two-thirds of the work of the nation, and ranking first in fuel energy resources, the Southeast not only affords a fifth of the nation's soft coal, but has an even higher ratio of quality than of quantity in the nation's reserves. Of the world's reserves, estimated at the long, long count of 8,154,322,500,000 short tons, the portion of the United States is no less than 4,231,352,000,000 or a little more than half of the total. The Southeast's possible reserves might represent nearly a tenth of this. Such are the stupendous reserve resources that it is estimated that at the rate of consumption of the 1930's there is coal enough to last the region hundreds if not thousands of years. Thus it has been estimated that less than two per cent of the total southeastern coal seams have been tapped.

Location of Phosphate Resources

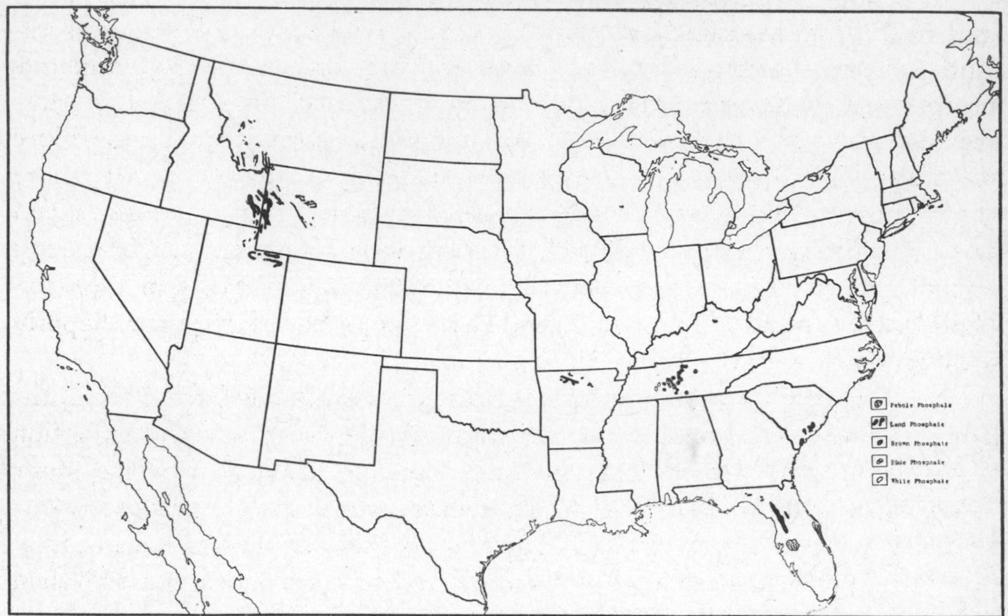

Florida and Tennessee produced nearly 99 per cent of the phosphate mined in the United States in 1929; Florida alone, 82.1 per cent. *Below:* The increase in value of mineral products was greater in the Southwest and the Southeast than in any other region except the Far West.

Change in Value of Mineral Products, 1909-1929

STATE AND REGION	1909 (000 omitted)	1919 (000 omitted)	1929 (000 omitted)	STATE AND REGION	1909 (000 omitted)	1919 (000 omitted)	1929 (000 omitted)
United States	$1,238,410	$3,158,464†	$5,164,880†	*Middle States*	*$ 341,743*	*$ 662,721*	*$ 927,265*
				Ohio	63,767	134,518	220,061
Southeast	*83,424*	*276,575*	*429,803*	Indiana	21,934	52,840	96,962
Virginia	8,796	29,363	39,753	Illinois	76,659	178,673	182,791
North Carolina	1,359	2,737	10,964	Michigan	67,714	103,870	151,976
South Carolina	1,253	1,351	3,592	Wisconsin	7,459	10,581	24,222
Georgia	2,875	4,082	15,294	Minnesota	58,665	130,399	136,350
Florida	8,847	8,976	14,804	Iowa	13,878	18,474	35,955
Kentucky	12,100	98,487	132,650	Missouri	31,667	33,366	78,948
Tennessee	12,692	23,292	40,720				
Alabama	24,351	59,866	65,402	*Northwest*	*168,018*	*294,293*	*489,382*
Mississippi	....	*	2,573	North Dakota	565	1,927	3,466
Arkansas	4,604	8,405	41,325	South Dakota	6,432	5,314	8,914
Louisiana	6,547	40,016	62,726	Nebraska	322	293	4,845
				Kansas	18,723	90,338	124,472
Southwest	*76,186*	*549,657*	*1,207,593*	Montana	54,992	49,924	93,842
Oklahoma	25,638	281,928	516,685	Idaho	8,649	11,840	32,143
Texas	10,742	160,378	495,820	Wyoming	10,572	41,929	51,237
New Mexico	5,588	18,873	37,128	Colorado	45,680	51,217	55,332
Arizona	34,218	88,478	157,960	Utah	22,083	41,511	115,131
Northeast	*470,656*	*1,178,164*	*1,488,771*	*Far West*	*98,383*	*197,038*	*621,089*
Maine	2,056	1,823	6,749	Nevada	23,272	18,054	36,776
New Hampshire	1,309	1,568	3,726	Washington	10,538	13,329	22,435
Vermont	8,221	8,555	14,603	Oregon	1,191	1,885	6,877
Massachusetts	3,468	4,176	16,031	California	63,382	163,770	555,001
Rhode Island	898	952	940				
Connecticut	1,376	1,649	7,053				
New York	13,335	25,131	109,361				
New Jersey	8,347	9,309	71,892				
Delaware	516	244	467				
Pennsylvania	349,060	819,451	892,914				
Maryland	5,782	9,699	18,470				
West Virginia	76,288	295,607	346,565				

*Included in Louisiana. †Here as elsewhere the totals include the District of Columbia.

80. The Southeast not only affords immeasurable resources of energy and fuel through power and coal, but it could afford also the perfect setting for great buildings, for beautiful homes, as well as for roads and bridges, reservoirs and dams. Here again is abundance of steel and stone, marble and granite, concrete, and metals. Iron and steel, king of fabricated structures, and basic to modern civilization, appear in abundance in the picture. Of the world's requirement of about 100,000,000 tons of steel a year the United States furnishes a little more than half of the supply. Of the 58,000,000 tons of iron ore mined in 1930 in the United States the Southeast produced 5,800,000, and of the 30,000,000 tons of pig iron production the Southeast produced nearly a tenth.

81. More immediate for the building industry, however, is the regional abundance of limestone, granite, sandstone, basalt, slate, marble, of which the Southeast has important supplies and reserves. In limestone, Virginia, Alabama, Kentucky, and Tennessee rank in the upper quartile. In granite, North Carolina by 1929 was second, South Carolina third, Virginia fourth, and Georgia sixth. In marble, Tennessee had replaced Vermont in first place while Georgia and Alabama follow in close succession. In 1919 the Southeastern States accounted for 37 per cent of the total marble production, and by 1929 they had increased to 61 per cent.

82. Other samplings of minerals in the region will indicate the region's capacity to match its geographical endowment further with the tools necessary for the highest type of industry and culture. Copper and manganese and bauxite and all manner of domestic clay, sand and gravel, cement and lime continue the list available for the reconstruction of the region's building standards. Most of the world's soapstone comes from Virginia. There are 350,000,000 long tons of phosphate deposits in five Southeastern States, while Florida and Tennessee actually produce 98 per cent of all the phosphate in the nation. Texas produces approximately 85 per cent of the world's supply of sulphur and 99.9 per cent of the nation's supply, while Georgia and Tennessee furnish 43 per cent of the nation's barite.

83. In three other major groups of mineral resources superabundance must be measured in special relationship to other factors. In the case of petroleum and natural gas the catalogue must be made in connection with the Southwest which with Louisiana produces more than 65 per cent of the nation's more than 696,000,000 barrels of petroleum and more than 50 per cent of its nearly 2,000,000,000,000 cubic feet of natural gas. This stupendous capacity constitutes a separate inventory of the total development of the southern regions in relation to the whole Mississippi Valley and the Tennessee Valley subregions. The other great reserve power not summarized here is found in the abundant chemical resources of the region, a part of

General Distribution of Erosion, 1933

Adapted from the U. S. Bureau of Agricultural Economics

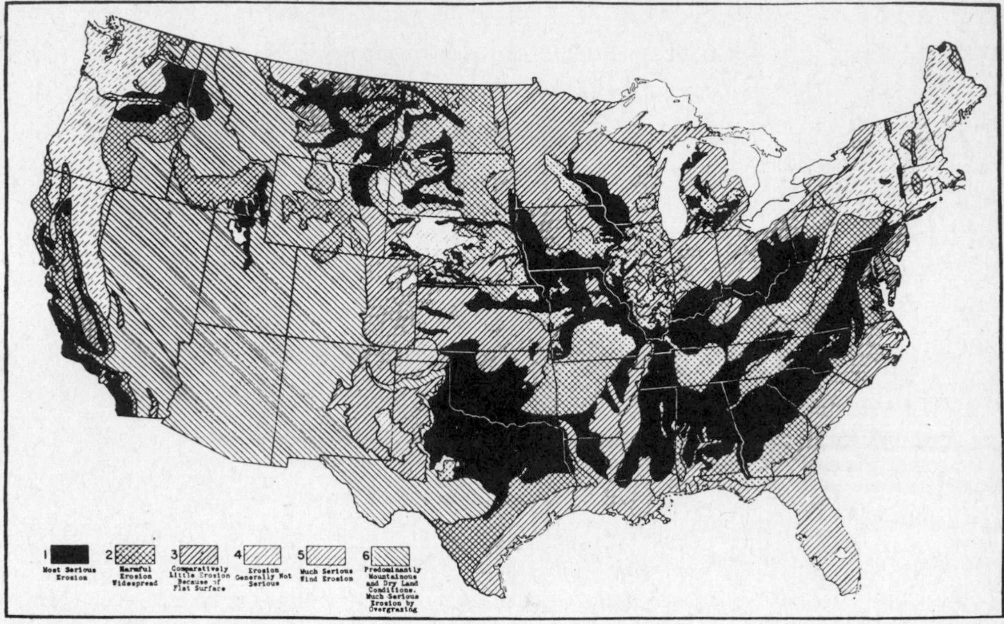

A distinguished anthropogeographer returning to the Southeast recently wrote as follows: "I must say that the cotton Piedmont is a lot farther gone than I had expected. The problem appears to me to be perfectly staggering. The erosive qualities of the greater part of the soils appear much lower than anticipated. That is, I think the popular theme that these southern uplands are peculiarly sensitive to wash is a myth. On the other hand, their abuse is well-nigh incredible under the cotton economy, and the necessary breaking of that socio-economic pattern if the country is not ultimately to be left to the foxes and briars is about as tough a task of regeneration as one can imagine."

Preliminary Estimate of Soil Impoverishment and Destruction by Erosion
(Areas in Acres)

REGION	Approximate Area of Region	Severely Impoverished or Soil Washed off	Devastated	Total Erosion	Per Cent
Piedmont	46,000,000	12,000,000	4,500,000	16,500,000	35.8
Triassic Piedmont	5,000,000	1,200,000	400,000	1,600,000	32.0
Appalachian Mountains	78,000,000	12,000,000	3,000,000	15,000,000	19.2
Mississippi-Alabama-Georgia Sandy Lands	27,000,000	6,500,000	2,000,000	8,500,000	31.4
Southern Brown Loam	17,000,000	4,500,000	1,800,000	6,300,000	37.0
Texas-Arkansas-Louisiana Sandy Lands	33,000,000	9,500,000	1,500,000	11,000,000	33.3
Texas-Alabama-Mississippi Black Belt	12,000,000	4,500,000	1,000,000	5,500,000	45.8
Red Plains of Texas, Oklahoma	36,000,000	15,000,000	3,000,000	18,000,000	50.0
Total	254,000,000	65,200,000	17,200,000	82,400,000	32.4
Estimates of other southern areas, e. g., Ozarks, coastal plain*	....	10,000,000	5,000,000	15,000,000	....
Grand Total, South	254,000,000	75,200,000	22,200,000	97,400,000	....
Total for Nation	....	125,000,000	34,200,000	159,200,000	....
Per Cent which South is of Total	....	....	....	....	61.1

*The above table except the estimates in this line adapted from H. H. Bennett, *American Geographic Review*, May, 1933.

which belongs to technological equipment and a part to nature's endowment. Omitting the undeveloped possibilities of pine products in paper and rayon and cellulose, estimated at a possible two billion dollar output, the units in which the Southeast excels would include naval stores with 100 per cent; cotton-seed products of great richness and variety with more than 95 per cent; carbon black with three-fourths; fertilizers with more than two-thirds; rayon with nearly two-thirds; lime with about a fourth; and a large ratio of clay products. Of other chemical resources a large number will be dependent upon mineral resources; such as, phosphates and sulphur, pyrites and salt, rayon and pulp, paints and papers; and another large number will depend almost entirely for their uses upon the adequate development through technology of all natural resources and of industry.

VII. REGIONAL TECHNOLOGY, DEFICIENCY, AND WASTE

84. Impressive alongside the extraordinary regional potentialities in natural resources is a similar catalogue of products of technological lag and economic and social waste. A first measure of waste and related deficiencies in technology may be applied to the basic resources of land and climate. To begin with two of the greatest of all geographic assets, soil and rainfall, there are the uncounted millions of acres of eroded land threatening to make the regions impotent for a rich agrarian culture and incapable of supporting industrial and commercial activities. To the southern regions may be accredited no less than 97,000,000, or 61 per cent, of the nation's total 150,000,000 acres of eroded lands. Of this, again, perhaps three-fourths belongs to the Southeast, in parts of which as high as 50 per cent of arable land has been denuded of its topsoil and in other portions a half has been actually lost to cultivation.

85. Yet the total losses of land use and soil fertility are not limited to lost acres or wasted topsoil. There are other millions, perhaps five million acres, of bottom land that have been affected by the filling of stream beds and consequent overflow, and other thousands of acres of arable land that have been handicapped by sand and gravel from the hillsides. And still other immeasurable losses through soil drainage and depletion, due to the single crop system of the region, are augmented by shortage of moisture due to the rapid running off of water from the overtilled fields needing rotation cultivation. If an estimated annual loss of more than 20,000,000 tons of potash, nitrogen, and phosphoric acid, the three most important elements for plant growth, be multiplied by the number of recent years in which the waste has been going on, something of the stupendous drain can be pictured.

Regional Distribution of Tonnage and Expenditures for Bought Fertilizer, 1929

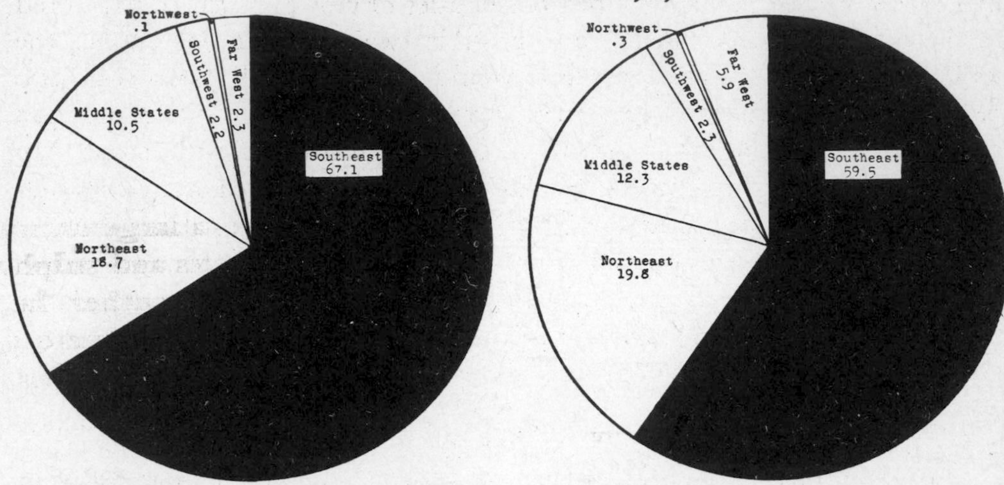

Regional Distribution of the Total Tons of Commercial Fertilizer Bought in the United States During the Crop Year of 1929

Regional Distribution of the Total Expenditure by United States Farmers for All Types of Bought Fertilizers During the Crop Year of 1929

Regional Importance of Expenditures for Fertilizers, Feed and Labor, 1929

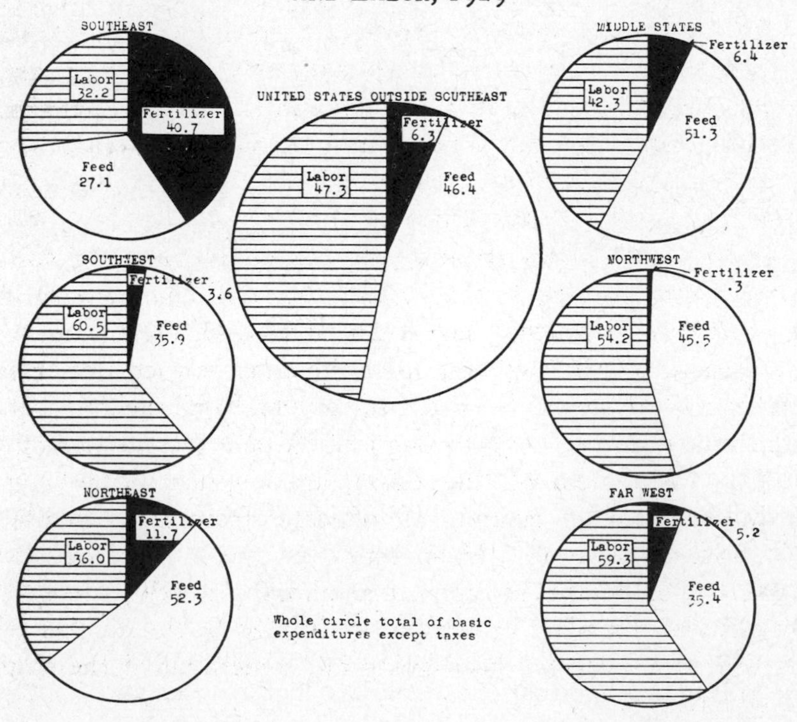

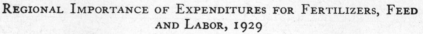

86. Waste from profitless land, however, is not measured only through the inventory of its nature and amount. In addition to the human drain of submarginal land upon the folk, there is, for instance, the annual purchase by the Southeast of no less than 5,500,000 tons of commercial fertilizer at a cost of $161,000,000 as compared with all the rest of the nation's 2,500,000 tons. This expenditure represents a per acre cost of $2.71 as compared with a 30 cents per acre cost in the great farming region of the Middle States. Now it is not the cost or the use of fertilizer which represents waste and drain; for the Southeast is rich in resources for the making of fertilizer, and under proper technology there is a great future for such industry. It is rather the whole economy of leached and eroded lands, continuously drained by more cultivation of fertilizer money crops, and the contrariwise absence of conservation and of other crops and technologies for the increase of value and output and for the elimination of waste.

87. Some of the actual measures of this waste and lack of technology are found in deficiency indices, such as the lowest per capita farm income, the lowest income per worker, the lowest return per unit of horse power, the lowest ratio of income from livestock production, the lowest per capita purebred livestock, the lowest production of milk and dairy products, a low ratio of pasture land, a low carrying capacity for pasture lands. Proceeding to other selected facts, there has been a decrease in the last decade in the number of most livestock. There is a low evaluation of livestock and a low evaluation of their products. The total number of purebred cattle in the Southeastern States as reported in the most recent figures was 8,360,888, the lowest of any region, and with the Southeast showing every state with a deficiency and the total with an aggregate deficiency of 18,540,216. There is a corresponding deficit of 121,000,000 gallons of milk based upon the average per capita national consumption.

88. On the other hand, there is still other deficiency in land use and management. If even one-half of the cattle deficiency should be added to the Southeast, there would be required, according to present estimated carrying capacity of grazing lands in most of the Southeastern States, four times the total number of acres now listed as total pasture lands. The present 45,000,000 acres would, therefore, be challenged to an improvement which would transform its ten acre carrying capacity into that of two or three acres together with the acquisition of another 40,000,000 acres taken over from the 170,000,000 acres in farm lands and from other lands not in use. Similar computations with reference to the amount of feed stuffs raised and consumed, of hays grown and imported, should show equally radical transformations necessary before any such optimum esti-

Per Cent of Farms Having Tractors, 1930

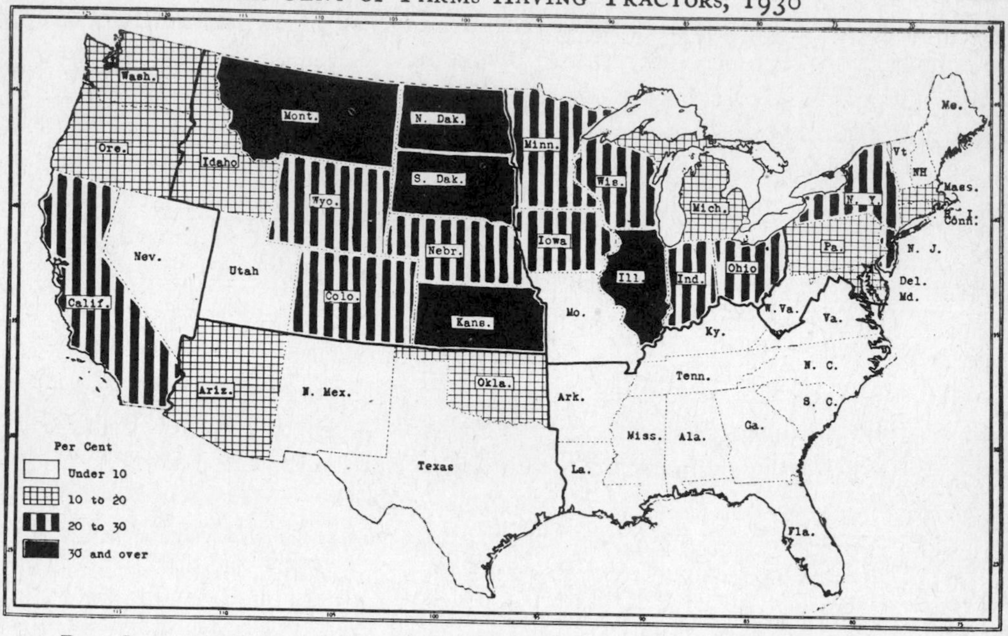

Per Cent of Farms Having Modern Tools and Conveniences, 1930

STATE	Tractors		Electric Motors		Gas Engines		Electric Lights		Piped Water		Implements and Machinery	
	Rank	%	Rank	%	Rank	%	Rank	%	Rank	%	Rank	Per Farm
North Dakota	1	43.8	26	4.1	3	45.2	31	7.9	38	7.5	1	$1,523
South Dakota	2	37.2	28	3.9	5	35.8	30	10.9	28	14.5	3	1,291
Montana	3	36.0	32	2.3	16	24.4	34	7.5	34	11.3	2	1,307
Kansas	4	35.6	30	3.1	18	20.7	28	12.5	25	16.9	10	1,010
Illinois	5	30.8	22	4.9	9	31.1	25	16.0	24	19.4	21	748
Iowa	6	29.4	16	8.0	4	44.1	19	21.4	19	24.0	4	1,259
Nebraska	7	29.3	24	4.5	7	32.4	23	16.5	15	29.6	6	1,166
New Jersey	8	28.5	5	16.2	11	27.4	5	53.0	8	48.7	9	1,067
California	9	27.6	1	32.2	23	19.3	1	63.3	4	72.0	11	1,000
Wisconsin	10	26.8	8	12.6	2	48.6	17	25.6	26	15.7	14	937
Minnesota	11	24.9	19	6.3	1	50.4	27	12.6	31	12.5	12	981
New York	12	23.6	13	10.0	8	31.3	9	34.4	13	37.1	8	1,086
Wyoming	13	23.4	33	2.0	24	18.3	35	7.2	31	12.5	7	1,100
Ohio	14	23.1	18	6.4	19	20.6	16	25.9	16	29.2	32	470
Indiana	15	22.3	25	4.3	22	19.4	22	16.7	23	19.5	31	478
Colorado	16	20.1	29	3.8	28	16.6	26	15.7	22	20.5	16	838
Michigan	17	19.5	20	6.1	10	27.5	21	20.5	18	24.1	27	623
Pennsylvania	18	18.4	17	7.1	12	27.1	15	26.5	12	37.2	15	898
Oregon	19	16.6	9	11.0	15	24.7	10	33.4	10	44.0	19	772
Maryland	20	15.6	21	5.9	25	18.1	20	21.2	19	24.0	29	594
Rhode Island	21	15.5	2	19.4	30	16.4	4	57.5	6	56.8	18	818
Delaware	22	14.9	27	4.0	31	15.0	24	16.1	27	15.5	20	751
Arizona	23	14.4	12	10.1	28	16.6	18	23.9	17	28.8	22	735
Connecticut	24	14.3	7	14.6	13	26.1	6	52.7	5	62.3	25	719
Massachusetts	25	13.9	3	16.7	27	16.9	2	62.6	1	74.5	23	732
Oklahoma	26	11.4	38	0.8	37	4.2	42	4.0	39	5.3	33	455
Washington	27	11.1	6	15.2	17	21.7	7	48.0	9	48.6	26	712
Idaho	28	10.5	10	10.6	21	19.8	13	30.7	21	23.9	13	954
Vermont	29	9.4	14	9.5	6	33.9	14	30.4	3	72.3	17	834
Nevada	30	9.2	4	16.4	13	26.1	11	33.1	14	35.3	5	1,226
Missouri	30	9.2	34	1.4	32	10.7	31	7.9	37	8.3	35	369
Maine	32	8.2	15	8.8	26	18.0	11	33.1	7	49.0	24	728
Florida	33	7.4	31	2.7	33	6.1	29	11.0	30	12.8	37	262
New Mexico	34	7.1	36	1.3	35	5.0	37	5.4	36	8.9	34	414
New Hampshire	35	6.8	11	10.5	20	20.3	8	41.3	2	73.8	28	598
Texas	36	6.4	38	0.8	39	3.3	39	4.6	29	13.9	36	368
Virginia	37	5.4	34	1.4	34	5.3	33	7.6	35	9.0	38	260
Utah	38	4.9	23	4.7	38	4.1	3	58.1	11	38.9	30	502
North Carolina	39	3.9	40	0.6	42	1.6	37	5.4	41	3.3	42	151
West Virginia	40	3.2	37	1.1	36	4.5	36	6.4	33	11.7	40	185
Kentucky	41	2.8	41	0.5	40	2.0	40	4.3	40	3.4	43	148
Tennessee	42	2.7	41	0.5	41	1.8	41	4.1	41	3.3	39	186
Louisiana	43	2.4	47	0.3	46	1.3	45	2.6	44	3.1	41	175
Georgia	44	2.1	44	0.4	42	1.6	44	2.9	44	3.1	48	122
South Carolina	45	2.0	41	0.5	45	1.5	43	3.8	41	3.3	45	136
Arkansas	46	1.8	44	0.4	42	1.6	47	2.1	48	1.5	44	137
Alabama	47	1.7	46	0.3	47	0.8	46	2.5	46	2.0	47	130
Mississippi	48	1.5	48	0.2	48	0.6	48	1.5	47	1.8	46	133

mates could be even suggested. Likewise, deficiencies in type of labor management and technique required for the care of high grade cattle, for the construction of fences, for the improvement of lands, for the seeding of poor and rich lands for field and pasture, and for the curing and processing of hay and grains would have to be met.

89. Other measures of technological deficiencies relating to the land and its cultivation and to farm equipment will be found in the percentage of farms lacking modern tools and conveniences. Here the Southeast is uniformly deficient, ranking as follows in selected items: farms with tractors, the Southeast averaging around two per cent, contrasted to the highest states around 40 per cent; the Southeast contrasted with the highest of other states in other conveniences ranks as follows: electric motors, less than 0.5 and as high as 32 per cent; gas engines, as low as one per cent and as high as 48 per cent; electric lights, as low as 1.5 per cent and as high as 63 per cent; piped water as low as 1.8 and as high as 74.5; value of implements and machinery, as low as $133 and as high as $1,523. Or in terms of averages for the Southeast compared with the national average: tractors, 2.4 and 14; electric motors, 0.4 and 4.5; gasoline engines, 1.6 and 18.3; electric lights, 3.8 and 16.1; piped water, 3.3 and 18.7; passenger cars, 33.0 and 62.0; motor trucks, 5.0 and 18.5; telephones, 7.1 and 40.3.

90. This deficiency in farm equipment is representative further of a long catalogue of similar deficiencies in the neglect of farm tools and animals, in harvesting and processing of commodities, in the conservation of perishable produce and marketing of crops, the waste from which aggregates annually enough millions of dollars to afford a substantial margin between the present scarcity economy and an early attainable abundance. Examples approximate the whole range of activities. To cite a few, there are losses of millions of tons of hay uncut, matched by other millions wasted through inadequate techniques of curing and storing. Multiplied similar losses from other fruits of the soil and products of a varied livestock industry are reflected in wasted, ungathered or unpreserved produce and underfed livestock. These deficiencies constitute not only a drain upon the region, but impede self-development at home and an interregional trade sufficient to stabilize to a considerable degree the flow of capital and goods.

91. Two other major deficiencies are found in the fields of farm management and coöperative activities. The former, measured in composites of values and output, comprehends the whole range of farm activities—cost accounting, land use, crop rotation, pasture rotation, seasonal work planning, animal and plant breeding programs, woodland crops and conservation, and harvesting of crops. Sample measures of such deficiency are found in comparison of the lowest southeastern state with the highest of

Value of All Farm Property Per Farm, 1930

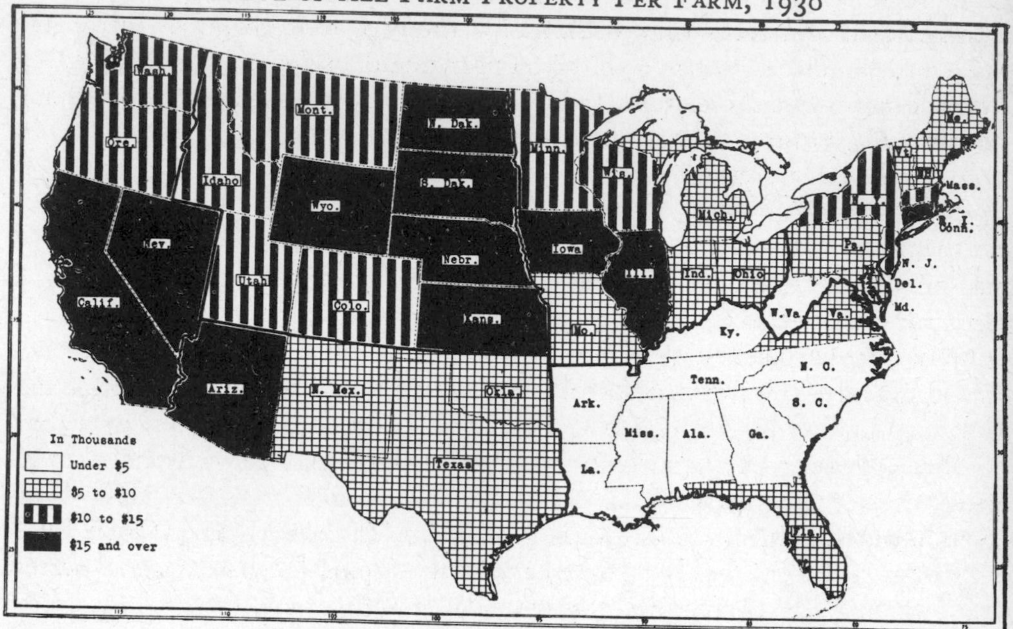

Value of Farm Property, 1930

STATE	All Farm Property		Value of Dwelling		Value of Land and Building		Land and Dwellings		Land and Buildings		Value of Land and Buildings	
	Rank	Per Farm	Rank	Per Farm	Rank	Per Farm	Rank	PerOwned Farm	Rank	Per Tenant Farm	Rank	Per Acre
Nevada	1	$28,236	17	$1,624	4	$18,626	4	$16,361	4	$18,223	45	$ 15.71
California	2	27,680	9	1,895	1	25,203	1	21,663	1	25,871	6	112.33
Iowa	3	23,229	6	2,212	2	19,655	3	19,019	2	20,150	4	124.18
Nebraska	4	22,671	15	1,719	3	19,274	2	20,194	5	18,022	19	55.81
Wyoming	5	19,149	33	991	10	12,919	7	13,002	18	9,963	47	8.79
South Dakota	6	18,991	21	1,432	6	15,455	5	15,895	8	14,734	36	35.24
Illinois	7	17,654	11	1,803	5	15,553	8	12,949	3	18,381	7	108.68
Arizona	8	17,178	32	1,011	9	12,999	18	9,685	6	15,016	44	17.50
Kansas	9	16,234	26	1,271	7	13,738	6	14,290	11	12,743	22	48.56
North Dakota	10	15,218	22	1,408	11	12,199	9	12,721	14	11,071	42	24.61
Connecticut	11	15,136	1	3,708	8	13,226	10	11,893	7	14,756	2	151.38
Montana	12	14,914	35	910	15	11,109	11	11,292	21	9,114	46	11.81
Minnesota	13	14,079	16	1,704	13	11,471	13	10,715	10	12,871	16	68.74
New Jersey	14	14,004	2	3,218	12	11,776	14	10,695	13	11,816	1	169.99
Oregon	15	13,705	25	1,317	14	11,438	12	10,783	12	12,385	32	38.12
Colorado	16	13,266	31	1,074	17	10,497	15	9,996	16	10,453	43	21.79
Idaho	17	12,692	29	1,117	20	10,012	17	9,694	17	10,144	25	44.64
Washington	18	12,522	24	1,318	16	10,911	16	9,789	19	9,845	18	57.17
Rhode Island	19	12,376	4	2,965	18	10,388	19	9,412	9	14,527	5	123.52
Wisconsin	20	12,156	10	1,888	21	9,526	22	9,065	15	10,884	10	79.16
Massachusetts	21	11,870	3	3,050	19	10,205	21	9,104	27	7,794	3	130.26
New York	22	10,712	5	2,296	23	8,234	25	7,645	22	8,971	14	73.19
Utah	23	10,645	28	1,189	24	8,145	23	7,998	28	7,637	30	39.41
Maryland	24	9,843	7	2,051	22	8,244	26	7,358	24	8,484	9	81.42
New Mexico	25	9,334	42	526	33	6,619	34	5,905	31	6,394	48	6.74
Indiana	26	9,242	23	1,358	25	7,796	29	6,917	20	9,468	15	71.90
Ohio	27	9,179	18	1,619	26	7,720	28	7,042	23	8,797	11	78.69
Pennsylvania	28	8,906	8	2,038	30	6,977	31	6,356	26	8,032	12	78.58
Delaware	29	8,579	12	1,789	31	6,896	32	6,319	29	6,750	13	74.31
Texas	30	8,546	37	708	27	7,260	20	9,210	33	5,265	39	28.85
Michigan	31	8,436	19	1,596	32	6,853	33	6,269	25	8,362	17	67.80
Missouri	32	8,398	30	1,099	29	7,018	27	7,068	30	6,588	20	53.23
Vermont	33	8,147	14	1,727	35	5,861	35	5,552	32	6,363	33	37.46
Florida	34	7,843	36	807	28	7,179	30	6,820	41	2,233	8	84.22
Oklahoma	35	7,249	40	620	34	6,096	24	7,884	34	4,836	34	36.78
New Hampshire	36	6,682	13	1,738	36	5,190	38	4,808	35	4,245	29	39.47
Maine	37	6,376	20	1,450	38	4,981	37	4,884	36	4,057	27	41.87
Virginia	38	5,819	27	1,226	37	5,016	36	5,278	37	3,441	21	51.16
West Virginia	39	4,983	34	941	39	4,138	39	4,170	38	3,313	31	38.85
Kentucky	40	4,177	38	664	40	3,535	40	3,939	39	2,597	26	43.73
Tennessee	41	3,639	41	602	41	3,025	42	3,621	42	2,198	28	41.28
North Carolina	42	3,451	39	653	42	3,018	43	3,492	40	2,427	23	46.75
Louisiana	43	3,108	45	447	43	2,590	41	3,718	44	1,728	24	44.70
South Carolina	44	2,784	43	519	44	2,401	44	3,490	45	1,692	35	36.48
Arkansas	45	2,682	47	391	45	2,261	46	2,907	43	1,801	37	34.13
Georgia	46	2,674	44	483	46	2,259	45	3,236	46	1,629	41	26.15
Alabama	47	2,375	46	408	47	1,952	47	2,795	47	1,420	40	28.62
Mississippi	48	2,216	48	377	48	1,818	48	2,721	48	1,358	38	32.79

other regions: value of domestic animals per farm $247 and $8,385; gross income from livestock, $209 and $4,371; value of farm lands and buildings, $1,800 and $25,000; gallons of milk per farm, 333 and 6,829. Deficiencies in coöperatives are measured in terms of the exceedingly small number and variety of organizations and by the small ratio of sales. In 1930 around two per cent of the farms in the region were selling through coöperatives as opposed to 51 per cent in Minnesota; while the lowest southeastern state showed less than one per cent of all cash sales from coöperatives as opposed to 30 per cent for the highest state of the nation.

92. Composite deficiencies which relate to the land and its products are reflected again in such vivid examples as Christmas trees shipped from Pacific states to the Carolinas, land of green trees; spinach and carrots from California, a chief supply for southeastern towns, 3,000 miles away; or southern farmers buying winter rutabagas from Canada and cabbage from everywhere; California's 589,000 cases of eggs shipped annually to New York compared with quantities shipped from the nearby Carolinas so negligible as not to be recorded; carload lots of milk and cheese and butter from the Middle States' dairy regions into southern areas, disgracefully deficient in dairy cows; or less than six per cent of the cheese factories in a region admirably equipped for production; or retail prices of southern farm products far below those of imported ones. Similar deficiency is found in the millions of dollars expended for importing into the Southeast from western states hay and corn and other feed stuffs, the retail price for which to the southern farmer must include the increment for freight and handling sometimes nearly equivalent to the farm price of the commodity. Still another deficiency is found in the shortage of all plant seed for field crops, garden, grasses, and legumes. A $20,000,000 shortage of field peas reflects a threefold remediable deficiency in land improvement, feed production, and cash income or outgo.

93. The long roll of technological lag and waste will be continued in the subsequent inventory of the agrarian South. Yet even for the present purpose of summary, the catalogue is not complete without reference to another major group of deficiencies which involve also the basic consumption of producers' goods. This is the great deficiency reflected in millions of rural homes and farm buildings, unpainted and out of repair, and basically below any adequate standard of culture, alongside waste of lumber and superabundance of labor. Here is deficiency enough to provide unemployment insurance for a long time to come provided organization, finance, management, and technology can be harnessed together. Further shortage of producers' goods exists in facilities and equipment for sanitation and water supply, and for storing and processing of products. So, too,

Per Cent Geographic Distribution of the Aggregate Personal Income of the Farm and Non-Farm Population, 1929

Adapted from Leven, Moulton, Warburton. *America's Capacity to Consume*, Table 16, p. 172.

State and Region	Income of Entire Population	Income of Non-Farm Population	Income of Farm Population *
Southeast	*10.00*	*8.60*	*24.30*
Virginia	1.14	1.04	2.12
North Carolina	1.09	0.88	3.21
South Carolina	0.50	0.40	1.44
Georgia	1.09	0.95	2.55
Florida	0.86	0.81	1.40
Kentucky	1.13	1.04	2.13
Tennessee	0.99	0.88	2.02
Alabama	0.95	0.82	2.29
Mississippi	0.63	0.41	2.82
Arkansas	0.63	0.44	2.51
Louisiana	1.00	0.92	1.85
Southwest	*5.20*	*4.40*	*12.70*
Oklahoma	1.31	1.14	3.00
Texas	3.34	2.83	8.44
New Mexico	0.22	0.17	0.68
Arizona	0.35	0.32	0.68
Northeast	*42.50*	*45.40*	*13.60*
Maine	0.56	0.53	0.93
New Hampshire	0.33	0.34	0.25
Vermont	0.25	0.23	0.49
Massachusetts	4.51	4.87	0.86
Rhode Island	0.66	0.71	0.11
Connecticut	1.76	1.87	0.62
New York	18.61	20.03	4.25
New Jersey	4.37	4.71	1.04
Delaware	0.34	0.36	0.21
Pennsylvania	8.56	9.09	3.15
Maryland	1.42	1.46	0.93
West Virginia	0.91	0.91	0.86

State and Region	Income of Entire Population	Income of Non-Farm Population	Income of Farm Population *
Middle States	*28.50*	*29.00*	*23.40*
Ohio	5.74	6.00	3.13
Indiana	2.17	2.17	2.18
Illinois	8.17	8.62	3.62
Michigan	4.53	4.72	2.68
Wisconsin	2.18	1.99	4.13
Minnesota	1.71	1.61	2.66
Iowa	1.31	1.19	2.49
Missouri	2.57	2.57	2.56
Northwest	*4.60*	*3.70*	*13.00*
North Dakota	0.31	0.20	1.45
South Dakota	0.32	0.22	1.26
Nebraska	0.78	0.67	1.99
Kansas	1.17	0.97	3.21
Montana	0.41	0.35	1.09
Idaho	0.30	0.20	1.26
Wyoming	0.19	0.15	0.57
Colorado	0.78	0.70	1.58
Utah	0.33	0.30	0.65
Far West	*8.90*	*8.50*	*12.60*
Nevada	0.10	0.09	0.16
Washington	1.43	1.34	2.35
Oregon	0.78	0.71	1.50
California	6.56	6.35	8.64

*Includes income from non-agricultural sources.

Per Capita Personal Income, by Geographic Divisions and States, 1929

Adapted from Leven, Moulton, Warburton. *America's Capacity to Consume*, Table 17, p. 173.

State and Region	Entire Population	Non-Farm Population	Farm Population
Southeast	*$365*	*$535*	*$183*
Virginia	431	594	182
North Carolina	317	472	167
South Carolina	261	412	129
Georgia	343	532	147
Florida	548	577	419
Kentucky	398	605	148
Tennessee	346	529	137
Alabama	331	527	141
Mississippi	287	530	173
Arkansas	311	503	185
Louisiana	438	603	186
Southwest	*564*	*683*	*366*
Oklahoma	503	699	243
Texas	531	690	298
New Mexico	476	549	354
Arizona	744	795	567
Northeast	*881*	*946*	*366*
Maine	645	689	474
New Hampshire	652	689	379
Vermont	633	761	351
Massachusetts	975	976	898
Rhode Island	881	881	859
Connecticut	1,008	1,028	630
New York	1,365	1,417	493
New Jersey	1,002	1,011	704
Delaware	1,315	1,550	368
Pennsylvania	815	865	305
Maryland	799	881	323
West Virginia	485	602	157

State and Region	Entire Population	Non-Farm Population	Farm Population
Middle States	*$715*	*$854*	*$262*
Ohio	795	893	255
Indiana	614	748	221
Illinois	987	1,091	299
Michigan	869	983	283
Wisconsin	682	807	389
Minnesota	610	802	248
Iowa	485	659	214
Missouri	675	851	189
Northwest	*590*	*703*	*426*
North Dakota	422	588	302
South Dakota	420	614	268
Nebraska	521	698	281
Kansas	569	686	376
Montana	698	856	435
Idaho	609	647	559
Wyoming	777	841	648
Colorado	690	772	470
Utah	600	629	496
Far West	*921*	*953*	*818*
Nevada	1,000	1,041	811
Washington	841	887	651
Oregon	757	817	563
California	1,085	1,066	1,246

the region is short millions of dollars worth of fencing materials for making usable millions of acres for pasturage to help supply its shortage of millions of livestock in a new reconstructed southern economy which must point the "way on" from an increasingly inadequate cotton economy.

94. To hazard a general summary in terms of an adequate farming economy, capable of actual measurement by numbers of farms, the Southeast, in comparison with the mode of other regions, lags in every item of a twelve-point scale. These include farm ownership, balanced animal and plant production, balanced plant crops, enrichment of land and increasing of values, adequate home-grown feeds, efficient cultivation, adequate fencing, well planned fields and forest areas, adequate housing for animals and tools, farm management and accounting, care in preparation of commodities for market, motivation for the enrichment of farm life, measured by the type of housing, household equipment, and coöperative arrangements. Since the physical and human resources for the raising of standards in all of these are available and since these deficiencies are the natural products of chronological and technological lag, reflecting rural and pioneer heritage, the analysis may well point to immediate programs of progress.

95. The significance of this technological lag in the agrarian South is emphasized again by contrast with a certain superior technology in the building and maintenance of roads, in the development of transportation facilities, in the expansion of light and power, and in certain aspects of industrial development which in turn must be contrasted again with lag in finance, science, institutional leadership, and in the human-use aspects of industrial technology, basic to optimum development of the region. Indeed the measure of what used to be called "the New South" is largely a measure of change wrought by industrial technology.

96. In expenditure for highways and in the character of the best roads, the Southeast excels, while in railroad mileage and equipment the Southeast shows 9.5 square miles to the rail mile as compared with 11.9 for the nation. Or for each 10,000 persons in the United States there are 34 miles of railroad compared to 39 in the Southeast. In industry the Southeast has made unusual advances. For instance, from 1914 to 1929, the index of value of products per horse power of industrial machinery in the textiles had increased from 56 per cent of the national product to 67 per cent, providing almost 60 per cent of the nation's spindles. In furniture and tobacco manufacture the region set new paces with its technology, producing 84 per cent of the nation's cigarettes with 17.2 per cent of its factories. In technology of iron and steel the region excels as it does also in hydroelectric plants, petroleum refineries, rayon and paper mills, and in certain shipyards, sawmills, fertilizer factories, and other selected industries.

Estimated Tangible Wealth Per Capita of Total Population By States, 1930

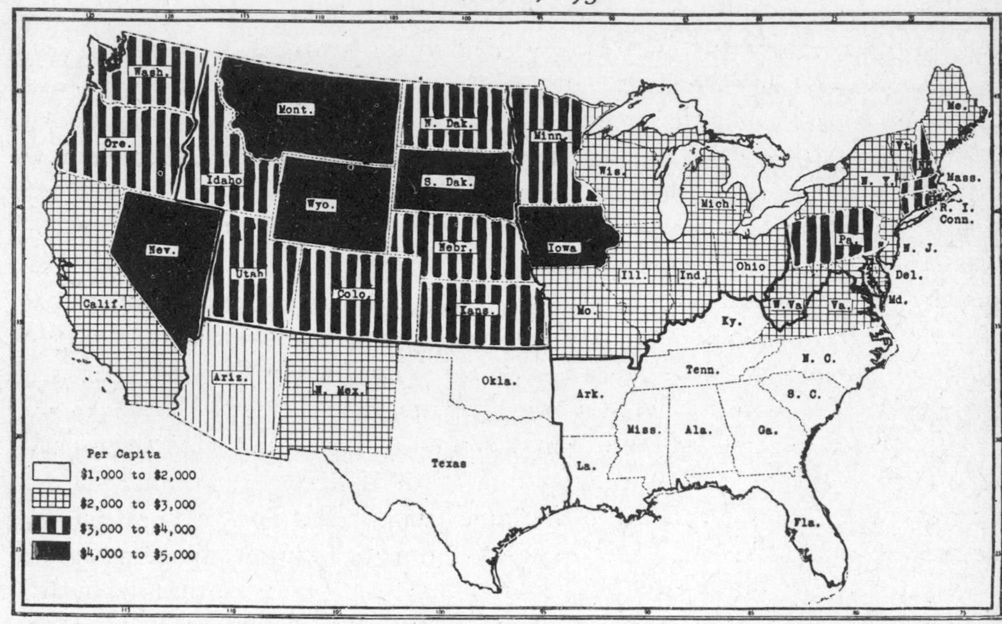

It should be noted that, for the most part, maps on upper page represent different data from the tables below. This is important both to give greater variety and for the reader to avoid confusion.

Differentials in Per Capita Wealth in the United States

STATE	Per Capita Estimated True Wealth 1930	Inhabitants Per Income Tax Return 1930	Bank Resources Per Capita 1928	Average Federal Income Tax Paid 1928
Southeast				
Virginia	$2,081	62.6	$267.91	$117.20
North Carolina	1,482	109.0	176.88	195.23
South Carolina	1,423	131.4	131.45	52.21
Georgia	1,377	90.0	149.31	115.63
Florida	1,710	48.8	345.24	239.91
Kentucky	1,399	75.5	248.12	159.45
Tennessee	1,667	75.4	219.56	160.51
Alabama	1,155	102.1	144.94	150.08
Mississippi	1,110	128.1	158.39	47.32
Arkansas	1,430	117.2	138.40	52.69
Louisiana	1,662	59.0	274.42	118.44
Southwest				
Oklahoma	1,683	64.7	219.30	173.00
Texas	1,720	51.2	257.31	128.28
New Mexico	2,057	61.5	121.75	69.46
Arizona	3,118	34.9	206.94	138.83
Northeast				
Maine	2,591	41.5	636.40	229.03
New Hampshire	3,044	32.4	705.97	140.95
Vermont	2,399	37.5	790.57	112.38
Massachusetts	3,144	19.9	1,226.35	277.14
Rhode Island	2,875	25.9	816.96	313.67
Connecticut	3,389	19.5	857.07	285.02
New York	2,987	16.6	1,735.34	578.67
New Jersey	2,990	20.6	736.32	263.82
Delaware	2,706	24.3	673.10	1,104.35
Pennsylvania	3,068	26.4	693.65	267.90
Maryland	2,506	23.7	598.74	247.12
West Virginia	2,775	58.0	256.54	95.32
Middle States				
Ohio	$2,859	30.7	$494.73	$253.54
Indiana	2,786	42.2	384.52	134.01
Illinois	2,985	20.6	662.12	296.18
Michigan	2,419	27.2	524.47	281.29
Wisconsin	2,774	28.5	385.54	126.51
Minnesota	3,403	42.2	422.37	196.29
Iowa	4,322	54.8	419.86	152.40
Missouri	2,819	36.8	459.40	190.45
Northwest				
North Dakota	3,653	74.2	253.14	21.57
South Dakota	4,356	66.3	254.59	30.19
Nebraska	3,927	44.5	385.50	67.12
Kansas	3,381	50.0	296.24	88.92
Montana	4,262	31.4	348.02	75.85
Idaho	3,577	45.2	193.61	28.87
Wyoming	4,480	27.7	295.55	43.16
Colorado	3,165	33.1	318.78	143.42
Utah	3,106	38.5	351.83	82.63
Far West				
Nevada	5,985	17.6	633.90	106.69
Washington	3,342	23.9	348.67	67.48
Oregon	3,658	33.8	373.10	81.39
California	2,692	18.0	883.05	201.14
United States	2,620	....	593.51	176.97

97. It is in the regional balance and range of technology, in the human-use aspects, and in the representation of corporate control that the region's technology lags again. Of an aggregate of 161 units in the 29 great concentration centers of iron and steel industries, only five are in the Southeast, representing only four of the industries. Of an aggregate of 195 units in major concentration of food industries only 28 are in the Southeast, 16 of these being devoted to manufactured ice and beverages. Of the 30 great industrial areas where workers are concentrated, none is in the South; of more than 6,700 milk processing plants in the nation, only 236, or 3.5 per cent, are in the South. Of the great corporate bodies in finance and commerce, the South's share is negligible. In manufacturing the South fails to produce more than twenty of the major commodities, while its manufacturing processes are largely confined to the more elementary products.

98. Income and wages rank uniformly from 30 to 50 per cent below the national level. This differential corresponds to some extent to a similar differential in skill and training of workers and of machinery in the region adapted to its resources and to the better training of its workers. The lag in human use is illustrated by the case of furniture manufacture, where the Southeast furnished 17 per cent of the nation's workers, 11 per cent of the pay roll, 12 per cent of value added to products. As compared with the nation's $3,600, the Southeast's value added per wage earner was less than $2,000. Also from 1914 to 1929 the real wages of the southeastern worker tended to decrease by one-third. Thus, while there has been some consistent absolute mechanical gain in the region, there has been a progressive lag. In those cases where cash return per technological unit is higher than the average, it may denote man power use instead of inanimate power and a higher degree of pre-technological use in competition with technological production.

99. A major deficiency is the lack of invested capital and surplus wealth to develop requisite industry. Of the 100 largest banks in the nation, the Southeast has three with less than one and one-half per cent of the total deposits. The Southeast in 1929 reported only seven of the 513 individuals with an income of one million dollars; 34 out of 1,482 with income of a half million; 96 out of 4,053 with an income of a quarter million; and only 441 out of 14,677 with an income of $100,000. The Southeast's contracted access to capital is expressed in a differential of a third more in rates of interest. The South is also a debtor region, accentuating scarcity of capital wealth through its imports from other regions of great quantities of luxuries and equipment at excess speed alongside great inequalities of income, as compared with the richer regions.

Per Cent Which Net Gain or Loss by Interstate Migration Forms of Number Born in the State, 1930

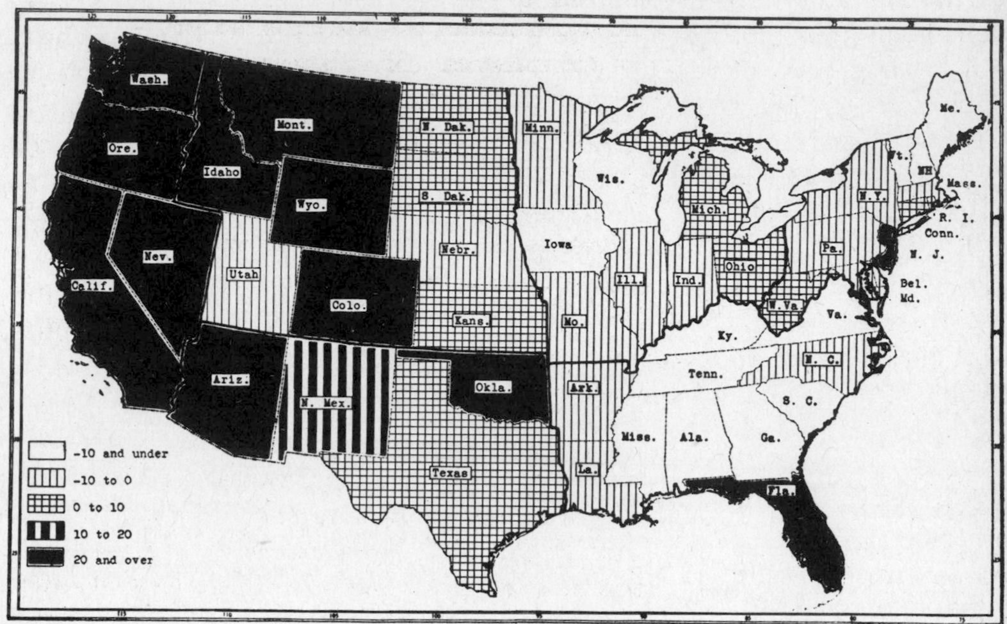

Percentage Measure of Interstate Migration, 1930

Adapted from Galpin and Manny, *Interstate Migrations among the Native White Population as Indicated by Differences between State of Birth and State of Residence*, pp. 6-7

STATE AND REGION	Natives of Each State Living in Other States	Migrants Born in Other States Living in Each State
Southeast		
Virginia	25.3	14.8
North Carolina	14.2	9.2
South Carolina	18.7	12.7
Georgia	23.0	12.4
Florida	16.5	50.6
Kentucky	28.9	10.7
Tennessee	27.9	14.6
Alabama	23.5	14.8
Mississippi	27.4	13.9
Arkansas	35.9	26.1
Louisiana	16.6	16.0
Southwest		
Oklahoma	28.6	51.9
Texas	16.5	24.5
New Mexico	26.9	42.3
Arizona	40.4	72.7
Northeast		
Maine	26.3	9.0
New Hampshire	34.9	26.8
Vermont	38.5	18.8
Massachusetts	17.8	15.7
Rhode Island	22.3	22.6
Connecticut	20.6	24.3
New York	16.2	12.9
New Jersey	16.2	30.6
Delaware	31.1	28.8
Pennsylvania	18.7	8.6
Maryland	21.2	19.9
West Virginia	22.3	17.8
Middle States		
Ohio	20.3	20.3
Indiana	27.7	20.6
Illinois	25.9	21.7
Michigan	16.9	26.3
Wisconsin	24.4	14.6
Minnesota	26.5	23.2
Iowa	37.6	21.3
Missouri	34.7	24.0
Northwest		
North Dakota	31.2	31.9
South Dakota	33.9	38.3
Nebraska	34.0	29.4
Kansas	39.2	36.3
Montana	37.9	53.6
Idaho	37.6	53.8
Wyoming	44.6	64.7
Colorado	38.6	55.7
Utah	27.4	16.9
Far West		
Nevada	53.7	64.7
Washington	24.0	56.6
Oregon	28.5	54.7
California	8.7	59.1

100. These deficiencies in the balance of wealth and trade are matched by the migratory flow of people from the South which shows a net loss of more than 3,400,000 people since the turn of the century. Among these was a large ratio of its best equipped workers, educators, and scientists. This is reflected in the negligible part which the South has in nearly all national organizations and agencies of science, education, and social welfare, and in positions of leadership in national affairs other than current politics. The measure of the region's leadership in national management is generally considerably less than five per cent as compared with its approximately 21 per cent of population, 17 per cent of area, and 12 per cent of wealth. In the great majority of the dominant national groups the southern representation on the executive or controlling boards is negligible. The same is true in most of the New Deal units of administration in contrast to the large representation in Congress.

101. A part of the region's deficiency in organization and personnel is due to migration as is indicated by the positions of leadership which southern folk have attained in other regions and by constant call of superior appointments; a part is due to the deficiency in institutions for higher education and technical training; a part to the deficiency in organizations and technical equipment necessary for apprenticeship and development; a part to lack of cultural experience and to the inhibiting influence of a constricting intellectual environment; a part to the inhibiting influences of a physical environment, standards of housing, of diet, of work. Poverty and isolation, lack of medical attention, and lack of economic opportunity constrict millions in cultural and economic experience. Greatest waste of all is reflected in the vast potential power of millions of youth, undeveloped and untrained, moving through life without sensing their abilities or maturing their capacities, oblivious of the wide reaches of opportunity.

102. The measure of human waste will be found in the later inventory of institutions. These are shown in the ranking of the Southeastern States in the lowest quartile of nearly all indices of health and education, of government and public welfare, and of the multiple cultural equipment of the people. Certain aspects of this waste, however, represent such elemental factors in the composite picture as to require cataloguing here. Such is the pathology of submarginal folk, of killings and homicides, of state conflicts and rivalries, of sectarian strife, of race conflict, of lynchings and mobs, of drain and strain in intemperate work and living for men, women, and children. Partial samplings from the field of health and diet will illustrate the case. Pellagra, a form of malnutrition, demonstrably curable or preventable, has occurred in the past in perhaps two per cent of the whole population and within subregions in very large ratios. From 50 to 90

Per Cent Coöperative Sales Were of Cash Farm Income, 1929

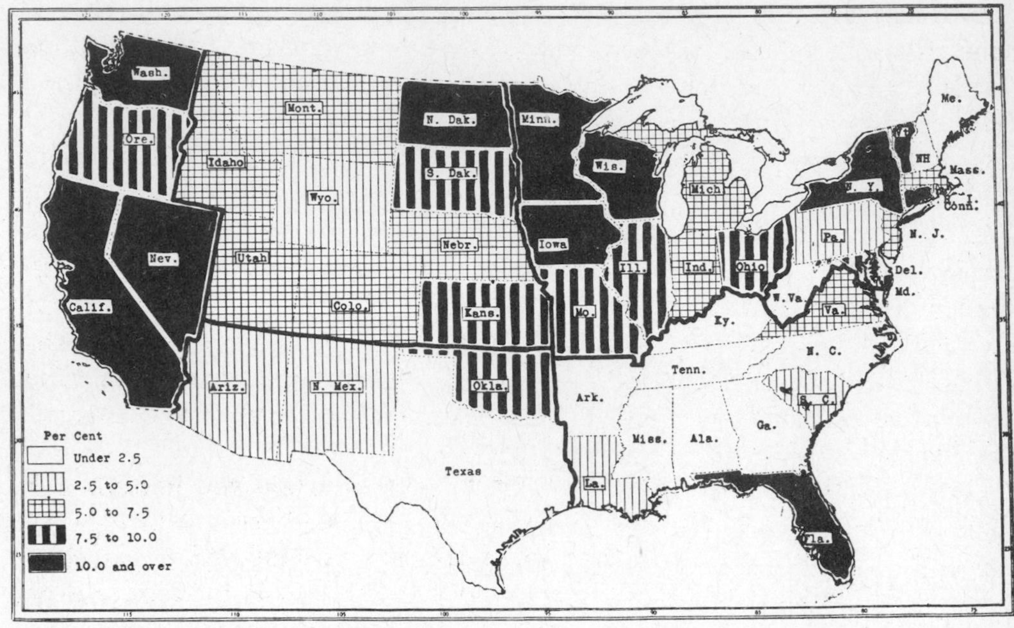

Average Annual Wage Per Wage Earner in All Manufactures, 1929

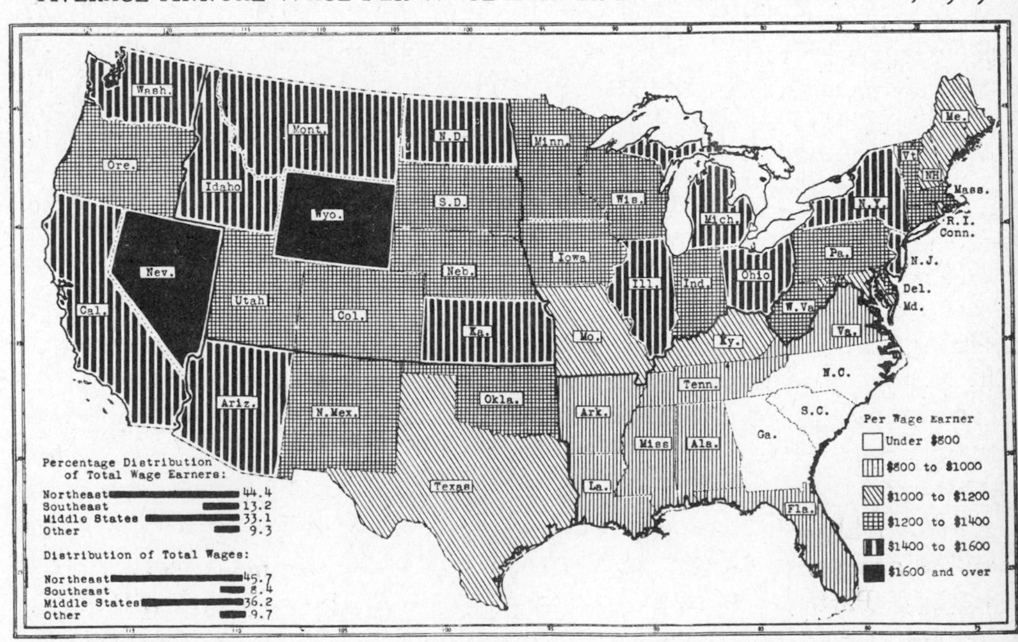

per cent of southern children in large areas receive inadequate diets for any normal health standard; perhaps more than 50 per cent of all school children examined show carious teeth; standard tests show inadequacy of minerals and proteins in most food. There is large waste in tuberculosis, rickets, anemia, and many other results of poor diet. All of this in a land peculiarly fitted for a superabundance of food of all sorts, rich in minerals, vitamines, and proteins. In addition to these basic deficiencies, there is the other side of the picture which reflects waste in malnutrition, unbalanced diet, richness of foods, and other allied factors, to which must be added an enormous waste in the money value of human life and morbidity, estimated in billions of dollars.

103. Inventory of technological lag and waste must, however, be in terms of perspective and of regional and subregional interrelationship. Minimum considerations will include attainable standards of life and culture, measured partly by economic indices, partly by physiological optima, partly by a congruous set of values, which, within the bounds of inside and outside influences, fix the conditions and capacities of human life. All of these, inventoried with due regard to equilibrium and balance, are measures of the difficulties and prospects of planning. They must, moreover, be measured in relation to new reaches in practical technological wealth, such as will yield millions of dollars in value from the pine tree and cotton stalk, from chemical transformations of corn and wheat, and a seemingly unlimited development of "the farm chemurgic" calculated to return the farm to its basic place in regional economy. Here are involved also the mandatory technics for the development of skills in both old and new occupational opportunities and for increasing basic home consumption of goods and for balancing thereby a larger production economy.

104. Irreducible minimum for technological development must be abundance of capital wealth necessary for factory or farm, for tools and science, for laboratory experimentation, for metropolitan concentration, for transportation facilities and port development, for rural electrification, for the flow of men and money into a region in which much of deficiency in technology is explained partly not as southern or regional but as chronological lag. This may be illustrated in many instances of southeastern deficiency which conforms to the status of the whole nation only a few generations ago. Much of it again is rural rather than primarily southern, and the solution of this problem must be found partly in the measure of the new agrarian South. In addition to these basic factors of chronological lag, rural lag, and capital wealth deficiencies, there remain the very dynamic essentials of drawing power and of specific opportunities

Regional Distribution of Agricultural Commodities

Per Cent Gross Value Each Commodity Is of the Total in Each State and Region

STATE AND REGION	Cereals	Other Grains and Seeds	Hay and Forage	Vegetables (including all potatoes)	Fruits and Nuts	All other field crops	Farm Garden Vegetables	Dairy Products	Chicken Eggs Produced	Chickens Raised	Wool	Beef Cattle (gross income)	Hogs (gross income)
Southeast	*15.83*	*1.51*	*4.08*	*6.00*	*3.98*	*41.59*	*3.61*	*6.37*	*4.24*	*3.58*	*.12*	*2.90*	*6.17*
Virginia	19.26	2.53	7.77	12.92	8.10	10.71	4.39	9.14	7.16	5.96	.32	4.66	6.90
North Carolina	13.37	2.91	3.01	5.28	2.19	47.66	3.66	5.32	3.80	3.70	.04	1.39	7.58
South Carolina	12.93	.90	2.04	6.91	1.04	54.87	3.20	4.48	3.04	3.39	.01	1.37	5.77
Georgia	12.75	3.44	1.53	4.99	2.35	49.76	2.77	5.90	3.17	2.97	.01	1.86	8.41
Florida	5.10	1.34	.71	21.67	41.06	7.78	1.71	6.06	4.24	2.75	.03	1.92	5.49
Kentucky	21.98	.39	7.95	3.37	1.45	23.96	4.83	10.13	5.61	4.72	.54	6.12	9.13
Tennessee	21.75	.66	8.58	5.00	1.89	25.85	3.87	9.08	5.73	4.18	.17	4.78	8.36
Alabama	15.93	2.47	2.97	4.86	1.58	56.77	4.37	7.68	4.33	3.21	.02	2.33	6.27
Mississippi	10.65	.45	2.36	3.90	.63	62.04	3.87	5.48	2.69	2.31	.03	2.02	3.53
Arkansas	12.88	.39	3.87	2.84	2.73	54.33	3.01	6.25	4.00	3.02	.02	2.32	4.27
Louisiana	18.40	.75	2.03	5.53	3.01	50.37	3.22	4.16	3.49	2.98	.07	2.95	2.97
Southwest	*18.75*	*.82*	*5.35*	*2.56*	*1.21*	*39.30*	*1.48*	*7.17*	*4.69*	*3.17*	*1.16*	*9.36*	*4.39*
Oklahoma	27.53	.49	5.06	1.62	1.03	30.01	1.67	8.75	5.53	4.44	.06	7.16	6.70
Texas	16.22	.45	4.80	2.55	1.03	45.49	1.51	6.49	4.50	2.83	1.28	8.32	3.77
New Mexico	14.29	6.65	9.44	2.73	2.72	15.67	.94	5.24	3.03	1.66	4.67	30.53	1.84
Arizona	2.41	1.67	11.33	9.39	3.64	35.00	.42	10.08	3.85	1.74	2.58	16.01	1.10
Northeast	*10.08*	*.50*	*12.93*	*14.73*	*5.31*	*2.23*	*1.98*	*27.24*	*9.30*	*6.62*	*.24*	*4.80*	*3.90*
Maine	3.01	.44	9.13	54.99	3.26	.09	1.73	13.01	5.48	4.17	.16	2.62	1.86
New Hampshire	.72	.02	16.70	7.81	4.53	1.02	2.59	31.87	13.25	13.90	.12	4.96	2.39
Vermont	1.79	.18	22.63	4.45	2.54	3.44	1.51	45.35	4.17	2.81	.15	7.89	2.97
Massachusetts	.57	.02	10.40	12.06	8.87	6.30	1.78	30.82	11.63	10.53	.03	2.08	4.87
Rhode Island	1.01	.18	10.92	10.49	5.49	......	1.92	45.33	12.11	9.67	.03	.35	2.43
Connecticut	1.12	.12	12.07	7.02	3.33	20.85	1.74	30.48	10.49	8.61	.03	2.26	1.81
New York	5.36	1.18	16.67	12.03	5.84	.31	1.07	36.69	7.97	4.92	.23	5.52	2.02
New Jersey	7.12	.12	7.17	26.82	7.97	......	1.41	20.31	14.80	10.89	.01	1.63	1.67
Delaware	20.16	1.92	5.24	14.36	11.42	......	1.93	11.83	14.91	12.95	.02	2.30	2.89
Pennsylvania	17.40	.08	12.17	9.88	3.38	1.50	1.97	24.43	10.08	6.96	.25	5.45	6.32
Maryland	22.62	.46	7.32	16.08	4.93	5.29	2.06	17.28	8.30	6.75	.18	3.37	5.28
West Virginia	16.89	.20	12.27	6.70	9.87	1.33	7.89	12.43	9.56	5.24	1.06	8.80	7.54
Middle States	*28.07*	*1.57*	*9.28*	*3.60*	*1.28*	*1.08*	*1.14*	*15.94*	*6.05*	*4.60*	*.34*	*8.28*	*18.66*
Ohio	27.29	.89	8.53	5.36	1.72	1.67	1.93	16.00	8.78	6.38	1.01	5.47	14.84
Indiana	29.94	1.28	6.82	3.26	1.06	1.04	1.50	11.96	6.87	6.09	.31	6.72	23.04
Illinois	39.72	1.44	6.80	2.00	1.45	.16	1.02	10.88	5.40	4.75	.16	6.46	19.65
Michigan	14.87	6.73	13.49	8.86	5.01	1.04	1.04	21.75	7.07	5.12	.80	7.70	6.28
Wisconsin	12.21	.80	16.75	5.69	.79	1.26	.79	37.72	4.40	2.95	.14	7.92	8.56
Minnesota	28.30	2.67	11.32	4.99	.38	.36	.65	18.98	4.55	3.26	.21	8.44	15.69
Iowa	35.06	.61	6.17	1.19	.44	.09	.81	8.29	4.83	3.83	.20	11.00	27.40
Missouri	23.13	.68	8.01	1.76	1.64	4.57	2.05	9.30	9.30	6.24	.40	9.78	23.04
Northwest	*36.23*	*2.76*	*9.66*	*3.35*	*.93*	*1.77*	*.62*	*8.04*	*4.13*	*3.05*	*1.50*	*13.57*	*14.29*
North Dakota	50.92	6.91	7.39	2.92	.03	.16	.35	11.06	2.54	2.01	.56	6.61	8.47
South Dakota	38.16	3.32	7.19	1.47	.11	.25	.51	8.64	4.00	3.16	.55	12.32	20.23
Nebraska	38.12	.28	6.84	1.84	.28	1.13	.57	5.80	3.53	3.20	.11	14.64	23.63
Kansas	43.49	.35	6.83	1.13	.65	.22	.67	7.47	6.17	4.34	.11	14.73	13.79
Montana	29.94	5.47	17.02	2.36	.70	1.77	.80	8.11	2.81	1.74	6.10	17.80	5.25
Idaho	22.82	9.73	17.28	11.66	4.83	2.66	.90	10.14	3.07	1.75	3.86	6.99	4.12
Wyoming	12.19	3.59	19.62	3.78	.17	5.51	.99	7.52	2.56	1.45	11.44	26.55	4.35
Colorado	19.04	3.60	14.72	11.05	2.80	9.50	.60	7.83	3.62	2.34	1.68	16.20	6.79
Utah	11.11	1.39	21.17	6.62	3.61	5.52	.80	14.25	7.57	3.99	8.32	12.54	2.55
Far West	*10.70*	*2.72*	*10.42*	*7.98*	*30.63*	*2.91*	*.56*	*12.65*	*7.09*	*3.61*	*1.17*	*6.93*	*2.54*
Nevada	3.74	.23	32.03	5.39	.57	.01	.72	9.88	3.35	2.08	10.11	27.90	3.75
Washington	22.93	.93	10.86	6.73	21.40	.46	1.10	13.08	10.03	4.49	.65	4.52	2.76
Oregon	20.60	.84	16.83	5.18	11.96	1.85	1.61	14.53	6.02	2.79	3.46	9.33	4.75
California	5.47	3.66	8.50	8.94	37.65	3.89	.19	12.23	6.55	3.55	.67	6.61	2.02
United States	22.58	1.67	8.46	5.54	4.67	13.01	1.61	12.95	5.69	4.14	.64	7.74	11.14

and occasions for redirecting the flow of resources and technics into the region, and in relation to the people and their institutions.

105. Further aspects of technology, deficiency, and waste will appear in their relation to the agrarian South, to the industry and wealth of the region and to the people and their institutions.

VIII. AN AGRARIAN COUNTRY

106. Key to the Southeast is the agrarian South, old and new. This is true not only because of the economic and romantic aspects of the Old South, but because of more recent developments and the prospects for regional agricultural reconstruction. On the one hand, it is often assumed that the South is the most fertile field in the Union for agrarian recovery; and, on the other, it is known that internal agricultural readjustment is an irreducible minimum for survival on any adequate cultural basis. In addition to deficiency units in agricultural production and farm and home standards already catalogued, there are certain other aspects of the agrarian heritage and promise which give definitive character to the region.

107. Inherent in its dynamic part in the region's past and future are the meanings and implications of agrarian culture. There was, of course, the spell of the old plantation economy, significant not only for its way of life but for its subsequent influence upon the tenant system and other aspects of cotton economy. To many, agrarianism means a trend back toward the glory that was the Old South. Yet the substance of the nostalgic yearnings of this particular group of agrarians is little more than this: the culture of the Old South, if it had been what it was purported to be, which it was not, would have constituted a magnificent contribution to a richer civilization; therefore, go to, let us turn back to that agrarian ideal as relief from the maladjusted industrialism of the new era. Manifestly, there is little realism here.

108. There remain, however, some aspects of this agrarian ideal which yet retain the motivation of agriculture as a way of life, to be adapted to a new equilibrium between rural and urban, between agricultural and industrial life. Here are included the ideals of those who, as Julia Peterkin points out, yearn for the peace and quiet of country places with leisure to possess their own souls and with abundance of things for the comfort of minds and bodies. "To realize the earth's generosity to those who have joy in sowing and reaping," so runs the theme, "gives a deep sense of security and a faith in the rightness of things." For such an ideal the Southeast is peculiarly well equipped by nature and awaits that new planning which will transvaluate the poverty-breeding system of tenant and landlord into that abundant life so pictured.

Per Cent of Total Population Living on Farms, 1930

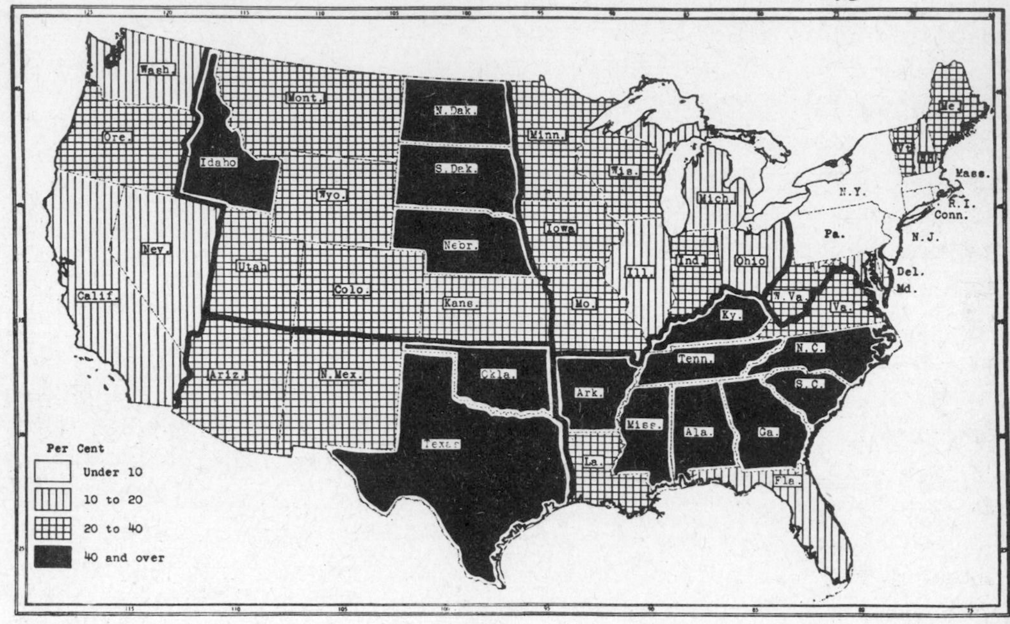

Regional Variation in Number of Agricultural Extension Workers, 1934

STATE AND REGION	Counties	Farm Agents	Home Demonstration Agents	Boys' and Girls' Club Agents	All Others	Total
Southeast	*977*	*1,192*	*718*	*32*	*882*	*2,824*
Virginia	100	138	54	2	58	252
North Carolina	100	133	106	1	93	333
South Carolina	46	68	59	3	71	201
Georgia	161	176	101	3	166	446
Florida	67	52	36	1	33	122
Kentucky	120	135	30	7	42	214
Tennessee	95	109	49	1	59	218
Alabama	67	100	65	3	97	265
Mississippi	82	107	78	7	111	303
Arkansas	75	94	78	2	84	258
Louisiana	64	80	62	2	68	212
Southwest	*376*	*417*	*283*	*5*	*330*	*1,035*
Oklahoma	77	102	89	3	87	281
Texas	254	277	178	1	214	670
New Mexico	31	21	10	...	15	46
Arizona	14	17	6	1	14	38
Northeast	*298*	*344*	*235*	*162*	*330*	*1,071*
Maine	16	17	15	9	15	56
New Hampshire	10	12	11	15	19	57
Vermont	14	15	10	13	11	49
Massachusetts	14	19	15	29	24	87
Rhode Island	5	3	4	4	8	19
Connecticut	8	10	9	15	25	59
New York	62	86	48	45	85	264
New Jersey	21	24	19	8	23	74
Delaware	3	3	4	3	7	17
Pennsylvania	67	72	48	6	44	170
Maryland	23	33	27	2	37	99
West Virginia	55	50	25	13	32	120

STATE AND REGION	Counties	Farm Agents	Home Demonstration Agents	Boys' and Girls' Club Agents	All Others	Total
Middle States	*736*	*787*	*142*	*119*	*344*	*1,392*
Ohio	88	88	24	15	46	173
Indiana	92	98	12	12	34	156
Illinois	102	99	37	9	34	179
Michigan	83	70	6	18	45	139
Wisconsin	71	66	9	11	49	135
Minnesota	87	88	15	44	29	176
Iowa	99	140	23	6	70	239
Missouri	114	138	16	4	37	195
Northwest	*535*	*512*	*109*	*28*	*175*	*824*
North Dakota	53	67	9	2	13	91
South Dakota	69	74	16	5	15	110
Nebraska	93	99	16	7	30	152
Kansas	105	114	31	6	38	189
Montana	56	33	10	2	14	59
Idaho	44	33	7	2	18	60
Wyoming	23	21	6	1	9	37
Colorado	63	46	7	1	23	77
Utah	29	25	7	2	15	49
Far West	*150*	*230*	*53*	*19*	*70*	*372*
Nevada	17	13	5	...	5	23
Washington	39	55	10	5	14	84
Oregon	36	52	8	11	17	88
California	58	110	30	3	34	177

109. Another meaning is that which sets the agricultural economy simply but clearly over against industrialism. This envisages the imbalance between country life and urban trends and their contrasting character of life and labor. Such an ideal, however, allows liberally for suitable industrial development, decentralized and featuring the coördination of small industries and village industrial centers with small-scale farming. It allows for new developments in subsistence farming and in the great natural increase of basic consumption of farm commodities. The new agrarian culture, furthermore, is fabricated upon the assumption of reasonable advances in rural electrification, good roads, and ample tools and facilities for richer living. Here again the Southeast excels in its natural equipment and awaits only the technics of a new day.

110. The most realistic implication of the agrarian South, however, is found in the actual picture of the present Southeast. After all, the region is primarily rural, constituting in area almost the whole landscape; in people, three-fourths and more of the population, either in actuality or in experience and interest. The region ranks second only to the great agricultural Middle States in composite measure of its commodity production. Moreover, the Southeast receives more than 25 per cent of its income from agriculture as opposed to about 12.5 per cent for the nation. Its percentage of gainfully employed in extractive work, 45.7, is the highest of any region, as is its ratio of farm population to the total. The burden and implications of agrarianism include further the processes of change and conflict reflected in a heavy migration cityward and the whole recent decade of country life bankruptcy. Likewise, part of the agrarian problem is that of attaining an enduring balance between rural and urban civilization. A part is the reconstruction of cotton economy. A part is the problem of securing the southeastern farmer in a normal procedure whereby he adapts his crops to climate, soil, transportation, human-use requirements, rather than primarily to a colonial, commercial agriculture. A part is the marginal standard of living and housing of five millions of the region's rural folk; a part is the prospect of a new sort of American peasantry. In fine and in sum, the agrarian problem is *the region*, for better or for worse, and the agrarian statecraft which is involved.

111. Among the important neglected factors in the interpretation of the agrarian South is that of the large number of upper middle class, non-slave-owning white folk who constituted the backbone of reconstruction and recovery. Their contributions were definitive in the regional culture. It was upon their sturdy character and persistent work that the "New South" was largely built. They illustrated the Sumner theory that "the share which the upper strata (the large middle group) of the masses have

PROPORTION OF GAINFULLY OCCUPIED PERSONS ENGAGED IN EXTRACTIVE GROUP

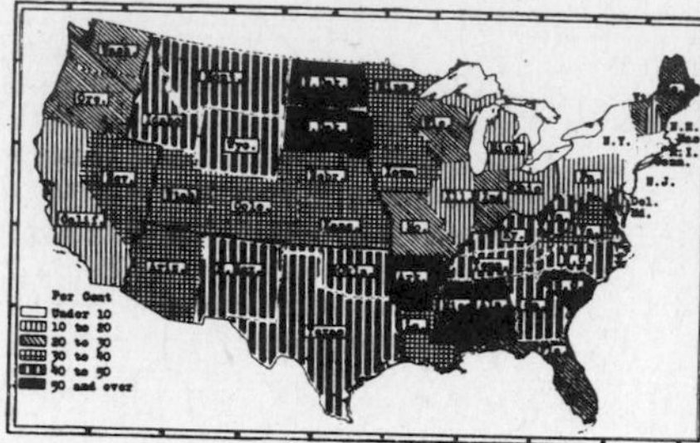

PROPORTION OF GAINFULLY OCCUPIED PERSONS ENGAGED IN MANUFACTURING AND MECHANICAL GROUP

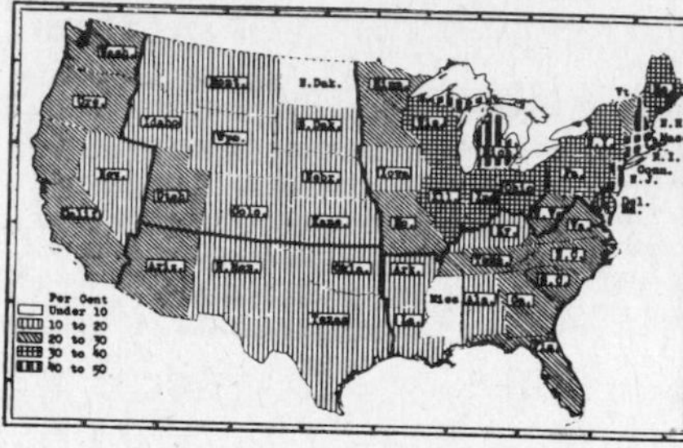

PROPORTION OF GAINFULLY OCCUPIED PERSONS ENGAGED IN DISTRIBUTIVE AND SOCIAL GROUP

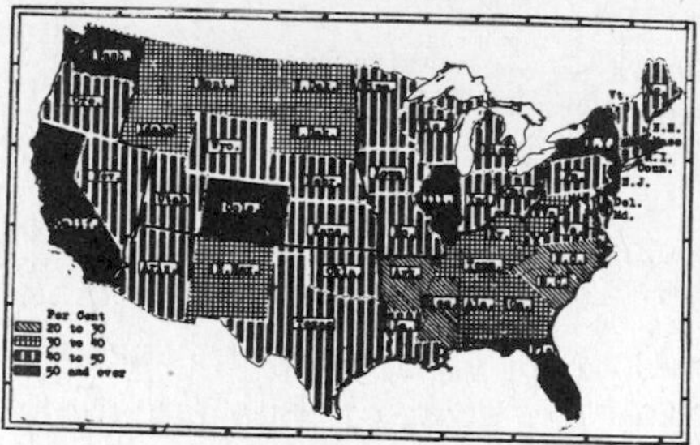

REGIONAL DISTRIBUTION OF OCCUPATIONAL GROUPS

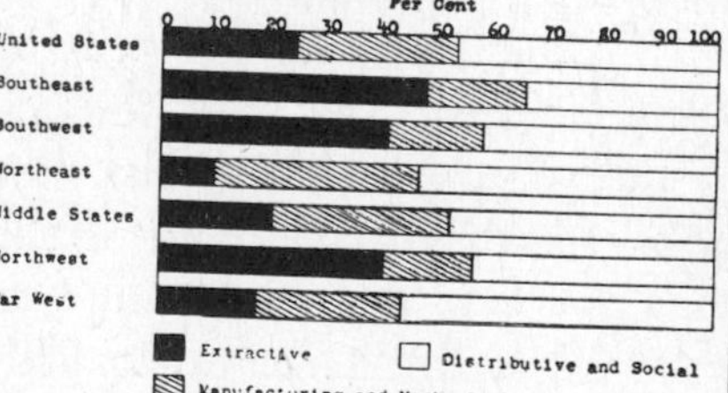

OCCUPATIONS OF GAINFULLY OCCUPIED PERSONS 10 YEARS AND OVER BY FUNDAMENTAL OCCUPATIONAL GROUPS, 1930

	Extractive		Manufacturing and Mechanical		Distributive and Social	
	Number	Per Cent	Number	Per Cent	Number	Per Cent
United States	11,706,790	23.8	14,110,652	29.0	23,012,438	47.2
Southeast						
Virginia	298,060	33.9	212,855	24.2	369,296	41,9
North Carolina	511,728	44.8	290,719	25.5	338,524	29.7
South Carolina	348,908	50.6	147,590	21.5	191,239	27.8
Georgia	506,542	43.5	233,060	20.1	422,556	36.4
Florida	148,630	24.8	141,951	23.7	308,358	51.6
Kentucky	422,445	46.5	162,873	18.0	321,777	35.6
Tennessee	395,872	41.3	201,614	21.0	360,900	37.5
Alabama	529,652	51.6	185,681	18.1	310,962	30.5
Mississippi	565,223	66.9	82,464	9.8	197,218	23.3
Arkansas	398,772	59.7	81,960	12.3	187,113	28.1
Louisiana	317,324	38.9	154,889	19.0	343,403	42.1
Total	4,443,156	45.7	1,895,656	19.6	3,351,346	34.7
Southwest						
Oklahoma	349,588	42.3	139,923	16.9	338,493	40.9
Texas	882,665	40.0	385,307	17.5	938,795	42.6
New Mexico	67,054	47.0	23,322	16.4	52,231	36.7
Arizona	53,214	32.2	34,704	21.0	77,378	46.8
Total	1,352,521	40.6	583,256	17.4	1,406,897	42.0
Northeast						
Maine	62,009	20.2	113,985	36.9	132,609	42.9
New Hampshire	24,762	12.9	89,303	46.4	78,601	40.7
Vermont	41,213	29.2	41,450	29.4	58,540	41.4
Massachusetts	64,769	3.6	773,293	42.6	976,253	53.8
Rhode Island	10,138	3.5	151,462	51.0	135,572	45.7
Connecticut	38,356	5.7	309,465	45.7	329,387	48.7
New York	281,804	5.1	1,866,374	33.8	3,375,159	61.1
New Jersey	70,546	4.1	689,715	40.3	951,845	55.5
Pennsylvania	555,513	14.8	1,416,590	38.1	1,750,000	46.9
Delaware	17,731	18.2	33,604	34.3	46,769	47.7
Maryland	95,164	14.1	223,412	33.2	354,303	52.7
D. of Columbia	1,221	.4	46,658	19.1	195,974	80.3
West Virginia	233,331	40.9	133,698	23.4	203,423	35.7
Total	1,496,557	9.4	5,889,009	37.0	8,588.435	53.6
Middle States						
Ohio	353,277	13.5	991.242	37.9	1,271,245	48.5
Indiana	272,280	21.8	433,095	34.6	545,690	43.6
Illinois	414,902	13.1	1,035,696	32.5	1,734,086	54.4
Michigan	280,703	14.6	786,031	40.8	860,613	44.6
Wisconsin	300,466	26.6	364,511	32.3	464,484	41.1
Minnesota	320,380	32.3	206,139	20.8	466,279	47.0
Iowa	340,317	37.1	173,149	19.0	399,369	43.7
Missouri	390,964	26.8	361,227	24.8	705,777	48.4
Total	2,673,289	19.8	4,351,090	32.3	6,447,543	47.9
Northwest						
North Dakota	135,516	56.4	21,995	9.2	82,792	34.4
South Dakota	132,457	53.5	27,682	11.2	87,514	35.4
Nebraska	197,924	39.0	80,989	16.0	228,095	44.9
Kansas	243,850	35.1	131,715	19.0	318,667	45.9
Montana	97,088	44.8	33,618	15.5	85,773	39.7
Idaho	76,578	47.2	26,652	16.4	59,002	36.4
Wyoming	37,922	41.0	15,155	16.4	39,371	42.7
Colorado	124,806	30.9	76,734	19.0	201,327	50.0
Utah	51,996	30.6	36,969	21.7	81,035	47.7
Total	1,098,137	40.2	451,509	16.5	1,183,576	43.3
Far West						
Washington	141,718	21.4	188,411	28.3	334,601	50.4
Oregon	102,678	25.0	107,166	26.2	199,801	48.8
California	384,711	15.4	636,564	25.5	1,479,369	59.2
Nevada	14,023	32.8	7,991	18.6	20,870	48.7
Total	**643,130**	**17.7**	**940,132**	**26.0**	**2,034,641**	**56.3**

in determining the policy of the masses is therefore often decisive of public welfare." This group stands out in contrast to the "planter class," to which so much attention has been given, who numbered for the Southeastern States less than 200,000 as compared with no less than a million and a half of those farm folk corresponding to the upper farmer class in the earlier East and Middle West. This group, however, constricted round about by Negro and tenant, on the one hand, and artificial patterns, on the other, has not been normally articulate. Yet in all the averages and distributions of deficiencies and lags this group still constitutes the norm around which judgments should be made and plans developed.

112. This preëminently rural Southeast enumerates a larger number of farm families than any other region of the nation. Of the 6,266,000 odd farms in the United States, the Southeast has 2,380,000 compared with the other regions: in round numbers the Far West, 265,000; the Northwest, 648,000; the Northeast, 618,000; the Southwest, 744,000; and the Middle States, 1,622,000. Mississippi alone has a larger number of farms than all of the great agricultural Far West. The Southeast is different, among other respects, in having the lowest average acreage per farm; namely, 71 acres. Mississippi averages only 53 acres per farm. A similar small farm division is found in the other "plantation states"; in Louisiana where the average size is scarcely 58 acres; in Arkansas, only 66; and in Alabama, only 68. For the whole Southeast nearly 80 per cent of the total farms are under 100 acres and less than one per cent over 500 acres. Moreover, the size of these farms has been steadily decreasing since 1900. And before that time the break-up of the plantation system into small farms constituted an unprecedented revolution in the economic and cultural ways of the region.

113. The visible ends of this revolution have been manifest primarily in cotton economy, which is the most dominant and definitive factor of all the region's agrarian culture. Basic to any adequate regional analysis and reconstruction are the understanding and mastery of this situation. First of all, there is the dominance over all other crops of cotton culture in eight cotton states, including Oklahoma and Texas of the Southwest, with conflicting patterns of production, harvesting, marketing. The Southeast produces nearly 60 per cent and the Southwest nearly 40 per cent of the nation's annual cotton crop, which ranges from 12,500,000 to 17,000,000 bales, with the Southwest's meteor-like rise within the last few decades. Of this crop in 1932-33, 66.2 per cent was exported. And of the 24,800,000 bales world consumption of the same year, 58.2 per cent was American grown. Furthermore, this raw cotton constitutes about a fifth of the total exports of the United States.

THE COTTON BELT

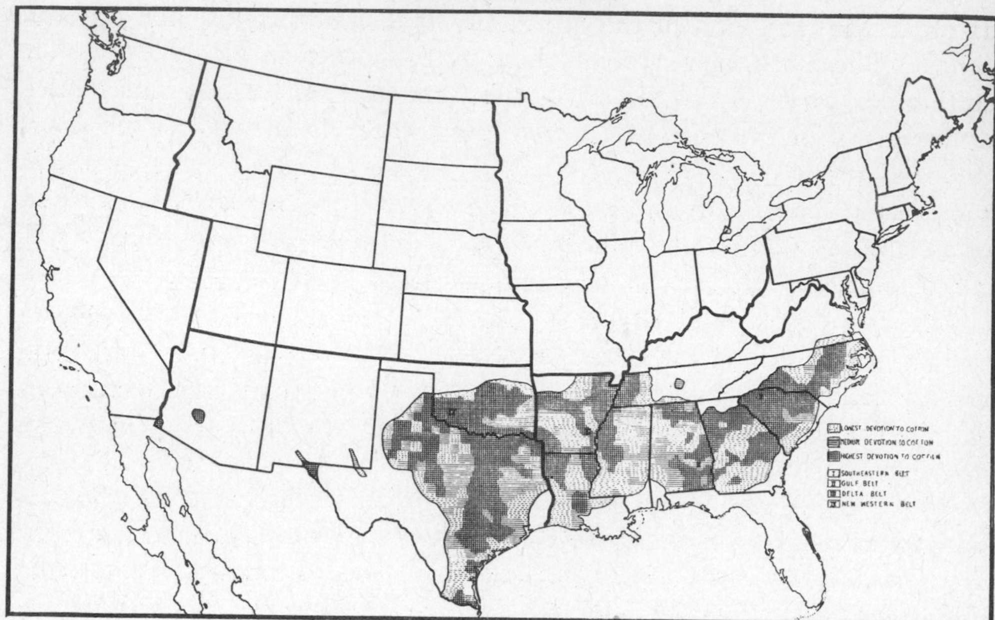

STATE AND REGIONAL DISTRIBUTION OF THE 1929 NATIONAL COTTON CROP

STATE AND REGION	Value (000 omitted)	Per Cent of Total	Number of Bales (000 omitted)	STATE AND REGION	Value (000 omitted)	Per Cent of Total	Number of Bales (000 omitted)
Southeast	*$745,211*		*9,043*	*Southwest*	*$430,103*		*5,726*
Virginia..........	4,080	.33	44	Oklahoma........	89,726	7.37	1,072
North Carolina.....	62,374	5.12	766	Texas...........	315,200	25.88	4,416
South Carolina.....	68,060	5.59	949	New Mexico......	7,965	.65	96
Georgia..........	106,097	8.71	1,444	Arizona..........	17,212	1.41	142
Florida..........	2,422	.20	41				
Kentucky.........	....	....	....	*Far West*	*23,400*		*235*
Tennessee........	42,488	3.49	499	California........	23,400	1.92	235
Alabama..........	108,031	8.87	1,415				
Mississippi........	164,690	13.52	1,701	*Middle States*	*18,370*		*214*
Arkansas..........	119,822	9.84	1,388	Missouri.........	18,370	1.51	214
Louisiana.........	67,147	5.51	796				

COTTON: PRODUCTION BY STATES IN 500-POUND GROSS-WEIGHT BALES, MINIMUM AND MAXIMUM YEARS 1914-1931 (IN 1,000 BALES)

STATE	1914	1921	1922	1923	1925	1926	1931
Virginia..............	25	21	16	27	53	51	43
North Carolina.........	931	776	852	1,020	1,102	1,213	775
South Carolina.........	1,534	755	493	770	889	1,008	1,015
Georgia...............	2,718	787	715	588	1,164	1,496	1,395
Florida...............	81	11	25	12	38	32	43
Tennessee.............	384	302	391	226	515	451	605
Alabama..............	1,751	580	824	587	1,357	1,498	1,430
Mississippi............	1,246	813	989	604	1,991	1,888	1,725
Arkansas..............	1,016	797	1,011	622	1,600	1,548	1,855
Louisiana.............	449	279	343	368	910	829	865
Oklahoma.............	1,262	481	627	656	1,691	1,773	1,220
Texas................	4,592	2,198	3,222	4,340	4,163	5,628	5,220
New Mexico...........	......	6	12	30	66	75	98
Arizona..............	......	45	47	78	119	122	119
United States..........	16,135	7,954	9,755	10,140	16,104	17,612	16,408

114. In the production of this gigantic cash-crop commodity more than half of all the crop land of the region involved is utilized at one time or another. There are, moreover, in these states more than 2,000,000 cotton farm families or nearly a third of all the farm families in the nation. Furthermore, half of the people and more depend for their cash income upon cotton and its related economy, which in turn is a hard master over the whole human culture of the region. For one thing, over half of these farmer families are tenants and their number and ratio are increasing, white tenancy increasing faster than Negro. In some of the subregions of the Southeast the proportion of tenants is much larger. Thus, in the Delta it is 90 per cent; in the Red River Bottoms it is 80 per cent; in the Bluffs it is 75 per cent; in the Black Belt, 73; in the Cotton Piedmont, 64; in the Interior Plain, 61; in Southern Cotton and Tobacco, 60. In at least ten of the subregions white tenancy averages more than 50 per cent.

115. The Negro tenant constitutes a special aspect of this agrarian situation, although in many ways he may play a quite different rôle from that commonly assumed. The Negro tenant numbers at least a quarter million fewer than the whites, and during the last decade his number actually decreased, while white tenants increased nearly a quarter million. In certain subregions of the Southeast, however, the concentration of Negro tenancy still constitutes a more acute problem than in others. Thus, the Delta shows 95 per cent Negro tenancy; the Red River Bottoms, 89; the Black Belt, 88; the Bluffs, 86; the Cotton Piedmont, 85; the Interior Plain, 79; and the semi-tropical, Interior Ridge, both the southern and northern Cotton and Tobacco, more than 70 per cent. The increase of tobacco growing has accentuated the trends toward tenancy, giving the region two major money crops especially suited to tenant cropping instead of one. The size of this factor is indicated by the fact that of the 1,600,000,000 pounds of the American weed grown annually the Southeastern States account for 85 per cent.

116. The picture of the cotton-tobacco agrarian South may almost be described as a landscape of dilemmas. The tenant type bordering on poverty and hopelessness is only one. The human factors of waste, product of the single-crop system, have already been enumerated, as have the waste of land and forests. The instability that comes from great mobility and lack of purpose on the part of millions of citizens is another problem. Disgracefully low standards of housing follow a logical shiftlessness and irresponsibility. Instability of prices and income, speculation and tragedy of lost fortunes, lack of capital for efficient farm management and machinery, the low standard of wages due partly to the Negro, the debtor character

Regional Distribution of Agricultural Production Compared with Population, Area, and Wealth, 1929

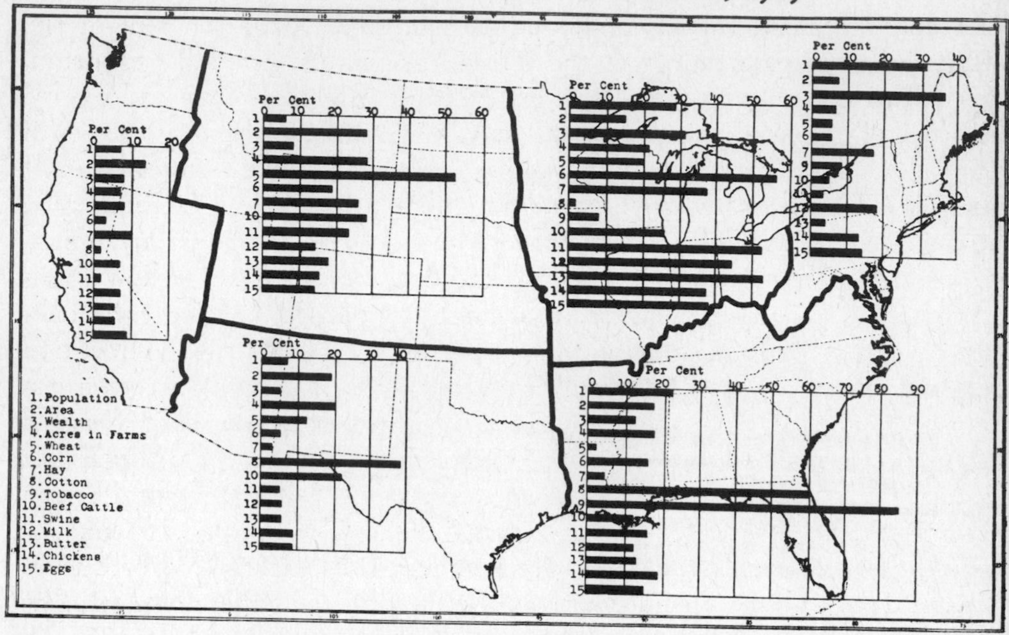

State Percentage of the 1929 National Total Value of Certain Commodities

STATE AND REGION	Dairy Products	Hogs	Wheat	Corn	Beef Cattle
Southeast					
Virginia	1.20	1.06	1.28	1.79	1.03
North Carolina	.95	1.58	.61	1.92	.41
South Carolina	.42	.63	.09	1.02	.21
Georgia	.97	1.61	.08	1.85	.51
Florida	.38	.40	....	.29	.20
Kentucky	1.53	1.60	.38	3.10	1.54
Tennessee	1.39	1.48	.39	3.00	1.22
Alabama	.98	.93	....	1.84	.50
Mississippi	.97	.73	....	1.68	.60
Arkansas	.90	.72	.02	1.44	.56
Louisiana	.41	.34	....	.86	.49
Southwest					
Oklahoma	1.75	1.56	6.03	1.85	2.37
Texas	3.06	2.08	5.56	3.04	6.57
New Mexico	.19	.08	.50	.20	1.86
Arizona	.28	.03	.07	.03	.75
Northeast					
Maine	.76	.12	.01	.03	.26
New Hampshire	.51	.04	....	.03	.47
Vermont	1.62	.12	....	.14	.13
Massachusetts	1.29	.24	....	.11	.15
Rhode Island	.25	.02	....	.03	....
Connecticut	1.02	.07	....	.12	.13
New York	9.38	.60	.57	.92	2.36
New Jersey	1.16	.11	.16	.32	.16
Delaware	.18	.05	.28	.16	.06
Pennsylvania	5.71	1.72	2.48	2.32	2.13
Maryland	1.06	.38	1.28	.70	.35
West Virginia	.64	.45	.21	.67	.76
Middle States					
Ohio	4.32	4.66	4.21	4.76	2.47
Indiana	2.90	6.49	3.45	4.97	2.72
Illinois	4.41	9.25	4.06	11.17	4.38
Michigan	4.11	1.38	1.84	1.36	2.43
Wisconsin	12.35	3.21	.25	2.87	4.34
Minnesota	6.64	6.38	2.59	5.19	5.01
Iowa	4.79	18.40	1.00	15.84	10.64
Missouri	2.62	7.55	2.07	5.73	4.61
Northwest					
North Dakota	1.60	1.43	11.61	.52	1.60
South Dakota	1.60	4.34	3.86	3.81	3.81
Nebraska	1.94	9.21	6.51	8.53	8.22
Kansas	2.30	4.94	17.65	4.38	7.60
Montana	.67	.51	4.67	.07	2.47
Idaho	.83	.39	3.27	.05	.96
Wyoming	.26	.18	.46	.09	1.56
Colorado	.88	.88	1.98	.85	3.03
Utah	.55	.11	.64	.02	.81
Far West					
Nevada	.11	.05	.05	....	.52
Washington	1.62	.40	5.41	.06	.93
Oregon	1.21	.46	2.83	.10	1.30
California	5.29	1.02	1.57	.14	4.78

of the southern economy—these and others cry out for a more adequate analysis and long-time planning.

117. The region's dilemmas are increased by the falling off of exports and the trend toward economic nationalism. Sixty per cent of the cotton and perhaps a fourth of the tobacco grown are normally exported. This falling off of exports itself offers multiple dilemmas. It may deprive the South of its place in the world markets. It will certainly throw the South back into intolerable deficiency of income, throwing a million and a half farm families tragically out of gear and forfeiting millions of dollars in equipment and good will. On the other hand, if there should be maximization of exports and domestic demand, the South will resort to new highs in production and consequent drain of land and people, slaves to the one-crop system. There is, moreover, the dilemma of ineffective competition with southwestern cotton culture, or inventions which may make cotton less exclusively necessary for world markets. Still other dilemmas envisage a better machine cultivation and harvesting which will throw millions out of employment and the spectacle of an already over-populated rural cotton South unable to absorb any of the stranded folk set free from city and industry. To these are added the great agrarian discontent, partly due to the cumulative plight of the depression years with the cotton farmer's few dollars worth about 42 cents each, and none left to pay taxes, debts, and interest, or to recoup his depreciated tools and buildings.

118. What then is the picture and the promise of the agricultural South in the production of other commodities? First of all, the inventory of its natural resources presented justifies the conclusion that the region now featuring commercial farming in a sort of continuing colonial policy is peculiarly well adapted to a more balanced agriculture in subsistence and self-sufficing economy. In the meantime, here is the Southeast's quota of the nation's major farm commodities: wheat, less than 2 per cent; corn, about 15 per cent; beef cattle, nearly 12 per cent; milk, about 12 per cent; butter, about 13 per cent; eggs, about 15 per cent; hay, not quite 8 per cent. The Southeast's ratio of vegetables, exclusive of potatoes, nearly 20 per cent; cabbage, cantaloupes, and onions, nearly 10 per cent; white and sweet potatoes, nearly 23 per cent. The ratio of fruits: apples, peaches, and pears, about 18 per cent; grapes and strawberries, about 5 per cent; oranges and grape fruit, about 43 per cent. The corresponding ratio of farm animals: sheep and lambs, about 4 per cent; horses and colts, nearly 9 per cent; mules and mule colts, 52 per cent; milk cows and heifers, nearly 16 per cent; all cattle and calves, 13 per cent; hogs and pigs, 15 per cent.

119. Set over against these is the Southeast's 85 per cent of all tobacco production; 60 per cent of cotton, yielding recently to the great South-

Total Pasturage, Acreage, 1929

Adapted from the U. S. Bureau of Agricultural Economics.

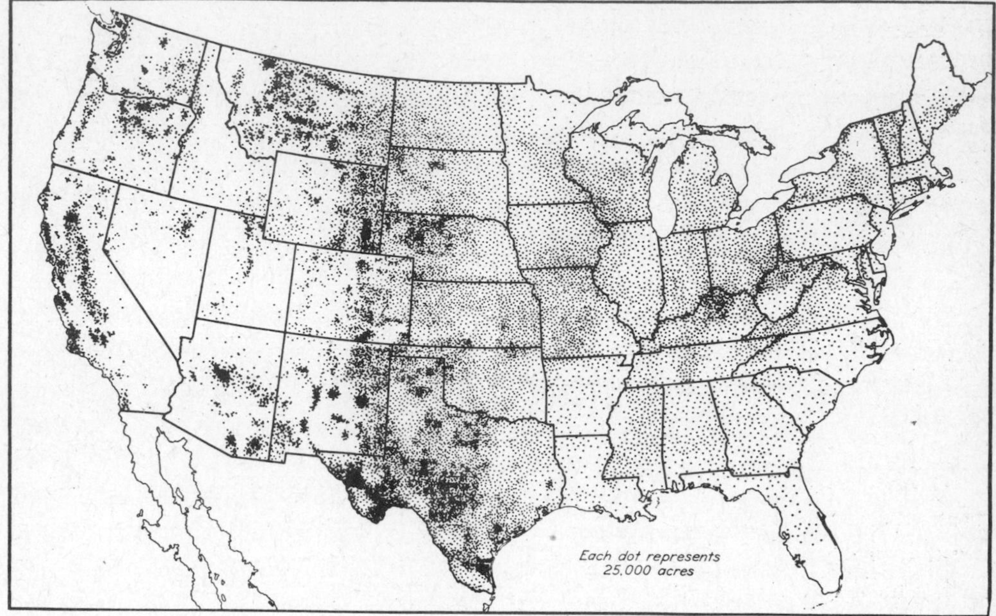

Regional Differentials in Dairy Cattle and Milk Production, 1929

State and Region	Farms Reporting Cows Milked		Average number of gallons per animal milked	Per Cent of whole milk sold	Number of Purebred Registered Dairy cattle per farm reporting cows milked
	Number	Per Cent			
Southeast	*1,489,272*	*62.0*	*394**	*34.7*	*0.08*
Virginia	128,453	75.3	431	52.2	0.11
North Carolina	152,609	54.6	447	33.4	0.08
South Carolina	82,594	52.3	400	28.2	0.07
Georgia	154,964	60.6	380	36.0	0.05
Florida	22,613	38.3	355	61.6	0.13
Kentucky	190,060	77.1	431	51.0	0.09
Tennessee	183,928	74.9	411	46.0	0.10
Alabama	179,623	69.8	392	25.5	0.04
Mississippi	167,492	53.6	340	34.1	0.09
Arkansas	144,827	59.8	394	34.7	0.05
Louisiana	82,109	50.9	309	31.6	0.05
Southwest	*520,309*	*69.0*	*416**	*57.5*	*0.12*
Oklahoma	158,766	77.9	425	54.5	0.10
Texas	339,635	68.5	408	44.5	0.12
New Mexico	15,824	50.4	392	60.6	0.08
Arizona	6,084	42.9	607	78.2	0.56
Northeast	*486,691*	*79.0*	*618**	*87.8*	*0.82*
Maine	30,427	78.0	541	71.2	0.53
New Hampshire	11,314	75.9	568	84.3	0.99
Vermont	21,587	86.7	544	89.1	1.20
Massachusetts	17,271	67.5	654	89.7	1.13
Rhode Island	2,376	71.5	725	92.3	1.34
Connecticut	13,045	75.9	653	88.9	0.94
New York	130,142	81.4	644	91.0	1.20
New Jersey	14,158	55.8	732	91.6	1.21
Pennsylvania	139,684	81.0	594	87.0	0.78
Delaware	6,335	65.3	491	82.9	0.46
Maryland	30,725	71.1	527	84.1	0.63
West Virginia	69,627	84.3	425	46.8	0.10
Middle States	*1,431,862*	*88.0*	*530**	*81.2*	*0.39*
Ohio	187,772	85.6	535	83.2	0.44
Indiana	156,197	86.0	502	79.3	0.23
Illinois	190,861	89.0	525	78.6	0.31
Michigan	141,390	83.5	603	83.9	0.51
Wisconsin	168,890	92.9	664	93.2	0.90
Minnesota	170,317	91.9	567	86.9	0.46
Iowa	198,316	92.3	499	78.0	0.22
Missouri	218,119	85.2	409	61.9	0.14
Northwest	*541,764*	*83.0*	*504**	*70.6*	*0.16*
North Dakota	68,617	88.0	477	70.5	0.14
South Dakota	71,081	85.5	468	72.2	0.13
Nebraska	115,435	89.2	471	70.6	0.10
Kansas	142,967	86.1	451	70.6	0.19
Montana	34,412	72.5	504	66.0	0.13
Idaho	32,872	78.9	623	77.8	0.29
Wyoming	11,905	74.4	504	68.4	0.13
Colorado	43,306	72.2	520	74.3	0.19
Utah	21,169	77.9	634	79.5	0.32
Far West	*145,593*	*54.0*	*638**	*83.3*	*0.45*
Nevada	2,364	68.7	594	83.6	0.44
Washington	49,019	69.1	673	83.2	0.40
Oregon	41,405	75.1	602	78.5	0.53
California	52,805	38.9	755	91.0	0.44
United States	†4,615,529	73.4	523	75.4	0.2

*The median of the states of the region. †Includes 38 in the District of Columbia.

west's nearly 38 per cent. In contrast to this abundance of cotton and tobacco are the scarcity of special commodities necessary for health and vitality and for balancing the agricultural program of seasonal work, land conservation and enrichment, and seasonal stability. Thus, the production requirement deficit in eggs for the Southeastern States shows an increase of from 90 per cent in Virginia to 374 per cent in South Carolina needed to meet reasonable standards. The other greatest deficits are found in the states listed below as requiring the following percentage of increase necessary for meeting the minimum dietary standards: Florida, 341; Georgia, 313; Louisiana, 302; North Carolina, 250.

120. The situation with reference to dairy products merits special treatment in view of not only the production-requirement deficits but also because of the relation to the whole program of balanced agriculture. Some of the deficiencies and problems have already been noted. The production requirement is met in only the state of Kentucky with the other states requiring percentages of increase from ,30 per cent for Tennessee to 403 for Florida. The other four low states are Louisiana, 224; South Carolina, 198; North Carolina, 139; Georgia, 130. The minimum dietary requirements for the whole Southeast may be set at 2,450,000,000 gallons, of which there is a production deficit of no less than 1,161,455,000, which is more than a tenth of the nation's total milk production. Thus the deficit must be made up at home.

121. Some of the explanations of this deficit will indicate also the practicability of reconstructing the whole dairy industry such that within so short a time as ten years the whole region can be remade. Thus, only 62 per cent of all farms in the Southeast reported cows milked and the average number of gallons per animal was only 394 as compared with 618 for the Northeast, 638 for the Far West, and 530 for the Middle States. So, too, the number of purebred cattle per farm is less than one per cent as compared with 28 per cent for the nation. Furthermore, the low ratio of pasture land, the excellent conditions for dairying and other factors make it clear that the problem presents no insurmountable obstacles, but requires special emphasis upon initiating, financing, and management. Yet the fact that one answer to the question often asked as to why millions of southern folk working on the richest land in the world are living on standards close to the margin of slow starvation and deterioration may be found in this deficit of dairy products, eggs, and vegetables, indicates the critical nature of this phase of southern agrarian life.

122. The place of commercial fertilizer as a leading factor in human culture also deserves a special twofold appraisal. One is the quantitative problem and the other is its relation to the whole farm economy of the

State Percentage of Fertilizer Consumption in the United States, 1910-1930

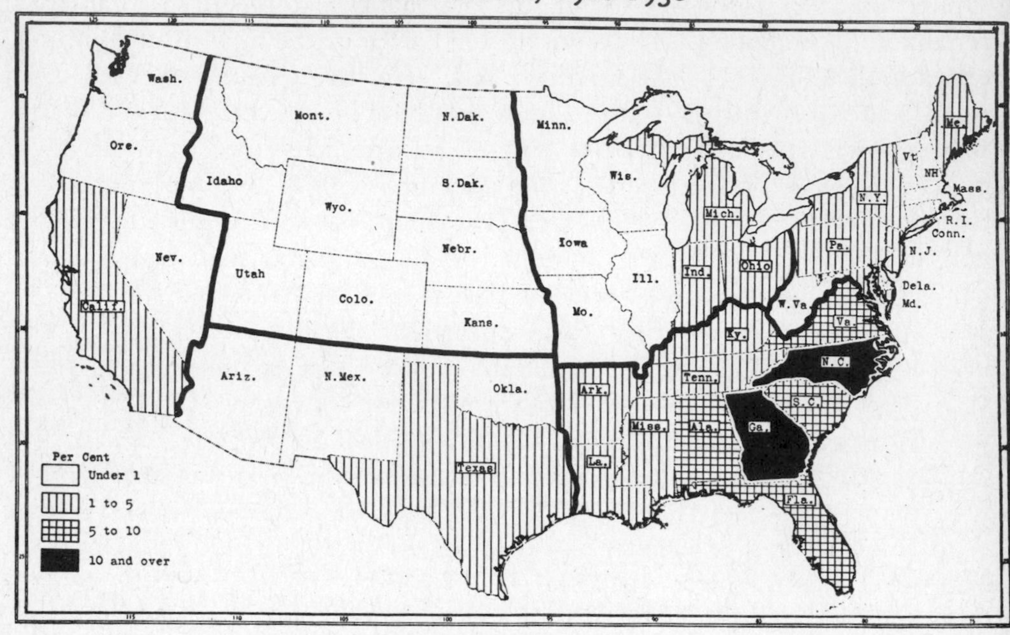

Percentage of Farm Income Spent for Fertilizer, 1929

STATE AND REGION	Farm Income	Fertilizer Bill	Per Cent for Fertilizer
Southeast	*$2,277,739,000*	*$161,062,000*	*7.07*
Virginia	204,653,000	11,781,000	5.75
North Carolina	278,480,000	34,887,000	12.52
South Carolina	140,605,000	22,080,000	15.12
Georgia	241,186,000	27,533,000	11.40
Florida	92,009,000	15,153,000	16.47
Kentucky	228,699,000	2,298,000	1.01
Tennessee	219,256,000	4,110,000	1.87
Alabama	212,280,000	21,830,000	10.30
Mississippi	274,213,000	11,555,000	4.21
Arkansas	225,279,000	4,607,000	2.05
Louisiana	161,079,000	5,228,000	3.23
Southwest	*1,166,434,000*	*6,131,000*	*.53*
Oklahoma	307,060,000	225,500	.08
Texas	749,324,000	5,631,000	.75
New Mexico	61,165,000	98,500	.16
Arizona	48,885,000	176,000	.36
Northeast	*1,304,886,000*	*53,598,200*	*4.10*
Maine	92,372,000	7,288,000	7.90
New Hampshire	28,583,000	439,000	1.54
Vermont	55,873,000	681,200	1.22
Massachusetts	75,199,000	3,014,000	4.01
Rhode Island	9,910,000	336,000	3.39
Connecticut	53,009,000	3,653,000	6.88
New York	384,192,000	11,505,000	2.99
New Jersey	90,018,000	6,583,000	7.17
Delaware	21,202,000	1,300,000	6.12
Pennsylvania	323,551,000	12,113,000	3.75
Maryland	89,828,000	5,525,000	6.15
West Virginia	81,149,000	1,161,000	1.43
Middle States	*3,348,628,000*	*33,198,000*	*.99*
Ohio	367,809,000	11,028,000	3.00
Indiana	306,671,000	7,054,000	2.30
Illinois	509,866,000	3,594,000	.71
Michigan	266,154,000	5,474,000	2.05
Wisconsin	400,104,000	2,133,000	.53
Minnesota	418,801,000	714,000	.17
Iowa	690,302,000	1,171,000	.17
Missouri	388,921,000	2,030,000	.52
Northwest	*1,935,429,000*	*905,200*	*.05*
North Dakota	216,685,000	51,800	.02
South Dakota	233,480,000	21,400	.01
Nebraska	437,250,000	53,700	.01
Kansas	458,530,000	428,600	.09
Montana	138,513,000	29,900	.02
Idaho	135,802,000	80,600	.06
Wyoming	63,293,000	25,400	.04
Colorado	187,299,000	165,000	.08
Utah	64,577,000	48,800	.07
Far West	*977,731,000*	*2,539,120*	*.26*
Nevada	19,875,000	5,500	.28
Washington	197,744,000	1,194,000	.60
Oregon	137,009,000	669,810	.49
California	623,103,000	669,810	.11

region. Both are fundamental. First, as to the size of the fertilizer bill, the Southeast, cultivating barely a sixth of all crop lands harvested in the United States, uses two-thirds of the total national tonnage of commercial fertilizer. The Southeast, accounting for a fifth of the agricultural income, expends three-fifths of the fertilizer bill. Further comparison with other regions shows that although the Far West, the Northwest, and the Southwest account for nearly 50 per cent of all crop land and nearly 40 per cent of all agricultural income, they account for only five per cent of the total fertilizer tonnage. Furthermore, the Southeast spends more than seven per cent of its gross income for fertilizer as compared with less than one per cent for the Northwest and Southwest and only one per cent for the Middle States. In costs for farm operation, the Southeast shows a still greater preponderance with 41 per cent for fertilizer, 27 per cent for feed, and 32 per cent for labor as contrasted with the great Middle States farming areas of 6 per cent for fertilizer, 51 per cent for feed, and 42 per cent for labor; or contrasted with the Southwest with less than 4 per cent for fertilizer, 36 per cent for feed, and 60 per cent for labor. Thus, exclusive of debt service and taxes, the fertilizer bill amounts to nearly a half of the base cost of operation for southeastern agriculture, and has nearly four times the importance as for the Northeast, seven times as for the Middle States, and about 150 times that of the Northwest.

123. The significance of this to the cultural region is manifold. In the first place, this tremendous expenditure is not reflected in crop yields except in relation to commercial crops of cotton and tobacco, and, even with these, they have a very special significance in comparison with southwestern culture of cotton, where, with little fertilizer, yields are far greater than on millions of acres of run-down land in the Southeast. The southeastern yield for corn is only 15 bushels per acre compared to 43 for the Northeast, 36 for the Middle States, and 28 for the nation. Similar comparison for other crops and for fruits and vegetables mark striking contrasts to other regions and indicate the relation of fertilizer, not only to the past development of the Southeast, but to any adequate reconstruction which departs from the present commercial-colonial policy supported by the tenancy system.

124. From these premises it is possible to characterize the whole regional cash-crop agriculture which is carried on with the minimum amount of mechanical assistance. The sum total of potential productive energy in southeastern agriculture is practically confined to the muscles of work animals and agricultural workers. In the Southeast, then, the expenditure for feed is, in a direct sense, largely analogous to the alternative of spending for fuel to run farm machinery in other regions. Notably in the North-

Per Cent of Urban Population in the Total Population, 1910-1930

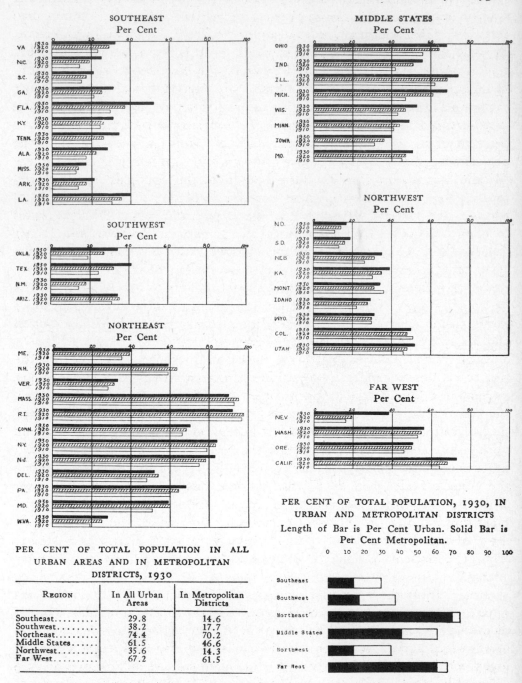

SOUTHEAST
Per Cent

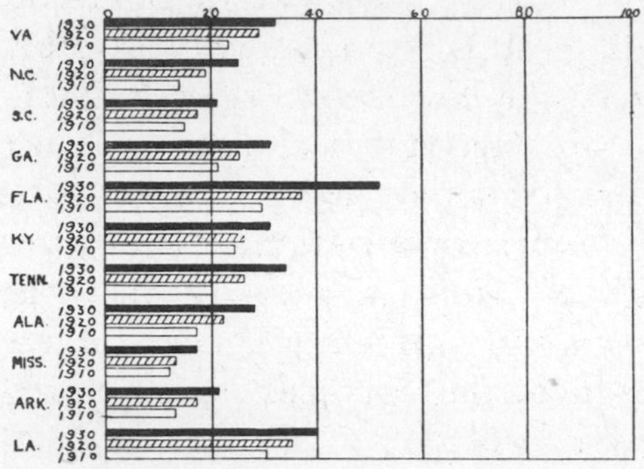

VA. N.C. S.C. GA. FLA. KY. TENN. ALA. MISS. ARK. LA.

SOUTHWEST
Per Cent

OKLA. TEX. N.M. ARIZ.

NORTHEAST
Per Cent

ME. N.H. VER. MASS. R.I. CONN. N.Y. N.J. DEL. PA. MD. W.VA.

MIDDLE STATES
Per Cent

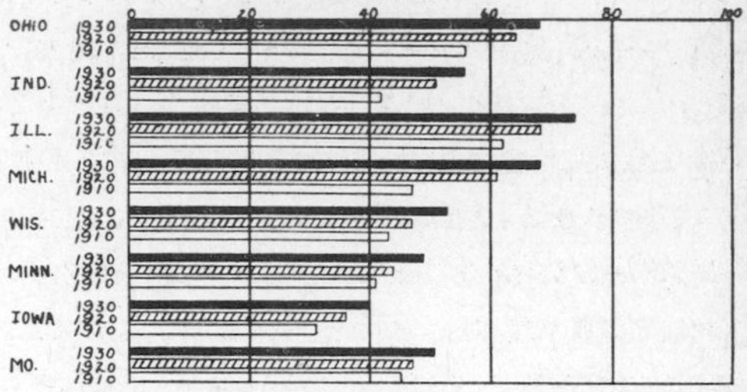

OHIO IND. ILL. MICH. WIS. MINN. IOWA MO.

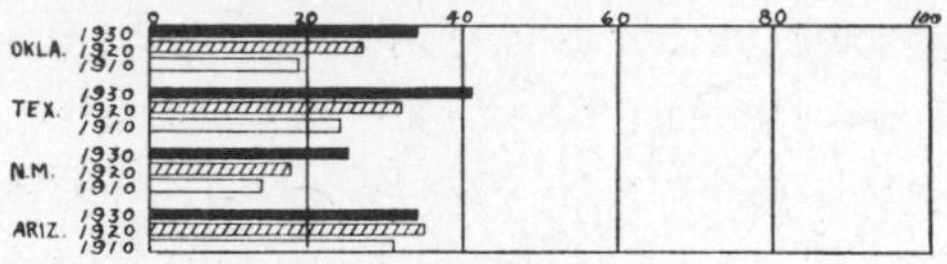

NORTHWEST
Per Cent

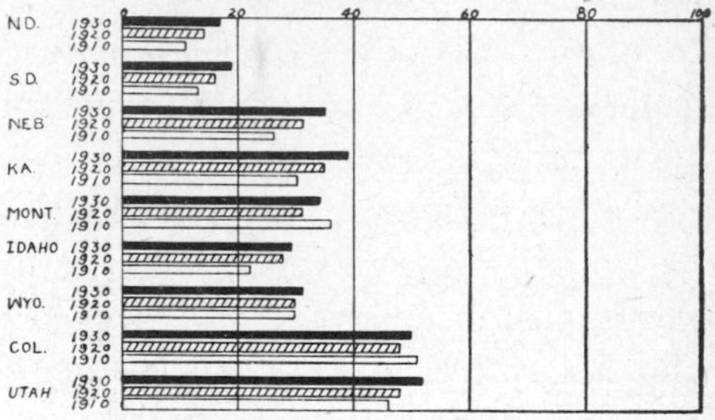

N.D. S.D. NEB. KA. MONT. IDAHO WYO. COL. UTAH

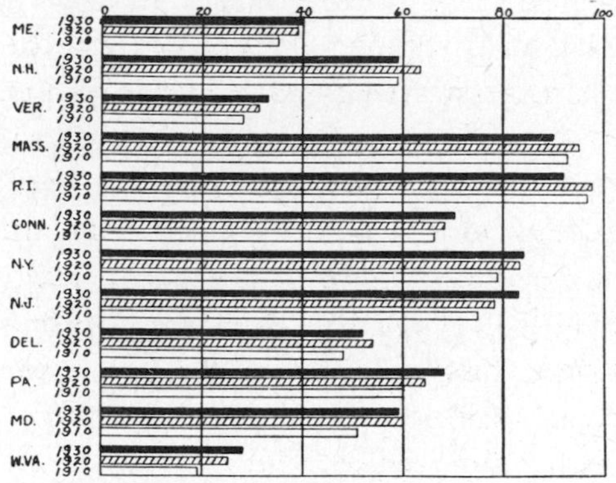

FAR WEST
Per Cent

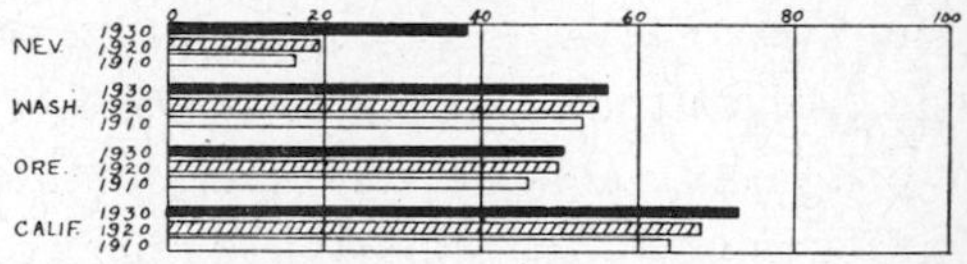

NEV. WASH. ORE. CALIF.

PER CENT OF TOTAL POPULATION IN ALL URBAN AREAS AND IN METROPOLITAN DISTRICTS, 1930

Region	In All Urban Areas	In Metropolitan Districts
Southeast..........	29.8	14.6
Southwest..........	38.2	17.7
Northeast..........	74.4	70.2
Middle States......	61.5	46.6
Northwest..........	35.6	14.3
Far West...........	67.2	61.5

PER CENT OF TOTAL POPULATION, 1930, IN URBAN AND METROPOLITAN DISTRICTS

Length of Bar is Per Cent Urban. Solid Bar is Per Cent Metropolitan.

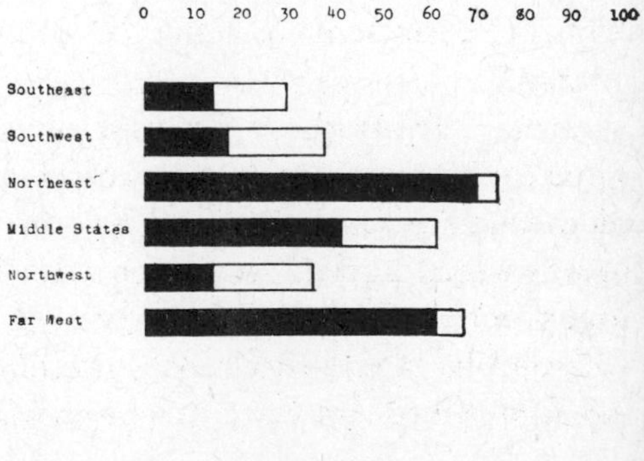

0 10 20 30 40 50 60 70 80 90 100

east and the Middle States, expenditure for feed must be considered as a short-term investment in dairy or other livestock for cash sale, with the buying of feed for work stock a relatively smaller item than in the Southeast. To compare with other regions, the southeastern economy operates on a basis of cheap labor, animal power, and plentiful fertilizer, which becomes clearly a major factor, not an incidental one. Its presence cannot be dismissed as an important detail merely, for the bill for it reaches totals remarkably close to the regional expenditure for all types of education and multiplies several times over the expenditure for all other social services combined. It may be conceded, therefore, that commercial fertilizer is probably the one material factor which has been most directly instrumental in determining the direction of southeastern social-economic trends during the past half century. Without it, there can be no doubt that the cash-crop system would have failed to survive into this century of worn-out lands.

125. Other basic aspects of the agrarian South, some of which have been pointed up as elemental factors in the whole regional structure, include a larger list than can be envisaged in a single factorial syllabus or summary. Among them are forestry and forestry crops; the whole question of markets and marketing, with special emphasis upon coöperatives; the problem of agricultural credit and of interest rates; the problem of tariffs and free trade; the developing culture of decentralized industry and comparative appraisals of tenant and mill worker; the Negro farmer and his future; together with a considerable number of phases in which special advantages are reflected in the region. Among these, in addition to the natural endowments enumerated, are elements of stability in an economy requiring much human labor; the extraordinary progress that has been made, as measured from a scale of recent developments; the extraordinary record of the region in the work of its home and farm demonstration agents; the unrivalled opportunities in the development of special crops peculiarly adapted to the region; and the basic power and capacity in the rural pattern of the people.

IX. MEASURES OF INDUSTRY AND WEALTH

126. Although the Southeast has been and still is preëminently rural, there was from 1920 to 1930 a considerable decreasing ratio in rural farm population and a larger ratio of increase in urban population than for the nation as a whole. Virginia, Georgia, Kentucky, Tennessee, and Arkansas showed an actual decrease of rural farm population from 2.4 per cent to 10.5 per cent, while the increases for other states were much below that of urban population. In all states except Georgia and Virginia the increase in urban population was more than 25 per cent, a ratio found in only six other states

COUNTIES IN THE UNITED STATES HAVING MORE THAN 100,000 COTTON SPINDLES EACH, 1929

County	State	Spindles (number)
Bristol	Massachusetts	6,144,328
Providence	Rhode Island	1,525,952
Gaston	North Carolina	1,184,298
Spartanburg	South Carolina	975,608
Hillsborough	New Hampshire	879,836
Greenville	South Carolina	766,316
Anderson	South Carolina	647,024
Windham	Connecticut	592,456
Hampden	Massachusetts	486,948
Berkshire	Massachusetts	477,684
New London	Connecticut	473,772
Worcester	Massachusetts	472,152
Pittsylvania	Virginia	467,440
Cabarrus	North Carolina	454,208
Kent	Rhode Island	444,920
Muskogee	Georgia	444,106
Androscoggin	Maine	427,212
Essex	Massachusetts	412,252
Middlesex	Massachusetts	348,534
Union	South Carolina	347,100
Yo-k	Maine	332,984
Madison	Alabama	314,716
Strafford	New Hampshire	307,180
Guilford	North Carolina	305,548
Oneida	New York	302,796
Mecklenburg	North Carolina	294,324
Greenwood	South Carolina	289,116
York	South Carolina	270,434
Richmond	North Carolina	267,816
Laurens	South Carolina	264,616
Pickens	South Carolina	254,732
Richland	South Carolina	252,792
Cherokee	South Carolina	233,764
Albany	New York	229,960
Hudson	New Jersey	222,080
Rowan	North Carolina	220,440
Bristol	Rhode Island	217,900
Rutherford	North Carolina	209,380
Fulton	Georgia	207,850
Rockingham	North Carolina	202,852
Chambers	Alabama	199,178
Cleveland	North Carolina	195,854
Troup	Georgia	195,192
Newberry	South Carolina	194,232
Richmond	Georgia	191,720
Aiken	South Carolina	189,948
Knox	Tennessee	187,236
Tallapoosa	Alabama	184,456
Stanly	North Carolina	180,248
Calhoun	Alabama	175,602
Durham	North Carolina	174,928
Talladega	Alabama	170,574
Lancaster	South Carolina	163,928
Floyd	Georgia	162,188
Kennebec	Maine	160,704
Alamance	North Carolina	160,500
Chester	South Carolina	148,648
Halifax	North Carolina	147,080
Hall	Georgia	146,520
Spalding	Georgia	143,344
Cumberland	Maine	138,400
Hampshire	Massachusetts	137,906
Upson	Georgia	134,256
Catawba	North Carolina	130,848
Davidson	North Carolina	130,656
Lincoln	North Carolina	128,936
Iredell	North Carolina	127,160
Caldwell	North Carolina	118,444
Chattooga	Georgia	117,648
Hamilton	Tennessee	116,264
McDowell	North Carolina	115,474
Coweta	Georgia	113,240
Robeson	North Carolina	109,856
Oconee	South Carolina	106,828
Polk	Georgia	106,454
Merrimack	New Hampshire	105,404
Newton	Georgia	104,568
Essex	New Jersey	104,348
Vance	North Carolina	101,184

CONCENTRATION OF COTTON SPINDLES

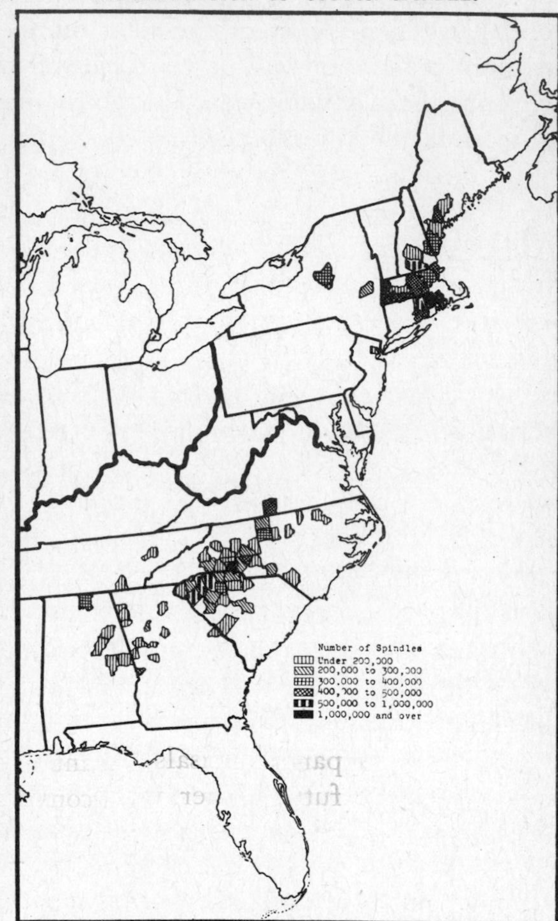

REGIONAL DISTRIBUTION OF PRODUCING SPINDLES

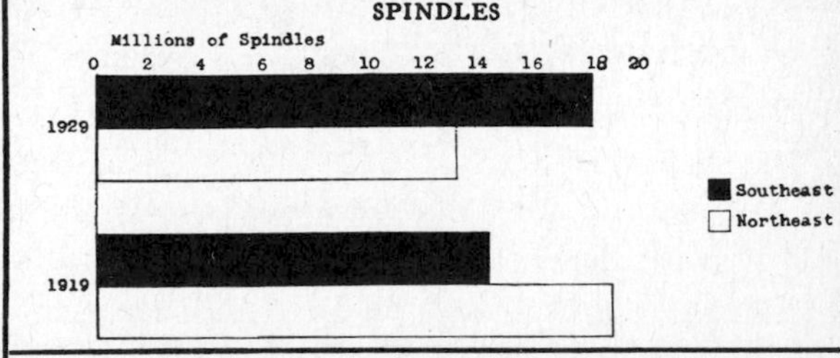

PRODUCING SPINDLES, ACTIVE AT SOME TIME DURING THE YEAR

	1929	Per Cent	1919	Per Cent
United States	31,583,588	100.0	33,718,953	100.0
Cotton Growing States	18,318,642	58.1	14,568,272	43.2
Northeast	13,264,946	41.9	19,150,681	56.8

outside of the Southwest and Far West. By 1930 the Southeast had no less than thirteen cities with a population of 100,000 or more; or a little more than ten per cent of the total number. This increase of urban and industrial population was partly a natural technological product and partly a chronological development, in which metropolitan centers, chain stores, and manufactures were changing the regional landscape and capacity.

127. Industries, like cities, have grown in the midst of an agrarian setting. The Southeast can exhibit a rural county with a hundred cotton mills having the third largest number of spindles of any county in the nation. Thus, the rapid industrialization of the South, like its urbanization, has been a relative measure. In textiles, from small beginnings the Southeast by 1919 had gained 43 per cent of the producing spindles and by 1929, 58 per cent. In 1929 the Southeast accounted for 56 of the 79 counties in the nation with a concentration of more than 100,000 cotton spindles each. In the consumption of tobacco in domestic manufacture the Southeast uses about 60 per cent and for cigarette manufacture nearer 90 per cent. In furniture manufacturing the Southeast has attained a number of concentrations comparable to the best in the nation and accounted for a little more than 13 per cent of the nation's total value of product. Yet the Southeast receives less than a fourth of its income from manufacturing; and, with the exception of the Carolinas and Georgia, the density of wage earners per 1,000 population is scarcely more than half of that for the nation and less than one-fourth of that of the northeastern manufacturing states. On the other hand, the highest rate of relative density of employment for North Carolina is 92.3 as compared with 100 for the nation and 254 for Massachusetts, the highest of any state.

128. Further comparisons of occupations within the region and of its manufacturing status with the other regions will give a fair picture of this aspect of the Southeast's present capacity and status. The total number of the Southeast's gainfully occupied persons in manufacturing and mechanical pursuits is a little less than 1,900,000 as compared to 4,440,000 in the extractive services, and 2,350,000 in the distributive and social. Yet, next to the significance of the mere quantitative measure of the regional rôle of manufacturing is the relative importance of the Southeast and the other regions. In industries the Northeast is easily the leader with roughly 43 per cent, Middle States is second with 35 per cent, and the Southeast is a poor third with about 10 per cent. The remaining 10 to 12 per cent is divided among the other three regions, the Far West having about as much as the other two together.

129. Somewhat less obvious, but more significant, are comparisons between the ability of the industries in the various regions to create and dis-

Wage Earners in Manufacturing Industries of the United States, 1929

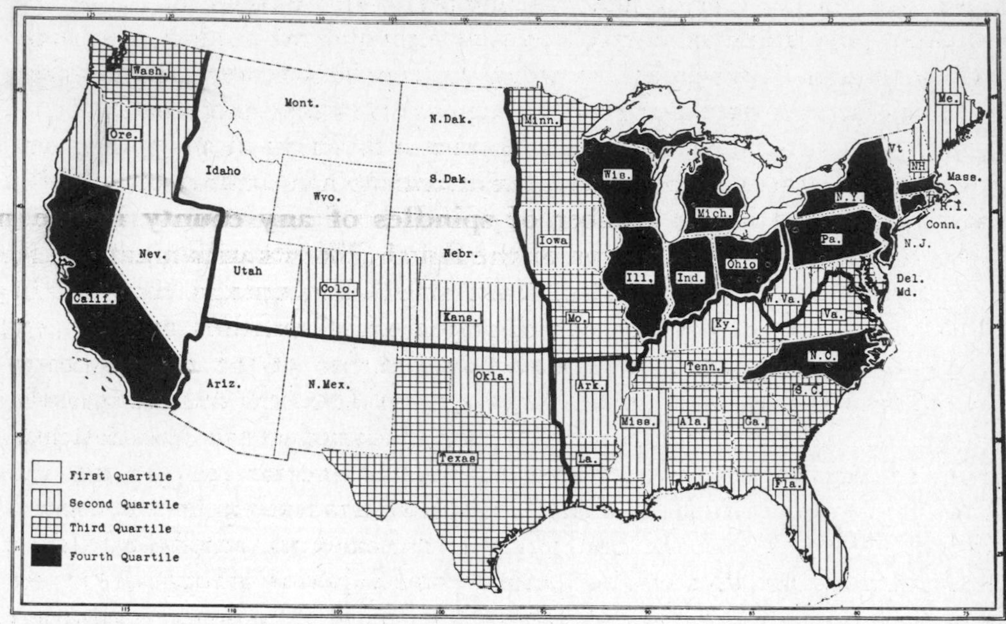

Number and Proportion of Wage Earners in Manufacturing, 1929

STATE AND REGION	Number of Wage Earners	Per Cent of Total Wage Earners in U. S.	Per Cent of Total Population	STATE AND REGION	Number of Wage Earners	Per Cent of Total Wage Earners in U. S.	Per Cent of Total Population
Southeast	1,165,092	13.2	20.8	*Middle States*	2,917,985	33.1	27.6
Virginia	118,399	1.3	2.0	Ohio	737,469	8.3	5.4
North Carolina	208,068	2.3	2.6	Indiana	313,829	3.5	2.6
South Carolina	108,600	1.2	1.4	Illinois	687,917	7.8	6.2
Georgia	158,280	1.8	2.4	Michigan	528,512	6.0	3.9
Florida	64,936	.7	1.2	Wisconsin	264,061	3.0	2.4
Kentucky	76,201	.8	2.1	Minnesota	102,408	1.1	2.1
Tennessee	126,921	1.4	2.1	Iowa	82,615	.9	2.0
Alabama	120,064	1.3	2.2	Missouri	201,174	2.2	3.0
Mississippi	52,039	.6	1.6				
Arkansas	44,073	.5	1.5	*Northwest*	169,678	1.9	6.0
Louisiana	87,511	.9	1.7	North Dakota	4,033	.0	.6
				South Dakota	6,518	.0	.6
Southwest	177,772	2.0	7.4	Nebraska	28,219	.3	1.1
Oklahoma	31,279	.3	2.0	Kansas	46,906	.5	1.5
Texas	131,503	1.4	4.7	Montana	13,673	.1	.4
New Mexico	4,490	.0	.3	Idaho	15,656	.1	.4
Arizona	10,500	.1	.4	Wyoming	6,288	.0	.2
				Colorado	32,735	.3	.8
Northeast	3,903,994	44.4	31.4	Utah	15,650	.1	.4
Maine	69,593	.7	.6				
New Hampshire	65,119	.7	.4	*Far West*	473,015	5.4	6.8
Vermont	27,582	.3	.3	Washington	114,591	1.3	1.3
Massachusetts	559,443	6.3	3.5	Oregon	65,521	.7	.8
Rhode Island	124,838	1.4	.6	California	290,702	3.3	4.6
Connecticut	253,468	2.8	1.3	Nevada	2,201	.0	.1
New York	1,106,976	12.5	10.3				
New Jersey	441,105	5.0	3.3	United States	8,807,536	100.0	100.0
Pennsylvania	1,006,946	11.4	7.8				
Delaware	23,382	.2	.2				
Maryland	131,399	1.4	1.3				
Dist. of Columbia	9,683	.1	.4				
West Virginia	84,460	.9	1.4				

tribute the means of social well-being. Thus, in 1929 the Southeast with 13.6 per cent of the establishments and 13.2 per cent of the wage earners in the United States distributed only 8.4 per cent of the total manufacturing wage bill of the country, or $844 per wage earner as against $1,364 for the Northeast and $1,447 for the Middle States. So, too, the Southeast ranked far below the other regions in value of product. It had only 8.9 per cent of the value of the national product with 13.2 per cent of the wage earners, while the Northeast had 42.2 per cent with 44.4 per cent of the wage earners and the Middle States had 36.4 per cent of the product with 33.1 per cent of the wage earners. Stated in other terms, the industry of the Southeast produced $5,355 worth of products per wage earner as against $7,577 for the Northeast and $8,744 for the Middle States. The smaller industrial regions went far beyond these.

130. If "Value Added by Manufacture" be taken as an index, the Southeast again ranks low with only 9.1 per cent of the national total for its 13.2 per cent of the wage earners, while the Northeast has 45 per cent for 44.4 per cent and the Middle States has 35 per cent for 33.1 per cent, in both cases a larger proportion than their proportion of the wage earners. The Southeast had a per wage earner average of $2,481 as against $3,674 for the Northeast and $3,881 for the Middle States. Yet in the nature and cost of raw materials, the patterns of work and living, the relative technical efficiency, all have a bearing upon the ultimate capacity here both for employment and production.

131. In the development of water power the Southeast has made more rapid strides than any other region, having developed 3,916,000 of its 3,980,000 horse power available 90 per cent of the time, and having a reserve of 6,304,000 horse power available 50 per cent of the time. It is around the continuing utilization of power that much of the newly developed capacity of the region is likely to revolve. The Southeast is peculiarly well adapted, from the engineering viewpoint, to the development and utilization of water power. In horse power the Southeast excels in ratio to wage earners, having 13.4 per cent as compared to 13.2 per cent wage earners, whereas the other regions show less horse power ratio than of wage earners: the Middle States, 32.9 and 33.1; the Northeast, 41.6 and 44.4. The same general ratios obtain if comparisons are made in terms of horse power per wage earner, the Southeast showing 4.82 horse power to 4.56 for the Northeast. In potential capacity, however, the Southeast is short of three other regions. In round numbers, the Southeast's 10 billion potential horse power contrasts with the Far West's 40 billion, the Northwest's 21 billion, and the Northeast's 15 billion.

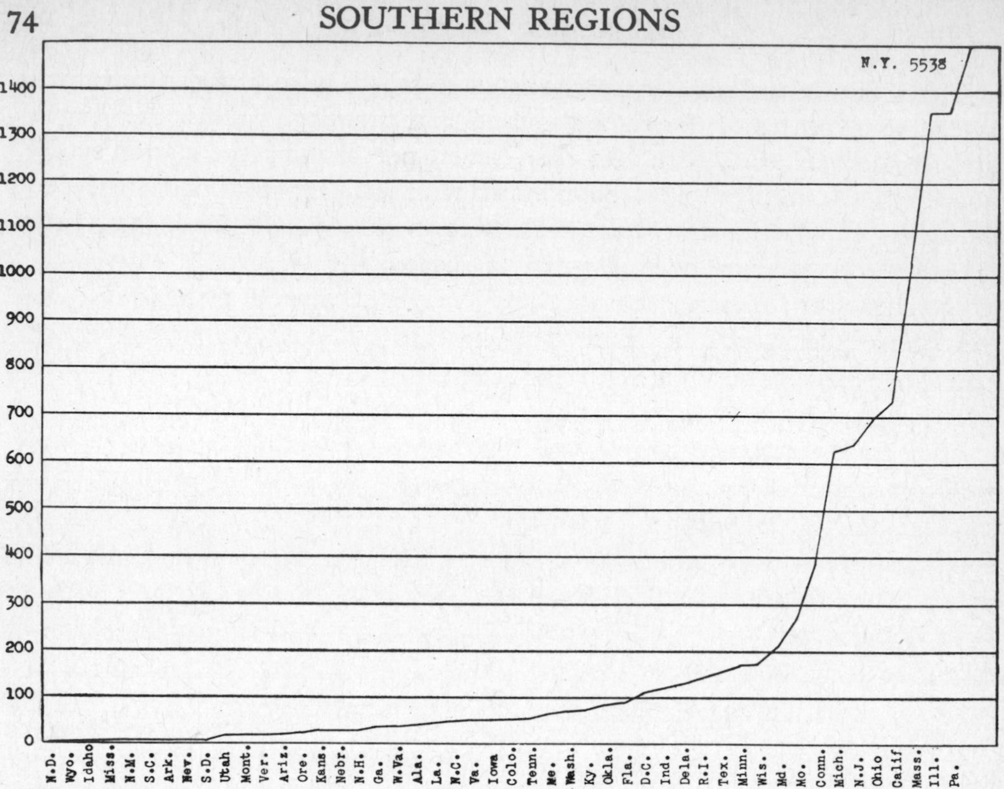

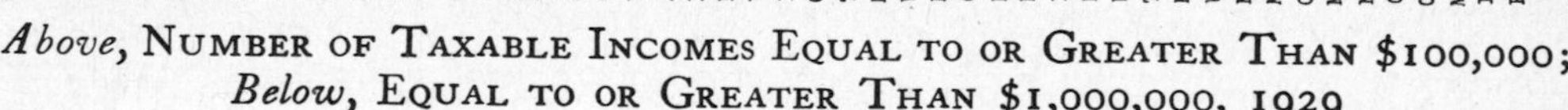
Above, Number of Taxable Incomes Equal to or Greater Than $100,000; *Below*, Equal to or Greater Than $1,000,000, 1929

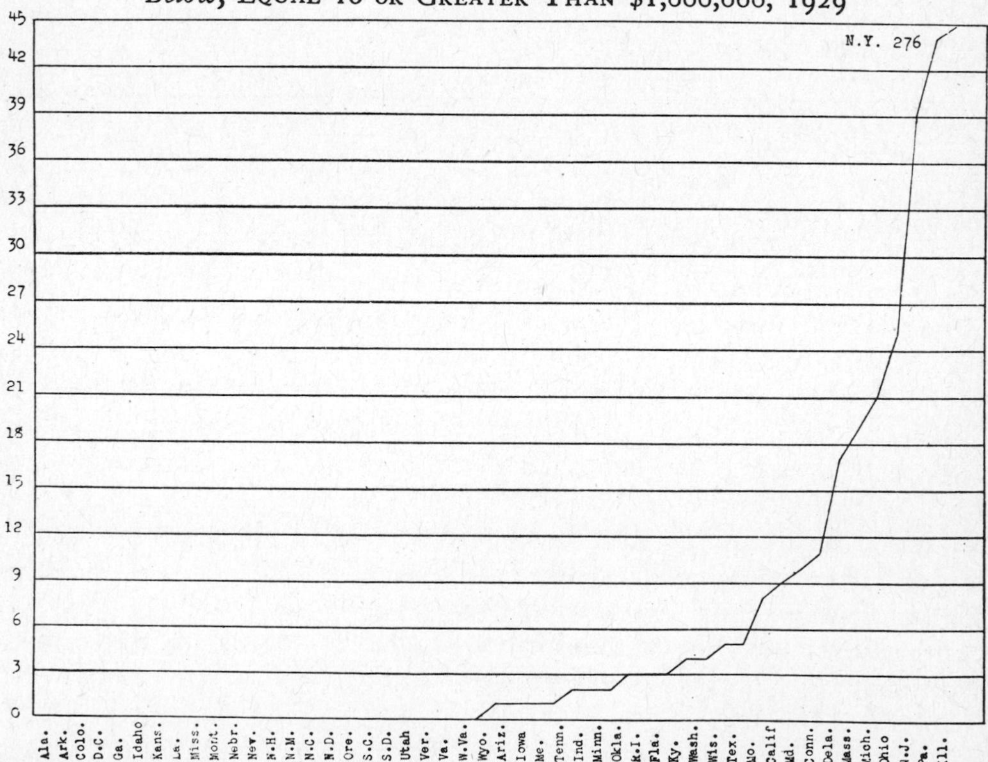

132. Similar relative comparisons extended to wealth and income will give further indices of the region's status and capacity. Thus, the Northeast, smallest in area, with less than seven per cent of the nation's total square miles, ranking first in population, with 31.4 per cent of all the people, shows 35.8 per cent or more than twice as much wealth as the aggregate of both the Southeast and Southwest. That is, the Southwest with nearly 20 per cent of the nation's area has only 7.4 per cent of its people, and only a little more than five per cent of its wealth, while the Southeast with a little less than 20 per cent of the area and 20 per cent of the people has a little less than twelve per cent of the total wealth. Or to turn the figures around, the Southeast and the Southwest with about six times the area of the Northeast and nearly as many people have a little less than half of the total wealth. Compared with the Far West, with 14 per cent of the nation's area and a little less than seven per cent of its people and 7.7 per cent of the total wealth, the southern regions fared somewhat better, as is also the case with the Northwest which, with more than 25 per cent of the nation's area has eight per cent of its wealth and six per cent of its people. On the other hand, the Middle States constituted a sort of upper norm for the nation, with about a sixth of its area, with 27.6 per cent of its population and more than 30 per cent of its wealth.

133. The ranking of the states in the distribution of large incomes is perhaps as characteristic a picture as any that can be found. For instance, there are only three Southeastern States which reported in 1929 taxable incomes equal to or greater than $1,000,000. These are Tennessee, Kentucky, and Florida, with no more than 7 compared to the Northeast's total of 513 such incomes, of which over half or 276 were in New York. Of the total incomes equal to or greater than $100,000 eight states boast 12,000 of the nearly 15,000 in the nation. New York has more than a third of them all, with 5,538; Pennsylvania is next with 1,354; Illinois and Massachusetts follow with 1,352 and 1,027. Four other states have more than 500 each of such taxable incomes—California, Michigan, New Jersey, Ohio. Thus, a sixth of the states, none of which is in the South, approximate five-sixths of the large fortunes. Among the non-southern states which reported no incomes up to a million dollars are Colorado, Idaho, Kansas, Montana, Nebraska, Nevada, New Hampshire, North Dakota, Oregon, South Dakota, Utah, Vermont, and West Virginia.

134. In per capita wealth the Southeast ranks lowest of the six regions, in general no state outside of the southern regions ranking as low as the highest southeastern. In tangible wealth the Southeast is $1,498; the Southwest, $1,801; the Middle States, $2,974; the Far West, $2,984; the Northeast, $3,004; and the Northwest, $3,665. In per capita estimated

Net Income Per Capita, 1930

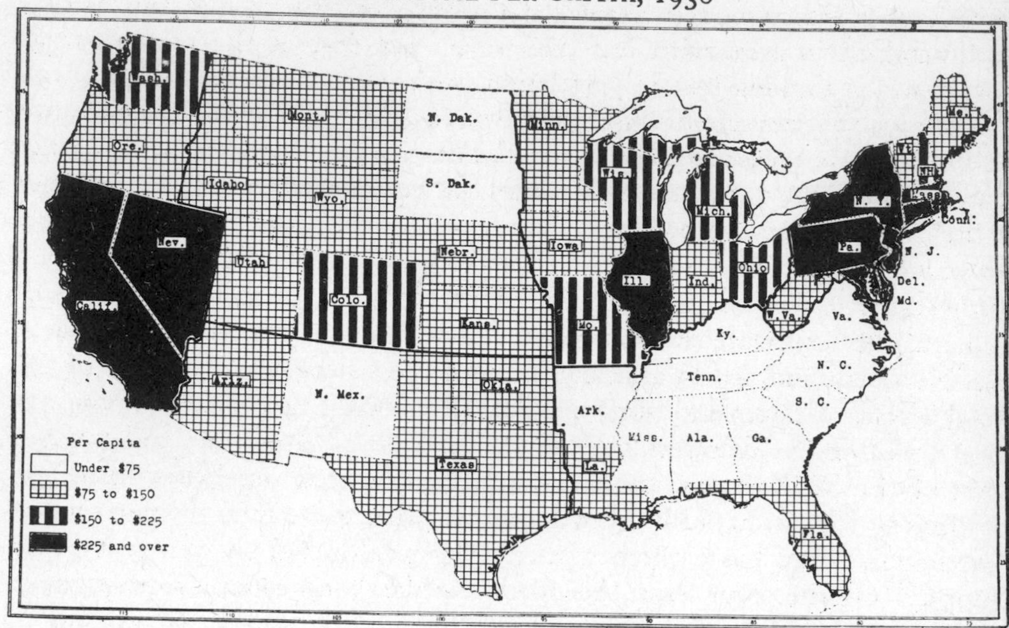

State Differentials in Financial Capacity

STATE	Per Capita Net Income of Corporations, 1928	Taxable Property Per Capita, 1928	Ratio of All Local Taxes to True Wealth 1927	Per Capita State Governmental Cost Payments 1929
Southeast				
Virginia........	$49.32	$1,044.25	0.78	$10.87
North Carolina .	31.49	937.21	1.21	9.78
South Carolina..	10.30	245.20	1.29	8.98
Georgia........	22.33	451.80	0.89	6.02
Florida........	19.57	418.00	2.82	11.31
Kentucky......	29.12	1,061.73	1.26	7.53
Tennessee......	25.65	678.24	0.96	8.99
Alabama.......	12.04	470.15	0.81	10.30
Mississippi.....	6.32	385.54	2.11	9.26
Arkansas.......	9.29	673.31	0.70	11.11
Louisiana......	29.38	835.92	1.38	11.64
Southwest				
Oklahoma......	33.96	807.08	1.68	9.73
Texas.........	30.92	722.80	1.04	12.01
New Mexico....	11.19	808.60	0.87	15.25
Arizona........	23.47	16,441.39	1.00	18.20
Northeast				
Maine........	44.08	932.61	1.08	16.52
New Hampshire.	24.67	1,338.88	1.08	17.23
Vermont.......	28.81	777.93	1.19	27.36
Massachusetts..	98.64	1,676.44	1.71	10.81
Rhode Island...	76.87	2,025.99	1.16	11.57
Connecticut....	113.18	1,744.43	1.06	12.81
New York.....	266.04	2,241.52	1.77	16.01
New Jersey.....	96.72	1,689.80	1.69	14.74
Delaware.......	304.17	1,158.47	0.74	24.89
Pennsylvania...	95.58	1,414.43	1.10	10.86
Maryland......	97.72	1,772.01	1.03	12.22
West Virginia...	30.93	1,176.25	0.97	10.39
Middle States				
Ohio..........	$ 90.83	$2,030.74	1.40	$ 7.93
Indiana........	38.48	1,595.45	1.27	9.21
Illinois........	136.23	1,096.28	1.18	6.82
Michigan......	138.48	1,693.69	1.76	14.51
Wisconsin.....	63.93	2,006.26	1.44	12.17
Minnesota.....	61.42	759.65	1.18	16.01
Iowa..........	26.63	1,569.24	0.87	10.54
Missouri.......	71.51	1,369.99	0.95	8.87
Northwest				
North Dakota ..	8.43	1,469.70	1.00	21.24
South Dakota...	9.12	2,439.00	0.93	18.81
Nebraska.......	22.45	2,251.18	0.92	9.27
Kansas........	58.07	1,958.36	1.35	8.69
Montana.......	27.12	26,344.61	0.93	13.69
Idaho.........	15.00	1,093.41	1.14	11.25
Wyoming......	26.07	1,936.59	0.99	25.11
Colorado.......	58.81	1,531.29	1.31	12.59
Utah..........	40.89	1,434.21	1.06	19.40
Far West				
Nevada........	78.24	2,382.40	0.84	29.83
Washington....	49.34	809.55	1.07	15.58
Oregon.........	31.77	1,179.49	1.25	16.67
California......	104.34	1,742.21	1.74	13.96
United States...	88.58	2,137.98	1.32	11.62

true wealth, the lowest states are in the Southeast, ranging from $1,100 to $2,000 with no state in any other region except the Southwest as low as the highest southeastern state, Virginia, and the highest states in the Union ranging from $4,000 to $6,000. In per capita bank resources seven southeastern states record under $150. No other states are so low. No southeastern state exceeds $275, and only the Dakotas, West Virginia, Idaho, and Kansas outside of the southern regions are so low. In comparison the highest per capita bank resources are $1,850 for New York, while at least eight states show three times as much as the highest, and twenty-three states show three times as much as the lowest southeastern state. In per capita savings deposits the differences are similar. Seven of the Southeastern States record per capita savings of less than $50, while at least six Northeastern States show ten times as much. With the exception of Kansas and the Dakotas no other state outside of the southern regions has as low as the highest southern. In per capita postal receipts again no state outside of the southern regions, except the Dakotas and Idaho, show as low per capita as the southern. The same comparisons hold true in the per capita life insurance, the additional exceptional state being Wyoming.

135. In the several measures of income the story is much the same. In a ten-year average, 1920 to 1930, the only state which shows as low per capita annual income as the highest southeastern state is Washington. Income measured by federal income tax payments shows still greater contrasts. Thus, Delaware, the highest state, records a per capita personal income tax payment of total population of $44.93, which is just about 100 times that of 39 cents reported by Mississippi. The exceptionally low states outside of the southern regions are the Dakotas, Idaho, Nebraska, and West Virginia. For personal and corporate payments the contrast continues to grow, with Delaware recording a per capita of about 120 times Mississippi, but with the Dakotas a little below Mississippi. Virginia, Florida, and North Carolina, however, rank above Kansas, Washington, Indiana, Utah, Vermont, New Hampshire, and Oregon. The greatest contrast is found in the per capita income as measured by the aggregate of net incomes of $50,000 or over worked out for the total population. Thus, Mississippi's per capita is $1, while Delaware's is $429 and New York's $193. Florida of the South has $25, while the Dakotas, Wyoming, Idaho, Kansas, Iowa, Oregon, and Nebraska show less than $10. One other index may be cited. In a ten-year average cash farm income all of the Southeastern States except Florida fall under the $1,000 mark, and no other state except West Virginia has so low a record. The highest states are California, Arizona, and Nevada, averaging about $4,000, and thirteen other states averaging about $2,500.

PER CAPITA BANK RESOURCES, 1930

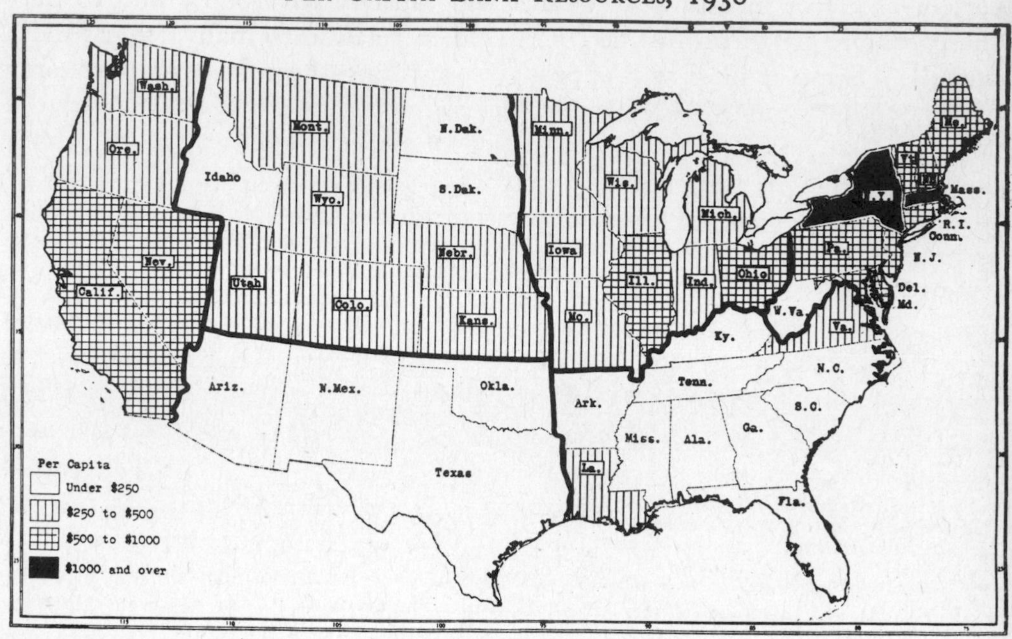

PER CAPITA SAVINGS DEPOSITS, 1930

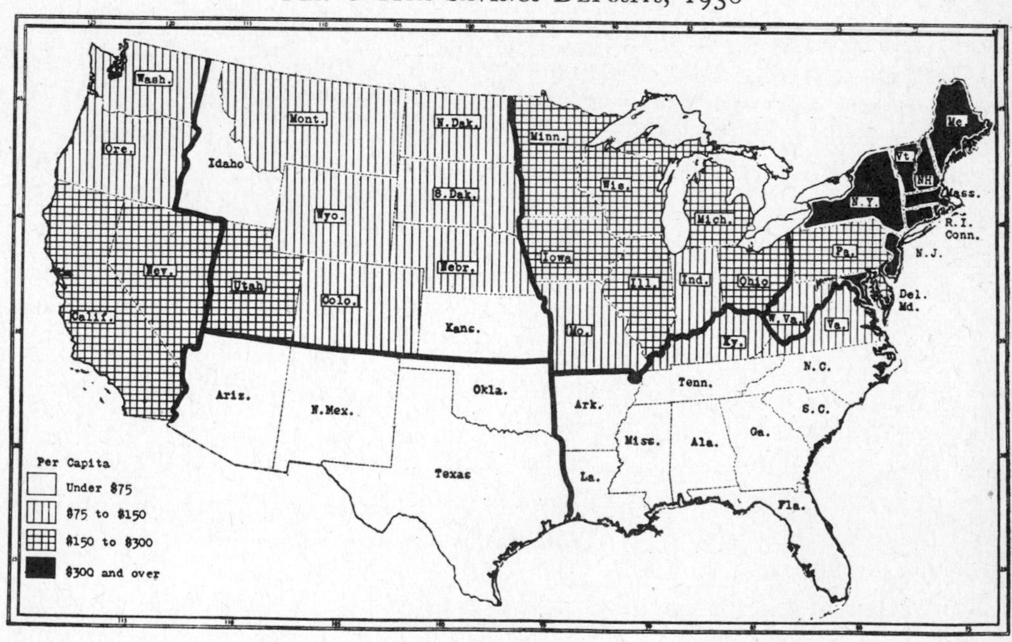

136. While these comparisons are fundamental and indicate clearly certain objective measures of wealth and capacity to produce and to purchase, manifestly they must be considered in relation to many other fundamentals. Some of these will appear in contrasting the culture and economy of the two low Southeastern States, Mississippi and South Carolina, with the two Dakotas, or again in the comparison of Florida and the coastal resorts of South Carolina and Mississippi with California. Or, again, there is the high ranking of certain Southeastern States in the aggregate value of agricultural output alongside low per capita or per farm standards and a poorly balanced economy. Critical studies of incidence and resources, of maximization and optimization of developments, lie at the basis of any final judgments. Or to put the question in another form, is the culture and civilization of North Carolina inferior in the composite and in specified cultural activities to Nevada which outranks it in many of the standard economic indices?

137. A type of measure susceptible to a number of comparative estimates is found in the portion which the Southeast has in the greatest industries of the nation. Mention has been made of the Southeast's total of only 5 out of 161 concentrations of 29 iron and steel industries. Yet this does not represent the potentiality which may grow out of the new regional developments of the Birmingham area in connection with the eventualities of the Tennessee Valley, the Mississippi Valley developments, the possible growth of decentralized industry, the increase of technology on the farm, the increase of purchasing power for automobiles and trucks, and many other factors. The same may be true of a changing ratio of the Southeast's present 28 of 195 concentrations of the nation's 16 greatest food products industries. Or to take another series, of the 102 major industrial, public utility, and railroad corporations, utilized as samples by Mills in his picture of economic tendencies, not more than four are quartered in the South. These include 12 railroads, 18 public utilities, 72 industrial corporations. Similarly, of the 56 main raw materials only three may be said to belong to the South with major concentration. The same negligible representation is shown in Berle's list of 200 corporations owning nearly half of the nation's corporate wealth. The South has a bare handful of the 40 to 50 utilities, 40 or more railroads, 27 chemical industries, 13 food, drugs, and tobacco, 10 machinery, 4 automobile, 17 metal, 20 petroleum, and the lesser number of paper, glass, leather, textile, transportation, mercantile, real estate.

138. The picture of the Southeast's place in the nation and its opportunities as measured by availability of resources, power, transportation, labor, may be continued further by checking with the nation's "ten major

THE YELLOW PINE BELT

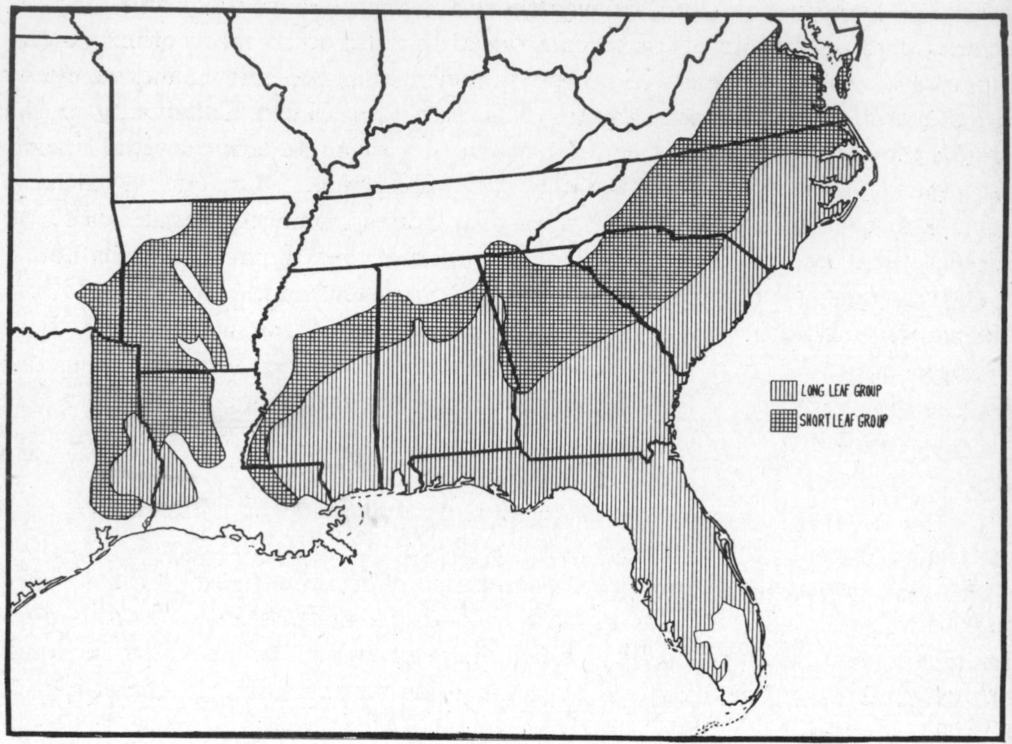

SOUTHERN YELLOW PINE REGION—CLASSIFICATION OF PINE LAND BY CHARACTER OF GROWTH, 1919 AND 1927

STATE	Total Pine Area	Area Old Growth	Cut-Over Lands: Restocking to saw timber	Restocking to cordwood	Not Restocking
	Thousand Acres	*Thousand Acres*	*Thousand Acres*	*Thousand Acres*	*Thousand Acres*
1919					
Alabama	15,500	1,500	3,500	4,000	6,500
Arkansas	9,500	1,150	2,000	5,500	850
Florida	18,000	11,000	700	1,000	5,300
Georgia	15,500	700	3,800	6,000	5,000
Louisiana	11,750	2,510	4,500	1,200	3,540
Mississippi	12,000	3,000	5,000	1,000	3,000
North Carolina	10,700	500	3,600	5,400	1,200
Oklahoma	2,250	500	560	550	640
South Carolina	8,000	600	2,500	3,000	1,900
Texas	7,800	2,000	1,700	1,000	3,100
Virginia	4,000	......	1,500	2,200	300
Total	115,000	23,460	29,360	30,850	31,330
1927					
Alabama	15,500	1,350	3,900	5,100	5,150
Arkansas	9,500	650	2,750	5,250	850
Florida	18,000	5,450	3,150	4,300	5,100
Georgia	15,500	350	6,200	5,900	3,050
Louisiana	11,750	1,400	2,150	4,000	4,200
Mississippi	12,000	1,350	2,950	2,500	5,200
North Carolina	10,700	250	5,350	3,900	1,200
Oklahoma	2,250	350	250	1,150	500
South Carolina	8,000	200	4,150	2,100	1,550
Texas	7,800	1,300	1,650	1,700	3,150
Virginia	4,000	......	1,950	1,850	200
Total	115,000	12,650	34,450	37,750	30,150

industries." If the test is employment of labor in manufacturing industries, the Southeast does not now assume leadership in any one of the ten: cotton goods, foundry and machine shops, steam railroad repair shops, steel works and rolling mills, lumber and lumber products, boots and shoes, bread and bakery products, electrical machinery, knit goods, and women's clothing. Or to take the value of products as the measure, consider ten with an average annual product of more than a billion dollars: meat packing, motor vehicles, petroleum refining, printing and publishing, steel works and rolling mills, women's clothing, foundry and machine shops, bread and baking products, electrical machinery, cigars and cigarettes. Within this frame of great industries the Southeast with technological development in both men and machines might well be a region for revolutionary developments.

139. If to these be added others of the non-manufacturing kind, there would appear, in addition to the public utilities, the electric railroad and motor bus operation, forest products, construction and building, mining and quarrying, food and kindred products, and transportation equipment, including air, water, and land. In contrast to the Southeast's present status, these might well open up new avenues of development for which the region's position and resources are peculiarly favorable.

140. In addition to sources of wealth previously catalogued in natural resources, among the sources which demand special attention at the present time is that of the southern pines, the long leaf, the short leaf, the loblolly, the slash, and certain others, such as sand or scrub pine. This source of wealth has constituted also one of the chief examples of exploitation and waste. Now because of the growing tendency towards conservation, because of the rapid growing qualities of many of the pines and of the abundance of submarginal lands in the Southeast suitable for the growing of pine crops, and because of the new uses for them, the southern pine again looms large in the picture. Among the great sources of wealth is that of the paper industry, which in very recent years, due to chemical techniques, is assuming the proportions of a billion dollar industry. The nature and possibilities of this industry together with the use of wood pulp for rayon, which increased from 9,000,000 pounds in 1920 to nearly 100,000,000 pounds by 1930, will be set forth in later chapters. In 1930, 26 of the 200 pulp mills in the United States were in the South. Yet the South with 40 per cent of the pulp supply of the nation is manufacturing only seven per cent of the paper, which is of the nature, of course, of wrapping paper and boards. Lumbering still constitutes a basic source of wealth, employing more than 200,000 workers with a potential payroll of $200,000,000, with value of products approximating $500,000,000 and value added by

Regional Variations in Forests and Principal Types of Forests

Adapted from the U. S. Bureau of Agricultural Economics

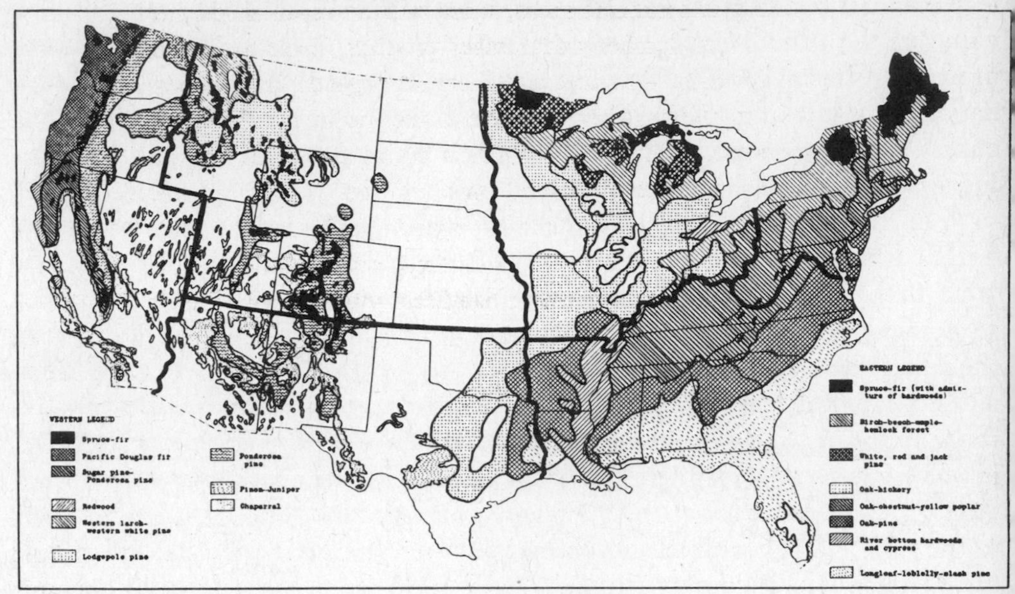

Commercial Forest Area of the United States, Stand of Saw-Timber, and Total Stand on Saw-Timber and Cordwood Areas

REGIONS	Present forest area (1000 acres)	Saw-timber stand (Million feet b.m.)	Total stand, saw-timber and cordwood areas (Million cubic feet)
Southeast	*199,173*	*194,847*	*108,970*
Virginia	14,857	11,086	9,234
North Carolina	20,216	19,443	13,944
South Carolina	12,415	18,462	9,711
Georgia	22,872	20,870	14,039
Florida	23,600	15,312	8,602
Kentucky	10,296	5,574	3,714
Tennessee	14,041	9,683	8,296
Alabama	21,680	21,176	9,474
Mississippi	18,293	20,481	7,459
Arkansas	22,000	24,170	13,241
Louisiana	18,903	28,590	11,256
Southwest	*24,360*	*53,923*	*15,514*
Oklahoma	4,279	3,542	1,866
Texas	12,624	16,165	7,104
New Mexico	3,806	14,389	2,919
Wisconsin	3,651	19,827	3,625
Northeast	*64,181*	*89,087*	*49,346*
Maine	14,490	39,750	14,309
New Hampshire	4,435	6,956	2,661
Vermont	3,232	8,306	3,841
Massachusetts	3,255	2,042	1,486
Rhode Island	279	91	78
Connecticut	1,582	730	1,200
New York	9,593	18,015	9,201
New Jersey	1,973	857	888
Delaware	320	107	333
Pennsylvania	13,085	5,897	8,363
Maryland	2,168	1,274	1,812
West Virginia	9,769	5,062	5,174
Middle States	*85,543*	*50,137*	*33,053*
Ohio	4,651	4,194	2,895
Indiana	3,438	2,182	1,384
Illinois	3,196	3,131	1,815
Michigan	19,000	16,430	8,898
Wisconsin	16,200	10,824	6,923
Minnesota	20,200	8,580	5,634
Iowa	2,358	1,107	524
Missouri	16,500	3,689	4,980
Northwest	*55,560*	*237,403*	*71,665*
North Dakota	495	53	95
South Dakota	1,284	3,208	911
Nebraska	......	......	......
Kansas	......	......	......
Montana	14,865	49,796	21,191
Idaho	17,464	96,592	23,843
Wyoming	5,588	32,584	10,855
Colorado	12,516	47,379	12,442
Utah	3,348	7,791	2,328
Far West	*67,062*	*1,042,406*	*189,751*
Nevada	377	778	219
Washington	20,309	321,316	59,535
Oregon	28,838	437,852	80,495
California	17,538	282,460	49,502
United States	495,879	1,667,803	468,299

manufacture nearly $300,000,000. The Southeast had a little more than half of the mills in the United States, nearly half of the workers, a little less than 40 per cent of the payroll, a little less than 40 per cent of the value of the products, and about 40 per cent of the value added by manufacture. In addition to this, the region produces more than half of the national output of cooperage stock and about 20 per cent of the wooden boxes, thus giving additional employment to thousands and adding millions of dollars to the value of the product.

141. The special forest products industry, namely, naval stores, being confined exclusively to the South, constitutes a special source of wealth. In 1929 there was a production of spirits of turpentine amounting to more than 31,000,000 gallons and approximately 2,000,000 barrels of rosin. For the years 1927 to 1929, the average exports of turpentine to Europe were 247,000 barrels, or only 42,000 barrels less than the annual average for the ten years preceding the World War. Countries outside of Europe have in recent years shown little variation in their consumption of turpentine. In 1913 the exports of rosin to Europe amounted to 1,120,000 barrels and to the rest of the world 338,000 barrels. In the five-year period 1922-1926, the average annual exportation of rosin to Europe was 677,000 barrels, and to countries outside of Europe 446,000 barrels. The expansion outside of Europe has been mainly in the Far East. In pre-war years, 1910-1913, the approximate annual production of turpentine was 52,000,000 gallons, of which the United States furnished 33,000,000. France and Russia produced about 7,000,000 gallons each, and the balance came in small quantities from a dozen or more countries. Of the total annual consumption, the United States accounted for only about 25 per cent. The annual pre-war production of rosin was about 2,900,000 barrels, about three-fourths of which came from the United States. As in the case of turpentine, the United States consumed about 25 per cent. At the present time the proportions are not greatly different, the southern pine producing approximately 70 per cent of the total world supply of naval stores.

142. Retail and wholesale stores and sales represent another measure of capacity and wealth. Of the 168 head offices of major chain stores in the nation, none is in the Southeast. In the number of retail stores per 1,000 population, Mississippi ranks lowest with 8.1, with most of the other southeastern states under 11, except Florida, which leads the nation with 15.3, and no other state outside the South lower than 11. Louisiana with 11.1 and Virginia with 10.8 lead the Southeast. In retail sales per capita the ten lowest states in the Southeast average under $250 compared with a dozen states averaging more than $500. South Carolina, Mississippi, and Alabama are the lowest, while California, New York,

Per Capita State Governmental Cost Payments, 1929

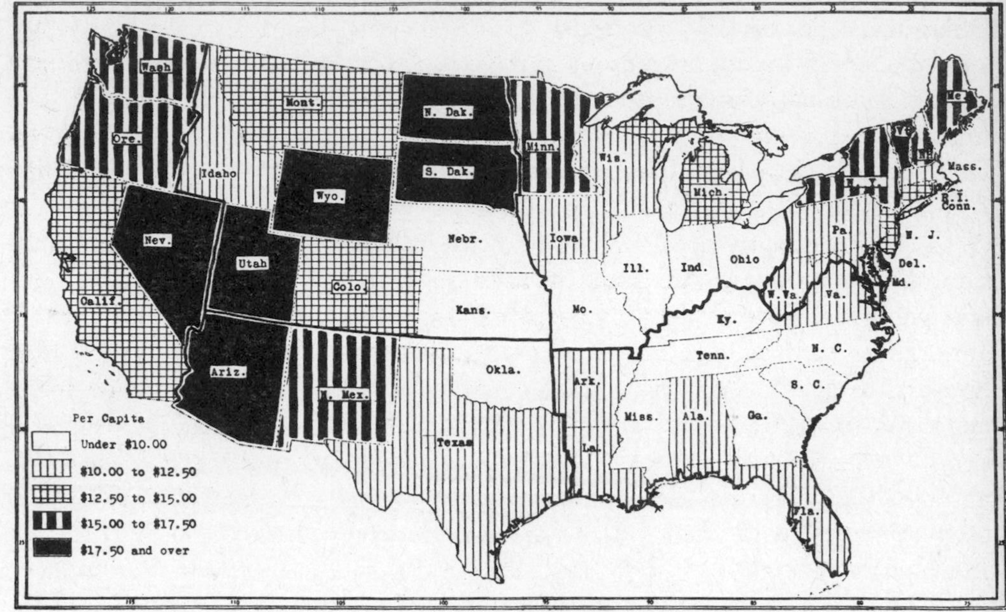

Relative Proportions of Total State and Local Tax Collections Applied to State and Local Roads, 1930

State and Region	Taxes and Appropriations for State and Local Roads (000 Omitted)	Ratio of Taxes for Roads to Total State and Local Tax Collections
Southeast	*237,095*	*20.7*
Virginia	23,835	30.0
North Carolina	25,783	25.3
South Carolina	14,072	29.5
Georgia	24,035	36.0
Florida	24,985	28.8
Kentucky	19,515	23.4
Tennessee	25,238	34.1
Alabama	15,441	28.6
Mississippi	23,714	37.5
Arkansas	18,830	42.8
Louisiana	21,646	28.2
Southwest	*89,572*	*26.2*
Oklahoma	26,697	28.2
Texas	53,820	26.2
New Mexico	3,907	26.2
Arizona	5,148	19.1
Northeast	*397,181*	*14.9*
Maine	11,822	26.8
New Hampshire	8,108	30.0
Vermont	5,836	30.1
Massachusetts	29,074	09.0
Rhode Island	3,815	09.7
Connecticut	16,723	16.0
New York	101,677	08.9
New Jersey	60,777	18.5
Delaware	9,342	51.8
Pennsylvania	114,863	24.4
Maryland	14,870	19.6
West Virginia	20,273	28.5
Middle States	*466,879*	*23.8*
Ohio	78,480	20.4
Indiana	49,363	25.4
Illinois	95,911	23.3
Michigan	79,990	23.3
Wisconsin	50,382	27.4
Minnesota	43,440	26.9
Iowa	40,876	28.8
Missouri	28,438	19.8
Northwest	*102,268*	*24.4*
North Dakota	5,943	16.6
South Dakota	11,053	25.5
Nebraska	19,538	25.3
Kansas	31,563	30.1
Montana	7,323	'1.3
Idaho	8,817	34.9
Wyoming	2,902	20.8
Colorado	10,692	17.8
Utah	4,437	17.7
Far West	*107,889*	*17.9*
Nevada	1,796	23.8
Washington	24,502	26.0
Oregon	18,640	28.3
California	62,951	14.5
United States	1,400,884	20.7

and Nevada are the highest. In retail sales per store, the eleven Southeastern States are again lowest, with the exception of West Virginia and Delaware. South Carolina with $19,000 contrasts with Michigan with $39,000. In wholesale trade per capita the Southeast ranks better, with the leaders Louisiana and Tennessee with $405 and $411, ranking above no less than 17 other states. The higher rates are: for New York, $1,403; Delaware, $991; Illinois, $899; and with California, Washington, Nebraska, and Massachusetts over $700 each.

143. In exports the South ranks high and, with the probability of considerable shifts in trade routes, there is possible a new pattern for industry and wealth. Cotton accounts for about a fifth of all exports, sometimes amounting to nearly a billion dollars annually. Its importance to the South is indicated by the fact that the total value of agricultural products exported in 1930 was only about $1,200,000,000. Other southeastern products are tobacco, of which more than a third is exported; turpentine, about 50 per cent; and rosin, nearly 60 per cent. Of the exports from 47 seaport towns in the east and southeast, 24 southern ports accounted for a little more than 60 per cent, and about the same ratio for shipments in coastwise shipping. Of these ports ten are Atlantic Seaboard and fourteen are Gulf ports. Here, again, potential exceeds present realization of opportunities. Nearness to market, nearness to resources, a great inland waterway system, a great array of ocean ports, and the Panama Canal make the capacity of the region measurable only by the realities of development.

144. Other measures of visible regional wealth may be found in governmental expenditures and tax collections and in ratios of recent state and federal relief expenditures. In per capita state and local tax collections every Southeastern State except Florida is in the lowest quartile, and no state outside of the two southern regions is so low. The five states having a per capita under $30 are Alabama, Georgia, Arkansas, South Carolina, and Tennessee contrasted with the five top states having more than $75; namely, New York, Nevada, New Jersey, California, and Massachusetts. Yet for nine of the eleven states this represented an increase from 1922 to 1930 of over 60 per cent with no other state in the Union, except Delaware, ranking so high. For South Carolina and Arkansas the increase was over 100 per cent. In per capita cost of state government all the Southeastern States, except Florida, rank within the lower half with $10 or less. Lower than any Southern States, however, except Georgia with $5.11, are Illinois with $6.33 and Ohio with $6.35 contrasted with Nevada's $34.81 and five other states between $15 and $20. Other similar indices will appear in the inventory of special governmental expenditures, as, for instance, in the per capita total expenditure for public day schools, in which

Per Cent Federal Contribution to Relief Is of Total Contribution, July and August, 1933

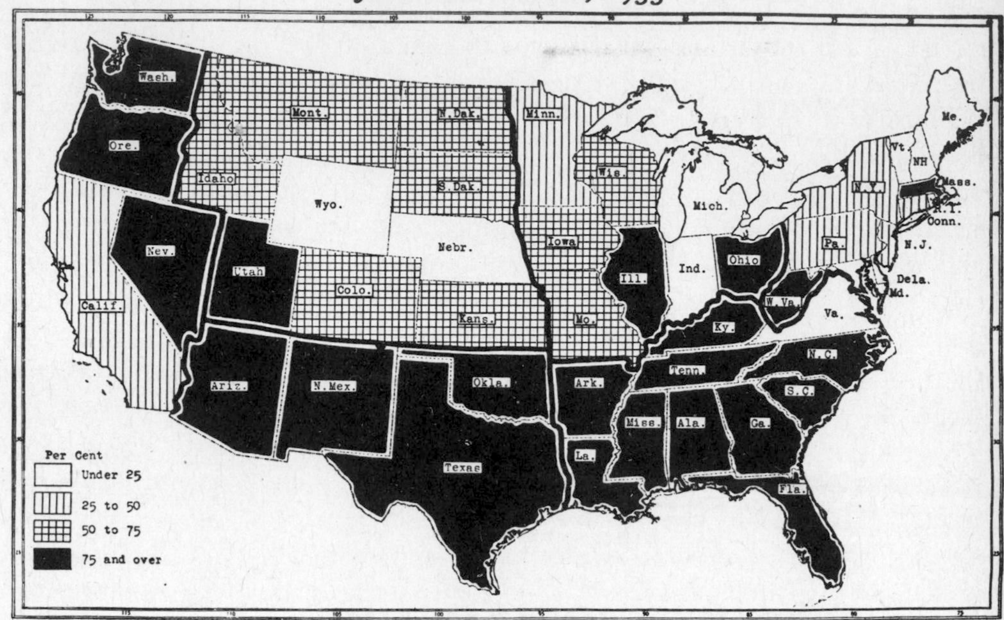

Per Cent of Total Families in Each State Receiving Unemployment Relief From Public Funds, September, 1933

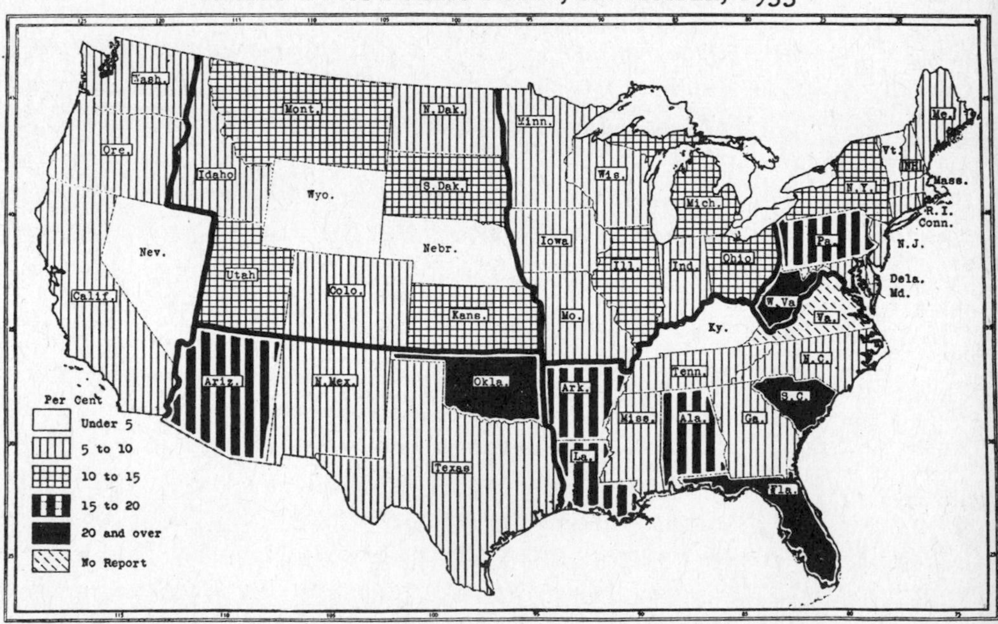

These should be compared with later variations (see also p. 136) and with the per capita contributions and also with state pro rata of all relief funds. So compared the absolute amounts to most of the Southern States appears small compared to New York or Pennsylvania.

all of the states except Florida fall within the lowest quartile. Eight of the Southeastern States show less than $10 as compared to 20 other states with more than $20.

145. An important poverty-wealth index of the region may possibly be found in the analysis of federal emergency relief obligations and expenditures in relation to total state funds for the same purpose. Measured by this index the Southeastern Region ranks lowest with seven of the states showing no state contribution in 1933, with two others less than one-tenth of one per cent, and only Kentucky and Tennessee contributing 2.3 and 2.4 per cent respectively to the total of more than $100,000,000. Yet the Southeastern States with 20 per cent of the population and contributing 20 per cent of the federal internal revenue received less than 17 per cent of the federal relief funds. Once again the Southeast's proportion of farm crop rentals and individual farm loans was large. The Southeast accounted for 71.6 per cent of the 385,000 loans of 1931 and 69.1 per cent of the $47,000,000 of loan money, while the two southern regions accounted for more than 80 per cent of the first year's crop rentals under the AAA. Once again in the index of contributions for philanthropic purposes the Southeast is the lowest, reporting a per capita contribution of $1.58 as compared with the Northeast's $7.51; the Middle States' $4.08; the Far West's $3.30; the Northwest's $1.96; and the Southwest's $1.92.

146. Other similar indices may be examined in the later analysis of the institutional wealth of the region as found in education, health, politics, religion, public welfare, and social work. Still others will be reflected in the opportunities for new developments, catalogued as basic to regional planning, including a long list such as the production of forest products, clay and mineral uses, increased manufacturing of special commodities, increased interregional and international trade, increased basic consumption of commodities, and still other increase in the ratio of production over this increased consumption.

X. THE SOUTHERN PEOPLE

147. Center and symbol of all the region's culture and capacity are its more than twenty-five million vibrant folk, 20 per cent of the nation's human wealth. More than the mere census count of 25,550,890 of the nation's 122,775,046 melting pot, they represent the living, striving, creative wealth of the region, reflecting the epic of those "giants in the earth" whose episodes and conquests are perpetually reminiscent of the exterior appearance and the inner psychological realities in the American picture. Yet, also like the nation, they reflect great contrasts and heterogeneity as well as similarities and homogeneity. As for any democracy, so here and

Percentage Gain or Loss in Negro Population, 1920-1930

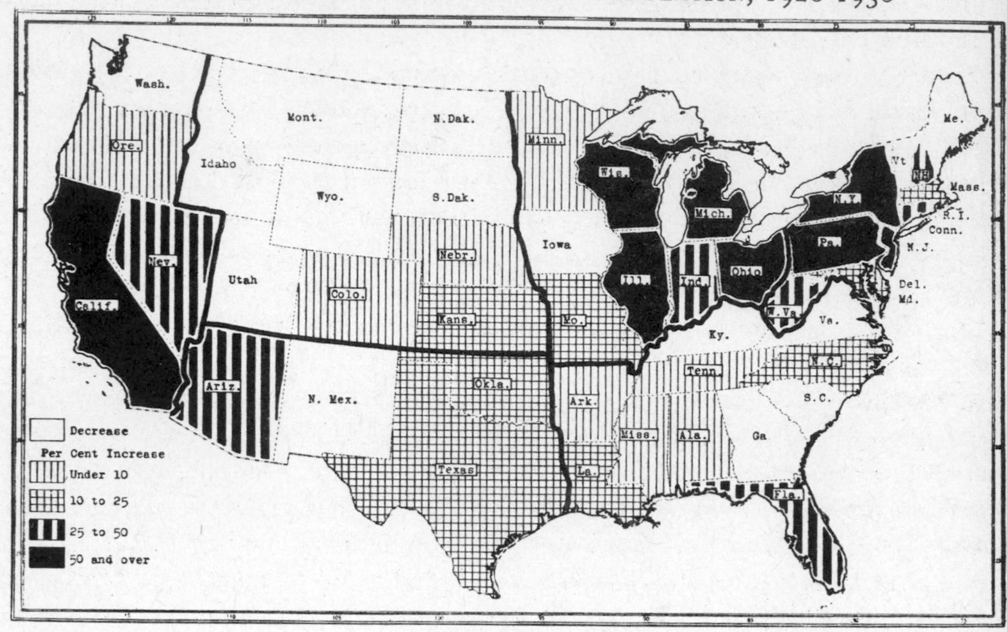

Percentage of Negroes in Population, 1930

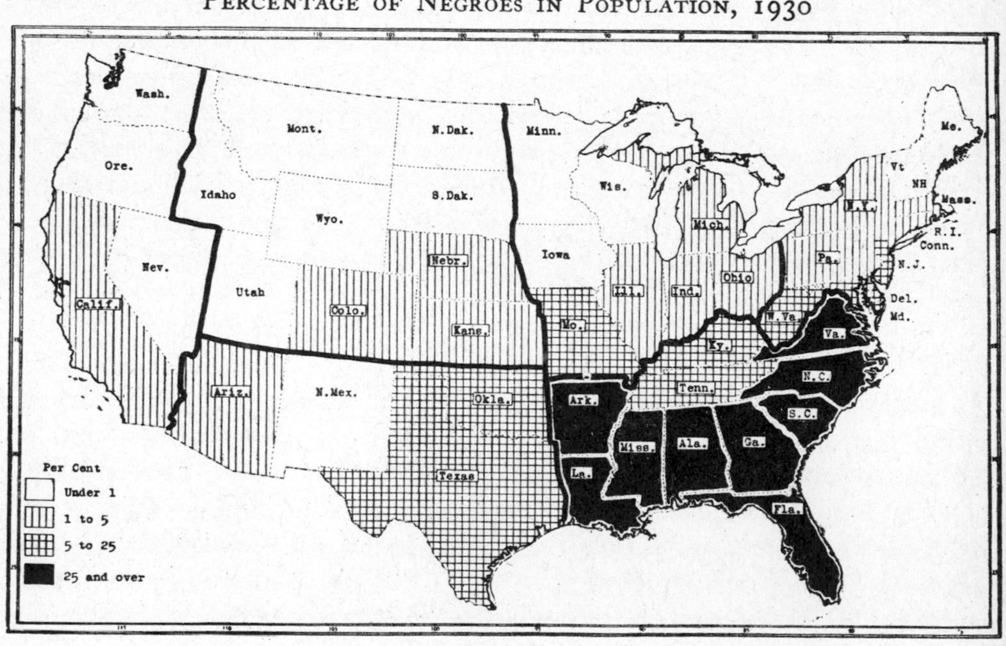

perhaps more so than for the nation as a whole, they are alike the hope and the despair of the region. Paradox again, they represent too many people in a region which is constantly complaining of its losses of millions of migrants to other regions of the nation. They reflect too many people on farms in a region recommended for the increased farm life. Yet the real measure of this human wealth is determined not only by the number but by the kind of folks they are; by the number and kind of their increase, decrease and mobility; by their ethnic composition; and by the cumulative character of their institutions and culture. What the people do and how they do it; what they want and how they go about getting what they want; how they lead and how they follow; and what they purpose in their hearts to do for the future—all of these are basic indices to the most definitive of all cultural wealth.

148. Of all these "southern people" nearly 8,000,000, or 30 per cent, are Negroes. No southeastern state except Kentucky and Tennessee has fewer than a fourth of its population Negroes, while Mississippi has half, and four other states, Alabama, Louisiana, Georgia, and South Carolina, have more than a third. There are, however, yet other four million Negroes in the nation outside of the Southeast, or approximately as many as were all the people of the nation in Jefferson's day. Of these a million are in the Southwest, a million and a half in the Northeast, a little more than a million in the Middle States, and a hundred thousand each in the Northwest and the Far West. This interregional contact of races is one of the important elements in the regional cultural landscape. Likewise the ratio of Negro to white population constitutes one of the indices by which the border states are classified as Southeast or otherwise and by which the Southeast is logically differentiated from the Southwest. Thus, Missouri and West Virginia each has only about 6 per cent Negro population, while Texas and Maryland show respectively less than 15 and 17 per cent, with Oklahoma barely 7 per cent.

149. The changing landscape of the nation with reference to its Negro population represents an extraordinary spectacle of cultural evolution. The Negro assumes an increasingly important place in spite of the fact that in the Southeast every one of the eleven states showed substantial decrease in the ratio of Negroes to the total population with the percentage of Negro increase considerably below that of the white population, and with absolute decrease in the Negro population itself in Virginia, South Carolina, Georgia, Kentucky. On the other hand, there was a notable increase both in the percentage of the Negro population itself and in their ratio to the total in many of the states outside of the South, especially of the Northeast and Middle States. Thus, in Michigan there was an in-

Population of Southeastern States, 1910, 1920, and 1930

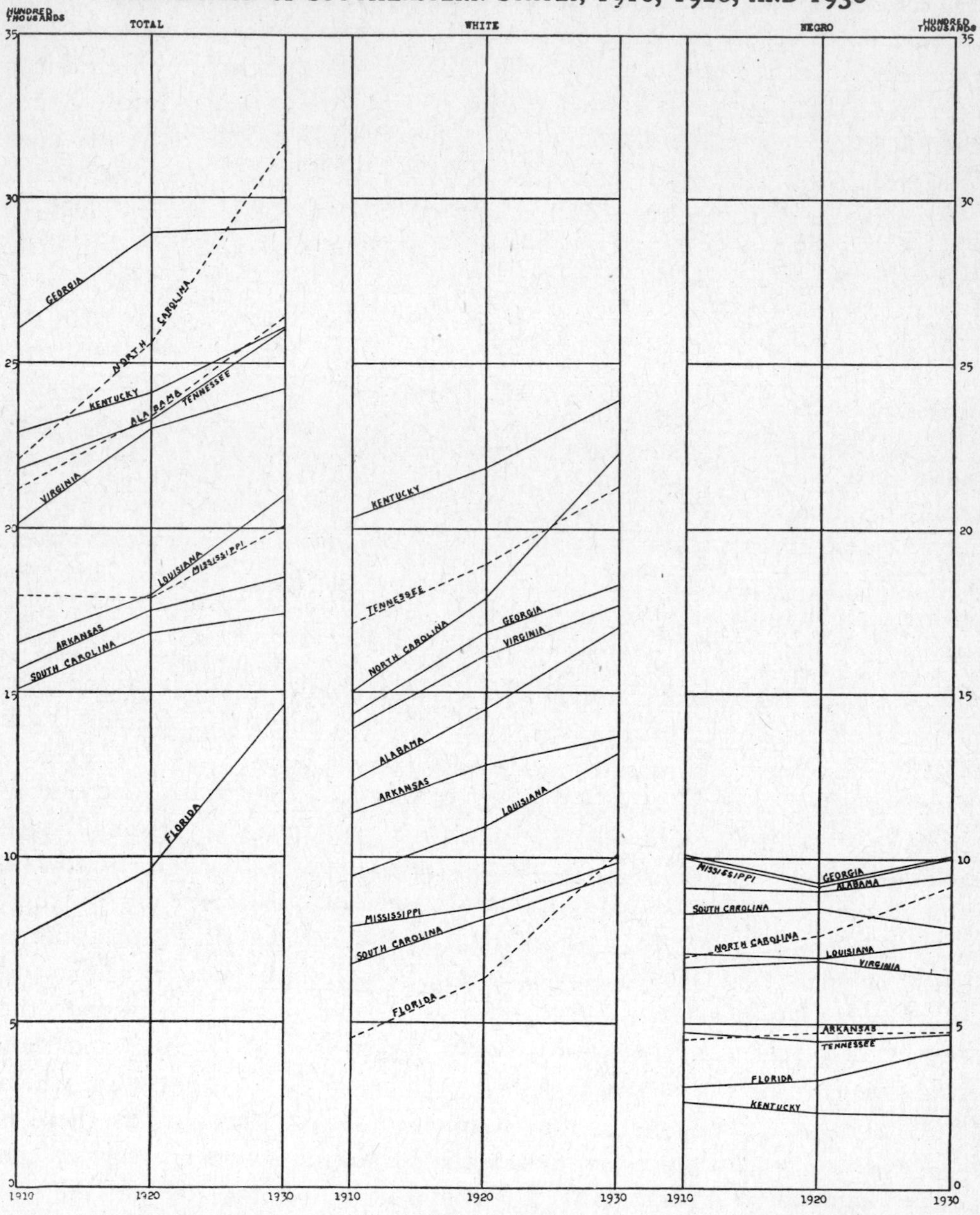

Regional Increase in Population by Decades, 1860-1930

STATE AND REGION	1870	1880	1890	1900	1910	1920	1930
Southeast	*3.5*	*30.6*	*17.5*	*18.0*	*15.0*	*10.0*	*11.8*
Virginia	−23.3	23.5	9.5	12.0	11.2	12.0	4.9
North Carolina	7.9	30.7	15.6	17.1	16.5	16.0	23.9
South Carolina	0.3	41.1	15.6	16.4	13.1	11.1	3.3
Georgia	12.0	30.2	19.1	20.6	17.7	11.0	0.4
Florida	33.7	43.5	45.2	35.0	42.4	28.7	51.6
Kentucky	14.3	24.8	12.7	15.5	6.6	5.5	8.2
Tennessee	13.4	22.6	14.6	14.3	8.1	7.0	11.9
Alabama	3.4	26.6	19.9	20.8	16.9	9.8	12.7
Mississippi	4.6	36.7	14.0	20.3	15.8	−0.4	12.2
Arkansas	11.3	65.6	40.6	16.3	20.0	11.3	5.8
Louisiana	2.7	29.3	19.0	23.5	19.9	8.6	16.9

crease in Negro population of 182 per cent; in Wisconsin, 106 per cent; in Illinois, 80 per cent; in Ohio, 60 per cent; in New York, 108 per cent. In some of the eastern and western cities the increase was three or four times as great as the increase in southern cities. High cities in the Middle States include four with more than 200 per cent. The Far West showed four California cities with more than 100 per cent increase. On the other hand, no southeastern city except Chattanooga and Miami reported as much as 75 per cent increase, while Richmond showed an actual decrease of a little more than one per cent. Yet, like the white urban increase, the Negro population in southeastern cities as a whole increased more rapidly than the rural.

150. Of the total population, the Southeast has the smallest ratio of native white of any region. These percentages are: the Southeast, 68.6; Southwest, 74.8; Far West, 77; Northwest, 87; Middle States, 75; Northeast, 73. Nearly all of the white population in the Southeast, however, is native born, the Carolinas recording less than one-half of one per cent otherwise. Almost the same ratios apply to the foreign born, the Southeastern States continuing to show the smallest ratio of foreign-born folk with a consistent decrease even in this small number. Thus all of the Southeastern States, except Virginia, Louisiana, and Florida, still show less than one per cent foreign-born population. This is in contrast to such states as New York with 26.3 per cent; Rhode Island with 25.3; Massachusetts, 25.1; Connecticut, 24.3; New Jersey, 22. During the last decade there was a decrease in foreign-born population in the following states: Virginia, 5.8 per cent; South Carolina, 8.2; Georgia, 13.9; Kentucky, 28.9; Tennessee, 15.4; Alabama, 10.8; Missouri, 11.1; Arkansas, 26.2. Of this white population, further, at least 4,000,000 abide in the hill country of the Southern Appalachians; 4,900,000 in all the Southern Appalachians including West Virginia and the western fringe. These millions represent the original gateway to the west; they continue a gateway between the past and the future; and they constitute one of several blocks of the population of the Southeast, which afford abundant evidence to support the conclusion that, just as there is no longer a "South," so any blanket classification, "southern people," no longer constitutes an authentic characterization. Even within the restricted Southern Appalachian Region of some 200 counties in six states with an area of a half hundred million acres, there is considerable diversity of people and culture. Another distinctive block of white folks of the Southeast outside of the Appalachian Highlands are the four million and more farm tenants already catalogued as elemental factors in the agrarian South.

Effective Fertility and Net Reproduction Trend of Native Whites by Geographical Divisions and by States. Data of 1920 and 1930

Adapted from Frank Lorimer and Frederick Osborn, *Dynamics of Population*

STATE AND REGION	Children under 5 with native white mothers per 1,000 native white women aged 20-44 years			Index of net reproduction per generation. (1.00 = trend toward stationary population).		
	Data of 1920(*) (a)	Data of 1930(†) (b)	Value for 1930 as *per cent* of value for 1920 ($\frac{b^*}{a}$)	Data of 1920(**) (Permanent replacement ratio: 472) (c)	Data of 1930(‡) (Permanent replacement ratio: 443) (d)	Value for 1930 as *per cent* of value for 1920 ($\frac{d^*}{c}$)
Southeat						
Virginia	688	594	86	1.46	1.34	92
North Carolina	827	694	84	1.75	1.57	90
South Carolina	777	648	83	1.65	1.46	89
Georgia	731	598	82	1.55	1.35	87
Florida	627	520	83	1.33	1.17	88
Kentucky	722	674	94	1.53	1.52	100
Tennessee	706	615	87	1.50	1.39	93
Alabama	786	682	87	1.67	1.54	92
Mississippi	740	659	89	1.57	1.49	95
Arkansas	798	672	84	1.69	1.52	90
Louisiana	659	583	89	1.40	1.32	94
Southwest						
Oklahoma	722	599	83	1.53	1.35	88
Texas	630	514	82	1.33	1.16	87
New Mexico	757	688	91	1.60	1.55	97
Arizona	580	472	81	1.23	1.07	87
Northeast						
Maine	515	539	105	1.09	1.22	112
New Hampshire	435	463	106	.92	1.04	113
Vermont	525	539	103	1.11	1.22	109
Massachusetts	359	374	105	.76	.84	112
Rhode Island	363	393	108	.77	.89	115
Connecticut	371	374	101	.79	.84	107
New York	362	351	97	.77	.79	104
New Jersey	402	372	93	.85	.84	99
Delaware	491	421	86	1.04	.95	91
Pennsylvania	512	478	93	1.08	1.08	100
Maryland	507	453	89	1.07	1.02	95
West Virginia	788	712	90	1.67	1.61	96
Dist. of Columbia	240	262	109	.51	.59	116
Middle States						
Ohio	482	446	93	1.02	1.01	99
Indiana	519	483	93	1.10	1.09	99
Illinois	450	395	88	.95	.89	94
Michigan	524	505	96	1.11	1.14	103
Wisconsin	548	502	92	1.16	1.13	97
Minnesota	538	477	89	1.14	1.08	95
Iowa	546	491	90	1.16	1.11	96
Missouri	510	445	87	1.08	1.00	93
Northwest						
North Dakota	722	634	88	1.53	1.43	94
South Dakota	670	573	86	1.42	1.29	91
Nebraska	578	506	88	1.22	1.14	93
Kansas	574	498	87	1.22	1.12	92
Montana	620	514	83	1.31	1.16	88
Idaho	729	619	85	1.54	1.40	90
Wyoming	593	534	90	1.26	1.21	96
Colorado	516	465	90	1.09	1.05	96
Utah	788	677	86	1.67	1.53	92
Far West						
Nevada	477	423	95	.95	.95	90
Washington	462	388	84	.98	.88	89
Oregon	463	383	83	.98	.86	88
California	341	305	89	.72	.69	95
United States	538	479	89	1.14	1.08	95

* Ratios by Thompson, *Ratio of Children to Women*, 1920, pp. 200-201.
† Based on Census data.
** Permanent replacement quota based on *United States Abridged Life Tables*, 1919-1920. (See Prefatory Note, Appendix 2, above.)
‡ Permanent replacement quota based on life tables prepared by the Statistical Bureau of the Metropolitan Life Insurance Company. (See Prefatory Note, Appendix 2, above.)

151. Yet an increasing number of southern people live in urban communities. In 1930 the Southeast had nearly as many of its people residing in cities as there were total Negroes in the population. These nearly eight million urban folk, constituting nearly 30 per cent, have grown quickly since the turn of the century from two and three-quarter millions or 15 per cent of the total at that time. Florida with 51.7 per cent followed by Louisiana with 39.7 per cent and Tennessee with 34.3 are the only states with as many as a third of the people living in the cities. This is in contrast to such states as Rhode Island with 92.4 per cent; Massachusetts, 90.2; and New York's 83.6 is almost the exact ratio which Mississippi has of rural population. On the other hand, the percentage increase of urban population in the Southeast from 1920 to 1930 was greater than for the nation, being respectively 39.6 for the last decade and 175.9 since 1900 as compared to 26.9 and 126.9 for the nation as a whole. Except for the Far West and the Southwest, the Southeast had the largest ratio of urban increase. Of the southern people in cities, two and a half million or a little over a third live in cities of 100,000 or more, such cities increasing in the Southeast from three in 1900 to 13 in 1930, being an increase of 333 per cent as compared with the other regions: Northeast, 94 per cent; Middle States, 92; Northwest, 150; Far West, 400. In the Southwest there were seven cities of 100,000 or more population in 1930 and none in 1900. The Southeast by 1930 had developed 16 metropolitan districts with an aggregate population of 3,708,182, or about half of all its urban population.

152. The white population of the Southeast tends to reproduce at a higher rate and has a larger ratio of children and young people than any other region. The ratio is much larger than for the nation as a whole and nearly twice as high as for a number of states. For instance, the average for all the Southeastern States shows more than double the number of children under five years of age, with native white mothers per 1,000 native white women 20-44 years, as for the State of California. California's 341 stands in stark contrast to North Carolina's 827. Connecticut's 371, Rhode Island's 363, New York's 362, and Massachusetts' 359 are more than doubled by Alabama's 786, South Carolina's 777, Mississippi's 740, and Arkansas' 798. Or to cite an index of net reproduction per generation in which 100 represents the trend toward a stationary population, all the Southeastern States, except Florida, show an index of over 130 with four states over 150 as compared to all of the Far Western States, six of the Northeastern States, and Illinois in the Middle States, below the 100 index.

153. The Southeastern States afford a superabundance of youth and a small proportion of the aged; heavy burden, on the one hand, for educa-

Rural Farm Population Under 5 Years Old Per Thousand Women 15 to 44 Years Old, April 1, 1930

Adapted from the U. S. Bureau of Agricultural Economics

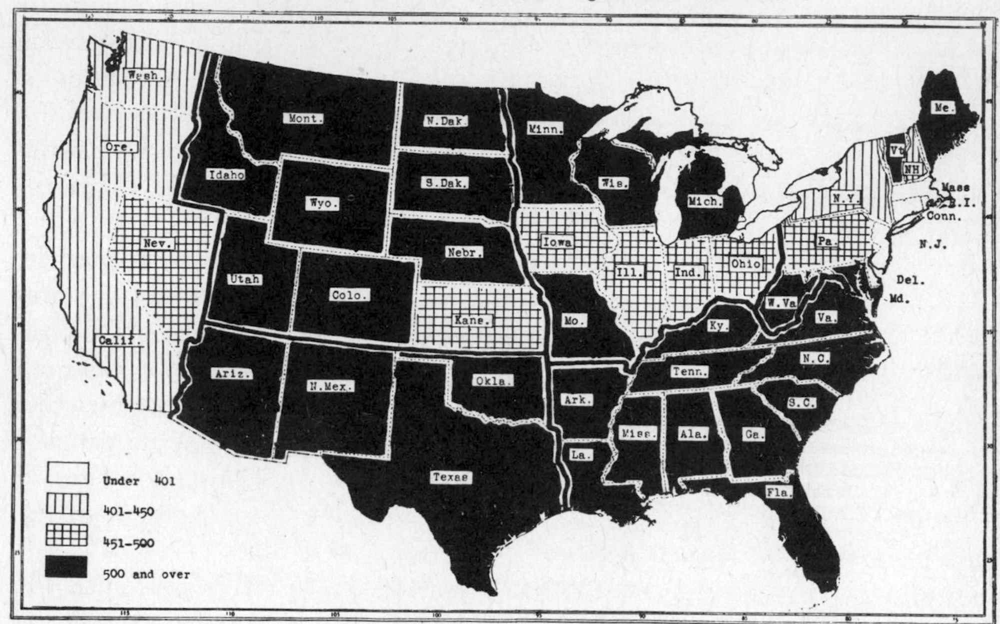

Per Cent of Total Population Fifty-Five Years of Age and Over, 1930

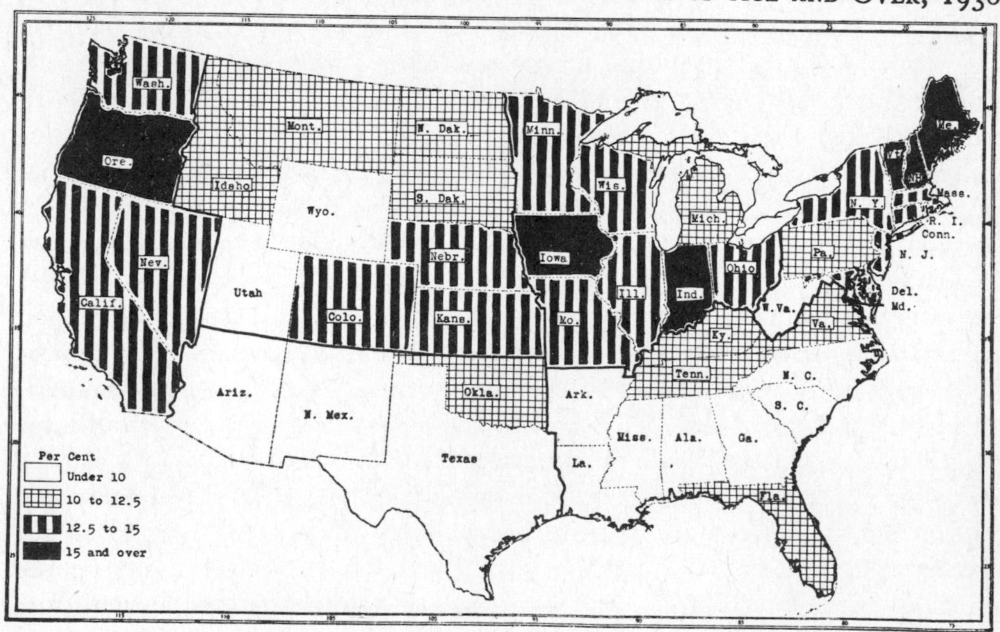

tion, and lighter, on the other, for old age security. Thus, with the exception of the Dakotas, Idaho, and West Virginia, no state outside of the southern regions records as much as 40 per cent of its population under 19 years of age, and no Southeastern State, except Florida, shows a ratio as low as 40 per cent. In contrast to the low states of California and Nevada with 30 and 31 per cent are the Carolinas with 50 and 49. In ratios of people 55 years of age and over, the Carolinas again with 7.9 and 8.4 per cent contrast with New Hampshire and Maine with 18.6 and 17.8 per cent respectively. Again, the Southeastern States are below the other regions in the proportion of people in the prime of work age, from 20 to 54 years, at least eight of the eleven states falling within the lowest quartile. The Carolinas with 41 and 42 per cent again contrast with the high states of Nevada and California with approximately 55 per cent each. Of population 15 years of age or older who are married, the Southeast ranks high in the number of females, seven of the eleven states in the highest quartile, but no southeastern state ranks among the topmost twelve in the ratio of married men. This and the relatively small ratio of men at the ages of 20 to 55 may have its relation to the large migration of people from the Southeastern States.

154. The people of the Southeastern States continue to replenish the other regions. The birth rate of all the Southeastern States except Florida and Tennessee is over 20 per 1,000 population, while no other states outside of the southern regions rank so high except Utah, West Virginia, North Dakota, and Michigan. North Carolina, Alabama, New Mexico, and Utah are the four with a birth rate of 24 or more, while the four states of the Far West are the only ones with a ratio below 15. In excess of births over deaths the Southeast outranks any other, with an index of 9.5 compared to 8.1 for the Southwest, 6.1 for the Northeast, 6.4 for the Middle States, 8.9 for the Northwest, and 3.1 for the Far West. In the meantime, more than 3,500,000 of those born in the Southeast have moved to states outside the region between 1900 and 1930. What the estimated money value of this human wealth would be to the region depends upon the per capita estimate of capital wealth and upon opportunities offered by the region for its human capital wealth. At an appraisal of half of the maximum rate used by economists the aggregate would approach the present stupendous national debt.

155. Of the twenty-five million people in the Southeast nearly ten million are at work in the gainful occupations. This constitutes 49.6 per cent as compared with the nation's ratio of 49.4 per cent of all its people gainfully occupied. Nearly four and a quarter million are in agriculture; nearly two million in manufacturing; a million and a quarter in trade and

PROPORTION OF THE POPULATION 10 YEARS OLD AND OVER GAINFULLY OCCUPIED

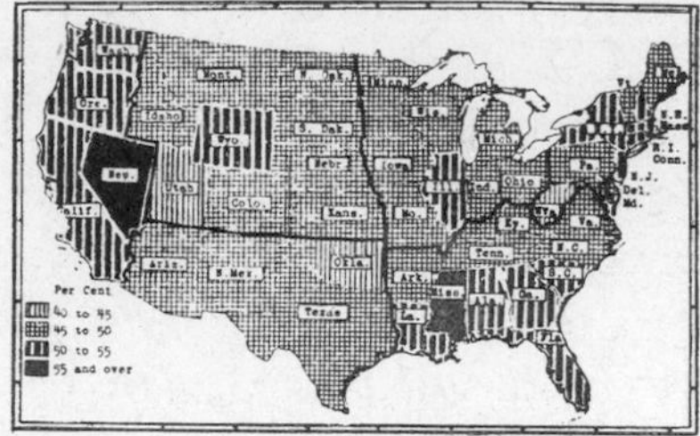

PROPORTION OF FEMALES 10 YEARS OLD AND OVER GAINFULLY OCCUPIED

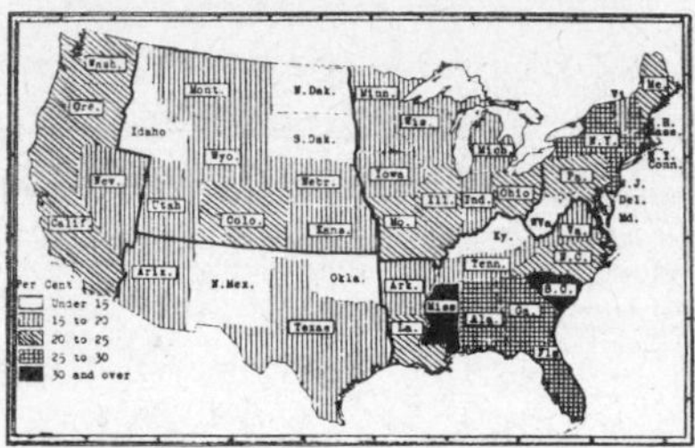

PROPORTION OF CHILDREN 10-17 YEARS OLD GAINFULLY OCCUPIED

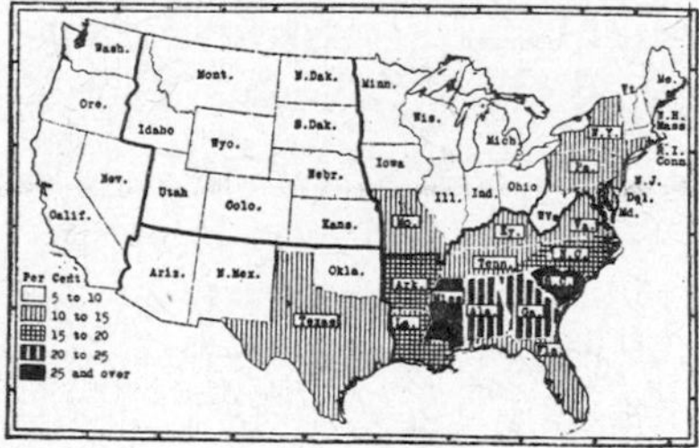

PROPORTION OF THE POPULATION GAINFULLY OCCUPIED, BY REGIONS

General Population

Per Cent

0 10 20 30 40 50

United States
Southeast
Southwest
Northeast
Middle States
Northwest
Far West

FEMALES

United States
Southeast
Southwest
Northeast
Middle States
Northwest
Far West

CHILDREN

United States
Southeast
Southwest
Northeast
Middle States
Northwest
Far West

PROPORTION OF GAINFULLY OCCUPIED, 1930, AMONG: THE GENERAL POPULATION 10 YEARS AND OVER, FEMALES 10 YEARS AND OVER, AND CHILDREN 10-17 YEARS

	General Population		Females		Children	
	Number Gainfully Occupied	Per Cent of Total Population 10 Years and Over	Number Gainfully Occupied	Per Cent of Total Females 10 Years and Over	Number Gainfully Occupied	Per Cent of Total Children 10-17 Years
United States	48,829,880	49.4	10,752,076	22.1	2,145,960	11.3
Southeast						
Virginia	880,211	47.0	182,267	19.5	48,641	11.5
North Carolina	1,140,971	48.5	272,965	22.9	111,897	18.6
South Carolina	687,737	53.2	206,761	31.2	92,447	26.3
Georgia	1,162,158	51.9	311,939	27.4	121,408	22.4
Florida	598,939	51.0	149,984	25.7	29,587	13.1
Kentucky	907,095	45.2	146,678	14.8	48,997	11.2
Tennessee	958,386	47.3	195,324	19.1	62,918	14.1
Alabama	1,026,295	51.3	254,014	25.1	116,667	24.0
Mississippi	844,905	55.4	231,728	30.3	111,073	30.5
Arkansas	667,845	47.0	119,193	17.0	57,318	17.1
Louisiana	815,616	50.3	191,420	23.5	59,455	16.6
Total	9,690,158	49.6	2,262,273	23.0	860,408	18.8
Southwest						
Oklahoma	828,004	44.9	129,346	14.5	31,796	7.8
Texas	2,206,767	48.5	421,708	18.9	125,744	13.1
New Mexico	142,607	45.4	22,101	14.7	5,920	8.2
Arizona	165,296	49.3	29,971	19.4	5,595	8.4
Total	3,342,674	47.4	603,126	17.7	169,055	11.2
Northeast						
Maine	308,603	48.0	68,493	21.4	8,141	7.0
New Hampshire	192,666	50.4	49,956	25.9	5,852	8.9
Vermont	141,203	48.4	28,397	19.9	4,494	8.5
Massachusetts	1,814,315	51.7	528,999	29.2	60,524	9.9
Rhode Island	297,172	53.0	87,829	30.4	16,144	15.8
Connecticut	677,208	51.2	178,007	26.8	32,129	12.8
New York	5,523,337	52.5	1,415,105	26.9	174,359	10.2
New Jersey	1,712,106	51.4	416,512	25.1	75,779	12.5
Pennsylvania	3,722,103	48.1	803,892	20.9	156,351	10.1
Delaware	98,104	49.9	20,883	21.6	3,480	9.9
Maryland	672,879	50.8	157,692	23.9	30,656	12.8
D. of Columbia	243,853	58.2	88,825	40.1	3,855	7.3
West Virginia	570,452	43.8	82,198	13.1	20,707	6.9
Total	15,974,001	50.6	3,926,788	24.9	592,471	10.4
Middle States						
Ohio	2,615,764	48.1	539,606	20.1	58,097	6.0
Indiana	1,251,065	47.4	235,304	18.1	31,404	6.7
Illinois	3,184,684	50.3	715,468	22.9	95,780	8.8
Michigan	1,927,347	49.5	359,822	19.4	47,967	6.8
Wisconsin	1,129,461	47.5	215,214	18.7	35,183	7.8
Minnesota	992,798	47.8	200,965	19.9	31,145	7.8
Iowa	912,835	45.5	163,522	16.5	28,236	7.6
Missouri	1,457,968	48.9	299,234	20.1	57,606	11.1
Total	13,471,922	48.6	2,729,135	20.0	385,418	7.7
Northwest						
North Dakota	240,303	45.6	36,213	14.8	10,036	8.0
South Dakota	247,653	45.6	37,310	14.6	8,478	7.2
Nebraska	507,008	45.8	89,721	16.7	16,285	7.6
Kansas	694,232	45.7	119,160	16.1	19,407	6.8
Montana	216,479	49.8	32,274	16.7	5,673	6.5
Idaho	162,232	46.5	22,286	13.9	4,624	6.0
Wyoming	92,448	51.7	12,739	16.4	2,288	6.8
Colorado	402,867	48.2	80,993	20.0	13,315	8.5
Utah	170,000	44.0	28,984	15.4	4,938	5.4
Total	2,733,222	46.5	459,680	16.3	85,044	7.2
Far West						
Washington	664,730	50.6	126,676	20.6	12,246	5.5
Oregon	409,645	51.0	81,142	21.3	9,530	7.2
California	2,500,644	52.0	557,354	24.2	31,195	4.6
Nevada	42,884	56.4	5,902	19.3	593	5.3
Total	3,617,903	51.7	771,074	23.3	53,564	5.1

transportation; another million in domestic and personal service. As compared with the nation the Southeast has a larger ratio in domestic and personal service. As compared with the nation, the Southeast has a larger ratio in agriculture, 43.5 per cent compared with 21.4 per cent; a little higher in forestry and fishing with 0.8 per cent and 0.5 per cent respectively. In all others there is a lower ratio; manufacturing 19.6 and 29.0; professional service, 4.5 and 10.1; clerical occupations, 3.8 and 8.2; or to group all the distributive and social service occupations, 34.7 per cent of the southeastern workers compare with 47.2 for the nation.

156. Relatively more children and women work in the Southeast than in the nation at large. Of children, 18.8 per cent or nearly a million are at work in the Southeast as compared with 11.3 per cent for the nation and lesser ratios for the Far West, 5.1; the Northwest, 7.2; the Middle States, 7.7; the Northeast, 10.4; and the Southwest, 11.2. The largest percentage of children from 10 to 17 years of age employed is in Mississippi with 30 per cent; South Carolina with 26 per cent; and Alabama with 24. Of these children, nearly three-fourths are engaged in agricultural work, a little over 11 per cent in industry, and about 14 per cent in distributive and social. This is in contrast to the Northeastern Region with 41 per cent of all children gainfully occupied in manufacturing and mechanical services and 48 per cent in distributive and social. The Southeast contrasts with other regions also in that 30 per cent of its women workers are on the farm as opposed to less than one per cent in the Northeast, 2.4 per cent in the Middle States, 2.5 in the Far West, 5.1 in the Northwest, and 16.1 in the Southwest. Compared with the Southeast's 37 per cent of women occupied with distributive and social service are the Far West's 87.2, the Northwest's 88.4, the Middle States' 80.6, the Southwest's 76.8, and the Northeast's 76.8. The Southeast, however, does not have as high ratio of total women employed as do the Northeast and Far West. The highest percentages for any states are South Carolina with 31.2 per cent; Rhode Island, 30.4; Mississippi, 30.3. Then follow Massachusetts, New York, Connecticut, New Hampshire, and Georgia, showing the contrasting emphasis upon industry and agriculture.

157. The further character of the people will be indicated by their institutions and their ways of doing things. Not susceptible to clear-cut objective measurement are the regional folkways of the people, their like-mindedness, and their regional conditioning. Reputed to be the most individualistic of all the regions, they coöperate most fully with the New Deal techniques. The richness of personality in mountain folk and Negro, the contrasting class distinction between farm tenant and cotton mill worker and many of the urban and more aristocratic folk of the South, and all

The Relative Standing of the States in Wealth

General indices from S. H. Hobbs representing the composite picture in 1930

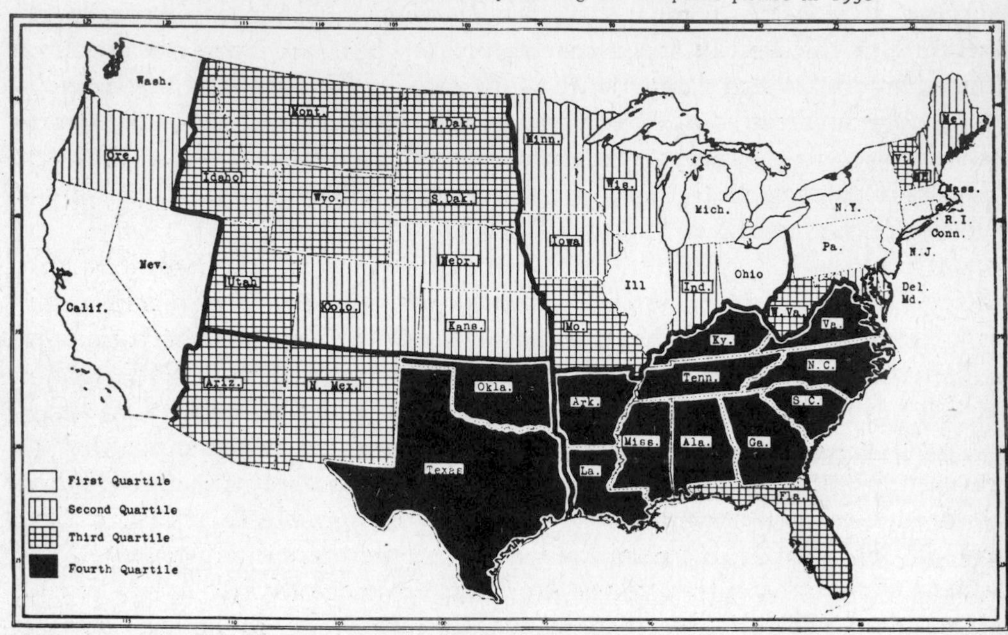

The Relative Standing of the States in Education

General indices from S. H. Hobbs representing the composite picture in 1930

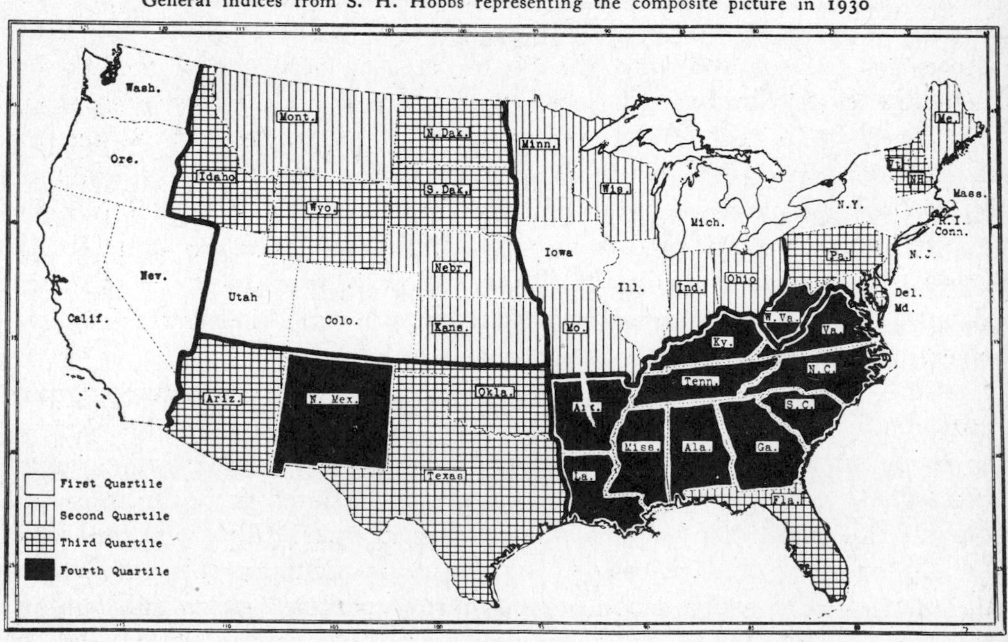

those qualities and situations which lift "the story of simple scattered localities, engaged in the homely tasks of living and living better into the dignity of world history"—these are elemental factors in any social inventory of the people and their culture. These are question marks in the appraisal of the comparative cultures of a Nevada ranking often in the upper brackets of the usual measurable average indices and a North Carolina ranking equally often in the lowest quartile of such measurement. These are factors in the culture product of a Southeast which stood out against public education, yet which ranks first in relative public educational efforts.

XI. THE EDUCATION OF THE PEOPLE

158. The story of the South's education, like that of its cultural development, is both complex and compound, yet simple enough in the telling, provided the chief elements of its drama and struggle are envisaged. "Historical relativity" is the first essential. Here as elsewhere, therefore, the mixed picture abounds in contrasts and paradoxes, requiring critical analysis and interpretation. Hidden in the realities of the region and scarcely measurable by the usual comparative indices are the heroic and sometimes poignant efforts of the people to make their education universal and potent, to build their schoolhouses and reconstruct their curricula according to the standards set down by the nation's leaders in education, some of which lacked regional balance and perspective. It is the story of what the people have accomplished through hard work and combative persistence by and among themselves and with substantial aid from philanthropy and federal grants from outside the region.

159. Perhaps the best framework around which to project the principal specific inventories may be found in three general conclusions. The first is that the region measured by any absolute standards has made great strides in its educational endeavors, increasing its quantitative achievement a hundredfold, straining its financial capacities to the limit, and making distinctive contributions in creative effort. The second is that, nevertheless, the region now ranks lowest of all the regions in most aspects of its educational equipment and work. It does not, therefore, develop its students, nor equip them equally for the competitive work of the nation and its regions. The third is that its catalogue of deficiencies represents the logical product of certain distinctive regional conditions, other than those already implied in cultural backgrounds, chronological lag, and rural economy. One of these is the basic load which is measured by the largest proportion of children of school age to the total population alongside the smallest income and wealth with which to educate them. Thus, the burden of supporting schools on a property tax in a poor state with a large ratio of

Per Cent of Public School Enrollment in High Schools

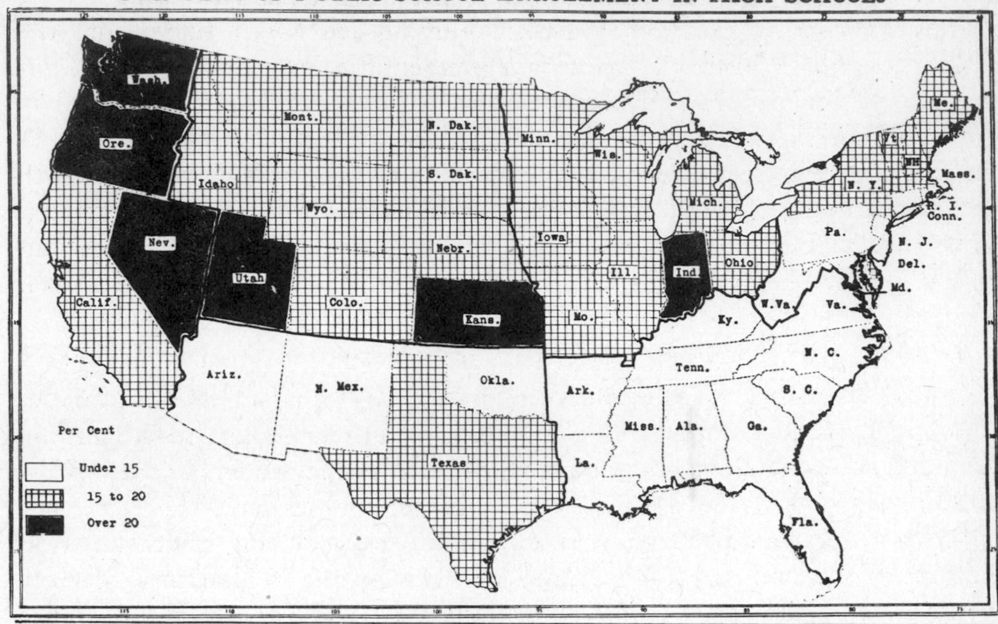

STATE AND REGION	Per Cent Total Enrollment in High Schools	Total Number of Graduates 1928	Per Cent Increase in Graduates 1911–1928
Southeast			
Virginia	10.2	5,877	463
North Carolina	12.1	9,533	980
South Carolina	11.3	3,363	284
Georgia	10.2	5,000	247
Florida	11.3	3,660	1,212
Kentucky	9.5	7,172	601
Tennessee	9.7	6,108	687
Alabama	8.6	5,113	650
Mississippi	8.3	3,191	303
Arkansas	8.1	3,250	384
Louisiana	11.5	4,379	511
Southwest			
Oklahoma	13.5	9,848	1,045
Texas	17.5	16,254	382
New Mexico	10.4	1,071	743
Arizona	13.5	1,523	864
Northeast			
Maine	18.7	3,683	127
New Hampshire	17.9	2,099	135
Vermont	17.1	1,367	88
Massachusetts	19.9	20,641	156
Rhode Island	14.3	2,096	248
Connecticut	14.8	6,056	220
New York	17.4	37,908	291
New Jersey	14.0	12,432	366
Delaware	15.5	704	263
Pennsylvania	13.9	35,976	232
Maryland	13.4	4,245	283
West Virginia	11.0	5,212	940
Middle States			
Ohio	18.7	31,010	220
Indiana	20.1	18,339	178
Illinois	19.5	32,444	308
Michigan	15.5	17,711	210
Wisconsin	17.8	14,490	213
Minnesota	16.2	14.411	302
Iowa	19.9	18,427	217
Missouri	18.4	13,723	205
Northwest			
North Dakota	15.5	3,505	429
South Dakota	17.0	4,275	368
Nebraska	20.0	10,987	261
Kansas	20.4	15,041	339
Montana	18.8	3,389	933
Idaho	19.7	3,267	703
Wyoming	20.0	1,279	948
Colorado	18.5	5,660	258
Utah	20.5	2,799	610
Far West			
Nevada	23.9	488	495
Washington	23.1	10,667	414
Oregon	22.6	5,875	496
California	19.8	27,293	534

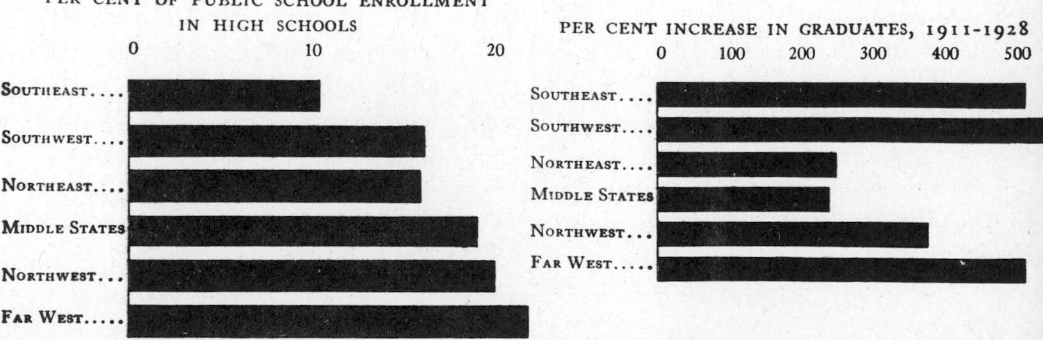

children may be more than ten times as heavy as for a rich state with fewer children. Important also is the dual load of a regional dichotomy of education. The chief phase of this dual load is that relating to Negro and white and applies to all education, from the lowest to the highest schools, as well as to libraries, playgrounds, and other cultural agencies. For institutions of higher learning the dichotomy of separate institutions goes further: for Negroes and whites; for men and women; for technical and liberal training; and all along the line, public and private. This handicap is accentuated by the further multiplicity of institutions representative of religious denominations within and without the region and of political and geographical subregions within the various states. Out of these arrangements have grown certain distinctive contributions, but also among the resulting products are overlapping duplication, competition, inadequate support, low standards, outmoded arrangements, lack of concentration of needed bodies of knowledge and services, uniform deficiencies in the techniques and tools necessary for the development and utilization of the human wealth of the region.

160. Turning to the first general conclusion, it is relatively easy to point up samplings of recent educational advance. First of all, the region has made extraordinary progress measured not only since reconstruction days but compared with the last three decades, 1900, 1910, 1920. There have been notable achievements in expenditures for education, in buildings, enrollment, curricula, not only in terms of comparison with its own early stages but also compared with the earlier nation. Thus, with its 25,000,000 people, just a third as many as the nation's 75,000,000 in 1900, the size of the Southeast's educational job in 1928 to 1930 was larger than that of the whole nation in many of its aspects at the turn of the century. Even with its relative shortage of high school students the region still enrolls more than all the nation did, and there are more accredited high schools in the region than all the nation had in 1900. From the viewpoint of its own progress and efforts the situation is equally impressive. The 60,000 high school graduates represent an increase of more than 500 per cent for the last two decades, while some of the states spend more on Negro education than they did for all education two or three decades ago. In the percentage of high school graduates continuing their education, seven of the Southeastern States are in the highest quartile and only two in the lowest.

161. Alongside low ranking in most financial indices there are exceptions in the upper measures. With less than 12 per cent of the nation's wealth the Southeast accounts for 20 per cent of the total expenditures for state supported institutions of higher learning, and has a little more than 20 per

Average Length of School Term in Days, 1927-1928

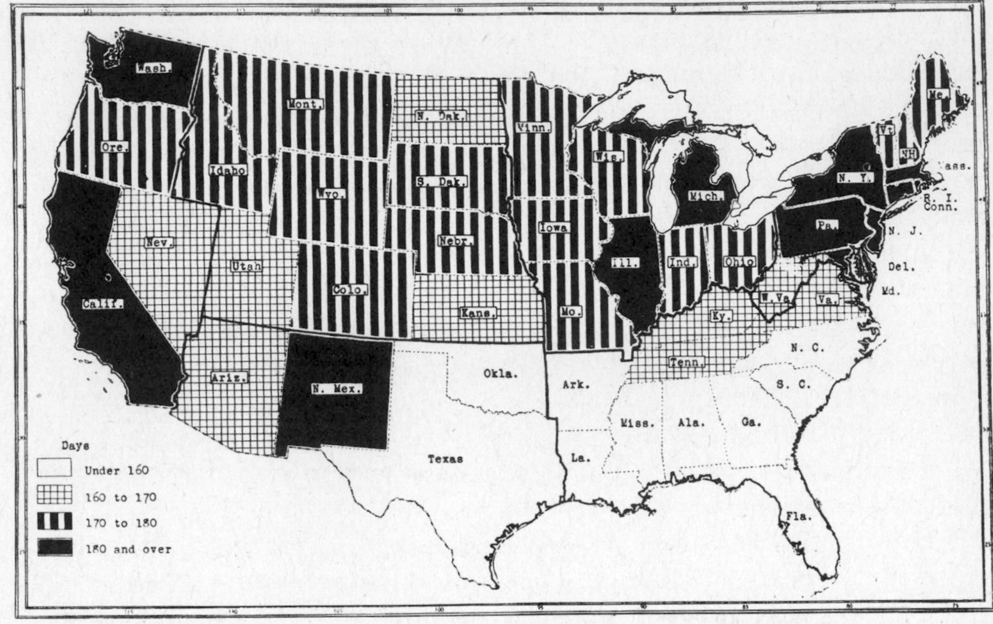

Rated according to a scale of national uniformities, Mississippi would have to expend 99.4 per cent of its tax moneys in order to reach the national average in educational standards.

Average Length of School Term in Days, 1927-1928

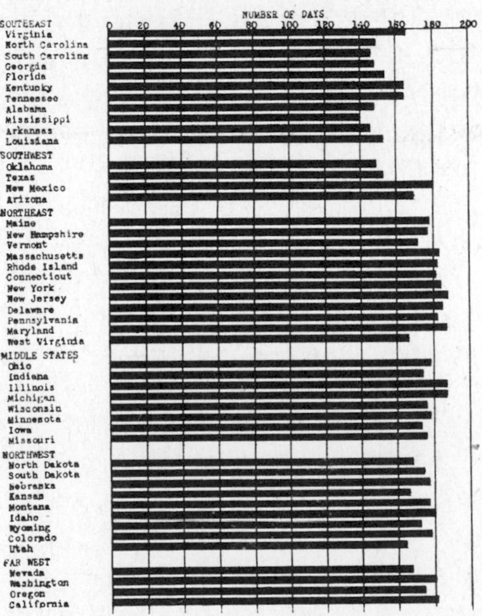

Average Number of Days Attended by Each Pupil Enrolled in 1920 and 1930

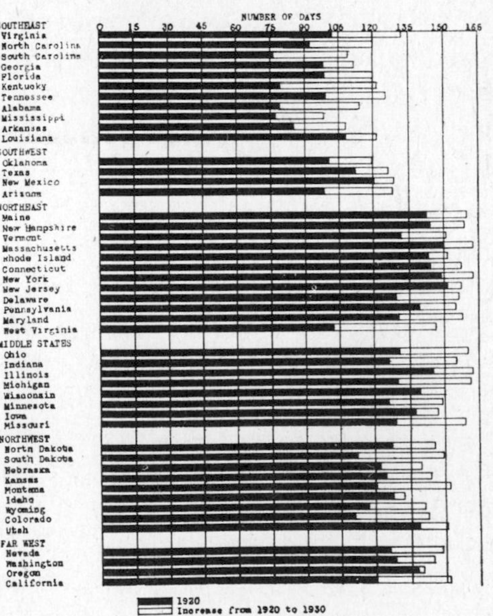

cent of the colleges and universities publicly supported and nearly 24 per cent of those privately supported. Furthermore, the Southeast appropriates a greater percentage of its total income for higher education than the rest of the nation, its ratio being .30 per cent compared to .19 per cent for the Middle States. In the highest quartile of states, in the percentage which investment in public school property is of wealth, are North Carolina, Mississippi, Florida, with only three states in the lowest. Five southern states rank higher than the average for the nation in the percentage of total wealth and total income appropriated for school purposes. Eighteen other states rank lower than the highest southern states in the appropriation per inhabitant for state support of colleges and universities for maintenance, the six states below any southern state being Pennsylvania, New York, Massachusetts, Connecticut, Rhode Island, and New Jersey. Again, although representing only a fifth of the people, the Southeast accounts for about a third of the public schools, about a third of the pupils transported over a similar ratio of miles and in more than a third of the school busses of the nation. Of these samplings of special achievements one other will suffice. The Southeastern States also show a larger ratio of total population enrolled in public schools than any other region, Mississippi showing nearly 34 per cent as contrasted with Rhode Island, New Hampshire, and Delaware with less than half as many.

162. Yet, turning to the other side of the picture, the average daily attendance per 100 pupils enrolled is lower in the Southeastern States. Thus, the two high states in enrollment, Mississippi and Tennessee, become low states with a daily attendance of 70 per 100 pupils enrolled compared to the two low states in enrollment, Rhode Island and New Hampshire, which become high states in attendance, with above 86. In average number of days attended, the Southeastern States are again in the lowest quartile, Mississippi ranking lowest with 98 days contrasted with Michigan with 171. The same is true in the average length of the school term, the range of difference being as much as 50 days. Still again, in the percentage of total enrollment in the high schools the lowest eight Southeastern States report less than half that of the eight highest states of the nation. The total picture shows the score card heavily against the region in length of school term, some children having two months' schooling less than the nation's mode; in high school facilities, thousands of children without access to high school advantages; and below national standards in equipment, facilities, teacher training; teachers' salaries 40 to 70 per cent of the nation's average; and the separate count against it for Negro schools, a story in itself.

163. The comparative deficiency continues in financial indices. In the value of school property per pupil enrolled, in the salary of teachers, in

Per Cent Total Illiteracy Ten Years of Age and Over, 1930

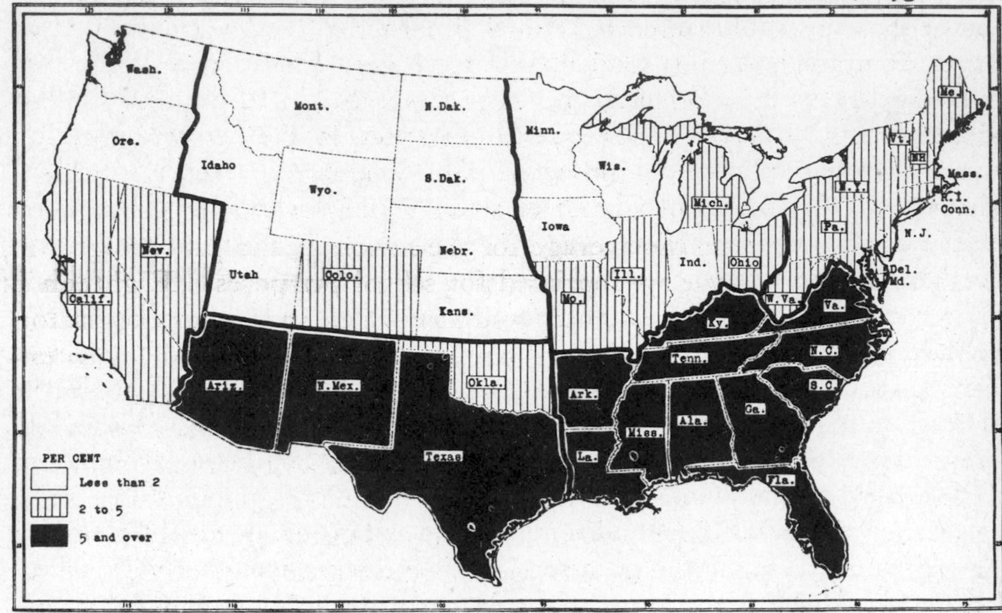

Per Cent Illiteracy Ten Years of Age and Over, 1930

STATE	Total		Native White		Negro		Male		Female		21 and Over, Male		21 and Over, Female	
	Rank	%	Rank	%	Rank	%	Rank	%	Rank	%	Rank	%	Rank	%
Iowa	1	0.8	7	0.4	2	2.0	1	0.8	1	0.7	1	1.0	1	.9
Oregon	2	1.0	32	1.5	5	2.5	2	1.0	2	0.9	3	1.3	2	1.1
Washington	2	1.0	2	0.3	7	2.9	2	1.0	3	1.0	2	1.2	3	1.3
Idaho	4	1.1	7	0.4	17	4.2	6	1.2	3	1.0	6	1.5	3	1.3
South Dakota	5	1.2	7	0.4	4	2.2	4	1.1	9	1.4	4	1.4	9	1.9
Nebraska	5	1.2	7	0.4	13	3.9	4	1.1	6	1.2	4	1.4	7	1.6
Kansas	5	1.2	15	0.5	27	5.9	8	1.3	6	1.2	7	1.6	6	1.5
Utah	5	1.2	2	0.3	10	3.2	8	1.3	5	1.1	9	1.7	5	1.4
Minnesota	9	1.3	7	0.4	2	2.0	6	1.2	8	1.3	7	1.6	8	1.7
North Dakota	10	1.5	7	0.4	11	3.4	10	1.4	11	1.6	10	1.8	13	2.3
Wyoming	11	1.6	2	0.3	17	4.2	11	1.7	11	1.6	11	2.0	11	2.0
Indiana	12	1.7	27	0.9	28	6.0	13	1.8	10	1.5	13	2.3	9	1.9
Montana	12	1.7	2	0.3	21	4.6	11	1.7	13	1.7	12	2.1	13	2.3
Wisconsin	14	1.9	19	0.6	20	4.4	13	1.8	15	1.9	14	2.4	15	2.5
Michigan	15	2.0	22	0.7	8	3.0	15	1.9	17	2.1	14	2.4	17	2.7
Vermont	16	2.2	29	1.3	23	4.9	19	2.6	13	1.7	21	3.2	12	2.2
Missouri	17	2.3	32	1.5	32	8.8	19	2.6	16	2.0	19	3.1	15	2.5
Ohio	17	2.3	22	0.7	30	6.4	16	2.3	19	2.2	16	2.9	19	2.9
Illinois	19	2.4	19	0.6	12	3.6	16	2.3	22	2.6	16	2.9	23	3.3
California	20	2.6	2	0.3	9	3.1	19	2.6	22	2.6	18	3.0	21	3.2
Maine	21	2.7	34	1.6	22	4.8	26	3.2	17	2.1	23	3.9	17	2.7
New Hampshire	21	2.7	25	0.8	13	3.9	22	2.8	21	2.5	22	3.5	21	3.2
Oklahoma	23	2.8	35	1.7	33	9.3	26	3.2	20	2.4	23	3.9	20	3.1
Colorado	23	2.8	25	0.8	13	3.9	18	2.5	24	3.1	19	3.1	24	3.9
Pennsylvania	25	3.1	19	0.6	17	4.2	23	2.9	25	3.3	23	3.9	25	4.4
Massachusetts	26	3.5	7	0.4	26	5.4	24	3.1	28	3.9	27	4.0	28	5.0
New York	27	3.7	15	0.5	5	2.5	24	3.1	31	4.3	23	3.9	29	5.4
New Jersey	28	3.8	15	0.5	25	5.1	28	3.5	30	4.2	28	4.4	30	5.5
Maryland	28	3.8	29	1.3	36	11.4	30	4.1	26	3.5	29	5.0	25	4.4
Delaware	30	4.0	28	1.2	37	13.2	31	4.2	27	3.8	31	5.2	27	4.9
Nevada	31	4.5	1	0.2	1	1.5	32	4.3	32	4.5	29	5.0	32	5.6
Connecticut	31	4.5	7	0.4	23	4.9	29	3.9	33	5.1	31	5.2	33	6.8
West Virginia	33	4.8	40	3.7	34	11.3	34	5.5	29	4.1	34	7.0	30	5.5
Rhode Island	34	4.9	22	0.7	31	8.1	33	4.4	34	5.4	33	5.8	35	7.0
Kentucky	35	6.6	46	5.7	40	15.4	37	7.7	34	5.4	38	9.3	33	6.8
Arkansas	36	6.8	39	3.5	41	16.1	36	7.4	37	6.2	37	9.2	39	8.2
Texas	36	6.8	31	1.4	38	13.4	35	6.8	39	6.8	35	7.8	38	8.0
Florida	38	7.1	36	1.9	42	18.8	37	7.7	38	6.5	36	8.7	37	7.8
Tennessee	39	7.2	44	5.4	39	14.9	39	8.4	36	6.0	39	10.3	36	7.7
Virginia	40	8.7	40	3.7	34	11.3	41	10.0	40	7.4	41	12.1	40	9.5
Georgia	41	9.4	38	3.3	43	19.9	42	10.6	41	8.3	42	12.5	41	10.9
North Carolina	42	10.0	45	5.6	44	20.6	43	11.2	42	8.9	44	14.2	42	12.0
Arizona	43	10.1	15	0.5	16	4.0	40	9.0	43	11.4	40	10.4	43	13.7
Alabama	44	12.6	42	4.8	47	26.2	45	13.5	44	11.6	46	16.6	44	15.2
Mississippi	45	13.1	37	2.7	45	23.2	47	14.4	45	11.8	47	18.0	45	15.6
New Mexico	46	13.3	48	7.7	28	6.0	43	11.2	48	15.7	43	13.6	48	20.3
Louisiana	47	13.5	47	7.3	46	23.3	46	13.6	46	13.5	45	16.5	46	17.2
South Carolina	48	14.9	43	5.1	48	26.9	48	15.8	47	14.1	48	18.8	47	18.4

the per capita expenditures in public day schools, and other indices the Southern States rank uniformly in the lowest quartile. Georgia, for instance, contrasts with California: Average annual teachers' salaries $546 and $2,337; value of school property $46 and $386; per capita total expenditures, $6.11 and $25.43. Similarly in a count of a dozen other aspects the region ranks lowest, with a final composite ranking in more than 20 indices, listing the lowest quartile states as follows: Mississippi, Alabama, Arkansas, Georgia, South Carolina, Louisiana, North Carolina, New Mexico, Arizona, Tennessee, Virginia, and Kentucky. Perhaps the most commonly cited indices are those of illiteracy, reading, and library facilities, where there is again uniform ranking in the lowest quartile. The range in illiteracy, for instance, is from South Carolina with nearly 15 per cent to Iowa with less than one per cent; from ten Southeastern States averaging more than ten per cent to more than a dozen other states with less than 2 per cent. More marked is the excessive ratio of illiterate population 21 years of age and over, eight or more Southeastern States having as many as 12 per cent and two with more than 18 per cent. In population per library every Southeastern State is within the lowest fourth, six states with an index of more than 40,000 people to each library of 3,000 volumes compared to the six high states with less than 10,000. In general reading indices of books and of newspapers and magazines the differences continue at about the same level.

164. These deficiencies have been cited so often that they have come to be characterized as commonplace lags. In reality they are not lags in any accurate sense, because the region has made extraordinary strides in all of them and, in nearly all, greater advance than for the rest of the country. The same is true in colleges, universities, and professional schools. From earlier measures of endowment, expenditures, equipment, number and salaries of faculties, the increase has been in the hundredfolds. Yet the realities of the case are usually overshadowed by the marked comparative deficiencies. For in spite of this advance which is undoubtedly a reliable index of capacity, the actual measure of present status again shows great variation with the southeastern mode below the national median. Thus, the two lowest states of Arkansas and Alabama show per capita total receipts of universities, colleges, and professional schools of $1.31 and $1.95 compared to the two high states, Connecticut and Massachusetts, $9.08 and $8.13. Even so, the record has many elements that are creditable. For instance, nearly half of the Southeastern States are above the lowest quartile in enrollment of total collegiate students, in total graduate students, in enrollment in all colleges, in all students of all institutions of higher learning combined, in both natives and residents in *American Men of*

Proportion of Out of State and Out of Region Enrollment in Colleges and Universities in the United States, 1929-1930

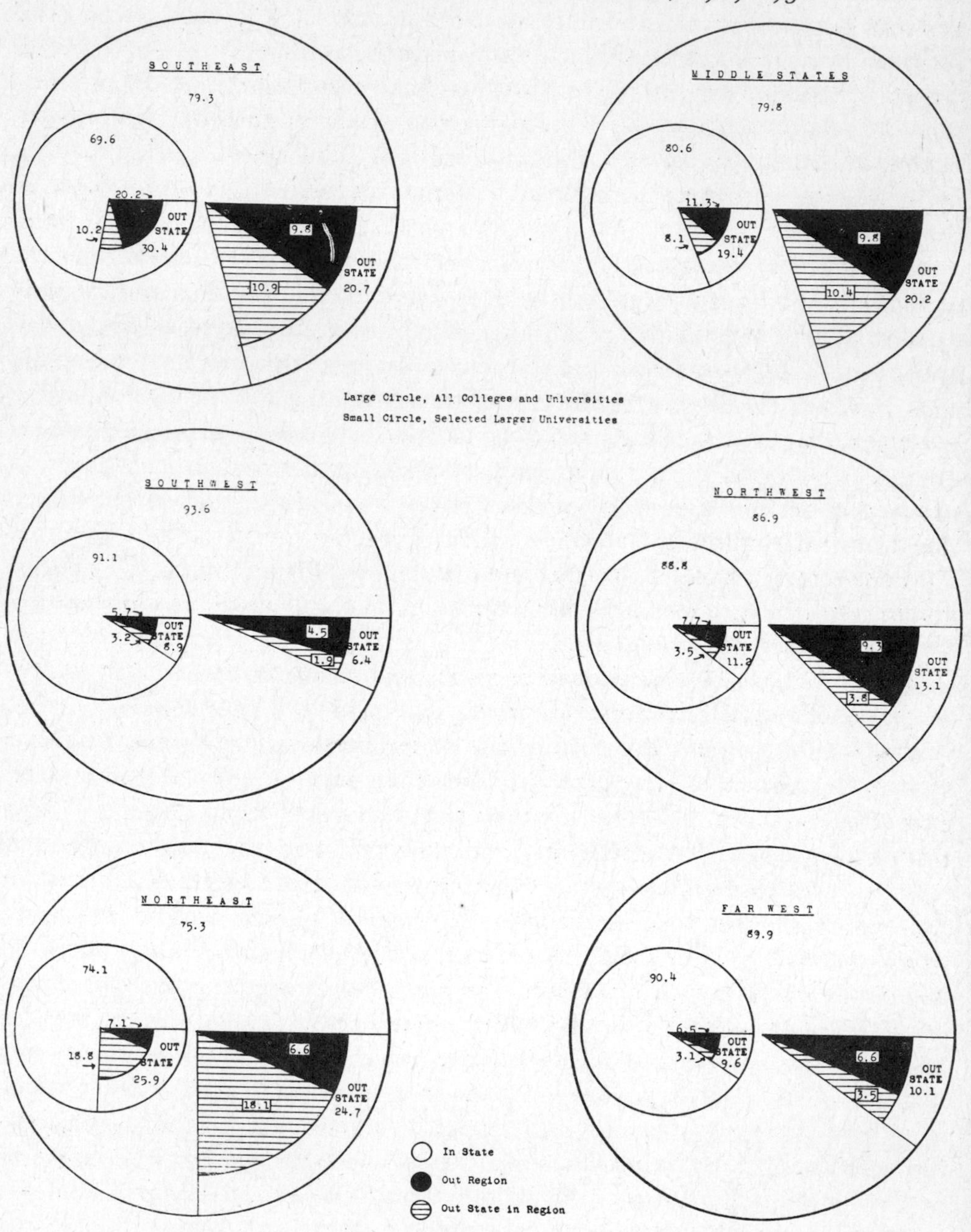

Science and in *Who's Who in America*, and in the recent gains in college enrollment. If, moreover, to the Southeast's record of nearly a third of all colleges, including junior colleges, be added the enrollment in the larger universities augmented by a relatively large number of students from the Northeast and Middle States, the total picture is impressive. In this new record of student migration the Southeastern States show the largest percentage of any region of its total university students enrolled from states outside the states of its own region. Such a migratory movement may be in the way of a cultural revolution as compared with so short a period as that just before 1920.

165. For the most part, however, the relative status of the institutions of higher learning is similar to that of public elementary and secondary education in that, although expenditures, enrollment, the number of faculty members, buildings and facilities have increased a hundredfold, they still rank low in comparison with the best of the nation. It borders on monotony to repeat that the Southeast has no university or college of agriculture or engineering school of the first rank, and affords no advanced instruction of the highest order in many of the subjects now demanded in the newer developments in politics, business, agriculture, industry, land utilization. The teaching load of faculty members is about a third heavier and salaries about a third less than for the best of the nation's colleges and universities. So, too, in terms of the highest degree less than fifty per cent of the faculties hold the doctor's degree compared with about 75 per cent of the corresponding schools elsewhere.

166. Yet, again, the record of the Southeast is noteworthy enough for special recording. Its increase in college students, faculty members, and expenditures has been several hundred per cent since 1900. Quantitatively, the picture is reflected in the fact that total receipts from universities and colleges exceeded those of the New England States; they amounted to four times those of the census division of the Mountain States; and three times as much as the Pacific States. Two special features, in contrast to what is commonly assumed, is the large ratio of faculty members and students in southern institutions who are not native to the region. As to quantity, the Southeast ranks with the Northeast in the number of private and denominational colleges. It contrasts with the Northeast in its public support of higher education. A little more than one-fifth of its 250 universities, colleges, and professional schools are publicly supported, whereas a little more than four-fifths of its normal schools and teachers' colleges are state supported. Student fees accounted for only about a tenth of the total receipts as compared with a fifth in the Northeast. Like the Northeast, again, a large number, nearly a third, of its colleges and universities

Total Number of Graduate Students per 100,000 Population, 1928

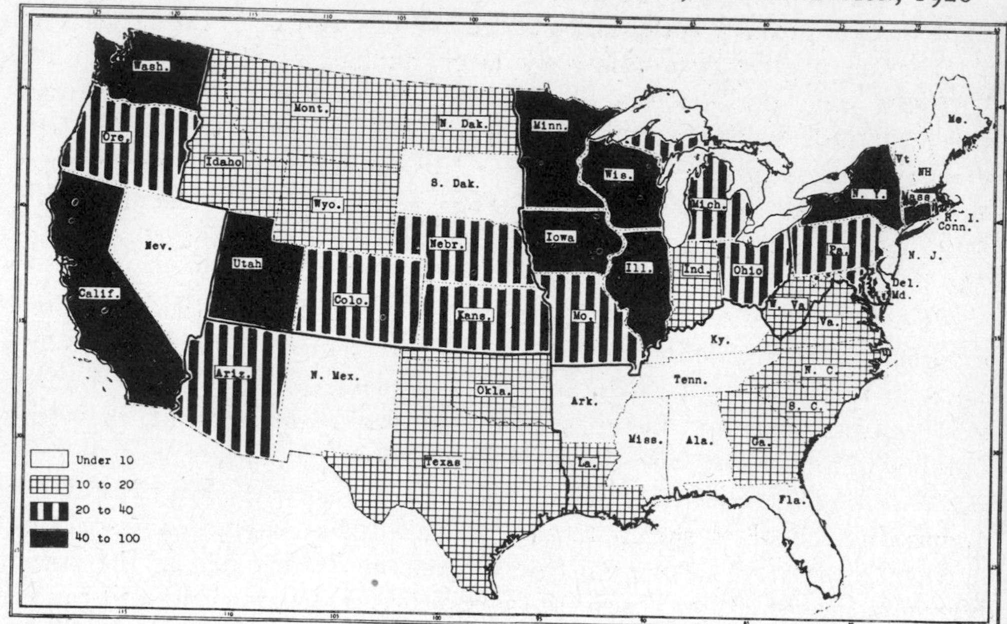

Total Number of Professional Students per 100,000 Population, 1928

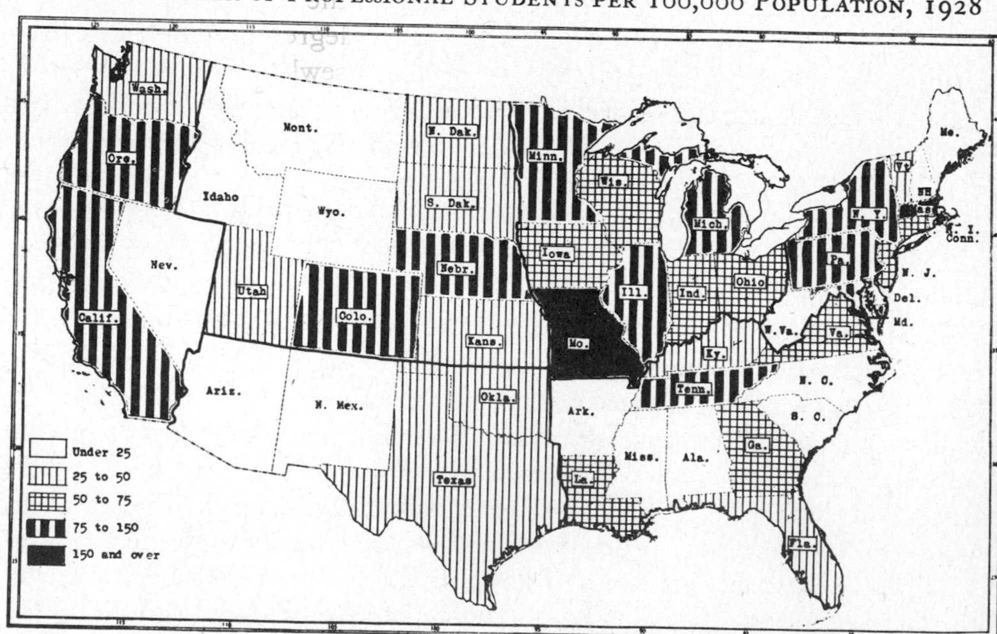

are women's colleges. Of the ten largest colleges for women, the Southeast has four, all being state colleges for women—North Carolina, Florida, Georgia, South Carolina; and the Southwest, one—Texas. Although in the rate of collegiate students per 100,000 population the Southeast does not excel, neither does it lag lowest, only a small number of the states being in the lowest quartile, other southern states ranking as high as 21st, 27th, 33d, and 34th. In per capita investment in universities, colleges, and professional schools, North Carolina is the only state above the national average, although five are above the fourth quartile, and in this ratio to total tax monies these states are higher. In the number of graduate students six Southeastern States are above the lowest fourth, while all states send relatively large ratios of their best graduate students to the Northeast and Middle States universities. These, added to their own graduate students, make an excellent record. In the professional field the region ranks relatively high, in the number of schools and students only three states being as low as the lowest quartile with other states ranking as high as 13th, 17th, 21st, 22d, 28th, and 30th. Again, the region ranks well up in the ratio of students in normal schools and teachers' colleges with rankings as high as 6th, 9th, 11th, 17th, and only one state in the lowest quartile.

167. Two elemental factors in determining the character of southern education have been the extraordinary variety, number, and nature of institutions of higher learning, and the source of their support and the directive influence from agencies and individuals outside the South. For one thing there was and is the almost uniform pattern through which each of the principal southern denominations provided for each state at least one college for men and one for women. There were numerous additional finishing schools, academies, and junior colleges. To these were added denominational schools set up and supported by northern denominational groups, there being more than one hundred and fifty such minor schools in the Appalachian regions alone. These varying institutions resulted in a number of marked trends. One was the religious and classical nature of prevailing education. Another was the early policy of separate state institutions for men and women and the almost exclusive emphasis on the part of state institutions for women upon the vocational aspects of education, particularly the normal schools and home economics teaching. For a long time there was clear-cut division between education for women, on the one hand, for leisure and "culture" and, on the other, for those who expected "to have to work." Perhaps coeducation in the state universities has been most responsible for the diminishing emphasis upon this class education which has been one of the distinguishing marks of southern institutions. Among the divisive factors in southern higher education was not

Negro Institutions of Higher Education and Negro Enrollment in White Institutions, 1929-1930

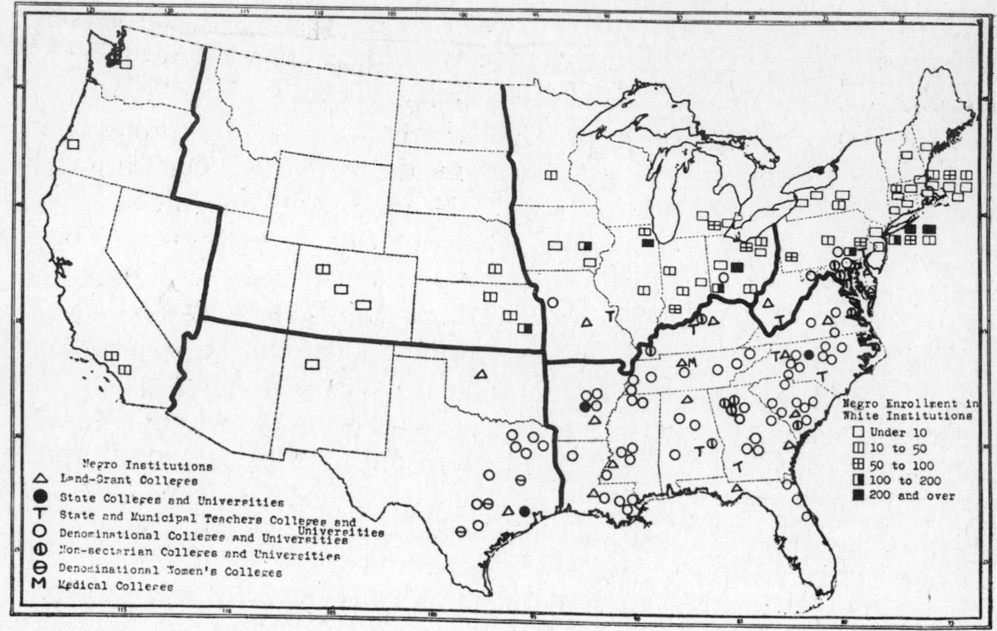

Teachers and Attendance of Negro Schools in Seventeen States and the District of Columbia, 1929-1930

State and Region	Teachers in Elementary Schools			Teachers in Secondary Schools			Grand Total	Average Daily Attendance in All Negro Schools	Aggregate Days Attended in All Negro Schools
	Men	Women	Total	Men	Women	Total			
Southeast	*4,850*	*31,860*	*36,710*	*1,562*	*1,908*	*3,470*	*41,180*	*1,370,194*	*176,161,572*
Virginia	329	2,162	2,491	133	179	312	3,803	115,048	17,725,389
North Carolina	676	4,674	5,350	251	285	536	5,886	186,298	26,317,414
South Carolina	611	3,655	4,266	151	175	326	4,592	156,005	18,252,585
Georgia	361	4,607	4,968	183	176	359	5,327	178,423	24,265,529
Florida	230	1,917	2,147	51	108	159	2,306	71,203	9,419,549
Kentucky	174	1,028	1,202	122	137	259	1,461	33,218	5,295,720
Tennessee	374	1,687	2,061	79	81	160	2,221	86,412	13,473,790
Alabama	384	3,308	3,692	175	360	535	4,227	145,589	18,913,012
Mississippi	789	4,632	5,421	305	206	511	5,932	205,565	20,301,140
Arkansas	558	1,738	2,296	43	58	101	2,397	71,005	9,326,076
Louisiana	364	2,452	2,816	69	143	212	3,028	121,428	12,871,368
Southwest									
Oklahoma	218	1,042	1,260	133	91	224	1,484	31,836	5,381,340
Texas	779	3,725	4,504	259	378	637	5,141	154,705	20,575,744
Northeast									
Delaware	20	164	184	10	9	19	203	5,234	959,451
Maryland	142	1,098	1,240	117	138	255	1,495	40,637	7,221,918
West Virginia	*43	*460	*503	70	70	140	*643	20,613	3,536,327
Dist. of Columbia	63	605	668	81	123	204	872	22,299	3,917,992
Middle States									
Missouri	131	847	978	163	119	282	1,260	......	....

*Estimated.

only the conflict between church and state schools, but between the older state universities and the new colleges of agriculture and engineering, again setting the one over against the other, the "liberal" education and the "practical". A third basis of the multiplicity of institutions was the geographic distribution within the several states of state supported schools, the number of separate institutions in a single state reaching as high as fifty or sixty, if district and county agricultural schools be included.

168. These basic factors related primarily to schools for the whites. Negro education, both higher and elementary, was and is a separate problem and process. The size and complexity of the problem may be illustrated by noting that the number of Negro children and youth to be educated in the Southeast is larger than that of all the children of the Far West, or Northwest, or Southwest, or of all the New England States, and that the taxable property and income of the whole Negro population of the Southeast is negligible in comparison. A part of the low ranking in "average" indices of the Southeast is, of course, due to the Negro pro rata which, however, is nevertheless of the essence of the whole composite situation of the region. It is a product of matured policies. The status of Negro education parallels in a much lower bracket the ranking of southern education in general. That is, from almost no beginnings Negro education has grown into many multiples of its earlier status, reflecting unprecedented progress. Yet, in the setting of the Southeast, many of whose indices reflect about half the achievement of the nation, the Negro's measures are no more than a fourth. From more than four-fifths illiteracy to less than one-fifth, from no public schools to nearly 2,000,000 pupils enrolled with 40,000 teachers, is no small achievement. In the field of higher education, from slavery to a roll call in the Southeast of eighty colleges of all ranks with some ten to twelve thousand college students and endowments of nearly $25,000,000 is also a notable achievement. Accentuating this progress is the recent ratio of increases: in value of land and buildings, from eight to ten million dollars in 1915 to more than forty million in 1932; in income from less than two million to more than eight million; and the rapid rise of public appropriations to approximate other receipts. Yet, with the exception of institutions supported from outside the South, no Negro college approximates the best white colleges. For a state such as North Carolina to expend more for its Negro schools than it did for all its schools in 1900 is an achievement not altogether overshadowed by the comparatively lower salaries of Negro teachers than of whites, themselves near the bottom of the states. For the purpose of vividness and planning for the future the dilemma of the Southeast, however, may be measured in terms of dollars by pointing out that it would require a million annual

Per Cent of All Income Expended For Schools, 1928

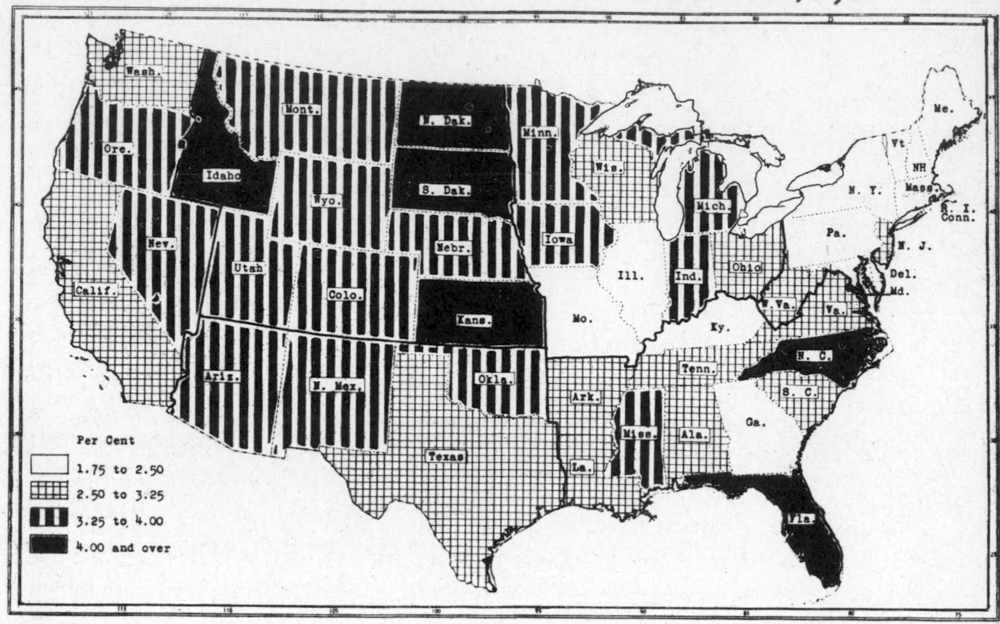

Differentials in Regional Educational Load and Economic Capacity

State and Region	Per Cent Population Under 19 Years of Age 1930	Per Cent of Total Population Attending School 1930	Per Capita Net Income 1929*	Per Capita Total Expenditures in Public Day Schools 1927-28	Per Cent School Expenditures are of all income 1928
Southeast					
Virginia	44.4	21.9	$74	$ 9.23	2.61
North Carolina	49.3	24.1	42	12.28	4.38
South Carolina	50.6	24.1	29	9.10	3.16
Georgia	46.3	21.7	56	6.11	1.75
Florida	39.2	19.7	117	20.76	5.76
Kentucky	43.9	21.5	74	8.58	2.29
Tennessee	43.8	21.9	69	8.72	2.57
Alabama	47.0	22.5	47	7.60	2.74
Mississippi	46.6	23.5	32	9.04	3.94
Arkansas	45.8	23.2	37	7.63	2.55
Louisiana	44.0	21.5	83	10.32	2.61
Southwest					
Oklahoma	44.2	23.7	92	12.24	3.27
Texas	42.6	21.1	94	11.32	2.57
New Mexico	46.8	22.7	74	12.36	3.40
Arizona	42.1	20.7	143	19.06	3.67
Northeast					
Maine	37.3	20.2	146	13.50	1.93
New Hampshire	35.2	19.4	160	14.42	2.14
Vermont	37.0	19.8	139	14.14	2.24
Massachusetts	35.1	20.3	326	19.55	1.85
Rhode Island	37.0	19.6	272	18.30	1.89
Connecticut	37.0	29.4	355	20.44	2.46
New York	33.6	19.0	506	23.86	2.11
New Jersey	36.1	19.9	308	25.82	3.20
Delaware	35.9	19.7	629	13.54	1.91
Pennsylvania	39.4	21.2	233	18.40	2.20
Maryland	37.2	19.1	264	13.20	1.97
West Virginia	46.1	23.1	80	14.91	3.21
Middle States					
Ohio	36.1	20.8	$ 192	$21.03	3.05
Indiana	36.5	20.3	114	22.04	3.93
Illinois	34.9	19.6	301	19.28	2.28
Michigan	37.7	20.7	219	22.57	3.92
Wisconsin	38.0	21.2	155	16.32	2.95
Minnesota	38.3	21.8	133	19.30	3.55
Iowa	37.2	21.1	90	20.18	3.82
Missouri	35.7	19.1	155	14.57	2.46
Northwest					
North Dakota	45.4	24.9	46	22.77	6.13
South Dakota	42.5	23.7	58	21.61	5.78
Nebraska	39.3	22.1	102	19.50	3.95
Kansas	38.1	21.9	97	22.82	4.24
Montana	39.0	22.8	133	24.24	3.96
Idaho	42.8	25.1	87	23.44	4.02
Wyoming	39.2	21.8	139	27.25	3.30
Colorado	38.0	21.6	155	24.02	3.29
Utah	46.1	27.1	119	21.17	3.91
Far West					
Nevada	31.8	18.1	241	25.24	3.33
Washington	33.7	21.2	186	57.91	2.80
Oregon	33.1	20.8	138	20.98	3.31
California	30.4	19.3	313	25.43	3.25

*Based on aggregate net income as reported in Federal individual income tax returns for 1929.

expenditure to bring the educational facilities of the Negroes up to the present status of the whites and a million dollars annually to bring both the white and Negro schools up to the national average.

169. The situation with reference to Negro education is illustrative of the part which direction and resources from outside the region have played in the development of the South. Thus the Jeanes Fund, the Slater Fund, and the Rosenwald Fund were leverages helping to lift the whole level of Negro common school education. The grants and endowments of the General Education Board and the Rockefeller Foundation and the denominational groups of the East constituted the great body of support for Negro colleges, while the federal land grant college funds were stimuli to the agricultural education of the whole region and the heart of the program for Negroes in each of the states. Turning from the special field of Negro education to the earlier South, the Peabody Fund proved a powerful stimulus to teacher training and upraising standards of education by special grants for special purposes, by providing in state universities buildings for schools of education, and finally through the enlarging of the George Peabody College for Teachers. For all purposes the Rockefeller groups have contributed more than $100,000,000. The General Education Board up to June 30, 1932, had appropriated $39,805,000 for education for the whites in the Southeast and $25,717,000 for Negroes. A total of $68,777,000 had been appropriated for both Southeast and Southwest. The Carnegie Corporation has allocated half of all its grants to the South. For experimentation, for supplementary resources, and for research, these and other funds were often both the genesis and the continuing stimulus. So, too, the federal grants for agricultural education, for general extension work, for experimentation, for boys' and girls' club work, both by actual contribution and by securing larger funds for matching federal grants, have been responsible for the greater part of this work. In the field of agricultural and home demonstration agents and boys' and girls' club work the Southeast ranks first.

170. These factors of outside participation, cooperation, and supplement are elemental to the understanding of the present situation, to the appraisal of the region's capacity, and to the planning of the future. In addition to the large federal grants for health, sanitation, and child welfare, similar momentum in the general cultural aspects of the southern states have obtained in library work and endowment, in adult education, in research and public administration, and in the sustaining power of outside fellowships, grants-in-aid to individuals, periodicals, publishing houses, theatres, universities, to support and encourage creative work in the region. The same influences, however, have stimulated the migration from the

Permanent State Universities and Women's Colleges Founded Before the Civil War

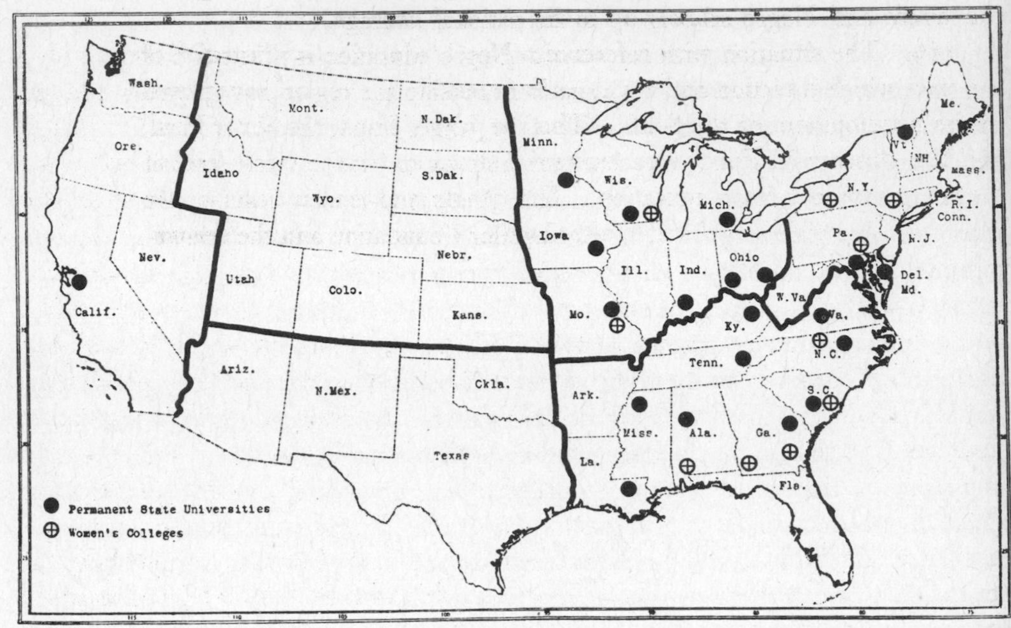

Regional Distribution of Institutions of Higher Learning in Which Women Are Located, 1928-1929

State and Region	Accredited		Unaccredited		Total
	Coeducational	Women's Colleges	Coeducational	Women's Colleges	
Southeast	*63*	*28*	*71*	*47*	*209*
Virginia	9	5	2	10	26
North Carolina	5	5	9	9	28
South Carolina	3	4	2	5	14
Georgia	3	7	13	3	26
Florida	1	1	3	0	5
Kentucky	10	0	11	6	27
Tennessee	11	0	13	4	28
Alabama	5	2	6	1	14
Mississippi	3	4	5	5	17
Arkansas	5	0	7	2	14
Louisiana	8	0	0	2	10
Southwest	*26*	*5*	*61*	*7*	*99*
Oklahoma	4	1	15	2	22
Texas	16	4	42	5	67
New Mexico	3	0	2	0	5
Arizona	3	0	2	0	5
Northeast	*65*	*36*	*94*	*42*	*237*
Maine	3	0	7	0	10
New Hampshire	1	0	1	1	3
Vermont	2	0	0	1	3
Massachusetts	6	6	12	17	41
Rhode Island	2	0	1	0	3
Connecticut	2	2	3	4	11
New York	17	16	21	8	62
New Jersey	1	1	11	0	13
Delaware	1	0	0	0	1
Pennsylvania	21	7	22	9	59
Maryland	4	4	5	1	14
West Virginia	5	0	11	1	17

State and Region	Accredited		Unaccredited		Total
	Coeducational	Women's Colleges	Coeducational	Women's Colleges	
Middle States	*121*	*17*	*138*	*20*	*296*
Ohio	24	4	17	4	49
Indiana	11	2	10	1	24
Illinois	26	2	21	5	54
Michigan	16	1	13	1	31
Wisconsin	9	2	11	0	22
Minnesota	7	3	17	1	28
Iowa	13	1	25	1	40
Missouri	15	2	24	7	48
Northwest	*41*	*1*	*64*	*8*	*114*
North Dakota	3	0	3	0	6
South Dakota	7	0	7	1	15
Nebraska	5	0	15	1	21
Kansas	12	0	20	4	36
Montana	2	0	4	0	6
Idaho	2	0	5	0	7
Wyoming	1	0	0	0	1
Colorado	6	1	6	1	14
Utah	3	0	4	1	8
Far West	*21*	*3*	*64*	*9*	*97*
Nevada	1	0	0	0	1
Washington	5	0	8	2	15
Oregon	7	1	6	2	16
California	8	2	50	5	65
United States	337	90	492	133	1,052

South of its men of science, its representatives in *Who's Who in America*, its educational leaders.

171. One of the distinctive aspects of education in the Southeast has been its special education for women and its late adoption of coeducation for men and women in the institutions of higher learning. From the earlier premise that higher education was not needed for women, by 1930 there were approximately as many women in universities and colleges as there were men. The two types of education have already been mentioned, the one emphasizing the liberal arts and "finishing school" type and the other in extraordinary contrast to southern tradition, namely the practical and occupational type. Perhaps the best summary of distinctive features of recent southern education for women is found in the contrast between its largest colleges for women and women's colleges in general in the United States. Thus, of the ten largest colleges for women in the United States five are southern state colleges for women in striking contrast to the following conclusion about women's colleges in general in the United States. "The women's colleges as a group are predominantly of liberal arts type; they assume that a broad cultural education, not based on sex differentiation, is desirable for women as for men. The educational opportunities compare favorably with those offered in liberal arts colleges for men and in coeducational colleges. The formal requirements for the degree are almost identical. There is remarkably little consideration given to any special needs of women in preparation for professional life and for vocations in general." In contrast to the Middle States where there are no publicly supported institutions for women, the Southeast enrolled about the same number of women as men in separate state schools, although the expenditures for men were double that for women. Of the nation's 105 women's colleges, 35, or exactly one-third, are in the Southeast. Of these, all but seven are private or denominational, and of the remaining 28 all but seven are denominational. There were, on the other hand, more than twice as many men in coeducational institutions as women. In private and denominational institutions the number of women in separate schools exceeded that of men. Of women enrolled in accredited institutions there were nearly three times as many in private and denominational colleges as in public institutions contrasted with the Middle States which had four times as many in public institutions as in private. In the number of institutions similar comparisons can be made. Of colleges in the Southeast in which women are enrolled, 75 of its slightly more than 200 are women's colleges contrasted with the Middle States which have only 37 out of their nearly 300 total colleges, the Northwest with only 9 out of 114, the Far West with 12 out of 97, and the Southwest with 12 out of 99. The North-

PERCENTAGE OF FACULTY MEMBERS IN LAND GRANT COLLEGES AND UNIVERSITIES WHO SECURED ALL, PART, OR NONE OF THEIR UNDERGRADUATE AND GRADUATE TRAINING AT INSTITUTIONS WHERE EMPLOYED

Adapted from John H. McNeely, *Faculty Inbreeding in Land-Grant Colleges and Universities*

INSTITUTION	Undergraduate Training			Graduate Training		
	All	Part	None	All	Part	None
Southeast						
Virginia A. & M. College	36.2	11.2	52.6	17.4	28.9	53.7
N. C. State College	20.8	4.7	74.5	16.3	30.4	53.3
Clemson College	13.7	10.9	75.4	5.3	....	94.7
Georgia State College of Agriculture	17.5	5.0	77.5	12.9	3.2	83.9
University of Florida	10.3	5.2	84.5	3.6	12.5	83.9
University of Kentucky	26.2	2.9	70.9	13.9	15.4	70.7
University of Tennessee	14.6	9.7	75.7	13.0	9.6	77.4
Alabama Polytechnic Institute	33.6	7.9	58.5	8.2	17.6	74.2
Mississippi A. & M. College	37.9	9.9	52.2	1.9	26.4	71.7
University of Arkansas	8.8	3.2	88.0	.9	5.2	93.9
Louisiana State University	29.9	9.4	60.7	9.9	22.8	67.3
Southwest						
Oklahoma A. & M. College	12.6	15.7	71.7	5.9	15.4	78.7
A. & M. College of Texas	13.8	17.9	68.3	13.6	16.9	69.5
University of Arizona	6.8	7.7	85.5	1.9	15.5	82.6
Northeast						
University of Maine	38.7	4.7	56.6	27.5	16.4	56.1
University of New Hampshire	11.9	2.4	85.7	2.9	8.8	88.3
Massachusetts State College	26.2	3.6	70.2	8.4	23.9	67.7
Massachusetts Institute of Technology	45.8	4.9	49.3	26.5	18.3	55.2
Rhode Island State College	20.5	5.1	74.4	....	10.0	90.0
Connecticut Agricultural College	18.9	8.6	72.5	6.9	2.3	90.8
University of Delaware	17.3	1.9	80.8	11.1	4.4	84.5
Pennsylvania State College	20.9	9.8	69.3	28.4	20.4	51.2
University of Maryland	20.4	2.0	77.6	4.5	25.0	70.5
West Virginia University	18.3	9.8	71.9	8.1	17.0	74.9
Rutgers University	9.8	5.2	85.0	9.1	3.5	87.4
Cornell University	32.2	8.9	58.9	42.2	26.5	31.3
Middle States						
Ohio State University	25.9	11.0	63.1	23.2	23.7	53.1
Purdue University	20.2	4.7	75.1	19.8	12.6	67.6
University of Illinois	14.4	11.9	73.7	31.6	23.0	45.4
Michigan State College	20.0	7.3	72.7	19.1	9.5	71.4
University of Wisconsin	28.8	13.0	58.2	39.2	35.9	24.9
University of Minnesota	28.0	9.0	63.0	26.6	24.6	48.8
Iowa State College	20.7	4.2	75.1	30.3	21.5	48.2
University of Missouri	26.7	9.7	63.6	14.6	30.7	54.7
Northwest						
North Dakota Agricultural College	9.7	9.7	80.6	4.8	9.7	85.5
South Dakota State College	18.5	5.7	75.8	5.4	12.5	82.1
University of Nebraska	14.5	5.5	80.0	19.3	26.9	53.8
Kansas State Agricultural College	24.6	5.2	70.2	17.2	29.1	53.7
Montana State College	14.6	5.9	79.5	7.1	16.1	76.8
University of Idaho	14.2	7.1	78.7	25.9	11.1	63.0
University of Wyoming	15.2	10.1	74.7	5.8	15.9	78.3
Colorado Agricultural College	16.4	5.5	78.1	17.6	13.3	69.1
Utah State Agricultural College	27.1	28.8	54.1	9.8	33.3	56.8
Far West						
University of Nevada	14.5	5.5	80.0	4.2	12.5	83.3
State College of Washington	14.9	7.4	77.7	18.6	6.2	75.2
Oregon State College	19.2	14.3	66.5	8.9	8.9	82.2
University of California	18.3	4.5	77.2	14.0	19.0	67.0

east, on the other hand, shows about the same ratio of women's colleges to the Southeast, namely 78 out of 237. Or to make the comparison of accredited institutions by regions, the Northwest has only 2 per cent women's colleges, the Far West and Middle States 12 per cent, the Southwest 16 per cent, and the Southeast and Northeast respectively 31 and 36 per cent. The dual educational program of the Southeast and its probable future development may be studied further in relation to the region's number of employed women and the nature of their work and opportunities.

172. The work of the agricultural colleges has contributed another special chapter. Two types of separate institutions are provided. First, there are eleven Negro state agricultural and mechanical colleges, with variations in names and courses; second, in Virginia, North Carolina, South Carolina, Georgia, Alabama, and Mississippi, the colleges of agriculture were set up separately and in special contradistinction to the state universities which came to be regarded by legislatures not only as liberal arts colleges, but as institutions for the "wealthy". The Virginia and older southern cultural educational influence was strong in the state universities of these states as compared with the later developments in Florida, Louisiana, Arkansas, Kentucky, and Tennessee. This separateness in education for the whites, alongside the earlier absence of coeducation, was a distinguishing mark between southern higher education and that of the great universities of the Middle States. This separation of liberal from occupational interests was analogous to the establishment of state normal schools and colleges for women. Recent trends, however, tend to bring all institutions closer together and to break down these class distinctions. While it is not yet possible to make a satisfactory appraisal of the work of the agricultural colleges, it is very clear that they, in collaboration with federal agricultural extension agencies, have made distinctive contributions and should have a still greater role to play in the future. Of the total 69 land grant colleges, 22, or about one-third, are in the Southeast.

173. Of special significance is the part which federal influences have had in their development. In every state except Florida the ratio of federal funds to receipts is higher than for the nation, and in six states more than double. A special feature of the agricultural and technical colleges differing from the other institutions of higher learning is the large proportion of their faculties who received all or nearly all of their specialized education outside of the region. Thus, in the Southeastern States more than 75 per cent of the faculty members received no graduate training in the institutions in which they were employed, and nearly as large a percentage received no part of their undergraduate instruction at home. The highest percentages were Arkansas and South Carolina, over

Public Library Facilities, by Counties, 1933

Counties without public libraries

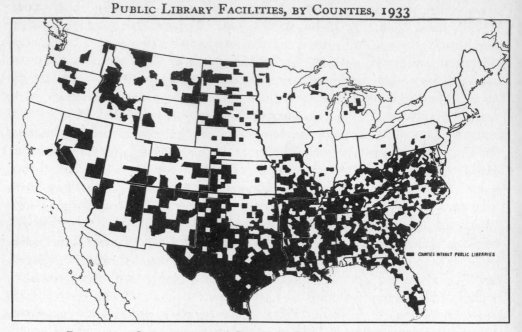

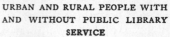

Regional Comparison of Present Library Standards with National Library Standards

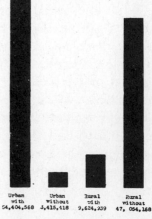

INCOME PER CAPITA

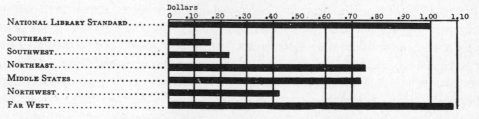

Dollars
0 .10 .20 .30 .40 .50 .60 .70 .80 .90 1.00 1.10

National Library Standard........
Southeast........................
Southwest........................
Northeast........................
Middle States....................
Northwest........................
Far West.........................

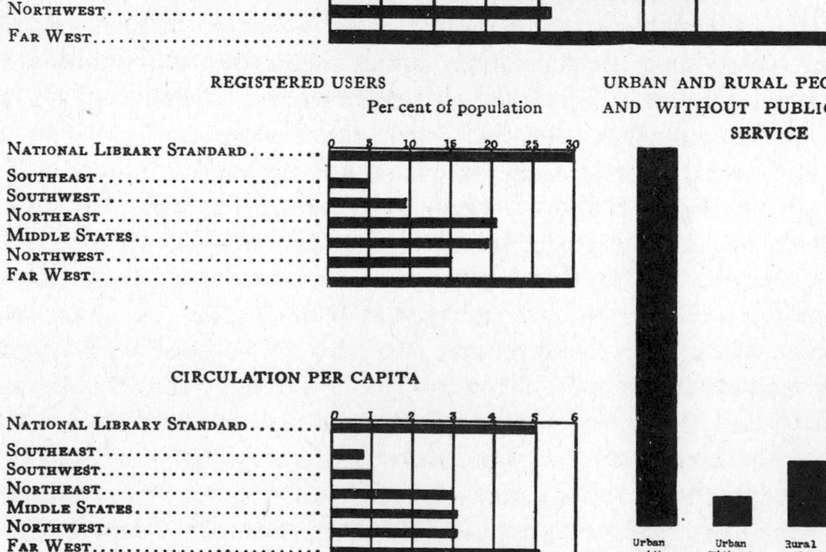

90 per cent; Georgia and Florida, over 80 per cent; Kentucky, Tennessee, Alabama, and Mississippi, over 70 per cent. These are in contrast to such states as Wisconsin, with 24 per cent; Illinois, with 45 per cent; and Minnesota and Iowa, with 48 per cent. This cross fertilization from outside has had a very important part in the nature of the work done and in the relationship between these institutions and the older colleges.

174. Another distinguishing feature is found in the fact that in the number of extension workers in cooperative extension work with the United States Department of Agriculture the Southeast exceeds all other regions. Thus, of the total workers the eleven Southeastern States had 2,834 of the 7,545. Another thousand in the Southwest gives the two southern regions more than half of all extension agricultural workers. Only New York, outside the South as compared to seven Southern States, has as many as 250 workers. One reason for the large number is that among the workers are nearly 300 Negro agents and several hundred assistants in cotton adjustment work. Another reason is that the two southern regions have nearly 1,400 of the 3,000 odd counties in the United States. The county as the chief unit of administration affords opportunity for both effectiveness in work and drain in resources.

175. Perhaps no deficiency in the Southeast is more marked than its lack of books and libraries and the consequent absence of reading habits. What lack of many techniques on farm and in factory is to the development of wealth, the lack of reading may very well be to the development of the youth of the land. Although this deficiency has not commonly been appraised as adequately as lack of school equipment, shortness of school terms, imbalance of diet, it is possible to point up the picture sufficiently to make clear the problem. Measured by the American Library Association's threefold national library standards, the Southeast compares with the other regions as follows: The index of income for libraries is $1.00 per capita. The Southeast has 16 cents, the Southwest 23, the Northwest 42, the Middle States 73, the Northeast 75, and the Far West $1.08. The standard for population registration of readers is 30 per cent of the total. The Southeast has 5 per cent, the Southwest 9, the Northwest 15, the Middle States 19, the Northeast 20.6, and the Far West 29.9. If the standard of five books circulated per capita be used, the Far West again leads with a little above the standard; the Middle States, the Northeast, and the Northwest have about 3.5; while the Southwest has about one and the Southeast less than one book per capita, the percentage for the latter being .77. Comparison of the ratio of library expenditures with general educational expenditures gives similar results: the Southeast 1 per cent, the Southwest 1.5, the Northwest 1.8, the Northeast, the Middle States,

Members of the National Association of Accredited Commercial Schools, 1929-1930

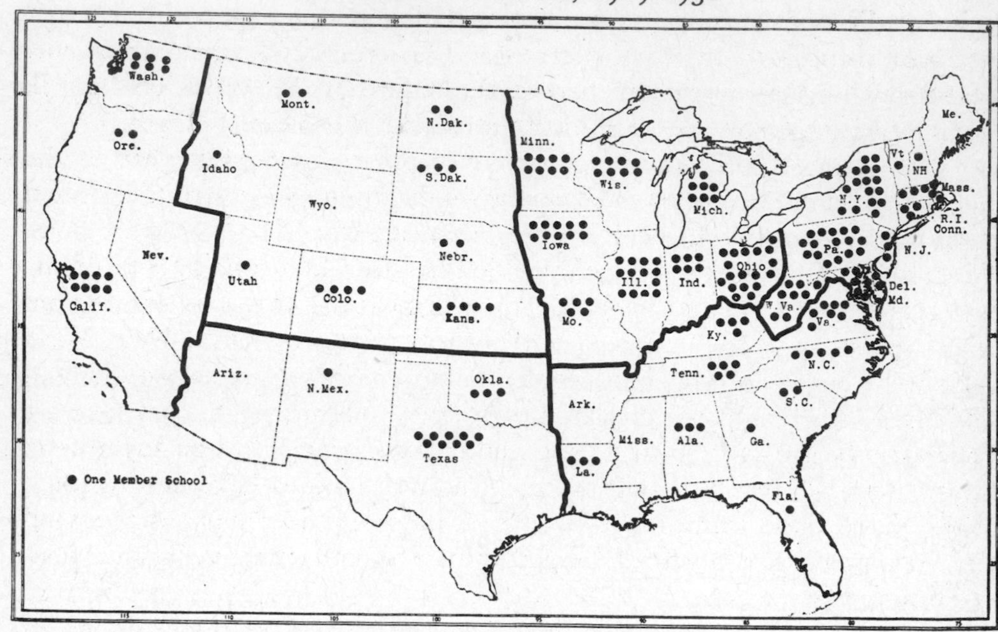

Collegiate Schools and Departments of Commerce and Business in the United States, 1929-1930

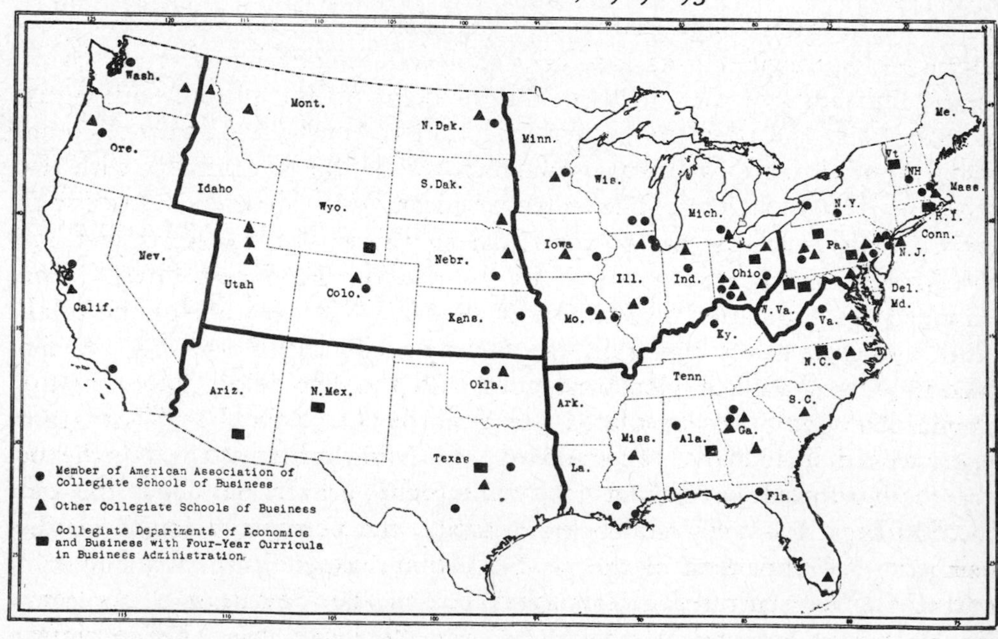

the Far West 3 per cent. Furthermore, there were in 1930 more than 600 counties in the Southeast without library facilities, 257 in the Southwest, 142 in the Northwest, 85 in the Middle States, 46 in the Northeast, and 19 in the Far West. Here again, however, two important factors are everywhere apparent. The one is the extraordinary progress within recent years and the other is the stimulus and cooperative resources which come from outside the region. Indices of these may be seen in the fact that four of the thirteen states having library commissions are in the South, in the many state activities, and in the organization and functioning of the Southeastern and Southwestern Library Associations. Of special significance is the work of the American Library Association and of four of the larger foundations in the support of various library activities.

176. Among the special aspects of southern specialized training looking toward the new technical developments is that of commercial education. There are several measures of activity. Of the 46 members of the American Association of Collegiate Schools of Business, 11 are in the Southeast, 3 in the Southwest, 5 in the Far West, 4 in the Northwest, 14 in the Middle States, and 9 in the Northeast. Of the 15 collegiate departments of commerce and business, 2 are in the Southeast, 3 in the Southwest, 3 in the Northwest, 1 in the Middle States, and 6 in the Northeast. Of the 42 other collegiate schools of business, 8 are in the Southeast, 2 in the Southwest, 3 in the Far West, 9 in the Northwest, 12 in the Middle States, and 8 in the Northeast. Of the 703 private high schools and academies reporting to the United States Office of Education in 1929-1930, about one-seventh reported from the Southeast. The Northeast reported the largest number of schools, the Middle States the second largest, and the Southeast the third largest. The 703 schools in the United States reported a total of 26,287 students. The Northeast stood first in the total number of students reported, the Middle States second, and the Southeast third. On the other hand, the number of private commercial and business schools in 1928-1929 per 1,000,000 population in the United States was 5.3, while for the Southeast the number was only 4.3. Aside from the Southwest and the Middle States every other region in the United States has a larger number of private commercial and business schools per 1,000,000 population than that of the Southeast. The Southeast also stands at the bottom of the list as measured by the number of students enrolled per 100,000 population. Whereas the Middle States has 193 students, the Southeast has only 70. Even the Southwest has 90. Finally, out of a total of 220 members of the National Association of Accredited Commercial Schools, 31 are located in the Southeast, 13 in the Southwest, 16 in the Far

Per Capita Total Expenditures in Public Day Schools, 1927-28

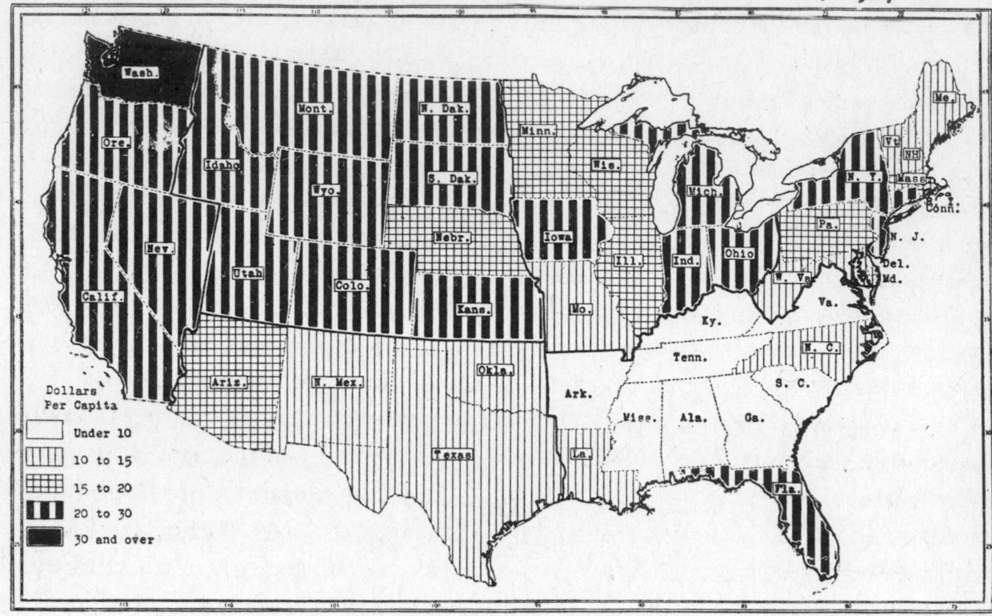

Percentage of Revenue for Public Education Derived from Taxes Other Than General Property Taxes, 1930

Adapted from Mort's *State Support of Education.*

STATE AND REGION	Percentage of state taxes from other than general property taxes	Percentage of revenue for public education from state sources	Percentage of revenue for public education from taxes other than general property taxes
Southeast			
Virginia	88.3	26.9	23.7
North Carolina	100.0	20.1	20.1
South Carolina	85.0	24.1	20.4
Georgia	77.3	34.4	26.6
Florida	65.5	21.8	14.3
Kentucky	62.2	25.2	15.7
Tennessee	86.8	23.7	20.6
Alabama	63.5	39.7	25.2
Mississippi	56.3	32.3	18.2
Arkansas	76.6	32.3	24.7
Louisiana	64.3	26.2	16.8
Southwest			
Oklahoma	83.5	10.1	8.4
Texas	65.7	42.3	27.8
New Mexico	59.2	21.2	12.6
Arizona	32.3	19.2	6.2
Northeast			
Maine	67.3	28.1	18.9
New Hampshire	66.7	8.7	5.8
Vermont	85.9	12.0	10.3
Massachusetts	86.9	9.2	8.0
Rhode Island	91.8	8.4	7.7
Connecticut	94.6	7.8	7.3
New York	99.3	27.4	27.2
New Jersey	55.5	21.1	11.7
Delaware	99.8	87.2	87.0
Pennsylvania	100.0	13.5	13.5
Maryland	71.6	17.2	12.3
West Virginia	84.5	7.9	6.7
Middle States			
Ohio	90.6	3.7	3.3
Indiana	68.1	5.3	3.6
Illinois	84.5	14.8	12.5
Michigan	57.6	18.0	10.4
Wisconsin	75.4	16.6	12.5
Minnesota	80.0	20.3	16.2
Iowa	31.0	3.9	1.2
Missouri	84.7	10.1	8.5
Northwest			
North Dakota	56.2	10.9	6.1
South Dakota	57.3	9.9	5.7
Nebraska	54.7	4.7	2.6
Kansas	74.9	1.4	1.0
Montana	72.2	13.7	9.9
Idaho	63.7	7.5	4.7
Wyoming	54.2	26.7	14.5
Colorado	61.3	3.1	1.9
Utah	46.5	33.3	15.5
Far West			
Nevada	46.7	18.0	8.4
Washington	55.8	28.6	15.9
Oregon	78.5	2.1	1.6
California	100.0	25.5	25.5

West, 20 in the Northwest, 79 in the Middle States, and 61 in the Northeast.

177. One of the most interesting phases of the southern educational picture is reflected in the long catalogue of original projects in education and related activities. These include a wide range from such beginnings as farm demonstration work, boys' and girls' club work, Smith-Hughes projects, all the way through to many private adventures. The list includes experimental schools, schools that are quite unique and original or designed to meet some special need, and educational movements and organizations involving such special features as adult education, art, music, vocational guidance, rural development, Negro schools, mountain schools, and new "colleges" not founded to be hid under a bushel. Typical of the special schools were the early distinctive industrial high school of Columbus, Georgia, the Mississippi county agricultural high schools, and the district agricultural schools in Georgia, Alabama, and Arkansas; the moonlight schools in Kentucky and the "Organic School" at Fairhope, Alabama. There were many pioneering mill schools, such as those at Pacolet, South Carolina, and Gainesville, Georgia. In addition to the missionary mountain schools, there were notable experiments in the Berry School in Georgia, Berea College in Kentucky, the Alvin York School and the Farragut School in Tennessee, the Tallulah Falls and the Rabun Gap Schools in Georgia, the John C. Campbell Folk School and others in North Carolina. In Negro education there were scores of experiments, while the eleven grade system of schools was a regional contribution. There were also fantastic dreams of great schools, such as the Woodrow Wilson College at Valdosta, Georgia, the Bryan University at Dayton, Tennessee, and the Lanier University at Atlanta. The catalogue of several hundred would itself be groundwork for a powerful human story, reminiscent of creative effort, wasted energy, and diluted support.

178. There were other special problems, many of which are scarcely susceptible to measurement. The problem of finance was accentuated through the depression years, making the region and the nation aware of its cumulative deficit in resources and standards. The realities of the situation were measured by the actualities of capacity, on the one hand, and, on the other, by the rising tide of agitation and disorganization consequent upon a chaotic attempt to throttle the whole educational system. What had been gained at so great a price seemed in the way of being lost. Other problems emphasized by the depression were the lack of educational backgrounds on the part of the people and their leaders, the assumption of administrative functions by boards and committees, the revivification of politics in education, the retardation of the movement to develop a number

Estimated State and Local Tax Collections Per Capita, By States, 1930, and Per Cent Increase in Per Capita State and Local Tax Collections, By States, 1922-1930

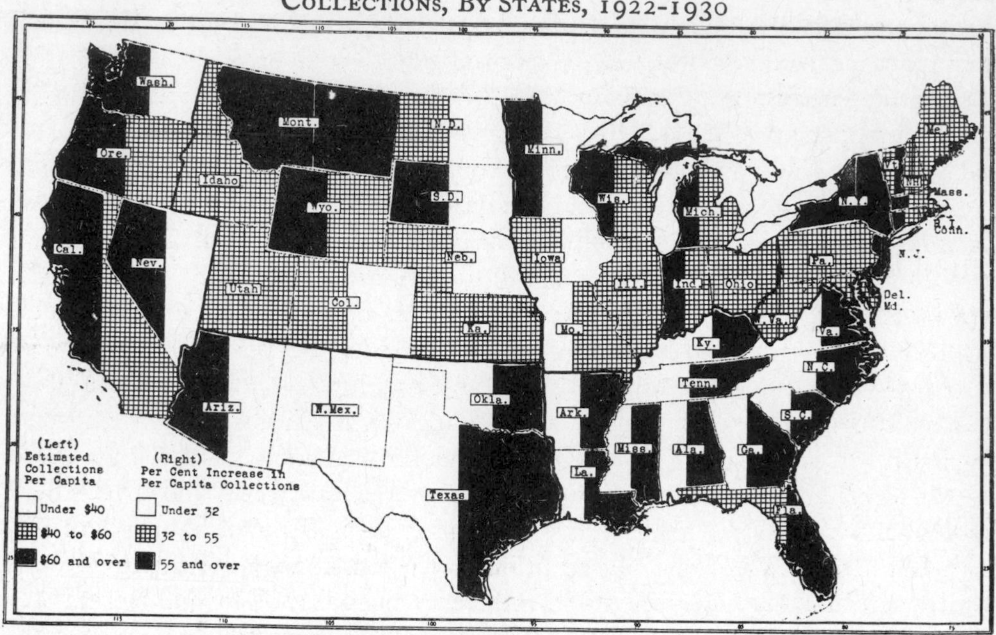

State and Local Tax Collections

State	Collections, 1930		Per Cent Increase			
			1922-1930		1913-1930	
	Rank	Per Capita	Rank	Per Capita	Rank	Per Capita
New York	1	$90.64	12	61.9	29	216.4
Nevada	2	82.82	49	11.2	38	197.2
New Jersey	3	81.33	7	71.3	8	297.7
California	4	76.44	37	34.3	47	150.6
Massachusetts	5	76.05	28	44.5	46	161.4
Delaware	6	75.73	1	115.7	1	564.0
Michigan	7	70.75	27	45.7	7	299.3
Oregon	8	69.18	36	35.2	42	183.6
Connecticut	9	64.90	25	46.9	26	223.0
Montana	10	63.93	18	56.0	49	108.9
Minnesota	11	62.91	41	27.2	37	199.9
Wisconsin	12	62.65	35	35.7	13	261.3
South Dakota	13	62.45	42	27.0	17	255.2
Arizona	14	61.75	48	13.2	40	189.8
Wyoming	15	61.73	21	49.5	20	246.6
Washington	16	60.21	44	23.1	48	135.6
Indiana	17	60.03	23	47.6	22	241.7
Florida	18	59.04	6	76.3	5	393.6
New Hampshire	19	58.15	38	34.0	33	211.3
Colorado	20	58.00	45	22.8	44	178.0
Ohio	21	57.75	33	37.2	32	212.0
Iowa	22	57.52	43	26.1	27	221.7
Rhode Island	23	57.17	22	47.7	30	214.3
Idaho	24	56.74	32	38.4	41	184.7
Nebraska	25	56.03	40	27.7	25	224.4
Kansas	26	55.71	31	39.8	23	240.9
Maine	27	55.33	19	53.2	16	257.7
Illinois	28	53.96	29	44.4	31	213.4
Vermont	29	53.89	14	57.6	19	248.8
North Dakota	30	52.59	46	18.5	43	183.4
Utah	31	49.41	34	35.9	45	166.2
Pennsylvania	32	48.94	26	46.5	28	216.6
Maryland	33	46.56	20	51.2	36	202.7
West Virginia	34	41.09	24	47.1	6	336.2
Missouri	35	39.60	30	43.1	35	203.2
Oklahoma	36	39.53	15	56.7	10	276.1
Louisiana	37	36.56	39	31.5	12	265.6
Texas	38	35.31	16	56.7	9	295.4
New Mexico	39	35.26	47	17.7	18	250.5
Virginia	40	32.77	10	66.4	11	267.4
North Carolina	41	32.10	5	84.1	2	553.8
Kentucky	42	31.90	9	67.2	21	246.0
Mississippi	43	$31.45	13	57.6	4	411.4
Tennessee	44	28.30	17	56.3	15	258.2
South Carolina	45	27.41	3	102.1	3	448.2
Arkansas	46	23.74	2	107.5	24	236.3
Georgia	47	22.97	11	64.2	39	196.0
Alabama	48	20.43	8	67.6	14	259.1

Per Capita State and Local Tax Collections

Per Cent Increase in Per Capita, 1913-1930

State: New York, Nevada, New Jersey, California, Massachusetts, Delaware, Michigan, Oregon, Connecticut, Montana, Minnesota, Wisconsin, South Dakota, Arizona, Wyoming, Washington, Indiana, Florida, New Hampshire, Colorado, Ohio, Iowa, Rhode Island, Idaho, Nebraska, Kansas, Maine, Illinois, Vermont, North Dakota, Utah, Pennsylvania, Maryland, West Virginia, Missouri, Oklahoma, Louisiana, Texas, New Mexico, Virginia, North Carolina, Kentucky, Mississippi, Tennessee, South Carolina, Arkansas, Georgia, Alabama

0 100 200 300 400 500 600

of institutions of higher learning to approximate the best. Accentuated also was the need for cooperative assistance from federal and from philanthropic agencies and the need of a well planned, cooperative program on their part, as well as within the South itself. Some of these factors will appear in the picture of politics, governmental finance, public welfare, public health, and general cultural movements.

XII. POLITICAL GENIUS AND GOVERNMENTAL FINANCE

179. The story of the South's politics is again reminiscent of its cultural background of conflict and crisis, while its present status can be explained only in terms of its historical-geographical setting. The South, so it is represented, had a genius for politics. Yet the first task here as elsewhere is to begin with present basic factors which condition government and politics as instrumentalities of progress. Just as the key to the region's ultimate capacity for educational and social development must be found in its economic capacity, attained and measured by technological development of its incomparable resources, so the problem of public support of the essential institutions of civilization is bound up in governmental finance and political leadership. The stark reality of regional dilemma here may be illustrated by a continuation of the educational picture in which the Southeast is shown to have increased its index of educational expenditures from something like 300 in 1900 to an analogous more than 6,000 in 1930, yet, in order to bring its standards up to the best of the nation, must double its current annual expenditures and approximate a third of its taxable income for education. More and still more grows the demand; less and still less seem the relative tangible liquid resources, under the present economy, emphasizing again the irreducible minimum of increasing values, augmenting wealth, and raising the standards of wages, salaries, and other income. Some of the most important factors can be summarized in relative measures.

180. Perhaps the first measure is that of taxation. To begin with the percentage increase in per capita state and local tax collection, the Southeast leads the list, both in increase from 1913 to 1930, and from 1922 to 1930. The relative ratios for the six regions are respectively for the two periods: the Southeast, 307.5 per cent and 70.2 per cent; the Southwest, 281.9 and 50.5; the Northeast, 222.3 and 57.3; the Middle States, 232.4 and 39.9; the Northwest, 203 and 30.6; and the Far West, 158.2 and 36.0. So, too, the Southeast ranks at the top in percentage ratio of total tax collections to aggregate private income, the regions in the above order beginning with the Southeast being 12.4, 10.1, 10.4, 8.7, 9.6, and 11.5. Again in the ratio of general property to total state and local collections, eight of

PERCENTAGE EXPENDITURE OF STATE GOVERNMENT BY FUNCTIONS, 1930

Adapted from Mort's *State Support of Education.*

STATE AND REGION	General Government	Protection to Person and Property	Development and Conservation of Natural Resources	Conservation of Health and Sanitation	Highways	Charities, Hospitals, and Corrections	Education	Recreation	Public Service	Miscellaneous
Southeast										
Virginia	7.0	2.7	1.3	1.0	40.6	9.9	32.0	0.1	....	5.4
North Carolina	2.7	2.3	1.0	1.8	48.3	7.2	27.2	1.1	0.9	7.5
South Carolina	4.6	2.0	0.4	1.2	57.9	5.5	23.7	....	....	4.7
Georgia	4.6	2.2	3.0	1.4	46.7	5.3	30.6	....	0.5	5.7
Florida	8.3	3.1	5.5	1.4	32.3	8.9	32.4	....	....	8.1
Kentucky	10.6	2.1	1.6	1.1	43.0	8.1	30.2	0.2	0.1	3.0
Tennessee	2.9	1.3	0.7	1.0	69.7	5.6	14.5	1.2	....	3.1
Alabama	5.2	2.6	0.8	2.0	24.3	12.6	41.4	....	3.6	7.5
Mississippi	6.0	1.3	1.7	3.0	19.2	11.7	45.3	....	....	11.8
Arkansas	3.0	1.1	0.4	1.1	62.7	2.8	15.8	....	4.8	8.3
Louisiana	4.7	3.4	0.9	1.3	56.8	9.2	19.4	0.1	0.1	4.1
Southwest										
Oklahoma	4.6	2.4	1.3	2.1	41.8	13.9	29.3	0.1	....	4.5
Texas	5.0	2.4	0.6	0.6	43.0	5.9	39.2	....	....	3.3
New Mexico	5.2	2.4	2.7	0.7	55.1	5.4	26.8	0.2	....	1.5
Arizona	5.3	3.3	4.4	0.7	42.1	6.1	35.3	....	....	2.9
Northeast										
Maine	2.9	4.5	2.4	2.9	53.5	10.7	18.8	0.1	1.3	2.9
New Hampshire	3.7	4.5	3.4	2.1	55.9	10.4	17.8	0.1	....	2.1
Vermont	5.6	3.3	2.6	2.4	61.8	9.0	10.6	....	....	4.7
Massachusetts	10.0	6.7	2.4	4.5	24.9	32.5	10.7	2.3	1.2	4.8
Rhode Island	19.6	4.0	1.9	3.5	39.4	14.5	10.5	1.9	0.4	4.3
Connecticut	8.6	6.9	2.3	5.2	36.6	17.7	14.7	2.2	....	5.8
New York	6.6	3.7	2.7	1.1	26.3	18.8	34.9	2.9	0.7	2.3
New Jersey	5.6	4.7	1.1	1.9	39.7	14.4	28.0	0.5	2.8	1.3
Delaware	3.6	3.5	1.5	1.8	27.1	8.6	53.1	....	....	0.8
Pennsylvania	6.0	5.1	4.3	1.9	37.8	13.4	29.8	0.2	0.2	1.3
Maryland	6.4	3.8	1.4	3.4	49.7	11.9	21.2	....	0.3	1.9
West Virginia	6.0	4.1	0.9	2.4	58.6	6.7	19.7	0.1	....	1.5
Middle States										
Ohio	5.1	4.1	1.8	0.7	49.5	15.4	20.8	0.4	0.1	2.1
Indiana	2.9	3.1	1.7	0.9	49.5	10.4	28.1	1.9	....	1.5
Illinois	7.5	6.6	3.0	1.0	42.1	20.3	16.0	0.4	....	3.1
Michigan	3.0	3.4	2.0	1.4	34.9	14.3	37.0	0.3	0.2	3.5
Wisconsin	5.0	3.5	4.2	2.4	38.5	9.4	34.5	0.3	....	2.2
Minnesota	5.4	4.1	6.9	2.2	29.4	10.6	34.3	0.2	5.9	1.0
Iowa	3.8	1.3	4.6	1.8	49.9	11.3	24.0	0.4	....	2.9
Missouri	4.3	2.0	1.1	1.1	61.8	9.1	19.2	0.1	....	1.3
Northwest										
North Dakota	3.9	2.7	1.5	2.3	21.3	8.1	27.4	0.1	31.7	1.0
South Dakota	5.1	2.2	2.3	2.0	33.1	8.1	25.3	0.8	17.6	3.5
Nebraska	7.0	3.2	2.6	1.0	46.1	10.4	27.7	0.1	....	1.9
Kansas	2.9	2.5	2.3	1.3	55.0	10.4	19.0	0.4	0.5	5.7
Montana	4.4	3.5	4.0	1.5	46.9	8.5	28.3	....	....	2.9
Idaho	5.7	5.7	4.1	0.6	51.4	8.1	20.8	0.3	....	3.3
Wyoming	4.3	2.8	4.3	1.0	41.8	8.6	33.7	0.7	....	2.8
Colorado	4.3	3.8	3.6	0.7	43.8	14.8	26.6	0.1	....	2.3
Utah	10.6	3.5	3.4	0.4	32.5	4.5	43.8	0.1	....	1.2
Far West										
Nevada	4.8	2.0	4.0	1.0	54.8	6.7	25.2	0.1	....	1.4
Washington	4.3	3.9	2.0	0.6	39.6	7.1	39.5	....	....	3.0
Oregon	5.7	4.7	3.5	1.3	54.4	5.9	19.1	0.1	0.3	5.0
California	4.6	5.3	2.7	1.2	30.5	10.3	39.2	0.6	4.2	1.4
United States	5.5	3.7	2.4	1.6	41.1	12.4	28.3	0.7	1.2	3.1

the first ten states are in the Southeast. Yet these and other indices of strain and drain on resources give the net result of leaving the per capita expenditures of state governments for operation, maintenance, and interest low, with at least six states in the lowest quartile and all states less than half of the highest. The averages for the regions beginning with the Southeast are: $30.44, $37.69, $70.04, $57.83, $56.85, $72.62. At the same time the ratio of per capita taxes to per capita private income is highest of any of the regions. Yet once again the net indebtedness of state governments per capita of total population finds four of the first five high states in the Southeast. By entire regions the Southeast ranks first with $23.48 per capita indebtedness followed by the Far West with $19.92, the Northeast with $15.98, the Middle States with $11.44, the Northwest with $7.87, and the Southwest with $1.73.

181. Another measure of capacity and prospects is found in the extent to which the various sources of tax moneys have been tapped. The relative status of the Southeast in some of these follows: of the 21 states having personal income taxes seven are in the Southeast, leaving only Alabama, Louisiana, Kentucky, and Florida out of the picture. Of the nine states having a sales tax in 1932, five were southeastern states. Of thirteen states having cigarette and tobacco taxes, nine are southeastern, only Arkansas and Louisiana with its radio anti-chain store propagandist out of the picture. Four of the fourteen states having severance taxes are Alabama, Arkansas, Kentucky, and Louisiana. Again the Southeastern States feature the poll tax as a key to voting, although, for the most part, the other states in the Union make no such demands for franchise privilege. Likewise, the use of special consumption excise taxes has been featured more than elsewhere. Once again the Southeastern States have drawn heavily upon motor vehicles and gasoline licenses. Nine of the Southeastern States are in the top twelve of states in the ratio of motor vehicle license and gasoline tax to total state and local tax collections, in 1930. Likewise the eight top states in rate of taxation per gallon of gasoline are southeastern with also Kentucky and Louisiana in the first quartile, leaving only Virginia below with still a score no higher than fifteenth place in the roll of states. The regional averages for gasoline taxes are: the Southeast 5.8 cents, the Southwest 4.5, the Northeast 3.2, the Middle States 3.3, the Northwest and Far West 4 cents. The regional averages for license fees are Southeast $15.07, Southwest $10.98, Northeast $18.16, Middle States $13.05, Northwest $10.85, Far West $18.16. In the index number of farm real estate taxes, the Southeastern States are again above the national, the three highest being in the Southeast, and six of the twelve states of the United States with an index of more than 250 being in the Southeast.

Taxes, Debts, Bonded Indebtedness, and Expenditures of Combined State and Local Governments for Given Years

STATE AND REGION	Ratio of Total Taxes to Private Income, 1930[1]	Ratio of General Property to Tax Collections 1930[2]	Average License Fee, 1930[3]	Gross Receipts from License Fees, 1930[3]	Gasoline Tax Rates in Cents 1932	Ratio License and Gas Tax to Total Tax Collections 1930	Per Capita: Tax Collections 1930[4]	Per Capita: Net Debt 1930[5]	Per Capita: Bonded Debt 1927[6]	Per Capita: Operation and Maintenance Expenditures 1930
Southeast										
Virginia	10.4	48.9	$ 17.28	$ 6,493,989	5	$ 21.61	$ 32.77	$ 10.93	$ 62.13	$ 11.89
North Carolina	11.7	61.6	15.08	6,835,743	6	19.04	32.10	52.28	143.58	11.62
South Carolina	14.1	61.7	13.18	2,878,352	6	20.85	27.41	32.46	47.62	9.52
Georgia	10.4	64.6	13.12	4,482,257	6	26.76	22.97	2.50	21.89	7.18
Florida	17.4	74.3	14.69	4,813,495	7	21.24	59.04	.12	341.26	12.58
Kentucky	12.3	66.1	16.76	5,547,069	5	16.62	31.90	.77	23.22	8.66
Tennessee	10.5	66.2	12.95	4,767,239	7	20.91	28.30	32.34	72.26	10.03
Alabama	9.7	59.8	13.71	3,799,761	5	19.80	20.43	25.58	49.38	10.30
Mississippi	18.0	73.0	12.85	3,046,393	5½	15.57	31.45	15.66	74.76	8.90
Arkansas	12.2	60.8	19.45	4,283,959	6	24.32	23.74	65.03	20.60	12.20
Louisiana	13.8	73.4	16.74	4,609,042	5	15.80	36.56	17.71	92.80	12.12
Southwest										
Oklahoma	10.5	67.8	11.88	6,536,361	4	19.67	39.53	.81	60.33	9.67
Texas	9.8	70.4	10.22	13,961,362	4	20.91	35.31	.75	105.89	12.16
New Mexico	10.3	70.2	15.20	1,279,623	5	26.79	35.26	21.48	65.56	16.96
Arizona	10.2	83.0	6.65	734,626	5	12.05	61.75	.68	142.90	18.01
Northeast										
Maine	11.0	66.3	17.01	3,166,642	4	16.10	55.33	27.36	59.18	17.80
New Hampshire	11.1	69.6	20.42	2,290,435	4	17.39	58.15	10.96	33.38	20.37
Vermont	8.0	61.9	27.62	2,392,152	4	21.79	53.89	26.90	24.93	20.36
Massachusetts	11.7	66.8	8.41	7,120,583	3	5.17	76.05	4.06	88.36	11.33
Rhode Island	9.3	73.7	16.72	2,280,849	2	9.95	57.17	25.24	93.93	12.37
Connecticut	8.2	66.8	25.04	8,290,404	2	11.68	64.90	.78	67.94	13.35
New York	12.1	70.0	17.70	40,857,715	2	5.99	90.64	22.09	176.18	17.41
New Jersey	11.7	81.1	18.04	15,382,456	3	7.87	81.33	16.89	152.61	15.44
Delaware	12.0	29.6	19.79	1,110,047	3	11.55	75.73	20.91	131.15	26.13
Pennsylvania	7.3	79.6	18.88	33,112,371	3	13.18	48.94	8.50	95.66	12.01
Maryland	9.1	75.5	10.69	3,437,796	4	13.14	46.56	19.16	119.37	14.10
West Virginia	9.8	74.9	17.66	4,702,812	4	13.87	41.09	42.10	75.25	10.64
Middle States										
Ohio	8.3	79.0	7.55	13,287,352	4	13.04	57.75	1.43	105.04	8.49
Indiana	10.0	85.0	7.25	6,346,879	4	11.96	60.03	.77	64.25	9.55
Illinois	7.1	78.1	11.26	18,444,247	3	11.02	53.96	26.54	66.12	7.05
Michigan	10.7	80.7	16.93	22,482,412	3	12.60	70.75	13.37	133.36	14.78
Wisconsin	8.8	66.4	16.72	13,083,521	4	11.52	62.65	.47	50.73	12.20
Minnesota	11.4	75.8	15.09	11,062,150	3	13.26	62.91	1.57	74.39	15.94
Iowa	7.9	77.6	16.31	12,693,621	3	15.97	57.52	5.75	71.56	9.98
Missouri	7.9	74.6	13.33	10,150,000	2	13.07	39.60	24.95	61.62	9.49
Northwest										
North Dakota	12.0	86.0	10.70	1,958,662	3	10.97	52.59	3.59	17.98	21.78
South Dakota	11.0	80.1	14.43	2,959,913	4	14.86	62.45	14.90	61.57	18.70
Nebraska	8.1	79.6	8.93	3,804,950	4	16.51	56.03	.17	80.34	10.87
Kansas	8.9	83.5	10.23	6,084,348	3	14.51	55.71	12.34	82.96	9.36
Montana	9.7	79.0	11.71	1,583,276	5	13.00	63.93	5.80	80.00	14.53
Idaho	10.2	77.4	16.78	1,998,290	5	18.44	56.74	8.72	88.40	13.14
Wyoming	10.2	80.2	11.24	691,509	4	15.36	61.73	7.02	112.51	26.72
Colorado	10.3	82.6	6.16	1,901,230	4	13.28	58.00	7.85	131.17	12.98
Utah	11.1	85.6	7.51	855,584	4	11.80	49.41	10.40	79.66	19.70
Far West										
Nevada	11.4	79.6	12.61	373,966	4	12.84	82.82	9.96	97.70	29.64
Washington	10.5	80.9	17.08	7,616,676	5	15.78	60.21	7.41	111.58	15.51
Oregon	12.9	74.9	38.15	9,617,930	4	23.36	69.18	31.42	165.39	17.29
California	11.2	74.4	4.83	9,858,810	3	10.16	76.44	21.81	190.20	14.68

[1] Total Taxes from *Trends in Taxation and Finance;* Income from Brookmire's Economic Service.
[2] From *Trends in Taxation and Finance*, p. 53.
[3] Elmer D. Fagan and C. Ward Macy, *Public Finance*, p. 144.
[4] *Trends in Taxation and Finance*, p. 9.
[5] Source: U. S. Department of Commerce, Bureau of the Census, *Financial Statistics of State Governments, 1930.*
[6] Source: National Industrial Conference Board, *Cost of Government in the United States, 1927-1928*, p. 46.

182. Other comparative measures are significant. Some of these relate to regional and some to national policies. There is the multiple dilemma of most of the Southeastern States, seeking to increase wealth and income through a balanced industry and agriculture and enacting tax exemption legislation designed to encourage industrial development, later contemplating the task of making the still new and immature industry shoulder an increasingly larger cost of nursing a sick agriculture. There was the case of North Carolina ranking second in the amount of federal internal revenue, yet in general measures of federal aid ranking lowest. There was the cumulative load of a region which had increased in the first quarter century its per capita wealth about 250 per cent, its value of manufactured products more than 400 per cent, its value of agricultural products nearly 200 per cent; yet its expenditure for schools was more than 1,200 per cent, with correspondingly large increases in expenditures for roads, public health, public welfare, and the other broadening functions of government. For state and local roads the Southeast expended, in 1930, $237,000,000, which constituted 30.5 per cent of total state and local tax collections. This was the highest proportion of any region, the national average being 20.7 per cent, the Northeast being as low as 14.9, and the Far West as low as 17.9 per cent. The Southwest and Northwest were next highest with 26.2 and 24.4, the Middle West median with 23.8. For these and other functions all of the Southeastern States except Florida had less than $40.00 estimated state and local tax collections per capita as compared with New York, New Jersey, California, and Massachusetts with more than double that amount. More specifically, sixteen states showed a rating three times Alabama's $20.43, while New York's rate is more than four times that of each of the four lowest states. There were similar problems facing the counties, all the Southeastern States featuring many smaller counties as opposed to the fewer larger counties of the more westerly states.

183. These were the problems which the 1,290 state representatives and the 455 state senators of the Southeast were called upon to meet, for the most part without precedent or guide posts, and with little experience, training, or broader education. These were problems of the new government requiring attention, special techniques and policies as opposed to the old politics of personalities and generalities. For the election of these representatives to work out these problems only five million people were registered to vote. Whereas the Southeast comprises 20 per cent of the nation's population, it had only 10 per cent of the total registration of persons eligible to vote and a much smaller actual vote. And here was the 1932 roll call of legislators. Of 1,745 members there were less than 100 Republicans; 953 from rural homes and less than 200 from cities of over

SOUTHERN "PRINCIPLES" IN POLITICS

Adapted from *The Atlas of the Historical Geography of the United States*, pp. 121-124

STATE AND REGION	Woman Suffrage 1919		Prohibition 1917		Fordney Tariff 1921		Smoot-Hawley Tariff 1930		Underwood Tariff 1913	
	For	Against	For	Against	For	Against	For	Against	For	Against
Southeast	*31*	*55*	*82*	*15*	*12*	*83*	*24*	*72*	*86*	*9*
Virginia	1	8	10	..	1	9	3	7	9	1
North Carolina	2	8	8	2	..	10	2	8	10	..
South Carolina	..	7	6	1	..	7	..	7	6	..
Georgia	1	9	12	..	..	12	..	12	12	..
Florida	3	1	4	..	..	3	3	..	4	..
Kentucky	9	1	8	3	2	8	7	4	9	2
Tennessee	7	3	10	..	5	5	2	8	7	2
Alabama	1	7	5	5	..	10	..	10	10	..
Mississippi	..	6	8	..	..	8	..	8	8	..
Arkansas	6	..	7	..	..	7	..	7	7	..
Louisiana	1	5	4	4	4	4	7	1	4	4
Southwest	*19*	*7*	*18*	*8*	*7*	*20*	*5*	*23*	*26*	*2*
Oklahoma	7	..	8	..	5	3	2	6	6	2
Texas	10	7	8	8	1	16	2	16	18	..
New Mexico	1	..	1	..	1	..	1	..	1	..
Arizona	1	..	1	..	..	1	..	1	1	..
Northeast	*97*	*24*	*57*	*76*	*116*	*15*	*96*	*35*	*78*	*54*
Maine	4	..	4	..	4	..	4	..	1	3
New Hampshire	2	..	2	..	2	..	2	..	2	..
Vermont	..	1	1	1	2	..	2	..	..	2
Massachusetts	8	5	6	8	11	2	13	3	8	8
Rhode Island	3	..	1	2	2	..	2	..	2	1
Connecticut	3	1	..	5	5	..	4	..	5	..
New York	37	3	14	28	33	10	18	25	28	13
New Jersey	8	3	2	10	11	1	9	2	10	1
Delaware	1	..	1	..	1	..	1	..	1	..
Pennsylvania	22	8	18	18	35	..	36	..	13	23
Maryland	3	3	2	4	4	2	1	4	6	..
West Virginia	6	..	6	..	6	..	4	1	2	3
Middle States	*112*	*6*	*89*	*28*	*109*	*12*	*81*	*37*	*73*	*45*
Ohio	19	2	12	8	20	2	18	3	18	3
Indiana	13	..	13	..	13	..	10	3	12	..
Illinois	27	..	17	7	23	3	18	6	18	6
Michigan	11	1	11	2	13	..	12	..	2	11
Wisconsin	8	2	6	5	7	4	2	9	5	6
Minnesota	9	..	8	2	9	1	2	8	1	9
Iowa	10	1	10	1	10	..	10	1	3	8
Missouri	15	..	12	3	14	2	9	7	14	2
Northwest	*30*	..	*31*	..	*28*	*1*	*21*	*8*	*14*	*17*
North Dakota	3	..	3	..	2	1	2	..	..	3
South Dakota	3	..	3	..	3	..	1	2	..	3
Nebraska	6	..	6	..	6	..	4	2	3	3
Kansas	8	..	8	..	8	..	5	3	5	3
Montana	2	..	2	..	2	..	1	1	2	..
Idaho	1	..	2	..	2	..	2	..	..	2
Wyoming	1	..	1	..	1	..	1	..	..	1
Colorado	4	..	4	..	2	..	4	..	4	..
Utah	2	..	2	..	2	..	1	..	..	2
Far West	*19*	..	*12*	*7*	*20*	..	*18*	*1*	*6*	*14*
Nevada	1	..	..	1	1	..	1	..	..	1
Washington	5	..	5	..	5	..	5	..	1	4
Oregon	3	..	2	1	3	..	3	..	..	3
California	10	..	5	5	11	..	9	1	5	6

40,000 inhabitants, with the other 580 from towns in between. No more than fifty were born outside the region with ten foreign-born and forty mostly from adjacent states. There were nine women only. Of the senators, somewhat over half were college men and of the representatives somewhat less than 50 per cent. Of 1,435 legislators for whom the records were available, 1,255 were church members, representing 27 different denominations with Methodists and Baptists about equally divided, 419 and 416 respectively. There were 175 Presbyterians, 77 Episcopalians, 66 Christians, 18 Catholics, 9 Jews, and others from 20 other communions, including Holiness and Latter Day Saints. There were 650 lawyers with allied interests, 173 other professional folk, 374 farmers and planters, 35 labor representatives, and some 50 miscellaneous occupations, among which were sheriff, jailer, bus operator, teacher, preacher, undertaker, football coach, veterinarian, barber, locomotive engineer, pawnbroker, carpenter, editor, music teacher, bricklayer, and almost literally "the butcher, baker, and candlestick maker." Counting all vocational and professional activities and various ways of making a living, past and present, here is democracy in which more than 300 different occupational combinations are represented. Only about one-third of the members had previously been officeholders and somewhat less had had actual experience in the legislature.

184. The historical background of the political South comprehends a twofold setting, both aspects of which are essential to the understanding of and working with the present régime. The one was the "Old South" before 1850-1860; the other was the "New South," after 1860-1870. The present southern politics is in great contrast to the first period and is a logical product of the complex conditioning of the second. The later records of demagoguery in low places is in contrast to the earlier statesmanship in high places which had the remarkable record of having native and resident sons fill 14 out of the first 17 presidential administrations to 1850 and since then has had none save the incidental stormy Andrew Johnson. For more than three score years the chief justice of the United States was a southern man. Of those men in politics deemed worthy of permanent biographies by the *Encyclopaedia of the Social Sciences* all but 14 of 41 Americans "important in domestic affairs before the Civil War" were southern. Of those "figures important for the development of political theory" the Southeast had 27 as opposed to 25 from all the other states. Since the Civil War there was only the rabble rouser Tom Watson, who stands as sign and symbol of the South's political dilemma. Yet the contrast between the old and the new is not primarily one of before-the-war

SUBREGIONS OF THE SOUTHEAST ACCORDING TO REPUBLICAN VOTE IN THE 1920 PRESIDENTIAL ELECTION

Adapted from *The Atlas of the Historical Geography of the United States*

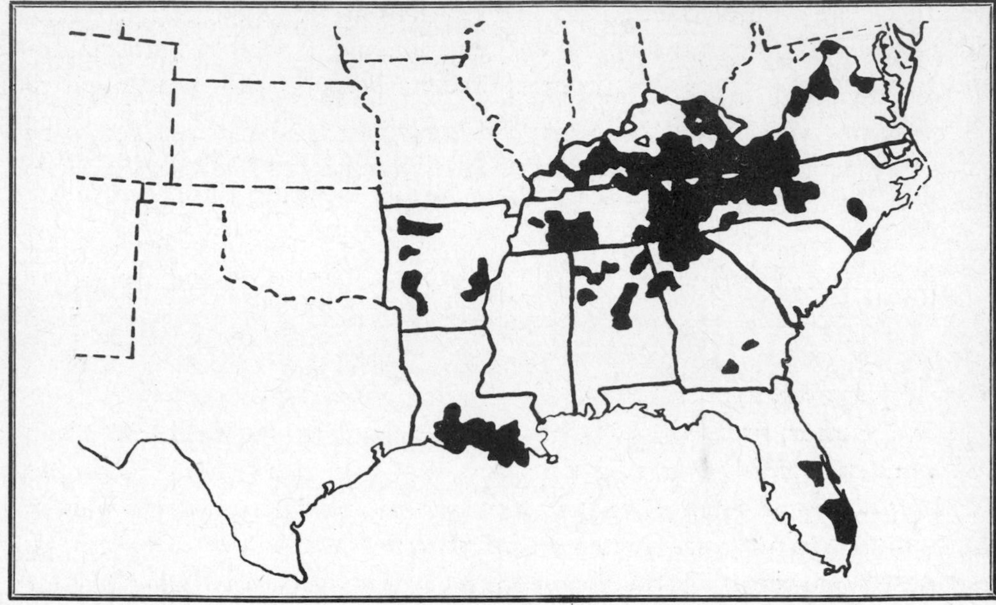

SUBREGIONS OF THE SOUTHEAST ACCORDING TO REPUBLICAN VOTE IN THE 1924 PRESIDENTIAL ELECTION

Adapted from *The Atlas of the Historical Geography of the United States*

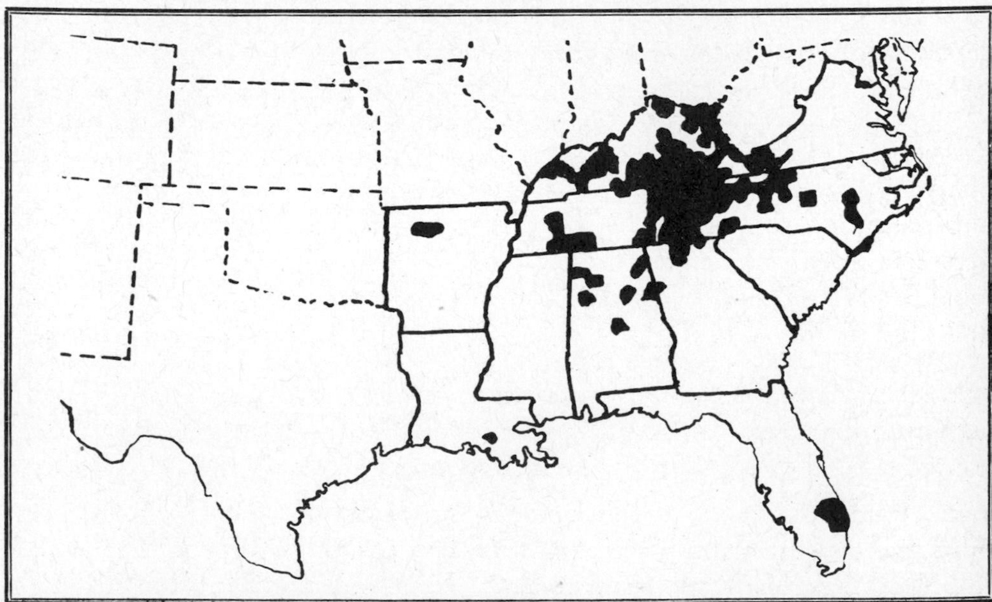

and since, but an inevitable logical consequence of extraordinary forces. First of all, it must be remembered that, while the South's ratio of rulers was large in the earlier period, its proportion of area, population, and wealth of the whole country was greater than at any later period. Next, the South lost by the war its place in the nation and its leaders both matured and prospective. It lost its property and its bearing, and in addition the national political and economic pattern changed radically. The South followed in line with industrial expansion and the rise of the common man so rapidly that new leaders were not available or being raised up to take the place of the old. Then, too, the old agrarian culture in the Jeffersonian sense the Southeast knows no longer. Rather it is the agrarian culture of the small owner and of the tenant, white and Negro. These were not only the numerical inheritors of the Old South, but were fashioned by the conflict of reconstruction as were their leaders and the patterns of political control. Product and process was the solid Democratic South with its demagogic quota of great ones beginning with Jeff Davis of Arkansas, Huey Long of Louisiana, Vardeman and Bilbo of Mississippi, Heflin of Alabama, Tom Watson and Talmadge of Georgia, Catts of Florida, Blease of South Carolina. And in the state legislatures records tragic and comic enough to overshadow much that was original, fine, and statesmanlike.

185. No picture of southern politics, however, could be adequate without a long catalogue of personalities. There have been many strong governors, wise in their day and generation, wielding effective home-made tools of administration in situations far more difficult than appear to the outside critic. They have many times shown high qualities of statesmanship. There have been in every state legislature notable examples of struggle and courage and wisdom, as there have been also in the national congress. There are the chronicles of such personalities at large as John Sharp Williams and L. Q. C. Lamar of Mississippi. Finally, there is the unprecedented record of the South in the national congress holding the great majority of senior committee positions with a group of veteran personalities whose influence and power approximate major ranking for the first time similar to that of the Old South, and in contrast to the economic, educational, and general representation of the South in the nation. Glass and Byrnes, Garner and Robinson, Hull and Swanson represent reality in American politics.

186. Back of both the federal and state politics was always the Negro, made commonplace by repetition and discussion, yet representing every third man as having no place in government except to impede the reasonable workings of white government. In round numbers, in the stark

COUNTIES HAVING FIFTY PER CENT OR MORE NEGRO POPULATION, 1900

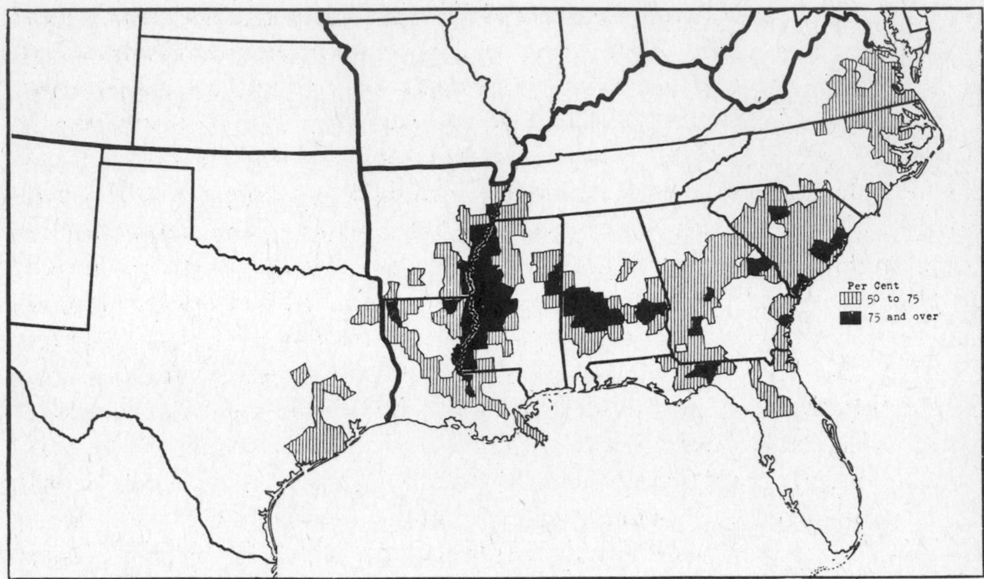

The changing ratio of Negro-white population in the Southeast is significant for politics as well as for the general culture of the region. The contrast between 1920 and 1930 is striking in the decrease of counties having as many as half of their population Negroes. It is still more striking in the decrease of counties having three-fourths Negroes.

COUNTIES HAVING FIFTY PER CENT OR MORE NEGRO POPULATION, 1930

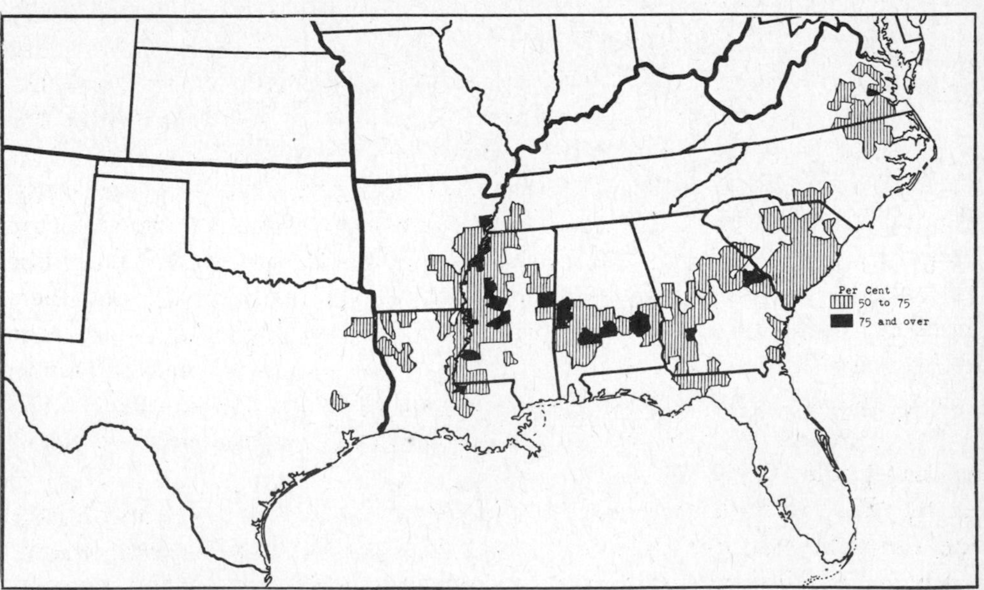

reality of the facts, the Negro population in the Southeast is about the same as all the stirring folks of the whole Far West—California, Oregon, Washington, and Nevada's restless tribe; or nearly as many as all the people of the Northwest or of the emerging Southwest. Next to these are nearly as many in the families of farm tenants and marginal white folk who, with the Negro, represent not only class and mass distinction, but who are the balance of power, the white classes by votes, the Negro as an issue. A third group approximating a social class is the mill village worker, who has emerged through the new and distinctive decentralized industry which has followed some of the patterns of the Old South in the control and dominance of its workers. Other factors which have determined the nature of the Southeast's politics are its rapid increase in urban population and its lack of adjustment, the conservative attitude of the people as well as their leaders, and the continuing emphasis upon personalities and shibboleths in politics.

187. The emerging picture is thus a logical one—the absence of economic issues in politics, the lack of experience and training in fiscal affairs, the political "machine" politics of a solid South, the dilemmas of modern issues to be attacked, and the whole question of the place of large race and propertyless classes in a region theoretically the most democratic in its clamor for the rights of the common man. Yet a large ratio of Southeastern States has undertaken reorganization of state government, the study of county reform, and many important administrative reforms. In the South, too, were the early beginnings of city manager government and of the techniques of public welfare and other progressive moves, which in turn have been retarded by the same economic and political limitations which characterize the region in most of its activities.

XIII. PUBLIC AND PRIVATE SOCIAL SERVICES

188. The political philosophy of the Old South and the incidence of its later political and religious life have been responsible for much of the nature and amount of social and public services in the present Southeast. Here again, however, much of the limitation of the region's program is explained by the oft-repeated factor of chronological lag. Illustration is found in a region, the most predominantly religious of all, which sometimes appears to be least generous with its children. Or featuring chivalry, it has neglected its age of consent laws and has the largest ratio of women in agricultural work. Or, genuinely professing neighborliness, it registers the lowest ratio of per capita contributions for religious and social services. Yet, again, measurable deficiencies are explained to a great extent in the lack of technical institutions and agencies well matured, and in the inade-

Federal Emergency Relief Administration Grants Through September 30, 1933

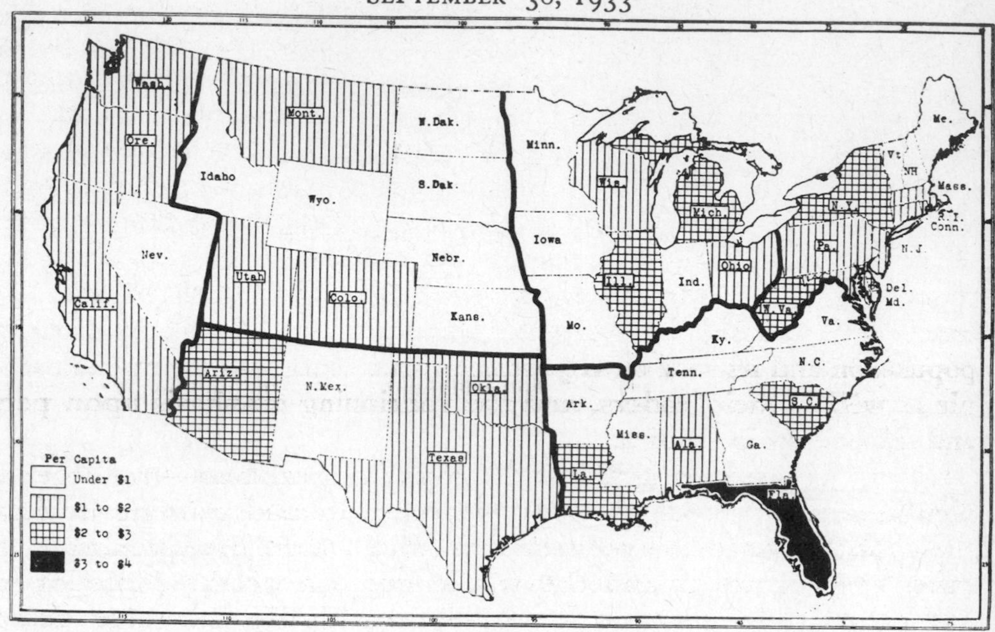

Per Cent of Public Unemployment Relief Funds Supplied by the Federal Government April Through September, 1933

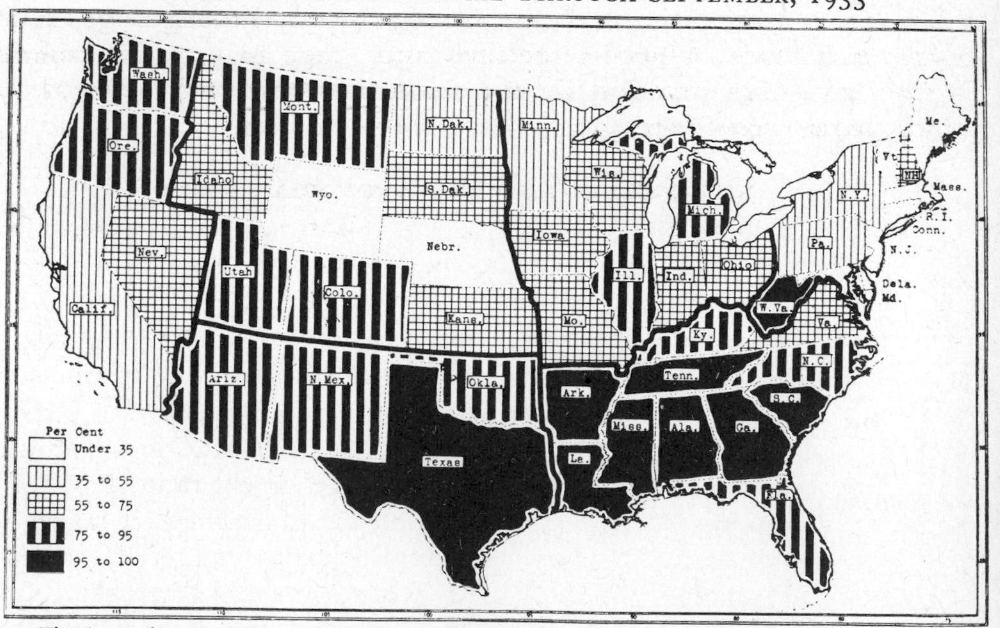

The later pictures will of course show a different ratio. See also page 86.

quate income already emphasized. Yet, here as in the case of education and government there have been many examples of distinctive contributions and pioneering efforts, such as those in public welfare administration, social service conferences, and community organization and citizens' committees. Potential resources here as elsewhere have lacked development. The story of this undeveloped potential is a long one comprehending not only the ever dominant backgrounds, but a framework of southern charities and welfare, the work of organized women's groups, social legislation, civic and fraternal institutions, state systems of public welfare, and state conferences of social service. These rank, for the purpose of interpretation, alongside the religious and general cultural forces.

189. In substance the chief tenets in the philosophical backgrounds of the Old South and their products centered around the following foci: the dominance of the few commonly assumed to be superior; the resulting inherent responsibility for the welfare of the dependent; the religious coloring of action and policies; the stern hard doctrine of punishment for the criminal; the ideologies of self-righteousness; the development of democratic ideals of education in contrast to the older aristocratic ideals; the Negro and the convict system; the establishment of institutions for the deficient; general civic movements looking toward reform and social legislation; and many organizations for the promotion of many causes. The three most significant south-wide organizations were the Conference for Education in the South, functioning in the first decade of the century, followed by the Conference on Education and Industry, and by the Southern Sociological Conference. Each of these reflected the religious and revival motivation in program, each was greatly influenced in origin and objectives by leaders and agencies outside the South, and each sought to develop higher standards of civic and social welfare through a broad general attack. The state conferences of social work in the Southeast were also more nearly civic conferences than technical social work. This was a logical need for attacking evils such as those of the chain gang and racial discrimination and for promoting constructive measures for general public welfare and social work. Two examples will indicate the nature and need of the work which was to be done.

190. The first illustration of the "social service" objectives of state conferences is that of penal reform and especially that relating to county chain gangs and jails, both of which had constituted evils of incredible proportions, ameliorated only after tragedy and publicity had shocked the public into reform. The chain gang was the result of disciplinary measures deemed appropriate for the control of unruly Negroes who were but yesterday slaves of masters. Stern discipline, officials and employees

PERCENTAGE RATIO OF TOTAL STATE AND LOCAL TAX COLLECTIONS TO AGGREGATE PRIVATE INCOME, 1929

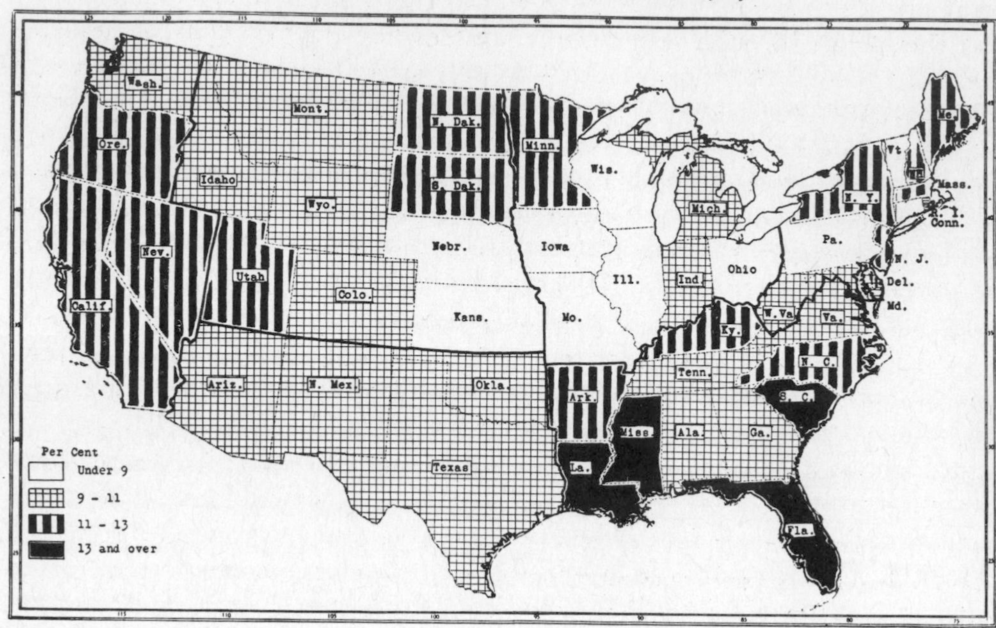

CONTRIBUTIONS FOR RELIGIOUS, EDUCATIONAL, CHARITABLE AND PHILANTHROPIC PURPOSES, PER CAPITA OF TOTAL POPULATION, AS REPORTED IN FEDERAL INDIVIDUAL INCOME TAX RETURNS, 1929

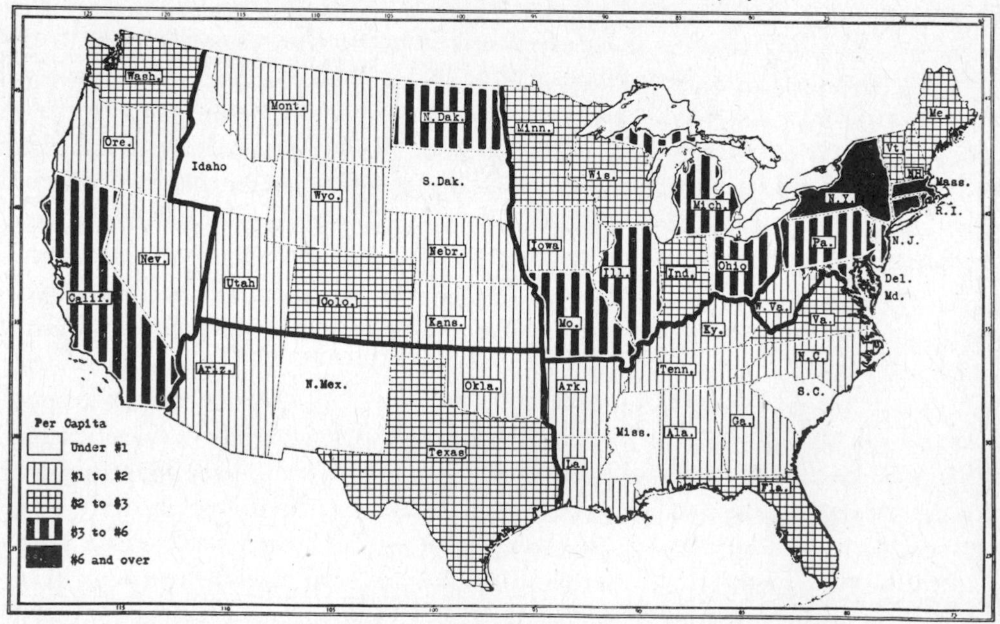

hardened by experience, the economic factor of maintenance and subsequent private profit motives, together with the indifference of the people, were the factors through which the region developed its unenviable reputation. To these factors were added a high rate of crime, the tragedy of lynching, and the failure of criminal justice in many places. The state conferences, following an earlier program of the Southern Sociological Congress and of the National Conference of Charities and Correction (in 1917 the National Conference of Social Work) were instrumental in promoting needed measures. The second illustration is that of state and county public welfare administration. The state and county system, sponsored by the North Carolina Conference for Social Service, inaugurated in that state in 1918-1919, had a great deal of influence in the nation and later in the Southeast. In these movements another influence of great significance was the American Red Cross with its civilian relief and its post-war social work program under the direction of Joseph C. Logan and Harry L. Hopkins, who was head of the Southern Division.

191. Here, again, the Southeast's relative ranking is consistent with other indices. First, in contributions for religious, educational, charitable, and philanthropic purposes, Mississippi and South Carolina, alongside Idaho and South Dakota, report less than $1.00 per capita compared with seven Northeastern States with over $5.00. In public welfare expenditures the Southeast's per capita for all purposes is $2.05 as compared with $2.88 for the nation; yet of this, 28.9 per cent is for veterans as compared with only 8.6 for the nation, leaving the ordinary welfare services much below the average. A summary of all ordinary welfare expenditures reveals the Southeast with the lowest per capita expenditure, approximately one-third that of the Northeastern Region. The region has lagged noticeably in the matter of old age pension legislation. Although the Southeast has the lowest per capita expenditure for child welfare, the region places relatively more emphasis on this phase of public welfare work than upon other aspects. The region, along with all other regions except the Northeast, is decidedly backward in the matter of mothers' aid, only North Carolina and Virginia having state systems in operation in 1933. As to care of the blind, deaf and mute, the Southeast ranks only slightly below the average. Again, the Southeast, along with the Southwest, is found ranking far below the other regions, this time in regard to expenditures for hospitals—general, insane, and feeble-minded—with a per capita figure of approximately one-fourth that of the Northeastern Region. Although the Southeast has the lowest per capita expenditure for corrections, when considered from the point of view of the percentage devoted to corrections, it jumps to a ranking of second. As to the percentage devoted to juvenile delinquency, the Southeast ranks only slightly below the

Percentage of Methodists and Baptists in Total Church Membership, 1926

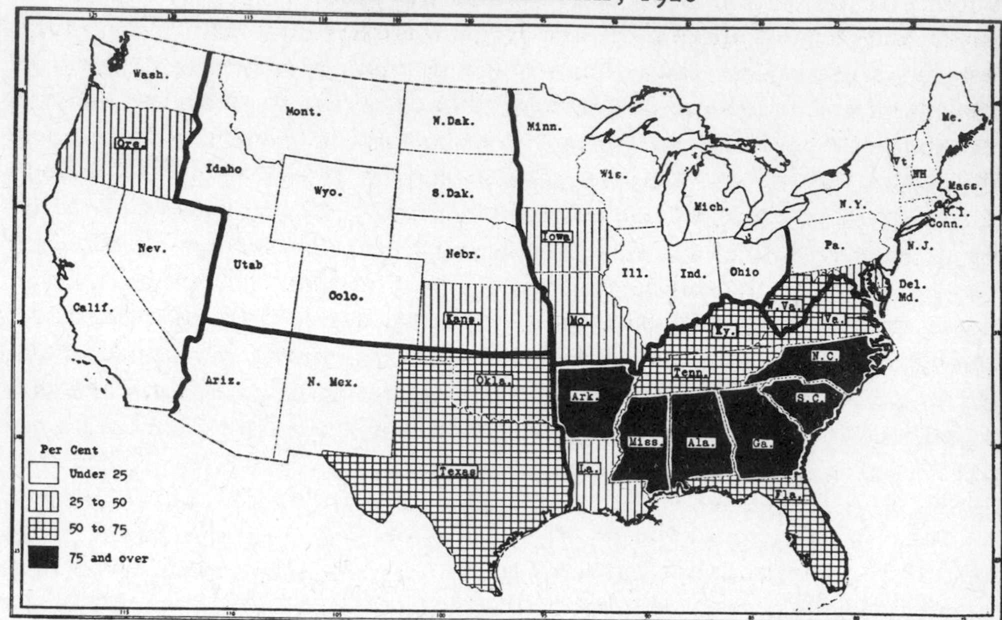

Distribution of Jews, Adult Catholics, and Adult Members of Church of Jesus Christ of Latter-Day Saints, by States and Regions, 1926*

STATE	Jews	Adult Catholics	Adult Members Church of Jesus Christ of Latter-Day Saints
Southeast	*125,850*	*693,341*	*17,869*
Virginia	22,414	27,298	1,456
North Carolina	3,724	4,851	1,631
South Carolina	3,956	6,221	2,581
Georgia	18,366	13,178	2,662
Florida	11,975	28,838	2,037
Kentucky	15,548	126,047	1,656
Tennessee	18,993	18,566	1,857
Alabama	9,218	27,213	1,561
Mississippi	2,871	22,557	1,256
Arkansas	4,940	17,027	183
Louisiana	13,845	401,545	989
Southwest	*44,487*	*603,539*	*15,926*
Oklahoma	4,098	33,313	422
Texas	39,089	390,952	2,112
New Mexico	367	115,005	1,084
Arizona	933	64,269	12,308
Northeast	*2,930,907*	*6,826,261*	*3,849*
Maine	7,582	118,197	......
New Hampshire	2,129	106,651	......
Vermont	1,433	64,841	......
Massachusetts	213,085	1,206,999	407
Rhode Island	24,034	235,511	......
Connecticut	90,165	409,513	122
New York	1,899,597	2,289,093	1,106
New Jersey	219,455	749,422	......
Delaware	5,000	27,422	......
Pennsylvania	393,517	1,399,153	723
Maryland	69,974	170,284	479
West Virginia	4,936	49,175	1,012
Middle States	*773,749*	*3,876,261*	*6,868*
Ohio	166,154	678,851	550
Indiana	23,622	224,789	828
Illinois	339,730	970,853	1,822
Michigan	83,161	591,672	765
Wisconsin	31,839	453,888	478
Minnesota	39,925	333,133	492
Iowa	12,714	207,277	438
Missouri	76,604	415,798	1,495
Northwest	42,311	544,068	343,428
North Dakota	1,626	65,278	100
South Dakota	380	67,592	539
Nebraska	12,271	109,170	523
Kansas	4,973	121,358	......
Montana	671	49,577	1,763
Idaho	316	16,268	64,042
Wyoming	834	13,352	8,511
Colorado	18,950	90,498	4,273
Utah	2,290	10,975	263,677
Far West	147,938	685,715	28,205
Nevada	164	6,066	3,402
Washington	13,050	88,415	4,100
Oregon	12,000	40,997	5,159
California	122,724	550,237	15,544
United States	4,081,242†	13,278,900†	417,810†

**Census of Religious Bodies*, 1926. These three faiths are classified as non-protestant, all others being protestant according to the census definition. Jewish congregations did not report members according to age distribution.

†District of Columbia included.

average. In the percentage devoted to pardon and parole work, the region is found at the bottom along with the Southwest and the Northwest. The pardon and parole work of these three regions is extremely small. The Southeast has slightly less than the average per capita expenditure for the prevention and treatment of communicable diseases. In industrial welfare the Southeast ranks at the bottom in per capita expenditure, both when figured on the basis of total population and on the basis of the number of industrial wage earners in the region. Expenditures devoted to regulation of immigration in the Southeast are of no consequence. In vocational rehabilitation the Southeast ranks along with other regions in per capita expenditures and has approximately an average rank as to staffing of state vocational rehabilitation agencies. The tendency for states to grant subsidies to private welfare organizations seems to be more marked in the Southeast than in any other region except the Northeast.

XIV. RELIGION AND CULTURE

192. Like politics, religion is closely interwoven in the fabric of southern culture. In its church membership, in its Protestant representation, in its church colleges, in the position which the church holds in the community, and in its general influence upon social policy, the Southeast outranks the other regions of the nation. In most of the indices relating to these factors, with the exception of Louisiana, the southern Baptist and Methodist bodies are to the Southeast what the Catholic Church is to certain subregions of the Northeast. This factor is a key to many of the general culture patterns of the region. Of the more than 4,000,000 white adult members of Protestant churches in the Southeast, nearly 2,500,000 belong to the Southern Baptist Convention and a little over 1,500,000 to the General Conference of the Methodist Episcopal Church, South. To these are added more than 2,000,000 Negro Baptists and nearly a million Negro Methodists. The denominational numerical superiority by states is shown in the following priority ranking: Southern Baptist Convention: North Carolina, Florida, Kentucky, Tennessee; Negro Baptists: Virginia, South Carolina, Alabama, Mississippi, and Arkansas. The Roman Catholic Church leads in Louisiana and Kentucky.

193. In the United States as a whole 54.3 per cent of the adult population is enrolled in some denomination. The Southeast has 61.4 per cent, the Southwest 48.3, the Northeast 60.2, the Middle States 50.8, the Northwest 47.4, and the Far West 32.8. The Southeast is the stronghold of Protestantism in the United States. With 19.7 per cent of the adult population of the nation, the Southeast has 33.4 per cent or slightly over one-third of the adult Protestant Church membership and 22.3 of the total church membership. The Southwest is more nearly balanced in popula-

Southern Baptists and Southern Methodists in the Adult White Population in the Southeast and the Southwest, 1926

STATE AND REGION	Adult White Population	Per Cent of Adult White Population in Southern Baptist Church	Per Cent of Adult White Population in Southern Methodist Church	Per Cent of Population in Southern Baptist and Southern Methodist Churches
Southeast				
Virginia	1,153,925	17.96	18.45	36.41
North Carolina	1,287,813	28.03	17.25	45.28
South Carolina	568,851	35.57	20.83	56.40
Georgia	1,182,921	32.71	18.51	51.22
Florida	585,960	16.24	11.15	27.39
Kentucky	1,549,819	19.01	7.02	26.03
Tennessee	1,367,700	18.74	12.40	31.14
Alabama	1,029,839	24.78	16.80	41.58
Mississippi	608,493	32.39	19.31	51.70
Arkansas	877,492	10.78	12.63	23.41
Louisiana	820,415	13.12	6.06	19.18
Southwest				
Oklahoma	1,368,584	8.79	4.83	13.62
Texas	3,042,831	13.89	10.95	24.84
New Mexico	253,225	3.51	3.14	6.65
Arizona	258,121	.42	1.81	2.23

Adult Negro Population and Negro Baptists and Methodists in the Southeast and the Southwest, 1926

STATE AND REGION	Adult Negro Population	Adult Negro Baptists	Adult African Methodist Episcopal Church	Adult African Methodist Episcopal Zion Church	Adult Colored Methodist Episcopal Church
Southeast	*4,983,478*	*2,119,797*	*304,216*	*303,874*	*133,722*
Virginia	441,749	289,129	14,080	14,774	1,934
North Carolina	530,109	188,976	16,568	117,571	4,306
South Carolina	509,320	213,171	51,781	33,457	4,096
Georgia	729,248	345,126	66,562	6,808	27,833
Florida	276,768	88,965	42,988	12,052	4,540
Kentucky	151,048	78,116	9,843	6,088	7,045
Tennessee	308,731	130,301	18,031	12,959	23,433
Alabama	593,709	324,034	31,014	70,132	17,765
Mississippi	638,263	216,029	19,827	15,901	22,439
Arkansas	310,012	124,712	22,385	12,545	9,973
Louisiana	494,521	121,238	11,137	1,587	10,358
Southwest	*666,246*	*254,919*	*36,095*	*8,442*	*24,349*
Oklahoma	107,484	42,939	5,472	6,885	3,450
Texas	549,743	210,941	30,623	1,259	20,657
New Mexico	2,529	388	0	0	50
Arizona	6,490	651	0	298	192

Members of Non-Protestant Churches in the Southeast and the Southwest, 1926

STATE AND REGION	Members Catholic Church	Members Jewish Congregations	Members Church of Jesus Christ of Latter-day Saints	Total Members Non-Protestant Churches	Per Cent of Adult Population in Non-Protestant Churches
Southeast	*693,341*	*125,850*	*17,869*	*837,060*	*5.22*
Virginia	27,298	22,414	1,456	51,168	3.20
North Carolina	4,851	3,724	1,631	10,206	.56
South Carolina	6,221	3,956	2,581	12,758	1.17
Georgia	13,178	18,366	2,662	34,206	1.75
Florida	28,838	11,975	2,037	42,850	4.96
Kentucky	126,047	15,548	1,656	143,251	8.42
Tennessee	18,566	18,993	1,857	39,416	2.35
Alabama	27,213	9,218	1,561	37,992	2.34
Mississippi	22,557	2,871	1,256	26,684	2.14
Arkansas	17,027	4,940	183	22,150	1.86
Louisiana	401,545	13,845	989	416,379	31.66
Southwest	*603,539*	*44,487*	*15,926*	*663,952*	*11.87*
Oklahoma	33,313	4,098	422	37,833	2.56
Texas	390,952	39,089	2,112	432,153	12.02
New Mexico	115,005	367	1,084	116,456	45.53
Arizona	64,269	933	12,308	77,510	29.29

tion, church membership and Protestant membership ratios, with 6.9 per cent of the adult population, 6.1 per cent of the total church membership, and 7.6 per cent of the Protestant Church affiliates. In the Northeast, adult population, total church membership, and Protestant membership are distributed as follows: 31.9 per cent of the population, 35.3 per cent of the church members, and 21.7 per cent of Protestants, there being here a higher percentage of church members than adult population. The Middle States have 28.7 per cent of the total population, 26.9 per cent of the church members, and 26.7 per cent of registered Protestants. The Northwest, with 6.2 per cent of the population, has 5.4 per cent of the church members and 7.2 per cent of Protestants. The Far West, with 6.6 per cent of the population, has 4 per cent of the church members and 3.4 per cent of Protestant church membership.

194. The Southeast's large church membership is divided into many small church bodies with an average of 137 persons per congregation. The Southwest, with 179 members per congregation, also falls far behind the United States average of 235 members for each church edifice. Northeastern churches, with 418 members, are largest in membership, followed next by churches of the Middle States with 265 persons per congregation. Northwestern churches have an average of 196 members each and Far West churches follow closely with 193. Thus, Southeastern churches have one-third as many members as Northeastern churches and 58 per cent of the average total for all churches. There are 31.9 churches in rural United States per 10,000 population as contrasted with 10.4 churches for the same number of urban population. The combined urban and rural figures give an average of 20.3 churches per 10,000 population. Southeastern states have 18.2 churches per 10,000 urban population, 40.6 per 10,000 rural population, and 34.6 for combined urban and rural areas. The Southwest has 16.1 churches for each 10,000 urban population, 32.4 for rural, and 26.8 for total population. In Northeastern cities there are 7.9 churches for each unit of 10,000 urban population, 26.2 for the rural, and 12.7 for the total. Middle States have 9.8 churches for the urban and 27.9 churches for each 10,000 rural population, with an average of 17.3 for the region. The Northwest has 16.3 churches for each 10,000 urban population, 28.4 for rural, and 24.2 for each 10,000 of the total population. Far Western States have 9.8 churches for urban, 17.4 for rural, and 12.4 for each 10,000 combined population.

195. That areas having a small ratio of churches to population should have high average expenditures per church per year is not surprising. Each of the 12.7 churches per 10,000 population in the Northeast spends annually $6,621. In contrast, the Southeastern churches, two and a half

Per Cent of Church Membership in the Total Population, 1926

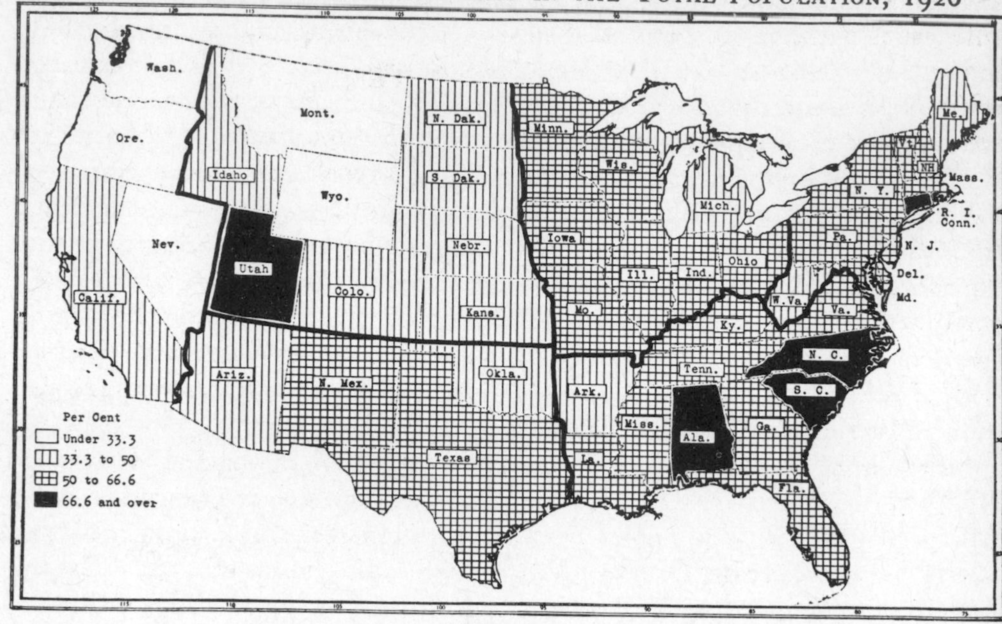

Churches in the United States, 1926

	Value Church Edifices per $1,000 Land Value	Number of Churches per 10,000 Population			Per Cent of Population in Church
		Urban	Rural	Total	
United States	$27.02	10.4	31.9	20.3	54.3
District of Columbia	.....	8.6	....	8.6	54.3
Southeast	34.37	18.2	40.6	34.6	61.4
Virginia	34.20	14.9	39.6	32.0	65.8
North Carolina	28.75	22.6	39.8	35.9	69.6
South Carolina	87.34	24.3	35.8	33.6	72.3
Georgia	41.66	17.6	45.3	37.6	63.8
Florida	87.45	17.2	55.7	38.1	54.2
Kentucky	20.54	15.9	33.7	28.6	55.5
Tennessee	32.21	19.2	41.3	34.5	55.8
Alabama	44.56	17.8	47.0	39.6	67.0
Mississippi	36.75	26.0	44.1	41.4	57.5
Arkansas	44.75	23.6	41.0	37.7	47.4
Louisiana	10.81	11.8	27.5	21.6	61.1
Southwest	24.84	16.1	32.4	26.8	48.3
Oklahoma	22.46	17.6	26.7	23.9	34.7
Texas	29.86	15.4	36.6	28.7	53.5
New Mexico	13.91	18.9	30.6	28.1	59.3
Arizona	7.69	17.3	14.2	15.3	42.3
Northeast	31.20	7.9	26.2	12.7	60.2
Maine	27.39	10.0	24.0	18.5	39.9
New Hampshire	22.45	11.4	28.4	18.1	52.4
Vermont	38.58	11.2	26.1	21.3	50.1
Massachusetts	25.70	7.3	19.9	8.3	64.3
Rhode Island	19.38	7.3	30.6	8.5	71.8
Connecticut	30.49	7.5	16.6	10.3	68.1
New York	31.50	6.1	25.0	9.3	60.1
New Jersey	28.18	7.5	21.4	10.2	57.7
Delaware	44.74	12.5	32.7	22.0	54.2
Pennsylvania	40.01	10.2	24.6	15.1	63.3
Maryland	29.99	9.6	33.6	19.2	55.0
West Virginia	19.22	15.6	36.8	31.1	44.7
Middle States	25.15	9.8	27.9	17.3	50.8
Ohio	20.12	9.6	27.8	15.8	50.7
Indiana	20.60	13.4	31.7	22.0	51.7
Illinois	63.58	8.1	26.9	13.5	51.0
Michigan	15.57	8.1	23.3	13.4	44.7
Wisconsin	15.88	10.5	24.6	17.5	55.1
Minnesota	34.85	11.2	29.1	20.7	53.9
Iowa	50.86	15.1	25.0	21.2	50.1
Missouri	22.70	10.4	34.3	22.6	52.2
Northwest	13.56	16.3	28.4	24.2	46.9
North Dakota	14.75	19.4	39.8	36.7	49.4
South Dakota	9.21	16.4	36.9	33.4	48.7
Nebraska	11.90	14.6	26.5	22.5	47.1
Kansas	15.05	18.4	28.6	24.8	47.7
Montana	19.46	14.9	28.2	23.9	29.6
Idaho	15.07	23.3	22.7	22.9	35.8
Wyoming	8.43	17.9	22.2	20.9	33.2
Colorado	14.68	15.1	19.1	17.1	40.0
Utah	20.26	11.5	18.4	14.9	92.3
Far West	17.22	9.8	17.4	12.4	32.8
Nevada	5.02	8.8	22.9	18.8	22.5
Washington	22.17	12.0	20.2	15.6	28.8
Oregon	15.96	13.9	22.2	18.0	30.0
California	16.92	8.7	14.2	10.2	34.8

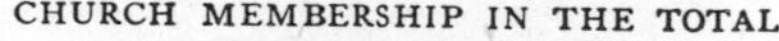

CHURCH MEMBERSHIP IN THE TOTAL POPULATION BY REGIONS, 1926

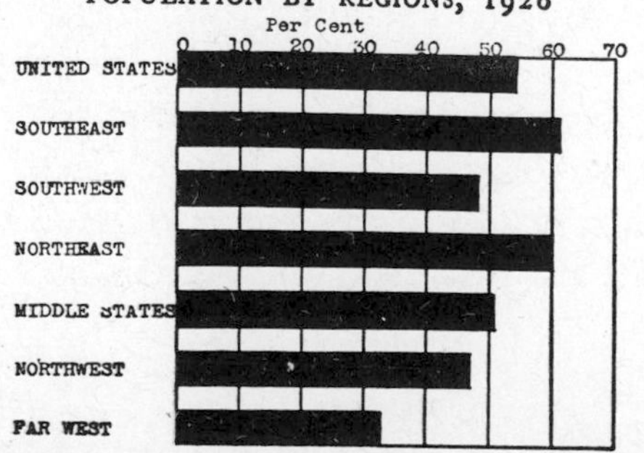

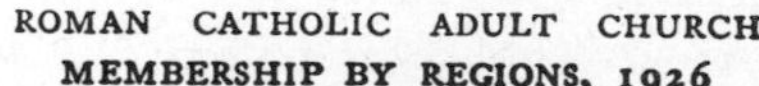

ROMAN CATHOLIC ADULT CHURCH MEMBERSHIP BY REGIONS, 1926

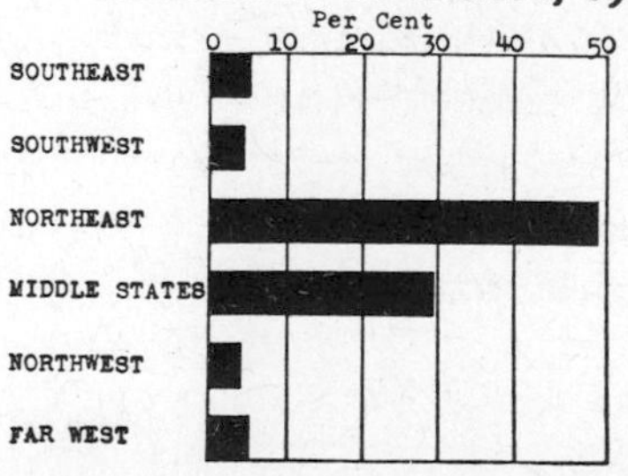

times as numerous, have an average expenditure of $1,749 per year. Southwestern churches spend $2,099, Middle States churches $4,419, Northwestern churches $2,586, and Far Western churches $4,084 each year. Yet the ranking of regions is quite different when total church expenditures are seen in relation to per capita income of the states rather than in amounts spent alone. The Southeast has the highest relative annual expenditure, $16.02 of each $1,000 of income going into church coffers. Ranking the regions in order of church expenditures per $1,000 income: Southeast, $16.02; Northeast, $10.68; Southwest, $10.48; Northwest, $9.68; Middle States, $9.48; Far West, $7.31. It may be noted that, in general, regions with high per capita incomes have proportionately low church expenditures. Equally as significant as the proportionate expenditure of income through the churches is the value of church edifices per thousand dollars land value. Ranking the regions according to value of churches per thousand dollars land value the Southeast has $34.37 invested in church property for each $1,000 land value, the Northeast $31.20, Middle States $25.15, the Southwest $24.84, Far West $17.22, and Northwest $13.56. The value of church edifices per adult member, while not so illuminating as investments in church property in relation to total land value, is somewhat revealing in regional comparisons. With large membership and few but expensive church buildings, church edifices of the Northeast are valued at $97.35 per member. Middle States churches are valued at $90.95 per member, Far West churches at $84.36, Northwest churches at $72.79, Southeast churches at $58.05, and Southwest churches have a value of $50.87 for each member.

196. Between the Southeast and the Southwest there is a wider difference in church mores than between the Southeast and the Northeast. With a church membership less than one-half the total adult population, the Southwest ranks fourth among the six regions in membership. Only the Northwest and Far West have fewer adults in church. There is also a difference in the composition of the church membership of the regions, the proportion of non-protestants in the Southwest being nearly two and one-half times that in the Southeast. West of Texas, Southern Baptist and Southern Methodist churches have not added converts in large numbers, although Arizona, New Mexico, and Oklahoma are in the territory of the Southern Baptist Convention and the General Conference of the Methodist Episcopal Church South. It should be added, however, that the stronghold of southern Protestantism does not extend into Louisiana and Kentucky in the Southeast. In Louisiana the proportion of non-protestants is more than six times that of the Southeast as a whole and Kentucky churches have a large Catholic following. In the Southwest, New Mexico has an adult

Homicides, 1918-1927

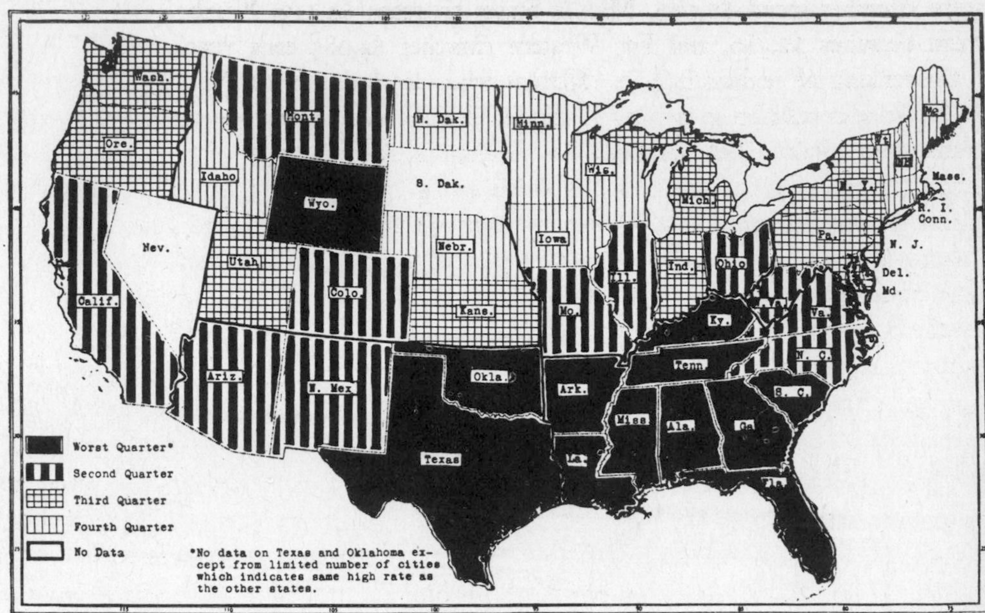

The Southeast reflects the Protestant preponderance, being characterized somewhat as early American in its religion and stocks of people, other than Negroes. The folkways of the frontier, of "honor", of white supremacy, however, have not hitherto run contrary to the religious motivation of the region.

Lynchings, 1889-1932

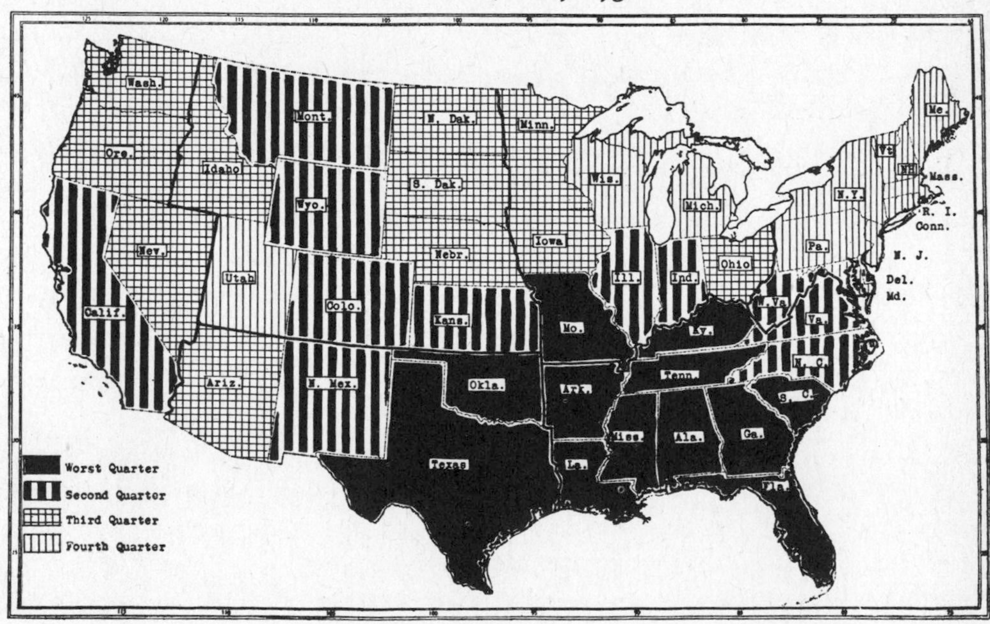

population over 45 per cent non-protestant, most of whom are affiliated with the Catholic Church. Oklahoma's church membership is less concentrated within a few religious bodies than other southern states. There are 62 denominational groups which claim 99.4 per cent of the church population of the state. Only Texas, with nearly three times as many churches, has a membership distribution among a larger number of faiths with 64 denominational groups accounting for 99.8 per cent of the church population. Within other Southeastern and Southwestern States there are fewer churches represented, and in most instances less than four church bodies claim a majority of church followers.

197. Differences between the Southeast and the Southwest also appear in the value of church edifices in relation to property value and church expenditures related to income. The relative value of church property in the Southeast is highest for the six regions; in the Southwest the relative value of church property falls below the averages of the Southeast, Northeast, and Middle States churches. A regional comparison of church expenditures per $1,000 income discloses another regional difference between Southeast and Southwest, for here again the Southwest falls below both the Southeast and Northeast averages. In distribution of churches per 10,000 population the Southeast and Southwest rank first and second respectively, and in the circulation of religious periodicals regional differences are not so pronounced between the Southeast and Southwest as between the Southeast and other regions.

198. The relative strength of leading denominations varies in the Southeast and Southwest. In Oklahoma the Southern Baptist Convention has the largest membership, but in Texas, New Mexico, and Arizona, the Roman Catholic Church ranks first in size among religious bodies. The Southern Baptist Convention has the greatest number of members in five Southeastern States, the second largest number in three other states, and takes third place in all the remaining states. The Methodist Episcopal Church South, is first in membership in none of the southern states, but this body is second in size in five states, and third in seven other states. Although Roman Catholics rank first in Louisiana and Kentucky, the only other denomination listed among the three strongest in the Southeast is the Disciples of Christ, which is third in size in Kentucky. The denominational homogeneity of the Southeast is apparent when it is pointed out that in ten of the eleven states Baptist bodies have the largest following, and in Louisiana, where Roman Catholics rank first, Negro Baptists are second in size and the Southern Baptist Convention third. Two new bodies enter the first three ranking bodies of Southwestern States. The Church of Jesus Christ of

COMPARATIVE DISTRIBUTION OF "WHO'S WHO" NOTABLES PER 100,000 POPULATION, 1910 AND 1930

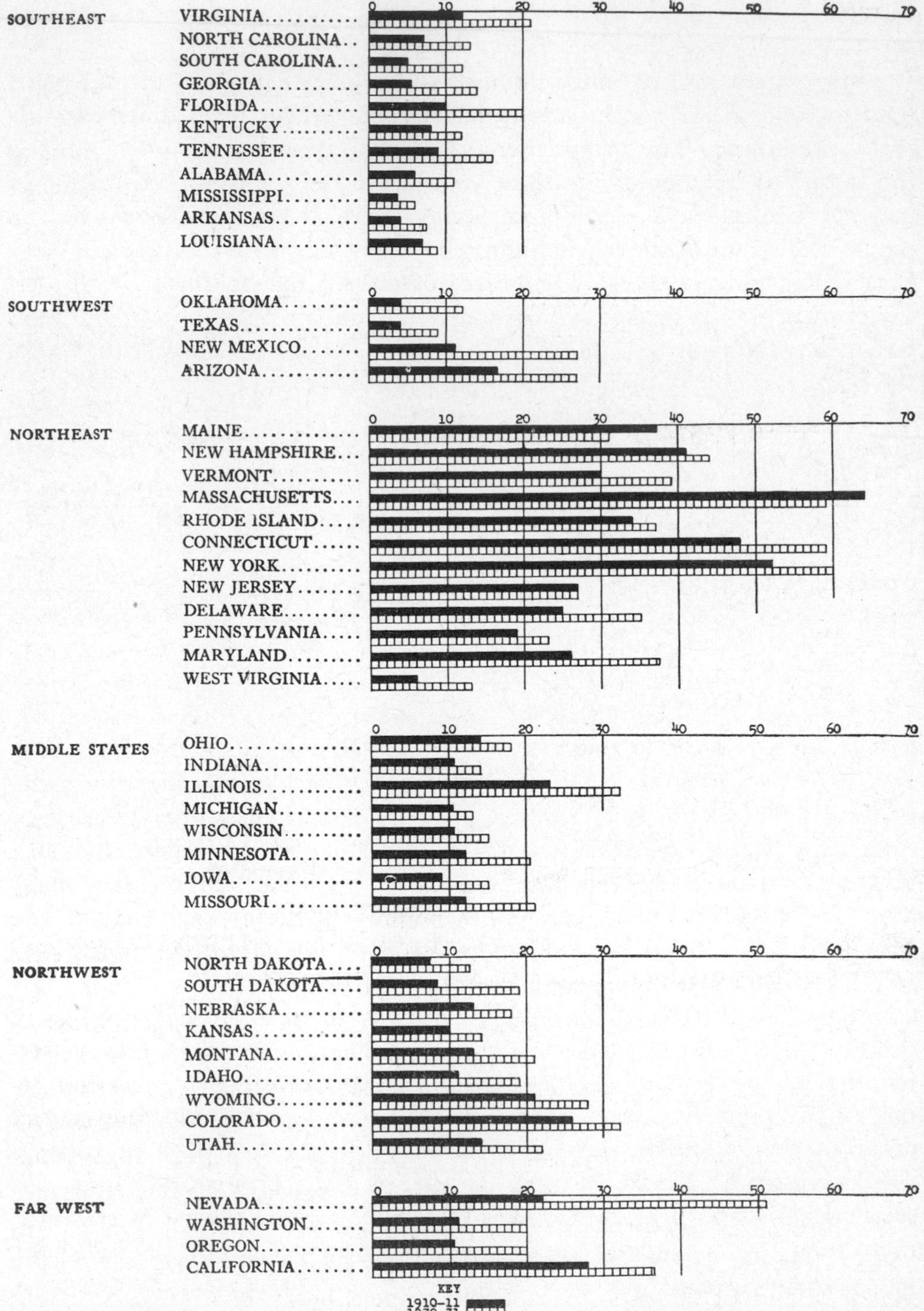

Latter-Day Saints has the second largest following in Arizona, and the Presbyterian Church, United States of America, is third in this state.

XV. ASPECTS OF GENERAL CULTURE

199. Many indices commonly utilized to indicate general cultural status tend to confirm the conclusions which may be drawn from summaries already presented. The picture here as elsewhere is a mixed one. Among the factors to be sampled are those relating to the region's participation in national currents and control, in literary and dramatic achievements, in public health and vitality, in family relationships and in crime, in law-abidingness and violence. The representation of the Southeast in the national codes is representative of the general ratio. With more than 3,000 code representatives both the Southeast and Southwest have less than 300, the Southeast having perhaps less than seven per cent of the total. Of 364 special codes the South has no representation on 243. In national groups, samplings of control representation are the National Research Council with 3.8 per cent, the Social Science Research Council with 7.5, the American Council of Learned Societies with no representation. The White House Conference on Child Health and Protection had 6.8 per cent; the President's Conference on Home Building and Home Ownership, 8.9; the Committee on the Cost of Medical Care, 9.3, *The Encyclopaedia of the Social Sciences* had no southern representation; *Social Science Abstracts* had 7.1 per cent; *The Social Work Year Book* had 5.6; the *Dictionary of American Biography*, 14.3; and the *Linguistic Atlas*, 10 per cent. Of national educational periodicals, exclusive of state organs and of Negro periodicals, the South has none in 19 out of twenty classes. For state journals of state educational associations, however, it has 25.6 per cent, 16.7 per cent of the journals issued by state departments of education, 50 per cent Negro and Indian, and 26.8 per cent of parent-teacher bulletins in state branches. Here as in many other instances the South emphasizes state organization and action. In national organizations, the region either does not have the trained personnel available or they are not articulate.

200. The picture of the region's more than three million net loss of people in interstate migration has been presented, as have the relative status of the states in native and resident men of distinction. A further index of the region's capacity and status may be found in the measure of drain in specific fields such as social and physical scientists in colleges and universities. Thus, Wilson Gee shows that, of approximately 200 social scientists born in the South and listed in *Who's Who in America*, more than 100 are located in the South and nearly 100 outside, indicating an approximately 45 per cent "drag" out of the region. According to fields of specialization, the loss is least with the historians, greater among

Offenses Per 100,000 Population Reported in 1933*

STATE AND REGION	Criminal Murder	Homicide Manslaughter by Negligence	Rape	Robbery	Aggravated Assault	Burglary	Larceny	Auto Theft
Southeast								
Virginia	16.3	9.0	11.2	74.3	193.9	479.0	1,244.2	250.7
North Carolina	23.4	16.6	7.2	67.9	566.6	470.0	846.0	376.3
South Carolina	8.0	0.0	3.2	53.4	126.9	36.9	2,258.1	67.5
Georgia	19.7	3.1	6.2	47.6	97.2	393.0	1,657.8	221.5
Florida	20.8	6.9	2.9	107.1	233.3	727.2	957.4	302.6
Kentucky	19.0	3.8	5.8	156.6	209.7	562.9	987.9	284.9
Tennessee	22.6	6.5	3.3	136.3	229.1	518.8	623.4	308.0
Alabama	34.5	15.0	2.5	98.9	140.3	673.9	488.2	413.0
Mississippi	11.8	4.3	4.3	23.6	165.4	229.9	545.6	61.2
Arkansas	17.6	8.8	1.5	179.3	17.6	526.8	1,146.1	477.5
Louisiana	13.5	1.9	3.6	50.8	33.4	241.8	315.6	201.0
Southwest								
Oklahoma	10.5	1.4	2.9	133.7	40.7	576.3	1,195.8	299.6
Texas	18.2	6.8	7.0	87.9	82.1	616.6	1,418.4	516.3
New Mexico	3.0	0.0	0.0	38.7	3.0	532.9	1,104.5	247.1
Arizona	19.8	3.8	10.4	92.5	54.7	578.6	1,619.7	591.8
Northeast								
Maine	1.7	2.9	3.7	20.4	35.8	227.8	395.6	184.9
New Hampshire	0.6	0.0	6.2	8.0	4.9	160.9	300.3	102.4
Vermont	0.0	0.0	1.0	2.1	7.2	73.9	174.4	50.3
Massachusetts	2.5	3.4	6.5	31.2	17.8	293.0	543.3	317.1
Rhode Island	1.7	1.9	0.2	7.4	21.0	250.8	636.0	98.9
Connecticut	1.2	2.2	4.2	21.3	16.3	328.6	655.7	218.6
New York	2.4	2.7	5.6	18.0	29.9	200.1	417.0	131.1
New Jersey	6.0	14.5	6.2	56.9	71.7	375.7	443.7	218.5
Delaware	9.2	1.8	10.1	42.2	64.1	353.7	604.8	208.0
Pennsylvania	5.3	11.4	5.4	53.5	36.5	167.7	217.5	161.6
Maryland	5.7	0.9	9.6	63.4	6.2	265.6	457.6	323.2
West Virginia	7.2	2.3	5.7	73.3	50.9	279.6	596.3	257.9
Middle States								
Ohio	7.8	3.0	4.6	97.5	43.0	330.5	865.3	260.9
Indiana	4.9	2.1	7.2	102.2	52.3	419.0	981.5	340.4
Illinois	8.4	3.6	4.6	339.7	58.8	528.5	566.9	615.3
Michigan	3.3	2.2	11.3	75.1	32.0	267.8	1,130.8	206.1
Wisconsin	1.1	0.2	3.3	19.3	6.4	175.7	619.0	134.0
Minnesota	2.1	0.6	1.5	86.5	11.6	391.8	440.8	478.4
Iowa	2.9	0.8	2.2	73.0	15.6	384.5	754.1	293.9
Missouri	13.1	7.3	6.8	128.5	31.7	286.5	869.5	307.1
Northwest								
North Dakota	2.0	1.0	3.0	54.4	3.0	403.8	641.3	155.4
South Dakota	1.9	0.0	6.7	82.8	2.9	293.5	701.5	240.6
Nebraska	4.1	0.2	1.2	66.2	26.7	263.3	741.1	562.4
Kansas	8.0	2.4	5.0	121.8	25.0	479.9	1,123.7	305.3
Montana	0.0	0.0	6.6	27.9	8.2	272.3	1,164.5	126.3
Idaho	0.0	0.0	14.8	37.0	22.2	233.0	569.6	144.2
Wyoming	11.7	0.0	11.7	23.3	11.7	110.8	408.3	35.0
Colorado	6.6	0.7	6.2	149.8	15.7	769.3	1,172.6	393.4
Utah	4.7	0.0	2.3	80.1	15.0	629.8	924.4	487.0
Far West								
Nevada	19.9	0.0	0.0	99.3	87.4	774.9	2,133.9	472.9
Washington	3.2	0.6	2.0	132.9	17.9	713.7	1,504.6	508.1
Oregon	1.8	1.6	2.7	139.1	15.0	828.6	1,491.2	303.0
California	5.1	5.1	9.3	111.8	26.0	532.1	1,202.2	457.6

*Rates are based on reports from 1,264 cities with over 49,500,000 population.

the economists, psychologists, and political scientists, and quite high among sociologists, anthropologists, and statisticians. This reflects comparative opportunities for employment in and out of the South. Fifty-eight northern- and western-born social scientists have migrated to the South. This makes a net loss for the South of 31. Of the southern-born social scientists, about 150 or almost 75 per cent pursued their undergraduate training in the South. Among 188 who received graduate training, there were 160 or approximately 86 per cent who were awarded the highest degrees which they earned from northern and western institutions. Nearly half or 48 per cent of those who left the South for graduate training did not return to the South; while 75 per cent of those receiving graduate training in the South remained at home. Of about 1,100 natural scientists born in the South, there is about a 60 per cent "drag" out of the South. Seven hundred and seventy natural scientists born in the North and West have moved into the South, making a net gain of 110 for the South. The South is, however, unsuccessful in holding its scientists of superior talent, approximately four-fifths having left the region of their birth, with less than two-fifths starred scientists born elsewhere found in the South, leaving a net loss of about two-fifths.

201. In the field of literature and drama the Southeast has achieved an increasingly merited distinction. Of more than 1,000 volumes of fiction in the decade from 1920 to 1930 featuring regional Americana, the Southeast predominated in titles largely by southern authors in which the folk-regional character of the Negro, the poorer whites, the old South, the conflict between the old and the new South, and between the Negro and the whites was depicted variously. There were no less than a dozen Pulitzer awards in fiction, drama, and editorial effort, and more than that many adoptions and awards by book clubs and others. In more than 90 per cent of distinguished awards, however, distinction came after the author had left the region or had been conditioned and motivated largely from without the region. The record, however, is clear evidence of capacity and cultural setting for achievement.

202. The Southeast still reflects the frontier in its homicide and crime rates and in its mob action. The highest rates of homicide are in southeastern cities. The 1929 homicide rate for the registration area of the United States was 8.5 per 100,000 population. For the Southeastern States the rates were: 19.5, 15.4, 25.8, 18.3, 16.7, 16.6, 23.2, 16.7, 14.1, with only North Carolina and Virginia as low as 10 per cent. Urban rates are still higher with at least four states with over 40 per 100,000 of population, while the highest crime rates in the nation are in southeastern cities. The Southeast was responsible for more than 90 per cent of the lynchings during the five-

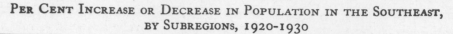

Per Cent Increase or Decrease in Population in the Southeast, by Subregions, 1920-1930

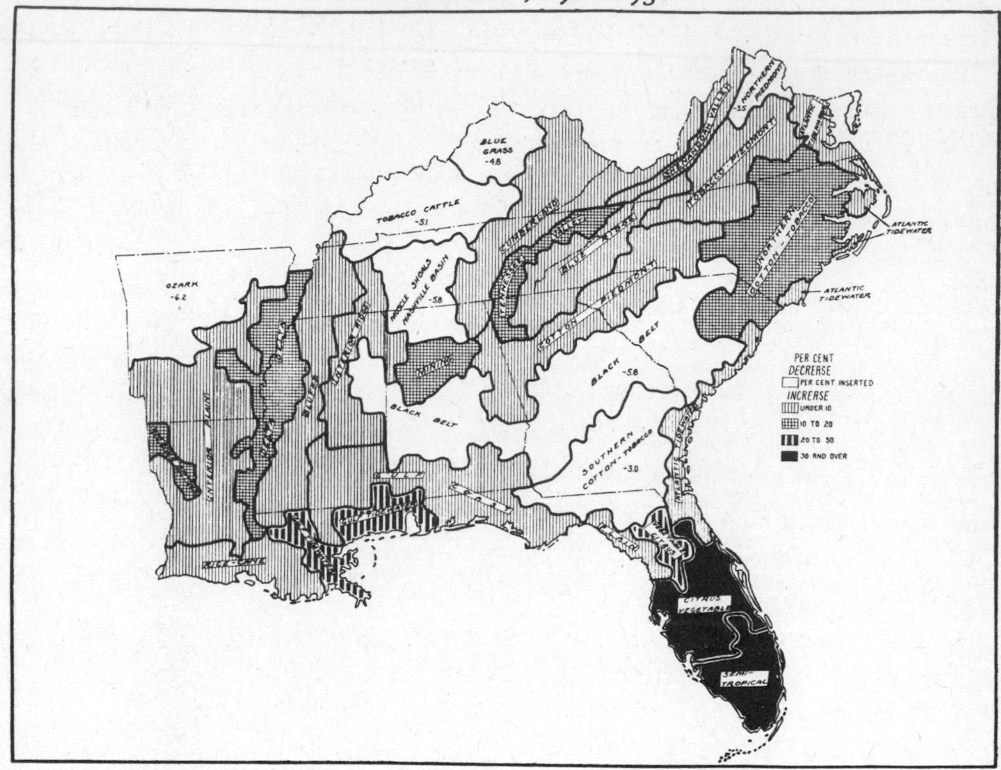

County Medians of Selected Indices of the Subregions in the Southeastern Region of the United States: Population

Subregion	Per Cent Increase in Population 1920-30	Per Cent Population Under 19 Years	Per Cent Males Gainfully Employed	Per Cent Native White Illiteracy	Per Cent Negro
Cotton Piedmont	5.8	49.7	57.0	4.9	19.5
Shenandoah Valley	2.8	45.5	54.5	5.7	9.8
Tennessee Valley	10.4	48.1	55.7	6.0	6.4
Atlantic Tidewater	.1	45.3	57.7	2.9	42.4
Northern Piedmont	-3.5	45.0	57.7	5.1	24.3
Tobacco Piedmont	5.0	48.9	55.7	4.5	32.6
Blue Ridge Mountains	6.0	50.7	53.6	7.6	2.5
Cumberland Mountains	6.3	52.7	52.2	8.9	1.8
Blue Grass	-4.8	39.8	60.1	4.3	9.5
Tobacco-Cattle	-5.1	44.2	59.1	7.1	6.2
Muscle Shoals-Nashville Basin	-5.8	47.6	57.2	6.5	16.0
Bluffs	3.9	46.5	60.9	2.2	51.1
Northern Cotton and Tobacco	11.3	52.1	54.3	5.2	46.9
Southern Cotton and Tobacco	-3.0*	51.1	57.9	4.3	34.5
Black Belt	-5.8	49.6	58.2	2.9	56.4
Citrus-Vegetable	77.1**	38.3	60.7	1.0	27.8
Vegetable-Citrus	25.7**	43.7	59.5	2.6	34.3
Semi-Tropical	165.0**	36.3	64.2	0.6	29.1
Gulf Coast Plain	5.7†	49.4	58.3	4.5	33.4
Mining	17.5	49.9	57.7	5.5	14.3
Gulf Tidewater	28.3	46.3	58.0	3.9	25.0
Interior Ridge	9.4	49.5	59.5	3.2	19.8
Delta	11.6	44.2	64.4	2.8	68.0
Ozarks	-6.2	48.5	56 6	4.3	1.4††
Interior Plain	6.6	47.7	57.6	2.5	31.4
Red River Bottoms	16.3	46.6	63.1	2.9	49.0
Rice-Cane	4.5	48.2	56.3	21.8	36.4

†Thirteen Florida and Louisiana counties omitted. **Actual increase for region—not median of counties.

*Three Florida counties omitted—one change in county lines across region lines—Gulf from Lafayette in Southern Cotton and Tobacco. ††More than 10 per cent of counties with no Negro population.

year period before 1930. Regional distributions of these factors as well as others relating to prisoners and to prohibition enforcement may be seen from the maps and tables. Even the briefest summary, however, reveals the Southeast as extraordinarily out of step and inexcusably backward, wasteful of its human resources, a significant commentary on its religious culture.

XVI. SUBREGIONS OF THE SOUTHEAST

203. Just as it is not possible to understand American people and their institutions through the "national average," independent of the richer regional variations and distributions, so it is not possible to gain a fair picture of the several regions except through subregional variations and homogeneity within the larger framework of regional homogeneity. And just as the larger regions of the nation afford practical workable areas for general analysis and planning, so many subregions within the major regional divisions are necessary for more exhaustive study and for planning the total area involved.

204. A single illustration as found in population will serve to summarize this twofold value of regional and subregional measurement. The Southeastern States, comprising the eleven states of Virginia, the Carolinas, Georgia and Florida, Alabama and Mississippi, Louisiana and Arkansas, Tennessee and Kentucky, according to the most commonly used major population indices appear as homogeneous. Moreover, they are the only grouping of "Southern" States that can be so clustered. This homogeneity is indicated as follows: First, these 14 indices were checked with each of the eleven states: density of population, rural-urban composition, age composition, racial composition, native-born composition, occupation, religion, education, general cultural equipment, wealth, politics, vital statistics, migration, institutional composition. The result was that, with the exception of Florida, homogeneity was indicated by an average of more than 13 of the 14 indices. When applied to the border states the results were as follows: Maryland ranks with the Southeast in only one out of 14; Missouri, three; Texas, three; Oklahoma, five; and West Virginia, six.

205. Yet within this larger regional homogeneity there is subregional heterogeneity of great importance. The old cotton South is different from the Appalachian and Ozark hills. The Black Belt is different from the Piedmont Cotton Region. The black man is different from mountain folk; the tenant farmer in the lower South is different from mountain or western tenant. A half dozen subregions having a tenancy rate from 80 to more than 90 per cent differ greatly from those with less than one-third, while areas of poor land with high tenant rates are different from

The Cotton Southeast

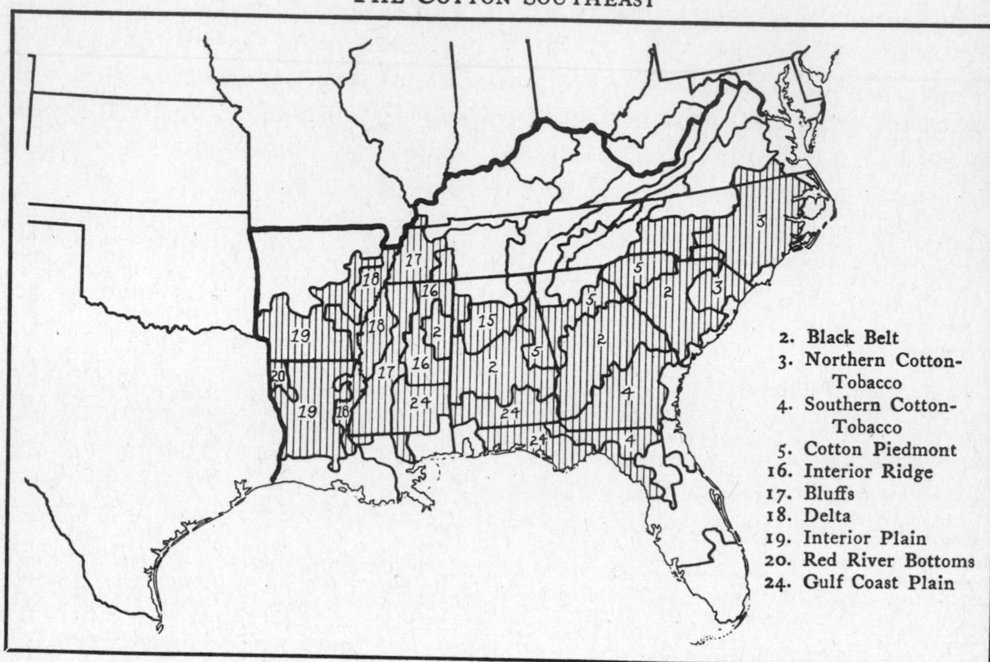

The Fruit and Vegetable Southeast

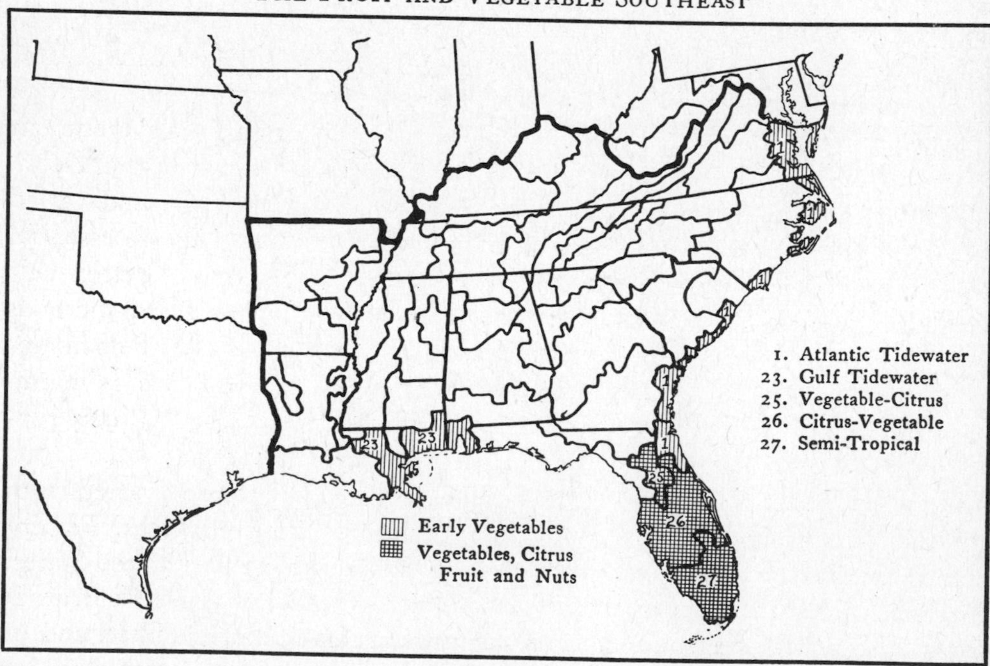

those of rich lands. So in other indices. In rates of increase and decrease in population the range is from three to six per cent decrease in seven subregions to an increase of 165 and 77 per cent in the Semi-Tropical and Citrus-Vegetable subregions. And in the ratio of Negro population there are variations from two per cent, three per cent, six per cent in a half dozen subregions, such as the Cumberland and Blue Ridge and Ozarks subregions, to 68 per cent in the Delta and 56 per cent in the Black Belt.

206. Subregions vary in size and number according to the purposes for which they are classified. Some are historical and cultural, and some are functional. Within the Southeast there are several general groupings of subregions which present the whole picture of diversification and serve as effective units for planning. There is, for instance, the Appalachian Subregion, which L. C. Gray and associates have recently analyzed in great detail. There is the Tennessee Valley, which is the subject of a special division. There are, besides, a number of larger geographic-agricultural subregions, such as are described by Rupert B. Vance, and there are the 27 subregions set up by T. J. Woofter, Jr., as embodying sufficient diversity and homogeneity as to warrant separate functional analysis. There is, again, the old smaller local cultural areas, such as New Orleans and Savannah and Charleston, which may be characterized as distinctive subregional phenomena.

207. Again, "the deep South" is no longer characteristic of both cultural and geographic indices, since Florida and the coastal fringe of South Carolina, Georgia, Alabama, and Mississippi rank higher in general economic and cultural status than do other cross-beltings higher up. So, too, the "Cotton Belt" itself is not one but several subregions—the Piedmont Cotton, the Upper and Lower Piedmont, the Black Belt, and the Delta. These in turn may change in accordance with shifting economy and varied geography, affording basic differentials as well as uniformities essential to effective organization and future development. Or, again, cotton culture, for instance, in New Mexico and Arizona, with specialized methods and higher yields may become an index of southwestern cotton-belt homogeneity. Once again, the Piedmont may denote a cotton culture or manufacturing region or a tobacco culture or manufacturing region, or it may represent a geographic-cultural fringe of the Appalachian South.

208. Once more, within the Southeast there are many varied subdivisions for functional or commercial or administrative purposes. For instance, the Southeast is a part of three census subregions of the United States: the South Atlantic, the East South Central, and the West South Central. It shows also certain metropolitan regions more or less clearly defined and of great importance in an understanding of the region, with greater major

Subregions Around the Tennessee River Basin and the Two Piedmont Regions—Textile and Mountain

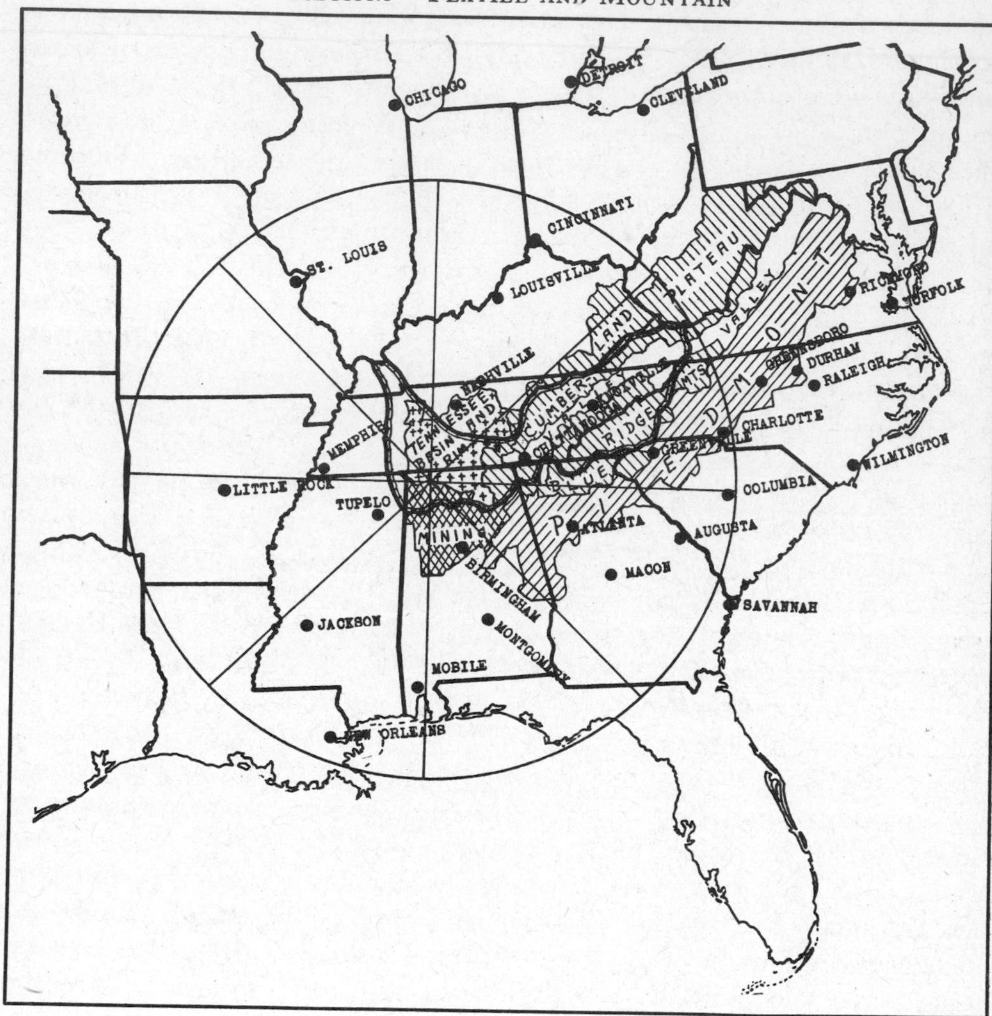

Tennessee Basin—Percentage Distribution of Population

STATE	Urban		Rural-Farm		Rural Non-Farm	
	Number	Per Cent	Number	Per Cent	Number	Per Cent
Tennessee	401,680	26.7	750,205	49.9	352,261	23.4
Kentucky	63,416	21.1	116,324	38.7	121,055	40.2
West Virginia	5,376	5.9	8,759	9.7	76,344	84.4
Virginia	38,243	12.3	155,651	49.9	117,777	37.8
North Carolina	73,516	17.2	221,028	51.8	131,999	31.0
Georgia	14,201	15.5	52,532	57.4	24,847	27.1
Alabama	65,931	15.4	296,844	69.2	66,307	15.4
Mississippi	6,220	8.0	59,772	77.1	11,562	14.9
Total Tennessee Basin	668,583	20.7	1,661,115	51.4	902,152	27.9

regions centering around Atlanta, New Orleans, or Memphis. It shows many subregional divisions for newspaper circulation and for retail and wholesale trade. Thus, the Department of Commerce has arranged the Southeast into thirty or more subregions according to combinations of urban and wholesale grocery territories, with a subregion centering around each of the major cities—Charlottesville, Richmond, Norfolk, Petersburg, Lynchburg, and Roanoke, in Virginia; in North Carolina, the regions are Winston-Salem, Raleigh, Wilmington, Charlotte, Asheville; in South Carolina, Spartanburg, Greenville, Columbia, Charleston; in Georgia, Atlanta, Augusta, Macon, Columbus, Albany, Savannah; in Florida, Miami, Tampa, Orlando, Jacksonville, Pensacola; in Alabama, Birmingham, Selma, Mobile; in Mississippi, Jackson, Vicksburg, Meridian, Natchez; in Arkansas, Fort Smith, Little Rock, Pine Bluff, Texarkana; in Louisiana, Shreveport, Alexandria, Lake Charles, New Orleans; in Tennessee, Memphis, Nashville, Chattanooga, Knoxville; in Kentucky, Paducah, Louisville, Lexington. The significance of subregions, however, is emphasized by the overlapping of state lines of many of these regions. Thus, the Memphis region includes about 30 counties comprehending all of the north of Mississippi, as well as about 20 counties in Northeast Arkansas. The Chattanooga area includes counties in both Georgia and Alabama. The Norfolk Region includes a large part of the northeastern area of North Carolina. A part of Kentucky is included in the Evansville, Illinois, subregion.

209. To continue more specifically with the Southern Appalachians, there is need only to point to Dr. Gray's study just now being published, which comprehends a greater Southern Appalachian area embracing parts of nine states, or 70,000,000 acres, and a lesser Appalachian subregion, embracing parts of six states with a little more than 55,000,000 acres. Even here the still smaller subregional analysis is of great importance. These regions may be compared with certain of the Tennessee Valley areas or with other special subregions of the Southeast or with the Southeast as a whole for various purposes of analysis or planning. Thus, the more than two hundred maps portray a vivid homogeneity and a striking diversity as well, in area, population, land utilization, types of farming, standards of living, industries, taxation, public expenditures, education, social conditions. From the vast amount of data gathered it is possible to measure here, as for the whole South, something of the natural wealth, the technological wealth, the artificial wealth, the human wealth, and the institutional arrangements which give distinctive character to the people and delimit their prospects for the future. From these data emerge not only a comprehensive picture but certain definite conclusions with reference to the movement of the people, new industries, land utilization, and social legislation. From them

Subregions of the Southeast

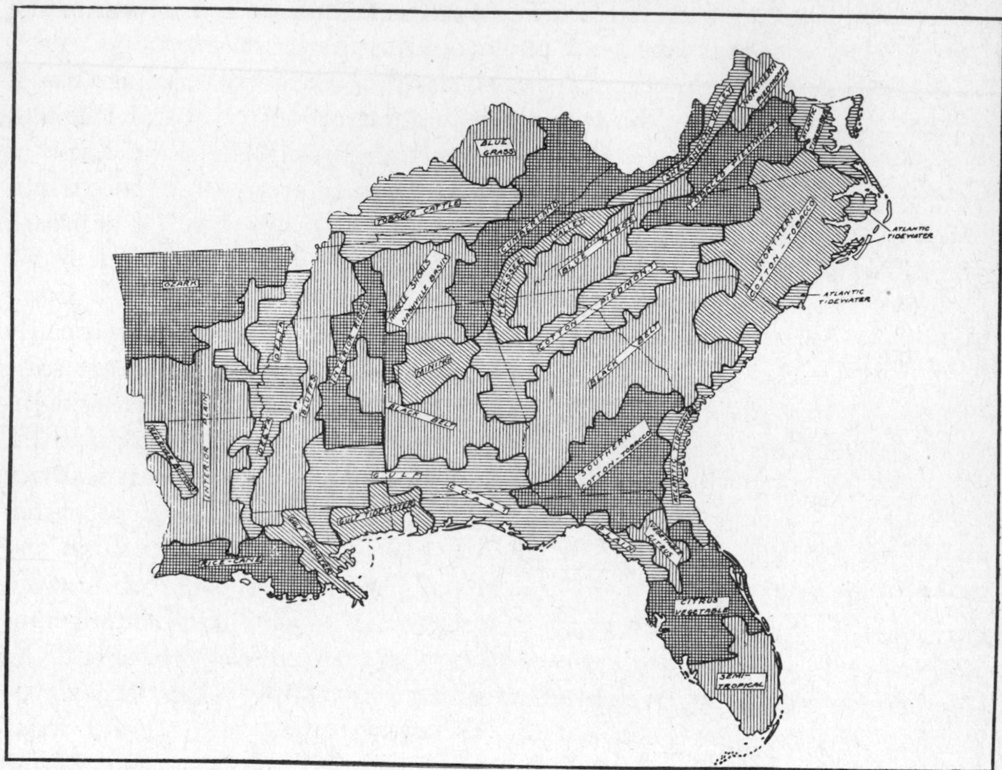

County Medians of Selected Indices of the Subregions in the Southern Region of the United States: Agriculture

Subregion	Per Cent Tenancy	Per Cent White Tenancy	Per Cent Negro Tenancy	Per Cent Land in Farms	Average Size Farms (Acres)	Value Land and Buildings Per Farm	Value Land and Buildings Per Acre
Cotton Piedmont	63.9	55.5	85.1	71.9	65.1	$ 2,269	$36
Shenandoah Valley	16.6	17.0	12.5	65.3	110.4	7,728	74
Tennessee Valley	37.2	37.0	43.4	78.7	79.6	3,556	37
Atlantic Tidewater	18.5	19.2	18.5	37.6	79.3	3,823	47
Northern Piedmont	15.4	16.0	12.5	75.5	129.8	7,997	54
Tobacco Piedmont	31.5	26.9	41.0	70.0	92.6	3,105	34
Blue Ridge Mountains	30.9	30.0	23.1*	53.1	76.8	2,420	35
Cumberland Mountains	28.7	28.7	12.1	64.0	79.0	2,199	27
Blue Grass	41.0	40.7	44.5	88.5	79.7	5,137	71
Tobacco-Cattle	38.8	37.6	50.9	81.3	83.4	2,354	27
Muscle Shoals-Nashville Basin	44.2	43.9	57.1	74.5	80.4	2,747	41
Bluffs	74.7	51.4	86.6	69.0	65.8	1,627	26
Northern Cotton and Tobacco	58.3	47.5	73.5	58.2	61.5	2,775	43
Southern Cotton and Tobacco	60.4	55.0	71.6	58.0	104.5	2,479	24
Black Belt	73.5	49.4	88.3	58.3	79.9	1,875	24
Citrus-Vegetable	8.6	10.0	25.0	8.7	51.3	14,703	205
Vegetable-Citrus	30.1	29.9	28.8	30.9	100.0	3,720	41
Semi-Tropical	34.9	32.6	75.0	3.1	43.2	7,532	156
Gulf Coast Plain	41.7	34.0	55.7	36.6	76.3	2,012	25
Mining	50.8	49.6	63.9	49.4	64.8	1,859	26
Gulf Tidewater	25.2	24.3	43.6	15.4	72.5	3,824	53
Interior Ridge	57.0	48.6	71.7	70.7	70.9	1,398	19
Delta	90.3	75.5	95.3	50.6	34.5	2,271	57
Ozarks	42.7	42.6	46.2*	53.3	89.7	2,092	25
Interior Plain	61.2	49.3	79.1	39.0	60.8	1,875	31
Red River Bottoms	80.0	54.5	89.0	43.2	41.8	2,015	48
Rice-Cane	51.9	42.1	67.8	33.7	138.9	7,004	49

*More than 10 per cent of counties with no Negro tenancy.

also emerge new definitions of marginal land and folk and new plans for adaptation of man to land, featuring man more and land less within the bounds of reasonable margins of physical adjustment.

210. In delimiting southern areas it has proved possible to make use of several regional indices. The approach to American Agricultural Regions, first developed by O. E. Baker and now lately amplified in the Type of Farming Areas, shows the South largely given over to cotton, tobacco, subtropical crops, and subsistence farming areas. A related type of approach based on studies by the United States Geological Survey is found in the delimitation of the physiographic areas of the United States by a Committee headed by Nevin M. Fenneman. Interpreting these areas broadly in the light of the soil surveys, Hugh H. Bennett mapped the large scale regions of the South in relation to agriculture. These were Coastal and Interior Flatwoods; Middle, Interior, and Upper Coastal Plains; Sand Hills, Piedmont, Appalachians, Clay Hills, Bluffs, Silt Loam Uplands, Black Prairies, and River Bottoms making up the Southeast; while the Coastal, Black Waxy, Grand, Eastern Oklahoma, and Red Prairies, the High and Staked Plains, and the Edwards Plateau make up the Southwest.

211. In an attempt to integrate these areas in a minimum number of homogeneous human-use regions, Rupert B. Vance has presented the regional economy and the pattern of life in some fifteen southern zones. These areas include the Fishing and Trucking Fringes; the Rice and Sugar Bowls; the Piney Woods and Cut Over Areas; the Southern Highlands of Appalachians and Ozarks; Tobacco Zones; the Piedmont Industrial Crescent of minerals, water power, textiles, tobacco, and furniture manufacturing; and the Great Cotton Belt. The Cotton Belt splits into Atlantic, Gulf, Delta, and Southwestern areas. The Southwest includes a Ranching Zone, a Cotton Empire, an Oil Region, with special Sulphur, Gulf Ports, and Rio Grande Valley areas. The emphasis in this analysis is found in the attempt to present the patterns of regional housekeeping rather than in the exact delimitation of the various areas.

212. Another grouping of subregions extending across state lines is that of T. J. Woofter, Jr., in which 27 subregions are differentiated by indices of physical, demographic, agricultural, trade, and industrial character, recognizing, however, only those subregions which are large enough to constitute important socio-economic entities, yet which exhibit sufficient distinctive characteristics to warrant differentiation from neighboring regions. The regions thus approximating homogeneity are Cotton Piedmont, Shenandoah Valley, Tennessee Valley, Atlantic Tidewater, Northern Piedmont, Tobacco Piedmont, Blue Ridge Mountains, Cumberland Mountains, Blue Grass, Tobacco-Cattle, Muscle Shoals-Nashville Basin, Bluffs, Northern

Submarginal Counties of the Southeast

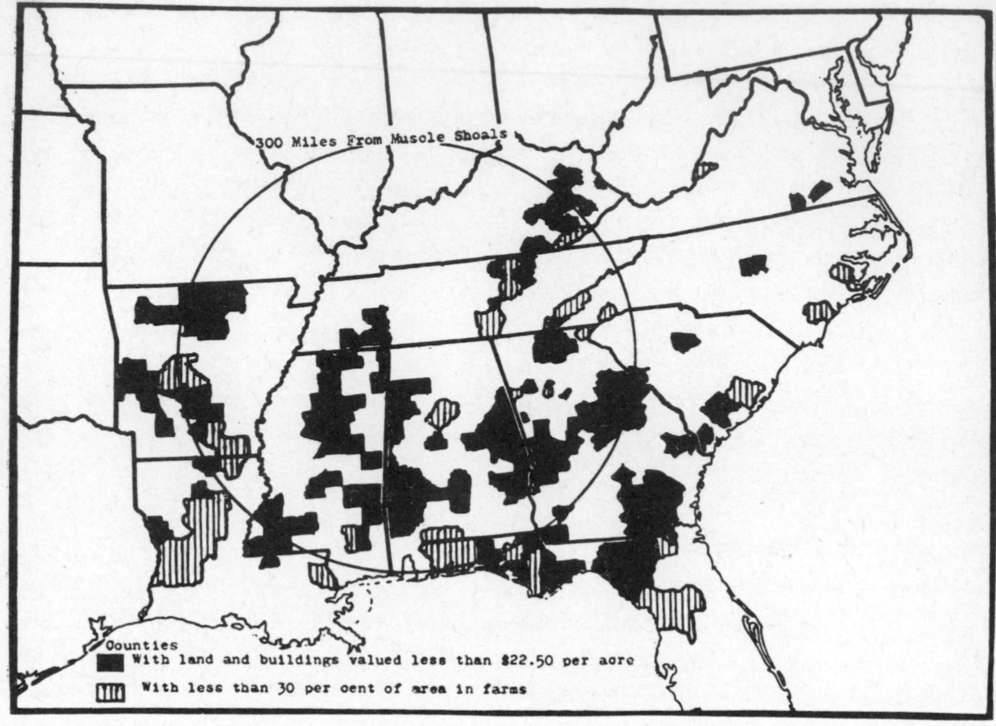

Submarginal Counties by States and Subregions, Exclusive of Virginia

REGIONS	Arkansas	Alabama	Florida	Georgia	Kentucky	Louisiana	Mississippi	North Carolina	South Carolina	Tennessee	Totals
Black Belt	..	12	..	32	..	..	1	..	4	..	49
Blue Ridge	..	..	..	8	..	..	..	4	..	..	12
Bluffs	..	..	..	..	..	1	10	..	..	2	13
Cumberland	..	..	..	..	18	..	..	..	..	10	28
Cotton Piedmont	..	4	..	4	..	..	..	..	..	..	8
Gulf Coast	..	3	14	..	..	..	8	..	..	..	25
Interior Plain	7	..	..	..	..	11	..	..	..	..	18
Mining	..	2	..	..	..	..	..	..	..	..	2
Ozark	16	..	..	..	..	..	..	..	..	..	16
Ridge	..	2	..	..	..	..	12	..	..	4	18
Southern Cotton and Tobacco	..	..	7	16	..	..	..	..	..	..	23
Total	23	23	21	60	18	12	31	4	4	16	212

The above is adapted from Woofter's special studies of the poorest counties. See further discussion in Chapter X and on pages 222 and 228. Other approaches to the study are suggested by Vance in relation to land utilization, standards of living and consumption, social inadequacy, and regional reconstruction and planning for optimum production. These studies depend, of course, upon various measures and concepts of submarginality, of standards of living as applied to submarginality, submarginal social groupings. The extension of studies of marginality and submarginality, again, must apply to both lands and people, to small areas and large, to special groups and to individual families. The studies will be somewhat related also to the picturization of abandoned land areas in the South, a field not yet developed.

Cotton and Tobacco, Southern Cotton and Tobacco, Black Belt, Citrus-Vegetable, Vegetable-Citrus, Semi-Tropical, Gulf Coast Plain, Mining, Gulf Tidewater, Interior Ridge, Delta, Ozarks, Interior Plain, Red River Bottoms, Rice-Cane.

213. One value inherent in such a classification as these 27 subregions is that they can be analyzed in varying states of change which may arise from shifting population or changing crop economy. Or they may also be subdivided into still smaller regions if more homogeneity is sought or if county lines be ignored or if more refined indices be used. For such inquiry and planning as might be required for soil improvement, for readjustment of marginal lands and people, or for reshaping the cotton economy, the subregional analysis is fundamental. Thus, in the distribution of crop-land acreage devoted to various crops such wide range is illustrated in the following: in cotton, from no cotton grown in four of the subregions, or less than one per cent in three others, up to 67 per cent in the Delta and the Red River Bottoms, over 50 per cent in the Interior Plain, and over 40 per cent in the Cotton Piedmont, the Interior Ridge, the Bluffs. Likewise, the whole tobacco economy is one of subregional base, while important planning for corn, hay, oats, orchards, vegetables, and dairy products can be effective only through some such subregional approach. The same is true of the tenant farmer and his problem where there is a variation in percentage of tenancy from more than 90 per cent in the Delta to less than 10 per cent in the Citrus-Vegetable, with subregions in between of 80, 73, 63, 60, 58 on down to 15, 16, 8.6 per cent. So also the percentage of land in farms ranges as low as 3.1 to as high as 88, while the value of land and buildings per acre varies from as low as $19 to as high as $205, and the value of land and buildings per farm from $1,300 to $14,000.

214. An illustration of more specific subregional analysis may be had in the study of submarginal counties measured by particular indices. Thus, Woofter, using the measures of $22.50 for value of land per acre and 30 per cent of the total area in farm lands in 1930, plotted 212 submarginal counties in the Southeast, of which 60 were in Georgia, 31 in Mississippi, 23 each in Arkansas and Alabama, 21 in Florida, 18 in Kentucky, 16 in Tennessee, 12 in Louisiana, and 4 each in the Carolinas. These submarginal counties also show a decrease in population and crop lands, less favorable indices of education and of situation on good roads, and many other characteristics. Within these submarginal counties and other still smaller submarginal areas may be found extraordinarily low standards of living, stamping the people as near the margin of subsistence. An examination of most of the data available indicates that there is in no other region of the United States such large areas where the value of crop land is so low. Yet

Southern Regions in Relation to the National Development of the Greater Mississippi Valley and the Tennessee Valley

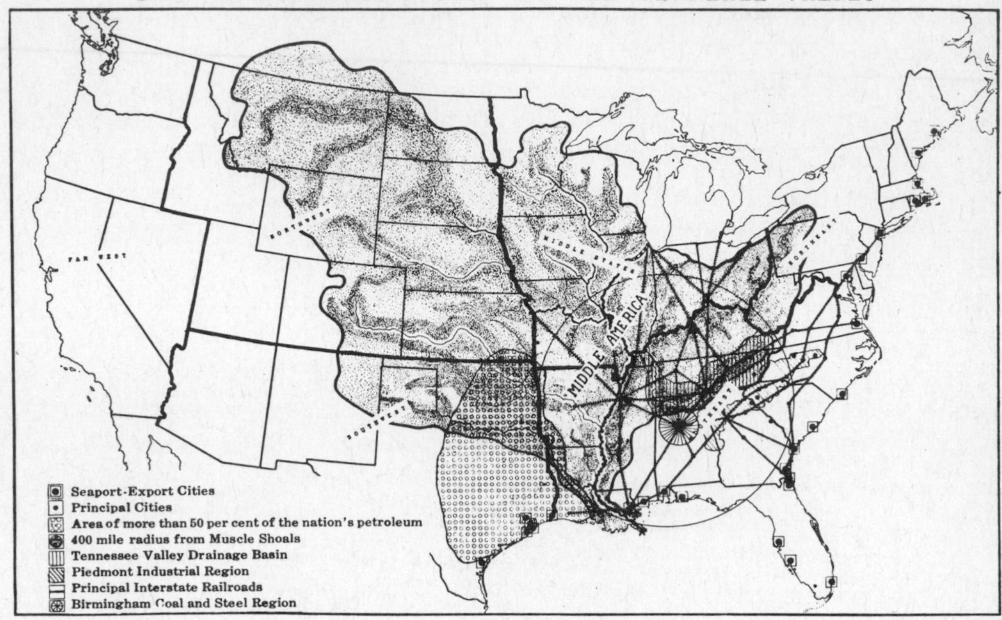

The significance to the Southeast of the development of its multiple river basins may be hazarded from an examination of the brilliantly illustrated report of the Mississippi Valley Committee of the Public Works Administration in 1934 and the cumulative work of the Tennessee Valley authority. *Below:* The Catawba Valley is illustrative of the smaller valley in which electrification has been highly developed.

River Basins of the Southeast

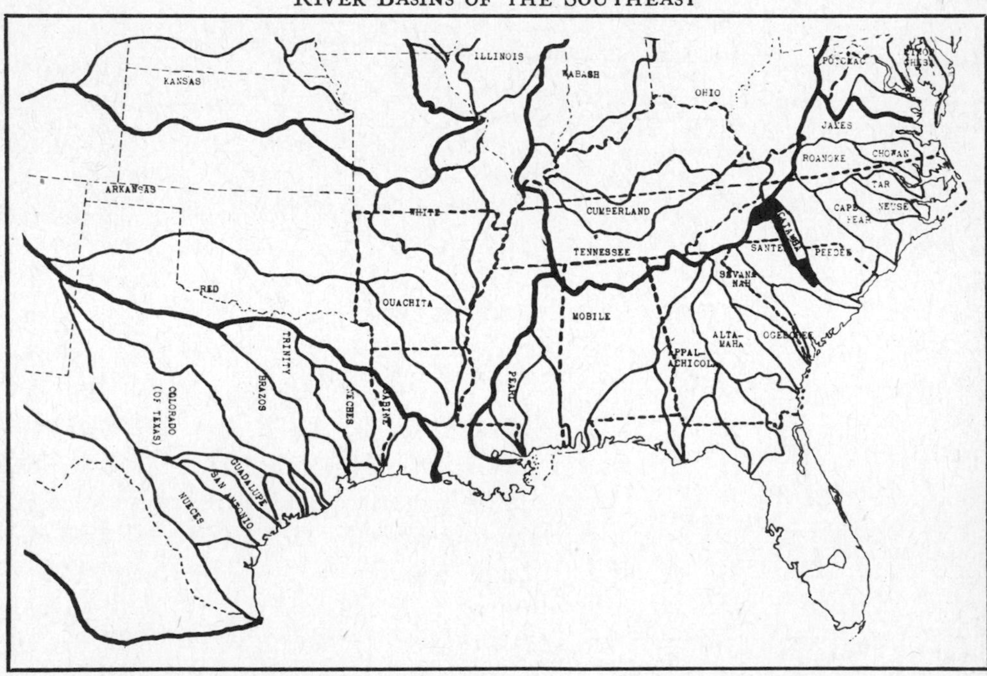

these 212 submarginal counties represent nearly a third of the total acreage of the region and its future use will be determined by special adjustments by subregions.

215. Further subregional analysis was continued through the classification of civil divisions according to farm land and buildings and resulting in new mapping of still lower values. Thus a belt across the Ozarks and on the Tennessee-Kentucky line in the Cumberland and a large area of the Georgia Blue Ridge falls below a value index of from $7.50 to $12.50 per acre. Still another concentrated subregion of low value is found in southeastern Georgia and Florida. Data on nearly 3,000 minor civil divisions were catalogued showing a little more than 1,000 with values between $17.50 and $22.50; a little over 1,100 with values from $12.50 to $17.50; 550 with values of $7.50 to $12.50; and less than 100 with values of $7.50 or under. The largest number of these was in the Black Belt, the next in the Ozark Mountains, and the next in the Southern Cotton and Tobacco Belt.

216. Other subregions will offer other special factors for consideration. Variations from the "Solid South" in politics, for instance, is a good illustration. One series of subregions may be seen from county and district voting in the presidential elections of 1920 and 1924, "normal" Republican years in which a large tri-state region centering in Tennessee, Kentucky, and North Carolina appears Republican, with some extension down into northern Alabama and Georgia. Still other subregional factors will be considered in relation to the Tennessee Valley and the different states which vary so greatly among themselves.

217. These are samples and summaries, adequate to indicate the place of subregions in the task of regional analysis and planning. Still other illustrations follow in the Sections on the Tennessee Valley, on the variations among the states, and the emerging Southwest.

XVII. THE TENNESSEE VALLEY

218. In the Tennessee Valley may be found all the elemental factors of the new American regionalism and a fair epitome of the range and complexity of the southern regions. Here indeed may be almost recapitulated the whole story of the southern regions, from physical and geographic range and variety to the multiple currents of historical and cultural incidence. In area touching seven states, in near physical contiguity bordering on four more states inseparably linked through wealth and welfare; within the bounds of a circle radiating four hundred miles from Muscle Shoals, parts of still other states; comprehending all told a population aggregating more than half the people of continental United States. In regional homogeneity

Distribution of Farms by Size in the Tennessee Basin, 1930: Part I, Tennessee

STATE AND COUNTY	Total Number	Under 3 Acres	3–9 Acres	10-19 Acres	20-49 Acres	50-99 Acres	100-174 Acres	175-259 Acres	260-499 Acres	500-999 Acres	1,000–4,999 Acres	5,000 Acres and Over
Total Tennessee	*144,634*	*237*	*8,570*	*16,276*	*39,851*	*39,130*	*26,258*	*8,462*	*4,674*	*991*	*180*	*5*
Anderson	1,445	.....	84	150	337	438	295	84	47	9	1	.....
Bedford	2,801	6	95	192	605	754	719	290	119	20	1	.....
Benton	1,751	.....	34	75	336	499	500	191	97	14	5	.....
Bledsoe	927	.....	14	102	250	228	174	83	55	17	3	1
Blount	2,417	3	219	280	611	664	397	136	89	14	4	.....
Bradley	1,780	.....	103	130	382	431	454	158	114	8	.....	.....
Campbell	1,754	1	128	224	548	527	246	40	34	5	1	.....
Carroll	4,310	8	217	451	1,198	1,374	803	174	75	9	1	.....
Carter	2,348	8	361	438	831	443	178	55	23	9	2	.....
Chester	1,891	2	30	205	622	482	365	120	59	5	1	.....
Claiborne	3,298	3	380	548	1,075	811	353	79	35	10	3	1
Cocke	2,707	2	203	411	834	707	345	100	70	25	10	.....
Coffee	2,112	8	83	182	511	634	458	147	70	16	3	.....
Cumberland	1,034	.....	56	130	320	287	146	47	27	18	3	.....
Decatur	1,654	14	62	142	453	405	371	117	76	12	2	.....
Dickson	2,487	3	214	374	402	632	568	204	72	18	.....	.....
Fentress	987	.....	54	118	239	288	200	45	31	9	3	.....
Franklin	2,553	15	130	250	677	713	504	166	83	11	4	.....
Giles	4,811	2	141	585	1,707	1,286	726	228	114	21	1	.....
Grainger	2,140	1	125	285	630	611	336	84	54	10	4	.....
Greene	5,004	23	311	654	1,631	1,367	735	189	89	5	.....	.....
Grundy	524	4	79	62	138	109	68	38	19	7	.....	.....
Hamblen	1,501	2	143	195	452	401	198	70	31	8	1	.....
Hamilton	2,407	5	203	326	686	589	372	123	80	20	2	1
Hancock	1,613	.....	138	187	396	476	291	79	35	11	.....	.....
Hardin	2,708	1	74	359	1,000	678	384	118	70	20	4	.....
Hawkins	3,505	7	298	500	975	934	524	148	84	30	5	.....
Henderson	3,290	6	72	267	1,010	870	777	197	83	8	.....	.....
Henry	3,296	7	71	250	778	1,017	820	227	111	13	2	.....
Hickman	1,647	.....	27	71	292	466	482	182	105	20	2	.....
Houston	789	.....	35	131	154	179	148	78	56	5	3	.....
Humphreys	1,452	.....	26	77	333	360	341	167	109	32	7	.....
Jefferson	2,204	8	168	282	615	552	347	131	84	16	1	.....
Johnson	1,593	12	157	209	506	395	186	61	49	16	2	.....
Knox	4,039	9	446	583	1,231	1,015	506	156	73	15	5	.....
Lawrence	3,845	2	106	356	1,357	1,191	600	139	80	10	4	.....
Lewis	507	.....	17	47	105	132	107	54	38	5	2	.....
Lincoln	4,131	6	148	485	1,400	1,060	678	209	115	25	5	.....
London	1,332	2	105	131	298	331	260	116	69	19	1	.....
McMinn	2,510	.....	112	169	555	736	657	177	91	11	2	.....
McNairy	3,414	3	77	335	1,129	917	619	206	113	14	1	.....
Marion	1,044	4	113	142	270	245	152	63	39	12	4	.....
Marshall	2,297	2	106	154	502	662	542	211	106	12	.....	.....
Maury	3,680	13	233	389	898	863	777	287	178	36	6	.....
Meigs	757	.....	14	20	95	159	226	115	106	19	3	.....
Monroe	2,800	1	179	308	670	806	566	184	72	12	2	.....
Moore	976	.....	19	162	323	256	155	35	23	2	1	.....
Morgan	1,074	1	59	93	311	326	186	45	38	10	5	.....
Overton	2,724	.....	207	341	651	803	503	137	63	17	2	.....
Perry	1,070	17	31	102	294	169	171	98	121	55	12	.....
Polk	1,082	1	42	103	274	328	227	63	34	7	3	.....
Putnam	2,913	1	245	364	809	839	455	122	63	10	5	.....
Rhea	1,206	1	75	142	302	340	212	70	47	12	3	2
Roane	1,304	.....	28	100	231	309	345	146	98	43	4	.....
Scott	1,124	1	90	132	355	314	158	46	20	4	4	.....
Sequatchie	537	.....	66	69	134	143	90	18	13	4	.....	.....
Sevier	2,931	3	166	317	757	921	544	146	64	10	3	.....
Stewart	1,902	.....	103	285	368	445	412	172	95	18	4	.....
Sullivan	3,186	.....	283	442	1,039	834	387	121	62	16	2	.....
Unicoi	860	1	128	148	273	205	76	17	8	3	1	.....
Union	1,966	1	114	169	569	691	346	58	17	1	.....	.....
Van Buren	488	.....	27	31	111	146	97	39	29	6	2	.....
Warren	2,615	1	127	216	556	869	615	159	54	15	3	.....
Washington	2,980	14	315	442	931	811	329	96	40	2	.....	.....
Wayne	1,635	.....	16	155	362	365	388	180	129	37	3	.....
White	1,960	1	103	211	510	572	363	128	53	14	5	.....
Williamson	3,005	1	135	291	647	720	698	293	174	44	2	.....

the valley ranks high, yet with such extraordinary range and variety of resources, people, and institutions as to afford ample subregional divisions and to constitute the perfect laboratory for social experiment and social planning. The Tennessee Valley now represents no mere river basin, but the skill and planning of a nation, the imagination of the people many times divided, and the on-goings of engineers, planners, educators, economists, sociologists, critics and patrons, politicians, manufacturers, dreamers and schemers, reformers and statesmen, common folks in the South and out. In the Valley are possible also most of the dangers and most of the virtues inherent in a great regional-national experiment. Here, too, are dangers and difficulties symbolic of the range and power, or the failure and futility of a possible abortive southern regionalism. Here are measures of what civilization has done to a people and by the same token what civilization should do for them in another era. Here is test for the southern people and test for the nation in a dozen fundamentals of economic and social reconstruction.

219. One of the requirements of satisfactory regional division, as stated in the earlier premise of the Southern Regional Study, was that the regions should be few enough, and therefore large enough, for general composite use, yet not too large or heterogeneous to preclude quantitative and qualitative analysis of important factors. Something of the same qualifications are required in the area for a national-regional experiment if it is to comprehend the largest possible number of prerequisites to success. Thus, Dr. Harcourt A. Morgan characterizes the Tennessee Valley in terms of a proving ground sought by the President to apply to the nation's whole complex development. Thus was needed a region which would "reflect all the important characteristics of our country—its agricultural, industrial, social, educational, and commercial features—and would embrace those features within an area small enough to be readily coördinated yet large enough to be truly typical of the whole." These characteristics of the Valley apply even more aptly to the whole of the Southeast, with its varying eleven states featuring the Tennessee Valley as a great cross section as well as a recapitulatory picture of regional culture.

220. Yet the Tennessee Valley is but a gateway to the great Ohio Valley and the greater Mississippi Valley, comprehending two-thirds of the nation. It is but one of the scores of river valleys of the Southeast where the engineers have estimated the possibilities of dam construction to cost not 50 millions, not 100 or 200 or 300 millions but 3,000 millions out of a national possible aggregate of 8,000 millions, for flood control and power and irrigation and restoration. Even the 42,000 square miles of basin territory is less than half as large as the Appalachian regions themselves.

Distribution of Farms by Size in the Tennessee Basin, 1930: Part II, States Exclusive of Tennessee

State and County	Total Number	Under 3 Acres	3–9 Acres	10-19 Acres	20-49 Acres	50-99 Acres	100-174 Acres	175-259 Acres	260-499 Acres	500-999 Acres	1,000–4,999 Acres	5,000 Acres and Over
West Virginia	*1,430*	*17*	*292*	*187*	*391*	*282*	*152*	*57*	*31*	*19*	*2*	*0*
McDowell	1,430	17	292	187	391	282	152	57	31	19	2	0
Virginia	*26,983*	*49*	*2,855*	*3,754*	*7,495*	*6,347*	*3,750*	*1,317*	*964*	*332*	*114*	*6*
Bland	693	.....	19	38	110	133	188	80	76	38	10	1
Buchanan	2,048	1	126	171	642	553	372	99	67	14	3	.....
Dickenson	1,558	.....	130	228	526	387	200	58	25	4	.....	.....
Grayson	2,557	.....	117	261	682	734	445	165	110	36	7	.....
Lee	2,439	3	298	411	642	561	291	119	81	24	9	.....
Russell	2,796	10	339	410	758	614	379	135	107	35	7	2
Scott	3,791	1	329	567	1,136	977	534	153	78	13	3	.....
Smythe	1,822	2	196	264	495	416	237	78	84	32	18	.....
Tazewell	1,748	.....	241	228	402	349	227	121	102	50	28	.....
Washington	3,813	6	529	605	1,057	837	458	163	111	37	10	.....
Wise	1,833	25	322	327	576	380	140	39	18	5	1	.....
Wythe	1,885	1	209	244	469	406	279	107	105	44	18	3
North Carolina	*40,481*	*52*	*4,064*	*5,453*	*12,653*	*10,396*	*5,262*	*1,479*	*846*	*213*	*61*	*2*
Ashe	3,660	5	372	479	1,108	1,006	457	132	77	21	3	.....
Avery	1,410	1	161	222	530	296	124	41	21	9	5	.....
Buncombe	3,895	16	606	634	1,175	832	415	115	79	16	7	.....
Burke	2,136	.....	120	266	656	591	330	101	61	9	2	.....
Cherokee	1,958	5	119	171	519	584	395	113	37	14	1	.....
Clay	898	4	75	107	284	247	124	35	14	8	.....	.....
Graham	692	.....	50	79	187	215	112	33	14	2	.....	.....
Haywood	2,125	10	285	358	562	466	266	84	56	26	12	.....
Henderson	1,983	1	255	326	614	436	237	66	36	11	1	.....
Jackson	2,117	1	231	275	657	548	292	68	37	6	2	.....
McDowell	1,268	2	85	126	324	357	233	73	56	11	1	.....
Macon	1,847	3	136	244	545	502	277	90	37	11	2	.....
Madison	3,267	.....	434	432	945	860	397	125	56	16	2	.....
Mitchell	1,887	.....	298	353	645	362	159	40	22	7	1	.....
Polk	1,229	1	61	147	413	344	185	38	28	8	4	.....
Rutherford	3,791	.....	151	446	1,483	1,079	444	108	68	11	1	.....
Swain	1,174	2	42	113	333	397	190	51	35	10	1	.....
Transylvania	730	.....	92	79	207	169	120	28	22	5	8	.....
Watauga	2,375	1	229	291	740	637	312	92	60	10	3	.....
Yancey	2,039	.....	262	305	726	468	193	46	30	2	5	2
Georgia	*10,127*	*28*	*376*	*1,007*	*2,765*	*2,808*	*2,075*	*662*	*332*	*61*	*13*	*0*
Catoosa	974	3	10	53	337	303	201	46	17	2	2	.....
Dade	486	5	12	48	151	110	103	30	19	7	1	.....
Fannin	1,472	3	100	153	340	354	342	124	50	5	1	.....
Gilmer	1,234	4	42	78	213	288	372	138	85	12	2	.....
Towns	663	.....	27	94	194	208	108	20	5	3	4	.....
Union	1,117	.....	17	57	281	389	257	82	28	6	.....	.....
Walker	2,370	11	125	311	726	639	378	93	68	16	3	.....
Whitfield	1,811	2	43	213	523	517	314	129	60	10	.....	.....
Alabama	*59,429*	*33*	*1,854*	*6,281*	*28,185*	*14,954*	*5,749*	*1,406*	*748*	*173*	*46*	*0*
Colbert	2,904	2	88	306	1,377	731	252	77	48	19	4	.....
DeKalb	6,586	7	95	512	3,254	1,949	587	125	48	6	3	.....
Franklin	3,429	2	55	302	1,511	893	459	130	64	12	1	.....
Jackson	5,337	2	175	529	2,322	1,358	591	179	131	39	11	.....
Lauderdale	5,246	4	162	465	2,595	1,375	487	95	45	14	4	.....
Lawrence	5,119	2	210	509	2,490	1,336	436	82	41	11	2	.....
Limestone	6,349	.....	206	779	3,489	1,376	397	61	26	12	3	.....
Madison	7,178	1	225	904	3,574	1,729	517	119	79	22	8	.....
Marion	3,746	2	75	355	1,156	1,077	751	204	113	12	1	.....
Marshall	6,279	6	268	865	3,363	1,276	340	94	49	12	6	.....
Morgan	5,079	3	252	575	2,371	1,241	466	108	50	11	2	.....
Winston	2,177	2	43	180	683	613	466	132	54	3	1	.....
Mississippi	*13,040*	*36*	*514*	*2,224*	*4,642*	*3,125*	*1,745*	*458*	*260*	*32*	*4*	*0*
Alcorn	3,334	13	183	624	1,186	767	384	104	66	6	1	.....
Itawamba	3,459	7	67	608	1,201	776	542	153	91	12	2	.....
Prentiss	3,713	2	192	625	1,401	917	414	109	43	10	.....	.....
Tishomingo	2,534	14	72	367	854	665	405	92	60	4	1	.....
Kentucky	*23,288*	*21*	*1,433*	*2,437*	*6,220*	*7,110*	*4,102*	*1,217*	*582*	*130*	*35*	*1*
Calloway	2,990	.....	49	137	874	1,276	543	85	20	4	2	.....
Graves	4,638	1	208	469	1,353	1,700	725	145	32	5	.....	.....
Harlan	786	10	150	112	196	151	112	26	13	12	4	.....
Letcher	1,674	4	155	258	538	403	207	56	41	7	5	.....
Livingston	1,339	.....	21	63	191	340	398	162	140	22	2	.....
Lyon	1,210	.....	89	161	237	279	261	120	51	8	3	1
McCracken	1,979	1	258	224	565	570	263	74	19	4	1	.....
Marshall	2,417	1	84	188	673	949	414	81	25	2	.....	.....
Pike	4,205	3	338	521	1,213	1,057	687	222	107	45	12	.....
Trigg	2,050	1	81	304	380	385	492	246	134	21	6	.....
Total, including Tennessee	319,412	473	19,958	37,619	102,202	84,152	49,093	15,058	8,437	1,951	455	14

The threefold significance, therefore, of the Tennessee Valley as a subregional symbol is: first, its availability for a national-regional laboratory, revolutionary in its methodology, heroic in its sweep; second, its tremendous significance in the framework of realistic southern regional analysis and planning; and, third, its reality as a type of actual subregion of the Southeast. These three features may be summarized briefly, the last, first, and the first, last.

221. The size and shape of the Tennessee River Basin has become so well known in American life as almost to become a popular symbol. A strangely meandering river, often appearing to run in the wrong direction, now making its famous Moccasin Bend, now drawing in its multiple smaller streams and turning round about again to become a part of the great Ohio, the river leaves a net product of a peculiarly complicated picture which ruthlessly ignores state lines. Thus the watershed begins with a county or two up in western West Virginia, then wide across the merging Tennessee-North Carolina Great Smokies and down to take a corner from Georgia and Alabama, and thence to provide the technical nucleus of the whole TVA, namely, Muscle Shoals; then, not to neglect Mississippi and its Tupelo, first power participator in the big measuring stick; then on up and up across Tennessee into blue grass Kentucky and back to the Ohio Valley proper. And somewhere in between a touch of the Old Dominion to give the Valley something more of the Old South, yet disdainfully leaving out South Carolina, which shares none of its physical representation, yet must surely be no less a participator in the works and implications of the Authority.

222. And of the character of the region, again, the nation has been told a thousand times in almost limitless ways. Picturesque and vivid; realistic and romantic; factual and speculative; descriptive and analytical; in pictures and in maps; in books and in papers; on the air and on the stage; in county and state, country and city; in conference and committee; almost all things to all men. In terminology the Valley and its Authority have ranged from the greatest national experiment in social and economic reconstruction to the pork barrel de luxe, "a river basin draining the seven states, an authority draining forty-eight states." The experiment is of the essence of Americanism; it is the quintessence of unamericanism. To the North it is sometimes seen as regional favoritism; to the South it has at times been characterized as federal dictation; yet in both North and South, it has appeared most often as a great and hopeful portent in the American scene. Perhaps its significance has been recognized almost uniformly as, first of all, southern, and yet more important, national, the great Appalachian Divide again serving as gateway to new social frontiers as to new

Basic Regional Areas for Re-Planning Dairy Farming in the Southeast in Relation to "New Dairy Region" Shown on Map on Page 194

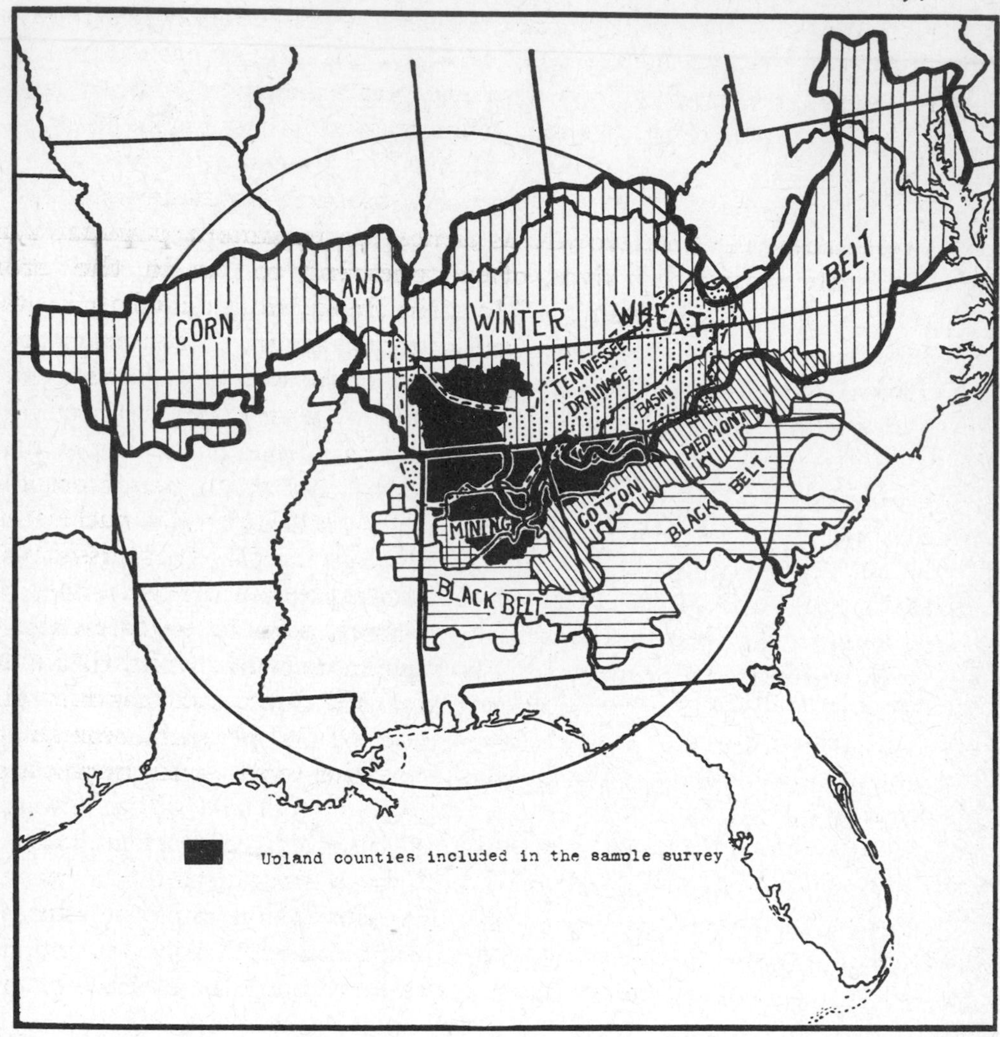

Regional Differentials in Dairy Cattle and Milk Production, 1929

REGION	Number Farms Reporting Cows Milked	Per Cent of All Farms	Average Number Gallons Per Animal Milked	Proportion of Whole Milk Sold	Number Purebred Registered Dairy Cattle per Farm Reporting Cows Milked
Southeast	1,489,272	62.0	394*	34.7	0.08
Southwest	520,309	69.0	416*	57.5	0.12
Northeast	486,691	79.0	618*	87.8	0.82
Middle States	1,431,862	88.0	530*	81.2	0.39
Northwest	541,764	83.0	504*	70.6	0.16
Far West	145,593	54.0	638*	83.3	0.45
United States	4,615,529†	73.4	523	75.4	0.28

*The median of the states of the region. †Includes 38 in the District of Columbia.

physical frontiers in the earlier days when Tennessee and Kentucky constituted the "Great West" of the nation.

223. But to summarize more of the details of the region, here are sample broadcasts—elevation from 250 feet above sea level to 6,000 feet . . . climate so rich and varied as to comprehend great lakes and mountains, subtropical in the Cotton South and, in between, the other ranges of abundance. . . . They can raise anything that grows from the Canada border to the Gulf. . . . The rainfall is heavy . . . the growing season long and moderate . . . the soil is varied, rich by nature, poor by exhaustion. . . . There are great wide rich valleys and mountain forests. . . . The minerals are rich and varied. . . . Tremendous hydro-electric power is inherent in the rivers. . . . Rocks and hills, valleys and sands, make for construction advantages . . . range of flora and fauna extraordinary, both wild and tame . . . hardwoods and timberlands . . . and all that combination of circumstances which brings forth the oft-repeated verdict, "No other comparable area in the United States offers the diversity of climate, soil, vegetation, and of other resources, which we find in the Tennessee Valley."

224. Yet the Valley recapitulates the southern regions in more ways than in situation and natural endowment. Its geographic conditioning, its historical backgrounds, and its cultural equipment are all peculiarly representative of the cultural evolution of the American South. Its people and their problems reflect dilemmas of long standing and those that have come upon the region in recent years. They are peculiarly rich in the complexities of transitional American democracy. The TVA affords the maximum opportunity for interregional interplay between North and South, testing the common sense, techniques, and realities of coöperative efforts on a new scale. It offers the perfect laboratory for the development of the more dynamic regionalism as opposed to the old state sectionalism. It affords abundant opportunity for the cross fertilization of South and North and West, to the enrichment of our common culture through the enrichment of regional ways of life.

225. The further recapitulatory aspects may be summarized briefly, recalling the framework upon which the present analysis is being made; namely, a fivefold premise in terms of wealth and capacity: natural wealth, technological wealth, artificial wealth, human wealth, institutional wealth. Applying the TVA as a yardstick over these, it is relatively easy to come to some general measures of values and attainments of the regional experiment. First, the foundation of the Authority rests upon the basis of the development of natural endowment through new reaches in many sorts of technological means, primarily physical and mechanical, yet also social. There is the objective of land conservation and development; of forestry

Types of Farms: Number by States

TYPE OF FARM	Virginia		North Carolina		South Carolina		Georgia		Florida		Kentucky	
	Number	Per Cent	Number	Per Cent	Number	Per Cent	Number	Per Cent	Number	Per Cent	Number	Per Cent
All Types	*170,610*	.....	*279,708*	.....	*157,931*	.....	*255,598*	.....	*58,916*	.....	*246,499*	.....
Cotton	3,458	2.0	77,116	27.6	109,900	70.0	172,395	67.4	5,622	9.5	575	0.2
General	34,309	20.1	26,956	9.6	7,630	4.8	16,724	6.5	8,503	14.4	46,982	19.1
Crop Specialty (Tobacco)	35,749	21.0	103,813	37.1	16,085	10.2	19,577	7.7	3,710	6.3	65,555	26.6
Self-Sufficing	44,149	2.6	34,422	12.3	6,978	4.4	12,762	5.0	6,188	10.5	70,506	28.6
Unclassified	7,128	4.2	12,032	4.3	7,547	4.8	17,130	6.7	4,725	8.0	18,683	7.7
Part Time	21,953	12.9	13,820	4.9	5,302	3.4	6,758	2.6	4,721	8.0	18,960	7.7
Cash Grain	1,868	1.1	1,058	0.4	626	0.4	300	0.1	134	0.2	2,721	1.1
Animal Specialty	6,497	3.8	1,985	0.7	404	0.1	1,428	0.6	1,632	2.8	11,620	4.7
Dairy	3,357	2.0	2,525	0.9	1,052	0.6	2,618	1.0	952	1.6	5,901	2.4
Fruit	2,716	1.6	1,655	0.6	168	0.1	1,487	0.6	13,631	23.1	564	0.2
Truck	2,301	1.3	1,226	0.4	1,190	0.7	2,170	0.8	6,714	11.4	786	0.3
Poultry	4,181	2.5	1,080	0.4	396	0.1	722	0.2	1,783	3.0	1,267	0.5
Stock Ranch	418	0.2	127	0.0	21	0.0	80	0.0	375	0.6	408	0.2
Forest Production	1,610	1.0	1,439	0.5	469	0.1	1,108	0.5	166	0.3	860	0.4

TYPE OF FARM	Tennessee		Alabama		Mississippi		Arkansas		Louisiana		United States	
	Number	Per Cent	Number	Per Cent	Number	Per Cent	Number	Per Cent	Number	Per Cent	Number	Per Cent
All Types	*245,657*	.....	*257,395*	.....	*312,663*	.....	*242,334*	.....	*161,445*	.....	*6,288,648*	.....
Cotton	63,076	27.3	206,835	80.4	259,198	82.9	168,701	69.2	115,123	69.6	1,640,025	16.5
General	47,887	19.5	13,220	5.1	14,503	4.6	23,789	9.8	8,309	5.1	1,044,266	16.6
Crop Specialty (Tobacco)	23,492	9.6	2,620	1.0	912	0.3	757	0.3	5,699	3.5	431,379	6.9
Self-Sufficing	53,822	21.9	12,941	5.0	10,342	3.3	17,098	7.1	6,972	4.2	498,019	7.9
Unclassified	13,552	5.5	9,400	3.7	11,493	3.7	14,295	5.8	7,449	4.6	288,766	4.6
Part Time	16,324	6.6	5,906	2.3	5,848	1.9	5,345	2.2	3,766	2.3	339,207	6.3
Cash Grain	4,120	1.7	90	0.0	58	0.0	1,529	0.6	4,135	2.6	454,726	7.2
Animal Specialty	10,853	4.4	938	0.4	820	0.3	1,921	0.8	850	0.5	479,042	7.6
Dairy	5,826	2.4	1,541	0.6	3,208	1.0	2,525	1.0	1,393	0.9	604,837	9.6
Fruit	1,128	0.5	951	0.4	442	0.1	3,190	1.3	5,084	3.1	141,418	2.2
Truck	1,754	0.7	923	0.4	4,265	1.4	1,083	0.4	1,625	1.0	84,561	0.1
Poultry	1,743	0.7	746	0.3	335	0.1	1,040	0.4	277	0.2	166,517	2.6
Stock Ranch	53	0.0	261	0.1	216	0.1	58	0.0	344	0.2	71,000	1.1
Forest Production	1,130	0.5	768	0.3	707	0.2	541	0.2	259	0.2	20,106	0.3

In the above tables the classifications do not always add to the total due to the fact that certain ones not relevant to the inquiry were omitted.

Tennessee Basin—Number and Per Cent of Farms by Size Groups

STATE	Under 100 Acres		100–174 Acres		175–259 Acres		260–499 Acres		500 Acres and Over		Total
	Number	Per Cent	Number	Per Cent	Number	Per Cent	Number	Per Cent	Number	Per Cent	Number
Tennessee	104,064	71.9	26,258	18.2	8,462	5.9	4,674	3.2	1,176	0.8	144,634
Kentucky	17,221	74.0	4,102	17.6	1,217	5.2	582	2.5	166	0.7	23,288
West Virginia	1,169	81.7	152	10.6	57	4.0	31	2.2	21	1.5	1,430
Virginia	20,500	76.0	3,750	13.9	1,317	4.9	964	3.5	452	1.7	26,983
North Carolina	32,618	80.6	5,262	13.0	1,479	3.6	846	2.1	276	0.7	40,481
Georgia	6,984	69.0	2,075	20.4	662	6.6	332	3.3	74	0.7	10,127
Alabama	51,307	86.3	5,749	9.7	1,406	2.4	748	1.2	219	0.4	59,429
Mississippi	10,541	80.8	1,745	13.4	458	3.5	260	2.0	36	0.3	13,040
Total Tennessee Basin	*244,404*	*76.5*	*49,093*	*15.4*	*15,058*	*4.7*	*8,437*	*2.6*	*2,420*	*0.8*	*319,412*

conservation and development; of water control and use; of power development and use; of fertilizer manufacture and use; of revolutionary sources of phosphorous supply and use; of the physical development of farms and rural homes, and of roads and rural electrification; of the physical equipment of home and farm through appliances, with a possible mechanical reserve attaining the tremendous total of more than 200 articles related to electric current. The technological wealth of the Valley will extend further into new inventions and procedures for new industries, for new occupations, for new equilibrium between agriculture and industry; and especially for those techniques which will contribute to the reconstruction of such fundamentals as the dairy industry and of optimum programs of production in basic commodities.

226. When we come to measure the wealth of capital goods in the Valley, there is again recapitulation of the region's poverty and capacity, potentiality and actuality. Through much research not only are statistical analyses available, but, through the planning approach, practical ways of increasing wealth and raising values are presented. Likewise, in the human wealth, the people of the Tennessee Valley offer a rare range of population resources suitable for the best of policy development, as well as for research. Likewise, the whole cultural equipment as reflected in the institutions of the people affords unsurpassed data for measuring, for appraising, and for planning a social economy which will bridge the distance between potential capacity and the actual working capacity of the present.

227. This brief summary deals with the significance of the Tennessee Valley and its Authority rather than with the facts and attainments, some of which will be given in the later chapter devoted to this subregion. The evidence is not yet adequate for an appraïsal of the experiment to date, a large part of the ultimate value being contingent upon the final range and scope of the experiment and upon the extent to which it can be continuously motivated, as planned and staffed with capable personnel chosen for skill and for capacity to function in the realities of the situation. Values and problems inherent in the TVA experiment will emerge in connection with the summaries of prospects and planning as discussed in the last chapter of the present volume. Fundamental issues involved in the transitional dilemmas of adjustment between public ownership of control of utilities and private holdings and distribution are an integral part of the experiment.

228. In summary, however, the TVA may be adjudged on the basis of the following considerations. It has made considerable progress in the general purposes and functions set forth in the original legislation and has made various readjustments and adaptations to test new deeds and new situations. It has promoted public discussion, not only of the Tennessee

Rank of States in Public Education, 1930

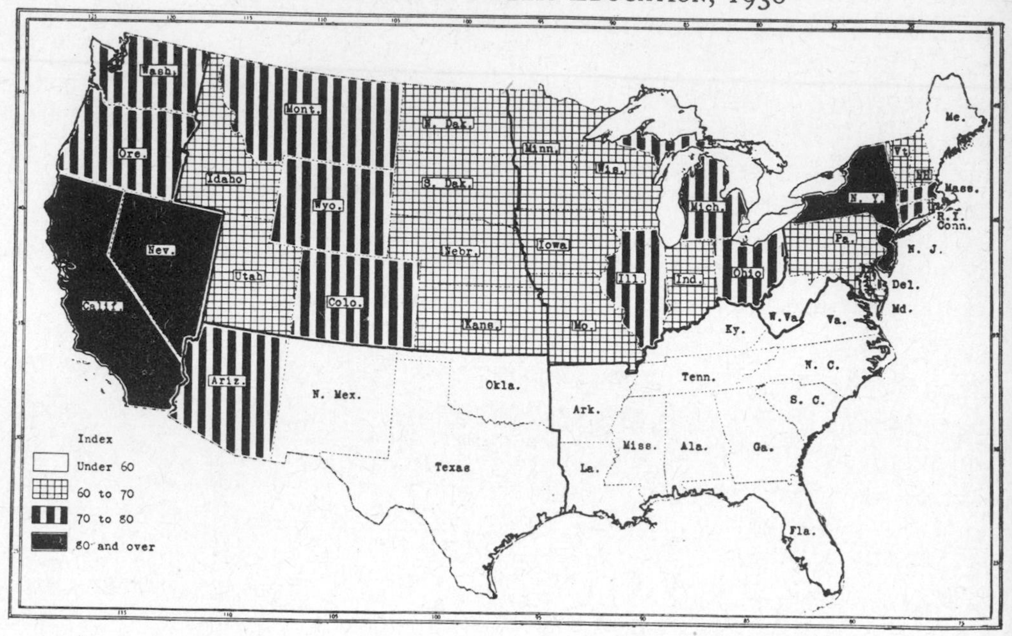

RANK OF STATES IN PUBLIC EDUCATION, 1930

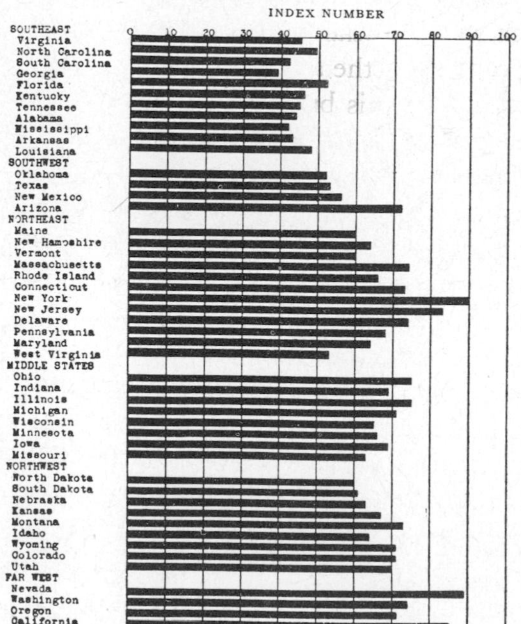

SCHOOL DEBT OUTSTANDING PER PUPIL IN AVERAGE DAILY ATTENDANCE, 1930

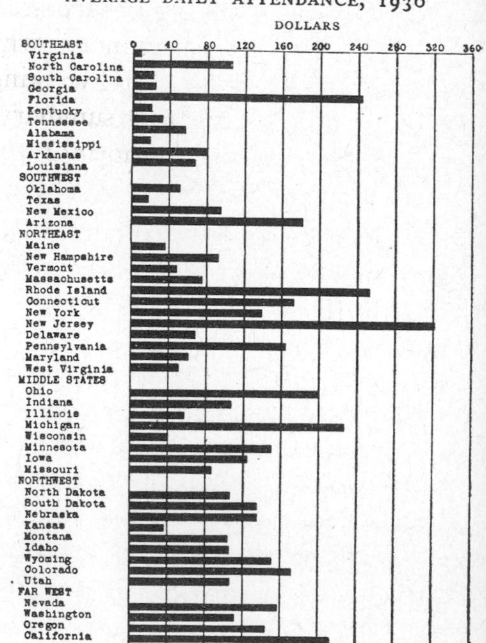

Valley Authority and its work, but of national and regional planning. It has done much toward making the public planning conscious, and it has set up a current of wide and varied discussions on a number of conflicting theories. It has worked out, in varying degrees of completeness, comprehensive programs centering around the development of the Authority itself and of the Tennessee Valley Subregion. It has sponsored many conferences on research and planning in many aspects of its work. It has experimented and explored with varying degrees of success many new angles of its work. It has undertaken and sponsored wide research and study. It has made rapid progress on the building of the Norris Dam, and it has experimented in the building of homes and communities. It has made new reaches in the development of electrification for the countryside. It has promoted rural electrification, and it has organized for the manufacture and distribution, at reasonable cost, of electrical equipment. It has raised fundamental issues with reference to natural resources and especially with reference to power and the public. It has experimented in the field of technology in relation to culture. It has trained personnel, promoted libraries, and developed social legislation. It has been a demonstration of the need for social and political wisdom. It has reflected caution and hesitation. It has participated to some extent in the arbitrary action which comes from authority of that sort. It has weathered many conflicts, attacks, and disturbances from without and from within. Its ratio of success appears to be substantially high in comparison both with actuality of results and with what might have been done or what could be done under different circumstances.

XVIII. STATES AND REGIONS

229. Perhaps the most interesting and elemental inventory of the region and the nation is found in state portraitures, each constituting its own world of culture and politics. Not one nation but forty-eight; not one patriotism but four dozen; not one government but multiplied political bodies, state, county, city within the states. And every state its pride and loyalty, its "first," its seal and flag; every state its popular name, its people their caricatured nomenclature; every state its official song, flag, motto, poem, bird, flower. And within the Southeast state folkways multiplied and constituting basic elements of regional homogeneity.

230. Outside of the specific values inherent in each state picture the significance of state differentials and state groupings within the regions is twofold. One is the measure of the wide range of state differentials within the framework of homogeneity already described and the significance of the states in the understanding and direction of regional evolution in the

Per Capita Postal Receipts, 1930

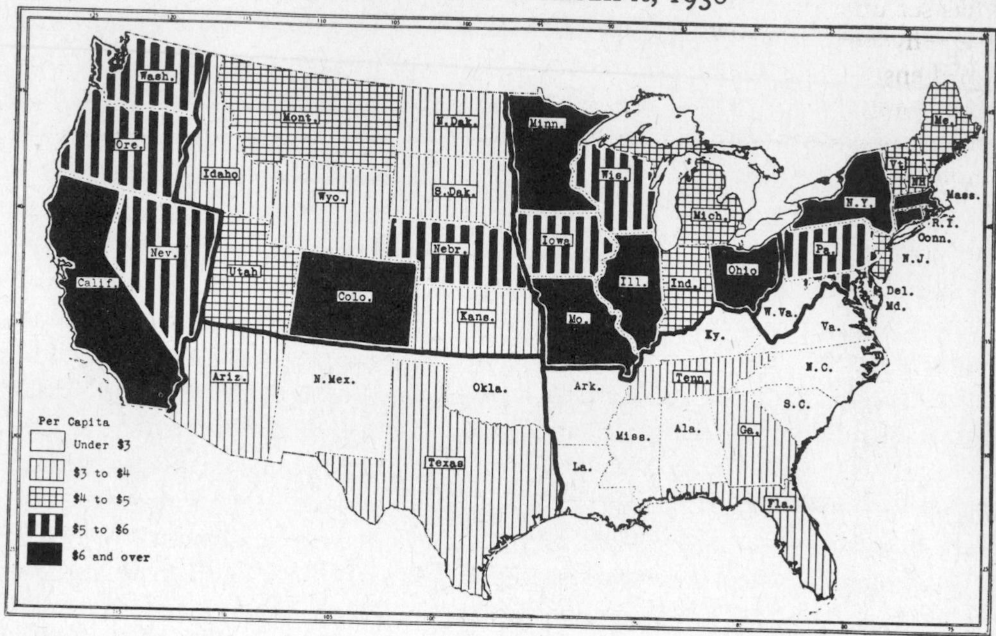

Per Capita Life Insurance in Force, 1929

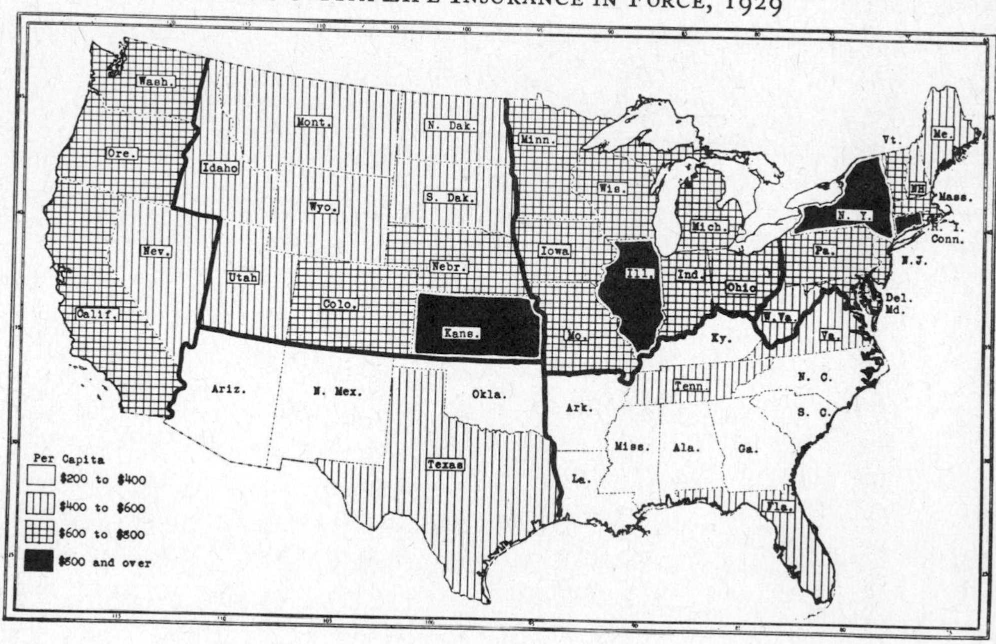

South. "Many States, Many Souths" has been symbolic of the great variation in southern culture as typified by states which sometimes approximate subregions of their own. This is especially true in their history and local traditions and in their local politics. No picture of the South can be complete or accurate without knowledge of the states as entities. How else could Jefferson's Virginia be appraised, or Calhoun's South Carolina, or Longstreet's Georgia?

231. The second very significant factor in the comparison of states is the clearer delineations and evaluations which emerge from comparison of individual southern states with individual states of other regions, or by contrasting aggregate achievements or wealth, as opposed to averages, in single states of the South with aggregates in states of other regions. This gives qualitative interpretation to mass figures, and features distribution instead of mass averages, which, at best, are usually poor measures of reality.

232. For those who anticipate an early diminishing rôle of states as definitive units of administration or who see an early breaking down of state lines, the Southeast offers as yet little in the way of encouragement or tangible prospects. For the Southeast is peculiarly articulate in matters of local state pride. The region is state conscious, state patriotism and pride vying with southern loyalty. State patriotism may very well be a part of the sectional heritage alongside the other cumulative bases for state consciousness. The "southern" emphasis upon "belonging" is manifest through state organization and activities. A part of this is characteristic "Americanism." A part reflects, along with other characteristics, the factors of chronological lag and relative isolation or lack of wider travel or social experience. A part appears to be due to the striking differences and rivalries which are found among the states within the region.

233. If the same sort of classification of Southeastern States within a scale of priority ranking be used, as was used in the case of the 48 states, similar variations on the map-picture will appear. First of all, Florida ranks outside any general pattern of southern homogeneity in nearly half of the indices selected. If then a new set of values be provided to comprehend the southeastern range so that a new quartile ranking is made, Florida appears outside the lowest or middle fourth regularly in many indices which tend to rank it with the Northeast and particularly with the border state, Maryland. There are exceptions to this in the case of certain "southern" patterns, such as racial composition of the population and many of the agricultural indices of general farming, such as value and ratio of livestock, value of hay and forage, size of farms, milk production, and others.

Variations Among the States of the Southeast Region

AVERAGE VALUE PER ACRE OF LAND AND BUILDINGS, FULL OWNERS, REPORTING MORTGAGE DEBT, 1930

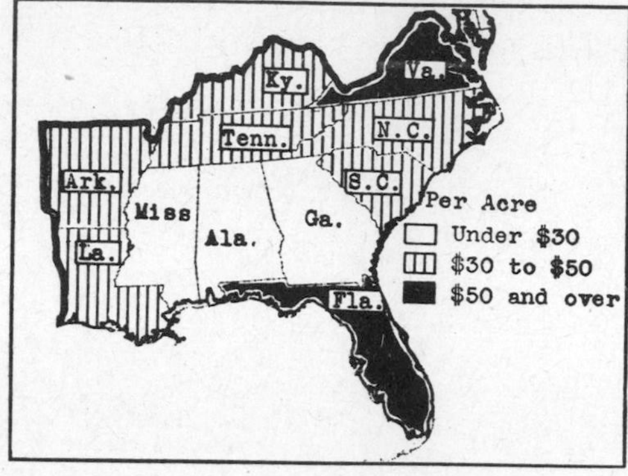

AVERAGE VALUE PER FARM OF LAND AND BUILDINGS, MANAGER-OPERATED FARMS, 1930

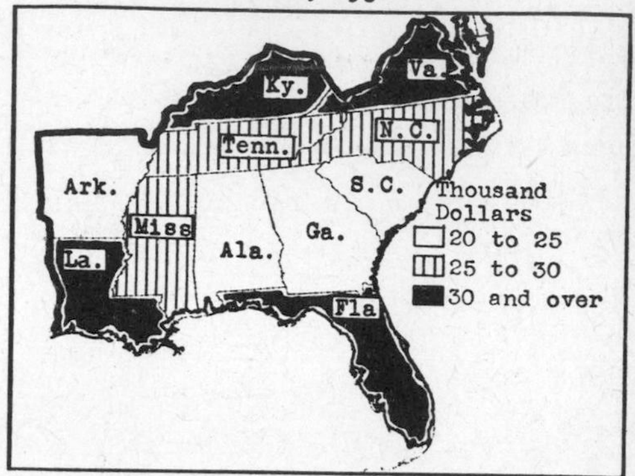

AVERAGE PER ACRE TAX ON FARM LAND AND BUILDINGS, FARMS OPERATED BY FULL OWNER, 1930

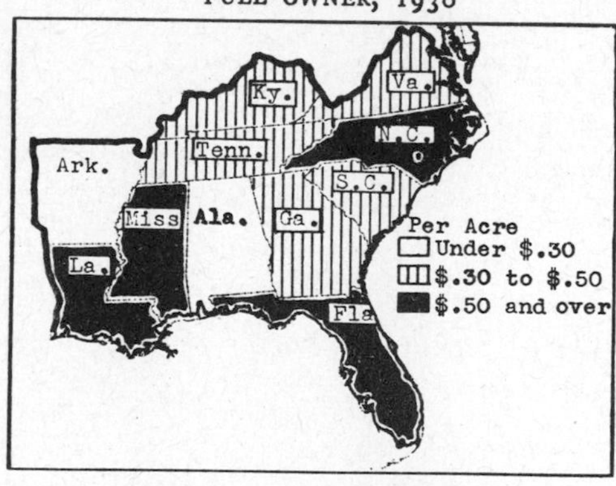

VALUE OF ALL FARM PROPERTY PER FARM, 1930

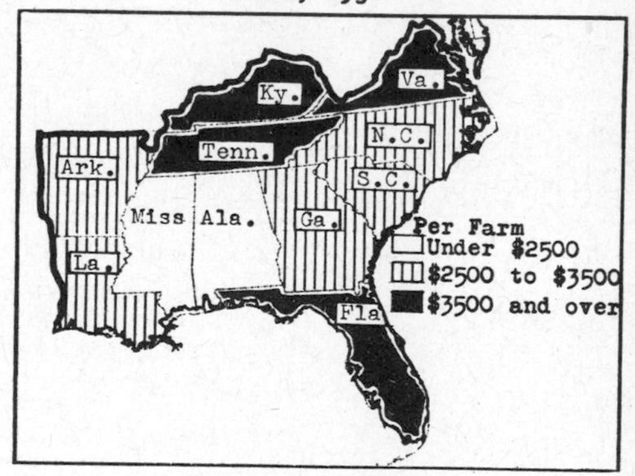

VALUE OF FARM IMPLEMENTS AND MACHINERY PER FARM, 1930

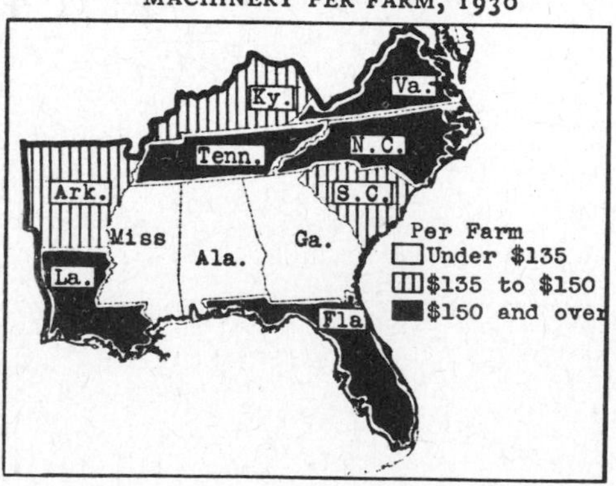

AVERAGE VALUE PER FARM OF DOMESTIC ANIMALS, 1930

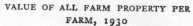

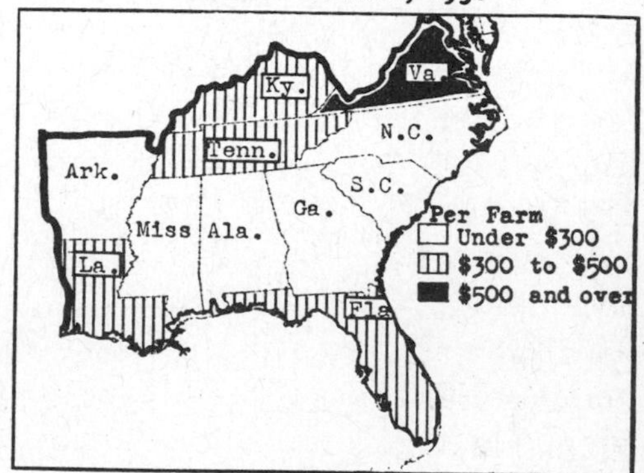

234. Virginia and Kentucky, and sometimes North Carolina, often form a sort of upper quartile of variation or fringe bordering the inner "South." So much is this true that if the southeastern map be pictured to indicate more detailed homogeneity, the result is the appearance of what may be denoted as a sort of "Middle South," comprising South Carolina, Georgia, Alabama, Mississippi, and Arkansas, and sometimes North Carolina. Such a Middle South is indicated by no less than 100 of the general indices, such as, value of all farm property per farm, value of land and buildings, value per farm of domestic animals, percentage of rural population in the total population, percentage of total population under 20 years, percentage of population 55 years or over, per capita bank resources, income, taxable property per capita, net income from corporations, expenditures for schools, and many others.

235. Illustrations of this heterogeneity of southern states appear clearly in the map picture. Thus Florida is white or black when the rest of the South is black or white in such indices as church membership in Methodist and Baptist churches, per capita income, wealth, gross farm income, value of farms and farm property, value of farms per acre, value of farm equipment, increase in population, ratio of urban population, percentage of the population living on farms, net gain in migration from other states, percentage of foreign born population, relative standing in health, in age of population—particularly in the ratio of population 55 years and over, percentage of income from sources other than agriculture, state and local bonded debt, percentage of coöperative sales of cash farm income, wholesale and retail sales, relative standing in wealth and education, motor cars per 1,000 inhabitants, families per radio, circulation of newspapers, and many others. A much wider range of differentials will appear if more refined indices be selected with a view to comparison only of Southeastern States with Southeastern States. In the case of Virginia there is a considerable trend toward the northeastern grouping in farm tenancy, in health, education, wealth, income, farm values, farm income, livestock, manufacturing, and many general cultural indices.

236. The fabric of the general political, economic, and social life of the region likewise is scarcely discernible except in multiples of the different states. James K. Vardaman was Mississippi; Thomas E. Watson was Georgia; Jeff Davis was Arkansas; Heflin and Catts and Blease and Long were and are of the political folkways of Alabama and Florida and South Carolina and Louisiana. So also is the long roll of local leaders and historical contributions to the region's background. So also is the long catalogue of "first" and distinguishing features and contributions of each state to its region and nation. These, however, can scarcely be summarized from

The Southwest Distinctive from the Southeast

The samples below are in addition to two large "blocks" of indices. One is the general "cultural" background, such as Spanish, Indian, Mexican influence, and the rapid growth of the "spirit of the Southwest." Another is the peculiar physical environment with its many measures of soil, rainfall, crop usage, agricultural engineering problems, etc.

1. Average total acreage per farm, 1930
2. Amount of vegetables grown for sale
3. Amount of vegetables grown for home use
4. Swine on farms
5. Amount of hay per unit area
6. Difference in soil composition
7. Average value of farms, including land, buildings, livestock, and equipment
8. Average size of farms
9. Farms operated by croppers and tenants
10. Improved land relative to total land area
11. Methods of farming
12. Farm population per farm
13. Average value per farm of land and buildings—farms operated by tenants
14. Per cent total farms under 100 acres
15. Farms 500 acres or more
16. Value of all farm property per farm
17. Per cent of fertilizer consumption
18. Per cent total pasture land is of all land on farms
19. Gross farm income per capita—also cash income
20. Average gross income per farm per year
21. Annual precipitation
22. Total pasturage acreage, 1929
23. Annual wage per wage earner, 1929
24. Number and value of sheep
25. Plowable pasture acreage
26. Horse power available per worker, 1924
27. Increase of land in harvested crops, 1920-1930
28. Increase in cotton
29. Increase in wheat
30. Ratio of mortgaged debt to values
31. Per cent of farms having tractors
32. Population per square mile
33. Negro population
34. Mexican population
35. Indian population
36. Per cent increase in total population
37. Deaths under one year per 1,000 population, 1929
38. Per cent of females 15 years of age or over married
39. Net gain by interstate migration, 1920
40. Per cent children 10-17 years gainfully occupied
41. Proportion females ten years or over gainfully occupied
42. Wages in manufacturing industries, 1929
43. Total pounds of tobacco used in manufacturing
44. Also in manufacturing of cigars and cigarettes
45. Per capita total expenditure in day schools, 1927-1928
46. Accredited denominational schools
47. Students in normal schools per 10,000 population, 1930
48. Per cent total income from manufacturing, 1928
49. Net income per capita
50. Personal income per capita of total population
51. Retail sales per capita
52. Per capita total federal aid to states, 1930
53. Net indebtedness of state governments, 1930
54. Ratio of total state and local tax collections to aggregate private income
55. Per capita annual 11 year income
56. Relative standing in education
57. Public, society, and school libraries
58. Prisoners received by federal prisons and reformatories per 100,000, 1929
59. Net income per capita, 1930
60. Flora, forests, and plants
61. Milk production
62. Religion, multi-Protestant faiths, 29 per cent Catholic in Southwest
63. Characteristic culture traits of population (Southwest progressives and liberal)
64. Climatic differences other than rainfall
65. Revenue from motor vehicles, registration, and gasoline tax
66. State gasoline tax
67. General ranking in public education
68. Families per radio
69. Circulation of newspapers and periodicals
70. Per capita value of mineral products
71. Per capita cost of state government
72. Per inhabitant estimated true wealth
73. Retail sales per store and per inhabitant retail trade
74. Supply of physicians per 10,000 population
75. Per cent of rural poulation served by whole-time health units
76. Clinical medicine
77. Motor cars per 1,000 inhabitants
78. Per capita annual income
79. Different cultural influences (Spanish and western in Southwest)
80. Farm diversity
81. Petroleum production and mineral wealth
82. Increase in urban metropolitan areas
83. Loss of population through migration
84. Land topography

And the following fifty additional *per capita differentials:*

85. Number of dairy cattle
86. Value of dairy cattle (1920)
87. Number of all cattle
88. Number of horses
89. Value of horses
90. Number of mules
91. Number of acres in wheat
92. Production of wheat
93. Value of wheat produced
94. Number of acres of oats
95. Production of oats
96. Value of oats
97. Production of rice
98. Value of rice produced
99. Number of acres of barley
100. Production of barley
101. Value of barley
102. Number of acres of grain sorghums
103. Production of grain sorghums
104. Value of grain sorghums
105. Number of sheep
106. Value of sheep
107. Wool—number of fleeces
108. Production of wool—pounds
109. Number of acres of corn
110. Production of corn
111. Number of acres in cotton
112. Number of bales of cotton produced
113. Canteloupes—car lot shipments
114. Tomatoes—car lot shipments
115. Production of petroleum
116. Production of natural gas
117. Production of natural gasoline
118. Production of gold, silver, lead, zinc, sulphur, and copper
119. Flour mill and grist mill products—value of products
120. Animal slaughter, meat packing—value of products
121. Petroleum refining—value of products
122. Dairy products—value of products
123. Value of all tangible property
124. Value of real property
125. Value of livestock
126. Value of farm implements
127. Value of manufacturing equipment
128. Value of railroads and equipment
129. Miles of railways
130. Number of residence telephones per 1,000 population
131. Postal receipts
132. Net retail sales
133. Total wholesale sales
134. Motor vehicles registered per 1,000 population
135. Total loans and discounts in state and national banks
136. Rate of increase of bank loans and discounts
137. Net individual incomes
138. Gross corporate incomes

the detailed pictures which must remain largely within the bounds of state characterization.

237. Again the comparison of individual states within the Southeast with individual states of other regions, clearly lifted out of average or aggregate, is of great importance. Thus North Carolina and Nevada, the one ranking low in per capita indices and high in totals; the other at the top in averages and at the bottom of the states in many absolute measurements. Thus North Carolina with twenty times as many people, more than twenty times as many colleges and institutions, forty times as much internal revenue tax to the nation, with a more balanced economy, more cultural stability. So Virginia and Utah, South Carolina and Idaho, Georgia and Wyoming, rural states all, yet widely differing in their definitive cultures, if compared separately, yet conforming to the general homogeneity of their respective regions. Does Nevada rank higher in civilization and culture than Virginia, the Mother of Presidents? Or agrarian North Dakota rate higher than agrarian-industrial North Carolina? So the per capita rankings indicate.

XIX. THE SOUTHWEST AND THE SOUTHEAST

238. From this inventory of the southern United States, the picture of Texas, Oklahoma, New Mexico, and Arizona as the new emerging Southwest is clear. Part of the significance of such a regional classification is found in its designation as one of the six major regional units of the nation; a part is found in its peculiar importance in study and planning in relation to the Southeast; while still another part inheres in the peculiar promise of the Southwest to the national culture. Brief and inadequate as a preliminary summary must be, it is possible to indicate something of the extraordinary range, variety, and size of the great Southwest empire of the nation and to project the region as one for special study and analysis. Its main differentials from the Southeast have already been indicated. In general, those who characterize the Southwest begin with its great expanse, its distinctive geographic character, and the quick sweep of its recent development. Next come the historical and cultural backgrounds, upon which this superstructure was built, and thirdly the emerging "spirit of the Southwest" which is reflected among the cumulative products of the region. Thus "Fort Worth and Dallas are as western as Duluth." Raymond D. Thomas has made a special study of the economic backgrounds and prospects of the Southwest. J. J. Rhyne and Clyde Russell Rhyne have made for the Southern Regional Study some exploratory researches into the human wealth of the region. Since the Southwest has been constituted a special field for further study, it is necessary here only to point up the general

State Differentials and Percentage of Federal Internal Revenue and Federal Relief, 1933, Compared With Population

STATE AND REGION	Relief Funds	Internal Revenue	Population*
Southeast	*16.96*	*22.53*	*20.8*
Virginia	1.95	5.35	2.0
North Carolina	1.41	11.40	2.6
South Carolina	1.00	0.41	1.4
Georgia	1.04	0.75	2.4
Florida	0.93	0.47	1.2
Kentucky	1.12	2.37	2.1
Tennessee	2.00	0.59	2.1
Alabama	1.14	0.33	2.2
Mississippi	1.14	0.07	1.6
Arkansas	1.32	0.15	1.5
Louisiana	3.50	0.64	1.7
Southwest	*6.89*	*4.44*	*7.4*
Oklahoma	1.08	1.78	2.0
Texas	4.41	2.31	4.7
New Mexico	0.43	0.30	.3
Arizona	0.08	0.05	.4
Northeast	*27.91*	*42.75*	*31.0*
Maine	1.00	0.26	.6
New Hampshire	0.25	0.15	.4
Vermont	0.43	0.05	.3
Massachusetts	2.25	3.40	3.5
Rhode Island	0.25	0.50	.6
Connecticut	0.80	1.16	1.3
New York	11.94	22.66	10.3
New Jersey	2.88	4.26	3.3
Delaware	0.20	0.72	.2
Pennsylvania	4.61	7.37	7.8
Maryland	1.97	1.88	1.3
West Virginia	0.97	0.34	1.4

STATE AND REGION	Relief Funds	Internal Revenue	Population*
Middle States	*29.92*	*21.68*	*27.6*
Ohio	7.70	4.69	5.4
Indiana	1.59	0.98	2.6
Illinois	6.67	6.55	6.2
Michigan	5.71	3.27	3.9
Wisconsin	3.07	1.60	2.4
Minnesota	1.61	1.41	2.1
Iowa	2.16	0.39	2.0
Missouri	1.93	2.79	3.0
Northwest	*7.16*	*1.77*	*6.0*
North Dakota	0.62	0.05	.6
South Dakota	0.64	0.04	.6
Nebraska	1.22	0.29	1.1
Kansas	1.09	0.70	1.5
Montana	0.91	0.11	.4
Idaho	0.55	0.03	.4
Wyoming	0.45	0.03	.2
Colorado	0.75	0.43	.8
Utah	0.61	0.09	.4
Far West	*11.16*	*6.77*	*6.8*
Nevada	0.51	0.09	.1
Washington	1.61	0.42	1.3
Oregon	0.89	0.22	.8
California	7.91	6.04	4.6

*Population for 1930.

Per Capita Public Welfare Gross Expenditures in the Southeast and Southwest by States and Regions, 1930

STATE AND REGION	All Public Welfare Services	Ordinary Public Welfare Services	Aid to Soldiers and Sailors	Charities	Hospitals	Corrections	Prevention and Treatment of Communicable Diseases	Conservation of Child Life	Industrial Welfare	Vocational Rehabilitation	Supervision of Welfare Department
Southeast	*2.05*	*1.46*	*.593*	*.129*	*.652*	*.483*	*.143*	*.022*	*.008*	*.014*	*.008*
Virginia	2.53	2.09	.440	.104	.975	.669	.262	.026	.039	.012	.005
North Carolina	1.84	1.44	.405	.150	.542	.439	.185	.052	.028	.017	.013
South Carolina	1.63	1.11	.522	.112	.683	.164	.127	.016	.0002	.005	....
Georgia	1.31	.74	.564	.043	.492	.068	.104	.010	....	.014	.014
Florida	2.50	1.65	.848	.114	.912	.550	.021	.031	.002	.010	.007
Kentucky	1.23	1.12	.119	.202	.484	.347	.035	.011	....	.015	.023
Tennessee	1.87	1.44	.432	.206	.524	.606	.045	.024	.006	.017	.008
Alabama	2.56	1.89	.663	.096	.407	1.192	.145	.037	.002	.015	....
Mississippi	2.23	1.55	.674	.076	.789	.381	.272	.014	....	.019	....
Arkansas	2.73	.95	1.780	.102	.302	.292	.237	.004	.001	.011	....
Louisiana	2.74	2.19	.547	.196	1.312	.473	.139	.006	....	.010	.005
Southwest	*2.19*	*1.68*	*.520*	*.216*	*.698*	*.586*	*.131*	*.013*	*.021*	*.008*	*.002*
Oklahoma	3.44	2.80	.640	.298	1.032	1.106	.301	.012	.023	.018	.008
Texas	1.75	1.20	.545	.170	.564	.365	.077	.010	.017	.002	....
New Mexico	1.63	1.62	.007	.379	.677	.491	.008	.042	....	.024	....
Arizona	1.87	1.85	.023	.217	.691	.778	.029	.028	.085	.023	....
United States	*2.88*	*2.64*	*.249*	*.233*	*1.442*	*.656*	*.177*	*.018*	*.046*	*.014*	*.020*
Southeast	2.05	1.46	.593	.129	.652	.483	.143	.022	.008	.014	.008
Southwest	2.19	1.68	.520	.216	.698	.586	.131	.013	.021	.008	.002
Northeast	3.97	3.91	.065	.266	2.451	.718	.274	.020	.068	.013	.028
Middle States	2.67	2.51	.164	.245	1.294	.730	.126	.017	.051	.016	.027
Northwest	2.45	2.24	.208	.251	1.027	.726	.170	.012	.022	.014	.014
Far West	2.48	2.35	.128	.354	1.129	.620	.109	.009	.084	.015	.024

character and perspective of the Southwest in relation to the "South" as a whole. This is done largely in terms of Thomas' characterizations.

239. The historical uniformities of the Gulf Southwest go back to a very old Indian civilization in the broad southwestern country. Particularly in New Mexico and Arizona there still remain concrete results of the blending processes between the old Indian and early Spanish civilizations which have continued since the sixteenth century. Little evidence of this Indian-Spanish influence is to be discovered in Oklahoma and Texas. The "push" of American settlers into the Southwest came with the southwestward and westward trends of migration after 1825. The westward migration from the Old South penetrated first into the Texas area, which became one of the states of the Federal Union in 1845, the present boundaries of which were determined soon after the close of the Mexican War in 1848. The retarded development of the Southwest is evidenced in the late admission into the Union of Oklahoma, New Mexico, and Arizona. With the admission of Oklahoma in 1907 and both Arizona and New Mexico in 1912, the whole southwest country came within the fold of states. Excepting limited community areas in eastern Texas and the old Spanish settlements in the New Mexico-Arizona region, the Gulf Southwest is historically young, yet in the stage of cultural infancy. Long after the culture of the Old South had matured the Southwest Region was a wild country. The industrial revolution in the United States which came after the Civil War met resistance to change in the conservative and more or less tradition-bound Old South. But the emerging culture of the Southwest was receptive to the new social, political, and economic spirit which came with the industrialization movement after 1875.

240. The difference between the two southern regions cannot be mistaken by anyone who travels today through the Southwest country. Traveling westward from the eastern boundaries of Oklahoma and Texas, one moves gradually into the vast open spaces. Unending stretches of prairies and plains reach toward the horizon. Signs of the "cattle country" era still remain. The ranching areas still afford scenes of thousands of grazing cattle. Large areas of "desert country" are included in the Arizona-New Mexico region. A combination of physical conditions and remains of the pioneering type in the population generates and keeps alive the adventurous spirit which is characteristically southwestern. Louisiana joined the Union in 1812, while the area to the west did not become a part of the nation until 1845. Arkansas was made a state in 1836, but the wild territory to its west did not become the State of Oklahoma until 1907. Missouri on the northeastern border of Oklahoma was a state after 1821; Kansas to the north of Oklahoma was admitted in 1861. Colorado bordering northwest-

ern Oklahoma and immediately to the north of New Mexico (a state in 1912) was in the Union after 1876. Utah to the north of Arizona (a state in 1912) passed from territorial status to statehood in 1896, and California on the western border came into the Union in 1850. This boundary embracing the four states of the Southwest Region—Texas, Oklahoma, New Mexico, and Arizona—separates a relatively new cultural region from the more mature surrounding states.

241. Decades before the southwest area arrived at the status of political partnership as sister states in the Federal Union, the flow of economic and cultural life in the surrounding area had marked out fairly definite channels. The "economic nerves" of Louisiana and Arkansas centered along the Mississippi River, converging on New Orleans. Up in Missouri and Kansas, transportation and financial connections were established with Kansas City and St. Louis toward the east and northeast. In the mountain states of Colorado and Utah, Denver and Salt Lake City were the points of cultural concentration. The desert region west of the Colorado River formed a natural barrier to cultural relations between southern California and Arizona. Accordingly, the cultural life of southern California centered along the Pacific Coast.

242. Conditions within the Southwest draw the cultural currents toward points of concentration within the region. The transportation routes—railways and highways—head at the Gulf ports in Texas, which are the gateways leading from the Southwest into the Gulf and Latin American commercial areas. El Paso is an important connecting point between the Southwest and Mexico. The valleys of the Rio Grande and of the Pecos River lead southward from the high plateaus of northern New Mexico. These rivers with important railways tend to turn the flow of economic intercourse to the east and southeast into the Texas and Oklahoma region. The cities of Tulsa, Oklahoma City, Dallas, and Fort Worth draw the currents of trade southward and southwestward from the northern and eastern borders of the Southwest Region.

243. The boundaries of the Southwest surround an area of 568,125 square miles. The region is larger than the area comprising the eleven states of the Southeast and one and one half times larger than the Middle States Region. Texas alone constitutes one-twelfth of the total area of the United States.

244. The variety of topography, temperature, rainfall, and soil conditions makes the Southwest a region of variations in agricultural pursuits. In the subregions of broken hill country in the northern and southern Ozarks in Oklahoma, small-scale and largely self-sufficing diversified

farming is typical. In the Black Belt of Texas and in eastern Texas, also in the lower Red Valley and in central and eastern Oklahoma, mixed farming is the principal occupation with relatively small scale cotton culture as the chief source of income. Large scale cotton farming by machine methods has grown rapidly, particularly during and since the World War, in southwestern Oklahoma and in the Corpus Christi area and the west Texas area around Lubbock. An important sector of the nation's hard winter wheat belt lies in northwest Oklahoma and northwest Texas. All over this vast plains area wheat farming is a large scale activity. Single wheat "ranches" of thousands of acres are not uncommon in this region. Cattle and sheep ranching on a large scale is one of the important agricultural operations in the Southwest. The Edwards plateau in Texas and the plateau areas in New Mexico and Arizona are the centers of the sheep industry. Irrigation farming for the production of fruits, vegetables, and small grains is practiced in the lower Rio Grande Valley in Texas and in favored valleys in New Mexico and Arizona. Another type of agricultural activity, which has grown quite rapidly during the past ten or twenty years, is that of dry farming in the 100th meridian region where drought resisting crops like kaffir and grain sorghums are grown with fair success.

245. The Southwest is spotted with relatively small areas of specialized crops. White potatoes are produced commercially in the Arkansas River Valley near Muskogee in Oklahoma. Broom corn yields abundantly in Garvin, Grady, McClain counties in southwestern Oklahoma, also in smaller districts in northwest Oklahoma, and in the tier of counties in New Mexico along the northern half of the eastern boundary of that state and in Bee County in southern Texas. In Wilson and Atascosa counties in southern Texas, in Parker and Wise counties in north-central Texas, in Grady County in Oklahoma, and in Willacy County on the lower Texas Gulf coast are important commercial watermelon districts. Other small crop areas include pecans in Bryan County in the lower Oklahoma Red River Valley and in Comanche and Eastland counties in central Texas; blackberries in Tarrant County in north-central Texas, in Smith County in eastern Texas, and in Comanche County in central Texas; strawberries in the northern Ozark district in Oklahoma, in Atascosa County in southern Texas, and in the Houston district on the Gulf coast.

246. The urban cultural centers of the Southwest are quite distinctly regional in their foundations and development. Like the general region from which they draw their strength, they are comparatively new. The urban area along the Texas Gulf coast, the Houston-Galveston-Beaumont district, has had a phenomenal growth during the past quarter of a century.

The principal economic bases of this district are petroleum production and refining, cotton compresses, and foreign shipping.

247. On the southern fringe of the Texas Black Belt, the San Antonio-Austin area is growing to an important position as a distributing point and resort center. The Dallas-Fort Worth district in the northern Black Belt is a strong urban center with meat packing, general merchandise distribution, and manufacturing as the principal sources of economic support. El Paso on the Mexican border in west Texas is a distribution point for a broad area and an important center of contact for over-land trade with Mexico across the Rio Grande. The urban life of Oklahoma is concentrating in Tulsa, the "Oil Capital of the World," and in Oklahoma City, the state capital and a rapidly growing center of manufacturing and wholesale distribution. In New Mexico the flow is toward the Albuquerque-Santa Fe district, and in Arizona principally toward Phoenix.

248. The Southwestern Region is a rich empire of natural resources. The heart of the mid-continent oil and gas fields is within the area. In 1930 the United States produced about two-thirds of the world's output of crude petroleum, and nearly two-thirds of this total of 898 million barrels produced by the United States came from the fields of Texas and Oklahoma. At the present time the major portion of the world's production of commercially used natural gas comes from the Texas-Oklahoma fields. The story of the Mineral Empire of the Southwest can perhaps best be told in figures. Take Texas as the chief example. The total value of the mineral production in Texas in 1929 amounted to close to a half billion dollars, which was approximately ten per cent of the total mineral wealth production of the nation in that year. This vast Texas production came from the following principal sources: petroleum, $322,520,000; natural gas, $67,474,000; sulphur, $43,811,000; natural gasoline, $26,561,000. Other minerals of importance in Texas are cement, clay products, sand and gravel, gypsum, and stone. The total mineral production, measured in dollars for Oklahoma for 1929, went slightly beyond a half billion dollars, or ten per cent of the total for the nation—petroleum, $364,650,000; natural gasoline, $42,766,000; zinc, $25,349,544; coal, $11,481,000; lead, $5,860,638; gypsum, $2,255,374; with lesser amounts from clay products, sand and gravel and asphalt.

249. The Southwest is rapidly developing its own ports. The rise to first rank importance of Beaumont, Port Arthur, Houston, Galveston, and Texas City as shipping ports is one of the interesting new aspects of the developing foreign trade of the Southwest. These ports are among the nation's chief outlets for the shipping of cotton, grains, and petroleum.

The traffic through the Houston harbor alone amounted in 1930 to more than five hundred million dollars.

250. The regional subdivisions of the Southwest and the comparison of the Southeast and the Southwest in special indices are shown in the tables and maps. The keynote here as in the Southeast is one of future trends and planning. Thomas sees many advantages. Natural advantages of soil, crop adaptation, climate, and human factors will sustain agriculture, even if mineral production and manufacturing activities should increase. The newness of the Southwest as an agricultural area offers a regional advantage in a new era of more intelligent utilization of land. Soil conservation and restoration methods can be practiced before destructive erosion has gone beyond repair. Certain sections of the region are already badly eroded. But the soil ruin pictures in the Southwest do not compare in magnitude with the gullied landscapes in the Old South. Getting on the job of soil conservation and restoration in good time will save the Southwest literally millions of dollars in soil resources. Oklahoma and Texas are already among the leading states in the soils management program of the nation. The culture of the Southwest is quite substantially endowed by vast stores of mineral resources—petroleum, gas, coal, zinc, lead, copper, gold, asphalt, gypsum, sand and gravel, and other minerals of less importance. The socialization of the income from this rich gift of nature presents perhaps the most perplexing problem of the region for the immediate future.

251. The processing of the products of the farms and mines of the Southwest will build a reasonably strong manufacturing structure within the region. The four necessary requirements of manufacturing are available; namely, raw materials, power, population, and market outlets. These conditions, however, point strongly toward regionally adapted types of secondary industries. Abundant raw materials and power are at hand for petroleum refining, flour milling, meat packing, cotton ginning and compressing, and cement manufacturing. Despite the availability of apparently inexhaustible sources of cheap fuel for power in the form of crude oil, natural gas, and coal, it seems doubtful if manufacturing in this region will be developed far beyond the regionally adapted type.

252. The Southwest Region is much too large in area and its physiographic, demographic, and economic characteristics too varied for regional homogeneity except in rather generalized aspects. Preliminary studies have resulted in the tentative delineation of some twenty cultural subregions. In separating and designating these twenty subregions, broad general principles of comparison and differentiation have been followed.

Subregions of the Southwest

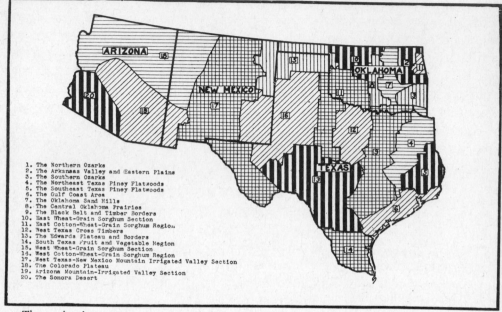

1. The Northern Ozarks
2. The Arkansas Valley and Eastern Plains
3. The Southern Ozarks
4. The Northeast Texas Piney Flatwoods
5. The Southeast Texas Piney Flatwoods
6. The Gulf Coast Area
7. The Oklahoma Sand Hills
8. The Central Oklahoma Prairies
9. The Black Belt and Timber Borders
10. East Wheat-Grain Sorghum Section
11. East Cotton-Wheat-Grain Sorghum Region
12. West Texas Cross Timbers
13. The Edwards Plateau and Borders
14. South Texas Fruit and Vegetable Region
15. West Wheat-Grain Sorghum Section
16. West Cotton-Wheat-Grain Sorghum Region
17. West Texas-New Mexico Mountain Irrigated Valley Section
18. The Colorado Plateau
19. Arizona Mountain-Irrigated Valley Section
20. The Sonora Desert

These subregions, analogous to those represented by Woofter for the Southeast, were designated as tentative subdivisions by Raymond Thomas. They are discussed at length by him in his special study of the Southwest. See Thomas' special viewpoint on subregions and state lines in Chapter X.

Population and Area of Subregions of the Southwest

REGION	Area in Sq. Mi.	Population	Urban Population	Rural Population	Population Per Sq. Mi.	Per Cent Urban	Per Cent Rural
No. 1	3,000	60,000	....	60,000	20.	....	100
No. 2	7,500	520,000	241,244	278,756	69.7	46.3	53.7
No. 3	5,743	86,928	....	86,928	15.1	....	100
No. 4	18,634	651,391	117,261	534,130	34.9	18.0	82.0
No. 5	14,025	284,111	23,929	260,182	20.2	8.4	91.6
No. 6	14,762	825,639	528,105	297,533	55.9	63.9	36.1
No. 7	9,963	454,175	133,653	320,522	45.5	29.4	70.6
No. 8	6,949	446,116	251,641	194,475	64.1	56.4	43.6
No. 9	37,782	2,245,563	1,039,764	1,205,799	59.4	46.3	53.7
No. 10	12,015	255,747	77,654	178,091	21.2	30.3	69.7
No. 11	27,855	665,570	160,064	505,506	23.9	24.0	76.0
No. 12	18,611	382,585	120,642	261,943	20.5	31.5	68.5
No. 13	53,317	283,326	74,336	208,990	5.3	26.2	73.8
No. 14	17,217	271,057	126,400	144,657	15.7	46.6	53.4
No. 15	28,800	133,109	30,047	103,062	4.6	22.5	77.5
No. 16	58,947	465,507	133,217	332,290	7.9	28.6	71.4
No. 17	83,691	405,781	183,119	222,662	4.8	45.1	54.9
No. 18	88,266	144,410	13,800	130,610	1.6	9.5	90.5
No. 19	37,960	370,753	140,675	230,078	9.7	37.9	62.1
No. 20	21,987	29,816	4,892	24,924	1.4	16.4	83.6
Total	567,024	8,981,584	3,400,443	5,581,138	15.8	37.8	62.2

The criteria include soil, elevation, topography, mineral products, climate, precipitation, temperature, winds, growing season, drainage, vegetation, agricultural products, livestock, transportation, urbanization, manufacturing, population, education, economic development, and social conditions. The decision as to regions and boundaries was made as objective and scientific as possible with the preliminary studies that have been made. Over one hundred dot and cross-hatched maps of more than 40 characteristics of these regions were made and carefully and objectively compared together with all other available information from other and previous studies and from personal travel and acquaintance with the conditions within the various sections. The present classification of subregions should, however, be considered purely *tentative*, and whenever new and additional information justifies it, alterations in classification can be made. The boundaries designated in this study generally follow county lines in order to make use of census data. Later refinements upon these borders may be possible.

XX. TOWARD REGIONAL PLANNING

253. The facts which have been presented are adequate for a fair analysis of the Southeastern Region and its relation to the Southwest and to the nation. They have been summarized in this syllabus. More details, distribution, and illustration will be found in the several chapters and in the maps and tables. The effort has been made to present a balanced picture of basic facts, exclusive of the most vivid extremes. From these facts it seems possible to focus upon strategic factors in terms of what is to be done. Some of these relate to general underlying principles and policies, some to the differentials between the Southeast and the Southwest, some to specific problems of the Southeast, and some to organization and means for attaining desired ends.

254. The first general conclusion is that the task of planning the "way on" for the Southeast is an extraordinarily difficult one, but that all the elements necessary for success are present provided they can be focused in the right ways and combinations. On the other hand, there is ample evidence to warrant the conclusion that unless there is a definite change in regional economy there will be retrogression in agriculture, in industry, and in general culture and institutions. Some aspects of this prospect are alarming, indicating that the South can ill afford to make many more mistakes. The situation is all the more tragic in view of the extraordinarily contrasting possibilities.

255. Another general conclusion is that regional reconstruction can be successfully achieved only in relation to national integration and interregional adjustments. By the same token national social planning must be

PUBLIC, SOCIETY, AND SCHOOL LIBRARIES IN THE UNITED STATES, 1929

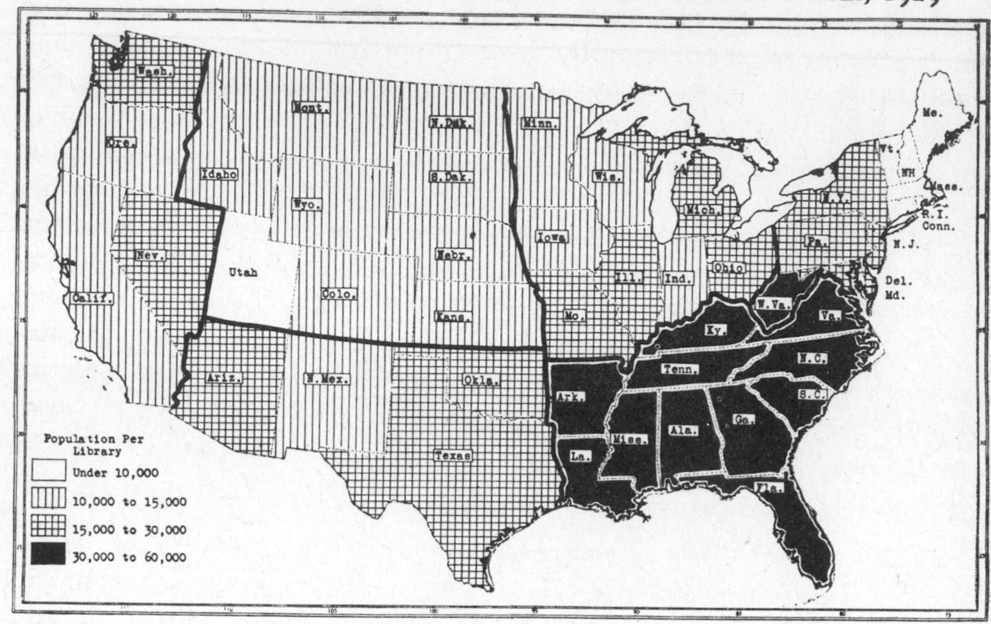

INHABITANTS PER VOLUME IN ALL COLLEGE LIBRARIES, 1928

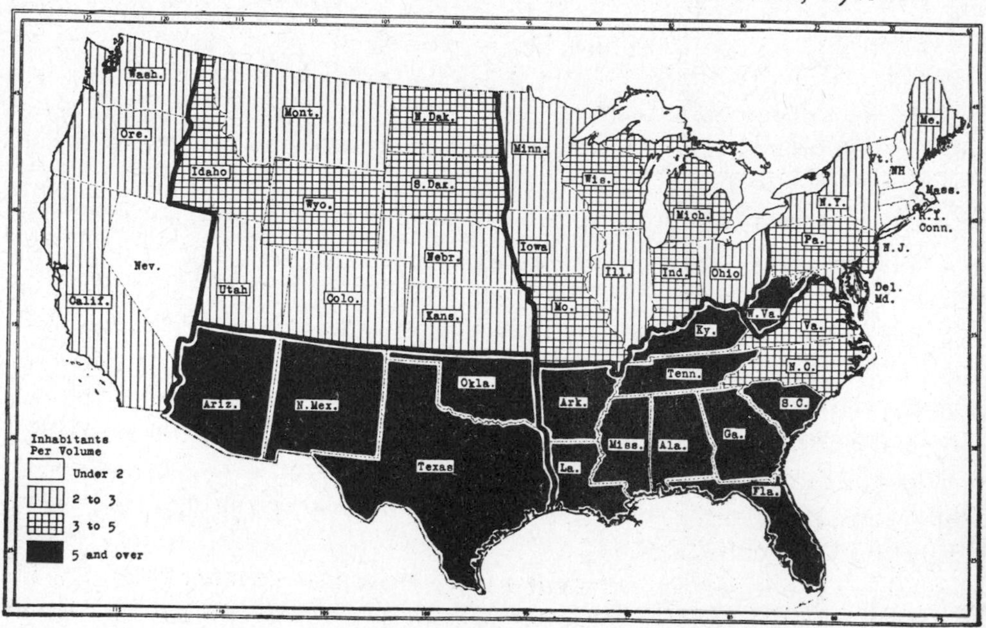

based upon regional analysis and functioning, giving logical values to regional differentials and distribution. Realistic and stable results can be attained, however, only through approximate delimitation and definition of the regions on the basis of scientific and functional analysis, subdividing the South into southeastern and southwestern groupings, reclassifying such states as Maryland and Missouri, and providing for adequate functional subregional divisions to meet the practical needs of overlapping areas and specialized activities. In this regional classification there is need for more approximate uniformity among the many national and regional boards, agencies, consultants, and less accidental and arbitrary allocation of areas and functions.

256. It is assumed that, both because of basic needs and trends and because of the fact that all states are now setting up state planning boards in coöperation with federal agencies, increasing emphasis will be placed upon social planning. It is assumed further that social planning so applied to the region will be a gradual, coöperative, flexible program comprehending varied institutional activities in contradistinction to a rigid planned economic order. The objectives of the new planning envisage no Utopias or quick magic changes; yet they do look toward the rehabilitation of the people, toward the reconstruction of cotton economy, toward increasing the South's revenue to the nation as well as its own wealth, and toward general regional, cultural adjustment. It means a goal ahead definitely to be achieved through gradual growth and through intelligence and skill. Such emphasis in the Southeast ought to serve as a new regional motivation, as well as to point the way to tangible, visible next steps.

257. While it is assumed further that there must be a certain boldness and magnitude adequate to start the flow of new currents and processes, the task is a step-by-step procedure adapted to flexible democracy. Gradual progress will be made through state planning boards and through the stimulation of a national planning board and through general promotion and educational work. While continuous emphasis must be placed upon state planning, a regional planning board can contribute wisely to many special aspects and to the general regional development. This is especially true in agricultural reconstruction, in land and other resources utilization, in institutions of higher learning and research, and in social legislation needed as adequate framework for practical planning. A regional advisory board comprehending all of the eleven Southeastern States might assist the TVA in helping to plan for all these states rather than for the seven states arbitrarily selected because of points of contact within the Basin. Such a southeastern regional planning board would be composed

Taxable Property Per Capita, 1930

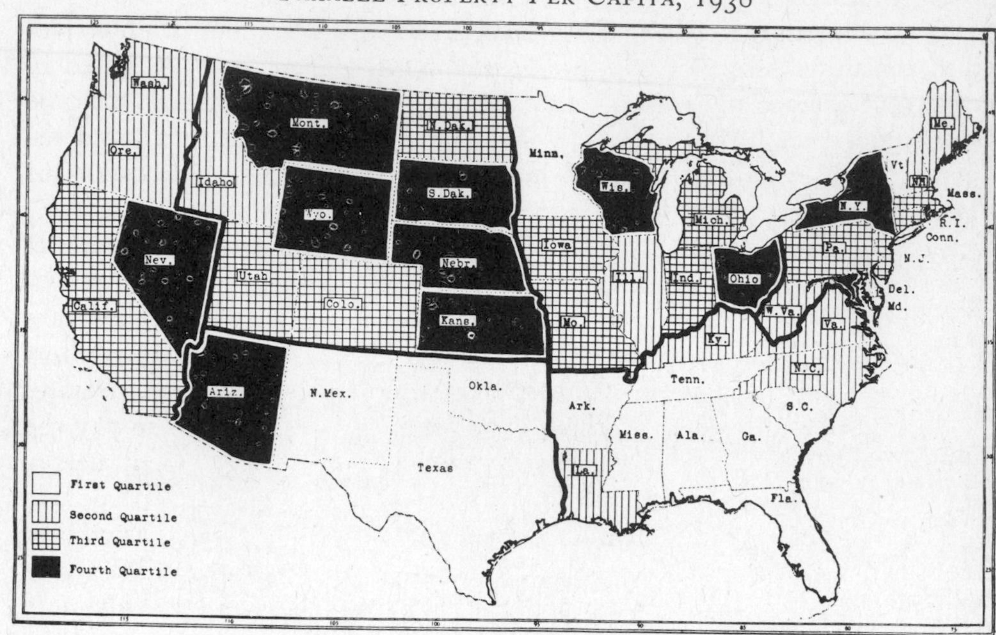

Per Inhabitant Estimated True Wealth, 1930

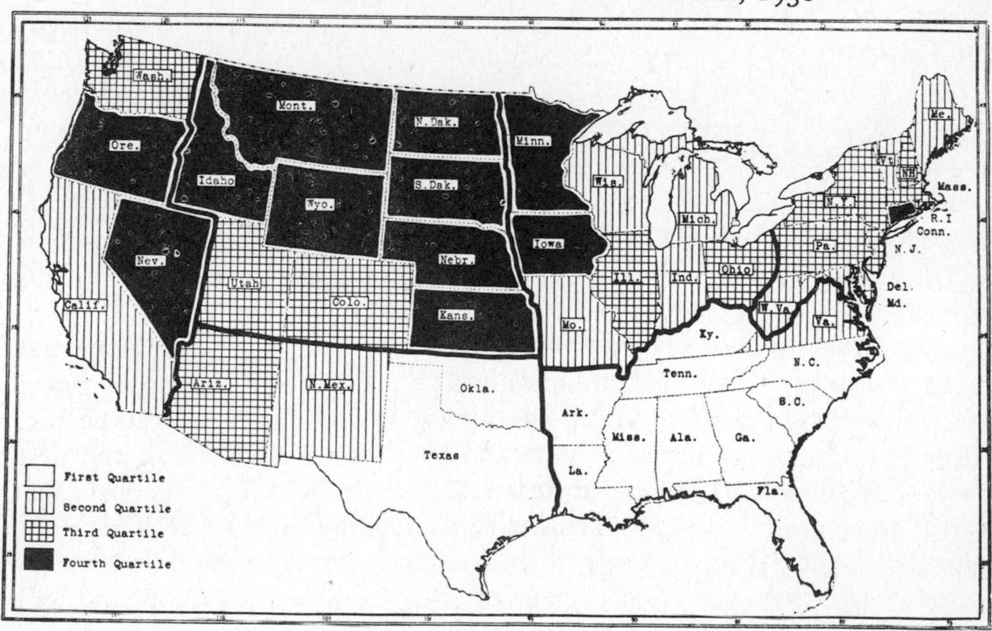

of a representative from each state board and a small number selected at large.

258. It seems possible to focus upon a reasonable number of objectives which constitute a sort of irreducible minimum. These may be stated in varied terms, some more specific and some more general. There must be some logical repetition and overlapping necessary to conform to the summary of facts already catalogued and to reëmphasize strategic points of approach. Thus, preliminary to physical and visible objectives there is need to emphasize again cultural attitudes and understanding. On the part of the South, three essentials stand out. One is a more realistic facing of facts than has yet been attained. The South does not appear cognizant of the critical nature of its dilemmas. Another is a greater unity of effort with a resulting diminution of internal jealousies and rivalries of states and institutional interests. A third is an intelligent willingness to pay the price of progress. This means work, trained people, and patient persistence.

259. On the part of the nation at large there also appear three essentials. One is the recognition of the logical, inevitable, evolutionary nature of the South's culture. The South cannot be arbitrarily relegated through mere stage characterizations. Another is an understanding of the size and the time quality of the regional problem involved. For instance, the region's Negro child population to be educated is larger than all the children of the Far West. Its farm tenant families are more than half of all the farm families outside the two southern regions. The money income from these groups is as one to a hundred compared to the highest brackets of selected areas in other regions. The third is the need for wiser counsel than the growing body of critics who tend to incite the South's marginal folk to violent revolution. This is an elemental factor in planning for reconstruction. In place of these, however, is the also increasing and promising trend toward orderly planning and federal cooperative participation, this in itself constituting one of the chief objectives.

260. Proceeding to the more measurable economic ends, an elemental objective is a substantial increase of values and wealth, the raising of wages and income, and the expansion of basic consumption capacity of the people. A part of this new value can be added by existing labor. Yet the first essential is substantial increase in technology aptly applied to the development and use of the region's extraordinary natural endowment. This technology will comprehend a wide range from much needed scientific research to such fundamentals as farm management and social organization, and will be directed toward such objectives as farm credit and the reconstruction of the farm tenant system in the South. More specifically, one irreducible

Fertilizer Consumption in the United States, 1910-1930
Expressed in Short Tons

STATE AND REGION	1910-1914*	1915-1919*	1920-1924*	1925	1926	1927	1928	1929	1930
Southeast									
Virginia	385,353	424,769	429,785	451,656	435,223	408,008	437,709	429,886	449,178
North Carolina	750,252	806,023	1,012,353	1,217,822	1,218,176	1,171,499	1,349,360	1,293,572	1,242,036
South Carolina	984,826	890,759	752,361	873,255	840,128	726,736	788,293	760,069	749,230
Georgia	1,146,283	884,832	683,013	778,808	780,302	713,047	883,274	868,911	928,606
Florida	199,709	216,737	334,066	358,463	398,480	417,438	468,907	427,224	487,324
Kentucky	69,200	94,200	82,400	93,000	91,500	70,500	90,500	93,000	114,000
Tennessee	75,739	98,094	94,731	142,174	156,336	112,473	150,726	142,745	163,909
Alabama	476,829	261,249	346,444	598,115	615,364	478,400	681,100	675,450	643,700
Mississippi	131,235	90,500	149,871	258,028	278,075	218,750	333,350	327,806	403,718
Arkansas	51,370	60,665	62,451	123,387	126,175	75,487	126,391	156,582	157,648
Louisiana	88,880	89,372	90,278	110,784	114,347	92,866	143,693	174,278	175,560
Southwest									
Arizona	(†)	300	425	500	500	700	1,000	1,200	1,800
New Mexico	(†)	400	780	1,200	1,566	1,256	1,400	1,500	1,787
Oklahoma	1,500	3,000	3,220	5,000	5,418	4,263	8,203	9,422	6,613
Texas	56,967	40,369	63,503	101,008	125,150	80,521	144,643	192,133	145,218
Northeast									
Maine	113,760	118,968	168,275	185,000	147,000	183,750	178,750	185,650	195,650
New Hampshire	15,050	15,766	15,800	16,000	14,680	16,875	16,900	16,900	17,000
Vermont	13,040	15,400	17,200	18,000	18,000	15,663	16,911	14,905	16,069
Massachusetts	48,140	60,400	62,819	62,656	58,920	71,734	70,458	62,491	66,621
Rhode Island	7,300	8,900	8,860	9,000	8,100	10,125	10,100	10,100	10,200
Connecticut	54,200	75,200	71,000	70,000	70,000	65,000	72,000	69,000	69,000
New York	257,580	284,972	246,000	253,000	234,000	260,000	260,000	250,000	250,000
New Jersey	142,415	152,408	163,012	146,686	135,141	141,635	143,574	141,981	156,445
Pennsylvania	331,123	319,996	320,970	328,462	328,904	326,514	339,984	332,396	332,000
Delaware	36,600	44,880	42,542	41,006	43,084	41,126	40,817	41,000	43,000
Maryland	163,670	172,280	155,006	165,474	163,285	165,174	173,159	165,443	177,021
West Virginia	30,680	32,260	36,466	41,000	43,000	43,500	49,700	49,700	50,000
Middle States									
Illinois	6,200	9,800	14,991	24,582	25,227	26,000	30,509	38,056	40,818
Indiana	177,654	185,930	204,004	226,148	228,280	240,498	221,082	250,201	224,055
Iowa	(†)	1,100	3,700	6,000	6,021	7,181	10,000	17,000	24,597
Michigan	48,786	78,300	92,116	109,327	105,014	117,227	150,213	152,812	130,000
Minnesota	1,800	3,600	6,000	9,000	11,316	11,387	14,211	13,024	15,500
Missouri	47,326	68,800	58,596	63,939	56,891	56,100	64,922	58,892	59,810
Ohio	165,652	220,650	298,058	321,966	304,480	312,703	320,866	338,662	327,179
Wisconsin	3,300	6,800	13,800	12,500	16,000	22,520	33,041	40,671	51,222
Northwest									
Colorado	(†)	(†)	230	250	337	607	728	800	900
Idaho	(†)	(†)	340	400	420	450	500	550	1,250
Kansas	4,910	10,107	6,111	4,138	7,746	7,800	9,162	9,943	6,355
Montana	(†)	(†)	(†)	(†)	50	90	100	100	100
Nebraska	(†)	140	470	500	500	500	600	700	1,000
North Dakota	(†)	(†)	160	225	250	398	450	550	1,548
South Dakota	(†)	(†)	145	150	200	220	250	250	250
Utah	(†)	(†)	300	500	500	500	500	550	550
Wyoming	(†)	(†)	(†)	100	150	200	300	600	650
Far West									
California	43,234	35,998	70,384	85,933	93,845	102,524	121,183	130,477	142,489
Nevada	(†)	(†)	28	30	30	30	30	30	30
Oregon	3,960	6,700	6,900	8,000	8,000	9,000	10,000	10,000	10,500
Washington	1,300	2,100	5,400	10,000	12,207	14,244	15,500	17,500	17,500
United States	6,135,854	5,892,944	6,195,364	7,333,166	7,328,268	6,843,199	7,985,019	7,974,712	8,109,636

(*) Five-year average tonnage. (†) No report or negligible quantity reported.

minimum is that of stopping the gigantic soil erosion process, to conserve what is still left, to restore millions of acres of marginal or submarginal lands, and to retard the present process which will not only be fatal to agriculture, but to industry and water power resources.

261. This means a very realistic program of inquiry and action, comprehending the whole problem of land use and planning and of optimum programs of agricultural production in relation to population, to industry, and to total capacity of the region, its interregional relations, and its foreign markets. This, again, involves the measure and use of present surplus people and labor as well as land; of readjusted crop production and land improvement; of programs of rural housing and rural electrification. It implies new emphasis upon special activities, such as dairying and livestock industry, small industries and part-time farming, new occupations and new crops, new industries, and it assumes new reaches in expanded cooperative organizations and endeavor.

262. The substance of the whole situation, however, as well as the planning approach to these problems, can best be illustrated through a comprehensive view of the crisis now in prospect in the Southeast due to the diminishing ratio of cotton in the total regional economy of the future. The problem may be stated in a sequence of factors somewhat as follows. First of all, as to the fact, such a crisis, already impending, seems inevitable for a half dozen major reasons, to each of which a number of special factors contribute. First, the decreasing exports of cotton appear to be due to various factors of international relations and tariff policies, to the increase of cotton production in foreign countries, and to possible reduced consumption abroad due to several factors. Second, reduced home consumption of cotton appears likely to be due to the high cost of producing and processing, to substitutes of other fibres or of newly invented processes or materials, and to further reaches of technology. Third, new inventions relating to cultivation, picking, and manufacturing appear to point toward a reduced ratio of people needed to cultivate and harvest the cotton crop and also of those who are employed in textile industries. Fourth, at the current rate of soil depletion through cash-crop-fertilizer farming, the Southeast cannot long survive on its present basis of quantitative production. Fifth, progress in social standards will not permit of cotton production on the present level of living standards which obtain among half of the cotton farmers of the region. And sixth, the Southwest will continue so advantaged in cotton culture as to make southeastern competition except on moderate and specialized bases unsuccessful.

263. Next is the characterization of the situation which appears to be threefold. First, there is the size of the problem; second, there is the quick-

A New Dairy Region for the Southeast

Adapted from the U. S. Bureau of Agricultural Economics

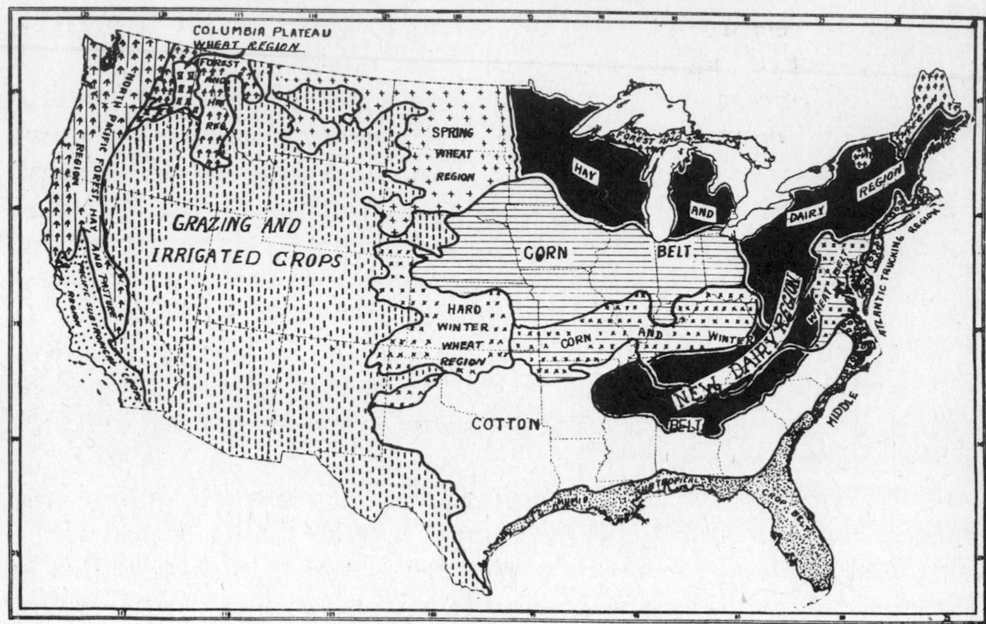

Percentage of Gross Income from All Farm Products Derived from Milk, 1929-1932

State and Region	Per Cent of Gross Income From Milk 1929	1930	1931	1932
Southeast				
Virginia	16.2	19.4	20.8	23.5
North Carolina	11.5	13.3	16.7	17.0
South Carolina	11.5	13.2	16.1	17.3
Georgia	10.9	12.6	16.6	19.2
Florida	8.6	7.5	10.0	10.4
Kentucky	18.6	20.9	21.1	19.9
Tennessee	16.7	19.1	18.9	19.0
Alabama	14.0	17.5	20.4	20.7
Mississippi	10.1	15.7	16.0	15.9
Arkansas	11.6	18.8	15.8	16.2
Louisiana	11.0	14.5	15.2	14.6
Southwest				
Oklahoma	15.1	20.6	21.0	20.9
Texas	11.4	13.8	14.2	13.8
New Mexico	9.7	13.1	13.7	14.9
Arizona	11.9	16.2	20.4	19.0
Northeast				
Maine	18.9	24.8	32.9	33.8
New Hampshire	42.2	43.9	43.7	45.0
Vermont	58.9	59.7	61.8	61.2
Massachusetts	33.3	36.0	36.6	38.8
Rhode Island	44.9	48.1	48.8	51.5
Connecticut	36.1	37.8	43.3	44.8
New York	45.8	45.8	46.9	46.6
New Jersey	25.6	25.9	29.2	28.3
Delaware	17.5	19.7	21.9	23.2
Pennsylvania	36.7	39.7	40.7	42.2
Maryland	24.7	30.4	31.0	34.0
West Virginia	27.3	31.4	30.3	34.2
Middle States				
Ohio	25.1	26.2	25.7	28.8
Indiana	19.5	20.7	22.0	24.4
Illinois	18.2	19.5	22.3	26.3
Michigan	31.4	32.2	33.8	32.9
Wisconsin	51.4	50.4	52.2	54.2
Minnesota	30.1	29.2	31.6	34.1
Iowa	14.0	13.9	15.2	17.7
Missouri	16.3	17.3	18.5	19.0
Northwest				
North Dakota	16.3	18.6	29.4	22.0
South Dakota	14.5	14.5	16.5	20.2
Nebraska	10.1	10.1	12.0	14.1
Kansas	11.8	13.1	14.9	17.8
Montana	12.4	14.4	16.9	15.2
Idaho	14.2	16.9	19.9	19.6
Wyoming	11.0	11.6	12.0	13.8
Colorado	12.4	10.9	13.7	15.2
Utah	17.8	17.8	19.4	20.2
Far West				
Nevada	11.7	16.7	17.1	18.9
Washington	17.5	19.9	21.9	22.3
Oregon	19.4	22.6	24.0	24.4
California	14.3	16.4	17.9	17.9
United States	19.5	21.6	23.4	24.5

ness with which the shift must be made; and third, there are the emerging next steps which must be taken in order to meet the crisis. The size of the problem may be seen by anticipating the nature of the dilemma in which half of the people of the Southeast, who now depend for their cash income upon cotton and its related economies, will find some sort of readjustment necessary. This readjustment will apply to ginning, manufacturing, marketing, merchandising, as well as farming. Of the farm families thus dependent more than half are tenants who have not means of their own for making a transition. Furthermore, the present cotton crop involves the use of more than half of all crop lands in the region, and the ratio of most of the other farm commodities produced is very small, requiring almost complete re-regimentation of millions of people. The dilemma of such a quick-changing economy may be imagined by comparing the situation with similar historic changes which have required several centuries to make such a shift. Yet a part of the dilemma of the Southeast must be charged to the cumulative complexities of the two other recent quick shifts; namely, from slave to free labor, from agriculture to industry.

264. The key to this regional reconstruction appears to be a straightaway planning for a new diversity in both crops and types of farming; a new quality both in amounts of production and in types of commodities; and within these bounds a literally unrestricted production, gauged for a period of twelve years to new reaches in basic regional consumer's power. This means that, in order to make the transition more gradual, home consumption of better quality cotton produced at a lower cost must be one objective alongside the planning for substitution and diversification. Specifications for the needed readjustment inhere in detailed plans themselves, yet enough of specific information is at hand to indicate a practical interrelation of sufficient fundamental factors to insure concreteness and stability of results. Thus, there must be changed in the Southeast an economy which produces too much of cotton, a commodity of which there is too much, and too little of commodities of which there is too little in the region. In such a changed economy one strategy is to reduce the cost of cotton production by planting a much smaller acreage of continuously enriched land, adjusted to other crops for feed and food and for land improvement. In this way only can the marginal amount of cotton needed be produced on an adequate living standard in competition with foreign production. This means a readjusted standard of diet and of farm and home regimen, geared to a higher standard of living. It means a readjusted seasonal occupational management and redirected programs of work in food and feed harvesting, processing, storing, and marketing. It means in aggregate a shifting from the southeastern

Average Value Per Farm of Domestic Animals, 1930

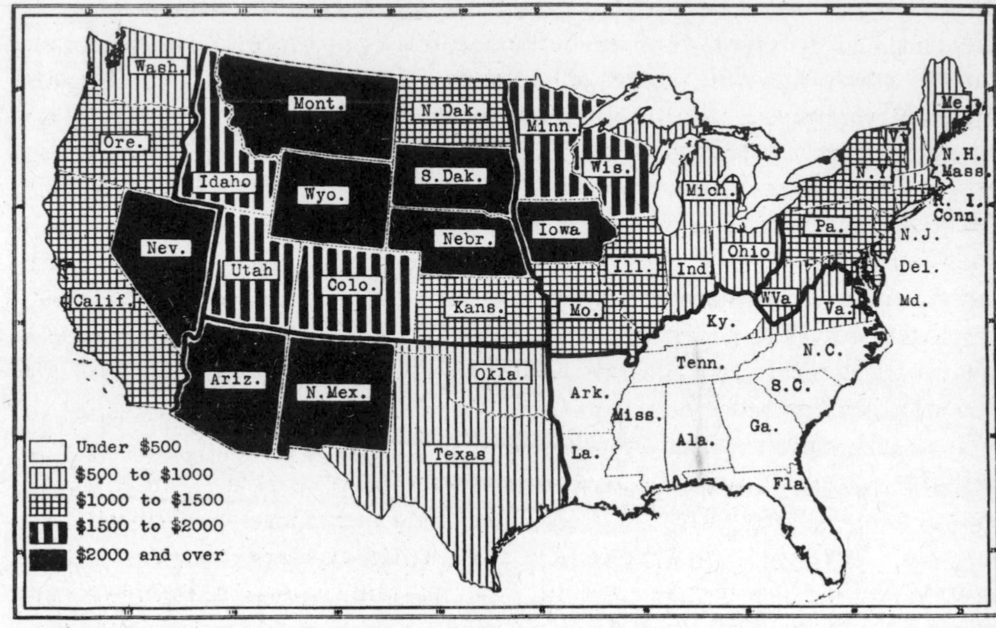

Purebred Cattle by Regions and Per Capita Rural Population, 1929

REGION	Total Farms in Region	No. Farms Reporting	Per Cent Total Farms Reporting	Total No. Cattle in Region	Rural Population 1930	Cattle per Capita
Southeast	2,397,776	37,754	1.57	8,360,888	17,934,067	.4
Southwest	744,932	29,986	4.02	10,455,724	5,611,944	1.9
Northeast	616,079	65,073	10.56	6,095,724	9,730,000	.6
Middle States	1,622,625	167,844	10.34	20,710,226	13,070,509	1.5
Northwest	648,927	75,199	11.59	14,436,139	4,757,557	3.0
Far West	266,175	17,839	6.70	3,839,574	2,716,146	1.4
United States	6,296,514	393,695	6.25	63,898,275	53,820,223	1.2

Per Cent Total Number Farm Animals in Each Region, 1932

Classification	Southeast	Southwest	Northeast	Middle States	Northwest	Far West
Sheep and lambs	4.2	21.7	3.5	17.3	38.4	14.9
Milk cows and heifers	15.7	8.7	15.0	40.8	14.8	5.0
Mules and mule colts	52.4	25.2	2.1	12.7	6.1	1.5
Chickens*	17.6	8.7	13.0	39.7	14.4	6.6
All cattle and calves	13.1	16.5	8.9	32.2	23.5	5.8
Hogs, including pigs	15.5	5.7	2.6	52.7	21.5	2.0
Horses and horse colts	8.8	10.7	8.0	38.8	29.3	4.4

See also maps and tables in Chapter VI.

single cash crop, fertilizer-land-washing and bleaching economy to livestock and rotation.

265. Of special importance is a strategy which will take advantage of the southern differentials in favor of many special crops, such as forestry and forestry products; of new sugar canes and sorghums; of lespedezas and the other legumes; of peanuts and pecans; of sweet potatoes and special vegetables; of figs and grapes and other fruits; of climate and man power; of flora and fauna extraordinary; and of agricultural chemistry peculiarly adapted to the region. But most of all it means land ownership for hundreds of thousands of tenant farmers through definitely planned state-federal-county programs of cooperative organization and agencies, and in particular for the development of adequate rural credits. This involves special state rural rehabilitation corporations with adequate provisions and power to start at the "bottom".

266. Such a revitalized economy would mould a new setting for an extraordinary expansion of new smaller industries and markets at least for a period of years. Crop seeds adequately processed are needed by the million bushels; oats and peas and potatoes and corn; pounds upon pounds of grass seeds for the remaking of the landscape; storage and marketing centers for various commodities; creosoting and processing plants for a million poles for rural electrification and other millions of fence posts; concrete and lime for farm and road equipment; (limestone and new technics of fertilizer production;) wire fencing and paint; wood-pulp products and farm chemical industries; other chemical products; wild-game breeding; botanical and biological specialization; landscaping and gardening; many border projects between farm and factory, in addition to another catalogue of possible new industries or new arrangements in special industrial activities or in the field of coal and iron and power.

267. A catalogue of measurable deficiencies indicates that new markets likewise are almost unlimited for a period of years: cotton goods, enough to run all the mills if only tenant and farmer could buy an extra pair of overalls or socks and women folk could venture a half of what they need in personal apparel and household goods; of feedstuffs, hay and corn and wheat, the farmer needs four times what he has; of food, almost everything is short—cheese by the million pounds, butter, milk, eggs, pork products, basic to home consumption; and of outside imports from the regions, clothes and shoes and equipment for home and farm and factory. Yet, for the Southeast to import corn from Mexico, rutabagas and paper pulp from Canada, and meats from South America, reflects the *nth* degree of unplanned economy which results in incredible everyday scarcity of what could

WAGES IN MANUFACTURING INDUSTRIES OF THE UNITED STATES, 1929

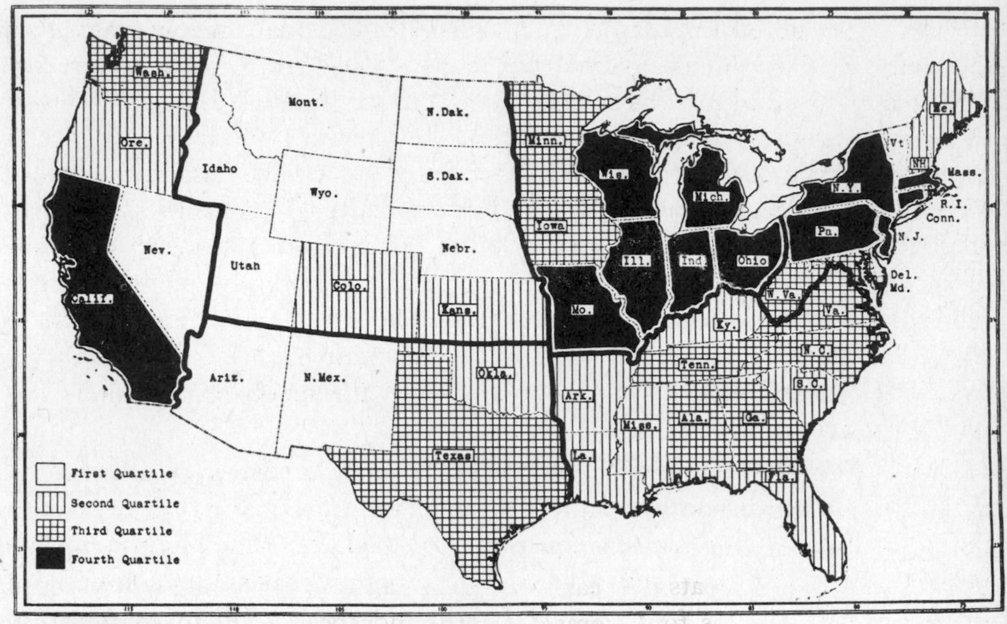

MANUFACTURING INDUSTRIES OF THE UNITED STATES, 1929

STATE	Wages Paid (000 Omitted)	Value of Products (000 Omitted)	Value Added by Manufacture (000 Omitted)
Southeast	$ 983,443	$ 6,237,292	$ 2,890,371
Virginia	116,847	727,606	368,857
North Carolina	159,795	1,301,319	687,179
South Carolina	73,232	385,339	158,236
Georgia	109,552	718,603	288,576
Florida	54,662	232,912	135,810
Kentucky	87,518	490,492	227,935
Tennessee	114,078	706,054	318,433
Alabama	102,040	560,975	261,456
Mississippi	42,508	220,209	107,116
Arkansas	39,221	208,897	93,867
Louisiana	83,990	684,886	242,906
Southwest	209,328	2,123,094	668,430
Oklahoma	40,722	452,161	145,171
Texas	147,888	1,449,802	451,870
New Mexico	5,640	21,760	11,275
Arizona	15,078	199,371	60,114
Northeast	5,322,579	29,581,391	14,341,741
Maine	73,601	392,096	173,111
New Hampshire	70,107	331,366	145,990
Vermont	34,035	144,156	77,633
Massachusetts	695,351	3,392,149	1,706,564
Rhode Island	142,341	664,216	322,138
Connecticut	329,657	1,495,635	828,502
New York	1,651,134	9,979,959	4,961,727
New Jersey	628,098	3,937,656	1,809,488
Delaware	28,847	146,856	69,805
Pennsylvania	1,390,782	7,387,857	3,387,183
Maryland	149,051	1,120,409	560,226
Dist. of Columbia	15,444	88,643	52,590
West Virginia	114,131	500,393	246,784
Middle States	$ 4,223,457	$25,516,819	$ 11,324,797
Ohio	1,103,939	5,999,124	2,871,956
Indiana	416,714	2,534,717	1,129,851
Illinois	1,038,833	6,232,438	2,830,843
Michigan	838,242	4,636,361	2,057,543
Wisconsin	352,814	2,158,400	953,261
Minnesota	130,950	1,171,710	402,233
Iowa	103,532	907,929	327,938
Missouri	238,433	1,876,140	751,172
Northwest	240,972	2,334,584	680,523
North Dakota	5,688	55,347	15,655
South Dakota	8,086	97,769	22,602
Nebraska	36,883	484,263	119,957
Kansas	72,628	734,919	190,909
Montana	21,719	247,953	74,358
Idaho	22,468	96,683	44,552
Wyoming	10,306	96,466	32,950
Colorado	43,429	304,655	122,202
Utah	19,765	216,529	57,338
Far West	669,761	4,344,277	1,938,061
Nevada	3,585	33,717	19,821
Washington	160,514	794,143	367,300
Oregon	86,865	412,331	206,783
California	418,797	3,104,086	1,344,157
United States	11,649,537	70,137,459	31,843,926

abound without limit. There is no way to supply these needs except through a bold declaration of war against the present extraordinary scarcity accompanied by a strategy that is not afraid of abundance.

268. Further evidence of the opportunity for expanded production and consumption is found in the catalogue of manufacturing establishments in the Southeast. And while well balanced planning programs project no great industrial development over and above natural needs and capacities, any reasonable inventory shows marked deficiency in certain industries where there should clearly be greater participation if not leadership. Thus, in the whole Southeast there are only 45 manufacturing establishments for cheese production out of 2,758 for the nation, or less than 2 per cent; for butter there are only 166 out of 3,527. Of 29 food industries catalogued there are 13 in which the Southeast might excel, yet in which at the present time there can be found scarcely 5 per cent of the aggregate. Even in textiles the Southeast has only 6.8 per cent of the total. Other examples include paper and allied products with only 5.3 per cent; printing and publishing, 9.5; chemical products, 16.2; products of petroleum and coal, 11.6; leather, 3.6; stone, clay, and glass products, 11.1; iron and steel, 4.6; and of 1,636 cigar and cigarette manufactures the Southeast has only 153. Yet an increase in these fields might be undesirable without the requisite planning for a richer agriculture and farm purchasing power, and for natural increase in regional consumer's power over and above the mere surplus existing in other regions.

269. Alongside this reconstruction of agriculture and industry and markets must go coordinate efforts for the development and training of the people for better work and better pay. There is needed not only an abundant labor supply, but there must be developed in both races the skills and quality of workers necessary to meet the needs of competitive industry. This means new standards of training, of work, of wages, of hours, rather than cheap labor. The Southeast, if it thus develops its people, can provide also a surplus of workers adequate to meet any shortage which may arise from limited immigration. In this way, too, alongside other means, the region can reduce its marginal and submarginal folk, plan wisely the redistribution of its rural population, and direct its public welfare programs, looking toward balanced rates of increase. In such programs may be found also new approaches to the better adjustment of its dual Negro and white population problem.

270. Planning strategy in the field of cultural relations appears to require two major approaches. One relates to the population and one to cultural institutions. With reference to population one basic factor is found in the large number of people, their high rate of increase, and their uneven

ACCREDITED COLLEGES AND UNIVERSITIES, 1929-1930

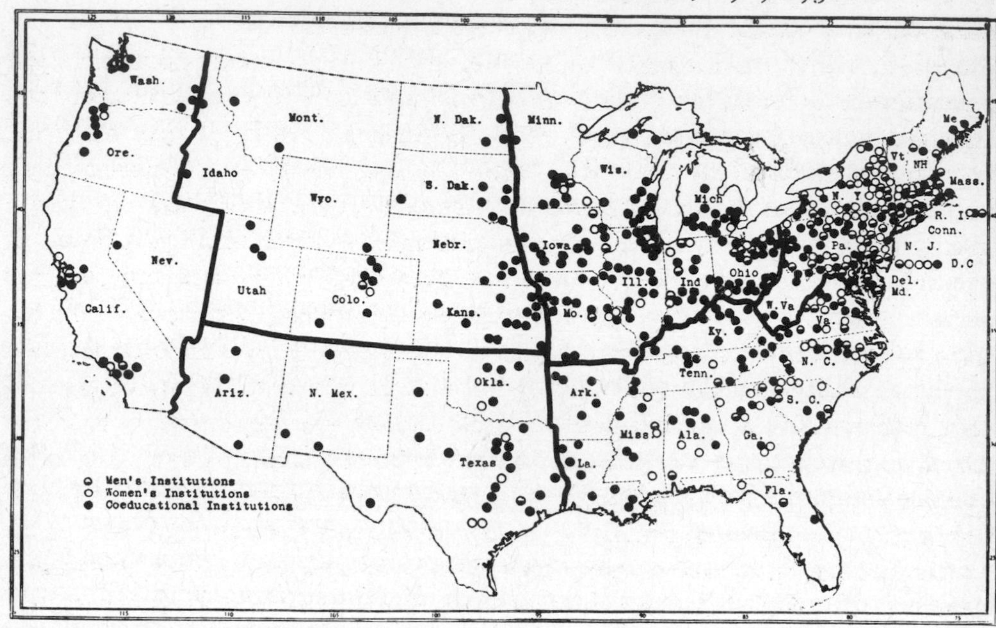

ACCREDITED DENOMINATIONAL COLLEGES AND UNIVERSITIES, 1929-1930

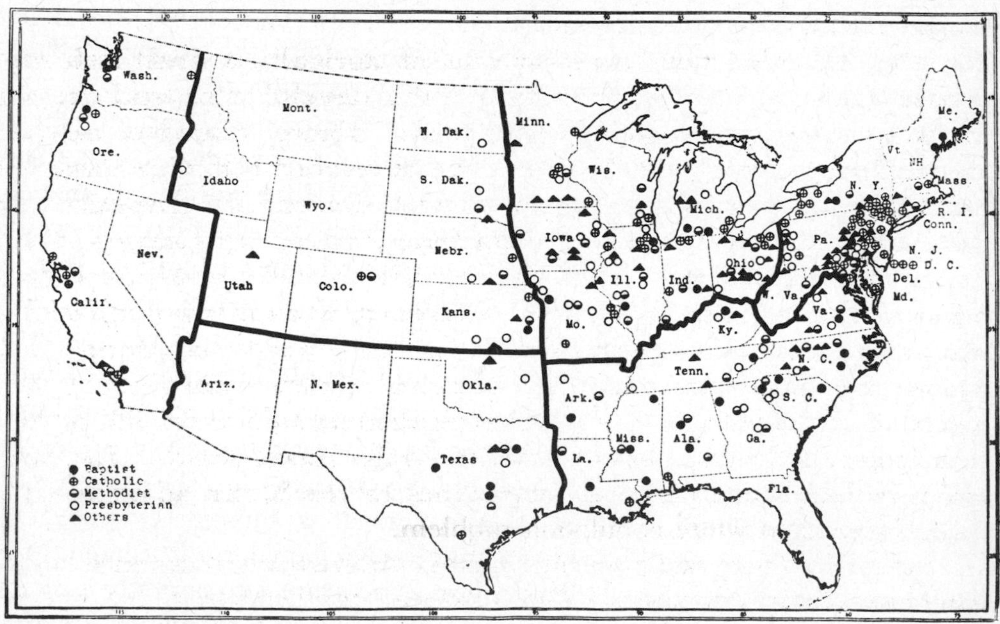

geographic and occupational distribution. The other relates to the human waste involved in ignorance and lack of equipment for which institutions must be developed. Such institutions cannot be developed without special planning, which will involve: the concentration in a few subregions of educational and research centers of the first rank; providing funds for such regional centers over a period of years sufficiently long to insure the necessary momentum; planning these regional concentrations to comprehend the necessary fields of technology and general educational leadership; and providing for a revitalized adult education program capable of interpreting the newer social developments basic to social needs. Specifications for all of these activities can be set up on the basis of present information and trends.

271. A number of requisites appear to be basic to next steps, in addition to the actualities already cited. The first is a considerable amount of further research into a limited number of fields, some of which have been cited. Of very special significance is the opportunity for unprecedented agricultural research as well as extraordinary demands for research in the basic sciences. The fields include, further, population, marginal and submarginal land and people, theory and instrumentation for optimum programs of production, the general but critical problem of reintegrating agrarian culture in the life of the people. The second requisite is to project actual experimentation in selected areas, testing both facts and hypotheses and utilizing the vast amount of facts and experience, cumulated from recent years' work. The third requirement is to work out increasingly effective plans for states' relations, interregional equilibrium, and federal participation and cooperation in all regional developments and readjustment.

272. These general requirements apply to both specific and to general comprehensive programs, which may be expanded to provide for as many fields of effort, projected in as many ways and time periods as may be best suited to each state. Thus the field of educational planning would comprehend, in addition to the major fields of higher education, that of elementary, secondary, and adult education, within which fields Negro education will require special planning. Rural electrification and soil erosion service supplying services to millions of people in every part of the countryside, and adding millions of dollars in value, could be planned on a fraction of the billions of dollars which the engineers propose to utilize for an incredibly big national playhouse of federal dams for specialized purposes. Another small fraction of the stupendous amounts proposed for forced public works would, through state and regional rural rehabilitation programs, reconstruct the whole southern agriculture into not only a reintegrated agrarian culture but into a wealth and revenue producing economy such as has been demonstrated as possible in tobacco and cotton culture

Percentage Distribution of Total Taxes and Appropriations Applied to Education Among Various Types of Educational Institutions, 1929-30

STATE AND REGION	Elementary and Secondary Education	Teachers Colleges and Normal Schools	Universities Colleges and Professional Schools	STATE AND REGION	Elementary and Secondary Education	Teachers Colleges and Normal Schools	Universities Colleges and Professional Schools
Southeast	*90.3*	*2.0*	*7.7*	*Middle States*	*91.8*	*1.8*	*6.4*
Virginia	90.5	2.1	7.4	Ohio	94.3	0.6	5.1
North Carolina	93.2	1.0	5.8	Indiana	94.3	0.9	4.8
South Carolina	87.0	.7	12.3	Illinois	91.7	2.0	6.3
Georgia	90.1	1.7	8.2	Michigan	90.6	2.5	6.9
Florida	90.8	0.0	9.2	Wisconsin	88.0	4.1	7.9
Kentucky	87.7	5.6	6.7	Minnesota	88.3	1.7	10.0
Tennessee	91.0	3.3	5.7	Iowa	89.7	1.2	9.1
Alabama	88.3	2.6	9.1	Missouri	93.2	2.8	4.0
Mississippi	92.2	1.6	6.2	*Northwest*	*89.5*	*2.5*	*8.0*
Arkansas	87.7	1.5	10.8	North Dakota	85.5	3.9	10.6
Louisiana	91.6	1.7	6.7	South Dakota	90.9	2.8	6.3
Southwest	*88.5*	*3.3*	*8.2*	Nebraska	88.7	3.1	8.2
Oklahoma	86.5	4.0	9.5	Kansas	89.5	2.3	8.2
Texas	89.4	2.9	7.7	Montana	91.8	1.6	6.6
New Mexico	88.7	3.4	7.9	Idaho	88.5	4.3	7.2
Arizona	89.2	3.4	7.4	Wyoming	95.3	0.0	4.7
Northeast	*97.0*	*1.3*	*1.7*	Colorado	88.5	2.5	9.0
Maine	91.5	2.1	6.4	Utah	92.3	0.0	7.7
New Hampshire	91.9	2.4	5.7	*Far West*	*90.3*	*1.6*	*8.1*
Vermont	95.2	1.0	3.8	Nevada	88.9	0.0	11.1
Massachusetts	97.2	1.4	1.4	Washington	87.5	2.5	10.0
Rhode Island	97.2	1.1	1.7	Oregon	83.6	1.6	14.8
Connecticut	97.0	1.7	1.3	California	92.2	1.4	6.4
New York	97.5	.7	1.8	United States	93.1	1.8	5.1
New Jersey	98.7	1.2	.1				
Delaware	95.6	0.0	4.4				
Pennsylvania	96.7	2.3	1.0				
Maryland	95.0	1.8	3.2				
West Virginia	91.1	2.8	6.1				

Relative Proportion of Total State and Local Tax Collections Applied to Education, 1929-1930

STATE AND REGION	Total State and Local Tax Collections (000 omitted)	Total Taxes and Appropriations applied to Education (000 omitted)	Ratio of Taxes for Education to Total State and Local Taxes (000 omitted)	STATE AND REGION	Total State and Local Tax Collections (000 omitted)	Total Taxes and Appropriations applied to Education (000 omitted)	Ratio of Taxes for Education to Total State and Local Taxes (000 omitted)
Southeast	*777,842*	*214,105*	*27.5*	*Middle States*	*1,963,861*	*569,864*	*29.0*
Virginia	79,371	20,871	26.3	Ohio	383,820	133,963	34.9
North Carolina	101,754	33,525	32.9	Indiana	194,399	78,508	40.4
South Carolina	47,653	13,947	29.3	Illinois	411,770	73,601	17.9
Georgia	66,794	17,315	25.9	Michigan	342,584	99,056	28.9
Florida	86,684	20,234	23.3	Wisconsin	184,121	45,415	24.7
Kentucky	83,402	20,758	24.9	Minnesota	161,305	43,059	26.7
Tennessee	74,052	21,087	28.5	Iowa	142,136	48,220	33.9
Alabama	54,060	17,945	33.2	Missouri	143,726	48,042	33.4
Mississippi	63,201	18,000	28.5	*Northwest*	*419,799*	*142,956*	*34.1*
Arkansas	44,034	10,924	24.8	North Dakota	35,808	11,548	32.2
Louisiana	76,837	19,499	25.4	South Dakota	43,266	14,403	33.3
Southwest	*342,226*	*107,633*	*31.5*	Nebraska	77,214	22,358	29.0
Oklahoma	94,712	29,741	31.4	Kansas	104,795	35,154	33.5
Texas	205,690	61,346	29.8	Montana	34,368	12,113	35.2
New Mexico	14,928	5,722	38.3	Idaho	25,250	9,246	36.6
Arizona	26,896	10,824	40.2	Wyoming	13,925	4,503	32.3
Northeast	*2,663,428*	*780,943*	*29.3*	Colorado	60,078	22,963	38.2
Maine	44,121	10,677	24.2	Utah	25,095	10,668	42.5
New Hampshire	27,056	6,988	25.8	*Far West*	*601,641*	*147,399*	*24.5*
Vermont	19,379	4,906	25.3	Nevada	7,541	2,228	29.5
Massachusetts	323,175	85,521	26.5	Washington	94,130	26,584	28.2
Rhode Island	39,305	13,879	35.3	Oregon	65,980	15,084	22.9
Connecticut	104,286	31,283	30.0	California	433,990	103,503	23.8
New York	1,140,986	309,180	27.1	United States	6,768,797	1,962,900	29.1
New Jersey	328,689	99,934	30.4				
Delaware	18,028	5,035	27.9				
Pennsylvania	471,393	165,219	35.0				
Maryland	75,964	22,172	29.2				
West Virginia	71,046	26,149	36.8				

geared with their manufacture in the same regions. This is in contrast to the specific figures in which nearly $3,000,000,000 is the estimated cost of flood control dams alone in the Southeastern Region where the wealth of soil is not only being wasted but adding to flood hazard; where the hearts and bodies of millions of wealth-making farmers are being broken in poverty-making economy; and where both physical and cultural resources are being warped through temporizing processes which with moderate subsidy and planning can be replaced with permanent measures.

273. Toward the attainment of these ends there must, of course, be practical ways and means such as have been indicated in advisory planning boards and in specific programs of action. Among the first of all practical considerations is the clear recognition of the limitations of all planning programs and the necessity for relativity of both arrangements and results. In a democratic order such programs need to be presented to the people both for their understanding and to the end that during the special periods selected for civic education and planning there may be attempted a sort of moratorium on violent industrial and race conflict. Keeping in mind the realistic nature of prevailing difficulties, the changing fortunes of democratic institutions, the need for flexibility of programs, and the special regional peculiarities of the people, of the land and of problems, it seems likely that the minimum special periods needed for both experimental reference and for actual results should comprehend two six-year priority schedules. Such schedules would be practically geared to state and regional adaptations and would feature not only public works, economic objectives and national resources, but human and cultural factors as well. And although effective planning would provide for flexibility in time sequences as well as in working specifications, it seems possible to set certain goals, to fix certain beginning dates, and to set up continuing priority schedules which contemplate periods of measuring results toward which major efforts are directed. On this basis the first six-year priority schedules would extend from 1936-37-38 to 1942-43-44. Such a period would afford an optimum number of practical factors which might apply to all programs whether of agricultural reconstruction or of institutions of higher learning. Thus from the viewpoint of legislation, there would be from two to three biennial legislative periods for the states, parts of three federal administrations at Washington, and a new decennial period. In agriculture, land utilization, and forestry there would be suitable periods for crop rotation, soil erosion service, rural rehabilitation cycles for transfer of tenant to land ownership, and for various experimentation in livestock and seed breeding. In industry, experimentation in part-time industry and farming, in small new industries, in training and apprenticing workers for both old and new skills would

PER CAPITA NET INCOME OF CORPORATIONS, 1928

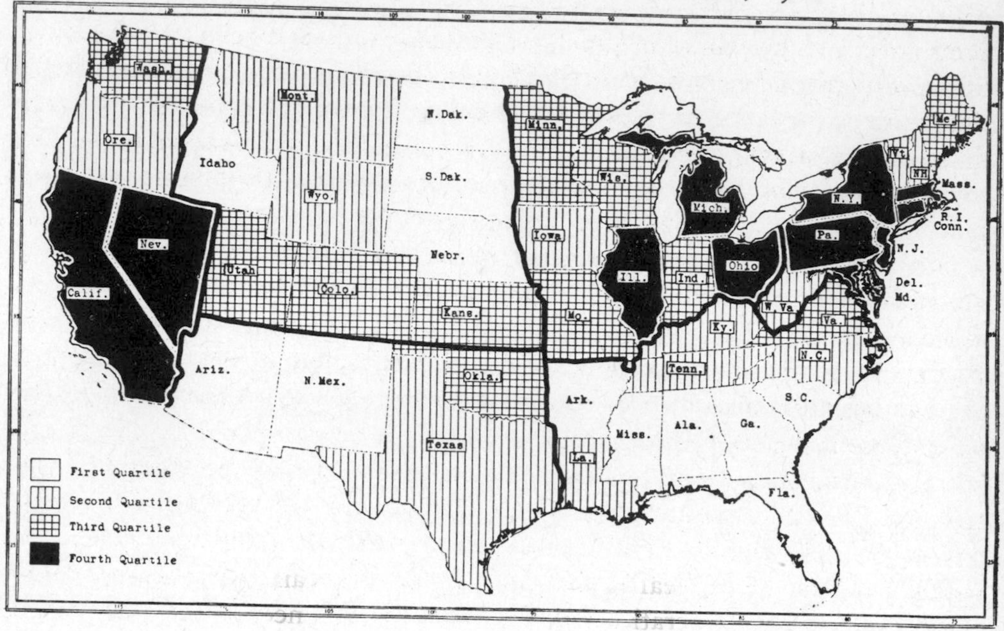

TOTAL PERSONAL INCOME OF THOSE FILING FEDERAL INCOME TAX RETURNS REDUCED TO PER CAPITA OF TOTAL POPULATION, 1928

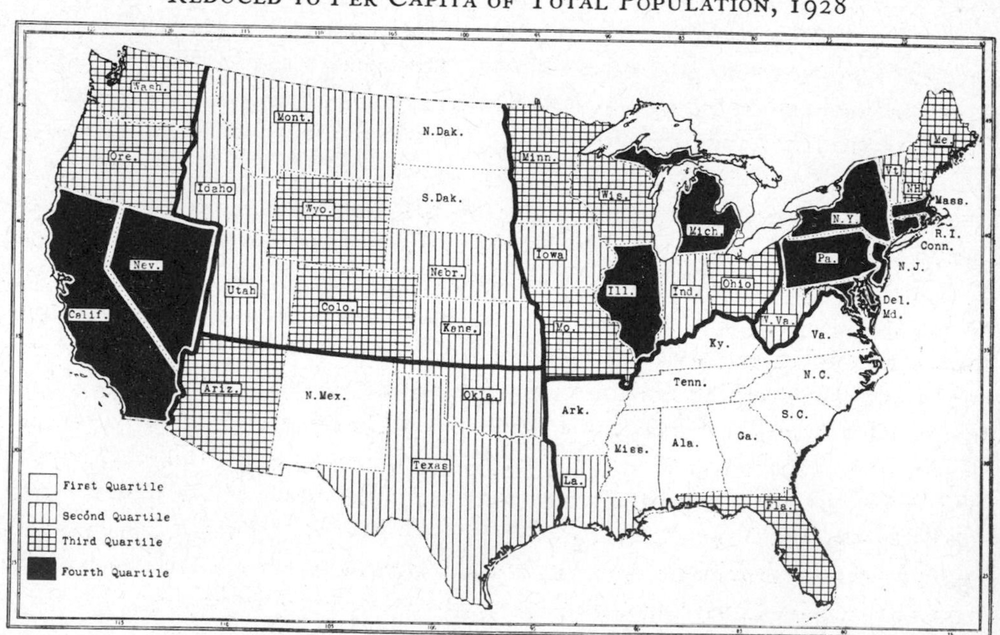

be facilitated. In education new arrangements in high schools and junior colleges, in upper and lower college curricula, in the projecting of research programs, and in the enlarging of endowments could be promoted most effectively through some such time limit, five years being too short and ten years too long for a practical utility period of work. Following the first period would be a second similar six-year priority schedule pointing to the mid-century. Such a schedule would conform to the same general plan as the first but profiting by logical developments and experience. It would focus upon some special motivation preparatory to a mid-century inventory, comprehending a more adequate local, state, regional, and national measurement of all aspects of American life than had yet been undertaken. More specifically, such a period is the minimum time within which the Southeast might attain its early maturity or, failing that, give evidence of what place it will henceforth hold in the nation.

PART II

Thomas Jefferson's Agrarian America

Adapted from the U. S. Bureau of Agricultural Economics

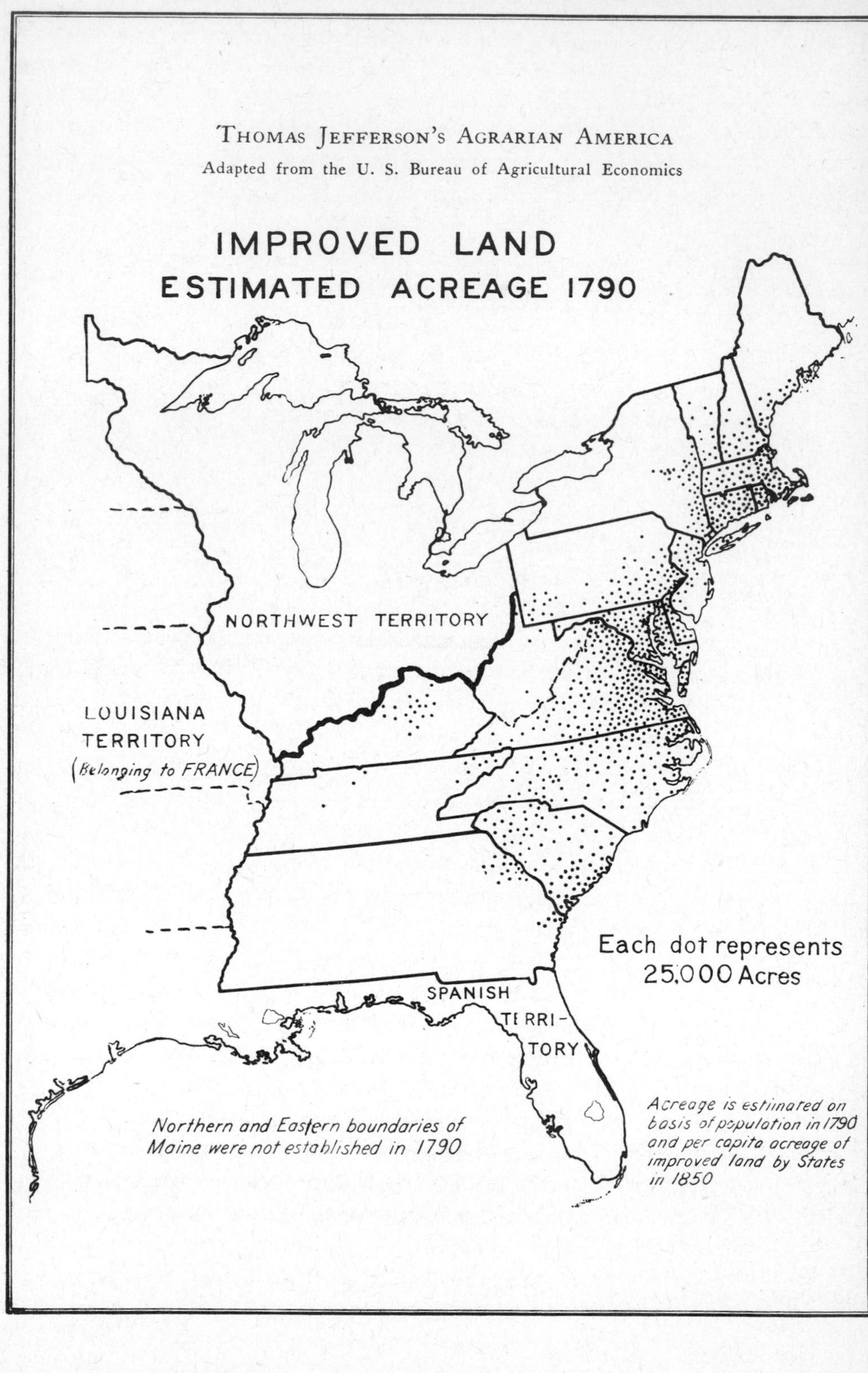

CHAPTER II

A GENERAL MEASURE OF THE SOUTHERN REGIONS

THIS IS A PICTURE of the southern United States of America, formerly designated as "the South," now characterized in this work as southern regions, clearly differentiated into the older Southeast and the emerging new Southwest, together with something of the multiple subregions of each. Its inventory of actualities will indicate the place of these regions in the changing nation and will explain much of the dramatic struggle of a large and powerful segment of the American people for mastery over an environment capable of producing a superior civilization, yet so conditioned by complexity of culture and cumulative handicaps as to make doubtful the nature of their future development. The picture is, however, first of all a part of the total American drama of development and of social and economic reconstruction. Its appraisal and its problems, therefore, must be in terms of national, regional, and interregional concern. If such realistic pictures as may be presented between the covers of the present work are not likely to please either the South or its critics, it should be a reasonable expectation to hope that both will be prepared to face the facts, and, what is more important, to act wisely upon their teachings. These facts in their relational implications and perspective constitute a long story, difficult and complicated in its telling, even as are the regional realities upon which the story must be based.

We begin with the statement of a difficult and comprehensive question. Can the southern regions of the United States, set in the midst of superabundance of nature's wealth, abounding in the other multiple resources of geography, of human stocks, and of American cultural backgrounds, occupying strategic positions within the nation and with reference to the nations of the world, continue to feature deficiency, marginality, and immaturity, framed in isolated sections separate from the rest of the nation, except as a peculiar phenomenon of cultural pathology? Such a query, however, no matter how challenging or dramatic it may be made to appear, has little meaning except as it can be approximately answered in terms of realistic inventory of fact and of the actualities of what is to be done. The time has come to follow up the earlier broadsides and critical

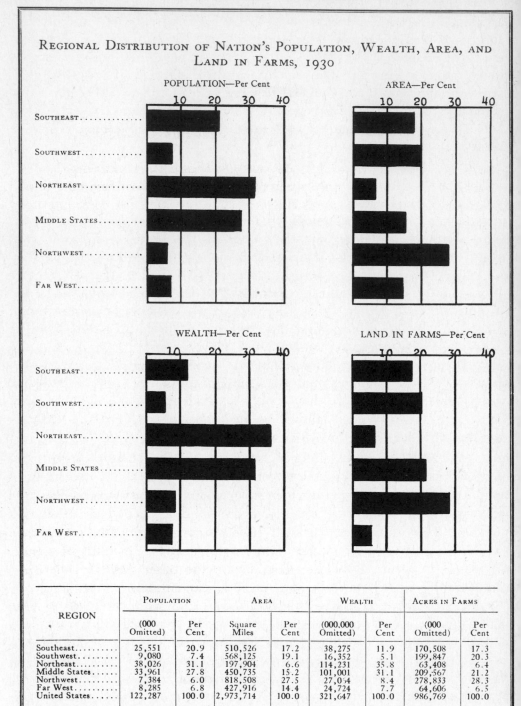

REGIONAL DISTRIBUTION OF NATION'S POPULATION, WEALTH, AREA, AND LAND IN FARMS, 1930

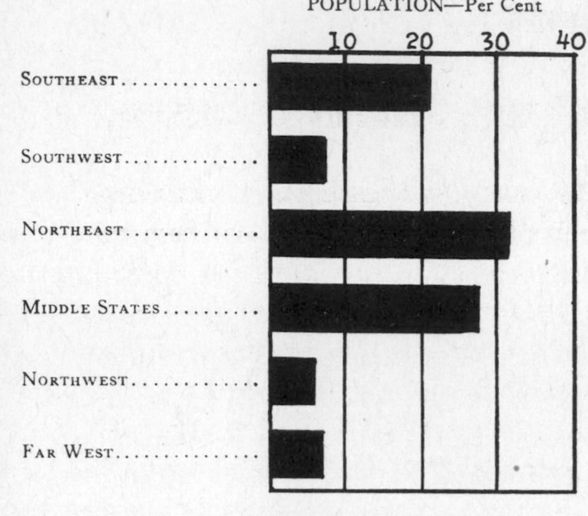

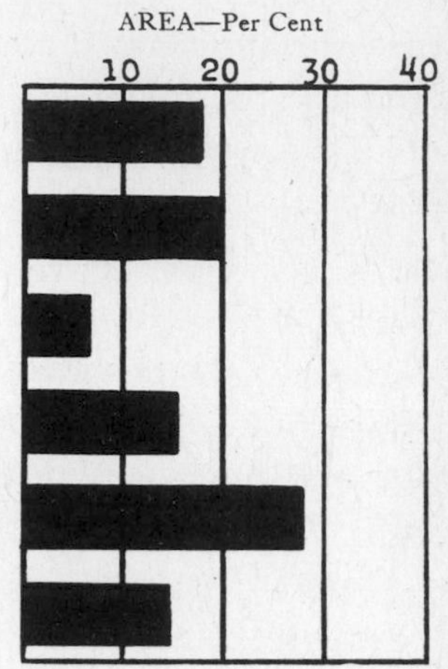

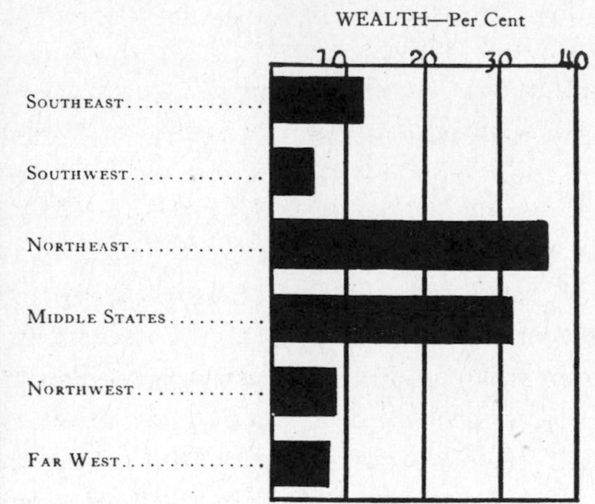

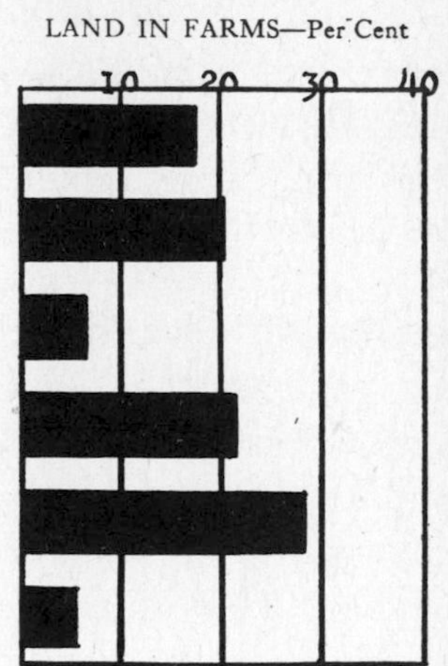

REGION	POPULATION		AREA		WEALTH		ACRES IN FARMS	
	(000 Omitted)	Per Cent	Square Miles	Per Cent	(000,000 Omitted)	Per Cent	(000 Omitted)	Per Cent
Southeast	25,551	20.9	510,526	17.2	38,275	11.9	170,508	17.3
Southwest	9,080	7.4	568,125	19.1	16,352	5.1	199,847	20.3
Northeast	38,026	31.1	197,904	6.6	114,231	35.8	63,408	6.4
Middle States	33,961	27.8	450,735	15.2	101,001	31.1	209,567	21.2
Northwest	7,384	6.0	818,508	27.5	27,064	8.4	278,833	28.3
Far West	8,285	6.8	427,916	14.4	24,724	7.7	64,606	6.5
United States	122,287	100.0	2,973,714	100.0	321,647	100.0	986,769	100.0

appraisals of southern culture with something more nearly approaching functional analysis and working specifications. Basic to such an objective are three essentials. The first is to understand the realities and the exceedingly complex nature of the regional culture involved. The second is to sense the immensity and the time-quality of cultural reconstruction. The third and the most immediate task is to focus upon a relatively small number of elemental factors toward which practical study and planning may be directed.

"The American South," wrote Sherwood Anderson, "should be America's garden spot. It should be one of the very lovely lands of the world." After the same manner, wrote also a geographer, in those earlier days of transformation when technology was making of the world an open book. The South, he said, was "one of two regions on this earth and only two, which eventually will outdistance all others as to the number of people they will support by agriculture and factory production. . . . Above all the other regions, they are the gardens of the world." So Walter Lippmann, in the middle 1920's, wrote that many observers were of the opinion that "nothing, since the opening of the West, has so great a meaning to the future of America as the profound transformation which is now taking place in the United States. . . . Everything that was ever possible for civilized man is possible here. If the South fails she will have only herself to blame and if she succeeds she will have only herself to thank." And a few years later, at the crest of regional and national achievement he risked the feeling that "the adventure of American life today is in the South."

Yet something was wanting in these enthusiastic verdicts. In the first place, the evidence would seem to indicate the inability of the southern regions to develop their capacities independent of resources, coöperative effort, and conditioning attitudes of other regions and of the nation as a whole. The South, when it shall have succeeded, will have more than itself to thank, and if it fails, unfortunately more than itself to blame. In the next place, it was not possible longer to characterize the region merely in terms of "the South" or of isolated totality of resources, or to explain it in terms of one or two or three forces, such as geography, climate, slavery, cotton, tariff, or even the range of natural and human resources. For, in the next place, the measure of achievement must be found in the gearing together of cultural and technical resources with natural wealth. And here the picture was complete only when, to the superabundance of its endowment, were added the inventory of its deficiencies. Among these were the necessary initial leverage of invested capital and technology and the cultural handicaps reflected in social waste, in fear

PER CAPITA TOTAL FEDERAL AID TO STATES, 1930

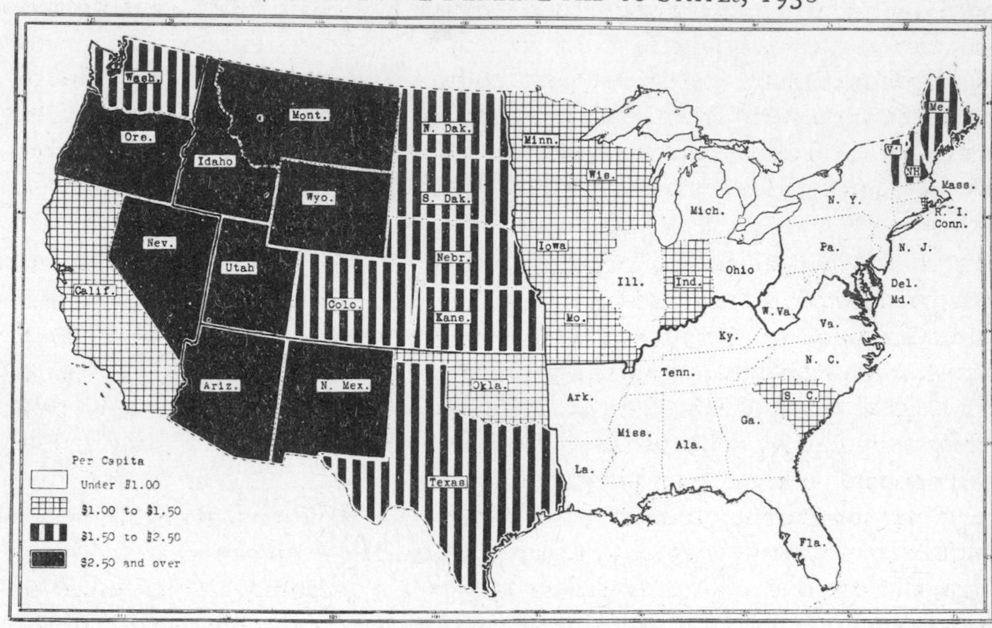

NET INDEBTEDNESS OF STATE GOVERNMENTS, PER CAPITA OF TOTAL POPULATION, 1930

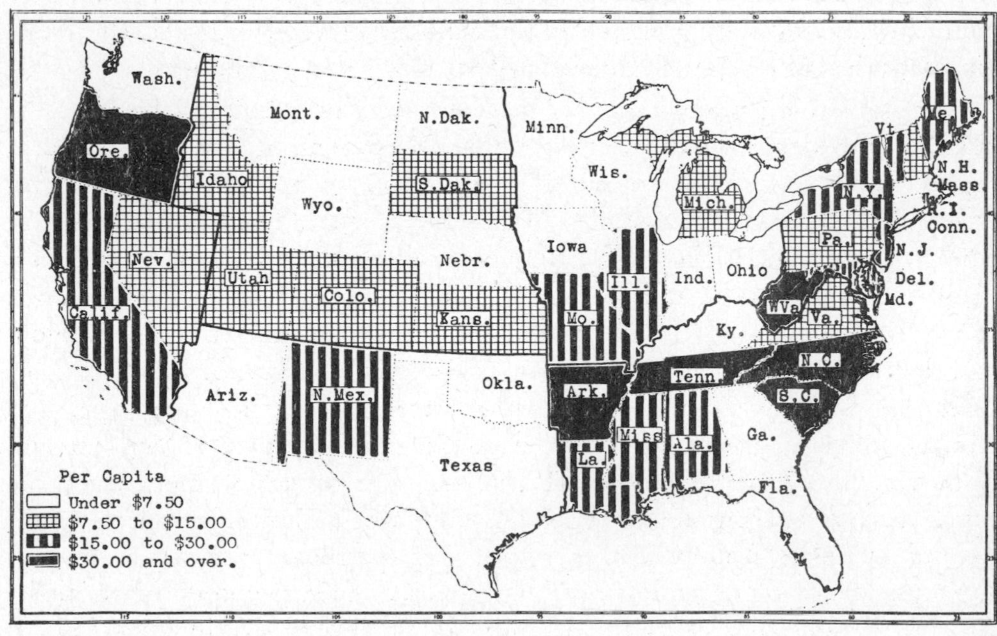

and race conflict, in superficial standards of work and leisure, in political patterns, and in numerous and varied manifestations of submarginality and lack of social equilibrium.

Here, then, was at once southern picture and national prospect. Here was challenge and promise for the enrichment of the national culture in the next American epoch through the development of regional empires which, while capable of making a very great contribution, also revealed the capacity for augmenting conflict and drain. For there was, moreover, not one empire, but two, a vast *Southeast* and another vast *Southwest* both of which, while differing from each other in the aggregate of economic and cultural indices, reflected certain general characteristics more in common with each other than with the other regions of the nation.

That there was, therefore, no more important or difficult task, no more dramatic phase of American life, before the people of the United States than the adequate readjustment of the nation's southern regions to the new America had been the assumption underlying a decade of special southern regional study begun at Chapel Hill in the early 1920's. There was abundant evidence to indicate that these Southern States, because of their incredibly rich resources, were capable of almost unlimited development provided they could eliminate the stupendous economic and social waste which kept them drained to poverty levels; could develop adequate technology for the utilization of physical wealth; could provide adequate education and cultural institutions for the enrichment of human life; and could face more realistically and maturely than they had yet done the fact and action requirements necessary for these attainments. These tasks had not yet been accomplished with either sufficient zeal or skill. On the other hand, the southern regions, on the threshold of great promise, and having made tremendous strides forward, were by the late 1920's apparently unable to hold the position that they had gained with so much difficulty. There were also unmistakable signs of a revivification of sectional conflicts, constituting one of the most interesting phenomena of American culture.

There was evidence to indicate that much of the South was again veering rightward toward the old type of state and sectional mindedness, wistful of its own peculiar civilization limited by geographical and traditional boundaries rather than seeking to develop a richer regional culture, merged into the national picture, but gaining strength from its normal regional advantages. There were also hidden evidences in certain peculiar sectional phenomena of possible trends, now toward unsuspected fascistic principles and now symptomatic of revolution. For instance, before Hitler's Nazi Germany, parts of the South were revivifying an emotional culture through attack upon universities and intellectual life; through reli-

Population Per Square Mile, 1930

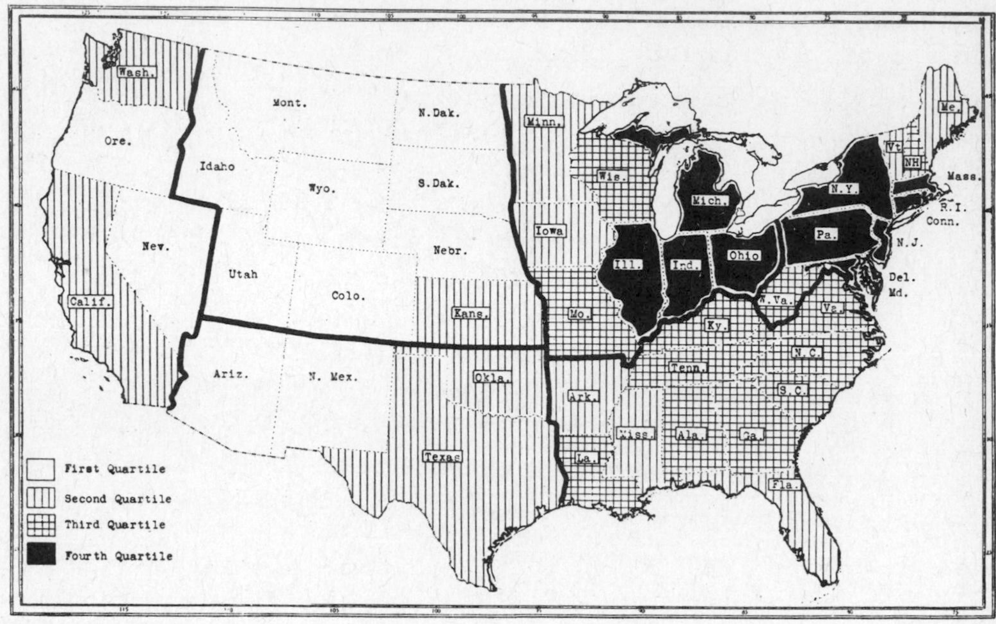

Area and Population of States Per Unit of Local Government, 1930

Adapted from William Anderson, *Units of Government in the United States*

STATE AND REGION	Number of Local Units	Area per Local Unit in Square Miles	Population per Local Unit
Southeast	*20,191*	*25.28*	*1,255.55*
Virginia	317	127.00	7,639.00
North Carolina	2,008	24.27	1,578.82
South Carolina	2,116	14.41	821.72
Georgia	754	77.88	3,857.43
Florida	1,456	37.67	1,008.38
Kentucky	898	44.74	2,911.56
Tennessee	536	77.77	4,881.63
Alabama	475	107.90	5,571.00
Mississippi	6,639	6.98	302.72
Arkansas	4,491	11.69	412.93
Louisiana	501	90.63	4,194.79
Southwest	*15,875*	*35.79*	*571.95*
Oklahoma	6,430	10.79	372.63
Texas	8,676	30.24	671.35
New Mexico	195	628.22	2,170.85
Arizona	574	198.27	758.83
Northeast	*21,574*	*9.19*	*1,762.59*
Maine	562	53.19	1,418.90
New Hampshire	489	18.46	951.51
Vermont	626	14.57	574.75
Massachusetts	431	18.65	9,859.89
Rhode Island	93	11.47	7,392.44
Connecticut	355	13.57	4,526.48
New York	11,184	4.26	1,125.54
New Jersey	1,149	6.53	3,517.26
Delaware	268	7.33	889.47
Pennsylvania	5,583	8.03	1,725.12
Maryland	161	61.74	10,133.70
West Virginia	673	35.69	2,569.39

STATE AND REGION	Number of Local Units	Area per Local Unit in Square Miles	Population per Local Unit
Middle States	*71,987*	*6.26*	*471.77*
Ohio	4,487	9.07	1,481.32
Indiana	1,830	19.69	1,769.67
Illinois	17,336	3.23	440.16
Michigan	8,905	6.45	543.77
Wisconsin	9,762	5.66	301.06
Minnesota	10,544	7.66	243.16
Iowa	7,497	7.41	329.59
Missouri	11,626	5.91	312.17
Northwest	*36,177*	*22.62*	*201.24*
North Dakota	4,080	17.20	166.87
South Dakota	4,981	15.43	139.09
Nebraska	8,455	9.08	162.97
Kansas	11,072	7.38	169.88
Montana	2,667	54.79	201.57
Idaho	1,679	49.64	265.05
Wyoming	547	178.33	412.36
Colorado	2,429	42.67	426.42
Utah	267	307.80	1,902.04
Far West	*9,564*	*44.74*	*866.32*
Nevada	364	301.70	250.15
Washington	2,423	27.58	645.23
Oregon	2,500	38.24	381.51
California	4,277	36.39	1,327.39
United States	175,368	16.96	700.17

gious coloring of politics and statescraft; through appeal to sectional patriotism; through intolerance of criticism and opposition; and through continuing emphasis upon racial issues, Nordic superiority, and one hundred per cent Americanism. There was lacking, however, sufficient sectional isolation and strong leadership to furnish good soil for open outbreaks. Dictatorships of demagogues were ample but localized. The seeds of revolution appeared also to be local and scattered, but abundant. They were found in mob action, in class conflict, in mass protests against various activities of government, in conflicting political units of administration, in frontier individualism, and in a considerable volume of radical rumblings under the guise of patriotic protest and traditional loyalties. There had been no inventory of this regional discontent, even as there had been no authentic measure of the South's economic actualities in which, through gradual, inevitable, logical processes, millions of marginal folk, white and black, had in reality no semblance of equality of opportunity or even of living much above the subsistence level.

Of any such verdicts the southern regions were, of course, largely unaware. This was a part of the realism of the situation. Certainly the idea of revolution would be ridiculed. Most of the prominent folk of industry and farm never recognized the poverty and suffering level of the five million tenant folk. "I guess nobody ever starves in the South, anyway"; so quoth the average commentator. There always would be shiftless poor people. There always had been. Most of the people of whatever groups had thought little about ways of improvement, and they took the recommendations of agricultural colleges and of a few leaders as a sort of matter of fact service. Yet here were American regional cultures, vibrant with the emotions and unplanned activities of a great people working heroically to overcome multiple handicaps, conscious of their power, yet also sometimes conscious of their limitations and need of help; now boastful, now discouraged, now troubled, now fretted by the severity of their critics and the handicaps and hazards of their fortunes. It was, all told, a paradoxical South, now single-minded, now of multiple trends, now one South, now many Souths, now rapidly developing, now receding, an eager and a puzzled South trying to take stock of itself and its rôle in the changing nation.

In all these aspects of regional culture it seemed clear that what neither the nation nor the South appeared to comprehend in the practical way was the fact that this was first of all a national problem. That is, the key to the situation was to be found in the phenomenon as a normal problem of complex social development, essentially of American civilization, secondarily of southern culture. The story of both the settlement and evolu-

Chronological and Rural Variations in Natural Population Increase

Number of White Children Under 5 Years of Age to 1,000 White Women 15 to 49 Years of Age, 1800-1930

Adapted from the U. S. Bureau of Agricultural Economics

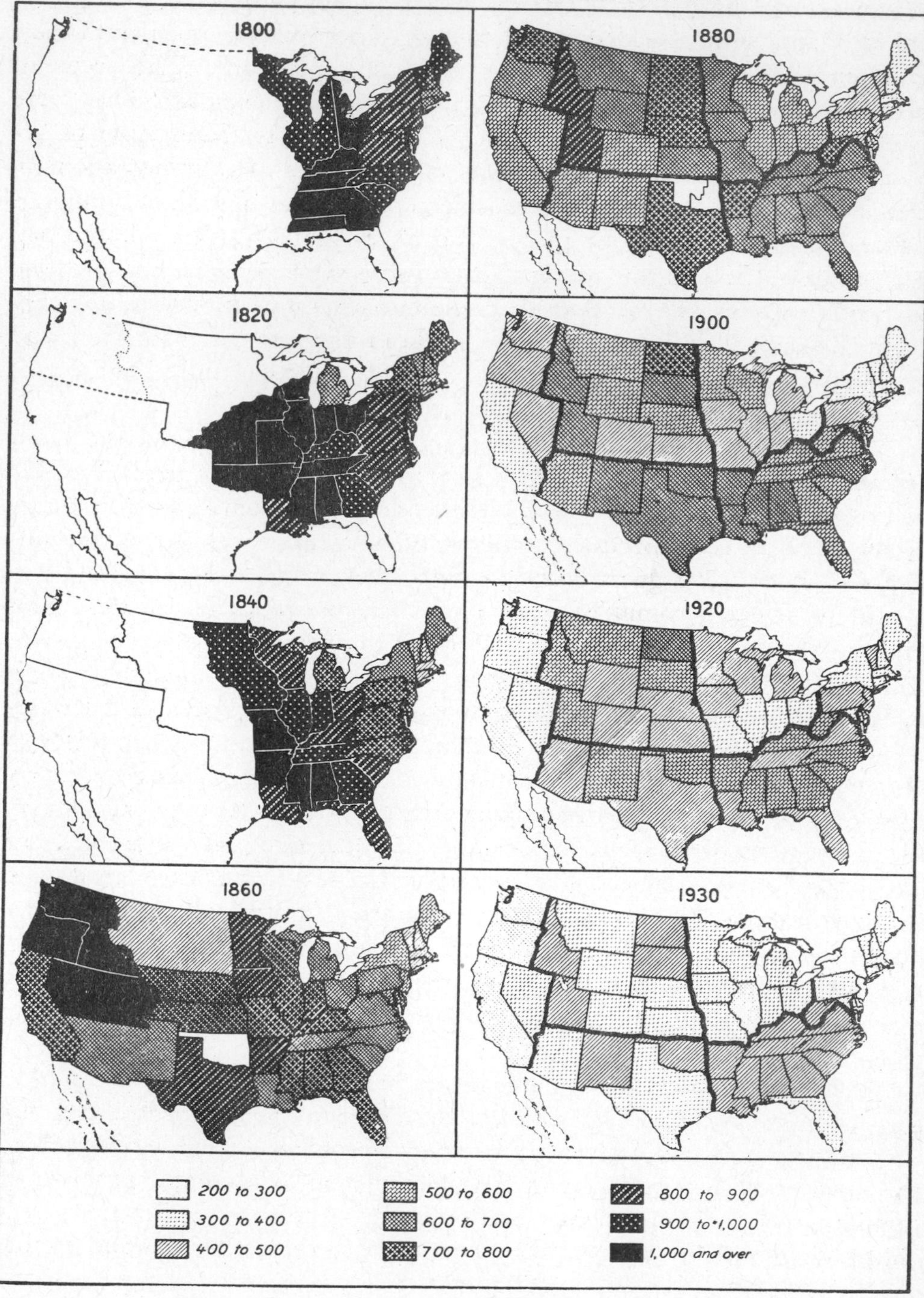

tion of the Southern States and of their subsequent development was first of all an American story. More than that, the epic of how these states came to be what they were in early territorial expansion and divisions, in population and its distribution, in the great range and variety of resources and activities, in the preëminence of economic and social waste, and in their later development into a peculiar culture region, might well be appraised as one of the most dramatic stories, not only of American but of modern civilization. And as for the future, what the South did and how it developed was important to the South, but of much greater significance to the nation—basic contribution to the regional planning of national reconstruction and to the theoretical understanding of a changing nation.

Yet everywhere the tendency persisted to make of the South a single arbitrary sectional issue and to make the regional character of the problem synonymous with the whole complex problem itself. The final result would be inevitable if both the nation and the South insisted on this interpretation and action. The South would be in fact a sectional division of the nation, continuing outmoded sectional conflicts, isolation, deficiency. The South needed to reconstruct its place in the nation by building upon its own physical and cultural resources. The South itself must be largely instrumental in accomplishing this task. Yet the South could not succeed without the liberal and intelligent coöperation and understanding on the part of the other regions of the nation. This the southern regions had not yet gained. Furthermore, there could never be adequate regional development through sectional isolation. The situation was in the way of becoming a crisis for both the South and the nation. Literature and discussions about the South had become extraordinarily voluminous. There was extraordinary range and variety to the southern picture. There was much that was scientific and objective. There was much that was platitudinous, monotonous, featuring flight from reality where achievement was demanded. Perhaps also in both the "North" and "South," there were good reasons for a certain fatigue and impatience with the continuous talk about southern problems. Yet there was still little unity, little integration of effort, little knowledge adequately interpreted in realistic perspective, and practically no approach to orderly research and planning. There was, therefore, need for a much more realistic analysis and synthesis of facts, a more penetrating insight into the total meaning of the situation, and a clearer focusing upon action and planning programs of the future.

So much for the general aspects of earlier hypotheses. This was, in substance, the situation in 1930 when the Southern Regional Study was authorized for the purpose of making available a more synthetic and practical inventory of the South's capacity for development and for larger par-

Rank of States Based on Twenty-three Cultural Tables

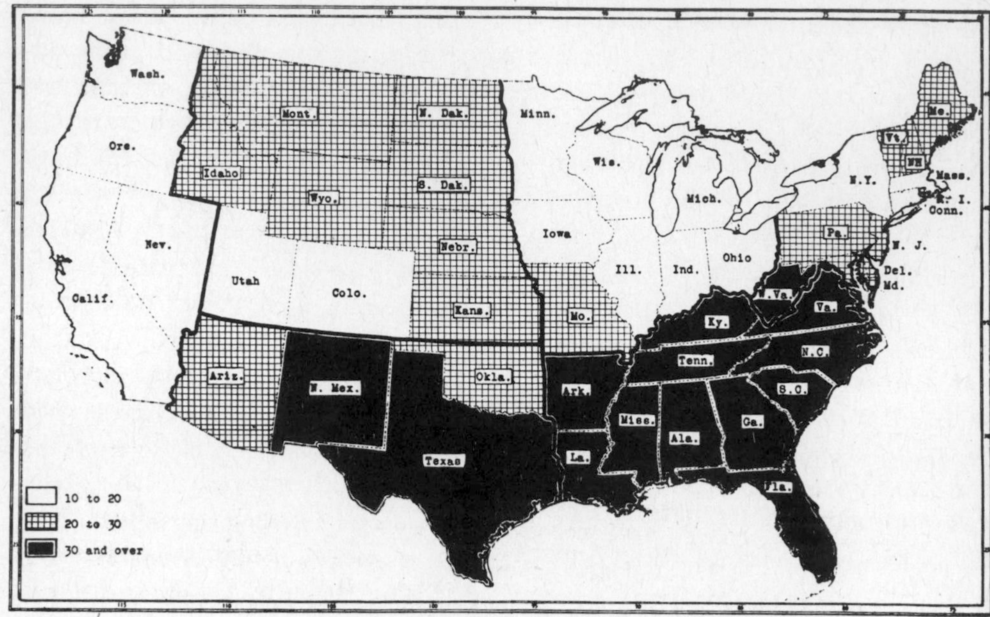

State Quartile Distribution in 152 Cultural Items

STATE AND REGION	Number of Times in Lowest Quartile	Number of Times Outside the Lowest Quartile	Number of Times in the Highest Quartile
Southeast	*89*	*63*	*15*
Virginia	62	90	11
North Carolina	79	73	27
South Carolina	107	45	13
Georgia	114	38	10
Florida	56	96	30
Kentucky	88	64	10
Tennessee	78	74	7
Alabama	104	48	13
Mississippi	104	48	21
Arkansas	111	41	10
Louisiana	76	76	14
Southwest	*45*	*107*	*23*
Oklahoma	39	113	15
Texas	45	107	17
New Mexico	65	87	18
Arizona	30	122	41
Northeast	*24*	*128*	*46*
Maine	31	121	26
New Hampshire	30	122	44
Vermont	28	124	37
Massachusetts	16	136	78
Rhode Island	20	132	51
Connecticut	17	135	72
New York	15	137	70
New Jersey	21	131	61
Delaware	33	119	26
Pennsylvania	12	140	35
Maryland	13	139	32
West Virginia	48	104	19

STATE AND REGION	Number of Times in Lowest Quartile	Number of Times Outside the Lowest Quartile	Number of Times in the Highest Quartile
Middle States	*15*	*137*	*40*
Ohio	13	139	34
Indiana	13	139	24
Illinois	13	139	57
Michigan	8	144	52
Wisconsin	12	140	38
Minnesota	13	139	40
Iowa	23	129	59
Missouri	22	130	17
Northwest	*26*	*126*	*39*
North Dakota	40	112	45
South Dakota	28	124	42
Nebraska	23	129	51
Kansas	15	137	38
Montana	33	119	32
Idaho	34	118	25
Wyoming	24	128	50
Colorado	12	140	34
Utah	23	129	38
Far West	*16*	*136*	*68*
Nevada	24	128	66
Washington	10	142	54
Oregon	13	139	60
California	15	137	93

See representative list of indices on pp. 4, 292, 332, 376, 432, 462, 496. The above table makes no allowance for refined or weighted indices. It represents only a common mode of comparison which indicates in a broad way conventional measures of the contrast between physical resources and cultural reality.

ticipation in the national culture. There is now abundant evidence from this reëxamination of a vast amount of data already available, from more recent special studies of the South's capacity and prospects, and from observations of national and regional recovery measures, to support these hypotheses and to give them and others restatement in more concrete terms. A supporting corollary is that the task of regional reconstruction and readjustment is all the more urgent because the South, now facing its own peculiar crises in the midst of and in relation to national recovery, appears almost equally capable of making the best or the worst of all possible contributions to the national culture of the next generation. That is, its contribution might be of the lowest as well as of the highest order; might add to the nation's burden as well as enhance its riches; might contribute to national conflict as well as national unity; might afford the shortest road to revolution or the quickest steps to fascism, as well as a logical part of an orderly planned reconstruction economy.

Nowhere is this merely an academic problem. It is stark reality. The Southern States, like the nation, are in the remaking; they have their big chance. How long will the option last? The South has reflected a peculiar fortune and social heritage often likened unto Germany in the sense that facing a crisis it has a tendency to take the wrong road. In this respect there was very great practical significance to the cultural changes which resulted in the evolution of two "new Souths" instead of one. Both Southeast and Southwest are at new crossroads of crisis. It follows, of course, that the contribution which these regions make to the nation will determine the quality of their own civilization, and that axiomatically the quality of their own development will determine the measure of their national contribution. A second corollary is to the effect that the chances in favor of the southern regions enriching rather than impoverishing both regional and national life appear to depend upon a much more realistic facing of facts and a much more comprehensive and equally realistic regional-national planning program than have been anywhere attempted heretofore. The regions, so the hypothesis assumes, must supplement idealistic pictures and wishes and demands with deep and clear understanding of what is involved, with actual technical ways of doing the things recommended, and with the will and capacity to support what it takes to succeed. Such programs, furthermore, must be begun at once and must encompass definite objectives in the major activities and institutions of the region and for regional interaction; and for both periodic priority schedules and for aggregates of a minimum six to twelve-year period. Adequate planning, moreover, while magnifying the regional approach, will point to an increasingly effective integration with the national reconstruction. It

PER CAPITA ANNUAL INCOME, ELEVEN-YEAR AVERAGE, 1920-1930 INCLUSIVE

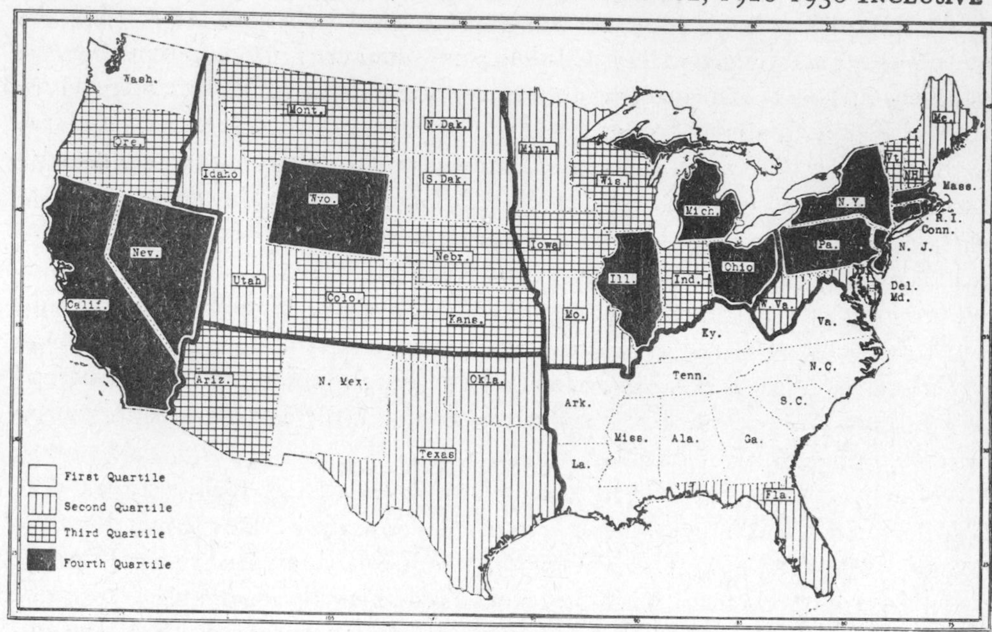

GOVERNMENTAL OUTLAY FOR EDUCATION, HOSPITALS, ROADS, ETC., 1929

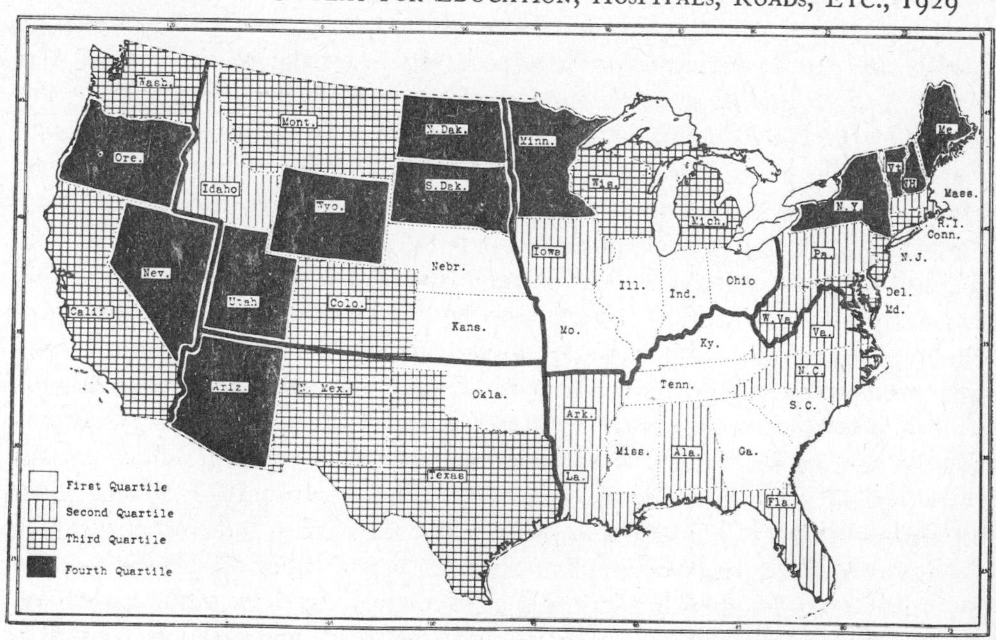

is this featuring of action and reality which gives special emphasis to the approach to social planning implied in the present appraisal.

A part of the reality is the recognition that conditions and situations are the products of certain geographic and economic forces and of special historical and cultural factors, an understanding of which is essential to intelligent planning and action. This cultural background, as is also notably the case of New England, for instance, reflects much of the basic explanation of the South's civilization and constitutes a separate story in itself. In the case of the southern regions their cultural experience includes a series of regional crises featuring emergency and struggle extraordinary—not only slavery and war and destruction of its wealth and people and its more recent burden of bi-racial culture, tenancy, political conflict within a solid South, its boll weevil, land erosion, and agrarian bankruptcy and discouragement, but its earlier crisis of indigo and rice and sugar and depleted cotton lands, its cattle fever and malaria, and other multiple handicaps which had not been subjected to technical mastery.

The main task, however, is not the catalogue of handicaps and the backward look, but to turn regional potential into regional reality and national power. There is only one main question: how achieve the attainable ends in view? The evidence, including past experience and present probabilities, indicates that the South cannot approximate these ends without considerable outside coöperation and assistance through well designed plans which will meet the peculiar specifications involved. The evidence of need for supplementary resources will appear from many sources. In addition to the past record of its colonial economy and of millions of supplementary dollars which have come to the South from philanthropy and federal aid, there is the very realistic incapacity of half of the farming population to produce enough either for their own standards of living or for the support of adequate culture. There is the dual load of bi-racial culture; a heavy responsibility of young industry to equalize fiscal demands of impoverished agriculture; an extraordinarily heavy load of education with neither money nor institutions available to carry on; and a continuous flow of money to other regions. Such coöperative interregional and national efforts, however, must be based upon standards and designed arrangements that will hold the southern regions alike with all others to the hard and fast rules of self-development, permanency, and adequacy of results, and other realistic tests of survival values.

Continuing the preliminary inventory, there are other still more specific and distinctive problems in the southern regions. One is that of planning for the utilization of an unusually large amount of submarginal land and the closely related problem of planning for the readjustment, some in

PER CAPITA SAVINGS DEPOSITS, 1930

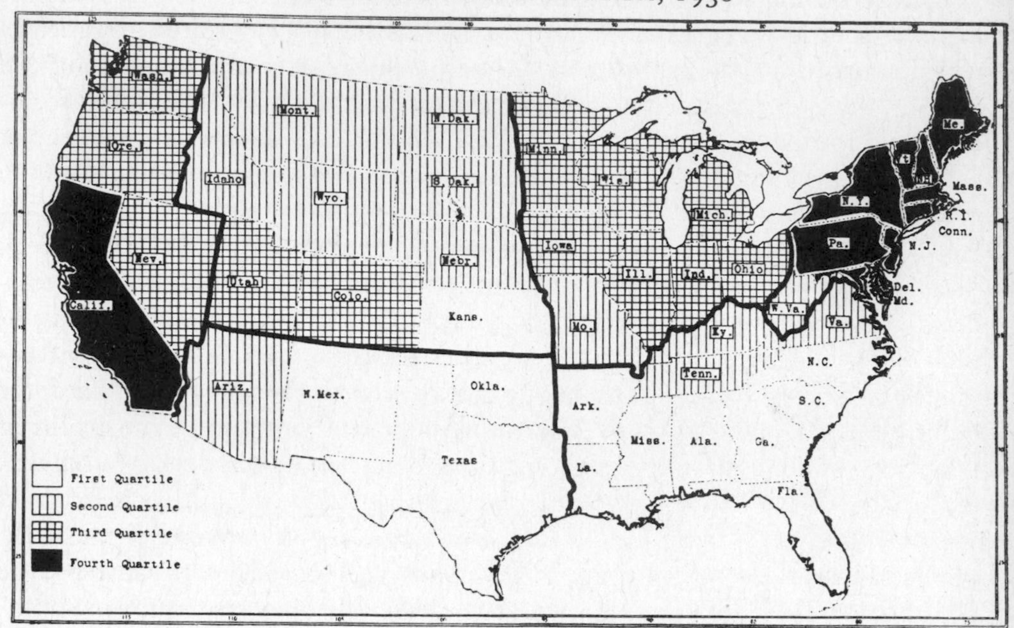

PER CAPITA ASSETS, BUILDING AND LOAN ASSOCIATIONS, 1929

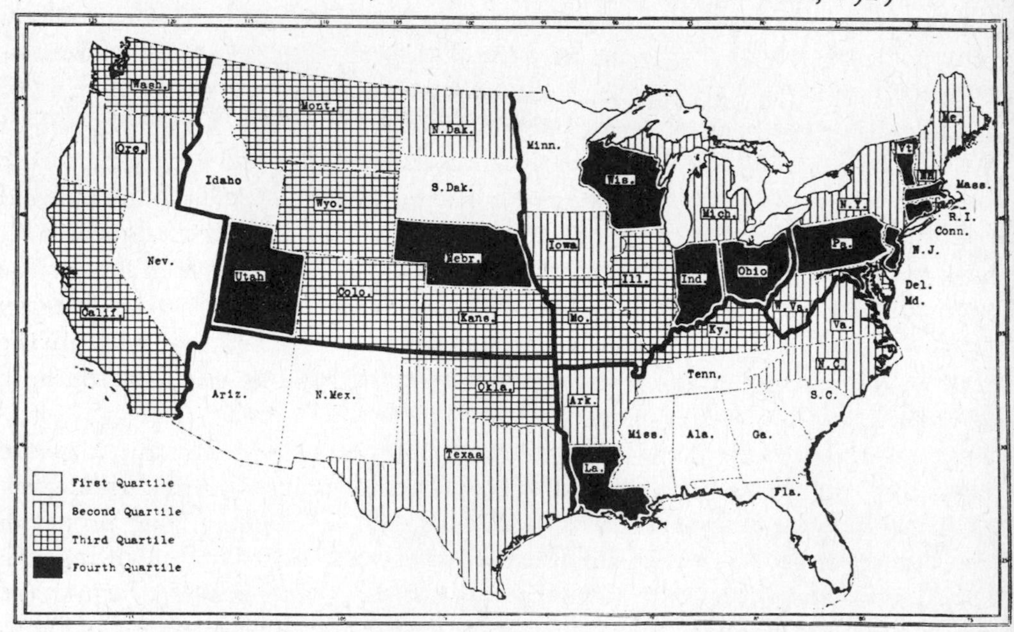

their present habitat and some elsewhere, of displaced or marginal families. It may be estimated that more than half of the eroded land of the nation is in these southern regions. There are no less than six hundred counties in which more than 50 per cent of farmer folk are tenants. The southern regions, furthermore, have distinctive problems in a type of dual socio-economic load—farm owner and tenant; white man and Negro; white man and Mexican; reputation and reality; and other class-mass aspects of uneven cultural development.

The South's experience with the decentralization of industry has given rise to new and distinctive problems of community standards and dependency. These are yet to be fully appraised. Yet more, rather than less, of such industries appear from the evidence to be essential to any sort of regional balance. Some of the background factors pointing to the need for more industry, better planned, include: a surplus of land in use, a surplus of people on the land; of these an unbalanced ratio between owners and tenants, and between good land and poor, with an apparent increase of land area in farms now in process. Likewise the economy of the southern regions is especially bound up with international relations due to the large exports of cotton and tobacco and of the dominance of these crops in southern agriculture.

The southern regions, in many subregions and among many of their people, are characterized by a low standard of consumption of both the principal agricultural commodities and manufactured products. A special problem, therefore, is that of providing for increased local consumption of commodities and goods. Increased standards of consumption are essential to both economic and cultural adequacy. There is an extraordinarily large ratio of the people of the regions whose standards of living and culture, whose homes and surroundings range from marginal subsistence to submarginal deficiency according to not only the usual mechanical patterns but according to any composite norm of American life. By the same token one of the remediable elemental deficiencies of the regions is found in the extraordinary part which malnutrition and the regimen of diet and hygiene play in the waste and drain upon work and creative effort throughout the southern regions.

As relates to agricultural economy, the southern regions have a special problem in their large ratio of cash crop farming and its related dilemmas. Closely related to this is the special problem of planning new programs of optimum production in the agricultural commodities, of balancing this production with new decentralized industry and self-sufficing farms, and of promoting interregional trade and exchange for the adjustment of interregional optima. Special tasks, therefore, are involved in the planning for

Submarginal Counties in the Southeast as Measured by Value of Land and Buildings Per Acre, 1930

Adapted from Woofter's Studies of Submarginal Counties

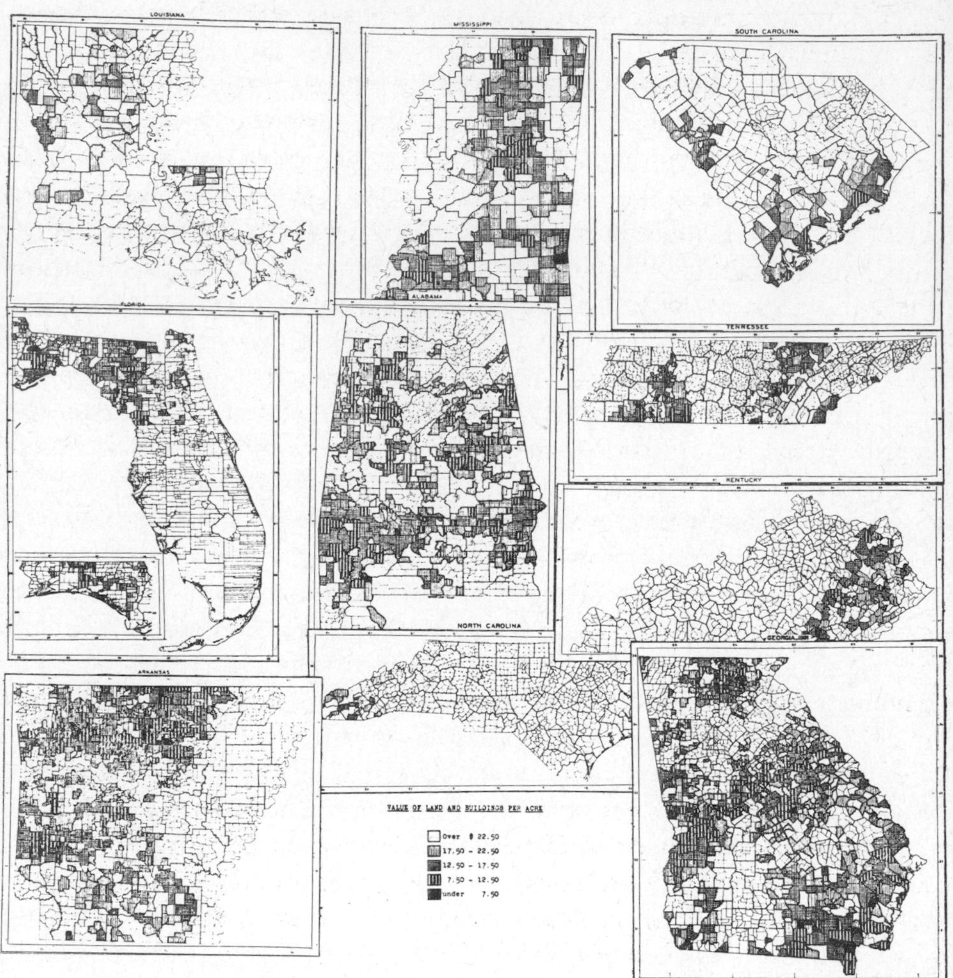

Facts about submarginal areas in the Southeast are of the greatest importance in both understanding and planning for the region's chief problems. In Chapter V which deals with deficiencies and waste and Chapter X which is devoted to states and subregions evidence of submarginal lands, marginal folk, marginal standards of living and housing is presented. Likewise many other contrasting conditions in the counties are shown.

new industries and new occupations and for the reëmployment of tenants and other workers in the South who are being thrown out of employment by the new economies.

Of special urgency are the problems of deficiency of institutions and tools of science, education, organization, management. The dual load of dichotomous education for Negroes and for whites, for men and for women, technical and liberal, public and private, and for geographical and denominational representation, constitutes a special problem as yet comparatively unexplored. The special problem of almost complete readjustment of "mountain schools" is paramount. There is the special problem of federal coöperation with states in an equalization effort. In higher education the region affords no university of the first rank, while nine of the eleven states composing the Southeastern Region have no universities rated by the American Council on Education as capable of giving the Ph.D. degree. No southern university is rated competent to give this degree in civil, chemical, mechanical, electrical, or mining engineering, or in bacteriology, entomology, geography, geology, plant pathology, plant physiology, soil science. There is, therefore, no institution equipped for advanced instruction and training for land study and use or for other highest technical equipment necessary for the development of an agrarian culture. Nor is there anywhere in the South a technical engineering school of the first rank.

There are other distinctive tasks straining regional capacity to the breaking point, such as the economic and educational load of an extraordinarily large ratio of children per thousand women; the largest ratio of any region of children to be educated from the smallest aggregate and per capita wealth; the new tension due to new demands for higher and professional education of Negroes and to culture conflicts arising from the impatience and enthusiasm of the younger generation of Negroes. In addition to these illustrations of special situations involving regional differentials, the assumption is that many of the standard problems of taxation and of governmental expenditures and reorganization must be approached through critical programs of regional study and planning.

Indeed, perhaps the chief point of departure in the study and planning of public finance in the South is the fact that the fiscal problems of the regions are derivative in the sense that they grow out of special economic and social conditions. For instance, the problem of submarginal areas and groups already designated as an elemental factor is reflected in governmental finance through the absolute certainty that the people do not produce enough to pay for adequate services of any sort. Thus the financial dilemmas are often demonstrably due to lack of planning as well as to deficiency in current capacity. Likewise the financial plight of southern cities

Distribution of English-Language "Country" Weekly Newspapers in the United States, 1900, 1910, 1920, and 1930, by States and Regions

Adapted from Malcolm M. Willey and William Weinfeld, "The Country Weekly: Trends in Number and Distribution, 1900-1930." *Social Forces*, October, 1934, p. 53

STATE AND REGION	1900		1910		1920		1930	
	Number	Per Cent	Number	Per Cent	Number	Per Cent	Number	Per Cent
Southeast	*1,724*	*15.3*	*1,729*	*14.7*	*1,461*	*13.9*	*1,436*	*15.2*
Virginia	134	1.2	140	1.2	117	1.1	115	1.2
North Carolina	153	1.4	151	1.3	138	1.3	141	1.5
South Carolina	77	0.7	82	0.7	73	0.7	67	0.7
Georgia	230	2.0	230	1.9	183	1.8	193	2.0
Florida	106	0.9	97	0.8	100	1.0	134	1.4
Kentucky	183	1.6	186	1.6	157	1.5	148	1.6
Tennessee	187	1.6	168	1.4	145	1.4	133	1.4
Alabama	167	1.5	155	1.3	115	1.1	126	1.3
Mississippi	180	1.6	179	1.5	138	1.3	113	1.2
Arkansas	188	1.7	214	1.8	196	1.9	163	1.7
Louisiana	119	1.0	127	1.1	99	0.9	103	1.1
Southwest	*727*	*6.4*	*1,199*	*10.1*	*973*	*9.3*	*897*	*9.5*
Oklahoma	112	1.0	474	4.0	335	3.2	304	3.2
Texas	556	4.9	611	5.2	529	5.1	5.6	5.3
New Mexico	32	0.3	84	0.7	70	0.7	52	0.5
Arizona	27	0.2	30	0.3	39	0.4	35	0.4
Northeast	*2,036*	*18.0*	*1,840*	*15.6*	*1,559*	*15.0*	*1,520*	*15.9*
Maine	79	0.7	71	0.6	50	0.5	43	0.5
New Hampshire	58	0.5	52	0.4	43	0.4	41	0.4
Vermont	48	0.4	44	0.4	39	0.3	34	0.4
Massachusetts	139	1.2	119	1.0	104	1.0	92	1.0
Rhode Island	14	0.1	12	0.1	9	0.1	9	0.0
Connecticut	51	0.5	46	0.4	40	0.4	40	0.4
New York	614	5.4	567	4.8	499	4.8	526	5.5
New Jersey	175	1.6	174	1.5	173	1.6	198	2.1
Delaware	19	0.2	20	0.2	21	0.2	17	0.2
Pennsylvania	600	5.3	509	4.3	386	3.7	334	3.5
Maryland	102	0.9	90	0.8	76	0.7	76	0.8
West Virginia	137	1.2	136	1.1	119	1.1	110	1.2
Middle States	*4,492*	*39.6*	*4,166*	*35.3*	*3,609*	*34.4*	*3,211*	*33.7*
Ohio	549	4.9	458	3.9	356	3.4	324	3.4
Indiana	454	4.0	363	3.1	312	3.0	274	2.9
Illinois	764	6.8	707	6.0	615	5.9	558	5.9
Michigan	503	4.4	436	3.7	362	3.4	319	3.3
Wisconsin	349	3.1	396	3.3	364	3.5	318	3.3
Minnesota	455	4.0	518	4.4	508	4.8	460	4.8
Iowa	776	6.9	686	5.8	593	5.7	507	5.3
Missouri	642	5.7	602	5.1	499	4.8	451	4.7
Northwest	*1,787*	*15.8*	*2,176*	*18.4*	*2,151*	*20.6*	*1,728*	*18.1*
North Dakota	136	1.2	308	2.6	265	2.5	189	2.0
South Dakota	226	2.0	355	3.0	299	2.9	249	2.6
Nebraska	479	4.2	462	3.9	440	4.2	380	4.1
Kansas	565	5.0	552	4.7	477	4.6	419	4.4
Montana	60	0.5	85	0.7	209	2.0	122	1.3
Idaho	61	0.5	100	0.8	117	1.1	94	1.0
Wyoming	37	0.3	54	0.5	68	0.6	56	0.6
Colorado	178	1.7	210	1.8	217	2.1	168	1.7
Utah	45	0.4	50	0.4	59	0.6	51	0.5
Far West	*546*	*4.9*	*692*	*5.9*	*709*	*6.8*	*730*	*7.6*
Nevada	20	0.2	30	0.3	27	0.2	17	0.2
Washington	138	1.2	214	1.8	197	1.9	184	1.9
Oregon	123	1.1	137	1.2	136	1.3	131	1.4
California	265	2.3	311	2.6	349	3.3	398	4.2
United States	11,310	100.0	11,802	100.0	10,462	100.0	9,522	100.0

rests largely upon undesigned expansion with no sort of measuring rod of industrial development and growth for the future.

Again, the special elemental problem of replanning agriculture with a view to optimum programs of production in relation to a certain increment of technological and industrial production through new small industries and new occupations reflects the present financial dilemma of attempting to make the South's immature and new industry shoulder the cost of nursing its sick agriculture. Thus are involved not only the planning within the region, but because of the overwhelming agricultural population, the planning for federal coöperation and subsidy through the mobilization of the resources of the nation. Accordingly, this problem of reconstructing the agricultural economy of the South must feature the *increase of values* of farm lands, buildings, and property; the increase in permanent producing capacity; the increase in both cash and total farm income; the increase in the standards of living conditions in a new agrarian culture; increase, in fine, of the attractiveness and profitableness of southern farm life; unless indeed it is expected the present order will continue southern deficiency and national drain in preference to regional abundance and federal income. The conclusion seems justified, therefore, that it is hopeless to try to meet these fiscal deficiencies without some sort of planned direction or control of the South's economic development such as has not yet been approached.

The southern picture includes more than the long list of economic and cultural problems and deficiencies. It includes a long catalogue of other regional differentials many of which are discussed in Benjamin B. Kendrick's special volume giving the historical development of the South. A part of the South's distinctiveness is found in its rural predominance which, in contradistinction to its present plight, might make possible the revival of the ideal of the southern regions as still a Jeffersonian America of agrarian culture. Either the Southeast or the Southwest could spare from cultivation the whole 40,000,000 acres of harvested crop lands commonly estimated as the war surplus and become better off thereby. There is, therefore, the specialized problem of land planning and utilization which will point to a new and more vital realization of agriculture as a way of rural and village life, such as will constitute fundamental next steps in the American experiment which seeks more of the value economy and less of the money economy. Once again, the southern regions still abound in great possessions characterized by non-liquidity. Perhaps their greatest wealth is not liquid now. Yet for this reason it ought to be made capable of affording richness and stability of life and a powerful reserve culture for the enrichment of the national fabric.

There are many who are committed to the task of rebuilding the agra-

Subregions of the Southeast

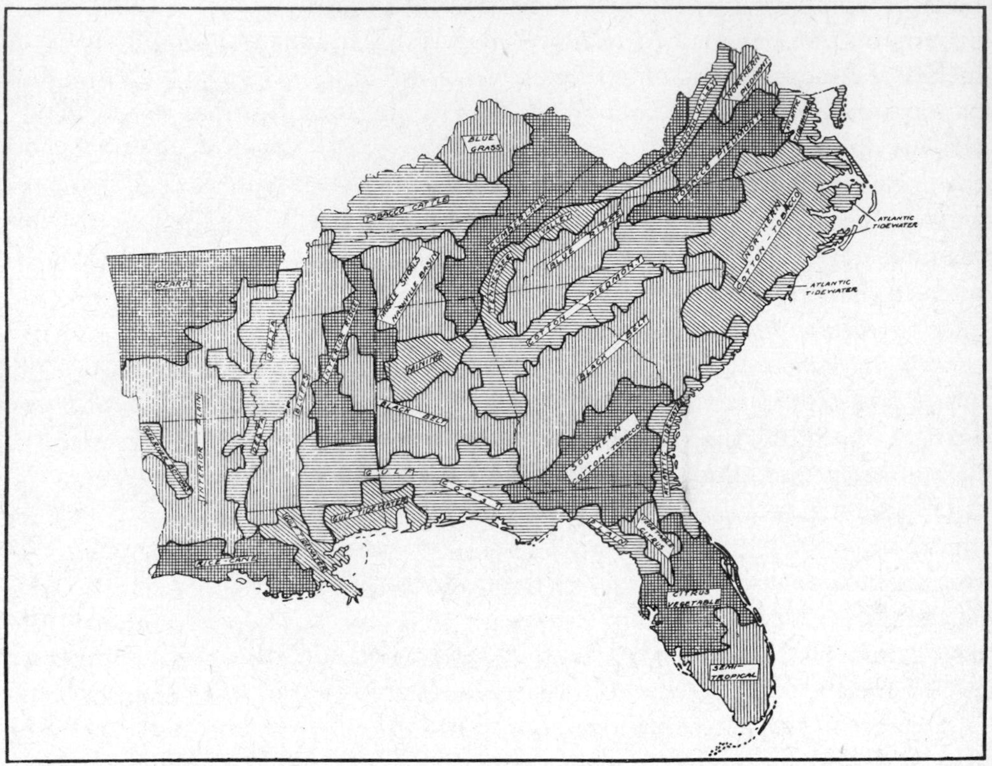

Distribution of Acreage in Subregions of the Southeast According to Percentage of Total Crop Land, 1929-1930

SUBREGION	Number of Counties in Region	Cotton	Tobacco	Corn	Oats	Wheat	Hay Crops	Irish and Sweet Potatoes	Vegetables Harvested for Sale	Orchards	Idle or Fallow Land
The Tidewater	46	4.09	.53	37.11	1.02	3.81	12.82	12.60	6.03	1.13	16.43
The Black Belt	122	37.86	.04	29.88	3.43	.55	3.93	.82	.73	1.68	17.30
The Northern Cotton and Tobacco	55	27.74	13.17	29.31	2.85	1.00	9.21	1.69	.59	.68	10.48
The Southern Cotton and Tobacco	51	22.32	2.67	40.10	2.30	.01	4.15	1.38	1.87	1.44	15.84
The Cotton Piedmont	64	41.00	.18	26.04	3.92	3.81	2.88	.79	.39	1.27	17.78
The Tobacco Piedmont	39	.73	10.80	27.14	1.39	1.07	9.14	1.09	.71	2.82	31.36
The Northern Piedmont	13	.00	.01	32.52	2.21	18.86	22.60	.57	.38	7.70	11.40
The Shenandoah Valley	15	.00	.46	24.71	2.95	26.25	24.01	.78	.87	9.12	6.90
The Tennessee Valley	21	10.61	1.21	29.79	.97	6.35	19.78	.96	.86	2.54	22.00
The Blue Ridge	43	6.03	.44	33.48	3.27	4.68	16.36	1.76	.81	5.43	22.63
The Cumberland Mountains	72	4.90	.87	40.27	3.53	1.94	16.31	1.85	.35	3.28	23.09
The Blue Grass	39	.00	12.20	36.93	3.15	5.69	26.17	.92	.63	1.12	8.99
The Tobacco Cattle Region	55	.50	6.49	40.98	2.25	2.69	16.97	.89	.15	1.16	24.08
The Muscle Shoals Nashville Basin	29	23.99	.61	38.95	1.38	2.57	13.95	.66	.27	.81	14.22
The Mining Region	9	39.31	.00	34.50	1.23	.00	3.80	1.48	.97	1.23	13.57
The Interior Ridge	27	41.84	.00	35.82	.53	.00	4.93	.90	.16	.70	12.23
The Bluffs	40	45.16	.10	30.93	.37	.34	7.39	.94	.95	.43	14.19
The Delta	29	67.72	.00	14.64	.29	.01	3.34	.25	.06	.17	6.48
The Interior Plain	50	50.35	.00	24.42	.53	.02	3.68	1.30	.37	.82	11.70
The Red River Region	4	66.97	.00	17.33	.11	.00	3.36	.88	.20	.75	8.85
The Ozark Mountains	38	28.24	.00	28.36	2.00	.45	13.09	.82	.78	3.12	17.22
The Rice-Cane Region	16	11.94	.00	21.47	.03	.00	3.73	2.36	1.19	.27	14.36
The Gulf Tidewater	18	15.01	.02	34.26	.85	.00	8.15	5.35	7.39	10.95	15.73
The Gulf Coast	46	38.65	.02	36.22	.87	.00	5.58	1.37	.83	1.36	9.71
The Vegetable-Citrus Region	..	1.36	.60	42.20	.37	.00	3.45	1.42	12.82	6.67	27.55
The Citrus-Vegetable Region	..	.03	.00	8.93	.01	.00	1.91	2.19	8.58	59.91	17.15
The Semi-Tropical Region	..	.00	.00	1.51	.00	.00	.66	2.37	39.28	17.21	20.16

rian South through the revitalized dream of Henry Grady. His specifications of a half century ago, they pointed out, are not only peculiarly appropriate now, but may have more abundant fulfilment through the joint means of practical technology and a designed order of state, regional, and national coöperation. "Then shall be breaking the fullness of our day," was his often quoted and little heeded admonition, "when every farmer in the South shall eat bread from his own fields and meat from his own pastures and, disturbed by no creditor and enslaved by no debt, shall sit among his teeming gardens and orchards and vineyards and dairies and barnyards, pitching his crops in his own wisdom and growing them in independence, making cotton his clean surplus, and selling it in his own time and in his chosen market and not at a master's bidding—getting his pay in cash and not in a receipted mortgage." "Why not?" both the new and old agrarians asked. Quoting the Jeffersonian dictum, they affirm that we still have "lands enough to employ an infinite number of people in their cultivation." And are not "cultivators of the land the most notable citizens . . . the most vigorous, the most independent, the most virtuous . . . tied to their country and wedded to its liberty and interests by the most lasting bonds"? And further, does not this present need of agricultural reconstruction in the South demand "a noble response to a national call"?

There are other aspects of culture in the southern regions, in addition to agrarian interests, which characterize them as the most "American" of all the regions, if by "American" we mean the culture and people of early America. This is more than merely cultural lag behind the rest of the nation. For here were major regions, greater in territory than all the earlier colonies, with five times as many people as Jefferson's beloved America, still reflecting the mode of life which the early nation boasted. Are not its white people still more than 90 per cent of the earlier stocks? Are they not of protestant faith, Sabbath observing, family loving and patriarchal, of religious intensity, "quarrelling" with government, individualists taking their politics, their honor, and their drinking hard? Was not all the nation so a century ago? Their attitudes toward work and play, toward women and property, toward children and their work, toward the dominant leader are still much the same as was the early vintage. Both Southeast and Southwest are still frontier folk; the Southeast, parts of which are of the oldest of the United States culture, reflecting a sort of arrested frontier pattern of life. Such a culture not only affords a realistic historical picture but also offers still a base line from which to explore the possibility of a sort of "recovery of the past" through projecting an American culture that might have been. The fact that the hazards of sectionalism and isolation may threaten the whole structure but adds to the significance

SUBMARGINAL COUNTIES IN CERTAIN SOUTHEASTERN STATES AS INDICATED BY LOW OCCUPANCY IN MINOR CIVIL DIVISIONS

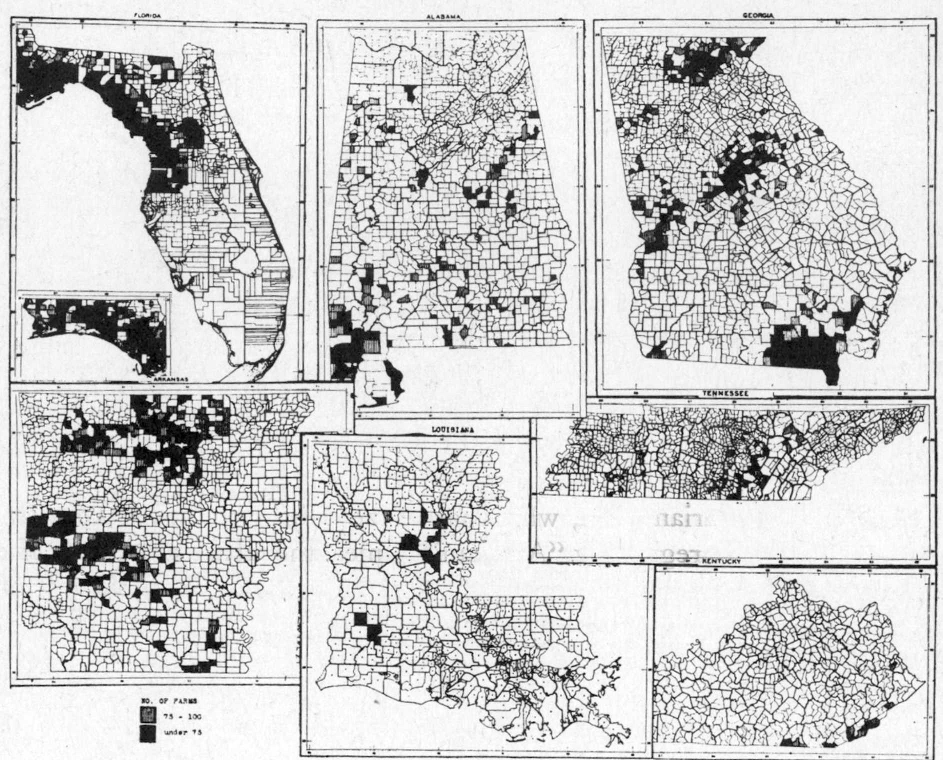

Woofter's approach to the location of large submarginal areas within 300 miles of Muscle Shoals isolates poor areas only if they comprise less than two contiguous counties. "To deal with the concept of submarginality in a clearcut manner" he points out, "implies an objectively stated margin. Various margins could be fixed for various uses. Land might be below the profitable margin for highly intensive truck or orchard crops but excellent for field crops. It might be below the margin for field crops but well adapted to grazing. It might be below the margin for grazing but well adapted for forests. The margins selected in this study are those more applicable to profitable culture of general field crops. A dual concept has been used, low land values and sparse occupancy of land even though the value of the occupied land may be somewhat above the margin. The value margin selected was $22.50 per acre for *land and buildings* in 1930. The use margin was 30 per cent of the total area in farms."

of regional differentials and national obligation. The southern regions, moreover, are reputed rich in folk reserves, where resides a great seed bed of population for renewing the national stream. They are thus rich in the sheer organic vitality of the folk life and society which has always been a definitive force in the rise of new cultures.

Many of these regional differentials have been emphasized in various ways by the depression years and the various problems and procedures of the National Recovery Administration. Among them are: the mass unthinking acceptance of federal bounty by the South; the growing critical protest by other regions; the profound questioning of values; the actualities of planning and enforcing relief measures; the unforeseen by-products and the notable differences and points of conflict; the competitive activities of industry; the scramble for political position; the deficiencies in exports and international trade; the very realistic recognition of the need for regional analysis in the national program—these are some of the factors which accentuate the importance of regional inventory and planning. Other more specific observable recent developments include an increase in the numbers of northern and western students attending southern institutions; a decrease in the ratio of northern and western faculty members in white southern universities; an increase in the number of distinguished Negro faculty members from outside the South teaching in southern Negro colleges; a decrease in the opportunities for both southern students and faculties to affiliate with eastern and western institutions; a decrease in the economic and cultural opportunities for southern folk in the North and West; an increase in the political representation of the southern regions in the routine work of the government; an increase in government subsidy with a particularly high ratio of total federal funds going to the South in farm payments both from cotton and tobacco crop reduction and for loans to farmers for seed and feed and stock. For instance, a single state in the Southwest was credited with almost a third of the nation's 1933 bill for crop payments, while the Southeast received approximately 60 per cent, excluding the special funds for the purchase of commodities for distribution through relief agencies. Of the $47,000,000 in loans in the early 1930's to more than 385,000 farmers for seed, fertilizer, feed, agricultural rehabilitation following drought, more than $40,000,000 went to 325,000 of these same farmers in the southern regions.

Another series of considerations centers around the viewpoint and nature of the inventory attempted in the present volume. In addition to the oft-repeated emphasis upon the regional viewpoint rather than the sectional, the special merits of which are presented in the next chapter, and upon the approach to social planning in the moderate sense featured by

Denominational and Independent Mountain Schools

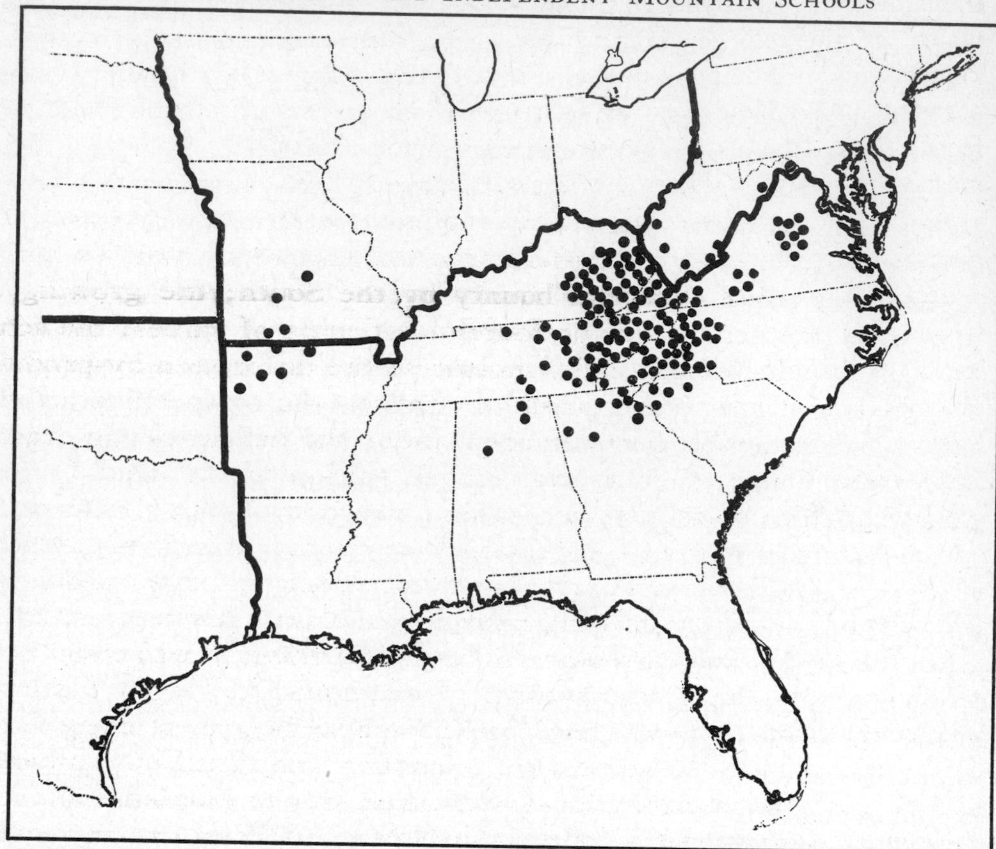

The above map is an adaptation from Miss Fannie W. Dunn's special study of Appalachian Philanthropic schools, Chapter IX in *Religion in the Highlands,* by Elizabeth R. Hooker, and published in 1933 by the Home Mission Council. Dr. Dunn's list of schools was made up from the earlier list of 150 such schools listed by the Russell Sage Foundation. Of these located on the map, Dr. Dunn estimates that there are some thirty which are doubtful. By 1933 or 1935, there had been many readjustments. Yet the total picture is illustrative of the problem of religious schools and education in the region.

The Southeast's Dichotomous Education in White Institutions

STATE AND REGION	Private and Denominational						State Supported						Total White Institutions
	For Men		For Women		Coeducational		For Men		For Women		Coeducational		
	Liberal	Technical*	Liberal	Technical*	Liberal	Technical*	Liberal	Technical*	Liberal	Technical*	Liberal	Technical*	
Southeast	*13*	*12*	*66*	*2*	*73*	*4*	*5*	*8*	*6*	*6*	*22*	*27*	*244*
Virginia	..	1	13	..	5	..	4	2	..	2	2	4	33
North Carolina	3	..	12	1	11	..	..	1	1	2	1	..	32
South Carolina	3	1	7	..	2	..	..	2	1	..	2	1	19
Georgia	1	4	8	..	5	1	..	2	2	1	3	4	31
Florida	..	..	..	..	4	..	1	..	1	..	..	..	6
Kentucky	1	4	7	..	11	2	..	..	..	..	2	4	31
Tennessee	2	1	4	1	17	1	..	..	..	..	2	3	31
Alabama	3	..	3	..	3	..	..	..	..	1	2	6	18
Mississippi	..	..	8	..	3	..	..	1	1	..	2	2	17
Arkansas	..	1	2	..	8	..	..	..	..	..	4	1	16
Louisiana	..	..	2	..	4	..	..	..	..	..	2	2	10

*Includes Professional and Normal Schools.

the American reconstruction programs, there are a number of other features which are the essence of the picture. The historical perspective must be kept in mind. The powerful onrush of time and technology is no respecter of what might have been or what is wished or of stubborn blindness to facts. The attempt has, therefore, been made to make the viewpoint and method objective. There are several ways in which objectivity has been sought. One was by comparison of the southern regions with other regions in a large number of items. Another was the moderate use of statistics and graphical methods of presenting various aspects of the picture, of which only a very small part can, from the nature of the data, be presented in a single volume. The historical approach has afforded something of objectivity as have the general methods of observation and description. Since it was neither possible nor desirable to include all the data available and since an unusual storehouse of regional facts already is available, the attempt has been made to effect a fair synthesis of what has gone before and to feature in this book selected data with a view to total analysis, to vivid portraiture and to instrumental or functional purposes, especially with reference to regional capacity. Finally, the attempt has been made to see the picture of the southern regions in the whole national setting and in relation to the fundamental social reconstruction now going on. And there is the sort of objectivity in which Pearl Buck, looking back at America, values distance as the invaluable aid to clear vision and space as the great lens for portraiture.

Still another way of achieving objectivity is that of looking at the picture both in relation to its past evolution and to the demands of the future as being essentially a product and a process of time. It seems difficult for the nation and in particular the southern regions to sense the immensity and the time qualities of the tasks of reconstruction; to understand that not all of time is now. It must be clear also that it is no longer possible to cover over stark reality with incurable romanticism, no longer possible to ignore the actualities of the past, the realities of the present, or the prospects of the future.

The specific time base line around which the inventory of the southern regions has focused its inquiry mainly is the decade of the 1920's, crest years of achievement and beginnings of recession for both southern regions and nation alike. Back of that were the premises of the cultural history of the South, and beyond the 1920's were the early 1930's of depression years from which comparative data and supplementary observations were made. For the suggested planning program one, and perhaps two, six-year periods constitute the best hypothesis, the first period being

Per Capita Expenditures for Public Libraries, 1929

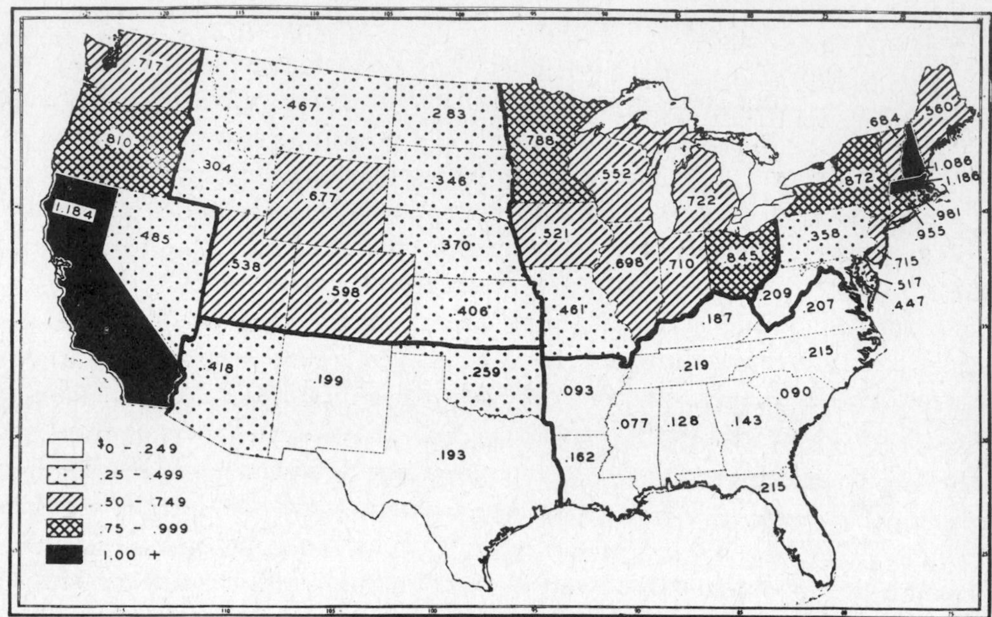

The two maps on this page are adapted from L. R. Wilson's studies of regional library facilities in the United States which are to be published at an early date. Although made independently of the sixfold regional division, the Southeast and the Southwest differentials are clearly demonstrated in accordance with Dr. Wilson's indices.

Per Cent of Population Registered as Library Borrowers, 1929

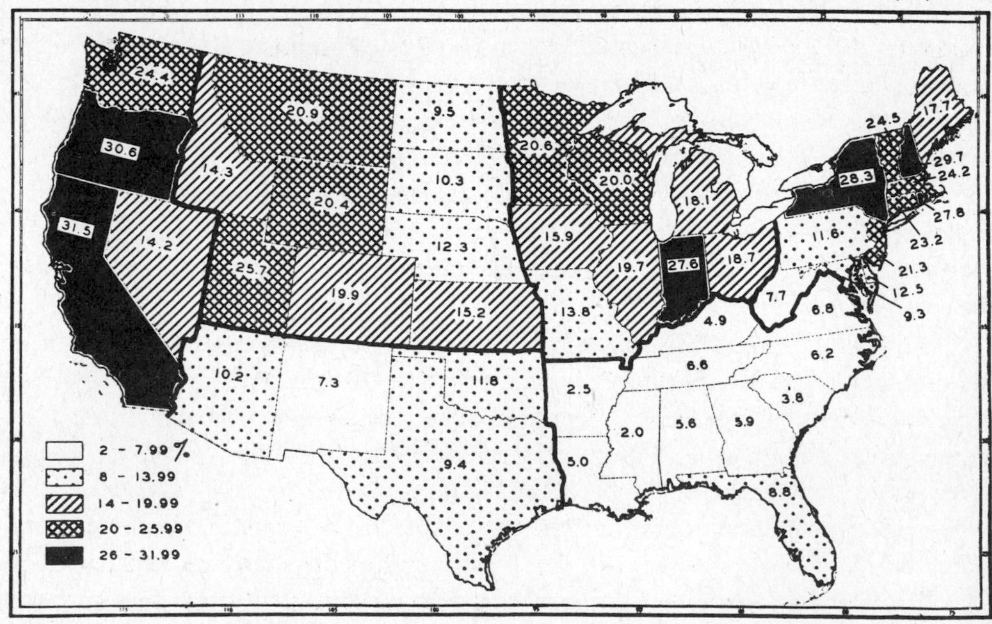

from 1936-37-38 to 1942-43-44, for reasons which will be set forth in the later chapter emphasizing the planning approach.

The clear-cut delineation of the South into two distinctive major southern regions, the Southeast and the Southwest, with the present volume featuring the Southeast more specifically is an important part of the picture. The significance of this and the reasons and indices upon which the division was made will be apparent from the subsequent catalogue of indices and from the many mapographs and other data. There is ample evidence to indicate that for some time there has been no clearly demarcated South composed of such divergent and border margin states as Missouri, Maryland, Delaware, West Virginia, Oklahoma, and that there is an emerging new Southwest consistently different and of a notable quality, ranking well alongside other major regions. So, also, the present classification of the United States into six cultural regions as explained in Chapter III is an approach to what Rupert B. Vance, regretting the lack of any formulation of regionalism as a social policy, has termed the practice of regional housekeeping. The New Deal with its projection of planning hypotheses and of administrative problems has greatly augmented the need for regional analysis, and more regional analysis.

The inventory, further, is predicated upon the assumptions of certain theoretical implications and framework. Some of these point to the premise that in the next period of development in American culture there will be an increasing emphasis, in both social study and social action, upon the concept and techniques of social planning. Such social planning, however, will comprehend a working equilibrium in the whole culture process and function, featuring a series of priority schedules, in contradistinction to a mere social *plan* or to a planned economic order constituted as a single project in which inheres the sovereign power to execute. It will utilize the full capacity of a social engineering competent to build not only new structures for the nation but to carry in the meantime the traffic of all the institutions in a transitional society. On these assumptions the next premise is that, due to the bigness of the nation and to its cultural backgrounds and motivations, as well as to technological considerations, the regional approach and analysis are fundamental to any successful permanent social planning program or procedure in the United States.

Other assumptions concern the theoretical framework upon which the study was projected, something of which has been described in Chapter I. The chief divisions of the work tend to follow and extend the classification used earlier in *An American Epoch*, *Man's Quest for Social Guidance*, and *An Introduction to Social Research*; and later in *Recent Social Trends*. The elemental factors thus catalogued include social change and social

Sample Pictures of Wage Differentials With Non-Identifiable Lines in Food Groups, Quarrying and Finishing

These maps are presented to show only the broad outlines of regional divisions, differentiating clearly "South" from "North."

Adapted from Research Division, N. R. A.

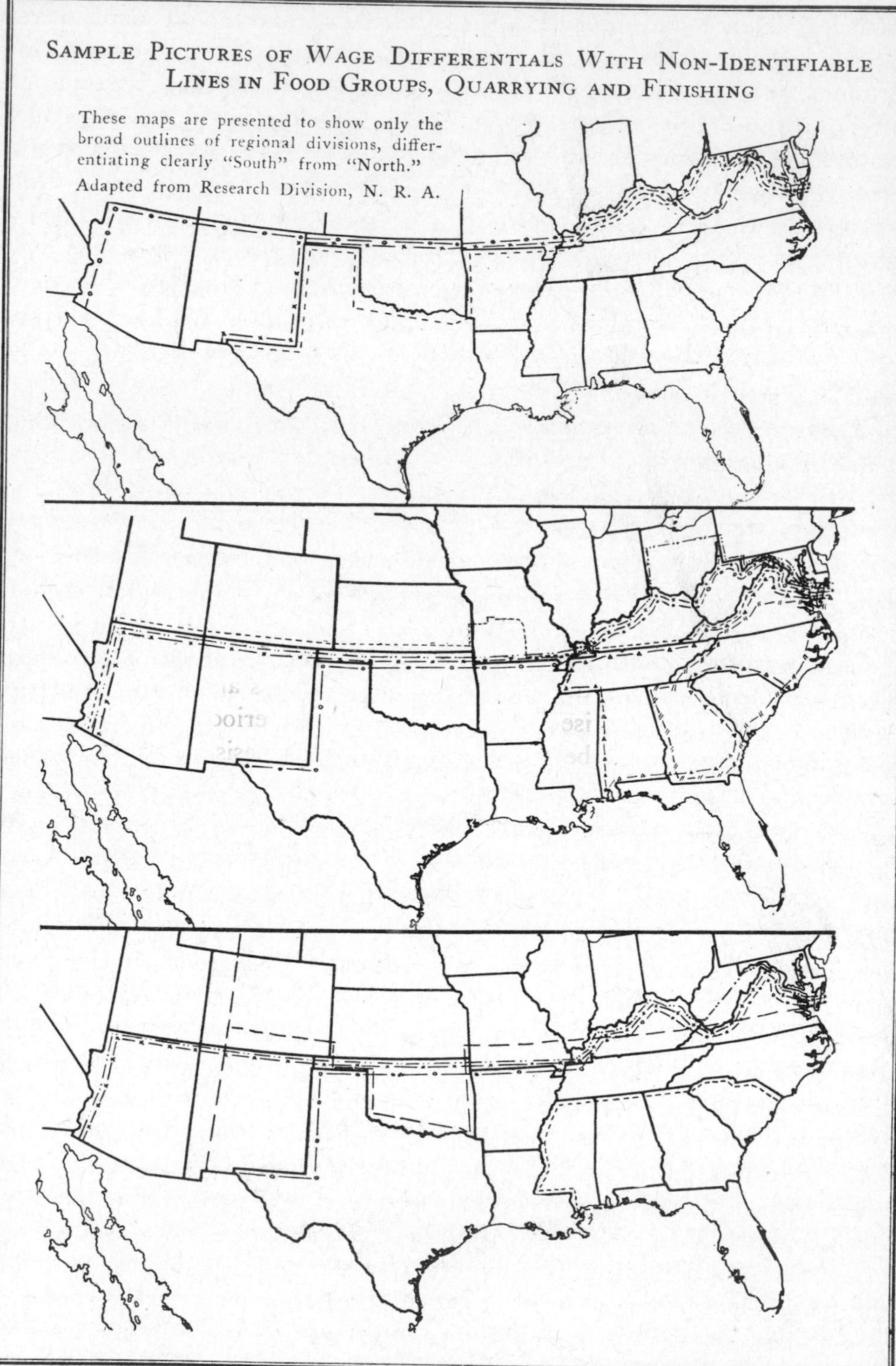

incidence, science and invention, physical backgrounds and natural resources, technological progress, human and artificial wealth, the major institutional modes of life, and the forces of social science, social technology, social guidance. Further assumptions of theoretical values in regional study are found in the hypotheses that cultures evolve and can be understood only through the study of regional areas, that society always has grown up thus and will continue to do so, and that capacities and directions are always determined by regional situations. The assumptions are in line, not only with cultural anthropology and sociology, but with the popular historical and cultural pictures of America, as, for example, New England and her culture. And they reëmphasize the growing significance of the geographic factor in human affairs.

This recognition of the place of the historical and cultural backgrounds in determining the kind of attitudes and culture in the southern regions emphasizes forcibly a factor in social planning too often overlooked; namely, the cultural foundations and implications. That is, the regional planning program must provide not only the detailed specifications for carrying out plans or policies already determined, but must also set in motion stimuli or movements from which will mature new policies and procedures. If, for instance, many aspects of southern culture in relation to the Negro were first set to growing from the social incidence of climate, cotton and the cotton gin, slavery and war and reconstruction, the presumption would be that the time has come to design events or practices which should now set in motion processes which will result in the desired transformation of certain of the present regional unfair practices. Examples might be found somewhere in the midst of race segregation practices, in the economic and cultural relations between the whites and Negroes in the South, or in the practices relating to the millions of farm tenants, or in the differential wage rate and standards of living and housing. These are samples from many, which illustrate the necessity of more than general education or propaganda or exhortation; on the contrary, the need is for specific, technical units of codes or plans from which the new order may arise. Such units are essential not only to insure actual beginnings, but as measures of trial and error. Not only in aspects of regional life appraised as deficient or immature does this apply, but to the possibilities of developing and testing new values and ideals. Sometime, somewhere, somehow, the nation is accustomed to embark on new adventures and epochs; the present is such a period. It ought to be a reasonable presumption that the southern regions, through realistic regional planning, might make a contribution of the first order.

This consideration is of importance in connection with the methods of regional and state comparison utilized in this inventory. The comparison

State Percentage of the Total Population, 1930

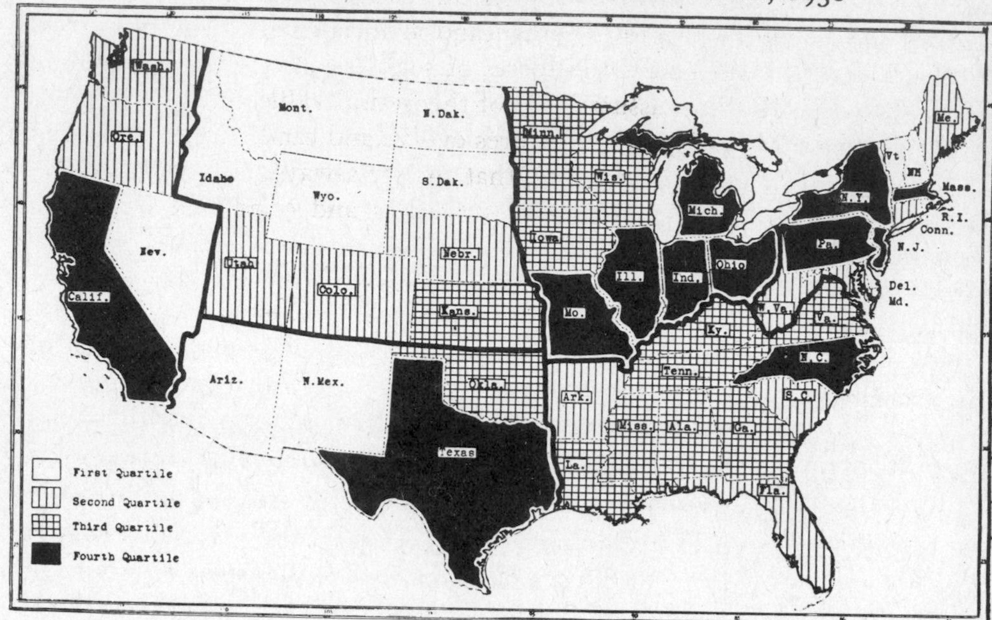

Among the most interesting of the state comparisons are those which show the relative standing of the states in their proportion of people and area in the nation.

Above, the population picture is seen to follow the westward trend of industry and wealth just after the Civil War and these heavily populated states make a regional pattern of their own which may be compared to the other maps showing present trends in industry.

Below, the great wide spaces of the "WEST" are shown vividly. See discussions of state character in Chapter X.

State Percentage of the Total Area

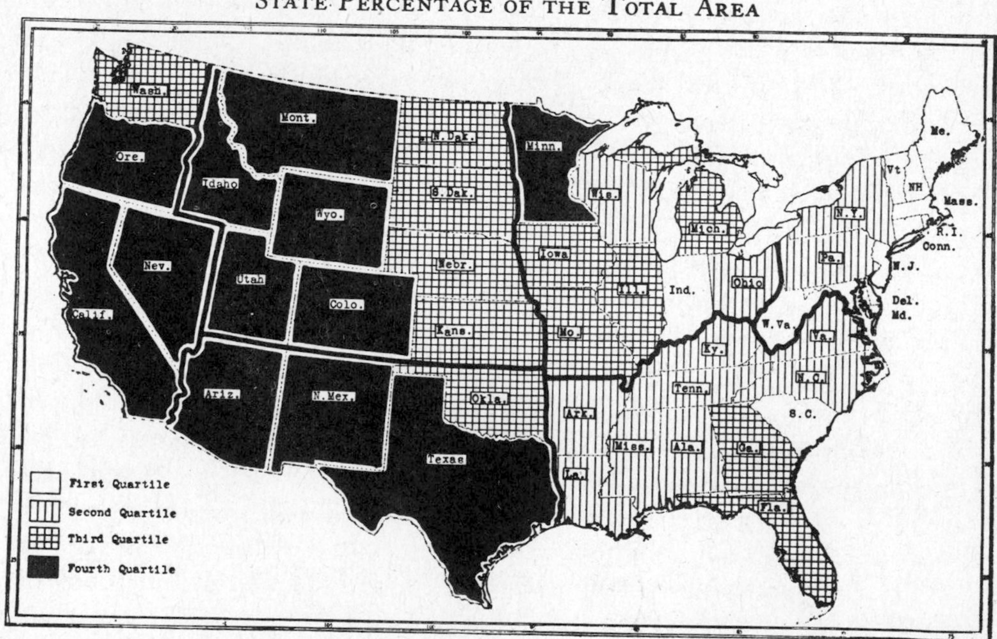

of the southern regions with other regions is exactly what it implies—an inventory of certain characteristics in terms of uniform statistical indices most commonly utilized and applied to all states. By rearrangement and groupings, the aggregates for each of the six regions may be obtained. The methodology of comparison itself has no reference to the uniformity or validity of standards used, to the accuracy or perspective of the indices, or to the desirability of seeking a national average. It is of the essence of a different appraisal to know that a high value of farm and lands in one area might mean rich wheat, corn, and alfalfa lands with a stack of alfalfa hay bigger than the owner's house, compared to a low value in another region where farm lands have deteriorated and cash money goes for the family automobile. Yet the facts are as they are and provide one type of irreducible minimum of comparative measurement from which, for the purpose intended, there is no appeal. Without such comparisons, data for a single region are often not only useless but misleading.

On the other hand, such comparisons, if utilized as the sole criteria of measurement, negate the whole theory and practice of the regional approach to study and planning. It becomes necessary both to question the meaning, accuracy, and applicability of many indices and to reduce them to the regional denominator. Greater waste, for instance, could scarcely be fabricated than for the small interior or upland farmers of the Southeast to be "sold" the giant tractor-combine or other machine method of farming which makes of the western fields models of efficiency. Yet the aggregate deficiency in farming technology in the southern regions constitutes a major problem for technical planning. But it must be special regional planning based upon the realities of the region and need and ends in view. The incongruity of measuring standards of living by the number of automobiles and radios must be clear in an economy where such forced sales drain the very heart of the family resources.

Again there must surely be room enough in the regional cultures of America for experimentation, for exploration, for the genuine liberalism that strives to maintain a quality civilization in a quantity world. The mechanized perfections of light and heat, of water and bath, of clothes and moving pictures, of spending money and automobiles of the mill village economy, may not rank higher than the vigorous satisfaction of the mountain folk, deep in the living experience of their music and liberty, who look for no new horizons save in the promised land. Folk beauty in the hills may transcend technological pathology. Yet progress and capacity in a technological age must somehow be inventoried by means of certain objective measures which neither permit pathological lag nor become mere propaganda standardization.

Per Cent of Rural Farm Population in the Total Population, 1930

Per Cent
Under 12½
12½ to 25
25 to 37½
37½ to 50
50 and over

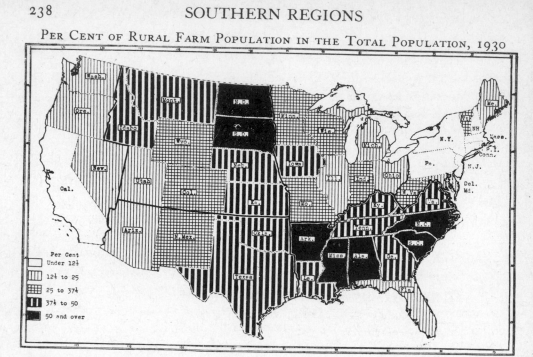

RURAL FARM POPULATION 1930 AND PER CENT INCREASE 1920-1930 BY STATES AND REGIONS

STATES	Rural Farm Population 1930	Per Cent Increase 1920-1930
Southeast		
Virginia	948,746	-10.5
North Carolina	1,597,220	6.5
South Carolina	914,098	14.8
Georgia	1,413,719	-15.9
Florida	274,949	1.6
Kentucky	1,174,232	- 9.8
Tennessee	1,213,065	- 4.5
Alabama	1,336,409	.1
Mississippi	1,360,729	7.2
Arkansas	1,117,330	- 2.4
Louisiana	826,882	5.4
Southwest		
Oklahoma	1,021,174	.5
Texas	2,342,553	3.4
New Mexico	157,906	- 1.6
Arizona	98,189	8.9
Northeast		
Maine	161,429	-14.6
New Hampshire	54,911	-15.0
Vermont	111,898	-10.1
Massachusetts	80,309	30.3
Rhode Island	10,289	9.4
Connecticut	80,247	-11.1
New York	706,446	- 9.8
New Jersey	121,008	-11.6
Delaware	46,302	- 9.5
Pennsylvania	846,240	10.1
Maryland	236,172	-14.9
West Virginia	447,750	- 6.1
Middle States		
Ohio	1,004,288	-11.4
Indiana	808,981	-10.4
Illinois	991,401	- 9.1
Michigan	775,436	- 8.2
Wisconsin	873,008	- 8.5
Minnesota	888,049	- 6.1
Iowa	964,659	- 1.3
Missouri	1,108,969	- 8.2
Northwest		
North Dakota	396,871	.8
South Dakota	389,431	7.6
Nebraska	582,981	.0
Kansas	704,601	4.2
Montana	203,962	- 9.5
Northwest (cont.)		
Idaho	186,100	- 5.3
Wyoming	72,905	8.7
Colorado	281,038	5.9
Utah	106,667	19.1
Far West		
Nevada	16,296	1.2
Washington	300,143	7.2
Oregon	221,545	4.5
California	579,350	17.4

RURAL-FARM POPULATION, 1930

HUNDREDS OF THOUSANDS

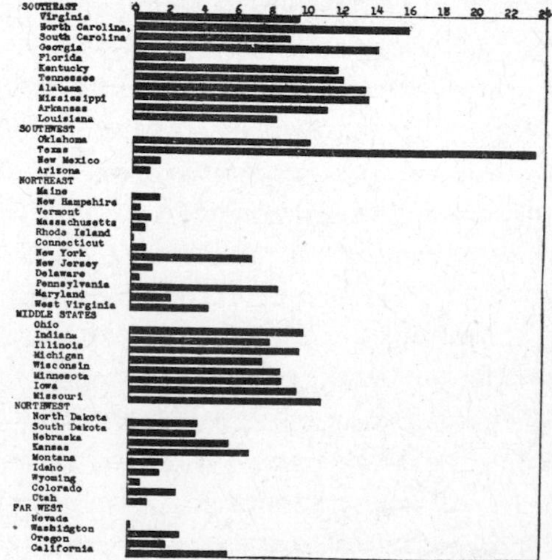

There is another way in which mere comparison is a poor index of status and capacity. There is, for instance, a subregion which reflects a low scoring with reference to the number and ratio of Negro high schools and high school students, yet which has increased 1,400 per cent since the turn of the century. The base comparison neither tells the story nor measures immediate capacity for further expansion. Or compare two units with reference to taxation payments, one in which the rating is low but represents an extraordinary increase and also a very large ratio to total income, with another region where the index is high but represents a recent decrease and a lower ratio to per capita income and wealth. Or to compare the educational equipment of two states in one of which the same tax rate yields eight times as much as it does in the other is a very poor index. The comparative measure while utilized for one purpose may sometimes find its chief value in the relative meanings involved. In either case it is necessary to know the realities of the case in order to work out specifications for next steps.

When we come now to test our fivefold measures of abundance, deficiency, waste, immaturity, and lag, as larger indices of the regions, the same values and limitations of the comparative method apply. Abundance and superabundance of natural resources can be measured in absolute terms and in comparison with other regions. When it comes to the measure of the abundance of human resources, new and varied indices are needed. There are, for instance, immeasurable undeveloped resources in the capacity of millions of southern folk to learn about and work with peoples from the rest of the nation. Such capacity has neither been measured nor developed. Another test might be found in the conflict patterns of the southern people. Still another measure of human resources might be made, for instance, in connection with technical deficiency by working out varied relationships between the phenomenon of ten million black folk whose health and professional welfare are provided for by an infinitesimally small percentage of trained Negro doctors, dentists, lawyers, and other professional folk, and by an almost disgracefully negligible provision of any sort. The same phenomenon illustrates the large measure of human waste as well as the extraordinary immaturity of Negro culture which, nevertheless, has changed phenomenally within even so short a time as the last decade.

Again, the measure of technological deficiencies is found not only in the physical realm but in the cultural indices of libraries, skills, universities, technical institutions, which may also indicate measures of cultural immaturity. So also with reference to the immaturity of regional cultures as measured by, let us say, universities. In the southern regions there

Average Annual Salaries Paid Public School Teachers, 1928

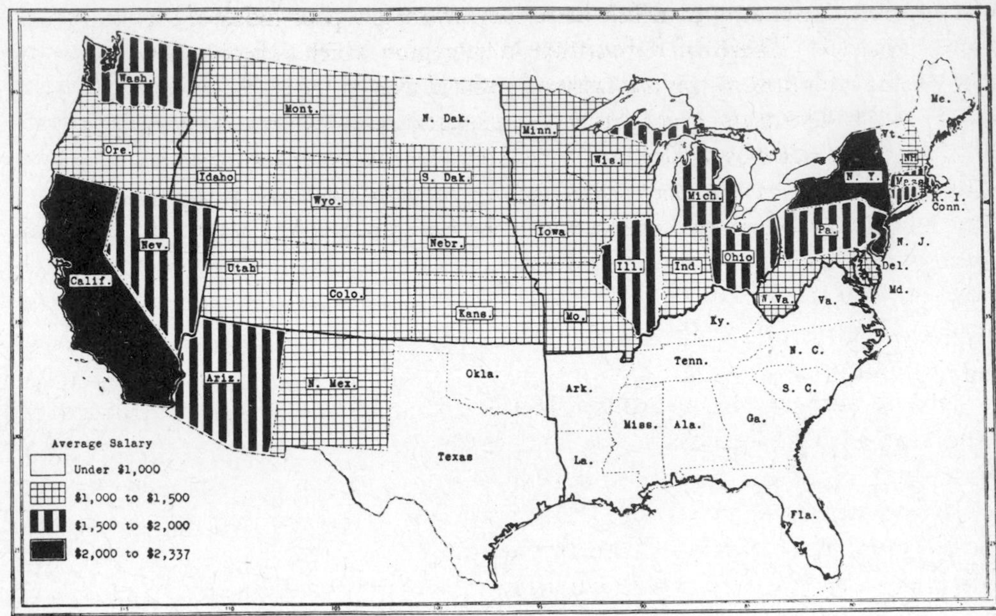

Expenditures for Public Education, 1930

Adapted from *American School Board Journal*, February, 1932

STATE	Per Child Attending		Per Child of School Age		Per Teacher Employed		Per Pupil Excluding Teachers' Salaries		Per Teacher for Salaries			Average Per Pupil in Attendance		Per Capita of Adult Population		Wealth Per School Dollar
	Rank	Index	Rank	Index	Rank	Index	Rank	Index	Rank	Index	Rank		Rank		Rank	
New York	1	112.19	3	74.98	1	106.14	2	107.79	1	110.30	1	$191.85	8	$43.92	47	$115.17
Nevada	2	108.54	1	89.84	3	87.63	1	127.54	15	72.29	2	185.60	3	48.03	12	191.01
New Jersey	3	102.53	4	69.13	2	104.42	12	68.97	2	106.43	3	175.32	6	46.37	46	118.49
California	4	94.90	2	75.70	5	86.80	5	80.62	3	99.57	4	162.28	14	38.16	45	119.05
Wyoming	5	86.52	5	65.60	25	53.01	13	68.83	20	68.83	5	147.94	1	48.76	38	143.32
Montana	6	85.59	6	61.93	21	60.47	4	87.35	25	59.23	6	146.36	4	46.98	26	170.80
Arizona	7	83.54	11	54.15	10	74.85	7	76.96	7	80.75	7	142.85	2	48.43	35	147.91
Delaware	8	82.44	12	53.19	4	87.04	3	92.40	12	76.53	8	140.98	17	35.22	40	139.03
Colorado	9	80.37	7	58.79	15	65.10	9	71.58	16	72.21	9	137.43	9	42.04	41	135.04
Connecticut	10	76.27	16	51.57	8	79.81	14	68.16	5	88.30	10	130.43	16	36.03	21	176.02
Michigan	11	75.64	8	58.38	39	39.87	6	79.58	8	79.75	11	129.35	10	40.59	48	113.42
Massachusetts	12	75.50	18	50.29	7	80.54	19	62.13	4	94.81	12	129.10	24	32.00	20	176.07
Illinois	13	74.73	17	50.65	9	76.20	10	71.54	9	79.46	13	127.78	25	31.67	7	210.40
Rhode Island	14	74.39	28	40.39	17	63.90	15	67.01	18	70.01	14	127.20	30	27.85	16	190.56
Ohio	15	74.36	13	53.06	6	81.74	8	74.95	6	81.05	15	127.16	18	35.12	34	148.71
Iowa	16	71.53	9	54.68	23	55.97	11	69.59	27	57.48	16	122.31	13	38.17	11	198.50
Washington	17	69.64	10	54.46	13	69.19	18	62.97	13	75.81	17	119.08	21	32.91	23	173.90
Oregon	18	68.68	14	52.21	14	66.94	26	56.75	11	78.56	18	117.44	28	30.77	10	203.69
Kansas	19	67.60	15	52.01	26	52.12	21	61.96	26	57.74	19	115.60	15	37.50	31	160.94
Wisconsin	20	66.33	26	42.19	20	60.90	27	56.23	17	70.16	20	113.42	29	30.34	28	168.29
Minnesota	21	65.99	23	45.85	22	56.67	24	59.16	24	62.54	22	112.85	19	33.52	17	185.53
Pennsylvania	22	64.61	27	42.02	11	73.33	23	59.66	10	78.94	23	110.48	23	32.39	19	179.98
South Dakota	23	64.52	22	45.74	37	41.66	25	56.80	34	46.65	24	110.32	11	39.63	3	224.92
North Dakota	24	63.24	21	46.06	34	42.98	16	64.18	41	42.36	25	108.14	7	44.86	30	161.14
Maryland	25	63.18	32	36.77	12	71.52	20	62.09	14	72.74	26	108.03	35	25.39	18	180.79
Nebraska	26	61.93	24	44.34	33	43.63	32	49.32	30	52.51	27	105.90	20	33.38	5	215.50
New Hampshire	27	61.10	29	40.04	19	61.55	17	63.54	22	63.93	21	113.03	34	25.44	6	213.93
Indiana	28	60.46	20	46.99	18	63.52	28	54.42	19	69.81	28	103.39	26	31.44	33	158.54
Idaho	29	60.22	25	44.08	27	48.54	30	49.87	28	56.88	29	102.97	12	38.85	15	191.23
Utah	30	59.94	19	47.03	16	65.09	22	60.70	21	64.26	30	102.51	5	46.73	37	144.00
Vermont	31	55.56	31	37.54	30	45.93	29	54.36	33	46.91	31	95.00	33	25.50	27	168.71
Missouri	32	54.77	30	37.71	24	55.84	33	47.55	23	63.19	32	93.65	36	24.44	8	204.91
New Mexico	33	54.64	34	32.74	28	48.17	34	45.67	29	56.08	33	93.44	22	32.86	29	166.27
Maine	34	49.28	33	34.95	29	46.05	31	49.45	35	45.89	34	84.27	38	24.02	13	193.87
West Virginia	35	47.13	35	31.72	40	38.10	40	31.24	31	50.95	35	80.59	27	31.32	14	192.59
Texas	36	44.90	38	28.10	32	44.56	35	44.15	37	45.01	36	76.78	37	24.29	39	141.92
Oklahoma	37	42.82	37	28.22	36	41.78	38	36.23	32	48.21	37	73.22	32	26.06	44	128.78
Florida	38	40.46	36	28.63	38	40.46	36	39.24	42	41.68	38	69.19	39	21.39	32	160.78
Louisiana	39	38.75	40	22.01	31	45.68	37	38.62	36	45.83	39	66.26	40	20.11	25	171.09
North Carolina	40	36.12	39	23.63	35	42.65	39	35.79	39	43.04	40	61.76	31	27.00	42	132.29
Kentucky	41	31.08	43	17.81	41	36.48	43	21.57	38	47.64	41	53.15	45	16.13	22	175.14
Virginia	42	30.65	41	19.11	42	33.38	42	22.22	40	42.56	42	52.41	43	17.99	1	242.96
Alabama	43	27.97	45	16.21	43	32.63	41	22.94	45	38.50	43	47.83	44	16.80	36	147.66
Tennessee	44	27.79	44	17.61	47	28.97	47	16.30	43	40.94	44	47.52	46	15.97	4	220.44
South Carolina	45	27.16	46	15.99	45	29.26	44	19.15	46	37.90	45	46.45	41	19.76	24	171.11
Mississippi	46	26.30	42	18.30	46	29.13	45	19.13	47	37.06	46	44.97	42	18.60	43	130.05
Arkansas	47	24.68	47	14.77	44	32.23	46	18.28	44	40.58	47	42.20	47	14.61	9	204.06
Georgia	48	20.05	48	12.06	48	22.81	48	11.56	48	32.47	48	34.29	48	12.32	2	240.63

has been a phenomenal increase in enrollment and facilities for higher education. Yet immaturity is registered by the small number of people in each state, active in the control of state policies, who know or care what a first-class university is or should be. Or to point the inquiry, is it possible to have a mature culture where there are no universities of the first order? Such a query manifestly can be partly answered by comparative reference to the Old South or to other regions of the nation. So also the relative degree of cultural immaturity reflected in the attitudes and experiences of the people with reference to race contacts and culture, to the higher brackets of intellectual endeavor, and to wider participation in national affairs.

If the sum of the measures of resources, technology, and culture be expressed in terms of deficiency and inadequacy, the negative measure of prevailing economy may best be expressed in terms of waste. For the southern regions show a very large ratio of waste of both physical and social resources, resulting in an immeasurable drain in land and men and morale. The realities of the situation, therefore, are essentially paradoxical. No matter what the hidden possibilities may be, the South under the present economy is not capable of attaining the highest economic and cultural development. Yet an examination of the whole range of evidence indicates that both the limitations and the waste may be practically remediable through normal processes provided social study, social planning, and social action be extended to comprehend the more recently recognized institutional and cultural foundations of planning as well as the economic and political factors immediately involved.

Unevenness, deficiencies, excellencies, possibilities, may all be indicated on a comparative score card. In a series of 152 indices in which the states and regions are ranked in their order of priority in the nation, the Southeast falls within the lowest quartile in 89 instances, with five states ranking above 100, while the average for the highest quartile is only about 15 out of the 152, low states ranking 7, 10, 11, 13. Similar rankings of other regions show for the lowest quartile, Southwest 45, Northeast 24, Middle States 15, Northwest 26, Far West 16, while for the highest quartile the Southwest is 23, Northeast 46, Middle States 40, Northwest 39, and Far West 68. Or to make the comparison in another way, the Southeast with a possible aggregate of 1672 points registers only 167 or approximately 8 per cent in the top brackets; the Southwest with a possible 608 points shows 91 or 14 per cent as compared with the Far West's 273 or 43 per cent of the same number. On the same basis the Northwest registers 25 per cent, the Middle States 25 per cent, the Northeast nearly 30 per cent.

Regional Distribution of All College Students in the United States With Special Reference to Residence as Reported by the United States Office of Education, 1932

State and Region of Institution Attended	Total Number of Students From								
	State	Region (Exclusive of State)	South-east	South-west	North-east	Middle States	North-west	Far West	Total
Southeast	......	......	*130,163*	*1,760*	*8,179*	*3,647*	*356*	*233*	*144,338*
Virginia	12,037	2,245	14,282	309	3,457	579	57	36	18,720
North Carolina	14,538	1,250	15,788	38	1,424	169	8	8	17,435
South Carolina	9,521	2,600	12,121	16	142	55	7	1	12,342
Georgia	11,107	2,461	13,568	121	356	208	33	7	14,293
Florida	5,307	359	5,666	16	374	228	15	9	6,308
Kentucky	16,086	805	16,891	80	550	939	66	55	18,581
Tennessee	12,415	3,031	15,446	388	499	647	75	30	17,085
Alabama	9,649	1,572	11,221	214	1,156	492	28	46	13,157
Mississippi	8,345	248	8,593	64	38	109	5	2	8,811
Arkansas	5,271	160	5,431	190	111	111	34	18	5,895
Louisiana	10,258	898	11,156	324	72	110	28	21	11,711
Southwest	......	......	*1,214*	*71,832*	*297*	*887*	*616*	*393*	*75,239*
Oklahoma	26,366	668	210	27,034	70	260	351	35	27,960
Texas	39,417	425	948	39,842	119	272	117	73	41,371
New Mexico	1,972	197	30	2,169	40	94	78	70	2,481
Arizona	2,685	102	26	2,787	68	261	70	215	3,427
Northeast	......	......	*4,745*	*1,134*	*289,777*	*10,802*	*1,987*	*1,929*	*310,374*
Maine	3,165	1,176	61	......	4,341	26	4	3	4,435
New Hampshire	2,125	1,498	44	14	3,623	424	57	34	4,196
Vermont	1,308	1,191	8	1	2,499	10	3	2	2,523
Massachusetts	27,602	12,383	735	257	39,985	3,040	454	631	45,102
Rhode Island	1,515	1,104	8	4	2,619	116	4	3	2,754
Connecticut	3,880	3,345	289	85	7,225	995	123	173	8,890
New York	93,023	17,509	1,518	410	110,532	2,988	813	554	116,815
New Jersey	8,749	3,178	184	42	11,927	496	66	57	12,772
Delaware	367	74	2	21	441	......	......	......	464
Pennsylvania	71,426	9,762	749	137	81,188	1,671	216	249	84,210
Maryland	9,428	4,188	887	146	13,616	728	224	218	15,819
West Virginia	11,002	779	260	17	11,781	308	23	5	12,394
Middle States	......	......	*4,465*	*2,165*	*11,712*	*245,568*	*6,971*	*1,349*	*272,230*
Ohio	40,936	2,429	1,477	113	4,377	43,365	275	116	49,723
Indiana	20,166	4,074	494	134	1,411	24,240	253	119	26,651
Illinois	46,155	6,229	836	462	1,797	52,384	1,519	480	57,478
Michigan	29,510	3,723	527	154	2,357	33,233	384	121	36,776
Wisconsin	17,044	3,039	148	257	701	20,083	429	82	21,700
Minnesota	22,105	2,378	139	53	208	24,483	1,758	120	26,761
Iowa	20,758	2,318	203	196	382	23,076	1,013	104	24,974
Missouri	21,488	3,216	641	796	479	24,704	1,340	207	28,167
Northwest	......	......	*271*	*963*	*482*	*5,871*	*82,735*	*929*	*91,251*
North Dakota	8,448	198	3	4	41	773	8,646	13	9,480
South Dakota	5,803	197	16	6	11	348	6,000	12	6,393
Nebraska	16,625	1,231	59	107	114	2,444	17,856	137	20,717
Kansas	23,800	423	94	515	65	1,708	24,223	102	26,707
Montana	4,540	120	8	7	31	103	4,660	65	4,874
Idaho	3,908	85	4	6	14	25	3,993	285	4,327
Wyoming	1,018	122	11	9	27	38	1,140	15	1,240
Colorado	10,006	599	69	263	172	403	10,605	161	11,673
Utah	5,130	482	7	46	7	29	5,612	139	5,840
Far West	......	......	*254*	*901*	*694*	*1,517*	*2,440*	*81,391*	*87,197*
Nevada	832	156	......	28	3	6	......	988	1,025
Washington	16,507	824	39	66	57	198	841	17,331	18,532
Oregon	9,375	1,034	5	18	19	56	226	10,409	10,733
California	51,649	1,014	210	789	615	1,257	1,373	52,663	56,907

The facts above shown are represented graphically on page 106 where they are also compared with similar ratios for selected larger institutions in the Southeast. In both instances the proportions of out-of-region students is greatest in the Southeast.

These indices are, of course, in no sense definitive or reliable measures except in multiple perspective. And of those indices in which the Southeast ranks high they are more often than not either measures of potential resources or of drain upon capacity. Illustrations include the largest proportion of total population enrolled in schools but with lowest per capita wealth and income to support the schools; or the largest proportion of population living on farms and the lowest per capita man power and income returns on farms; or the highest birth rate, the highest ratio of taxes to value of property, or high ratio of mileage and expenditures for roads. Others in the highest quartile which indicate drain and strain, as well as excellence, include a high ratio of local taxes to true wealth; a high ratio of total population attending school; a large percentage for school expenditures; a large percentage of Negro population; a large increase in taxes and indebtedness for public improvement; a large expenditure of money for automobiles. The specific nature of needs and measures for planning will be apparent from even the hastiest purview of the low-high rankings, such as the lowest ratio of purebred stock and lowest income from dairy products alongside the highest ratio of expenditures for commercial fertilizer and the largest area of eroded lands. Yet the total inventory presents an extraordinary array of variations and contrasts, with always a long list of indices of potential abundance.

As bearing upon the chasm between reality and possibility and also upon great cultural differentials in both quantity and meaning of indices, a state ranking highest in the largest number of indices of wealth, estates, capital, population increase will likely rank highest also in the ratio of federal relief funds to all relief expenditures, while a state with a high ranking in mineral resources and land abundances may more nearly approximate bankruptcy, or receive the highest rates of federal land rentals. Or there may be high ratios of income alongside low contribution for agencies for the development of general cultural development or the public weal.

Or again the southern regions having the richest of possibilities in land, streams, agriculture, climate, rainfall, growing season, afford unreasonably large ratios of the erosion lands of the nation. Or to turn to human resources of the southern regions, their one-third of the population produces less than five per cent of the nation's leaders, with an aggregate net drainage of population to other regions of nearly 3,500,000 since the turn of the century. If the South's personnel were not capable of first rank achievement, that would be a special problem. If, however, it is capable and the region does not develop capacities, or having produced abundantly there is a failure to realize results, that is a problem even more susceptible to treatment. But for whatever reason, the South in the early 1930's had but a fragmentary representation upon the major national control groups—economic, social, educational—approximating perhaps from three to five per cent; and what is more there could not be found throughout the whole region proportionate numbers of individuals now equipped by education and experience to fill the quota. Again, on the basis of the costs of education, the economic earning capacity and the drain in inherited estates, the South may well be poorer by 15 to 20 billion dollars from its net loss by migration of more than three and a half million of its people to other parts of the nation.

The several hundred mapographs and statistical pictures accompanying them will provide a fair inventory of the situation as indicated. It is when we come to the more difficult task of pointing up, from an understanding of these elemental backgrounds and problems, actual specifications upon which to construct the more adequate regional culture, that the test of reality must be met. There are difficulties of focusing upon basic factors, of selecting the most available units, of relating each to the fabric of the whole, of making specifications properly geared in with time and action settings, and of determining both the outlines and priority schedules of a new order, against which the whole heart of the southern regions must protest and in favor of which there is no guide of experience. These problems will emerge as the study unfolds and will be treated specifically in the chapters that follow.

CHAPTER III

A NEW REGIONAL ANALYSIS: SOUTHERN REGIONS IN THE NATIONAL PICTURE

WE APPROACH our regional analysis in this chapter by inquiring further into the relation of the southern regions to other regions of the nation. In addition to such portraiture as may result from description and statistical inventory, it is hoped that there may emerge gradually, through the continuing series of map pictures, a clear-cut cumulative picture of the southern regions which could not be attained in any other way. The premise of this study is that there can be no adequate analysis of the southern regions without a corresponding interregional and national perspective. What the southern regions are, what the other analogous regions are and how they have been determined, how they compare with one another and with the southern regions, what all these regions mean in the fabric of American culture, and how important it is for the nation to transvaluate its earlier sectionalism into a new realistic regionalism—these are questions which are basic to method and content of any reliable and useful appraisal of regional capacity and trends. For just as it is not possible to understand or to plan for the next period of American development without a vivid sensing of great regional differences, so it is not possible to attain superior regional achievements without a very realistic sensing of national unity and culture. Romance no less than realism, culture no less than technology, convenience no less than commerce, politics no less than business, history no less than current dilemma, are all bound up in regions of land and stream, sunshine and rain, oil and ore, flora and fauna, in multiplied abundance and from mountain crag to shores of sand, from lakes to gulf, east and west, north and south, and in the middle places roundabout. For, calculated upon these indices, there is not merely one vast nation but a half dozen empires within its borders, definitive of the length and breadth and depth of the whole drama of a changing nation. What these regions are, what they mean in the fabric of the nation's culture is to be an increasingly important part of the changing Northeast, Southeast, Northwest, Southwest, Middle States, and Far West, all of which, except the Northeast and the South-

Illustrations of Current Regional Divisions of the United States

THE SIX MAJOR DIVISIONS BASIC TO THE SOUTHERN REGIONAL STUDY

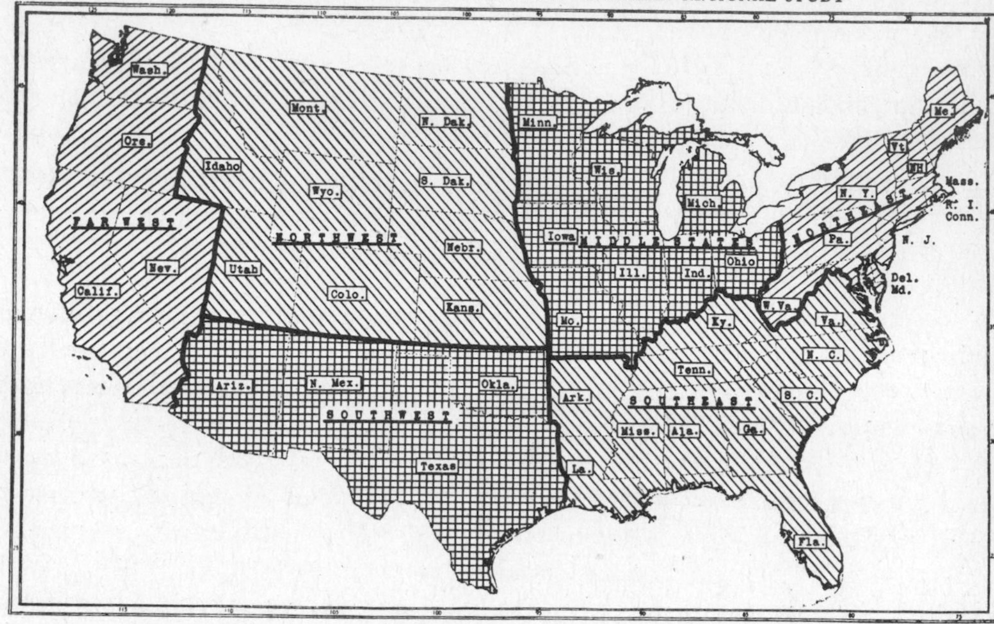

THE UNITED STATES FEDERAL RESERVE DISTRICTS

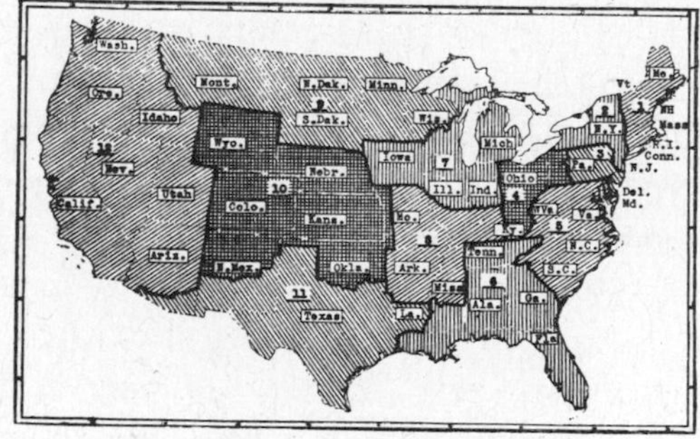

THE UNITED STATES CENSUS DIVISIONS

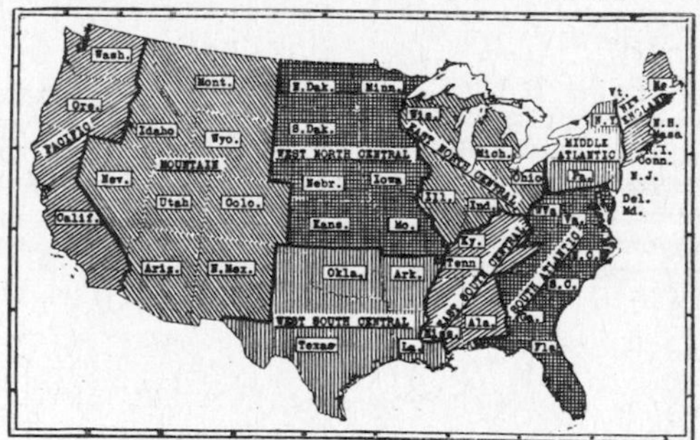

COMMERCIAL SURVEY REGIONS USED BY THE UNITED STATES DEPARTMENT OF COMMERCE

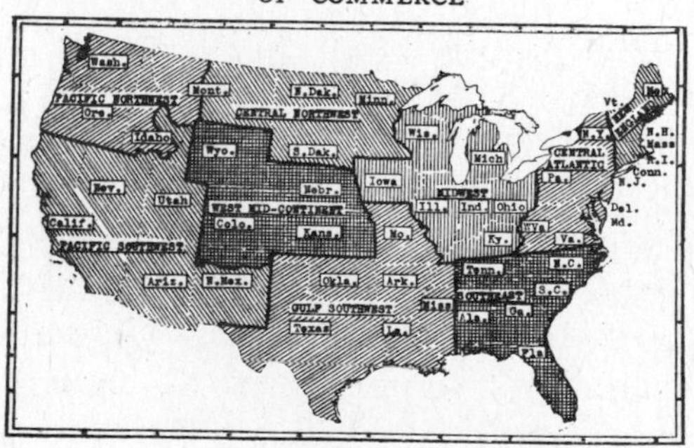

THE UNITED STATES CHAMBER OF COMMERCE GEOGRAPHIC REGIONS

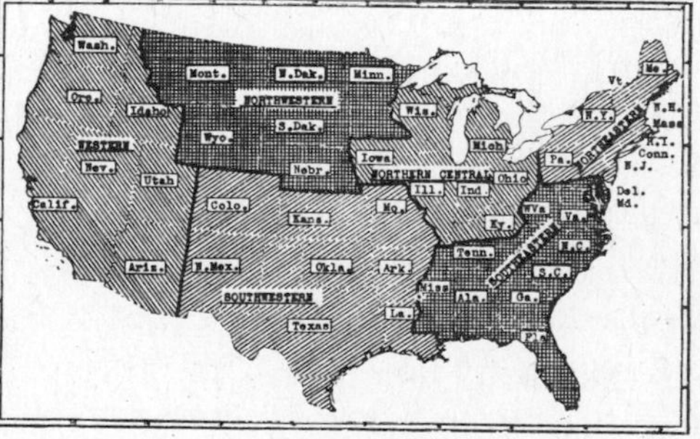

east are incredibly young in the annals of the new western culture and inseparably interwoven in the fabric of the nation's history.

Here are not only the southern states and regions but all the states, forty-eight of them, each with its rich historical backgrounds, institutional character, and interstate cultural conditioning. No matter what might be desirable or what might have been under other conditions the facts are that legally, constitutionally, historically, the American states are living realities. Here are groupings of states, tending to constitute relatively homogeneous areas of culture and geography. Here are other demographic groupings transcending state lines and reflecting through various indices of occupation, population, politics, religion, folkways, soil, climate, similarities enough to indicate a regional society distinctive in some ways from the rest of the country. Once again there are regions so differentiated primarily because of geographic, soil, or agricultural character, while others are functional regions looking to practical applications of commerce, trade, newspaper circulation, politics, financial organization, census enumerations, army organization, postal regulations. Moreover, there are still larger implications of regionalism in the traditional divisions of North and South, East and West, and in the perennial twofold division of the nation—half rural and half urban, with the urban half suddenly grown to two-thirds and comprising nearly a hundred metropolitan subregions of over a hundred thousand people each; and the tragedy of the transfer of rural regionalism in old frontier America to the rise of industrialism, "a regional story with a different epic theme for the same tragic circumstances in every regional landscape."

One of the most important of the new implications of regionalism in the nation reflects a trend contrary to what has often been predicted and finds a sort of counterpart in the increasing tendency toward economic nationalism. It had been freely predicted that modern communication, technology, and standardization processes would tend to minimize regional and national differences. There is, however, the important fact that certain economic aspects of both regionalism and nationalism have been accentuated by modern technology. Communication, transportation, and invention bring regions and nations closer together, but they may also solidify groups and standardize production. In the older days, for instance, the manufacture of finer fabrics, cloths, and paper was centered in northern and eastern regions of the United States. The progress of science and invention later made it possible for the South to compete on more favorable terms. Continued development easily leads to competitive rivalries which accentuate regional or sectional interests. The same sort of thing is likely to apply in other regions and to other commodities, setting, for instance, the Middle

Sample Pictures of Wage Differentials With Non-Identifiable Lines in Textile Fabrics, Apparel, Lumber and Timber Products

These maps are presented to show only the broad outlines of regional divisions exhibiting confusion between Southeast and Southwest.

Adapted from Research Division, N. R. A.

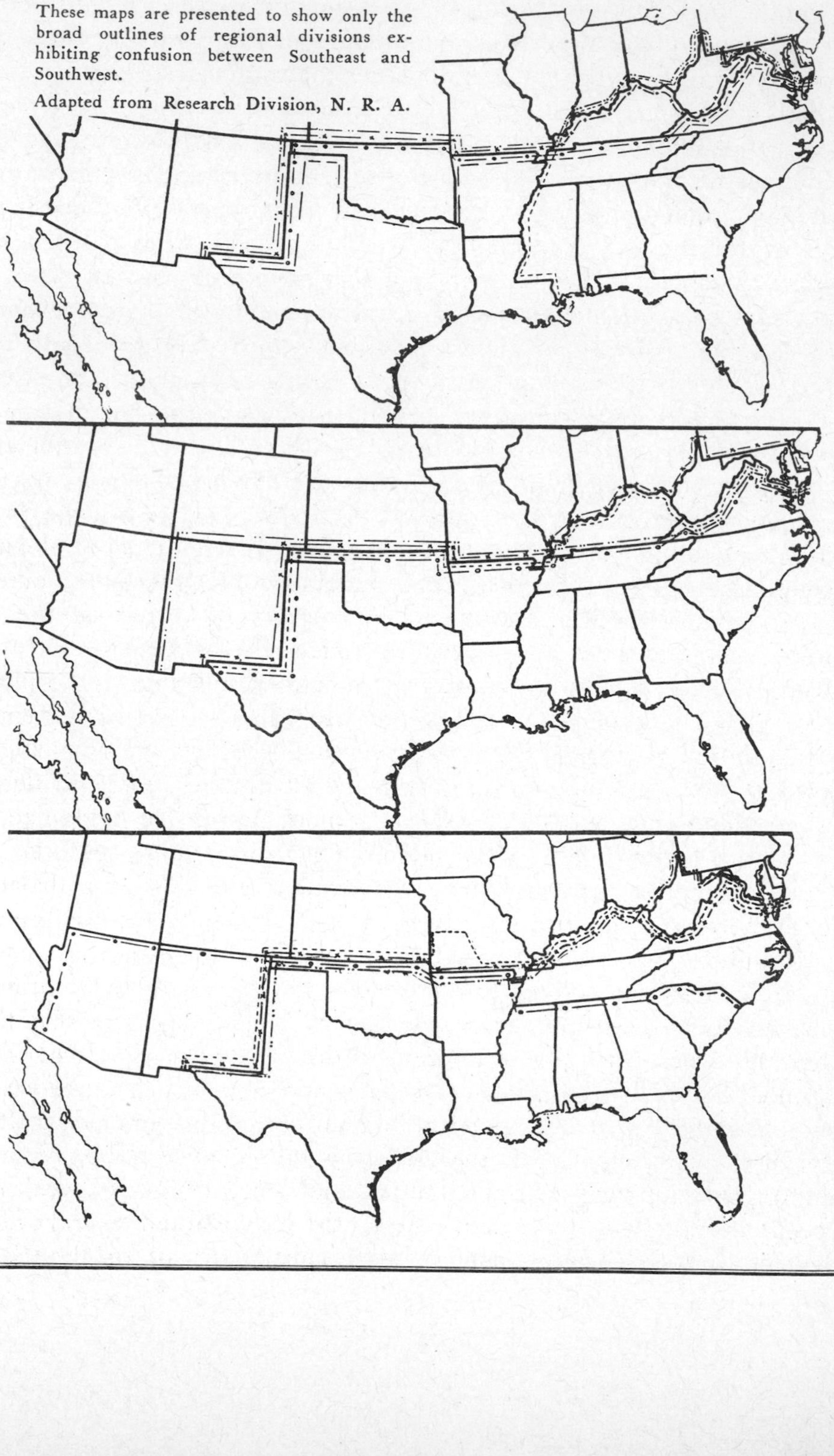

States and the Southeast in regional rivalry in furniture making and the dairy industry, or the Southwest and the Far West in citrus fruits, or the Southwest and the Southeast in cotton growing and manufacture. It applies also to other nations—the production of cotton and cotton goods, of oil, of many things originally imported or exported; so that a new type of economic planning will be necessary to gear together interregional and international programs.

As if in substantiation of this hypothesis, there has been growing up a considerable movement for America to be "self-contained." A great array of data is presented to show how science and technology have made it possible now for the nation to produce what is needed, even to such basic materials as rubber. The assumption is that science has broken down the old division between manufacturing countries and raw material countries and is reducing the number of raw materials which come primarily from nature. The further assumption is that general cultural factors, science, ideas, literature, travel, recreation, should be international, but that goods, finance, economic processes should be primarily national. The same presumptions are applicable to regions within the nation, changing many of the earlier assumptions and in particular affecting especially both the Southeast and the Southwest. What this might mean to steel and petroleum in the southern regions might easily be imagined. Furthermore, even if economic nationalism were desired, the inventory of regions is the first essential to the inventory of capacity for national self-sufficiency.

In the United States, therefore, from whatever motivation, the picture of the regions of the nation is increasingly important. The earlier simple assumption that regionalism was only a glorified localism now appears completely outdated. Regionalism as a key to attaining balanced democracy and the redistribution of wealth is more and more recognized as sound theory as well as practice. Resources, differences, conflicts, cultural development, interregional free trade, planning for balanced regional optimum production programs and for interregional optima, for "the more perfect union," the historical and theoretical understanding of American society—all are elemental factors in the continuing reconstruction of the nation. For a long time it has been clear that there has been no America but many Americas of the North Americas, and within the United States it is an America of states and regions. Natural wealth, technological wealth, artificial wealth, human wealth, institutional wealth—every one is richly regional in origin or implication or distribution or conditioning or functioning. The distribution and concentration of wealth, of the people, of immigrant and native stock; the romance and drama of their settlements, and the conditioning of their culture are of the essence of

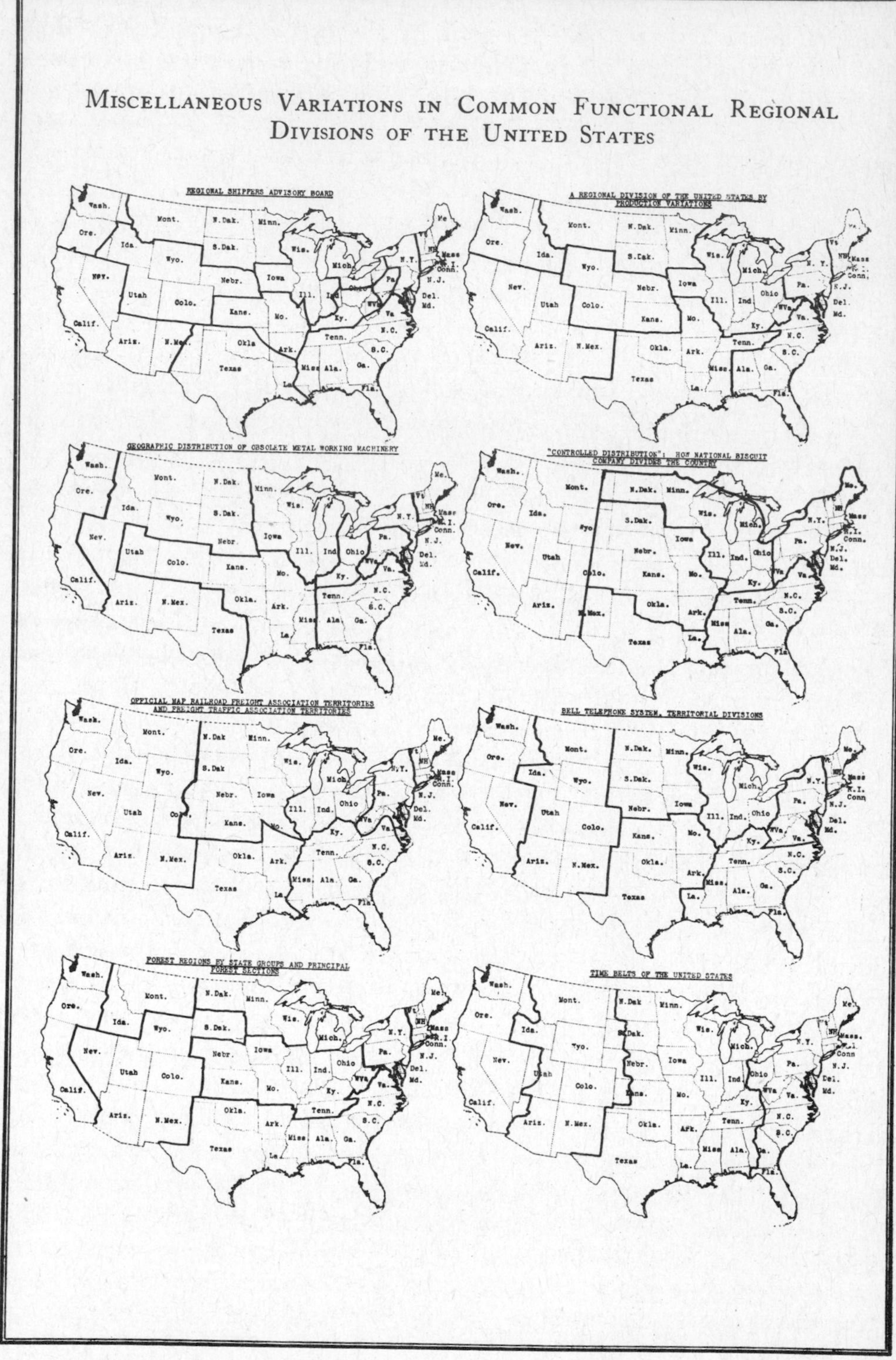
MISCELLANEOUS VARIATIONS IN COMMON FUNCTIONAL REGIONAL DIVISIONS OF THE UNITED STATES
REGIONAL SHIPPERS ADVISORY BOARD
A REGIONAL DIVISION OF THE UNITED STATES BY PRODUCTION VARIATIONS
GEOGRAPHIC DISTRIBUTION OF OBSOLETE METAL WORKING MACHINERY
"CONTROLLED DISTRIBUTION": HOW NATIONAL BISCUIT COMPANY DIVIDES THE COUNTRY
OFFICIAL MAP RAILROAD FREIGHT ASSOCIATION TERRITORIES AND FREIGHT TRAFFIC ASSOCIATION TERRITORIES
BELL TELEPHONE SYSTEM, TERRITORIAL DIVISIONS
FOREST REGIONS BY STATE GROUPS AND PRINCIPAL FOREST SECTIONS
TIME BELTS OF THE UNITED STATES

regional America, which in turn reflects a remarkable richness and variety of culture and of institutional ways of life. So, too, science, invention, technology, management, play a widely varying rôle in many different parts of the nation and in different aspects of life. These reflections are peculiarly applicable to the southern regions and the need for defining them in relation to each other and to the other major regions of the nation.

Thus, Sir William Beveridge wrote after a month's visit to the United States, "If I had to sum up my impressions, I should think in terms of drama; I should choose a parody from Pirandello: 'Six Americas in search of a Faith.'" These regions, he thought, are characterized by "profound divisions of race and history with opposed economic interests, with different ways of life and thought." And within each region, inventory of capacity and character, prospects and reasonable attainments and autonomy are of the utmost importance. Moreover, there are fundamental readjustments to be made in land utilization, in redistribution of deficiency groups and areas, and in multiple tasks for transforming cultural sterility into the sense and action of a more abundant life, a nearer approximation to human adequacy. In fine, it does not seem possible, without the regional approach, to build permanent foundations for national unity, to attain social and mental freedom, to develop creative research and discovery, or to achieve economic rehabilitation, sound legislation aptly adapted, and strong autonomous movements well integrated with the new public administration.

The merits of the regional approach to national study and planning inhere not only in this greater probability of attaining a national and interregional balanced social and political economy, but also in the opportunity for a better understanding and more effective and orderly development of each regional unit based upon essential differences, capacities, needs, fitness. In the case of the South, whatever else may be true, whatever may be its place in the national economy, it is "different" from the rest of the nation in much of its quantitative distribution of wealth, management, and labor, and in many of its folkways and institutional modes of life. These differences can be ascertained, stated, measured, plotted. Their significance, often quite different from what is commonly assumed, can be appraised in relation to regional capacities and cultural developments and to readjustment to other regions and to the whole national picture.

Finally, the American regional picture is rich in historical and theoretical backgrounds, interpretative and reminiscent of how civilizations grow and change, rise and fall, basic to the planning of a balanced political and social economy. Perhaps there is no need to elaborate further except to keep on emphasizing the theoretical significance of the region and folk society in the development of all civilization, whether it be in institutional

Examples of Variation in Federal Administrative Districts in which State Lines are Largely Ignored

Adapted from *Regional Factors in National Planning and Development* by the National Resources Committee

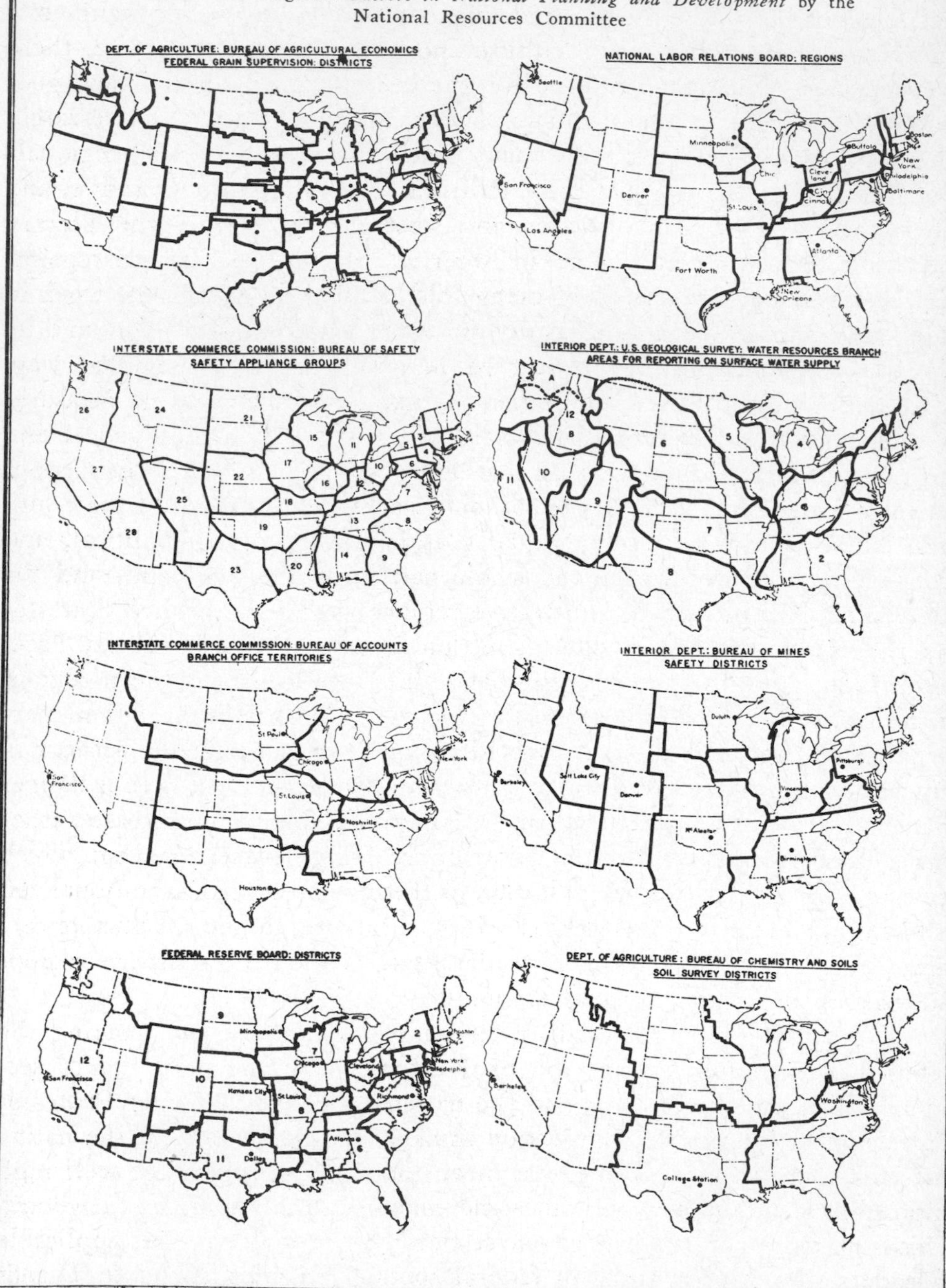

culture or in the long road from province to empire, and to emphasize the phenomenal ignorance concerning the various regions of the United States. It is amazing to observe how common it is to ignore the actualities of sound social theory and of the historical development of peoples. It must be clear that it is not possible either to understand or direct any society without a knowledge of its folk-regional culture and backgrounds. Likewise, there is everywhere abundant evidence for the reëmphasis upon the new geographical and demographical points of view in interpretation and research. These are all interlinked with the many practical aspects of current regionalism, such as regional mercantilism; industrial, political, administrative, and other phases of regional function and strategy; as well as the literary and artistic aspects of regionalism in America. As for the southern regions, the rest of the nation is tired of being told it must do missionary work in the South. The South is certainly no more enthusiastic. The middle ground of coöperative effort must be found through the regional way.

There is yet, however, one other premise upon which these measures of regional status and trend are based, which involves both practical and theoretical considerations. It is that there are fundamental distinctions between sectionalism, such as the authentic earlier sectionalism of the South or Frederick Jackson Turner's equally authentic, historical, political, and economic sectionalism within the whole nation, on the one hand, and the developing cultural and administrative regionalism of the United States of the 1930's, on the other. The distinction is not in the least merely "academic," but is of the greatest possible significance to the southern regions in the formation of their new policies and in the probabilities of their participation in new national and regional planning programs. For, without in any way accepting or rejecting the Turner sectional theories, there is danger that his prophecy that sectionalism in America is likely to increase rather than decrease may be realized in a sort of recurring new sectionalism, which appears to be primarily a revivification of the older sectionalism rationalized in terms of the "new regionalism." It is, therefore, important to note certain distinctions which have a particular bearing upon the southern regions and their place in the national economy.

In the first place, regionalism envisages the nation first, making the national culture and welfare the final arbiter. On the other hand, sectionalism sees the region first and the nation afterwards. Or, in Professor Turner's characterization, the section thinks "in other words, of the nation in terms of itself." This does not mean that regionalism is not well nigh impossible of attainment without some change in the American viewpoint. This is no more nor less true of one section than another; no less applicable if leaders who happen to be in federal control interpret, to quote Turner

Counties in the Southern Regions (Shown in Black) Having a Negro Population of Less Than 2500, 1930

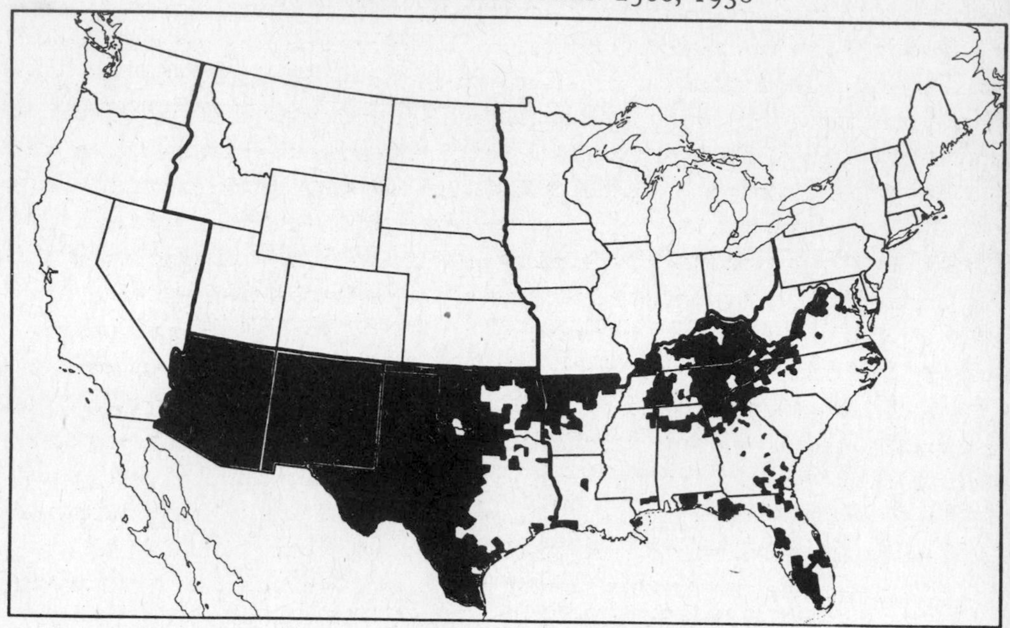

Counties in the United States in Which One Half or More of All Farmers Are Tenants, 1930

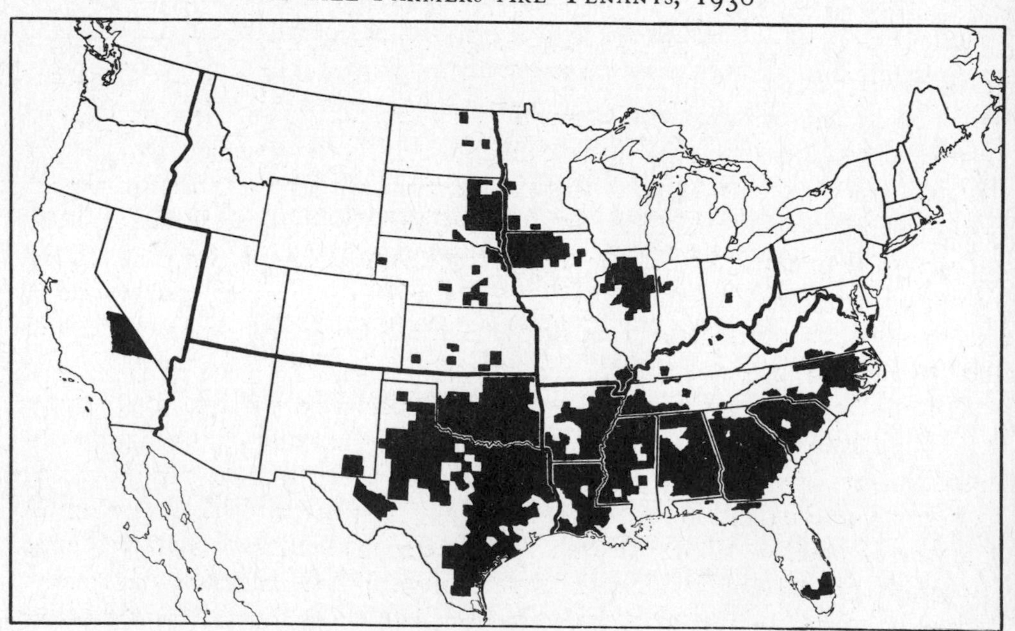

again, their own particular sectional "culture, economics, politics, and well-being as best for all the nation." Illustrations are abundant. One of the best may be found in the problem of race development and relations in the South. The evidence all indicates that it is not possible to make adjustments or work out solutions on any purely "southern," sectional basis, which logically would have in mind primarily the interests of the white South. On the other hand, in view of the dominance of folkways over stateways, of the actualities already existent, and of the cultural and historical backgrounds of the several regions and of the American principles of government, it is not possible to effect immediate readjustments through complete federal coercion and control, which would be analogous in many ways to the extreme sectional viewpoint. What is needed is a comprehensive approach looking to the facts and welfare of the nation, of the North and the South, of white and Negro, all according to the regional-national approach inseparably involved both in ultimate ends and in methods of attainment. There are fundamental differences involving both cultural and technical difficulties based upon sound, historical, and philosophical grounds.

A specific illustration of a real regional-national approach as opposed to the earlier narrow sectional may be found in the upbuilding of Negro institutions of higher learning in the South, in which southern institutions are being developed through interregional cooperation and aid, approximating mutual satisfaction to the South, the North, the Negroes, and the whites, as nearly as is possible under the circumstances. Thus the most eminent Negro men of science and letters in the nation have come to southern Negro colleges to develop a new era. This new educational statesmanship is a maturer development than the earlier limitations set by the South, in which it sought little education for the Negro, on the one hand, and the missionary spirit of the philanthropists from the North, on the other. It also represents the best thought and effort of the Negro race, whose personnel, skill, and training are being brought more and more to bear upon the problems in hand. A similar illustration might be cited in the case of public and elementary education in many of the southern states, in which such out of the region funds as Rosenwald, Slater, and Jeanes have contributed to a richer regional culture and a broader interregional contact.

In the second place, sectionalism emphasizes political boundaries and state sovereignties, technical legislation, local loyalties, and confederation of states "with common interests, menaced by federal action." Where sectionalism features separateness, regionalism connotes component and constituent parts of the larger national culture. Or, to use Turner's definition again, sectionalism is characterized by "those manifestations of economic and social separateness involved in the existence in a given region of a set of

Families Per Radio, 1930

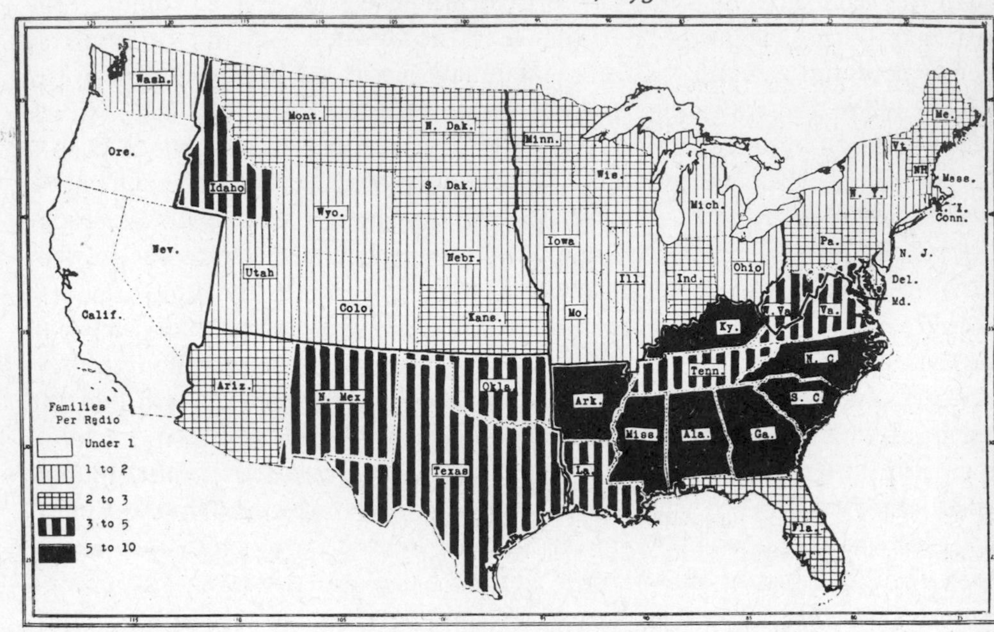

Per Cent of Farms Having Telephones, 1930

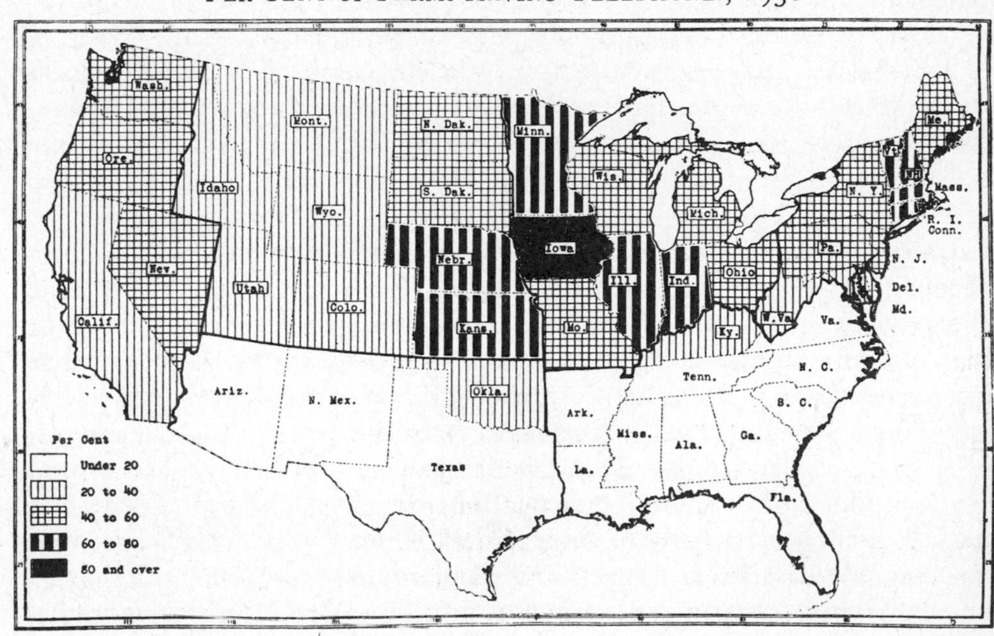

fundamental assumptions, a mental and emotional attitude which segregates the section from other sections or from the nation as a whole." Or still again, "the various sections of which the country is composed are thus seen as potential nations," and "the imagination stirs at the possibilities of the future, when these sections shall be fully matured and populated to the extent of the nations of the Old World." An illustration in point is that of the Old South of the Southern Confederacy and those states which feature certain sectional legislative enactments, such as requiring native teachers, in contrast to the present designated cultural and demographic regions of the Southeast and the Southwest.

Woodrow Wilson gave a clear interpretation of this sectionalism as opposed to realistic regionalism from the viewpoint of the citizen and the nation at large. Although a southerner and ever eager to emphasize the merits of the southern genius and culture, he had little patience with sectionalism. "Any man," he said, "who revives the issue of sectionalism in this country, is unworthy of the government of the nation; he shows himself a provincial; he shows that he himself does not know the various sections of his own country; he shows that he has shut his heart up in a little province and that those who do not see the special interests of that province are to him sectional, while he alone is national. That is the depth of unpatriotic feeling." This has no reference to geographic representation which recognizes the actualities of groups, occupations, aptitudes, cultures, and the special parts which they must play in the national drama.

In the third place, sectionalism may be likened unto cultural inbreeding, in which only home stocks and cultures are advocated, whereas regionalism is line-breeding, in which the regional cultures constitute the base but not the whole of new evolving cultures. As I have pointed out elsewhere, "In the one case only the local viewpoint, contacts, materials, and resources are utilized, while in the other local resources are utilized with reference to all other possible materials; and, if matters of social policy are involved, local resources are utilized and developed through skills made available through outside cooperation and cross fertilization of ideas. Sectionalism inbreeds to stagnation by ignoring time, technology, and collaboration; regionalism develops new strength from old power through progressive line breeding of new cultures, built upon the old." Another way of distinguishing the two is that regionalism may be conceived as a sort of cultural specialization within geographical bounds in an age which continuously demands wider contacts and standardized activities; or it may be the much desired way of quality in a quantity world. An illustration here was the prediction of the late Professor Giddings that one or more southern universities were destined to be the greatest in the nation if and when they

Eighteenth Amendment Voting

Adapted from the *New York Times*

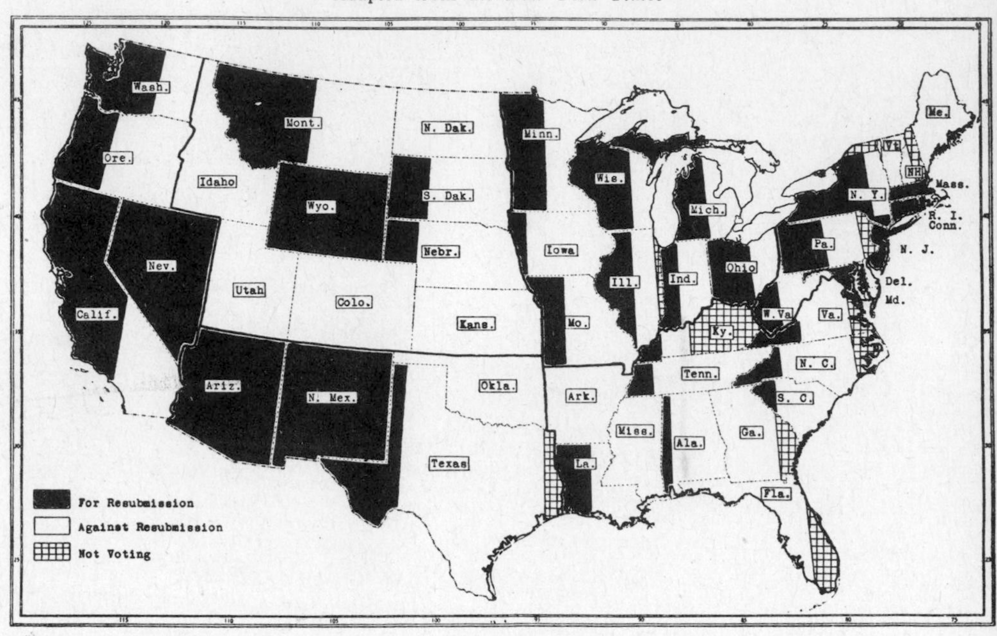

The Solid South

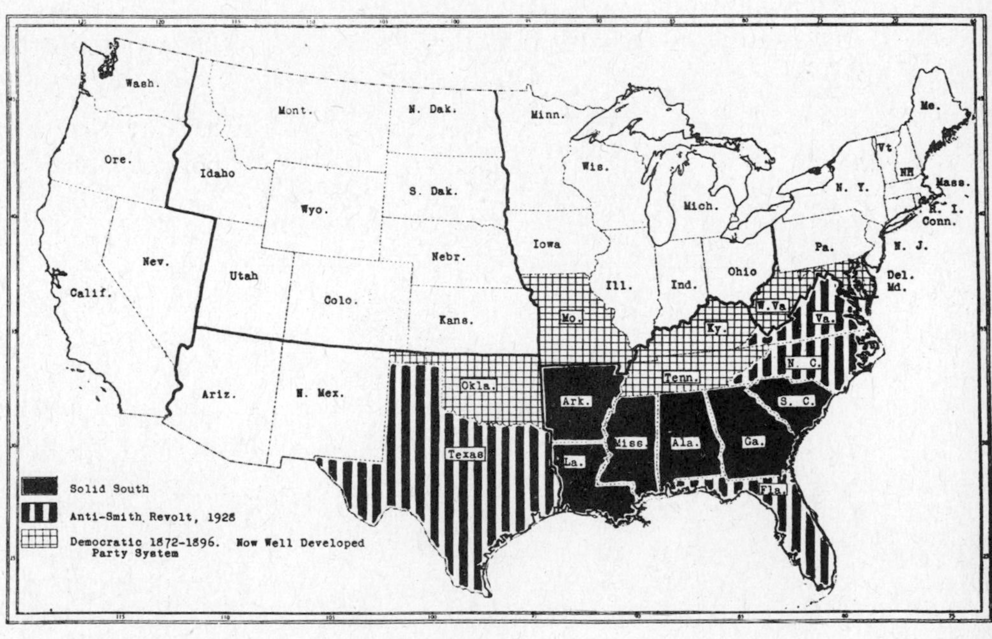

would command the best of faculty talent of North and South, because they could merge all regions on a new cultural border frontier, and could feature climate and finance and fellowship adequate to insure the best possible balance of desirable factors. This ideal he set up as opposed, on the one hand, to the older southern sectional colleges and, on the other, to mere quantity standardization of university work, with inferior standards imitative of other regions.

In the fourth place, regionalism by the very nature of its regional, interregional, and national cooperative processes implies more of the designed and planned society than sectionalism, which is the group correspondent to individualism. Whereas sectionalism would abound in conflict, making necessary buffer issues or areas or fighting grounds "for breaking the impact of sections and of affording a means of accommodating rival interests and shifting the balance of power," regionalism would find its buffer and adjustments through the well planned, interregional balanced economy. Instead of the old and recent recurring questions, will the South or the West "fight," there would be substituted the inquiry as to whether the South or the West or any other region will *plan* and *work together* for the mutually better ordering of the common good. Fundamental also is the significance of accommodating the many subregions within each of the major regions through the regional and interregional approach of social planning as opposed to the revivification of provincial cultures and selfish interests. As is everywhere agreed, the old American unlimited free competition must now be replaced by something better, so also the old sectionalism of the nation must be replaced by a realistic, social regionalism. Because the southern regions reflect strong individualism and a well-nigh invulnerable background of sectional pride and patterns, it has seemed necessary to incorporate the item of attitudes as our first approach to regional planning.

Finally, one of the most critical aspects of sectionalism is the fact that it must have its counterpart in a potential, and in the full flowering of its development, an inevitable coercive federalism, which is contrary to the stated ideals of American democracy. Not only does sectionalism sooner or later, as Turner points out, constitute "potential bases for forceful resistance," and thus necessitate federal coercion, but it gives excuse for the theory and practice of dictatorship which ignores regional, cultural, and geographical differentials, and almost inevitably goes too far in coercion and regimentation. Just as within the nation coercive federalism may become the objectionable counterpart to sectionalism, so sectionalism is analogous to the new economic nationalism as related to international economy.

Manifestly, these fundamental issues, always of the greatest importance, are accentuated in the new period of recovery and reconstruction.

Retail Sales Per Capita, 1929

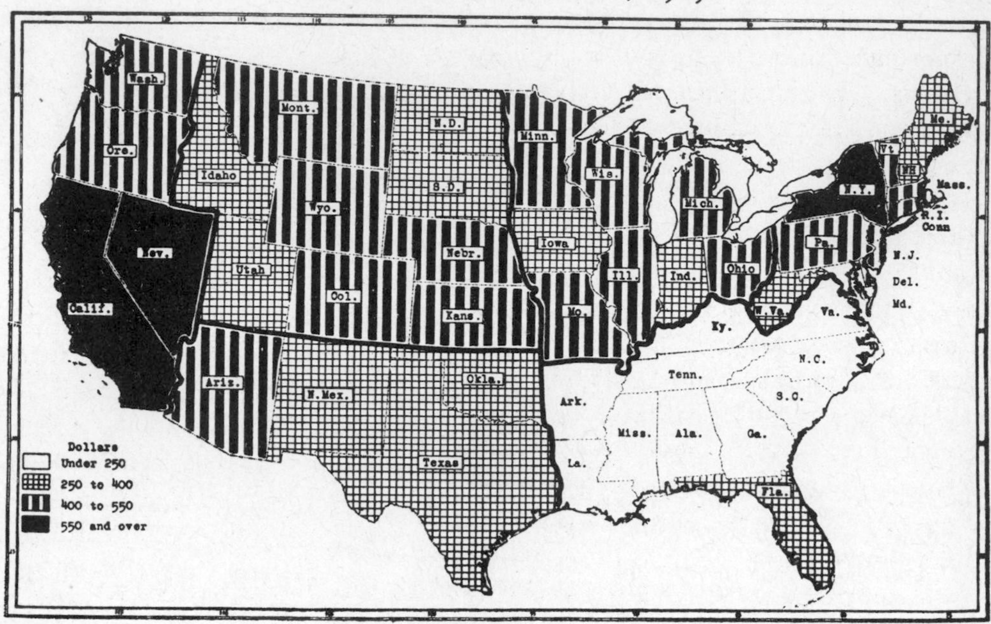

Wholesale and Retail Trade in the United States

STATE	Wholesale Trade Per Capita 1929	Retail Sales Per Store 1929	Retail Stores Per 1,000 Population 1930
Southeast			
Virginia	$270.97	$22,759	10.8
North Carolina	227.15	25,697	9.1
South Carolina	191.79	19,827	8.7
Georgia	349.87	21,466	9.9
Florida	317.69	22,203	15.3
Kentucky	204.31	21,712	10.4
Tennessee	411.82	27,656	9.0
Alabama	216.98	24,471	8.6
Mississippi	191.65	23,880	8.1
Arkansas	201.22	22,810	9.7
Louisiana	405.86	20,082	11.1
Southwest			
Oklahoma	324.24	28,878	11.5
Texas	481.46	30,839	11.5
New Mexico	126.58	28,748	9.9
Arizona	228.87	38,148	11.6
Northeast			
Maine	238.36	27,932	14.0
New Hampshire	132.81	27,867	14.0
Vermont	159.42	29,420	14.4
Massachusetts	727.48	38,230	12.7
Rhode Island	437.68	33,366	13.8
Connecticut	322.06	34,651	13.7
New York	1,403.28	38,119	15.1
New Jersey	251.04	30,753	14.9
Delaware	991.87	27,378	15.2
Pennsylvania	494.42	29,590	14.2
Maryland	454.44	29,051	13.0
Dist. of Columbia	720.23	56,088	12.1
West Virginia	200.60	25,581	10.0
Middle States			
Ohio	$465.54	$36,372	12.6
Indiana	284.60	29,412	12.9
Illinois	899.79	37,985	12.7
Michigan	449.03	39,715	11.6
Wisconsin	333.20	31,110	13.5
Minnesota	669.61	31,027	12.1
Iowa	427.76	32,991	13.4
Missouri	926.34	31,560	13.0
Northwest			
North Dakota	385.40	28,632	11.9
South Dakota	341.25	29,160	13.0
Nebraska	764.86	32,677	13.3
Kansas	542.62	30,691	13.8
Montana	294.69	34,317	13.0
Idaho	272.34	34,257	11.1
Wyoming	153.36	34,315	13.1
Colorado	521.62	35,402	13.6
Utah	355.56	37,808	10.4
Far West			
Nevada	150.75	38,177	14.4
Washington	733.88	34,866	14.2
Oregon	489.35	31,432	15.3
California	732.60	37,995	15.1
United States	567.12	32,297	12.6

They are important in the attempts to achieve a better balance between agriculture and industry, between man and machine, between the vitality of old cultures and the dominance of the new. They are of peculiar importance and of dramatic significance in the case of the southern regions. How important the issue is may be seen from many recent developments. Illustrations of current viewpoints which appear to lend support to the drift toward the "new sectionalism," include: "A Southern Confederation of Learning" by Benjamin B. Kendrick and "The Southern Philosophy of States' Rights" by Charles W. Pipkin, in the January, 1934, *Southwest Review;* an illuminating series by Donald Davidson, "The Dilemma of the Southern Liberals" in the February, 1934, *American Mercury;* "Sectionalism in the United States" in the July-September, 1933, *Hound and Horn;* "Where Regionalism and Sectionalism Meet" in the October, 1934, *Social Forces;* "Nationalism and the South" by Claudius T. Murchison in the January, 1934, *Virginia Quarterly Review;* "The Aesthetic of Regionalism" by John Crowe Ransom in *The American Review,* January, 1934; "Is This the Voice of the South" by John Gould Fletcher in *The Nation* for December 27, 1933; "What Economic Nationalism Means to the South" and a series of ten or twelve 1934 discussions by Peter Molyneaux in the *Texas Weekly*.

Now in the case of the southern United States, regions most complex and paradoxical, it must be clear that the situation is peculiarly difficult. The South not only differs from the rest of the country, but also, and radically, within its own former bounds. Its perpetual paradox must be emphasized again and again. There is no longer "the South" but many Souths. In addition to its multiple smaller subregions, which will be utilized for the purpose of more detailed analysis and planning, there are its two major regions, comprising the *Southeast*, with eleven states approxmately coinciding with the "Old South;" and the *Southwest*, with the four states of Texas, Oklahoma, Arizona, and New Mexico, comprising a new and evolving culture, already radically different from the Southeastern States in most respects and developing more and more into a regional culture distinctive from any other.

In order both to make adequate analyses and appraisals of the southern regions and to make due comparative studies basic to regional development, it was equally important to determine other major regions of the nation comparable in area and the other selected indices to those of the Southeast and the Southwest. During recent years various classifications of the states of the union into regional divisions for specific and practical purposes have been utilized. From a careful examination of these and many others, it is clear at once that they are not suitable for a statistical

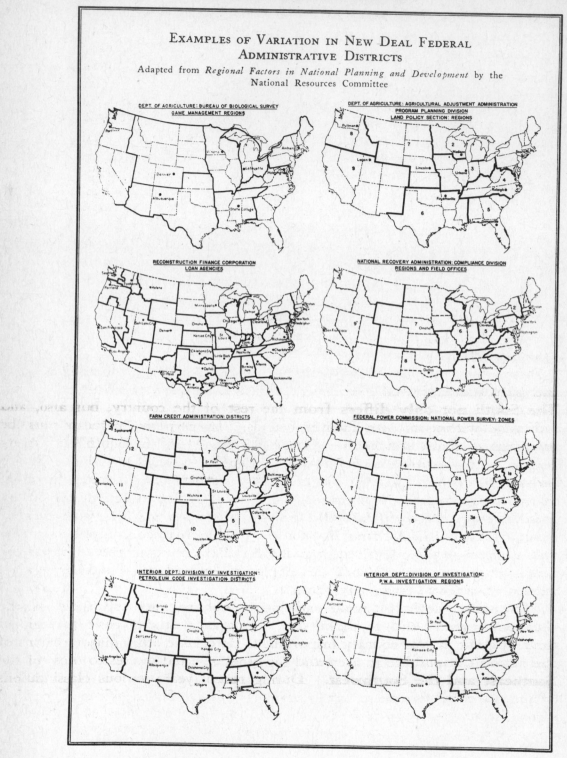

Examples of Variation in New Deal Federal Administrative Districts

Adapted from *Regional Factors in National Planning and Development* by the National Resources Committee

DEPT. OF AGRICULTURE: BUREAU OF BIOLOGICAL SURVEY GAME MANAGEMENT REGIONS

DEPT. OF AGRICULTURE: AGRICULTURAL ADJUSTMENT ADMINISTRATION PROGRAM PLANNING DIVISION LAND POLICY SECTION: REGIONS

RECONSTRUCTION FINANCE CORPORATION LOAN AGENCIES

NATIONAL RECOVERY ADMINISTRATION: COMPLIANCE DIVISION REGIONS AND FIELD OFFICES

FARM CREDIT ADMINISTRATION: DISTRICTS

FEDERAL POWER COMMISSION: NATIONAL POWER SURVEY: ZONES

INTERIOR DEPT.: DIVISION OF INVESTIGATION: PETROLEUM CODE INVESTIGATION DISTRICTS

INTERIOR DEPT.: DIVISION OF INVESTIGATION: P.W.A. INVESTIGATION REGIONS

and cultural study of contemporary changing regional society in the United States. A special grouping is, therefore, necessary if the desired results are to be obtained. For the purpose of such study, the designation of major regional divisions of the United States must meet a number of specific requirements: the number of regions must not be too large, nor, on the other hand, must the regions themselves be too large for effective study and unity. Each region should combine the largest number of geographic, economic, and cultural factors possible for the purpose of classification and study. Such classification must take into consideration historical factors, present trends and movements toward new developments, and a large number of elemental focusing indices, such as population, urban and rural trends, production and consumption of commodities, occupational and industrial factors, educational and philanthropic developments, special institutional character, political uniformities, and other measurable factors.

For a number of years the United States has been pointing toward regional analyses of its work and domain out of pure necessity of coping with magnitude and distances. More than 100 such administrative regions have been mapped out for functional use in banking, commerce, military strategy, power, relief. One group of these regional divisions served to focus varying interests and to enrich the amazing picture of the agricultural regions, veritable empires of the nation. Thirteen such regions there were: the corn belt, the hay and dairy region, the great expanse of grazing and irrigated crops region, the cotton belt, the corn and winter wheat belt, the hard winter wheat region, the spring wheat region, the humid subtropical crop belt, the North Pacific forest, the hay and pasture region, the Pacific subtropical crop region, the Columbia Plateau wheat region, and the Middle Atlantic trucking region. And in these a vast network of interrelated factors of growing season, rainfall, temperature, flora, fauna, accessibility.

The best known regional classification was the Census picture of the nation, long since a pattern recitative for statistical arrays and providing some remarkably inapt combinations. There were nine divisions of states: New England, Middle Atlantic, East North Central, West North Central, South Atlantic, East South Central, West South Central, Mountain, Pacific. There were paradoxical factors inherent in a division called Mountain, extending all the way from north to south and coinciding to a great extent with the agricultural region designated as grazing and irrigated farming country, and including much of the vast desert plains of America. Likewise, there was little in common between Delaware and many another state of the South Atlantic Division, such as South Carolina or Georgia. Certainly the District of Columbia was not "southern." Yet because of its

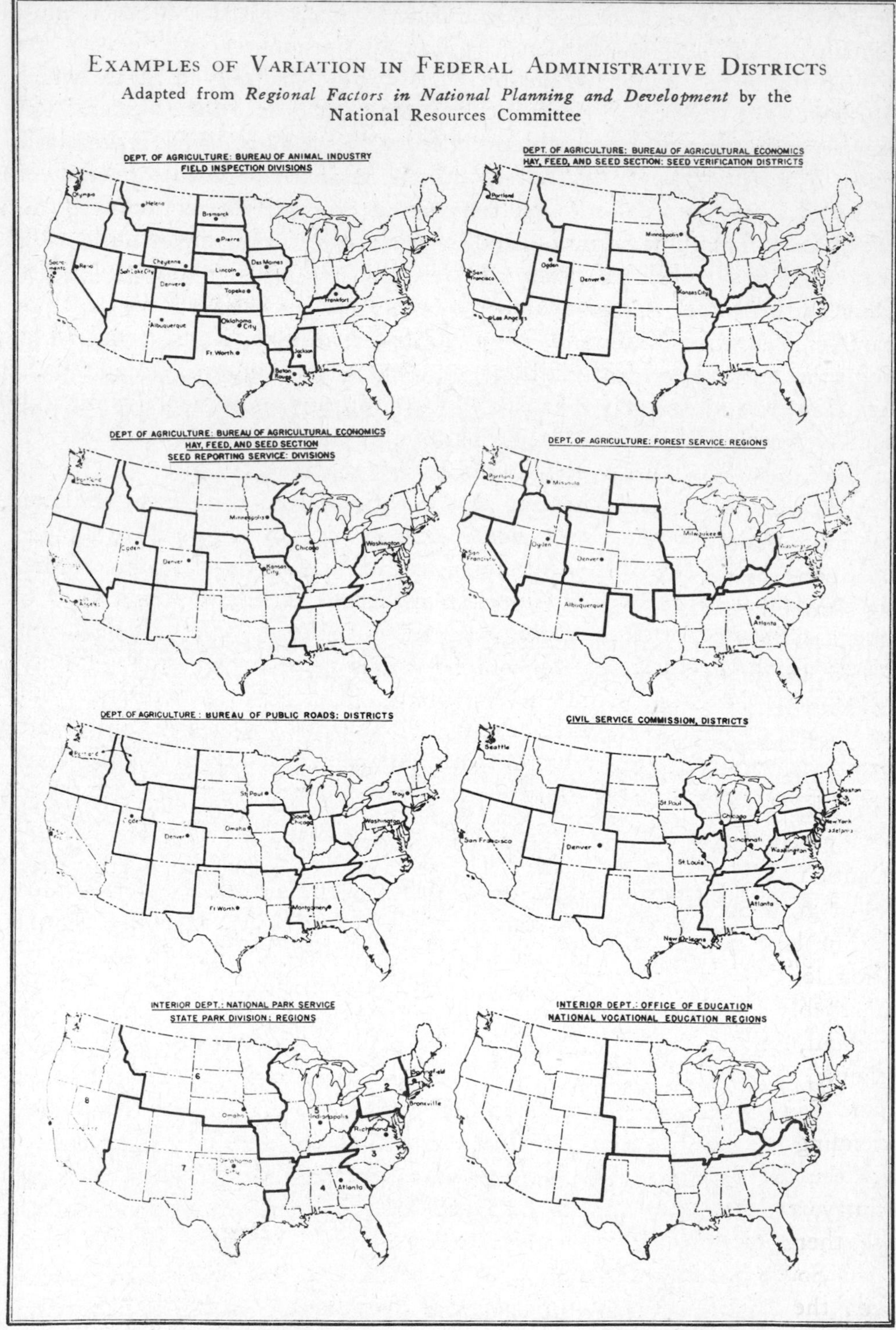

EXAMPLES OF VARIATION IN FEDERAL ADMINISTRATIVE DISTRICTS
Adapted from *Regional Factors in National Planning and Development* by the National Resources Committee

decades of usage and because of comparative data this classification must remain the simplest standard mechanical subdivision.

An important regional-functional division of the United States which illustrated the necessity for regional groupings was that of the Federal Reserve organization, which operated under twelve regions, varying greatly in size. Manifestly, however, there was little emphasis upon cultural indices. New York was a region unto itself as was also the metropolitan area focusing upon Philadelphia, Trenton, and the eastern part of Pennsylvania, while western Pennsylvania and most of Ohio comprised another separate region. On the other hand, Region Number 10 was large enough in area to include parts of Wyoming, Colorado, New Mexico, Nebraska, Kansas, and Oklahoma; and Number 12 was still larger, serving Washington, Oregon, California, Idaho, Utah, and Arizona. The incongruity is evident from a cultural viewpoint, of linking California, one of the richest of states, with so many states of such wide areas and differing wealth.

Two other regional divisions of the nation, from the scores available, are illustrative of the great range and variety of regional groupings. One was made the basis of the commercial survey of the United States Department of Commerce, and the other was the United States Chamber of Commerce geographic regions. The former comprised nine regions as follows: New England, Central Atlantic, Southeast, Midwest, Central Northwest, West Mid-Continent, Gulf Southwest, Pacific Southwest, Pacific Northwest. How Missouri, parts of which were near the center of the nation and a thousand miles from the healing water of the Gulf, could be included in the Gulf Southwest does not appear. The United States Chamber of Commerce division comprised only six divisions—the Northeastern, the Southeastern, the Southwestern, the Northern Central, the Northwestern, and the Western. Here again, Colorado and Kansas scarcely rate as Southwest. Another similar illustration of regional America was Goode's political map of the nation, cutting across state lines and composed of nineteen regions. In general, the Northeast included three or four subregions; the Southeast about the same number; the Middle States four; the Southwest two; the Northwest and Far West combined in five. These political boundaries were based upon economic areas and served to show the clarity of interrelated economic and political pictures so characteristic of the nation in the 1930's. More recently the varied votings on prohibition and upon national issues have made possible other useful regional groupings for the student of American morals and politics.

One of the best illustrations of both the need for satisfactory cultural regional analysis and also of examples of the most varied and confusing

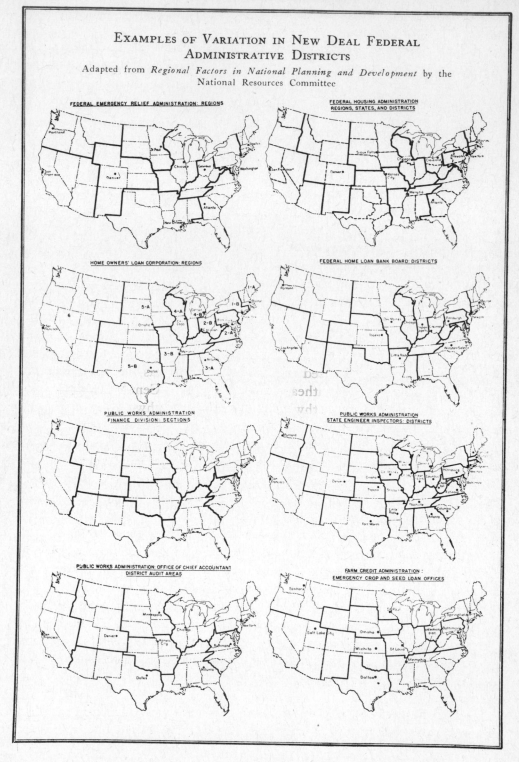

Examples of Variation in New Deal Federal Administrative Districts

Adapted from *Regional Factors in National Planning and Development* by the National Resources Committee

FEDERAL EMERGENCY RELIEF ADMINISTRATION: REGIONS

FEDERAL HOUSING ADMINISTRATION REGIONS, STATES, AND DISTRICTS

HOME OWNERS' LOAN CORPORATION: REGIONS

FEDERAL HOME LOAN BANK BOARD: DISTRICTS

PUBLIC WORKS ADMINISTRATION FINANCE DIVISION: SECTIONS

PUBLIC WORKS ADMINISTRATION STATE ENGINEER INSPECTORS: DISTRICTS

PUBLIC WORKS ADMINISTRATION: OFFICE OF CHIEF ACCOUNTANT DISTRICT AUDIT AREAS

FARM CREDIT ADMINISTRATION: EMERGENCY CROP AND SEED LOAN OFFICES

of all regional Americas is found in the multiple regional administrative divisions of the nation in the New Deal. First the National Planning Board, then the National Resources Board, then the National Resources Committee, experimented with and later studied the range, implication, and prospects of a more unified regional classification. Yet the countings are still being made, the functional indices multiplying, the names and areas still changing and overlapping. The National Planning Board included in some regions such varying states as Ohio and Virginia, Colorado and Missouri. The Tennessee Valley combined arbitrarily those states which were so much as touched by the Tennessee River drainage basin, omitting other states equally necessary to its framework of reconstruction. Again, the Mississippi Valley Committee gave expression to the verdict that the more than a score of states involved, because of their physical location within the great drainage valley, found their problems common problems. Thus Dayton, Ohio and Dayton, Tennessee, mountain village of Montana, and delta town of Mississippi. The Internal Revenue Bureau of the Treasury Department showed an extraordinarily wide range and density of regions. In one, El Paso, Texas and Louisville, Kentucky would contrast with the western part of Pennsylvania constituting an entire region in itself.

Other regional classifications were legion. During the early 1920's there were samplings enough to plot the map-picture of the nation in sufficient variety as to show the necessity for more satisfactory regional analysis of the nation. Another type of arrangement for a specific purpose was the Domestic Commerce Division of the United States Department of Commerce which listed 183 metropolitan and small city areas in the United States. These divisions, based upon indices of geographic territory, freight rates, zones of truck delivery, data from salesmen, and number of accounts in each county covered from 2,303 cities, constituted an excellent basis for study of economic circulation, and, especially if done from decade to decade, would indicate changing areas. It was also of importance in showing a picture of intercorrelations with newspaper circulation and other items.

As indicative of the possibilities of multiple subdivisions a somewhat similar map plotted by the J. Walter Thompson Company for retail shopping areas grouped 683 retail shopping zones about the same number of centers, to which were appended yet other 642 subcenters. A similar charting of metropolitan regions by Batten, Barton, Durstine, and Osborne divided the United States into 187 local area divisions comprising 745 subdivisions, in which the index used was the area covered by Sunday newspapers circulating out of major centers, and for subareas circulation of daily news-

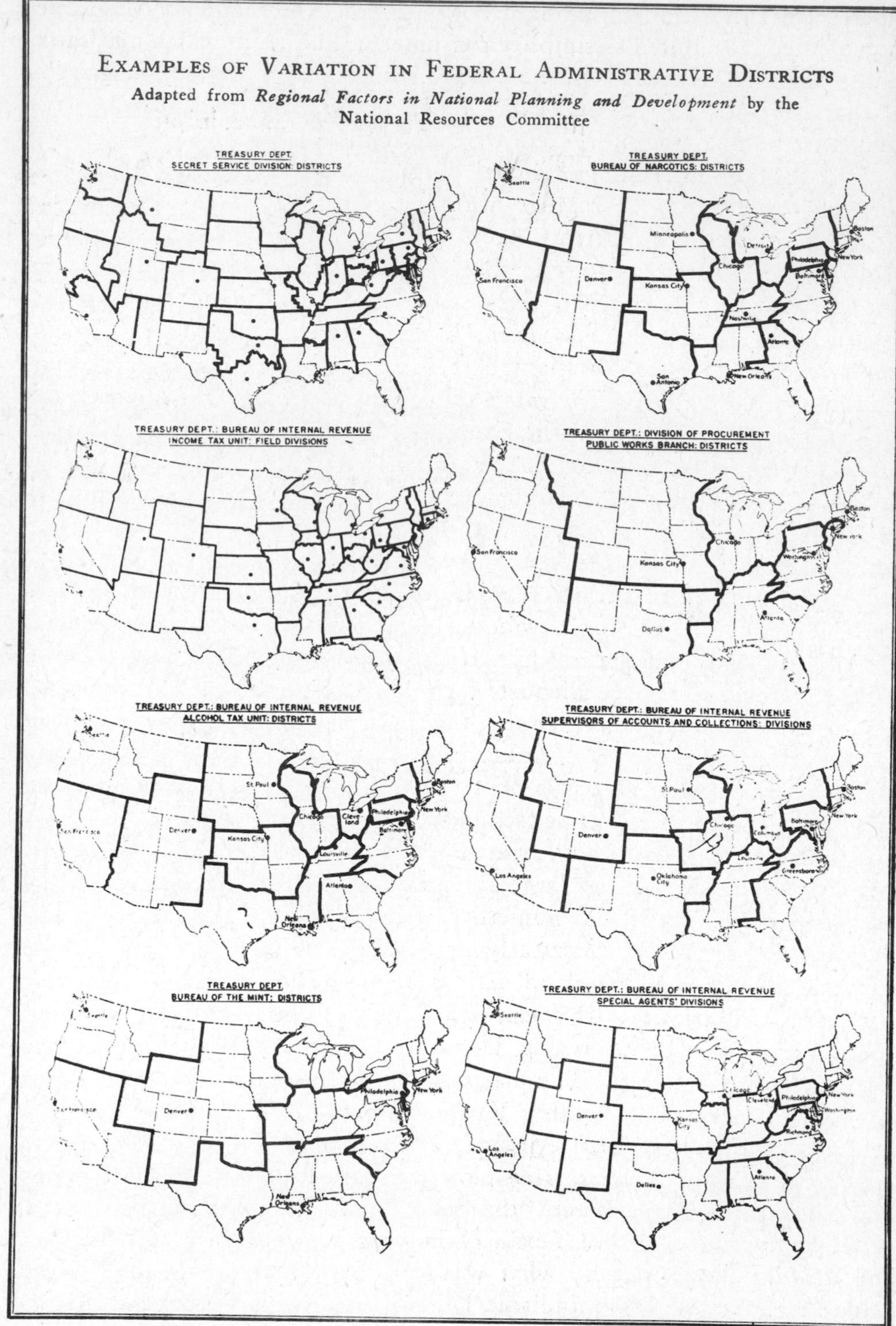

EXAMPLES OF VARIATION IN FEDERAL ADMINISTRATIVE DISTRICTS

Adapted from *Regional Factors in National Planning and Development* by the National Resources Committee

papers. In 1920 the Marketing Division of the International Magazine, Incorporated, attempted to simplify consumer selling from which maximum results might be secured. On the basis of studies of population, geographical characteristics, sources of wealth, trade outlets, and transportation, the boundaries of 632 trading centers were delimited.

Still another interesting regional division was that of the Army and Corps Areas plotted for regular army activities. This consisted of the First, Second, and Third Army Areas with three Corps Areas under each Army Area. There was considerable variation here, as, for instance, the Second Army Area comprised eight states of the southeastern group, but also included Michigan, Wisconsin, Ohio, Indiana, and West Virginia. Scores of other regional divisions bore further witness to the region consciousness of the nation. The range of activity was wide. In football, the big ten, the East, the South, the Southeast, the Far West, the Southwest, the Mountain. Regions for Rotary and Kiwanis, for Y. M. C. A. and Y. W. C. A., for church and religious bodies, for educational associations and historical groups, for lawyers and engineers, and the traditional banker and baker and candlestick maker.

From the study of various regions as found in the many map pictures available and by combining a wide range of factors, based upon general historical, cultural, and several hundred statistical indices, it was possible to construct a regional picture adequate for comparative purposes and in particular for understanding and planning the southern regions. For the present and for practical purposes of measurement it is, of course, necessary to designate each region in terms of a number of states, although in many instances cultural and economic factors transcend state boundaries. On such a basis six major regions approximate characteristics suitable for adequate portraiture; regions not too large for measurement and distinctive characterization, not so small and numerous as to complicate the picture. The *Northeastern* picture is practically synonymous with Frederick Jackson Turner's greater New England and includes twelve states: Maine, Vermont, New Hampshire, Massachusetts, Rhode Island, Connecticut, New Jersey, New York, Pennsylvania, Delaware, Maryland, West Virginia, and the District of Columbia. The *Southeastern* picture includes eleven states, approximating the "Old South": Virginia, North Carolina, South Carolina, Georgia, Florida, Alabama, Mississippi, Louisiana, Arkansas, Tennessee, and Kentucky. The *Southwestern* picture represents a new cultural region long since differentiated from "the South" and nearer West than South, including the four states of Texas, Oklahoma, New Mexico, and Arizona. The *Middle States,* largely what was long known as the Middle West, include eight states: Ohio, Indiana, Illinois, Michigan, Wisconsin, Minne-

Examples of Variation in New Deal Federal Administrative Districts

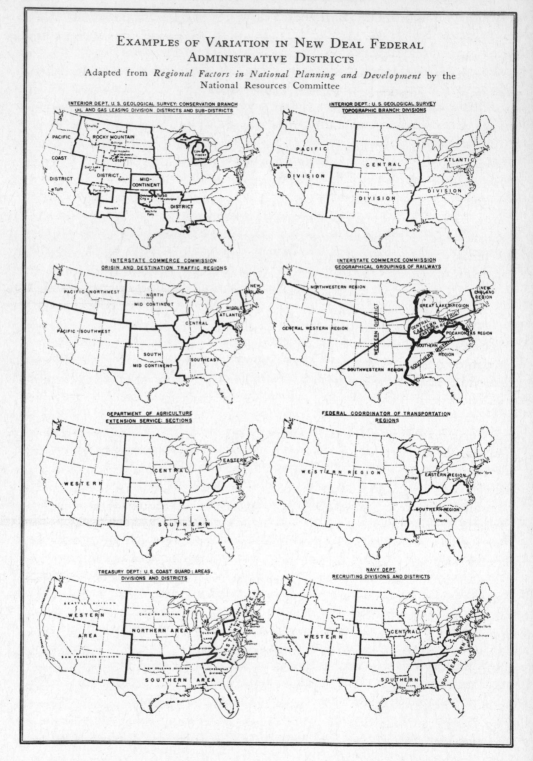

Adapted from *Regional Factors in National Planning and Development* by the National Resources Committee

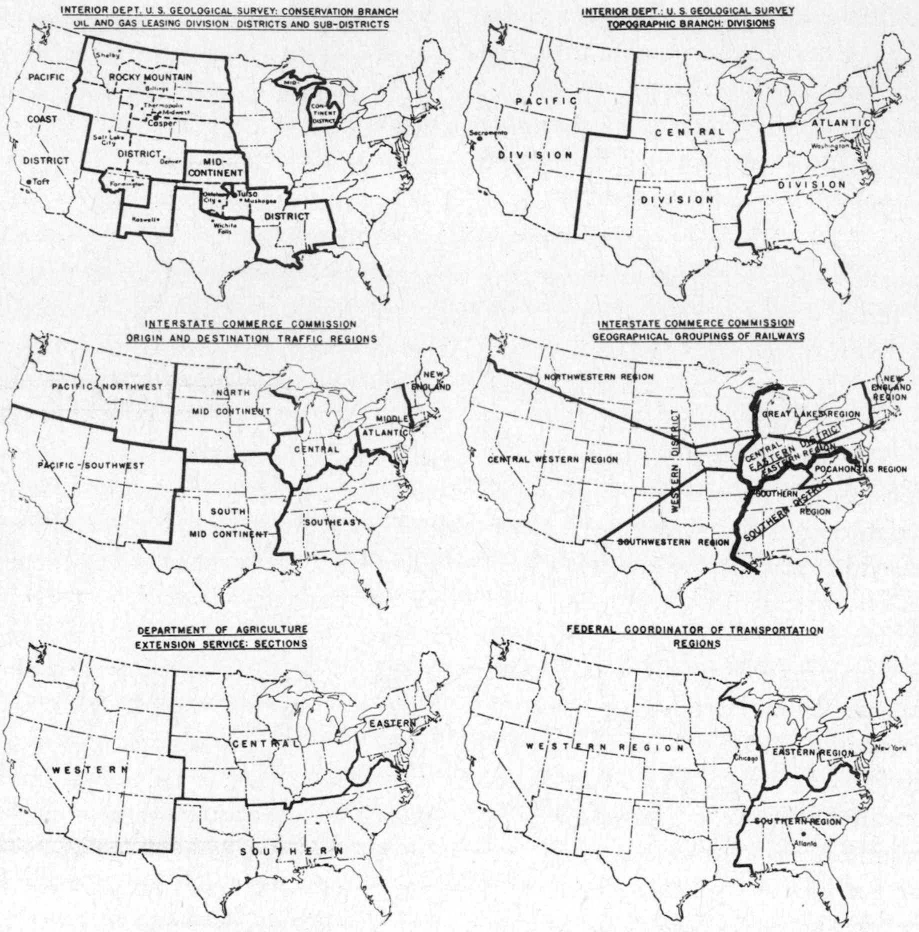

INTERIOR DEPT. U. S. GEOLOGICAL SURVEY: CONSERVATION BRANCH
OIL AND GAS LEASING DIVISION DISTRICTS AND SUB-DISTRICTS

PACIFIC COAST DISTRICT
ROCKY MOUNTAIN DISTRICT
MID-CONTINENT DISTRICT
Casper
Tulsa

INTERIOR DEPT.: U. S. GEOLOGICAL SURVEY
TOPOGRAPHIC BRANCH: DIVISIONS

PACIFIC DIVISION
CENTRAL DIVISION
ATLANTIC DIVISION

INTERSTATE COMMERCE COMMISSION
ORIGIN AND DESTINATION TRAFFIC REGIONS

PACIFIC NORTHWEST
PACIFIC SOUTHWEST
NORTH MID CONTINENT
SOUTH MID CONTINENT
CENTRAL
SOUTHEAST
MIDDLE ATLANTIC
NEW ENGLAND

INTERSTATE COMMERCE COMMISSION
GEOGRAPHICAL GROUPINGS OF RAILWAYS

NORTHWESTERN REGION
CENTRAL WESTERN REGION
SOUTHWESTERN REGION
WESTERN DISTRICT
GREAT LAKES REGION
CENTRAL EASTERN REGION
EASTERN DISTRICT
POCAHONTAS REGION
SOUTHERN REGION
SOUTHERN DISTRICT
NEW ENGLAND REGION

DEPARTMENT OF AGRICULTURE
EXTENSION SERVICE: SECTIONS

WESTERN
CENTRAL
EASTERN
SOUTHERN

FEDERAL COORDINATOR OF TRANSPORTATION
REGIONS

WESTERN REGION
EASTERN REGION
SOUTHERN REGION
Chicago
New York
Atlanta

TREASURY DEPT: U. S. COAST GUARD: AREAS, DIVISIONS AND DISTRICTS

WESTERN AREA
SEATTLE DIVISION
SAN FRANCISCO DIVISION
NORTHERN AREA
CHICAGO DIVISION
EASTERN AREA
SOUTHERN AREA
NEW ORLEANS DIVISION
JACKSONVILLE DIVISION

NAVY DEPT.
RECRUITING DIVISIONS AND DISTRICTS

WESTERN
CENTRAL
NORTHEASTERN
SOUTHEASTERN
SOUTHERN
San Francisco
New York
Baltimore
New Orleans

sota, Iowa, and Missouri. The new *Northwest,* comprising much of what was called the Mountain States, includes nine states: North Dakota, South Dakota, Nebraska, Kansas, Montana, Idaho, Wyoming, Colorado, Utah. Finally, the *Far Western* picture includes the four states: Washington, Oregon, California, and Nevada.

If it were not necesary to adhere to state lines, the same general sixfold division could be made more nearly to approximate a cultural division combining nearly all of the desired indices. Thus the eastern border of the proposed 100 mile belt of forest planting would represent the western boundary of both the Middle States and of the Southeast, adding to the Middle States a part of the Dakotas, Nebraska, and Kansas, while to the Southeast would go a small part of Oklahoma and Texas. So the borders of the Northeast would change to acquire a small part of Ohio, Kentucky, and Virginia, and to give up a part of West Virginia to the Southeast. The border of the Far West, too, would shift to leave most of Nevada and parts of Oregon and Washington to the Northwest. It would be possible, too, that the Southwest would annex a part of California's "Southland," while other shiftings would conform to specialized indices or functional analysis in accordance with the nature of the classification wanted or the focusing of indices.

Illustrative of this more informal cultural division, Guy-Harold Smith writes in *The Saturday Review of Literature,* January 6, 1934, in answer to the question, "What is Middlewestern?" "Probably the southern boundary of the Middle West lies somewhere near where the pronunciation changes from 'down' to 'daown,' or perhaps where the expression 'damn Yankee' becomes 'damnyankee.' The indefinite boundary between corn and cotton is a boundary which is no respecter of the political borders. While these three boundaries are not coincident we can be reasonably sure that a line representing the mean or average position is very close to the southern limit of the Middle West. On the west the Middle West ends at the twenty-inch mean annual isohyet. Near here a railway company posted Indians at the stations so the tourists might observe where the West begins. Where the tall grass of the prairie is replaced by the bunch grass of the plains is an indefinite line which separates the cornhusker from the cowpuncher. This boundary lies near the center of the Dakotas, Nebraska and Kansas at the hundredth meridian, which is labeled by such a convenient whole number. The northern boundary of the Middle West may be the Canadian border, but I believe it lies farther south near the center of Minnesota, Wisconsin and Michigan. . . . The eastern boundary is uncertain, though I believe that at or near Columbus, Ohio, the Middle West begins. Near here corn begins to occupy more land than any other crop. Also the

North Dakota, South Dakota, Kansas, Nebraska Are Not "Middle States"

The common designation of "Middle West," like that of "The South", is no longer definitive of the realities of the regions. Utilizing state lines, necessary because of statistical data available for analysis, North Dakota, South Dakota, Kansas, and Nebraska rank with the Northwest of the present regional classification, rather than with the Middle States, as indicated by a hundred or more indices listed below. In fifty or more these states might as well rank with the Middle States, or Minnesota, Iowa, and Missouri, might lean toward the further western group.

If state lines are omitted, then the regional division will be easily defined. Thus, the eastern portion of the Dakotas and Kansas and Nebraska are clearly homogeneous with the Middle States in soil regions, forestry belt, precipitation, land use, agricultural provinces, types of farming regions, natural vegetation, quality of land, submarginal land, as classified by the National Resources Board. Here also county medians indicate other indices which would give similar results.

Samplings of indices definitive of such ranking are given below.

1. Average daily attendance per 100 pupils enrolled in school
2. Average number of days attended by each pupil enrolled in school
3. Average annual salaries paid public school teachers
4. Per capita total expenditures in public day schools
5. Per cent of total enrollment in high schools
6. Per cent of total population enrolled in public schools
7. Per cent total illiteracy ten years of age and over
8. Native white illiterates ten years of age and over
9. Public society, and school libraries, population per library
10. Net paid circulation daily newspapers per 1,000 inhabitants
11. Rank of states based on twenty-three cultural tables
12. Composite rank in public education in the states
13. Per cent of school population 5-17 years of age in daily attendance
14. Ratio of population 21 years of age and over to those 5-17, inclusive
15. Average expenditure per teacher employed
16. Per capita cost for each adult, all expenditures
17. Per cent boys were to girls in high school
18. Total professional students per 100,000 population
19. Enrollment in all colleges per 100,000 population
20. Total graduate students per 100,000 population
21. Per cent of total population attending school
22. Passport applications per 1,000 population
23. Expenditure per teacher for salaries
24. Per cent school expenditures were of all income
25. State support of colleges and universities for maintenance
26. Circulation of the *Nation* per 100,000 population
27. Circulation of the *Atlantic Monthly* per 1,000 population
28. Circulation of the *Saturday Evening Post* per 1,000 population
29. Inhabitants per woman's magazine
30. Inhabitants per daily newspaper
31. Per cent of total income from agriculture
32. Per cent of income from manufacture
33. Per cent of income from mining
34. Per cent of income from sources other than agriculture, manufacturing, and mining
35. Per cent of total income from construction
36. Per cent of income from all other sources, exclusive of agriculture, manufacture, mining, and construction
37. Per capita production of electric power, all public utility plants
38. Per capita cost of state government
39. Federal personal income tax payments per capita of total population
40. Per inhabitant estimated true wealth
41. Per capita net income, federal personal and corporation income tax returns
42. Total personal income of those filing federal income tax returns reduced to per capita of total population
43. Per capita federal income tax payments
44. Bank resources per inhabitant
45. Per capita savings deposits
46. Per capita postal receipts
47. Per capita life insurance in force
48. Aggregate net income as reported in federal individual income tax returns for 1929, per capita of total population
49. Death rate per 1,000 population (South Dakota not given)
50. Deaths from typhoid fever per 1,000 inhabitants
51. Deaths from tuberculosis per 1,000 population
52. Cases of smallpox per 1,000 population
53. First admissions to hospitals for mental diseases per 100,000 population
54. Per cent of counties having hospitals
55. Death rate per 1,000 population
56. Supply of physicians per 1,000 population
57. Per cent increase in total population
58. Per cent increase or decrease in rural population
59. Per cent increase in native white population
60. Per cent increase or decrease in native whites of foreign parentage
61. Per cent increase or decrease in foreign-born whites
62. Per cent increase or decrease in Negro population
63. Per cent of males fifteen years of age and over married
64. Per cent males ten years of age and over gainfully employed
65. Per cent females ten years of age and over gainfully employed
66. Per cent of total population living on farms
67. Per cent increase or decrease in the rural non-farm population
68. Per cent of population 21 years of age and over Negro
69. Per cent of total population fifty-five years of age and over
70. Per cent of total population 19 years of age or less
71. Per cent increase in white population
72. Per cent increase or decrease in population, native white of foreign or mixed parentage
73. Per cent of total population urban
74. Per cent of Negroes in total population
75. Per cent native white of total white population
76. Per cent of foreign born in total population (not North Dakota)
77. Average per acre tax on farm land and buildings, farms operated by full owners
78. Ratio of mortgaged debt to value, farms operated by full owners
79. Ratio of taxes to value of land and buildings, farms operated by full owners
80. Per cent of farms having electric lights
81. Per cent of farms having electric motors
82. Average annual cash farm income per farm
83. Average value per farm of domestic animals
84. Value of land and buildings per acre of farm land
85. Ratio of charges to debt, mortgaged farms operated by farmers owning no other farm land (not South Dakota)
86. Average value per acre of land and buildings, full owners reporting mortgaged debt
87. Average value of land and buildings, owner operated farms
88. Per cent of owner operated farms mortgaged
89. Average gross income per farm per year
90. Average gross income from livestock per farm per year (North Dakota Midwest)
91. Per capita production of milk
92. Average total acreage per farm
93. Railway mileage per 1,000 square miles
94. Railway mileage, square miles of area per mile of line
95. Per cent of farms having telephones (not South Dakota)
96. Telephones per 100 inhabitants
97. Inhabitants per residence telephone
98. Prisoners received by federal prisons and reformatories per 100,000 population
99. Lynchings per 100,000 population

land is spread out in a terrain of low relief, as though there were not enough surface to permit the making of a rugged topography so characteristic of the Appalachian plateau."

In the case of the Southwest, the justification for the present four-state grouping does not rest solely upon the cultural and statistical indices presented in a later chapter of this volume. Fort Worth and Dallas are self-designated gateways to the great Southwest. They no longer answer to the roll call of "The South." Illustrative of the more general viewpoint, Paul Horgan writes "About the Southwest. A Panorama of Neuva Granada," in the *Southwest Review*, in the Summer Number, 1933: "A French map in the year 1679 showed the new land explored as far as the *terra incognita* of present-time Utah. The groaning wagons and horses had tried the terrain of Nueva Granada, that embraced everything we know now as New Mexico, Texas, Arizona, and part of Oklahoma. . . . His chart of what he found suggests that we use his name for the territory, since it so easily indicates the boundaries of the Southwest as we now regard it. In area, then, Texas, New Mexico, Arizona, and Oklahoma will constitute the Southwest of our time. . . .

"The Southwest is large enough to include the widest varieties of terrain, and thus of weather and of human pursuits. It is a country of one of two characters: either there are immense plains flat alike to the tempests and the endless days of sunlight, or there are mountains that challenge the zenith with the power of a legend. Only in the littlest local sense are there pastoral regions, with bounding green hills and. sustained valleys. This meant that, looking for natural securities and havens, the early people found none; and the resultant exercise of human ingenuity and faith produced that crew of pioneers whose philosophy so often seemed almost geological in its simplicity and its strength. The great river, Rio Grande, went slowly and widely down to the Gulf of Mexico, hardly oozing enough water in summer to slake a traveled animal train, going brown and reedy in the winter under its red banks, tearing away from the course of mountains in the spring, and changing the face of the deserts through which it went with the high breast of flood. So, either sleepy and endlessly peaceful, or sudden and terrible with storm and change, the life in the valley of the Rio Grande affords an easy figure for the life of the entire region."

When it comes to a satisfactory designation of the Far West, the problem is more difficult. To those who would rate California as a distinct and separate Pacific region comes the quick recognition that even California would divide itself into North and South and that there is a movement to add a part of California's "Southland" to the State of Arizona. We are thus reminded again and again that it is not possible to satisfy everybody

Indices Indicating that Nevada Ranks with the Far West More than with the Northwest

Nevada is an excellent example of Dr. Willis H. Miller's statement that in the creation of "groups of States" regions "there are no possible combinations of States which will serve ultimate aims, although they will serve certain designated proximate aims with entire adequacy. For example, Missouri, Illinois, and Indiana might be grouped with their northern neighbors to form a north-central region. This would result from considering the characteristics of the northern portions of these three States. But if attention be focused upon the characteristics of the southern parts of Missouri, Illinois, and Indiana, one can make just as valid a claim for grouping these States with their neighbors on the south. There is no known or possible grouping of States which would provide for Texas, which lies partly on the Great Plains and partly in the Cotton Belt, and both western and southern in its characteristics. The same may be said regarding Missouri, of which, part is southern and part is midwestern; part is forest and part is prairie; part is plain and part is Ozark; part is Corn Belt and part is general farming." The same is true to some extent for Arizona and New Mexico; while West Virginia easily qualifies for each of three regions—the Northeast, the Southeast, the Middle States, with perhaps a majority of the economic and deficiency indices ranking it with the Southeast. Again, for that matter there can be no completely satisfactory classification of parts of the same states such as east and west Oregon and Washington, northern and southern California, southern and northern Florida.

With these qualifications, the case for Nevada can be made to approximate a classification. First of all, it tends to rank with California and parts of Oregon and Washington in a generally high average in the indices represented by twenty-six items relating to wealth and twenty-four relating to education. In per capita wealth it is sixth and in education within the first quartile alongside California, Washington, and Oregon, the region composing those states commonly reputed to reflect the highest standard of culture in the world. Samplings from the conventional measures include the following:

1. Annual wage per wage earner all manufactures 1929
2. Per capita value mineral products
3. Per cent total income from agriculture
4. Ratio of farm tenancy
5. Average value farm land and buildings
6. Average gross income per farm per year
7. Gross income per farm per capita
8. Per cent cooperative sales were of cash farm income
9. Value of all farm property
10. Per cent total pasture land
11. Horse power available per worker
12. Per cent foreign born white
13. Per cent increase in urban population
14. Excess of births over deaths
15. Deaths under one year per 1,000 live births
16. Per cent total population under 20 years
17. Per cent total population 55 years of age or over
18. Per cent total population living on farms
19. Per cent males 15 years or over married
20. Per cent total illiteracy
21. Per cent net gain by interstate migration
22. Proportion females 10 years or over gainfully occupied
23. Proportion children 10-17 years gainfully occupied
24. Per capita total expenditures in public day schools
25. Average annual teachers' salaries
26. Daily expenditure per pupil in average daily attendance
27. Percentage total school enrollment in secondary schools
28. Ratio of aggregate days attended to total population 5-17 years
29. Value school property per pupil enrolled
30. Rank in public education
31. Per cent total population enrolled
32. Relative standing of states in education
33. Index of library development: number and circulation of books, registration of readers, annual expenditures, etc.
34. Net annual income per capita
35. 11-year per capita annual income
36. Value of homes owned
37. Per capita bank resources
38. Per capita postal receipts
39. Per cent savings deposits
40. Life insurance per capita
41. Per capita net income of corporations
42. Per capita true wealth
43. Personal incomes federal taxes
44. Retail sales per capita
45. Ratio of total state and local tax collections to private income
46. Relative standing of states in wealth
47. Supply of physicians per 10,000
48. Suicides per 100,000 population
49. Patients in hospitals for mental diseases
50. Families per radio
51. Number residence telephones per hundred population
52. Percentage urban families having radio sets
53. Percentage rural families having radio sets
54. Percentage rural-non-farm families having radio sets
55. Number farm telephones per 100 population
56. Hotel rooms per thousand population
57. Percentage farms on hard surfaced roads
58. Number air ports per million people
59. Combined circulation per thousand population of 47 national magazines

or to designate regions which qualify with all indices. In the case of the Far West the simplest way would be to make the usual arbitrary classification to include only the three Pacific states. Yet Nevada, in addition to being literally bound to California by the beautiful Lake Tahoe, shows more than a half hundred indices in which it ranks with California rather than with either the Northwestern or Southwestern States. Again, Nevada is uniform in physiography with eastern California's and Oregon's grazing and irrigated crop lands, and, if this be ruled out as the dominant index, the preponderance of other indices is clearly in favor of the Far Western Region being better balanced with Nevada than without it. Likewise, such an addition is of importance in effecting better equilibrium between southern California and northern California, and between California and the protesting parts of Oregon and Washington. Among the cultural indices which indicate Nevada's alignment with the Far Western Region are a number of population indices, some relating to Reno and Carson City and urban increase, its rural population, its percentage of foreign born white, its percentage of increase of births over deaths, its age groups, its ratio of people living on farms, its percentage of illiteracy, its percentage of children gainfully occupied, its ratio of children enrolled in schools, its percentage of increase in population from interstate migration. Still others are those relating to income from minerals, ratio of farm ownership and tenancy, value of farms, wealth, income, rank in education, health, savings, bank deposits, state and local tax collections, and two score more. It does not qualify by position or other compelling indices as Northwest or Southwest, so that both by positive factors and by the process of preferential elimination it ranks with the Far West decidedly more than with any other region.

Originally mooted points with reference to the Southeast concerned the limits of the Northeast and of the Southwest and of the Middle States centering around certain border states. Missouri is not Southeast by any plurality count, certainly not by location, while its preponderance of indices differing from "the South" rules it out from almost every viewpoint. Its farms and its folkways are not southern. It lies almost literally at the center of the nation. St. Louis and Kansas City, for instance, are not southern cities. The other border state giving most trouble is West Virginia, which ranks now with the Southeast and now with the Northeast. In perhaps forty indices commonly connoting deficiency in culture and institutional standards it tends to rank with the Southeast. Thus in value of farms, lands, property; in horse power per worker, machine farming; in population under twenty years, over fifty years; in wage earners and wages paid; in value of manufactured products; in rank in education and other services. On the other hand, in its industries, its educational institu-

Per Cent of Land in Farms in the Southeast, by Subregions, 1930

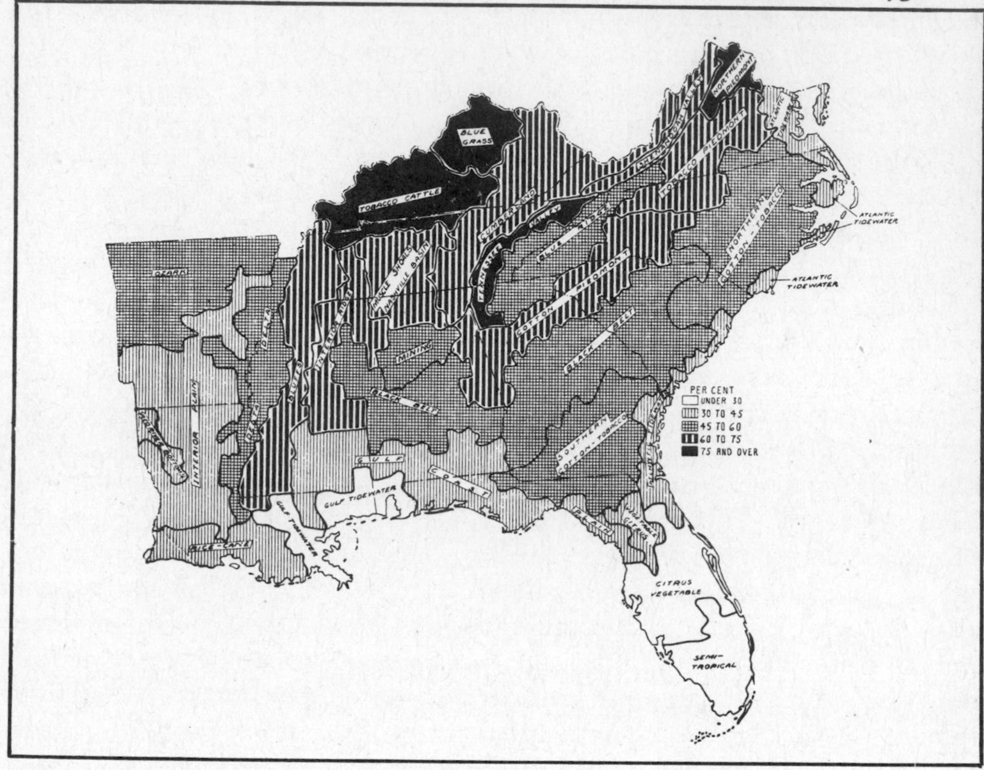

Rural-Value Indices on Southern Farms, Per Farm, 1930

STATE AND REGION	Value Farm Implements and Machinery	Value Dwellings	Average Annual Cash Income 1920–1930
Southeast			
Virginia	$ 260	$ 1,226	$ 871
North Carolina	151	653	994
South Carolina	136	519	784
Georgia	122	483	677
Florida	262	807	1,665
Kentucky	148	664	664
Tennessee	186	602	710
Alabama	130	408	629
Mississippi	133	377	604
Arkansas	137	391	749
Louisiana	175	447	849
Southwest			
Oklahoma	455	620	1,329
Texas	368	708	1,594
New Mexico	414	526	1,368
Arizona	735	1,011	3,519
Northeast			
Maine	722	1,450	1,588
New Hampshire	598	1,738	1,396
Vermont	834	1,727	2,073
Massachusetts	732	3,050	2,072
Rhode Island	818	2,965	1,988
Connecticut	719	3,708	2,289
New York	1,086	2,296	2,077
New Jersey	1,067	3,218	2,814
Delaware	751	1,789	1,634
Pennsylvania	898	2,038	1,476
Maryland	594	2,051	1,601
West Virginia	185	941	674
Middle States			
Ohio	$ 470	$ 1,619	$ 1,471
Indiana	478	1,358	1,505
Illinois	748	1,803	2,237
Michigan	623	1,596	1,405
Wisconsin	937	1,888	2,072
Minnesota	981	1,704	2,016
Iowa	1,259	2,212	3,048
Missouri	369	1,099	1,292
Northwest			
North Dakota	1,523	1,358	2,492
South Dakota	1,291	......	2,486
Nebraska	1,166	1,719	2,856
Kansas	1,010	1,271	2,388
Montana	1,307	910	2,317
Idaho	954	1,117	2,332
Wyoming	1,100	991	2,621
Colorado	838	1,074	2,424
Utah	502	1,189	1,853
Far West			
Nevada	1,226	1,624	3,861
Washington	712	1,318	2,511
Oregon	772	1,317	2,170
California	1,000	1,895	4,235

tions of higher learning, its Negro population, its foreign born, its wealth and income, its fertilizer consumption, and many others it ranks with the Northeast. Yet, it is practically always apart from Ohio. There are varying indices characterizing Kentucky, yet its population, folkways, culture, history, cities, rank it without serious question in the southeastern group.

With reference to the Southeast and the Southwest, and a comparison of the Southwest with the Middle States, some of the several indices have been cited in Chapter I, while others will be discussed at length in later chapters. It is important to note here, however, that the most common assumption is that Texas is "southern" in the sense of the Old South. So it is in parts of its cultural heritage, the date of its admission to the Union, its settlement by farm folk from the Southeast, its eastern population, some of its folkways of race and honor, its cotton economy, and some of its tropical crops. Yet its cotton culture is radically different by means of its Mexican versus Negro labor, its machine cultivation and its tenant system; while many of its folkways of western hustle and drive, its widening divergence from the Southeast, and many other factors separate it from the older Southern States. In addition, its older Spanish culture, much of its small urban patterns, its great expanse, its gigantic petroleum industry make it the major unit of the great Southwest as well as the essential eastern border of this great empire. These are general considerations in addition to several score of economic indices in which the Southeast and the Southwest differ. Even when Texas ranks as part of the "Cotton Belt" it is different and increasingly so.

Within these six major regions there are, of course, subregions of varying number, size, and distinction. Within the Northeastern Region, there is the old New England indescribably American in the old days, indescribably mixed in the new, yet still New England. The American Geographic Society has presented a picture of *New England's Prospect*, 1933, as a sort of commemoration of a similar title by William Wood in 1634. In the Far West there are the "Southland" of California and the divergent "Pacific Northwest." Within the South, there are not only the old cultural subregions, such as Charleston and New Orleans, Savannah and Vicksburg, Virginia and the Deep South, but more than a score of demographic subregions, including the Black Belt, the Cotton Piedmont, Tobacco Piedmont, Northern Cotton-Tobacco, Blue Ridge, Atlantic Tidewater, Semi-Tropical, Citrus-Vegetable, Vegetable-Citrus, Southern Cotton-Tobacco, Northern Piedmont, Tennessee Valley, Cumberland, Blue Grass, Tobacco-Cattle, Muscle Shoals-Nashville Basin, Mining, Gulf Coast Plain, Gulf Tidewater, Rice-Sugar, Bluffs, Interior Ridge, Delta, Interior Plain, Ozark, Red River Bottoms, Shenandoah Valley. And Florida Spanish and South-

GENERAL LOCATION OF IRON ORES IN THE UNITED STATES

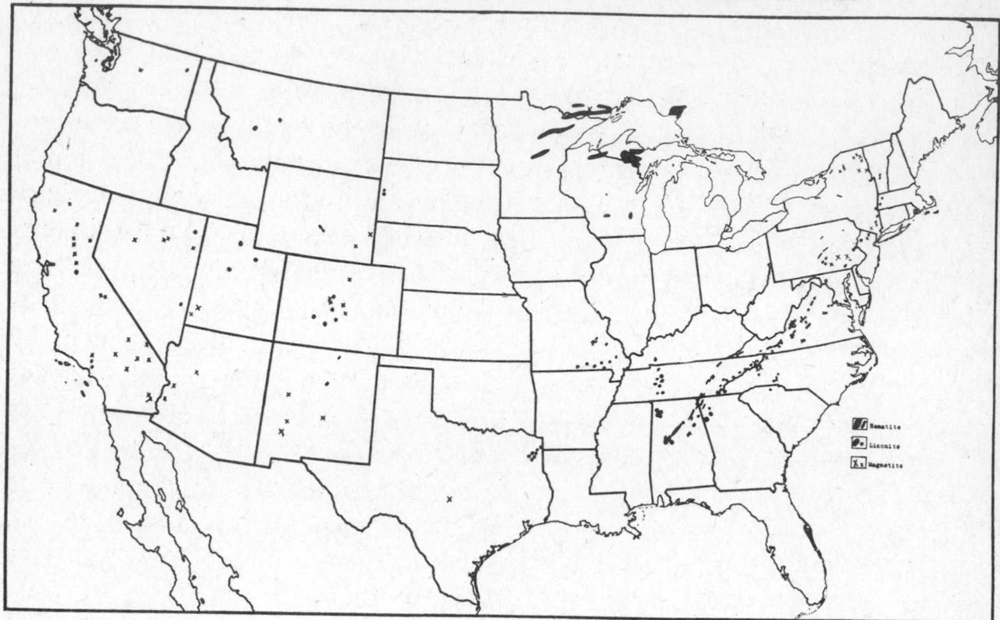

GEOGRAPHIC BACKGROUND OF THE U. S. IRON ORE MOVEMENT, 1929

Adapted from the Wisconsin Planning Board.

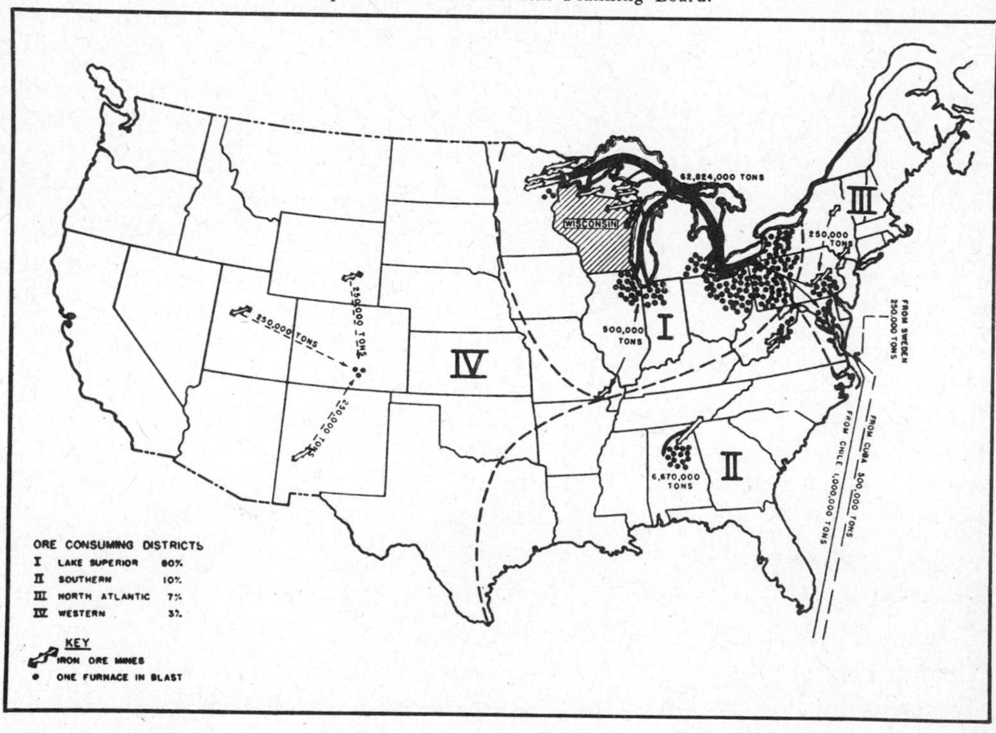

western Spanish culture, Westward Hollywood, Old Northwest, and on and on to this and that "garden spot of the nation," this and that "best in the world."

As corollaries to these regions, shifting boundaries of cultural and economic life might presage the development of a far eastern and a lower southern region, somewhat after the manner of the present far western area. Virginia, parts of North Carolina, parts of the coast line of South Carolina and Georgia, and much of Florida now rank with the "East" in many cultural indices. A great "Middle America," corresponding somewhat to the great Mississippi Valley drainage area, within appropriate parallels, might develop with its subregions into new possibilities for a dynamic transformation of American commerce and business, featuring movement north and south instead of east and west. Thus Lakes to Gulf, North America to South America. Towards such a development the Tennessee Valley experiment, the possible expansion of the Birmingham steel area and the petroleum industry of the east of the Southwest appear to be possible major contributions. The southern regions would be inseparably bound up with any such turn of the nation.

There are innumerable other portraitures of regions past, of regions present, and of regions to come. Many of them cannot be bound by state lines, county lines, or metropolitan boundaries, and, therefore, cannot be measured in statistical analyses at the present time. For instance, there is an imaginary eastern picture of a region so rich and culturally mixed that its boundaries and influences can no more be fixed than its definitive qualities can be measured. Such a region might begin with Boston and extend through New Haven, New York, New Jersey, eastern Pennsylvania, and the cities of Philadelphia, Wilmington, Baltimore, and Washington. Here would be the super-centers of cities, industries, surplus wealth, philanthropic foundations, propaganda organizations, universities, publishing houses. This would be a picture of transcendental culture, practically dominating the culture of the nation, even so far as the furthermost regions. Here is workshop and experimental laboratory for the development and utilization of all of the nation's fivefold wealth—a social laboratory *de luxe*.

If the observer continues the semi-real and semi-imaginary pictures of regions, he would project a second great region of financial-industrial-cultural dominances which might tend both to duplicate and to rival the great eastern one. This would center in Chicago and would include the great state universities of the old Middle West and the metropolitan centers, with a tendency to bring more national propaganda organizations and philanthropy and surplus wealth within the radius. An illustration of that is found in the clustering of certain organizations for the study of government,

Types of Farms in the Southern Appalachians

Adapted from *Economic and Social Problems and Conditions of the Southern Appalachians*

NUMBER OF SELF-SUFFICING FARMS, APRIL 1, 1930

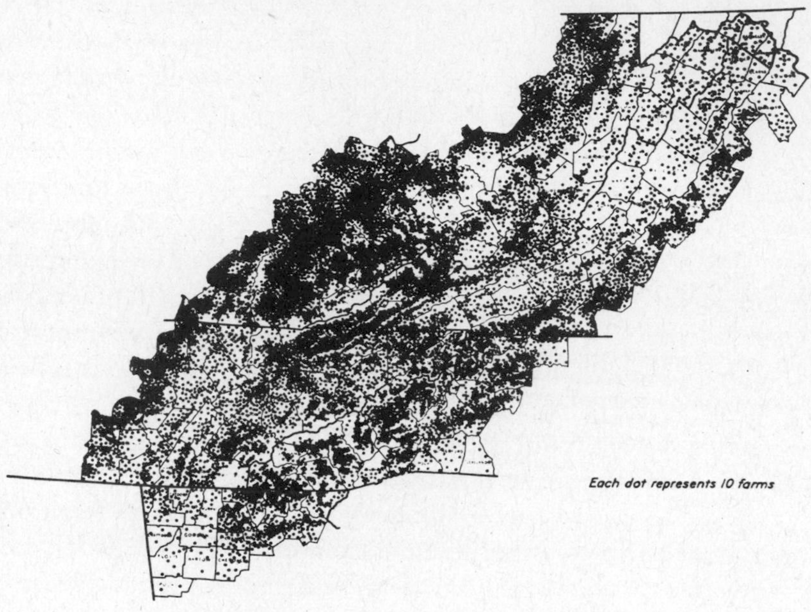

NUMBER OF PART-TIME FARMS, 1930

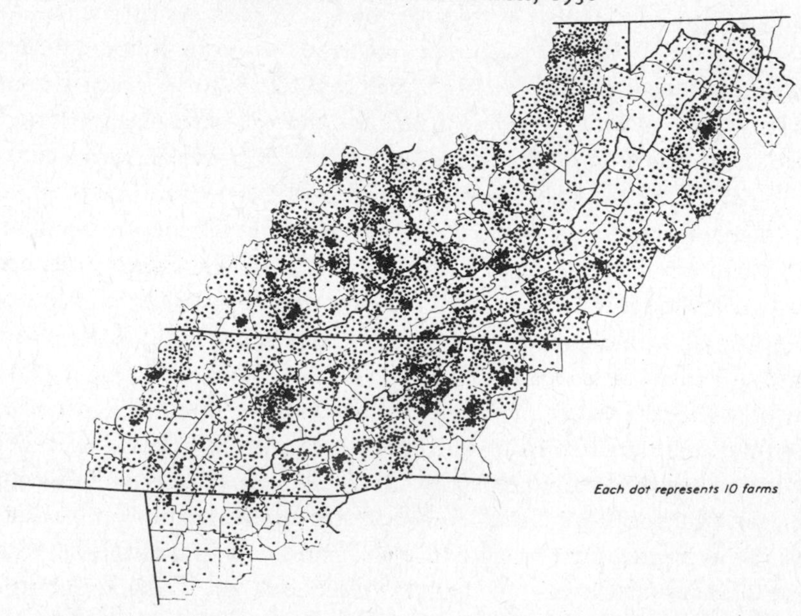

public administration, land planning, in Chicago, and the common assertion that this region would determine the definitive culture of future America. Two powerful setbacks to such a regional development have been the plight of agriculture and the financial and political demoralization of Chicago. Such regional culture as is evident in the United States is likely to continue even if the nation should turn away from its system of economics which tends to center the control of wealth in the hands of the few, because in planned society control and organization are even more important.

Another type of region which might rival these two, under the planned order, would be a third great industrial-cultural empire extending down from the upper Pennsylvania great valley, circling from the Piedmont industrial south, crescent-like, through the Tennessee River Basin, and transforming completely such an area as north Mississippi-Alabama and west Tennessee into a new region which, in turn, would draw on the limitless wealth of power of the Southeast and of oil-energy of the Southwest and start a new epoch in the flow of commerce north-south instead of east-west. This is different from the special picture of the Appalachian South which has been made under the direction of L. C. Gray and described in a later chapter dealing with the subregions of the South. Concerning the influence and possibilities of the Piedmont plains, Frederick Jackson Turner, a good many years ago, wrote in his *Sections in American History* that "no one has attacked the problem of the settlement, development, and influence of the Piedmont Plains as a whole. This peninsula, as we may conceive it, thrust down through the Great Valley from Pennsylvania, between the mountains and the seaboard, the land that received the German, Scotch-Irish, and poorer white English settlers, developed, in the second half of the eighteenth century, an independent social, economic, and political character. It was a region of free labor upon small farms. It was devoted to cereals rather than to the great staple crops of the seaboard. In its social structure it was more like Pennsylvania than the Southern commonwealths with which it was politically connected. It struggled for just representation in the legislatures, and for adequate local self-government. The domestic history of the South is for many years the history of a contest between these eastern and western sections. When the cotton belt, with slavery as its labor element, spread across this Piedmont area, the region became assimilated to the seaboard. The small farmers, raising crops by the labor of their own families, were compelled either to adjust themselves to the plantation economy, or to migrate. The process of this transformation and its effects constitute a problem not yet worked out in details. A migration of small farmers from the Piedmont across the Ohio and

Regional Variations in Certain Indices of Distribution and Character of the Population, 1930

PERCENTAGE INDICES	Southeast	Southwest	Northeast	Middle States	Northwest	Far West	United States
Per Cent in Each Region							
Increase in Urban Population (1900-1930)	175.9	453.9	84.1	119.4	131.4	393.0	126.9
Increase in Rural Population (1900-1930)	17.1	58.9	21.1	- 3.5	38.4	104.3	18.0
Increase in Total Population (1900-1930)	*41.3*	*118.4*	*62.7*	*47.1*	*61.5*	*236.9*	*61.5*
Urban Population	29.8	38.2	74.7	61.5	35.6	67.2	56.1
Per Cent in Each Region							
Increase of Cities of 100,000 or more (1900-1930)	333.3	—(*)	94.1	92.3	150.0	400.0	144.7
Increase of Places of 25,000-100,000 (1900-1930)	141.2	220.0	87.7	193.5	42.9	216.7	130.1
Increase of Places of 10,000-25,000 (1900-1930)	152.9	277.8	93.0	64.5	193.3	514.3	112.6
Increase of Places of 5,000-10,000 (1900-1930)	168.6	295.0	40.6	41.4	111.1	376.9	112.6
Increase of Places of 2,500-5,000 (1900-1930)	94.6	163.0	-3.3	19.4	48.6	132.5	37.5
Per Cent Each Group Is of the Regional Total							
Urban Population in Cities of 100,000 or more	33.9	39.7	57.5	55.5	33.3	59.9	52.7
Urban Population in Places of 25,000-100,000	24.7	17.9	17.8	19.2	16.0	15.3	18.7
Urban Population in Places of 10,000-25,000	16.3	13.9	13.4	10.9	22.7	11.3	13.2
Urban Population in Places of 5,000-10,000	12.0	15.8	6.8	7.9	14.6	7.8	8.6
Urban Population in Places of 2,500-5,000	13.1	9.3	4.4	6.4	13.3	5.7	6.8
Per Cent of the National Total							
Distribution of Urban Population in Cities of 100,000 or more	7.1	3.8	45.6	31.9	2.4	9.2	*100.0*
Distribution of Urban Population in Places of 25,000-100,000	14.5	4.8	39.7	31.1	3.3	6.6	*100.0*
Distribution of Urban Population in Places of 10,000-25,000	13.7	5.3	42.4	25.1	6.6	6.9	*100.0*
Distribution of Urban Population in Places of 5,000-10,000	15.5	9.3	33.3	28.0	6.5	7.4	*100.0*
Distribution of Urban Population in Places of 2,500-5,000	21.1	9.3	27.1	28.4	4.4	6.7	*100.0*
Distribution of Total Urban Population	*11.0*	*5.0*	*41.8*	*30.3*	*3.8*	*8.1*	*100.0*
Per Cent in Each Region							
Total Population in Cities of 100,000 or more	10.1	15.2	43.0	34.2	11.9	40.3	29.6
Total Population Places of 25,000-100,000	7.3	6.9	13.3	11.8	5.7	10.3	10.5
Total Population in Places of 10,000-25,000	4.9	5.3	10.0	6.7	8.1	7.6	7.4
Total Population in Places of 5,000-10,000	3.6	6.0	5.1	4.8	5.2	5.3	4.8
Total Population in Places of 2,500-5,000	3.9	4.8	3.3	4.0	4.7	3.7	3.8
Total Population—Urban	*29.8*	*38.2*	*74.7*	*61.5*	*35.6*	*67.2*	*56.1*
Total Population—Rural-farm	*47.7*	*39.9*	*7.5*	*21.8*	*39.6*	*13.5*	*24.5*
Total Population—Rural-nonfarm	*22.5*	*21.9*	*17.8*	*16.7*	*24.8*	*19.3*	*19.3*
Per Cent Each Group Is of the Regional Total of That Group							
Native White Population—Urban	29.8	37.8	71.3	58.1	35.1	66.9	54.6
Native Population—Rural-farm	46.0	39.5	9.0	24.1	40.3	13.3	24.9
Native White Population—Rural-nonfarm	24.2	22.7	19.7	17.8	24.6	19.8	20.5
Foreign-born White Population—Urban	72.1	52.5	87.3	78.2	36.0	71.3	80.3
Foreign-born White Population—Rural-farm	10.8	28.3	2.7	11.2	37.8	13.0	8.1
Foreign-born White Population—Rural-nonfarm	17.1	19.2	10.0	10.6	26.2	15.7	11.6
Negro Population—Urban	28.7	38.9	79.8	88.3	81.0	86.7	43.7
Negro Population—Rural-farm	52.2	47.2	3.9	4.1	5.6	4.2	39.4
Negro Population—Rural-nonfarm	19.1	13.9	16.3	7.6	13.4	9.1	16.9
All Other Races—Urban Population	12.6	37.9	79.7	67.3	25.2	60.1	45.8
All Other Races—Rural-farm Population	69.7	36.7	5.1	8.2	39.2	17.6	29.3
All Other Races—Rural-nonfarm Population	17.7	25.4	15.2	24.5	35.6	22.3	24.9
Per Cent Each Group Is of the Total							
Urban Population—Native White	68.7	74.8	73.1	79.9	87.0	77.0	75.6
Urban Population—Foreign-born White	.8	2.2	22.1	14.7	8.3	15.0	15.6
Urban Population—Negro	30.4	11.7	4.7	5.0	3.0	1.4	7.5
Urban Population—All Other Races	.1	11.3	.1	.4	1.7	6.6	1.3

*No cities of 100,000 or more in 1900; 5 in 1930.

Although the Southeast is characterized as rural and agrarian, it is important to note changes in rural-urban ratios and the nature and distribution of migration. Thus in all states, except Virginia and Georgia, the urban increase was more than 25 per cent, a ratio found in only six states outside of the Southwest and Far West. Equally significant was the decrease in rural population in many counties, Georgia, for instance having an actual decrease in more than 100 of its counties, and Kentucky a similar proportion. These data are discussed further in Chapter X. These factors are also discussed in Section 126; and in 106 to 125, pages 55 to 69; and again in Chapter VI.

into the Gulf region followed. Many had moral and religious objections to slavery; many were unable to change their agricultural habits to meet the new conditions; many lacked the necessary capital for a slave plantation and preferred to accept the price for their lands offered by the planters, and to migrate to the public lands where they could continue their old industrial and social type of society. In this expansion of the South into the Ohio Valley and the Gulf Plains we have a colonization demanding study."

This regional basis of social study constitutes one of the remaining aspects of regional analysis to be illustrated before we proceed to the more definitive presentation of the southern regions in the national picture. *New England's Prospects,* to which reference has already been made, comprised the six states of Maine, New Hampshire, Vermont, Massachusetts, Connecticut, and Rhode Island, and presented three score varied pictures by nearly as many authors. These included historical and cultural backgrounds, rural and city life, industry and manufacturing, agriculture and forests, food supply and fisheries, railroads and highways, government and trade, land use and social planning, and the New England changing geography and culture.

Another example of the region selected for special study is that designated by the Central Northwest Survey Committee at the University of Minnesota, in which parts of the Dakotas together with Minnesota constituted the heart of a region demarcated by historical, social, and economic conditions. This study comprehended a wide variety of inquiries including some of the more recent emergency problems of land utilization, balanced industries, and the reallocation of governmental units. Another well known regional concentration is that of the University of Chicago's ecological studies, in which the metropolitan region constitutes the base. On a larger picture background R. D. McKenzie has presented studies of major metropolitan regions centering around the ninety-six communities of more than a hundred thousand population. Still another type of study is that proposed by Dickinson in the metropolitan regions of the United States, in which the basic indices are those of trade and transit, produce and finance, with corollaries of administration and culture organization. These and other study-regions are similar to those subregions of the Southeast and the Southwest which are pictured in later chapters of this book.

It remains to call attention to the many specialized geographical and physical regional classifications of the United States and to emphasize the impracticability of attempting to utilize them exclusively for social and economic inventories and analysis. This is not to underestimate their value and their more precise and scientific definitions of more exact, dominant, and selective realities. It must be clear, however, that such master maps

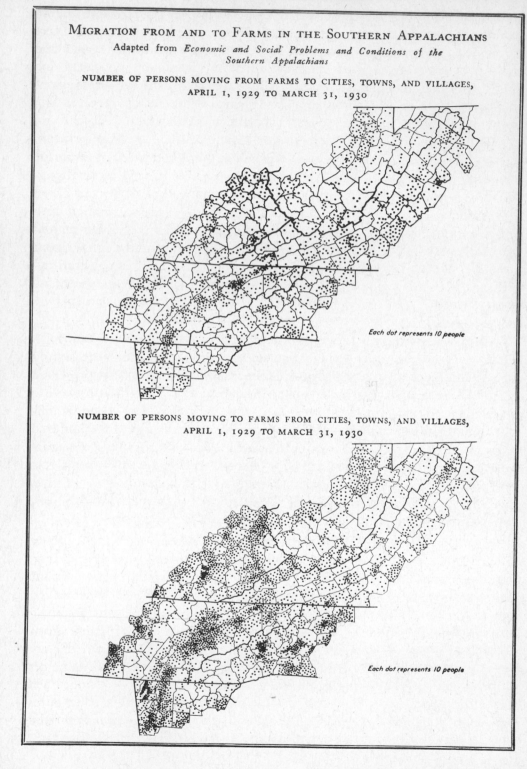

Migration from and to Farms in the Southern Appalachians

Adapted from *Economic and Social Problems and Conditions of the Southern Appalachians*

NUMBER OF PERSONS MOVING FROM FARMS TO CITIES, TOWNS, AND VILLAGES, APRIL 1, 1929 TO MARCH 31, 1930

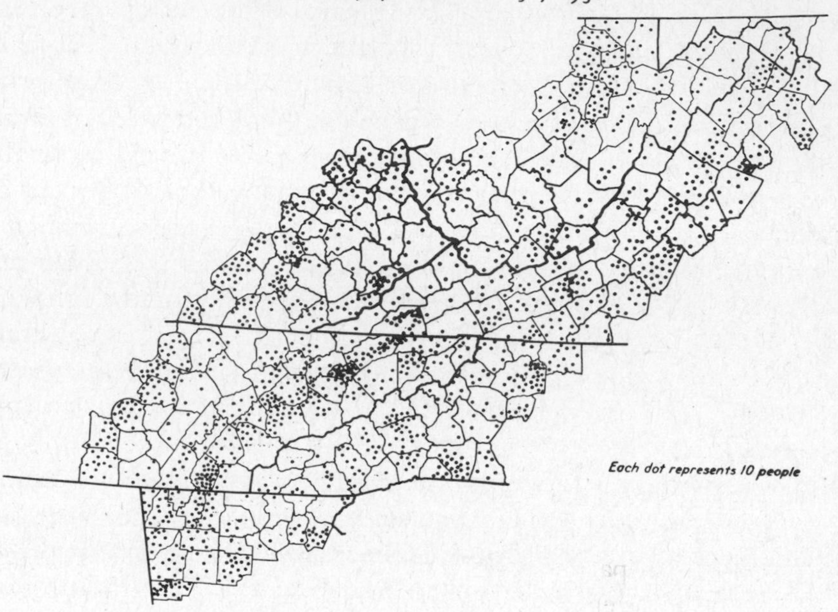

NUMBER OF PERSONS MOVING TO FARMS FROM CITIES, TOWNS, AND VILLAGES, APRIL 1, 1929 TO MARCH 31, 1930

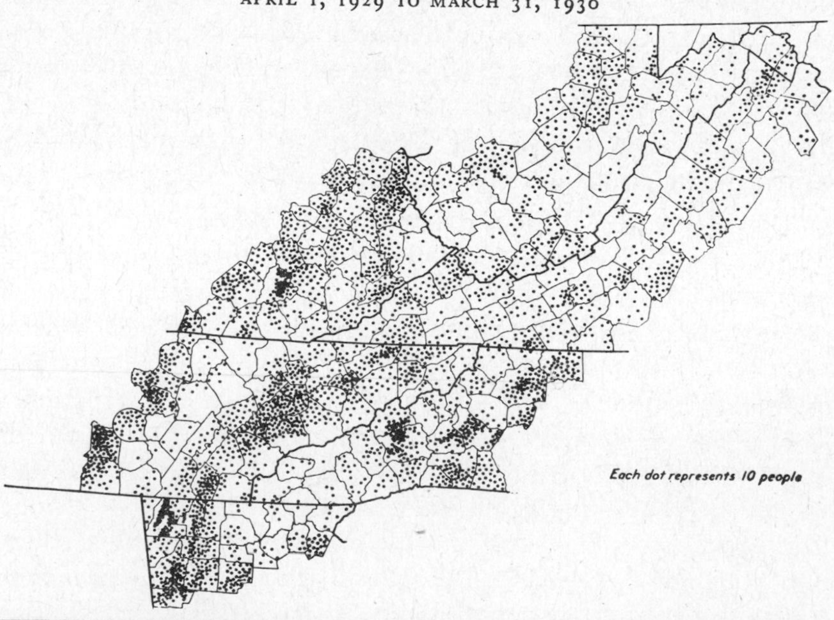

as that representing the 25 physical divisions of the nation with an 80 subdivision classification is in no way available for cultural inventory. Here are joined Alabama, Georgia, and the Carolinas with Pennsylvania and New York through a grand combination of the Piedmont provinces and the Appalachian plateaus. So, too, the 12 natural agricultural regions of Marbut feature, for instance, a dry plains region narrowly extending from lowest south to farthest north, conforming to no state or cultural or civic units, as also the "Mountainous Region", which defies any reasonable uniformity of cultural analysis. Again, the Mississippi Valley drainage area comprises a multiple and heterogeneous group of regions challenging any solidarity of cultural indices. So also temperature belts cut across the continent dividing the same regions into many belts and binding East and West together, just as contrariwise rainfall and humidity cut regions north and south. Or to take a different sort of example, although Arizona and New Mexico may be ranked with California in certain physical and early cultural indices, they do not even approximate the great southland of California in the dominant indices of population, wealth, occupation, institutions, and other current economic and social activities.

Adequate illustrations have now been presented to make the case for a better regional analysis of the nation and to support the present sixfold regional division of the nation. No other classification has been presented which will approximate so many of the desired points or conform so well to the largest number of those now in use for specific purposes. And assuming the necessity of utilizing state units, no valid objections have been offered to the present classification, provided further refinements of subregional study are continued and provided the effort is continued to break across state lines as indicated in the hypothetical division so presented. These, then, are the "Six Americas in search of a faith,"—Northeast and Southeast, Northwest and Southwest, Middle States and Far West.

Turning now to the six major regions designated, each is an empire of territory and wealth in itself. Each is greater and more self-sufficing than many nations of the world. Each is incurably sentimental and patriotic about its own virtues and assets. Each is colossally ignorant and provincial with reference to other regions, believing everything it hears and inquiring into the truth only when impelled by necessity or specific advantage. Each can honestly boast of a surprisingly large number of superior and distinctive advantages, resources, cultural backgrounds. Each has its strong points and weak points, foci of motivation and crisis, of advance and recession. Each bears its integral part in the burden of the nation, and each, alas, contributes its load to the nation's burden of problems. Each wants much from the

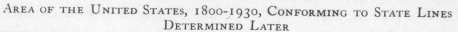

Area of the United States, 1800-1930, Conforming to State Lines Determined Later

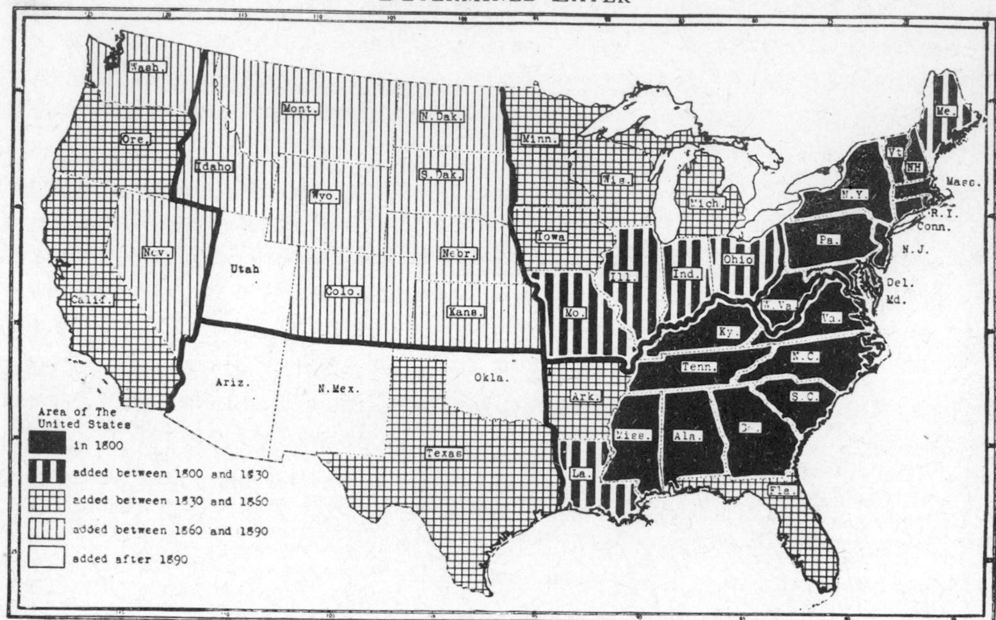

Above: In noting the earlier priority of the South in national matters it is important to recall that for a long time the "Old South" constituted a major part of the area and population.

Below: The chronological picture of the states indicates how extraordinarily new, after all, are the regions except the Northeast and the Southeast. A part of the lack of national equilibrium is reflected in the continuing rearrangements between and among the regions.

Date of Entrance of the States Into the Union

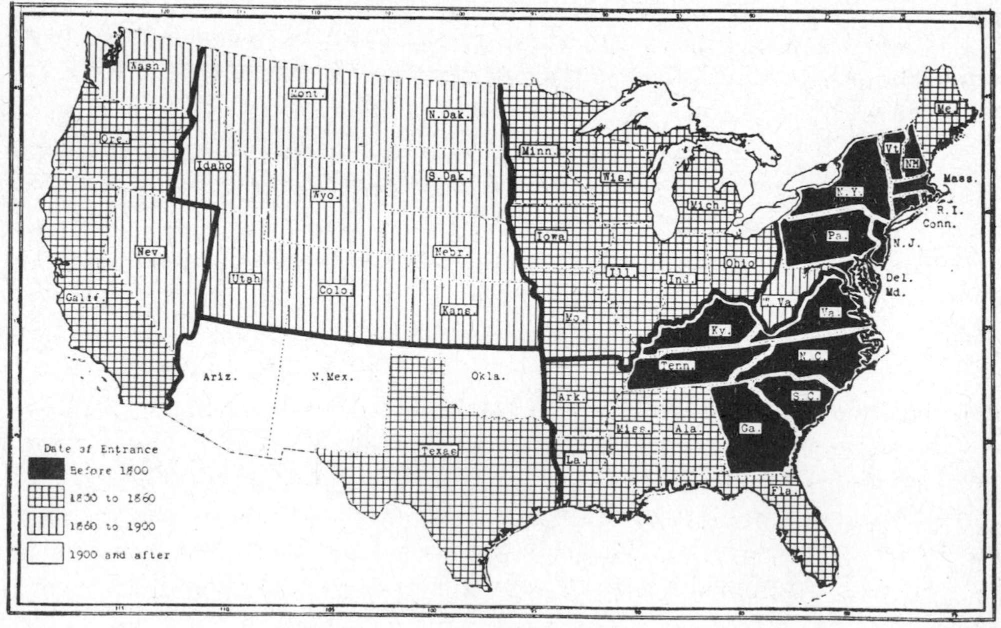

federal government, and each presents a marvelous array of evidence to support its claims. The Deal at Washington was learning as never before the significance of regions and the measure of common ignorance concerning their complicated folkways and institutions.

Again, each region has its distinctive historical backgrounds rich in romance and contributing materially to the total national pattern and inseparably interwoven with the economic and political fabric of the nation. How new and young, after all, were the more westerly regions: Middle States, Southwest, Northwest, Far West—cultures fabricated by and in the memory of living men and women. Chicago, rival of New York, was just a hundred years old and was celebrating its birthday through the picturesque "Century of Progress," colorful portraiture of what the people had done since 1833—more colorful picture of what they were doing in 1933. There was in 1833 a letter from Douglas predicting a rivalry between Chicago and New York—at the time seemingly a far prophecy. No state of this great region of Middle States was admitted to the union before the turn of the nineteenth century, while the baby giant of them all, Minnesota, with its magic Twin City metropolitan area came in after the Civil War. The others: Wisconsin, 1848; Iowa, 1846; Michigan, 1837; Missouri, 1821; Illinois, 1818; Indiana, 1816; Ohio, 1803. And of the northwestern group, an unbelievably young region, most of which were admitted just before the turn of the twentieth century—Utah as late as 1896; Idaho and Wyoming, 1890; Montana and the Dakotas, 1889; with Nebraska and Kansas belonging to the more eastern group of Middle States in time, 1867 and 1861. And still younger members of the new Southwest, Oklahoma in 1907, Arizona and New Mexico in 1912. Beyond and below these, however, product of the earlier westward movement, California was as old as 1850; Oregon, 1859; and Washington, 1889; while Texas belonged back again in the pre-Civil War period of 1845.

Here, then, are the four youthful regions in contrast to the two eastern, North and South, patriarchial groups, thirteen of which constituted the first original empire. It is essential if one is to understand the unevenness of development, the rugged and ragged dynamics of action, the contrasts between Southwest and Southeast, and the instability of the 1930's to see the American picture in terms of its regional chronology. The Northeast groups all charter members of the nation in 1787 to 1790, except West Virginia which was a war debt from Virginia to the union in 1863. And the Southeast, largely of the Old South, charter states of the nation—Virginia, South Carolina, Georgia, 1788, North Carolina 1789, and Tennessee of 1796 vintage, followed then by early acquisitions,—Mississippi, 1817; Alabama, 1819; Louisiana, 1812; Arkansas, 1812; and

New Interstate Highways of Communication

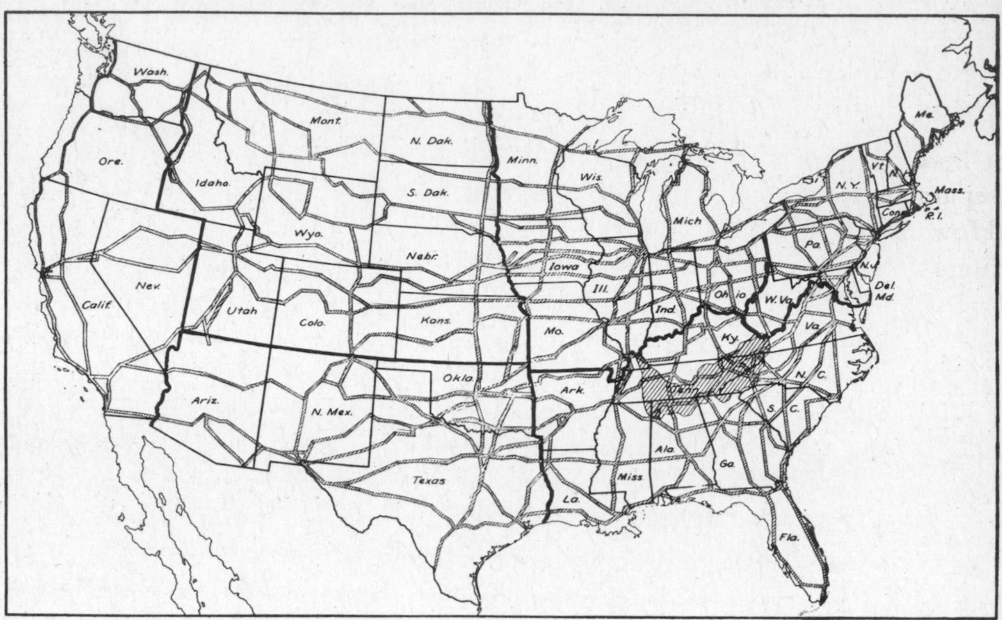

Perhaps there is no greater contrast between the present "Wests" and those earlier frontiers around which centered the crises of early American expansion than between the old trails and the present highways, airways, and railways of quick communication. The two maps presented here are illustrative of the general picture of communication in the late 1920's. The Tennessee Valley area is featured, as in some other maps, to indicate its place in regional-national position.

Interstate Airway Communication

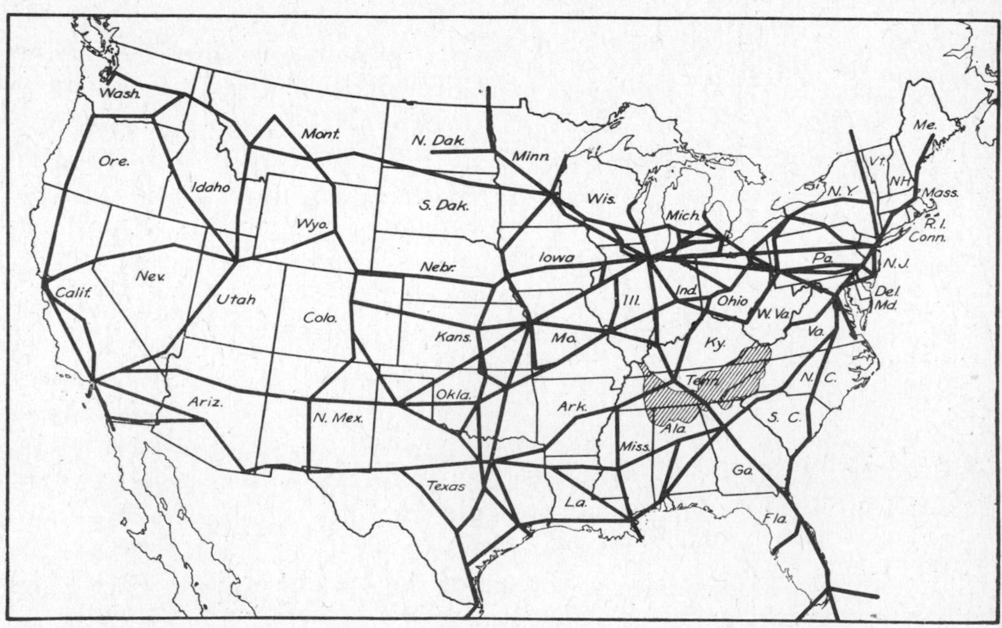

Florida in a class of its own in history, culture, and chronology, in 1845.

It is this newness and variety which justify the conclusion that there is perhaps no part of the American picture more characteristically dramatic than the regional expansion of an evolving nation. The stock pictures are those of the Louisiana Purchase, the Texas acquisition, the "Winning of the West," the gold rush to California, covered wagons, and cavalcades; German migration of the 1840's, romance and tragedy, Indian wars, French traders, epic and epoch of a nation. There are other fundamental pictures of the ways in which the nation came to be as it was. The historical nomenclature of the regions, like some strata evidence of an old civilization, reveals the growing changing nation. Thus, at one time or another the designation of "the great West" or "West" signified an extraordinarily large number of western regions. It might in recent years mean anything from Buffalo or Pittsburgh to the golden gates of California. In earlier days, Tennessee at one time constituted the great western lands, while at the turn of Jefferson's century most of all the western lands were in Kentucky and Tennessee. The "Middle West" in the early 1930's is scarcely west at all, and the great Northwest is at most a North Central Region, challenging new alignments with national cooperative endeavor.

It is in the interrelation of economics and politics, religion and conquest, in the winning of these "Wests" that an organic part of the national picture is found. In the South's contribution there was drain from the South and cultural influence upon the new regions. The South was the great gateway to "the West." These "Wests" and "Southwests" were frontiers, experimenters with regional and sectional expansion, debtor regions to the East, which in turn was sponsor and financier for great developments which were to be profitable. They were likewise moulders of culture which would constitute the outlying provinces, rural and religious, adventurous, and gradually becoming a different America. Contests for empire and wealth conditioned the nation for its future economic development: North and South, East and West, railroad and canal, slave and free, cities and country —it was a grand picture, prophetic of the confusion and corruption of later days when the nation, caught up with its free lands and new territory, and dependent upon eastern capital and control, turned back into the making of a fearfully mixed composite of interrelated yet separate regions. Frederick Jackson Turner had painted many pictures of the significance of the frontier and of sections in the American picture. William E. Dodd and others had pictured the gigantic struggle for economic control, and many others had interpreted the devious ways by which government had contributed to the advance and advantage of the various regions. Samplings only—land grabbing and manipulation, tariff and freight rates, subsidy and federal grants, Lakes to Gulf waterway, concessions and franchises, drainage and irrigation, flood control and giant dams, parks and highways, power and oil, colossal land ownership of railroads, utilities, and private corporations, war-time camps and camp cities. And, then, latest reconstruction aids to wheat and cotton and fruits and tobacco and dairying and corn, public works and civil works, and whatever must balance the regional claim.

But what were the regional divisions of people and area and wealth and welfare of the nation in the 1930's? What was the comparative picture of Southeast and Southwest? What were their relative standing in the nation and their rates of progress or retrogression? What were the dramatic features of the several regions? What were the "believe it or not" inventories of nature and wealth and people? In fine, how did the regions rank in each of the major storehouses of wealth—natural, technological, artificial, human, institutional? And, in particular, for the purposes of this study, what were the capacities and prospect of the southern regions? The answers to some of these questions are presented in the following chapters.

CHAPTER IV

REGIONS OF NATURAL RICHNESS AND ABUNDANCE

THE TWO MAJOR pictures of the natural resources of the southern regions can best be presented in separate chapters, featuring again regional culture and demography in the national setting. There is, first of all, the superabundance of nature's endowment; and there is the other story of the uses and misuses which have been and are being made of it. The measure of the region's culture and wealth must be found in a working balance between these, achieved through an optimum realization of its incomparable resources and an abundant enjoyment of the fruits of toil and technology. The present chapter, therefore, will present a simple and quick-moving inventory of the range and nature of the natural resources of the Southeastern Region, while the following chapter will present the case of regional deficiencies in technology and in the utilization of these resources together with some elemental catalogue of the factors of waste. A comparative picture of the Southwest, sketched in another chapter, will indicate a similar major task for that great emerging region.

Inventory of the natural "wealth," of both southern regions, if adequate, must be in terms of enormous aggregates as it relates to range and quantity and in terms of superlatives as it relates to quality and possibilities. There is not only no objection to presenting such a picture in authentic glowing terms, but such full appraisal is fundamental to competent regional analysis, provided the picture is also interpreted in relation to capacity for utilization and actualities of waste and in some comparative relation to other regions. Thus in this particular case of the South, a realistic picture can be had only through the portraiture of the superabundance of resources alongside deficiencies in technology, waste in economy, immaturity in culture, and lack of unity in action. It is this measuring and bridging of the chasm between possibilities and actualities which constitutes a definitive quality of this whole southern regional appraisal, which must bring to its task both the sweep of imaginative exploration and the solid base of factual support.

We proceed, then, to the picture of abundance. In contrast to the dry regions of the nation and the sometimes drought-parched fields of a great

Samplings of Indices Relating to Natural Resources

Number of Indices	Classification
1.	Distribution of potential water power available 90 per cent of the time.
2.	Potential water power, horse power available 90 per cent of the time, 1928.
3.	Distribution of potential water power available 50 per cent of the time.
4.	Potential water power, horse power available 50 per cent of the time, 1928.
5.	Distribution of surveyed water power locations, 1929.
6.	Distribution of developed water power.
7.	Distribution of water power development: Amount of horse power, 1929.
8.	Distribution of total developed water power: Capacity, 1932.
9.	Variations in influence of forests on watershed protection.
10.	Location of major streams and lakes.
11.	Distribution of completed waterways, 1929.
12.	Distribution of projected, but not completed, waterways, 1929.
13.	Distribution of state, foreign, and privately owned waterways, completed, 1929.
14.	Distribution of state, foreign, and privately owned waterways, projected, but not completed, 1929.
15.	Distribution of improved rivers, 1929.
16.	Distribution of canals in use, 1929.
17.	Distribution of abandoned canals, 1929.
18.	Southern regions in relation to the national development of the Greater Mississippi Valley and the Tennessee Valley.
19.	River basins of the Southeast.
20.	Distribution of coal.
21.	Sources and production of anthracite coal.
22.	Sources and production of bituminous coal, workable.
23.	Sources and production of bituminous coal, not workable.
24.	Sources and production of sub-bituminous coal, workable.
25.	Sources and production of sub-bituminous coal, not workable.
26.	Sources and production of lignite, workable.
27.	Sources and production of lignite, not workable.
28.	Estimated original tonnage of bituminous coal in the Southeastern States.
29.	Estimated original tonnage of semi-bituminous coal in the Southeastern States.
30.	Estimated original tonnage of semi-anthracite coal in the Southeastern States.
31.	Estimated original tonnage of total production of coal in the Southeastern States from earliest record to end of 1929.
32.	Number of operating commercial coal mines in the Southeastern States, 1929.
33.	Total production in net tons of operating commercial coal mines in the Southeastern States, 1929.
34.	Location of phosphate resources.
35.	Sources and production of building stone.
36.	Value of building stones in the Southeast, 1930.
37.	Value of sand and gravel used in building in the Southeast, 1930.
38.	Comparative production of petroleum, 1930.
39.	Comparative production of natural gas, 1930.
40.	Comparative production of natural gasoline, 1930.
41.	Differential values, by regions, of limestone products.
42.	Differential values, by regions, of granite products.
43.	Changing status of twelve leading states in granite sales and value of granite, 1919-1929.
44.	Comparative value of granite production, 1919-1929.
45.	Comparative value for different uses of granite production, 1913-1929.
46.	Comparative value of marble production, 1919-1929.
47.	Location of iron ores.
48.	Change in value of mineral products, 1909-1929.
49.	Value, and per cent of U. S. total value, of mineral products, 1929.
50.	Per capita value of mineral products, 1929.
51.	Comparative value of mineral products, 1909, 1919, 1929.
52.	Differential values, by regions, of mineral products.

Number of Indices	Classification
53.	Uncritical list of some 300 varieties of minerals of the Southeast.
54.	Distribution of the present forest area.
55.	Variations in principal types of forests.
56.	Location of land devoted to forests.
57.	Extent of the long leaf group in the yellow pine belt of the Southeast.
58.	Extent of the short leaf group in the yellow pine belt of the Southeast.
59.	Total yellow pine area in the Southeast, 1919, 1927.
60.	Area of old growth of yellow pine in the Southeast, 1919, 1927.
61.	Area of restocking to saw timber on cut-over lands of yellow pine in the Southeast, 1919, 1927.
62.	Area of restocking to cordwood on cut-over lands of yellow pine in the Southeast, 1919, 1927.
63.	Area of no restocking on cut-over lands of yellow pine in the Southeast, 1919, 1927.
64.	Comparative lumber production, 1923-1930.
65.	Distribution of the total timber stand.
66.	Distribution of the saw-timber stand.
67.	Distribution of the total stand, saw-timber and cordwood areas.
68.	Number and per cent of forest production farms.
69.	Value of forest products cut on farms, 1929.
70.	Quantity of saw logs and veneer logs cut on farms, 1929.
71.	Quantity of firewood cut on farms, 1929.
72.	Quantity of pulp wood cut on farms, 1929.
73.	Number of fence posts cut on farms, 1929.
74.	Number of railroad ties cut on farms, 1929.
75.	Number of poles and piles cut on farms, 1929.
76.	Estimate of destruction by erosion—extent of area with severely impoverished soil or soil washed off.
77.	Estimate of destruction by erosion—extent of area devastated.
78.	Estimate of destruction by erosion—extent of total erosion.
79.	Estimate of per cent of soil impoverishment and destruction by erosion.
80.	Distribution of most serious erosion, 1933.
81.	Distribution of harmful erosion widespread, 1933.
82.	Distribution of comparatively little erosion because of flat surface, 1933.
83.	Distribution of erosion generally, not serious, 1933.
84.	Distribution of much serious wind erosion, 1933.
85.	Distribution of much serious erosion by overgrazing in predominantly mountainous and dry land conditions, 1933.
86.	Land productivity classes—number of acres, Grade 1.
87.	Land productivity classes—number of acres, Grade 2.
88.	Land productivity classes—number of acres, Grade 3.
89.	Land productivity classes—number of acres, Grade 4.
90.	Land productivity classes—number of acres, Grade 5.
91.	Land productivity classes—per cent of Grades 4 and 5.
92.	Location of land used for crops.
93.	Distribution of crop land lying idle or fallow, 1929.
94.	Location of land used for grazing-hay.
95.	Location of arid-grazing land.
96.	Location of desert land.
97.	Location of irrigated land.
98.	Distribution of total pasturage acreage, 1929.
99.	Distribution of plowable pasture acreage, 1929.
100.	Acreage, and per cent of the total, of crop land, 1930.
101.	Acreage, and per cent of the total, of pasture land, 1930
102.	Acreage, and per cent of the total, of woodland pasture, 1930.
103.	Acreage, and per cent of the total, of woodland not used for pasture, 1930.
104.	Acreage, and per cent of the total, of all other land in farms, 1930.
105.	Variations in average length of the growing season.
106.	Variations in average annual precipitation.
107.	Average annual number of clear days.
108.	Average annual number of partly cloudy days.
109.	Average annual number of cloudy days.
110.	Average annual number of days with one inch or more of rain in twenty-four hours.
111.	Average annual number of days with thunderstorms.

middle belt of America, the abundant rainfall of the Southeast, its ever-flowing streams, and its long growing season in the midst of its happy medium climate may well serve as vivid reminder of that large part of regional abundance which is so commonly taken for granted. Yet here is the most entrancing of southern pictures—multiplied hundreds of miles of ocean front and gulf coastline, fringed with inflowing rivers and rivulets, brooks and branches, springs and freshets. Here is natural wealth of the first order, the most potent of all geographical influences—life-giving waters from abundant clouds and from swift moving streams from mountain to shore, nature's endowment for land and crops, for power and commerce, for man and beast, a regional keynote to health and happiness, inspiration and wealth, beauty and utility, work and play. Here is a map picture *de luxe*—big river basins and lesser valleys, wheels within wheels, most influential of all nature's relief features—Mississippi and Ohio in their lower sweep, Arkansas and Red, Tennessee and Cumberland, Holston and French Broad, Catawba and Yadkin, Ocmulgee and Savannah; multiplied miles of waterways, multiplied millions of water power; multiplied hundreds of little streams with their lowland and bottoms, tributaries to the richness and beauty and uninventoried possibilities of agrarian life.

The rapid rise of the automobile and of new modes of rapid transportation and communication has obscured for most Americans the important aspects of the nation's physical wealth as found in its hundreds of rivers. Yet to counteract this is the new dominance of power in which streams are again keys to wealth and development. There are yet other inventories in the countless little lakes and streams which dot its landscape and the limitless reaches of its thousands of miles of gulf and ocean water front. What the lakes to gulf development may be is still problematical, yet, with the new reaches of building upon the Tennessee, the Cumberland, and other rivers farther west, there are powerful resources available. There are four great rivers in the picture which would average more than two thousand miles in length; another four, more than a thousand miles; and of the four score and more navigable streams in the nation, the Southeast shares more than a half, capable of adding richly to its scenic beauty and commercial assets. Pictures of Showboat and river romance are lost in the past, yet the modern picture is more dynamic: power dams and factories, rivers of waters with towns on their shores, barges on their bosoms; big rivers laden with commerce, little rivers from the hills store streams for power, mountain streams and lakes, water reservoirs for the cities. Yet, not overlooking these modern sources of power and wealth, it is unfortunate to forget so easily what these rivers have been in the romance and practical techniques of earlier developments, whether as practical routes of discovery and commerce or travel-

Canals and Improved Waterways of United States. Completed and Projected by 1929 With Depth at Low Water

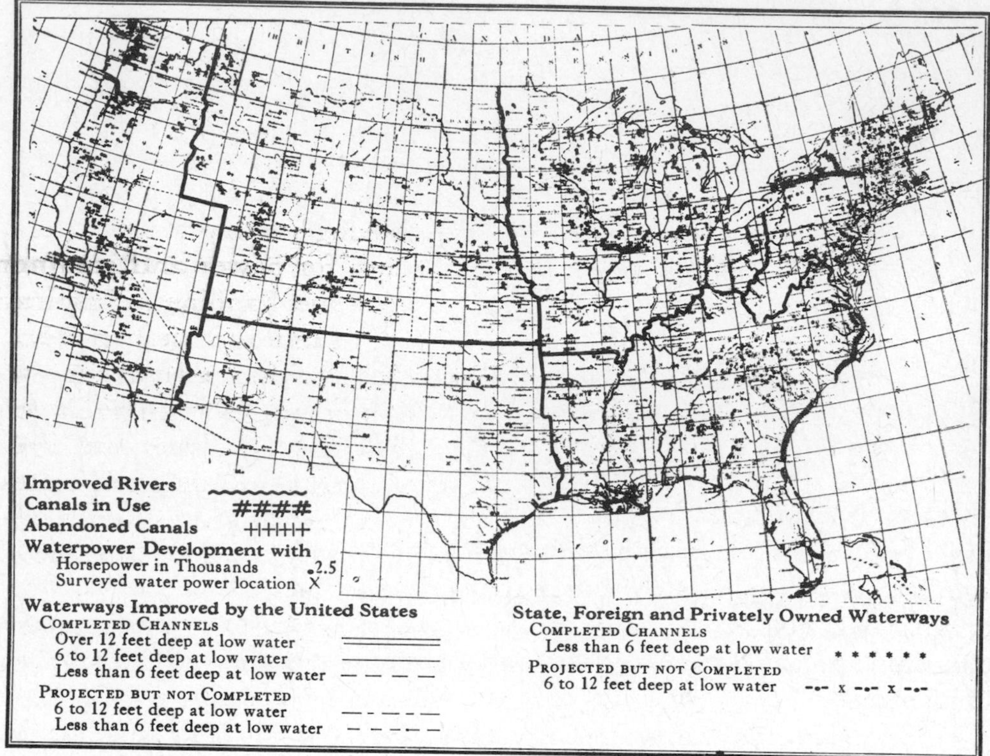

Picture of the Nation's Wealth of Streams of Water

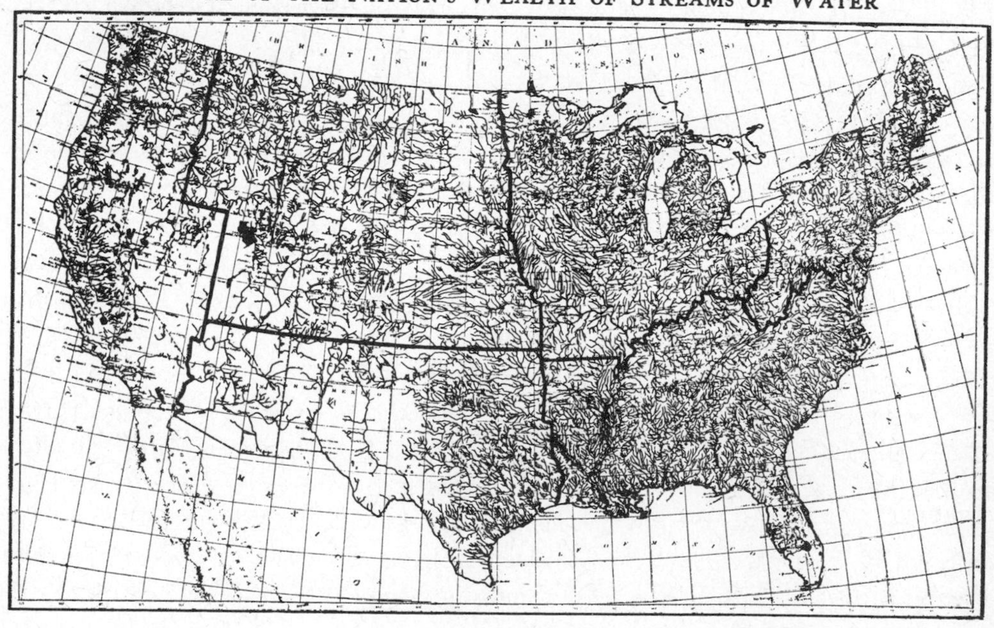

ways for intrepid trappers whose trading posts penetrated far into the depths of the forest frontier. This is particularly true of the Southeast with its romantic culture of the past, its Spanish and Indian trails, and its continuing frontier gateways to the West and Southwest.

To rivers and oceans add rainfall; to abundant waters add long, frostless growing seasons and land of variety and richness—thus is projected boldly the basic vein of natural resources stretching across and throughout this Southeastern Region of eleven states no one of which is outside the range of superior advantage. In the measure of its rainfall, the whole of the Southeast lies within the bounds of that magic area which measures more than 40 inches average annual precipitation, and much of it, as in the Tennessee Valley and lower South, has upwards of 60 and 80 and more. Of the 27 per cent of the nation's total land area with a precipitation of 40 or more inches, the Southeast's own part is nearly two-thirds, or 17 of the 27 per cent. Again, of the 55 per cent of the nation's area, in which a frostless growing season of six months or more is available, the Southeast itself has nearly a third, while the Southeast and the Southwest together aggregate more than two-thirds of the total. Thus the Southeast belongs to that minority ten per cent of the earth's surface where rainfall and temperature abound alongside the other optimum conditions most favorable to mankind.

Once again the realism and romance of the nation are bound up in regional differentials. Compare, for instance, the rainfall and water supply of the Southeast with the rest of the nation and especially with the Southwest. In precipitation, there is range from a few inches to more than a hundred inches, while in the distribution of water supply, other than for power, the Southeast excels almost uniformly. About a half of the total land acreage of the nation has a median of between 15 and 40 inches annual rainfall with ratios about as follows: nearly 10 per cent shows less than 10 inches, 30 per cent between 10 and 20 inches, 16 per cent each between 20 and 30 and between 40 and 50 inches, while the areas of 50 to 60 inches are again about the same as those under 10 inches. The highest rainfall prevails in the southeast and extreme west to northwest, with special winter recreational areas, such as Florida, conveniently providing low precipitation in winter and high in summer. In general, rainfall provides another one of those picturesque dividing lines between the East with more and the West with less precipitation, with the exception of the Far West coast line. Bisecting the nation almost exactly in the middle is a uniform belt of three or four hundred miles width with a sort of median precipitation of 20 to 30 inches. Shading off to the east the precipitation

Average Annual Precipitation

Adapted from the U. S. Bureau of Agricultural Economics

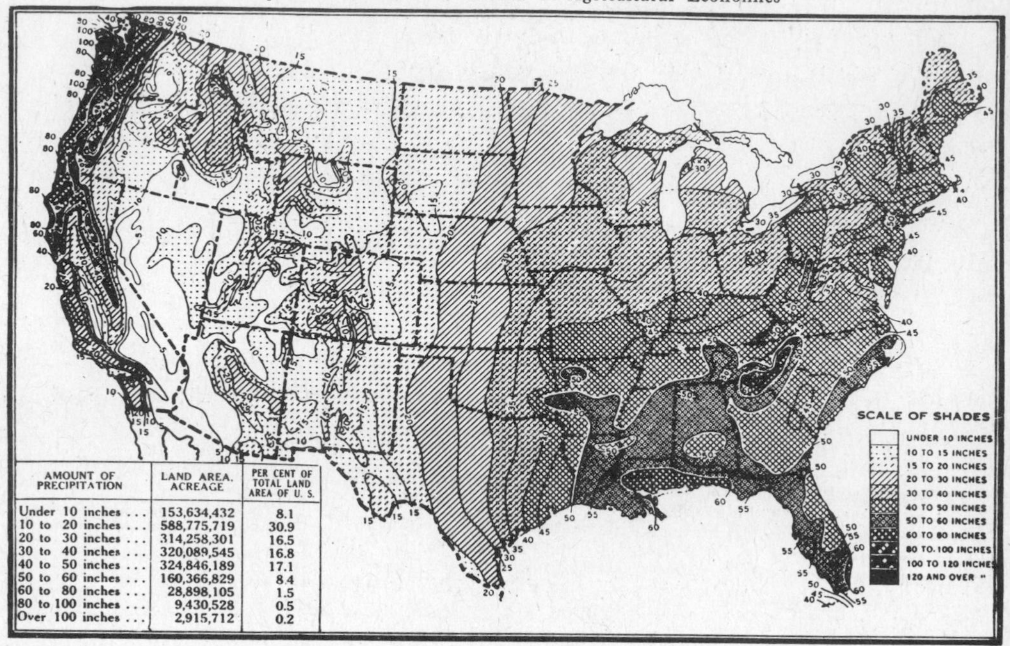

AMOUNT OF PRECIPITATION	LAND AREA, ACREAGE	PER CENT OF TOTAL LAND AREA OF U. S.
Under 10 inches . . .	153,634,432	8.1
10 to 20 inches . . .	588,775,719	30.9
20 to 30 inches . . .	314,258,301	16.5
30 to 40 inches . . .	320,089,545	16.8
40 to 50 inches . . .	324,846,189	17.1
50 to 60 inches . . .	160,366,829	8.4
60 to 80 inches . . .	28,898,105	1.5
80 to 100 inches . . .	9,430,528	0.5
Over 100 inches . . .	2,915,712	0.2

Clear Days and Heavy Rainfall by States

Minimum Average Annual Number of Days Adapted from Airway Information

STATE AND REGION	Number Clear Days	Partly Cloudy	Cloudy	One Inch or More Rain in 24 hours	Days with Thunderstorms
Southeast					
Virginia	144	120	108	7	40
North Carolina	126	114	96	13	40
South Carolina	173	98	94	12	50
Georgia	132	118	115	12	60
Florida	130	145	90	15	61
Kentucky	161	87	117	12	50
Tennessee	127	124	114	14	55
Alabama	161	95	109	15	60
Mississippi	...	...	132	18	60
Arkansas	146	111	108	12	60
Louisiana	142	119	104	15	50
Southwest					
Oklahoma	195	90	80	12	50
Texas	140	111	54	1	20
New Mexico	210	93	37	1	40
Arizona	166	89	40	1	7
Northeast					
Maine	114	127	124	3	16
New Hampshire	150	100	115	12	25
Vermont	100	120	145	2	30
Massachusetts	112	116	137	12	20
Rhode Island	137	104	124	8	19
Connecticut	120	117	128	12	28
New York	93	118	154	1	30
New Jersey	114	110	141	8	30
Delaware	194	81	90	10	35
Pennsylvania	86	118	131	6	34
Maryland	113	93	88	10	35
West Virginia	100	113	147	8	46
Middle States					
Ohio	94	122	128	6	40
Indiana	146	101	118	10	40
Illinois	127	123	115	10	40
Michigan	86	103	141	2	20
Wisconsin	102	112	151	7	30
Minnesota	116	124	125	4	30
Iowa	167	100	98	6	40
Missouri	148	114	103	8	50
Northwest					
North Dakota	122	116	120	2	30
South Dakota	176	101	88	5	30
Nebraska	138	122	105	6	40
Kansas	153	114	63	4	40
Montana	113	124	79	1	25
Idaho	...	...	...	1	10
Wyoming	180	120	65	1	20
Colorado	144	119	61	2	50
Utah	153	113	72	4	33
Far West					
Nevada	200	100	65	1	12
Washington	...	...	...	1	2
Oregon	75	93	130	1	4
California	195	68	63	1	3

increases, while to the west it decreases into the great desert picture which again merges into the luxurious Far West belt of greater moisture.

Coincident with this east and west division of the nation in terms of rainfall is a similar division of east and west according to soils and crops. Almost coincident with this belt of uniformly medium precipitation is a bisecting belt of black lands, extraordinarily rich, from which shade east the brown and west the lighter shades of soil, grey white in desert, grey drab in forest lands. Thus the very climate and soils themselves add richness to the colorful, natural, regional pictures of the nation. Especially is the romance of the Southwest fabricated into its distinctive pattern because of contrasting lack of moisture, lack of trees, and other climatic and soil differentials, while Florida, a state apart and a major subregion in itself, is sunshine and gold largely because of its climatic assets. Still another comparison of regions and water may be made by noting that the eleven western states commonly credited with twenty times as much water power resources per capita as the rest of the nation also include the greater part of the great arid regions of America. This is in contrast to the Southeast, the least of the four great power regions in potential water power, which nevertheless provides the richest distribution of its water for crops and pasture lands and reflects also basic waste of water and land as well as great potential advantage.

These elemental illustrations of the superabundance of climatic natural wealth are indicative for the whole Southeastern Region of some such exclusive characterization as was made for the Tennessee River drainage basin by the chairman of the Tennessee Valley Authority. "No other comparable area in the United States," he said, "offers the diversity of climate, of soil, of vegetation and of resources which we find in the Tennessee Valley. . . . The climate runs all the way from that of the Great Lakes in the mountain sections to subtropical in the cotton country of the Gulf States. . . . They can raise anything that grows between Canada and the Gulf of Mexico." If climate is the master of man's destiny in economics, politics, manners, religion, and in the comfort of their culture, then the Southeastern Region follows a generous master.

Yet climate's example is indicative also of the superabundance of the other well-nigh limitless sources of natural wealth. Call the long roll: land and forests; minerals and mines, coal and iron and phosphate and hundreds of other minerals from the land undug; sticks and stones of fabulous quality and quantity for the fabrication of great buildings and for the construction of roads and bridges; energy and power, dominant or surging from oil and gas and electricity; sea water minerals and tidal power; iodine and phosphorous and nitrogen wealth, overhead basic potential of

Average Length of Growing Season

Adapted from the U. S. Bureau of Agricultural Economics

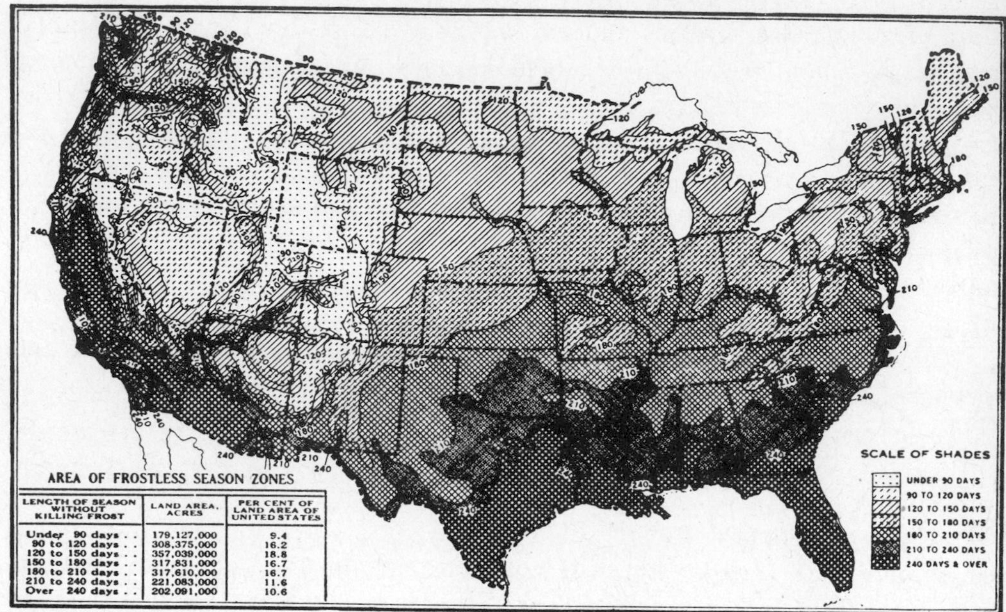

AREA OF FROSTLESS SEASON ZONES

LENGTH OF SEASON WITHOUT KILLING FROST	LAND AREA, ACRES	PER CENT OF LAND AREA OF UNITED STATES
Under 90 days . .	179,127,000	9.4
90 to 120 days . .	308,375,000	16.2
120 to 150 days . .	357,039,000	18.8
150 to 180 days . .	317,831,000	16.7
180 to 210 days . .	317,610,000	16.7
210 to 240 days . .	221,083,000	11.6
Over 240 days . .	202,091,000	10.6

State Percentage of the 1929 National Total Value of Garden Vegetables as Opposed to Commercial Production

STATE AND REGION	Value (in thousands)	Per Cent
Southeast		
Virginia	$10,483	4.64
North Carolina	11,900	5.26
South Carolina	5,445	2.41
Georgia	8,315	3.68
Florida	1,948	.86
Kentucky	13,263	5.87
Tennessee	10,759	4.76
Alabama	10,183	4.50
Mississippi	12,472	5.52
Arkansas	7,900	3.49
Louisiana	5,798	2.56
Southwest		
Oklahoma	6,080	2.69
Texas	12,955	5.73
New Mexico	621	.27
Arizona	217	.09
Northeast		
Maine	1,841	.81
New Hampshire	757	.33
Vermont	982	.43
Massachusetts	1,362	.60
Rhode Island	194	.09
Connecticut	1,062	.47
New York	4,981	2.20
New Jersey	1,463	.65
Delaware	527	.23
Pennsylvania	8,380	3.71
Maryland	2,303	1.02
West Virginia	7,418	3.28
Middle States		
Ohio	$9,479	4.19
Indiana	6,602	2.92
Illinois	7,519	3.33
Michigan	3,591	1.59
Wisconsin	4,724	2.09
Minnesota	4,159	1.84
Iowa	8,496	3.76
Missouri	10,429	4.61
Northwest		
North Dakota	942	.41
South Dakota	1,713	.76
Nebraska	3,472	1.54
Kansas	3,738	1.65
Montana	1,206	.53
Idaho	1,344	.59
Wyoming	635	.28
Colorado	1,217	.54
Utah	564	.25
Far West		
Nevada	147	.07
Washington	2,474	1.09
Oregon	2,438	1.08
California	1,533	.68
United States	226,046	100.00

10,210,000,000,000 uncountable tons for the upbuilding and up-clearing of lands; parks and playgrounds, mountain and seashore, summer and winter resorts, play places of a nation; nature reserves and sanctuaries for wild life; flora extraordinary, grasses and cultivated plants to feed man and animal and land; fauna of the woods and fields, millions of game, for commerce and recreation; domesticated animals on farm and grazing land, race horses and work mules, makers of a culture; and many other tangibles and intangibles of geography's situation, relief, and area, inseparably interrelated to time and space relationships, biological backgrounds and genetic reserves of the people. Thus, justifiable basis for geographers' and anthropologists' and economists' and sociologists' portraiture of the region as "garden spot of the world."

The first of American pictures has been that of land, the source and power of all the Jeffersonian dream of the greater domain and democracy. This has been especially true of the southern agrarian culture. The heart of the southerner has been in his land, the early richness of which, like the prodigality of his rainfall and climate, he has nonchalantly taken for granted. Yet the region's extraordinary resources in land, with the companion forces of climate and accessibility, still constitute its incomparable basic power, but, like most other aspects of the American situation, they challenge to a new sort of utilization and planning economy as a result of the great changes of recent years. Land there is in abundance and more, but the epic of free land and frontier domain, the trek of Virginians and Carolinians south and west for new virgin lands; the plight of Ruffin and Jefferson and a thousand early southern bankrupt plantation prospects have been transcended by the complicated problems of the new agricultural crisis, the problem of mortgaged and submarginal lands, the land problem of cities, and the back-sweep from frontier and city to newer rural life and to new ways of using the land. Forestry land there is in abundance, but not the primeval limitless woods for prodigal cutting and lumbering; on the contrary, new forestry policies and developments anticipate the utilization of millions of acres for other uses, such as erosion prevention, moisture conservation and drought alleviation, recreation, parks, game conservation, and new resources of energy and materials, pulp and paper, rayon and oil. The old frontier of the section and the half section of land has gone, but a new and expanding domain of county, state, and nation-owned lands challenges new utilization policies, extraordinary economic and social planning and great obligations for a new agrarian economy. All in all it would be difficult to find any phase of the American or southern situation in which the foundations of great natural resources are the same as formerly, which, nevertheless, reflects a greater difference in status and use or treatment and requires greater science,

Regions of Major Rural Land Uses

Adapted from the U. S. Bureau of Agricultural Economics.

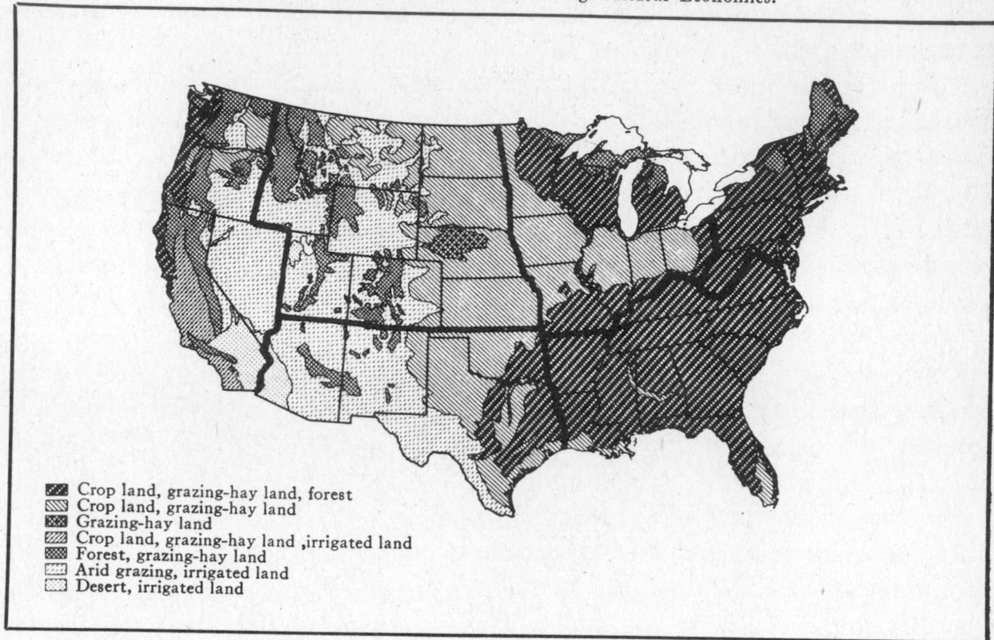

Carrying Capacity of Pasture and Rangeland

Adapted from the U. S. Bureau of Agricultural Economics

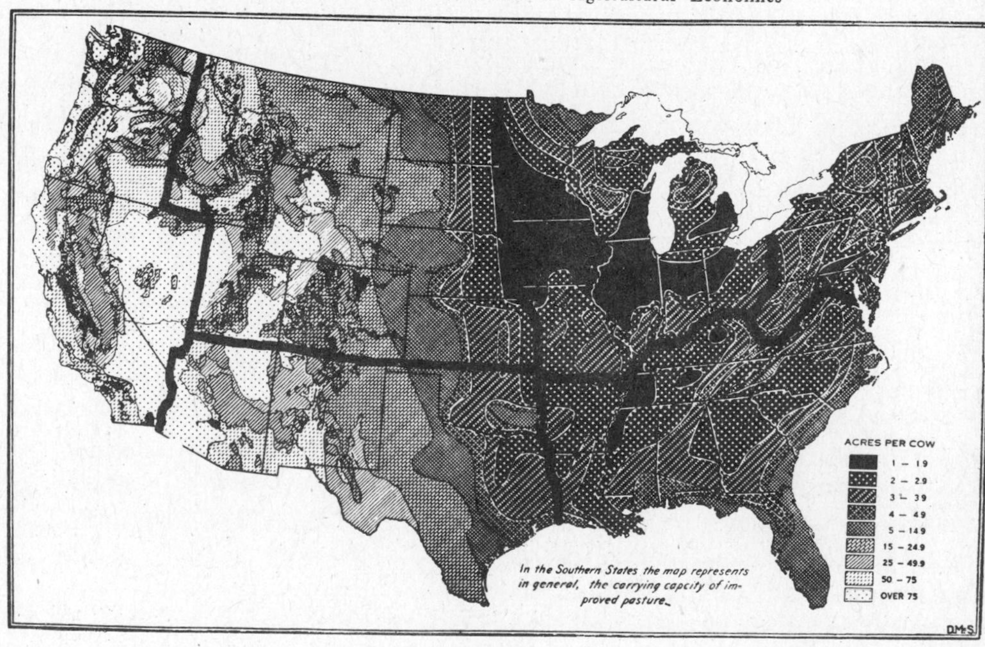

skill, and foresight, than that of the utilization of land. This problem in the Southeast is reflected in its nearly 325,000,000 acres of the nation's 1,900,000,000; this southern land expanse alone comprehending an area many times greater than all of Jefferson's early America.

Some indication of the superabundance in the Southeast of land resources, the original region of the Jeffersonian dream of a great agrarian America, may be indicated by the fact that this region alone might easily add forty million acres, the commonly quoted post-war surplus of harvested crop lands in the nation, to its present area; or just as easily take out of cultivation that amount and still, through better utilization and management, enrich its agricultural capacity and output. For in spite of its millions of acres of submarginal lands and its incredible landscape of gullies and red hills of waste, it still boasts other millions of acres of unused fertile lands and still other millions as yet so undeveloped as to defy measurement of capacity for cotton and cattle, corn and tobacco, vegetables and fruits. There is available for replanning and sale no less than 100,000,000 acres within the former area of the South's piney woods alone. Of the nation's nearly 100,000,000 acres of drainable land suitable for cultivation after reclamation, the Southeast has nearly two-thirds. There is another illustration of a single southern regional land bank, which served three states only, with the prospect of owning and managing 2,000,000 and more acres of farm lands whose titles the fortunes of depression had poured into its vaults. This was more than all the cultivated lands of Georgia or of New York state at the turn of Jefferson's century.

The size of the southern land picture may be further envisaged by comparing its area with the rest of the country, by counting and classifying its millions of acres in farm lands, or by hypothetical maximum comparison of its uses and capacities with crop areas of the world. In measures of general land area, the Southeast constitutes in itself an empire of more than 500,000 square miles or slightly more than 17 per cent of the nation's total, as compared with the Southwest's slightly more than 19 per cent, the two southern regions aggregating more than a third of America's vast domain. Such separate regional measures are important in contradistinction to the customary way of blocking out a large general "South," comprising such states as Missouri, Maryland, West Virginia, Oklahoma, and Texas, in order to "claim" for the South a major ratio of population, wealth, and area. Such mass aggregates, shifted and varied and set up for special argument or advantage, contribute little to dependable regional analysis or planning. This is especially true with reference to the Southeast's land in farms, its number and kinds of farms, and its land-man ratio. Of the more than 6,250,000 farms in the United States in 1930 the Southeast has a little

Percentage Distribution of Acres in Farms, Number of Farms, Farms Under 100 Acres, and Farms 500 Acres and Over, by Regions, 1930

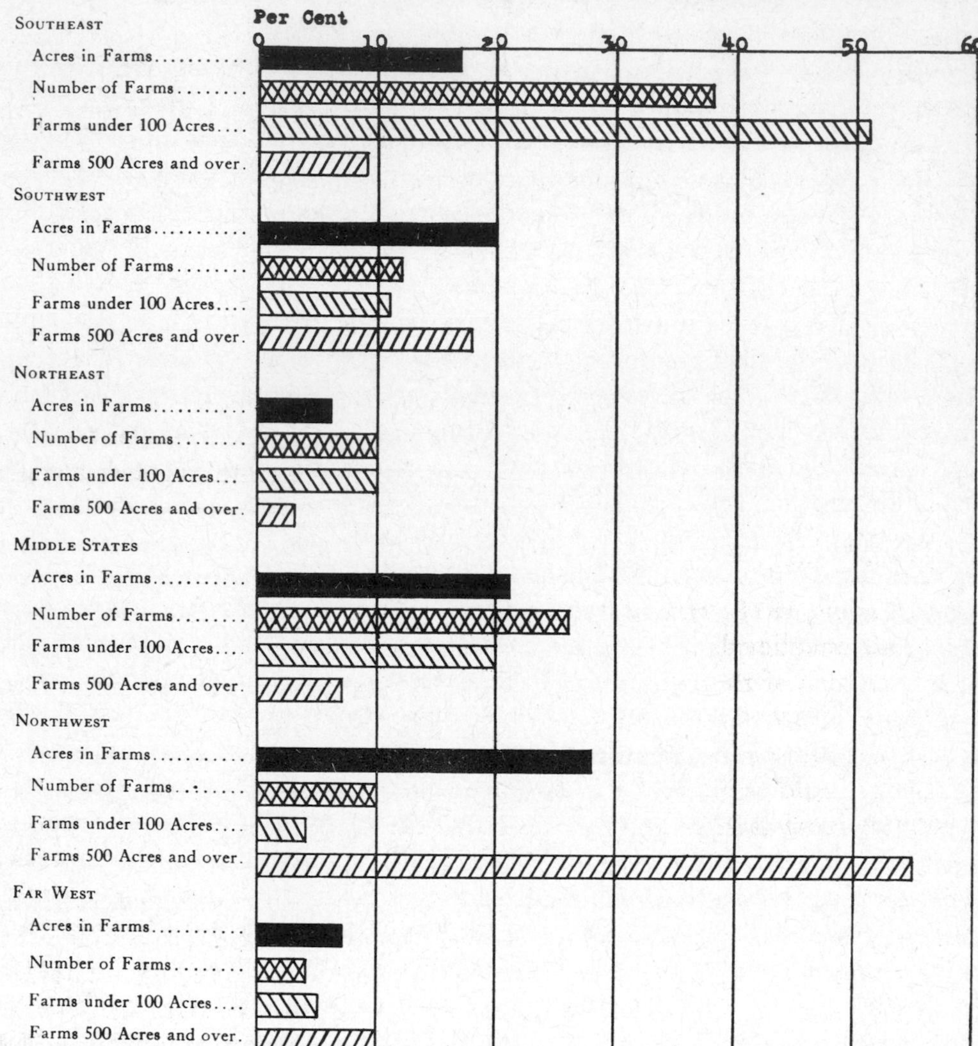

Regional Distribution of Acres in Farms, 1930

Region	Per Cent of Total Crop Land	Per Cent of Total Pasture Land	Per Cent of Total Woodland Pasture Land	Per Cent Woodland not Used for Pasture	Per Cent All Other Land in Farms
Southeast	42.5	26.4	41.8	24.3	6.8
Southwest	27.3	69.9	14.6	0.9	1.9
Northeast	40.2	38.0	32.5	16.4	5.4
Middle States	57.9	32.6	34.3	4.0	5.5
Northwest	43.1	52.4	4.7	0.4	4.1
Far West	29.9	63.3	19.8	2.3	4.5

more than 2,380,000, or nearly 40 per cent. Its acreage in farms is of a lesser ratio with 170,507,839 of which the total crop land was a little more than 70,000,000, the total pasture land nearly 45,000,000, woodland not used as pasture 41,000,000, and all other land in farms a little more than 11,500,000. The map picture of the land uses of the Southeast shows practically the entire region classified as featuring the highest multiple land use; namely, "crop land, grazing-hay land, forest." Yet the uses of the land vary in both the size of farms and in the crops grown. Here again is measure of the region's culture and capacity. There are, for instance, more than 300,000 farms in Mississippi which average only 53 acres per farm; there are scarcely 16,000 farms in Wyoming but they average nearly 1,500 acres each. Here again there are great regional differences, with the Southeast clearly distinctive, with an average acreage per farm of 71 acres contrasted with the Northeast's 102, the Middle States' 123, the Far West's 243, the Southwest's 268, and the Northwest's 429 acres.

A glance at regional priorities in the major agricultural commodities will suggest other comparisons and indicate something of the regional dominance of land use, the details of which may be studied in subsequent chapters. Old King Cotton, periodically reported in ill health, still rules in the Southeast and the Southwest, which produce respectively nearly 60 and nearly 40 per cent of the nation's maximum of 15,000,000 bales. And tobacco, a newly crowned queen of the land in manufacture, in advertising, in internal revenue, and in new manners and mores, hails mostly from the Southeastern States which produce 85 per cent of the nearly 1,600,000,000 pounds of the American weed. Yet wheat is king of the great Northwest, which produces a little over half of the nation's more than 850,000,000 bushels. Corn is king of the Middle States, which produces a little more than half of the nation's 2,384,000 bushels, with hay and hogs runners-up for leadership in the Middle States and Northwest which aggregate 60 per cent of the nation's 86,000,000 tons of hay and 75 per cent of its 56,000,000 swine.

The Far West dominates the picture in abundance and variety of fruits and vegetables, yet the Southeast follows in close succession. The Southeast and the Middle States lead the procession of the foster mother of the race, the dairy cow, which flourishes on three-fourths of all the nation's farms, aggregating more than 30,000,000 on 4,615,000 farms, pastured on wooded lot and meadow, on hillsides and by the waters, or languishing on barren lands. The Southeast and the Middle States each report milk cows on more than 1,480,000 farms, which aggregate nearly half of the nation's total cows milked, the Southeast leading by nearly 3,000 farms but lagging in the number of cows by nearly 6,000,000. And what a picture and what

Percentage Distribution of Agricultural Commodities, by Regions

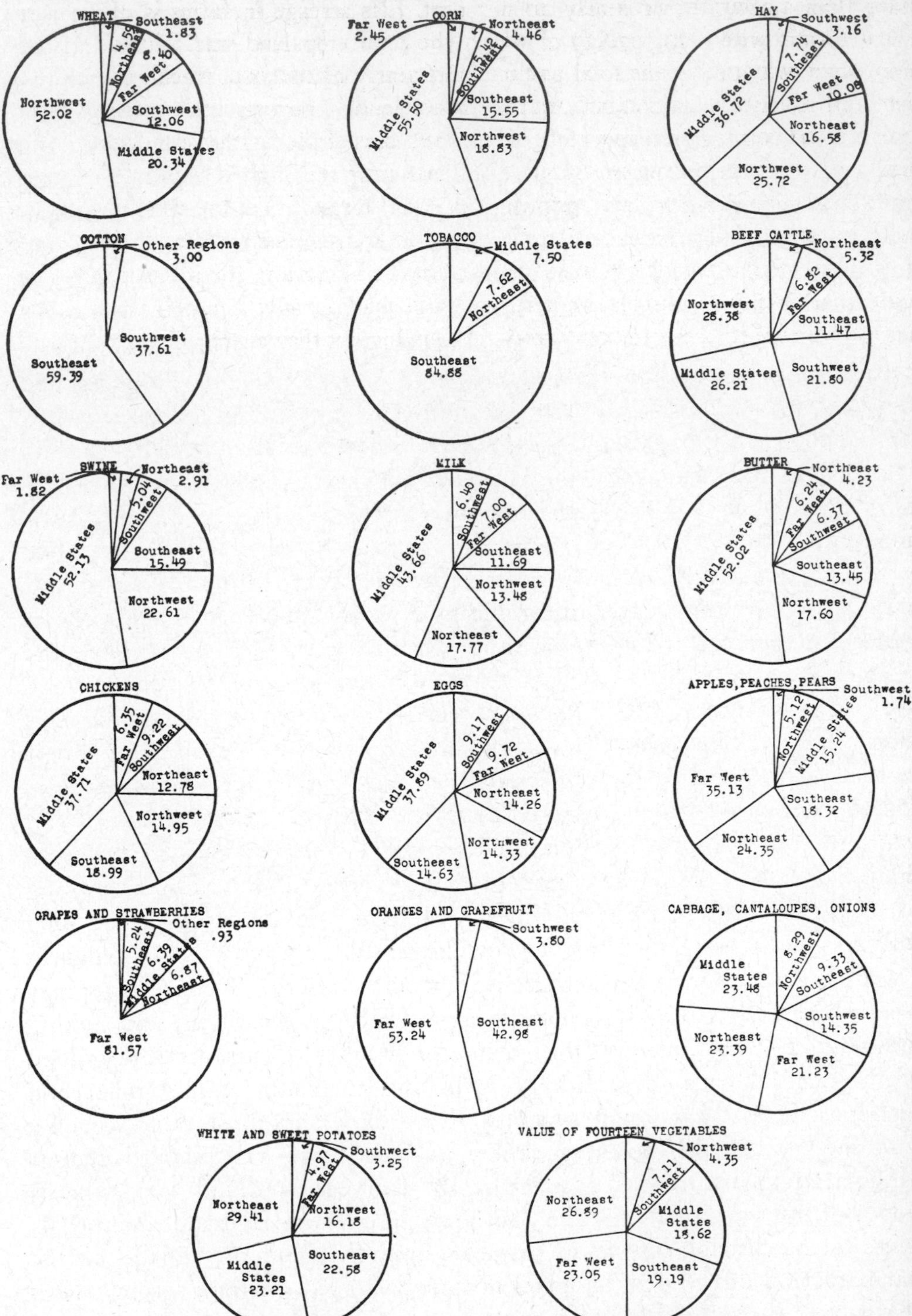
WHEAT
Southeast 1.83
4.59 Northeast
8.40 Far West
Southwest 12.06
Middle States 20.34
Northwest 52.02
CORN
Far West 2.45
Northeast 4.46
5.42 Southwest
Southeast 15.55
Northwest 18.83
Middle States 55.50
HAY
Southwest 3.16
7.74 Southeast
Far West 10.08
Northeast 16.58
Northwest 25.72
Middle States 36.72
COTTON
Other Regions 3.00
Southwest 37.61
Southeast 59.39
TOBACCO
Middle States 7.50
7.62 Northeast
Southeast 84.88
BEEF CATTLE
Northeast 5.32
6.82 Far West
Southeast 11.47
Southwest 21.80
Middle States 26.21
Northwest 28.38
SWINE
Far West 1.82
Northeast 2.91
5.04 Southwest
Southeast 15.49
Northwest 22.61
Middle States 52.13
MILK
6.40 Southwest
7.00 Far West
Southeast 11.69
Northwest 13.48
Northeast 17.77
Middle States 43.66
BUTTER
Northeast 4.23
6.24 Far West
6.37 Southwest
Southeast 13.45
Northwest 17.60
Middle States 52.02
CHICKENS
6.35 Far West
9.22 Southwest
Northeast 12.78
Northwest 14.95
Southeast 18.99
Middle States 37.71
EGGS
9.17 Southwest
9.72 Far West
Northeast 14.26
Northwest 14.33
Southeast 14.63
Middle States 37.89
APPLES, PEACHES, PEARS
Southwest 1.74
5.12 Northwest
Middle States 15.24
Southeast 18.32
Northeast 24.35
Far West 35.13
GRAPES AND STRAWBERRIES
Other Regions .93
5.24 Southeast
6.39 Middle States
6.87 Northeast
Far West 81.57
ORANGES AND GRAPEFRUIT
Southwest 3.80
Southeast 42.98
Far West 53.24
CABBAGE, CANTALOUPES, ONIONS
8.29 Northwest
9.33 Southeast
Southwest 14.35
Far West 21.23
Northeast 23.39
Middle States 23.48
WHITE AND SWEET POTATOES
Southwest 3.25
4.97 Far West
Northwest 16.18
Southeast 22.58
Middle States 23.21
Northeast 29.41
VALUE OF FOURTEEN VEGETABLES
Northwest 4.35
7.11 Southwest
Middle States 18.62
Southeast 19.19
Far West 23.05
Northeast 26.89

variety—the South with its transplanted Islands of Jersey and Guernsey with their golden and spotted fawns, vying with the Middle States and the Northeast with other millions of big handsome Holsteins, black and whites, for new world records of production and new standards of food values.

Yet the composite spectacle of 40,000,000 acres of cotton, bloom and boll, of 100,000,000 acres of tasseling corn, of 60,000,000 acres of wheat, golden wave on wave, or 100,000,000 cattle on a thousand hills, gorgeous and stupendous as it is, constitutes but a small part of the possible picture for all available lands. To make southern comparison, all of the harvested wheat land in the world would scarcely exceed an area equal to the seven westerly states of the Southeast. The world's total harvested land in cotton could be superimposed upon North Carolina, South Carolina, and Georgia, while an area less than the mid-central South would be sufficient for all the present corn lands of the universe. The well-watered grazing lands of the Southeast, were they utilized for nature's most important of all plant families, the grasses, wild and tame, could pasture a continent's cattle and more.

Of the land is the forest, "nature's preferred crop." And just as forests and forest lore have played a significant and romantic rôle in the story of general human culture as well as in its specific aspects of literature, art, and religion, so also in the United States it is in nowise possible to understand the national culture and background without sensing the tremendous part which its more than 800,000,000 acres of primeval forest land have played in the development of the American people. "The richest forest lands in the world," so geographers have described America's heritage, and of this vast area the Southeast has excelled in many ways. "The Southeastern States," wrote A. N. Polk as late as 1932, "represent the most interesting of all regional forestry possibilities. Here are the great areas of long leaf and short leaf pine with a growing season of almost twelve months a year." As in other aspects, there is, however, variety. Deep, dark, piney woods with their tall, graceful, and compact millions of swaying and sighing lumber trees, fragrant with the incense of woodland moisture and golden brown needles, rich in wealth of rosin and turpentine and lumber and timbers contrast with great swamps, forest-dark and mysterious, echoing with the cry of wild cat and panther, owl and hawk, tall gnarled cypress silhouetted against the sky or river bank. Immense midland woods, hardwoods of interior uplands of the Southeast, bisected by rivers, original challenge to the clearing instinct of pioneers, ambush places for Indians on the war path, now afford new resources in time and need. Million acre expanses of cut-over timbers afford reforestation possibilities for the next period of

Regional Variations in Influence of Forests on Watershed Protection

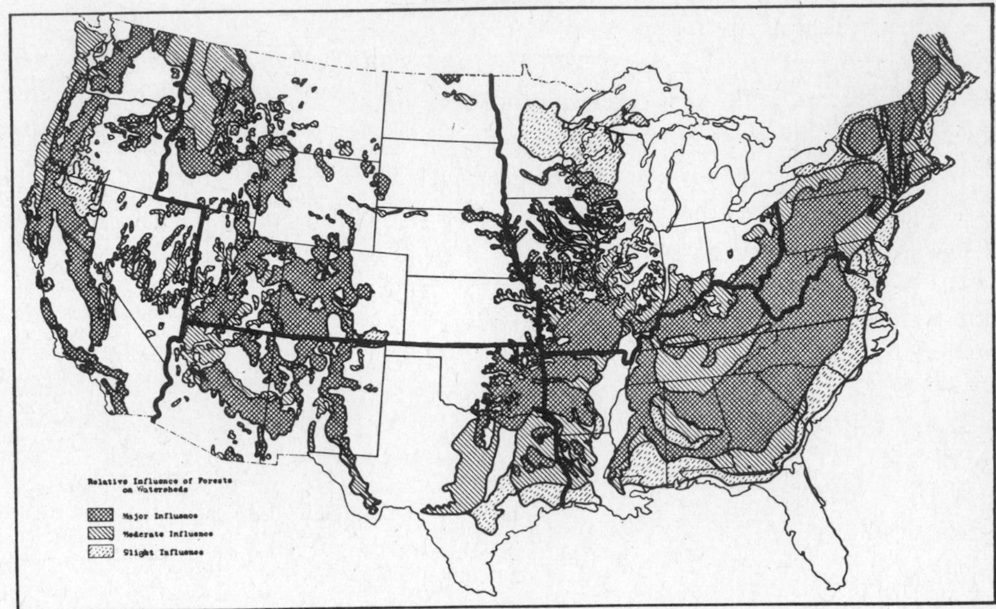

Forest Area of Southeast, by Character of Growth, 1930[1]

STATE	Total Area	Saw-timber Area	Cordwood Area	Fair to Satisfactory Restocking Areas	Poor to Non-stocking Areas
	Thousand Acres	Thousand Acres	Thousand Acres	Thousand Acres	Thousand Acres
Virginia	14,857	2,859	5,582	3,298	3,118
North Carolina	20,216	4,192	7,890	3,455	4,679
South Carolina	12,415	3,757	3,947	1,558	3,153
Georgia	22,872	6,900	7,566	5,010	3,396
Florida	23,600	6,030	6,921	3,164	7,485
Kentucky	10,296	2,767	4,441	1,705	1,383
Tennessee	14,041	5,067	7,170	874	930
Alabama	21,680	7,427	4,407	5,174	4,672
Mississippi	18,293	5,067	2,446	3,674	7,106
Arkansas	22,000	7,700	7,000	5,000	2,300
Louisiana	18,903	7,383	2,459	2,833	6,228
Total	199,173	59,149	59,829	35,745	44,450

[1] Embraces only commercial forest land, or land capable of producing commercial timber in commercial quantities, and does not include the commercial forest land withdrawn from commodity use, which amounts to nearly one million acres, or the new-commercial forest land which amounts to nearly 25 million acres.

Total Stand (in Cubic Feet) in the Southeast, 1930[1]

STATE	Combined Area			Saw-Timber Area[2]		Cordwood Area	
	Total Million Cu. ft.	Softwood Million Cu. ft.	Hardwood Million Cu. ft.	Softwood Million Cu. ft.	Hardwood Million Cu. ft.	Softwood Million Cu. ft.	Hardwood Million Cu. ft.
Virginia	9,234	3,837	5,397	1,589	2,480	2,248	2,917
North Carolina	13,944	7,795	6,149	3,314	3,042	4,481	3,107
South Carolina	9,711	5,030	4,681	2,792	3,155	2,238	1,426
Georgia	14,039	9,976	4,063	4,571	2,409	5,405	1,654
Florida	8,602	7,075	1,527	4,217	1,172	2,858	355
Kentucky	3,714	378	3,336	204	1,503	174	1,833
Tennessee	8,296	779	7,517	440	3,621	339	3,896
Alabama	9,474	6,550	2,924	5,106	2,247	1,444	677
Mississippi	7,459	4,010	3,449	3,302	2,710	708	739
Arkansas	13,241	5,615	7,626	3,714	5,104	1,901	2,522
Louisiana	11,256	4,457	6,799	3,745	6,113	712	686
Total	108,970	55,502	53,468	32,994	33,556	22,508	19,812

[1] Includes volumes of all material of cordwood size or larger on commercial forest area, excluding that on restocking areas, but does not include the materials on commercial forest areas withdrawn from commodity use, that on non-commercial forest areas, or that on the restocking land of the commodity forest area. The material on the restocking and non-restocking areas is negligible.

[2] Includes saw-log material, tops and limbs (only tops in the case of softwood), stumps, long butts, breakage, etc., of saw-timber trees; also trees of less than saw-timber size but large enough to produce cordwood.

development and add to the vast panorama of wealth and beauty, inventory of the southern scene.

Until recently with the revival of the conservation movement, of land planning and reforestation, the forest lands were still for the most part empires for commercial lumber and cordwood. Yet there need be no conflict between the vast economic wealth inherent in the forest and reforestation programs and the larger aspect of forest development in the nation. Here again the Southeast with 40 per cent of the nation's forest area ranks high in potentiality. The statistics of the situation are still eloquent if adequately interpreted. There is still magic in the remaining more than 495,000,000 acres of commercial forests, of which the Southeast has its nearly 200,000,000. There are challenging problems and reserve power in the millions of acres of low-grade woodland and scrub and in the millions of acres of forest land which have been withdrawn for uses other than timber production. Of the commercial forests, there is stark contrast between the old days and the 1930 era, with only about one-fifth in virgin stands and with less than 40 per cent constituting saw-timber area. Yet lumbering can still constitute the second industry of the Southeast, based upon its incomparable natural resources. There are still great mills and markets for the fruits of the forest, and there is still left some small remnant of the romance of logging communities and lumber towns and many a lost village with scarcely a surviving trace to tell its tale.

Of the total commercial forest area, the Southeastern Region contains 198,000,000 acres, or about 40 per cent. However, the region contains only 30 per cent of the saw-timber area and only 15 per cent of the old-growth, or virgin, area. Nearly half of the total saw-timber area and about three-fourths of the virgin area are found in the Pacific Coast and Rocky Mountain regions. Nearly one-half of the country's second-growth saw-timber area and 44 per cent of the cordwood area are in the Southeast Region. On the other hand, of its 82,000,000 acres of cut-over land only 37,000,000, or 45 per cent is in a fair to satisfactory restocking condition.

The present stand of saw timber in continental United States is estimated at 1,668 billion board feet, or about one-third of the amount in the original stand. Of this total, 1,346 billion feet, or 80 per cent, is in virgin stands. The Pacific Coast Region, with 13 per cent of the forest area, has 62 per cent of the saw timber, including 71 per cent of the old growth. The Southeast Region, with 40 per cent of the forest area, has 12 per cent of the saw timber but only 5 per cent of the old growth. Of the total stand of saw timber, 1,486 billion board feet, or 89 per cent, are softwood and 182 billion feet are hardwood. At present, the Southeast Region contains 78 billion board feet, or 43 per cent, of the hardwood of saw-timber size, and

Lumber Production in the United States and the Southeast, 1923-1930

(Millions of Board Feet)

STATE	1923	1924	1925	1926	1927	1928	1929	1930
United States	37,166	35,931	38,339	36,936	34,532	34,142	36,886	26,051
Virginia	771	696	709	677	536	547	709	495
North Carolina	1,096	1,072	1,041	971	1,055	1,021	1,202	815
South Carolina	1,070	879	980	921	817	822	1,068	707
Georgia	1,149	1,207	1,365	1,146	1,201	1,039	1,386	753
Florida	1,110	1,089	1,064	921	907	995	1,137	876
Kentucky	196	194	207	217	198	174	339	189
Tennessee	661	659	642	683	595	530	764	414
Alabama	1,787	1,873	2,236	2,105	2,172	1,980	2,059	1,342
Mississippi	2,691	2,807	3,128	2,895	2,557	2,524	2,670	1,484
Arkansas	1,538	1,536	1,597	1,441	1,229	1,130	1,348	869
Louisiana	3,554	3,397	3,293	2,890	2,386	2,279	2,232	1,607
Regional Total	15,623	15,409	16,264	14,867	13,653	13,041	14,914	9,551

Distribution of Lumber Produced by Southeastern States, 1926

(Thousand Board Feet)

STATE	Within the State	To Other Southern States		To States Outside the South		To Foreign Countries	Total Distribution
		No. of States	Quantity	No. of States	Quantity		
Softwood							
Virginia	126,687	2	675	15	291,126	7,506	425,994
North Carolina	305,294	7	70,726	15	406,504	465	782,989
South Carolina	115,748	6	121,457	17	536,804	5,135	779,144
Georgia	284,574	8	210,286	18	619,730	7,656	1,122,246
Florida	442,080	9	56,875	20	232,042	105,204	836,201
Kentucky	15,905	0	0	3	2,606	......	18,511
Tennessee	38,451	7	25,398	17	59,968	1,291	125,108
Alabama	661,584	9	292,693	21	839,015	56,238	1,848,530
Mississippi	400,858	10	551,650	30	1,086,267	323,712	2,362,487
Arkansas	177,180	7	21,447	29	673,475	377	872,479
Louisiana	408,308	10	114,237	31	1,441,025	203,641	2,167,211
Total	2,976,669	..	1,465,444	..	6,188,562	711,225	11,340,900
Hardwood							
Virginia	65,604	3	18,624	14	144,606	17,673	246,507
North Carolina	10,492	7	19,439	15	170,068	1,921	201,920
South Carolina	19,029	6	45,349	17	79,170	3,167	146,715
Georgia	32,918	6	24,113	17	47,163	1,904	106,098
Florida	6,210	5	1,108	16	12,949	59	20,326
Kentucky	83,065	4	6,138	18	107,107	1,321	197,631
Tennessee	182,763	10	60,746	14	285,063	16,244	544,816
Alabama	39,605	10	75,081	24	147,368	28,122	290,176
Mississippi	55,682	10	125,121	31	238,902	37,436	457,141
Arkansas	159,687	7	30,067	30	331,527	3,073	524,354
Louisiana	136,917	8	158,900	32	341,811	62,404	700,032
Total	791,972	..	564,686	..	1,905,734	173,324	3,435,716

Forest Products Cut on Farms in United States and the Southeast, 1929

STATE	Saw Logs and Veneer Logs	Firewood	Pulpwood	Fence Posts	Railroad Ties	Poles and Piles	Value of Products	Rank of State
	M. bd. ft.	Cords	Cords	Number	Number	Number		
United States	5,042,926	34,110,529	1,485,759	98,664,249	15,338,786	3,2[illegible]8,415	$242,042,245	
Virginia	329,010	1,533,297	220,879	1,434,686	850,124	286,420	12,028,661	5
North Carolina	485,520	2,638,271	104,083	794,817	579,056	147,529	15,184,145	3
South Carolina	207,352	1,079,973	20,212	498,622	277,815	57,278	5,824,378	17
Georgia	328,679	1,737,476	13,842	2,303,301	422,770	118,321	8,861,877	9
Florida	59,158	132,863	4,097	567,902	171,118	24,542	1,262,546	35
Kentucky	156,583	1,319,281	24,[illegible]45	2,984,863	922,950	116,368	6,662,901	16
Tennessee	478,630	1,960,679	73,366	3,002,578	1,051,871	165,655	13,021,166	4
Alabama	408,899	1,561,519	33,975	2,626,481	580,303	103,512	8,504,708	11
Mississippi	365,613	1,400,377	30,396	3,957,535	1,079,088	164,228	9,280,785	8
Arkansas	154,903	1,559,570	58,129	4,712,272	1,325,879	59,269	7,769,391	14
Louisiana	80,078	505,927	58,044	2,291,326	692,384	63,221	3,231,438	26
Regional total	3,054,425	15,429,233	641,168	25,174,383	7,953,358	1,306,343	31,631,996	

121 billion, or 8 per cent, of the softwood. Ninety-eight per cent of the 118 billion feet of southern yellow pine is in the Southeast. Practically all of the hardwood saw timber is in the East, and about 43 per cent of it is in the Southeast. The region has 33 billion feet of old-growth hardwood, comprising the only large reserve of old-growth hardwood timber left in the United States. Oak is the leading hardwood of the country. There is a total stand of about 60 billion board feet, more than half of which is in the Southeast Region. Of the 50 billion feet of beech, birch, and maple, the Southeast has only 2,500 million, but it has 43 million feet of other hardwoods, principally red gum, tupelo, poplar, and hickory.

Returning again to the farm land picture, about 72,000,000 acres, or about 42 per cent of the forest land of the Southeast is in farms and about the same amount of the farm land is forest or potential forest, a situation in striking contrast to the situation in the United States as a whole. In the entire nation there are 987 million acres in farms of which only 195 million acres, 19.7 per cent of the total farm area, are woodland. In the Southeast the farm woodland may be classified as follows: woodland not used for pasture, 41,429,543 acres; woodland pasture, 18,586,643 acres; waste and potential woodland, 11,694,842 acres; making a total farm woodland of 71,711,028 acres. From map pictures and statistics the South's profile still presents the forest predominance, a region in which as yet not more than a third is cleared ground and one in which 95 per cent of all the forest land is privately owned. Of the 191,739,000 acres of forest land in the southeast forest region, 182,245,000 acres, or 95 per cent, are in private ownership. Moreover, much of the 6,281,000 acres that is reported as belonging to the states, counties, or municipalities is tax delinquent land to which absolute title has not been taken. There are only 3,213,000 acres that are owned or managed by the Federal Government. In contrast with the 95 per cent in private ownership in the Southeast, the average for the rest of the country is 69 per cent. Stated differently, 46.5 per cent of the privately-owned forest land of the country is in the northeast forest region. Singularly, the proportion of the privately-owned forest land in farm woodlots is exactly the same in the Southeast as for the country as a whole, 31.8 per cent.

Other measures of the southeastern forest resources will appear from the inventories of its production and distribution of lumber, pulp, naval stores, and other products. There is an important regional differential which needs to be recorded alongside the elemental natural resources, and that is the quick-growing possibilities of the southern forests and the potentials which they offer for commercial purposes and for the restoration and conservation of southern lands. There is yet another significant picture to

Ownership of Forest Areas and Timber Stands in United States and in the Southeast Forest Region, 1930

Adapted from a Special Report to the Timber Conservation Board, 1932, Tables 9-14

		Federally Owned or Managed					Private		
	All Areas Thousand Acres	Total Thousand Acres	National Forest Thousand Acres	Indian Reservation Thousand Acres	Other Thousand Acres	State, County and Municipal Thousand Acres	Total Thousand Acres	Farm Woodlot Thousand Acres	Other Thousand Acres
United States	*495,879*	*88,029*	*74,680*	*7,428*	*5,921*	*16,633*	*391,217*	*124,678*	*266,539*
Saw-timber areas	188,645	59,277	49,795	5,304	4,178	3,103	126,265	35,640	90,625
Cordwood areas	120,881	13,706	12,069	846	791	2,283	104,892	43,299	61,593
Fair to satisfactory restocking areas	102,073	7,917	6,495	854	568	5,440	88,716	26,488	62,228
Poor to non-restocking areas	84,280	7,129	6,321	424	384	5,807	71,344	19,251	52,093
Southeast Forest Region	*191,739*	*3,213*	*3,137*	*56*	*20*	*6,281*	*182,245*	*57,866*	*124,379*
Saw-timber areas	57,265	1,941	1,884	49	8	104	55,220	13,729	41,491
Cordwood areas	52,702	638	631	3	4	421	51,643	19,789	31,854
Fair to satisfactory restocking areas	37,236	373	366	3	4	1,711	35,152	12,084	23,068
Poor to non-restocking areas	44,536	261	256	1	4	4,045	40,230	12,264	27,966
	Per Cent	Per Cent	Per Cent	Per Cent	Per Cent	Per Cent	Per Cent	Per Cent	Per Cent
Portion of Total in Southeast	*38.6*	*3.6*	*4.2*	*0.7*	*0.3*	*37.7*	*46.5*	*46.4*	*46.6*
Saw-timber areas	30.4	3.3	3.7	0.9	0.2	3.3	43.7	38.5	45.7
Cordwood areas	43.5	4.6	5.2	0.4	0.5	1.8	49.2	45.7	51.7
Fair to satisfactory restocking areas	36.4	4.7	5.6	0.3	0.7	31.4	39.6	45.6	37.1
Poor to non-restocking areas	52.8	3.6	4.0	0.2	1.0	69.6	56.4	63.7	53.6

Woodland in Farms, 1930

		All Land in Farms			Woodland					
State and Region	Approximate Land Area (000 omitted)	Area (000 omitted)	Per Cent of Total Land Area	Crop Land and Pasture (Exclusive of Woodland Pasture) (000 omitted)	Woodland not Used for Pasture (000 omitted)	Woodland Pasture (000 omitted)	Waste and Potential (000 omitted)	Total (000 omitted)	Per Cent of Farm Area	Per Cent of Approximate Land Area
United States	1,903,216	986,771	51.8	792,068	64,623	85,321	44,756	194,702	19.7	**10.2**
Southeast	*319,736*	*170,507*	*53.3*	*98,628*	*41,429*	*18,586*	*11,694*	*71,711*	*42.0*	*22.4*
Virginia	25,767	16,728	64.9	9,150	5,167	1,527	909	7,604	45.7	30.0
North Carolina	31,193	18,055	57.9	8,433	6,902	1,423	1,295	9,621	53.3	30.8
South Carolina	19,516	10.393	53.3	5,778	2,850	1,051	712	4,614	44.4	23.6
Georgia	37,584	22,078	58.7	12,217	5,492	2,880	1,487	9,860	44.7	26.2
Florida	35,111	5,026	14.3	2,446	1,050	840	687	2,579	51.3	7.4
Kentucky	25,715	19,927	77.5	13,644	3,393	1,207	1,486	6,087	30.6	23.7
Tennessee	26,679	18,003	67.5	11,304	3,884	1,528	1,284	6,698	37.2	25.1
Alabama	32,818	17,554	53.5	10,013	4,195	2,290	1,055	7,541	43.0	23.0
Mississippi	22,671	17,332	58.4	9,945	3,370	2,853	1,162	7,386	42.6	32.6
Arkansas	33,616	16,052	47.8	9,635	3,378	2,064	974	6,417	39.9	19.0
Louisiana	29,061	9,355	32.2	6,057	1,741	917	638	3,297	35.2	11.3

Lumber Production in the United States and the Southern States, and the Rank of Each Southern State, 1870-1929

(Quantity expressed in millions of board feet)

	1870		1880		1890		1899		1909		1919		1929	
	Quantity	Rank	Quantity	Rank	Quantity	Rank	Quantity	Rank	Quantity	Rank	Quantity	Rank	Quantity	Rank
United States	12,756	..	18,091	..	23,498	..	34,787	..	44,510	..	34,552	..	......	..
Southeast	*1,540*	..	*2,780*	..	*4,841*	..	*11,510*	..	*19,734*	..	*15,834*	..	*14,914*	..
Virginia	144	20	316	15	410	22	956	15	2,102	6	1,098	12	709	14
North Carolina	125	22	242	22	509	16	1,278	8	2,178	4	1,654	7	1,202	10
South Carolina	95	..	186	24	198	..	466	..	898	20	622	20	1,068	12
Georgia	245	13	452	9	573	10	1,309	7	1,342	15	894	13	1,386	8
Florida	159	19	248	21	411	21	789	18	1,202	17	1,137	10	1,137	11
Kentucky	214	15	306	16	421	20	765	21	861	21	512	22	339	21
Tennessee	205	16	303	18	450	18	939	16	1,224	16	792	15	764	16
Alabama	97	..	252	20	586	9	1,097	12	1,691	11	1,799	5	2,059	6
Mississippi	161	18	169	..	453	17	1,202	10	2,573	3	2,390	4	2,670	3
Arkansas	79	..	173	..	526	14	1,596	5	2,111	5	1,772	6	1,348	9
Louisiana	16	..	133	..	304	25	1,113	11	3,552	2	3,164	2	2,232	4

be found in the ever-growing federal national forest enterprise. Although no less than four-fifths of all timber-growing land, and 90 per cent of the possible growing capacity, are privately owned, the federal forest lands total more than 160,000,000 acres, of which 140,000,000 acres are in the Continental United States. These acres contain 83,000,000 acres or 12 per cent of all the western range lands. They contain the major mountain ranges of the nation, 75 per cent of the big game range of the west, and nearly one-sixth of the nation's commercial forest area, of which all is under timber management.

Like the rest of the nation, the South has begun to reckon its resources in national forests and playgrounds and in the conservation and development of field and stream for the enrichment and recreation of its people. There is an increasing recognition of the new resources in the out-of-doors, a sort of back-to-nature movement, with the emphasis upon recreation, leisure time, physical reconstruction, picturesque and historical heritage. Parks and playgrounds, national, state, municipal, have multiplied a hundredfold, national forests and bird sanctuaries have become a public interest, and a thousand organizations attend to the promotion and educational features of the new good life. Here is scenic beauty unparalleled, a picture unsurpassed. Yet the southeastern picture includes but two out of the 21 national parks with scarcely more than two per cent of the over 8,000,000 acres. The Great Smokies, however, contain the finest virgin hardwood and red spruce in the nation and the greatest variety of plant life known. Of the national forests of 185,000,000 acres in twenty-six states, the Southeast has less than 4,000,000 in nine states. The names and places of these forests are folknames from Indian lore, reminiscent of primeval forests: Ouachita and Ozark, Choctawhatchee and Ocala, Cherokee and Nantahala, Kisatchie and Unaka, Pisgah and Monongahela. What these parks and forests may mean in the Southeast when developed may be surmised from the great American moving picture which records more than 35,000,000 visitors to such places in the decade from 1920 to 1930, or from the fact that the new Great Smokies were reported as being the most popular of parks in attendance in 1933. Of state parks and forests, almost 600, covering more than 4,250,000 acres, the Southeast as yet records no more than a score and little more than 20,000 acres. Of municipal parks and playgrounds, the Southeast, compared to cities of 5,000 population and over, at least half of which have one or more, recorded less than two score, with an aggregate acreage of scarcely more than 6,000. Yet, of the 2,053,169 acres of land to be added to the national forests as approved in late 1934 by the National Forest Preservation Commission for eastern United States,

MUNICIPAL PARKS: PARKS IN 898 MUNICIPALITIES OF 5000 POPULATION AND OVER, 1930

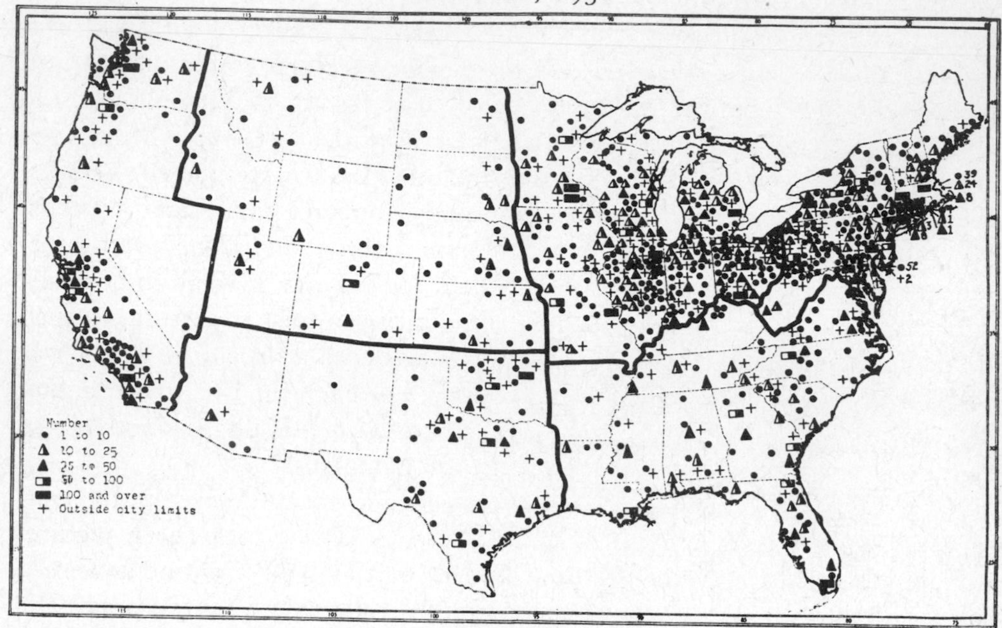

NATIONAL, STATE, COUNTY—PARKS, MONUMENTS, GAME PRESERVES, 1930

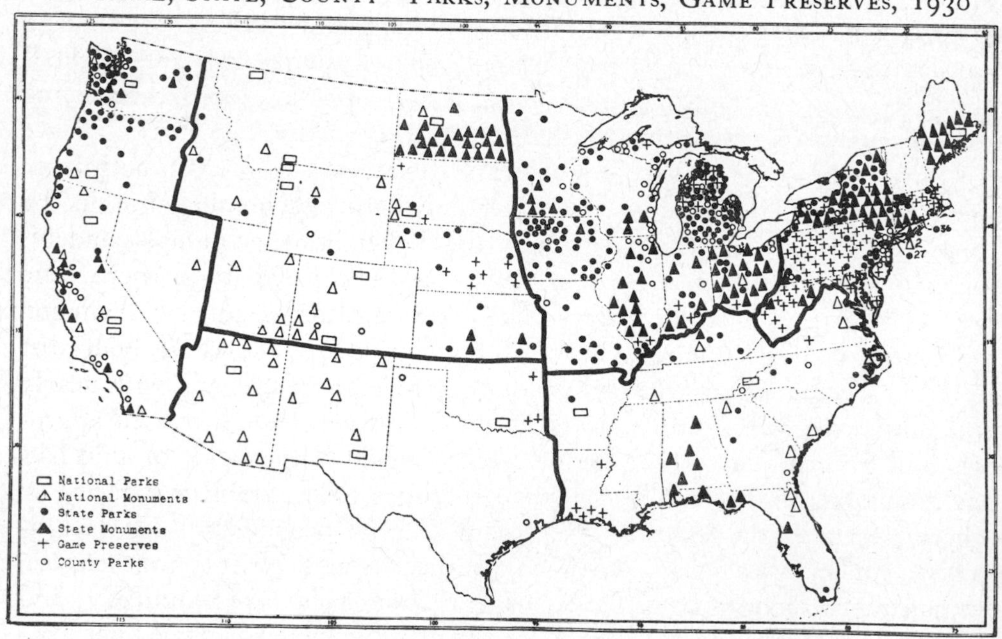

a little more than 1,000,000 are in the Southeast, while most of the Southern States are planning additional parks.

In the wealth of physical resources for summer and winter resorts, the Southeast is coming again into its own with its thousands of coast and interior resorts contributing to one of the most colorful of all American pictures. Samplings include hundreds of coast resorts of Virginia and the Carolinas, of Georgia and east and west Florida, of south Mississippi and Alabama. Other special samplings include Hot Springs and the Ozarks, the Great Smokies and Chickamauga, Stone Mountain and Warm Springs, Pinehurst and Aiken, Charleston and Mount Vernon, and a thousand hunting lodges and play places, on coastal island or old rice plantation or abandoned indigo lands of yesteryear. The picture must record also such hectic episode as the Florida boom of the 1920's as a dream in which was envisioned a physical play place big enough not only for the whole nation but for a large part of the world. The optimum utilization of all these resources constitutes itself a rare picture of potentiality.

Another part of the nature picture reflects a growing interest in the conservation and development of wild life. In the earlier American picture, the abundance and variety of the wild life of the New Continent were a constant marvel wherever they were not taken for granted by the pragmatic pioneers. Here again the most extravagant terms were always needed for these pioneer pictures, of which the South boasted a superabundance: buffalo and bear, turkey and deer; fox and beaver, marten and mink, fur-bearing gold mines; clouds of wild pigeons, millions of ducks, millions of small game, rabbit and squirrel, bobwhite and dove. These again are becoming in new reality one of the most interesting of all natural resources. Since the turn of the century there has been a great revival of interest, both from the aesthetic and recreational viewpoint and that of economic value, in the conservation and breeding of game birds, of fur-bearing animals, and all manner of wild life and of fish in stream and lake. By 1930 there were no less than four score federal refuges and sanctuaries and 29 Audubon sanctuaries throughout the country. The map picture shows the Southeast leading all regions here with no less than 30 federal refuges and with nearly two-thirds of all the Audubon sanctuaries. The states have increased appropriations for game farms and for the protection and conservation of wild life, and thousands of individuals or private groups have established farms or sanctuaries until the industry has assumed large proportions. It is estimated, for instance, that in eleven southern states of the Southeastern Region more than 10,000,000 bobwhites alone were taken annually, and that the aggregate food value of these and other game birds would approximate $10,000,000. Or sample again, Alabama's game crop of birds and ani-

Preliminary Inventory of Land Productivity Classes of the United States

Adapted from National Resources Board, Report, Part II.

STATE AND REGION	Grade 1 Acres	Grade 2 Acres	Grade 3 Acres	Grade 4 Acres	Grade 5 Acres	Per Cent of Grades 4 and 5
Southeast	*5,423,479*	*36,955,099*	*100,234,769*	*104,992,387*	*78,757,366*	*56.3*
Virginia	....	3,653,134	9,279,761	7,312,200	5,399,769	49.6
North Carolina	....	1,166,506	11,360,152	9,381,729	9,285,453	59.8
South Carolina	....	296,359	7,069,969	7,127,990	5,022,890	62.3
Georgia	....	1,851,537	15,614,067	9,750,361	10,368,603	53.5
Florida	71,161	933,187	3,928,412	12,892,726	17,077,968	85.9
Kentucky	863,916	5,020,424	8,956,319	7,905,826	2,877,195	42.1
Tennessee	902,258	4,769,847	9,305,437	8,239,726	3,412,108	43.8
Alabama	....	3,002,499	9,528,183	10,730,251	9,490,887	61.7
Mississippi	844,230	5,336,459	8,614,697	10,928,882	4,090,950	25.7
Arkansas	1,452,484	7,952,405	9,231,149	8,299,905	6,707,425	44.6
Louisiana	1,289,430	2,972,742	7,346,623	12,422,991	5,024,118	60.1
Southwest	*3,291,751*	*32,255,668*	*71,157,460*	*50,785,773*	*266,297,180*	*74.7*
Oklahoma	1,700,604	12,795,160	15,268,765	7,825,536	6,856,079	33.0
Texas	1,591,147	19,460,508	54,974,391	35,950,166	56,098,156	54.8
New Mexico	....	....	914,304	6,060,758	71,426,858	98.8
Arizona	....	....	....	949,313	71,916,087	100.0
Northeast	*905,648*	*21,378,863*	*31,424,615*	*29,709,934*	*32,584,672*	*53.7*
Maine	....	1,615,033	3,788,506	5,791,456	7,977,805	71.8
New Hampshire	2,330	237,212	370,426	1,671,601	3,478,271	89.4
Vermont	33,217	900,588	1,268,238	2,185,398	1,451,919	77.4
Massachusetts	11,906	759,807	1,274,906	1,644,453	1,367,488	59.5
Rhode Island	....	5,463	228,082	71,019	378,316	65.8
Connecticut	48,452	338,620	902,062	962,120	850,826	58.4
New York	94,037	6,863,934	9,248,628	9,172,273	4,925,960	46.5
New Jersey	6,272	943,268	963,896	1,379,108	1,471,016	59.8
Delaware	....	222,080	350,784	417,216	273,280	54.7
Pennsylvania	177,151	6,268,104	9,496,900	5,908,804	6,909,469	44.6
Maryland	143,732	1,874,527	1,445,544	1,859,409	972,532	45.0
West Virginia	388,551	1,350,227	2,986,643	7,647,077	2,827,790	68.9
Middle States	*76,005,150*	*75,888,929*	*59,397,840*	*36,826,916*	*40,387,438*	*26.8*
Ohio	4,214,074	6,234,205	10,439,723	3,809,973	1,374,625	19.9
Indiana	5,262,498	6,438,377	7,743,581	2,436,801	1,153,367	15.6
Illinois	14,777,030	6,847,145	6,223,171	6,621,568	960,998	21.4
Michigan	2,251,155	8,961,198	5,386,738	7,228,991	13,223,254	55.2
Wisconsin	2,820,276	14,529,981	8,396,995	4,564,307	5,271,021	27.6
Minnesota	12,022,243	12,138,815	7,511,325	6,898,992	13,144,839	38.8
Iowa	25,983,110	6,906,158	1,392,680	1,007,416	344,556	3.8
Missouri	8,674,763	13,833,050	12,303,627	4,258,868	4,914,778	20.9
Northwest	*14,938,514*	*41,376,309*	*68,160,714*	*105,537,864*	*293,448,979*	*76.2*
North Dakota	....	7,365,682	17,715,865	14,151,534	5,679,955	44.2
South Dakota	3,052,320	8,775,365	8,960,392	15,552,419	12,821,104	57.7
Nebraska	8,120,907	9,690,068	9,639,648	10,908,321	10,757,984	44.1
Kansas	3,765,287	15,172,236	15,964,703	11,207,323	6,094,867	33.1
Montana	....	....	7,366,681	30,438,292	55,565,267	92.1
Idaho	....	87,288	949,208	3,728,908	48,581,156	98.1
Wyoming	....	....	522,936	4,577,769	57,314,015	99.2
Colorado	....	285,670	7,041,281	13,743,839	45,270,330	89.0
Utah	....	....	....	1,233,459	51,364,301	100.0
Far West	*473,032*	*3,079,860*	*14,596,402*	*25,682,099*	*229,959,779*	*93.4*
Nevada	....	....	....	76,900	70,208,480	100.0
Washington	83,520	542,138	6,537,431	6,760,172	28,836,291	83.2
Oregon	342,536	2,059,425	4,694,454	5,464,700	48,567,845	88.4
California	46,976	478,297	3,364,517	13,380,327	82,347,163	96.1
United States	101,037,573	210,934,728	345,871,800	362,559,173	881,735,414	65.5
Percentages	5.3	11.1	18.1	19.1	46.4	....

mals is estimated at more than $3,000,000, while no less than 6,000,000 muskrat furs alone are taken in Louisiana in a single year.

Ever since John James Audubon and Alexander Wilson, each in his own solitary way, wandered down the Mississippi Valley and along the Gulf and Atlantic coast equipped with gun, pen, and brush, the South has been known for its bird life. Even before this, early explorers and settlers were awed by the countless abundance and variety of birds in the southern regions. Thousands of beautiful paraquets, millions of herons, turkeys, waterfowl, and even billions of wild pigeons were on every hand throughout the region. The value of this teeming life to the early explorers and inhabitants was mainly their economic or food value, but even then there were rough, bearded explorers and scientists who were interested in naming these beautiful and fascinating creatures, in forming some concept of their relation, and in studying their habits. From tropical Florida to the tops of high mountains, along its more than 2,000 miles of seacoast, the Southeast has a greater variety and abundance of bird life than any other region of the United States, except possibly certain areas on the Pacific coast. In southern Florida and along the southern border, tropical and Mexican species reach the United States. On the tops of the higher mountains, Canadian species are found. Many species are found only or most commonly in the South, and most of the northern species reach the South through migrations. Thus, in Florida no less than 423 forms, species, and subspecies have been recorded; in North Carolina, 352, in Alabama, 314, and in Tennessee, 280.

Regional abundance in bird and animal life may be illustrated by further samplings from the states. For instance, since early times Florida has been the mecca of students, explorers, and adventurers, who have visited this unique state in search of new and rare species. The roll of Florida ornithologists would include many of the best known in the United States. A large number of birds found in the United States were first discovered in Florida and several species and a number of subspecies are not found anywhere else. More species are found in Florida than any other southeastern state, due to the special geography of the state. Florida is largely flat and sandy, there being no elevation of any consequence. The southern tip is the only part of the United States that is in the tropical zone. However, the strictly tropical bird life is not as numerous or pronounced as the tropical plant life. The greater part of the state is in the Lower Austral Zone, being subdivided into the western portion, and the eastern and central portion. The physiographic regions are recognized as follows: flatwoods, high pinelands, hammocks, sand scrub, swamps, Everglades, salt marshes, sea beaches, prairies, and the Keys. The Everglades are a dis-

Location of Plant Nurseries in the United States, 1929

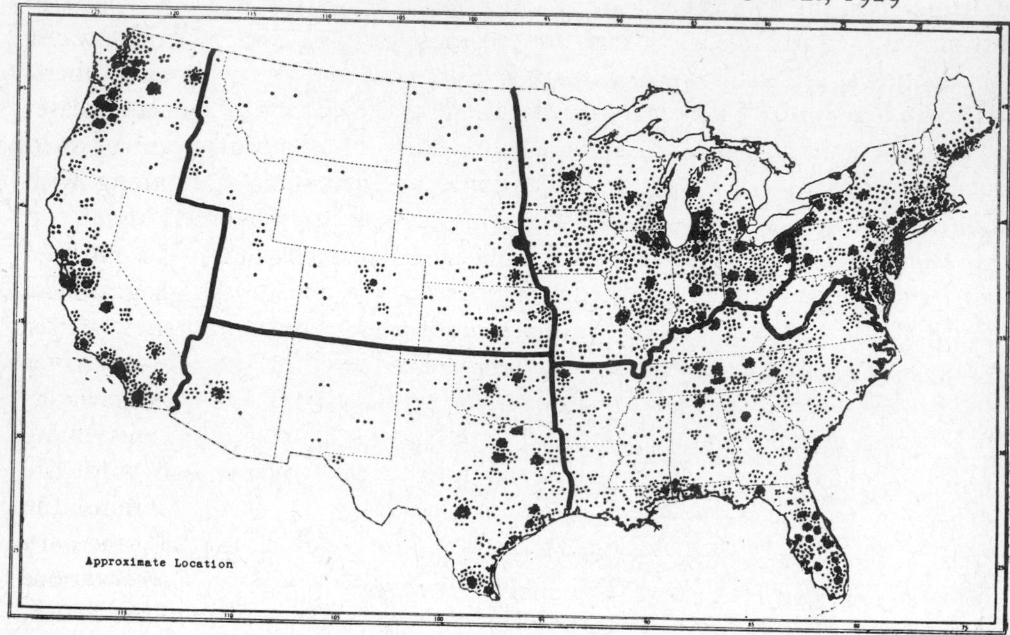

Nurseries: Establishments and Value of Stock

State	Number Establishments Reporting			Value of Land, Buildings and Equipment, 1929	Expenditures, 1929	Receipts From Sales of Products Amount		
	1929	1919	1909			1929	1919	1909
Southest	1,431	693	914	$ 9,023,668	$ 4,914,439	$ 6,597,485	$ 3,047,297	$ 2,709,867
Virginia	91	47	69	787,780	626,098	827,399	100,256	159,992
North Carolina	109	62	125	842,389	594,799	657,868	334,977	266,968
South Carolina	46	18	22	143,033	106,256	138,886	106,871	4,409
Georgia	154	104	54	834,879	426,145	631,402	257,491	366,433
Florida	487	127	133	2,259,960	1,074,247	1,399,786	935,843	478,174
Alabama	89	48	62	1,473,831	666,710	961,284	234,670	259,057
Mississippi	106	37	34	181,942	82,293	133,229	56,959	74,946
Tennessee	165	109	145	1,014,783	627,916	925,301	666,028	697,703
Kentucky	64	47	77	668,951	304,248	369,687	67,245	115,963
Arkansas	65	59	133	285,526	194,859	279,307	185,860	198,579
Louisiana	55	35	60	530,594	210,868	273,336	101,097	87,643
Southwest	545	279	351	4,182,769	2,704,890	3,931,927	986,195	1,438,779
Texas	418	181	233	3,341,739	2,233,104	3,218,203	871,192	1,253,110
Oklahoma	74	76	90	609,072	340,222	449,688	79,222	171,952
Arizona	45	14	11	186,233	125,628	253,371	23,481	4,535
New Mexico	8	8	17	45,725	5,936	10,665	2,300	9,182
Total South	1,976	972	1,265	13,206,437	7,619,329	10,529,412	4,023,492	4,148,646
United States	7,207	4,049	5,582	78,360,468	45,106,709	58,182,562	20,434,389	21,050,822

tinctive feature of Florida as also are the hammocks and the Keys. The longest seacoast of any state in the United States, the many miles of beaches and salt marshes, the extensive swamps and Everglades, make Florida especially attractive to water birds. Many of the most striking and beautiful water birds, such as herons, cranes, ibis, spoonbills, now find their center of abundance in the state. Florida also ranks along the forefront of southern states as a game state. It probably has a better stock of unmixed strain of wild turkeys than any other. Quail and doves are abundant and, along with Louisiana, Florida ranks first as a wintering ground for waterfowl.

Like Florida, a great many of Louisiana's resident birds and most of her winter visitors are water birds. This is largely due to her geographical position. The state is situated in a region of a great many marshes. Over 3,000 square miles are taken up with land-locked bays, inland lakes, or river surface. Situated as it is on the Gulf coast, with so much area under water, in the path of a migratory route, it serves as a stop-over place for many migratory water birds. Louisiana operates 234,300 acres of wild life refuges. Besides these, the National Audubon Society maintains the Rainey Wild Life Sanctuary with 26,000 acres and 11 small sanctuary islands and lakes, and the government has created seven bird reservations in the state. Louisiana is also among the best states for hunting in the South. Besides her upland game, every winter, because of its geographical position, long coast line, and seven million acres of marshes, the state is host to vast quantities of migratory ducks and geese. One branch of the game industry that annually is worth to the state and its citizens several million dollars is the muskrat trapping industry. The marshes offer a good habitat for muskrats, and they are found there in great enough numbers to warrant extensive trapping every year. It is estimated that about 6,000,000 furs are taken in Louisiana every year by some 20,000 trappers.

North Carolina, with its four life zones of the seven in North America, represents another type of abundance for fauna and flora. Each is marked by its characteristic bird, animal, and plant life. The Canadian Zone is found on the tops of the highest mountains in the western section of the state. The greater portion of the mountainous region is occupied by the Alleghanian or Transition Zone. The Carolinian or Upper Austral Zone occupies in a diagonal fashion the central part of the state, while the Lower Austral or Austro-riparian Zone, ranging over the Coastal Plain and part of the Piedmont Plateau, is the most extensive. Containing these four life areas and lying in the path of one of the main routes of bird migration, the state affords abundant resources for science or use.

The growing interest in bird and animal life is reflected in the selection of state birds, in the multiple activities of bird clubs, in the publication of

Minerals of the Region: Undifferentiated Picture, Samplings and Variety

albite
agate
alum
antimony
actinolite
apatite
asbestos
amethyst
anglesite
arsenopyrite
aragonite
autunite
albite
azurite
argentite
alunogen
amphibole
andesine
altaite
agate
auerlite
anthophyllite
autunite
amazon stone
automolite
amphibole
aegirite
astrophyllite
apophyllite
alisonite
allophane

bauxite
barytes
bronzite
bornite
boulangerite
barite
beryl
biotite
black garnet
brookite
breunnerite
barnhardtite
bismite
bismutite
bismuthinite
bismuth carbonate
brucite
braunite
bournonite
bindheimite
breccia marble

copper
coal
clay
chalk
corundum
columbite
calcite
chalcopyrite
cyanite
chlorite
chromite
cerargyrite
chloritoid
cassiterite
cerussite
calamine
cuprite
chalcosite
chrysolite
chrysocolla
culsageeite
cyrtolite
cuproscheelite
chrysotile
chalcanthite
covellite
chalcedony
chiastilite
copperas
clausthilite
cantonite
corals
cobalt
celestite crystals
cancrinite
calamine
chalcotrichite

dolomite
diamonds
diatomaceous earth
dufrenite
dudleyite
deweylite
damourite

epidote
emerald
enstatite
electrum
energite
eleolite
eudialyte
eleonorite
epsomite

feldspar
fluorite
felsyte
fergusonite
fossil wood
fire-opal

gold
graphite
granite
green sand
gypsite
garnet
galena
gypsum
glauconite
genthite
goslarite
gothite
gahnite
gadolinite

hematite
helvite
hisingerite
hornblende
hornstone
hydrofergusonite
halloysite
hyalite
hatchetolite
hitchcockite
harrisite
hessonite
hydrotitanite
hydrozincite

iron
ilmenite
itacolumyte

jasper
jefferisite
jamesonite

kaolin
kyanite
kaolinite
kammererite
kerrite

lignite
limestone
lead
limonite
labradorite
leuceopyrite
lazulite
lucasite
leadhillite
lanthanite

marl
marble
mineral waters
mica
manganese
muck
monazite
microlite
magnetite
melaconite
muscovite
malachite
minium
molybdenite
malacon
marmolite
margarite
melanterite
montanite
montmorillionite
martite
millerite
molybdite
microcline
manganopectolite
monticellite
melanterite

novalculite
nagyagite
niter
nivenite
natrolite
natroxonolite
newtonite
nacrite
nitrocalcite

ocher
opal
orthoclase
octahedrite
oligoclase
ozarkitte

phosphate Rock
pyrites
peat
phenacite
pyrolusite
psilomelane
pyrrhotite
prase
pyromorphite
plumbic ocher
prochlorite
psilomelane
picrolite
phlogopite
prochlorite
pycnite
polycrase
penninite
pleonaste
pyrope
phosphuranylite
pyroxene
plumbogummite
perovskite

quartz crystals

ruby
rose quartz
rhodochrosite
rogersite
red jasper
ripidolite
rowlandite
rectorite
rahtite

sulphur
soapstone
salt cake
silica
shale
sand and gravel
sandstone
silver
slate
staurolite
sapphire
sphalerite
serpentine
spessartite
sipylite
siderite
stalactites
smithsonite
strengite
scorodite
smoky quartz
spodumene
siderite
samarskite
steatite
scheelite
smaragdite
stolzite
stibnite
stilbite
semi-bituminous coal
spodumene
silicified shells
schorlomite
sodalite-syenite
stibiconite
stilpnosiderite
selenite
soda alum

tripoli
topazolite
tennantite
tourmaline
tetradymite
tabular quartz
talc
tscheffkinite
tantalite
tremolite
titanite
thorite
tetrahedrite
thulite
thorogummite
tengerite
thuringite

uranotil
uraninite

vivianite
vermiculite
vesuvianite
variscite
variegated marbles

white beryl
willcoxite
wavellite
whetstone
witherite
wulfenite
wolframite
wollastonite

yttrialite

zinc
zircon
zenotime
zoisite
zanthitane
zinkenite

a rapidly growing literature, as well as in the official departments and boards in the various states which feature game conservation and breeding. Of the state adopted birds, all the Southeastern States have either a formal or informal bird adoption. Thus the mocking bird for Florida, Mississippi, Arkansas, and Tennessee. There are the Carolina chickadee and the Carolina wren for North and South Carolina, the "red bird" cardinal for Kentucky, the brown thrasher for Georgia, the flicker for Alabama, and the brown pelican for Louisiana. Of books there is a fine library ready and in the making. There are Howell's *Birds of Alabama;* Bailey and Howell's *Florida Birds;* Pearson and Brimley's *Birds of North Carolina,* Gamer's *Birds of Tennessee,* and various lists and bulletins by state conservation departments. There are innumerable bird census reports from all over the region.

Once again the resources of "nature" are represented in the increasing interest and number of plant nurseries, in the value of their equipment and in the sale of their products, as well as in the south-wide sweeping movement of garden clubs. Of the more than 7,000 establishments reporting upon the value of equipment and sale of stocks, the Southeast had in 1929 approximately one-fifth. The Southeast's 1,431 in 1929 was an increase from 693 in 1919, or more than 100 per cent as compared with the increase for the whole nation from 4,040 to 7,207. An indication of the basic possibilities may be seen in the case of Florida, which had but 133 nurseries in 1920, yet had more than 530 by 1932. A part of this picture belongs to the inventory of wealth and agriculture, but it is also a part of the natural plant capacity of the region as is further abundantly illustrated in the extraordinary number and variety of fruit trees, nut-bearing trees, berries, vegetables, and grasses as yet uninventoried.

In the plant realm of general horticulture could be listed more than 100 specimens; garden resources incomparable, celery and cabbage, potatoes and spinach, lettuce and carrots, strawberries and dewberries, sugar cane and sorghum; more than 200 medicinal plants from alum root to witch-hazel and all the long alphabet between; raspberry and rosinwood, pumpkin and pennyroyal, hellebore and huckleberry, catnip and cotton bark, bittersweet and boneset; more than 200 trees, fruit bearing, ornamental, and otherwise. The list reads like a perpetual catalogue or a mouth-watering inventory of nature's endowment. Of fruit trees the Southeast grows a third of all peach trees, a third of the orange trees, four-fifths of the grapefruit, and nearly half of the pecan trees in the nation; and of apple trees and pears and figs and plums, a great number and variety. Likewise, of non-fruit bearing trees, yellow pine and pitch, loblolly and long leaf, locust and walnut, dogwood and holly, chinquapin and chestnut, oaks and oaks—white oak and post, live oak and willow, black jack and red—hickory nut and wild plum.

Per Capita Value of Mineral Products, 1929

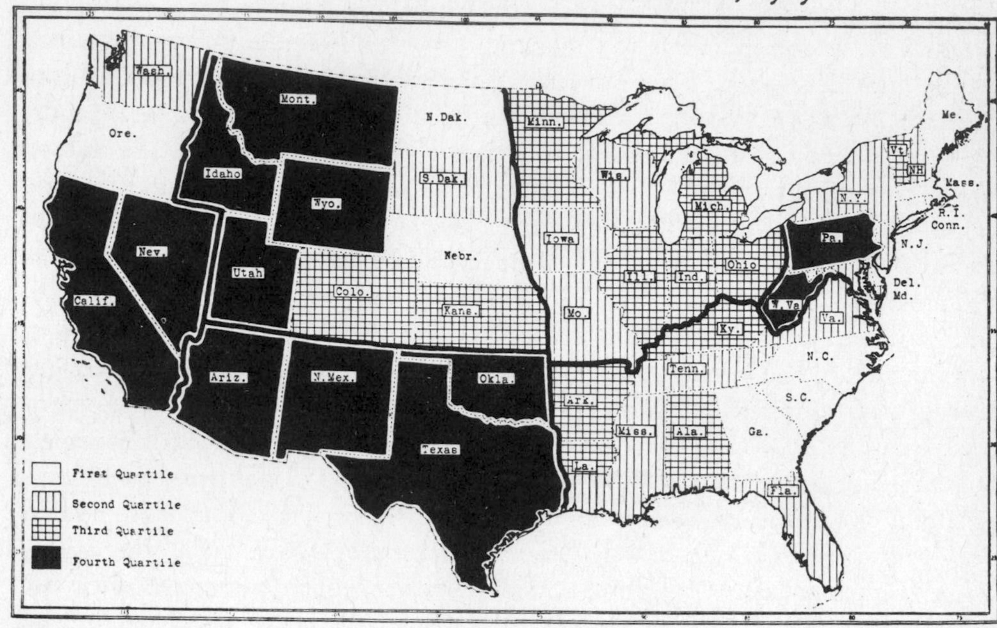

Value of Mineral Products by Regions, 1929

STATE AND REGION	Value	Per Cent of U. S. Total
Southeast	*$ 429,803,000*	*8.31*
Virginia	39,753,000	.76
North Carolina	10,964,000	.21
South Carolina	3,592,000	.08
Georgia	15,294,000	.29
Florida	14,804,000	.27
Kentucky	132,650,000	2.58
Tennessee	40,720,000	.79
Alabama	65,402,000	1.26
Mississippi	2,573,000	.06
Arkansas	41,325,000	.79
Louisiana	62,726,000	1.22
Southwest	*1,207,593,000*	*23.38*
Oklahoma	516,685,000	10.00
Texas	495,820,000	9.60
New Mexico	37,128,000	.72
Arizona	157,960,000	3.06
Northeast	*1,488,771,000*	*28.83*
Maine	6,749,000	.14
New Hampshire	3,726,000	.08
Vermont	14,603,000	.27
Massachusetts	16,031,000	.31
Rhode Island	940,000	.02
Connecticut	7,053,000	.14
New York	109,361,000	2.11
New Jersey	71,892,000	1.39
Delaware	467,000	.01
Pennsylvania	892,914,000	17.29
Maryland	18,470,000	.35
West Virginia	346,565,000	6.72
Middle States	*$ 927,265,000*	*17.94*
Ohio	220,061,000	4.26
Indiana	96,962,000	1.88
Illinois	182,791,000	3.54
Michigan	151,976,000	2.94
Wisconsin	24,222,000	.46
Minnesota	136,350,000	2.63
Iowa	35,955,000	.70
Missouri	78,948,000	1.53
Northwest	*489,382,000*	*9.47*
North Dakota	3,466,000	.08
South Dakota	8,914,000	.17
Nebraska	4,845,000	.10
Kansas	124,472,000	2.40
Montana	93,842,000	1.82
Idaho	32,143,000	.62
Wyoming	51,237,000	.99
Colorado	55,332,000	1.06
Utah	115,131,000	2.23
Far West	*621,004,000*	*12.04*
Nevada	36,776,000	.72
Washington	22,435,000	.43
Oregon	6,877,000	.14
California	554,916,000	10.75
United States	5,164,883,000*	100.00

*Includes 1065 in the District of Columbia.

In the realm of grasses the South, trained to fight grass to the death, has unmeasured resources in the nation and tame grasses with which it may build pasture lands and grow hays to balance its feed rations. The story of these again is a part of the South's agriculture and agrarian life. Yet part and parcel of climate and land are the peculiar resources for land building and conservation and for balancing agriculture as found in the legumes, such as soy beans and cow peas, velvet beans and peanuts, and some of the grasses which give promise of making over whole areas into new dairy regions of rare possibilities and into new garden spots of the nation: clovers and alfalfa, vetches and field peas, lespedezas and ryes. Thus, all told, for experimentation, for commercial and aesthetic purposes, for the regional balance of crops, the Southeast's flora constitutes still an uninventoried wealth awaiting further development.

Superabundance and variety again characterize the resources of the Southeast for fish and for fishing in the waters of the Atlantic and of the Gulf, in sounds and lakes, in rivers and bayous, in mountain streams and flat-land marshes. This is also another of the undeveloped resources which can be multiplied at will through planning and technology. Some of the Carolina Atlantic-coast sounds possess resources exceeding any known similar regions, while Florida has for another example a clam bed of forty miles in length. Shrimp and shad, oysters and clam, mullet and mackerel, menhaden and sponge, mountain trout and perch, and all that long roll call of fish for sport and home-farm food constitute another extraordinary unit of the region's natural resources: black bass and blue fish, catfish and eel, pickerel and pike, suckers and perch, frog's legs and turtle. The actual measure of the region's commercial fisheries in terms of 1929 values showed the Southeast with a little more than a fifth of the nation's total. The whole measure, however, is found in the map picture of coast and sound and stream and lake in conjunction with the actual commercial value of $22,000,000 as the Southeast's part of the nation's $104,000,000, and compared with the Northeast's $47,000,000, the Far West's $25,000,000, the Middle State's $8,000,000. With the exception of Massachusetts and New Jersey, Virginia and Florida lead all states with a little more than $7,000,000 and $6,000,000 respectively, while North Carolina and Louisiana report more than two and a half million dollars worth. Similar to the Southeast is borderland Maryland's value of a little more than four and a quarter million.

All this abundant endowment of natural resources of land and trees, of climate and water, of things that grow and enrich the region, reflect what may be characterized as optimum conditions for the development of vitality in culture and abundance in economy. Thus, of the land and crops, there

Per Capita Production of Electric Power, All Public Utility Plants, 1930

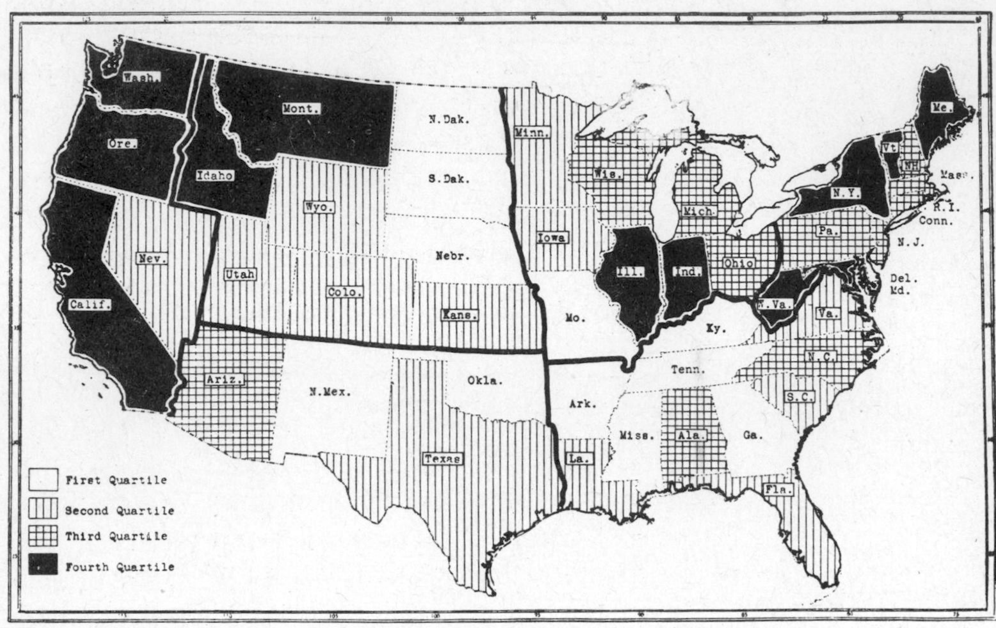

Potential and Developed Water Power

STATE AND REGION	Potential Water Power: 1928 — h.p Available 90 Per Cent of the Time (000)	Potential Water Power: 1928 — h.p Available 50 Per Cent of the Time (000)	Total Developed Water Power — Capacity: 1932
Southeast	*3,987*	*6,394*	*3,916,746*
Virginia	459	812	153,364
North Carolina	852	1,160	961,416
South Carolina	555	860	809,978
Georgia	572	958	512,455
Florida	20	30	21,325
Kentucky	172	280	144,665
Tennessee	654	882	287,563
Alabama	472	1,050	931,450
Mississippi	30	60	0
Arkansas	200	300	94,530
Louisiana	1	2	0
Southwest	*3,233*	*3,881*	*177,805*
Oklahoma	70	194	2,533
Texas	288	614	36,724
New Mexico	116	186	1,488
Arizona	2,759	2,887	137,060
Northeast	*5,837*	*9,256*	*4,744,606*
Maine	536	1,074	612,561
New Hampshire	186	350	558,822
Vermont	80	169	202,327
Massachusetts	106	235	362,123
Rhode Island	25	40	30,188
Connecticut	65	110	172,480
New York	4,010	4,960	1,892,464
New Jersey	50	90	17,229
Delaware	5	10	1,200
Pennsylvania	313	1,000	392,467
Maryland	106*	238*	415,755
West Virginia	355	980	86,990
Middle States	*1,181*	*2,374*	*1,807,604*
Ohio	55	166	20,901
Indiana	45	145	53,945
Illinois	189	361	94,428
Michigan	168	274	414,103
Wisconsin	285	480	519,816
Minnesota	203	401	287,289
Iowa	169	395	181,924
Missouri	67	152	235,198
Northwest	*8,159*	*13,057*	*1,124,258*
North Dakota	82	152	245
South Dakota	121	203	19,853
Nebraska	183	342	24,499
Kansas	104	251	16,254
Montana	2,550	3,700	428,434
Idaho	2,122	4,032	354,674
Wyoming	704	1,182	24,663
Colorado	873	1,609	98,136
Utah	1,420	1,586	157,500
Far West	*15,713*	*24,163*	*3,786,032*
Nevada	300	370	13,650
Washington	7,145	11,225	1,011,306
Oregon	3,665	5,894	354,042
California	4,603	6,674	2,407,034
United States	38,110	59,125	15,562,801**

*Includes District of Columbia. **District of Columbia 5,750.

are the rare concurrence of that optimum quartette of temperature, moisture, surface, and soil, with variety and abundance of sunshine, winds, and of growing seasons, with also such variety and complexity as to challenge initiative and technology on the part of the people. In the matter of extreme range and variety of climate and life zones and of soil and topography, as well as of other resources listed, there are the intangible and as yet unmeasured combinations which afford the region a superabundance of opportunities for richness of culture, of leisure, and optimum ways of living, such as perhaps obtain in no other region of the nation, provided the component elements of resources, space, time, and cultural equipment can be adequately correlated.

In the regional picture of natural abundance there must necessarily appear early those other special blocks of resources essential to the flowering of a culture of the first order, namely, minerals and power. Here are minerals of inanimate energy, minerals of fabrication and construction, minerals of life-giving and aesthetic qualities, multiplied minerals as yet scarcely developed at all. Here are more than three hundred, big and little, important and incidental, catalogue again of an extraordinary richness and variety. Word picture and map picture, copper and gold, iron and coal, mica and slate, jasper and agate, blue marble and white, granite enough for unlimited buildings. And with them all, twin resources of fuel and water power of such regional excellence as exists in no other region of the country, thus again combining one group of resources happily with another.

An example of the extension of river resources available for the strengthening of a regional economy for industrial development, for reconstruction of agriculture, and for the enrichment of agrarian life is that of the water power capacity in the Southeast which appears ample for all purposes without drawing upon outside forces. Thus Thorndike Saville has pointed out that the Appalachian subregions of the Southeast are more favored than any other part of the United States in having a topography adapted to the construction of dams and a relatively high rainfall well distributed throughout the year. The result is that both large fall and high stream flow make water-power development particularly attractive. Alongside this is also the abundance of granite and sand suitable to the construction of dams. Moreover, the states of North Carolina, South Carolina, Georgia, and Alabama are among the upper quartile of all states of the nation, ranking third, fourth, sixth, and ninth in developed water power.

Yet the full significance of the picture can be gained only from an understanding of the significance of power in the present national and regional civilization. Such was the growth of water power in the United States up to the early 1930's that there was a developed water power capacity of at

Sources and Production of Coal Resources in the United States

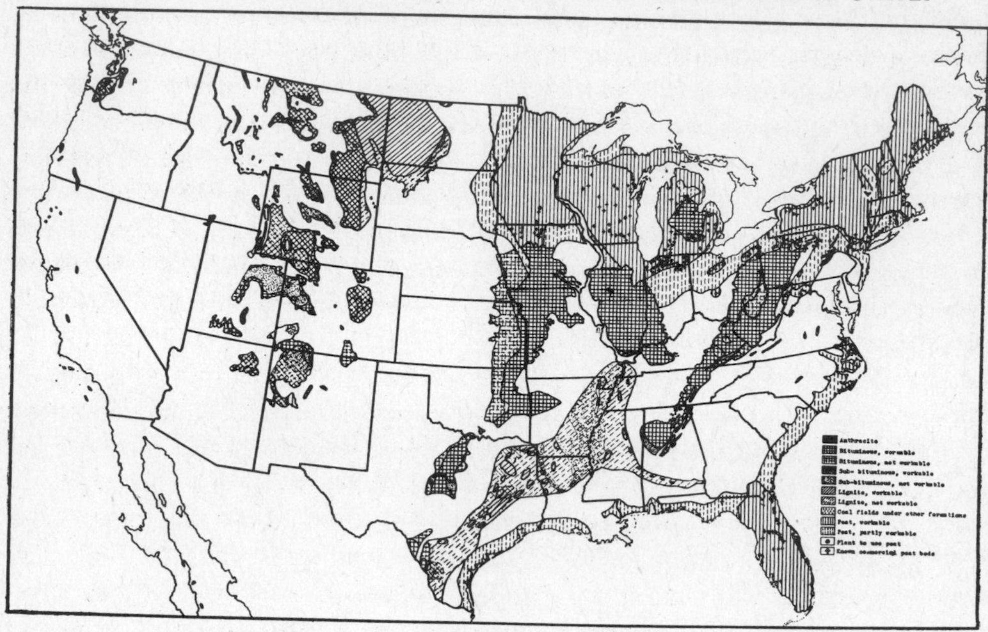

Estimated Original Tonnage of Coal in the Southeastern States

STATE AND REGION	Bituminous	Semi-bituminous	Semi-anthracite	Total Production from Earliest Record to End of 1929
Southeast	*237,524,000*	*1,333,000*	*400,000*	*1,909,222*
Virginia	20,749,000	400,000	400,000	268,096
North Carolina	200,000	....	....	982
Georgia	....	933,000	....	10,740
Kentucky	123,327,000	....	....	873,502
Tennessee	25,665,000	....	....	214,438
Alabama	67,583,000	....	....	541,464

Number of Operating Commercial Mines, Production, Value, Men Employed, Days Worked, and Output Per Man Per Day at Coal Mines in Southeastern States, 1929

STATE AND REGION	Number of Active Mines	Total Production (Net Tons)	Value* Total	Value* Average Per Ton	Number of Employees	Average Number of Days Worked	Average Tons Per Man Per Day
Southeast	*879*	*96,657,109*	*$160,969,000*	*$1.66*	*103,791*	*241*	*3.85*
Virginia	91	12,748,306	20,942,000	1.64	12,053	249	4.24
North Carolina	1	52,180	177,000	3.39	160	260	1.25
Georgia	1	44,636	136,000	3.05	102	260	1.68
Kentucky	501	60,462,600	93,283,000	1.54	58,649	222	4.64
Tennessee	83	5,405,464	9,122,000	1.69	7,619	228	3.11
Alabama	202	17,943,923	37,309,000	2.08	25,208	231	3.08
Total U. S. bituminous	6,057	534,988,593	952,781,000	1.78	502,993	219	4.85

*The value given in this table represents the amount received at the mines f.o.b. cars, minus the selling expense.

least 16,000,000 horse power, exclusive of the new Norris and Wheeler dams and other smaller units which would be constructed by the Tennessee Valley Authority and of other construction in prospect. Of this amount the Southeast provided approximately one-fourth. This capacity, however, has been estimated by the United States Geological Survey as being less than 40 per cent of the total potential water power, exclusive again of possible new technical construction which could multiply it several times over. And it was easily demonstrable that the Southeast could itself provide in plant capacity a full 16,000,000 horse power, and, if to the Southeast be added West Virginia to make what Saville has called the "southern power province," the aggregate potential is manifestly adequate for the optimum development of industry, agriculture, and the up-building of home standards in city and country.

Perhaps the magic of "natural" endowment had scarcely begun to appear until the great new energy resources of oil and gas were in the way of being developed. Something of this colorful picture of the colossal power of minerals might be glimpsed by contemplating the new civilization constantly being transformed from the crudest of crude resources—oil and natural gas. Here the Southwest with nearly a half of the nation's crude oil and the Southeast with as much natural gas made a combination challenging the new developments of these regions and the Mississippi Valley. A part of the picture is the marvel of production. There is eastern Texas projecting no less than 9,300 producing wells which in two hours of open flow could provide 50 per cent more oil than the daily consumption of the whole nation. Or if one wished to sense the colossal nature of such a picture, he might imagine a review of more than 30,000,000 automobiles, trucks and tractors, busses and boats, airplanes and engines, picture *de luxe* of the great American mobility, product of the new engine, dethroner of steam. And in the Southeast, the automobile changing the whole face of the region with its more than 4,000,000 cars and its extraordinary network of hard-surfaced roads.

Or, once again, if one wishes to see first hand, let him visit a single cluster of Oklahoma fields which could reach a peak of daily output of 527,400 barrels. And the total production in 1930 of gasoline, 436,217,000 barrels; of fuel oil, 340,000,000; of lubricating oils, 34,000,000; and of natural gas, multiple pictures of pipe lines to St. Louis and Chicago, to Memphis and Atlanta, east and west, north and south, a vast new source of wealth and use. Such are the increasing production and uses, by-products and refinements, that, of the total oil reserves in the southern regions, no man has appraised their power and influence in America or in the family of nations. Yet something further of the size and reach of this specific energy

Sources and Production of Building Stone in the United States

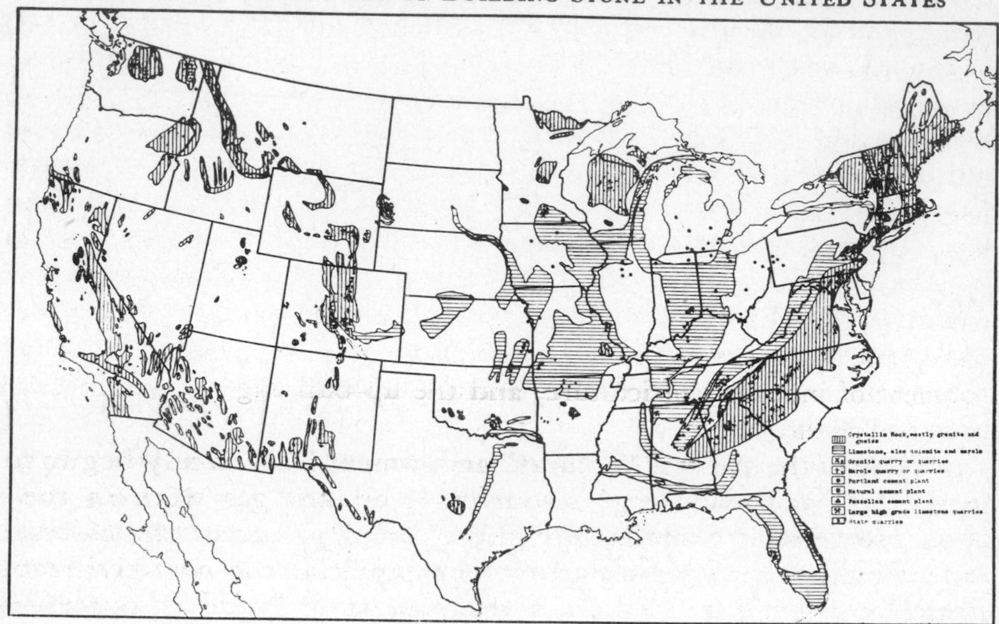

Changing Status of Twelve Leading States in Granite Sales, 1919-1929

TWELVE LEADING STATES, SHORT TONS

RANK	1919	1920	1921	1922	1923	1924	1925	1926	1927	1928	1929
1	Cal.	Cal.	Cal.	Cal.	Cal.	Cal.	Cal.	Cal.	Cal.	Cal.	Cal.
2	N. C.	N. C.	N. C.	N. C.	N. C.	N. C.	N. C.	N. C.	N. C.	N. C.	N. C.
3	S. C.	Mass.	S. C.	S. C.	S. C.	S. C.	S. C.	S. C.	S. C.	S. C.	S. C.
4	Mass.	S. C.	Mass.	Mass.	Mass.	Mass.	Mass.	Mass.	Mass.	Va.	Va.
5	Ariz.	Ga.	Wis.	Pa.	Ga.	Ga.	Ga.	Ariz.	Ariz.	Mass.	Mass.
6	Wis.	Ariz.	Ga.	Ga.	Me.	Pa.	Ariz.	Ga.	Ga.	Ga.	Ga.
7	Pa.	Wis.	Me.	Ariz.	Wis.	Md.	Me.	Md.	Md.	Wis.	Md.
8	Ga.	Ore.	Ariz.	Md.	Md.	Me.	Pa.	Pa.	Pa.	Pa.	Pa.
9	Me.	Me.	Va.	Wis.	Pa.	Wis.	Md.	Va.	Va.	Md.	Me.
10	Md.	Md.	Md.	Me.	Ariz.	Va.	Wis.	Wis.	Wis.	Md.	N. Y.
11	Vt.	Vt.	Pa.	N. Y.	Vt.	R. I.	Va.	Me.	Me.	Vt.	Vt.
12	N. H.	Minn.	Vt.	Minn.	Va.	Vt.	N. H.	N. H.	N. H.	N. H.	N. H.

TWELVE LEADING STATES BY VALUES

RANK	1919	1920	1921	1922	1923	1924	1925	1926	1927	1928	1929
1	Vt.	Vt.	Vt.	Cal.	Vt.	Vt.	Mass.	Mass.	Mass.	Mass.	Mass.
2	Mass.	Mass.	Mass.	Mass.	Mass.	Mass.	Vt.	Vt.	N. C.	Vt.	Vt.
3	Minn.	Minn.	Cal.	N. C.	N. C.	N. C.	Cal.	N. C.	Vt.	N. C.	N. C.
4	Wis.	Cal.	N. C.	Minn.	Me.	Cal.	N. C.	Cal.	Cal.	Minn.	Minn.
5	N. C.	N. H.	Wis.	Me.	Minn.	Minn.	Me.	Ga.	Ga.	Me.	Cal.
6	N. H.	N. C.	Me.	Vt.	Cal.	Me.	Minn.	Me.	Minn.	Ga.	Me.
7	Me.	Me.	N. H.	Wis.	Wis.	Wis.	Ga.	Minn.	Me.	S. C.	Ga.
8	Cal.	Wis.	Minn.	S. C.	N. H.	N. H.	Wis.	Wis.	S. C.	Cal.	Wis.
9	Ga.	Ga.	Ga.	Ga.	S. C.	S. C.	N. H.	N. H.	N. H.	Wis.	S. C.
10	S. C.	S. C.	S. C.	N. H.	Ga.	Ga.	S. C.	S. C.	Pa.	N. H.	N. H.
11	Pa.	R. I.	R. I.	Pa.	Pa.	Pa.	Pa.	Pa.	Conn.	N. Y.	Va.
12	R. I.	Pa.	Md.	Md.	R. I.	R. I.	Conn.	R. I.	Md.	Va.	Md.

During this 10-year period in amount of sales, North Carolina and South Carolina have held second and third places respectively; Georgia has risen from eighth to sixth, and Virginia has come into the list and risen to fourth place. During this same period in values, North Carolina has risen from fifth to second or third place; Georgia from ninth to seventh; South Carolina from tenth to ninth, and Virginia has come into the list and risen to eleventh position. The value of granite sold in the New England States is accounted for by the much higher percentage of the stone sold as finished stone or monuments.

picture might be envisaged by noting the rapid rise of mineral indices in comparison to other American activities. Using the index number of 100 in 1899, *Recent Social Trends in the United States* fixed the index of horse-power equipment in 1929, including all automobiles, as 2,610. Agricultural increase is represented by 148, manufacture by 310, transportation in railroad miles by 338, and all mining physical volume by 386. So paramount is the picture of oil that it has constituted already the basis for federal and state regulation and price fixing and for interregional balance of trade.

Yet coal, doing two-thirds of the work of the nation, ranks first in fuel energy resources, and the Southeast not only affords a fifth of the nation's soft coal, but has an even higher ratio of quality than of quantity in the nation's reserves. Of the world's reserves, estimated at the long, long count of 8,154,322,500,000 short tons, the portion of the United States is no less than 4,231,352,000,000 or a little more than half of the total. The Southeast's possible reserves might represent nearly a tenth of this. Such is the stupendous reserve resources that it is estimated that, at the rate of consumption of the 1930's, there is coal enough to last the region hundreds if not thousands of years. Thus it has been estimated that less than two per cent of the total southeastern coal seams have been tapped. The map picture and the statistical accompaniments show with what powerful reserve the region may develop. In the same way there is great range in quality and in the opulence of coal products: annual 3,000,000 and more of tons of coke of the nation's 30 millions, of peat a hundred by-products of gas, of ammonia and light oils, and of tar; and of tar products alone, again hundreds of by-products and uses, fields for the chemist.

The Southeast not only affords immeasurable resources of energy and fuel through power and coal, but it could afford also the perfect setting for great buildings, for beautiful homes, as well as for roads and bridges, reservoirs and dams. Here again is abundance of steel and stone, marble and granites, concrete, and metals. Iron and steel, king of fabricated structures, and basic to modern civilization, appear in the picture almost a hundred times as much as any other one metal. The per capita annual requirement of new iron and steel is nearly one hundred times the amount upon which nearly half of the world operates. Of the world's requirement of about 100,000,000 tons of steel a year the United States furnishes a little more than half of the supply. Of the 58,000,000 tons of iron ore mined in 1930 in the United States, the Southeast produced 5,800,000, and of the 30,000,000 tons of pig iron production the Southeast produced nearly a tenth. The reorganization of the Birmingham region for production and distribution gives promise of developing a new era in southern iron and steel capacity.

MARBLE

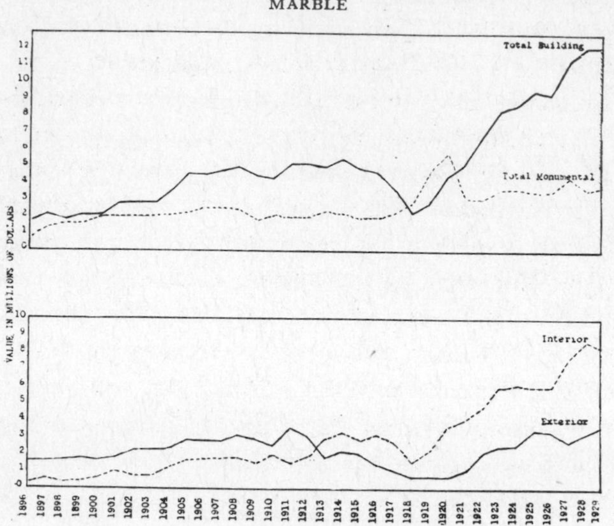

VALUE OF MARBLE PRODUCTION IN UNITED STATES AND SOUTHEASTERN STATES, 1919-29

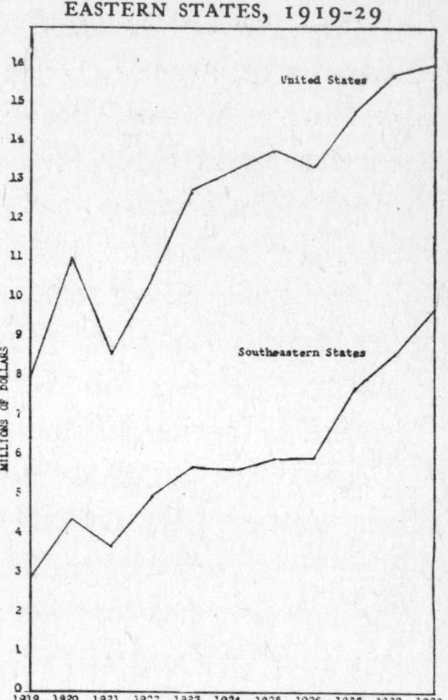

GRANITE PRODUCTION IN UNITED STATES 1913-29 VALUE FOR DIFFERENT USES

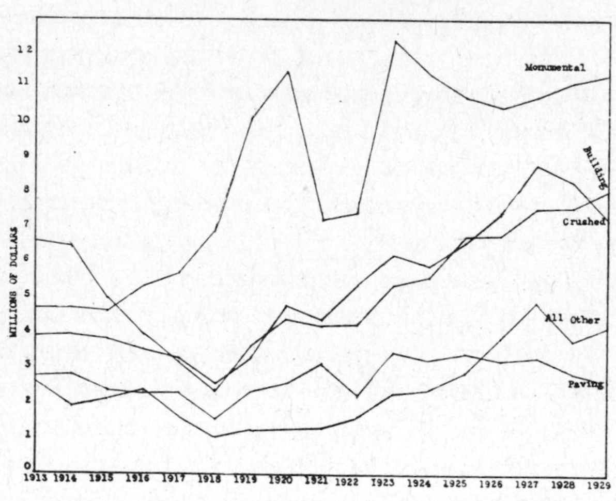

GRANITE PRODUCTION 1919-29 UNITED STATES AND SOUTHEASTERN STATES

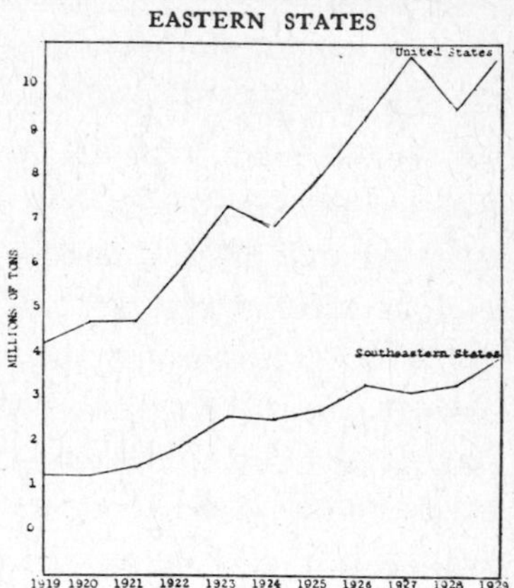

VALUE OF CERTAIN BUILDING MATERIALS IN THE SOUTHEAST, 1930

STATE AND REGION	Stone	Sand and Gravel	Common Brick
Southeast	*$23,358,000*	*$11,130,000*	*$5,764,699*
Virginia	3,853,000	997,000	1,103,990
North Carolina	2,457,000	438,000	978,856
South Carolina	2,021,000	475,000	401,419
Georgia	2,375,000	228,000	623,549
Florida	1,490,000	269,000	76,292
Kentucky	2,635,000	1,554,000	289,867
Tennessee	5,187,000	1,436,000	566,663
Alabama	2,111,000	901,000	753,253
Mississippi	25,000	1,051,000	399,373
Arkansas	1,204,000	1,556,000	257,181
Louisiana	....	2,225,000	314,256

More immediate for the building industry, however, is the regional abundance of limestone, granite, sandstone, basalt, slate, marble, of which the Southeast has important supplies and reserves. In limestone, Virginia, Alabama, Kentucky, and Tennessee rank in the upper quartile. In granite, North Carolina by 1929 was second, South Carolina third, Virginia fourth, and Georgia sixth. In marble, Tennessee had replaced Vermont in first place, while Georgia and Alabama follow in close succession. In 1919 the Southeastern States produced 37 per cent of the total marble production, and by 1929 they had increased to 61 per cent.

The map pictures, the statistical samplings, and the undifferentiated list of minerals in the region will be adequate to illustrate the region's capacity to match its geographical endowment further with the tools necessary for the highest type of industry and culture. Copper and manganese and bauxite and all manner of domestic clay, sand and gravel, cement and lime, continue the list available for the reconstruction of the region's building standards. Most of the world's soapstone comes from Virginia. There are 350,000,000 long tons of phosphate deposits in five southeastern states, while Florida and Tennessee actually produced 98 per cent of all the phosphate in the nation. Texas produced approximately 85 per cent of the world's supply of sulphur and 99.9 per cent of the nation's supply, while Georgia and Tennessee furnished 43 per cent of the nation's barite.

The four principal mineral products in the order of their value in 1929 for each of the Southeastern States were about as follows: Virginia—coal, stone, clay products, zinc; North Carolina—stone, clay products, copper, sand and gravel; South Carolina—stone, clay products, sand and gravel, barite; Georgia—stone, clay products, fuller's earth, cement; Florida—phosphate rock, stone, fuller's earth, cement; Kentucky—coal, petroleum, natural gas, clay products; Tennessee—coal, stone, cement, clay products; Alabama—coal, iron ore, cement, clay products; Mississippi—sand and gravel, clay products, stone, natural gas; Arkansas—petroleum, coal, natural gas, natural gasoline; Louisiana—natural gas, petroleum, natural gasoline, salt.

Of the abundant chemical resources of the region part belong to technological equipment and a part to nature's endowment. Omitting the undeveloped possibilities of paper making and allied industries, the units in which the Southeast excels would include naval stores with 100 per cent, cotton-seed products of great richness and variety with more than 95 per cent, carbon black with three-fourths, fertilizers with more than two-thirds, rayon with nearly two-thirds, lime with about a fourth, and with a large ratio of clay products. Of other chemical resources a large number are dependent upon mineral resources, such as phosphates and sulphur, pyrites and salt, rayon and pulp, paints and papers, and another large number depend almost entirely for their uses upon the adequate development of all natural resources and of industry. The measure of use and development of the region's wealth is, however, the subject for subsequent analysis of technological resources and waste.

Somewhere between the realm of natural endowment and technological efficiency lie the great resources of transportation—railroads, highways, water ways. These represent the utilization of technology and geographic factors through invested capital and will be presented as a part of the region's technology and part of its economic and social development.

CHAPTER V

REGIONAL TECHNOLOGY, DEFICIENCY, AND WASTE

THE PICTURE which we have presented of the abundance of the natural resources of the Southeast is such as clearly to indicate the possibility of almost unlimited achievement for the region, provided it can develop adequate technology for the optimum use of these resources, can avoid in the future the stupendous waste which in the past has kept it near the marginal level, can provide cultural institutions adequate for the enrichment of human life, and can face more realistically and maturely, than it has yet done, its cumulative deficiencies of will and action necessary for the attainment of these ends. The continuing picture, however, indicates that the region does not now afford adequate technological facilities—science, invention, skills, management, organization—for the conservation, development, and use of its resources, and that there is a large and unnecessary amount of actual waste and of non-use of regional reserves. We have pointed out that in reality, therefore, the region is an area of deficiency and scarcity in contrast to its abundance possibilities. The measuring and bridging of this chasm between actualities and potentialities constitutes, therefore, the major task of regional study and development.

One of the simplest ways to picture the region's technological equipment is to view it upon the backgrounds of the theoretical implications of modern technology and of a comparative view of the nation as a whole. The common interpretation of a nation's progress is that it is due, not to its extraordinary natural resources, but to its successful development and use of these resources through the advances of science and technology. Thus, it would be pointed out, the differences between a civilization such as America's and that of China, in addition to differences of race and age, are largely due to different applications of scientific discoveries and mechanical inventions. The picture of the United States, therefore, is a reflection of what science and invention have done to and with its great natural wealth during the previous century. In agriculture, for instance, it has multiplied the work capacity of a man many fold and has made possible some accomplishments which no number of men could do. A monster tractor driven by one man could pull enough deep furrow grain drills to seed more than 300 acres in one day.

Samplings of Indices Relating to Technology and Waste

Number of Indices	Classification
1.	Distribution of manufacturing establishments—iron and steel and their products, not including machinery.
2.	Distribution of manufacturing establishments—non-ferrous metals and their products.
3.	Distribution of manufacturing establishments—stone, clay, and glass products.
4.	Distribution of manufacturing establishments—products of coal and petroleum.
5.	Regional distribution of manufacturing establishments—paper and allied products.
6.	Regional distribution of manufacturing establishments—forest products.
7.	Distribution of developed water power.
8.	Distribution of water power development—amount of horse power, 1929.
9.	Distribution of total developed water power—capacity, 1932.
10.	Distribution of surveyed water power locations, 1929.
11.	Per capita production of electric power, all public utility plants, 1930.
12.	Distribution of completed waterways, 1929.
13.	Distribution of projected, but not completed, waterways, 1929.
14.	Distribution of state, foreign, and privately owned waterways, completed, 1929.
15.	Distribution of state, foreign, and privately owned waterways, projected, but not completed, 1929.
16.	Distribution of improved rivers, 1929.
17.	Distribution of canals in use, 1929.
18.	Distribution of abandoned canals, 1929.
19.	Value, and per cent of U. S. total value, of mineral products, 1929.
20.	Comparative value of mineral products, 1909, 1919, 1929.
21.	Differential values, by regions, of mineral products.
22.	Production of anthracite coal.
23.	Production of bituminous coal, workable.
24.	Production of bituminous coal, not workable.
25.	Production of sub-bituminous coal, workable.
26.	Production of sub-bituminous coal, not workable.
27.	Production of lignite, workable.
28.	Production of lignite, not workable.
29.	Comparative production of petroleum, 1930.
30.	Comparative production of natural gas, 1930.
31.	Comparative production of natural gasoline, 1930.
32.	Differential values, by regions, of limestone products.
33.	Differential values, by regions, of granite products.
34.	Changing status of 12 leading states in granite sales and value of granite, 1919-1929.
35.	Comparative value of granite production, 1919-1929.
36.	Comparative value for different uses of granite production, 1913-1929.
37.	Comparative value of marble production, 1919-1929.
38.	Distribution of the total timber stand.
39.	Distribution of the saw-timber stand.
40.	Distribution of the total stand, saw-timber and cordwood areas.
41.	Total number of farms, 1930.
42.	Per cent increase and decrease in farms, 1920-1930.
43.	Average acreage per farm, 1930.
44.	Percentage distribution of farms under 100 acres, 1930.
45.	Percentage distribution of farms of 100-499 acres, 1930.
46.	Percentage distribution of farms of 500 acres and over, 1930.
47.	Change in percentage distribution of farms by size groups, 1900-1930.
48.	Comparative number of planter farmers, 1900-1930.
49.	Comparative number of middle-class farmers, 1900–1930.
50.	Comparative number of small-owner farmers, 1900–1930.
51.	Comparative number of tenant farmers, 1900-1930.
52.	Variations in ratio of farm tenancy.
53.	Per cent of total crop land harvested, operated by tenants, 1930.
54.	Decrease and increase in acreage of land in harvested crops.
55.	Average agricultural production per full-time worker (year of labor) 1924-1928.
56.	Horse power available per worker, 1924.
57.	Ten-year average cash farm income, 1920-1921—1930-1931.
58.	Five-year average gross crop income, 1924-1928.
59.	Cooperative sales—per cent of cash farm income, 1929.
60.	Value per farm of farm implements and machinery, 1930.
61.	Per cent of farms having tractors, 1930.
62.	Per cent of farms having electric motors, 1930.
63.	Per cent of farms having gas engines, 1930.
64.	Per cent of farms having electric lights, 1930.
65.	Per cent of farms having piped water, 1930.
66.	Per cent of farms having telephones, 1930.
67.	Number and per cent of vehicles on farms.
68.	Number and per cent of trucks on farms.
69.	Number of farm agents, 1934.
70.	Number of home demonstration agents, 1934.
71.	Enrollment in federally aided agricultural schools and classes, 1933.
72.	Amount, and per cent of the total, of rental and benefit payments of the Agricultural Adjustment Association, through December 31, 1933.
73.	Number and per cent of loans made to farmers in states most seriously affected by drought, 1931.
74.	Amount and per cent of dollars loaned to farmers in states most seriously affected by drought, 1931.
75.	Estimate of destruction by erosion—extent of area with severely impoverished soil or soil washed off.
76.	Estimate of destruction by erosion—extent of area devastated.
77.	Estimate of destruction by erosion—extent of total erosion.
78.	Estimate of per cent of soil impoverishment and destruction by erosion.
79.	Tonnage, and per cent of the total, fertilizer consumption, 1910-1930.
80.	Amount, and per cent of farm income spent for fertilizer, 1929.
81.	Distribution of total tons of commercial fertilizer bought during the crop year of 1929.
82.	Distribution of total expenditure for all types of bought fertilizers during the crop year of 1929.
83.	Comparative expenditures for fertilizers, feed, and labor, 1929.
84.	Relative density of employment.
85.	Percentage distribution of total wage earners, 1929.
86.	Percentage distribution of income from agriculture, 1928.
87.	Percentage distribution of income from manufacture, 1928.
88.	Percentage distribution of income from mining, 1928.
89.	Percentage distribution of income from sources other than agriculture, manufacturing, and mining, 1928.
90.	Distribution of wages paid in manufacturing industries, 1929.
91.	Average annual wage per wage earner in all manufactures, 1929.
92.	Relative increase in amount of wages per wage earner in manufacturing, in three chief manufacturing regions, 1914-1929.
93.	Relative increase in value of product added by manufacture, per wage earner in manufacturing, 1914-1929.
94.	Relative increase in value of product added by manufacture, per horse power, 1914-1929.
95.	Distribution of general industrial resources — horse power.
96.	Distribution of general industrial resources — value of product.
97.	Distribution of general industrial resources — value added by manufacture.
98.	Amount and per cent of value of product added by manufacture, 1929.
99.	Ratio of taxes to value of land and buildings, farms operated by full owners, owning no other farm land, 1930.
100.	Ratio of mortgaged debt to values, farms operated by full owners, 1930.
101.	Federal contribution to relief—per cent of total contribution, July and August, 1933.
102.	Percentage distribution of Federal relief funds, compared with population, 1933.
103.	Federal Emergency Relief Administration grants per capita through September 30, 1933.
104.	Per cent of public unemployment relief funds supplied by the Federal Government, April-September, 1933.
105.	Per capita total federal aid to states, 1930.

One man riding the newest corn cultivator could "plow" from 30 to 65 acres a day. The proposed cotton picker, when perfected, would do the work of from 16 to 48 hand pickers. The tractor-drawn combine machinery, harvesting the wheat in the fields by the hundreds of bushels—cutting, binding, threshing, filling the bags—is in brilliant contrast to the earlier pictures of a single man swinging the old "cradle," sweeping in with his fingers the gathered grain, piling it on the ground in small "hands" to be garnered later and tied by hand in bundles, these bundles to be shocked and later hauled by wagon to some central place where the day's threshing was to be done. Indeed few American episodes have been more dramatic than the evolution of the harvester from McCormick's first efforts to the last supermodel machine at A Century of Progress. Scarcely less revolutionary was the transportation of farm products by truck and fast-moving refrigerator trains, representative of technology's transformation of agriculture, markets, and consumption habits.

There are many who see in the future a new agrarian culture made possible by still greater progress in technology, such that cheap light, power, heat, water, and transportation services would make possible a new type of rural comfort and culture. New inventions and skill would reduce the cost of equipment, such as electric ranges, frigidaires, household conveniences, to such an extent that they would be available for the common man on a small self-sufficing farm, or in small groups clustered around plants of decentralized industry. This indeed is a new picture and a fascinating one to anticipate in contrast to that other devastating prospect of the farmer who is to be made peasant by a great sweep of mechanized agriculture, of over-production, and poor markets. Science, invention, technology are also mightily at work upon the other natural resources and their utilization. In forestry, in lumber industries, in mining and mineral processing; in the transformation of great quantities of crude resources into materials for the building of roads and bridges; in the development of large areas for recreation, hunting, fishing—the nation's measure of wealth was largely a measure of its technology. Perhaps still more vivid was technology's multiplication of products from all and sundry natural resources. There were a hundred products from the lowly sweet potato—sugar and meal and beverage and glue; other hundreds of products from peanuts and cotton, wood pulp and corn stalks, clay and rosin, cotton stalks and new fibres, and a long catalogue of farm "chemurgic."

The picture of technology at work, furthermore, is far more inclusive than merely an inventory of science, discoveries, machines, and ways of spending money and time. It goes further to comprehend the whole scheme of scientific management in the uses of invested capital, which in turn

Value Added by Manufactures in Manufacturing Industries of the United States, 1929

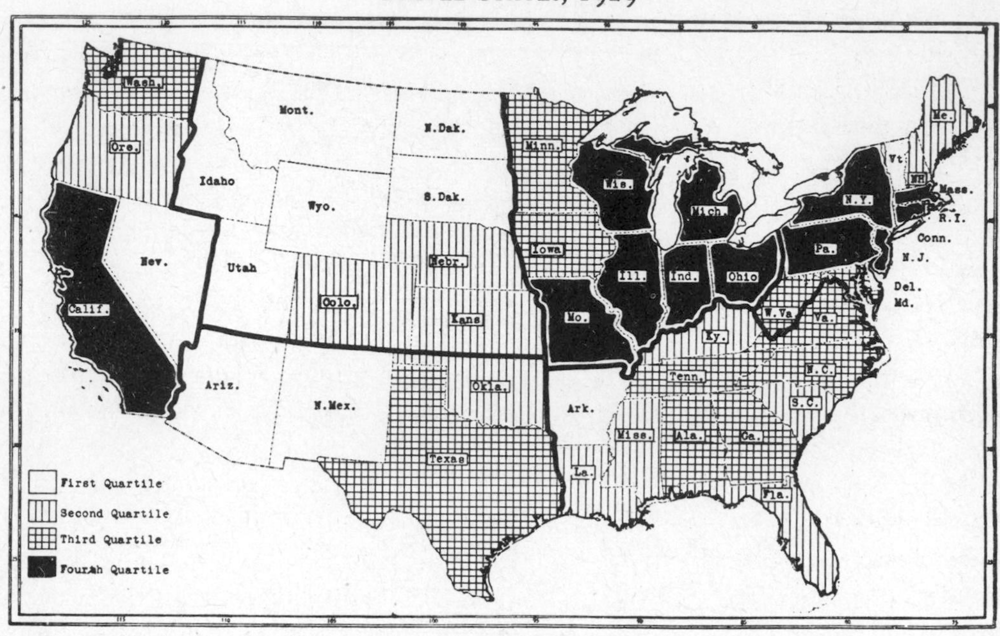

Value of Products in Manufacturing Industries of the United States, 1929

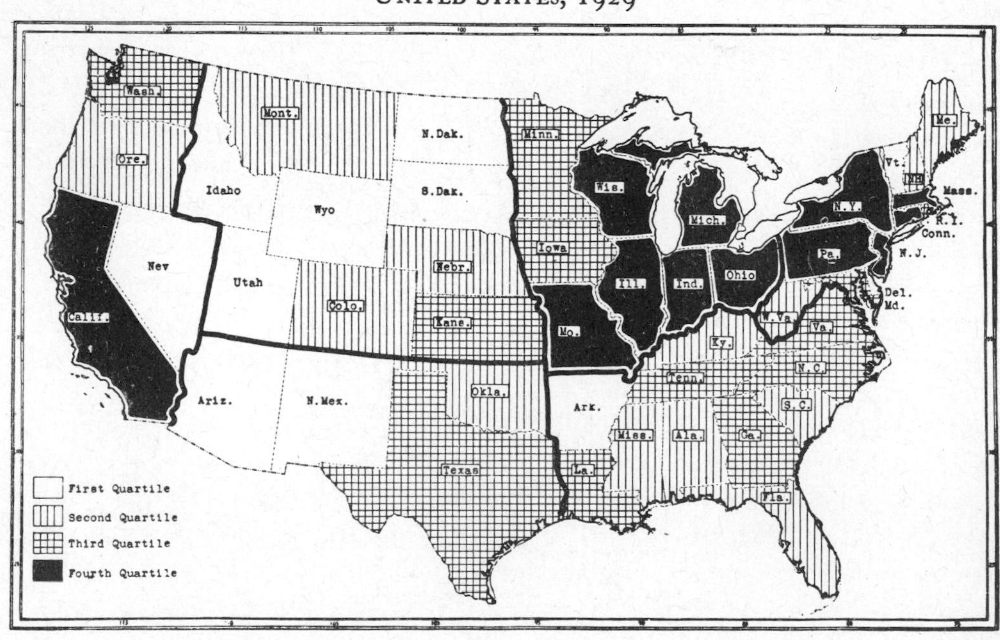

multiplies the ways and means for the practical application of science. It includes also new research into the best ways of speeding up industry and of supplying the world with comforts, luxuries, necessities, and of encouraging consumption. Management no less than discovery has become a part of the technological equipment of the nation. Indeed the common definition of management is that it is an art or science or technique of organizing and directing human effort, applied to control the forces and to utilize the materials of nature for the benefit of mankind. Management at its best is intended to promote the optimum utilization of productive resources; in practice it often becomes, as many other technologies, a form of supertechnology for competitive practices, for the multiplying of profits, a spread-out for the reduction of man power.

The startling nature of inventions and discovery and the extent of their extraordinary diffusion and application, however, still do not alone constitute the main picture, which is that of a world of invention transforming at breathtaking speed the whole life and culture of the people. The quantitative achievement of science and technology, with their brilliant discoveries and inventions, represents one side of the picture. Upon the other side is to be viewed the picture of what the future is likely to hold in store. Culture is to be remade, regions replanned through the new technology of power. For this technology it is often claimed that it can do for the community all that it wants done—raise standards of living, give the people new work and new play, end drudgery, banish noise and smoke, and contribute much to the enrichment of a universal culture.

Another general background upon which to view the picture of the Southeast and its technological development may be found in the rapid development of technological changes in industry and industrial inventions which appear of especial importance to the region. Among these are the continuing increase of automotive power which will release large quantities of food crops, formerly fed to work animals, for human consumption. Additional technologies in the processing of food and feed stuffs may have a similar effect. So, also, the development of hydrogenization for the making available of more fats from vegetable oil and the organized movement for the production of such products. The continuing development of rayon as a substitute for cotton, the further development of new fibers from plants now under experiment or likely to become available will make many important changes necessary. Another major development is that of paper making from new wood and of various other new products from wood industry. The movement for quantitative production of fabricated houses and the discovery and development of important minerals which may take the place of iron and steel may be of great significance. The possibilities for great

AVERAGE AGRICULTURAL PRODUCTION PER FULL-TIME WORKER (YEAR OF LABOR), 1924-1928

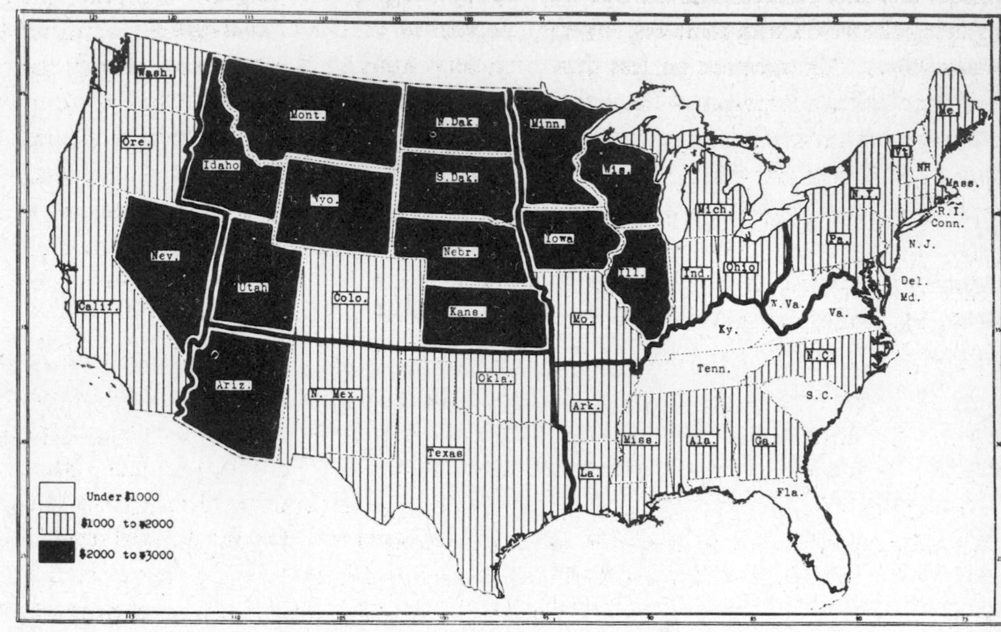

HORSE POWER AVAILABLE PER WORKER, 1924

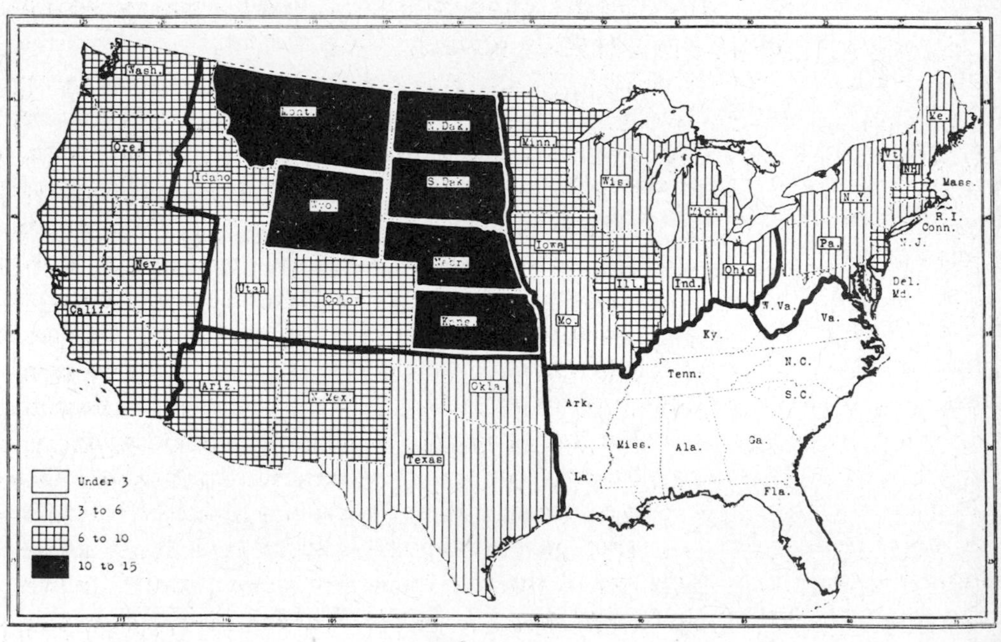

technological strides in air-cooling processes for homes and offices is usually listed as a field for possible revolutionary development, especially in the southern regions. These, together with whatever developments may come in the changing situation with reference to centralized or decentralized industry or the relative importance of large bodies of capital for large integrated plants and expensive machinery as opposed to smaller units, are sufficient to provide a checking background for technology in the Southeast.

What then is the perspective of the Southeast in this new picture of technology and what are the measures of its technological deficiency? Some of these measures will be in terms of interregional comparisons or regional factors measured by national indices. Some will be in terms of general comparisons, which give the region a definitive position within a scale of accepted standards. In seeking effective measures of deficiency or excellence, however, it is important to emphasize again and again the relative values of comparative indices. Comparisons are fundamental; they represent visible ways of measuring factors; they help to fix status within accepted frames of changing standards; they stimulate further study and planning; and they challenge original thinking and initiative. Yet, like the old fallacies of aggregate figures describing the nation or averages for men and wealth, measures fabricated from arbitrary comparative indices fall short of either scientific accuracy or practical application to living society. To demand of an agriculture of small farms in rolling lands of multiple specialized crops a technology of costly tractors, little used, is to make comparative figures ridiculous. Yet the region as a whole must still be ranked for particular purposes with reference to its machine technology. And in all comparisons we must keep in mind regional and functional specialization and prospects, and superior, as well as inferior, comparisons, featuring what we have termed the optimum development of cultural specialization in an age which demands standardization. Regional individuation may often attain this end.

With these qualifications in mind we may proceed, then, to emphasize the region's general deficiencies in terms of certain comparative standards. Thus, if Stuart Chase's six fundamental factors in production be used as a measuring rod, the Southeast excels in the first, namely, *natural resources available*, but lags in the other five; namely, the *use of inanimate energy*, the *use of skilled labor*, the *employment of technical management*, the presence of an *adequate culture heritage of technical arts*, and the *production plant itself*. Or if another general type of comparative measures be sought, the South excels in two of the five major sources of wealth, as we have sought to group them, and lags in three. That is, it excels in the superabundance of its *natural resources* and *its human resources*, and lags in the measure of its *technological wealth*, its *artificial wealth*, its industries,

Total Carload Lots of Nineteen Fruits and Vegetables Received in 66 Cities

ORIGIN, STATE AND REGION	Destination of Unloadings in Cities by Regions							
	Southeast	Southwest	Northeast	Middle States	Northwest	Far West	Total	Per Cent of U. S. Total
Southeast	*9,900*	*753*	*85,195*	*40,538*	*750*	*301*	*137,437*	*28.70*
Virginia	1,059	6	10,639	2,815	1		14,520	3.03
North Carolina	118	1	6,761	2,171	4		9,055	1.89
South Carolina	90	1	6,926	643			7,660	1.60
Georgia	1,012	59	5,543	6,865	32		13,511	2.82
Florida	4,788	470	50,594	16,857	331	195	73,235	15.29
Kentucky	35		250	963			1,248	.26
Tennessee	1,362	1	1,354	3,821	17	21	6,576	1.37
Alabama	882	1	374	2,084	5		3,346	.70
Mississippi	217	3	1,489	128	10	1	1,848	.39
Arkansas	84	95	162	1,160	109	32	1,642	.34
Louisiana	253	116	1,103	3,031	241	52	4,796	1.00
Southwest	*1,166*	*1,514*	*10,378*	*11,686*	*1,074*	*356*	*26,174*	*5.47*
Oklahoma	29	7	7	736	76	5	860	.18
Texas	810	1,196	7,031	7,914	788	101	17,840	3.73
New Mexico	9	2	96	91	5	80	283	.06
Arizona	318	309	3,244	2,945	205	170	7,191	1.50
Northeast	*4,176*	*32*	*51,817*	*10,489*	*1*		*66,515*	*13.89*
Maine	2,180	31	31,468	1,077			34,756	7.26
New Hampshire	2		91	52			145	.03
Vermont			471				471	.10
Massachusetts	9		598	55			662	.14
Rhode Island								
Connecticut			44				44	.01
New York	1,230	1	11,884	4,903			18,018	3.76
New Jersey	265		2,094	2,924	1		5,284	1.10
Delaware	36		1,018	232			1,286	.27
Pennsylvania	128		1,386	243			1,757	.37
Maryland	86		2,329	707			3,122	.65
West Virginia	240		434	296			970	.20
Middle States	*3,577*	*264*	*6,344*	*25,787*	*420*	*4*	*36,396*	*7.60*
Ohio	106	6	1,020	424			1,556	.32
Indiana	386	10	1,497	1,150	1		3,044	.64
Illinois	70	38	158	2,480	23		2,769	.58
Michigan	879	6	3,333	6,425	20		10,663	2.23
Wisconsin	1,034	24	15	5,252	33		6,358	1.33
Minnesota	877	102	105	5,916	146	2	7,148	1.49
Iowa	149	5	56	880	36		1,126	.24
Missouri	76	73	160	3,260	161	2	3,732	.77
Northwest	*3,597*	*4,474*	*3,888*	*20,205*	*1,996*	*3,499*	*37,659*	*7.86*
North Dakota	106	44	27	2,372	41		2,590	.54
South Dakota	2	1		299	1		303	.06
Nebraska	331	267	7	1,652	240		2,497	.52
Kansas	944	130		12	15	2	1,103	.23
Montana		4	86	121			211	.04
Idaho	797	2,383	1,281	11,573	724	3,359	20,117	4.20
Wyoming	219	70		280	17		586	.12
Colorado	1,079	1,422	2,252	3,645	910	22	9,330	1.95
Utah	119	153	235	251	48	116	922	.19
Far West	*7,416*	*7,384*	*78,961*	*50,369*	*3,852*	*26,674*	*174,656*	*36.48*
Nevada		12		1	16	118	147	.03
Washington	1,274	1,450	7,123	8,012	393	5,855	24,107	5.03
Oregon	181	218	1,649	1,042	110	1,282	4,482	.94
California	5,961	5,704	70,189	41,314	3,333	19,419	145,920	30.47

California ships more carloads of vegetables to the Southeast than Florida; the Far West nearly as many carloads to the Northeast as the whole Southeast. Yet the aggregate of the Southeast's unloadings is more than a fourth of the nation's shipping.

Calculated from *Carlot Unloads of Certain Fruits and Vegetables in 66 Cities, 1933.*

and its *institutional modes of life and culture.* This means that in all aspects of its potential resources it reflects the technological lag. For it does not afford the technical institutions for the development and use of its human resources any more than it does for its physical resources.

These appraisals, as well as other illustrations of comparative status and standards, will appear from the cumulative map pictures of the region and their accompanying statistical arrays. They are more vivid in such illustrations as the extraordinary spectacle of Christmas trees and carrots and spinach from California actually being marketed in the Carolinas, lands of many green trees and of garden soil *de luxe;* or of fifty times more poultry produce rolling in to New York from California than from the near-by neighboring Carolinas. Here are erstwhile incredible feats of technology—present incredible feats of regional deficiency in technology and intelligent action. Thus abide twin deficiencies of production and of consumption with resultant multiple deficiencies in standards of living, in health, in vitality and initiative.

Or to make the tests according to the several factors of land and soil, rivers and rain, and the other units of natural endowment, we begin with an appalling regional harvest of deficiency which flows from the richest of endowments; namely, soil, rainfall, rivers and streams. This waste is measured in terms of more than half of all the nation's erosion toll. Of the nation's more than 150,000,000 acres of eroded land, the two major southern regions furnish more than 97,000,000, or 61 per cent. Of this perhaps three-fourths is in the Southeast. To select the worst eroded lands only, Bennett's estimates, based upon the actualities of accurate samplings, indicated that, of Alabama's approximately 9,100,000 acres in cultivation in 1930, approximately 4,000,000 have been largely denuded of the top soil. Of the total of denuded lands in the other Southeastern States, there were 5,000,000 acres for Georgia, 4,000,000 for Mississippi, 2,500,000 for North Carolina, 2,000,000 each for South Carolina and Louisiana, probably more than 3,000,000 each for Arkansas and Tennessee, and 1,500,000 for Virginia. A single county in the South Carolina Piedmont had actually lost by erosion 277,000 acres of land from cultivation.

Yet the total losses of land use and soil fertility are not limited to lost acres or wasted top soil. There are other millions, perhaps five million acres, of stream bottomland that have been affected by the filling of stream beds and consequent overflow and other thousands of acres of arable land have been handicapped by sand and gravel from the hillsides. And still other immeasurable loss through soil drainage and depletion, due to the single crop systems of the region, are augmented by the rapid running off of water from the over-tilled fields lacking in rotation cultivation. No one

State Percentage of the 1929 National Total Value of Selected Agricultural Commodities

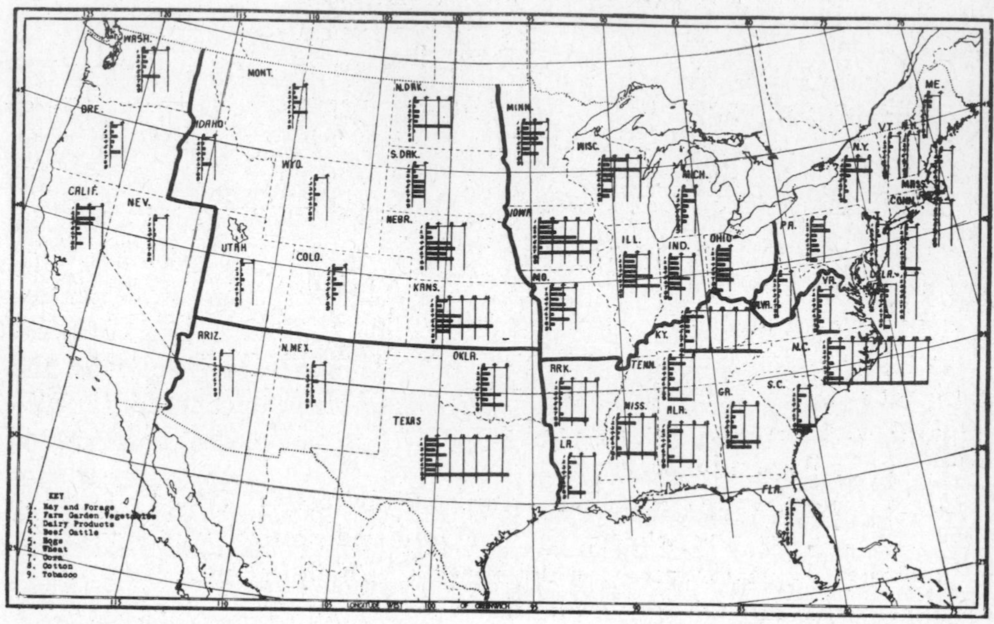

Per Cent in Each State of Major Agricultural Products Produced

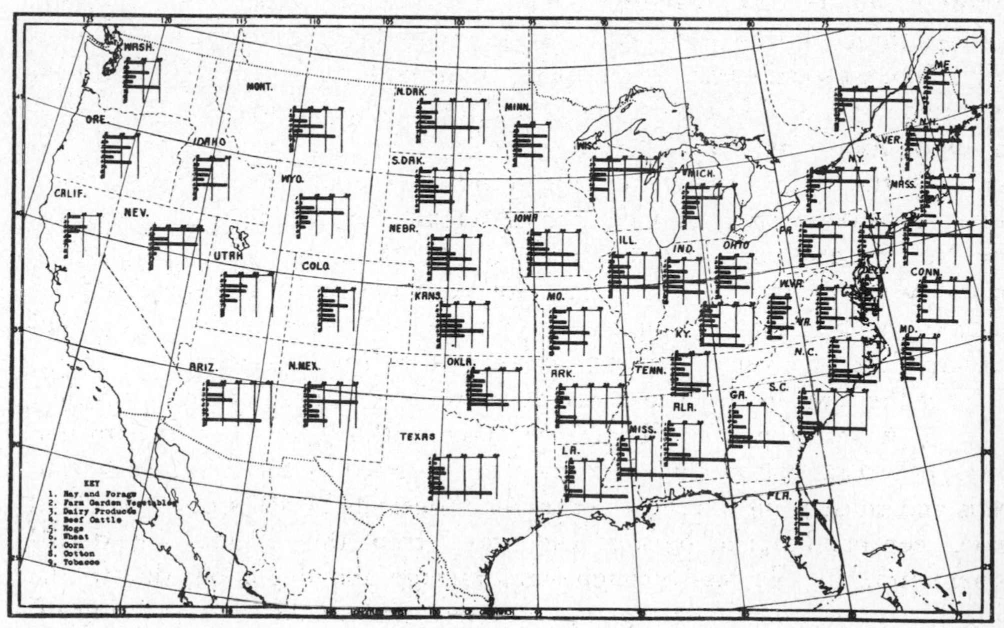

has estimated the total loss for the Southeast, yet from the estimated aggregates of the nation its preponderant part may be appraised adequately for reconstruction purposes. Annual net losses by crop removal have been estimated at from 3,000,000 to 4,000,000 tons of nitrogen, nearly 2,000,000 tons of phosphoric acid, and nearly 5,000,000 tons of potash. Losses by solution or leaching were estimated to be of no less than 3,500,000 tons of potash and more than 500,000 tons of nitrogen and phosphoric acid. From erosion it was estimated that the losses included more than 20,000,000 tons of potash, 1,500,000 tons of nitrogen, and more than 2,000,000 tons of phosphoric acid. If to this annual loss of more than 35,000,000 tons of the three most important elements for plant growth be added the aggregate of recent years, something of the stupendous drain can be pictured. In the last decade alone the staggering cost would run into the billions. But after all, the worst part of the picture is that of the destroyed land itself and the long chain of consequences to the region. Vast gullies and gulches, wagon wide and tree deep, spotty hillsides and great stretches of fields marred like some battle field—each year destroyed more and more, each decade added ugliness and havoc to the landscape. If continued, this process would make the region impotent for agrarian culture or to supply wealth adequate to support industry and mercantile interests.

The measure of drain from profitless land has, of course, but begun to be made with the inventory of its nature and amount. There is, for instance, the annual purchase by the Southeast of 5,514,000 tons of commercial fertilizer as compared with all the rest of the nation's 2,594,000 tons, at a cost of $161,000,000. This expenditure represents a per acre cost of $2.71 as compared with a 30 cents per acre cost in the great farming region of the Middle States. Now it is not the cost or the use of fertilizer which represents waste and drain—for the Southeast is rich in resources for the making of fertilizer, and under proper technology there is a great future for such industry. It is rather the whole economy of leached and eroded lands, continuously drained by more cultivation of fertilizer money crops and the contrariwise absence of conservation and of other crops and technologies for the increase of value and output and the decrease of waste. These points, however, will be presented in the next chapter dealing with the agrarian South. The measure of outgo can be, in the meantime, pictured from the accompanying map pictures and tables.

In the same way something of the agricultural deficiency will be pictured in the comparison of potentialities with actualities in the field of livestock and dairy production, and other aspects of agriculture closely correlated with the land drainage and technological deficiencies of the Southeast. Suffice it to point out here the consistently uniform deficiencies in number

Decrease in Livestock in the United States, 1919-1929

ANIMAL UNITS ON FARMS AND RANGES

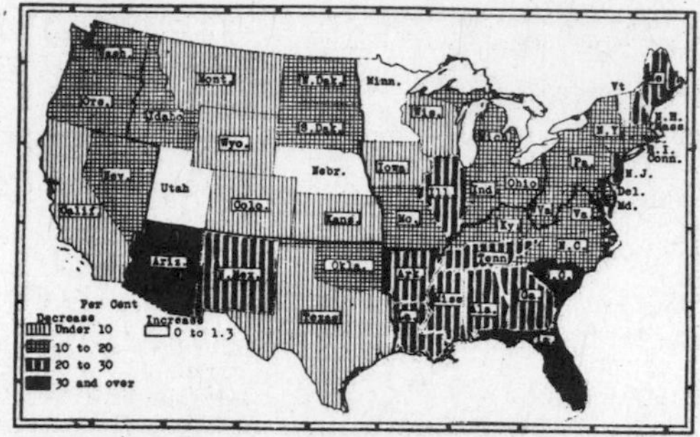

ALL CATTLE ON FARMS AND RANGES

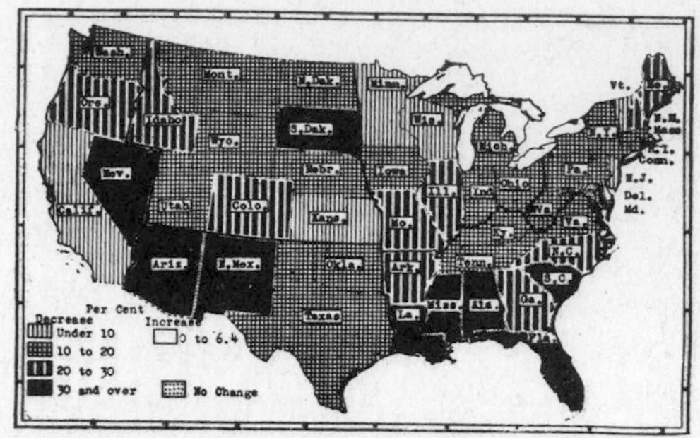

CATTLE OTHER THAN MILK COWS AND HEIFERS ON FARMS

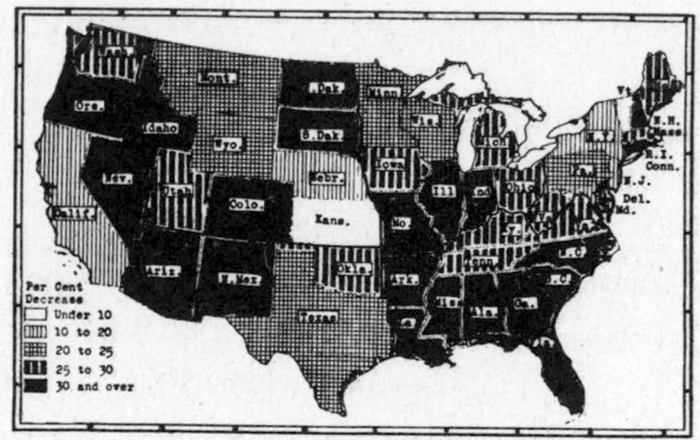

SHEEP AND LAMBS ON FARMS

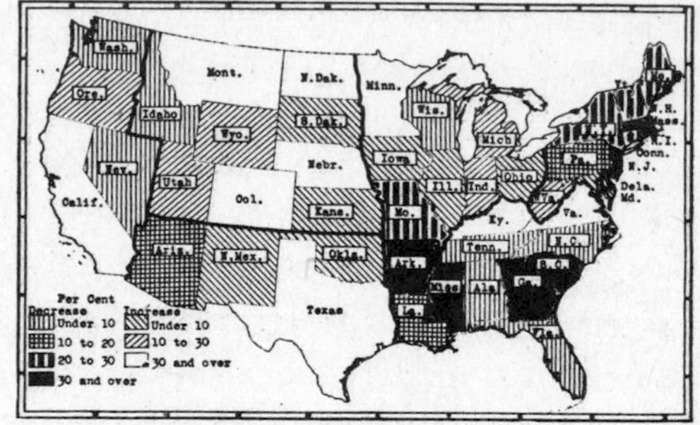

SWINE ON FARMS

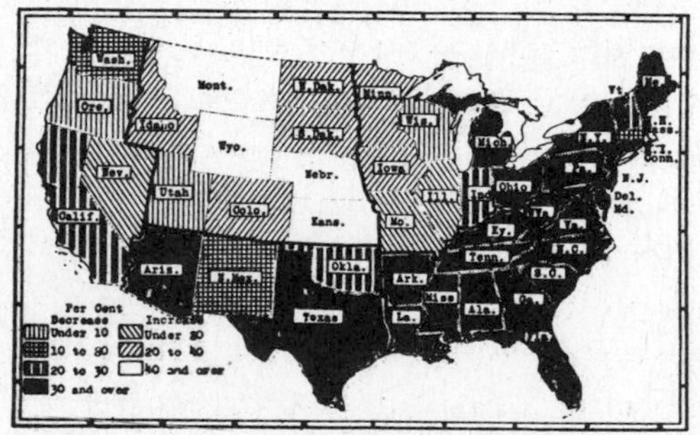

CHICKENS ON FARMS

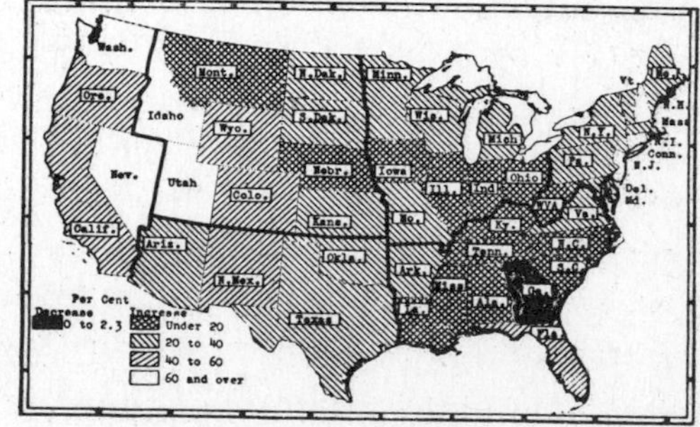

and value of livestock production, and in the consequent low return in money and in man power output and in the similar deficiencies of soil improving crops, and in cooperative activities which would result from a reconstructed land use and land conservation. A sample contrasting picture, product of more technology and planning, might be found in the development of a new dairy region in the Southeast which would serve the threefold purpose of rebuilding the soil, of avoiding the drain from fertilizer and fertilizer farming economy, and of coordinating the balanced program of agriculture and industry in the Piedmont South. Here again, however, technological deficiencies double back in the dilemma of a regional deficiency of workers, white and black, who have either the skills or the wills to make of dairying a profitable industry. Other aspects of this and similar dilemmas will appear in the cumulative picture and in the final chapter pointing toward regional planning programs.

Yet this particular picture of deficiency may well be continued here to the extent that it illustrates the margin between potentialities and the present status as well as the multiple interrelated indices involved. Thus deficiencies relating to this particular picture include the lowest per capita farm income, the lowest income per worker, the lowest return per unit of horse power, the lowest ratio of income from livestock production, the lowest percentage of total sales coming from coöperative sales, the lowest per capita purebred livestock, the lowest production of milk and dairy products, a low ratio of pasture land, a low carrying capacity for pasture lands, an extraordinarily large drain from erosion and waste lands, a phenomenally high expenditure for commercial fertilizers, a low ranking in the various mechanical techniques of farming and living, such as tractors, water, lights, telephone, and many others, in addition to deficiencies in health, literacy, education, and general cultural activities.

Proceeding to other selected facts, we note that the South has decreased in the last decade in the number of most livestock, and that the ratio of decrease is of considerable significance. We note also its low production of milk and its lower consumption than the average for the nation. We note also the low evaluation of its livestock, the low evaluation of their products, and, on the other hand, the high ratio between cost of fertilizer and the depleted land and low farm crop returns per acre. And we also note in those counties and parts of states showing large deficiencies in this respect a correspondingly large burden of public relief services, and of other indices of inadequacy. But we also note great variation in different counties and different states, with here and there not only a high degree of success but great increase within recent years, such as to indicate possibilities of immediate improvement through the proper use and technology.

Percentage of Purebred Dairy Cattle Which Are Jerseys, 1930

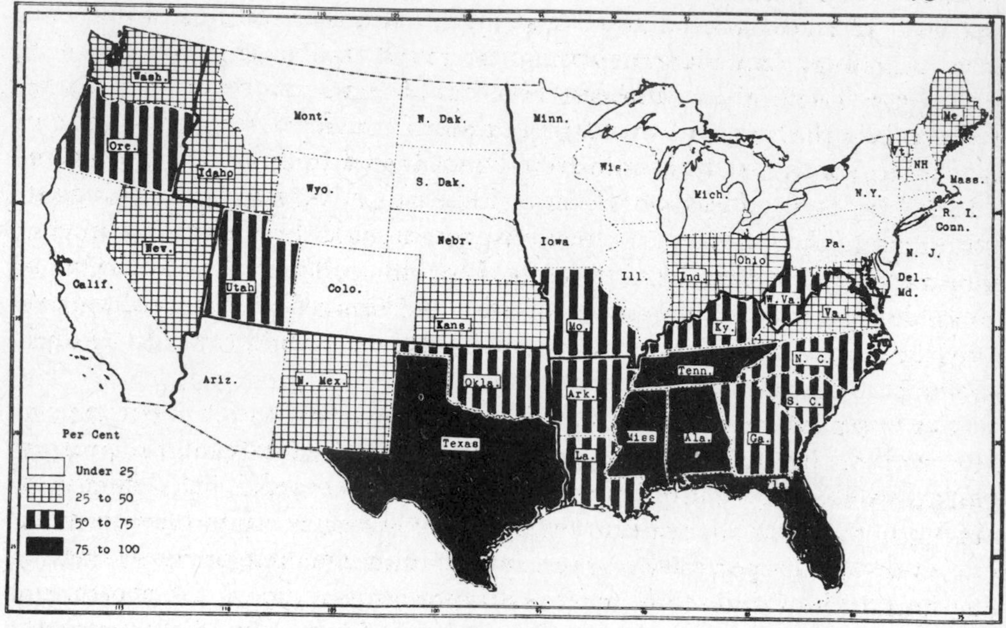

Increase of Breeders and Owners of Purebred Jersey Cattle Per Capita, Based Upon 1930, for Mississippi

STATE	Total Population 1930	Actual Breeders and Owners	Breeders and Owners per Capita	Actual Number Jerseys	Jerseys per Capita	On the Basis of Mississippi Per Capita*	
						Breeders and Owners	Jerseys
Southeast	*25,550,898*	*26,283*	*.0010*	*82,972*	*.0032*	*63,823*	*181,373*
Virginia	2,421,851	550	.0002	2,989	.0012	6,055	17,195
North Carolina	3,170,276	2,391	.0007	7,054	.0022	7,926	22,509
South Carolina	1,738,765	949	.0005	2,776	.0016	4,347	12,345
Georgia	2,908,506	2,352	.0008	7,092	.0024	7,271	20,650
Florida	1,468,211	244	.0002	2,017	.0014	3,671	10,424
Kentucky	2,614,589	4,739	.0018	13,281	.0051	6,536	18,564
Tennessee	2,616,556	4,818	.0018	17,729	.0068	6,541	18,578
Alabama	2,646,248	2,135	.0008	6,386	.0024	6,616	18,788
Mississippi	2,009,821	4,970	.0025	14,232	.0071	......	......
Arkansas	1,854,482	1,863	.0010	5,737	.0031	4,636	13,167
Louisiana	2,101,593	1,272	.0006	3,679	.0018	5,254	14,921
Southwest	*9,079,645*	*16,220*	*.0018*	*49,833*	*.0055*	*22,699*	*64,465*
Oklahoma	2,396,040	3,055	.0012	11,167	.0047	5,990	17,012
Texas	5,824,715	12,714	.0022	36,875	.0063	14,562	41,355
New Mexico	423,317	241	.0006	777	.0018	1,058	3,006
Arizona	435,573	210	.0005	1,014	.0023	1,089	3,092

*Used gross per capita.

Since the jersey, beginning with importations to Tennessee, was the pioneer purebred dairy breed in the Southeast, and since for a long time the figures on jerseys were typical of both status and possibilities, the above table and charts give one index of remediable deficiencies if other states should increase up to the standards of Tennessee, the early forerunner, and Mississippi, the latest to make special increases. These figures are discussed at length in Chapter VII.

The total number of purebred cattle in the Southeastern States as reported in the most recent figures was 8,360,888, the lowest of any region. Calculated according to rural population this shows a per capita of 0.4 for each rural dweller. Two states, North and South Carolina, rank as low as 0.2. If we fix the optimum number as 1.5 per capita, the Southeast shows every state with a deficiency and the total with an aggregate deficiency of 18,540,216. Such a deficiency represents, of course, a value in millions of dollars for the cattle and more millions for their products. On the other hand, were this number or one-half of it added to the Southeast, there would be required, according to present estimated carrying capacity of grazing lands in most of the Southeastern States, four times the total number of acres now listed as total pasture lands. The present 45,000,000 acres would, therefore, be challenged to an improvement which would transform its ten acres' carrying capacity into that of two or three acres together with the acquisition of another 40,000,000 acres taken over from the 170,000,000 acres in farm lands and from other lands not in use. Similar computations with reference to the amount of feed stuffs raised and consumed, of hays grown and imported, would show equally radical transformations necessary before any such optimum estimates could be even suggested. Likewise, a new type of labor management and technique required for the care of high-grade cattle, for the construction of fences, for the improvement of lands, for the seeding of poor and rich lands for field and pasture, and for the curing and processing of hay and grains would constitute another difficult and important problem.

Turning to a still more specialized aspect of the industry, we may examine the situation in the South with reference to breeders and owners of purebred Jerseys and the number of Jerseys in the Southeast by states. Since the Jersey is the predominant purebred dairy breed in the Southeast, a study of this particular breed will constitute a representative view of the whole industry. In 1932 the Southwest reported a total of 26,283 breeders and owners of purebred Jerseys, owning 82,972 purebred cattle. The per capita Jersey owners and breeders from this total is .001 and of the number of Jerseys .003. On the other hand, Kentucky, Tennessee, and Mississippi show a much larger per capita for cattle, Mississippi with .007, Tennessee with .006, and Kentucky with .005. If North Carolina should increase her purebred Jerseys to the approximate standard of Mississippi, the number would be increased from 7,054 to 22,509, and, if the entire Southeast should increase at the same rate, the total number would be 181,373 instead of 82,972. A later more detailed examination of the situation in Mississippi will indicate the reason for selecting that state as an index of deficiency in purebred dairy cattle and will show something of the

Milk Production, 1929

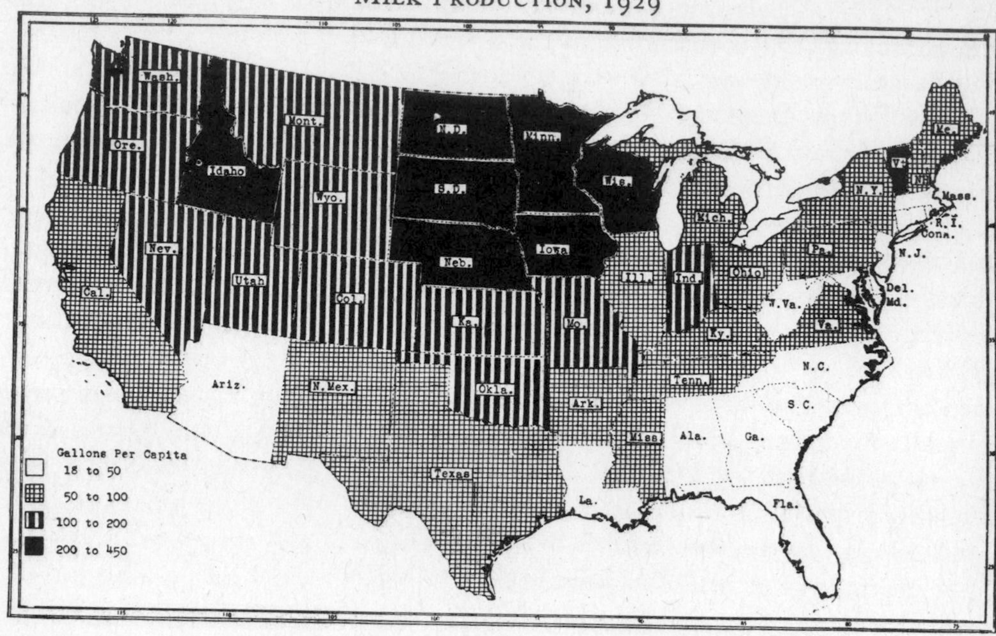

Milk Production in Gallons, 1929

STATE	Rank	Per Capita Gallons	Rank	Gallons Per Farm
Wisconsin	1	423	1	6,829
Vermont	2	359	2	5,886
South Dakota	3	334	14	2,780
North Dakota	4	333	12	2,922
Minnesota	5	322	5	4,456
Idaho	6	235	18	2,512
Iowa	7	221	11	3,011
Nebraska	8	213	22	2,263
Kansas	9	173	27	1,965
Montana	10	160	28	1,840
Wyoming	11	145	24	2,054
Oregon	12	142	19	2,455
Nevada	13	133	7	3,518
Utah	14	128	20	2,395
Colorado	15	118	25	2,033
Washington	16	115	17	2,540
Oklahoma	17	104	34	1,223
Indiana	18	103	29	1,830
Missouri	19	102	33	1,442
Michigan	20	93	15	2,655
Maine	21	89	30	1,823
New Hampshire	22	88	16	2,559
Kentucky	23	81	36	854
California	24	78	9	3,284
Texas	25	71	38	833
Ohio	26	70	23	2,071
Tennessee	27	69	40	740
Arkansas	28	68	41	531
Illinois	29	66	21	2,361
Mississippi	30	65	46	418
New York	31	63	3	5,009
Delaware	32	62	31	1,520
Virginia	33	61	37	853
New Mexico	34	58	39	780
Maryland	35	54	26	2,032
Pennsylvania	36	50	13	2,784
Arizona	37	48	32	1,482
Alabama	38	47	42	480
West Virginia	39	46	35	1,015
Connecticut	40	40	6	3,730
Georgia	41	39	44	445
North Carolina	42	33	45	429
South Carolina	43	30	48	333
Louisiana	44	28	47	361
Rhode Island	45	22	4	4,482
New Jersey	46	20	10	3,222
Massachusetts	46	20	8	3,337
Florida	48	18	43	446

MILK PRODUCTION
Percentage Change, 1919-1924

Decrease Per Cent Increase

20 10 0 10 20 30 40 50 60 70 80 90

State
Wisconsin
Vermont
South Dakota
North Dakota
Minnesota
Idaho
Iowa
Nebraska
Kansas
Montana
Wyoming
Oregon
Nevada
Utah
Colorado
Washington
Oklahoma
Indiana
Missouri
Michigan
Maine
New Hampshire
Kentucky
California
Texas
Ohio
Tennessee
Arkansas
Illinois
Mississippi
New York
Delaware
Virginia
New Mexico
Maryland
Pennsylvania
Arizona
Alabama
West Virginia
Connecticut
Georgia
North Carolina
South Carolina
Louisiana
Rhode Island
New Jersey
Massachusetts
Florida

practicability of absorbing 100,000 additional such cattle and a proportionate amount of other purebred dairy cattle within the next ten years in the Southeast.

The figures further reveal the South with a low per capita milk production and there are many areas in the Southeast where milk appears almost unobtainable to any reasonable extent. The estimated production of milk in the Southeastern States in 1929 was 1,291,430,023 gallons. This is a deficit of 121 million gallons needed if the national annual average per capita consumption obtained in this area. Or if the 90 gallons a year or the daily quart were produced, it would mean a shortage of a billion gallons. If to an estimate of the amount of milk needed based upon recommended standards of living for health and vitality should be added proportionate amounts of other dairy products, the deficiency would be still larger. If, on the other hand, planning for milk production is pursued on the basis of supply and demand as measured only by the commercial market and commercial dairying, or on the basis of a possible national allotment plan irrespective of state and regional needs and capacities, the result might very well be far below a reasonable standard for both production and consumption. The spectacle of carload shipments of milk from Middle States' territory to Florida at a loss to the producers while the prevailing condition of south Georgia and Florida farm families is one of poverty, poor use of lands and time, the people malnurtured for lack of dairy products, working on depleted soils for cash crops that they must produce at a loss, is one to challenge somebody somewhere and somehow to attempt some planning.

That successful planning can be done has been proved by the state colleges of agriculture and the national cooperative extension work and by the examination of certain subregions which have made the experiments. What has not been done is to work out an interrelated optimum production plan which comprehends the whole region and its many parts. In the meantime, an examination of the maps showing breeders in the two states of North Carolina and Mississippi is illuminating with respect to distribution. The whole eastern half of North Carolina reflects a large deficiency as compared to the more central and western counties, although it might be shown that more favorable conditions for the development of dairy farming and for the increase of dairy cattle on individual farms are found in the east than in the west. A glance at the Mississippi map shows a similar development—in the northeast and east where the greatest increase in recent years has made a transformation in the state, there appear less favorable conditions than might be found in many of the lower counties and some of the Delta areas, if developed under proper planning. It is of importance here to

PER CENT TOTAL PASTURE LAND IS OF ALL LAND IN FARMS, 1930

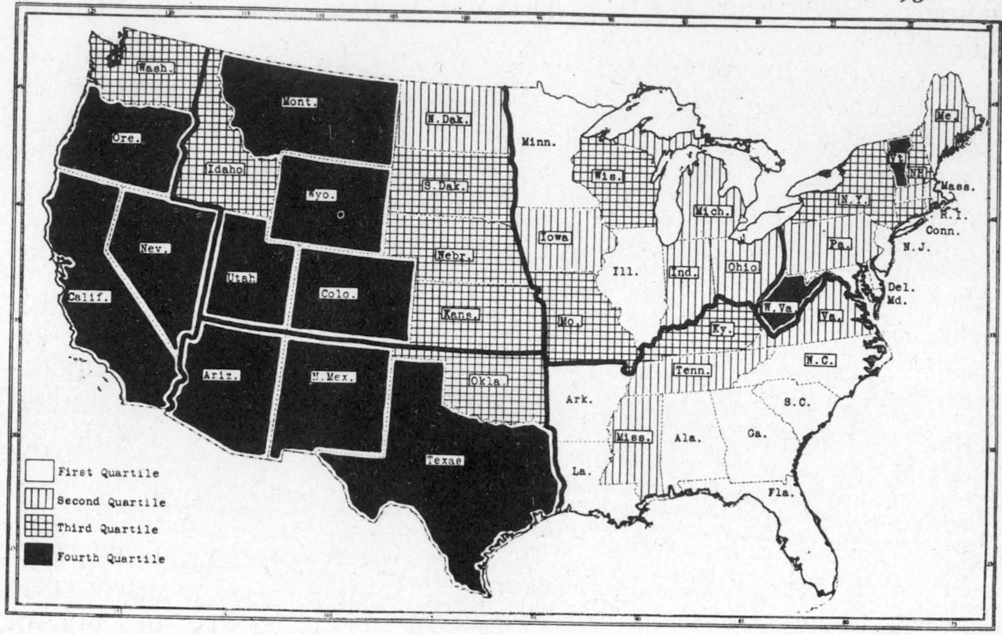

PER CENT OF FARMS REPORTING PUREBRED LIVESTOCK, 1930

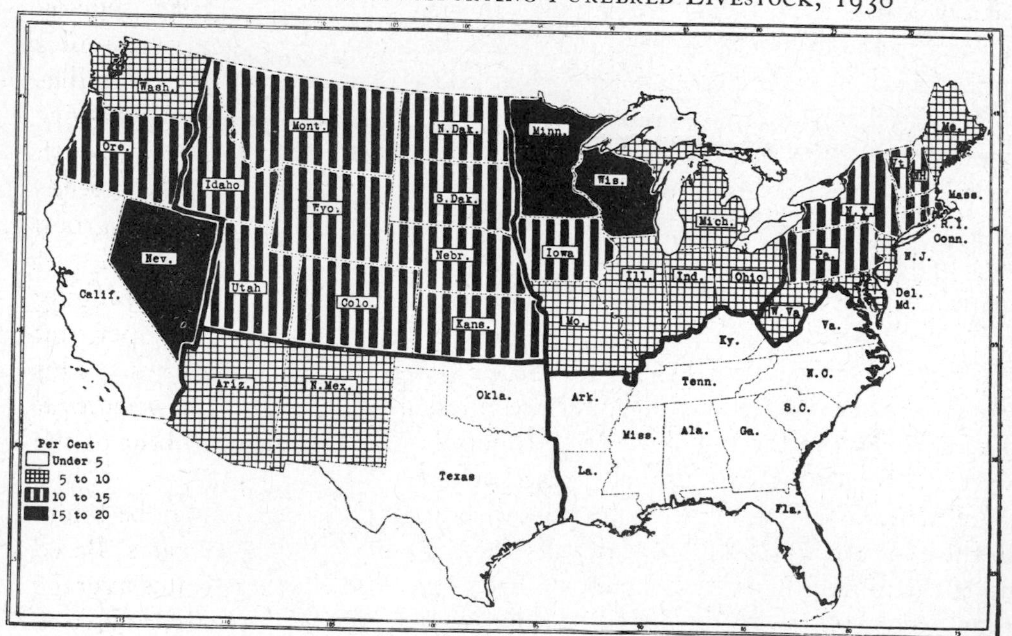

note only that the optimum production record, if it might be temporarily designated, has been attained in some counties and not in others, and that indications are that the best areas have not yet been planned for. This is substantial evidence of the attainability of such optimum development.

If we look further into the problem, we are again confronted with other facts of great significance. The states of the Southeast have the lowest percentage of total pasture land, the average being 26.4 as opposed to 69 for the Southwest, 38 for the Northeast, 32 for the Middle States, 52 for the Northwest, and 63 for the Far West. It is not to be implied arbitrarily, of course, that uniformity is either possible or desirable, yet, when North Carolina shows a percentage of only 15.8 and South Carolina 17.2, it must be clear that such a deficiency is a first obstacle to attack in seeking the optimum program. To this small acreage of pasture lands must be added the other handicap of a very low carrying capacity for most of the pasture lands. This example will be pointed up further in connection with the development of the agrarian South.

This illustration of deficiency may be continued further in the case of diet, which involves both the present standards of consumption and basic possibilities. The rural family illustrates the particular type of deficiency most pertinent to the present picture. Standard of living studies of southern rural families have shown that almost half of the total family budget goes for food. The proportion ranges from around 42 per cent for owner families to more than 55 per cent for tenant families. In regions of the country outside the South there is a natural tendency for more prosperous families to purchase a larger proportion of their food supply than poorer families who must follow more of a subsistence live-at-home routine. The tendency for poorer farm families to raise a larger part of their food has in the South been offset by the system of exclusive cash cropping and commissary feeding, so that families with very lowest cash incomes have been also the group raising least of the family food supply. A table including 52 samples of farm families shows ratios of food purchased in southern families ranging from only two to seven per cent in mountain areas, from 25 to 36 per cent for farm owners, and from 40 to 58 per cent for cropper families. This is in contrast to an itemized budget recommended in the 1933 *Agricultural Yearbook* by the Bureau of Home Economics that about 83 per cent of the value of an adequate diet can be raised at home.

Further illustration of needed food products in the region may be found in the production-requirement deficits for eggs in the southern states. Based upon the minimum dietary standard of ten eggs a week, these states average nearly 70 million dozen deficit as compared with their actual production record. The percentage increase necessary to meet this standard ranges

TOTAL POUNDS OF TOBACCO USED IN DOMESTIC MANUFACTURE, 1929

POUNDS OF TOBACCO USED IN MANUFACTURE OF CIGARETTES, 1929

POUNDS OF TOBACCO USED IN MANUFACTURE OF CIGARS, 1929

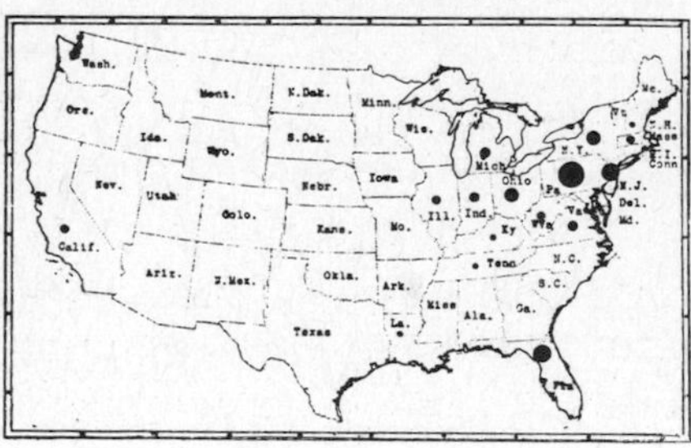

POUNDS OF TOBACCO USED IN MANUFACTURED TOBACCO, 1929

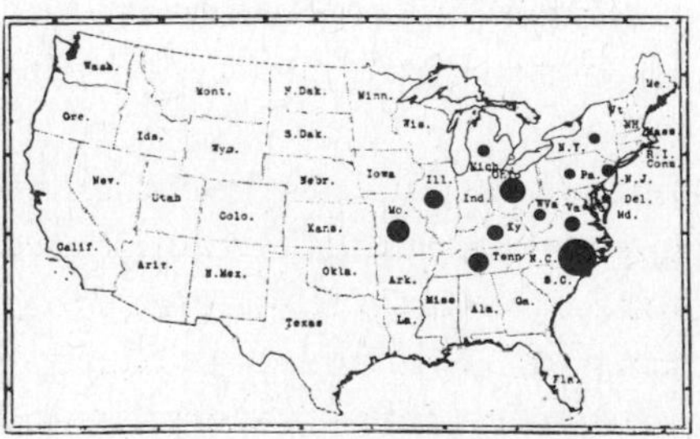

CONSUMPTION OF TOBACCO IN DOMESTIC MANUFACTURE, 1929

	Pounds of Tobacco Used In Manufacture of			
	Cigarettes*	Cigars**	Manufactured Tobacco	Grand Total
United States	270,735,485	128,544,467†	283,124,477	682,404,429
Southeast				
Virginia	53,489,883	5,261,322	14,713,024	73,464,229
North Carolina	163,356,479	262,337	98,443,148	262,061,964
South Carolina		405,876	18,285	424,161
Georgia		446,829	4,391	451,220
Florida	9,933	12,560,210	5,107	12,575,250
Kentucky	8,971,324	1,148,482	16,338,753	26,458,559
Tennessee		1,128,801	24,503,929	25,632,730
Alabama		67,468		67,468
Mississippi		1,279		1,279
Arkansas		6,228	274	6,502
Louisiana	6,203	1,381,567	74,796	1,462,566
Total	225,833,822	22,670,399	154,101,707	402,605,928
Southwest				
Oklahoma		21,132		21,132
Texas		414,186	193,102	607,288
New Mexico		697	220	917
Arizona		585		585
Total		436,600	193,322	629,922
Northeast				
Maine		135,387		135,387
New Hampshire		1,234,483	636	1,235,119
Vermont		3,899		3,899
Massachusetts	14,437	1,927,645	371,543	2,313,625
Rhode Island		154,679	18,256	172,935
Connecticut		803,789	57,384	861,173
New York	17,269,762	11,629,452	5,359,333	34,249,547
New Jersey	13,184,431	15,531,301	10,241,493	38,957,225
Pennsylvania	3,309,841	46,193,236	4,830,295	54,333,372
Delaware		232,712	3,105,958	3,338,670
Maryland		668,506	1,751	670,257
West Virginia	806	1,839,201	8,499,537	10,339,544
Total	33,770,277	80,354,290	32,486,186	146,610,753
Middle States				
Ohio		9,220,873	33,830,474	43,051,347
Indiana		3,981,805	329,337	4,311,142
Illinois	6,367	1,503,854	22,201,692	23,711,913
Michigan	8,225	5,845,157	8,290,216	14,143,598
Wisconsin		886,976	430,338	1,317,314
Minnesota	25	476,558	73,013	549,596
Iowa		393,463	232,501	625,964
Missouri	49,366	634,948	30,733,735	31,418,049
Total	63,983	22,943,634	96,121,306	119,128,923
Northwest				
North Dakota		5,105		5,105
South Dakota		32,500	3,051	35,551
Nebraska		165,331	41,788	207,119
Kansas		121,439	14,102	135,541
Montana		19,246	1,613	20,859
Idaho		8,174		8,174
Wyoming		2,881		2,881
Colorado		122,523	9,332	131,855
Utah		37,224	1,107	38,331
Total		514,423	70,993	585,416
Far West				
Washington		29,514	899	30,413
Oregon		22,824	4,198	27,022
California	11,067,403	1,570,401	145,866	12,783,670
Nevada		2,247		2,247
Total	11,067,403	1,624,986	150,963	12,843,352

*Tobacco used in cigarettes weighing not more than 3 pounds per thousand. Tobacco used in cigarettes weighing more than 3 pounds per thousand (92,284 pounds for whole U. S.) not included.

**Tobacco used in cigars weighing not more than 3 pounds per thousand. Tobacco used in cigars weighing less than 3 pounds per thousand (1,208,777 pounds for whole U. S.) not included.

†Hawaii, 135 pounds unstemmed.

Source: Annual Report of Commissioner of Internal Revenue, 1930, pp. 141 ff.

from 90 per cent in Virginia to 374 in South Carolina. Other large deficits are Florida with 341 per cent, Georgia with 313, Louisiana with 302, North Carolina with 250, and Alabama with 232. It is interesting to note that the five states showing the largest production-requirement deficit in milk are the same as for eggs, namely, Georgia, the Carolinas, Louisiana, and Florida.

The close relation of technology to deficiency and lag may be illustrated somewhat further, in addition to the summary in Chapter I. For example, we find that the agriculture of the Southeast produces a certain high fraction of the national agricultural product. The technological equipment and the annual capital expenditure of the Southeast, however, are demonstrated to be considerably less, relative to national norms, than the productivity of the region. It is then perfectly clear that the cash return per technological unit in southeastern agriculture is somewhat higher than that of the whole nation. But this in itself does not argue technological efficiency. It measures, rather, the extent to which pretechnological methods are used in the Southeast in what is ultimately a competition with technological means of production. Similarly a high index of value of manufactured product, or of value added, per unit of power or per dollar of investment in equipment, in southeastern industry, may indicate, rather than a high degree of industrial efficiency, a progressive burden on the worker. Here, as elsewhere, the Southeast continues its paradox and contrast, now in the first rank, now bringing up the rear.

In certain branches of industrial technology, the Southeast is well equipped, in others the region is almost destitute. The Southeast with 17.2 per cent of the nation's cigarette factories produces 84 per cent of the cigarettes, decisively indicative of an advanced technology in this industry. The South's textile mills, more recent in the aggregate than New England's, have the technological advantage in so far as mechanical equipment is concerned, although on the national scale the industry in its general productive and distributive set-up is a glaring example of the antithesis of technology. In coal, systematically efficient machine-mines sink their shafts next door to hazardous and wasteful "mule-mines" whose technology has not advanced beyond that of the early Industrial Revolution. The history of coal technology is thus concurrently recapitulated in a single field. John Beecher has estimated that in the technology of iron and steel the region's equipment is qualitatively supreme. Foreplanned Fairfield offers a striking contrast to haphazard, overcrowded, obsolescent Homestead, and surpasses even Gary in efficiency of layout and modernity of equipment. The technology of the region's hydroelectric plants, of southwestern petroleum refineries, Tennessee and North Carolina rayon and paper mills,

Rental and Benefit Payments of the Agricultural Adjustment Administration Through December 31, 1933

STATE AND REGION	Amount	Per Cent of Total	STATE AND REGION	Amount	Per Cent of Total
Southeast	*$54,834,397.01*	*41.8*	*Middle States*	*$6,787,490.61*	*5.2*
Virginia	460,013.12	0.3	Ohio	1,194,603.38	0.91
North Carolina	2,829,916.72	2.1	Indiana	956,733.22	0.73
South Carolina	4,684,930.19	3.6	Illinois	649,567.84	0.50
Georgia	7,926,220.87	6.0	Michigan	365,750.80	0.28
Florida	323,156.14	0.3	Wisconsin	359,773.44	0.28
Kentucky	153,425.80	0.1	Minnesota	529,682.31	0.41
Tennessee	3,357,447.59	2.6	Iowa	181,096.40	0.14
Alabama	9,537,007.25	7.3	Missouri	2,550,283.22	1.95
Mississippi	9,924,837.57	7.6			
Arkansas	10,667,598.82	8.1	*Northwest*	*9,679,509.38*	*7.4*
Louisiana	4,969,842.94	3.8	North Dakota	....	....
			South Dakota	699,725.60	0.5
Southwest	*58,122,325.13*	*44.3*	Nebraska	1,011,917.17	0.8
Oklahoma	12,745,521.26	9.7	Kansas	7,440,111.01	5.7
Texas	44,580,877.37	34.0	Montana	....	....
New Mexico	527,732.34	0.4	Idaho	12,380.80	0.01
Arizona	268,194.16	0.2	Wyoming	4,025.60	0.003
			Colorado	267,418.40	0.21
Northest	*1,316,369.70*	*1.0*	Utah	243,930.80	0.20
Maine	....	....			
New Hampshire	1,754.20	0.001	*Far West*	*336,395.67*	*0.3*
Vermont	2,384.45	0.002	Nevada	15,988.80	0.013
Massachusetts	78,313.10	0.059	Washington	16,091.60	0.013
Rhode Island	....	....	Oregon	60,961.80	0.05
Connecticut	169,757.99	0.129	California	243,353.47	0.2
New York	30,808.63	0.023			
New Jersey	6,147.60	0.005	United States	131,076,487.50	100.0
Delaware	66,431.40	0.051			
Pennsylvania	418,881.63	0.319			
Maryland	498,725.30	0.380			
West Virginia	43,165.40	0.032			

Loans Made to Individual Farmers in Each of the States Most Seriously Affected by Drought, 1931

STATE AND REGION	Loans		Dollars	
	Number	Per Cent	Number	Per Cent
Southeast	*275,963*	*71.6*	*$32,494,515*	*69.1*
Virginia	20,030	5.2	2,354,167	5.0
North Carolina	17,333	4.5	2,211,002	4.7
South Carolina	8,156	2.1	984,148	2.1
Georgia	17,678	4.6	2,537,070	5.4
Kentucky	33,237	8.6	2,588,076	5.5
Tennessee	24,067	6.2	2,306,572	4.9
Alabama	19,753	5.1	2,672,567	5.7
Mississippi	31,606	8.2	4,439,374	9.4
Arkansas	78,506	20.4	9,211,104	19.6
Louisiana	25,597	6.7	3,190,435	6.8
Southwest	*48,426*	*12.6*	*4,707,374*	*10.0*
Ohlahoma	18,869	4.9	1,621 889	3.4
Texas	29,557	7.7	3,085,485	6.6
All Other States	60,803	15.8	9,853,872	20.9
United States	385,192	100.0	47,055,761	100.0

Norfolk shipyards, and Louisiana sawmills reaches the highest standards.

The deficiency is found not in what industrial technology the South possesses, but in the incomplete range of technology. Until recently the South was a furnisher of raw materials to the manufacturing regions, essentially colonial in its economy. Although it now fabricates a considerable proportion of its raw materials, its manufacturing processes are still largely confined to the more elementary levels. The South makes cast iron pipe, steel rails, girders, bolts, wire, steel plate and sheet, fabricates its skyscrapers, its factories, its bridges, its oil and gas tanks, but imports its machinery, hardware, locomotives, and automobiles. Not among the South's products are, for example, radios and electric refrigerators, washing machines, vacuum cleaners, surgical instruments, fountain pens, garments (except overalls!), clocks and watches, boilers and dynamos, hats, shoes, typewriters, roller skates, sewing machines, musical instruments, radiators, drugs, cameras, wardrobe trunks, paints and abrasives. The region's industrial technology is admirable, as far as it goes, but it is not complete or balanced. The South's proportion of national manufacturing, as may be seen from the numerous figures and charts, is still far below its ratio of people and resources.

One of the chief causes of this uneven technology is the South's very contracted access to capital, expressing itself in a differential in rates of interest. If the rate for industrial borrowing of any given class is six per cent in the North and eight per cent here, that is to say one-third more in the South, any capital consuming project in the South must yield one-third more profit than a similar enterprise in the North, in order to pay its way at so much per cent on capital. Accordingly most sorts of manufacture involving elaborate technologies have avoided the South, because as a rule, the elaborate technology is expressed in expensive and elaborate plant; and the same drawback applies, for the same reason but to a less degree, on the farm or in the home.

Back of the rate of interest is the position of the South as a debtor region. The South has the general status of an agricultural country engaged in trade with industrial countries, importing both manufactures and its equipment, and paying for them chiefly by the export of raw produce. Most countries of this sort speedily get into debt so soon as inequalities of income develop. The proceeds of exports should be used to pay current debt service and buy necessary manufactured goods, but, in fact, a demand for luxuries from the richer elements of the population is added. This puts a strain on the mechanism of exchange, raising rates of interest or leading to the rationing of capital, both processes representing the inability of the region or country to live at the standards of an industrialized area when

Imports, 1920-1929

Adapted from the *Atlas of the Historical Geography of the United States*

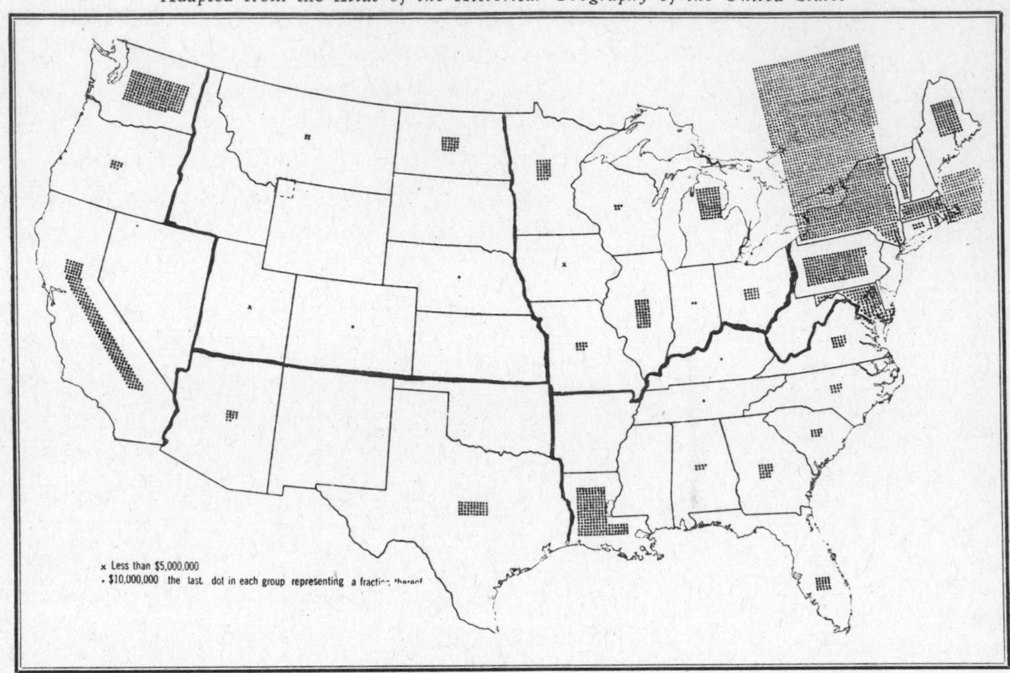

Exports, 1920-1929

Adapted from the *Atlas of the Historical Geography of the United States*

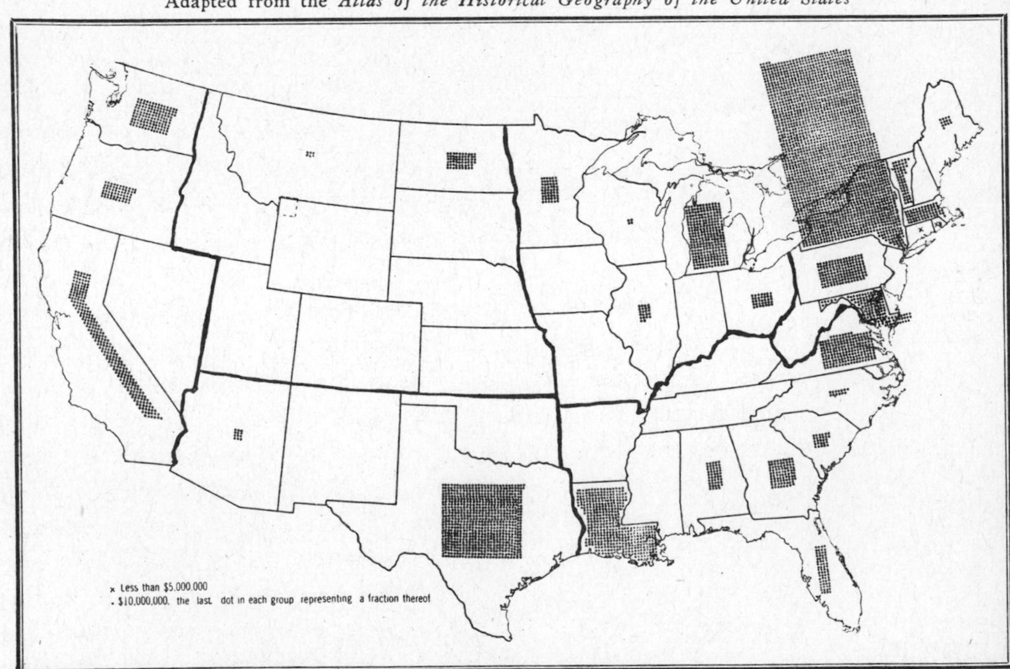

producing raw materials from which returns are less, and at the same time enlarge its capital.

Another factor is cheap labor. Wages in the Southeast are from 20 to 30 per cent lower than corresponding wages in the Northeast. This results in hand work rather than machine work, in roundabout methods of cultivation and processing, in piecemeal organization and set-up, and generally speaking, in the wasteful use of labor. Among the causes of low wages in the South are low skills and low standards of living, together with a tendency to wage deflation set up by the balance of trade situation already discussed. Still another technical factor is the fact that, compared with other regions, most products do not require so much processing, or, if they do, it is often better processed near large markets. Yet we should not exaggerate the insusceptibility of southern produce to industrial processing on the spot, since the increasing hydroelectric development and possibilities ought to make the South a leading industrial region. Looking at the matter historically, a large part of the region's technological lag is due to the lateness of the discovery of economical hydroelectric power, compared with coal, and to the apparent destitution, until the present time, of most of the South in power resources.

Illustrations of the region's technical achievements and problems may be found in such developments as railroads, highways, freight rates, and iron and steel industry. The text of the next eight pages follows Dan Lacy's special study of railways and motor development. First of all, he points out, topography represents the chief conditioning factor determining the basic trade routes of the region. The general picture shows: the extensive use of waterways before the development of modern techniques of land transportation, roads from the fall line to the mountains to bring the commerce of the Piedmont to the headwaters of the rivers, a north-south route through the Piedmont, roads around the mountains and through them at strategic points, and such roads as may be necessary to supplement the rivers of the transmontane section. Along the navigable rivers of the eastern coastal plain there early developed a staple economy, based on tobacco in Virginia and North Carolina and on rice and indigo in South Carolina and Georgia. The majority of the larger plantations had access to navigable water such as to enable them to trade directly with New England or Europe. Each plantation and farm tended to grow its own foodstuffs, each to produce the same staples for export. Hence, there was very little intraregional trade and slight need for commercial depots and trading centers or for improvement of the natural facilities for transportation.

During the course of the eighteenth century there was a heavy flow of population from the Tidewater and from Pennsylvania into the Piedmont

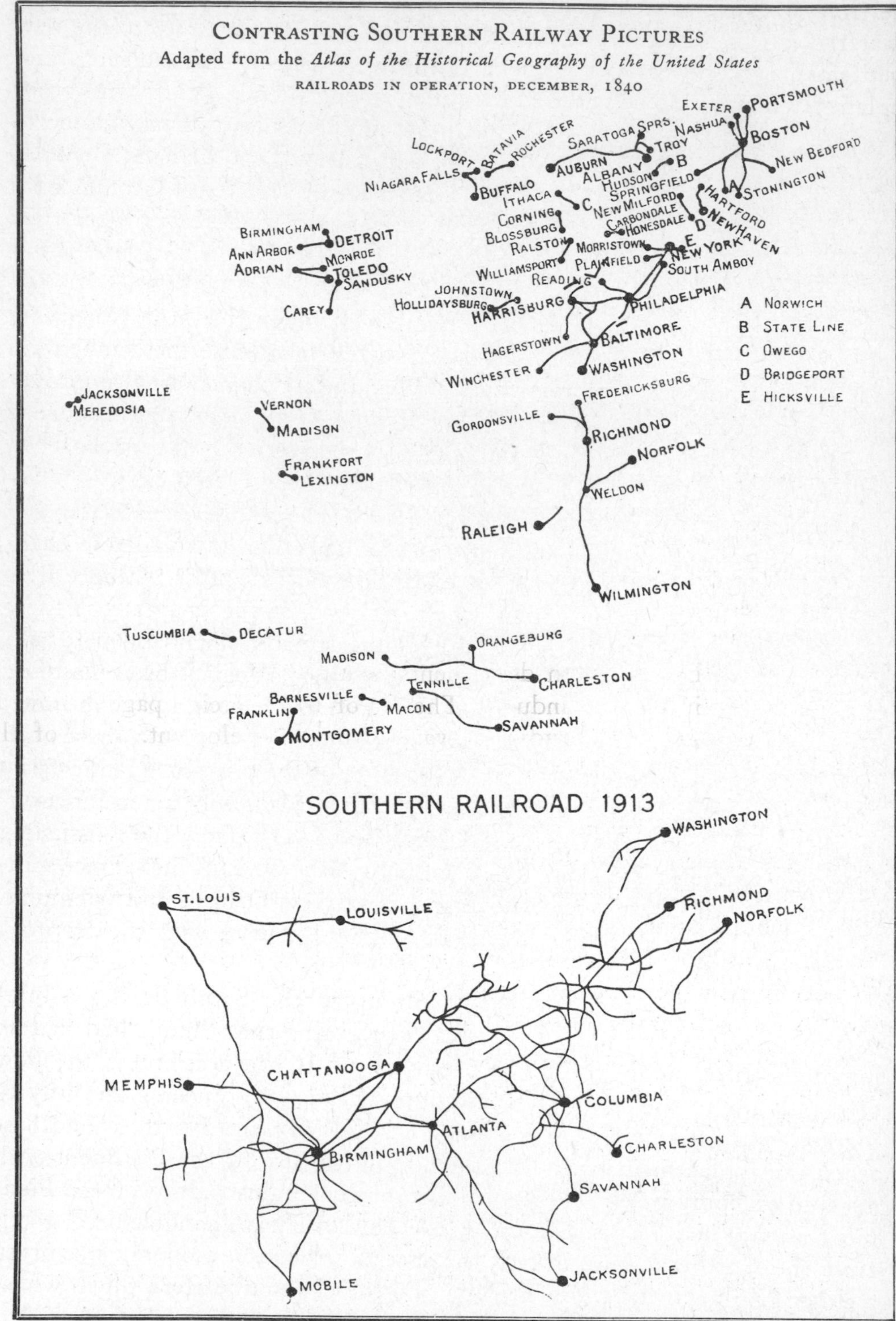

CONTRASTING SOUTHERN RAILWAY PICTURES
Adapted from the *Atlas of the Historical Geography of the United States*

territory. This greatly complicated the transportation problem, as the waterways which had served so well hitherto did not penetrate to the new settlements. The early Piedmont farms were largely self-sufficing, and relatively little trade was carried on either among themselves or with other regions. As the economy of the Piedmont matured, however, and came to be based more on the export of cotton and tobacco, the demand for adequate outlets became strong. The merchants of the coastal commercial towns joined the Piedmont farmers in their agitation, so eager were they to increase their trade with the up-country. The planters and farmers of the Coastal Plain were apathetic and in many cases even opposed, since their own transportation needs were fairly well satisfied by the waterways and since they were little disposed to pay taxes to increase the competition of Piedmont products with their own. This conflict over internal improvements was the most important factor in the intense political struggle between the Coastal Plain and the Piedmont in the Southeastern States between 1815 and 1835, a struggle which ended in the victory of the Piedmont.

The story of the historical development of the southeastern water and railway system constitutes one of the most interesting and valuable chapters in all the region's struggles for expansion and adequacy. Suffice it to say here only that from the coming of the railroads in the early 1830's there elapsed scarcely three decades until the Southeast had a fairly adequate railroad system. Not only had the barriers of the Appalachians been mastered through fine skill and technology, but the network of roads and connections made it possible for a traveller or a bill of goods to go down the coast from New York to Savannah much after the fashion of the present Atlantic Coast Line. Most of the Piedmont was accessible to railroads with a not unreasonable haul over roads which were still likely to be very poor; the Mississippi had been paralleled by a line which brought New Orleans into direct communication with Chicago and Cleveland; and New Orleans and Memphis, by somewhat indirect routes, were brought into contact with the territory east of the mountains.

This railroad system had been built up in the South during a brief twenty years, from 1840 to 1860, yet even during that time it had had an important effect upon the southern economy. It had accelerated the flow of population to the southern Mississippi Valley. By opening the way to market and to the sources of foodstuffs in the West and North, it had hastened the replacement of the subsistence agriculture of the Piedmont with a staple economy based on cotton. The nascent industrialism of the Piedmont as well had been stifled under the flow of cheap manufactured goods from the Northeast, and, in fact, the specialized cotton economy was given a closer grip upon the whole region. To the old southeastern towns whose

The Railroad Picture of the 1920's

Adapted from Edward C. Kirkland, *A History of American Economic Life*

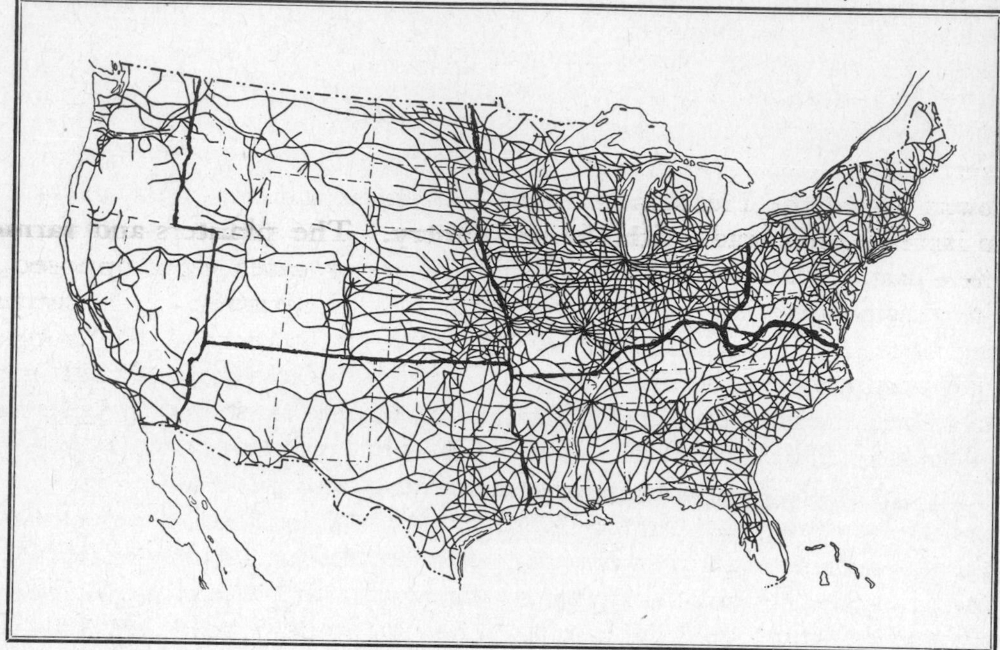

Miles of Railroad in the States and Regions, Year Ended December 31, 1933

(Excluding Switching and Terminal Companies)

STATE AND REGION	Total Miles	Per Cent total mileage in United States
Southeast	*35,512*	*20.97*
Virginia	3,478	1.80
North Carolina	3,031	2.02
South Carolina	2,354	1.52
Georgia	4,394	2.67
Florida	4,090	2.23
Kentucky	2,582	1.56
Tennessee	2,884	1.59
Alabama	4,219	2.11
Mississippi	2,958	1.66
Arkansas	3,478	1.94
Louisiana	2,044	1.87
Southwest	*15,977*	*11.76*
Oklahoma	5,231	2.74
Texas	8,589	6.87
New Mexico	1,771	1.20
Arizona	386	.95
Northeast	*18,945*	*14.14*
Maine	1,546	.88
New Hampshire	694	.46
Vermont	500	.42
Massachusetts	863	.81
Rhode Island	127	.08
Connecticut	777	.40
New York	4,668	3.36
New Jersey	725	.89
Delaware	......	.13
Pennsylvania	5,425	4.50
Maryland	596	.59
West Virginia	3,024	1.62
Middle States	*49,835*	*28.04*
Ohio	3,591	3.49
Indiana	3,351	2.87
Illinois	9,216	5.03
Michigan	5,051	3.14
Wisconsin	5,907	2.87
Minnesota	7,729	3.54
Iowa	8,119	3.90
Missouri	6,871	3.20
Northwest	*39,135*	*17.13*
North Dakota	5,142	2.15
South Dakota	4,153	1.72
Nebraska	5,755	2.48
Kansas	8,499	3.73
Montana	5,070	2.12
Idaho	2,621	1.19
Wyoming	1,839	.83
Colorado	4,268	2.02
Utah	1,788	.89
Far West	*10,822*	*7.95*
Nevada	980	.88
Washington	4,996	2.22
Oregon	2,405	1.48
California	2,441	3.37
United States	170,226	100.00

location was determined by water transportation, such as Norfolk, Richmond, Petersburg, Wilmington, Fayetteville, Charleston, Savannah, New Orleans, Vicksburg, Natchez, Nashville, Memphis, and Louisville, were added the new railroad towns, such as Knoxville, Chattanooga, and Atlanta.

Then came the automobile, which was the next great step in the evolution of the southern transportation system. This new agency of transportation, demanding roads passable in all weather and at high speeds, gave emphasis to the local agitation for good roads in the years before the World War. It was not until North Carolina passed her great Highway Act of 1921, however, that any of the Southeastern States began the building of a comprehensive state system. Other states soon followed, most of them financing their road construction with heavy bond issues, as North Carolina did. Some of them, such as Virginia, preferred to pay for the roads out of current revenue from gasoline and license taxes. North Carolina also established an example in providing that every county seat must be reached by a hard-surfaced state highway. Some such provision in the other states made it certain that the new transportation system would not serve only the wealthier metropolitan districts, but would reach the hitherto isolated rural sections as well. Construction proceeded at a rapid pace once the movement was launched, and by 1930 the Southeast was covered with a fairly adequate network of improved roads. North Carolina especially had an admirable system of fine concrete highways.

Turning now to a brief inventory of the transportation technology of the region, we begin with the railroads. In 1931, the Southeastern Region had 52,433.48 miles of railroad main track, or 2.05 miles per thousand population and 10.27 per hundred square miles. This compares well with the national total of 248,828.75 miles, or 2.03 per thousand population and 8.22 per hundred square miles. The Class I steam railroads of the Southern District (for which all following statistics will be given unless otherwise specifically stated) operated 46,116 miles of track. Numerically measured, the equipment of the southern railroads is about equal to that of other systems. On December 31, 1931, they owned 11,205 locomotives, 431,264 freight cars, and 7,979 passenger cars, a little less than a fifth of the locomotives and freight cars and a little less than a sixth of the national total of passenger cars. Although no statistics seem to be available to prove the point, it is probable that the roadbed and equipment of the southern roads is somewhat inferior in condition to the national standard.

Although the roads of the Southern District operate about a fifth of the track of the country, they did only 10.5 per cent of the passenger business in 1931, measured in passenger-miles; and passenger revenues comprised only 8.97 per cent of their total operating revenue, as compared with 13.14

State Variations in Automobile and Gas Figures

Adapted from *Automobile Facts and Figures*, 1934

STATE AND REGION	Total Motor Vehicle Registration, 1933	Gasoline Tax Receipts, 1933	Motor Vehicle Registration Receipts, 1933	Gasoline Tax Rates, 1933	Bus Census, 1933
Southeast	*2,897,865*	*$108,637,061*	*$ 38,169,498*		*26,156*
Virginia	344,704	11,080,040	6,090,279	5	2,401
North Carolina	382,308	14,769,602	5,356,126	6	4,714
South Carolina	162,735	6,679,326	2,503,367	6	1,634
Georgia	330,147	12,634,513	1,036,241	6	2,571
Florida	279,265	14,249,308	4,994,882	7	1,754
Kentucky	294,547	8,314,659	4,174,076	5	1,270
Tennessee	312,180	12,979,882	2,940,010	7	1,252
Alabama	206,361	8,033,141	3,382,455	6	2,391
Mississippi	164,688	5,801,725	1,870,396	6	4,089
Arkansas	188,242	5,989,429	1,768,850	6	1,357
Louisiana	232,688	8,155,436	4,052,816	5	2,723
Southwest	*1,819,613*	*43,488,577*	*17,444,508*		*7,083*
Oklahoma	451,712	10,064,685	3,382,455	4	2,270
Texas	1,201,762	28,479,350	12,747,489	4	3,347
New Mexico	76,643	2,265,510	666,748	5	639
Arizona	89,496	2,679,032	647,816	5	827
Northeast	*6,903,048*	*135,002,267*	*118,547,956*		*28,464*
Maine	168,173	4,080,371	2,909,237	4	564
New Hampshire	107,631	2,349,849	2,167,421	4	351
Vermont	73,576	1,766,152	2,072,717	4	369
Massachusetts	789,788	16,377,352	6,035,102	3	3,401
Rhode Island	136,261	1,880,972	2,198,342	2	357
Connecticut	314,751	4,811,630	7,850,589	2	1,196
New York	2,240,757	43,344,695	42,318,407	3	9,058
New Jersey	845,734	16,397,386	15,377,843	3	5,801
Delaware	51,099	1,127,330	1,014,333	3	272
Pennsylvania	1,635,019	30,739,117	29,184,792	3	4,777
Maryland	313,274	7,207,749	3,581,251	4	1,363
West Virginia	226,985	4,919,664	3,837,922	4	955
Middle States	*7,545,338*	*141,152,413*	*96,501,298*		*25,852*
Ohio	1,554,314	33,939,981	17,677,551	4	7,601
Indiana	770,071	16,283,202	7,846,883	4	7,144
Illinois	1,463,050	27,833,011	16,229,327	3	1,800
Michigan	1,077,209	19,458,458	18,560,314	3	2,027
Wisconsin	670,797	15,169,426	9,768,006	4	1,148
Minnesota	679,243	10,014,857	6,366,982	3	2,224
Iowa	632,292	9,372,343	10,695,407	3	1,990
Missouri	698,362	9,081,135	9,356,828	2	1,918
Northwest	*1,857,689*	*34,661,128*	*13,315,491*		*6,136*
North Dakota	153,889	1,923,951	1,382,008	3	598
South Dakota	169,249	3,346,015	1,459,027	4	396
Nebraska	390,651	7,706,261	1,721,834	4	948
Kansas	517,987	7,731,819	3,056,837	3	816
Montana	110,245	2,751,303	1,070,104	5	467
Idaho	96,255	2,282,370	1,401,849	5	425
Wyoming	52,560	1,405,415	679,411	4	867
Colorado	266,491	5,324,996	1,746,823	4	1,097
Utah	100,362	2,188,998	797,598	4	522
Far West	*2,653,947*	*53,119,920*	*17,985,978*		*7,799*
Nevada	28,324	695,653	299,634	4	230
Washington	427,406	10,863,214	2,482,768	5	2,512
Oregon	239,410	6,343,891	5,337,147	4–5	775
California	1,958,807	35,217,162	9,866,449	3	4,282
United States	23,677,500	516,061,366	301,964,729		101,490

per cent for the nation as a whole. This condition is further reflected in the fact that the southern roads received only $2,150 passenger revenue per mile of road as compared with $3,228 for the nation. Conditions appear to be somewhat better in the freight service, as Class I southern roads carried nearly 70 billion ton-miles of freight in 1931, or 20.2 per cent of the national total, and even received a slightly larger revenue per mile from the freight service than the national average—$13,430 as compared with $13,414. This is misleading, however, as it includes the heavy coal-bearing roads of the Pocahontas region which serve the mines of West Virginia and Kentucky and are not representative of typical southern railroads. These systems, the Chesapeake and Ohio, the Norfolk and Western, and the Virginian, together with the Richmond, Fredericksburg and Potomac, which is included by the Interstate Commerce Commission in the Pocahontas region, provided $200,000,000 of the Southern District's freight revenue in 1931, or nearly one-third of the total, although they operated much less than one-sixth of the track. Without the Pocahontas region, the average freight revenue of the Southern District was only $10,394 per mile, as contrasted with $25,590 for the Central Eastern region, for instance, or with $33,394 for the Pocahontas region itself.

This light freight traffic, from which the southern roads, because of the even greater scarcity of passenger traffic, must rely for six-sevenths of their revenue, leaves many of the southern roads in very bad condition financially. Of the 11,782 miles of road in receivership in 1931, 6,334, or 53.8 per cent, were in the South. Of the 29 Class I railroads in the Southern District, excluding the Pocahontas region, 22 were not able even to pay interest on their bonded indebtedness out of their 1931 operating income, the only major systems able to do so being the Atlantic Coast Line and the Louisville and Nashville.

Next is a similar and equally brief consideration of the other means of transportation available to the Southeast. Of these the chief is, of course, the highways. The building of the road system of the Southeast is one of the most brilliant chapters in the remarkable record of construction in the South since the Civil War. By 1933 there were two-thirds of a million miles of state and local highways in the Southeast, 22.1 per cent of the national total. Of this amount nearly 93,000 miles, or 26.0 per cent of the national total was incorporated into the state system. The more exacting test of surfaced highways finds the Southeast again excelling, with 70,638 miles, 26.6 per cent of all the surfaced highways in the United States and more than in any other great region. It is true that, although it still occupies a high place, the Southeast does not rank as well in the mileage of high-type highways of concrete or similar structure. It has nearly 21,000

Regional Variations in Motor Vehicles, Highways, Gasoline Taxes

STATE AND REGION	South-east	South-west	North-east	Middle States	North-west	Far West	United States
Total registration of motor vehicles	2,897,865	1,819,613	7,052,838	7,545,338	1,857,689	2,653,947	23,827,290
Per cent of total registration	12.2	7.6	29.6	31.7	7.8	11.1	100.0
Number of passenger cars	2,473,815	1,535,121	6,086,057	6,599,547	1,588,325	2,333,177	20,600,543
Per cent of passenger cars	12.0	7.5	29.6	32.0	7.7	11.3	100.0
Number of trucks	424,050	284,492	966,781	945,791	269,364	320,770	3,226,747
Per cent of trucks	13.1	8.8	29.9	29.3	8.3	9.9	100.0
Number of busses (also included in "passenger cars")	26,156	7,083	28,820	25,852	6,136	7,799	101,747
Per cent of busses	25.8	7.0	28.3	25.5	16.09	7.7	100.0
Number of vehicles on farms	980,981	537,835	670,084	1,766,892	765,281	313,987	5,035,060
Per cent of vehicles on farms	19.5	10.5	13.3	35.0	15.2	6.2	.....
Number of trucks on farms	139,002	84,900	180,554	287,530	137,610	70,789	900,385
Per cent of trucks on farms	15.4	9.4	20.1	32.0	15.3	7.9	.....
Number of school busses	23,955	4,859	12,579	17.764	3,733	4,430	66,320
Per cent of school busses	36.2	7.3	19.0	26.8	5.6	6.7	.....
Number persons per car	8.8	5.0	5.5	4.5	4.0	3.6	5.2
Per cent of total cars and trucks	14.6	15.1	13.7	12.5	14.5	12.1	13.6
Number of persons per dealer	2,120	1,340	1,290	990	770	695	1,210
Gallons of gas consumed per $1,000 income	207	244	138	180	266	214	180
Total highway funds available (000 omitted)	$ 210,271	$ 81,367	$ 407,291	$ 314,944	$ 71,936	$ 87,767	$1,173,576
Per cent of highway funds	17.9	6.9	35.3	26.8	6.1	7.5	.....
Funds per mile of State system	$ 226	$ 206	$ 584	$ 424	$ 116	$ 452	$ 328
Per cent of auto taxes	17.9	7.4	31.0	29.4	6.4	8.7	.....
Auto tax compared with total tax	55.9	54.1	42.3	57.5	56.5	50.1	51.2
Auto tax per capita	$ 5.79	$ 6.75	$ 6.60	$ 7.25	$ 7.24	$ 8.70	$ 6.78
Auto tax per $1,000 income	$ 16.10	$ 12.80	$ 7.20	$ 9.50	$ 12.70	$ 8.90	$ 9.80
Total state and local miles of highway	667,609	380,012	327,804	743,581	694,023	196,038	3,009,066
Per cent of state and local miles of highway	22.1	12.6	10.9	24.6	23.0	6.5	100.0
Miles of state systems	92,951	39,550	69,859	74,508	61,928	19,414	358,210
Per cent of state systems	26.0	11.1	19.5	20.8	17.3	5.4	100.0
Miles of surfaced highways	70,638	22,226	51,244	70,351	37,033	14,568	266,060
Per cent of surfaced highways	26.6	8.4	19.3	26.4	13.9	5.5	100.0
Miles of high-type surface	20,941	12,346	29,548	37,853	3,326	5,721	109,735
Per cent of high-type surface	19.1	11.2	26.9	34.6	3.0	5.2	100.0
Per cent of state system surfaced	76.0	56.4	73.3	94.5	60.0	75.3	74.3
Per cent of state system high-type	22.5	31.1	42.3	50.9	5.4	29.4	30.6
Miles of state system per 1,000 people	3.64	4.45	1.81	2.30	8.37	2.24	2.94
Miles surfaced per 1,000 people	2.77	2.44	1.33	2.08	5.01	1.76	2.16
Miles high-type surface per 1,000 people	.83	1.36	.77	1.12	.46	.69	.89
Use, in 1,000 gallons consumed, per mile of state system	20.3	29.3	69.3	62.5	18.1	89.6	42.9
Miles of state system per $1,000,000 wealth	2.42	2.42	.60	.74	2.28	.79	1.11
Miles surfaced per $1,000,000 wealth	1.85	1.36	.44	.70	1.36	.61	.82

The above figures are compiled largely from *Automobile Facts and Figures, 1934.* The years vary with some of the items. All data, however, apply to the period from the late 20's to 1933, and for comparative purposes by regions they are representative. Seven of the eleven Southeastern States expend a larger proportion of government funds for highways than does the nation as a whole: national percentage, 41.1; highest Southeastern States: Tennessee, 69; South Carolina, 57; Arkansas, 62; Louisiana, 56.8; North Carolina, 48.3. Low States: Mississippi, 19.2; Alabama, 24.3. See page 126. Note also the Southeast's highest rate per million dollars' wealth for surfaced highways: likewise the Southeast has the largest number of miles of surfaced highways of any of the six regions.

miles of this type of road, 19.1 per cent of the total in the country. Because of the lack of intraregional economic specialization and the peculiar distribution of the population pointed out above, the southeastern highways, like the railroads, bear light traffic. Some 20,300 gallons of gasoline per mile of state highway were consumed in 1933 in the Southeast, as compared with 42,900 gallons for the United States and 89,600 gallons for such a region as the Far West. This would indicate that the highways of the Southeast bear less than half as heavy a load as those of the rest of the country. In view of this light traffic and of the need of the Southeast for an extensive and, therefore, relatively inexpensive road system, it is probable that the highway commissions of the region acted wisely in investing a somewhat less proportion of the funds available in heavy highways than has been the practice in other regions.

To understand the problems of the Southeast's highway system, we must consider that system in relation to the region's wealth and income. And here the Southeast's achievement in highway construction becomes even more clear. In 1933 the region possessed 2.42 miles of state highway for each million dollars' wealth as compared with 1.11 for the United States as a whole; 1.85 miles surfaced as compared with .82; and .55 miles of high-type road as compared with .34 miles for the nation. These figures indicate that the Southeast's highway system has necessarily constituted a heavy financial burden on its people. It is true that automobile taxes, which are the source of highway revenue, are only $5.79 per capita in the Southeastern States and are $6.78 throughout the whole country; but, if again we turn to a comparison with wealth and income, we shall see that the burden has indeed been heavy. Automobile taxes constitute 55.9 per cent of the total state taxes in the Southeast, whereas they are but 51.2 per cent of the state taxes levied in the country. Again, 1.61 per cent of the Southeast's total income is consumed in automobile taxes, more than in any other region and over two-thirds again as much as the national average of .98 per cent. For all this heavy taxation, however, the Southeast is still somewhat deficient in funds available for construction and maintenance. In 1933 there was at hand in highway funds in the Southeast $226 for each mile of state highways, as compared with $328 for the United States as a whole and $528 for such a region as the Northeast.

It is necessary to consider the "rolling stock" of the highway system as well as the roads themselves. It is a common conception that the Southeast spends far too much of its money on cars and gasoline, but statistics hardly bear this out. Of the 23,800,000 cars in the United States in 1933, the Southeast had less than 2,900,000, or only 12.2 per cent. This deficiency in vehicles is shown further when we consider that there are 8.8

Regional Variations in Motor Vehicles for Special Purposes

Adapted from *Automobile Facts and Figures.* National Chamber of Commerce, 1934

STATES AND REGION	Total Passenger Cars 1933	Total Motor Trucks 1933	Passenger Cars on Farms 1930	Motor Trucks on Farms 1930	Trailer Registrations 1933	Number of School Busses 1933
United States	20,467,495	3,210,005	4,134,615	900,304	471,677	66,306
Southeast	*2,473,815*	*424,050*	*841,979*	*139,002*	*53,707*	*22,955*
Virginia	288,048	56,656	88,463	19,459	1,845	1,693
North Carolina	332,648	49,660	132,876	18,558	13,012	4,418
South Carolina	144,940	17,795	61,754	6,966	1,764	1,554
Georgia	278,935	51,212	88,479	15,967	5,836	2,304
Florida	234,246	45,019	26,387	12,203	9,567	1,348
Kentucky	262,436	32,111	86,784	7,188	......†	800
Tennessee	278,332	33,848	89,022	9,039	2,982	920
Alabama	176,523	29,838	73,634	12,838	4,007	2,255
Mississippi	131,764	32,924	85,563	16,503	850	4,010
Arkansas	155,262	32,980	65,935	11,000	6,887	1,265
Louisiana	190,681	42,007	43,082	9,281	6,957	2,388
Southwest	*1,535,121*	*284,492*	*452,935*	*84,900*	*43,229*	*4,859*
Oklahoma	385,755	65,957	127,448	23,930	4,184	1,770
Texas	1,013,086	188,676	300,176	52,580	36,073	2,150
New Mexico	61,353	15,290	15,395	5,328	983	433
Arizona	74,927	14,569	9,916	3,062	1,989	506
Northeast	*5,952,737*	*950,311*	*489,470*	*180,473*	*42,166*	*12,565*
Maine	132,902	35,271	26,227	10,781	5,893	475
New Hampshire	87,759	19,872	11,079	4,539	1,922	244
Vermont	65,652	7,924	18,620	5,035	683	217
Massachusetts	689,934	99,854	17,638	9,572	525	1,205
Rhode Island	118,296	17,965	2,569	1,701	92	100
Connecticut	262,187	52,564	13,154	6,344	1,816	635
New York	1,942,249	298,508	141,916	58,974	13,545	4,821
New Jersey	723,506	122,228	22,371	14,753	3,162	1,600
Delaware	42,614	8,485	8,724	2,996	912	208
Pennsylvania	1,415,522	212,497	152,222	47,062	10,139	1,760
Maryland	278,546	34,728	37,972	11,284	1,383	820
West Virginia	193,570	33,415	36,978	7,432	2,094	480
Middle States	*6,586,201*	*959,137*	*1,479,362*	*287,530*	*215,117*	*17,764*
Ohio	1,396,125*	158,189*	201,552	39,210	61,156	5,510
Indiana	653,710	116,361	154,556	30,037	27,996	6,500
Illinois	1,276,864*	186,186*	192,873	40,371	9,228	105
Michigan	955,570*	121,639*	150,922	36,768	78,998	850
Wisconsin	566,450	104,347	176,764	51,786	2,565	705
Minnesota	580,113	99,130	185,717	36,557	19,648	1,800
Iowa	562,802	69,490	240,512	32,669	2,416	1,772
Missouri	594,567*	103,795*	176,466	20,132	13,110	522
Northwest	*1,586,444*	*271,245*	*627,671*	*137,610*	*40,241*	*3,733*
North Dakota	128,547*	25,342*	78,798	16,990	143	552
South Dakota	146,485	22,764	81,923	14,816	9,693	300
Nebraska	336,704	53,947	141,144	26,045	14,727	156
Kansas	445,583*	72,404*	171,018	33,648	3,847	500
Montana	82,765*	27,480*	38,166	14,615	483	348
Idaho	81,371	14,884	33,966	6,281	10,039	377
Wyoming	41,917	10,643	12,824	4,108	20	523
Colorado	239,058	27,433	52,258	16,918	832	576
Utah	84,014	16,348	17,574	4,189	457	401
Far West	*2,333,177*	*320,770*	*243,198*	*70,789*	*77,217*	*4,430*
Nevada	22,397	5,927	2,921	1,241	631	126
Washington	364,858	62,548	55,995	18,836	4,849	1,770
Oregon	207,202	32,208**	47,440	9,741	1,750‡	450
California	1,738,720	220,087	136,842	40,971	69,987	2,084

*Busses not included. †Classified with trucks. **Includes 11,700 light delivery cars. ‡Estimated.

persons to each automobile in the Southeast and 5.2 to each in the country as a whole. Nor is an undue proportion of the wealth of the Southeast invested in motor cars. There are 75.5 vehicles for each $1,000,000 wealth in the Southeast; 73.3, in the nation. Residents of the Southeast seem to use their cars somewhat more than do those of other regions, consuming 652 gallons of gasoline per car in 1933 as compared with 645 for the whole country. Also a higher proportion of their income goes for the purchase of gasoline, 207 gallons out of each $1,000 income as compared with the nation's 180 gallons, but the difference is not great.

The distribution of these vehicles as to class and as to farm or city use is interesting. The motor transportation system of the Southeast would seem to be used slightly more for business and less for pleasure than in the rest of the country, as indicated by the fact that, in 1933, 14.6 per cent of the motor vehicles in the Southeast were trucks; in the United States, only 13.5 per cent. The heavy proportion of busses in the Southeast, over a fourth of those in the entire country, is a result of the use of motor transportation in an effort to solve the problem of providing adequate school facilities for a scattered rural population. Almost all the states of the Southeast have adopted the policy of consolidating their rural schools and providing the children with free transportation by bus to the school door. The extent of this practice is indicated by the fact that in the Southeast are nearly 24,000 school busses, well over a third of those in the nation. The predominance of the rural population is also shown in the proportion of cars on farms in the Southeast, 33.8 per cent as compared with 21.1 per cent in the United States. Only 14.2 per cent of the vehicles on farms in the Southeast are trucks, however, as compared with 17.9 per cent in the country as a whole.

Other forms of transportation in the Southeast are unimportant when compared with the railroads and highways. Waterways, other than the Mississippi, so significant in earlier periods, bear only a very small traffic. On the Mississippi itself, however, water transportation seems to have experienced something of a renascence in the last decade. The Department of Commerce presents the figures on river traffic in such a form that it is impossible to arrive at any exact total of tonnage carried, but it would seem that traffic on the lower Mississippi nearly doubled during the decade from 1923 to 1932. This is due chiefly to the great increase in petroleum carried on the river. Even so, the total is very, very small as compared with the tonnage by the Southern Railroad. Airways have penetrated the Southeast in good number, as is shown in the through airways picture, but this is still an experimental form of transportation bearing as yet little definitive relation to the region's economy.

Per Capita Value of Manufactured Products in the Southeast, by Subregions, 1930

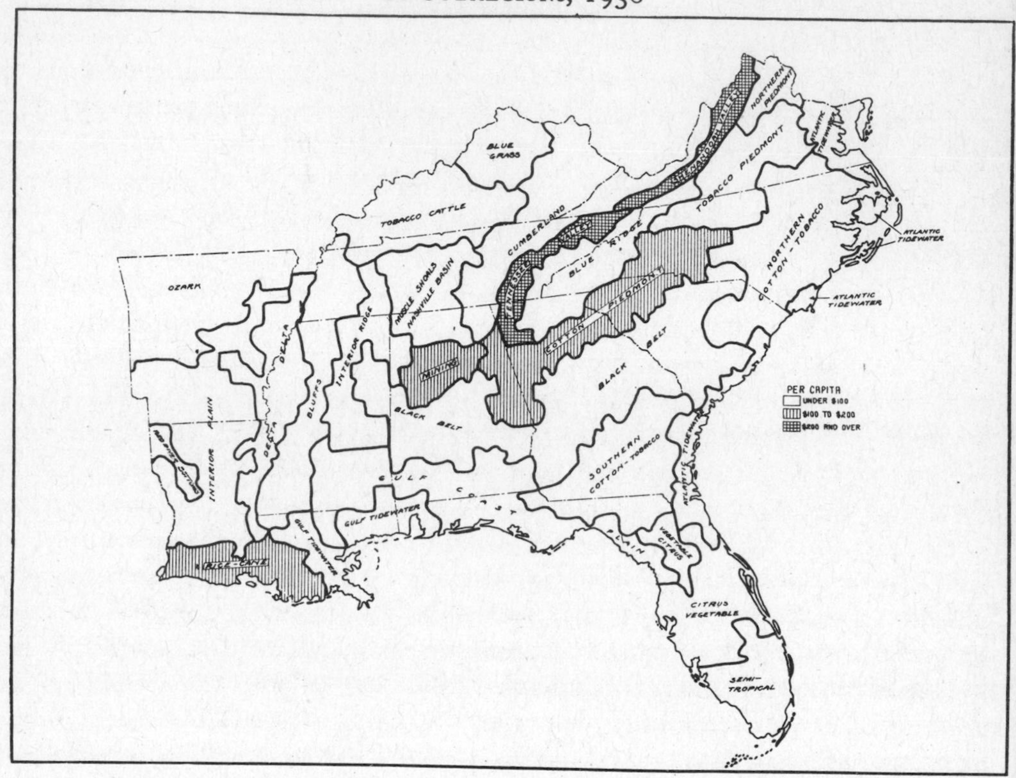

County Medians of Selected Indices of the Subregions in the Southern Region of the United States

Subregions	Per Capita Value Manufactured Products	Per Capita Retail Trade	Inhabitants Per Income Tax Return	Inhabitants Per Telephone	Inhabitants Per Passenger Car	Persons Per National Magazine
Cotton Piedmont	$143	$153	239.5	42.0	10.1	16.1
Shenandoah Valley	245	201	101.0	13.4	7.1	7.5
Tennessee Valley	240	196	175.0	29.4	9.4	15.7
Atlantic Tidewater	64*	138	198.5	44.6	7.9	15.1
Northern Piedmont	15*	170	108.0	19.1	6.3	11.6
Tobacco Piedmont	54*	131	181.0	42.7	8.5	16.1
Blue Ridge Mountains	17*	99	592.0	68.0	16.8	27.8
Cumberland Mountains	3*	92	515.5**	54.3	20.4	32.5
Blue Grass	16*	208	126.0	13.9	6.9	11.5
Tobacco-Cattle	25*	124	455.0	17.1	11.3	18.6
Muscle Shoals–Nashville Basin	29*	142	331.0	26.1	9.8	20.0
Bluffs	30*	170	206.5	38.5	10.9	20.0
Northern Cotton and Tobacco	88*	155	256.0	57.0	10.5	18.5
Southern Cotton and Tobacco	62	124	380.0	61.9	14.3	23.6
Black Belt	57*	121	342.0	55.0	13.5	21.8
Citrus-Vegetable	78	291	57.0	22.6	5.2	4.0
Vegetable-Citrus	55*	174	196.5	83.4	9.0	13.8
Semi-Tropical	52*	349	53.0	43.4	5.3	4.2
Gulf Coast Plain	70*	152	344.0	73.0	13.3	25.2
Mining	114	181	348.0	37.0	11.6	27.3
Gulf Tidewater	89*	167	144.5	53.2	11.0	14.3
Interior Ridge	38*	167	521.0	43.7	12.6	27.3
Delta	25*	178	151.0	68.6	13.5	25.2
Ozarks	25*	152	314.0	34.9	13.4	19.5
Interior Plain	53*	186	184.0	32.4	12.0	17.5
Red River Bottoms	0*	119	211.5	96.1	14.5	23.8
Rice-Cane	114*	136	70.0	62.1	13.3	29.6

*More than 10 per cent of counties with no manufacturing.
**More than 10 per cent of counties with one or no returns.

A special aspect of the region's technical relationships in the matter of transportation is that of freight rates and their relation to the economic development of the Southeast. Here again status and prospect are closely interrelated with problem. For differentials in freight levels have their bearing upon many of the socio-economic deficiencies catalogued against the region, such as wages and income, standards of living, and consumer's power. Some of these problems have been pointed up by G. L. Tillery in his studies and advocacy for the equalization of rate levels on behalf of southeastern development. Some of these may be illustrated on the background of regional freight rate territories and comparisons between specified regions.

For rate-making purposes, the whole country east of the Rockies is divided, roughly speaking, by the Mississippi River, and subdivided along a line from Norfolk via the Virginian Railway, Roanoke, the Norfolk & Western Railway, the Ohio River, up the Mississippi to St. Louis, and thence along the St. Louis-San Francisco Railway and the southern boundary lines of Missouri and Kansas. Basic first-class scales are lower north than south of the subdividing line. All other classes of freight take percentages of first-class, except where special rates apply. Taking the upper and lower Mississippi, respectively, the east bank territory has a lower rate level than the west bank territory. The territories have names which, given in the order of their rate levels from low to high, are as follows: the bottom level is the "Official" territory, east of the upper Mississippi River. Next in order are: the lower middle Western Trunk Line, west of the upper Mississippi River; upper middle Southeastern, east of the lower Mississippi River; top level Southwestern, west of the lower Mississippi River.

Something of the problem character of the situation may be illustrated by a simple comparison. From the North Carolina coast to Memphis and down to the Gulf is approximately 1500 miles, traversing North Carolina, Tennessee, and Mississippi, whose combined areas equal that of Illinois, Indiana, Ohio, Delaware, and Connecticut. The three Southeastern States have 141,313 square miles, inhabited by 7,796,653 people. But Illinois, with 56,665 square miles, has approximately the same population, the number being 7,630,654. According to the Census of Manufactures for 1929, Illinois has 15,333 establishments employing 691,555 wage earners, as against 8,563 establishments employing 390,312 wage earners in the Southeastern States named. In that same year the average wage earner produced a value added by the manufacture to the cost of his raw materials amounting to 102.5 per cent in these three Southeastern States as against 91.6 per cent in Illinois. In accomplishing this the southeastern wage earner

State and Regional Variations of Concentration of Twenty-nine Iron and Steel Industries and Sixteen Food Products Industries

Number of States in Each Concentration Determined by Number of Employees per 1,000 Population, 1929. Adapted from Frederic B. Garver and others, *The Location of Manufactures in the United States, 1899-1929.*

IRON AND STEEL INDUSTRIES	Southeast	Southwest	Northeast	Middle States	Northwest	Far West	Total
Iron and steel basic industry	..	..	1	1	..	..	2
Blast furnace	1	..	1	1	..	..	3
Steel works and rolling mills	..	..	1	1	..	..	2
Agricultural implements	..	..	..	4	..	..	4
Bolts, nuts, washers, and rivets	..	..	4	1	..	..	5
Cars, electric and steam railroad	..	..	3	3	..	..	6
Cash registers	..	..	..	2	..	..	2
Cast iron pipe	1	..	1	..	..	..	2
Electrical machinery	..	..	5	2	..	..	7
Engines	..	..	3	5	..	..	8
Forgings	..	..	3	4	..	..	7
Foundry and machine-shop products	..	..	6	5	..	..	11
Gas machines	..	..	5	1	..	..	6
Hardware	..	..	1	3	..	..	4
Machine tools	..	..	3	2	..	..	5
Motor vehicles	..	..	..	2	..	..	2
Motor-vehicle bodies	..	..	..	4	..	..	4
Plumbers' supplies	..	..	4	3	..	..	7
Pumps and pumping equipment	..	..	2	3	..	1	6
Ship- and boatbuilding	2	..	9	1	..	3	15
Steam fittings	..	..	5	1	..	..	6
Steel barrels	..	..	1	3	..	1	5
Stoves and ranges	1	..	..	5	..	..	6
Structural and ornamental iron and steel work	..	..	3	5	..	2	10
Textile machinery	..	..	2	..	..	..	2
Tin cans	..	..	3	2	..	1	6
Wire	..	..	3	2	..	..	5
Wirework	..	..	4	4	..	..	8
Wrought pipe	..	..	1	4	..	..	5
FOOD PRODUCTS INDUSTRIES							
Beverages	5	1	6	5	1	..	18
Bread and other bakery products	..	..	7	3	..	..	10
Butter	..	..	1	4	8	4	17
Canning and preserving	..	..	4	2	1	3	10
Cheese	..	..	2	1	..	1	4
Chocolate and cocoa products	..	..	3	..	..	..	3
Coffee and spice, roasting and grinding	2	..	4	4	2	2	14
Condensed and evaporated milk	..	1	2	3	3	3	12
Confectionery and chewing gum	..	..	4	3	1	1	9
Flour and other grain-mill products	2	1	1	6	8	3	21
Ice, manufactured	11	3	4	4	3	1	26
Ice cream	..	..	9	4	1	2	16
Salt	1	..	1	2	2	1	7
Slaughtering and meat packing	..	..	..	4	3	..	7
Sugar, entire industry	4	1	2	1	5	2	15
Tobacco, cigars, and cigarettes	3	..	3	..	..	..	6

Deficiencies in capital, in technology, in freight rates, in markets, in labor, are all involved in the prospect of readjustment in the industrial Southeast. Tennessee Valley and Birmingham steel area, Tennessee coal and Alabama coal, water power over against coal—these are some of the factors involved.

had at his disposal fuel and purchased electric energy costing $112, as against $221 per wage earner in Illinois.

The respective costs of the raw materials per wage earner were $2,808 and $4,626, and of the value added thereto by manufacture, $2,878 and $4,237. But the southeastern wage earner, in spite of the efficiency apparently indicated by his ability with less mechanical aid to more than double the value of his raw material, was held down by the cheap rawness of his materials, and was able to derive therefrom an average wage of only $817 as against the $1,482 of his Illinois neighbor. The latter was manipulating more valuable goods to a higher and finer finish with more mechanical help. Out of his higher wage the man in Illinois buys the cheap products of his southeastern neighbor. The latter, out of his lower wage, buys the costly products of his Illinois neighbor. Therefore, the South, wearing its economic strait-jacket of cotton, finds this another of its many problems. Basic to its solution are considerations relating to the Northeast, to technical problems involved, to political problems, and to regional planning, special aspects of which will be treated in the last chapter.

What the newer developments in power, or the work of the Tennessee Valley Authority, may mean to the Southeast is also largely a matter of technical development. So, too, is the possible development of the Birmingham steel region. A recent announcement of the United States Steel Corporation, which received but slight attention, has great significance for the future of the Birmingham district in relation to the entire southern regions. To obviate the anomalous competition which has prevailed in the past between its subsidiary companies, the corporation plans to rationalize its distributive machinery on a regional basis. The productive and administrative set-up of the dozen or so subsidiaries is to remain intact, but their separate sales organizations are to be coalesced in regional departments. Four regions are recognized, with sales headquarters for each established at Pittsburgh, Chicago, Birmingham, and San Francisco. Except in the Pacific Coast Region, which lacks extensive productive equipment, only products regionally manufactured are to be distributed within a certain region, so that no longer will subsidiaries be permitted to conduct wasteful raids back and forth in each other's territory. Extra-regional products will be barred from a region except where the demand arises for a product not manufactured by the subsidiary or subsidiaries whose plants are located within the region.

Since the Tennessee Coal, Iron and Railroad Company of Birmingham is the only corporation subsidiary within the region assigned to the Birmingham sales office, an area nearly coextensive with the Southern Region, corporation customers in the South will hereafter receive Birmingham

SUPPLY OF PHYSICIANS PER 10,000 POPULATION, 1930

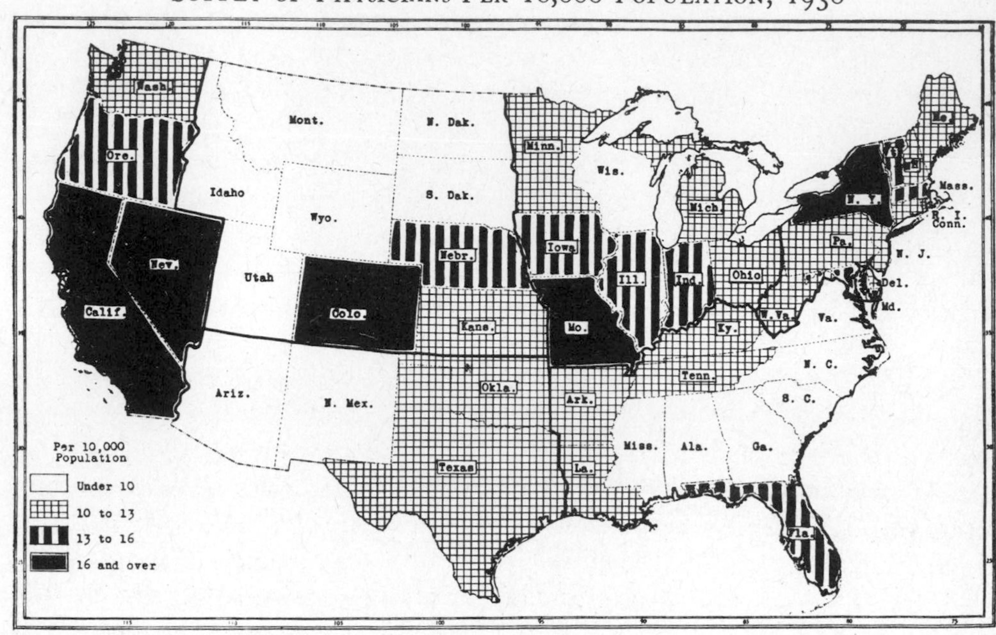

HOSPITAL BEDS PER 1,000 POPULATION, 1930

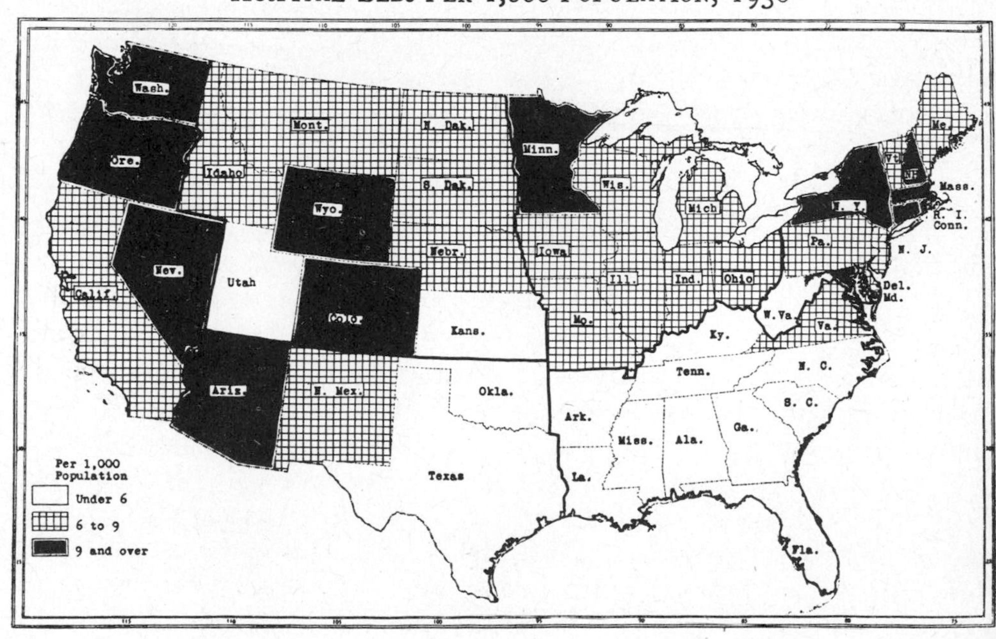

products exclusively, except in the case of a few products such as welded pipe and rolled steel car wheels, which the Tennessee Company at present lacks facilities to produce. This regional reorganization of the corporation is in effect a grant of autonomy to the Birmingham district, the development of which has been to a certain extent retarded in the interest of other producing centers.

Technology, however, after all is also a social product and process, resting upon the cultural heritage of technical arts and upon the conditioning social environment. In the current modern civilization, social science and social technology are increasingly important in the development of capacity and in the attainment of mastery over a rapidly changing environment.

Tremendous progress has been made in the application of the social sciences to human relationships and problems. The picture of such progress, however, has ordinarily not been viewed as one of social science and technology so much as it has been thought of as just another American institution or way of doing things. Thus, child welfare, with its extraordinary range, knowledge, and technical skill, has made its advances through technical and practical ways of promoting the public good through the special avenue of the child. Mothers' Aid in all the states, with its multiplied ways of contributing to the conservation of home and children, is an example of one phase of child welfare, which has been for a long time in America a very popular social technology. The prevention of delinquency, the elimination of physical defects, the care of the dependent, the cottage system of orphans' home administration, and scores of other ways of caring for children are no less techniques because they appear as popular institutional modes of work.

So, too, there are new *governmental techniques*: city and town planning, city manager and commission form of government, civil service, codes of law, court psychological clinics, hours of labor regulation, and a hundred more. There are many *economic techniques*, such as auditing and public accounting, Federal Reserve System of banks, state and national bank system, building and loan associations, company housing, corporations, cooperatives, workmen's compensation, farm tenancy and share cropping, holding company, income tax systems, inheritance laws, insurance and investment, minimum wage laws, and a hundred more. There are other *social welfare techniques*, such as institutions for the care of the handicapped, juvenile courts, probation, community chest, family case work, boys' and girls' clubs and camps, child welfare societies, civic and social centers, legal aid societies, marriage regulations, maternity clinics and hospitals, supervised playgrounds, visiting nurses, hospitals and clinics, and scores of others. The

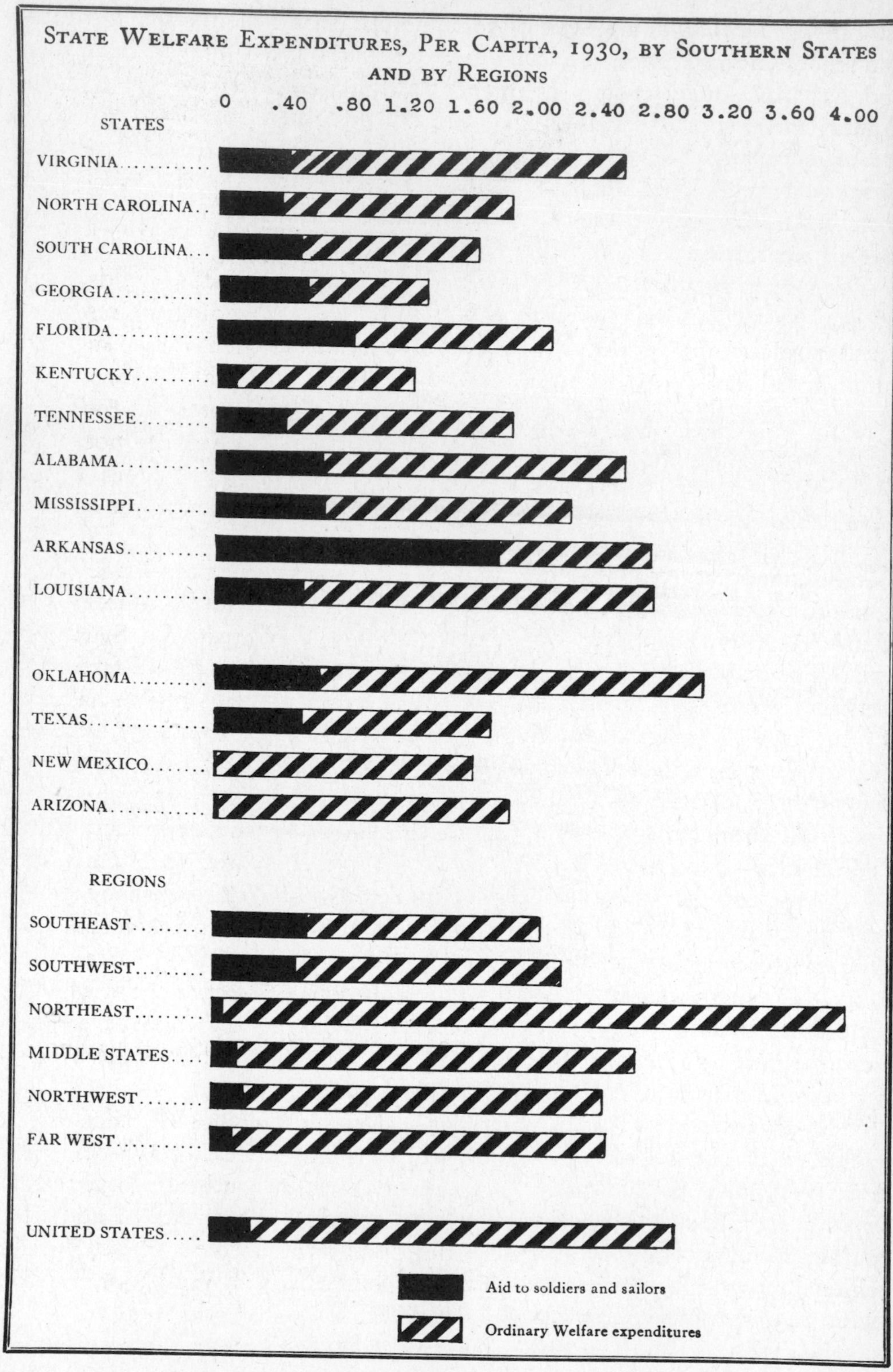

State Welfare Expenditures, Per Capita, 1930, by Southern States and by Regions

0 .40 .80 1.20 1.60 2.00 2.40 2.80 3.20 3.60 4.00

STATES

VIRGINIA

NORTH CAROLINA

SOUTH CAROLINA

GEORGIA

FLORIDA

KENTUCKY

TENNESSEE

ALABAMA

MISSISSIPPI

ARKANSAS

LOUISIANA

OKLAHOMA

TEXAS

NEW MEXICO

ARIZONA

REGIONS

SOUTHEAST

SOUTHWEST

NORTHEAST

MIDDLE STATES

NORTHWEST

FAR WEST

UNITED STATES

Aid to soldiers and sailors

Ordinary Welfare expenditures

educational techniques are even more numerous, such as university institutes and schools, adult education and university extension, graduate schools, state and national equalization, intelligence tests, parent-teachers' associations, kindergarten, special school taxes; and a score of other *special fields in which social technology* is the measure of the application of social science: social work, public welfare, public administration, public health, psychiatry, social insurance, jurisprudence, banking, business organization, the distribution of wealth, farming and the new agrarian culture.

Adequacy and deficiency in social technology, as in other fields, vary greatly by regions and in relation to natural and technological resources and the relation of the people and their institutions to them. The measure of technical lag is often most marked in terms of social waste. Some measures of such deficiency will be found in the later chapters on the institutions and folkways of the region. It is important, however, to note here samplings of deficiencies in the field of social technology. Thus, in the administrative part of public welfare, the adequacy of supervision of state welfare agencies may be measured by financial expenditures. In 1930 the Southeast lagged behind four of the other five regions, the percentage of the total cost devoted to supervision being as follows: Middle States 1.40, Far West 1.27, Northeast 1.15, Northwest .78, Southeast .69, Southwest .16. The Southeast lags also in the matter of staffing of state welfare institutions. As regards penal institutions, it is found that the region has next to the largest number of prisoners to each officer and employee, the figures for 1928 being: Northeast 7.9, Northwest 9.0, Middle States 11.7, Southwest 14.7, Southeast 16.4, Far West 17.8. In the number of psychologists and psychiatrists employed on prison staffs in 1928, the deficiency in the Southeast is clearly seen in the Southeast's two compared with 22 in the Northeast and 20 in the Middle States. Still another deficiency is the staffing of hospitals for the mentally sick. In 1927, 277 occupational therapists were found in the Northeast and 189 in the Middle States, while only 39 were found in the Southeast. So, too, with respect to social workers employed by state hospitals, the comparative deficiency may be seen in seven in the Southeast, with the Northeast and Middle States having together 118.

In the administration of parole to prisoners a similar deficiency is reflected in the following regional variations: Northeast 76.9 per cent, Far West 76.0, Middle States 73.0, Northwest 70.8, Southeast 26.3, Southwest 20.1. The Southeast also lags far behind in the matter of adequate parole administration, as shown by the number of paroles to each parole officer in 1928: Northeast 170, Middle States 214, Far West 239, Northwest 243, Southwest 657, Southeast 1,799.

The result of this deficiency in various aspects of social technology is reflected primarily in social waste. In anticipation of detailed comparative data, the following are samples: homicides among both whites and blacks, exceeding that of the highest records of larger cities of the North, waste and havoc wrought by false standards of "honor," wasted energies in factional and interstate jealousies, over-emphasis on intersectarian conflict, a large proportion of illiterates, absence of libraries, reading facilities, and reading habits, a lack of first rank universities, a lack of aesthetic influences, discouragement of original and creative work in literature, music, or other art, and a failure to regard distinguished effort; lack of interest in social and political science, lack of trained leadership for the industries and professions; poorly balanced work, strain on man power, waste in children and mothers on farm and in factory; waste in race conflict, in personal and feudal antagonisms, in fighting over small things; waste of intellectual power in emotional exhaustion, in stubborn opposition to progress; waste of vast possibilities of youth undeveloped and untrained, born, living, and moving through life without ever gaining a knowledge of their power and possibilities.

CHAPTER VI

AN AGRARIAN COUNTRY

In chapter i we have already discussed something of the meaning of agrarianism and certain of its aspects in the Southeast. We also presented a brief summary of the chief factors elemental to an understanding of the rural Southeast. We now continue our regional inventory through a somewhat more specialized consideration of the agrarian South. Here, as in other major aspects of the picture, several angles must be kept in mind. One of the first always is the regional picture on the screen of the whole national setting. Another must keep in mind the relation of the South to the international situation and to the present dilemma of agriculture in general in its conflict with industrial, scientific, and technological advance. It is not possible to isolate southern agriculture from the national or international picture if any sort of adequate inventory is to be provided. So also the rural predominance of the southern regions and the historical aspects of agrarianism in the Southeast are important in the problem of seeking balance between agriculture and industry in the nation.

Important also is the picturization of the southern regions in the total national picture, especially as compared with the other major regions selected as the basis for the Southern Regional Study. This offers an excellent opportunity for exploring also the possibilities of subregional classifications and is most important as a measuring scale for the main aspect of the study; namely, the inventory and characterization of the Southeast in representative aspects of its rural, agricultural, and agrarian life. Here as elsewhere a chief point of emphasis is that of capacity *versus* present deficiencies and the comparative indices of efficiency in the several regions. This comparative picture, again, emphasizes another important angle, namely, the characterization of the Southwest which tends to differentiate it from the Southeast. Thus, looking at the two southern regions in comparison with the other four regions, the rural picture everywhere predominates. In the Southeast there are more than two and a quarter million farms; in the Southwest nearly another million; and in the two about half of the farms and farm folk in the whole nation. So, too, in both southern regions, the chief industry, occupation, and income reflect the rural

Samplings of Indices Relating to Agrarian Culture

Number of Indices	Classification
1.	Value of all farm property per farm, 1930.
2.	Value per farm of farm implements and machinery, 1930.
3.	Value per farm of rural dwellings, 1930.
4.	Value of land and buildings per farm, 1930.
5.	Value of land and dwellings per owned farm, 1930.
6.	Value of land and buildings per tenant farm, 1930.
7.	Value of land and buildings per acre, 1930.
8.	Per cent increase and decrease in value per acre of farm real estate.
9.	Average value, by quartile distribution, per farm, of land and buildings, farms operated by tenants, 1930.
10.	Variations in ratio of farm tenancy.
11.	Comparative number of tenant farmers, 1900-1930.
12.	Comparative number of small-owner farmers, 1900-1930.
13.	Comparative number of middle class farmers, 1900-1930.
14.	Comparative number of planter farmers, 1900-1930.
15.	Average agricultural production per full-time worker (year of labor) 1924-1928.
16.	Horse power available per worker, 1924.
17.	Percentage distribution of income from agriculture, 1928.
18.	Percentage distribution of income of the farm population, 1929.
19.	Average gross income per farm per year, 1924-1928.
20.	Ratio of farm income to the total income, 1930.
21.	Gross farm income per capita, 1930.
22.	Cooperative sales—per cent of cash farm income, 1929.
23.	Ratio of taxes to value of land and buildings, farms operated by full owners, owning no other farm land, 1930.
24.	Ratio of mortgaged debt to values, farms operated by full owners, 1930.
25.	Acreage and per cent of total land in farms, 1930.
26.	Acreage, and per cent of the total, of crop land, 1930.
27.	Distribution of crop land lying idle or fallow, 1929.
28.	Per cent of total crop land harvested, operated by tenants, 1930.
29.	Acreage, and per cent of the total, of pasture land, 1930.
30.	Distribution of acreage of total pasturage, 1929.
31.	Distribution of acreage of plowable pasture, 1929.
32.	Land productivity classes—number of acres, Grade 1.
33.	Land productivity classes—number of acres, Grade 2.
34.	Land productivity classes—number of acres, Grade 3.
35.	Land productivity classes—number of acres, Grade 4.
36.	Land productivity classes—number of acres, Grade 5.
37.	Number of farms, 1930.
38.	Per cent increase and decrease in farms, 1920-1930.
39.	Average acreage per farm, 1930.
40.	Percentage distribution of farms under 100 acres, 1930.
41.	Percentage distribution of farms of 100-499 acres, 1930.
42.	Percentage distribution of farms of 500 acres and over, 1930.
43.	Change in percentage distribution of farms by size groups, 1900-1930.
44.	Distribution of the rural farm population, 1930.
45.	Per cent of the total population living on farms, 1930.
46.	Per cent increase and decrease of the rural farm population, 1920-1930.
47.	Extent of the rural farm population under 5 years of age per 1000 women, 15-44 years of age, 1930.
48.	Number and per cent of gainfully occupied persons, 10 years of age and over, in the extractive occupational group, 1930.
49.	Location of land used for crops.
50.	Location of land used for grazing-hay.
51.	Location of irrigated land.
52.	Location of arid-grazing land.
53.	Location of desert land.
54.	Variations in average annual precipitation.
55.	Variations in average length of the growing season.
56.	Estimate of destruction by erosion—extent of area with severely impoverished soil or soil washed off.
57.	Estimate of per cent of soil impoverishment and destruction by erosion.
58.	Tonnage, and per cent of the total, fertilizer consumption, 1910-1930.
59.	Amount, and per cent of farm income spent for fertilizer, 1929.
60.	Distribution of total tons of commercial fertilizer bought during the crop year of 1929.
61.	Distribution of total expenditure for all types of bought fertilizers during crop year of 1929.
62.	Comparative expenditures for fertilizers, feed, and labor, 1929.
63.	Number and per cent of self-sufficing farms.
64.	Number and per cent of part-time farms.
65.	Number and per cent of cotton farms.
66.	Number and per cent of truck farms.
67.	Number and per cent of dairy farms.
68.	Per cent of cash farm income from livestock, average, 1928-1930.
69.	Average value per farm of domestic animals, 1930.
70.	Number, value per head, and total value of all cattle and calves, including cows and heifers kept for milk, 1932.
71.	Milk cows and heifers—estimated number on farms, and value per head, 1932.
72.	Milk cows and heifers—per cent of total number of farm animals, 1932.
73.	Total number of purebred cattle, and number of cattle per capita rural population, 1929 and 1930.
74.	Percentage of gross income from all farm products derived from milk, 1929-1932.
75.	Number, and per cent of all farms, of farms reporting cows milked, 1929.
76.	Percentage increase and decrease in milk production, 1919-1924.
77.	Gallons of milk produced per capita, 1929.
78.	Proportion of whole milk sold, 1929.
79.	Dairy products—per cent in each state, and state percentage of the 1929 national total value.
80.	Percentage distribution of agricultural commodities — milk and butter.
81.	Beef cattle—per cent in each state, and state percentage of the 1929 national total value.
82.	Beef cattle—Per cent of state and regional total commodity value (gross income).
83.	Ratio of number of cattle and calves to the total number of farm animals, 1932.
84.	Regional distribution of agricultural production—milk and butter, 1929.
85.	Increase and decrease in number of sheep and lambs on farms, 1919-1929.
86.	Sheep and lambs—estimated number on farms and value per head, 1932.
87.	Per cent increase and decrease in number of swine on farms, 1919-1929.
88.	Hogs—per cent of state and regional total commodity value (gross income).
89.	Per cent increase and decrease in number of chickens on farms, 1919-1929.
90.	Chickens—estimated number on farms, and value per head, 1932.
91.	Chicken eggs produced—per cent of state and regional total commodity value.
92.	Horses and horse colts—estimated number on farms, and value per head, 1932.
93.	Mules and mule colts—estimated number on farms and value per head, 1932.
94.	Farm garden vegetables—per cent of state and regional total commodity value.
. . . .	
106.	Corn—per cent in each state, and state percentage of the 1929 national total value.
107.	Hay and forage—per cent of state and regional total commodity value.
108.	Distribution of acreage of alfalfa cut for hay, 1929.
109.	Per cent of farms having tractors, 1930.
110.	Per cent of farms having electric motors, 1930.
111.	Per cent of farms having gas engines, 1930.
112.	Per cent of farms having electric lights, 1930.
113.	Per cent of farms having piped water, 1930.
114.	Per cent of farms having telephones, 1930.
115.	Number and per cent of vehicles on farms.
116.	Number and per cent of trucks on farms.
117.	Number of farm agents, 1934.
118.	Number of home demonstration agents, 1934.
119.	Number and per cent of loans made to farmers in states most seriously affected by drought, 1931.
120.	Amount, and per cent of the total, of rental and benefit payments of the Agricultural Adjustment Association, through December 31, 1933.

and agricultural emphasis in measurable terms. Yet neither the Southeast's more than a million tenant farmers nor the Southwest's newly developed farm economy reflect much of the historical ideal of Jeffersonian agrarianism or the dream of the new agrarians. Nor did the political and economic theories of the early agrarianism give much hint of the complexities of southern agrarian problems of the present time: the hazards of farm life on millions of small and poorly equipped farms; hazards of financing, high interest and poor credits; of erosion and depleted resources; hazards of weather and of crop and animal disease in competition with depressed markets and prices. There was little in the picture to predict the battles against the odds of technology, of unbalanced economy, of changing international relations. There was no unromantic picture of a million prospective squatters and migrants, of lowering standards of living, nigh unto the bottom margin; no catalogue of economic and social deficiencies endangering the very existence of the rural South.

But more of this later. The scope and range of the subject and the extraordinary amount and diversity of materials at hand are such that the task of depicting the rural South sometimes seems to take the proportions of the whole story. It is necessary, therefore, in addition to the summary in Chapter I, to select special aspects for such further treatment as will give an authentic picture of the more fundamental phases. Among these selected aspects are: the size of farms and their distribution, presented, not only as a picture of status and trends, but as a foundation of next steps in the reconstruction of the cotton economy; the general distribution within the region and in the several regions, of the chief crops; the prospects for more adequate production of many of these crops, with special adaptations to subregional homogeneity in the Southeast, and consequently their relation to the changing cotton economy; special examination of such important developments as the dairy and livestock industry; and some special consideration of the problem and prospect of agrarianism and of practical planning for programs of optimum production.

We present first, then, the picture of the people in relation to the land as it is measured by the size of their farms. Other aspects have already been presented on pages 57-69. There are the three pictures: first, the regional variations within the nation; second, the contrast between the Southeast and Southwest in particular; and third, the emerging characterization of the Southeast. There will be still more specialized examination of smaller regions, which are in many respects inseparable and show regional variations due to a number of basic factors: geographic factors, soil, climate, topography; general cultural and folk-regional conditioning; labor conditions and supply; the mechanization of agriculture; markets and

Percentage Distribution of Farms by Size Groups, 1900-1930

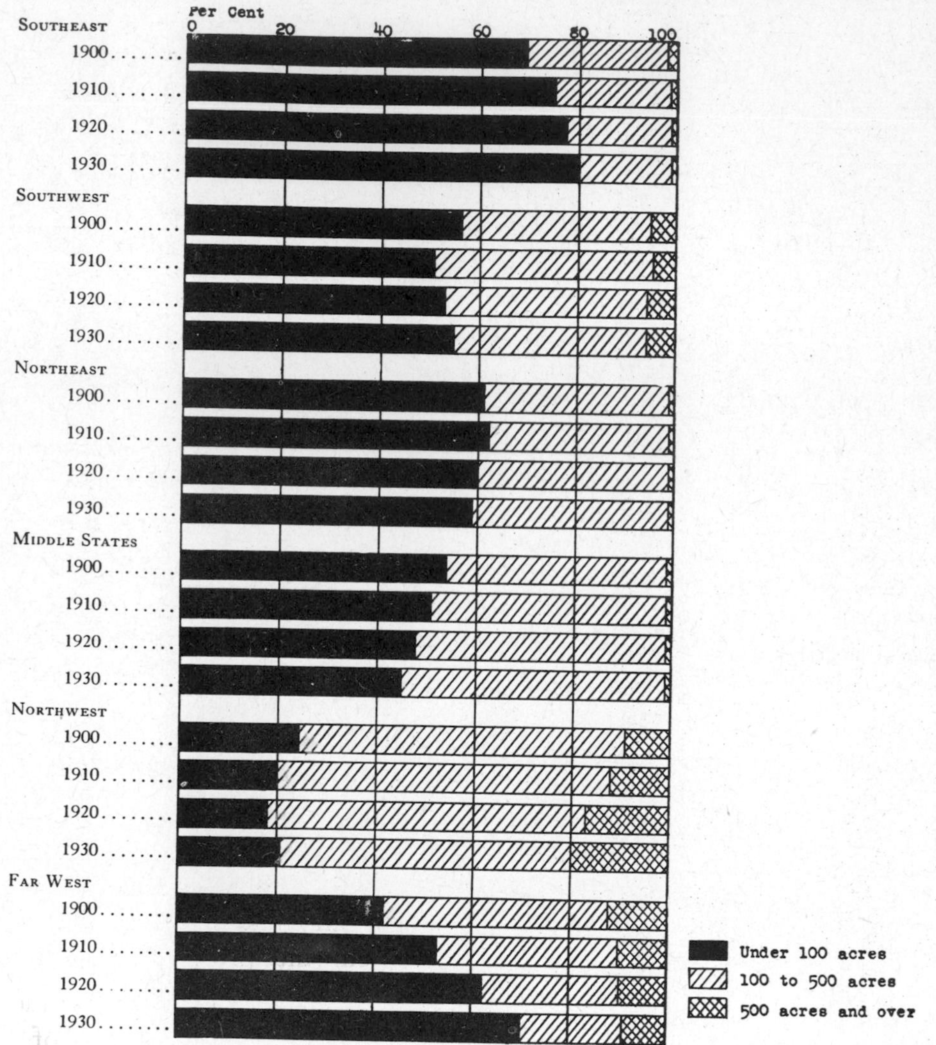

Percentage Distribution of Farms by Size, 1930

REGION	Under 100 Acres	100-499 Acres	Over 500 Acres
Southeast	79.7	19.4	.9
Southwest	54.9	39.5	5.6
Northeast	59.0	40.0	1.0
Middle States	45.4	53.6	1.0
Northwest	20.5	59.2	20.3
Far West	69.9	21.4	8.7

transportation, coöperatives; these and other factors affect the size of farms and in turn are affected by them. Edith Webb Williams has made a careful analysis of the size of farms in the several regions, the general findings of which follow.

Figures for the nation as a whole, however, here as in many other instances, have little significance because of such great variations. The Census of 1930 showed a decrease in the total number of farms in the United States since 1920; an increase in the number of acres in farms and consequently an increase in the average size of farms. Yet this is not true for the Southeast, and to some extent for the other older sections, the Northeast and the Middle States, which contributed to the total decrease in number of farms. Contrariwise, the number of farms increased in the Southwest, the Northwest, and in the Far West. The percentage increase in the three western regions has been smaller in each decade since 1900, with the exception of the Southwest, which showed a greater increase from 1920 to 1930 than in the previous decade.

The total number of acres in farms has decreased in the same regions of the country that have had a decrease in the number of farms. The decrease in area in farms has been constant throughout this century in the Northeast. In the Southeast there was a small increase in the first decade, with a steady decrease since then. A decrease appeared in the Middle States only in the last decade. In the three other regions there has been a steady increase in the number of acres in farms. For the whole nation the ratio of improved land to total land in farms was greater in 1930 than in 1900. The present tendency is toward a decreasing percentage of improved land. The Southeast and the Southwest, however, are exceptions. The actual number of improved acres in the Southeast decreased from 1920 to 1930, although the ratio went up. In the Northeast the actual number of improved acres has decreased along with the decrease in total acres in farms. The decreasing ratio in the Northwest is the result of the great increase in total acres in farms; the actual number of improved acres has increased throughout this century. The same thing was true of the Far West until the last decade, when there was some decrease in the number of improved acres.

More important than the average size of farms is the distribution of farms in the various size groups. The Census classifies farms into eleven size groups. For the purposes of this study the five groups under 100 acres and the two groups over 1,000 acres have been consolidated, leaving six groups: under 100 acres; 100 to 175 acres; 175 to 260 acres; 260 to 500 acres; 500 to 1,000 acres; and 1,000 acres and over. For the whole country the percentage of farms under 100 acres has slowly increased since

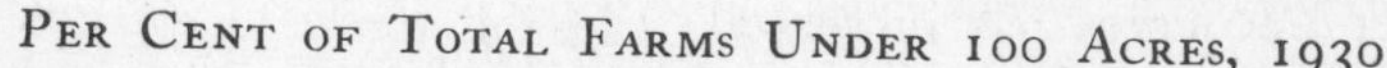

Per Cent of Total Farms Under 100 Acres, 1930

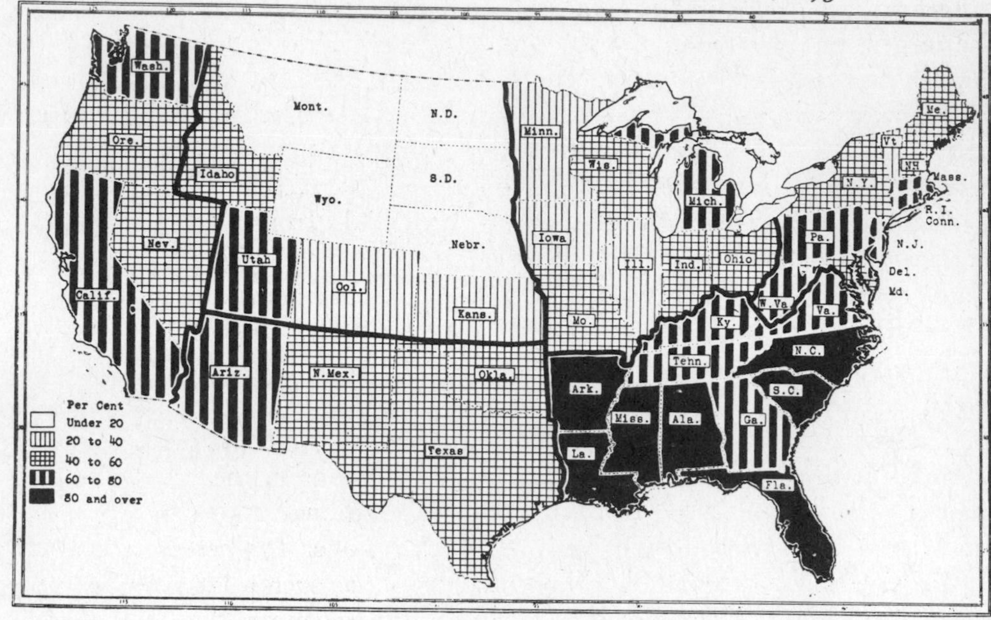

Chickens: Estimated Number on Farms and Value Per Head, 1931

STATE AND REGION	Number (in thousands)	Value Per Head	Total Value (in thousands)
Southeast	*80,624*	*$ .62*	*$ 50,123*
Virginia	10,214	.72	7,354
North Carolina	8,634	.70	6,043
South Carolina	4,167	.71	2,958
Georgia	7,355	.64	4,707
Florida	2,569	.85	2,183
Kentucky	11,039	.60	6,623
Tennessee	12,077	.57	6,883
Alabama	6,601	.54	3,564
Mississippi	6,590	.57	3,756
Arkansas	6,998	.47	3,289
Louisiana	4,380	.63	2,759
Southwest	*40,069*	*.56*	*22,426*
Oklahoma	14,653	.54	7,912
Texas	23,576	.56	13,202
New Mexico	1,128	.62	699
Arizona	712	.86	612
Northeast	*59,469*	*1.03*	*61,136*
Maine	2,159	1.25	2,698
New Hampshire	1,295	1.30	1,683
Vermont	1,064	1.15	1,223
Massachusetts	2,085	1.40	2,919
Rhode Island	382	1.35	515
Connecticut	2,197	1.20	2,636
New York	14,588	1.03	15,025
New Jersey	4,496	1.25	5,620
Delaware	1,454	.90	1,308
Pennsylvania	20,315	.98	19,908
Maryland	4,728	.90	4,255
West Virginia	4,706	.71	3,341
Middle States	*182,800*	*$ .69*	*$126,505*
Ohio	24,878	.75	18,658
Indiana	18,013	.71	12,789
Illinois	26,824	.73	19,581
Michigan	14,967	.81	12,123
Wisconsin	15,877	.72	11,431
Minnesota	17,783	.63	11,203
Iowa	34,050	.66	22,473
Missouri	30,408	.60	18,244
Northwest	*66,222*	*.57*	*37,761*
North Dakota	5,389	.52	2,802
South Dakota	8,923	.57	5,086
Nebraska	14,773	.57	8,420
Kansas	23,139	.54	12,495
Montana	2,690	.60	1,614
Idaho	2,789	.62	1,729
Wyoming	948	.68	644
Colorado	4,722	.63	2,974
Utah	2,849	.70	1,994
Far West	*30,182*	*.86*	*25,859*
Nevada	291	.90	261
Washington	8,751	.70	6,125
Oregon	4,073	.80	3,258
California	17,067	.95	16,213

1900; the percentage from 100 to 260 acres has decreased; and the percentage over 260 acres has increased. The changes in distribution of the different size groups in the total number of farms have not been marked, the largest increase being 1.9 per cent for farms under 100 acres, and the largest decrease being 3.5 per cent for farms from 100 to 175 acres. In spite of increases in the very small size groups, the total number of farms under 100 acres decreased slightly from 1920 to 1930. All other groups decreased at the same time, except those over 500 acres. From 1900 to 1910 the numbers in all the size groups increased; from 1910 to 1920 all except those from 100 to 175 acres and those from 175 to 260 acres; from 1920 to 1930 all groups decreased except those over 500 acres. These figures for the whole country give no indications of the changes in distribution by size groups that have occurred in the different regions, which in many cases have been marked.

Contrary to a widespread belief, the Southeast is, and has been, a region of small farms. In 1930, 79.9 per cent of all farms in the eleven Southeastern States were under 100 acres and an additional 12.9 per cent were from 100 to 175 acres, leaving only 7.4 per cent over 175 acres. Only 0.9 per cent were over 500 acres. No other region has such a large percentage of its farms in the smaller size groups. Furthermore, the number of farms under 100 acres has shown a constant increase since 1900, a condition found in no other part of the country except the Far West. In 1930 the Southeast had 51.0 per cent of the total farms in the United States under 100 acres, while it had only 38.0 per cent of the total number of farms, and 17.3 per cent of the total number of acres in farms. At the same time only 8.9 per cent of the farms 500 acres and over were in the Southeast. Even in 1900 no other region had as large a proportion of its farms under 100 acres as the Southeast, where the percentage was 68.9. The Northeast came next with 60.7 per cent. But these small farms have decreased in the Northeast in percentage since 1900 and in number since 1910. In the Southeast they have increased in number and percentage, the greatest increase (25 per cent or nearly 350,000 farms) occurring from 1900 to 1910. All larger farms in the Southeast have steadily decreased in actual numbers and in proportion to the total number of farms. The entire increase in the total number of farms, 16.0 per cent from 1900 to 1910 and 4.3 per cent from 1910 to 1920, is to be found in the under 100 acre group, and the decrease of 1.8 per cent from 1920 to 1930 is coupled with a 1.1 per cent increase in this group. Since 1910, there has been a decrease of 26 million acres in farms in the Southeast. However, in the decade when the greatest increase in small farms took place, 1900 to 1910, the total acreage in farms increased. This would

The National Farm Tenant Picture, 1930

State and Region	Number of Tenants			Per Cent of All Tenants	Per Cent of Farms in State and Region Operated by Tenants
	Total	White	Negro		
Southeast	*1,333,700*	*719,402*	*614,298*	*50.0*	*56.0*
Virginia	47,970	32,847	15,123	1.8	28.1
North Carolina	137,615	81,980	55,635	5.2	49.2
South Carolina	102,768	41,483	61,285	3.9	65.1
Georgia	174,390	98,755	75,635	6.5	68.2
Florida	16,737	11,375	5,362	.6	28.4
Kentucky	88,421	83,507	4,914	3.3	35.9
Tennessee	113,520	86,259	27,261	4.3	46.2
Alabama	166,420	88,567	77,853	6.2	64.7
Mississippi	225,617	65,660	159,957	8.4	72.2
Arkansas	152,691	84,610	68,081	5.7	63.0
Louisiana	107,551	44,359	63,192	4.0	66.6
Southwest	*435,650*	*358,608*	*77,042*	*16.4*	*58.5*
Oklahoma	125,329	113,635	11,694	4.7	61.5
Texas	301,660	236,385	65,275	11.3	60.9
New Mexico	6,330	6,301	29	.3	20.2
Arizona	2,331	2,287	44	.1	16.4
Northeast	*90,410*	*87,390*	*3,020*	*3.4*	*14.6*
Maine	1,755	1,754	1	.07	4.5
New Hampshire	796	795	1	.03	5.3
Vermont	2,409	2,405	4	.09	9.7
Massachusetts	1,442	1,439	3	.05	5.6
Rhode Island	415	415	....	.02	12.5
Connecticut	1,068	1,063	5	.04	6.2
New York	21,113	21,080	33	.79	13.2
New Jersey	3,948	3,822	126	.15	15.6
Delaware	3,282	2,867	415	.12	33.8
Pennsylvania	27,394	27,279	115	1.03	15.9
Maryland	11,441	9,235	2,206	.43	26.5
West Virginia	15,347	15,236	111	.58	18.6
Middle States	*512,306*	*506,437*	*5,869*	*19.2*	*31.5*
Ohio	57,604	57,166	438	2.2	26.3
Indiana	54,575	54,391	184	2.0	30.1
Illinois	92,482	92,054	428	3.5	43.1
Michigan	26,195	26,110	85	1.0	15.5
Wisconsin	33,121	33,107	14	1.2	18.2
Minnesota	57,638	57,630	8	2.2	31.1
Iowa	101,615	101,564	51	3.8	47.3
Missouri	89,076	84,415	4,661	3.3	34.8
Northwest	*245,560*	*245,088*	*472*	*9.2*	*37.8*
North Dakota	27,400	27,395	5	1.0	35.1
South Dakota	37,094	37,081	13	1.4	44.6
Nebraska	61,020	60,998	22	2.3	47.1
Kansas	70,326	69,935	391	2.7	42.4
Montana	11,628	11,622	6	.4	24.5
Idaho	10,559	10,552	7	.4	25.3
Wyoming	3,520	3,516	4	.1	22.0
Colorado	20,692	20,669	23	.8	34.5
Utah	3,321	3,320	1	.1	12.2
Far West	*46,715*	*46,507*	*208*	*1.7*	*17.6*
Nevada	445	444	1	.02	12.9
Washington	12,078	12,068	10	.5	17.0
Oregon	9,790	9,789	1	.3	17.8
California	24,402	24,206	196	.9	18.0
United States*	2,664,365	1,963,454	700,911	100.0	42.4

*Includes 22 white and 2 Negro tenants in the District of Columbia.

indicate that the land from the larger farms, in addition to the new land, was divided into small tracts which were listed as separate farms by the census takers. The additional acreage could have provided for only 13,764 farms of 50 acres, and there was an increase of 348,978 farms under 100 acres. Thus the break-up of the old plantations extended into the present century.

The more recent changes in southern agriculture should be emphasized. The number of small farms is still increasing slightly, while all other size groups and the total number of farms is decreasing. Millions of acres have been abandoned. The ratio of improved acres to total acres in farms is still increasing, but the actual number of improved acres decreased 7,618,444 from 1920 to 1930. Farming in the Southeast is decreasing, and it is being done more and more on small tracts of land. When these facts are coupled with increasing tenancy and decreasing livestock, they become more significant.

In the Southwest, farm operations have been increasing both in total extent and within each size group of farms. The decade from 1900 to 1910 saw an increase of 36.5 per cent in the total number of farms, and an increase as high as 84.0 per cent in one size group (260-500 acres). The only decrease in the ten years was in these farms of 1,000 acres and over, 445 of these disappearing. Between 1910 and 1920 there was a slowing up of the process of expansion, the increase in total number of farms being only 2.3 per cent. There was a decrease of 9.3 per cent in the 100 to 175 acre group, but every other group showed some increase. The trend toward increase continued through the last decade with a 11.5 per cent increase in total number of farms. Every size group increased in this decade. In this region the small farms under 100 acres do not constitute such a large percentage of the total, amounting to only 54.9 per cent in 1930; 5.6 per cent of the farms in 1930 were 500 acres or over, and this group of farms has increased in number throughout the 40 years since 1900. During this period while the total number of farms and the total number of acres in farms has been increasing the percentage of improved acres has gone from 17.3 in 1900 to 36.2 in 1930. This clearly indicates that this period has been one of expansion of farming in the Southwest, and that the late years of agricultural depression have not yet been reflected in changes in the size of farms in this region. Settlement of new land has brought many acres into farms, and the introduction of cotton and of truck farming in south Texas has brought much land formerly used only for grazing into farms. The prevalence of large farms is natural with the prevailing conditions. Ranching tends toward large units, and when crops are raised the

Distribution of Farms, 500 Acres and Over in the Two Southern Regions, by Counties, 1930

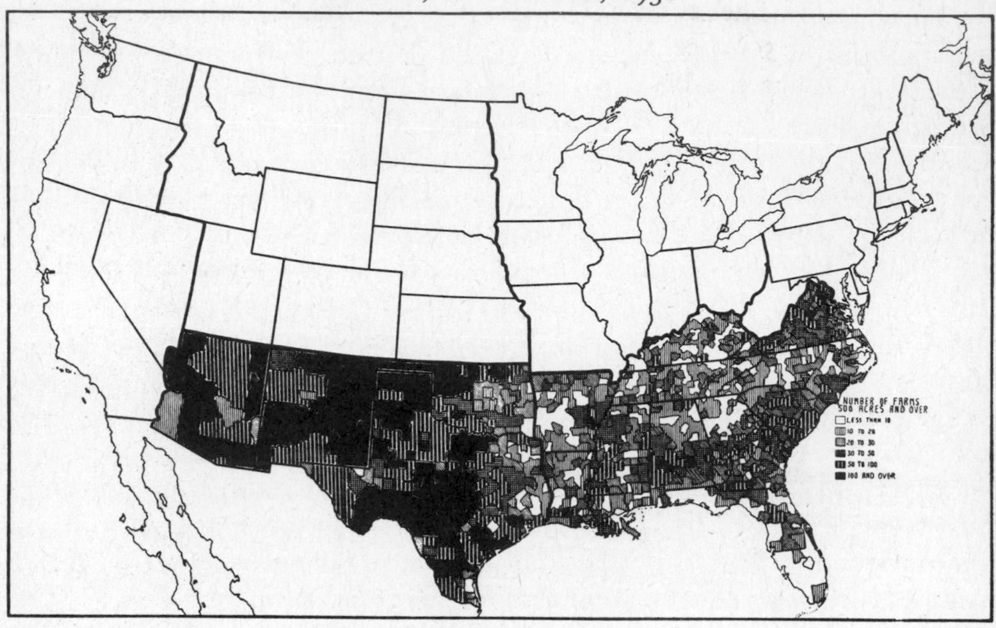

State Percentage of the 1929 National Total Value of Hay and Forage

STATE AND REGION	Value (in thousands)	Per Cent
Southeast		
Virginia	$18,570	1.56
North Carolina	9,797	.82
South Carolina	3,470	.29
Georgia	4,601	.39
Florida	813	.07
Kentucky	21,811	1.84
Tennessee	23,828	2.00
Alabama	6,915	.58
Mississippi	7,612	.64
Arkansas	10,166	.86
Louisiana	3,652	.31
Southwest		
Oklahoma	18,465	1.55
Texas	41,132	3.46
New Mexico	6,237	.53
Arizona	5,745	.48
Northeast		
Maine	9,688	.82
New Hampshire	4,901	.41
Vermont	14,674	1.23
Massachusetts	7,935	.67
Rhode Island	1,099	.09
Connecticut	7,350	.62
New York	77,572	6.53
New Jersey	7,415	.62
Delaware	1,430	.12
Pennsylvania	51,784	4.36
Maryland	8,200	.69
West Virginia	11,532	.97
Middle States		
Ohio	$41,915	3.53
Indiana	30,095	2.53
Illinois	50,044	4.21
Michigan	46,333	3.90
Wisconsin	99,744	8.39
Minnesota	72,081	6.07
Iowa	64,874	5.46
Missouri	41,066	3.46
Northwest		
North Dakota	19,510	1.64
South Dakota	24,146	2.03
Nebraska	41,733	3.51
Kansas	38,318	3.22
Montana	25,690	2.16
Idaho	25,730	2.17
Wyoming	12,564	1.06
Colorado	29,947	2.52
Utah	14,862	1.25
Far West		
Nevada	6,529	.55
Washington	24,434	2.06
Oregon	25,543	2.15
California	66,863	5.63
United States	1,188,415	100.00

country is well suited to mechanization of farming. This makes it possible for one man to handle many more acres here than in the Southeast.

Turning again to the regions other than southern, it is seen that farm operations in the Northeast have decreased to a degree comparable to that in the Southeast. The total number of farms and the number within each size group have steadily decreased in this century. This has not been marked by any shiftings between the groups like those in the Southeast, the proportion of farms in each size group remaining approximately the same. The decrease has been greater in the total and in all the smaller size groups for each successive decade. In the three groups over 260 acres the decrease from 1920 to 1930 has been somewhat smaller than that of the two previous decades. From this decrease in number of farms would be expected the constant decrease of acreage in farms, amounting to 18,892,002 acres in the 40 years. Both the actual number of improved acres and the ratio of improved to total acres has decreased. While the Northeast lost 18,892,002 acres from its farm land from 1900 to 1930, the Southeast lost 18,363,471 acres from 1920 to 1930, but the percentage loss in the Northeast has been greater than that in the Southeast. Farming in the Northeast shows a general decline, such as might be expected with the urbanization and concomitant industrialization of the region, together with the development of farming in the newer sections of the country.

In the Middle States the greatest decrease in number of farms has been in the under 100 acre group. The farms over 500 acres have also decreased in number, while the farms between these two groups have, with two exceptions, increased in number since 1900. The farms from 260 to 500 acres decreased slightly from 1910 to 1920, but there was a marked increase in the last decade in this group. The farms between 100 and 175 acres decreased from 1920 to 1930 to a number below that of 1910. This would seem to be a part of the general decrease in the number of small farms. The percentage of farms under 100 acres has decreased from 53.6 per cent in 1900 to 45.4 per cent in 1930. This has made a small decrease in the total number of farms, despite increases in other size groups. The change in the total number of farms has meant that, in spite of decreases in numbers, the farms over 500 acres still constitute as large a percentage of the total as they did in 1900; in the last decade even a larger percentage. In 1930 there were over 100,000 fewer farms in the Middle States than in 1920, and the acreage in farms had decreased by over six and a half million acres, and yet there were almost 13,000 more farms between 175 and 1,000 acres. True, there was a decrease in the number of farms over 1,000 acres, but if all this land went into the

Per Cent of Land Area in Farms, 1930

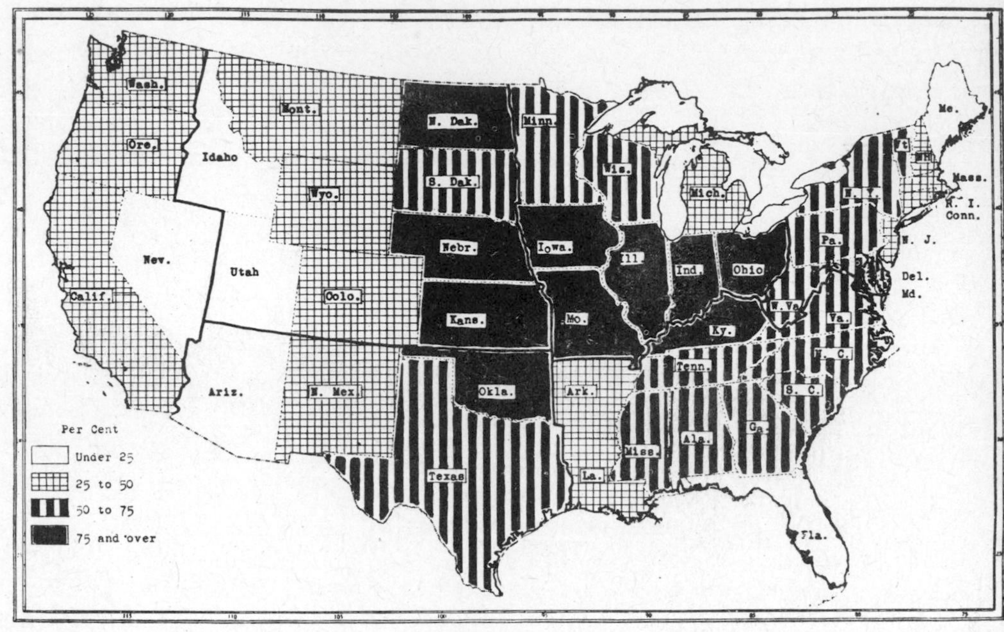

Horses and Horse Colts: Estimated Number on Farms and Value Per Head, 1932

STATE AND REGION	Number (in thousands)	Value Per Head	Total Value (in thousands)
Southeast	*1,111*	*$49.25*	*$ 54,715*
Virginia	187	66.00	12,342
North Carolina	77	65.00	5,005
South Carolina	26	54.00	1,404
Georgia	35	52.00	1,820
Florida	19	67.00	1,273
Kentucky	222	47.00	10,434
Tennessee	157	49.00	7,693
Alabama	58	46.00	2,668
Mississippi	92	43.00	3,956
Arkansas	132	31.00	4,092
Louisiana	106	38.00	4,028
Southwest	*1,359*	*29.94*	*40,688*
Oklahoma	453	30.00	13,590
Texas	704	30.00	21,120
New Mexico	128	23.00	2,944
Arizona	74	41.00	3,034
Northeast	*1,023*	*97.93*	*100,185*
Maine	57	114.00	6,498
New Hampshire	18	95.00	1,710
Vermont	50	102.00	5,100
Massachusetts	24	108.00	2,592
Rhode Island	4	100.00	400
Connecticut	21	110.00	2,310
New York	303	107.00	32,421
New Jersey	35	102.00	3,570
Delaware	17	64.00	1,088
Pennsylvania	297	104.00	30,888
Maryland	91	68.00	6,188
West Virginia	106	70.00	7,420
Middle States	*4,919*	*$64.57*	*$317,643*
Ohio	469	87.00	40,803
Indiana	425	73.00	31,025
Illinois	773	60.00	46,380
Michigan	373	97.00	36,181
Wisconsin	534	77.00	41,118
Minnesota	775	56.00	43,400
Iowa	996	56.00	55,776
Missouri	574	40.00	22,960
Northwest	*3,716*	*36.50*	*135,633*
North Dakota	586	41.00	24,026
South Dakota	581	36.00	20,916
Nebraska	697	44.00	30,668
Kansas	685	37.00	25,345
Montana	400	23.00	9,200
Idaho	190	36.00	6,840
Wyoming	166	26.00	4,316
Colorado	324	34.00	11,016
Utah	87	38.00	3,306
Far West	*551*	*50.77*	*27,975*
Nevada	38	46.00	1,748
Washington	161	49.00	7,889
Oregon	162	44,00	7,128
California	190	59.00	11,210

size farms which increased in number, it could account for only a small percentage of the increase, which must have come about through combinations of the smaller farms. It should also be noted that the farms under 100 acres have constantly decreased since 1900, while, for the most part, the larger farms have increased in number. The total acres in farms increased until 1920; since then there has been a sharp drop to a number below that of 1900. At the same time the number of improved acres dropped in actual number and in ratio to the total.

For the most part the Northwest shows an increase in number of farms for this period from 1900 to 1930. The increase was large from 1900 to 1910; since then it has become smaller, amounting to less than one per cent from 1920 to 1930. The increase has been mostly in the larger size groups, which constitute a larger percentage of the total here than in any other region. In 1930, 20.2 per cent of all farms were over 500 acres, a percentage equal to that of farms under 100 acres, and 45.5 per cent were over 260 acres. The increase in number of these larger farms accounts for the small increase in total number of farms at the same time that there has been a large increase in acreage in farms. The group of farms between 100 and 175 acres is the only one showing a tendency to decrease. These have decreased in actual numbers since 1910, and for each decade of this century have constituted a smaller percentage of the total farms of the region. The acreage in farms has almost doubled since 1900, and the improved acreage has more than doubled. In spite of this the ratio of improved to total acres in farms has decreased since 1910. The Northwest is the country's region of large farms. It has a larger percentage of the country's total area in farms than any other region, namely 28.3 per cent. It also has the largest percentage of the large farms in the country, 54.8 per cent of the farms 500 acres and over, at the same time that it has only 10.3 per cent of the total number of farms. Furthermore, the number of farms in the Northwest is still increasing, a condition found nowhere east of the Mississippi River.

In the Far West the number of farms has increased throughout the century, the largest increase occurring in the under 100 acre group. This group is larger by 125,000 farms than it was in 1900, and has risen from 42.0 per cent of the total number of farms to 69.9 per cent. This is of course commensurate with the population increase and the development of truck farming in this region. All the larger farms decreased in number in the last decade, except the group over 1,000 acres, which increased 15.6 per cent, or 1,518 farms. The decrease in all the middle groups caused the increase in total number to be smaller from 1920 to 1930 than previously. In spite of the increase in the number of very large farms, most of the farms

Changes in Status of Farm Lands and Commodities, 1919-1929

LAND IN HARVESTED CROPS

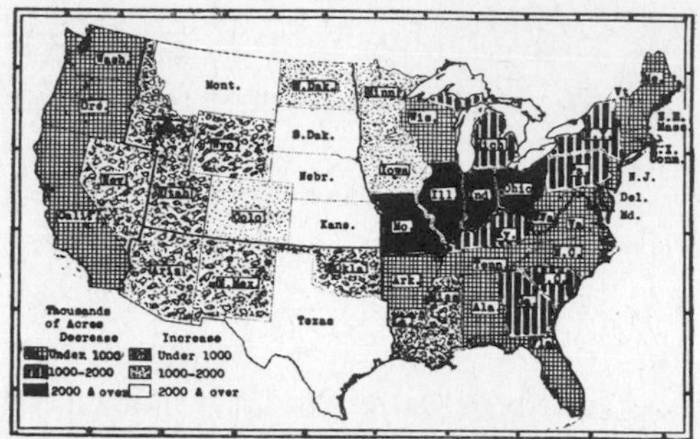

COTTON

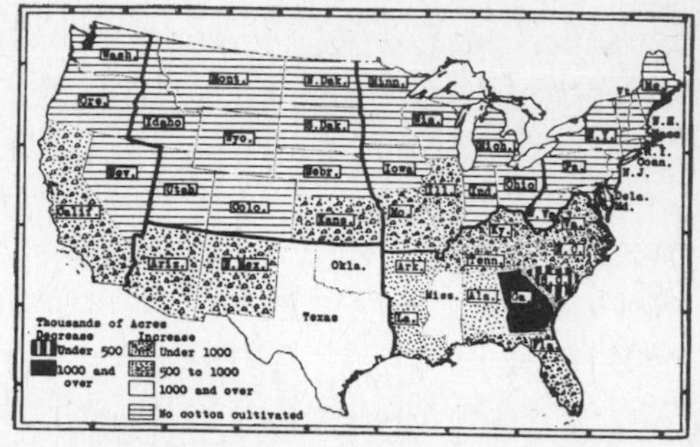

CORN

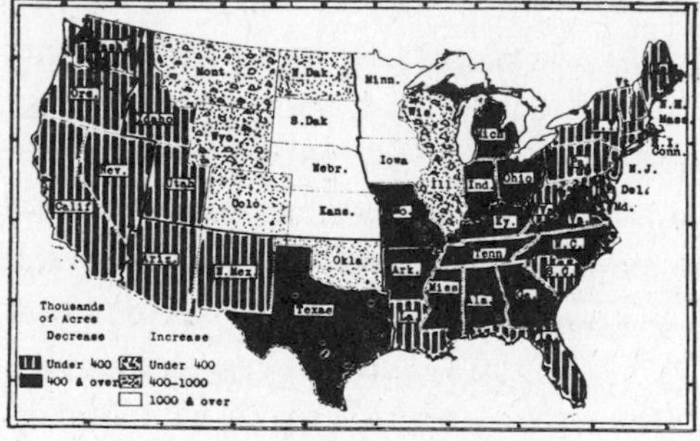

WHEAT

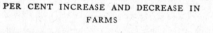

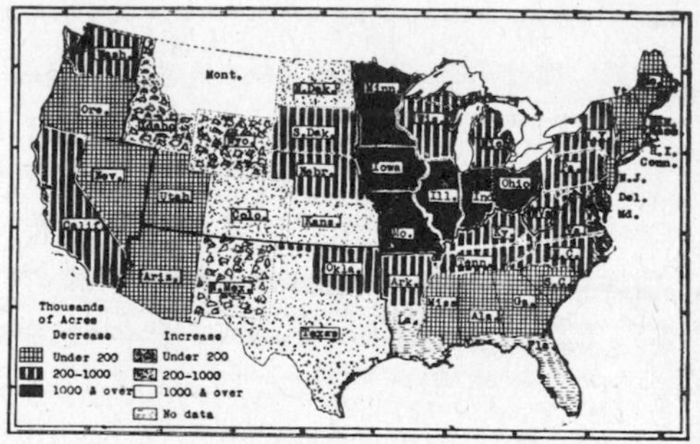

PER CENT INCREASE AND DECREASE IN FARMS

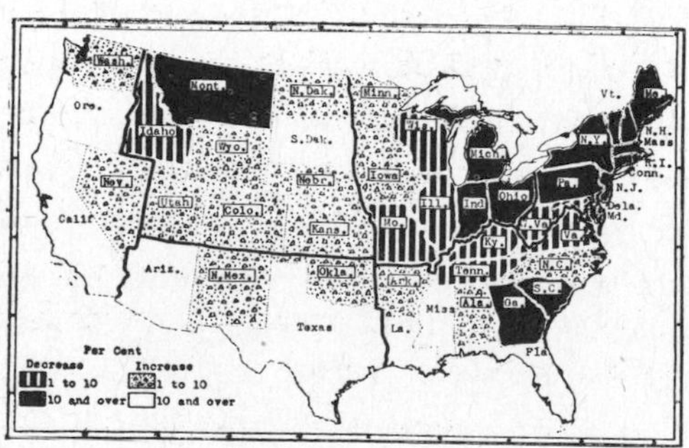

VALUE PER ACRE OF FARM REAL ESTATE

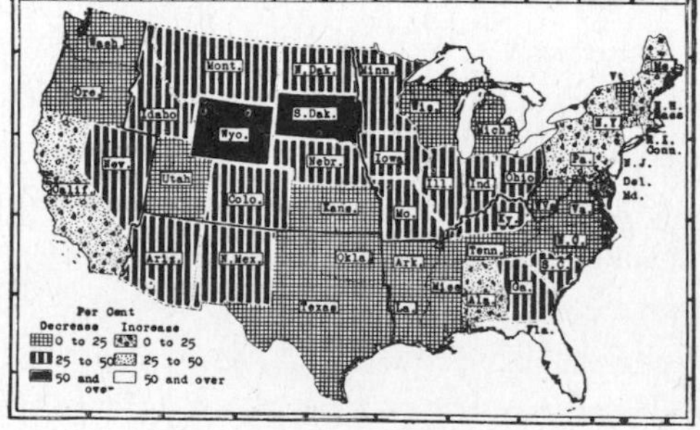

in the Far West are small, 80.7 per cent being under 175 acres. However, because of the small percentage of the total acreage in farms in the United States found in this region, it has only 5.0 per cent of the country's farms under 100 acres. The total acres in farms have increased each decade, but there was a decrease in improved acreage from 1920 to 1930. Changes in the number and size of farms in this region show a great deal of expansion in the early part of the century. This has tended to become less, and in the last decade there were decreases in the numbers of some of the middle size groups of farms. In the Far West there seems to be a tendency for the farms to concentrate in the very small and very large size groups, evidently due to farming along two quite different lines, vegetable and fruit culture, and ranching.

In general it may be said that farming in the United States as reflected by the size of farms and the acreage in farms has increased in extent in this century until the 1920-1930 decade. In this ten year period the number of farms decreased although the total acres and the improved acres in farms increased. This is obviously correlated with the fact that, while the number of farms in all other size groups decreased, the number over 500 acres increased. Farms under 100 acres have increased in number more since 1900 than any other one of the six size groups used in this study. The only size group smaller in 1930 than in 1900 is the 100 to 175 acre group. In the different regions changes have been more varied and more marked. The three regions east of the Mississippi River show a tendency toward a smaller number of farms, although this is true of the Southeast only in the last decade. In the same section of the country the total number of acres and the improved acres in farms are decreasing. The Northeast shows a consistent decline in the number of farms in all size groups. In the Southeast there has been a general decrease in all groups except that of the under 100 acre farms, which has shown a steady increase in number. In the Middle States the farms of both extremes of the size range are decreasing in number, while the farms in the middle groups are becoming more numerous. Farms of all sizes have increased in number in the Southwest, the largest actual increase occurring in the under 100 acre group. Although the Northwest shows the same general tendency toward expansion, farms between 100 and 175 acres are decreasing and are now fewer in number than in 1900. The larger farms, those over 260 acres, have shown the greatest increase in number. In the Far West, the third region of expansion, there has been a remarkable increase in the number of farms under 100 acres. Farms over 1,000 acres show the next largest increase for the 40 years. The last decade has seen a decrease in the four size groups between 100 and 1,000 acres.

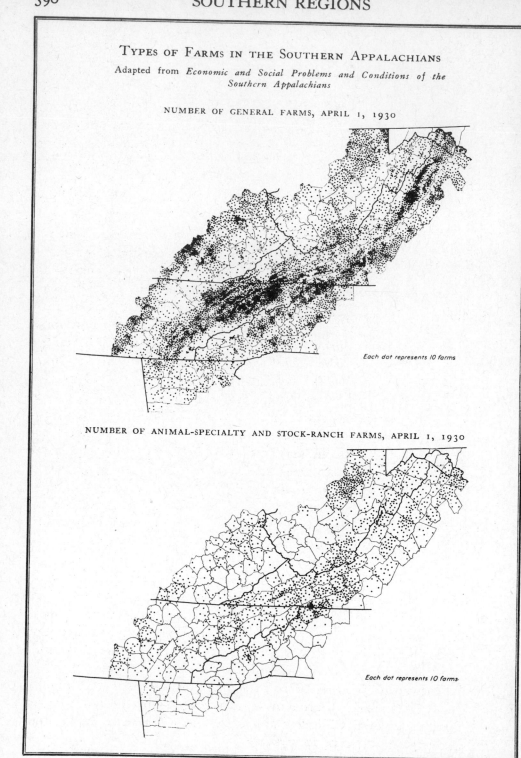

Types of Farms in the Southern Appalachians

Adapted from *Economic and Social Problems and Conditions of the Southern Appalachians*

NUMBER OF GENERAL FARMS, APRIL 1, 1930

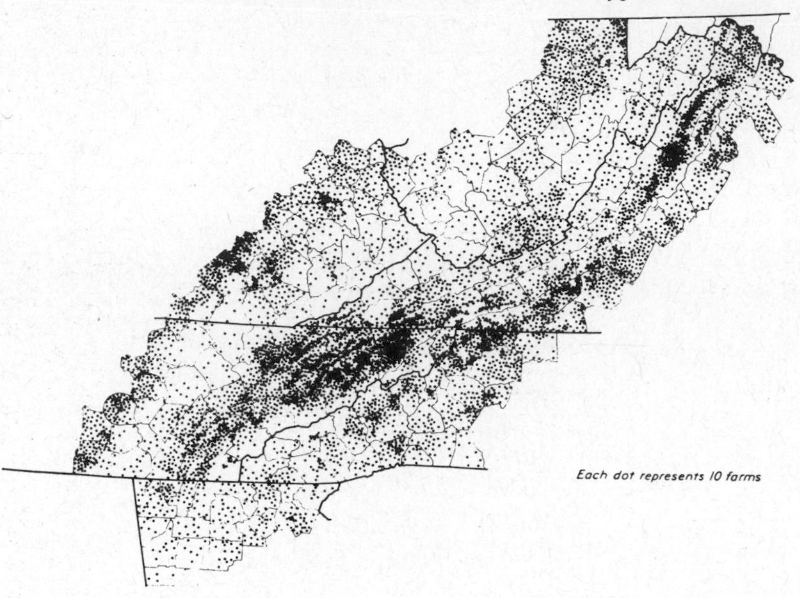

NUMBER OF ANIMAL-SPECIALTY AND STOCK-RANCH FARMS, APRIL 1, 1930

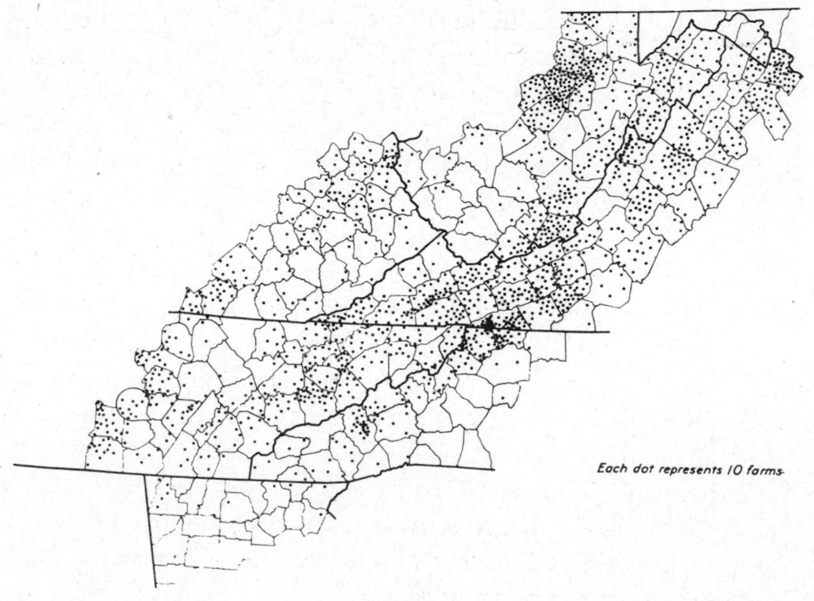

At present, the Southeast has a larger percentage of the total number of farms in the country—38.0 per cent—than any other region, and more than half of the farms under 100 acres—two and one-half times the number in the Middle States, which has the next highest percentage. The Southeast also has a relatively high percentage of the farms from 100 to 175 acres, although in this and all other groups the percentage is smaller than the percentage of the total number of farms. The Middle States have the second highest percentage of the country's farms and the percentages of this region in the three middle size groups (100 to 500 acres) are larger than its percentage of the total number. The Southwest comes third, and its percentage of the total is smaller than its percentages of the larger farms over 500 acres. The Northwest is fourth in percentage of the total number of farms, but it comes first in percentage of the three larger size groups. The Northeast ranks fifth in percentage of total farms, and last in the farms over 500 acres. The Far West has the smallest percentage of the total number, but ranks above the Southeast, Northeast, and Middle States in percentage of farms over 500 acres.

Thus it is evident that the Southeast is the nation's region of small farms, the Middle States predominate in the medium sized farms, while the Northwest and Southwest are regions of large farms. The Northeast and the Far West are not so easily typified; but the Northeast tends to line up with the Middle States, and the Far West with the Northwest and Southwest, although note should be made of the relatively large number of small farms in the Far West. Yet the contrast between the Southeast and the Far West, the region ranking second in small farms, offers an unusual basis for the study of farming methods, occupational aspects, and many other regional differences between southeastern farming and farming in the Far West.

It is not enough, however, to know only the size of farms; we must see them further in use. Here is a part of the picture. Of these farms in the Southeast, more than 1,100,000 are "cotton" farms. The next largest ratios are "general," "crop specialty," and dairy farms. Likewise, more than a million of the farms are tenant farms. Of the total crop land, by far the greatest part is devoted to cotton and corn culture, with other crops having relatively small ratios, with the exception of tobacco in North Carolina, Georgia, and Kentucky; fruits and vegetables in Florida; and hay in Virginia, Kentucky, and Tennessee; and wheat in Virginia. The cotton states show the following percentage, in round numbers, of total crop acreage in cotton: Mississippi, 54 per cent; Arkansas and Alabama, nearly 44; Louisiana, 41; South Carolina, 39; Georgia, 33; North Carolina, 23; with the lesser states, Tennessee, Florida, and Virginia, 14, 6, and 2 re-

Crop Land Lying Idle or Fallow, 1929

Adapted from the U. S. Bureau of Agricultural Economics

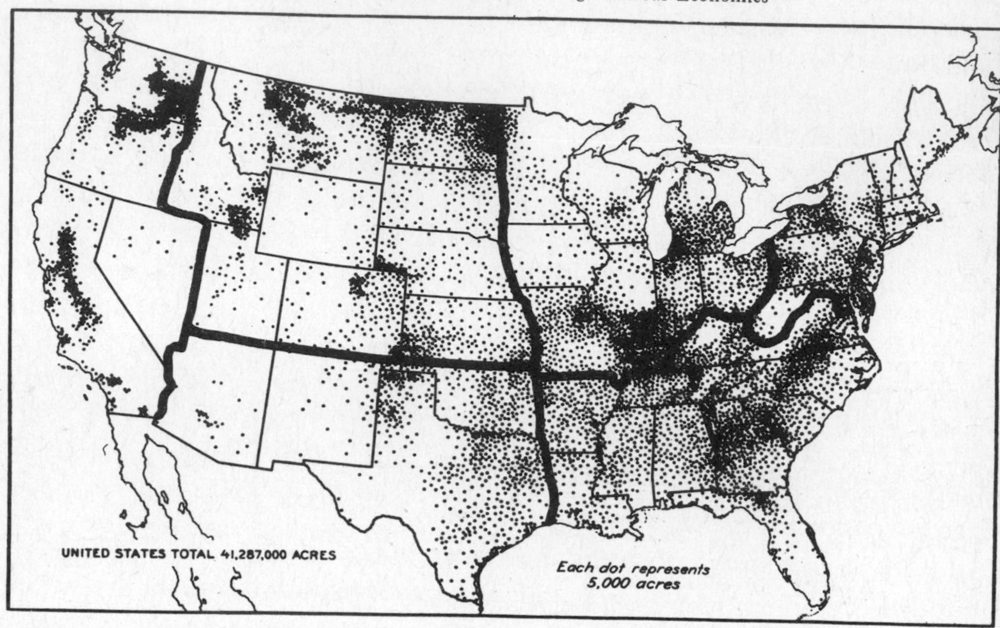

Sheep and Lambs: Estimated Number on Farms and Value Per Head, 1932

STATE AND REGION	Number (in thousands)	Value Per Head	Total Value (in thousands)	STATE AND REGION	Number (in thousands)	Value Per Head	Total Value (in thousands)
Southeast	*2,287*	*$4.10*	*$9,371*	*Middle States*	*9,307*	*$3.52*	*$32,731*
Virginia	485	4.60	2,231	Ohio	2,164	3.50	7,574
North Carolina	91	3.90	354	Indiana	826	4.00	3,304
South Carolina	14	3.70	51	Illinois	799	3.80	3,036
Georgia	37	2.30	85	Michigan	1,285	3.90	5,011
Florida	43	2.40	103	Wisconsin	546	3.20	1,747
Kentucky	875	4.70	4,112	Minnesota	1,084	3.20	3,468
Tennessee	393	4.00	1,572	Iowa	1,398	3.30	4,613
Alabama	50	2.60	130	Missouri	1,205	3.30	3,976
Mississippi	100	2.00	200				
Arkansas	59	2.60	153	*Northwest*	*20,669*	*3.37*	*69,706*
Louisiana	140	2.70	378	North Dakota	1,040	3.30	3,432
				South Dakota	1,465	3.30	4,834
Southwest	*11,724*	*2.68*	*31,467*	Nebraska	1,047	3.00	3,141
Oklahoma	164	3.00	492	Kansas	779	3.10	2,414
Texas	7,312	2.90	21,204	Montana	3,820	3.20	12,224
New Mexico	3,058	2.30	7,033	Idaho	2,274	3.60	8,186
Arizona	1,190	2.30	2,737	Wyoming	4,128	3.60	14,860
				Colorado	3,361	3.10	10,419
Northeast	*1,900*	*4.40*	*8,358*	Utah	2,755	3.70	10,193
Maine	81	3.50	283				
New Hampshire	18	4.50	81	*Far West*	*8,025*	*3.92*	*31,449*
Vermont	39	3.90	152	Nevada	1,152	4.00	4,608
Massachusetts	10	4.50	45	Washington	750	4.00	3,000
Rhode Island	2	4.50	9	Oregon	2,679	3.50	9,376
Connecticut	10	4.70	47	California	3,444	4.20	14,464
New York	473	4.40	2,081				
New Jersey	7	5.40	37				
Delaware	4	5.00	20				
Pennsylvania	491	4.40	2,160				
Maryland	108	5.10	550				
West Virginia	657	4.40	2,890				

spectively. Or if the percentage of cotton acreage to crop land harvested be figured, Alabama, Mississippi, and Arkansas all show more than 50 per cent, with Mississippi the highest with a little more than 60 per cent, and South Carolina and Louisiana nearly 50 per cent.

The distribution of crop lands in other crops may be examined more in detail from the accompanying table, as may also the number and types of farms, with their several ratios to the total. With the exception of Arkansas every one of the eleven Southeastern States shows a little more than a fourth of its total crop acreage in corn, and most of the states between 25 and 33 per cent, Kentucky and Tennessee alone going higher with 41 and 37 per cent respectively. With the exception of Tennessee, Kentucky, and Virginia, which have about 18 per cent each, the other states average under 5 per cent. The average for oats is less than 2 per cent if South Carolina's 7 per cent be excepted. Likewise, if Georgia's 8 per cent of Irish and sweet potatoes be excluded, the average for the other states is less than 2 per cent, while vegetables harvested for sale are grown on less than one per cent of the acreage if Florida's 7 per cent be excluded. Excluding Florida's 16 per cent and Virginia's 5 per cent, the acreage in orchard is considerably less than 2 per cent, although Georgia shows 2.27 per cent, both apples and peaches featuring this total. Of special importance are the tobacco states with their respective percentages of total crop acreage in tobacco about as follows: North Carolina, nearly 10 per cent; Georgia, nearly 9 per cent; Kentucky, nearly 7 per cent; and Virginia, about three and a half per cent; South Carolina, two and a quarter; and Tennessee, nearly two. Florida and Kentucky have the largest ratios of idle or fallow land, with a little more than 20 per cent each, while the average for the other states will be about 15, if Arkansas' low 9.53 be omitted. Of special importance also is the acreage devoted to legumes, including cowpeas, soybeans, velvet beans, peanuts, in which Florida's ratio is greatest with 26 per cent, Georgia and Alabama next with 16 and 11, respectively; and North Carolina, South Carolina, and Louisiana following with 10, 8, and 7 per cent respectively. Georgia, however, has the largest actual acreage by far with more than a million and a half acres.

This picture of the relative distribution of land usage in crops harvested or crop acreage is somewhat similar to the ratio of money value of these same crops as shown in the several tables. Still another similar ratio is reflected in the charts and tables showing ratios of quantities of these commodities as well as of a number of other staple agricultural crops, including livestock, dairy, and poultry products. It is sufficient here to note some of the aggregate ratios and regional variations, leaving the detailed distributions for special study as desired. Important in the pic-

Plowable Pasture, Acreage, 1929

Adapted from the U. S. Bureau of Agricultural Economics

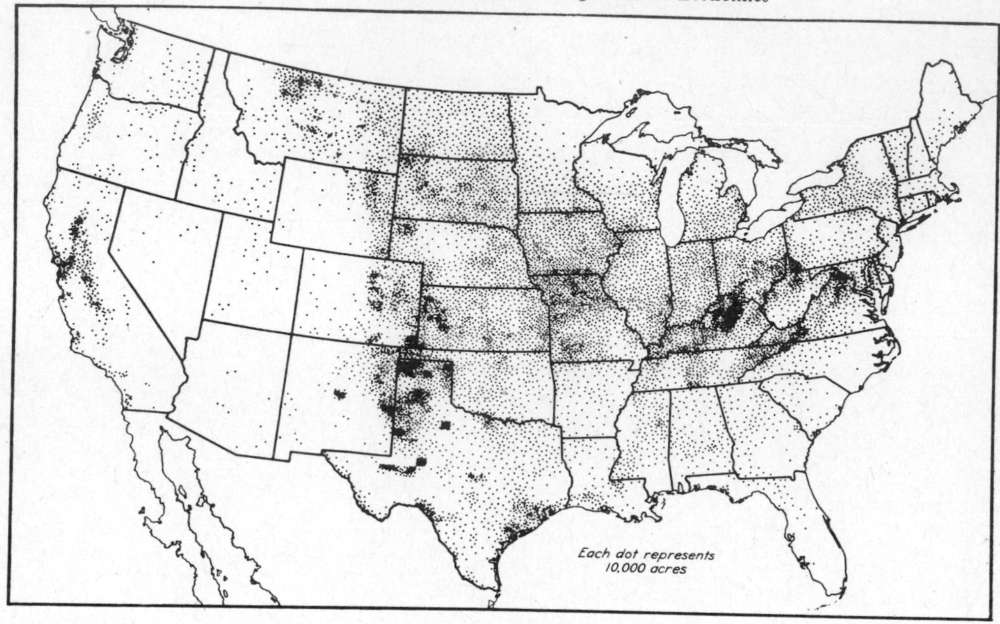

Milk Cows and Heifers: Estimated Number on Farms and Value Per Head, 1932

STATE AND REGION	Number (in thousands)	Value Per Head	Total Value (in thousands)
Southeast	*3,826*	*$28.73*	*$107,407*
Virginia	390	35.00	13,650
North Carolina	306	37.00	11,322
South Carolina	141	33.00	4,653
Georgia	336	25.00	8,400
Florida	88	38.00	3,344
Kentucky	518	30.00	15,540
Tennessee	507	28.00	14,196
Alabama	390	23.00	8,970
Mississippi	469	21.00	9,849
Arkansas	421	23.00	9,683
Louisiana	260	30.00	7,800
Southwest	*2,116*	*29.13*	*61,648*
Oklahoma	716	27.00	19,332
Texas	1,288	29.00	37,332
New Mexico	70	37.00	2,590
Arizona	42	57.00	2,394
Northeast	*3,651*	*57.54*	*210,064*
Maine	143	50.00	7,150
New Hampshire	81	61.00	4,941
Vermont	299	52.00	15,548
Massachusetts	131	88.00	11,528
Rhode Island	21	90.00	1,890
Connecticut	113	83.00	9,379
New York	1,411	61.00	86,071
New Jersey	120	89.00	1,068
Delaware	35	54.00	1,890
Pennsylvania	886	60.00	53,160
Maryland	186	49.00	9,114
West Virginia	225	37.00	8,325
Middle States	*9,982*	*$39.41*	*$393,427*
Ohio	938	44.00	41,272
Indiana	751	39.00	29,289
Illinois	1,099	42.00	46,158
Michigan	850	45.00	38,250
Wisconsin	2,150	43.00	92,450
Minnesota	1,708	35.00	59,780
Iowa	1,456	38.00	55,328
Missouri	1,030	30.00	30,900
Northwest	*3,596*	*34.17*	*122,872*
North Dakota	589	33.00	19,437
South Dakota	607	31.00	18,817
Nebraska	700	36.00	25,200
Kansas	860	33.00	28,380
Montana	195	36.00	7,020
Idaho	194	39.00	7,566
Wyoming	72	39.00	2,808
Colorado	266	36.00	9,576
Utah	113	36.00	4,068
Far West	*1,208*	*50.34*	*60,708*
Nevada	21	51.00	1,071
Washington	300	53.00	15,900
Oregon	250	45.00	11,250
California	637	51.00	32,487

turization of the region is the predominance of general crops and of "staples" in the Southeast as compared with other regions and the national average, and the relatively small ratio of gross value of livestock products. A major significance is, of course, in relation to the special studies of dairying which are presented in the following pages as one chief avenue of reconstructed agriculture. The high Southeastern States for gross value of crops as opposed to livestock products are Alabama, Mississippi, Louisiana, South Carolina, and Arkansas with the following percentages respectively: 89, 84, 83, 80, 82. The other states average around 70 per cent. These percentages are in contrast to the national average of 57 per cent; and of the lowest states under 40 per cent, such as New Hampshire, Vermont, Rhode Island, Wisconsin. Of similar contrast is the Southeast's large ratio of "staple" or money crops, including corn, wheat, cotton, tobacco. The nation's average is a little more than 30 per cent, while the Southeastern States range from more than 60 per cent in three states to the average for all of nearly 50 per cent, with the exception of Virginia which is about the national average. On the other hand, low states in other regions include a range from Maine of less than one per cent, several with less than 5 per cent, to such great states as California with 5 per cent, Wisconsin with 11, and Minnesota with 19 per cent.

Yet there are also important detailed ratios, such as vegetables for sale, including potatoes, where the South ranks a little above the national average with 6 per cent as opposed to 5.54, and considerably above the national average and also above every other region in farm garden vegetables raised, as opposed to commercial gardens. This is significant both in relation to certain common assumptions that the region does not use vegetables freely, and also with reference to the effectiveness of future programs of increased home consumption and dietary programs. In farm garden vegetables the Southeast shows a percentage of 3.61 contrasted with the nation's 1.61, and the other regions as follows: Southwest, Northeast, Middle States, Northwest, Far West respectively, 1.48, 1.98, 1.14, .62, and .56. In dairy products the Southeast ranks about a fourth as high as the Northeast and half that of the nation; in hay, about a half of the national average and a third of the three highest regions. About the same ratios are found for gross income from hogs. Creditable is the relative ratio of chickens raised as opposed to poultry products sold which is analogous to the vegetables sold in comparison with farm garden vegetables. These and other items indicate the relatively large dependence of the farm folk upon home produce. The Southeast also ranks considerably above the other regions in fruits and nuts, except that the Far West has nearly a third of its

Per Cent of Cash Farm Income From Livestock, Average, 1928-1930

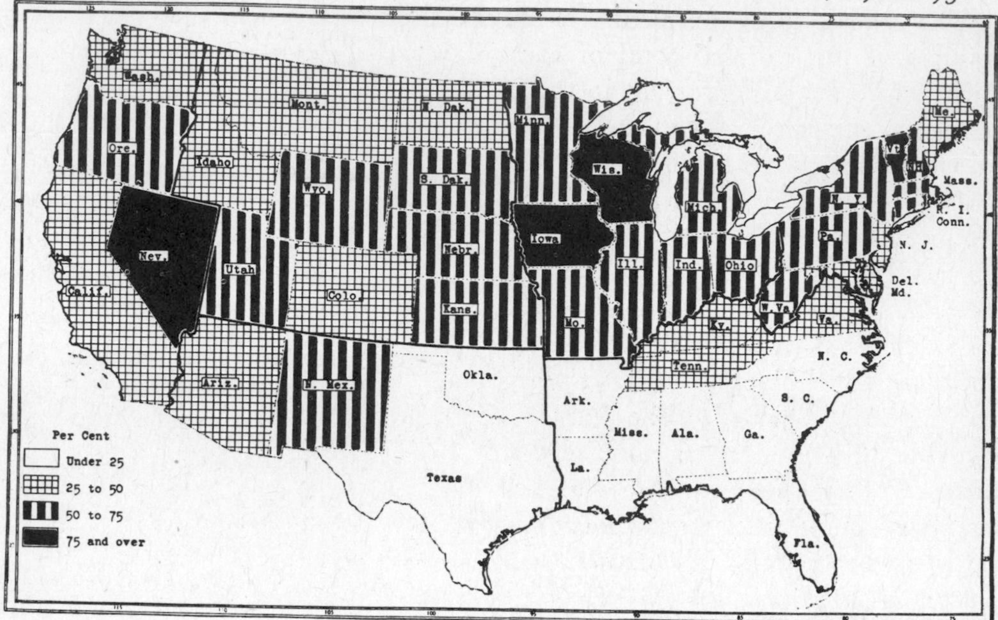

All Cattle and Calves, Including Cows and Heifers Kept for Milk, 1932

STATE AND REGION	Number (in thousands)	Value Per Head	Total Value (in thousands)
Southeast	*8,200*	*$18.28*	*$162,055*
Virginia	782	27.80	21,739
North Carolina	548	27.10	14,850
South Carolina	266	23.60	6,277
Georgia	789	16.60	13,097
Florida	441	18.00	7,938
Kentucky	978	23.70	23,178
Tennessee	1,032	20.50	21,156
Alabama	810	15.80	12,798
Mississippi	966	14.30	13,813
Arkansas	848	16.20	13,737
Louisiana	740	18.20	13,468
Southwest	*10,273*	*25.23*	*259,152*
Oklahoma	2,151	18.70	40,223
Texas	6,127	17.30	105,997
New Mexico	1,144	21.30	93,954
Arizona	851	22.30	18,977
Northeast	*5,561*	*47.21*	*262,535*
Maine	243	37.20	9,039
New Hampshire	131	45.00	5,895
Vermont	436	41.00	17,876
Massachusetts	179	70.30	12,583
Rhode Island	29	71.20	2,054
Connecticut	155	67.30	10,431
New York	1,976	49.70	98,207
New Jersey	163	73.50	11,980
Delaware	49	46.20	2,263
Pennsylvania	1,398	47.20	65,765
Maryland	277	41.20	11,412
West Virginia	525	28.60	15,015
Middle States	*20,104*	*$29.42*	*$591,493*
Ohio	1,610	34.60	55,706
Indiana	1,428	30.40	43,411
Illinois	2,401	31.70	76,111
Michigan	1,390	34.80	48,372
Wisconsin	3,184	34.60	110,166
Minnesota	3,246	25.60	83,097
Iowa	4,185	26.60	111,321
Missouri	2,660	23.80	63,308
Northwest	*14,663*	*23.03*	*337,725*
North Dakota	1,454	22.60	32,860
South Dakota	1,907	21.90	41,763
Nebraska	3,104	24.20	75,116
Kansas	3,392	22.00	74,624
Montana	1,250	24.10	30,125
Idaho	668	24.60	16,432
Wyoming	863	24.50	21,143
Colorado	1,541	22.50	34,672
Utah	484	22.70	10,986
Far West	*3,606*	*32.82*	*118,348*
Nevada	310	25.70	7,967
Washington	615	37.00	22,755
Oregon	795	29.80	23,691
California	1,886	33.90	63,935

gross value and the Northeast has a little over 5 per cent coming from this source, while the Southeast has about 4 per cent.

The other side of the picture is found in the ratio which the Southeast produces of the national total of each of these agricultural commodities, which, while not so important in the planning of the region, still has considerable significance in both the understanding of the problem and in interregional arrangements. Some detailed summary has been presented in section 118, page 63. The general picture shows wheat as king of the great Northwest, which produces a little more than half of the nation's 850,000,000 bushels. Corn is king of the Middle States, which produces a little more than half of the nation's 2,384,000 bushels. Yet hay and hogs are runners-up for leadership in the Northwest and Middle States, which produce 60 per cent of the nation's 86,000,000 tons of hay and 56,000,000 swine. The Far West is golden with oranges and the new rule of fruits, nuts, and vegetables. Old King Cotton, although periodically reported in the worst of health, still rules in the Southeast and the Southwest, which produce respectively nearly 60 and nearly 40 per cent of the nation's maximum fifteen million bales. And tobacco has become a sort of new queen of the Southeast, which produces about 85 per cent of the nation's 1,600,000,000 pounds. Joint queen, too, for the Middle States and the Southeast is the dairy cow, these two regions furnishing, on 1,400,000 farms, nearly half of the nation's 30,000,000 pastured on wooded lot and meadows, on hillsides and by running waters, or languishing on barren lands.

Of the 35 chief crops basic to the statistics in the *Graphic Summary of American Agriculture* at least 25 or 30 can be grown successfully in the Southeast. The staple crops of wheat and corn and cotton and tobacco and oats all do well; likewise the potatoes and most of the vegetables, especially onions, tomatoes, lettuce, and the melons. Fruits, apples, peaches, strawberries, pears, plums, grapes, figs, are examples of undeveloped crops; specials are also peanuts, the lespedezas, the other legumes, sugar cane, rice, together with some sub-specials such as tung nuts, the new growth of slash pine, and others. What part these will play in the reconstructed agriculture of the Southeast must depend upon many factors. But one thing is apparently clear, and that is that in the demand for expansion of both agriculture and industry, which must be essential to a surviving Southeast, they will play an important part.

It is important here to elaborate a little further the premise that cotton will assume an increasingly diminishing ratio in the total economy of the region. There appear at least seven reasons why cotton in the future will play an increasingly smaller rôle in the total economy of the Southeast,

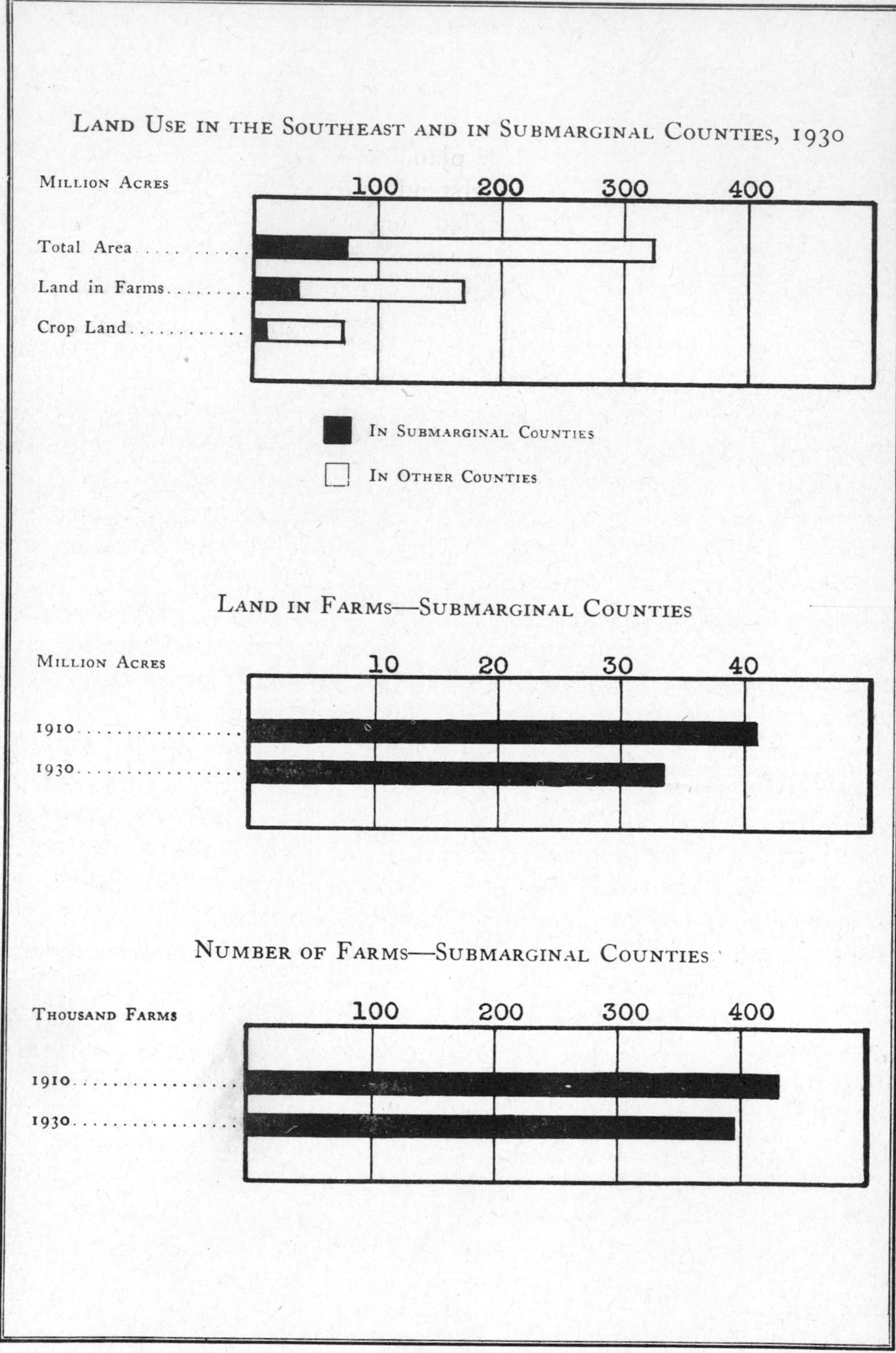
Land Use in the Southeast and in Submarginal Counties, 1930
Million Acres
100
200
300
400
Total Area
Land in Farms
Crop Land
In Submarginal Counties
In Other Counties
Land in Farms—Submarginal Counties
Million Acres
10
20
30
40
1910
1930
Number of Farms—Submarginal Counties
Thousand Farms
100
200
300
400
1910
1930

with each of these reflecting numerous minor considerations. The logical first reason is the reduction of exports. There is needed, however, considerably more research into the prospects with reference to general international relations and tariffs, with reference to increased foreign production and the possibility of a diminishing use of American quality of cotton. If a single European country can contract with a single non-American area for 1,000,000 bales of cotton to be manufactured with machinery different from that needed for American cotton, the implications call for a very specialized inquiry. Likewise, a decrease in American acreage from 1932 to 1933 of nearly 6,000,000 acres alongside an increase of foreign acreage of 4,000,000 acres gives an index of a trend away from American dominance.

A second major reason for accepting the hypothesis of diminishing ratio may be found in a diminishing ratio of home consumption due to high cost of production, to the high price of processing, due to substitutes, and due to further inventions and technology affecting the use of textile products and production processes. Thus, since the beginning of the depression the percentage of the cotton crop exported increased from 46 per cent in 1929-30 to 66.3 per cent in 1932-33, while the production of rayon increased nearly 200,000,000 pounds, which was also an increase of nearly fifty per cent. The extraordinary development of the paper industry will require special study from the viewpoint of substitutions for cotton goods as well as for affording a new base for diversification. A third basis for diminishing ratio may be found in the possibility of new technology in cultivating, picking, and manufacturing cotton, all of which may reduce the ratio of total workers required. Even though such inventions may make possible larger production, the human factors constitute an increasingly greater crisis in terms of the Southeast's more than two and a quarter million farm families and other workers.

A fourth reason for the diminishing cotton ratio may be found in the fact that at the present rate of soil depletion the Southeast could not long produce anything like the present maximum without the accompanying destruction of resources through the addition of new forest and drainage areas. In such case the cost of production will increase, whereas the demand of foreign competition is for the production at much lower cost, which suggests a fifth reason for a diminishing cotton rôle. This is, that modern social advance will not longer countenance such low standards of living as now emerge from cotton culture. Sixth, by the same token any return to the maximization of cotton would be detrimental to the South in that it would tend to reinslave the region to cotton, drainer of land and men. And seventh and finally, even should cotton consumption continue

PER CENT OF TOTAL INCOME FROM AGRICULTURE, 1928

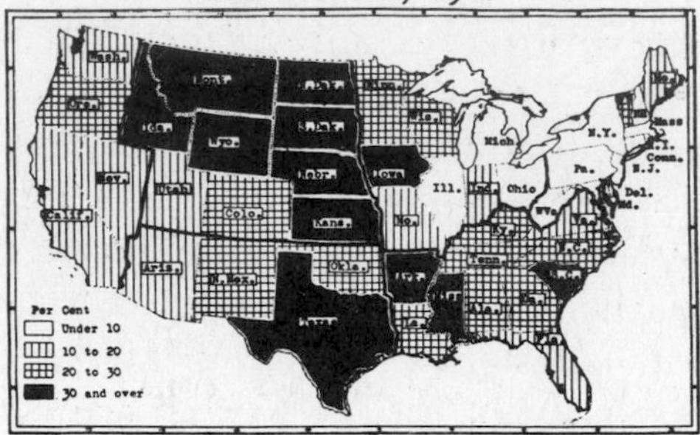

PER CENT OF TOTAL INCOME FROM MANUFACTURE, 1928

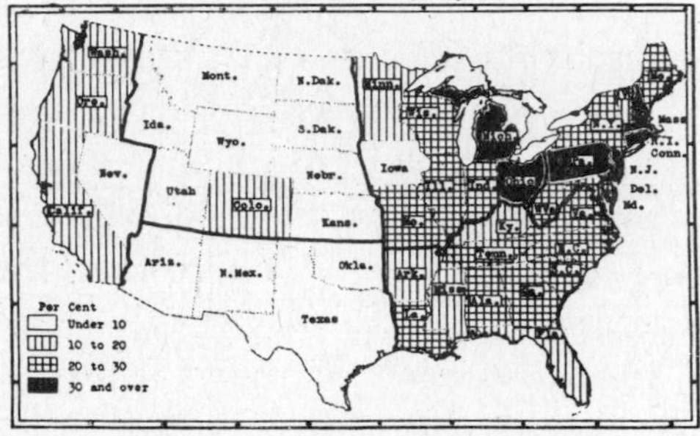

PER CENT OF TOTAL INCOME FROM MINING, 1928

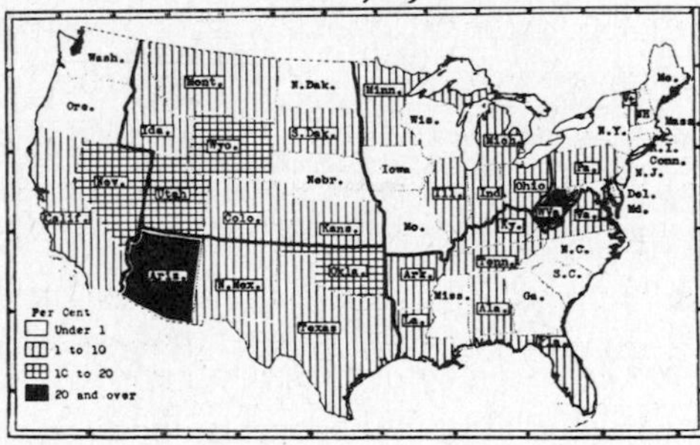

PER CENT OF TOTAL INCOME FROM SOURCES OTHER THAN AGRICULTURE, MANUFACTURING, AND MINING, 1928

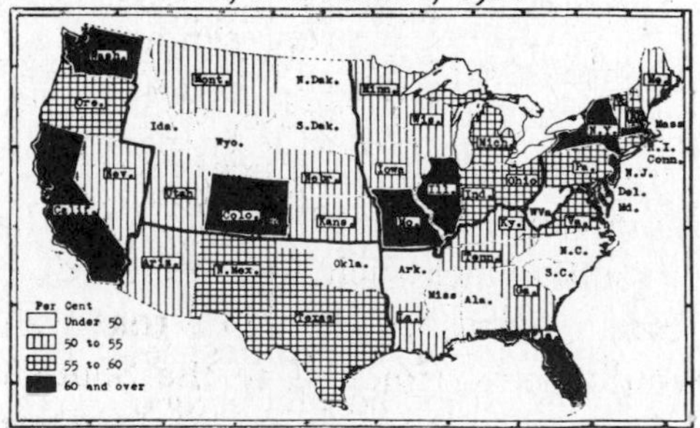

PERCENTAGE DISTRIBUTION OF THE SOURCES OF INCOME BY STATES, 1928

STATE	Rank	From Agriculture	Rank	From Manufacture	Rank	From Mining	Rank	From Other Sources
UNITED STATES	....	12.9	....	25.7	.. .	2.5	....	58.9
North Dakota	1	52.9	48	2.0	33	.5	42	44.6
South Dakota	2	52.5	47	2.8	27	1.0	44	44.0
Mississippi	3	46.8	32	14.3	46	....	48	38.9
Nebraska	4	41.9	44	6.2	46	....	34	51.9
Arkansas	5	39.4	33	11.7	13	4.9	44	44.0
Idaho	6	38.7	35	9.9	14	4.6	40	46.8
Iowa	7	38.4	38	9.3	30	.7	35	51.6
Kansas	8	35.3	41	8.4	18	3.5	31	52.8
Wyoming	9	32.2	42	8.2	6	15.8	46	43.8
Montana	10	31.5	43	7.1	9	6.5	23	54.9
South Carolina	11	31.4	17	26.2	38	.2	47	42.2
Texas	12	30.6	40	8.6	12	5.2	21	55.6
New Mexico	13	29.8	46	4.1	7	9.9	20	56.2
North Carolina	14	26.7	9	28.7	37	.3	43	44.3
Minnesota	15	26.5	31	15.4	15	4.5	28	53.6
Georgia	16	26.1	19	22.8	30	.7	37	50.4
Oklahoma	17	25.9	45	5.6	3	18.8	38	49.7
Vermont	18	25.6	26	18.8	19	3.4	32	52.2
Alabama	19	25.4	18	23.1	11	5.3	41	46.2
Colorado	21	24.4	34	10.8	16	4.0	10	60.8
Tennessee	20	24.4	20	21.8	21	1.8	33	52.0
Kentucky	22	22.9	29	17.1	8	9.1	36	50.9
Oregon	23	21.4	27	18.3	33	.5	12	59.3
Louisiana	24	20.6	22	21.4	20	3.2	25	54.8
Wisconsin	25	20.2	15	25.9	35	.4	29	53.5
Virginia	26	19.5	21	21.5	23	1.4	16	57.6
Nevada	27	18.8	37	9.4	3	18.8	30	53.0
Utah	28	18.6	36	9.6	5	17.2	26	54.6
Washington	29	17.9	25	19.8	32	.6	8	61.7
Florida	30	17.8	30	15.9	25	1.1	4	65.2
Missouri	31	17.7	24	20.8	29	.9	9	60.9
Maine	32	17.5	12	28.0	40	.1	27	54.4
Arizona	33	16.1	39	8.7	2	20.3	23	54.9
California	34	13.7	28	17.2	17	3.8	3	65.3
Indiana	35	12.2	9	28.7	22	1.6	17	57.5
Delaware	36	11.4	11	28.5	46	....	11	60.1
New Hampshire	37	9.9	4	34.8	40	.1	22	55.2
Maryland	38	8.4	14	26.6	35	.4	5	64.6
West Virginia	39	8.3	23	20.8	1	23.1	39	47.8
Illinois	40	7.3	16	25.7	24	1.2	2	66.3
Ohio	41	6.5	6	33.2	27	1.0	12	59.3
Michigan	42	6.3	3	35.8	25	1.1	19	56.8
Pennsylvania	43	4.0	8	30.7	10	6.4	14	58.9
Connecticut	44	3.6	2	37.6	40	.1	15	58.7
New York	45	3.4	13	26.9	38	.2	1	69.5
New Jersey	46	2.5	7	33.0	40	.1	7	64.4
Massachusetts	47	2.0	5	33.3	40	.1	5	64.6
Rhode Island	48	1.5	1	41.0	40	.1	18	57.4

PERCENTAGE DISTRIBUTION OF THE VALUE OF MANUFACTURED PRODUCTS, BY REGIONS, 1929

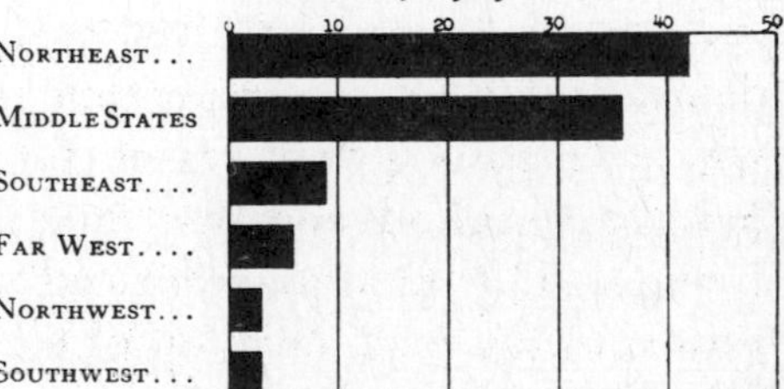

high, present indications are that the Southwest will continue in increasing advantage for cotton growing and export such that the Southeast cannot compete successfully.

Yet these assumptions based upon contingencies may be considerably altered by research programs which may strike at the heart of these problems. The seventh assumption above especially might be modified. New reaches in the quality of cotton produced, in the economies of production and manufacturing, in the wider uses of cotton products, in the increased consumer's capacity for present goods in relation to a balanced economy of self-sufficing farming and land improvement—all of these offer fields for new research methods and techniques combining the best that both physical and social sciences can afford.

The most important next step is to explore possible procedures for substitute economy which will effectively merge economic and social diversity with cotton economy. Such merging or replacement must meet the multiple needs of cash sales, subsistence farming, cultural development, regional and interregional balance. And, through enrichment of lands and diversification it must make possible the production of an optimum amount of cotton *at the lowest possible cost.* Our first and key example is that of dairying, in which our preliminary inquiry was predicated upon the basis of factual and experimental data. Special emphasis and effort were given to this enquiry because of its representation of the complexity and practical reconstruction of a regional economy. Results from the AAA have proved the applicability of this approach. We continue the assumption of regional development and specialization and such subsequent integration into the whole southeastern program as may be effective. Three approaches are illustrated. One is a proposal for a new dairy region to be projected down from the present designated northern and eastern dairy region to encompass the Piedmont South, touching also parts of the cotton belt and the Tennessee Valley. Supplementing this is a special subregional study of nearly a hundred counties in northern Alabama, Georgia, and Tennessee where actual data are available and where conditions are representative of subregional analysis. The third is illustrated in the case of a decade of recent developments in north Mississippi. The three coincide in part and illustrate both the problem and the method of approach. The studies were made by John Maclachlan for the purpose of answering the particular inquiries enumerated above.

The areas represented by the general regions and counties selected, classified according to physiographic subregions, may be characterized as "uplands." The particular counties in the sample survey included the following: In *Alabama:* Blount, Calhoun, Cherokee, Colbert, Cullman,

Gross Farm Income Per Capita, 1930

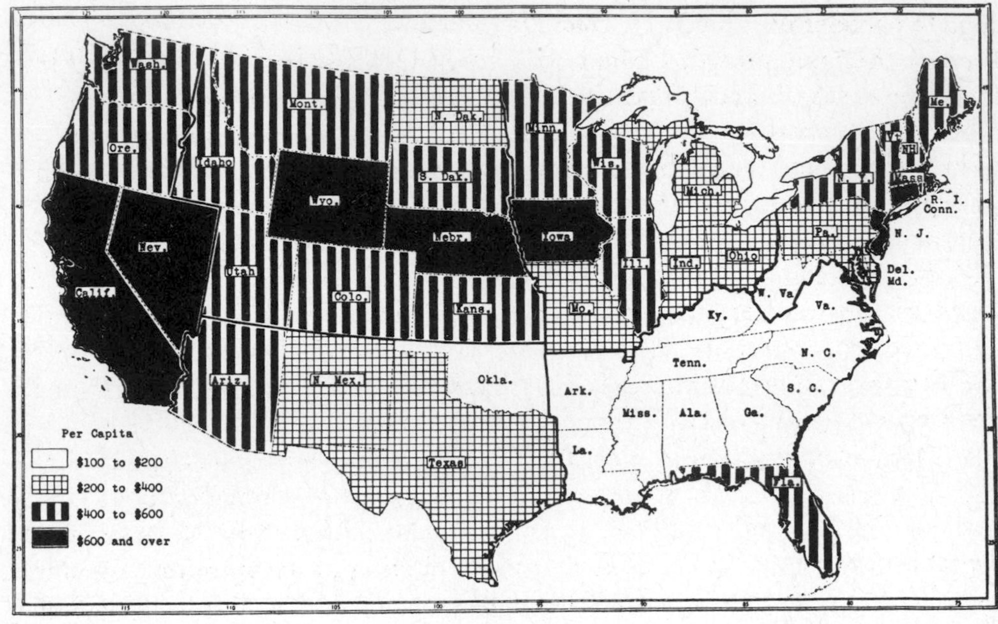

Relative Income Status of Farm Population by States, 1930

Rank in Ratio of Column 1	STATE	(1) Per Cent Farm Population Is of Total Population	(2) Per Cent Farm Income Is of Total Income	(3) Ratio of Column 2 to Column 1	(4) Gross Farm Income Per Capita	Rank in Ratio of Column 1	STATE	(1) Per Cent Farm Population Is of Total Population	(2) Per Cent Farm Income Is of Total Income	(3) Ratio of Column 2 to Column 1	(4) Gross Farm Income Per Capita
1	California	10.9	13.7	125.7	945	26	Wisconsin	30.0	20.2	67.3	416
2	Nevada	18.1	18.8	103.9	848	27	Connecticut	5.4	3.6	66.7	729
3	Wyoming	32.4	32.2	99.4	655	28	*Arkansas*	60.4	39.4	65.2	117
4	Nebraska	42.5	41.9	98.6	644	29	Rhode Island	2.4	1.5	62.5	566
5	Iowa	39.6	38.4	97.0	615	30	*Oklahoma*	42.7	25.9	60.7	184
6	Kansas	37.6	35.3	93.9	484	31	*South Carolina*	52.7	31.4	59.6	147
7	*Florida*	19.0	17.8	93.7	465	32	New York	5.7	3.4	59.6	555
8	South Dakota	56.3	52.2	92.7	483	33	Delaware	19.5	11.4	58.5	399
9	Washington	19.5	17.9	91.8	559	34	Missouri	30.7	17.7	57.7	296
10	Idaho	42.3	38.7	91.5	527	35	Maryland	14.6	8.4	57.5	328
11	Oregon	23.5	21.4	91.1	511	36	Illinois	13.1	7.3	55.7	475
12	North Dakota	58.4	52.9	90.6	381	37	*Georgia*	48.8	26.1	53.5	158
13	Colorado	27.3	24.4	89.4	549	38	*North Carolina*	50.5	26.7	52.9	166
14	Montana	38.1	31.5	82.7	453	39	*Tennessee*	46.5	24.4	52.5	142
15	Maine	21.4	17.5	81.8	448	40	*Louisiana*	39.5	20.6	52.2	146
16	Utah	22.8	18.6	81.6	458	41	*Kentucky*	45.0	22.9	50.9	152
17	Vermont	31.4	25.6	81.5	493	42	*Alabama*	50.6	25.4	50.2	130
18	New Mexico	37.5	29.8	79.5	263	43	*Virginia*	39.3	19.5	49.6	172
19	New Jersey	3.2	2.5	78.1	787	44	Indiana	25.1	12.2	48.6	355
20	Minnesota	34.9	26.5	75.9	422	45	Pennsylvania	8.9	4.0	44.9	374
21	*Texas*	40.4	30.6	75.7	226	46	Ohio	15.2	6.5	42.8	323
22	New Hampshire	13.5	9.9	73.3	505	47	Michigan	16.2	6.3	38.9	325
23	Arizona	22.7	16.1	70.9	498	48	West Virginia	26.0	8.3	31.9	172
24	Massachusetts	2.9	2.0	69.0	633						
25	*Mississippi*	67.8	46.8	69.0	120						

Dekalb, Etowah, Franklin, Jackson, Jefferson, Lauderdale, Lawrence, Limestone, Madison, Marion, Marshall, Morgan, St. Clair, Shelby, Talladega, Walker, Winston. In *Georgia:* Bartow, Catoosa, Chattooga, Dade, Dawson, Fannin, Floyd, Glimer, Gordon, Habersham, Lumpkin, Murray, Pickens, Polk, Rabun, Stephens, Towns, Union, Walker, White, Whitfield. In *Tennessee:* Bedford, Davidson, Dekalb, Dickson, Giles, Hickman, Lawrence, Lincoln, Marshall, Maury, Rutherford, Smith, Williamson, Wilson, Benton, Cheatham, Houston, Humphreys, Lewis, Perry, Trousdale, Wayne.

Mr. Maclachlan has pointed out that a realistic view of the Interior Uplands regions must take into account not only the peculiar problems incident to the geographic and cultural character of the regions themselves, but also, and very particularly, the modifying effect upon these problems of the adjacent regions. West and Northwest of the Interior Uplands lies the Middle States. East and Northeast is the commercial milk belt of the Northeast. To the south of the Uplands, from Virginia to Texas, extends the cotton-producing area of the Southeast and the Southwest. Definite limitations upon the economic wisdom of certain developments grow out of the nature of these neighbors, as well as out of the nature of the Uplands regions themselves.

The Uplands are generally characterized as a corn and winter wheat producing group of subregions. In view of the productive capacity of the Middle States and the northwestern regions, we can discard at once the possibility of making the Uplands larger producers of these crops. The commercial needs of the nation can be met with advantage in the corn and wheat belts. Beyond producing for their own consumption, and that within localized limits, the Uplands must not be led into extensive corn and wheat production. Yields of cotton and, over large territories, the practical impossibility of producing a profitable crop of the staple again restrict the possibilities of developing a cash-crop staple which is the peculiar product of other types of areas. Cotton growing is a losing game throughout the Uplands, when the cost of production in other areas is considered.

The several million persons dependent upon the land for their real income, however, must have cash resources. To argue for national-regional self-sufficiency is well enough; but to extend the argument too far is to invite disaster, if the general sufficiency of all the regions is to cut off the markets of each in its specialty. There cannot be a successful national agriculture in which all the farming regions produce all the necessities of their economic lives, disregarding the comparative advantages of certain regional specializations. Perhaps the most obvious cash crop of parts of the Uplands, tobacco, is a closed question. Surpluses of production in almost all

Farm and Home Work and Value of Current Living in the Southern Appalachians

Adapted from *Economic and Social Problems and Conditions of the Southern Appalachians*

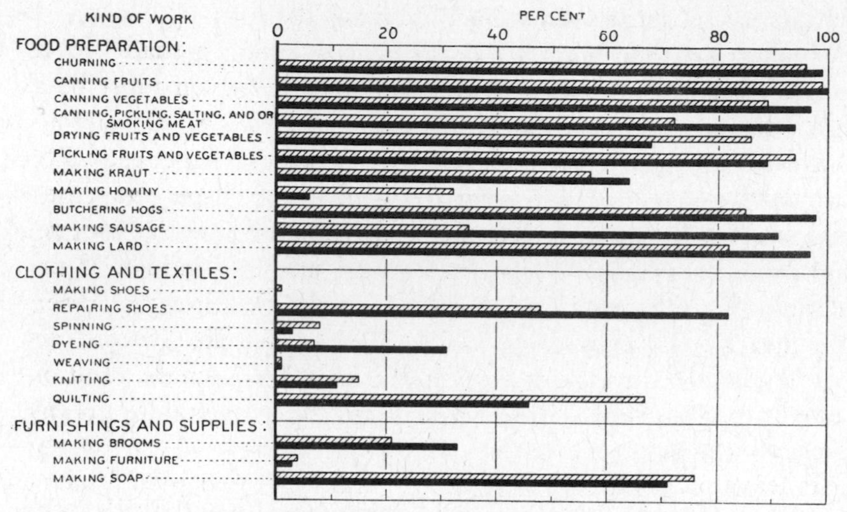

PERCENTAGE OF FAMILIES ENGAGED IN SPECIFIED TYPES OF HOUSEHOLD PRODUCTION (KNOTT COUNTY, KENTUCKY, 1929-30 AND GRAYSON COUNTY, VIRGINIA, 1930-31)

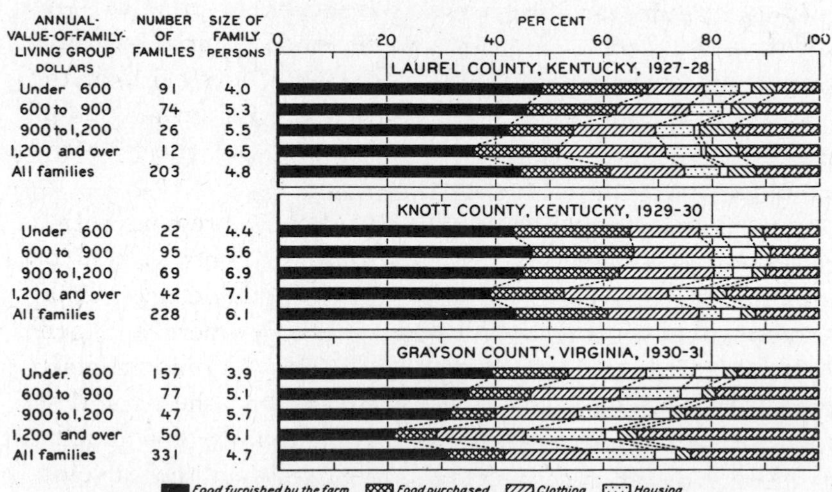

DISTRIBUTION OF THE VALUE OF CURRENT LIVING AMONG GOODS AND SERVICES OF SPECIFIED TYPES (LAUREL COUNTY, KENTUCKY, 1927-28, KNOTT COUNTY, KENTUCKY, 1929-30, AND GRAYSON COUNTY, VIRGINIA, 1930-31)

grades set aside the suggestion that we seek a wider regional distribution of dependence upon tobacco specialties.

These avenues being closed, what are the other ways out? The projected plan of supplementing agricultural income with part-time industrial activity, however excellent, encounters the simple fact that such non-competitive industrialization can at best affect only a small proportion of the population. The largest areas must remain dominantly agricultural, and reörganization of their agricultural practices must be made to meet the need for a healthful and healthy life. Industrialization must be arranged through some plan of interregional balance or must be reserved for those areas which can meet the demand for non-competitive products or can produce manufactures at a decided economic advantage over the existing national areas which produce goods of like description. The development of large units, or of large numbers of small units, of industrial production can be had, of course, only with reference to the capacities of present industrial regions. This limitation means, if we take into account actual net costs of production to society, that only a relatively small additional fraction of the national industrial income can be reallocated in any quick-changing economy.

This leaves us, then, to seek some definite general plan which will net a genuinely balanced regional real income. It is clear that certain modifications of national consumption habits, the potentialities of the lands and climate of the region and its cultural conditioning may offset the difficulties by providing a sufficient and marketable agricultural product. Indeed this study of dairying possibilities had for one of its assumptions an increased home consumption of local products. It assumed further that the wholesale evacuation of large areas of land now used for farming is untenable. What is needed, therefore, is a balanced program meeting the largest number of requirements.

Examination of the physical conditions of the subregions with an eye to the selection of crops which fit these conditions, points to non-commercial dairying, the growing of legumes, potatoes, vegetable and orchard crops. But recommendations and plans cannot be posited merely in general, nor can they be adapted uncritically to districts which are fundamentally administrative. The natural regions of the continent, and the natural subregions within them, are by definition the sole realistic units of planned reorganization. We find our authority for this premise in the development, in various of the subregions, of different possibilities. The Nashville Basin with its large development of milk production is not geographically or topographically better suited to such activity than other subregions in the Uplands. The large production of small field crops in certain areas has met

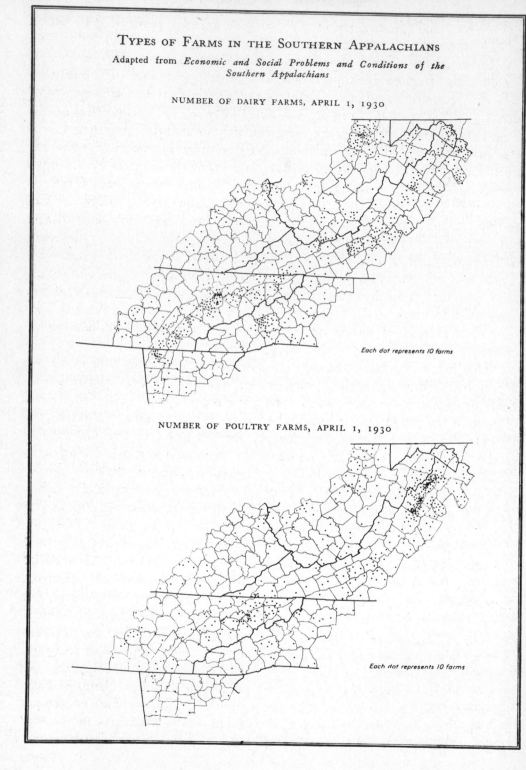

Types of Farms in the Southern Appalachians

Adapted from *Economic and Social Problems and Conditions of the Southern Appalachians*

NUMBER OF DAIRY FARMS, APRIL 1, 1930

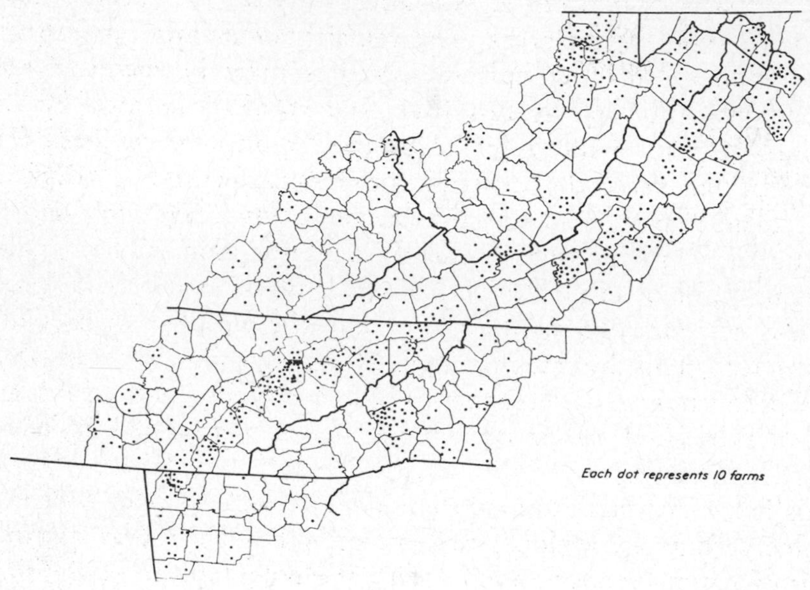

NUMBER OF POULTRY FARMS, APRIL 1, 1930

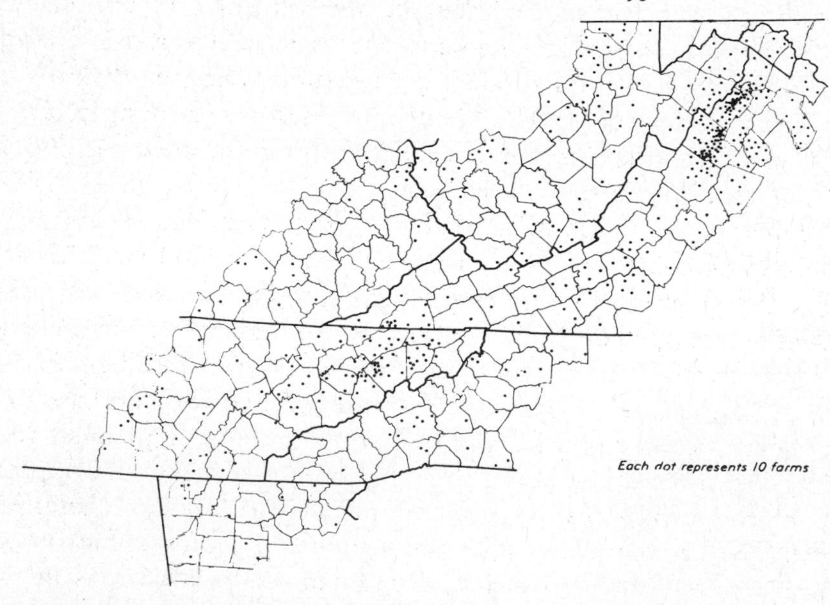

geographic obstacles greater than those prevailing elsewhere. The apple production of the Georgia Blue Ridge foothills is not based upon a superior *locale*, but rather points the moral that most of the Uplands can also produce certain varieties of apples profitably and in large quantities. In the same way the milk and butter fat production of north Mississippi, an extraordinary example of what can be done, must still be examined in the light of the fact that southern Mississippi has many superior advantages.

In a word, to analyze the specialties of many of the subregions, and to summarize these, is to point to the major possibilities of most of the subregions. We have in most such developments evidence of the virtue of local leadership in agricultural practices rather than of local physical advantages. This is clearly demonstrated in the case of northern Mississippi. The task of establishing these developments, of comparing their production with that of other areas, of estimating and analyzing their potential markets and their effect upon the national economy, is precisely the real task of establishing genuine attainable goals in realistic programs of optimum production.

Mr. Maclachlan follows the case further when he assumes that to consider the area as a physically homogeneous one and to generalize its possibilities without subregional exceptions would be a grievous mistake. But to consider it, alternatively, as a mere agglomeration of subregions would be equally bad. For certain basic problems are common to the whole area. The contour of the land is one. The presence of neighboring regions with diverse sources of agricultural income is another. The necessity for a constant source of cash income is another. The problems of transport to market, of institutional lacks, of cultural and economic isolation and dispersion of population; these and other parts of the situation of the Uplands subregions are similar, with exception made for infrequent concentrations of urban markets and local urban population. All these problems differ in kind from those of the plantation areas of the Southeast and the general-farming subregions of the Middle States. They become, on close observation, the unique problems of a buffer region. Hence we must consider the Uplands as a national unit as really as we must analyze the localized subregions. There must not be any tendency to confuse the real kinship between the several subregions which are separately analyzed, just as the danger of ignoring the special character of the individual subregion must not be disregarded in the formulation of social-agricultural objectives.

The study of geographical and cultural potentialities of the Uplands subregions must seek ways of development under three general headings. First of all in importance comes the question of the feasibility of extending present subregional specialties throughout the Uplands. Climate and

Regional Differentials, Purebred Registered Cattle, All Types, 1930

State and Region	Number Farms Reporting	Per Cent All Farms	Number Cattle Reported	Number Per Farm	Per Cent Dairy Breed
Southeast	*37,754*	*1.5*	*150,024*	*3.9*	*74.4*
Virginia	4,210	2.4	20,927	5.0	67.6
North Carolina	4,071	1.4	13,924	3.4	84.4
South Carolina	1,629	1.0	6,663	4.0	89.5
Georgia	2,740	1.1	10,528	3.8	80.1
Florida	675	1.1	3,304	5.0	85.9
Kentucky	6,477	2.6	27,118	4.1	62.3
Tennessee	5,606	2.2	26,717	4.8	70.6
Alabama	2,549	1.0	9,274	3.6	72.9
Mississippi	4,972	1.6	17,248	3.4	87.9
Arkansas	3,430	1.4	8,754	2.6	74.6
Louisiana	1,395	0.9	5,567	3.9	76.1
Southwest	*29,986*	*4.0*	*225,500*	*7.5*	*27.0*
Oklahoma	8,764	4.3	42,770	4.8	37.7
Texas	18,429	3.7	148,727	8.1	26.8
New Mexico	1,794	5.7	22,188	12.4	5.9
Arizona	999	7.0	11,815	11.8	34.4
Northeast	*65,065*	*10.5*	*438,892*	*6.7*	*90.6*
Maine	3,659	9.3	20,066	5.4	79.8
New Hampshire	1,986	13.3	13,561	6.8	83.4
Vermont	3,680	14.7	27,075	7.3	95.0
Massachusetts	2,619	10.2	22,112	8.4	88.4
Rhode Island	339	10.2	3,415	10.1	93.1
Connecticut	1,875	10.9	13,692	7.3	89.3
New York	21,024	13.1	165,160	7.9	94.2
New Jersey	2,432	9.5	17,906	7.3	95.4
Pennsylvania	18,757	10.8	116,370	6.2	93.1
Delaware	583	6.0	3,100	5.3	93.4
Maryland	3,945	9.1	20,773	5.3	92.8
West Virginia	4,166	5.0	15,662	3.8	43.8
Middle States	*167,844*	*10.3*	*830,602*	*4.9*	*66.8*
Ohio	17,293	7.9	98,079	5.6	83.7
Indiana	10,455	5.8	49,225	4.7	72.6
Illinois	18,755	8.7	92,992	5.0	64.1
Michigan	16,492	9.7	83,520	5.1	85.9
Wisconsin	31,931	17.5	165,871	5.2	91.7
Minnesota	28,581	15.4	117,570	4.1	66.8
Iowa	27,689	12.8	133,423	4.8	32.7
Missouri	16,648	6.5	89,922	5.4	35.1
Northwest	*75,199*	*11.6*	*397,945*	*5.3*	*22.2*
North Dakota	10,095	12.9	38,614	3.8	24.2
South Dakota	9,729	11.7	43,332	4.4	21.0
Nebraska	14,165	10.9	81,114	5.7	14.7
Kansas	18,416	11.1	103,339	5.6	26.6
Montana	6,235	13.1	34,309	5.5	13.2
Idaho	4,363	10.4	19,898	4.5	48.0
Wyoming	2,314	14.5	21,177	9.2	7.5
Colorado	6,567	11.0	41,916	6.4	19.4
Utah	3,315	12.2	14,246	4.3	48.1
Far West	*17,839*	*6.7*	*106,104*	*5.9*	*61.9*
Nevada	552	16.0	4,554	8.3	22.6
Washington	5,418	7.6	26,309	4.8	74.4
Oregon	6,585	11.9	33,312	5.1	65.3
California	5,284	3.9	41,929	7.9	55.1
United States	393,708	6.3	2,149,363	5.5	59.6

weather, topography and soil conditions, and the possession of a farming population prepared to undertake the projects must be surveyed and, most important, the existence of local or potential external markets must be inquired into. Can potato culture be introduced into the Limestone Valley or the Blue Ridge foothills? Is there any real impediment to the growth of milk production in the Uplands? What are the possibilities of establishing the production of apples as a widespread Upland specialty?

The second pertinent question in regard to extending production is that of non-competitive crops. The annual import of agricultural products into the United States has been known to approach a billion dollars in value. These products fall into two classes: food crops and industrial specialties, such as plants from which drugs are prepared. Many of these items require a careful cultivation and exact soil and climatic conditions. Can Uplands subregions provide these conditions? We know already that in some cases they can, and that such developments would be of considerable cash benefit to the subregions and the region as a whole.

The third question becomes that of eradicating crops now produced at a disadvantage in the Uplands, in favor of substituting for them crops of the above two classes. This is a practical question of shifting cash income, more or less immediately from one agricultural basis to another. It can be answered satisfactorily only in a study which brings together data ranging from market possibilities, local subregional conditions and costs of production, to the relation between pre-existing agricultural practices in the subregions. Only a factual answer is a useful one, but a simply agricultural analysis of possibilities becomes dangerous in the degree to which it fails to include social, geographic, national-economic materials.

The process of answering each of these questions in detail is not an impossibly large one, but without a complete and orderly technique it can become unwieldy. To record the physiographic, climatic, and demographic elements of the subregion succinctly, and to evaluate possibilities for various developments in view of the limits set by these data, is to provide a realistic picture of the possibilities of the subregions. Anything less than such a picture cannot be a safe basis for social planning.

But even a series of such social-physical analyses still suffers from a fatal weakness unless the whole Uplands area be pictured likewise. We have every reason for pointing out that the Uplands subregions are more nearly akin than any of them is to its northern or southern neighbors. By the same token we find that there is a danger of damaging competition between the subregions of the Uplands, which would succeed the present uneconomic competition of Uplands subregions with cotton and corn regions as an impediment to healthy regional and national economy. This is no

PUREBRED CATTLE BY STATES AND PER CAPITA RURAL POPULATION, 1930

STATE AND REGION	Total Farms in State	Number Farms Reporting	Per Cent of Total Farms Reporting	Total Number Cattle in State	Rural Population 1930	Cattle per Capita
Southeast	*2,397,776*	*37,754*	*1.57*	*8,360,888*	*17,934,067*	.4
Virginia	170,610	4,210	2.46	832,946	1,636,314	.5
North Carolina	279,708	4,071	1.45	532,631	2,360,429	.2
South Carolina	157,931	1,629	1.03	270,171	1,367,685	.2
Georgia	255,598	2,740	1.07	782,063	2,013,014	.4
Florida	58,966	675	1.14	431,448	708,433	.6
Kentucky	246,499	6,477	2.62	1,087,305	1,815,563	.6
Tennessee	245,657	5,606	2.28	1,073,899	1,720,018	.6
Alabama	257,395	2,549	.99	799,473	1,901,975	.4
Mississippi	321,633	4,972	1.55	1,008,672	1,670,971	.6
Arkansas	242,334	3,430	1.42	812,590	1,471,604	.6
Louisiana	161,445	1,395	.74	729,690	1,268,061	.6
Southwest	*744,932*	*29,986*	*4.02*	*10,455,724*	*5,611,944*	*1.9*
Oklahoma	203,866	8,764	4.29	2,097,576	1,574,359	1.3
Texas	495,489	18,429	3.72	6,602,703	3,435,367	1.9
New Mexico	31,404	1,794	5.39	1,060,327	316,501	3.3
Arizona	14,173	999	7.04	695,118	285,717	2.4
Northeast	*618,079*	*65,073*	*10.56*	*6,105,724*	*9,730,000*	.6
Maine	39,006	3,659	9.38	257,048	475,917	.5
New Hampshire	14,906	1,986	13.32	135,827	192,214	.7
Vermont	24,898	3,688	14.81	472,183	240,845	1.9
Massachusetts	25,598	2,619	10.23	207,389	418,188	.5
Rhode Island	3,322	339	10.20	31,633	52,068	.6
Connecticut	17,195	1,875	10.90	166,654	475,133	.4
New York	159,806	21,024	13.15	2,220,139	2,066,114	1.1
New Jersey	25,378	2,432	9.58	174,699	702,090	.2
Delaware	9,707	583	6.01	53,914	115,234	.5
Pennsylvania	172,419	18,757	10.87	1,511,202	3,097,839	.5
Maryland	43,203	3,945	9.13	318,779	656,657	.5
West Virginia	82,641	4,166	5.04	556,257	1,237,701	.4
Middle States	*1,622,625*	*167,844*	*10.34*	*20,710,226*	*13,070,509*	*1.5*
Ohio	219,296	17,293	7.88	1,772,856	2,139,326	.8
Indiana	181,570	10,455	5.75	1,446,747	1,442,611	1.0
Illinois	214,497	18,755	8.74	2,342,125	1,994,927	1.2
Michigan	169,372	16,492	9.74	1,528,161	1,540,250	.9
Wisconsin	181,767	31,931	17.57	3,536,603	1,385,163	2.6
Minnesota	185,255	28,581	15.42	3,165,178	1,306,337	2.4
Iowa	214,928	27,689	12.88	4,136,156	1,491,647	2.8
Missouri	255,940	16,648	6.50	2,782,400	1,770,248	1.6
Northwest	*648,927*	*75,199*	*11.59*	*14,436,139*	*4,757,557*	*3.0*
North Dakota	77,975	10,095	12.94	1,454,146	567,539	2.6
South Dakota	83,157	9,729	11.69	1,974,040	561,942	3.5
Nebraska	129,458	14,165	10.94	3,151,987	891,856	3.5
Kansas	166,042	18,416	11.09	3,223,772	1,151,165	2.8
Montana	47,495	6,235	13.13	1,290,383	356,570	3.6
Idaho	41,674	4,363	10.47	622,170	315,525	1.9
Wyoming	16,011	2,314	14.45	824,039	155,468	5.3
Colorado	59,956	6,567	10.95	1,453,952	515,909	2.8
Utah	27,159	3,315	12.20	441,650	241,583	1.8
Far West	*266,175*	*17,839*	*6.70*	*3,839,574*	*2,716,146*	*1.4*
Nevada	3,442	552	16.03	308,482	56,594	5.4
Washington	70,904	5,418	7.64	624,737	678,857	.9
Oregon	55,153	6,585	11.94	805,120	464,040	1.7
California	136,676	5,284	3.87	2,101,235	1,516,655	1.4
United States	6,298,514	393,695	6.25	62,908,275	53,820,223	1.2

merely theoretical point, but one of the utmost practical importance. Unless the effect upon the whole Uplands region be made a standard of criticism for the programs of the subregions, we can expect undesirable results from any extended plan.

Still another question lies before us. The consumption of agricultural products within the region and the subregions cannot be measured in terms of past consumption as if such data marked the ultimate limits. In the matter of milk, which will be discussed more fully, it may be pointed out that the Uplands should themselves consume more than twice as much as they now produce, despite the fact that a very considerable proportion of the present production is marketed. In the same fashion we must not consider national consumption totals to represent ultimate figures. There is no greater error than to presume that this nation has had at any time an actual overproduction of fruits, vegetables, eggs, small field crops, and milk. Changing trends in the national economy may mean that for the first time there is some prospect for a fair minimum national consumption of these products. In that case, which now seems alternative to chaos, the product of the regions which have hitherto specialized in such products will be insufficient to meet the national demand. The only risk of the Uplands in setting out toward a high degree of development in these necessities is that same risk which the entire nation faces, and which the region could not escape in any event. To seek the goals set forth here is the most reasonable manner of meeting the challenge of the national plan.

Selecting then strategically located Uplands subregions in Alabama, Georgia, and Tennessee, we undertake to discover their present development in regard to milk production with a view to getting at their potentialities. The elementary facts are about as follows:

In the *Tennessee Valley* area of Alabama, cotton and corn together cover about 75 per cent of the crop lands of the region. Hay and forage production is considerably above state ratios. The average present value per acre of farm lands is about 50 per cent above the state average, while the per farm value is exceeded only by the Gulf trucking area. The population is approximately three-fourths white, and tenancy exceeds 66 per cent. The fertility of the soil, as indicated in cotton and corn yields per acre, is consistently high. The index of local contour ranges from 30 to 40, with about 12 per cent of the total area ranging around 70.

The *Mineral District* of Alabama is an area of light cotton production, less than 15 per cent of the crop land being planted to the staple. Corn occupies almost half the crop land, while more than a third is devoted to other field crops. Potatoes are grown in commercial quantities in conjunction with local trucking. A per acre value of farm lands of $20.00

Per Cent of Total Crop Land Harvested Operated by Tenants, 1930

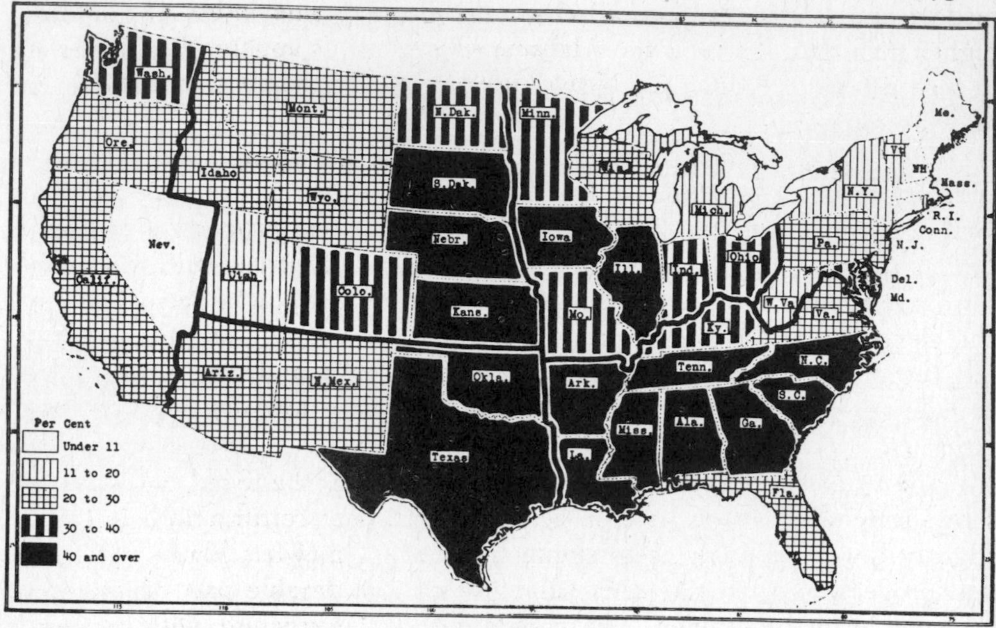

Mules and Mule Colts: Estimated Number on Farms and Value Per Head, 1932

STATE AND REGION	Number (in thousands)	Value Per Head	Total Value (in thousands)
Southeast	*2,663*	*$80.16*	*$213,466*
Virginia	93	84.00	7,812
North Carolina	273	89.00	24,297
South Carolina	176	74.00	12,802
Georgia	333	70.00	23,310
Florida	42	97.00	4,074
Kentucky	241	59.00	14,219
Tennessee	318	67.00	21,306
Alabama	319	62.00	56,606
Mississippi	347	63.00	21,861
Arkansas	332	46.00	15,272
Louisiana	189	63.00	11,907
Southwest	*1,281*	*46.07*	*59,015*
Oklahoma	287	43.00	12,341
Texas	960	47.00	45,120
New Mexico	22	39.00	858
Arizona	12	58.00	696
Northeast	*110*	*100.84*	*11,092*
Maine	...	.....	......
New Hampshire	...	.....	......
Vermont	...	.....	......
Massachusetts	...	.....	......
Rhode Island	...	.....	......
Connecticut	...	.....	......
New York	6	102.00	612
New Jersey	3	119.00	357
Delaware	10	93.00	930
Pennsylvania	50	111.00	5,550
Maryland	29	95.00	2,755
West Virginia	12	74.00	888
Middle States	*644*	*$64.17*	*$41,326*
Ohio	32	89.00	2,848
Indiana	83	77.00	6,391
Illinois	129	69.00	8,901
Michigan	6	89.00	534
Wisconsin	7	74.00	518
Minnesota	15	63.00	945
Iowa	81	64.00	5,184
Missouri	291	55.00	16,005
Northwest	*309*	*51.06*	*15,777*
North Dakota	8	45.00	360
South Dakota	18	46.00	828
Nebraska	91	57.00	5,187
Kansas	143	52.00	7,436
Montana	8	29.00	232
Idaho	7	45.00	315
Wyoming	4	45.00	180
Colorado	27	42.00	1,134
Utah	3	35.00	105
Far West	*75*	*59.25*	*4,444*
Nevada	3	44.00	132
Washington	20	54.00	1,080
Oregon	14	49.00	686
California	38	67.00	2,546

and per farm values of $2,151 for lands and buildings, of $236.00 for livestock indicate that the high income indicated in the 1930 Census proceeds from dairying and small-crop agriculture. The index of contour, higher than that of any of the Alabama subregions, is apparently no barrier to such a type of economy. Nearly 90 per cent of the rural population is of white stock.

The *Sand Mountain* subregion of Alabama is one of high yields of corn and cotton, which together occupy at present about 80 per cent of the crop land in roughly equal proportions. The values of real property are closely similar to those of the agriculture of the Mineral District, with crop performance somewhat higher. The farms of the area show a very considerable development of poultry production for home use, and are much nearer self-sustaining than those of the subregions South and Southeast. The population is almost entirely white, with relatively low tenancy and debt ratios.

The Alabama *Limestone Valley*, adjacent to the Sand Mountains, shows somewhat less of its crop acreage devoted to cotton and corn, with slightly lower yields of these staple crops and somewhat lower values of real property. As in the other subregions a considerable part of the area is available for pasturage. The population is mainly white, with no more than 20 per cent Negro in any part of the subregion. The index on contour for about two-thirds of the area is in the neighborhood of 60, with the remainder ranging near 100.

Of the Georgia subregions, the *Appalachian Plateau and Valley* plants very little cotton, the crops in general being those of a region with a shorter growing season and cooler climate than cotton can well withstand. The soils resemble closely those of the Alabama Limestone Valley, and about 40 per cent of the total area is classed as improved farm lands. Narrow ridges separate broad valleys, the altitude of the region ranging from 1,000 to 1,900 feet. The index of contour ranges below 75, a considerable proportion being at a figure of 30 or less. The population is very largely white, with most of the Negroes of the region concentrated in the towns.

The *Georgia Blue Ridge* ranges from 2,000 to nearly 4,800 feet above sea level, with numerous broad valleys, which keep the index contour in the neighborhood of 100. The altitude and location of the subregion result in its having a very high average rainfall, about 70 inches, with not less than four inches in any month. The typical annual average temperature, 57.5 degrees F., is significantly lower than that of other subregions of Georgia. Nearly the entire population is white, with many farms located in valleys too narrow and rocky for any profitable cultivation. Corn, apples, vegetables, potatoes, hay, and rye are the leading crops.

Alfalfa Cut for Hay
Acreage, 1929

Adapted from the U. S. Bureau of Agricultural Economics

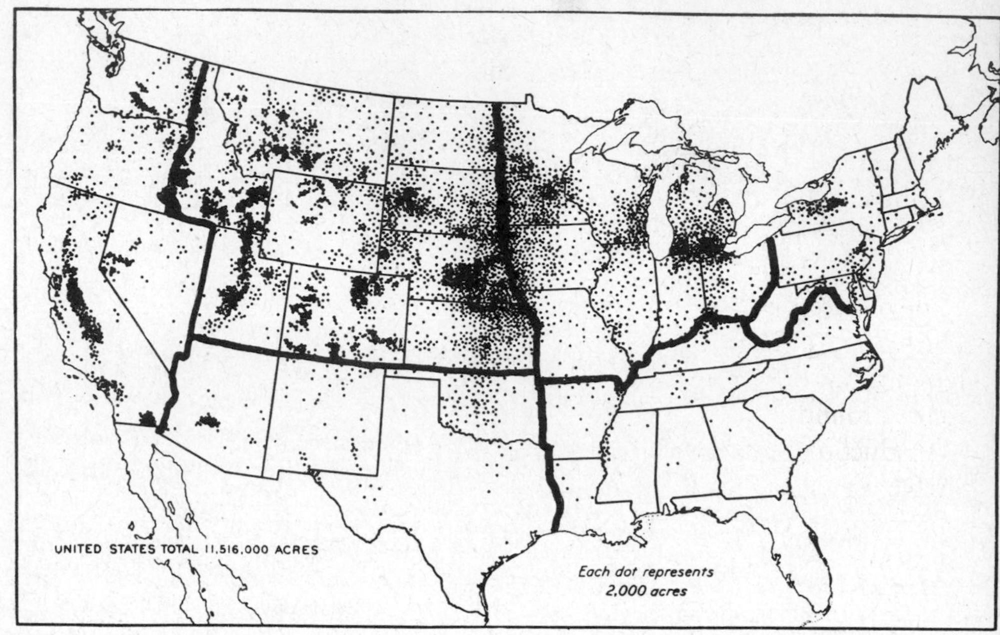

Sheep and Lambs: Number, April 1, 1930

Adapted from the U. S. Bureau of Agricultural Economics

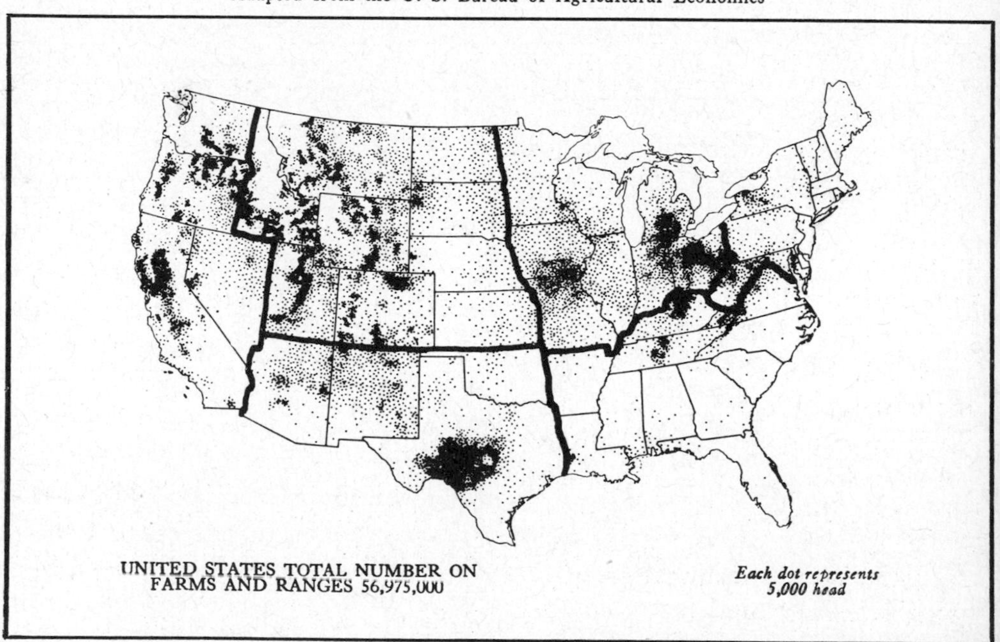

The *Blue Ridge Foothills and Upper Piedmont* of Georgia, lying south and southeast of the Blue Ridge, is somewhat lower than the latter, with an average altitude of about 1,500 feet and an index of contour something less than 50 except in some practically unpopulated areas. The soils contain a high percentage of acids except in the broader valleys. The crops are similar to those of the Blue Ridge, with somewhat more cotton produced. In Habersham County nearly 20 per cent of the annual Georgia apple crop is produced. The population is almost entirely white, with low values of real property and high rates of illiteracy.

Of the Tennessee subregions, the *Nashville Basin,* which is made the criterion of the subregions in this survey, has an index of contour ranging from 85 to 300 and above. The valleys are broad and broken by sharp declivities. The soils are fertile in the valleys, but do not assay out of the class of the better soils of the other subregions included here. The population has a higher proportion of Negroes than the other subregions, ranging to a third of the total in this datum. In the area of relatively retarded development the proportion of Negroes is considerably lower.

This subregion is notable for its livestock development. More than 80 per cent of all farms reported an average of 3.4 cows milked per farm, with cows milked totaling only 40 per cent of all cattle. The growing of potatoes, vegetables, feed crops, and field grains is well advanced. From five to ten per cent of all farms are listed as belonging to the owners or breeders of thoroughbred Jersey cattle.

Comparison of the objective conditions of the several subregions, which has been done above very sketchily, indicates that the Tennessee Valley dairying region possessed, in the period covered, two definite advantages over the other subregions here studied—an available and visible market, and adequate means of transport. Otherwise, in the matter of climate and weather, soil and topography, there is no effective superiority of the dairying subregion over the subregions where dairying is undeveloped and milk production carried out on a smaller scale. The size and value of farms and the value of farm equipment in the subregions, varying within limits of from $1,500 to $3,000 total per farm, with a high proportion of all farms falling close to the average, suggests the possibility of a program of stocking the area for increased milk production on a non-commercial scale. The local consumption of milk, if social pressure were applied, could with great benefit be doubled or trebled. The local production of milk products for sale, carried out through farmers' organizations, might well result in the development of a good cash income for the subregions. As has been observed before, surpluses in milk and milk products both locally and in the nation at large have been superficial commercial surpluses of production

Sorghums Harvested for Grain, Buckwheat, and Velvet Beans: Acreage, 1924

Adapted from the U. S. Bureau of Agricultural Economics

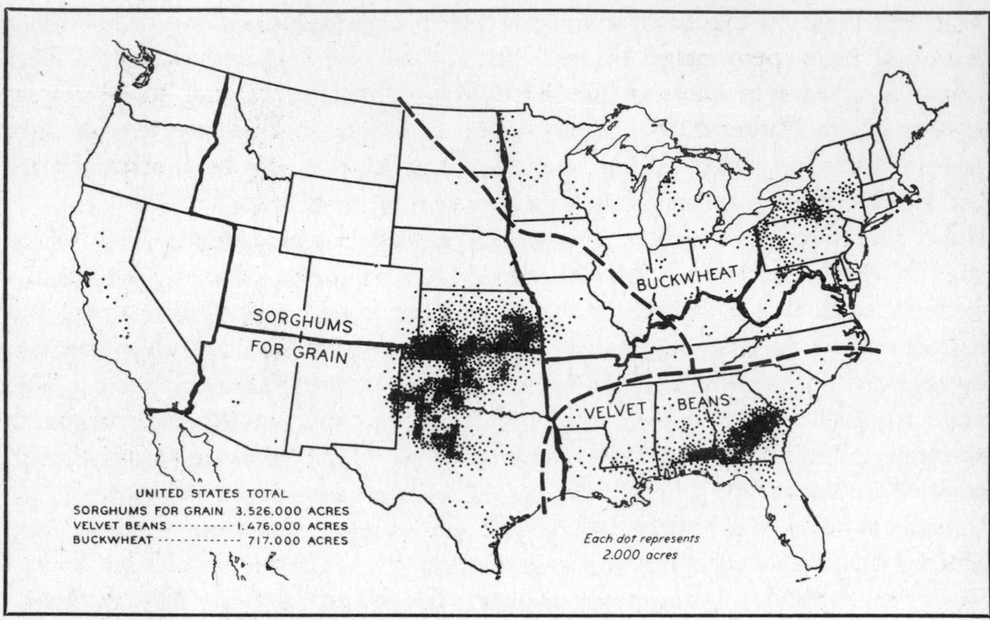

Field Beans and Peanuts: Acreage Harvested, 1924

Adapted from the U. S. Bureau of Agricultural Economics

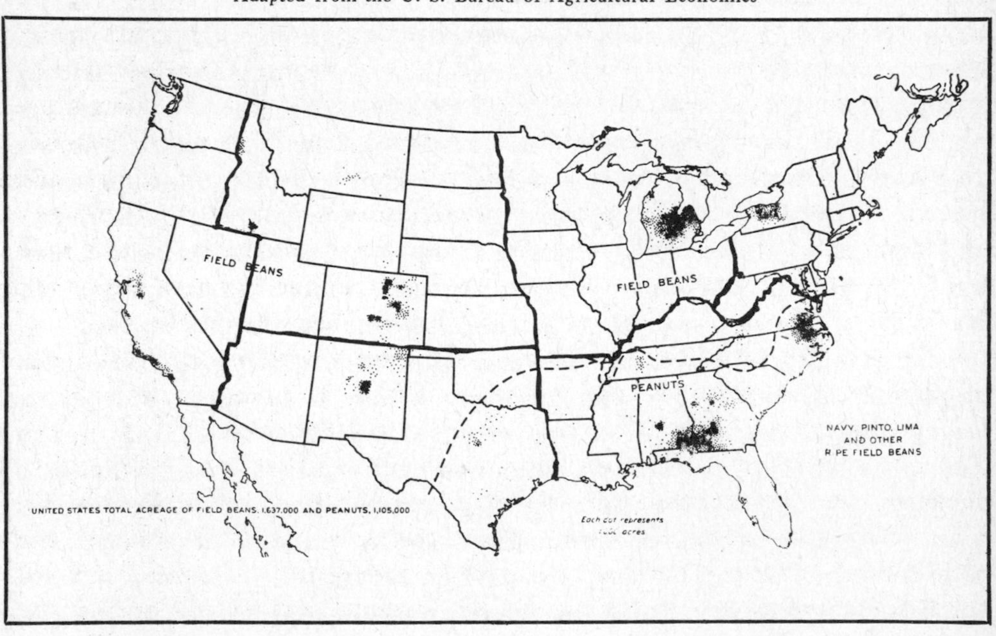

over effective demand. The great milk-producing areas of the northern regions could not supply sufficient of the fluid for the real demand, and in the Southeast particularly, where milk consumption is relatively infinitesimal, markets may be created under the national planned economy which have not been dreamed of before.

It is significant to point out that while only one-tenth of the land area in the Alabama and Georgia subregions is devoted to pastures, and one-fifth in the Tennessee subregions (nearly a third in the Nashville Basin), total crops harvested per square mile in the latter are even greater than in the former areas. This fact does not argue solely that the character of the soils of the latter subregions is intrinsically better than that of the former. Indeed, since the contour of the Tennessee areas as measured appears less suited to crop cultivation than the Georgia or Alabama areas, this fact may be seen as definite evidence of the direct value of cattle in protecting against erosion and washing of the lands. Soil analyses of the valley lands of the subregions do not indicate any original superiority of the Tennessee subregion; the superiority must be traced to the soil-building effect of the considerably greater number of cattle thereon and to the larger proportion of lands which are put under cover crops for pasturage.

In the event of attaining an adequate supply of cattle in the subregions we should find in the areas of the subregions of Alabama an average of 25 animals per square mile, in Georgia 23 per square mile, in the Nashville Basin approximately 60, and in the undeveloped area nearly 20. Maintaining present averages of milk production per cow milked, we should have a total production of 73,709,000 gallons of milk in the Alabama areas, 32,409,000 in the Georgia, and 84,450,000 in the Tennessee subregions of which 73,600,000 would come from the Nashville Basin and 10,850,000 from the undeveloped area. This rise in production would leave a deficit under minimum dietary requirements for local consumption of 39,993,000 gallons in the Alabama areas, and a surplus over the dietary figure of 5,168,000 in the Georgia subregion, about 24,209,440 in the Nashville Basin, and 4,320,000 in the undeveloped Tennessee area.

These figures demonstrate the feasibility of extending the production of milk in the subregions. In summary it may be pointed out that the largest production of milk in the subregions takes place in an area in Tennessee where the index of contour is superficially least favorable to dairying; that at least four-fifths of the farms in the subregions now milk cows, so that some degree of familiarity with the care of animals may be presumed; that the number of cattle per square mile of territory would not become excessive even at the point of attainment of the norms suggested, nor would the ratio between the number of cows and the acreage

Home Ownership, 1930

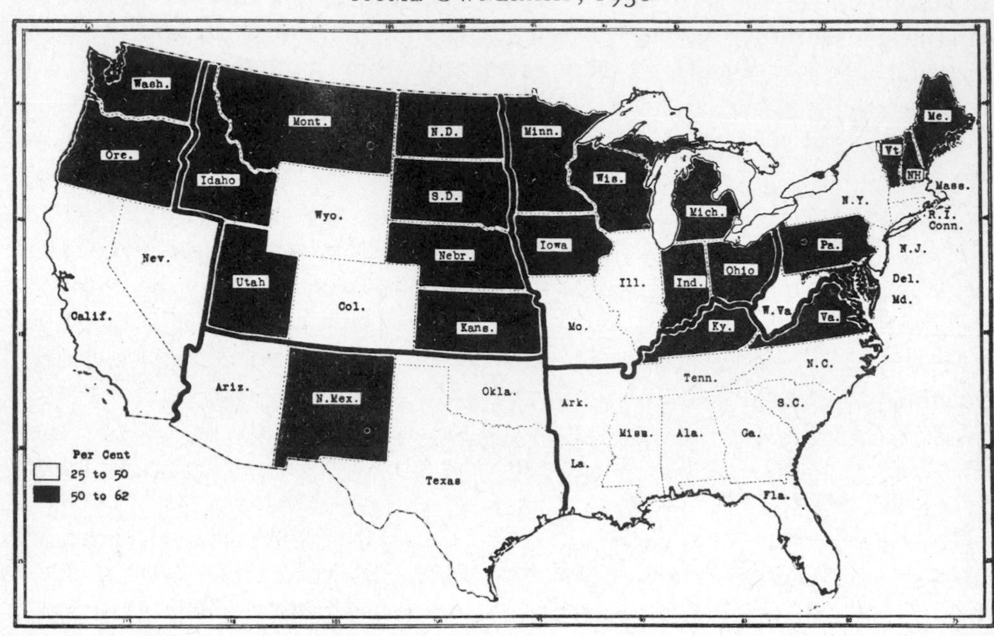

PERCENTAGE OF ALL HOMES OCCUPIED BY OWNERS, 1920 AND 1930

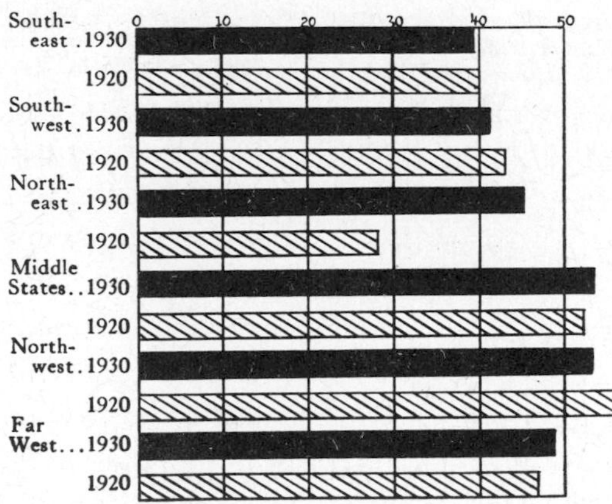

NUMBER OF FARMERS BY TYPES, IN THE SOUTHEAST, 1900-1930

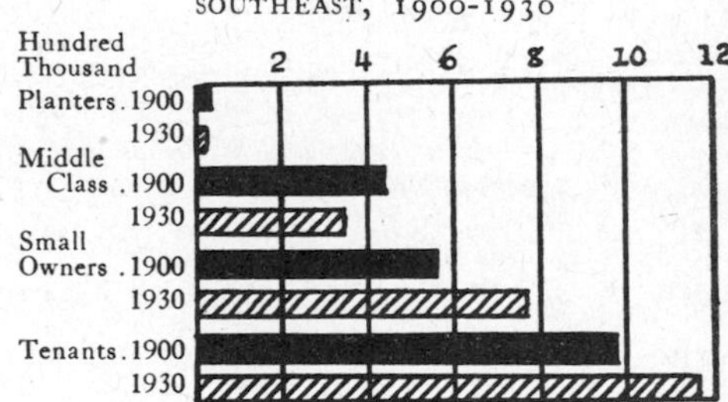

PERCENTAGE VARIATIONS IN AREAS, NUMBER AND SIZE OF FARMS

REGION	Total Acres	Total Number	Under 100 Acres	Over 500 Acres
Southeast	17.3	38.0	51.0	8.9
Southwest	20.3	11.8	10.9	17.5
Northeast	6.4	9.8	9.8	2.6
Middle States	21.2	25.8	19.7	6.6
Northwest	28.3	10.3	3.6	54.8
Far West	6.5	4.3	[illegible]	9.6

of farms or pasture lands be impracticable. Therefore, the obstacles to the development can only be those of marketing and of financing the development in the first place. As for the first point, it may be indicated that the minimum dietary requirements of the Southeast cannot be set lower than 2,450,000,000 gallons of milk per annum. The states of Tennessee, Alabama, and Georgia respectively require at least 251,189,000, 254,040,000, and 279,217,000 gallons per annum. Their production deficits as of 1930 are 1,161,455,187 gallons for the Southeast, 69,399,685 for Tennessee, 130,491,202 for Alabama, and 165,577,044 for Georgia.

As for the consideration that the Uplands might be thrown into competition with the existing dairying regions of the nation in selling their product, it may be pointed out that the production deficit of the Southeast (the excess of what is needed over what is produced) amounted in 1930 to more than one-tenth of the national total of milk produced. In other words, the present dairying areas could not carry more than a fraction of the task of supplying the Southeast with sufficient milk for the minimum needs of the people.

Granting any reasonable advance in the expansion of the Tennessee Valley and Piedmont areas, we must therefore assume the development of a market for milk and milk products in the Southeast which very nearly doubles present or normal (1929) consumption, a new demand which cannot be met by the product of the Middle States and the Northeast, or by that of the existing dairy industry in the Southeastern States. There will be clearly an outlet for an Uplands increase in production for sale of about 50 per cent, with sufficient leeway to provide for the utilization of the whole commercial total at any time. The salvation of the agriculture of the Uplands depends upon the creation there of a relatively self-sufficient life, with the production of crops and specialties which are in keeping with the objective situation of the region. The extension of milk production is entirely in keeping with the larger plan for the area.

Still another study was made of the northern counties of Mississippi where recent developments have been particularly successful. This study not only confirms the general hypotheses indicated in the proposed expansion in the Piedmont, Tennessee Valley, and other "uplands," but gives the results of an observable experiment which resulted in the northern counties of Mississippi, not so well adapted as the southern counties, reaching a high degree of success in both dairying and breeding of purebred Jerseys. Together with the Memphis area, this part of Mississippi has become well known for the number and quality of its Island-bred Jerseys, featuring both production and type. It also has a very large ratio of family milk cows on cotton farms. Seven of the Northeast Prairie counties produced 45 per

The Mississippi Land-Farm Picture

PROPORTION OF AREA TIMBERED OR UNCULTIVABLE

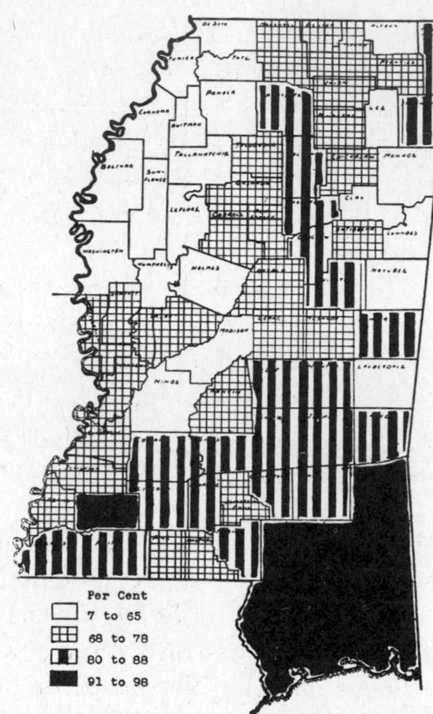

AVERAGE NUMBER OF ACRES, ALL FARMS, 1930

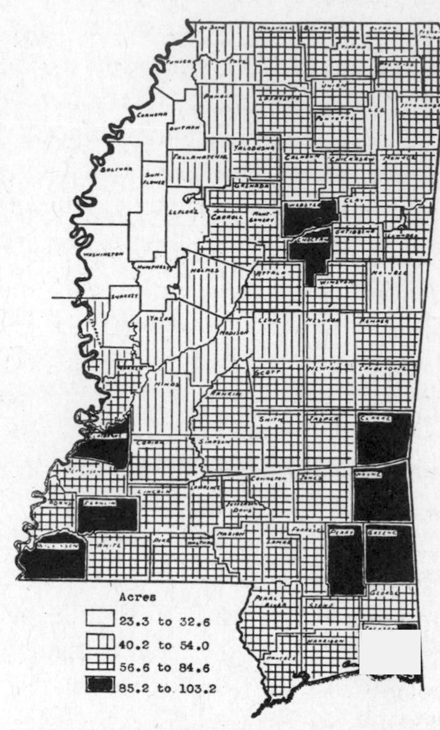

PER CENT OF FARM TENANCY AMONG WHITE FARMERS, 1930

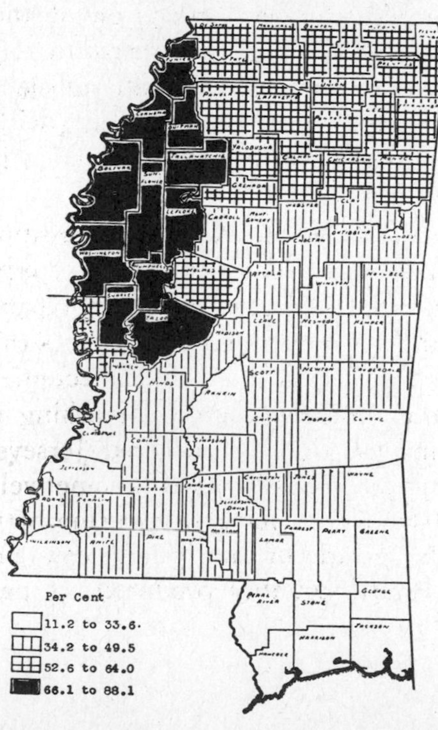

VALUE PER FARM OF ALL FARM PRODUCTS SOLD, TRADED OR USED, 1929

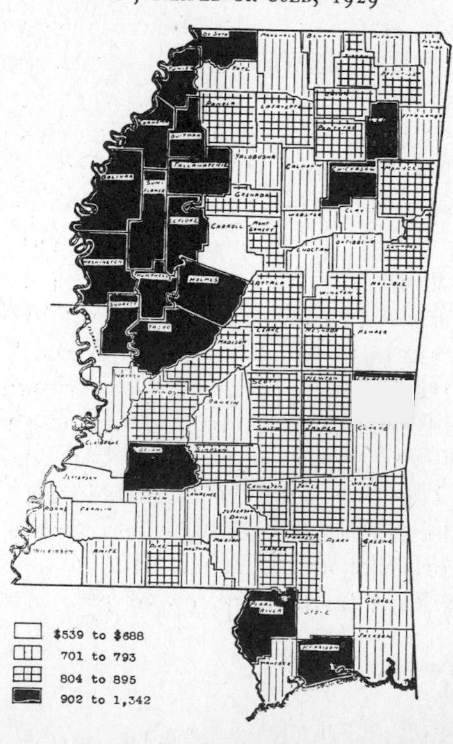

cent of the commercial butter fat. Another eight counties produced nearly 30 per cent. The same seven counties which produced 44.8 per cent of the state's butter fat total utilized in manufacture almost exactly 50 per cent of the state's total of butter fat manufactured into cheese, butter, and other finished products. The same eight other counties which produced 28 per cent of the state's butter fat manufactured 36.8 per cent of the total. The fifteen counties together produced three-fourths of the butter fat produced in the state, and manufactured more than 86 per cent. In the Northeast Highland and upper Shortleaf counties of Tippah, Union, Pontotoc, Calhoun, Webster, and Choctaw are 52 cream buying stations which ship most of their purchases into the Prairie for manufacture. Only two cheese factories and two commercial creameries are to be found in these counties. In the Northeast Prairie are six condensaries, four cheese factories, ten commercial creameries, and seven intermediate commercial handlers of whole milk.

Looking at the matter of the relation between the quantity of butter fat produced in the county and the quantity manufactured there, we find again that the counties already marked out are those of most significance. Four of the seven Prairie counties manufacture more than they produce, and the region as a whole imports 8.9 per cent of the state production from other counties for manufacture. Excepting Coahoma and Leflore counties in the Delta which, producing an inconsiderable proportion of state manufacture, still import several times their own production for manufacture, we find the upper Loess, the counties of Attala and Lauderdale and Hinds and Lincoln the heaviest importers outside the Prairie. As may be inferred from the figures for manufacture, the milk produced in other counties largely flows into these.

From what has been said it becomes clear that the dairying industry in Mississippi is a project of the northern half of the state, always excepting the three southerly Loess counties. This fact may be attributed to the influence of the A. & M. experiment stations and coöperatives and of numerous individuals who, upon the devastating invasion of the boll weevil, had vision enough and capital enough, in the Prairie and Loess regions, to branch out into dairying. The Longleaf region in south Mississippi, otherwise ideal for dairying, and formerly a notable area of cattle production, was for many years cursed with a superficially unconquerable infestation of ticks. It may be indicated with reference to the Longleaf country that the region is admirably suited to livestock production, that since the final eradication of the tick the great obstacle has been removed, that the region has a smaller proportion of farm population and hence a potentially greater local market for dairy products, a considerably better transporta-

Cotton Economy in the Mississippi Delta

PER CENT OF CROP LAND IN COTTON, 1930

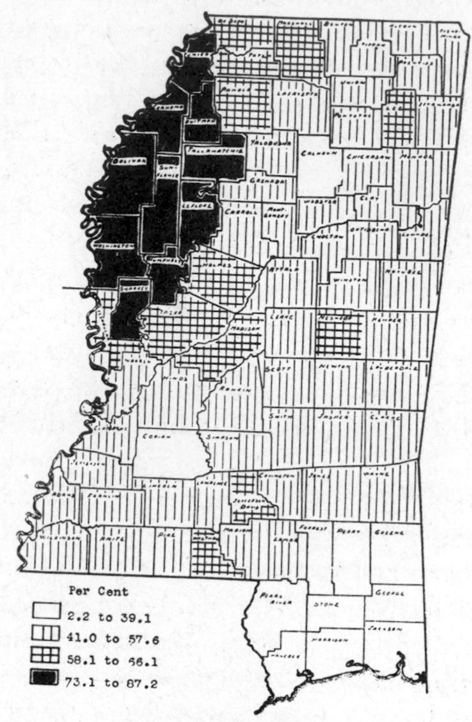

AVERAGE COTTON FARM INCOME, GROSS, 1929

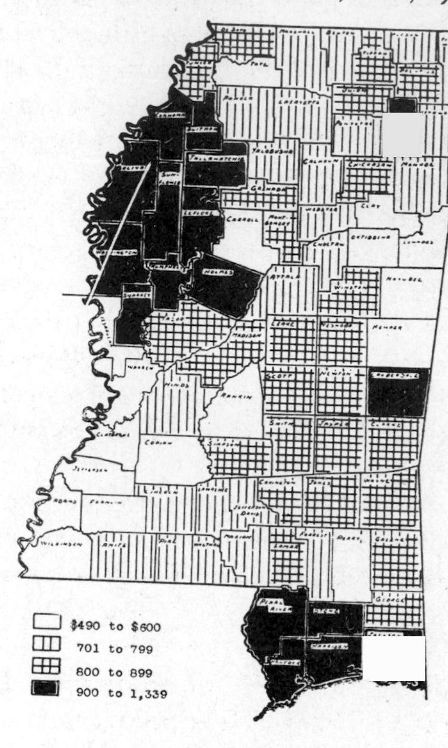

RECORDED CASES OF PELLAGRA PER 10,000 OF POPULATION, 1930

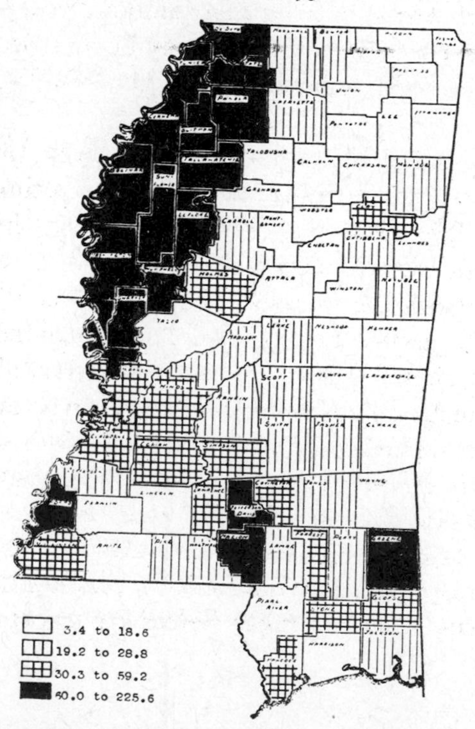

PER CENT TOTAL TENANCY, 1930

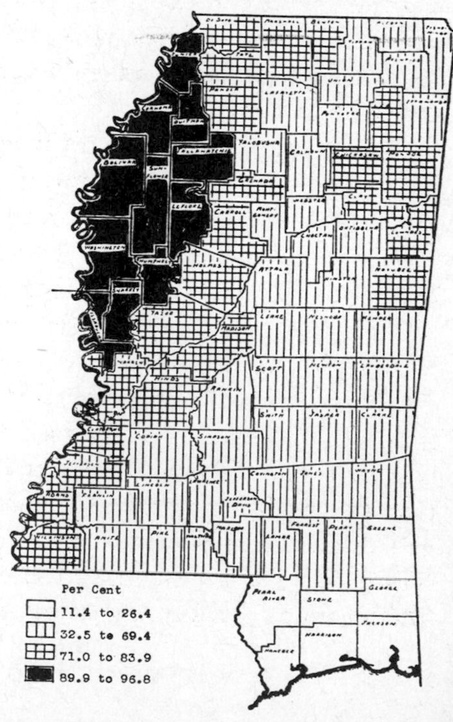

tion resource both of railways and highways than the northeastern areas of the state, and is nearer by many miles to large urban markets which might absorb manufactures. The transient population of the coast, the urban and suburban population of New Orleans and Mobile, constitute nearby markets wherein Mississippi products might compete very favorably with the dairy industries of the middle west. The general situation of the Longleaf, then, appears to be eminently suitable for an intensive dairy development, for, added to the advantages already mentioned, are those of the somewhat milder climate, which will add an average of about a month to the outdoor grazing season, and consequently, with the introduction of nourishing grasses, lower the gross cost of production by no little.

The Maclachlan studies may be used also to point to the quantitative aspect of livestock increase. Using the Mississippi per capita index of purebred Jerseys and multiplying the total population of the Southeast by this index, the result indicates the need for an increase of about 100,000 purebred Jerseys, and an increase of more than 50 per cent of Jersey breeders and owners. Almost the same ratio of increase would be necessary if we take the index of Tennessee and Kentucky. If to this index be added increases for other dairy breeds, Guernseys and Holsteins and Ayrshires, as well as the beef and dual purpose breeds, something of the size of the problem may be seen. As a matter of fact, although in the past the Jersey has predominated and the index of the Jersey might be a fair index of the region, there has been unusual increase in the last few years of Guernseys and Ayrshires. Or to make another sort of comparison, the region now has only about one-tenth as many purebred cattle per farm reporting as the Northeast and about one-tenth as many farms reporting as the three highest regions.

These studies of new prospects for dairying are fundamental to the whole question of agricultural reconstruction and agrarian life in the South. It is, indeed, through the very realistic, practical, subregion by subregion approach that the picture must be painted or success be attained, rather than through the ideological motivation for an abstract agrarian culture. To use Mississippi again as an example, at least half the people now live on tenant farms. Those counties having the largest ratios of tenancy also show the largest ratios of illiteracy and other measured deficiencies, yet show the smallest sized value of all farm products sold. This does not mean the highest ratio of vegetables raised in farm gardens, or chickens and eggs produced, or dairy cows on farms; but crops sold for cash, where in this case the cash does not go to the farm tenant. In the statistics for these four aspects of farm life—dairying, dairy cows on farms, farm vegetables grown in farm gardens, poultry produced and used at home—may

Ratio of Taxes to Value of Land and Buildings, Farms Operated by Full Owners Owning No Other Farm Land, 1930

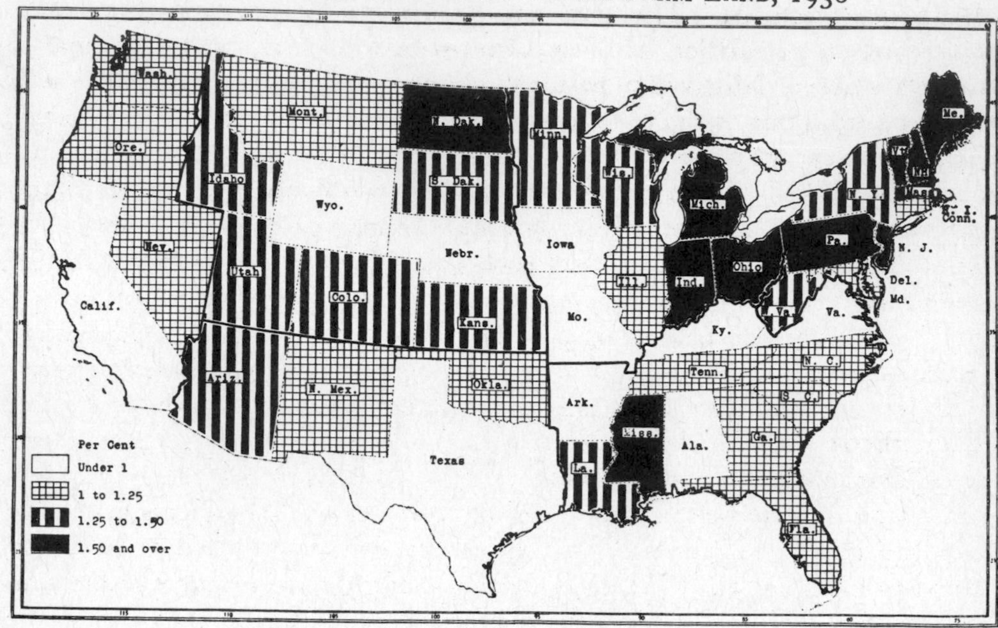

Ratio of Mortgaged Debt to Values, Farms Operated by Full Owners, 1930

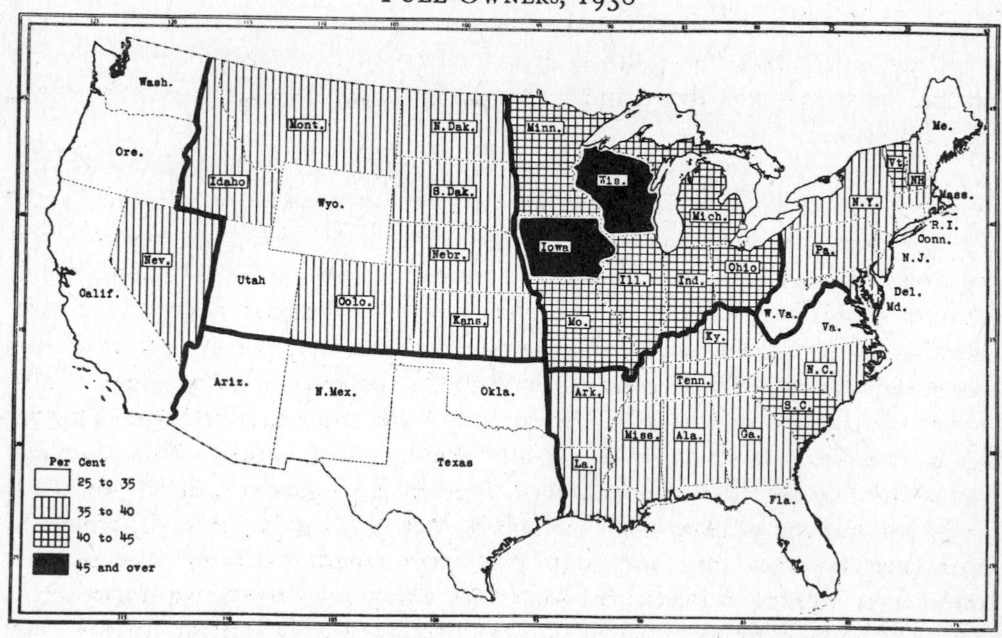

be found experimental demonstration of what may be accomplished through the reconstruction of farm life. Of special importance is the new program of county-state-federal coöperation in soil erosion and conservation of land. These factors are discussed in more detail in relation to planning and optimum programs of production, and a very large number of detailed series of figures are available for such further study and interpretation as may be desired.

The same is true of practically all other aspects of southern farm life, such as the low income, high tenant rates, low ratio of income from livestock, low ratios of domestic animals, high fertilizer consumption, deficiencies in farm tools and implements, in farm housing and conveniences, in low land and stock values, in waste from neglect and lack of coöperative effort. These deficiencies stand in the way of the dream of an immediate and invigorating agrarian life for the South, in contradistinction to either the present low levels of farming and living or to the growing industrial economy of the region. Yet, it is necessary to examine as carefully as possible, the claims of those who protest any increase in the industrialization of the South or who envisage immediately a newly reintegrated agrarian culture such that thousands and hundreds of thousands of urban and rural folk will choose the new agriculture as "a way of life," living happily ever after in this revitalized American economy.

Nevertheless, the dream of a revitalized agrarian culture in the Southeast must be given the fullest possible consideration, both because of inherent possibilities and because of the case which is being made for it on many sides. First of all, it must be urged again and again, the complexity and realities of the problem must be faced. For those who long easily "to recapture the past" for the Jeffersonian agrarianism, it must be pointed out that, in addition to many regional handicaps, the task is not so simple in the modern complex America. Compared with the earlier days, there was, for instance, the Jeffersonian eastern America in which the farmer was the bulwark of democracy; and there is the wide regional variation in the agriculture of the 1930's which, all told, provides less than 13 per cent of the nation's income. There was Thomas Jefferson proclaiming "the mob of great cities add just so much to the support of pure government, as sores do to the strength of the human body," and there is the 1930 America with more than 60 per cent of its people living within metropolitan areas, with 96 such regions each boasting over 100,000 population, with a single metropolitan region having twice as many people in it as all of Jefferson's beloved domain. There was Thomas Jefferson admonishing "to let our workshops remain in Europe," and there is the new American with more than 37,000,000 or 76.2 per cent of all its working folk occupied in manufacturing, mechanical distribution, and social services.

Or to focus the two pictures in a slightly different way, there was the Jeffersonian small nation of rural states, of one or two regions, of simple motivation, of homogeneity of people, of few occupations, with small individual fortunes centered chiefly in farm and forest, in land and homes; contrasted with the present very large nation of urban and industrial majorities, in greatly differing regions, with complex motivation and heterogeneity of population, with hundreds of varied occupations, large individual fortunes, fabulous salaries, corporate holdings and wealth, not only in farm lands and commodities, but in city real estate, factories, railroads, traction and steamship lines, coal and iron, stores and banks, utilities and amusements, food and tobacco, textiles and furniture, rubber and leather, glass and machinery, automobiles and metal, petroleum and power, soap and drugs, and multiplied consumers' goods.

Moreover, the total agricultural economy itself has come to be one of the most fundamental of the nation's critical points of tension because of an almost complete breakdown of what has hitherto been considered secure. Although there had been a steady decrease in the number of farms operated, in the number of acres of crop land, in the number of most livestock, especially hogs, horses, sheep, beef cattle, during the decade from 1920 to 1930, there was in the early 1930's still the most serious surplus that had yet existed. Practically all farm products were being produced at a loss. There was a still more serious situation in many regions, namely, that there was no market at any price. And since the old American adage that the nation depended upon the farmer for its food and prosperity still held true to a large degree, the nation was clearly in a paradoxical quandary with too much food, too many good farmers, too many poor farmers, but with the prosperity missing.

Nevertheless, agriculture was one of great size and of great range and variety. Samples of values of major commodities were adequate for comparisons with manufacturing and non-manufacturing industries. Agriculture's billions of dollars worth of products included, in 1929, hay and forage valued at $1,188,000,000; cotton lint about $1,218,000,000; dairy products, $1,800,000,000; corn, $1,962,000,000. The nation's hogs aggregated a billion and a half dollars worth; beef cattle with a little more than a billion; wheat worth $841,385,000; tobacco, $286,000,000; and garden vegetables, $226,000,000.

Aggregate figures, however, reflect little of the picture except to denote its size and general nature and to give bases for comparison and for reconstruction measures. Thus, more vivid than all the combined estimates of quantity or money value was the picture of a single week in October when 24,000 carloads of 27 varieties of vegetables rolled on and on in an incredible transfer of gardens to cities. It seemed perhaps more incredible that carrots and spinach, oranges and grapes should be pouring from California into a hundred cities and hamlets of the Carolinas, or that solid carloads of milk in glass refrigerator cars should be rushed from Wisconsin to Florida, than that solid trains of Florida produce should pour a steady stream from garden and grove into New York and Chicago. Yet the Southeast's ratio of car unloadings in the cities of the Northeast was scarcely more than a fraction of its logical capacity.

There were as usual contradictory pictures of the future of agriculture. One was a picture of the new agriculture as predominately machine farming, on large farms owned by commercial concerns with ever increasing use of inventions and the employment of fewer men. There would be the cotton picker which would do the work of forty Negroes or the multiple purpose corn harrow or threshing machine which might do the work of a hundred men. It was pointed out that, already by 1930, over half of all farms had automobiles, about 15 per cent trucks, besides a great many other types of mechanical farm equipment. On the other hand, the picture was presented, following actual trends, to show that, whenever the big farms owned by banks and insurance companies were sold, the tendency was invariably to break them up into smaller units. The statistics showed a regular decrease in the size of farms. Likewise, during the depression years the use of machine cultivation had decreased tremendously. The great decrease in exports threatened to make commercial farming unprofitable, while there seemed to be a definite trend toward self-sufficing farming, with a very large increase of the balanced live-at-home operations. These trends were as yet unmeasurable; yet the plight of the farmer was vivid and measurable enough.

Farm mortgages aggregated $8,500,000,000, nearly as much as the total money in circulation in the nation. Forty-two per cent of all farms were affected by mortgages which totaled about one-fourth of all farm land values. Here, as elsewhere, there were great regional differences. Sixty per cent of these mortgages were in eleven states, largely in the great Middle States farming area. The Southeast, with lower values and less money, was not quite so heavily loaded. Yet a large ratio of the farms were mortgaged up to three-fourths of their value. There was a picture of a single southeastern federal land bank owning 1,100,000 acres of land and operating more than 4,000 farms in three states only. Here were actual indices of the farmer's plight. How was he to pay debts which had more than doubled in an economy in which his income had been cut more than half? How could he pay interest with his products selling for less than cost with state, county, and federal authorities demanding more and more in costs of inspection, and confiscating his cattle in disease eradication programs? And all the while the urban intellectuals demanding a "standard of living" or standard of "economic well-being" which required more and more outlay for automobiles, telephones, radios, and other technologies which had come to signify blanket indices of well-being? And still again, the urban consumer protesting government assistance on the grounds that the urban consumer, being in the majority, should not have to pay the cost of helping the farmer folk who were in the minority. And finally, to this general picture must be added for the Southeast the cumulative handicap of the early 1920's when the farmer did not share the prosperity of the rest of the country, as well as the plight of the cotton economy which has already been depicted.

Yet this multiple dilemma of agriculture, so advocates in the new agrarian culture maintain, constitutes one of the basic reasons for a complete reconstruction of the whole agricultural-industrial economy. It is not only that a large group of folk discounts the wisdom of large scale agriculture and ascribes much of the present debacle to that turn of affairs in American life; or that a large group feels that the industrial system has forfeited its claim for dominance in the American scene; or that a considerable group of southern "Agrarians" is pleading for the region to develop a distinctiveness in this return to agriculture. These are all important elements. To these should be added two more; the one a general complaint against modern technology and bigness, with the implied ways of mastery through a more simple economy of agriculture and small industry; and the other the more tempered and better balanced claim for a realistic program which will bring about the reintegration of agriculture in American life, with the Southeast as an experimental laboratory on a large scale.

With reference to the first of these two major approaches, the complaint is frankly against the dominance of technology and bigness over human welfare and social evolution. It is a complaint against material technic ways of speeding up evolution helter-skelter and the lack of social technic ways to direct those forces. It is a search for some type of balanced economy which is also primarily a "culture" which will serve as a medium for the continuing sweep of science and technology which in turn can be made to serve mankind rather than exploit it. The complaint may be said to run somewhat as follows. All science has assumed social implications. Yet social applications in agriculture and in many of the human-labor relationships have not been made. Physical science has been the chief force in producing the rapid, social, economic, and political changes, which in turn have been the source of a world crisis. Science and invention, while making for progress in many fields, have developed a civilization which outstripped understanding and technique of control. This civilization, so the accusation goes, was top-heavy because of physical science, and it was lopsided because of the lopsidedness of science itself, and technology was a runaway. This rapid development of physical technology, outstripping progress in institutions and human relations, has resulted in a very great lack of equilibrium, so that material and culture factors are not geared together. This generated problems not only for mankind to keep pace with breath-taking inventions and discoveries, but to adjust social institutions to this breakneck speed. Man has conquered the machine in turn only to be conquered by the machine. Instead of the masterful direction of technology for the general well-being of mankind, much invention and discovery has been projected for the mere sake of mastery and conquest of some power or process. Invention for invention's sake, discovery for discovery's sake, multiplied thousands of achievements turned loose upon the world without any appraisal of problem or balance to be achieved in the social order. Agreed everywhere it was that something must be done about it, but what?

There were apparently uniform pictures which seemed to dominate the whole scene, pictures of an economic world torn asunder by something like an industrial tornado. The evils from which the world was suffering—depression, poverty, war, strife—had not grown out of electricity or steam technology, but out of the misuse and the maladjustment of these discoveries to impose supertechnology and artificial laws upon humanity. Machine industries swept on and on, slaves of colossal investments unable to direct the objectives of man and society, forced to seek artificial protection, monopolies, technologies which multiply hours and work and tensions. The catalogue of evils purported to come from this lack of adjustment was an extraordinary long and cheerless list: economic, moral, social, political crises; war and conflict between nations and classes and races; unemployment, insecurity, financial insolvency, over-taxation, high cost of living; physical exhaustion, weakening of the population, concentration in cities, depopulation of the countryside, confusion, superstandardization, artificial society, diminution of individual liberty and initiative, impotency of will.

Thus, this search for an attainable means of reconstructing regional agriculture rests on many fundamental needs. It assumes that the mere matching of modern technology with more technology is not the only way to meet cultural crisis. This assumption is supported by the facts of a realistic historical background, both of American culture and of racial development; and it is based upon current dilemmas. It assumes that American culture reflects a dangerous lack of equilibrium due to the preponderance of the urban-industrial factors over the natural agrarian elements. This is not merely economic imbalance of money and wealth. It has to do with regional distribution as well as personal. It has to do with the quality of the people and their increase. If, for instance, the strongest people, who under other circumstances would have succeeded on the farm, migrate to the city and fall heir to personal and social disorganization processes, depleting the countryside on the one hand, and to some extent failing in the city, on the other, there is needed some sort of culture economy which can restore the original balance in one way or another. In turn, urban life usurps much of rural institutions and withholds from it much of the advantages that come from modern civilization. What is wanted again is a merging or a converging or balancing of the two great types of culture. This applies to the biological aspects of population maintenance for which urban culture appears impotent; it seeks some new basis of selection of those who are to "inherit the earth" in both city and country. It involves the intellectual and social aspects of personality and culture, and the artificial influence of urban life whose multiple stimuli affect the individual differently from those in the country. It applies to regional variations within the nation and challenges the combination of political, economic, and cultural planning, the essentials of which constitute a separate subject for later treatment. In the meantime, the final measure and nature of agrarian emphasis must be determined by the nature of industrial and economic programs, and by the number and kind of people who continue to live in the region. These are discussed in the next two chapters.

CHAPTER VII

INDUSTRY AND WEALTH

In sections 126-146 we have presented a brief summary of some "measures of industry and wealth" in the Southeast, focusing upon a general framework calculated to feature elemental factors of regional status and trends. These showed a major trend in urban development and industrial growth as compared with both earlier and later agricultural and rural life and as compared with the other regions of the nation. The comparisons of regions showed an "average" distribution of establishments and their limited capacity to contribute to the means of social well-being. They reflected the region's small ratio of major industries and pointed to the region's special development of water power and of industries calculated to develop new wealth. The summary further attempted comparisons through a number of special indices, such as income, wealth, savings and bank deposits, retail and wholesale stores and sales, exports, governmental expenditures, emergency relief, and others. In sections 96-104 we pointed up representative technological deficiencies and waste in certain indices of income and wealth. So, too, in sections 179-182 some measures of capacity were indicated in taxation and government finance figures. In sections 84-94 special deficiencies in farm income and waste were cited, as were special educational expenditures in sections 163-170 and public welfare expenditures in section 192. These are partial indices of capacity to support cultural activities. On page 4 a partial list of the more than seven hundred indices utilized in the study indicates a wide range of measures of regional economics and industry, while throughout the volume a still more detailed picture can be had from selective figures available in the tables and graphs; in these absolute measures may be found, or regional and interregional comparisons may be made.

Since the purpose of this chapter is to present certain special aspects of the subject, it is not necessary to repeat general figures and ratings here except to note that according to a very large number of indices, which may be accepted as general measures of economic standards, economic well-being, capacity to buy, or levels of prosperity and living, it is possible to appraise the region with relatively clear cut pictures. This does not mean

Samplings of Indices Relating to Industry and Wealth

Number of Indices	Classification
1.	Relative standing of the states in wealth
2.	Regional wealth—per cent of total wealth.
3.	Estimated tangible wealth per capita of the total population, by states, 1930.
4.	Per capita estimated true wealth, 1930.
5.	Per capita bank resources, 1930.
6.	Per capita postal receipts, 1930.
7.	Per capita net income of corporations, 1928.
8.	Per capita annual income, eleven-year average, 1920-1930, inclusive.
9.	Percentage distribution of income of the entire population, 1929.
10.	Per capita personal income of the entire population, 1929.
11.	Percentage distribution of income from agriculture, 1928.
12.	Percentage distribution of income from manufacture, 1928.
13.	Percentage distribution of income from mining, 1928.
14.	Percentage distribution of income from sources other than agriculture, manufacturing, and mining, 1928.
15.	Number of taxable incomes equal to, or greater than, $100,000 by states.
16.	Number of taxable incomes equal to, or greater than, $1,000,000 by states.
17.	Average federal income tax paid, 1928.
18.	Number of taxable incomes equal to, or greater than, $100,000.
19.	Number of taxable incomes equal to, or greater than, $250,000.
20.	Number of taxable incomes equal to, or greater than, $500,000.
21.	Number of taxable incomes equal to, or greater than, $1,000,000.
22.	Distribution of taxable property per capita.
23.	Amount of taxable property per capita, 1928.
24.	Ratio of all local taxes to true wealth, 1927.
25.	Percentage ratio of total state and local tax collections to the aggregate private income.
26.	Estimated state and local tax collection per capita, by state, 1930.
27.	Combined state and local government, 1930—distribution of gross receipts from license fees.
28.	Combined state and local government, 1930—ratio of license and gasoline tax to total tax collections.
29.	Combined state and local government, 1930—per capita tax collections.
30.	Relative amount of taxes and appropriations for state and local roads, 1930.
31.	Distribution of the present forest area.
32.	Distribution of the total timber stand.
33.	Distribution of the total stand, saw-timber and cordwood areas.
34.	Mineral products—differential values, by regions.
35.	Mineral products—comparative value, 1909, 1919, 1929.
36.	Comparative production of petroleum, 1930.
37.	Comparative production of natural gas, 1930.
38.	Comparative production of natural gasoline, 1930.
39.	Production of anthracite coal.
40.	Production of bituminous coal, workable.
41.	Production of bituminous coal, not workable.
42.	Comparative ore-consuming districts, 1929.
43.	Variations of concentration in the iron and steel industries, 1929.
44.	Production of building stone.
45.	Limestone products—differential values, by regions.
46.	Changing status of 12 leading states in granite sales and value of granite, 1919-1929.
47.	Comparative value of marble production, 1919-1929.
48.	Distribution of water power development—amount of horse power, 1929.
49.	Distribution of total developed water power—capacity, 1932.
50.	Per capita production of electric power, all public utility plants, 1930.
51.	Percentage distribution of the value of manufactured products, 1929.
52.	Distribution of value of products in manufacturing industries, 1929.
53.	Distribution of value added to products by manufacture, 1929.
54.	Comparative value of products in manufacturing industries, 1929.
55.	Comparative value added by manufacture in manufacturing industries, 1929.
56.	Relative increase in value of manufactured product per wage earner in manufacturing, 1914-1929.
57.	Relative increase in value of product added by manufacture, per wage earner in manufacturing, 1914-1929.
58.	Relative increase in value of manufactured product per horse power, 1914-1929.
59.	Relative increase in value of product added by manufacture, per horse power, 1914-1929.
60.	Distribution of general industrial resources—horse power.
61.	Distribution of general industrial resources—value of product.
62.	Distribution of general industrial resources—value added by manufacture.
63.	Amount and per cent of value of product added by manufacture, 1929.
64.	Amount and per cent of value of product in furniture manufacturing, 1929.
65.	Value added by manufacturing, per wage earner, in furniture manufacturing, 1929.
66.	Amount and per cent of horse power used in furniture manufacturing, 1929.
67.	Value of manufactures per horse power used in furniture manufacturing, 1929.
68.	Value of manufacture added per horse power in furniture manufacturing, 1929.
69.	Distribution of industrial establishments.
70.	Regional distribution of manufacturing establishments—textiles and their products.
71.	Regional distribution of manufacturing establishments—forest products.
72.	Regional distribution of manufacturing establishments—paper and allied products.
73.	Regional distribution of manufacturing establishments—printing, publishing, and allied products.
74.	Regional distribution of manufacturing establishments—chemical and allied products.
75.	Regional distribution of manufacturing establishments—products of petroleum and coal.
76.	Regional distribution of manufacturing establishments—leather and its manufactures.
77.	Regional distribution of manufacturing establishments—stone, clay, and glass products.
78.	Regional distribution of manufacturing establishments—railroad repair shops.
79.	Distribution of wages.
80.	Distribution of wages paid in manufacturing industries, 1929.
81.	Average annual wage per wage earner in all manufactures, 1929.
82.	Relative increase in amount of wages per wage earner in manufacturing, in three chief manufacturing regions, 1914-1929.
83.	Amount and per cent of wages paid in furniture manufacturing, 1929.
84.	Per cent of total wages per wage earner in furniture manufacturing, 1929.
85.	Non-farm population—amount, and per cent of the total, of the aggregate personal income, 1929.
86.	Non-farm population—per capita personal income, 1929.
87.	Farm population—percentage distribution of income, 1929.
88.	Farm population—per capita personal income, 1929.
89.	Cooperative sales—per cent of cash farm income, 1929.
90.	Average annual rural cash income, 1920-1930.
91.	Ratio of farm income to total income, 1930.
92.	Value of all farm property per farm, 1930.
93.	Value of land and dwellings per owned farm, 1930.
94.	Value of land and buildings per tenant farm, 1930.
95.	Value per farm of farm implements and machinery, 1930.
96.	Average agricultural production per full-time worker (year of labor) 1924-1928.
97.	Number, value per head, and total value of all cattle and calves, including cows and heifers kept for milk, 1932.

that indices are adequate or absolute or that many more important measures are not needed. It means, however, that, by taking a large number of commonly accepted indices and massing them together more or less uncritically, there emerges one picture of regional status and comparison; then, by selecting more specialized indices and examining them more critically, a similar picture emerges. By checking these two then with other special means, it is possible to present a picture which, for the purposes in hand and for the time being, must be accepted as an authentic analysis of the region in most of its important economic and social aspects.

We may illustrate both the range and limitations of measures by referring to the catalogue of total indices previously mentioned and also to a special list on the accompanying page featuring the economic and industrial phases. These include the usual measures of income, wage differentials, savings and bank deposits, automobiles, telephone, and radio distribution, value added by manufacture and value of products, and also other and varied measures. It is clear, however, that while these measures are relative, in so many classifications errors tend to balance each other or to be eliminated through careful comparison and refinement of conclusions. Yet in a number of respects these figures are generally not reliable for the Southeast. An index of limitation in the matter of farm income may be found in the comparison of census figures with reference to farm produce in the following returns: the region ranks low in vegetables sold but high in farm garden vegetables raised; low in poultry products sold, but high in chickens raised on farm and lots; very low in ratio of total farm income derived from livestock, yet in certain aspects, such as milk cows on farms, the rating is quite different. The same would be true in uses of forest and woodland products. Thus, the real income of the farmer of the Southeast has not been measured with any reasonable accuracy.

So, too, in many of the measures of industrial wages and income, or value of product per wage earner, similar deficiencies abound in the limitation of statistics on rents, other costs of living, freight rates and the like. Once again, values and estimates are relative matters such that the same quality of goods or ability or work in one region may be listed as much lower than in another region where comparative factors are final arbiters. Real resources may be compounded of local materials and outside capital. Or to use a very specific example, a gold medal daughter of a gold medal imported dairy bull in a southeastern state will often be listed at only a percentage of the value of the same animal in the Northeast where values are uniformly higher in this classification. So, too, land capacity may not be measured always by its producing qualities. And finally, to select just one other, if we accept the premise everywhere indicated in our

Regional Variation and Trends in Total Manufactures: Establishments, Wage Earners, Wages

REGION	Year	Establishments		Wage Earners		Wages		
		Number	Per Cent of Total	Number	Per Cent of Total	Amount Dollars (.000 omitted)	Per Cent of Total	Per Wage Earner
United States..	1914	275,791	....	7,036,337	....	$ 4,078,332	....	$ 580
	1919	290,105	....	9,096,372	....	10,533,400	....	1,158
	1921	196,267	....	6,946,570	....	8,202,324	....	1,181
	1923	196,309	....	8,778,156	....	11,009,297	....	1,254
	1925	187,390	....	8,384,261	....	10,729,968	....	1,279
	1927	191,866	....	8,349,755	....	10,848,802	....	1,299
	1929	210,710	....	8,807,536	....	11,649,537	....	1,323
Southeast......	1914	39,282	14.3	855,669	12.2	356,319	8.7	416
	1919	41,186	14.2	1,031,762	11.3	918,167	8.7	890
	1921	21,202	10.7	830,049	12.0	673,244	8.2	811
	1923	21,866	11.2	1,071,054	12.2	872,626	7.9	815
	1925	22,119	11.8	1,089,920	13.0	912,151	8.5	837
	1927	21,969	11.5	1,125,876	13.4	954,381	8.8	848
	1929	28,666	13.6	1,165,092	13.2	983,443	8.4	844
Southwest......	1914	8,292	3.0	102,970	1.5	64,756	1.6	629
	1919	9,036	3.1	151,289	1.7	170,103	1.6	1,124
	1921	5,427	2.8	120,199	1.7	145,166	1.8	1,208
	1923	5,404	2.8	142,314	1.6	163,649	1.5	1,150
	1925	5,382	2.9	146,881	1.8	167,163	1.6	1,138
	1927	5,938	3.2	158,315	1.9	183,748	1.7	1,160
	1929	7,436	3.5	177,772	2.0	209,328	1.8	1,178
Northeast......	1914	119,527	43.3	3,709,868	52.7	2,113,567	51.8	570
	1919	122,873	42.4	4,486,987	49.3	5,201,527	49.4	1,159
	1921	91,866	42.8	3,511,818	50.6	4,153,624	50.7	1,183
	1923	90,796	46.3	4,195,949	47.7	5,355,940	48.6	1,276
	1925	82,604	44.2	3,850,199	45.9	5,058,794	47.2	1,313
	1927	85,488	44.5	3,801,712	45.6	5,106,554	47.0	1,343
	1929	88,632	42.1	3,903,994	44.4	5,322,579	45.7	1,364
Middle States..	1914	79,870	29.0	1,988,410	28.2	1,260,102	30.9	633
	1919	81,832	28.2	2,787,829	30.6	3,404,670	32.3	1,221
	1921	56,607	28.9	2,015,401	29.0	2,582,820	31.5	1,282
	1923	56,589	28.8	2,765,554	31.5	3,781,372	34.4	1,367
	1925	55,160	29.4	2,713,348	32.5	3,792,584	35.3	1,397
	1927	56,040	29.2	2,677,763	32.1	3,785,683	35.0	1,414
	1929	59,722	28.3	2,917,985	33.1	4,223,457	36.2	1,447
Middle West...	1914	12,434	4.5	140,250	2.0	101,763	2.5	725
	1919	15,245	5.3	200,257	2.2	251,343	2.4	1,255
	1921	7,724	3.9	150,691	2.2	210,490	2.6	1,397
	1923	7,392	3.8	178,147	2.0	236,526	2.1	1,328
	1925	7,261	3.9	166,219	2.0	219,531	2.0	1,320
	1927	7,126	3.7	159,207	1.9	214,649	2.0	1,348
	1929	7,997	3.8	169,678	1.9	240,972	2.1	1,420
Far West.......	1914	16,386	5.9	239,170	3.4	181,825	4.5	760
	1919	19,533	6.7	438,298	4.8	585,587	5.6	1,336
	1921	13,441	6.8	318,412	4.6	436,979	5.3	1,372
	1923	14,262	7.3	425,138	4.9	599,181	5.5	1,409
	1925	14,864	7.9	417,694	5.0	579,742	5.4	1,387
	1927	15,305	8.0	426,882	5.1	603,884	5.5	1,415
	1929	18,257	8.7	473,015	5.4	669,761	5.8	1,415

The above general summary is supplemented by full page tables showing horse-power, value of product, value added by manufacture, cost of material, etc., in Chapter VII.

data, namely, that the southern worker is less experienced, skilled, and dependable in technical tasks, we must also accept the conclusion that census data in the region are not as accurately gathered as in other regions. This factor, almost universally neglected, appears from some special exploration also, to diminish many differentials and to be of considerable importance in any final authentic regional comparisons.

Yet, for these reasons, as well as for others, it is all the more important for the Southeast to achieve a reasonably adequate appraisal of regional capacity, abundance, scarcity, deficiencies, prospects. If it cannot achieve certain "standard" attainments, either because of its own regional conditions or because of the traditional or established place of the region in the nation or because of preponderance of certain forces and resources militating against it, then it is important to appraise the region in terms of what it *can* do well. In so far as constraining environment impedes, it is important to know how much is permanent and how much temporary; how much is regional and how much fundamental in the larger national sense. Thus, it is peculiarly important, with reference to industry and wealth, to inventory resources in terms of both regional and interregional comparisons. This larger problem may well be illustrated in the case of manufactures in the United States, with special analysis of data on the Southeast. There are many angles from which to approach the problem. Harriet L. Herring has made a number of comprehensive studies of many aspects of the southern industrial situation. One is an analysis of the principal data of the manufacturing industries from 1914 to 1929, giving not only a cross section but a chronological view of the situation. In this picture certain conclusions are quite clear; other commonly accepted assumptions cannot be justified without further testing. For instance, regional differentials are quite obvious and demonstrable; the meaning of many tentative conclusions about southern industry is not clear due to the limitations of data and of unknown factors.

In total manufactures the Southeast ranks third in the rating of the six regions, with a bare ten per cent of the national total. The Northeast leads still with roughly 43 per cent and the Middle States follow with 35 per cent. The remaining tenth is divided among the Northwest, the Southwest, and the Far West, with about half of this now in the Far West. The Southeast, however, does not show up quite so well when it comes to the capacity or practice of creating and distributing what is commonly assumed to be the means of social well-being. Thus in the number of establishments and in the number of wage earners the region ranks higher than in total measures, having a little more than 13 per cent of the nation's total in each of these. Yet the Southeast distributed only a little more than eight

Regional Variation and Trends in Total Manufactures: Cost of Material, Value of Product, Value Added by Manufacture

REGION	Year	Cost of Material		Value of Product			Value Added By Manufacture		
		Amount Dollars (000 omitted)	Per Cent of Total	Amount Dollars (000 omitted)	Per Cent of Total	Per Wage Earner	Amount Dollars (000 omitted)	Per Cent of Total	Per Wage Earner
United States....	1914	$14,368,089	....	$24,246,435	....	$3,445	$ 9,878,346	....	$1,404
	1919	37,376,380	....	62,418,079	....	6,861	25,041,698	....	2,752
	1921	25,321,055	....	43,653,283	....	6,284	18,316,660	....	2,636
	1923	34,705,697	....	60,555,998	....	6,898	25,850,300	....	2,944
	1925	35,935,647	....	62,713,713	....	7,480	26,778,066	....	3,193
	1927	35,133,136	....	62,718,347	....	7,512	27,585,210	....	3,303
	1929	38,293,534	....	70,137,459	....	7,963	31,843,926	....	3,615
Southeast........	1914	1,199,979	8.4	2,066,646	8.5	2,415	866,668	8.8	1,012
	1919	3,171,645	8.5	5,394,761	8.6	5,228	2,222,587	8.9	2,154
	1921	2,122,329	8.4	3,574,719	8.2	4,306	1,452,389	7.9	1,750
	1923	2,993,037	8.6	5,153,114	8.5	4,810	2,160,078	8.4	2,016
	1925	3,237,438	9.0	5,643,126	9.0	5,177	2,405,688	9.0	2,207
	1927	3,122,666	8.9	5,642,965	9.0	5,012	2,520,300	9.1	2,238
	1929	3,346,923	8.8	6,237,292	8.9	5,353	2,890,371	9.1	2,481
Southwest.......	1914	367,827	2.6	536,695	2.2	5,212	168,867	1.7	1,640
	1919	1,114,152	3.0	1,539,985	2.5	10,179	425,835	1.7	2,814
	1921	806,498	3.2	1,179,209	2.7	9,810	372,710	2.0	3,100
	1923	968,661	2.8	1,438,199	2.4	10,105	469,538	1.8	3,299
	1925	1,248,245	3.5	1,799,487	2.9	12,250	551,242	2.1	3,752
	1927	1,200,200	3.4	1,716,105	2.7	10,840	515,905	1.9	3,258
	1929	1,454,663	3.8	2,123,094	3.0	11,942	668,430	2.1	3,760
Northeast.......	1914	6,731,560	46.9	11,636,594	48.0	3,136	4,905,034	49.7	1,322
	1919	16,312,666	43.7	28.617,661	45.8	6,378	12,304,991	49.1	2,742
	1921	11,292,434	44.6	20,593,558	47.2	5,864	9,285,562	50.7	2,644
	1923	15,346,561	44.3	27,743,944	45.8	6,612	12,397,384	47.9	2,954
	1925	14,840,812	41.3	27,176,556	43.2	7,058	12,335,740	46.1	3,239
	1927	14,459,831	41.0	27,180,466	43.3	7,150	12,720,636	46.2	3,346
	1929	15,240,650	39.8	29,581,391	42.2	7,577	14,341,741	45.0	3,674
Middle States....	1914	4,726,054	32.9	7,984,317	32.9	4,015	3,258,262	33.0	1,638
	1919	13,081,475	35.0	21,336,290	34.2	7,653	8,213,816	32.8	2,946
	1921	8,530,281	33.7	14,338,835	32.8	7,114	5,808,555	31.7	2,882
	1923	12,191,865	35.1	21,021,689	34.7	7,671	8,829,824	34.2	3,193
	1925	13,015,653	36.2	22,493,601	35.9	8,289	9,477,947	35.4	3,493
	1927	12,753,432	36.4	22,489,641	35.9	8,400	9,736,208	35.3	3,635
	1929	14,191,022	37.1	25,516,819	36.4	8,744	11,324,797	35.6	3,881
Northwest.......	1914	686,011	4.8	938,211	3.9	6,689	252,200	2.6	1,798
	1919	1,811,714	4.9	2,390,430	3.8	11,936	578,717	2.3	2,890
	1921	1,083,080	4.3	1,523,080	3.5	10,107	440,000	2.4	2,919
	1923	1,344,199	3.9	1,919,267	3.2	10,773	575,068	2.2	3,228
	1925	1,540,158	4.3	2,124,074	3.4	12,778	583,915	2.2	3,512
	1927	1,500,254	4.3	2,048,338	3.3	12,860	548,084	2.0	3,442
	1929	1,654,061	4.3	2,334,584	3.3	13,759	680,523	2.1	4,011
Far West........	1914	656,658	4.6	1,083,972	4.5	4,532	427,313	4.3	1,786
	1919	1,884,734	5.0	3,180,485	5.1	7,256	1,295,752	5.2	2,956
	1921	1,486,431	5.9	2,443,881	5.6	7,675	957,450	5.2	3,007
	1923	1,861,371	5.4	3,279,782	5.4	7,714	1,418,412	5.7	3,336
	1925	2,053,339	5.7	3,476,867	5.5	8,324	1,423,528	5.3	3,408
	1927	2,096,751	6.0	3,640,829	5.8	8,528	1,544,077	5.6	3,617
	1929	2,406,215	6.3	4,344,277	6.2	9,184	1,938,061	6.1	4,097

per cent of the total manufacturing wage bill of the nation. Or to make the comparison in terms of figures, the Southeast paid $844 per wage earner as contrasted with the Middle States' $1,447 and the Northeast's $1,364. Similar deficiency indices appear when measured by the value of product manufactured.

The Southeast had only 8.9 per cent of the value of the national product, although 13.2 per cent of the wage earners; the Northeast had 42.2 per cent of the value of product and 44.4 per cent of the wage earners; while the Middle States had 36.4 per cent of the product with 33.1 per cent of the wage earners. Stated in other terms, the industry of the Southeast produced $5,355 worth of products per wage earner as against $7,577 for the Northeast and $8,744 for the Middle States. The Southeast can be compared in this respect to the other three lesser industrial regions: the Southeast's $5,353 per wage earner contrasts with the Far West's $9,184; the Northwest's $13,759; and the Southwest's $11,942. In ratios of wage earners to wages, however, the Southwest, like the Southeast, has a less percentage of the total in earnings than in earners or establishments, in contrast to the other regions where earnings are greater than earners.

If it is said that, since industries vary greatly as to cost of raw materials, value of products is not a sound basis of comparison, it should be added that even the purchase of raw material means a distribution of wealth, and, with the exception of one or two industries in the Northeast and one or two in the Middle States, this purchasing is mainly within the region doing the manufacturing. Even so "Value Added by Manufacture" furnishes an index with this factor removed. Again the Southeast ranks low with only 9.1 per cent of the national total for its 13.2 per cent of the wage earners, while the Northeast has 45 per cent for 44.4 per cent and the Middle States has 35 per cent, in both cases a larger proportion than their proportion of the wage earners. The Southeast has a per wage earner average of $2,481 as against $3,674 for the Northeast and $3,881 for the Middle States.

The Census no longer collects statistics of "capital invested," so that it is impossible to say how the regions compare in that respect. The hypothesis is ventured here, subject to revision when more material is gathered and compared, that horse power forms, by and large, a rough index of investment in machinery and substantial buildings. If this is true the Southeast has its share, 13.4 per cent, compared with its share of the wage earners, so that it would seem to be relatively as expensively equipped as the Middle States with 32.9 H.P. and 33.1 per cent wage earners, and slightly more so than the Northeast with 41.6 H.P. and 44.4 per cent wage earners. If this is true the low value of product in the Southeast

Regional Variations and Trends in Total Manufactures: Horse Power

REGION	Year	Amount	Per Cent of Total	Per Wage Earner	Value of Product Per Horse Power	Value Added By Manufacture Per Horse Power
United States	1914	22,547,574	....	3.2	$1,075	$438
	1919	29,507,117	....	3.2	2,115	848
	1921	....	....	...	.....	....
	1923	33,094,228	....	3.8	1,829	782
	1925	35,772,628	....	4.3	1,753	748
	1927	38,825,681	....	4.7	1,615	710
	1929	42,798,911	....	4.9	1,638	744
Southeast	1914	3,377,668	15.0	4.0	612	257
	1919	3,959,820	13.4	3.8	1,362	561
	1921	....	....	...	.....	...
	1923	4,159,657	12.6	3.9	1,239	520
	1925	4,535,204	12.7	4.2	1,244	530
	1927	4,922,257	12.7	4.4	1,146	513
	1929	5,611,743	13 1	4.8	1,111	516
Southwest	1914	503,464	2.2	4.9	1,066	335
	1919	704,408	2.4	4.7	2,186	604
	1921	....	....	...	.....	...
	1923	846,649	2.6	6.0	1,699	554
	1925	850,593	2.4	5.8	2,115	648
	1927	943,043	2.4	6.0	1,819	547
	1929	1,256,336	2.9	7.1	1,689	532
Northeast	1914	10,456,640	46.4	2.8	1,112	469
	1919	13,188,156	44.7	2.9	2,170	933
	1921	....	....	...	.....	...
	1923	14,792,919	44.7	3.5	1,875	833
	1925	15,577,019	43.5	4.0	1,744	792
	1927	16,803,699	43.3	4.4	1,617	757
	1929	17,805,711	41.6	4.6	1,661	805
Middle States	1914	6,406,151	28.4	3.2	1,246	508
	1919	8,931,668	30.3	3.2	2,389	920
	1921	....	....	...	.....	...
	1923	10,357,538	31.3	3.8	2,030	851
	1925	11,454,302	32.0	4.2	1,963	827
	1927	12,628,145	32.5	4.7	1,780	772
	1929	14,095,546	32.9	4.8	1,810	803
Northwest	1914	775,089	3.4	5.5	1,210	325
	1919	945,393	3 2	4.7	2,528	612
	1921	....	....	...	.....	...
	1923	1,022,540	3.1	5.7	1,877	563
	1925	1,071,157	3.0	6.4	1,983	545
	1927	1,146,949	3.0	7.2	1,785	478
	1929	1,186,994	2.8	7.0	1,966	573
Far West	1914	1,128,562	5.0	4.7	960	378
	1919	1,777,672	6.0	4.1	1,791	729
	1921	....	....	...	.....	...
	1923	1,914,925	5.8	4.5	1,712	710
	1925	2,284,353	6.4	5.5	1,522	623
	1927	2,381,588	6.1	5.6	1,529	648
	1929	2,841,591	6.7	6.0	1,528	682

becomes even more out of line with the other regions. If horse power forms a rough index of mechanization of industry the Southeast with 4.82 H.P. per wage earner is somewhat more mechanized than the Northeast with 4.56 H.P. per wage earner and about the same as the Middle States with 4.83 H.P. per wage earner.

If these two hypotheses are correct then the Southeast is not nearly so efficient in the use of its capitalization and mechanization. For value of product per H.P. and value added by manufacture per H.P. the Southeast again falls considerably below the other great industrial regions. In value of product per H.P., the following comparisons may be drawn: the Southeast, $1,111; the Northeast, $1,661; the Middle States, $1,810. In value added by manufacture per H.P., the Southeast, $516; the Northeast, $805; and the Middle States, $803.

Measured by these several indices the manufacturing industry of the Southeast falls below the national average and below the other great industrial regions. There may be several explanations. One reason may lie in the fact that the Southeast has concentrated its efforts in industries that create and distribute relatively less than other industries wherever they are found. A comparison of the chief individual industries in the Southeastern States with the chief industries of other states will show to what extent this is true. In this case it will be desirable to examine briefly the reasons for this concentration: history, geography, climate, natural resources, and industrial experience, with possible trends in the future. On the other hand, it may appear that a given industry makes a low return only when found in the Southeast and ranks with its neighbors when found in other regions. If so, it will be necessary to search further for the reason for this: poor management, inefficient labor, unwillingness to distribute the return in better prices for raw material or wages, prevailing wage rates.

A third interpretation is that the return of manufacturing industries is as great relatively as any other form of economic endeavor in the Southeast. This is in general accord with the facts relating to the lower standard of living and achievement in the Southeast. Yet all these possibilities require further study of manufacturing and a correlation of these facts with those relating to agriculture, trade, and finance. Something of the situation may be implied from an illustration often used with reference to the textile industry of the Piedmont South. Certain of the economists accustomed to ascribe low wages to one or two factors only overlook other elements. There are the freight rate differentials for one thing; there is the large supply of labor clamoring for work at whatever might be offered, this being usually above the income of the farm kinfolks in the same com-

Regional Distribution of Manufacturing Establishments by Industries: I

INDUSTRIES	Southeast	Southwest	Northeast	Middle States	Northwest	Far West	Total United States
TEXTILES AND THEIR PRODUCTS							
Artificial leather	.....	.....	15	2	.....	.....	17
Asphalted-felt-base floor covering	.....	.....	12	1	.....	1	14
Awnings, tents, sails, and canvas covers	81	35	492	244	48	102	1,002
Bags, other than paper, not made in textile mills	38	13	77	55	5	14	202
Belting, other than leather or rubber, not textile product	.....	.....	6	3	.....	.....	9
Carpets and rugs, rag	4	.....	45	25	6	14	94
Carpets and rugs, wool, other than rag	1	.....	61	5	.....	.....	67
Clothing (except work) men, youth, boy, unclassified	85	18	2,804	660	16	108	3,691
Clothing, men's buttonholes	.....	.....	27	5	.....	.....	32
Clothing, women's not elsewhere classified	67	40	6,820	774	17	364	8,082
Clothing, work (shirts omitted) men's	88	41	174	160	15	33	511
Cloth sponging and refinishing	.....	.....	37	8	.....	1	46
Collars, men's	.....	.....	14	1	.....	.....	15
Cordage and twine	35	1	64	15	.....	8	123
Corsets and allied garments	1	.....	171	39	.....	2	213
Cotton goods	782	29	423	39	.....	8	1,281
Cotton small wares	13	.....	178	8	.....	3	202
Dyeing and finishing textiles	48	1	616	52	3	12	732
Embroideries	1	.....	737	61	.....	14	813
Felt goods, wool, hair, or jute	1	.....	43	8	.....	2	54
Flags and banners	4	.....	29	14	.....	7	54
Flax and hemp, dressed	.....	.....	.....	6	.....	.....	6
Furnishing goods, men's, not elsewhere classified	22	4	453	94	3	22	598
Gloves, mittens, cloth or cloth-leather, of purchased fabric	9	1	30	76	2	7	125
Haircloth	.....	.....	12	1	.....	.....	13
Handkerchiefs	6	3	91	2	.....	3	105
Hat and cap materials, men's	.....	.....	107	5	.....	.....	112
Hats and caps, except felt and straw, men's	11	5	368	146	7	39	576
Hats, fur-felt	4	3	126	17	1	8	159
Hats, wool-felt	.....	.....	14	.....	.....	.....	14
Horse blankets, fly nets, and related products	1	.....	6	7	.....	.....	14
House-furnishing goods, not elsewhere classified	27	7	605	221	2	102	964
Jute goods	8	.....	11	1	.....	.....	20
Knit goods	341	4	1,287	184	11	61	1,888
Lace goods	.....	.....	40	2	.....	.....	42
Linen goods	.....	.....	13	1	.....	2	16
Linoleum	.....	.....	7	.....	.....	.....	7
Mats and matting, grass and coir	.....	.....	3	3	.....	1	7
Millinery	10	20	942	205	9	107	1,293
Net and seines	2	.....	11	5	.....	1	19
Oilcloth	.....	.....	7	2	.....	.....	9
Regalia, badges and emblems	2	.....	43	27	2	3	77
Shirts	47	11	648	116	12	29	863
Silk and rayon manufactures	51	.....	1,423	12	.....	5	1,491
Suspenders, garters, elastic woven goods, purchased web	4	.....	60	24	1	2	91
Trimmings (not made in textile mills), stamp art goods	3	.....	526	77	3	30	639
Upholstering material, not elsewhere classified	24	1	13	10	.....	5	53
Waste	12	3	77	36	2	6	136
Woolen goods	30	1	352	61	2	14	460
Wool pulling	.....	.....	8	4	1	5	18
Wool scouring	.....	.....	15	3	.....	3	21
Wool shoddy	.....	.....	47	3	.....	.....	50
Worsted goods	7	1	249	5	.....	2	264
Totals	*1,870*	*242*	*20,439*	*3,535*	*168*	*1,150*	*27,404*
Percentage	*6.8*	*0.9*	*74.5*	*12.9*	*0.6*	*4.2*	*100*
FOREST PRODUCTS							
Baskets, rattan and willow ware (not furniture)	49	14	118	76	6	10	273
Billiards and pool tables, bowling alleys, etc.	1	.....	29	9	.....	1	40
Boxes, cigar, wooden	14	1	59	36	3	5	118
Boxes, wooden except cigar	133	29	278	249	17	86	792
Caskets, coffins, burial cases, etc.	79	19	105	161	17	33	414
Cooperage	214	14	194	133	9	22	586
Cork products	.....	.....	31	4	.....	.....	35
Excelsior	31	.....	16	14	1	4	66
Furniture, including store and office fixtures	406	53	1,521	1,296	51	451	3,778
Lasts and related products	.....	.....	48	10	.....	.....	58

munities. There is then the traditional low wage rate; the lower rates of professional and other incomes; the provision, at nominal rates, for houses and water and light; in other cases there are garden facilities. In still other instances the ownership and control of factories reside outside the region, and, the industry, having come South because of advantages in climate and labor, the owners or stockholders insist upon as large return as possible. And there is the factor of a wide range of quality in the labor employed, in experience and training of specialized workers, and in the types of management employed. And originally there was the factor of the quality of goods manufactured, the South limiting its major efforts to coarser goods. In other cases a large measure of risk was real or apparent where markets and continuity of production could not be guaranteed.

An important aspect of the regional-industrial situation is that of its development over a relatively large number of years as well as the picture of its more recent status. Figures are presented at length in several accompanying pages of tables and maps and graphs to show trends since the War, measured from the two extremes of just before the War and at the height of the prosperity period, or roughly from 1914 to 1929. The indices include those already reported in measuring present status; namely, number of establishments, number of wage earners, amount of wages, cost of material, value of product, value added by manufacture, together with the amount of horse power per wage earner and value of product, and value added by manufacture per horse power. This time-sequence is an illuminating picture, showing a gradual but sure gain by the Middle States, a gradual but sure loss by the Northeast, and a bare holding of its own by the Southeast. The Far West and the Southwest increased perceptibly while the Northwest decreased in all indices. Yet the Northeast is still predominant in actual quantitative measures, while the Southwest ranks below all regions except the Northwest. There are many other details which are important for more exhaustive study. For instance, there was a different trend in the Northeast and the Southeast in the 1921-1923 era. The Northeast, for instance, increased its number of establishments to the highest point of 46 per cent in 1923, whereas the Southeast decreased from 14 per cent to 11 per cent to return again in 1929 to about 14 per cent, while the Northeast decreased to 42 per cent. The same was true in value added by manufacture, although in the other indices advance and regression were relatively uniform over the fifteen-year period, 1914 to 1929.

This picture of shifting industry is reflected also in the statistics of the increase and decrease of the dollar value of manufactured products in the several regions. James W. Fesler has pointed up figures gathered by Colonel John P. Hasson in his study of regions in relation to War Depart-

Regional Distribution of Manufacturing Establishments by Industries: II

INDUSTRIES	Southeast	Southwest	Northeast	Middle States	Northwest	Far West	Total United States
FOREST PRODUCTS (Cont.)							
Lumber and timber products, unclassified elsewhere	7,959	436	1,580	1,093	318	1,529	12,915
Matches	.....	.....	8	11	.....	2	21
Mirror and picture frames	1	4	94	61	3	15	178
Planing mill products not made in planing-sawmills	1,216	174	1,479	1,219	164	597	4,849
Pulp goods	1	.....	25	16	.....	3	45
Refrigerators and refrig. cabinets, not mechanical	12	3	71	70	3	29	188
Turpentine and rosin	1,178	5	.....	.....	.....	.....	1,183
Window and door screens and weather stripping	25	16	103	110	5	21	280
Wood preserving	54	15	26	63	14	27	199
Wood turned and shaped, etc., unclassified elsewhere	182	8	426	226	1	51	894
Totals	*11,555*	*791*	*6,211*	*4,857*	*612*	*2,886*	*26,912*
Percentage	*43.0*	*2.9*	*23.1*	*18.0*	*2.3*	*10.7*	*100*
PAPER AND ALLIED PRODUCTS							
Bags, paper, not made in paper mills	10	1	56	25	.....	3	95
Boxes, paper, unclassified elsewhere	58	11	770	338	11	61	1,249
Cardboard, not made in paper mills	.....	.....	8	4	1	.....	13
Card cutting and designing	1	.....	50	18	.....	1	70
Envelopes	7	2	80	65	5	12	171
Labels and tags	9	1	86	44	.....	13	153
Paper	40	2	399	208	4	32	685
Paper goods, unclassified elsewhere	14	4	264	125	4	25	436
Pulp	26	1	98	49	.....	24	198
Wall paper	.....	.....	37	19	.....	.....	56
Totals	*165*	*22*	*1,848*	*895*	*25*	*171*	*3,126*
Percentage	*5.3*	*0.7*	*59.1*	*28.6*	*0.8*	*5.5*	*100*
PRINTING, PUBLISHING AND ALLIED INDUSTRIES							
Book-binding and blank book making	34	15	660	304	17	78	1,108
Engravers materials	.....	.....	13	5	.....	1	19
Engraving, chasing, etching, and diesinking	1	1	131	43	.....	13	189
Engraving, steel and copperplate, and plate printing	32	10	237	119	8	50	456
Engraving, wood	.....	.....	10	15	.....	2	27
Lithographing	11	6	196	134	6	23	376
Photo-engraving, not done in printing establishments	55	22	257	214	26	80	654
Printing and publishing, book and job	1,009	457	5,451	4,026	478	1,291	12,712
Printing and publishing, music	3	1	78	36	2	4	124
Printing and publishing, newspapers and periodicals	1,462	793	3,089	3,780	1,250	1,150	11,524
Printing materials, not including type and printing ink	7	2	33	37	1	4	84
Stereotyping and electrotyping, not done in printing estab.	9	4	99	102	3	13	230
Type founding	.....	.....	9	7	1	2	19
Totals	*2,623*	*1,311*	*10,263*	*8,822*	*1,792*	*2,711*	*27,522*
Percentage	*9.5*	*4.8*	*37.3*	*32.1*	*6.5*	*9.3*	*100*
CHEMICAL AND ALLIED PRODUCTS							
Alcohol, ethyl, and distilled liquors	11	.....	11	4	.....	4	30
Ammunition and related products	.....	.....	10	7	1	3	21
Baking powders, yeast, and other leavening compounds	2	.....	22	19	1	4	48
Blacking, stains, and dressings	3	2	109	42	1	13	170
Bluing	3	1	6	8	.....	2	20
Bone black, carbon black, and lampblack	30	34	7	.....	4	2	77
Candles	.....	.....	17	2	.....	1	20
Chemicals not elsewhere classified	39	8	312	130	8	54	551
Cleaning and polishing preparations	18	7	183	172	10	39	429
Compressed and liquefied gases	59	32	96	107	24	36	354
Druggists' preparations	25	7	195	145	35	22	429
Drug grinding	2	.....	18	6	.....	.....	26
Explosives	10	10	31	28	8	8	95
Fertilizers	415	13	127	52	6	25	638
Fireworks	2	1	30	12	2	3	50
Glue and gelatin	.....	.....	38	29	.....	7	74
Grease and tallow, not including lubricating grease	14	1	114	131	16	21	297

ment Procurement Districts. Almost the identical picture emerges from this and similar figures, showing six of the eight Middle States as being among the ten leading states in increase of the dollar value of manufactured products; while the Northeast had only one state, the Southeast one, the Southwest one, and the Far West one. The fact that North Carolina was one of the ten indicates also the special weight it has in the Southeast's barely holding its own, all the other Southeastern States except three having very small increase. The conclusion that the Northeast had lost steadily and continuously was again sustained in the figures which showed that the value of manufactured products of five of the six New England States was actually less in 1929 than in 1919, while Pennsylvania and New Jersey increased but slightly and West Virginia increased still less. In the Southeast, Alabama, Tennessee, and Kentucky were the three other states than North Carolina which showed perceptible increases. In the Middle States, in addition to six of the eight being among the first ten, Iowa was also among the first twenty, leaving only Minnesota to prevent the region from being solid in its maximum increase.

Manifestly, this may well have very important bearing upon developments in which the Mississippi Valley and the Southeast and the Southwest, including the TVA programs and the Southwest petroleum industry, will contribute to the remapping of the whole industrial nation. Contributing to certain of these developments would apparently be the great increase in mineral products in the Southeast and the Southwest, and in certain other special resources such as marble and granite. Thus from 1909 to 1929 the value of mineral products increased in the Southeast from 83 million dollars to 430 millions; in the Southwest from 76 million to about a billion and a quarter; whereas in the Northeast the increase was only about threefold. From 1919 to 1929 the Southeastern States thus increased from 37 to 61 per cent of the nation's total. As indices basic to the building of a greater economic civilization these are of special significance to the Southeast.

Of great importance also is an inventory of the number and kinds of industries, large and small, which go into the making of the total and the regional distribution of each general classified group. This is fundamental in the appraisal of the region's present capacity, especially with reference to small industries, and also in the planning of new and additional industries. It is accordingly also fundamental to any planning of the balanced agriculture in a new equilibrium between small and large industries and between agriculture and industry as a whole. The general picture here is not unlike the total in that the Northeast and the Middle States are the overwhelming leaders, with the Southeast a poor third. The detailed pic-

Regional Distribution of Manufacturing Establishments by Industries: III

INDUSTRIES	Southeast	Southwest	Northeast	Middle States	Northwest	Far West	Total United States
CHEMICAL AND ALLIED PRODUCTS (Cont.)							
Ink, printing	2	3	69	65	1	7	147
Ink, writing	1	.....	9	16	.....	3	29
Liquors, vinous	.....	.....	7	2	.....	15	24
Mucilage, paste, other adhesives, not glue or rubber	.....	1	38	34	2	9	84
Oil, cake, and meal, cottonseed	309	231	.....	5	.....	8	553
Oil, cake, and meal, linseed	1	.....	8	17	1	2	29
Oils, essentials	.....	.....	13	6	.....	3	22
Oils, not elsewhere classified	7	.....	39	11	2	16	75
Paints and varnishes	82	20	452	387	17	105	1,063
Patent and proprietary medicines and compounds	175	30	584	540	50	143	1,522
Perfumes, cosmetics, and other toilet preparations	51	14	437	231	16	66	815
Rayon and allied products	11	.....	14	4	.....	.....	29
Salt	3	2	12	17	13	11	58
Soap	8	4	129	93	7	41	282
Tanning material, natrl. dyestuffs, mordants and assistants, etc.	30	1	90	4	.....	1	126
Wood distillation and charcoal manufacture	29	1	40	15	.....	6	91
Totals	*1,342*	*423*	*3,267*	*2,341*	*225*	*680*	*8,278*
Percentage	*16.2*	*5.1*	*39.5*	*28.3*	*2.7*	*8.2*	*100*
PRODUCTS OF PETROLEUM AND COAL							
Coke, not including gas house coke	19	.....	94	33	6	1	153
Fuel, briquettes and boulets	2	1	9	5	2	4	23
Gas, manufactured, illuminating and heating	118	14	244	272	46	60	754
Lubricating oils and greases, not petroleum refinery	1	8	79	65	10	14	177
Petroleum refinery	34	136	78	34	54	54	390
Totals	*174*	*159*	*504*	*409*	*118*	*133*	*1,497*
Percentage	*11.6*	*10.6*	*33.7*	*27.3*	*7.9*	*8.9*	*100*
LEATHER AND ITS MANUFACTURES							
Belting leather	26	5	97	56	4	19	207
Boot and shoe stock not made in shoe factories	1	.....	184	21	1	3	210
Boot and shoe findings not made in shoe factories	2	.....	333	44	1	2	382
Boots and shoes other than rubber	27	9	1,017	256	7	25	1,341
Gloves and mittens, leather	1	.....	179	55	1	21	257
Leather goods, not elsewhere classified	8	2	270	76	4	32	392
Leather curried, tanned, and finished	31	2	334	87	.....	17	471
Pocketbooks, purses and card cases	2	2	245	28	1	12	290
Saddlery and harness	40	25	51	87	35	22	260
Trunks, suitcases and bags	15	7	243	140	11	51	467
Totals	*153*	*52*	*2,953*	*850*	*65*	*204*	*4,277*
Percentage	*3.6*	*1.2*	*69.0*	*19.9*	*1.5*	*4.8*	*100*
STONE, CLAY AND GLASS PRODUCTS							
Asbestos, not for steam packing, pipe and boiler covering	7	.....	31	22	.....	7	67
Cement	22	11	50	50	20	21	174
China firing, decorating, not pottery	.....	.....	16	8	1	2	27
Clay products (other than pottery), non-clay refractories	308	81	518	580	106	156	1,749
Concrete products	215	76	880	932	100	235	2,438
Crucibles	.....	.....	10	1	.....	.....	11
Emery wheels and other abrasive and polishing appliances	1	.....	38	27	.....	1	67
Glass	8	16	154	68	1	16	263
Glass products (except mirrors) made from purchased glass	8	6	258	123	4	32	431
Graphite, ground and refined	.....	1	5	4		1	11
Hones, whetstones, and similar products	.....	.....	4	2	.....	.....	6
Lime	54	8	73	75	13	14	237
Marble, granite, slate, etc.	231	79	946	472	61	92	1,881
Minerals and earths, ground or otherwise treated	11	2	44	19	2	10	88
Mirrors, framed and unframed	27	8	133	83	5	48	304
Pottery including porcelain ware	24	9	116	131	6	27	313
Sand-lime brick	4	2	10	21	2	1	40
Statuary and art products, factory product	12	1	68	53	6	31	171
Wall plaster, wall board, insulating board, floor composition	11	13	77	68	17	50	236
Totals	*943*	*313*	*3,431*	*2,739*	*344*	*744*	*8,514*
Percentage	*11.1*	*3.7*	*40.3*	*32.2*	*4.0*	*8.7*	*100.0*

ture, however, is often quite different, both in the picture of the Northeast as leader, the Middle States as increasing competitor, and the wide range and variety in the Southeast. The figures show that in the number of establishments the Northeast leads in textiles with nearly 75 per cent, paper products with nearly 60 per cent, printing and publishing with 37.3 per cent, chemical and allied products with about 40 per cent, products of petroleum and coal with a little more than a third, leather and its manufacture with nearly 70 per cent, stone, clay and glass products with 40 per cent, iron and steel products with 46 per cent, nonferrous metals with 50 per cent, and miscellaneous industries with 57.7 per cent. The Middle States lead in machinery with 40 per cent, transportation equipment with 38 per cent, railroad repair shops with 34 per cent. The Southeast leads only in forestry products with 43 per cent.

This predominance of the Northeast in number of establishments in most of the classifications is in accord with the ranking in previous indices of total manufactures in which the Northeast has led in number and has registered less loss in number of establishments than in the other indices of product, value, value added. In 1914, the Northeast had 43.3 per cent of the total number and in 1920, 42.1 per cent; the Middle States had in 1914 an even 29 per cent and 28.3 per cent in 1929; while the Southeast had 14.3 per cent in 1914 and 13.6 per cent in 1929. The Southeast, as would be expected, has a higher rating in small establishments than in large and in certain specialized aspects of manufacturing. Thus in textiles it has less than seven per cent of the total, although in cotton goods it has the largest number by far, 782 as opposed to the Northeast's 423. It excels the Middle States in knit goods and both Northeast and Middle States in upholstered goods. Outside of the textile field and of the forestry products in which it leads, the Southeast leads in a number of other specialties, including bone black, carbon black, and lampblack, in fertilizers, in mucilage and paste, in cast-iron pipe, in carriages. The Southeast is not even first in tobacco, chewing and snuff, nor pipes, nor soda water apparatus, although it leads in production of ice and drinks. Within these regional ranges there are, of course, great differences in the several states, details of which follow in a later chapter.

An intensive study of many of these industries would net essential facts and perspective necessary to either a current inventory or a planning program of optimum production. In addition to cotton textiles and forestry products the Southeast has developed rapidly in the field of furniture manufacture. Yet this is again specialized primarily in a small region, mostly in one state. The six leading states in order of ranking in dollar value of furniture products and value per wage earner are New York, Illinois,

Regional Distribution of Manufacturing Establishments by Industries: IV

INDUSTRIES	Southeast	Southwest	Northeast	Middle States	Northwest	Far West	Total United States
IRON AND STEEL AND THEIR PRODUCTS, NOT INCLUDING MACHINERY							
Bolts, nuts, washers, rivets, not made in rolling mills	2	.....	45	62	.....	8	117
Cast-iron pipe	38	.....	24	6	2	2	72
Cutlery	3	.....	161	65	1	9	239
Doors, shutters, window sash and frames, metal	4	1	80	46	.....	17	148
Files	.....	.....	19	14	.....	.....	33
Firearms	.....	1	17	2	1	.....	21
Forgings, iron and steel, not made in rolling mills	8	.....	100	95	2	13	218
Galvanizing and other coatings, not made in rolling mills	2	2	23	25	1	12	65
Hardware, not elsewhere classified	10	3	233	205	3	31	485
Iron and steel, blast furnaces	18	.....	42	43	2	.....	105
Iron and steel, processed	.....	.....	13	28	.....	5	46
Iron and steel, steel works and rolling mills	21	4	238	189	6	28	486
Nails, etc., not made in rolling mills	.....	.....	39	16	.....	.....	55
Plumbers' supplies not incl. pipe or vit. china sanitary ware	6	.....	119	114	1	15	255
Safe and vaults	1	1	8	16	.....	1	27
Saws	8	.....	42	26	.....	5	81
Screw-machine products and wood screws	.....	.....	115	149	.....	9	273
Springs, steel, except wire, not made in rolling mills	.....	3	35	36	1	11	86
Steam fittings and hot-water apparatus	8	.....	129	96	.....	7	240
Steel barrels, kegs, and drums	3	5	13	27	.....	5	53
Stoves and ranges	48	10	153	294	10	94	609
Structural and ornamental iron and steel work, not rolg. mill	90	48	689	450	41	164	1,482
Tin cans and other tinware, not elsewhere classified	12	4	117	70	3	26	232
Tools, not including edge or machine tools, saws and files	7	2	285	205	4	31	534
Wire, drawn from purchased bars or rods	1	1	47	30	.....	2	81
Wirework not elsewhere classified	14	7	269	210	10	37	547
Wrought pipe, welded and riveted, not made in rolling mills	.....	2	16	18	1	13	50
Totals	*304*	*94*	*3,071*	*2,537*	*89*	*545*	*6,640*
Percentage	*4.6*	*1.4*	*46.3*	*38.2*	*1.3*	*8.2*	*100.0*
NONFERROUS METALS AND THEIR PRODUCTS							
Aluminum manufactures	4	.....	39	87	.....	20	150
Clocks, clock movements, time recording devices, etc.	1	.....	34	19	.....	2	56
Collapsible tubes	.....	.....	15	2	.....	.....	17
Copper, tin and iron sheet work, etc.	148	100	694	750	68	401	2,161
Electroplating	8	5	228	226	3	64	534
Fire extinguishers, chemical	.....	1	10	14	1	2	28
Gas and electric fixtures, lamps, lanterns, etc.	5	4	313	190	4	98	614
Gold leaf and foil	.....	.....	61	8	.....	6	75
Gold, silver, platinum refining (not from ore)	.....	.....	55	6	.....	8	69
Jewelry	23	14	1,133	207	24	135	1,536
Needles, pins, hooks, eyes, snap fasteners	.....	.....	35	7	.....	1	43
Nonferrous-metal alloys and products (no aluminum)	29	15	614	447	20	100	1,225
Plated ware	1	.....	83	12	.....	.....	96
Silversmithing and silverware	1	.....	72	4	.....	6	83
Smelting and refining copper	2	11	5	3	.....	5	26
Smelting and refining lead	.....	1	1	7	9	1	19
Smelting and refining metals (no gold, silver, platinum)	1	1	41	52	3	8	106
Smelting and refining zinc	1	5	5	12	7	.....	30
Stamped ware, enameled ware, japaning, lacquering	9	.....	268	276	4	25	582
Tin and other foil, not including gold foil	2	.....	3	2	.....	.....	7
Watch and clock materials (not watch cases)	.....	.....	13	2	1	1	17
Watch cases	1	.....	34	4	.....	1	40
Watches and watch movements	.....	.....	5	3	.....	.....	8
Totals	*236*	*157*	*3,761*	*2,340*	*144*	*884*	*7,522*
Percentage	*3.1*	*2.1*	*50.0*	*31.1*	*1.9*	*11.7*	*100.0*
MACHINERY, NOT INCLUDING TRANSPORTATION EQUIPMENT							
Agricultural implements	41	2	45	160	21	24	293
Cash registers, adding, calculating, tabulating machines	1	.....	18	25	.....	2	46
Electrical machinery apparatus and supplies	50	23	784	754	26	165	1,802
Engines, turbines, tractors, and water wheels	3	3	65	108	2	18	199
Foundry and machine shop products, unclassified	558	305	3,195	3,287	252	1,008	8,605

Michigan and Ohio, Indiana, North Carolina. Regional comparisons in terms of percentages of indices previously used for all manufactures show the following: In wage earners, the Middle States leads with 46 per cent, followed by the Northeast with nearly 28 per cent and the Southeast with nearly 18 per cent. In amount of wages, however, the Southeast, as in other industries, shows a decreasing ratio of nearly 12 per cent, while the Northeast increases with 33 per cent. The same general order obtains in the other indices; namely, value of product, per cent and per wage earner, and in horse power, per cent, and value added.

Such further facts as may be needed for a general appraisal of the industrial status of the region are available in the tables and graphs and other data easily accessible. What is needed more, however, is special inquiry into particular industries, on the one hand, and on the other a look at the problem of developing the region's resources through more effective industrialization, and the development of this industrialization in accordance with agricultural needs, regional resources, and interregional arrangements. In the previous chapter we illustrated the possibilities of increased production and agricultural balance in the case of the dairy industry; other avenues have been discussed in our conferences on programs of optimum production and in the various sections on planning. The same general problem obtains in the field of industry; namely, to what extent there should be rearrangement of industry in the region, geared to a well planned program of optimum production which shall include industry as well as agriculture. Here as elsewhere there are many factors involved. In the case of dairying, for instance, it was pointed out that cultural conditions, the nature and training of the people, their capacity for sustained work and high standards, are important elements. So, too, in this and in the processing of foods and other similar industries we need not only a measure of what the region and the people can produce but also what they can and will likely consume. This is really the definitive keynote to next steps. Important also are matters of invested capital, management, labor and skills, transportation facilities, foreign and domestic markets, multiple comparisons with other regions, and a host of others, each requiring special study to match its special case. An examination of the total list of industries in the United States, together with their regional distribution, indicates that perhaps the Southeast could well develop, either new or increased plant capacity in a hundred or more industries, in addition to certain major fields to be noted specially, such as paper pulp from loblolly pine, fertilizer from special new processes, and various chemical industries which utilize raw materials of forest and field. Harriet L. Herring has set up a general framework for approaching the problem of planning for optimum

Regional Distribution of Manufacturing Establishments by Industries: V

INDUSTRIES	Southeast	Southwest	Northeast	Middle States	Northwest	Far West	Total United States
MACHINERY, NOT INCLUDING TRANSPORTATION EQUIPMENT (Cont.)							
Gas machines and gas and liquid meters	.....	3	37	25	1	6	72
Machine tools	3	.....	114	160	.....	3	280
Pumps and pumping equipment	13	7	94	134	9	65	322
Refrigerators, mechanical	.....	.....	8	19	1	6	34
Scales and balances	2	.....	27	27	2	1	59
Sewing machines and attachments	.....	.....	30	9	.....	.....	39
Textile machinery and parts	55	.....	313	8	.....	.....	376
Typewriters and parts	.....	.....	21	4	.....	1	26
Washing machines, wringers, driers, etc., household	.....	.....	14	45	1	5	65
Windmills, windmill towers	.....	.....	.....	10	5	.....	15
Machine tool accessories, etc., unclassified	3	2	259	426	1	31	722
Totals	*729*	*345*	*5,024*	*5,201*	*321*	*1,335*	*12,955*
Percentage	*5.6*	*2.7*	*38.8*	*40.1*	*2.5*	*10.3*	*100.0*
TRANSPORTATION EQUIPMENT, AIR, LAND, AND WATER							
Aircraft and parts	3	2	45	42	15	25	132
Carriage, wagon, sleigh, and sled materials	14	1	14	15	.....	1	45
Carriages and sleds, children's	1	.....	46	31	.....	1	79
Carriages, wagons, sleighs, and sleds	25	1	22	40	.....	.....	88
Cars, electric and steam RR, not built in RR shops	14	6	39	66	12	10	147
Locomotives not made in RR repair shops	4	.....	8	4	.....	.....	16
Motor vehicle bodies and body parts	74	20	394	524	21	121	1,154
Motor vehicles not including motor cycles	14	7	48	138	10	27	244
Motor cycles, bicycles and parts	1	.....	11	9	.....	.....	21
Ship and boat building, steel and wooden, also repair	88	9	295	105	1	126	624
Totals	*238*	*46*	*922*	*974*	*59*	*311*	*2,550*
Percentage	*9.3*	*1.8*	*36.1*	*38.1*	*2.3*	*12.4*	*100.0*
RAILROAD REPAIR SHOPS							
Car, construction and repair, electric RR	66	23	169	139	19	30	446
Car, construction and repair, steam RR	251	148	484	652	181	135	1,851
Totals	*317*	*171*	*653*	*791*	*200*	*165*	*2,297*
Percentage	*13.8*	*7.4*	*28.4*	*34.5*	*8.7*	*7.2*	*100.0*
MISCELLANEOUS INDUSTRIES							
Artificial and preserved flowers and plants	6	1	132	43	2	7	191
Artists' materials	1	.....	43	19	1	4	68
Brooms	68	47	100	140	23	29	407
Brushes, other than rubber	10	.....	184	84	8	17	303
Buttons	9	.....	148	84	.....	1	242
Carbon paper and inked ribbons	.....	.....	36	15	1	5	57
Cigars and cigarettes	153	3	917	485	35	43	1,636
Combs and hairpins not metal and rubber	.....	.....	21	3	.....	.....	24
Dairymen's, poultrymen's, creamery and factory supplies	15	5	35	90	7	20	172
Dental goods and equipment	.....	1	52	27	4	3	87
Fancy miscellaneous articles, unclassified elsewhere	11	2	582	154	5	60	814
Feathers, plumes, and manufactures thereof	.....	.....	34	2	.....	3	39
Foundry supplies	3	.....	21	34	1	.....	59
Fur goods	3	3	2,264	452	14	119	2,855
Furs, dressed	2	.....	220	20	2	4	248
Hair work	.....	.....	42	8	1	8	59
Hand stamps, stencils, and brands	25	10	140	110	8	39	332
Hats, straw, men's	.....	3	36	11	.....	.....	50
Instruments, professional and scientific	3	.....	176	75	5	17	276
Ivory, shell and bone work (not buttons, combs, hairpins)	1	.....	14	3	.....	3	21
Jewelry and instrument cases	1	.....	97	11	.....	4	113
Lapidary work	.....	.....	83	5	1	11	100
Mattresses and bed springs, unclassified elsewhere	141	92	402	201	33	82	951
Models and patterns, not including paper patterns	11	9	340	362	10	72	804
Motion pictures, not projection in theaters	3	2	47	27	2	61	142
Musical instrument parts and materials, piano and organ	1	.....	45	19	.....	2	67

production by classifying the industries under discussion into five main groups.

The first group represents bulky manufactures, contemplated for use both in the region and some extension out of it, for which the Southeast has abundant raw materials and suitable labor. These include such materials as sugar, vegetable oils, paper, clay products, cotton textiles, iron and certain of the metallic minerals. Under such expansion there might develop also subsidiary industries, such as containers, work clothes, heavy simple iron manufactures, and the like. The second group represents bulky manufactures, contemplated for the South only, for which the region could and should produce the raw materials. These include dairy and meat products, canning and preserving, various other food and feed processing industries, from which might grow up increased subsidiary industries such as meat packing, leather tanning, forest products. The third group represents certain industries, probably supplying part of the regional demand only, in which manufacture is to be determined by regional factors such as climate, market, special resources. Included here might be such industries as rubber, special types of machinery, new electrical apparatus, wire fencing, and many others.

The fourth and fifth groups represent industries which, from all apparent evidence, the region should not attempt to develop. These include manufactures in which special skills have already been built up in other regions, or bulky manufacture for which other regions have the raw materials and for which there are no justifiable reasons for development in new regions. Here might be classified such industries as advanced metal trades, women's clothing, and many others for which special skills are required. An exception might well be electrical apparatus if the TVA and other rural electrification agencies change the situation to conform to groups two and three above. In the group where raw materials are in other regions might be included all those in contrast to cotton, sugar, vegetable oils, that are produced in the several other regions. In this last grouping there might be other exceptions and the situation might often be complex and not so easy to decide by rule of thumb. The relative number of values inherent in the industry and its meaning to the nation or to international commerce or to the American standard of living might be of considerable importance.

There might also be injustices in the case of specific industries. The cost to society in the form of waste in transportation, in loss to a region involved in sacrificing an illogical industry and in profit to a section receiving a logical industry, should be balanced against each other. If the good of all is best served, for example, by having sugar and oil refined in the

Regional Distribution of Manufacturing Establishments by Industries: VI

INDUSTRIES	Southeast	Southwest	Northeast	Middle States	Northwest	Far West	Total United States
MISCELLANEOUS INDUSTRIES (Cont.)							
Musical instruments' parts and materials, unclassified	.....	.....	53	43	.....	10	106
Musical instruments, organs	1	.....	31	22	1	7	62
Musical instruments, pianos	.....	.....	47	34	.....	.....	81
Optical goods	1	.....	86	22	2	6	117
Paving materials, asphalts, tar, crushed slag, mixtures	14	1	55	50	1	5	126
Pencils, lead including mechanical	4	.....	25	8	.....	1	38
Pens, fountain and stylographic, pen points	2	.....	58	15	1	.....	76
Phonographs	.....	.....	32	21	1	5	59
Photographic materials and apparatus	.....	.....	54	47	.....	14	115
Pipes (tobacco)	1	.....	15	8	.....	.....	24
Roofing, asphalt shingles, roof coatings, (not paint)	9	.....	36	42	2	13	102
Sand paper, emery paper, abrasive paper and cloth	.....	.....	8	3	.....	.....	11
Signs and advertising novelties	66	44	480	475	43	131	1,239
Soda water apparatus	2	2	26	19	1	4	54
Sporting and athletic goods (not firearms and ammunition)	13	2	102	93	7	25	242
Stationery goods unclassified elsewhere	12	2	111	64	2	12	203
Steam and other packing, pipe coverings, gaskets, etc.	5	.....	89	55	4	18	171
Surgical and orthopedic appliances, artificial limbs	15	6	181	109	14	38	363
Theatrical scenery and stage equipment	1	4	23	15	2	10	55
Tobacco, chewing, smoking, and snuff	34	1	57	59	.....	1	152
Toys, games and playground equipment	4	3	317	124	8	20	476
Umbrellas, parasols, and canes	3	1	124	12	.....	1	141
Whips	.....	1	6	1	.....	.....	8
Window shades and fixtures	8	13	202	181	4	74	482
Totals	*647*	*273*	*8,429*	*4,006*	*256*	*1,009*	*14,620*
Percentage	*4.4*	*1.9*	*57.7*	*27.4*	*1.7*	*6.8*	*100.0*
Grand Total	*21,296*	*4,399*	*70,776*	*40,297*	*4,418*	*12,928*	*154,114*
Textiles and their products	1,870	242	20,439	3,535	168	1,150	27,404
Forest Products	11,555	791	6,211	4,857	612	2,886	26,912
Paper and allied products	165	22	1,848	895	25	171	3,126
Printing, publishing and allied industries	2,623	1,311	10,263	8,822	1,792	2,711	27,522
Chemical and allied products	1,342	423	3,267	2,341	225	680	8,278
Products of petroleum and coal	174	159	504	409	118	133	1,497
Leather and its manufactures	153	52	2,953	850	65	204	4,277
Stone, clay and glass products	943	313	3,431	2,739	344	744	8,514
Iron and steel and their products, not including machinery	304	94	3,071	2,537	89	545	6,640
Nonferrous metals and their products	236	157	3,761	2,340	144	884	7,522
Machinery, not including transportation Equipment	729	345	5,024	5,201	321	1,335	12,955
Transportation equipment, air, land, and water	238	46	922	974	59	311	2,550
Railroad repair shops	317	171	653	791	200	165	2,297
Miscellaneous industries	647	273	8,429	4,006	256	1,009	14,620

Northeast rather than in Louisiana or Texas, then let it continue to be concentrated there. Other considerations are clearly apparent. For instance, except in a few obvious cases, it would probably be better economics and better social policy to build up gradually a new industry that naturally belongs in a region. Expansion and replacement of obsolete and obsolescent plants give an opportunity for such gradual reallocation. This is what took place in the textile industry without planning because the advantages were so obvious. It would take place in other industries if many of the advantages were not hidden as at present.

The problem of expansion of industry in the region is thus a complex one involving a number of balances. We have already called attention to certain skeptical viewpoints as to large-scale industry in the South as opposed to a greater emphasis upon agrarian culture. There is, on the other hand, the obligation of the region, in any democratic program, of conserving and developing and protecting all of its people, to insure representative and adequate economic opportunity for earning a livelihood and also for reaping the collective rewards of industry. The Southeast being a heavily loaded debtor region faces an unusually adverse trade balance. It not only does not have adequate opportunity for earning, but its money, hard earned, flows out and out to enrich other regions, often contrary to its economic advantages and diminishing the income and purchasing power of the people. The remedying of this situation is the objective of all this planning for industrial development. The special task is to determine the largest number of criteria from which to judge the advisability of amounts and types of industrial expansion and of cultural conditions which will attract capital and leadership personnel from outside as well as within the region. Including the general tests, already enumerated in the above discussion of optimum programs, it seems possible to set up a relatively simple and clear-cut series of criteria. Thus, if the industry is a new one in the nation, not therefore involving competition with or injury to already established concerns in other regions; if it is both adapted to and needed in the region; if its development advances both technical aspects of industry and economic well-being; if it aids in balancing the regional economy; if it can also promote certain interregional advantages, such as economic distribution and manufacture of products and stimulate national industry; if it advances the general culture level of the region and stimulates the inflow of capital and personnel; then, the case is clear and awaits only the practical and technical ways of development.

The case may be illustrated by a half dozen types of industry which will meet, to varying degrees, the above conditions. One set of examples may be cited from among the proposed developments in the Tennessee

Geographic Distribution of the Aggregate Personal Income of the Non-Farm Population by Types of Income, 1929

Adapted from *America's Capacity to Consume*, pp. 172-173, 175-176.

State and Region	Total Income			Income from Occupations			Returns from Property			Profits from Sale of Property		
	Millions of Dollars	Per Cent of Total	Per Capita	Millions of Dollars	Per Cent of Total	Per Capita	Millions of Dollars	Per Cent of Total	Per Capita	Millions of Dollars	Per Cent of Total	Per Capita
Southeast												
Virginia	869	1.04	$ 594	$ 733	1.23	$ 501	$ 114	0.66	$ 78	$ 22	0.35	$ 15
North Carolina	729	0.88	472	632	1.06	409	84	0.49	55	13	0.21	8
South Carolina	335	0.40	412	300	0.50	369	29	0.17	36	6	0.10	7
Georgia	788	0.95	532	654	1.09	442	116	0.68	78	18	0.29	12
Florida	670	0.81	577	528	0.88	455	106	0.62	91	36	0.58	31
Kentucky	861	1.04	605	689	1.15	484	122	0.71	86	50	0.80	35
Tennessee	733	0.88	529	676	1.13	488	29	0.18	22	28	0.45	19
Alabama	683	0.82	527	589	0.99	455	78	0.45	61	16	0.26	12
Mississippi	341	0.41	530	300	0.50	466	38	0.22	59	3	0.05	5
Arkansas	368	0.44	503	320	0.54	437	42	0.25	59	6	0.10	7
Louisiana	761	0.92	603	622	1.04	493	118	0.69	93	21	0.34	17
Southwest												
Oklahoma	947	1.14	699	748	1.25	552	151	0.88	112	48	0.77	35
Texas	2,357	2.83	690	1,855	3.10	543	375	2.19	110	127	2.05	37
New Mexico	144	0.17	549	120	0.20	458	21	0.12	80	3	0.05	11
Arizona	263	0.32	795	209	0.35	633	40	0.23	121	14	0.23	41
Northeast												
Maine	437	0.53	689	326	0.55	514	83	0.48	131	28	0.45	44
New Hampshire	282	0.34	689	217	0.36	530	49	0.29	120	16	0.26	39
Massachusetts	4,053	4.87	976	2,709	4.53	652	914	5.33	220	430	6.94	104
Rhode Island	593	0.71	881	404	0.68	600	140	0.82	208	49	0.79	73
Connecticut	1,555	1.87	1,028	995	1.66	658	361	2.11	239	199	3.21	132
New York	16,652	20.03	1,417	9,906	16.57	843	4,792	27.98	408	1,954	31.51	166
New Jersey	3,910	4.71	1,011	2,752	4.60	712	876	5.11	226	282	4.55	73
Delaware	296	0.36	1,550	122	0.20	639	73	0.43	382	101	1.63	529
Pennsylvania	7,558	9.09	865	5,481	9.17	627	1,474	8.61	169	603	9.73	69
Maryland	1,218	1.46	881	800	1.34	578	309	1.80	224	109	1.76	79
West Virginia	760	0.91	602	657	1.10	520	82	0.48	65	21	0.34	17
Middle States												
Ohio	4,987	6.00	893	3,855	6.45	690	823	4.80	147	309	4.98	56
Indiana	1,801	2.17	748	1,512	2.53	628	236	1.38	98	53	0.85	22
Illinois	7,169	8.62	1,091	5,024	8.40	765	1,655	9.66	252	490	7.90	74
Michigan	3,921	4.72	983	3,000	5.01	752	646	3.77	162	275	4.44	69
Wisconsin	1,653	1.99	807	1,309	2.19	639	268	1.57	131	76	1.23	37
Minnesota	1,339	1.61	802	1,032	1.72	618	238	1.39	143	69	1.12	41
Iowa	993	1.19	659	819	1.37	543	146	0.85	97	28	0.45	19
Missouri	2,133	2.57	851	1,614	2.70	644	408	2.38	163	111	1.79	44
Northwest												
North Dakota	167	0.20	588	153	0.26	539	12	0.07	42	2	0.03	7
South Dakota	186	0.22	614	161	0.27	531	20	0.12	66	5	0.08	17
Nebraska	553	0.67	698	449	0.75	566	89	0.52	112	15	0.24	20
Kansas	803	0.97	686	658	1.10	562	119	0.69	102	26	0.42	22
Montana	286	0.35	856	237	0.40	710	41	0.24	123	8	0.13	23
Idaho	167	0.20	647	147	0.25	570	18	0.10	70	2	0.03	8
Wyoming	127	0.15	841	108	0.18	715	17	0.10	113	2	0.03	13
Colorado	580	0.70	772	445	0.74	592	111	0.65	148	24	0.39	32
Utah	249	0.30	629	203	0.34	513	37	0.22	93	9	0.14	23
Far West												
Nevada	77	0.09	1,041	61	0.10	824	13	0.08	176	3	0.05	41
Washington	1,111	1.34	887	891	1.49	711	157	0.92	125	63	1.02	51
Oregon	591	0.71	817	492	0.82	680	86	0.50	119	13	0.21	18
California	5,283	6.35	1,066	3,738	6.25	755	1,181	6.89	238	364	5.87	73

Valley Authority. Mr. David E. Lilienthal illustrates an opportunity in the case of the production of stainless steel, which will be essential to many manufactures and especially to many which the expansion of the Southeast will make profitable. Thus, stainless steel will be necessary for agricultural equipment, new types of high-speed streamline trains, new types of kitchen utensils. "Here is a new field of potential industrial production which has almost limitless possibilities. The industries associated with stainless steel would be new in their scope of operation and would not result in the transfer of industries from some other section of the country to the Tennessee Valley region. This area offers a unique location for this great new industry. We have here cheap hydro-electric power, which is essential. We have the various mineral resources which are requisite to such a development. Such an industry would be of particular benefit to Birmingham, because you produce under most satisfactory conditions vast quantities of the basic ingredients of the rustless iron industries."

We have already listed those industries in which power is an important item and have indicated the probability of a natural increase of all such industries in proportion as the region provides cheap and abundant power. We have listed the almost limitless possibilities of the chemical industries, especially as they relate to coal, iron, and agriculture. And we have indicated the possibilities which inhere in the vast mineral resources. We have already pointed out the significance of the new regional arrangements proposed for the production and distribution of steel products in the Birmingham area. It will suffice, perhaps, to indicate the place of other minerals in the regional development of industry by giving the mere catalogue of minerals whose values aggregate more than $300,000,000 in the Tennessee Valley states alone. Mr. Morgan has enumerated them somewhat as follows: "In fuels there is coal, lignite, petroleum and natural gas. Our heavy metals include iron ores, manganese, chromium and nickel, and our light metals are aluminum, magnesium and beryllium. There are other metals such as zinc, lead and tin. Of cement materials we produce limestone, shale, clay, gypsum, lime and slag. Similarly, this area has stone, sand, gravel, chert and asphalt. There is an abundance of fertilizers including phosphate, potash, schists and shales, green sand, niter, gypsum, lime, by-product ammonia and atmospheric nitrogen. There are the chemicals, salt, lime, alum, coal tar and pyrite. For ceramics we have clay, shales, kaolin and feldspar. Our pigments are ocher, metallic paint, pyrite, barite, carbon black, zinc white, coal tar colors and slate colors. Abrasives found here are bauxite, corundum, emery, garnet and sand. Refractories and insulators include cyanite, asbestos, mica, fire clays, bauxite, olivine

Distribution of Large Incomes, 1929

State and Region	Number of Taxable Incomes Equal to or Greater Than			
	$1,000,000	$500,000	$250,000	$100,000
Southeast	*7*	*34*	*96*	*441*
Virginia	...	2	8	50
North Carolina	...	6	12	48
South Carolina	...	....	....	4
Georgia	...	1	7	36
Florida	3	13	24	89
Kentucky	3	6	15	72
Tennessee	1	3	15	52
Alabama	...	1	6	39
Mississippi	...	....	....	3
Arkansas	...	1	2	5
Louisiana	...	1	7	43
Southwest	*8*	*22*	*62*	*260*
Oklahoma	2	8	15	87
Texas	5	13	44	152
New Mexico	...	....	....	4
Arizona	1	1	3	17
Northeast	*388*	*1,082*	*2,835*	*9,563*
Maine	1	3	12	66
New Hampshire	...	2	3	28
Vermont	...	....	5	16
Massachusetts	17	71	248	1,027
Rhode Island	3	12	35	139
Connecticut	10	32	83	386
New York	276	714	1,785	5,538
New Jersey	25	76	191	633
Delaware	11	29	51	130
Pennsylvania	36	125	353	1,354
Maryland	9	18	64	210
West Virginia	...	....	5	36

State and Region	Number of Taxable Incomes Equal to or Greater Than			
	$1,000,000	$500,000	$250,000	$100,000
Middle States	*98*	*290*	*857*	*3,448*
Ohio	21	69	194	694
Indiana	2	8	27	115
Illinois	44	126	333	1,352
Michigan	19	48	165	627
Wisconsin	4	12	33	171
Minnesota	2	7	29	169
Iowa	1	6	13	51
Missouri	5	14	63	269
Northwest	...	*8*	*33*	*138*
North Dakota	...	....	....	....
South Dakota	...	1	2	7
Nebraska	...	....	7	26
Kansas	...	2	7	25
Montana	...	2	3	15
Idaho	...	....	....	1
Wyoming	...	....	....	....
Colorado	...	3	12	52
Utah	...	....	2	12
Far West	*12*	*46*	*170*	*827*
Nevada	...	....	1	6
Washington	4	7	13	70
Oregon	...	....	3	20
California	8	39	153	731
United States	513	1,482	4,053	14,677

State Differentials and Percentage of Federal Internal Revenue and Federal Relief, 1933, Compared With Population

State and Region	Relief Funds	Internal Revenue	Population*
Southeast	*16.96*	*22.53*	*20.8*
Virginia	1.95	5.35	2.0
North Carolina	1.41	11.40	2.6
South Carolina	1.00	0.41	1.4
Georgia	1.04	0.75	2.4
Florida	0.93	0.47	1.2
Kentucky	1.12	2.37	2.1
Tennessee	2.00	0.59	2.1
Alabama	1.14	0.33	2.2
Mississippi	1.14	0.07	1.6
Arkansas	1.32	0.15	1.5
Louisiana	3.50	0.64	1.7
Southwest	*6.89*	*4.44*	*7.4*
Oklahoma	1.08	1.78	2.0
Texas	4.41	2.31	4.7
New Mexico	0.43	0.30	.3
Arizona	0.08	0.05	.4
Northeast	*27.91*	*42.75*	*31.0*
Maine	1.00	0.26	.6
New Hampshire	0.25	0.15	.4
Vermont	0.43	0.05	.3
Massachusetts	2.25	3.40	3.5
Rhode Island	0.25	0.50	.6
Connecticut	0.80	1.16	1.3
New York	11.94	22.66	10.3
New Jersey	2.88	4.26	3.3
Delaware	0.20	0.72	.2
Pennsylvania	4.61	7.37	7.8
Maryland	1.97	1.88	1.3
West Virginia	0.97	0.34	1.4

State and Region	Relief Funds	Internal Revenue	Population*
Middle States	*29.92*	*21.68*	*27.6*
Ohio	7.70	4.69	5.4
Indiana	1.59	0.98	2.6
Illinois	6.67	6.55	6.2
Michigan	5.71	3.27	3.9
Wisconsin	3.07	1.60	2.4
Minnesota	1.61	1.41	2.1
Iowa	2.16	0.39	2.0
Missouri	1.93	2.79	3.0
Northwest	*7.16*	*1.77*	*6.0*
North Dakota	0.62	0.05	.6
South Dakota	0.64	0.04	.6
Nebraska	1.22	0.29	1.1
Kansas	1.09	0.70	1.5
Montana	0.91	0.11	.4
Idaho	0.55	0.03	.4
Wyoming	0.45	0.03	.2
Colorado	0.75	0.43	.8
Utah	0.61	0.09	.4
Far West	*11.16*	*6.77*	*6.8*
Nevada	0.51	0.09	.1
Washington	1.61	0.42	1.3
Oregon	0.89	0.22	.8
California	7.91	6.04	4.6

*Population for 1930.

and vermiculite. In addition to these minerals there are the miscellaneous items of talc, graphite Fuller's earth, glass sand and bentonite."

Other "peculiar" industries in the Southeast include the vegetable oil industries, comprising products from cotton seed, soy beans, peanuts, pecans; tung oil of which the United States imports more than ten million dollars worth; products of medicinal plants of which perhaps three-fourths of the nation's supply is found in the region; food industries of which the region has great need and resources; paper and wood pulp as the basis for the production of millions of tons of newsprint; the ceramic industry for which there are abundant resources; a powerful fertilizer industry in both nitrates and phosphorous; and a score of small industries in wood and arts and crafts.

Here again, however, the picture of the Southeast must be presented in comparison with the rest of the nation and with the cumulative force of both earlier national industrial expansion and of the early depression period. It is important to inquire whether the industry and wealth of the region must continue with their deficiencies because of the overwhelming advantage which other regions already have. What is the place of the Southeast in the next period of development and what are the handicaps in terms of its present ratio in the nation? Has the Southeast lagged in its development as compared with the rest of the nation, on the one hand; and has it, on the other, also had less of disruption due to recent changes. What has happened as a whole seems clear; the South's reaction not so clear: giant industry taking the place of declining agricultural opportunity; rapid urbanization transforming a nation overnight; the development of early American free private enterprise into a gigantic modern industrial capitalistic system; the swift onrush of machine industry; the increase of specialization and the spreading out of labor; the concentration of business and industry into larger units with resulting scientific management and business organization; the organization of labor and the struggles between capital and labor; the rapid rise of speculative production and of the credit economy which has distinguished the nation.

What is relatively clear, however, is the negligible place of the region in, let us say, the ten major industries of the nation. If the picture is of manufacturing industries alone and features the employment of labor, these would appear to be in 1931 somewhat as follows: Cotton goods, foundry and machine shops, steam railroad repair shops, steel works and rolling mills, lumber and timber products, boots and shoes (not rubber), bread and bakery products, electrical machinery, knit goods, women's clothing. None of these is concentrated in the Southeast, even though the region leads in the number of industries classified as forest products.

Furniture Manufacturing, 1929

State and Region	Wage Earners		Wages			Value of Product			Value Added By Manufacturing			Horse Power		
	Number	Per Cent	Amount	Per Cent	Per Wage Earner	Amount	Per Cent	Per Wage Earner	Amount	Per Cent	Per Wage Earner	Amount	Per Cent	Value of Manufactures per H.P.
U. S.	193,399	100.0	$242,832,096	100.0	$1,256	$948,116,358	100.0	$4,902	$521,662,189	100.0	$2,697	$503,970	100.0	$1,881
S. E.	33,865	17.5	28,424,824	11.7	839	126,829,318	13.4	3,745	62,721,534	12.0	1,852	84,004	16.7	1,519
S. W.*	1,629	.8	1,979,669	.8	1,215	7,373,217	.8	4,526	4,031,213	.8	2,474	4,903	.9	1,504
N. E.**	55,428	28.7	81,090,715	33.5	1,463	302,715,484	32.0	5,461	170,503,161	32.7	3,076	144,790	28.7	2,091
M. S.	89,550	46.4	113,130,049	46.6	1,263	444,622,375	46.8	4,965	248,053,798	47.6	2,770	236,568	47.0	1,879
N. W.†	1,126	.6	1,298,208	.5	1,153	5,479,812	.6	4,866	2,781,319	.6	2,470	3,049	.6	1,797
F. W.	11,658	6.0	16,720,155	6.9	1,434	60,556,279	6.4	5,194	33,278,695	6.3	2,854	30,276	6.0	2,000
States Not Shown Separately	143	....	188,476	....	1,318	539,873	....	3,776	292,469	.. ..	2,045	680	....	1,421
SELECTED STATES IN ORDER OF IMPORTANCE														
N. Y.	25,220	13.0	$ 41,538,136	17.2	$1,647	$159,771,994	16.8	$6,335	$ 91,798,762	17.6	3,640	$ 61,093	12.2	$2,615
Illinois	23,767	12.3	32,453,867	13.3	1,365	130,535,112	13.8	5,492	71,754,086	13.8	3,019	50,730	10.1	2,574
Michigan	20,941	11.4	27,908,837	11.5	1,333	99,714,641	10.5	4,762	60,724,702	11.6	2,900	49,491	9.8	2,015
Indiana	18,700	9.7	20,344,735	8.4	1,088	83,495,716	8.8	4,463	42,328,233	8.1	2,263	64,335	12.7	1,298
Ohio	10,707	5.5	14,067,942	5.8	1,314	60,576,681	6.4	5,678	34,308,501	6.6	3,204	30,109	6.0	2,012
N. C.	15,609	8.1	12,822,796	5.3	821	56,737,489	6.0	3,635	27,012,621	5.2	1,730	38,165	7.6	1,487

*New Mexico and Arizona not separate.
**Delaware and District of Columbia not separate.
†Montana and Utah not separate.

Wages Per Wage Earner

COMPARISON OF CHIEF PRODUCING REGIONS WITH EACH OTHER AND WITH ALL MANUFACTURES IN UNITED STATES

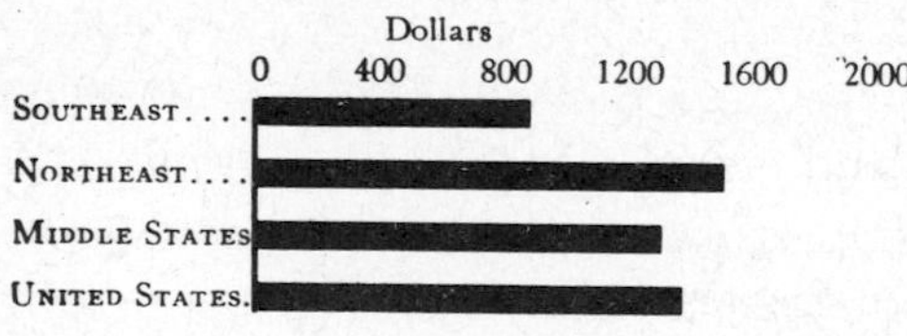

SELECTED STATES

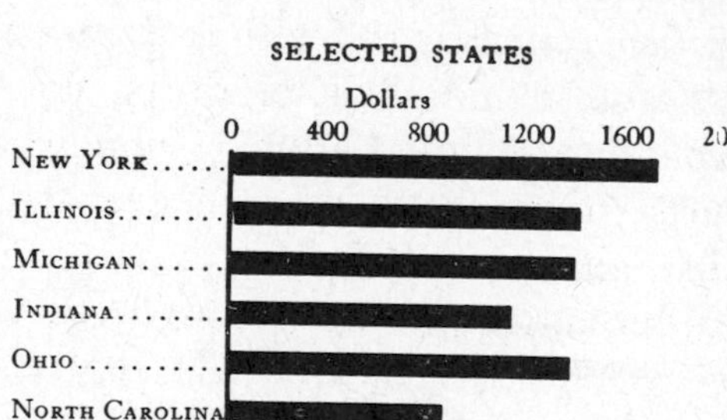

Value Added by Manufacturing, Per Wage Earner

COMPARISON OF CHIEF PRODUCING REGIONS WITH EACH OTHER AND WITH ALL MANUFACTURES IN THE UNITED STATES

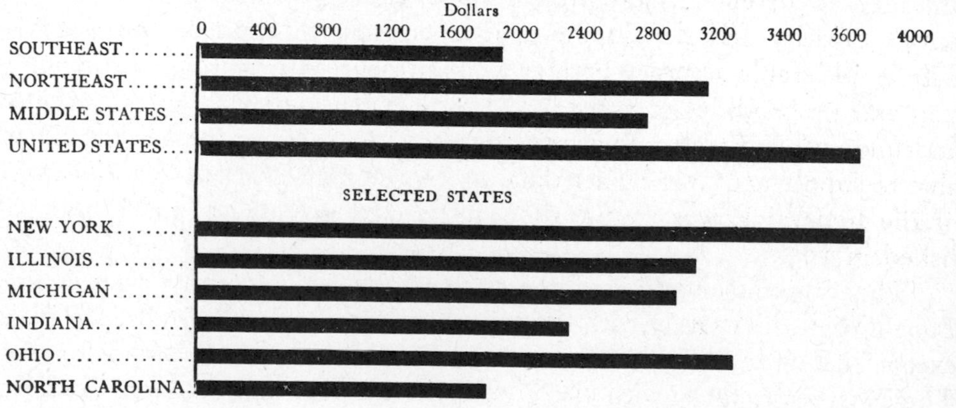

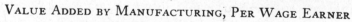

If, on the other hand, the index is one of value of products, the ranking is as follows, the first eight having products of more than a billion dollars worth: meat packing (wholesale), motor vehicles (excluding motorcycles), petroleum refining, printing and publishing (newspaper and periodical), steel works and rolling mills, women's clothing, foundry and machine shops, bread and baking products, electrical machinery, and cigars and cigarettes. If, again, another standard index were used, showing the value added by manufacture, the ranking would be still different: printing and publishing (newspaper and periodical), foundry and machine shops, cigars and cigarettes, bread and bakery products, electrical machinery, women's clothing, printing and publishing (book and job), steel works and rolling mills, motor vehicles (excluding motorcycles), and motor vehicle bodies and parts. In these groupings the region approaches priority in cigarette manufacturing.

Still another classification, showing the rank of industries including both manufacturing and non-manufacturing, would show the following: railroad; textiles and their products; machinery, not including transportation equipment; public utilities, including power and light, telegraph, telephone; electric-railroad and motor-bus operation and maintenance; iron and steel and their products, not including machinery; forest products; construction and building; mining and quarrying; food and kindred products; transportation equipment, air, land, and water. In this last composite list, although the region has no one of the major concentrations, under a different momentum it might have excelled in at least half.

One major index of the region's capacity, partly in the development of these industries and partly in its cultural advance, needs more exploration. We have referred to the Southeast's increasing mineral wealth; we have assumed that power is the index of the present technological age; and we have presented general pictures of the region's resources in water, coal, and electric current. If the measure of a region's civilization is found in its power capacity and development, it is possible to appraise the Southeast with considerable accuracy both as to its present status and as to the obligation and probabilities of future industrial expansion through its developed and undeveloped water power resources. The most important facts available to supplement our earlier data are those of the *National Power Survey* of the Federal Power Commission authorized in August, 1933, and published in 1935.

The Commission divided the nation into seven power zones. Their Zone 2 coincides exactly with the Southern Regional Study's Middle States, except that it includes the western part of Pennsylvania and Maryland. The Northeast, then, with these exceptions is the same as our Northeast.

Combined State and Local Net Bonded Debt, Per Capita of Total Population, by States, 1927

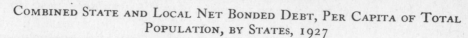

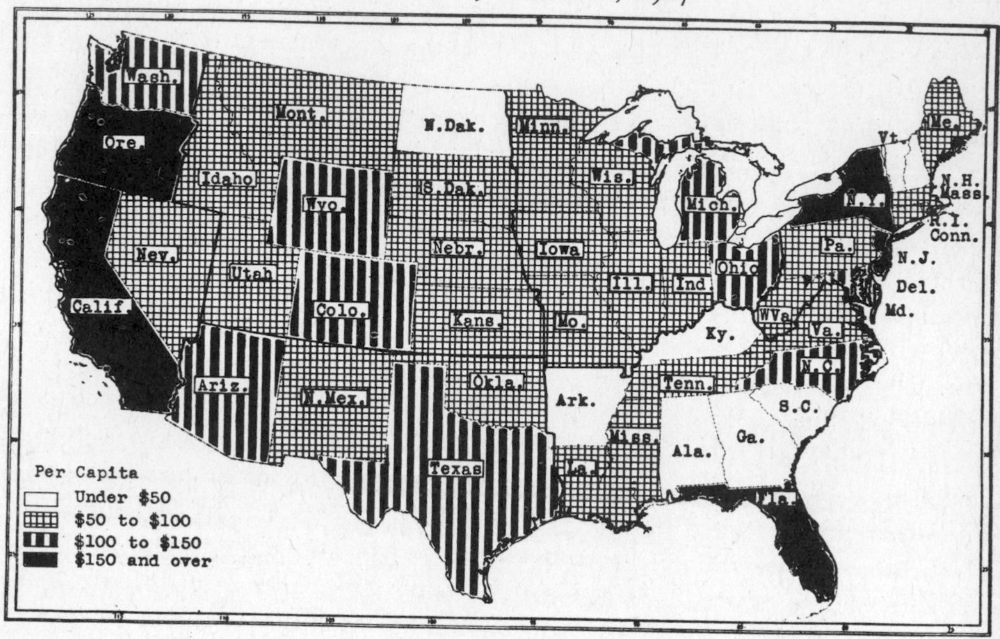

Summary of State and Municipal Defaults, 1933

Adapted from *The Bond Buyer*

REGION	Counties	Cities and Towns	School Districts	Other Districts	Total Number Municipalities	Reclamation, Levee, Irri., and Drainage Districts	Spec. Assmt.	*Grand Total* Municipalities and Spec. Districts
Southeast	*175*	*241*	*64*	*11*	*492**	*62*	*4*	*558*
Virginia	1	1	..	..	2	..	..	2
North Carolina	61	128	18	..	207	2	..	209
South Carolina	6	9	2	..	17	..	..	17
Georgia	1	1	4	..	6	..	..	6
Florida	33	74	16	11	134	14	..	148
Kentucky	29	6	4	..	39	..	2	41
Tennessee	20	6	..	..	26	5	..	31
Alabama	2	8	..	..	10	1	..	11
Mississippi	7	6	3	..	16	7	..	23
Arkansas	6	2	12	..	21*	23	..	44
Louisiana	9	..	5	..	14	10	2	26
Southwest	*37*	*45*	*18*	*12*	*112*	*15*	*8*	*135*
Oklahoma	4	14	3	..	21	..	2	23
Texas	31	26	11	12	80	12	2	94
New Mexico	..	3	2	..	5	..	2	7
Arizona	2	2	2	..	6	3	2	11
Northeast	*1*	*28*	*6*	*2*	*37*	..	..	*37*
Maine	..	1	..	..	1	..	..	1
New Hampshire	..	..	..	..	..	..	..	..
Vermont	..	..	..	..	..	..	..	..
Massachusetts	..	1	..	..	1	..	..	1
Rhode Island	..	..	..	..	..	..	..	..
Connecticut	..	2	..	..	2	..	..	2
New York	..	2	1	1	4	..	..	4
New Jersey	1	14	3	..	18	..	..	18
Delaware	..	..	..	..	..	..	..	..
Pennsylvania	..	8	2	1	11	..	..	11
Maryland	..	..	..	..	..	..	..	..
West Virginia	..	..	..	..	..	..	..	..
Middle States	*51*	*98*	*77*	*8*	*234*	*19*	*33*	*286*
Ohio	7	53	33	..	93	..	5	98
Indiana	15	..	..	..	15	..	5	20
Illinois	2	5	10	8	25	5	18	48
Michigan	11	24	15	..	50	2	3	55
Wisconsin	3	1	..	..	4	2	..	6
Minnesota	4	..	1	..	5	..	..	5
Iowa	2	6	2	..	10	1	2	13
Missouri	7	9	16	..	32	9	..	41
Northwest	*8*	*21*	*35*	*1*	*65*	*18*	*13*	*96*
North Dakota	..	3	4	..	7	..	1	8
South Dakota	1	..	15	..	16	1	..	17
Nebraska	..	1	5	..	6	2	1	9
Kansas	..	4	..	..	4	..	..	4
Montana	3	1	..	..	4	3	..	7
Idaho	2	1	..	1	4	2	6	12
Wyoming	..	2	..	..	2	1	2	5
Colorado	2	6	10	..	18	4	3	25
Utah	..	3	1	..	4	5	..	9
Far West	*10*	*24*	*9*	..	*43*	*89*	*17*	*149*
Nevada	..	..	..	..	..	2	..	2
Washington	1	3	..	..	4	4	13	21
Oregon	..	16	1	..	17	17	..	34
California	9	5	8	..	22	66	4	92
United States	282	457	209	34	983*	203	75	1261

*Includes default by State of Arkansas.

The Commission adds Arkansas and Louisiana to the Southwest, but places Arizona in the Pacific Southwest. A study of undeveloped water power shows the Far West to have nearly two-thirds and the Northeast and the Southeast to have about one-fourth. The Southeast itself is credited with nearly 400 undeveloped water power sites, with an estimated installed capacity of more than a fifth of the whole nation's undeveloped water power. At the same time the Southeast's actual developed power is relatively higher than its undeveloped power. That is, the Southeast's 1929 percentage of the nation's actual hydro-production was about 25 per cent, whereas its percentage of the nation's undeveloped hydro-production was considerably less than 20 per cent. The Southeast's ratio of total installed capacity as opposed to hydro-production is less, both for 1929 and 1934. For total installed capacity of undeveloped water power the Southeast was credited with a little more than 10 per cent in 1929 and 11 per cent in 1934. The study points out that, even with the South's relatively high development, there is deficiency in every state except Florida, Mississippi, Louisiana, and part of Alabama, based upon measured needs "with the resumption of normal industrial activity."

The Southeast's estimated increased need over 1929 generation will be about 25 per cent. A part of this shortage is due to the development of domestic uses of electricity, to the rural electrification movement, and to the extension of power to smaller industries. This is especially significant to the Southeast. Likewise, it is important to note that the "critical shortage of existing generating capacity most seriously affects the great industrial districts of the East and Middle West." This must have a decided bearing upon the relative industrial development of the Southeast from the viewpoint of the national welfare in case of war or other emergency. It is a measurable index of regional possibilities. If the Far West with its great undeveloped resources suffers by reason of situation and facilities for distribution to the rest of the nation, and if the great industrial regions of the Middle States and the Northeast are heavily developed, a reasonable expansion in the Southeast is the logical product. A greater flow of electricity in the Southeast is, therefore, one way of expansion which can scarcely be questioned. In addition to the rapidly increasing cultural aspects of a developing region in which "electric light and power has come to be almost as essential an element in our daily lives as the bread we eat and the water we drink," in the Southeast it is a measuring rod of immediate resources for the increase in industry, large and small, and for *bringing the region up to the standards already obtaining* in some other regions. The Southeast, for instance, has less than five per cent of its farms electrified as compared with the whole of the Northeast and the Far West with from 30 to 60 per cent.

Perhaps there is no need to illustrate further, except to reëmphasize the facts with reference to the agricultural Southeast and to reiterate the need for expansion in both agriculture and industry if the prospective rate of population is maintained and if the migration from the region slows down as now appears possible. It is important also to reëmphasize the rapid urbanization of parts of the region and to point toward that continuing trend. This will be discussed further in the following chapter on the southern people. It is important to emphasize again and again the minimum essentials for a reasonable development in industry and wealth, namely, increase in income and earning power; increase in values of land and goods; increase in consumers' power; increase in opportunities for occupational training and new occupations. And, finally, it is essential to understand that any enduring redistribution of wealth must be predicated upon regional adaptations and capacities rather than through any national, individual average allocation. All of these factors, however, are again related to the people of the region, the subject of our next chapter.

CHAPTER VIII

THE SOUTHERN PEOPLE

The story of the Southeast's economic prospects must be continued in the appraisal of its people and their prospects. The "wealth" of people in terms of increase excels any other region, yet offers problem and prospect alike confusing. For one thing, the region not only has an unfavorable balance of its trade with the resulting outflow of its wealth to contribute to other regional surplus, but a similar outflow of people whose economic evaluation may be estimated at widely varying figures; but in any estimate the aggregate runs into billions of dollars. Thus, if we take Woofter's figures of three and a quarter to three and a half million who have migrated to other regions since 1900 and use minimum and maximum actuarial estimates, the money value would range from five to ten billion dollars. Or if the estimate be made on the basis of the earning power of these millions there would accrue a similar aggregate in billions of wealth, assuming a region which, through the development of its capacities, could give adequate employment to all the people. Add to this further, the inheritance moneys which some of these migrants have carried with them to other regions and the total is increased again. Another way of estimating the drain upon the region and the possible gain to other regions is to appraise the cost to the Southeast of educating this large group, even with the scant education many receive. Thus, if the common estimate of a cost of from $2,000 to $3,000 to educate the individual up to eighteen or twenty years of age be accepted, the cost to the region again would approximate about the same amount as other estimates. This constitutes one basis upon which is predicated the premise for federal equalization funds for public education and substantial grants from the foundations or from individuals whose fortunes have been accumulated through national sources. This constitutes a part of the basis for the recommendation to get the money where the money is and use it where the demands for education are. This, however, will be discussed in relation to the educational picture of the region.

By some students, the problem of population-quantity lies at the heart of most southern economic dilemmas. To many the population problem is *the* problem. We may, therefore, very well continue our picture of

Samplings of Indices Relating to the Southern People

Number of Indices	Classification
1.	Population per square mile, 1930.
2.	Population per local unit.
3.	Amount, and per cent of the total, of population in the region.
4.	Per cent of the total population under 20 years of age, 1930.
5.	Per cent of the total population 20-55 years of age, 1930.
6.	Per cent of the total population 55 years of age and over, 1930.
7.	Per cent of males, 15 years of age and over, married, 1930.
8.	Per cent of females, 15 years of age and over, married, 1930.
9.	Percentage increase in the total population, 1900-1930.
10.	Percentage increase in the total population, 1920-1930
11.	Index of net reproduction per generation, 1920-1930.
12.	Number of children under 5, with native white mothers, per 1,000 native white women aged 20-44 years, 1920-1930.
13.	Population, and per cent increase in population by decades, 1860-1930.
14.	Chronological and rural variations in natural population increase, 1800-1930.
15.	Per cent increase in urban population, 1920-1930.
16.	Census urban population, 1930.
17.	Percentage of population that was urban, 1930.
18.	Metropolitan village population, 1930.
19.	Metropolitan unincorporated, population, 1930.
20.	Percentage increase in urban population, 1900-1930.
21.	Percentage of urban population in the total population, 1910-1930.
22.	Percentage increase in population of cities of 100,000 or more, 1900-1930.
23.	Percentage population increase, 1900-1930—places of 25,000-100,000.
24.	Percentage population increase, 1900-1930—places of 10,000-25,000.
25.	Percentage population increase, 1900-1930—places of 5,000-10,000.
26.	Percentage population increase, 1900-1930—places of 2,500-5,000.
27.	Percentage distribution of urban population, 1930—cities of 100,000 or more.
28.	Percentage distribution of urban population, 1930—places of 25,000-100,000.
29.	Percentage distribution of urban population, 1930—places of 10,000-25,000.
30.	Percentage distribution of urban population, 1930—places of 5,000-10,000.
31.	Percentage distribution of urban population, 1930—places of 2,500-5,000.
32.	Percentage increase in the rural population, 1900-1930.
33.	Per cent increase and decrease of the rural farm population, 1920-1930.
34.	Percentage of the rural farm population in the total population, 1930.
35.	Distribution of the rural farm population, 1930.
36.	Extent of the rural farm population under 5 years of age, per 1,000 women, 15-44 years of age, 1930.
37.	Number of urban white births per 1,000 population, 1930.
38.	Number of rural white births per 1,000 population, 1930.
39.	Number of urban colored births per 1,000 population, 1930.
40.	Number of rural colored births per 1,000 population, 1930.
41.	Number of urban white deaths per 1,000 population, 1930.
42.	Number of rural white deaths per 1,000 population, 1930.
43.	Number of urban colored deaths per 1,000 population, 1930.
44.	Number of rural colored deaths per 1,000 population, 1930.
45.	Urban white infant mortality per 1,000 live births, 1930.
46.	Rural white infant mortality per 1,000 live births, 1930.
47.	Urban colored infant mortality per 1,000 live births, 1930.
48.	Rural colored infant mortality per 1,000 live births, 1930.
49.	Number of maternal deaths in childbirth per 100,000 population, 1929.
50.	Number of deaths under 1 year of age per 1,000 live births, 1929.
51.	Excess of births over deaths per 1,000 population, 1929.
52.	Percentage distribution of native white population, 1930—urban.
53.	Percentage distribution of native white population, 9 —rural-farm.
54.	Percentage distribution of native white population, 1930—rural non-farm.
55.	Per cent of foreign-born white in the total population, 1930.
56.	Percentage distribution of foreign-born white population, 1930—urban.
57.	Percentage distribution of foreign-born white population, 1930—rural-farm.
58.	Percentage distribution of foreign-born white population, 1930—rural non-farm.
59.	Percentage of foreign-born in the total white population, 1930.
60.	Per cent of Negro population in the total population, 1930.
61.	Distribution of Negro population, 1930.
62.	Percentage distribution of Negroes in the total population, by counties, 1930.
63.	Per cent increase or decrease in the Negro population, 1920-1930.
64.	Percentage distribution of the Negro population, 1930—urban.
65.	Percentage distribution of the Negro population, 1930—rural-farm.
66.	Percentage distribution of the Negro population, 1930—rural non-farm.
67.	Percentage distribution of all other races, 1930—urban population.
68.	Percentage distribution of all other races, 1930—rural-farm.
69.	Percentage distribution of all other races, 1930—rural non-farm.
70.	Distribution of the Indian population, 1930.
71.	Distribution of the Mexican population, 1930.
72.	Distribution of the Japanese population, 1930.
73.	Distribution of the Chinese population, 1930.
74.	Per cent of gain or loss of the number born in each region, due to interregional migration, 1920.
75.	Net gain or loss by interregional migration, 1920.
76.	Per cent of gain or loss of population by interregional migration, 1930.
77.	Per cent of population remaining in the state of birth, 1920.
78.	Per cent of population born in other states of the section, 1920.
79.	Per cent of population born in other sections, 1920.
80.	Per cent of natives of each state living in other states, 1930.
81.	Per cent of migrants born in other states, living in each state, 1930.
82.	Distribution of Negroes living in and out of the states of birth, 1930.
83.	Comparative net gain or loss by inter-state migration, in white and Negro population, 1900-1920-1930.
84.	Number and per cent of the general population, 10 years and over, gainfully employed, 1930.
85.	Number of wage earners per 1000 population, 1929.
86.	Relative density of employment.
87.	Number and per cent of gainfully occupied persons, 10 years and over, in the extractive occupational group, 1930.
88.	Number and per cent of gainfully occupied persons, 10 years and over, in the manufacturing and mechanical occupational group, 1930.
89.	Number and per cent of gainfully occupied persons, 10 years and over, in the distributive and social occupational group, 1930.
90.	Number and per cent of gainfully occupied females, 10 years and over, in the extractive occupational group, 1930.
91.	Number and per cent of gainfully occupied females, 10 years and over, in the manufacturing and the mechanical occupational group, 1930.
92.	Number and per cent of gainfully occupied females, 10 years and over, in the distributive and social occupational group, 1930.
93.	Number and per cent of gainfully occupied children, 10-17 years, in the extractive occupational group, 1930.
94.	Number and per cent of gainfully occupied children, 10-17 years, in the manufacturing and mechanical occupational group, 1930.

regional wealth with some consideration of the problems of the quantity and movements of the population. For the Southeast, long the gateway to the "West," has continued to pour its stream of people into the Southwest and Far West, after adding considerable increments to the lower borders of the Middle States. Yet its present population, on the basis of its current culture economy, and especially in view of a diminishing cotton culture, is undoubtedly too large.

The story of the Southeast's migration is not only a continued story of the South's economics but also of its agrarian culture, since it is from the rural South that the people have moved most. This is true in the three major aspects of movement; namely, from rural to urban within the several states, from rural to urban in inter-southern state migration, and from rural to other regions than the Southeast. T. J. Woofter, Jr., has analyzed these movements in such way as not only to give the actual picture, but to make possible much needed interpretation of facts. We have already pointed out that the Southeast, especially parts of its rural districts, has perhaps the heaviest rates of natural increase of any section of the country, ranging as high as 22 per thousand in the mountain regions. Woofter points out the fact that this great excess has been produced in an agricultural economy which barely supported its present numbers, with the result that as the young people reach maturity they go to cities and to other sections of the country. The facts are that of the native born population of the United States in 1930, 28,700,000 were born in the Southeast, of whom 24,100,000 were born in rural districts and 4,600,000 in cities. Since only about 17,500,000 of these southeastern rural born live in the area of their birth, it is evident that over 6,500,000 have moved elsewhere. Of these, 3,800,000 have left the section entirely, while 2,900,000 have moved to southern cities. On the other hand, 400,000 have come into the region from elsewhere, still leaving a loss of 3,400,000. Thus, the rural districts of the Southeast have exported about a fourth of their natural population, have continued their own growth, and added much to the growth of southern cities, and have sent about 3,500,000 to other regions.

The extra high rate of natural population increase is an indication of the necessity both for an expanding industry and an expanding agriculture in the region unless indeed there must be more migration or lower standards of living. This problem may be studied further from the estimates of Thompson and Whelpton of the increase of population in the next quarter century, on the one hand, if this migration stops and, on the other, if it continues. One premise of the southern study is that the region can develop its potentialities in both natural and human resources in such way as to reduce the flow of men and capital. This premise can be tested out, how-

Percentage Which Net Gain or Loss by Interregional Migration Forms of Population in Region, 1930

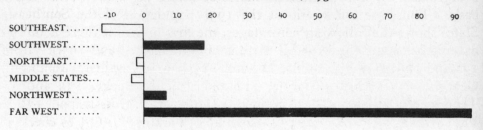

-10 0 10 20 30 40 50 60 70 80 90

SOUTHEAST........
SOUTHWEST.......
NORTHEAST.......
MIDDLE STATES...
NORTHWEST......
FAR WEST.........

NET GAIN OR LOSS BY INTERREGIONAL MIGRATION, 1930

SOUTHEAST	— 3,412,150
SOUTHWEST	+ 1,281,007
NORTHEAST	— 632,452
MIDDLE STATES	— 1,072,376
NORTHWEST	+ 394,542
FAR WEST	+ 3,263,866

Percentage Which Net Gain or Loss by Interregional Migration Forms of Number Born in Each Region, 1920

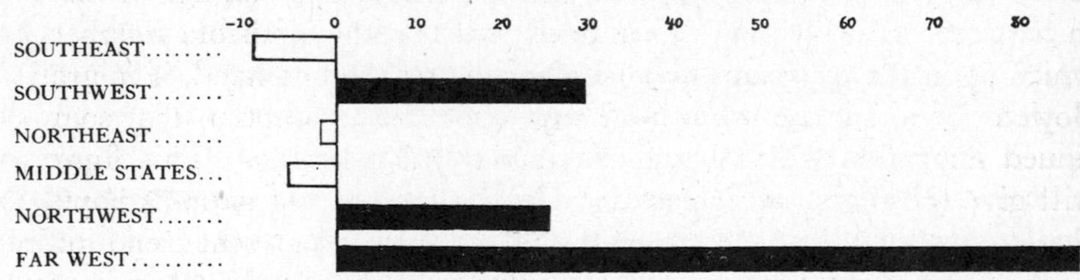

Population Born in Each Region by Place of Residence, 1920

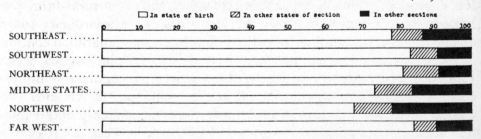

In state of birth · In other states of section · In other sections

0 10 20 30 40 50 60 70 80 90 100

SOUTHEAST........
SOUTHWEST.......
NORTHEAST.......
MIDDLE STATES...
NORTHWEST.......
FAR WEST.........

NET GAIN OR LOSS BY INTERREGIONAL MIGRATION, 1920

SOUTHEAST	— 2,378,639
SOUTHWEST	+ 1,502,362
NORTHEAST	— 1,036,253
MIDDLE STATES	— 1,514,788
NORTHWEST	+ 1,200,911
FAR WEST	+ 2,060,142

ever, only through estimates of optimum population and production on the backgrounds of probabilities. Estimates of future population constitute one basis. Thus, the 1960 ratio of the 1930 population of the Southeastern States shows the following percentages, the first figures if there is no internal migration and the second if there is migration like 1920-1930: Virginia, 131 and 106; North Carolina, 149 and 133; South Carolina, 146 and 107; Georgia, 139 and 99; Florida, 112 and 136; Kentucky, 139 and 112; Tennessee, 134 and 110; Alabama, 141 and 112; Mississippi, 139 and 114; Arkansas, 139 and 104; Louisiana, 133 and 117. Or, to check with actual population numbers, Virginia would have 3,176,000 people in 1960 with no internal migration and only 2,584,000 if migration continues at the rate of 1920-1930. So for the other states, North Carolina, 4,757,000 and 4,240,000; South Carolina, 2,544,000 and 1,862,000; Georgia, 4,062,000 and 2,906,000; Florida, 1,645,000 and 2,000,000; Kentucky, 3,643,000 and 2,952,000; Tennessee, 3,509,000 and 2,900,000; Alabama, 3,758,000 and 2,991,000; Mississippi, 2,806,000 and 2,304,000; Arkansas, 2,585,000 and 1,932,000; Louisiana, 2,806,000 and 2,476,000. For the whole Southeast there would be in 1960 a total of 35,291,000 without internal migration and 29,147,000 with migration continuing. Somewhere in between these, it may be assumed, will be the probable number upon which optimum programs may be planned; on the one hand, if migration is slowed down, but, on the other hand, upon the assumption that some continued migration will be both inevitable and desirable. This figure will still give the region an increasingly larger ratio of the nation's population, challenging a bolder economy of the future than the present trend indicates.

So much for the total southeastern population. If the trend is pursued further with reference to the rural population, the situation emphasizes more strikingly the problem of a balanced culture to be worked out with less migration. Thus Virginia's percentage of the 1930 rural-farm population which appears to be likely in 1960 shows the extraordinary contrast of 152 if there is no migration and only 83 if the same migration continues, or the difference in actual numbers of rural-farm folk in Virginia between 1,448,000 and 792,000, which would constitute a population difference enough to transform its culture. A similar difference in Alabama shows a 1960 ratio of 167 if there is no internal migration and only 100 if migration continues, or a difference in rural farm folk between 2,249,000 and 1,341,000. The Arkansas difference is nearly as great, with 158 and 96. Georgia's is still greater with an increase of rural farm folk of 171 without migration and a decrease to 73 if present migration continues, or more than double the rural-farm population of natural increase, 2,425,000, to that resulting from migration, namely, 1,041,000. Other Southeastern States:

Population Increase in the Southern Regions and the Nation, 1860-1930

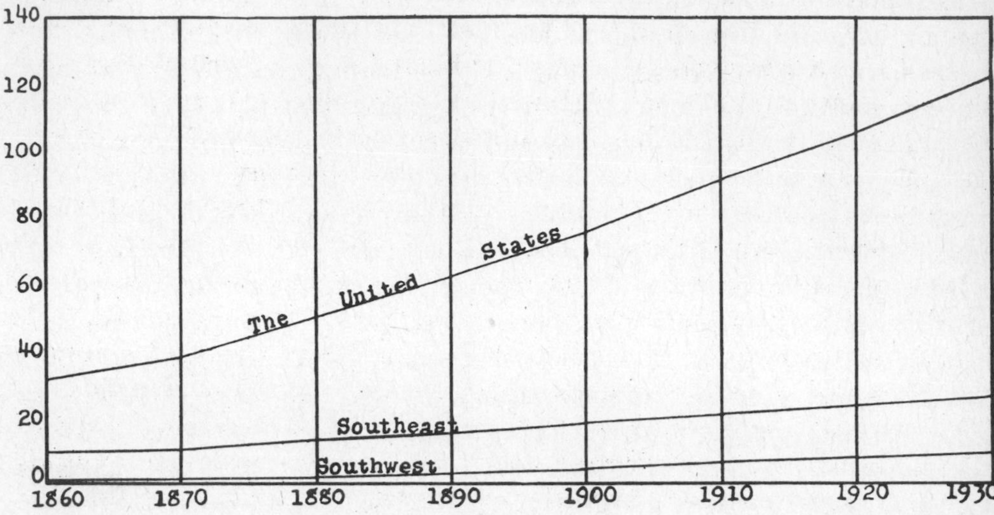

Population and Per Cent Increase by Decades in the United States and States in the Southern Regions, 1860-1930

Region and State	1860	1870		1880		1890	
	Population	Population	Per Cent Increase	Population	Per Cent Increase	Population	Per Cent Increase
United States	31,443,321	38,558,371	22.6	50,155,783	30.1	62,947,714	25.5
Southeast	9,654,801	9,989,818	3.5	13,047,187	30.6	15,329,806	17.5
Virginia	1,596,318	1,225,163*	-23.3*	1,512,565	23.5	1,655,980	9.5
North Carolina	992,622	1,071,361	7.9	1,399,750	30.7	1,617,749	15.6
South Carolina	703,708	705,606	0.3	995,577	41.1	1,151,149	15.6
Georgia	1,057,286	1,184,109	12.0	1,542,180	30.2	1,837,353	19.1
Florida	140,424	187,748	33.7	269,493	43.5	391,422	45.2
Kentucky	1,155,684	1,321,011	14.3	1,648,690	24.8	1,858,635	12.7
Tennessee	1,109,801	1,258,520	13.4	1,542,359	22.6	1,767,518	14.6
Alabama	964,201	996,992	3.4	1,262,505	26.6	1,513,401	19.9
Mississippi	791,305	827,922	4.6	1,131,597	36.7	1,289,600	14.0
Arkansas	435,450	484,471	11.3	802,525	65.6	1,128,211	40.6
Louisiana	708,002	726,915	2.7	939,946	29.3	1,118,588	19.0
Southwest	697,731	920,111	31.9	1,751,754	90.4	2,742,709	56.6
Oklahoma	...	...	...	...	...	258,657	...
Texas	604,215	818,579	35.5	1,591,749	94.5	2,235,527	40.4
New Mexico	93,516	91,874	-1.8	119,565	30.1	160,282	34.1
Arizona	...	9,658	...	40,440	318.7	88,243	118.2

*Western Virginia became West Virginia in 1863.

Region and State	1900		1910		1920		1930	
	Population	Per Cent Increase	Population	Per Cent Increase	Population	Per Cent Increase	Population	Per Cent Increase
United States	75,994,575	20.7	91,972,266	21.0	105,710,620	14.9	122,775,046	16.1
Southeast	18,074,129	18.0	20,785,777	15.0	22,860,356	10.0	25,550,898	11.8
Virginia	1,854,184	12.0	2,061,612	11.2	2,309,187	12.0	2,421,851	4.9
North Carolina	1,893,810	17.1	2,206,287	16.5	2,559,123	16.0	3,170,276	23.9
South Carolina	1,340,316	16.4	1,515,400	13.1	1,683,724	11.1	1,738,765	3.3
Georgia	2,216,331	20.6	2,609,121	17.7	2,895,832	11.0	2,908,506	0.4
Florida	528,542	35.0	752,619	42.4	968,470	28.7	1,468,211	51.6
Kentucky	2,147,174	15.5	2,289,905	6.6	2,416,630	5.5	2,614,589	8.2
Tennessee	2,020,616	14.3	2,184,789	8.1	2,337,885	7.0	2,616,556	11.9
Alabama	1,828,697	20.8	2,138,093	16.9	2,348,174	9.8	2,646,248	12.7
Mississippi	1,551,270	20.3	1,797,114	15.8	1,790,618	-0.4	2,009,821	12.2
Arkansas	1,311,564	16.3	1,574,449	20.0	1,752,204	11.3	1,854,482	5.8
Louisiana	1,381,625	23.5	1,656,388	19.9	1,798,509	8.6	2,101,593	16.9
Southwest	4,157,342	51.6	6,085,361	46.4	7,386,023	21.2	9,079,645	23.1
Oklahoma	790,391	205.6	1,657,155	109.7	2,028,283	22.4	2,396,040	18.1
Texas	3,048,710	36.4	3,896,542	27.8	4,663,228	19.7	5,824,715	24.9
New Mexico	195,310	21.9	327,310	67.6	360,350	10.1	423,317	17.5
Arizona	122,931	39.3	204,354	66.2	334,162	63.5	435,573	30.3

Florida, 146 and 96; Kentucky, 162 and 83; Louisiana, 168 and 110; Mississippi, 154 and 113; North Carolina, 172 and 113; South Carolina, 168 and 76; and Tennessee, 158 and 91. The Southwest, like the Southeast, showed a high ratio of increase of over 150 per cent and only three other states in the union give promise of so much.

What the problem will be if the present rural population is increased by 50 per cent or by about ten million people if the present migration stops must be determined by the future development of cotton economy, of industrialism, of any new agrarianism through which the balance of man and land can be attained. Already more than a million folk have returned South from the deficiency areas of industrial production. And often they have returned to deficiency agricultural areas, where the natural increase is still large. So, too, the protest in certain northern industrial cities against the influx of "hill-billy" labor is an index of what is likely to happen unless there is great industrial expansion in other regions. The nation will neither need nor welcome so large a supply of migrants from the Southeast as in the past. On the other hand, the popular estimates of the builder of metropolitan areas may offer an index of possible outlet for the rural population. Thus the Los Angeles area expects to double its population before the 1960 era. The continued increase of manufacturing industries in the great metropolitan areas of the Middle States affords another outlet. Yet still again the possibility of a gradual increase of industrialization in the Southeast will absorb a considerable portion of this continuing increasing population. Once again, however, to offset this there has been a relatively large migration into certain parts of the Southeast from other regions, with the indication that pressure of cities and industries in the North and West together with such developments as the TVA may increase the movement.

It is possible to study this prospect through the examination of migration from and into the Southeast, both within recent years and during the earlier decades. Thus the earlier decades following 1870 showed a strong flow of southern folk up into Indiana, Illinois, Missouri, and into Texas and Oklahoma, and then on further west. The figures for recent years show this outlet to have been relatively small. This is true both because of the relative saturation point and because of competition in skills and training. So, too, Texas and Oklahoma received increasingly larger increments from states further north and east, so that the same factors there as in the other states militate against unlimited migration. During the decade 1920-1930 the large migration of Negroes and others into a wide range of areas tended to meet all the demand for labor that those areas could support, leaving largely only a miscellaneous, widely distributed type of

Regional Distribution of Negroes, Mexicans, Indians, Japanese, Chinese, 1930

Adapted from Paul S. Taylor, *Mexican Labor in the United States Migration Statistics*. IV, pp. 32-34

STATE AND REGION	Negroes	Mexicans	Indians	Japanese	Chinese	Total
Southeast	*7,778,473*	*6,651*	*22,997*	*370*	*2,271*	*7,810,762*
Virginia	650,165	36	779	43	293	651,316
North Carolina	918,647	10	16,579	17	68	935,321
South Carollna	793,681	9	959	15	41	794,705
Georgia	1,071,125	47	43	32	253	1,071,500
Florida	431,828	185	587	153	200	432,953
Kentucky	226,040	88	22	9	60	226,219
Tennessee	477,646	25	161	11	70	477,913
Alabama	944,834	69	465	25	52	945,445
Mississippi	1,009,718	1,221	1,458	1	561	1,012,959
Arkansas	478,463	409	408	12	251	479,543
Louisiana	776,326	4,552	1,536	52	422	782,888
Southwest	*1,040,761*	*864,548*	*166,393*	*1,751*	*2,152*	*2,075,605*
Oklahoma	172,198	7,354	92,725	104	206	272,587
Texas	854,964	683,681	1,001	519	703	1,540,868
New Mexico	2,850	59,340	28,941	249	133	91,513
Arizona	10,749	114,173	43,726	879	1,110	170,637
Northeast	*1,570,459*	*7,201*	*10,248*	*4,069*	*18,415*	*1,610,392*
Maine	1,096	2	1,012	3	115	2,228
New Hampshire	790	1	64	....	84	939
Vermont	568	1	36	1	34	640
Massachusetts	52,365	66	874	201	2,973	56,479
Rhode Island	9,913	10	318	17	197	10,455
Connecticut	29,354	27	162	130	391	30,064
New York	412,814	2,898	6,973	2,930	9,665	435,280
New Jersey	208,828	454	213	439	1,783	211,717
Delaware	32,602	24	5	8	38	32,677
Pennsylvania	431,257	3,405	523	293	2,557	438,035
Maryland	276,379	56	50	38	492	277,015
West Virginia	114,493	257	18	9	86	114,863
Middle States	*1,181,115*	*71,227*	*32,132*	*1,204*	*7,651*	*1,293,329*
Ohio	309,304	4,037	435	187	1,425	315,388
Indiana	111,982	9,642	285	71	279	122,259
Illinois	328,972	28,906	469	564	3,192	362,103
Michigan	169,453	13,336	7,080	176	1,081	191,126
Wisconsin	10,739	2,396	11,548	24	363	25,070
Minnesota	9,445	3,626	11,077	69	524	24,741
Iowa	17,380	4,295	660	19	153	22,507
Missouri	223,840	4,989	578	94	634	230,135
Northwest	*97,229*	*99,606*	*60,475*	*10,503*	*1,953*	*269,766*
North Dakota	377	608	8,387	91	103	9,566
South Dakota	646	816	21,833	19	70	23,384
Nebraska	13,752	6,321	3,256	674	194	24,197
Kansas	66,344	19,150	2,454	37	60	88,045
Montana	1,256	2,571	14,798	753	486	19,864
Idaho	668	1,278	3,638	1,421	335	7,340
Wyoming	1,250	7,174	1,845	1,026	130	11,425
Colorado	11,828	57,676	1,395	3,213	233	74,345
Utah	1,108	4,012	2,869	3,269	342	11,600
Far West	*90,638*	*373,233*	*40,112*	*120,859*	*42,114*	*666,956*
Nevada	516	3,090	4,871	608	483	9,568
Washington	6,840	562	11,253	17,837	2,195	38,687
Oregon	2,234	1,568	4,776	4,958	2,075	15,611
California	81,048	368,013	19,212	97,456	37,361	603,090
United States	11,758,675	1,422,466	332,357	138,756	74,556	13,726,810

mobility for new movements of the future. Similar studies of the sources from which the half million people have come into the Southeast will indicate possible ways of predicting future trends. From every prospect, however, the indications are that the Southeast will have a continuing crisis in its increasingly large ratio of people such that the problem of optimum population for an agrarian region must, for a time at least, probably give way to the problem of optimum production and use in a very realistic given population, already in existence. This does not mean that the reduction of the population does not offer a field of the greatest importance but rather of lesser immediacy.

The net picture of the population of the Southeast then is one in contrast to the other regions in that, while they tend rapidly to a stabilized population, the Southeast largely through its rural predominance continues its rigorous multiplication and increase, with certain handicaps, in addition to numbers, due to the results of heavy migration and selection. Woofter has pointed out that this excess of population has been reared in an area where agriculture has declined rather than advanced. "Up to 1910, there was a gradual expansion in land in farms in the Southeast. Since 1910, owing to the above reasons, it has declined. In 1910, there were in the South Atlantic States 104,000,000 acres in farms, in 1930, 86,000,000, a decline of 18 per cent. In 1910 the rural population was about 16.5 million and in 1930 it was nearly 18,000,000. This increase of about a million and a half was largely in the rural non-farm group. The population within the farm area has therefore remained stationary. The Negro farm population has actually declined. The excess natural increase has drained off to the cities. Many of those who remained were producing the minimum for subsistence. The per capita gross farm income in southeastern states in 1930 (with the exception of Florida) ranged from $117 in Arkansas to $172 in Virginia. In no other state in the country was it so low. The southwestern states were next lowest, but outside these two southern sections, the lowest state average was $325, or nearly double the highest state average in the Southeast.

"To describe the situation before 1930 more exactly: of the 7.5 million people in southern cities, many were in small cities where the reproduction ratios were not as low as in metropolitan areas. The 17.8 million rural dwellers were divided into nearly 12.5 million white and 5.5 million Negro. Contrary to the popular impression, it is not the Negro group which contributes most heavily to the high southern natural increase. Their birth rate is higher but their death rate is so much higher that the Negro crude rate of natural increase between 1920 and 1930 was about ten and the white crude rate about 15 per thousand in rural districts. This higher crude rate

Natality and Mortality Rates for the Birth Registration Area by Registration States, Arranged by Regions, 1930

State and Region	Births Per 1,000 Population				Deaths Per 1,000 Population				Infant Mortality Per 1,000 Live Births			
	White		Colored		White		Colored		White		Colored	
	Urban	Rural	Urban	Rural	Urban	Rural	Urban	Rural	Urban	Rural	Urban	Rural
Southeast												
Virginia	20.1	22.6	20.0	25.8	12.2	9.9	21.4	16.6	63.8	65.6	128.5	100.6
North Carolina	24.1	23.7	20.8	25.9	12.6	9.0	20.2	13.7	74.9	65.4	140.8	97.6
South Carolina	22.7	20.9	23.5	26.0	16.3	8.6	29.3	15.0	80.0	66.8	160.2	102.2
Georgia	20.4	20.2	20.5	22.3	12.9	8.8	24.8	13.5	68.5	64.6	127.3	88.1
Florida	18.9	17.1	17.4	20.3	12.2	9.6	18.7	15.3	47.6	51.9	110.0	88.4
Kentucky	20.3	24.2	14.3	15.4	13.6	9.5	25.1	18.5	70.1	60.1	107.3	130.9
Tennessee	21.4	20.6	17.3	16.7	12.9	9.0	22.9	15.0	84.6	63.5	141.8	94.4
Alabama	21.0	24.6	19.9	25.6	12.7	8.5	20.0	13.7	62.6	59.3	121.7	87.2
Mississippi	26.1	22.8	23.7	24.6	15.3	8.1	27.5	13.4	61.4	49.2	99.3	81.7
Arkansas	18.5	23.9	15.0	19.4	15.9	8.1	26.4	11.9	55.8	49.5	72.0	54.9
Louisiana	19.6	19.8	22.7	20.8	14.2	7.1	24.0	12.3	70.7	57.4	120.3	96.9
Southwest												
Oklahoma	21.0	17.7	13.5	11.3	11.8	6.6	20.0	8.6	73.8	50.8	176.3	82.8
Texas*	....	....	....	....	....	....	....	....	....	....	....	....
New Mexico	27.8	28.6	**—	—	21.4	14.7	—	—	120.8	148.5	—	—
Arizona	32.3	21.7	—	—	25.4	12.9	—	—	116.2	116.7	—	—
Northeast												
Maine	21.0	20.0	—	—	15.3	13.3	—	—	82.9	72.7	—	—
New Hampshire	20.9	15.0	—	—	13.4	13.7	—	—	63.5	58.5	—	—
Vermont	27.0	17.9	—	—	14.7	12.7	—	—	68.5	63.8	—	—
Massachusetts	18.6	10.9	—	—	11.5	11.9	—	—	59.5	65.4	—	—
Rhode Island	18.2	13.7	—	—	11.7	11.2	—	—	61.1	68.4	—	—
Connecticut	20.3	10.7	—	—	11.2	9.7	—	—	56.5	54.3	—	—
New York	18.1	13.3	—	—	11.4	12.8	—	—	58.6	59.6	—	—
New Jersey	18.8	12.4	—	—	10.6	11.1	—	—	56.2	57.4	—	—
Delaware	21.6	16.4	—	—	14.6	12.8	—	—	70.7	86.7	—	—
Pennsylvania	20.2	18.9	—	—	12.3	10.6	—	—	66.3	70.3	—	—
Maryland	18.4	16.5	22.9	23.3	12.9	10.8	19.9	17.7	59.8	67.6	98.1	148.7
West Virginia	20.5	24.8	—	—	14.1	9.6	—	—	99.1	77.3	—	—
Middle States												
Ohio	18.7	16.3	—	—	11.6	11.1	—	—	61.6	59.2	—	—
Indiana	19.9	16.9	—	—	12.4	11.8	—	—	61.3	54.1	—	—
Illinois	17.8	14.7	—	—	10.9	10.9	—	—	54.3	59.3	—	—
Michigan	21.8	18.2	—	—	10.1	11.4	—	—	63.1	61.9	—	—
Wisconsin	21.7	17.4	—	—	10.7	10.1	—	—	54.3	57.1	—	—
Minnesota	19.1	18.0	—	—	11.7	8.9	—	—	51.7	53.0	—	—
Iowa	20.5	15.9	—	—	13.8	9.3	—	—	62.5	49.4	—	—
Missouri	16.9	17.3	—	—	13.6	10.5	—	—	58.7	58.6	—	—
Northwest												
North Dakota	34.4	20.1	—	—	14.8	7.0	—	—	54.6	63.2	—	—
South Dakota*	....	....	....	....	....	....	....	....	....	....	....	....
Nebraska	21.3	19.0	—	—	13.2	8.3	—	—	51.2	48.6	—	—
Kansas	20.0	17.0	—	—	13.0	9.3	—	—	58.1	49.9	—	—
Montana	23.1	17.2	—	—	15.3	8.6	—	—	51.7	61.2	—	—
Idaho	29.3	19.8	—	—	14.8	8.9	—	—	46.7	58.5	—	—
Wyoming	23.1	19.2	—	—	11.1	8.9	—	—	64.7	70.3	—	—
Colorado	18.0	18.2	—	—	14.9	11.2	—	—	89.0	98.1	—	—
Utah	26.0	25.1	—	—	12.8	8.2	—	—	54.2	59.5	—	—
Far West												
Nevada	15.2	14.5	—	—	17.8	11.4	—	—	49.3	73.5	—	—
Washington	17.7	11.6	—	—	11.9	9.3	—	—	41.7	59.8	—	—
Oregon	16.0	12.7	—	—	13.3	9.4	—	—	48.3	51.4	—	—
California	15.4	13.4	—	—	12.0	10.8	—	—	52.5	71.2	—	—
United States	19.1	18.7	—	—	12.3	10.5	—	—	62.8	66.3	—	—

*Not in registration area.

**No separate figures given for colored population, where dashes appear—hence figures under white population apply to total population.

of the whites applied to a larger base meant a gross natural increase from 1920 to 1930 of about 180,000 per year in the white rural element and about 75,000 a year in the Negro rural element, or a gross number of people produced for export to cities of about a quarter of a million annually."

Woofter also points out some of the far reaching implications of this expanding population. "*First*, it upsets race relations and the balance of white and Negro in urban employment. Formerly in the South, there were jobs known as Negro jobs at which the white man would not work. These included barbers, waiters, elevator tenders, and many manual occupations. *Second*, the population pressure is basic in determining the wage differentials between the South and other sections. The differentials recognized by the NRA have been long standing and even greater in extent than those set up by that body. Clarence Heer in his discerning study of incomes in the South has gone to the root of the matter in showing that these differentials are based on the low productivity of agriculture and the increase of population in agricultural areas. Any unskilled occupation which could be entered by a farm youth without an apprenticeship showed a wide differential between the South and other sections. In this category were the day laborers, sawmill roustabouts, railway maintenance men, etc. These occupations showed a differential of about 80 per cent in other sections over the South. On the other hand skilled occupations showed slight differentials, railway engineers none, skilled band-sawyers only around 20 per cent.

"*Third*, the fact that the excess of population has been draining off to other sections brings with it a whole series of phenomena common to areas losing by migration. There is the upset of the age distribution, drawing off the productive middle age groups and leaving behind the young and old. In my study of St. Helena Island in 1928 I found that a large proportion (about 30 per cent) of the households were headed by women past middle age who were widowed or deserted and who often were left with the care of growing children. Other studies of black belt areas have shown similar conditions. Before 1930 these female heads of households eked out a bare existence gardening, tending a few domestic animals and picking up spare cash at odd jobs. Since 1930, the majority have lost their casual income and gone on relief. Recent rural relief studies in the eastern cotton belt show 15 per cent of the relief households without a male over 16 and another 15 per cent without an employable male. This class may be characterized as the jetsam of migration.

"Migration further exerts a selective drag on the talent of the region. This is difficult to measure at the bottom of the scale, but its effect at the top is marked. Wilson Gee has shown a 45 per cent drag of social scien-

Death Rate Per 1,000 Population, 1930

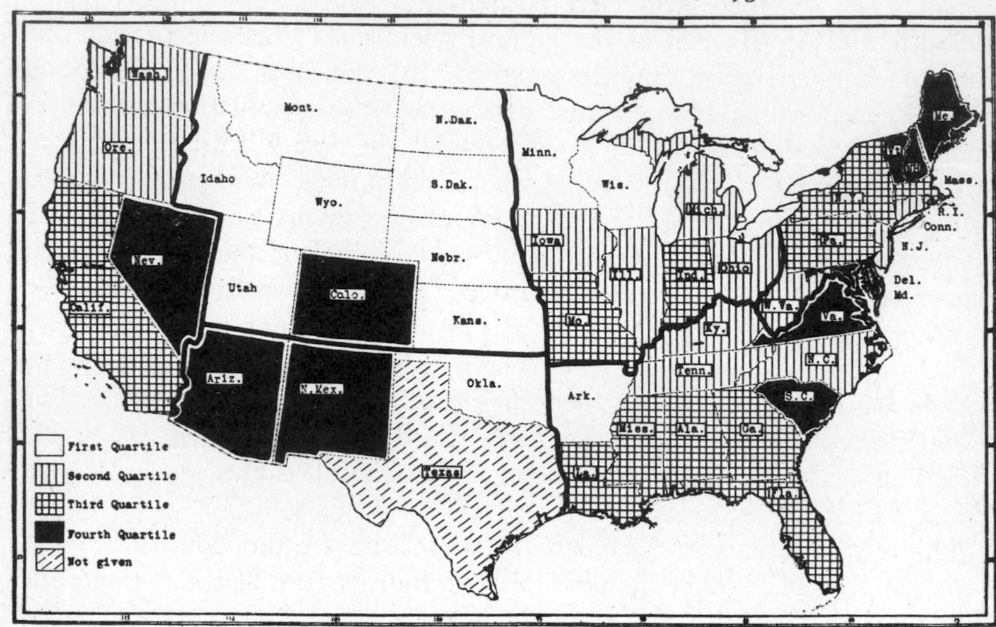

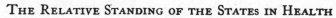

The Relative Standing of the States in Health

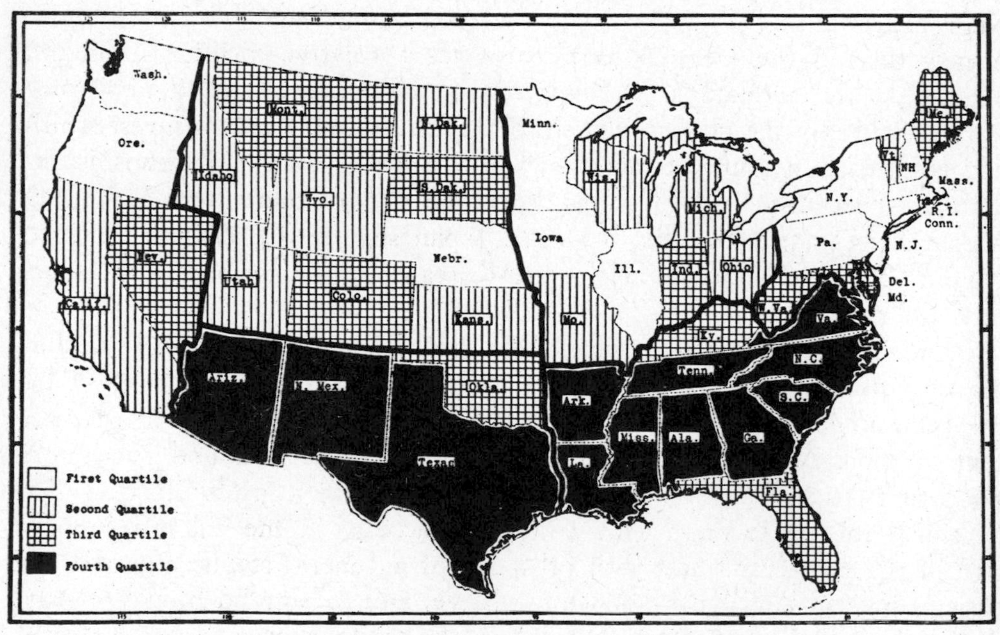

tists and 60 per cent of natural scientists. That is to say, 45 per cent of the eminent social scientists who were born in the South were living outside the South, and 60 per cent of the natural scientists. This selection of the most able and energetic doubtless extends all the way down the social scale. The educational implication of the southern population picture is seldom fully realized. Owing to migration, the South with meagre resources for taxation is left with a disproportionally large number of educable children. The rural states of the South must support nearly a third of their population in school, the industrial states less than one-fourth. This means that when an equal expenditure per dollar of wealth is made for education, a tremendous discrepancy in per capita remains.

"Also owing to migration, it is evident that a child born in Mississippi or Alabama has in about 12 per cent of the cases made his life contribution to some other section, say New York or Illinois. For this reason, the educational and cultural level of the southern population is almost as much of national as it is of sectional concern."

This picturization of the population problem of the Southeast must be compared, on the other hand, with the whole picture of the nation with many contrasting situations. In round numbers the American people, in 1930, were almost 90 per cent white with 108,000,000; in the Southeast less than 70 per cent, of whom, however, almost all were native born. There were almost as many Negroes as foreign born in the nation, the number of Negroes being 11,891,143 as against 14,204,149 foreign born population. A new turn in the 1920-1930 picture was a relative increase in Negro population and a decrease in foreign born. There was added new color to the picture by the new movement of Mexicans into the Southwest which had resulted in a count of more than four times as many Mexicans as Indians in the nation. Of the races other than Negro there were 1,423,533 Mexicans, 332,397 Indians, 138,834 Japanese, 74,954 Chinese, 45,000 Filipinos, 3,000 Hindus, nearly 2,000 Koreans, with a sprinkling of others here and there.

The significant factor, however, for the nation was the relative declining rate of the whole population and especially of the foreign born. Thus the percentage of increase which was foreign in 1930 was only two per cent as opposed to earlier rates of more than 50 per cent and even from 1900 to 1910 as much as 30 per cent. There was a gradually declining decennial rate of increase with a relative increase in the colored proportion of the population and with prospects of a general stabilization on the basis of present distribution of white, native, and foreign born, except that, due to the recent immigration legislation, the tendency was toward a slowly rising proportion of the people descended from populations of northern and

Per Cent of Total Population Under Twenty Years of Age, 1930

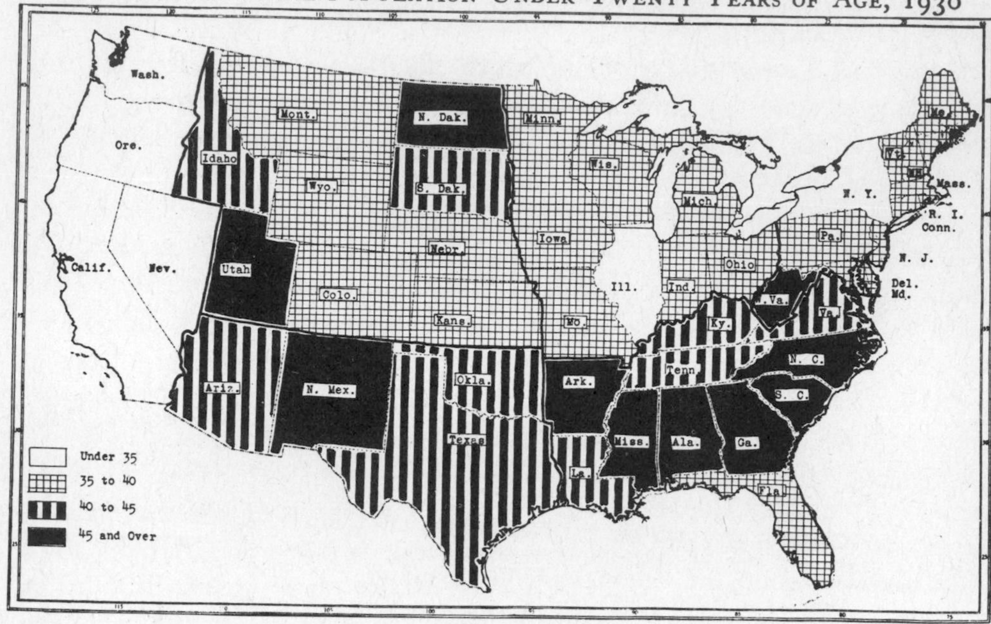

Percentage Distribution of Total Population, 1930

STATE AND REGION	Under 20	20 to 55	55 and Over
Southeast			
Virginia	44.4	44.6	11.0
North Carolina	49.3	42.2	8.5
South Carolina	50.6	41.5	7.9
Georgia	46.3	44.6	9.1
Florida	39.2	49.6	11.2
Kentucky	43.9	44.0	12.1
Tennessee	43.8	45.6	10.6
Alabama	47.0	44.3	8.7
Mississippi	46.6	44.4	9.0
Arkansas	45.8	44.6	9.6
Louisiana	44.0	47.2	8.8
Southwest			
Oklahoma	44.2	45.8	10.0
Texas	42.6	48.0	9.4
New Mexico	46.8	43.6	9.6
Arizona	42.1	48.9	9.0
Northeast			
Maine	37.3	44.9	17.8
New Hampshire	35.2	46.2	18.6
Vermont	37.0	45.2	17.8
Massachusetts	35.1	50.0	14.9
Rhode Island	37.0	49.1	13.9
Connecticut	37.0	49.5	13.5
New York	33.6	53.8	12.6
New Jersey	36.1	50.9	13.0
Delaware	35.9	49.3	14.8
Pennsylvania	39.4	48.2	12.4
Maryland	37.2	49.7	13.1
West Virginia	46.1	44.3	9.6
Middle States			
Ohio	36.1	50.1	13.8
Indiana	36.5	48.1	15.4
Illinois	34.9	52.4	12.7
Michigan	37.7	50.5	11.6
Wisconsin	38.0	48.0	14.0
Minnesota	38.3	48.1	13.6
Iowa	37.2	47.1	10.7
Missouri	35.7	49.5	14.8
Northwest			
North Dakota	45.4	44.3	10.3
South Dakota	42.5	47.9	1.6
Nebraska	39.3	47.7	13.0
Kansas	38.1	47.3	14.6
Montana	39.0	48.8	12.0
Idaho	42.8	45.5	11.7
Wyoming	39.2	51.2	9.6
Colorado	38.0	49.5	12.5
Utah	46.1	44.1	9.8
Far West			
Nevada	31.8	54.9	13.3
Washington	33.7	51.5	14.8
Oregon	33.1	51.3	15.6
California	30.4	54.8	14.8

PER CENT OF POPULATION UNDER 20 YEARS OF AGE, 1930

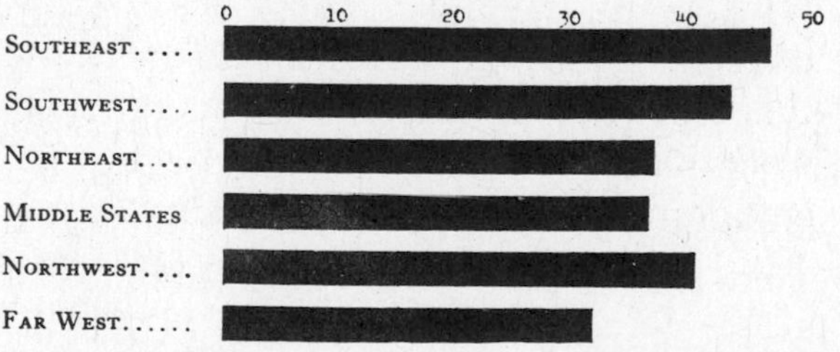

western Europe. Here the Southeast, exclusive of its Negroes, was the most "American."

Among the national factors in which the Southeast is different from the rest of the nation is the changing status with reference to age. For the first time in the history of the nation there were fewer persons under five years of age at the end of a decade than at the beginning. This was far from true in the Southeast. In the nation in 1920 there were 11,573,-230 children under five but nearly 129,000 less in 1930. Later census estimates have indicated a continuing decreasing ratio. This decrease in actual number of children tended toward a still more marked decrease in ratio of children to the total in view of the fact that the older groups from 45 to 75 years of age increased nearly one-third. A resulting characteristic of the population, therefore, was that of a greatly increasing ratio of old people with every prospect that the increase would continue. Here, again, the Southeast differs in that its smaller ratio of old people retards for a time the problem of a very large population of older people which, in an industrial era disposed to lay off its workers before the older age limit was reached, had already begun to assume puzzling proportions. The median age of the population had changed from the days of Jefferson from about 16 years to about 26 in 1930. The chief change, however, was being wrought in the ratio of the old and the young for both of whom in 1933 there was every indication that the nation was making inadequate provision for education and guidance, on the one hand, and for work and security, on the other. By 1950 or 1960 it was estimated that the proportion of people over 65 years and eligible for old age pensions would be half again as large as in 1930. Likewise, by 1960 the ratio of workers over 45 years of age, and thus subject to decreasing eligibility for employment, will probably have risen from the 22.8 per cent in 1930 to 30 per cent or more. On the other hand, the declining ratio of children and youth accentuated the significance to the Southeast of the old national ideal of measuring its wealth by the number, nurture, and education of its youth.

The most radical change of all, however, in the population picture of the nation was the complete surrender of the rural nation to that of an urban America. The picture was a clear-cut one of gradual, then rapid urbanization of the nation until in 1930, of all the more than 120 million people in the United States less than one-fourth were rural farm population. And the total of all who lived on farms and in rural villages was less than 40 per cent. Thus had a rural nation become one of cities and villages and of metropolitan regions. Here the rural variation is great in the southern regional groupings with no states except Florida, Louisiana,

Distribution of Negroes in Total Population, by Counties, 1930

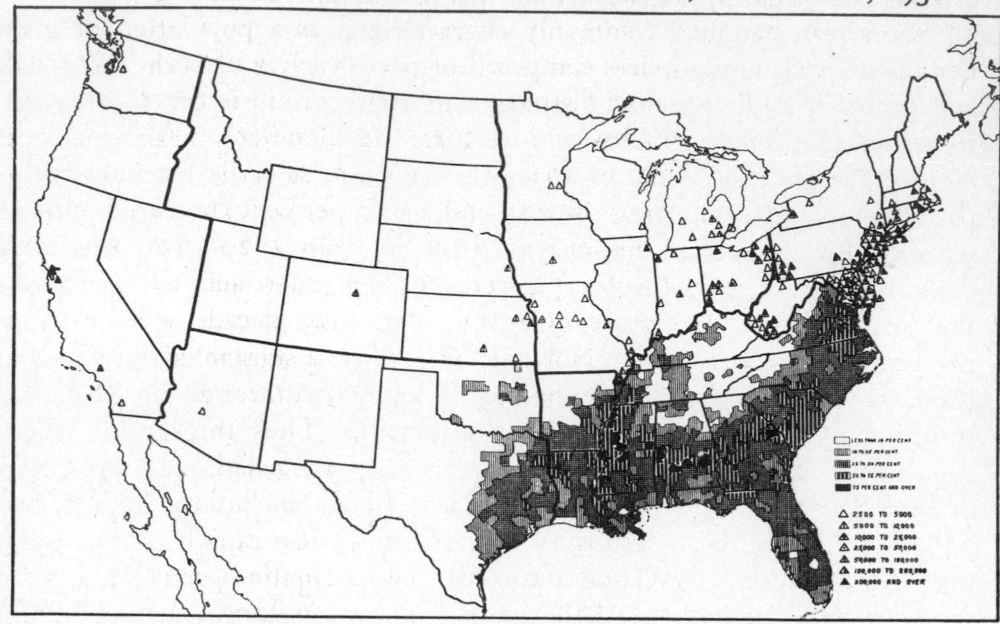

Negro Population in 1930 Living In and Out of States of Birth

Living in State	Born In					
	Virginia	North Carolina	South Carolina	Georgia	Florida	Kentucky
Virginia	*576,588*	44,354	8,711	2,479	593	526
North Carolina	9,578	*808,298*	79,368	13,272	1,074	196
South Carolina	617	6,913	*776,058*	6,924	793	40
Georgia	1,682	5,208	32,695	*996,411*	9,921	346
Florida	2,367	7,936	29,086	94,663	*259,635*	390
Kentucky	1,965	1,005	916	3,390	321	*185,051*
Tennessee	1,985	3,492	3,403	21,886	557	4,297
Alabama	1,123	1,444	2,258	28,374	3,667	545
Mississippi	920	2,197	1,177	3,806	716	513
Arkansas	704	3,336	3,926	4,987	190	877
Louisiana	815	1,117	725	2,060	805	401
Total Southeast out of State	21,756	77,002	162,265	181,841	18,637	8,131
Total outside State	331,963	220,240	319,156	407,445	55,053	107,314
Total outside Southeast	310,207	143,238	156,891	225,604	36,416	99,183

Living In State	Born In				
	Tennessee	Alabama	Mississippi	Arkansas	Louisiana
Virginia	1,507	1,493	234	66	183
North Carolina	821	1,206	340	82	125
South Carolina	199	435	119	29	75
Georgia	1,514	17,587	812	173	480
Florida	1,101	17,839	1,577	178	1,333
Kentucky	16,752	7,589	1,761	587	442
Tennessee	*363,704*	13,551	48,230	7,412	2,393
Alabama	4,282	*883,289*	13,425	594	1,485
Mississippi	6,271	25,237	*938,911*	7,129	18,099
Arkansas	16,432	9,142	57,229	*340,182*	28,886
Louisiana	1,047	5,925	30,515	8,706	*710,894*
Total Southeast out of State	49,926	100,004	154,242	24,956	53,501
Total outside State	175,852	250,482	288,846	109,269	171,130
Total outside Southeast	125,926	150,478	134,604	84,313	117,629

and Tennessee having as many as a third of its people urban. Yet the southern increase to cities was larger than was that of the nation as a whole.

"Southern people," commonly characterized as a population of great homogeneity, is nevertheless composed of great variety of both individuals and groups. And the most distinctive minority group is the Negro, who shows extraordinary vitality and cultural development. Although the Negro increase from 1920 to 1930 was not quite so large a percentage as the whole population, being thirteen and a half per cent compared with 16 per cent for the nation, his increase of 13.6 from 1920-1930, was more than twice as large as the 6.5 per cent between 1910 and 1920, whereas the total population increase over the 1910-1920 decade was only one per cent, from 15 to 16.1. Not only was there a substantial increase but there was a tendency to diffuse the Negro population throughout the nation, resulting in a number of important situations. Thus the largest Negro cities in the nation were not in the South. New York had 224,670; Philadelphia had 219,599, while Cook County, Illinois, including Chicago, had 246,992. While the Negro thus increased much less rapidly in the South than did the white population and constituted a smaller percentage of the southern population than a half century ago, a number of northern communities showed an increase in Negro population of several hundred per cent; many new centers of Negro population were established; there were no less than ten cities out of the South with Negro population of over 50,000; there were 149 northern or western counties with a Negro population of over 2,500. There developed increasingly an important middle class and in particular business and professional groups among the Negroes. Considerable progress had been made in improved race relations in the South, with new areas of race contact and conflict in the North.

The problem of racial minorities in the United States was adding to the complexity of social questions. The stoppage of immigration would lead to the more rapid assimilation of heterogeneous groups, but, on the other hand, the more recent mobility of the Negro and his northward movement created another issue of adjustment; and the immigration of the Mexican precipitated still others. The problem of the Negro in particular was one of intense interest from the point of view of a racial minority and from the viewpoint of the nation as a whole. Economic, cultural, and political questions were intertwined in such a manner as to set up problems of the utmost practical difficulty, thus far not successfully attacked on the whole. The increasing productivity of the soil and the use of machines for cotton cultivation and picking might complicate the position of the Negro still more in the future than in the 1930's. All this made the early and careful consideration of the whole problem more imperative.

DISTRIBUTION OF THE INDIAN POPULATION IN THE UNITED STATES, 1930

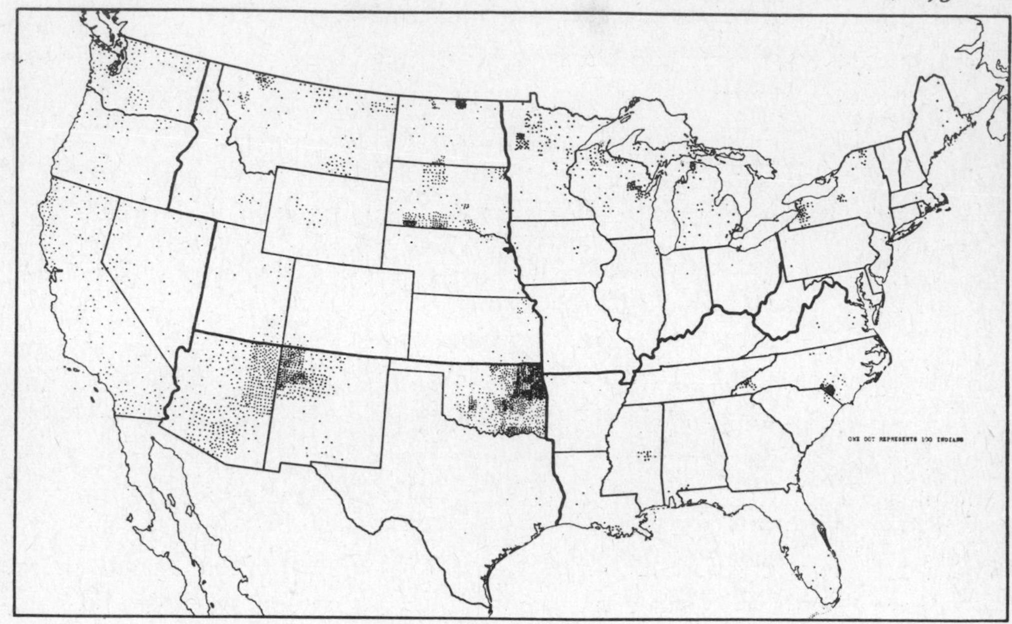

DISTRIBUTION OF MEXICAN POPULATION IN THE UNITED STATES, 1930

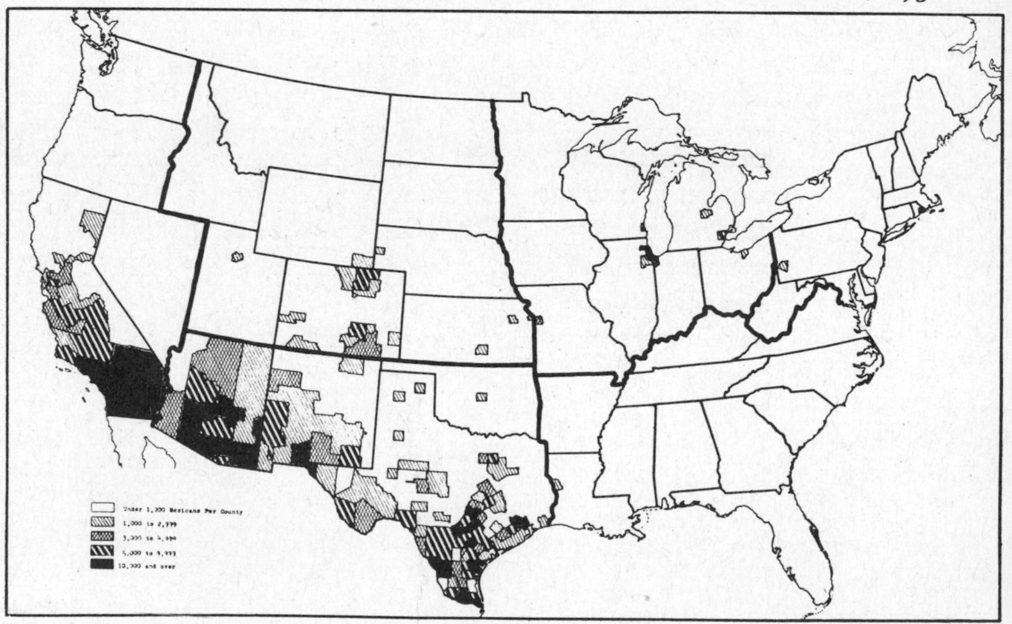

Predictions with reference to the Negro in the United States have been peculiarly unreliable in the past. There was, however, at the end of the first third of the century a different situation from that which had existed in any of the previous decennial periods. The four basic factors upon which prediction must be made and plans developed seemed to be: First, the ratio of Negro population to the total population was gradually decreasing and the experts estimated that this decline would be continuous until the maximum stabilization of population might occur in a half century hence. Second, the Negro population was being diffused throughout the nation so that the problem was national rather than southern. The Negroes complained that the North was "going southern." The third factor was the changing nature of the Negro population as it related to biological heritage. That is, there was growing up a "Brown America," a product of both selection and racial diffusion. The fourth element was found in the changing social character of the Negro as he expanded his activities and increased his cultural stature to higher levels. The future of the Negro was, therefore, essentially an American problem of development and assimilation. There would be need to take caution against riots and economic injustices, to provide for sensible political development, social representation and for educational and cultural advance. The picture was such as to justify the conclusion that, if the Negro be given a fair opportunity with his remarkable powers of adaptation and his attractive personality, he would become one of the most important of the basic elements of American culture. For the time being, however, there was no quick solution of his problem or the problem of the white man's relation to the Negro.

Four general and international factors make the problem of the Negro in the South and the nation increasingly dynamic. One is the general conclusion of the psychologists, sociologists, and anthropologists that evidence of inferior and superior races does not justify the world's previous appraisal and action in relation to races. This factor, communicated to all races, contributes to the dark races' as well as the white races' attitudes. A second factor has been the extension of learning and technology to all races and their consequent increasing use of common tools of economic and political development. A third factor is the increasing tendency toward racial and national consciousness. The fourth is the rapid rise and increasing articulation of the American Negro in contradistinction, on the one hand, to his earlier status, and, on the other, in relation to his proportionate part in southern life.

It thus happens that this racial situation is a second major population problem which must be met in more effective ways than has hitherto been done. This need is apparent on behalf of both whites and Negroes, neither

Per Cent of Negroes in the Total Population in the Southeast, by Subregions, 1930

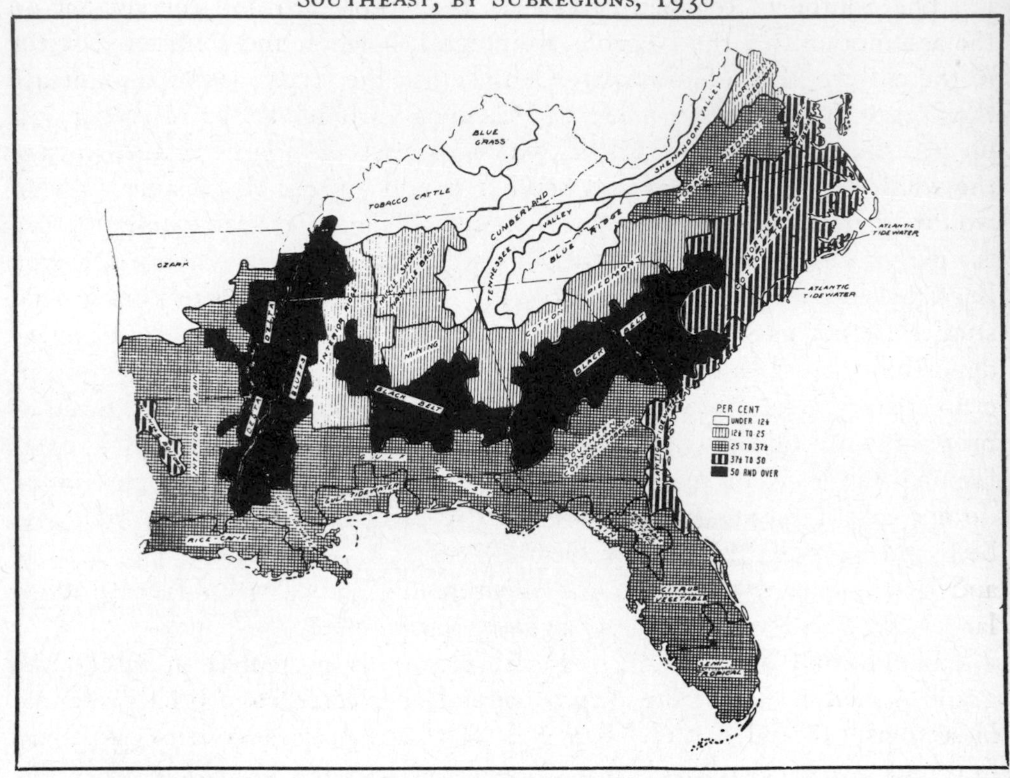

Per Cent Increase in Total Population, 1920-1930

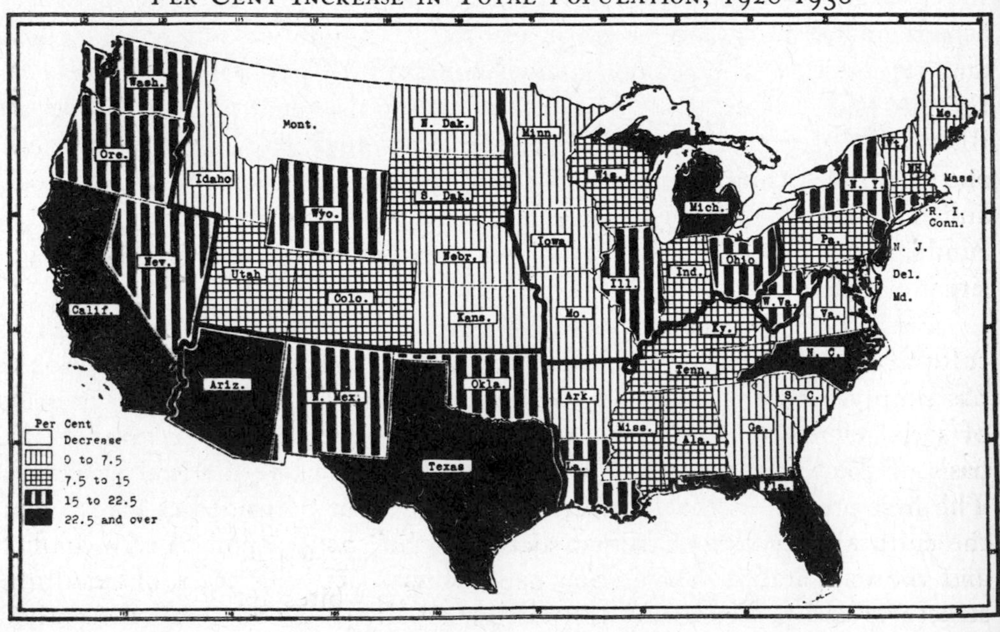

of whom functions normally under the present constraining conditioning.

The Southern Regional Study has been projected and carried out on the assumption that the Negro is an integral, normal, and continuing factor in the culture of the Southeast. Consistently the study, while recognizing the Negro as one of the chiefest of economic problems, has refused to set up a dichotomous framework in which one set of figures would present the whole southern picture and another would present the picture of what would be if the Negro were not included. The facts are that the Negro is a part, both creator and creature, of southern culture, for whom the region is responsible as for all other groups. This does not mean that special studies are not made of the Negro and his part in the region, or that every opportunity possible is not seized to give emphasis to this part of the southern people. What it does mean is that any realistic picture of the region or programs of action must assume the Negro to be exactly what he is in the regional fabric. The recognition of the handicaps to both Negro and white do not constitute any adequate basis for excuse and apology for what has been and what is. Here is the region's hardest problem; but it is of, for, and by the southern people, and the region's reality will be conditioned largely by the development of the next few decades.

The factual basis of the regional picture is presented in tables and graphs. Summaries of the Negro population picture have been presented in sections 148 and 149 of Chapter I. Other aspects have been presented in connection with educational, economic, and cultural developments. For the present purposes it seems important to present further two major aspects of the subject. One is the realistic long-time view of racial conflict and exploitation which have marked the cultural evolution of society in the past and have served to project the southern picture as a very concrete illustration of general societal behavior. The other is to point up the field and need for techniques of race relations through which the older methods and directions may be modified. The understanding of the first phase is fundamental to both the appraisal and reconstruction of present difficult situations in the Southeast.

First, if the South's racial situation be reflected upon the background of cultural evolution, its organic nature may be better understood. The South has simply been following on a specialized pattern the course of centuries of social evolution the world over. We may project this picture on the basis of four premises which seem acceptable to modern social scientists. The first premise is that high up in the catalogue of tragedies of error in the cultural evolution of human society is the phenomenon of race conflict and the exploitation of minority peoples with its long train of resulting structures and processes and cumulative conditioning and conflict. Another

REGIONAL AND RACIAL DISTRIBUTION OF POPULATION, 1930

STATE AND REGION	Total Population			Negro Population		
	Number	Per Cent of Total Population	Per Cent Each State Is of Its Regional Total	Number by States and Regions	Per Cent	Per Cent Each State Is of Its Regional Total
Southeast	*25,550,898*	*20.9*	*100.0*	*7,778,473*	*30.4*	*100.0*
Virginia	2,421,851	2.0	9.5	650,165	26.8	8.4
North Carolina	3,170,276	2.6	12.4	918,647	29.0	11.8
South Carolina	1,738,765	1.4	6.8	793,681	45.6	10.2
Georgia	2,908,506	2.4	11.4	1,071,125	36.8	13.8
Florida	1,468,211	1.2	5.7	431,828	29.4	5.6
Kentucky	2,614,589	2.1	10.2	226,040	8.6	2.9
Tennessee	2,616,556	2.1	10.2	477,646	18.3	6.1
Alabama	2,646,248	2.2	10.4	944,834	35.7	12.1
Mississippi	2,009,821	1.6	7.9	1,009,718	50.2	13.0
Arkansas	1,854,482	1.5	7.3	478,463	25.8	6.2
Louisiana	2,101,593	1.7	8.2	776,326	36.9	10.0
Southwest	*9,079,645*	*7.4*	*100.0*	*1,040,761*	*11.4*	*100.0*
Oklahoma	2,396,040	2.0	26.4	172,198	7.2	16.5
Texas	5,824,715	4.7	64.2	854,964	14.7	82.2
New Mexico	423,317	.3	4.7	2,850	0.7	0.3
Arizona	435,573	.4	4.6	10,749	2.5	1.0
Northeast	*38,026,202*	*31.1*	*100.0*	*1,570,859*	*4.1*	*100.00*
Maine	797,423	.6	2.1	1,096	0.1	.07
New Hampshire	465,293	.4	1.2	790	0.2	.05
Vermont	359,611	.3	1.0	568	0.2	.03
Massachusetts	4,249,614	3.5	11.2	52,365	1.2	3.33
Rhode Island	687,497	.6	1.8	9,913	1.4	.63
Connecticut	1,606,903	1.3	4.2	29,354	1.8	1.87
New York	12,588,066	10.3	33.1	412,814	3.3	26.28
New Jersey	4,041,334	3.3	10.6	208,828	5.2	13.29
Delaware	238,380	.2	.6	32,602	13.7	2.08
Pennsylvania	9,631,350	7.8	25.3	431,257	4.5	27.45
Maryland	1,631,526	1.3	4.3	276,379	16.9	17.59
West Virginia	1,729,205	1.4	4.5	114,893	6.6	7.31
Middle States	*33,961,444*	*27.8*	*100.0*	*1,181,115*	*3.4*	*100.00*
Ohio	6,646,697	5.4	19.6	309,304	4.7	26.19
Indiana	3,238,503	2.6	9.5	111,982	3.5	9.48
Illinois	7,630,654	6.2	22.5	328,972	4.3	27.85
Michigan	4,842,325	3.9	14.3	169,453	3.5	14.35
Wisconsin	2,939,006	2.4	8.7	10,739	0.4	.91
Minnesota	2,563,953	2.1	7.5	9,445	0.4	.80
Iowa	2,470,939	2.0	7.3	17,380	0.7	1.47
Missouri	3,629,367	3.0	10.7	223,840	6.2	18.95
Northwest	*7,384,497*	*6.0*	*100.0*	*97,229*	*1.3*	*100.00*
North Dakota	680,845	.6	9.2	377	0.1	.39
South Dakota	692,849	.6	9.4	646	0.1	.66
Nebraska	1,377,963	1.1	18.7	13,752	1.0	14.14
Kansas	1,880,999	1.5	25.5	66,344	3.5	68.23
Montana	537,606	.4	7.2	1,256	0.2	1.29
Idaho	445,032	.4	6.0	668	0.2	.69
Wyoming	225,565	.2	3.1	1,250	0.6	1.29
Colorado	1,035,791	.8	14.0	11,828	1.1	12.17
Utah	507,847	.4	6.9	1,108	0.2	1.14
Far West	*8,285,491*	*6.8*	*100.0*	*90,638*	*1.0*	*100.00*
Nevada	91,058	.1	1.0	516	0.6	.57
Washington	1,563,396	1.3	18.9	6,840	0.4	7.55
Oregon	953,786	.8	11.5	2,234	0.2	2.46
California	5,677,251	4.6	68.5	81,048	1.4	89.42

major error often made by the scientists, was the assumption that race was an entity in itself, a purely physical product rather than the result of long developed folk-regional culture. This took many forms. One was the assumption that races were inherently different rather than group products of differentials due to the cumulative power of regional and cultural conditioning. Another was the assumption of racial superiority and inferiority. A third error was the assumption that, because race conflict has constituted a major grouping of social phenomena, therefore, it was elemental and basic to social evolution and must always continue as a major societal force. A fourth error of assumption was that the Negro was an inferior race and that he was therefore available for exploitation and discrimination; that, because under certain regional and cultural conditions he had developed in certain ways, therefore he must always continue in those arrangements. On the contrary there is ample evidence to indicate many manifestations of superiority, of extraordinary personality and survival qualities, of capacity for intellectual and social achievement.

These assumptions are, of course, basic to an understanding of the difficulty of the South's problem. Manifestly, it is asking too much of a region to change over night the powerful folkways of long generations. Manifestly, too, it is too much to expect of a region to throw off its recent sectional conditioning of slavery and reconstruction without at the same time providing new ways of changing certain of its culture practices and arrangements. It is this problem that next faces the region. What the thousands of young white students want and the thousands of Negro students want is hard-boiled, realistic, evolutionary hope for the future, rather than closed doors of opportunity and change. What is needed is not to make the picture of southern treatment synonymous with all the black injustice of races, but rather to magnify the episode and the treatment of the Negro both South and North, as a supreme example of race tragedy under conditions which need not exist any more in civilized society. There can be no doubt about the enormity of the tragedies and injustices. But it is too big a burden to place upon one or two generations the task of changing the powerful folkways of the centuries at one stroke. It is unfair to characterize the southern pattern as one isolated and exclusive. It is too big an omission to ignore the great strides made by the Negro, by the nation, by the white South and the white North, contrasted with what was yesterday in the uttermost parts of the world and in particular before and during the reconstruction period in the United States.

While the historical view of the southern race situation tends to give it logical explanation, it also accentuates both the difficulties and obligations of the region in the tasks of better adjustment. For one thing the Negro

Per Cent Increase or Decrease in Negro Population, 1920-1930

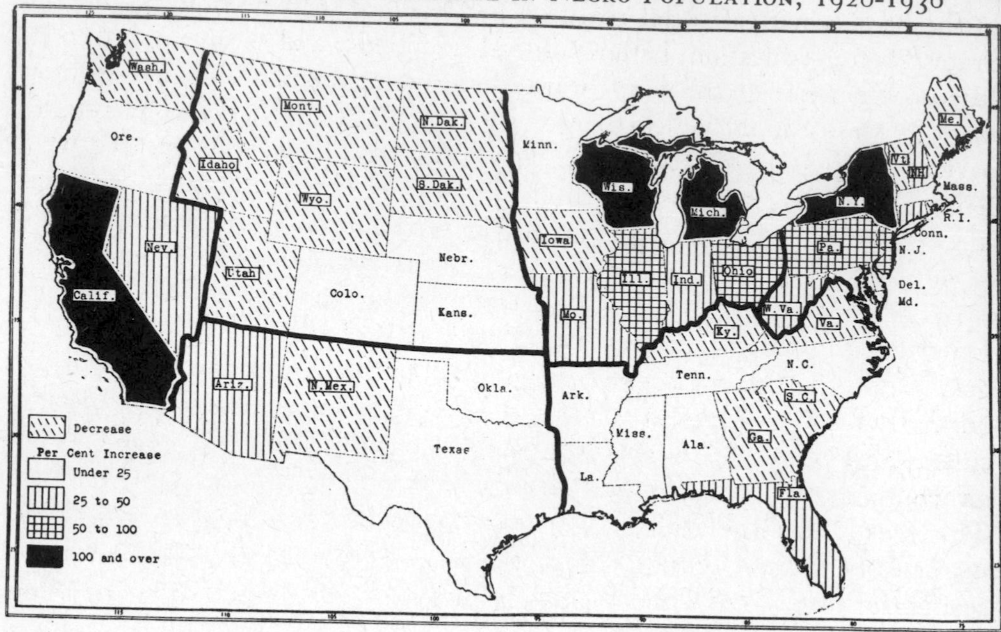

Net Gain or Loss by Inter-State Migration

SOUTHEAST

YEAR	Total Living In	Total Born In	Born in Living Outside	Living in Born Outside	Net Gain or Loss	Per Cent Born in Living Outside	Per Cent Gain or Loss
				Negro			
1900....	6,831,339	7,280,017	485,351	36,673	— 448,678	6.7	— 6.2
1920....	7,515,583	8,387,816	925,196	52,963	— 872,233	11.0	—10.4
1930....	7,766,013	8,914,763	1,905,489	64,731	—1,840,758	21.3	—20.6
				White			
1900....	10,996,099	12,257,972	1,750,548	488,675	—1,261,873	14.3	—10.3
1920....	15,027,730	16,546,570	2,339,164	822,324	—1,516,840	14.1	— 9.2
1930....	17,525,656	19,387,294	2,884,781	1,023,143	—1,861,638	14.9	— 9.6

SOUTHWEST

YEAR	Total Living In	Total Born In	Born in Living Outside	Living in Born Outside	Net Gain or Loss	Per Cent Born in Living Outside	Per Cent Gain or Loss
				Negro			
1900....	641,913	546,149	19,146	114,910	+ 95,764	3.5	17.5
1920....	897,603	813,336	53,846	138,113	+ 84,267	6.6	10.4
1930....	1,040,161	983,052	89,646	146,755	+ 57,109	9.1	5.8
				White			
1900....	2,383,462	1,940,395	166,283	1,064,350	+ 898,067	8.6	46.3
1920....	5,820,850	4,404,560	432,598	1,848,888	+1,416,290	9.8	32.2
1930....	6,854,511	5,546,410	675,525	1,983,626	+1,308,101	12.2	23.6

in three quarters of a century has made unbelievable progress and has earned in the hard school of social reality a better place than he now holds. He "rates" better education, better political, economic, and social opportunities. His problem lies at the very heart of the whole region's future development, a reality from which there is no escape. The Negro as an integral part of the population becomes a ten million unit of the Southeast's problem of numbers, standards of living, economic opportunity, agrarian culture. He constitutes a large part of the tenant problem. His inequalities of opportunity everywhere strike at the heart of any working democracy.

It seems possible to summarize the problem under two main divisions, somewhat mutually contradictory. The first is that the Negro is an integral regular part of the region's people and problem and must be naturally, normally taken into logical pro rata consideration in every aspect of regional culture. The second is that the region, in addition, must make special efforts in the field of new and more effective techniques of race relations. This means that the region must incorporate in its social planning special workable ways, not only of educating and developing the race, but of incorporating the Negro into a greater participation in the social control of the region. Guy B. Johnson has pointed up this problem for the Commission on Interracial Coöperation under nine major points. *First*, during their nearly seventy years of freedom, the Negroes in this country have made remarkable progress. It would probably not be exaggerating to say that in educational and economic attainments the average Negro today is better qualified to discharge the duties of citizenship than were the masses of white men when they were granted the right of full and free manhood suffrage. Yet there is not anywhere in the South today a full participation by Negroes in the rights and privileges which they as citizens are entitled to. *Second*, it is inevitable that Negroes will participate more and more in public affairs, particularly in the government under which they live. *Third*, the white race cannot go on forever excluding the Negro from such participation. *Fourth*, it is time for the leaders in the white race to make an honest effort to be fair to the Negro. *Fifth*, it is a matter of simple justice to a people who have earned well the right to have a voice in their own government for the South to take definite steps to usher Negroes into a larger participation in the rights and duties of citizenship in the broadest sense. *Sixth*, the tension among Negro leaders and spokesmen over the matter of political and civil rights is increasing. *Seventh*, the danger in conflicts over Negro rights is increasing. Negroes are less and less disposed to be content with what white people do about the race problem.

Dr. Johnson pointed out, in the eighth place, that "the policy of dis-

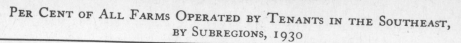

Per Cent of All Farms Operated by Tenants in the Southeast, by Subregions, 1930

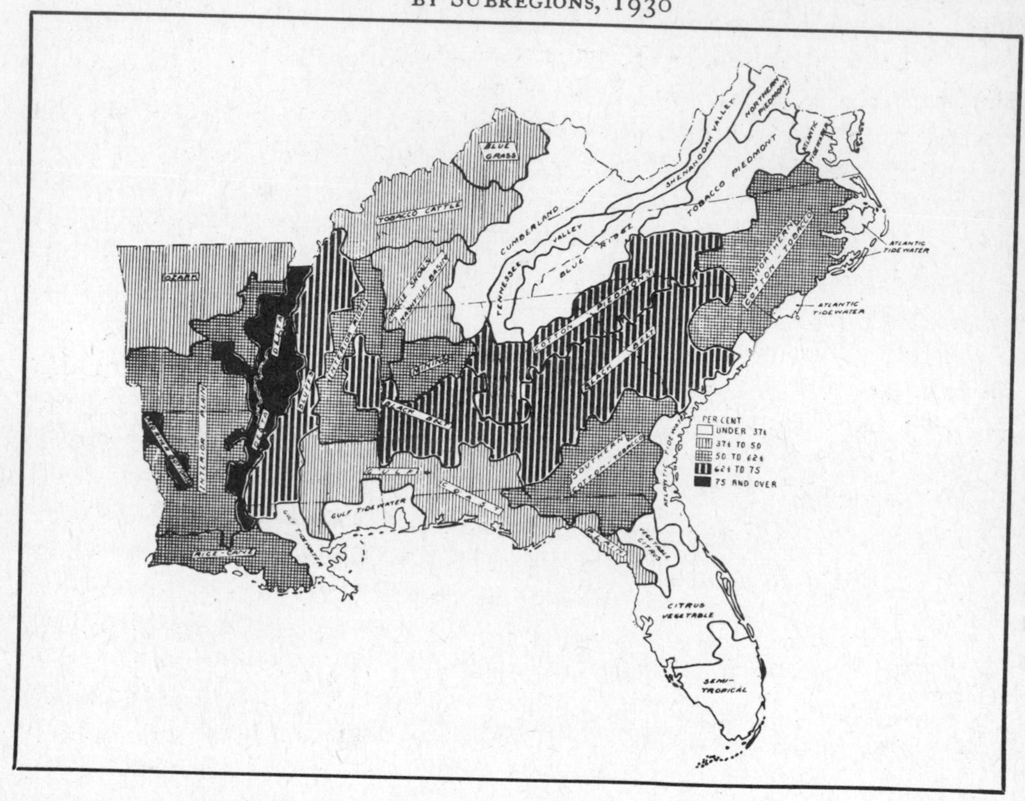

The Regional Picture of Farm Tenancy, 1930

STATE AND REGION	Number of Tenants
Southeast	*1,333,700*
Virginia	47,970
North Carolina	137,615
South Carolina	102,768
Georgia	174,390
Florida	16,737
Kentucky	88,421
Tennessee	113,520
Alabama	166,420
Mississippi	225,617
Arkansas	152,691
Louisiana	107,551
Southwest	*435,650*
Oklahoma	125,329
Texas	301,660
New Mexico	6,330
Arizona	2,331
Northeast	*90,410*
Maine	1,755
New Hampshire	796
Vermont	2,409
Massachusetts	1,442
Rhode Island	415
Connecticut	1,068
New York	21,113
New Jersey	3,948
Delaware	3,282
Pennsylvania	27,394
Maryland	11,441
West Virginia	15,347

STATE AND REGION	Number of Tenants
Middle States	*512,306*
Ohio	57,604
Indiana	54,575
Illinois	92,482
Michigan	26,195
Wisconsin	33,121
Minnesota	57,638
Iowa	101,615
Missouri	89,076
Northwest	*245,560*
North Dakota	27,400
South Dakota	37,094
Nebraska	61,020
Kansas	70,326
Montana	11,628
Idaho	10,559
Wyoming	3,520
Colorado	20,692
Utah	3,321
Far West	*46,715*
Nevada	445
Washington	12,078
Oregon	9,790
California	24,402
United States*	2,664,365

*Includes 24 tenants in the District of Columbia.

crimination and exclusion which the South has so long exercised against its Negro population had some justification from a purely practical point of view. That is, it has served to keep the peace, to adjust the races to each other with the minimum of friction. Like benevolent paternalism in the mill village, it has served a certain purpose well. But race relations are undergoing a change. The subordinate race has become acutely race conscious and is on the way to developing a nationalistic sentiment. This being true, the old policy of excluding Negroes from participation in political life will beget only an increasing ill-will and resentment on the part of the Negro race. The next step in race relations should be to take the inequalities out of the bi-racial system. The ninth point was that this step can be taken without destroying the integrity of the races. Negroes and whites have been meeting together in various organizations in the South for years now, and there is no evidence that either race is any the worse for the experience. The participation of Negroes in official or political functions would, of course, call for certain new conventionalities and codes of behavior on the part of both races, but these things are not impossible to attain. Furthermore, the increasing race pride among Negroes will act as a conserver of racial integrity as far as they are concerned. The old question of social equality is not necessarily involved, for there is no equality except that which is bestowed willingly in the attitudes and behavior of individuals. The races can go the whole way of political and civic equality without endangering their integrity."

The Southeast's "wealth" of people includes special groups other than the Negro. The most commonly portrayed is that of the southern Appalachian groups. L. C. Gray and collaborators have set forth the economic and social problems and conditions of this group in an extensive study over a period of five years and recently published. One point of emphasis only need be repeated here and that is the population pressure aspects, illustrating one unit of the larger regional problem already described. Dr. Gray summarized by pointing out that "Although population is sparse in some parts of the region if judged merely by statistical expression of population density, and although this sparseness makes for inadequate community facilities or high costs for providing them, the principal problems of the region as a whole grow out of an excess of population in relation to the economic opportunities to be found there under prevailing conditions. This population excess is the outgrowth of a high rate of population increase. From 1920 to 1930 population increased 16 percent in the Southern Appalachians, whereas, the increase in the six Appalachian States in counties outside of the Appalachian region was only 8 percent. For the

THE POOREST AGRICULTURAL COUNTIES OF THE SOUTHEAST

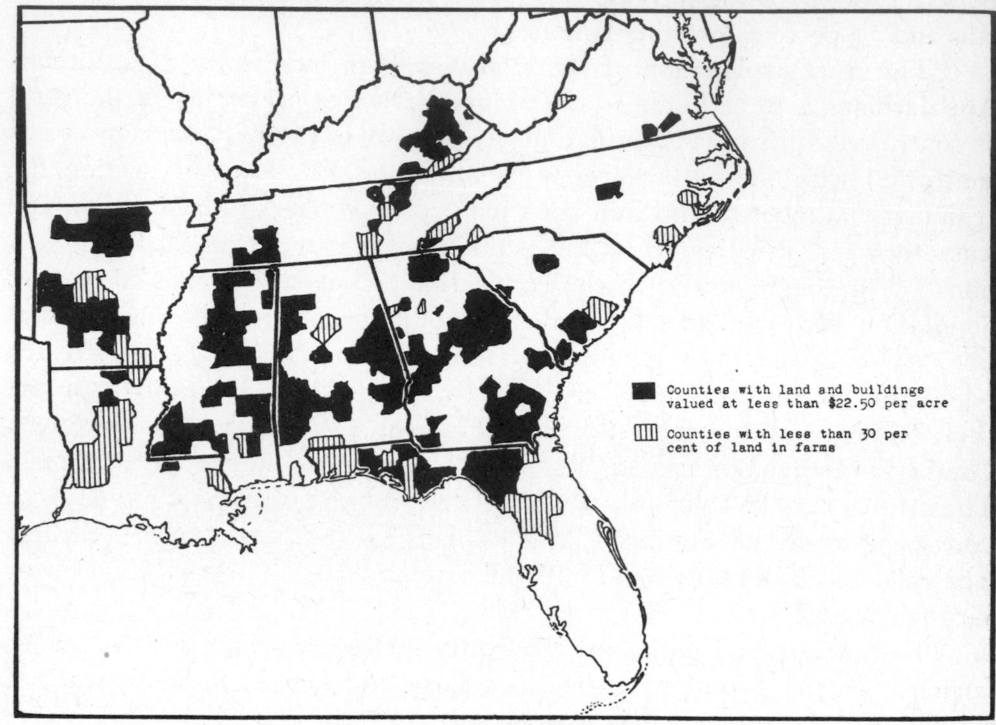

TYPES OF MEASUREMENT OF NEED AND DEFICIENCIES BASIC TO SPECIAL DAIRY INDUSTRY

MILK PRODUCTION IN GALLONS PER CAPITA IN THE SOUTHEASTERN REGIONS, 1930
(Minimum Requirement for Dietary Sufficiency: 90 Gallons Per Annum*)

STATE	Per Capita Production	Per Cent Whole Milk Sold	Deficiency Per Capita	Aggregate Deficiency
Virginia	60.1	52.2	29.9	72,413,345
North Carolina	37.8	33.4	52.2	165,488,307
South Carolina	30.2	28.2	59.8	103,977,147
Georgia	39.1	36.0	50.9	148,042,955
Florida	17.9	61.6	72.1	105,858,013
Kentucky	80.6	51.0	9.4	25,577,137
Tennessee	69.4	46.0	20.6	53,501,054
Alabama	46.7	25.5	43.3	114,582,538
Mississippi	65.0	34.1	23.0	50,245,525
Arkansas	69.3	34.7	20.7	38,387,777
Louisiana	27.7	31.6	62.3	130,929,244
Southeast	....	....	....	1,009,003,042

SURPLUS AND DEFICIT MILK PRODUCTION IN THE SOUTH
(Milk Required if State Consumed Annual Average National Per Capita Consumption of 55.3 Gallons*)

STATE	Amount Required	Gallons Produced 1929	Surplus or Deficit Gallons
Virginia	133,928,360.3	145,524,668	11,596,307.7
North Carolina	175,316,262.8	119,992,505	-55,323,757.8
South Carolina	96,153,704.5	52,525,520	-43,628,184.5
Georgia	160,840,381.8	113,639,532	-47,200,849.8
Florida	81,192,068.3	26,283,944	-54,908,124.3
Kentucky	144,586,771.7	210,623,997	66,037,225.3
Tennessee	144,695,546.8	181,789,691	37,094,144.2
Alabama	146,337,514.4	123,548,606	-22,788,908.4
Mississippi	111,143,101.3	130,644,269	19,501,167.7
Arkansas	102,552,854.6	128,568,652	26,015,797.4
Louisiana	116,218,092.9	58,289,639	-57,928,453.9
Southeast	1,412,964,659.4	1,291,431,023	-121,533,636.4

*Ninety gallons a year will meet the need for the quart a day per capita recommended by nutritionists but allows nothing or butter, cheese, ice cream, or milk used in cooking. For a family of five, two adults and three children, "2 cows freshening at different seasons, giving 2 gallons of milk each daily for a period of ten months will furnish requirements. Reserve 15 gallons per week for butter." (South Carolina's Live-at-Home-Plan for a Family of Five, Circular 125 of the S. C. Extension Service, Clemson College.) Such a program calls for an annual per capita production of *240* gallons.

period 1900-1930 the increase was 55 percent for the Southern Appalachians and 33 percent for other counties.

"The chief explanation of the relatively high increase in the Southern Appalachians is to be found in the higher birthrates prevailing in the rural as contrasted with urban population groups and in the mountain groups as contrasted with the valley groups or in cities. For example, within the region the number of children born per 1,000 women of childbearing age was much less in cities of 10,000 population and over than in other portions. For the region as a whole, the rate was 339 for cities of 10,000 population and over and 618 for the population outside of cities of that size. Taking the most mountainous portions, we find that the rate for population groups outside of cities of 10,000 population was 610 for the Blue Ridge, 613 for the Alleghany Plateau, 670 for the Northwestern Cumberland Plateau, and 746 for the Northeastern Cumberland Plateau. These rates may be compared with the rates for the corresponding population groups: in the Southern Appalachian Valleys, 532, in the Central Appalachian Valleys, 510, and in the Appalachian Valleys of Southwest Virginia, 504."

The other special group most recently in the foreground is the tenant farmer. In this group, of course, is a large number of Negroes, who, as elsewhere, constitute an integral part of the picture. This tenant white group, however, undoubtedly assumes more and more importance as the fortunes of cotton economy tend to shift, as unemployment increases, and as the group becomes increasingly a greater marginal factor in both economic and political life. What the situation might mean may be inferred from the fact that certain counties in the Southeast have more than three-fourths of their people tenants and in some nine out of every ten. In earlier days, and in other regions than the Southeast, the expectation was always that the children of the tenant would climb steadily higher upon the economic and social ladder. In recent years stark reality indicates the possibility of a new generation with lower developments and fewer prospects unless there is a change in the agricultural economy of the region. In summary, the size of the tenant picture is about as follows: A million families and five million people of the southeastern population are conditioned by the vicissitudes of tenancy. No one knows what their capacities are. No one knows who they are and what their backgrounds are, or what the potentialities of two million youth might be under changing circumstances.

It is an interesting comment that farm tenancy has just recently been "discovered" by so large a number of people both inside and outside the region of cotton farm tenancy. Rupert B. Vance points out that "until recently in this country no critical theory of tenancy has been developed

MATERNAL DEATHS IN CHILD BIRTH PER 100,000 POPULATION, 1929

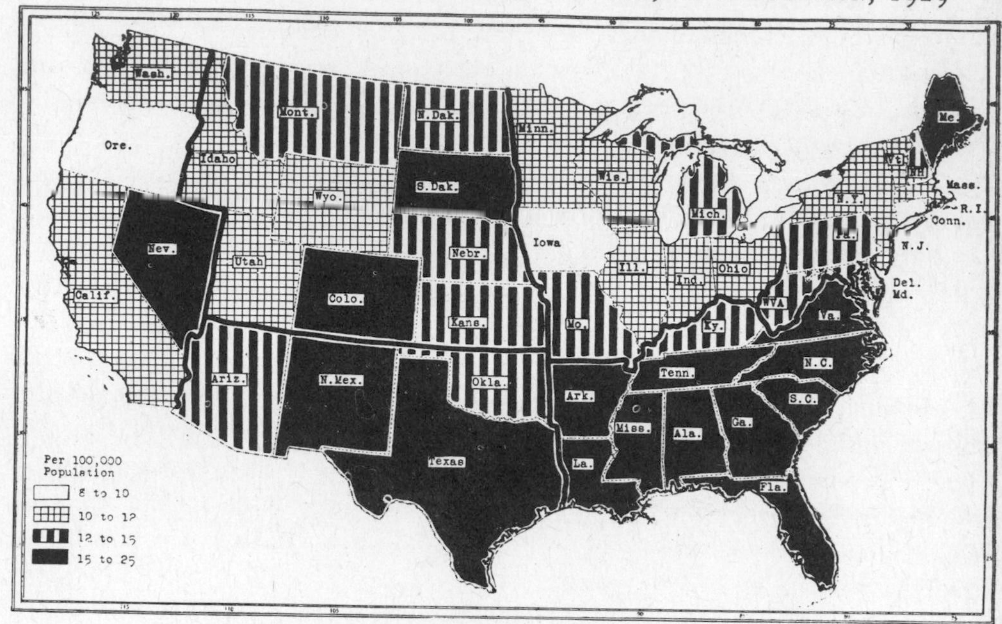

DEATHS UNDER ONE YEAR OF AGE PER 1,000 LIVE BIRTHS, 1929

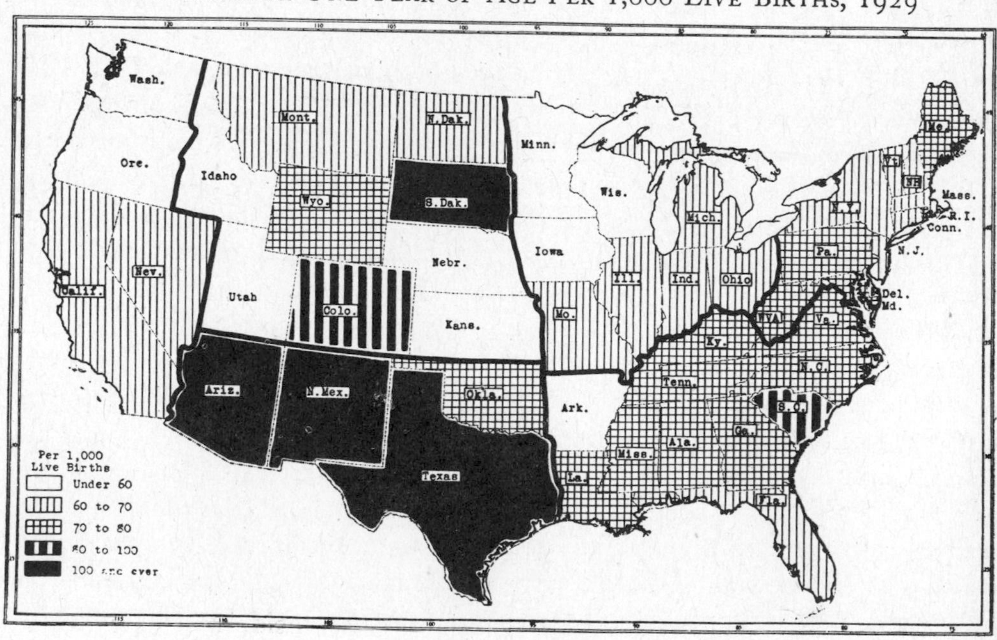

which takes into consideration the fact that while the United States is drifting into tenancy, certain European countries with semi-feudal backgrounds, notably Denmark, Ireland and France, have made the transitions to peasant proprietorship. The problem in America has been chiefly discussed either by Mid-Western economists to whom tenancy is an expression of capitalistic enterprise, or by Southern students with a definite racial bias, if not a predilection for the ante-bellum plantation. Of those acquainted with Mid Western conditions, T. N. Carver may be taken as representing the orthodox point of view. Tenancy is related to the inefficiency of farmers. Thus owing to his greater efficiency, the able farmer achieves ownership while the inefficient is forced to become a tenant and farm under supervision. Possibly the most able attempt to rationalize the system is found in the agricultural ladder theory developed by W. J. Spillman. According to this theory the young and inexperienced farmer has to go through a series of progressive stages represented by the system of wage labor and tenancy in order to acquire the capital and experience necessary to farm ownership. Tenancy is thus a stage through which farmers climb rather than a status into which they fall. Spillman contends that the ladder strengthens the system of land ownership. The ladder theory is sharply challenged by the fact that the percentage of tenants who are over 55 years old has been increasing for several decades. There are now about 375,000 who, as Secretary Wallace says, have struggled a lifetime toward ownership and in their old age possess no home of their own and no more security than when they started.

"The whole trend of the Mid-Western school" Vance continues, "has been to minimize the extent and increase of tenancy in the United States and to point to the South as a special case. As late as 1912 an able authority could write, 'With the exception of the Negroes in the South there is no tenant class of farmers in the United States.' With white tenancy increasing at a more rapid rate than Negro tenancy, and especially in consideration of its spread to the Southwestern cotton areas where few or no Negroes are found, this statement is now doubtful.

"It is also customary to hold that the Southern share tenant, and especially the cropper, is an agricultural laborer given a fictitious dignity by being called a tenant. Such procedure dismisses the problem from the category of tenancy and thus no doubt, serves to make the tenant situation seem immeasurably brighter. This is but an example of the practice, to which social scientists at times have proved addicted, of solving problems by shifting categories. It is best answered by pointing out that tenancy at its worst has tended to degrade its workers to lower levels and to deny their rights as tenants. Tenants with a fluctuating status are the best proof

Excess of Births Over Deaths Per 1000 Population, 1929

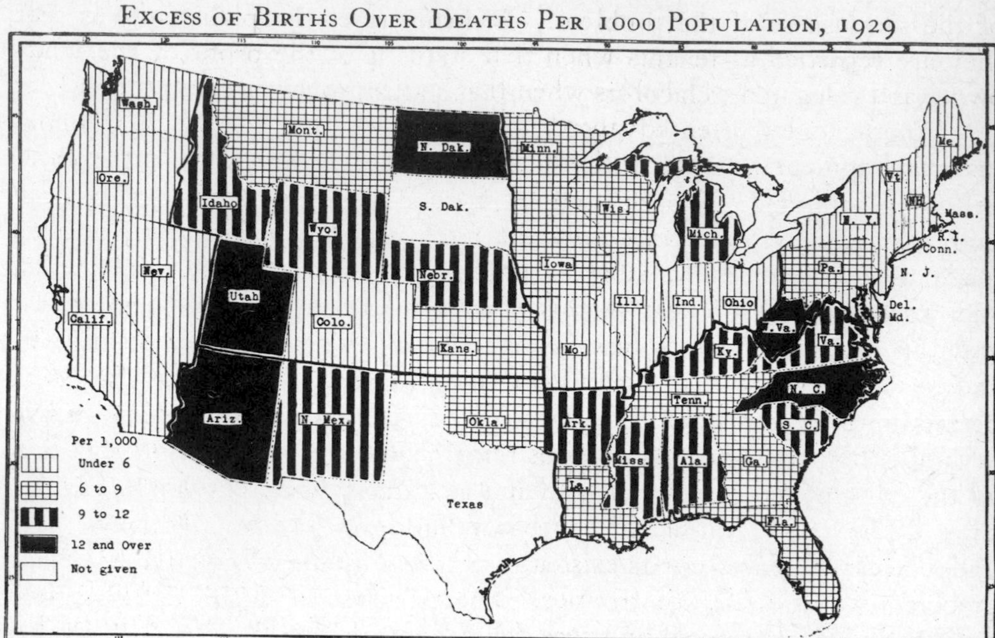

Births, Deaths, and Infant Mortality, 1929

REGIONS	Excess of Births Over Deaths	Birth Rate	Death Rate	Infant Mortality Per 1,000 Births
Southeast	*9.5*	*21.7*	*12.2*	*75*
Virginia	9.4	22.4	13.0	79
North Carolina	12.9	24.7	11.8	79
South Carolina	9.4	22.7	13.3	91
Georgia	7.9	20.1	12.2	76
Florida	6.1	18.8	12.7	66
Kentucky	9.7	21.7	12.0	71
Tennessee	7.3	19.5	12.2	77
Alabama	11.6	24.0	12.4	74
Mississippi	9.9	22.9	13.0	72
Arkansas	9.7	20.2	10.5	58
Louisiana	8.4	20.3	11.9	74
Southwest	*8.1*	*18.9*	*10.8*	*94*
Oklahoma	7.8	16.8	9.0	70
Texas (*)	....	....	....	..
New Mexico	11.7	27.1	15.4	146
Arizona	6.5	22.4	15.9	133
Northeast	*6.1*	*18.4*	*12.3*	*66*
Maine	5.7	20.0	14.3	77
New Hampshire	3.5	17.6	14.1	68
Vermont	4.0	18.7	14.7	66
Massachusetts	5.2	17.5	12.3	62
Rhode Island	4.9	18.0	13.1	72
Connecticut	5.6	17.1	11.5	64
New York	5.1	17.5	12.4	61
New Jersey	5.6	17.2	11.6	60
Delaware	4.9	18.1	13.2	81
Pennsylvania	7.5	19.8	12.3	71
Maryland	5.0	18.5	13.5	80
West Virginia	13.2	23.8	10.6	78
Middle States	*6.4*	*18.1*	*11.7*	*62*
Ohio	5.3	17.7	12.4	69
Indiana	5.6	18.3	12.7	64
Illinois	5.4	17.0	11.6	61
Michigan	8.9	20.8	11.9	66
Wisconsin	8.3	19.0	10.7	60
Minnesota	8.2	18.3	10.1	51
Iowa	6.7	17.1	10.4	53
Missouri	4.6	16.9	12.3	62
Northwest	*8.9*	*19.1*	*10.2*	*63*
North Dakota	13.6	21.6	8.0	67
South Dakota(*)	....	....	....	..
Northwest (Cont.)				
Nebraska	9.6	19.4	9.8	52
Kansas	7.0	17.4	10.4	58
Montana	8.0	18.7	10.7	64
Idaho	10.6	19.8	9.2	55
Wyoming	10.8	19.8	9.0	70
Colorado	4.9	17.4	12.5	91
Utah	14.5	24.6	10.1	59
Far West	*3.1*	*14.7*	*11.6*	*59*
Nevada	.9	14.2	13.3	67
Washington	4.0	14.6	10.6	49
Oregon	2.8	14.1	11.3	48
California	2.9	14.8	11.9	63

(*) Not in registration area.

BIRTH AND DEATH RATES, 1929

0 2 4 6 8 10 12 14 16 18 20 22

Excess of Births over Deaths
Southeast
White
Negro
Southwest
Northeast
Middle States
Northwest
Far West

Birth Rates
Southeast
White
Negro
Southwest
Northeast
Middle States
Northwest
Far West

Death Rates
Southeast
White
Negro
Southwest
Northeast
Middle States
Northwest
Far West

of the seriousness of the problem. In many cases the plain truth is that they are regarded as tenants when that status is to the profit of the landowner and relegated to laborers when that status proves more profitable.

"Another view often advanced holds that Southern tenancy is the normal development of the abolition of slavery and the break-up of the antebellum plantation. The shifting of former slaves into the metayer or share-cropping system was simply the method whereby large landholders made use of agricultural laborers lacking property in land, implements, and workstock. Moreover at this point the banker, the credit merchant and the farm mortgage companies crept in to furnish the credit needed and to dictate the type of agriculture to be practiced. This explanation is perfectly valid, but it should not be accepted as throwing the problem in any favorable light. Slavery, it must be remembered, had come to be regarded by the enlightened opinion of mankind as an abnormal industrial relationship. The concentration of large landholdings in the plantation was undoubtedly bolstered by its existence, as it was by the speculative and land grabbing activities of the frontier. The persistence of the pattern after sixty years, is, therefore, no cause for congratulation even as it refers to the Negro farmer. To those who see tenancy as an ideal system, the problem must be regarded as even more disconcerting when it is realized that white tenants have entered the cotton system on even terms with the ex-slaves, have secured their family living in the same extortionate credit system, have exceeded them in number, have carried tenancy into the Southwestern areas where few Negroes are found. In the disastrous period 1920-1930 the evidence is unmistakable that when Negro tenants fled from the blighted cotton area to the refuge of northern industry, white tenants crept in to take their places. Racial inefficiency, and the shadows of slavery and the plantation here seem to explain too much or else nothing at all.

"Behind the rallying defense of 'Let the Negro problem alone' the South has let and has forced the nation to let tenancy alone, until now it sees fastened upon itself the incubus of a degraded white tenancy. Yearning for the symbol of the old plantation, fearing the Negro, and held in thrall by credit institutions that enforce the commercial agriculture from which they take their toll, the section has long stood in the shadow of *laissez-faire* as regards land tenure—so long in fact that it has almost rejected the hope of an independent free-holding yeomanry, living self-sufficient lives on family-sized farms, for the chimera of land concentration and the commercialized farming of the cotton system."

Another group of people commonly pictured as a special class is the transitional groups embodied in the cotton mill village worker. Like the mountain folk, he has been stereotyped and pictured with great imagination and specialization. As a part of the urban-industrial South, the mill worker does, however, represent a special unit, although quantitatively less than 200,000. Yet the Southeast may well be performing a decided service to its population when it undertakes to compare the lot of the mill worker with that of his former state as farmer or farm tenant and to take stock of the marginal quality of both. This is, however, another particular situation which calls for more specialized study of a different sort than that commonly accorded it.

To other marginal groups in the flat woods or piney woods or isolated communities should be assigned special inquiries also. In all of these groups large increments of children are being added to the population. Two common impressions need authentic teaching by facts. One of these is that the majority of these children have the potential for strong physique and intellectual development under better environmental conditions. The contrary view is that many of them constitute submarginal elements of population bound for lower and lower status.

Finally, the key picture of the southern people must be found, as in the case of the region's physical resources, in the development and use of this human wealth. Like the physical resources, abounding in super-quantities, these human resources await adequate institutions for their development. As in the natural wealth, the chief fact is one of great deficiency between possibilities and actualities, so in the case of the region's superabundance of people and capacity, the outstanding fact seems to be that of undeveloped possibilities and of human waste. This situation, however, must be pictured more nearly in the story of the region's institutions and folkways, which is the subject of our next chapter. It is understood that the portraiture of rich personalities, of abiding loyalties, of the "peculiar" character of the southern people, and of other distinctive traits, does not come within the scope of the present work except in so far as the people and the institutional character of the region are inseparable.

CHAPTER IX

INSTITUTIONS AND FOLKWAYS

THE OBJECTIVES of the Southern Regional Study, as first set up, sought a twofold measure of the regions and their capacity for development, for supporting the institutions of a high type of civilization, and for contributing to the national culture and unity. The first measure was to appraise natural resources together with their mastery by technology and their availability for human use. This development and utilization would be manifest in wealth, industry, work, and standards of economic well-being. The second appraisal would inventory the population and "cultural" resources together with their mastery by social technology and their availability for social organization and achievement. This development and utilization would be manifest in the quantity, quality, and behavior of the people and in the nature of their institutions.

Our inventory of the physical and technological wealth of the region has been presented under the general divisions of natural resources; technological deficiencies and waste; agricultural resources and agrarian culture; industry and wealth. In this inventory were found great natural abundance and possibilities in general contrast to the actual development and use of resources and the creation of wealth. We have followed this, then, with an account of the human wealth as manifest in a vigorous, reproductive population but also with many indications of great human waste and undevelopment quite commensurate with the similar deficiencies in material culture. We come now to continue the story in terms of the region's major institutional modes of life and to inquire into the nature of social achievements and deficiencies here.

We have treated the institutions and folkways in a single chapter rather than devoting separate chapters to education, politics, religion, because the evidence justifies the conclusion that the composite institutional character of the region transcends any single aspect of culture or any single institutional influence. And it transcends completely the glamor and tragedy of the Old South. Appraisal is not so simple as a formula with merely so much religion, so much politics, so much education; or so much backwardness, so much progress, so much ignorance, so much enlightenment; nor

Samplings of Indices Relating to Institutions and Folkways

Number of Indices	Classification
1.	Rank of states based on 23 cultural tables.
2.	Quartile distribution in 152 cultural items.
3.	Per capita operation and maintenance expenditures, combined state and local government, 1930.
4.	State government—percentage expenditure for general government, 1930.
5.	State government—percentage expenditure for protection to life and property, 1930.
6.	State government—percentage expenditure for development and conservation of natural resources, 1930.
7.	State government—percentage expenditure for conservation of health and sanitation, 1930.
8.	State government—percentage expenditure for charities, hospitals, and corrections, 1930.
9.	State government—percentage expenditure for education, 1930.
10.	State government—percentage expenditure for recreation, 1930.
11.	State government—percentage expenditure for public service, 1930.
12.	Distribution of governmental outlay for education, hospitals, roads, etc., 1929.
13.	Per capita expenditures for ordinary public welfare services, 1930.
14.	Per capita expenditures for aid to soldiers and sailors, 1930.
15.	Per capita expenditures for charities, hospitals, and corrections, 1930.
16.	Per capita expenditures for prevention and treatment of communicable diseases, 1930.
17.	Per capita expenditures for conservation of child life, 1930.
18.	Per capita expenditures for vocational rehabilitation, 1930.
19.	Per capita expenditures for supervision of the welfare department, 1930.
20.	Relative amount of taxes and appropriations for state and local roads, 1930.
21.	Relative standing of the states in health.
22.	Supply of physicians per 10,000 population.
23.	Number of hospital beds per 1,000 population, 1930.
24.	Number of patients in hospitals for mental disease per 100,000 population, 1929.
25.	Number of mentally diseased in state institutions, 1932.
26.	Number of suicides per 100,000 population, 1929.
27.	Number of prisoners in state and federal prisons per 100,000 population, 1929.
28.	Number of offenses per 100,000 population, reported in 1933, criminal murder.
29.	Number of offenses per 100,000 population, reported in 1933—homicide and manslaughter by negligence.
30.	Number of offenses per 100,000 population, reported in 1933—burglary.
31.	Quartile distribution of number of homicides.
32.	Quartile distribution of number of lynchings.
33.	Comparative number and per cent of English-language "country" weekly newspapers, 1900, 1910, 1920, 1930.
34.	Net paid daily newspaper circulation per 1000 inhabitants, 1930.
35.	Number of inhabitants per daily newspaper, 1925.
36.	Number of inhabitants per 47 leading magazines, 1924.
37.	American Library Association Index—per cent of population registered readers.
38.	American Library Association Index—per capita circulation of books.
39.	Public library facilities, by counties, 1933.
40.	Number of urban people with and without public library service.
41.	Number of rural people with and without public library service.
42.	Relative standing of the states in education.
43.	Per cent total illiteracy, 10 years of age and over, 1930.
44.	Per cent of male illiterates, 1930.
45.	Per cent of female illiterates, 1930.
46.	Per cent of total population enrolled in public schools, 1930.
47.	Number of pupils enrolled in private and parochial elementary schools, 1927-1928.
48.	Number of pupils enrolled in private and parochial secondary schools, 1927-1928.
49.	Per cent of public school enrollment in high schools.

Number of Indices	Classification
50.	Per cent increase in number of high school graduates, 1911-1928.
51.	Per cent of high school graduates continuing education, 1930.
52.	Enrollment in federally aided home economics classes, 1933.
53.	Enrollment in federally aided agricultural schools and classes, 1933.
54.	Number of private commercial and business schools reporting, 1928-1929.
55.	Distribution of members of the National Association of Accredited Commercial Schools.
56.	Total number of collegiate students per 100,000 population, 1928.
57.	Number of professional students per 100,000 population, 1928.
58.	Number of graduate students per 100,000 population 1928.
59.	Number of students in normal schools and teachers' colleges, per 10,000 population, 1930.
60.	Number and per cent of colleges and universities.
61.	Distribution of accredited denominational colleges and universities.
62.	Distribution of women's colleges.
63.	Number of accredited institutions of higher learning in which women are located.
64.	Distribution of land grant colleges and state universities.
65.	Distribution of membership in the Association of American Universities, 1930.
66.	Proportion of students in all institutions enrolled from outside of region.
67.	Number of leaders in education born in the state, 1932.
68.	Number of leaders in education now in the state, 1932.
69.	Per cent of educational leaders born in state, now living in the state, 1932.
70.	Number and per cent of Negro colleges.
71.	Distribution of Negro state colleges and universities.
72.	Distribution of Negro denominational colleges and universities.
73.	Distribution of Negro enrollment in white institutions of higher education.
74.	Number of men and women teachers in Negro elementary schools, 1929-1930.
75.	Number of men and women teachers in Negro secondary schools, 1929-1930.
76.	Relative proportion of total state and local tax collections applied to education, 1929-1930.
77.	Percentage of total taxes and appropriations applied to education in universities, colleges, and professional schools, 1929-1930.
78.	Distribution of high schools having dramatic activities.
79.	Distribution of colleges and universities having dramatic activities.
80.	Distribution of Little Theater groups.
81.	Comparative distribution of "Who's Who" notables per 100,000 population, 1910 and 1930.
82.	Number of families per radio, 1930.
83.	Political affiliation, Democratic 1872-1896; now well-developed party system.
84.	Political affiliation, for the Solid South.
85.	Political affiliation, Anti-Smith Revolt, 1928.
86.	Political affiliation, votes for ratification of the eighteenth amendment.
87.	Political affiliation, votes against ratification of the eighteenth amendment.
. . . .	
105.	Per cent of church membership in the total population, 1926.
106.	Number of members of the Catholic Church, 1926.
107.	Number of members of Jewish congregation, 1926.
108.	Number and per cent of adult Protestant church membership, 1926.
112.	Circulation of church periodicals per 1,000 population, 1926.
113.	Per cent of churches whose pastors serve one church, 1926.
115.	Per cent of churches whose pastors serve six or more churches, 1926.
117.	Per capita contributions for religious, education, charitable, and philanthropic purposes, as reported in federal individual income tax returns, 1929.

again so much plantation and so much poor white. This conclusion is supported by the sound theoretical considerations which show all cultures as evolving through the folk-regional processes. It is supported by the realistic pictures of much "southern" culture as it reflects a regional cross-section or chronological strata of universal cultural development. It is indicated further in the interlapping and overlapping of many of the indices which characterize the special institutions, such as the church and religion, the state and politics, the school and education, rural life and culture, industrial development, and most of the general "southern" folkways. Of the more than 700 special measures of status which have been catalogued, no less than 400 appear in the list of technological deficiencies and waste. Many of them again overlap and repeat in most major aspects of southern culture. Thus, many of the same characteristic indices which qualify in the catalogue of politics must also go in the field of religion; many in politics and leadership must overlap with education; many in education explain much of industry and agriculture; and so on for the others. From the common occurrences it is possible to point out certain approximate "constants" in the midst of variables; to indicate much of the incidental and remediable nature of many deficiencies catalogued; and to indicate also the temporal quality as well as the inaccuracies of many characterizations.

Many of the characteristics of the Southeast are more nearly rural than regional; but not all, because the application of the same indices to the Northwest rural areas and again to the Middle States agricultural life shows marked contrasts and gives ample basis for regional differentials. An examination of the facts indicates further that much of the culture of the Southeast is more regional in the sense of a time lag than it is conditioned primarily by physiography or regional culture as a separate entity. In this sense it is more regional than southern in the sense that "southern" has changed and is changing to the extent that "the South" has changed and is changing. Here is one index which supports our hypothesis that the southern culture is immature rather than decadent—a most important key to the developing regional-national culture of the future. The real picture, therefore, must emerge here, as in other aspects, from a general comparison with other regions and with the earlier culture of the nation, and from the special examination of the several institutions and achievements in the region. From this viewpoint, it becomes apparent that "education," for instance, can neither carry the whole load of direction and reconstruction no more than it can be counted upon to characterize the whole region and its people in all aspects of enduring continuing culture. So to attempt to analyze and direct the region's politics without understanding and

PROPORTION OF GAINFULLY OCCUPIED CHILDREN 10-17 YEARS OLD ENGAGED IN EXTRACTIVE GROUP

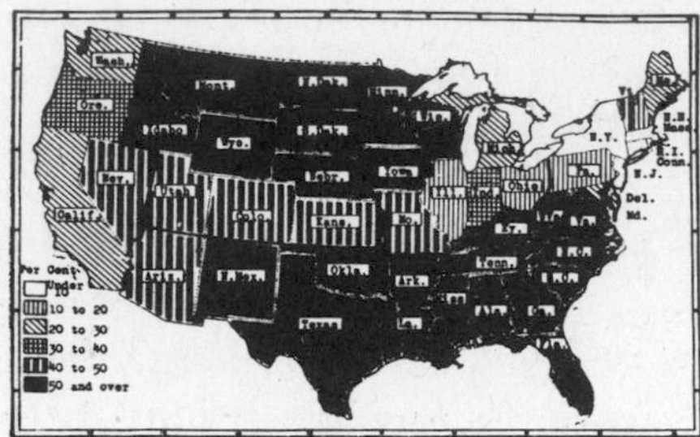

PROPORTION OF GAINFULLY OCCUPIED CHILDREN 10-17 YEARS OLD ENGAGED IN MANUFACTURING AND MECHANICAL GROUP

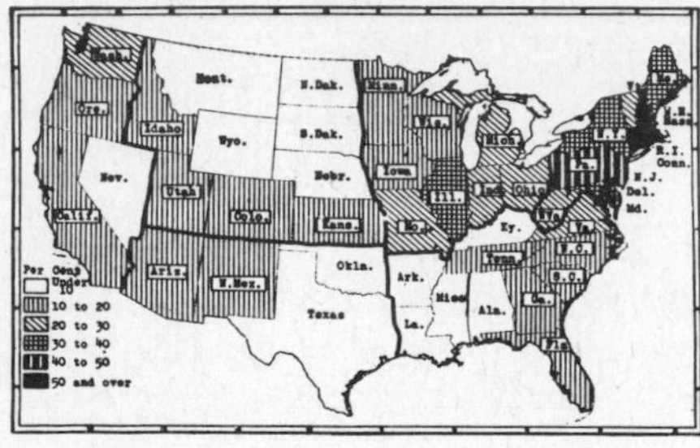

PROPORTION OF GAINFULLY OCCUPIED CHILDREN 10-17 YEARS OLD ENGAGED IN DISTRIBUTIVE AND SOCIAL GROUP

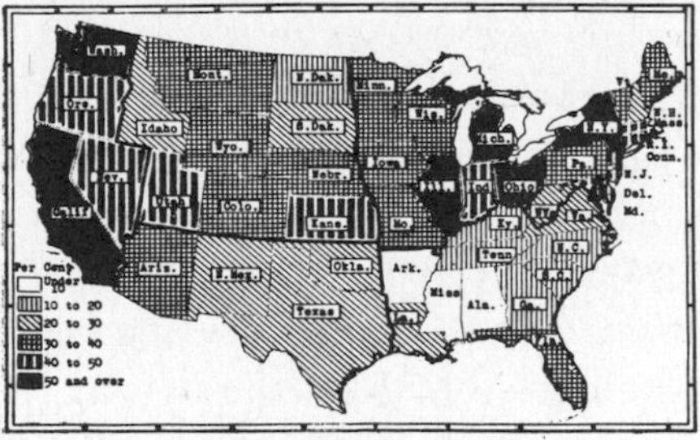

REGIONAL DISTRIBUTION OF GAINFULLY OCCUPIED CHILDREN

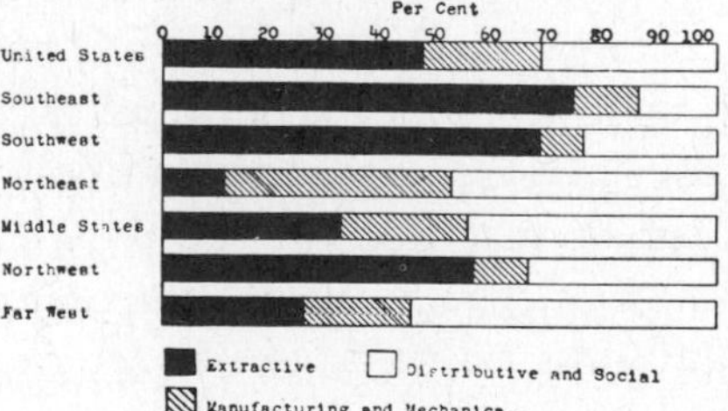

OCCUPATIONS OF GAINFULLY OCCUPIED CHILDREN 10-17 YEARS BY FUNDAMENTAL OCCUPATIONAL GROUPS, 1930

	Extractive		Manufacturing and Mechanical		Distributive and Social	
	Number	Per Cent	Number	Per Cent	Number	Per Cent
United States	1,002,535	46.7	466,251	21.7	677,174	31.6
Southeast						
Virginia	25,740	52.9	10,050	20.7	12,851	26.4
North Carolina	77,884	69.6	22,031	19.8	11,982	10.6
South Carolina	68,016	73.7	14,645	15.9	9,786	10.4
Georgia	84,924	69.8	16,429	13.6	20,055	16.6
Florida	15,163	51.4	4,925	16.7	9,499	31.9
Kentucky	34,755	71.1	4,764	9.7	9,478	19.2
Tennessee	43,725	69.5	8,740	13.9	10,453	16.6
Alabama	96,796	83.2	8,236	7.0	11,635	9.8
Mississippi	101,367	91.3	3,355	3.0	6,351	5.7
Arkansas	50,280	87.8	2,251	3.9	4,787	8.3
Louisiana	39,848	67.0	5,603	9.4	14,004	23.6
Total	638,498	74.2	101,029	11.7	120,881	14.1
Southwest						
Oklahoma	21,406	67.2	2,316	7.3	8,074	25.5
Texas	88,058	70.2	9,842	7.8	27,834	22.0
New Mexico	3,557	60.0	697	11.7	1,666	28.3
Arizona	2,645	47.3	727	13.0	2,223	37.7
Total	115,676	68.4	13,582	8.0	39,797	23.6
Northeast						
Maine	1,950	23.9	3,153	38.7	3,038	37.4
New Hampshire	716	12.2	3,417	58.5	1,719	29.3
Vermont	1,953	43.5	972	21.6	1,569	34.9
Massachusetts	3,273	5.3	32,281	53.5	24,970	41.2
Rhode Island	518	3.1+	10,524	65.2	5,102	31.7
Connecticut	1,955	5.9+	16,737	52.1	13,437	42.0
New York	10,769	6.2	53,086	30.4	110,504	63.4
New Jersey	3,221	4.1+	34,943	46.1	37,615	49.8
Pennsylvania	22,276	14.2	71,543	45.9	62,532	39.5
Delaware	1,019	29.1	1,213	35.0	1,248	35.9
Maryland	6,327	20.7	11,082	36.2	13,247	43.1
D. of Columbia	20	.4	622	16.2	3,213	83.4
West Virginia	10,536	51.0	4,158	20.1	6,013	28.9
Total	64,533	10.9	243,731	41.1	284,207	48.0
Middle States						
Ohio	10,877	18.7	15,300	26.3	31,920	55.0
Indiana	9,860	31.5	8,016	25.6	13,528	42.9
Illinois	16,886	17.6	29,090	30.4	49,804	52.0
Michigan	12,482	25.9	10,769	22.5	24,716	51.6
Wisconsin	17,891	50.8	6,178	17.6	11,114	31.6
Minnesota	16,001	51.5	3,799	12.2	11,345	36.3
Iowa	15,195	53.9	3,494	12.4	9,547	33.7
Missouri	23,197	40.2	12,480	21.7	21,929	38.1
Total	122,389	31.8	89,126	23.2	173,903	45.0
Northwest						
North Dakota	7,951	79.3	266	2.6	1,819	18.1
South Dakota	6,251	73.7	431	5.1	1,796	21.2
Nebraska	9,121	56.1	1,587	9.7	5,577	34.2
Kansas	8,678	44.7	2,583	13.3	8,146	42.0
Montana	3,227	56.9	510	9.0	1,936	34.1
Idaho	2,748	59.6	545	11.8	1,331	28.6
Wyoming	1,410	61.5	169	7.4	709	31.1
Colorado	6,359	47.6	1,676	12.6	5,280	39.8
Utah	2,042	41.4	657	13.3	2,239	45.3
Total	47,787	56.2	8,424	9.9	28,833	33.9
Far West						
Washington	3,311	26.9	2,820	23.0	6,115	50.1
Oregon	2,983	31.3	1,855	19.5	4,692	49.2
California	7,099	22.8	5,632	18.0	18,464	59.2
Nevada	259	43.7	52	8.8	282	47.5
Total	13,652	25.5	10,359	19.4	29,553	55.1

directing its agriculture and tenant economy or its educational backgrounds, or to reconstruct its agriculture and economy without coming to grips with its folk culture and attitudes would be quite as futile. The breaking up of the regional culture into its several elemental aspects is essential to see the whole picture, but also to make the needed comparisons in time and regional quality, and to appraise prospects of redirection and reconstruction. In this way only is it possible to appraise the folk culture of the region more realistically than through stereotypes or stage characterizations which persist throughout the country. In this way only can the picture of the region in the national development be projected into the future.

First, then the regional picture needs to be projected upon the screen of the past national culture and present trends. In the case of occupations in which the national trend is in contrast to the Southeast, there is evidence to indicate both the time lag and the rural character of the Southeast. That is, the Southeast is as the whole nation was in the earlier decades to the extent that agricultural occupation and ways of life and thought predominate. In the nation in 1930, Jefferson's earlier America of farmers had changed to a great economic empire in which only a little more than a fifth of the people or 10,242,000 were engaged in all agricultural and allied occupations. His much berated manufacturing and mechanical industries had grown to 13,790,000 or more than a fourth of the total, while trade and transportation had climbed to 9,963,000. The minor occupations were mining with 982,000 or two per cent; clerical service with 3,935,000 or about eight per cent; professional service 3,110,000 or six and a half per cent; domestic and personal service 5,448,000 or eleven per cent; with a miscellaneous and varied public service of not otherwise classified of 692,000 or nearly one and a half per cent. Or to focus the groups differently, a little less than a fourth were occupied in all extractive processes, a little less than thirty per cent in manufacturing and mechanical services, while nearly one-half of all gainfully occupied persons ten years of age and over were engaged in distributive and social service.

In some of the general cultural and "moral" aspects of regional behavior there is evidence to indicate again that the Southeast reflects much of the pattern of the earlier America. We have already pointed out something of its folkways of individualism, "honor," drinking, and other pioneer characteristics. So with the regional emphasis upon the family—from its earliest settlement throughout the early twentieth century flood of immigration the American people have been a unit in emphasizing the family as the basic institution of society. Old European stocks, new immigration stocks, Protestant, Catholic, refugees from debt, seekers after freedom from political bondage—all alike stressed the family as the foundation of

PROPORTION OF GAINFULLY OCCUPIED FEMALES 10 YEARS OLD AND OVER IN EXTRACTIVE GROUP

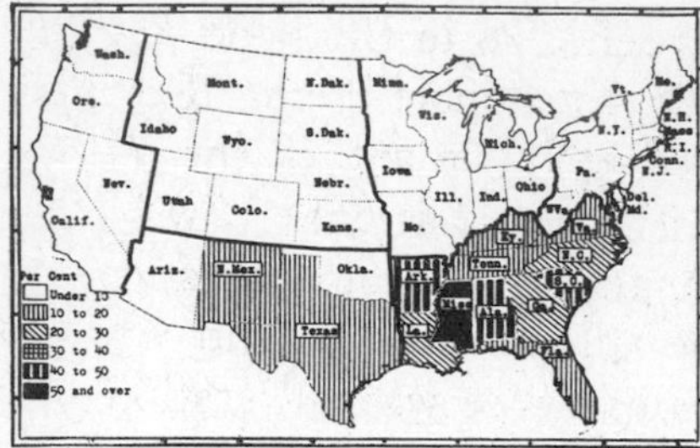

PROPORTION OF GAINFULLY OCCUPIED FEMALES 10 YEARS OLD AND OVER IN MANUFACTURING AND MECHANICAL GROUP

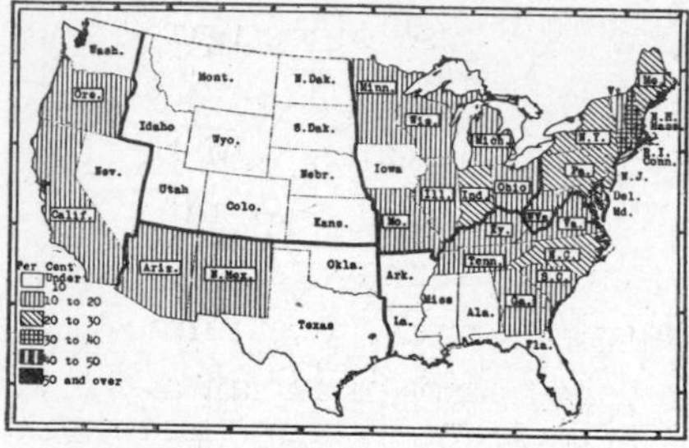

PROPORTION OF GAINFULLY OCCUPIED FEMALES 10 YEARS OLD AND OVER IN DISTRIBUTIVE AND SOCIAL GROUP

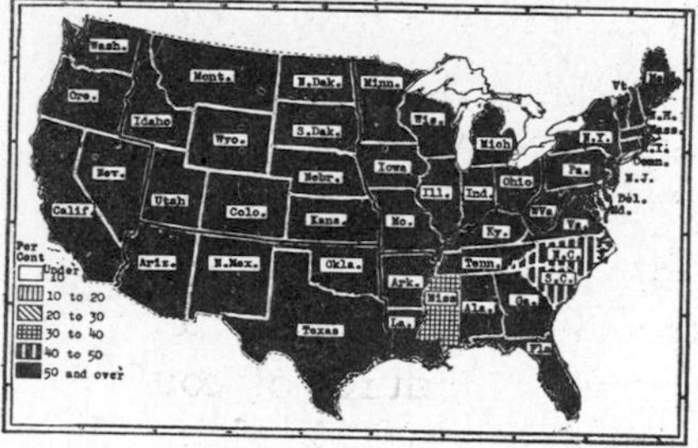

REGIONAL DISTRIBUTION OF GAINFULLY OCCUPIED FEMALES

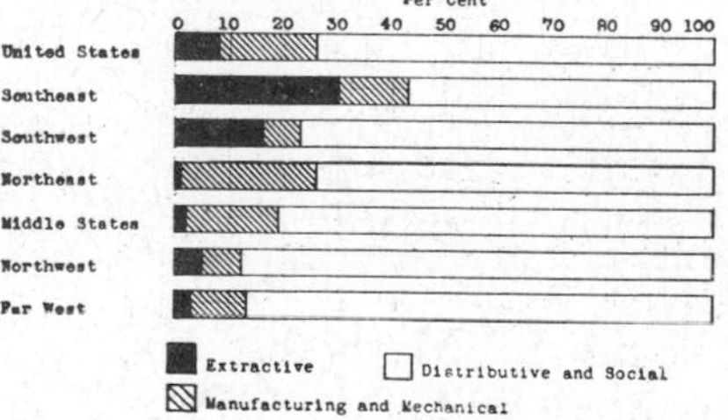

OCCUPATIONS OF GAINFULLY OCCUPIED FEMALES 10 YEARS AND OVER BY FUNDAMENTAL OCCUPATIONAL GROUPS, 1930

	Extractive		Manufacturing and Mechanical		Distributive and Social	
	Number	Per Cent	Number	Per Cent	Number	Per Cent
United States	911,027	8.4	1,886,307	17.6	7,954,742	74.
Southeast						
Virginia	18,169	10.0	33,022	18.1	131,076	71.9
North Carolina	70,690	25.9	68,789	25.1	133,486	49.0
South Carolina	88,597	42.8	32,665	15.8	85,499	41.4
Georgia	85,653	27.5	43,834	14.0	182,452	58.5
Florida	17,635	11.7	14,516	9.7	117,833	78.6
Kentucky	15,930	10.9	20,941	14.3	109,807	74.8
Tennessee	30,593	15.7	32,042	16.4	132,689	67.9
Alabama	104,473	41.1	21,950	8.6	127,591	50.3
Mississippi	142,204	61.4	6,628	2.9	82,896	35.7
Arkansas	48,050	40.3	4,834	4.1	66,309	55.6
Louisiana	48,253	25.2	14,803	7.7	128,364	67.1
Total	670,247	29.7	294,024	13.0	1,298,002	57.3
Southwest						
Oklahoma	12,829	9.9	5,998	4.6	110,519	85.5
Texas	79,871	18.9	29,189	6.9	312,648	74.2
New Mexico	2,221	10.0	3,164	14.3	16,716	75.7
Arizona	1,921	6.4	4,213	14.1	23,837	79.5
Total	96,842	16.1	42,564	7.1	463,720	76.8
Northeast						
Maine	1,499	2.2	18,719	27.3	48,275	70.5
New Hampshire	574	1.1	19,928	39.9	29,454	59.0
Vermont	880	3.1	4,345	15.3	23,172	81.6
Massachusetts	1,927	0.4	164,977	31.2	362,095	68.4
Rhode Island	229	0.3	39,831	45.4	47,769	54.3
Connecticut	1,192	0.7	55,399	31.1	121,416	68.2
New York	7,256	0.5	297,958	21.1	1,109,891	78.4
New Jersey	2,093	0.5	108,770	26.1	305,649	73.4
Pennsylvania	7,192	0.9	212,818	26.5	583,882	72.6
Delaware	579	2.8	4,075	19.5	16,229	77.7
Maryland	2,683	1.7	34,730	22.0	120,279	76.3
D. of Columbia	23	.0	4,792	5.4	84,010	94.6
West Virginia	5,456	6.6	11,634	14.2	65,108	79.2
Total	31,583	0.8	977,976	25.0	2,917,229	74.2
Middle States						
Ohio	8,108	1.5	101,791	18.9	429,707	79.6
Indiana	5,947	2.5	49,480	21.0	179,877	76.5
Illinois	8,243	1.2	125,324	17.5	581,901	81.3
Michigan	6,726	1.8	55,882	15.5	297,214	82.7
Wisconsin	9,131	4.2	41,057	19.1	165,026	76.7
Minnesota	9,311	4.6	20,581	10.2	171,073	85.2
Iowa	6,811	4.2	14,828	9.1	141,883	86.7
Missouri	12,652	4.2	53,085	17.7	233,497	78.1
Total	66,929	2.4	462,028	17.0	2,200,178	80.6
Northwest						
North Dakota	3,575	9.9	1,244	3.4	31,394	86.7
South Dakota	3,160	8.5	1,747	4.7	32,403	86.8
Nebraska	3,865	4.3	5,835	6.5	80,021	89.2
Kansas	5,459	4.6	9,428	7.9	104,273	87.5
Montana	2,114	6.5	1,220	3.8	28,940	89.7
Idaho	1,419	6.4	1,233	5.5	19,634	88.1
Wyoming	1,015	8.0	363	2.8	11,361	89.2
Colorado	4,084	5.0	5,973	7.4	70,936	87.6
Utah	971	3.3	2,701	9.3	25,312	87.4
Total	25,662	5.1	29,744	6.5	404,274	88.4
Far West						
Washington	4,740	3.7	11,502	9.1	110,434	87.2
Oregon	3,119	3.8	8,301	10.2	69,722	86.0
California	11,704	2.1	59,994	10.8	485,656	87.1
Nevada	201	3.4	174	3.0	5,527	93.6
Total	19,764	2.5	79,971	10.3	671,339	87.2

the nation. The family was also a religious sanction, based on scripture and revelation, and it was a great economic institution in the agrarian days of the republic and later. There were patriarchal rules of control; children were economic assets. Old age insurance was reflected in the good fortune which came to the elders who had large families to support them. Families were large, they lived in rural homes, worked at home and in the fields; young people married early, "two could live as cheaply as one;" "woman's place was in the home." Divorces were few, assuming proportions of discredit or scandal and were hard to get. The rule of the husband was assumed. Child labor was logical. Every man's home was his castle. By 1930 much of this had changed in metropolitan America, much more than in the Southeast with its continuing rural influence. In the American family of the 1930's one out of every six marriages was ending in divorce; one out of seven or eight married women earned money outside the home, not counting work in the fields. And the home as the base of occupation, of supplies and of industries had long since passed except in rural and isolated areas where home industries still survived on a small scale. On the contrary, there were ten million women in industry, nearly two million in clerical occupations, nearly two million in manufacturing, and a million and a quarter in the professions. Marriage came later; the family was more expensive. Children were no longer considered financial assets to the family since the days of compulsory education and of the elimination of child labor. Moreover, late marriage, the employment of women outside the home, greater freedom of women, increasing knowledge and practice of birth control, increasing standards and costs of living, decreasing earning capacity of children—all these had contributed to a greatly decreasing birth rate and to the multiplying of childless families in the nation.

So, too, the great change in the religious life of the nation is less marked in the Southeast than anywhere else in the nation. The picture of America in the earlier days was one with religion much in the foreground. The Constitution of the nation and of all the states, the procedures of courts, the language of laws, all paid homage to God as the guiding spirit of the nation. It was a nation of destiny, set forth by divine guidance to lead the world into a greater attainment of the good life and a greater glory to God. "For God and Country" was symbol of supreme patriotism. The Sabbath was holy, and in it there must be no work. Colleges and universities of the nation were founded by the church, and later state institutions were grounded deep in the religious faith. In 1780 the people were 99 per cent Protestant; by 1930 the Roman Catholics led with more than 13,000,000 members, the nearest single rival being the Methodist Episcopal Church with nearly 4,000,000. The 1930 predominance of Protestants

Per Cent of Total Population Enrolled in Public Schools, 1927-1928

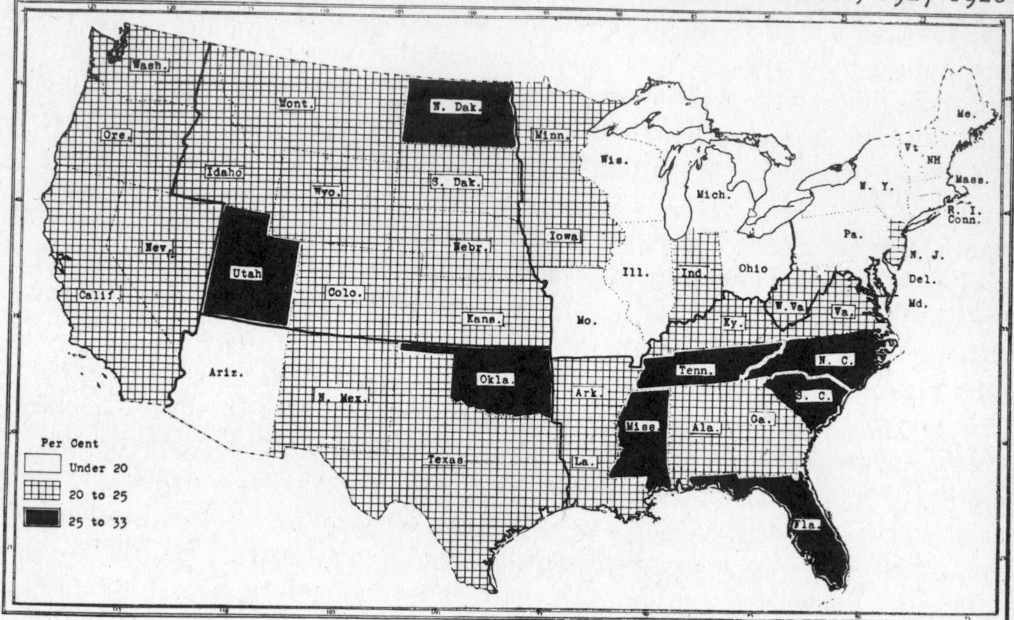

Rank in Public Education Attendance, 1930*

STATE	Daily Attendance		Average Days Attended		Average Days in School Session		Per Cent Enrollment in High School		Ratio of Boys to Girls in High School		Per Cent High School Graduates Continuing Education		Average Length of School Term		Ratio Adults to Children (†)	
	Rank	Index Per Cent	Rank	Index	Rank	Index	Rank	Index	Rank	Index Per Cent	Rank	Per Cent	Rank	Per Cent	Rank	Per Cent
Nevada	1	82.77	2	70.48	29	85.15	11	62.65	4	103.02	23	40.5	29	170.3	2	3.20
California	2	80.12	1	73.88	9	90.55	5	65.13	9	98.51	42	34.7	16	178.3	1	3.39
Utah	3	78.45	4	67.67	26	86.25	2	70.89	10	98.14	25	39.7	26	172.5	42	1.72
Washington	4	78.20	3	69.99	13	89.50	1	73.34	14	95.58	18	41.9	12	179.0	5	2.83
Indiana	5	77.73	8	66.07	30	85.00	6	64.74	11	97.91	28	38.6	30	170.0	12	2.56
Michigan	6	77.18	10	65.60	30	85.00	26	51.87	8	99.97	11	44.3	30	170.0	18	2.46
Kansas	7	76.94	11	65.02	32	84.50	8	63.75	19	91.20	30	38.4	32	169.0	23	2.37
Iowa	8	76.46	6	66.52	25	87.00	10	63.42	30	87.15	39	36.3	25	174.0	19	2.45
Oregon	9	76.03	7	66.26	24	87.15	3	70.62	24	89.85	41	35.2	24	174.3	4	2.90
Wyoming	10	75.82	5	66.69	21	87.85	14	61.44	40	82.03	46	30.3	21	175.7	25	2.30
Idaho	11	73.20	19	62.95	27	86.00	4	65.41	27	89.04	38	36.8	27	172.0	33	1.94
Colorado	12	73.15	9	65.84	10	90.00	27	50.52	20	90.85	27	39.3	9	180.0	21	2.39
North Dakota	13	72.84	25	60.35	36	82.85	25	52.62	48	73.23	36	37.3	36	165.7	34	1.89
Montana	14	72.36	12	64.66	14	89.35	13	61.80	37	83.36	12	44.1	13	178.7	28	2.25
Nebraska	15	71.61	15	63.48	20	88.65	9	63.63	31	86.71	48	27.1	20	177.3	27	2.27
Ohio	16	71.36	14	63.94	11	89.60	12	62.37	15	95.23	35	37.4	10	179.2	10	2.58
Maine	17	70.91	18	63.11	17	89.00	18	58.29	23	89.93	33	37.8	17	178.0	15	2.49
South Dakota	18	70.90	17	63.28	15	89.25	20	56.76	44	77.88	19	41.8	14	178.5	32	1.97
Florida	19	70.76	32	54.49	39	77.00	37	39.15	36	83.50	6	50.6	39	154.0	26	2.29
Mississippi	20	69.58	41	48.36	48	69.50	48	21.81	35	84.17	8	50.0	48	139.0	44	1.68
Minnesota	21	69.52	22	61.88	17	89.00	23	53.64	7	100.06	22	40.9	17	178.0	24	2.34
Missouri	22	68.86	24	60.49	21	87.85	15	60.39	17	93.25	15	43.2	22	175.7	9	2.64
Illinois	23	67.77	13	64.05	2	94.50	7	64.71	2	104.34	32	38.1	2	189.0	6	2.73
Connecticut	24	67.61	21	62.61	6	92.00	22	55.74	22	90.05	31	38.2	6	184.0	19	2.45
Vermont	25	67.57	29	56.76	33	84.00	24	52.95	5	102.48	26	39.5	33	168.0	14	2.52
New Jersey	26	67.43	16	63.39	3	94.00	32	45.42	1	106.43	47	28.5	3	188.0	13	2.55
West Virginia	27	67.31	31	55.73	37	82.80	36	40.08	29	87.78	9	49.2	37	165.6	40	1.73
New York	28	66.83	20	62.66	4	93.75	17	59.52	3	103.51	1	61.6	4	187.5	3	2.92
Massachusetts	29	66.61	23	60.95	7	91.50	16	59.58	16	95.06	45	30.8	7	183.0	7	2.69
Oklahoma	30	65.89	40	49.09	44	74.50	30	45.78	26	89.39	23	40.5	44	149.0	38	1.85
North Carolina	31	65.42	39	50.38	39	77.00	39	36.93	45	77.41	3	56.7	39	154.0	47	1.50
Pennsylvania	32	65.05	26	59.03	8	90.75	31	45.62	12	97.54	17	42.5	8	181.5	29	2.22
Arizona	33	64.82	30	56.75	23	87.55	34	44.10	6	100.59	21	41.3	23	175.1	30	2.08
Delaware	34	64.52	27	57.59	15	89.25	29	48.72	34	85.33	2	60.5	14	178.5	10	2.58
Wisconsin	35	63.62	28	57.00	11	89.60	21	56.55	25	89.74	34	37.7	10	179.2	22	2.38
Tennessee	36	63.38	36	52.29	38	82.50	47	29.25	42	78.29	9	49.2	38	165.0	34	1.89
Texas	37	62.99	42	48.16	42	76.45	28	49.58	21	90.37	5	53.1	42	152.9	31	1.98
Virginia	38	62.33	37	51.83	35	83.15	43	31.19	46	75.34	40	36.0	35	166.3	39	1.82
New Hampshire	39	60.58	34	53.87	19	88.93	19	56.91	18	92.60	20	41.7	19	177.9	7	2.69
Georgia	40	60.16	44	44.52	45	74.00	41	34.65	47	75.24	42	34.7	45	148.0	45	1.67
New Mexico	41	59.92	38	51.53	27	86.00	38	36.99	28	88.65	14	43.3	28	172.0	43	1.70
Arkansas	42	59.86	45	44.06	46	73.60	45	30.15	32	86.40	13	43.9	46	147.2	40	1.73
South Carolina	43	58.86	48	43.26	47	73.50	44	30.99	39	83.11	7	50.3	47	147.0	48	1.38
Maryland	44	58.19	33	54.44	5	93.55	33	44.20	33	85.81	44	33.7	5	187.1	16	2.48
Alabama	45	57.94	47	43.46	43	75.00	46	29.40	38	83.26	16	42.8	43	150.0	46	1.65
Kentucky	46	57.31	43	48.14	33	84.00	42	31.86	41	79.80	4	54.0	33	168.0	34	1.89
Louisiana	47	56.81	46	43.54	41	76.65	40	36.60	43	78.07	28	38.6	41	153.3	37	1.87
Rhode Island	48	54.29	35	52.93	1	97.50	35	43.95	13	96.67	37	37.2	1	195.0	16	2.48

*American School Board Journal, February, 1932. †Ratio of population 21 years of age and over to those 5-17 years, inclusive.

was in the Southeast, with the Southern Baptist Church enrolling a little more than 3,250,000, the Negro Baptist and the white Methodist Episcopal South, more than 2,000,000 adult members each.

In the realm of education the regional picture reflects the time lag doubly in that in much of its education the Southeast is now as the whole nation was earlier, and in that it shows the highest percentage of progress from an earlier stage to the present. Here, again, the characterization is that of immaturity. If the Southeast's educational deficiencies be ascribed to lack of money; lack of science, skills, and training; lack of understanding and experience; and lack of definite and guided motivation, then again it reflects the picture of the immaturity of all the nation only a few decades ago. Yet the Southeast has imitated the national mode in public education, which has long been acclaimed the great American institution just as equality of opportunity for the common man has been called the American ideal. What the South followed was essentially "American," with its own racial and regional variations. As America prospered, its education, public and private, had swept forward in a steady march of victory. Public schools, vocational education, universities, colleges, extension and adult education, professional education, commercial education—these had made the nation blossom like the rose. It was an amazing spectacle—beautiful buildings, artistic grounds, consolidated schools, transportation, the employment of millions of people in the promotion of construction work and community development. More than 30,000,000 people in the school business made education the nation's chiefest of industries. Upon its education by 1930 the nation was spending more of its tax money than upon any other general activity except that of war, which was, after all, an exception due to the World War and after. Of the total tax moneys collected from federal, state, and local sources, $2,164,598,000 or nearly 21 per cent was spent for education compared with $2,646,612,000 or 27.7 per cent, which went for war—the two making up nearly half of the nation's budget of tax money expenditures. Of expenditures of states for operation and maintenance 40 per cent was for education in 1931.

This picture of the educational expansion was relatively easy to present, such was its magnitude, so sweeping its advances, so clear cut its parts. The nation had grown and multiplied. Its children had multiplied in proportion. Not only that, but the nation tended more and more to decrease child labor and to compel schooling. Thus of children between ten and fifteen years of age the ratio employed ranged from 18.4 in 1910 to 4.7 in 1930. Add to these factors the rapidly increasing facilities for education, the expanding organization of educational forces, the organized labor movement, and the rapid increase in wealth and ability for sending children

Pupils Enrolled in Private and Parochial Schools, 1927-28

State and Region	Pupils in Elementary Schools			Pupils in Secondary Schools			Total Pupils in Elementary and Secondary Schools		
	Boys	Girls	Total	Boys	Girls	Total	Boys	Girls	Total
Southeast	*56,367*	*61,428*	*117,795*	*16,545*	*21,730*	*38,275*	*72,912*	*83,158*	*156,070*
Virginia	3,522	3,753	7,275	377	887	1,264	3,899	4,640	8,539
North Carolina	822	895	1,717	2,957	4,417	7,374	3,779	5,312	9,091
South Carolina	798	907	1,705	783	961	1,744	1,581	1,868	3,449
Georgia	2,052	2,243	4,295	1,533	1,902	3,435	3,585	4,145	7,730
Florida	2,386	2,906	5,292	550	764	1,314	2,936	3,670	6,606
Kentucky	15,235	16,027	31,262	2,339	3,941	6,280	17,574	19,968	37,542
Tennessee	2,404	2,679	5,083	752	774	1,526	3,156	3,453	6,609
Alabama	5,405	6,167	11,572	2,775	3,479	6,254	8,180	9,646	17,826
Mississippi	2,964	3,093	6,057	1,657	1,333	2,990	4,621	4,426	9,047
Arkansas	2,434	2,492	4,926	914	1,015	1,929	3,348	3,507	6,855
Louisiana	18,345	20,266	38,611	1,908	2,257	4,165	20,253	22,523	42,776
Southwest	*27,039*	*28,098*	*55,137*	*2,390*	*3,779*	*6,169*	*29,429*	*31,877*	*61,306*
Oklahoma	2,435	2,693	5,128	673	945	1,618	3,108	3,638	6,746
Texas	19,267	19,605	38,872	1,138	2,058	3,196	20,405	21,663	42,068
New Mexico	3,481	3,833	7,314	427	555	982	3,908	4,388	8,296
Arizona	1,856	1,967	3,823	152	221	373	2,008	2,188	4,196
Northeast	*531,081*	*542,582*	*1,073,663*	*73,000*	*72,806*	*145,906*	*604,081*	*615,388*	*1,219,569*
Maine	10,272	10,535	20,807	2,462	3,082	5,544	12,734	13,617	26,351
New Hampshire	11,163	11,329	22,492	2,671	1,405	4,076	13,834	12,734	26,568
Vermont	3,838	4,054	7,892	195	457	652	4,033	4,511	8,544
Massachusetts	78,178	79,534	158,712	19,862	23,762	43,624	98,040	103,296	201,336
Rhode Island	14,165	14,651	28,816	1,860	1,972	3,832	16,025	16,623	32,648
Connecticut	23,927	24,511	48,438	3,933	3,640	7,573	27,860	28,151	56,011
New York	168,866	172,697	341,563	21,168	18,594	39,762	190,034	191,291	381,325
New Jersey	57,652	58,273	115,925	6,363	5,107	11,470	64,015	63,380	127,395
Delaware	2,964	3,230	6,194	583	412	995	3,547	3,642	7,189
Pennsylvania	137,363	140,060	277,423	11,388	11,791	23,179	148,751	151,851	300,602
Maryland	19,195	19,965	39,160	2,032	1,972	4,004	21,227	21,937	43,164
West Virginia	3,498	3,743	7,241	483	612	1,095	3,981	4,355	8,336
Middle States	*404,421*	*412,744*	*817,165*	*49,682*	*59,014*	*108,696*	*454,103*	*471,758*	*925,861*
Ohio	74,728	75,899	150,627	8,892	11,544	20,436	83,620	87,443	171,063
Indiana	30,642	31,260	61,902	3,124	2,873	5,997	33,766	34,133	67,899
Illinois	114,822	118,528	233,350	17,586	19,883	37,469	132,408	138,411	270,819
Michigan	60,122	61,458	121,580	5,400	7,344	12,744	65,522	68,802	134,324
Wisconsin	48,789	49,198	97,987	2,927	3,409	6,336	51,716	52,607	104,323
Minnesota	25,279	25,380	50,659	4,374	5,000	9,374	29,653	30,380	60,033
Iowa	19,738	19,822	39,560	3,476	4,335	7,811	23,214	24,157	47,371
Missouri	30,301	3[illegible]199	61,500	3,903	4,626	8,529	34,204	35,825	70,029
Northwest	*46,713*	*47,689*	*94,402*	*7,696*	*12,152*	*19,848*	*54,409*	*59,841*	*114,250*
North Dakota	3,625	3,864	7,489	301	738	1,039	3,926	4,602	8,528
South Dakota	4,767	4,870	9,637	310	611	921	5,077	5,481	10,558
Nebraska	10,808	10,974	21,782	1,133	1,932	3,065	11,941	12,906	24,847
Kansas	16,053	15,454	31,507	3,183	4,660	7,843	19,236	20,114	39,350
Montana	4,111	4,399	8,510	501	681	1,182	4,612	5,080	9,692
Idaho	1,057	1,233	2,290	244	418	662	1,301	1,651	2,952
Wyoming	370	387	757	10	29	39	380	416	796
Colorado	5,413	5,693	11,106	678	935	1,613	6,091	6,628	12,719
Utah	509	815	1,324	1,336	2,148	3,484	1,845	2,963	4,808
Far West	*32,730*	*36,261*	*68,991*	*8,874*	*10,658*	*19,532*	*41,604*	*46,919*	*88,523*
Nevada	......	......	......	......	......	......	......	......	......
Washington	7,985	8,362	16,347	2,270	2,086	4,356	10,255	10,448	20,703
Oregon	4,448	4,504	8,[illegible]52	650	997	1,647	5,098	5,501	10,599
California	20,297	23,395	43,692	5,954	7,575	13,529	26,251	30,970	57,221
United States*	1,102,336	1,132,663	2,234,999	159,489	181,669	341,158	1,261,825	1,314,332	2,576,157

*Includes District of Columbia.

to school, and the result is easily understood. Thus, to begin with the lower schools, the enrollment in public elementary and secondary schools had increased from 15,500,000 to a little more than 25,500,000. The value of school property had multiplied many times faster, from a mere $550,000,000 in 1900 to the staggering amount of $6,211,327,000 in 1930.

The picture of higher education was in some ways even more pronounced. From 1900 to 1930 the attendance in institutions of higher learning had increased 314 per cent, as opposed to only 62 per cent increase in the population. And the Southeast reflected at times a greater acceleration than most of the nation. It was an amazing advance unprecedented in the annals of any educational system on record. There had been a similar increase in the nature and number of subjects of the curriculum, the nature and number of buildings and equipment, in the high standards required of teachers, and in the technical administration of school work. Million dollar high school buildings were the pride of small cities and large. Music rooms and play rooms, art studios and gymnasiums, swimming pools and cafeterias, workshops and playgrounds were brilliant items in the picture. Not the least impressive of all these pictures was that of library development, public, urban, college and university, the rise of the American Library Association, and the multiplication of books and reading. In all of these, measures of the Southeast reflect a relative time lag and represent regional distinctiveness primarily in that they reflect a general homogeneity and immaturity for the eleven states. This homogeneity is not invalidated by the record of the region for extraordinary advance, alongside the lowest standards in most phases of its educational achievements. It is, however, an index of composite culture, in which factors of economics, skills, understanding, and motivation share the responsibility for the relative lag and for the absolute deficiencies.

This character and power of the total regional culture is, of course, the key to the whole problem of appraising and reintegrating the southern culture into the national unity. The South is different; it reflects homogeneity in wealth, in population, in institutions, in technical deficiencies, in general institutional character. These, it is true, may be traced to the time lag, to historical conditioning, to agrarian culture, to economic and technological deficiencies, all of which presumably may be changed. In this assumption lies the prospect for the enrichment of the region's culture and contribution to the nation. Yet, what is not yet measurable is the degree to which the present regional homogeneity, due to whatever factors of folk-regional forces, has become sufficiently stable as to constitute in itself a fixed culture non-assimilable and not adapted to the national mode of in-

Sources and Expenditures of State Educational Funds, 1930

Adapted from Mort's *State Support of Education.*

State and Region	Percentage Distribution of Sources							Percentage Distribution of Expenditures					
	Dedicated General Property Taxes	Taxes Other than Dedicated General Property Taxes	Subventions	Institutional Receipts	Donations	Interest and Rent	Miscellaneous	Administration and Supervision	State Institutions	Apportionments	Other Institutions	Libraries	Interest on Debt
Southeast													
Virginia	....	66.5	4.3	20.4	....	5.9	2.9	1.4	48.6	48.1	0.7	0.4	0.8
North Carolina	....	75.3	5.2	15.8	3.6	0.1	....	1.3	43.9	46.8	2.2	0.5	5.3
South Carolina	....	80.3	7.0	11.5	0.8	0.1	0.3	0.7	44.2	54.2	0.7	0.2	....
Georgia	....	73.6	7.0	10.9	7.8	0.6	0.1	2.5	28.8	67.0	1.2	0.5	....
Florida	11.1	75.6	3.7	3.7	1.6	4.1	0.2	1.3	35.5	63.1	0.1	....	....
Kentucky*	54.0	31.7	5.3	7.0	1.5	0.3	0.2	1.0	43.1	55.5	0.4	....	....
Tennessee	25.1	53.5	6.6	12.8	0.8	1.0	0.2	0.7	39.8	56.0	0.7	0.4	2.4
Alabama	24.3	56.3	4.3	9.7	4.1	1.2	0.1	1.3	48.9	48.6	0.9	0.2	0.1
Mississippi	....	83.6	7.2	7.5	1.6	0.1	....	1.0	40.5	56.5	1.0	0.3	0.7
Arkansas	36.3	45.1	6.1	7.4	3.6	1.3	0.2	1.2	38.7	58.1	0.9	0.1	1.0
Louisiana*	59.8	29.3	5.2	4.5	0.4	0.5	0.3	1.4	28.2	60.0	9.9	0.5	....
Southwest													
Oklahoma	3.9	55.8	9.6	14.8	0.1	15.8	....	1.2	69.2	28.9	0.2	0.3	0.2
Texas	24.7	45.5	2.2	5.6	1.9	20.0	0.1	0.4	29.7	69.8	....	0.1	....
New Mexico	4.9	62.5	7.4	14.9	....	9.1	1.2	1.2	52.2	44.5	1.6	....	0.5
Arizona	43.1	33.9	6.4	6.6	0.4	9.3	0.3	1.5	47.5	50.4	....	0.6	....
Northeast													
Maine	65.1	5.8	5.6	21.4	....	1.3	0.8	1.5	38.5	54.6	4.0	1.2	0.2
New Hampshire	5.3	52.5	10.1	30.2	0.2	1.7	....	2.8	67.4	27.9	0.1	1.6	0.2
Vermont	27.0	38.4	21.0	6.4	2.7	3.5	1.0	2.9	32.6	45.7	14.9	1.8	2.1
Massachusetts	....	78.3	7.0	8.1	3.0	3.6	....	2.7	53.9	40.7	1.2	1.5	....
Rhode Island	....	74.1	16.3	7.5	....	1.6	0.5	3.3	49.4	38.4	2.7	2.6	3.6
Connecticut	....	78.7	6.7	10.6	0.1	3.3	0.6	7.3	55.1	33.8	....	3.8	....
New York	....	97.3	1.2	....	0.1	0.5	0.9	1.8	7.6	88.8	1.2	0.4	0.2
New Jersey	65.7	29.7	1.9	0.7	....	1.9	0.1	1.0	15.7	82.8	0.1	0.4	....
Delaware**	....	84.6	2.9	4.1	6.1	1.6	0.7	0.9	21.1	77.2	....	0.2	0.6
Pennsylvania	....	86.9	2.8	9.9	0.1	0.2	0.1	1.2	26.9	67.0	4.6	0.3	....
Maryland	32.1	42.3	4.7	20.2	0.6	0.1	....	4.3	49.3	40.8	4.6	0.6	0.4
West Virginia	2.1	74.8	6.8	10.9	....	4.0	1.4	2.4	63.2	33.9	0.3	0.2	....
Middle States													
Ohio	....	78.0	7.0	13.2	1.3	0.3	0.2	1.1	63.4	32.5	2.5	0.5	....
Indiana	32.2	32.3	3.9	14.5	4.5	7.0	5.6	0.8	64.4	33.4	0.3	0.7	0.4
Illinois	37.7	43.3	6.0	10.5	1.4	0.8	0.3	1.5	65.6	26.3	5.6	1.0	....
Michigan	15.1	71.5	1.5	8.2	2.4	1.3	....	0.5	38.2	60.9	0.1	0.3	....
Wisconsin	21.3	59.5	2.9	10.3	1.2	2.6	2.2	1.0	53.5	43.6	0.8	1.1	....
Minnesota	11.9	54.3	2.3	9.1	1.0	21.3	0.1	0.7	44.7	53.2	0.6	0.3	0.5
Iowa	....	65.0	4.7	25.5	2.0	2.6	0.2	1.0	89.7	7.7	0.2	1.1	0.3
Missouri	....	78.6	5.2	10.8	3.4	2.0	....	0.7	42.3	56.6	0.1	0.3	....
Northwest													
North Dakota	....	59.5	6.5	11.3	0.3	21.6	0.8	1.3	67.1	29.8	1.6	0.2	....
South Dakota	....	37.0	6.6	12.7	....	38.2	5.5	1.0	56.9	40.7	1.0	0.4	....
Nebraska	....	53.6	6.0	23.3	....	16.3	0.8	1.5	76.4	21.1	0.5	0.5	....
Kansas	....	59.1	5.4	24.8	....	10.1	0.6	2.5	87.5	9.1	....	0.9	....
Montana	25.4	19.1	6.9	6.4	0.1	41.8	0.3	1.4	45.2	48.1	1.3	0.1	3.9
Idaho	....	45.1	9.5	8.4	....	36.6	0.4	2.1	96.1	0.3	....	0.3	1.2
Wyoming	11.2	5.4	32.6	3.4	0.4	39.7	7.3	1.2	30.9	67.5	0.1	0.3	....
Colorado	46.8	10.4	5.5	22.0	0.5	14.7	0.1	0.6	82.8	15.6	0.9	0.1	....
Utah	71.7	10.9	5.2	12.0	....	0.2	....	1.1	32.8	65.8	0.1	....	0.2
Far West													
Nevada	22.9	37.9	18.6	5.4	2.1	11.9	1.2	5.1	51.4	42.0	0.5	0.7	0.3
Washington†	76.1	14.0	2.3	8.8	0.2	....	....	0.5	35.2	64.1	....	0.2	....
Oregon	42.7	7.3	5.3	29.4	5.4	8.6	1.3	0.8	87.7	8.8	1.0	1.0	0.7
California	....	84.1	1.8	7.0	3.7	3.3	0.1	0.5	37.2	60.3	1.0	0.1	1.0
United States	15.9	63.7	3.8	8.9	1.5	5.6	0.6	1.2	38.5	58.2	1.3	0.4	0.4

*Tax receipts are for fiscal year ending in 1929.
†Checked with Mort's, total percentage distribution of sources equals 101.4.
**Tax expenditures are for fiscal year ending in 1929.

dustry, commerce, and technology. What, for instance, is the relative place in the whole culture of the South's marginal groups and its millions of families maladjusted to the present environment? Perhaps the nearest approach to such a regional folk culture appears in the politics and religion of the region and in its folkways of race, state, and sectional loyalties, which come nearer conditioning all the culture of all the groups of the region than any other forces, not excepting education. Indeed, education reflects far more of the effect of politics, religion, and sectionalism than it appears as modifying influence upon them. Likewise, the premise is supportable that even the economic status and culture of the region, while underlying the incapacity to support institutions, nevertheless may be more the creature of these other cultural influences than their creator.

Here then is double and triple dilemma. It must be clear that the all-dependence so often placed upon education as the single institutional approach to progress was not enough. On the other hand, it seems clear that every major problem, from farm tenancy to political democracy, is bound up with the "culture" or "system" of economic and social ideologies and arrangements of the region, which in turn represent the realities of recent historical development more than the actual possibilities of the region under different conditioning and expansion. Manifestly, also, the strategy of mass attack upon the culture of a whole region conforms to neither common sense nor scientific specifications. Nor does pride or acquiescence in a regional culture as superior because of the "story" of its past or of its variation from national type or its conformity to certain early American traditions satisfy any of the realistic requirements of the present time. The more realistic approach as stated in the objectives of the Southern Regional Study, in addition to understanding the "exceedingly complex nature of the regional cultures involved and the immensity and time-quality of cultural reconstruction," is "to focus upon a relatively small number of elemental factors toward which practical study and planning may be directed," to the end that the whole culture may be best re-adapted to the needs and possibilities of the nation and of the region.

The desire for modifying the general culture through the approach to special aspects and interests must not be taken as a broadside assault or a blanket condemnation of the southern culture. On the contrary, our basic assumption is one of a vitally changing culture throughout the nation and the western world. The premise would be that this region need not lag, on the one hand, nor, on the other, follow blindly the paths of a hectic, urban, technological, transitional period of civilization. In this premise, what actual ways of modifying the regional culture appear? Some of such approaches appear in the Democratic New Deal. One is the AAA, which,

Enrollment in Federally Aided Schools and Classes, 1933

State and Region	Agricultural	Trade and Industrial	Home Economics	Total
Southeast	*113,480*	*56,258*	*69,952*	*239,690*
Virginia	10,979	9,711	3,685	24,375
North Carolina	13,499	5,984	8,733	28,216
South Carolina	15,967	5,377	7,798	29,142
Georgia	9,862	9,940	9,915	29,717
Florida	3,731	4,787	3,811	12,329
Kentucky	4,999	2,806	2,543	10,348
Tennessee	13,262	4,835	10,977	29,074
Alabama	7,722	5,148	8,416	21,286
Mississippi	14,826	2,294	3,863	20,983
Arkansas	9,234	1,132	4,537	14,903
Louisiana	9,399	4,244	5,674	19,317
Southwest	*31,133*	*14,494*	*36,989*	*82,616*
Oklahoma	6,420	4,278	15,250	25,948
Texas	23,246	9,669	17,887	50,802
New Mexico	683	179	1,501	2,363
Arizona	784	368	2,351	3,503
Northeast	*20,061*	*251,570*	*40,731*	*312,362*
Maine	760	294	814	1,868
New Hampshire	335	510	260	1,105
Vermont	326	305	189	820
Massachusetts	1,182	29,609	13,373	44,164
Rhode Island	617	1,534	560	2,711
Connecticut	621	6,613	1,734	8,968
New York	6,189	146,256	7,539	159,984
New Jersey	1,318	20,085	2,035	23,438
Delaware	274	1,326	343	1,943
Pennsylvania	5,820	39,008	11,325	56,153
Maryland	1,328	3,849	862	6,039
West Virginia	1,291	2,181	1,697	5,169
Middle States	*65,530*	*106,863*	*64,998*	*237,391*
Ohio	10,732	14,342	8,837	33,911
Indiana	4,743	10,431	5,478	20,652
Illinois	8,679	11,252	10,214	30,145
Michigan	13,129	18,711	8,126	39,966
Wisconsin	7,108	34,831	21,286	63,225
Minnesota	4,910	7,163	3,865	15,938
Iowa	9,399	3,519	2,470	15,388
Missouri	6,830	6,614	4,722	18,166
Northwest	*16,983*	*15,122*	*34,180*	*66,285*
North Dakota	1,495	568	2,301	4,364
South Dakota	1,637	198	2,313	4,148
Nebraska	3,068	2,439	10,253	15,760
Kansas	2,719	3,030	8,139	13,888
Montana	1,065	1,362	1,411	3,838
Idaho	1,462	605	814	2,881
Wyoming	1,223	508	587	2,318
Colorado	2,031	5,050	4,632	11,713
Utah	2,283	1,362	3,730	7,375
Far West	*13,841*	*44,253*	*25,716*	*83,810*
Nevada	181	449	224	854
Washington	2,753	3,868	1,506	8,127
Oregon	2,200	2,903	3,022	8,125
California	8,707	37,033	20,964	66,704

Junior Colleges in the United States, 1933

State and Region	Public		Private		Total	
	Number	Enrollment	Number	Enrollment	Number	Enrollment
Southeast	*33*	*6,516*	*103*	*11,913*	*136*	*18,429*
Virginia	1	—	12	1,569	13	1,569
North Carolina	2	278	21	2,553	23	2,831
South Carolina	0	0	3	283	3	283
Georgia	7	877	7	697	14	1,574
Florida	1	160	4	411	5	571
Kentucky	0	0	17	2,531	17	2,531
Tennessee	2	556	12	1,997	14	2,553
Alabama	1	100	4	282	5	382
Mississippi	11	2,109	9	776	20	2,885
Arkansas	6	2,022	7	631	13	2,653
Louisiana	2	414	7	183	9	597
Southwest	*36*	*9,128*	*28*	*3,285*	*64*	*12,413*
Oklahoma	14	2,859	3	110	17	2,969
Texas	20	5,475	24	3,070	44	8,545
New Mexico	1	218	0	0	1	218
Arizona	1	576	1	105	2	681
Northeast	*4*	*409*	*57*	*5,694*	*61*	*6,103*
Maine	0	0	3	147	3	147
New Hampshire	0	0	1	139	1	139
Vermont	0	0	1	69	1	69
Massachusetts	1	44	9	708	10	752
Rhode Island	0	0	1	25	1	25
Connecticut	0	0	5	351	5	351
New York	0	0	10	1,136	10	1,136
Pennsylvania	0	0	7	830	7	830
New Jersey	0	0	2	100	2	100
Delaware	1	51	2	875	3	926
Maryland	1	13	4	543	5	556
District of Col.	0	0	9	497	9	497
West Virginia	1	301	3	274	4	575
Middle States	*55*	*15,599*	*66*	*10,316*	*121*	*25,915*
Ohio	0	0	13	3,935	13	3,935
Indiana	0	0	4	341	4	341
Illinois	6	6,075	14	1,892	20	7,967
Michigan	8	2,982	2	113	10	3,095
Wisconsin	0	0	2	128	2	128
Minnesota	7	2,145	3	294	10	2,439
Iowa	27	1,911	10	826	37	2,737
Missouri	7	2,486	18	2,787	25	5,273
Northwest	*22*	*5,410*	*27*	*3,073*	*49*	*8,483*
North Dakota	2	407	0	0	2	407
South Dakota	0	0	6	306	6	306
Nebraska	2	156	6	629	8	785
Kansas	10	3,207	6	296	16	3,503
Montana	1	240	1	0	2	240
Idaho	3	772	2	345	5	1,117
Wyoming	0	0	0	0	0	0
Colorado	2	190	3	529	5	719
Utah	2	438	3	968	5	1,406
Far West	*39*	*30,858*	*23*	*1,929*	*62*	*32,787*
Washington	4	565	3	262	7	827
Oregon	0	0	1	42	1	42
California	35	30,293	19	1,625	54	31,918
Nevada	0	0	0	0	0	0

through special and technical action, instituted new coöperative endeavor which has resulted not only in certain changing attitudes but in an appreciable and measurable readjustment of farm economy. The reduction of cotton culture and the restriction of uses to which cereal crops grown on the retired acreage could be put has resulted not only in the increase of livestock temporarily but in the prospect of a new order of diversification far more effective than merely the educational teachings of the agricultural colleges and extension agents. Another is the popularity of the Democratic president, whose stated ideals in many policies such as prohibition, racial opportunity, immigration, public ownership of power, and others were quite different from those of the southern folk. Acquiescence by loyalties or opportunism, having given rise to practices, is apparently resulting in some continuing changes. The Tennessee Valley Authority, again, through special approaches bids fair to change a great deal of the cultural landscape of the whole Southeast. So far erosion prevention programs, forestry, and other aspects.

An example which indicates the capacity of the region to achieve distinction in a given field if it has money, motivation, understanding, and skill is the much lamented bigtime football of the colleges and universities. Reference to this involves no appraisal of the demerits of the case; it is cited to illustrate the point that when the South decided to play football it imported much of its skills in football coaches, it set up the necessary organizations and means, it built its stadia, and brought teachers and pupils from wherever they were found most appropriate to the purpose. Here, too, is illustrated the power of example, emulation, and competition, in that the setting of a pace by a few institutions was followed by many. The same example also illustrates one way of modifying attitudes in that it has been pointed out many times that the Notre Dame football system, through the introduction of coaches and popularization of the game, has done more to encourage good will to the Catholic following than anything else.

In the field of education, perhaps the most significant approaches to modifying the general culture through special avenues are found in Negro education, in the Federal grants to land grant colleges for extension service, research, and experimental stations, and in the endowments and grants made by the larger foundations. In the case of Negro education the change in status and attitude appears to be a gradual growth, partly a normal outgrowth of regional development but also accelerated mostly through the influence of Negro colleges, Negro teachers trained in other regions, grants from private individuals and foundations for Negro education, and the Negro's own significant achievements. Among the evidences of changing attitudes and procedures are new situations in race

Number of Private Commercial and Business Schools Reporting to the United States Office of Education in 1928-1930

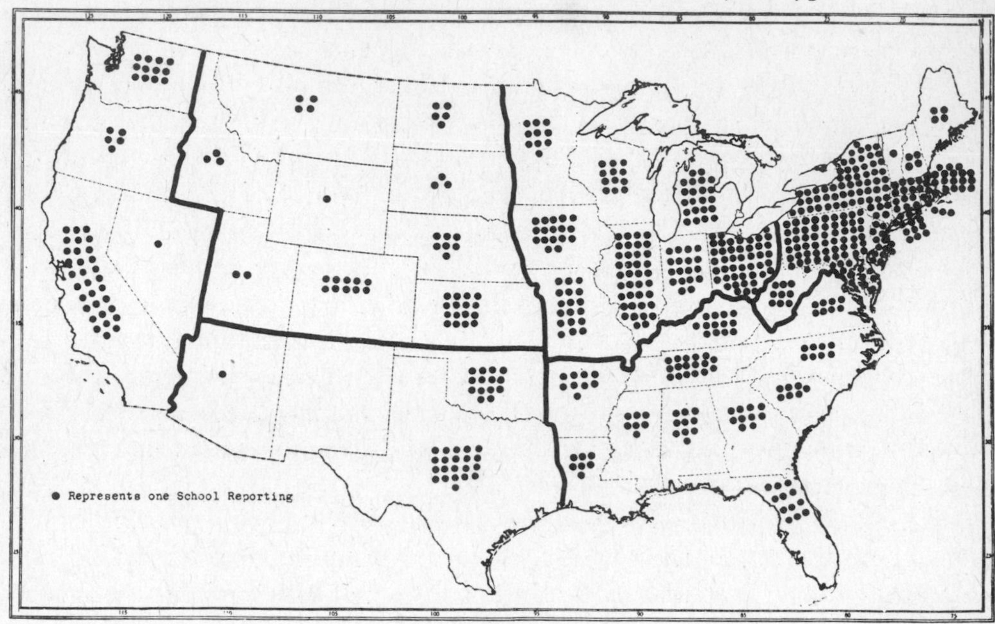

Number of Private High Schools and Academies in the United States Reporting Students Registered for Commerce and Business Courses in 1929-1930

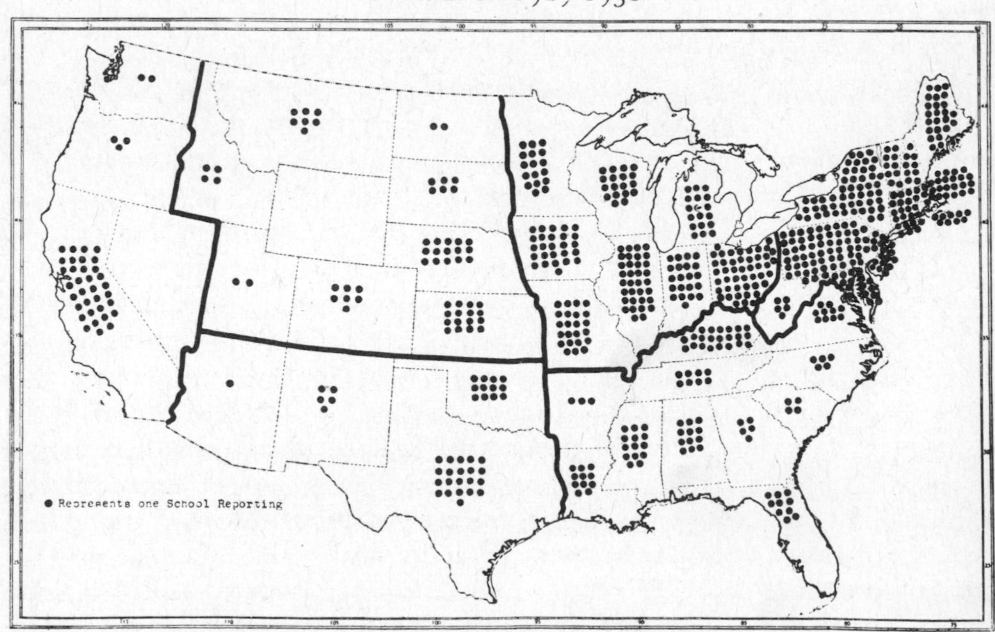

conferences and contacts, appreciation of the achievements of superior Negroes, greater respect for Negro personality, the rise of Negro college youth, the evolving of a new Negro culture. The land grant colleges, while for the most part standing afar off from the people, have made inroads into many of the old procedures in diet, home economics, farm management. Evidence of the forces involved may be seen in the figures for home and farm demonstration agents, faculty members, and in specific results in livestock farming. The national foundations have functioned broadly in the fields of higher education, public secondary education, Negro education, and in health and child welfare activities.

Perhaps in most of the general educational development in curricula, administration, buildings, and hygiene, the region has largely imitated the form and mechanics of the nation with little visible effect upon the regional culture. Something of routine imitation has been manifest in the over-emphasis upon illiteracy and in the weakness of adult education. It has been apparent in the over-emphasis upon wholesale consolidation and in the curriculum. The end results are probably as stated in spite of a very large number of educational ideologies, experiments, and "schools" which have marked the region's creative efforts, such as have been enumerated elsewhere. Perhaps most of the original proposals have assumed the form and ideology of ambitious plans, sectional schemes, or outlets for personal expression of leaders.

In colleges and universities, the influence of faculty members trained in eastern and western universities has been great, but for the most part these leaders have been conditioned to the southern culture more than they have contributed to fundamental modifications. This is one example of the dominance of the regional culture, and it has been especially apparent in race relations and attitudes. The strength and integrity of the southern culture have been more and more articulate as the ratio of southern men and women trained in other institutions and returning to major posts in southern colleges has increased to take the place of natives of other regions originally employed. This together with other factors, such as a certain revolt against industrialism, technology and cities; the romanticizing of the old southern culture; the experience of northern capitalists in southern industry; the attempt of northern idealists and reformers to coerce the region; the experience of the Negro in the North and West; and a certain revivification of sectional antagonisms have contributed to an apparent solidifying of the regional culture. The present visible ends of the entire election episode of 1928, with the subsequent magnanimous gestures and sympathy of President Hoover toward the region, appear to be a solidifying of the political democratic culture of the Southeast. So powerful is the "solid

Per Capita Total Receipts, Exclusive of Additions to Endowments, of Universities, Colleges, and Professional Schools, 1928

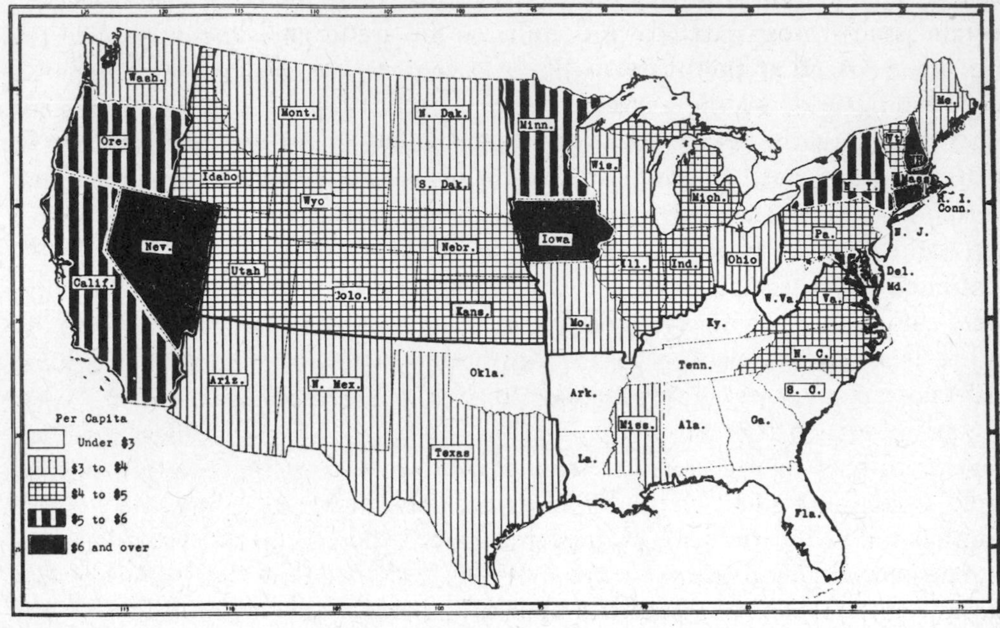

Per Capita Total Receipts, Exclusive of Additions to Endowments, Universities, Colleges and Professional Schools, 1928

STATE AND REGION	Rank	Total Receipts	Per Capita Receipts	STATE AND REGION	Rank	Total Receipts	Per Capita Receipts
Southeast				*Middle States*			
Virginia	12	$11,248	$4.68	Ohio	25	$25,323	$3.90
North Carolina	17	12,876	4.20	Indiana	16	13,517	4.24
South Carolina	36	5,388	3.12	Illinois	20	30,280	4.07
Georgia	42	7,877	2.71	Michigan	20	18,870	4.07
Florida	40	3,884	2.81	Wisconsin	24	11,422	3.96
Kentucky	44	5,701	2.21	Minnesota	7	14,650	5.78
Tennessee	39	7,688	2.99	Iowa	5	15,259	6.20
Alabama	47	5,080	1.95	Missouri	29	12,822	3.57
Mississippi	34	6,250	3.17				
Arkansas	48	2,412	1.31	*Northwest*			
Louisiana	43	4,707	2.30	North Dakota	31	2,305	3.41
				South Dakota	26	2,652	3.88
Southwest				Nebraska	22	5,501	4.03
Oklahoma	41	6,380	2.73	Kansas	18	7,807	4.19
Texas	38	16,918	3.01	Montana	36	1,684	3.12
New Mexico	28	1,482	3.59	Idaho	19	1,811	4.09
Arizona	35	1,323	3.16	Wyoming	14	968	4.40
				Colorado	13	4,657	4.57
Northeast				Utah	15	2,123	4.26
Maine	33	2,573	3.25				
New Hampshire	4	2,944	6.37	*Far West*			
Vermont	11	1,682	4.70	Nevada	3	680	7.64
Massachusetts	2	33,997	8.13	Washington	27	5,709	3.74
Rhode Island	32	2,197	3.26	Oregon	8	5,257	5.68
Connecticut	1	14,253	9.08	California	10	26,741	5.05
New York	9	64,616	5.29				
New Jersey	46	8,217	2.11				
Delaware	30	820	3.47				
Pennsylvania	23	38,106	4.02				
Maryland	6	9,361	5.85				
West Virginia	45	3,645	2.16				

South" and the Civil War republican tradition that the old order has continued unabated through the depression period, magnifying for the most part party and sectional acquisition over issues and men. In the case of certain issues the party culture dominates the traditional attitudes; in the case of AAA, the mob pattern of enforcement has often been evident.

Turning next to the several modes of institutional organization and achievement in the Southeast, perhaps relatively little more of the story of its education need be continued except to point up certain key situations. Certainly, there is no need to repeat the long catalogue of low rankings and deficiencies. Certainly, enough of these facts are available; their continued repetition may well be a smoke screen for realistic action. Of mere cataloguing of mechanical, self-evident indices we have had enough. What is needed, however, is to focus upon whatever elemental factors may appear as most fundamental to the understanding and direction of the region in its next period of development. One of these factors appears to be a relative retrogression of education in the region since those rapid gains of the first third of the present century. This relative loss of position which the region had appeared to be attaining with such difficulty is reflected in two principal ways. One is the fact that the Southeastern States registered greater penalties upon all phases of their education during the depression period than most of the other regions. Reductions and curtailments in institutions of higher learning and in public schools were greater; there were more articulate movements and attitudes advocating the turning of the clock backward. Here was illustration of the traditional "to him that hath not shall be taken even that which he hath," in that those states which had done least for education in the good years tended to take most from it in the lean years.

The other way in which the region appeared to accentuate its lag was in the decreasing influence and standing of its institutions and leaders in the national educational picture. Here are facts which, for the most part, the educational South appears not only unwilling to face but continues resentful of their presentation. It is not only that the region has no university of the first ranking, but it lacks college and university scholars and administrators of topmost distinction, measured by the usual standards of achievement and recognition. The statistics here, of course, measure status, not potential, and there are no data indicating what scholars or administrators might have done under different circumstances or had they been placed in equal competition. But the facts are incontrovertible that the region does not rank. Yet a wealth of evidence indicates that this region which needs such leadership more than the average region, not only for the development of its own incomparable physical and human resources, but for

Institutional Location of Women Who Are Pursuing Higher Education in the United States, 1930

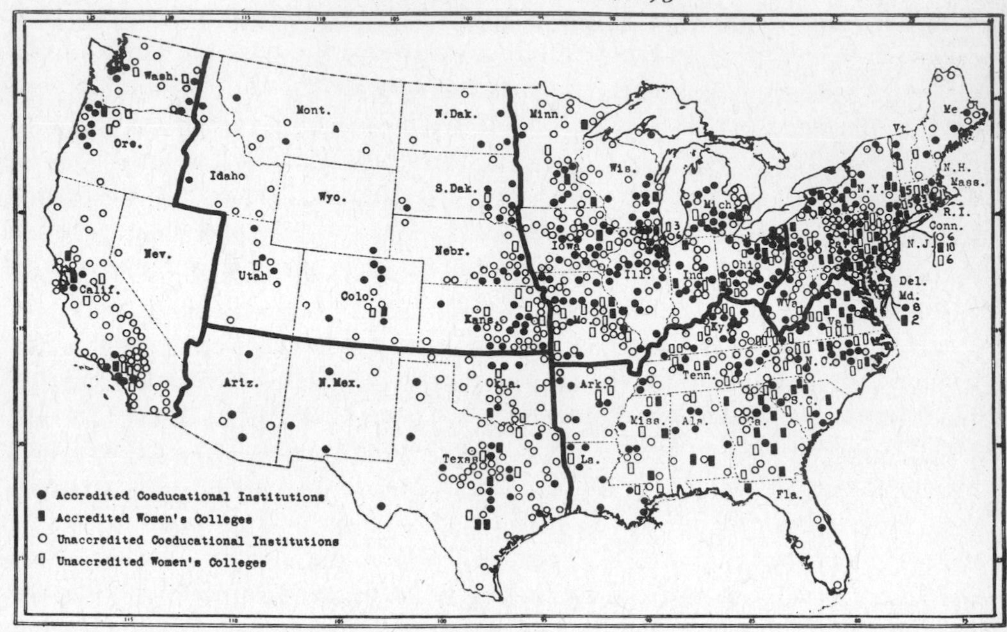

Students in Normal Schools and Teachers' Colleges Per 10,000 Population, 1930

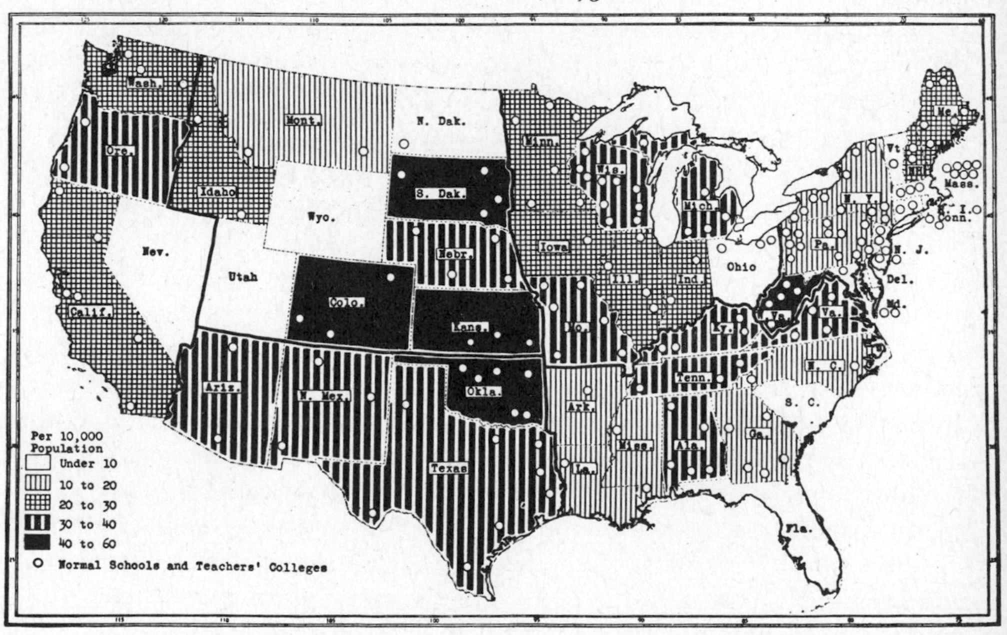

making its institutions articulate in the national culture and for obtaining a commensurate part in the nation's support, which it does not now have. There is one exception to this appraisal. The Southeast has gained in its Negro higher education and has in its institutions the best scholars and educational leaders of the race. Yet this is a result of the combined forces, on the one hand, of assistance from the outside, and, on the other, of the fact that colleges and universities of the East and West do not appoint Negro scholars on their faculties, and since they do not permit of separate institutions, the Negro scholar and teacher has nowhere else to go. In the meantime, the Negro is making an extraordinary contribution to the regional culture.

If one searches the field of education for forces that will modify, for instance, the region's personality-politics or its patterns of conflict, its mob tendencies, its homicide excesses, or its neglect of social science and the broader culture, the most promising prospect would apparently be the teachers and the teacher training institutions. Yet what do we find? A very large preponderance of former "normal" schools primarily for women whose chief emphasis was on the mechanics of curricula and methods with the added emphasis upon the superficial vocational training of women well mixed with sectional patriotism and loyalties. To expect the teacher thus trained to upraise standards and to modify a great traditional culture is to expect the impossible. So much for the women teachers. For the men teachers and administrators, for the most part, the region has gone to the opposite extreme of neglecting the teacher-training function and of sending out the great majority of its teachers from denominational colleges, nurtured and trained in the classical and patriotic-religious tradition of the South. It is pointed out, later, that there is here an extraordinarily fine record; in fact, one of the chief points of pride in most of the states. Yet it does not add stature to the teacher-training program. Moreover, there has been conflict between this body of teachers and those trained in the normal schools. And, furthermore, the regional promise of one or more great teacher-training universities of the South has tended toward sectional specialization and a strengthening of the old conservative regional culture. No great strength, liberalism, scholarship, or boldness has emerged from the great movement of which so much was expected. And how can teachers who have had no social science teach the principles needed? Or how can pupils be versed in sociology and economics through football coaches who must teach something in order to be placed upon the budget?

Again, the limitations of the natural sciences have been characteristic of education in the Southeast. Until very recently there was nowhere in the whole region a college or university science building or laboratory equal

Membership in the Association of American Universities, 1930

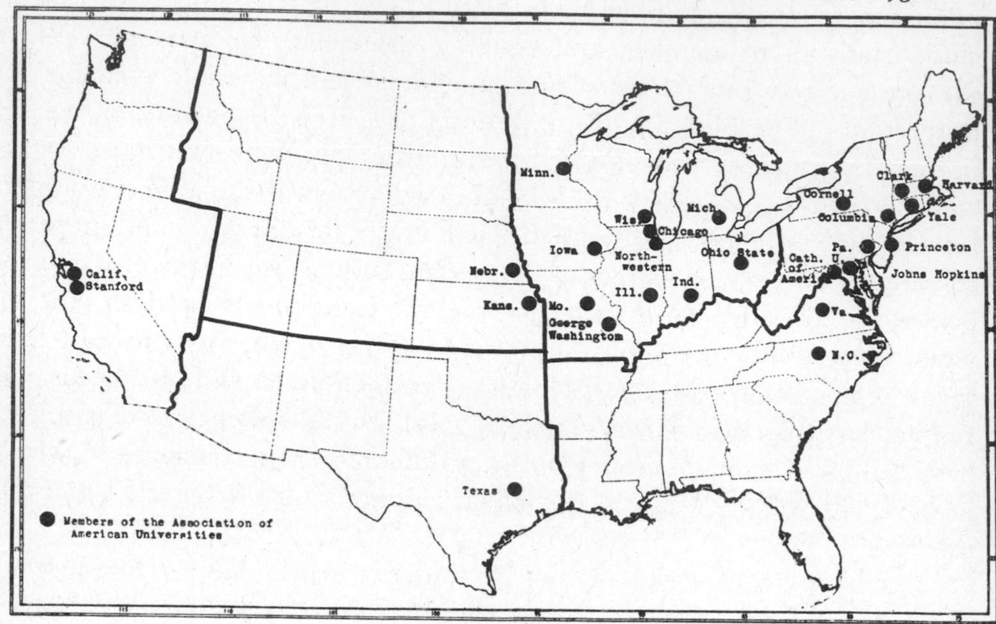

State Support for Agricultural Experiment Stations, 1932*

STATE AND REGION		STATE AND REGION	
Southeast	*$1,643,661.12*	*Middle States*	*$3,939,734.80*
Virginia	129,685.99	Ohio	1,162,788.18
North Carolina†	141,605.86	Indiana	657,694.98
South Carolina	131,467.80	Illinois	482,392.59
Georgia**	39,135.07	Michigan	350,694.93
Florida	360,497.66	Wisconsin	441,532.73
Kentucky	308,363.83	Minnesota	399,311.37
Tennessee	44,436.84	Iowa	301,695.80
Alabama	200,256.89	Missouri	143,624.22
Mississippi	34,401.42		
Arkansas	112,441.49	*Northwest*	*1,222,633.04*
Louisiana	141,368.27	North Dakota	211,641.55
		South Dakota	48,823.25
Southwest	*927,049.34*	Nebraska	214,075.26
Oklahoma	204,140.36	Kansas	217,958.02
Texas	557,663.81	Montana	133,025.82
New Mexico	51,350.41	Idaho	52,021.58
Arizona	113,894.76	Wyoming	85,889.85
		Colorado	163,712.14
Northeast	*3,314,135.32*	Utah	95,485.57
Maine	58,521.62		
New Hampshire	50,626.23	*Far West*	*1,670,771.52*
Vermont	24,011.87	Nevada	9,510.55
Massachusetts	277,943.28	Washington	126,560.63
Rhode Island	6,209.52	Oregon	241,616.80
Connecticut	321,072.85	California	1,293,083.54
New York	1,422,708.61		
New Jersey	721,277.66		
Delaware	37,148.87		
Pennsylvania	166,779.82		
Maryland	119,905.70		
West Virginia	107,929.29		

*Supplied by Office of Experiment Stations, U. S. Department of Agriculture.
†Including all expenditures of State Department of Agriculture and Experiment Station.
**Does not include work at the University of Georgia and two independent stations.

to many of the high school laboratories in the larger and better school systems of the country. Science was a disciplinary subject upon which certain minimum requirements must be fulfilled. The data in support of this include statistics of number and training of science faculties as well as the amount and kind of laboratory equipment and materials available for instruction. The high schools, it follows, are proportionally even weaker in their facilities and personnel. Strategically more important in the recent and forthcoming programs of regional development is the almost complete lack of major scientific and technical laboratories for discovery and invention relating to the great resources of the region, such as, for instance, was made possible by the support of Professor Herty's experiments on slash pine for paper pulp and its commercial production. Once again, the Southeast lacks great regional agricultural institutions commensurate with its needs and resources. Like the normal schools, most of the colleges of agriculture have followed a mechanical pattern of minimum requirements, in which, however, they have made extraordinary progress and achieved significant results.

Compared with those regions of America which have achieved most distinction in higher education, the Southeast reflects yet two other situations which call for special attention. The first of these is that it lacks a reasonable number of endowed institutions sufficiently free from state or church dominance to function independently in the best manner of university standards and sufficiently well endowed to set the pace for other regional universities and to keep interregional and national influences and participation constantly on the scene. This again is not the expression of opinion, but is simply a comparative picture of a region that has no Harvard or Yale or Chicago or Stanford as pacemakers or independent university influences of sufficient strength to maintain a continuous presumption for the best in science and education. The premise is, of course, one which assumes that these institutions in the other regions have, by measured fact, contributed largely to the standards, achievements, and status of university education in those regions and in the nation. The conclusion might be naturally drawn that one sure way to insure a continuing lower standard and status in the Southeast would be to continue the policy of having no great institutions in the region. The claim that the Southeast could or should set up its own pacemaking institutions is not in accord with historical developments in the other regions. Differing from the conditions in the Northeast, Middle States, and Far West, the Southeast has its powerful handicap of imbalance of trade and wealth which goes to enrich these other regions. Yet none of these considerations alter the reality of the situation,

PERCENTAGE OF WEALTH INVESTED IN PUBLIC SCHOOL PROPERTY, 1928

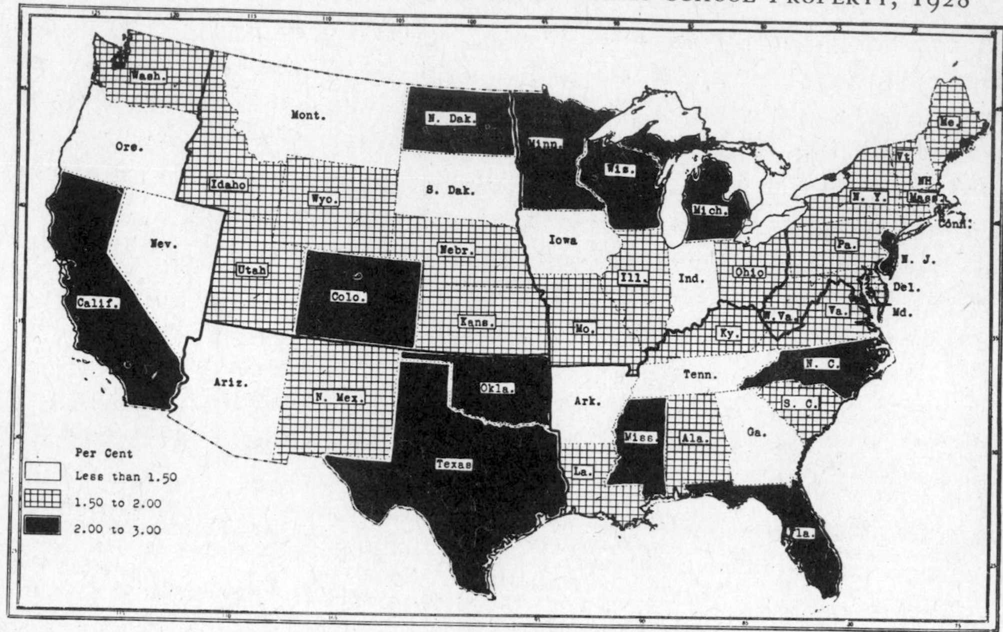

VALUE OF SCHOOL PROPERTY PER PUPIL ENROLLED, 1927-1928

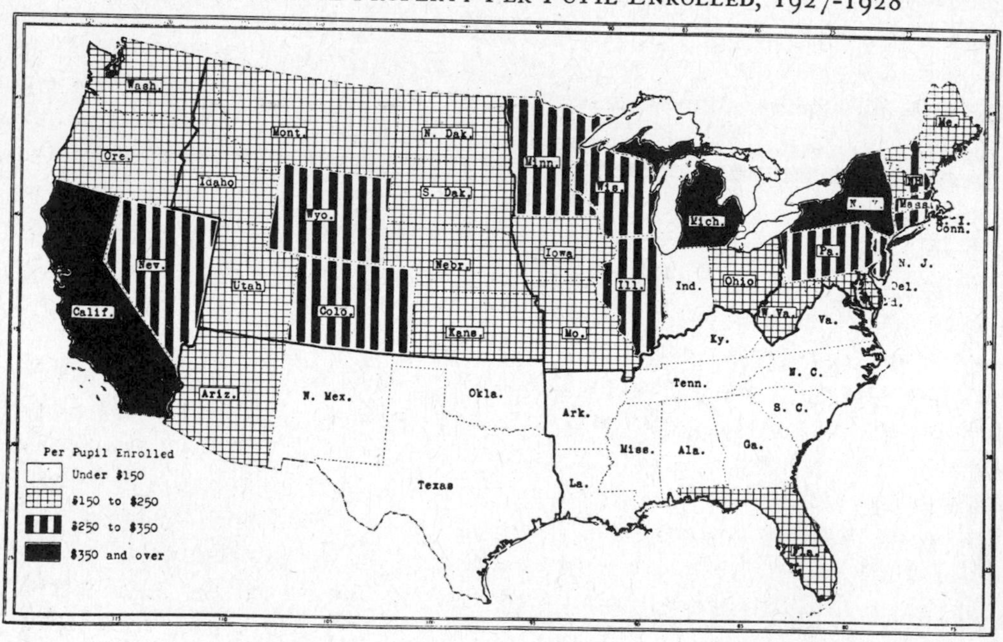

namely, that the Southeast has no institutions sufficiently endowed to lead the way.

A common response to the urge of the Southeast that it have a few strong universities comparable to the best in other regions is in substance about as follows: the Southeast is neither capable of nor deserving of such universities nor would the region support them either in funds or cultural constituency if it had them. Furthermore, instead of becoming national universities they would become sectional universities concentrating upon the regional culture, drawing a larger proportion of the students who now go into other universities. The present enrollment of southern students in northern, eastern, and western universities is perhaps the chief interregional cultural contact and should not be disturbed. Furthermore, it has not seemed possible to reach satisfactory agreements upon the universities to be endowed and the method of endowing them. In addition to this, some of the experiments in endowments and grants have not been convincing as to the feasibility of focusing upon large endowments. The alternative proposal has been that in both Federal equalization funds and in Foundation assistance the functional approach is the only feasible one. That is, there must be broad equalization of opportunity in science, in rural education, in higher education, in agriculture, to the end that the best results may be distributed most equitably.

The answer to this realistic situation and to these logical arguments is equally realistic. If the nation and the region, after appraising the extraordinary facts pointing to the abundance of natural, cultural, and human resources, still continues in the matured judgment that the region should not and cannot have its first class universities, then by all inductions and additions the region must remain continuously deficient. Such a final conclusion must reflect upon the national program and capacity as it must reflect upon the region. It must inevitably result in continued sectionalism and drain upon the national unity and resources. From any viewpoint of adequate culture and effective democracy the position is untenable. It is a record of defeatism. The more realistic and difficult the situation is, the more it reflects the necessity for working out an increasingly effective program of regional equilibrium, of balance, and of enrichment of culture. Equalization funds and supplementary endowments will still be needed as they are projected on the functional framework of statesmanlike programs.

Moreover, when it is suggested that the region have first class, privately endowed institutions, comparable to Stanford, Princeton, Chicago, and others, two assumptions are inherent. One is that the institutions will be in reality first class and national universities, taking advantage of the many regional opportunities and equipping themselves with facilities and person-

Total Collegiate Students Per 100,000 Population, 1928

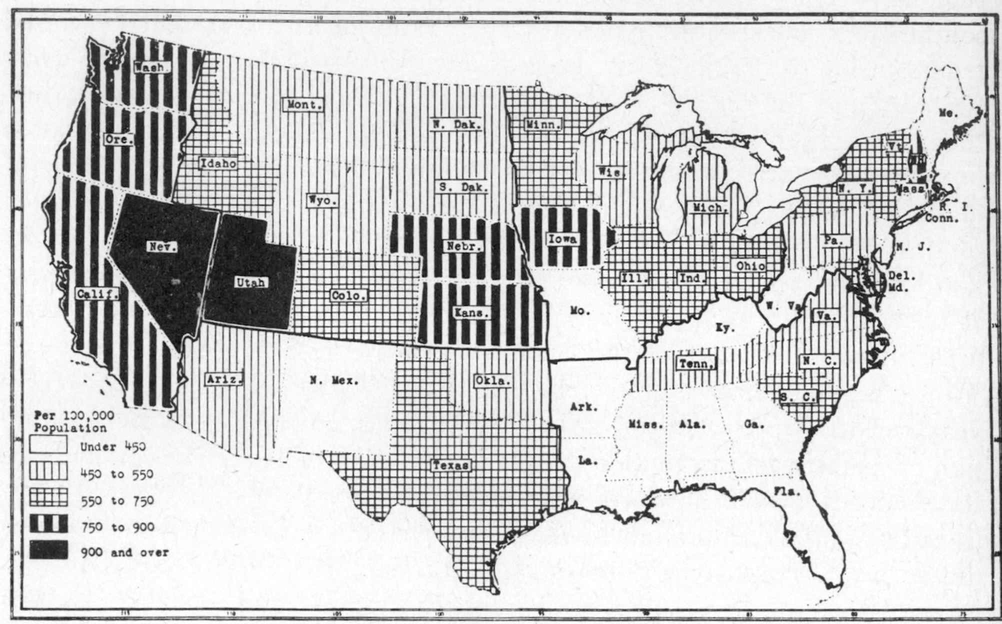

Distribution of Leaders in Education

Adapted from *School and Society*, December 3, 1932

STATE AND REGION	Number Born in	Number Now in	Per Cent of Number Born in Now Living in
Southeast	*1,434*	*1,358*	*94.7*
Virginia	277	216	77.9
North Carolina	180	207	115.0
South Carolina	134	95	70.9
Georgia	119	127	106.7
Florida	21	66	314.3
Kentucky	198	144	72.7
Tennessee	166	168	101.2
Alabama	122	120	98.4
Mississippi	87	54	62.1
Arkansas	78	80	102.6
Louisiana	52	81	155.8
Southwest	*202*	*502*	*248.5*
Oklahoma	16	123	768.7
Texas	174	291	167.2
New Mexico	6	36	600.0
Arizona	6	52	866.7
Northeast	*3,629*	*4,063*	*112.0*
Maine	201	85	42.3
New Hampshire	107	91	85.0
Vermont	117	48	41.0
Massachusetts	683	753	110.2
Rhode Island	70	79	112.9
Connecticut	170	291	171.2
New York	978	1,340	137.0
New Jersey	165	295	178.8
Delaware	24	25	104.2
Pennsylvania	811	776	95.7
Maryland	187	178	95.2
West Virginia	116	102	87.9
Middle States	*3,986*	*3,118*	*78.2*
Ohio	851	645	75.8
Indiana	584	268	45.9
Illinois	732	760	103.8
Michigan	368	355	96.5
Wisconsin	343	295	86.0
Minnesota	202	256	126.7
Iowa	491	237	48.3
Missouri	415	302	72.8
Northwest	*657*	*765*	*116.4*
North Dakota	28	70	250.0
South Dakota	42	77	183.3
Nebraska	171	138	80.7
Kansas	274	199	72.6
Montana	12	49	408.3
Idaho	10	35	350.0
Wyoming	11	32	290.9
Colorado	50	114	228.0
Utah	59	51	86.4
Far West	*210*	*887*	*424.4*
Nevada	3	16	533.3
Washington	27	130	481.5
Oregon	42	90	214.3
California	138	651	471.7

nel such that their enrollment would be to a considerable extent interregional. The statistics of the last ten years, which show that the leading southeastern universities have a larger ratio of their students enrolled from outside the region than those of any other region, indicates the practicability and the reality of such a premise. The assumptions provide further, as has been set forth in various memoranda, that one basic foundation in such universities would be provision for interregional exchange of students and faculty as an essential part of the university system. In addition to this, the assumption is that these universities would tend to have the same effect in the southern region as in other regions, namely, to accelerate at once, through example and competition, and in very appreciable measures, the development of standards and support in the state universities. Thus, the immediate logical goal would be, within the suggested twelve-year period of projected program, a probable membership in the Association of American Universities of at least five universities for whites and one for Negroes, in which, however, a special development would provide for inter-institutional education of Negroes in three or four of these regional universities. Based on the findings of the Southern Regional Study, with its picturization of resources, deficiencies, trends, and possibilities, this program represents a bold, but minimum and attainable end.

The other key situation which appears from the evidence is that of educational administration. As in the case of government and much of its business the greatest need of the region often appears to be that of administrative leadership. The region has no educational administrative leaders who participate freely in the nation's councils of learning or who have access to its larger sources of endowment and support. Manifestly, this conclusion is susceptible to objective measurement. Manifestly, too, without such administrative leadership it seems self-evident that adequate endowment, standards, and leadership may not be attained. This deficiency, however, appears as a product of the larger patterns of political, religious, and regional culture and of the lack of training and experience in administration. It is further a reflection of recent years in which there has been no apparent realistic and statesmanlike effort on the part of the nation or its leaders toward a comprehensive plan of educational equalization technique which would involve, besides funds, interregional exchange, conference, planning. Among other values such procedures would afford a broader motivation for regional achievement and a larger acquaintance with national and interregional personnel and movements.

One of the points of immaturity of many of the national programs is found in the failure to "balance" values, resources, opportunities in the region with those in other regions. When the accrediting agency or the

State Support of Colleges and Universities for Maintenance, 1927-1928

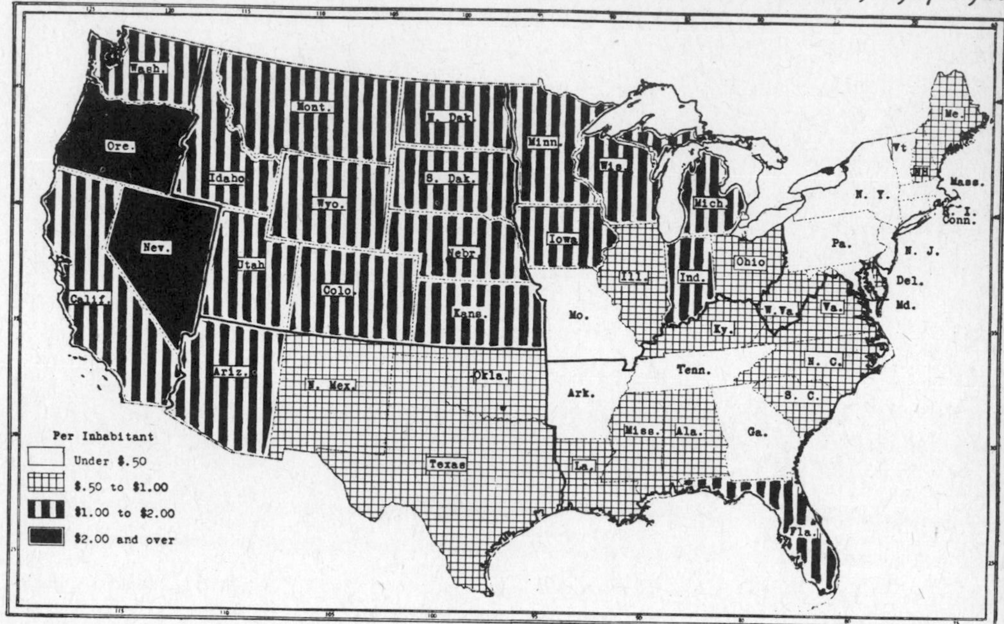

Percentage Distribution of Total Taxes and Appropriations Applied to Education Among Various Types of Educational Institutions, 1929-30, by States and Regions

STATE AND REGION	Elementary and Secondary Education	Teachers Colleges and Normal Schools	Universities Colleges and Professional Schools
Southeast	*90.3*	*2.0*	*7.7*
Virginia	90.5	2.1	7.4
North Carolina	93.2	1.0	5.8
South Carolina	87.0	.7	12.3
Georgia	90.1	1.7	8.2
Florida	90.8	0.0	9.2
Kentucky	87.7	5.6	6.7
Tennessee	91.0	3.3	5.7
Alabama	88.3	2.6	9.1
Mississippi	92.2	1.6	6.2
Arkansas	87.7	1.5	10.8
Louisiana	91.6	1.7	6.7
Southwest	*88.5*	*3.3*	*8.2*
Oklahoma	86.5	4.0	9.5
Texas	89.4	2.9	7.7
New Mexico	88.7	3.4	7.9
Arizona	89.2	3.4	7.4
Northeast	*97.0*	*1.3*	*1.7*
Maine	91.5	2.1	6.4
New Hampshire	91.9	2.4	5.7
Vermont	95.2	1.0	3.8
Massachusetts	97.2	1.4	1.4
Rhode Island	97.2	1.1	1.7
Connecticut	97.0	1.7	1.3
New York	97.5	.7	1.8
New Jersey	98.7	1.2	.1
Delaware	95.6	0.0	4.4
Pennsylvania	96.7	2.3	1.0
Maryland	95.0	1.8	3.2
West Virginia	91.1	2.8	6.1
Middle States	*91.8*	*1.8*	*6.4*
Ohio	94.3	0.6	5.1
Indiana	94.3	0.9	4.8
Illinois	91.7	2.0	6.3
Michigan	90.6	2.5	6.9
Wisconsin	88.0	4.1	7.9
Minnesota	88.3	1.7	10.0
Iowa	89.7	1.2	9.1
Missouri	93.2	2.8	4.0
Northwest	*89.5*	*2.5*	*8.0*
North Dakota	85.5	3.9	10.6
South Dakota	90.9	2.8	6.3
Nebraska	88.7	3.1	8.2
Kansas	89.5	2.3	8.2
Montana	91.8	1.6	6.6
Idaho	88.5	4.3	7.2
Wyoming	95.3	0.0	4.7
Colorado	88.5	2.5	9.0
Utah	92.3	0.0	7.7
Far West	*90.3*	*1.6*	*8.1*
Nevada	88.9	0.0	11.1
Washington	87.5	2.5	10.0
Oregon	83.6	1.6	14.8
California	92.2	1.4	6.4
United States	93.1	1.8	5.1

endowment advisers insist that standards of achievement must be equal they are, of course, following the only reasonable procedure. What they have generally not sought, however, is a fair equilibrium between the ends sought and the available means to those ends. Here, for instance, are some handicaps of the professor or administrator in all institutions of the Southeast where he is required to carry heavier teaching and administrative loads; to function through many local and state committees; to function in a conditioning environment where standards are not known or understood; to fight against inertia and antagonisms; to combat racial and religious conflicts; to stand for or against his own people in the midst of violent outside criticisms; to have less money, less intellectual contact and companionship; and to have fewer pacemaking institutions or leaders to give him leverage to lift and carry his load. And back of all this he has had less training and experience upon which to build his structure of scholarship or administration. It is, of course, an impossible basis upon which to plot comparable standards and achievements.

Some of the notable features of southern education which have reflected distinctive quality and culture character and have motivated the region are the extraordinary amount and quality of work and achievement done under these circumstances. This has been reflected especially in the output of graduate students for other institutions, South and North, of educational and religious leaders of the smaller colleges; and in the educational ideology of southern culture. The denominational colleges in particular, for both men and women, are examples. The denominational colleges for women have been particularly articulate in preserving and developing the southern culture. Because of the multiplicity of smaller colleges and their significant part in the past, because of diminishing financial support, and of the changing trend toward state education, the problem of standards and consolidation appears to be an imminent one. In the process of strengthening weaker centers, of consolidating institutions, and of seeking the most effective regional balance of colleges and universities, the Southeast may well consider the premise for one or more well supported municipal universities. And in the process of redistribution the old premise of women's education as distinctive from men, both in its conservative old southern view and in the later opposite extreme of vocational training, appears to be untenable. Some of the older order is being affected by the trend toward coeducation, some by the growing popularity of the state universities, and some by the influx of students from other regions of the nation.

In all summaries of data on education, the economic factor, of course, looms large and is usually reflected in indices of deficiency. Yet it does not appear that this situation can be remedied until two other factors, even

State Controlled Institutions

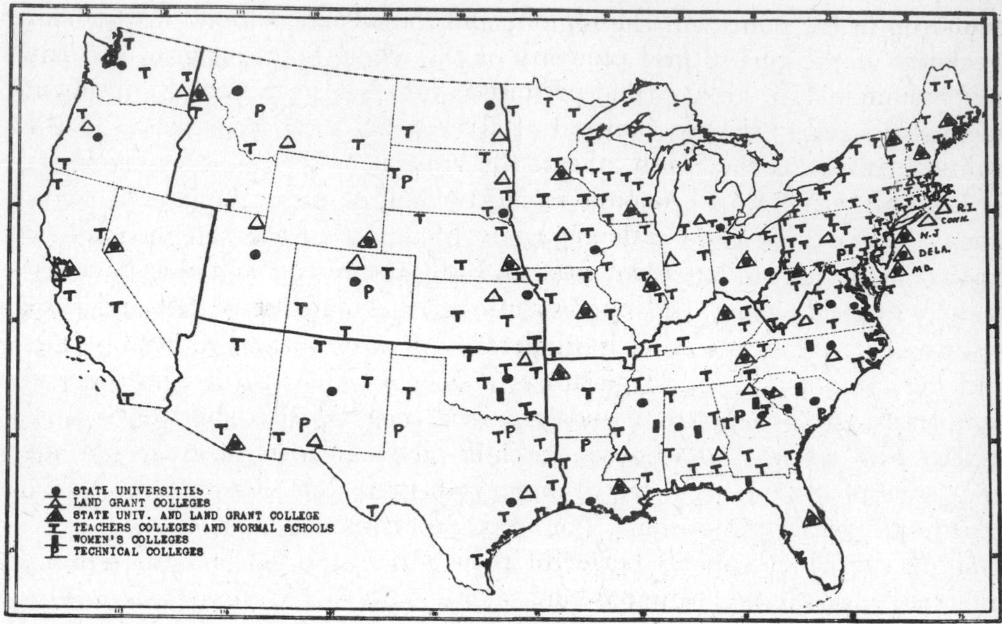

Institutions of Higher Learning in the United States, 1934

Adapted from *School and Society*, Volume 40, Number 1042

STATE AND REGION	Universities Colleges and Professional Schools		Teachers Colleges and Normal Schools	
	Public	Private	Public	Private
Southeast	*50*	*194*	*39*	*7*
Virginia	5	25	7	1
North Carolina	5	30	5	1
South Carolina	6	15	1	1
Georgia	8	25	6	1
Florida	3	5	0	0
Kentucky	2	26	6	0
Tennessee	2	28	5	2
Alabama	3	9	7	1
Mississippi	5	14	3	0
Arkansas	7	11	2	0
Louisiana	4	6	3	0
Southwest	*42*	*61*	*19*	*0*
Oklahoma	12	9	7	0
Texas	24	51	8	0
New Mexico	4	0	2	0
Arizona	2	1	2	0
Northeast	*21*	*218*	*81*	*25*
Maine	1	4	7	0
New Hampshire	1	2	3	0
Vermont	1	3	1	0
Massachusetts	2	31	11	7
Rhode Island	1	3	1	0
Connecticut	2	8	5	4
New York	4	57	16	8
Pennsylvania	1	63	17	3
New Jersey	1	14	6	2
Delaware	1	0	0	0
Maryland	2	15	5	0
Dist. of Columbia	1	9	2	1
West Virginia	4	9	7	0

STATE AND REGION	Universities Colleges and Professional Schools		Teachers Colleges and Normal Schools	
	Public	Private	Public	Private
Middle States	*58*	*239*	*92*	*15*
Ohio	6	47	5	2
Indiana	2	23	2	3
Illinois	5	53	7	6
Michigan	12	16	34	0
Wisconsin	1	13	28	0
Minnesota	7	21	6	2
Iowa	16	26	1	1
Missouri	9	40	9	1
Northwest	*34*	*65*	*23*	*56*
North Dakota	4	1	5	0
South Dakota	3	7	4	1
Nebraska	2	16	4	2
Kansas	12	23	3	0
Montana	3	2	2	0
Idaho	1	4	2	0
Wyoming	1	0	0	0
Colorado	6	7	3	1
Utah	2	5	0	1
Far West	*40*	*55*	*13*	*6*
Washington	5	9	3	2
Oregon	2	10	3	2
California	32	36	7	2
Nevada	1	0	0	0

more basic than education, have been mastered. The first of these is bound up in the politics of the region; and the second is found in the basic weakness of the agricultural economy of the whole South, cotton economy and mountain folk alike. The premise is here set forth that government and politics reflect the most critical of all regional social problems. In the political culture of the South inheres the limitations of educational support, of law enforcement, of economic reconstruction, of race relations, of traditional one-party control, of demagogic exploitation of the poor people—in fine, the politics of the recent past and of the present stands as a closed door to any reasonably full opportunity for the southern people and their institutions. The conclusion is supported by the statistics of state politics and state leaders, of state legislatures and appropriations, of elections and campaigns, and of legislation and leadership in high places and low. It is reflected in jails and almshouses, in child labor and the courts, in old age and unemployment security, in organization for public welfare, public health and public education. The very problems and policies of population are subject to this all powerful political culture which is inextricably interrelated with the religious and moral culture of the people. This political supremacy is found in county and local politics, in state and national politics, and in the regional demagogic exhibition which is always in some part of the South, before the public, reflecting the weakest chain in the whole southern culture as failure in government and law and public welfare.

The folkways of southern politics may be set up as perhaps the most powerful of all the culture rationalizations which serve to satisfy the people and "solve" their problems, being reinforced by the religious sanctions of protestantism, racial supremacy, and "anti-northern" righteousness. Republicans and yankees and northern city folks are meddlers and corrupters of the South. They afford demagogic thunder for the orator. "Northern brethren trying to purge our brains of ignorance and our stomach of worms." John Machlachlan has satirized the great party thusly: "democracy is something born only into the pure Anglo-Saxon. In his rugged veins, especially if a more rugged southern skin cover them, flows the essence of enlightened citizenship. . . . And so we have the Great Party. But if democracy is something born into us it must have come from God. And if the party comes from God—and everything does, of course, except what comes from the devil to the opposition—then we must be thankful unto Him. And our faith in the Great Godgiven Party must never waver. This is the weapon He gave us, and we must use it as He must have meant, against every alien and ugly kind of politics and for the sacred ways of our life. This brings us to something else. If the party is God-given, and politics is the business of the people, and if

Regional Variations in Indices of Religious Activity, 1926

INDEX	South east	South-west	North-east	Middle States	North-west	Far West	Continental United States
Debt load of churches, percent of total value of edifices	9.9	13.0	11.2	11.4	10.1	15.8	11.3
Value of church edifices per $1,000 land value	$ 34.37	$ 24.84	$ 31.20	$ 25.15	$ 13.56	$ 17.22	$ 27.02
Value of church edifices per adult member	$ 58.05	$ 50.87	$ 97.35	$ 90.95	$ 72.79	$ 84.36	$ 86.63
Average value of parsonages	$4,494.00	$2,977.00	$9,107.00	$6,037.00	$3,918.00	$4,963.00	$6,175.00
Average expenditures per church per year	$1,749.00	$2,099.00	$6,621.00	$4,419.00	$2,586.00	$4,084.00	$3,783.00
Total church expenditures per $1,000 income	$ 16.02	$ 10.48	$ 10.68	$ 9.48	$ 9.68	$ 7.3[illegible]	$ 10.50
Circulation of church periodicals per 1,000 population	8.1	2.7	12.7	10.9	2.8	2.4	9.2
Number of churches per 10,000 population	34.6	26.8	12.7	17.3	24.2	12.4	20.3
Average number of Sunday school scholars per church	84.0	85.0	134.0	126.0	107.0	117.0	114.0
Average number of members per church	137.0	179.0	418.0	265.0	196.0	193.0	235.0
Adult population, number	16,016,606	5,589,007	25,905,747	23,327,599	5,018,299	5,392,201	*81,249,459*
Adult population, percent of total	19.7	6.9	31.9	28.7	6.2	6.6	*100.0*
Adult church membership, number	9,832,357	2,699,399	15,584,803	11,850,515	2,380,526	1,769,504	*44,117,104*
Adult church membership, percent of total	22.3	6.1	35.3	26.9	5.4	4.0	*100.0*
Adult protestant church membership, number	8,995,297	2,035,848	5,823,786	7,193,637	1,929,509	907,646	*26,885,723*
Adult protestant church membership, percent of total	33.4	7.6	21.7	26.7	7.2	3.4	*100.0*
Percent of adult population in church	61.4	48.3	60.2	50.8	47.4	32.8	54.3
Percent of churches whose pastors serve one church	40.1	52.6	58.1	56.7	53.5	68.0	50.2
Percent of churches whose pastors serve two churches	22.1	18.5	19.7	21.8	23.2	15.7	21.1
Percent of churches whose pastors serve three churches	14.5	11.4	9.9	11.9	10.8	6.7	12.2
Percent of churches whose pastors serve four churches	10.5	7.1	5.9	5.8	5.3	4.1	7.8
Percent of churches whose pastors serve five churches	6.2	3.9	2.7	2.4	2.7	2.1	4.1
Percent of churches whose pastors serve six or more churches	6.6	6.5	3.7	1.4	4.5	3.4	4.6

Baptists and Methodists in Total Adult Population, 1926

STATE AND REGION	Combined White and Negro Baptists	Combined White and Negro Methodists	Per Cent Total Adult Population Baptist	Per Cent Total Adult Population Methodist	Per Cent Total Adult Population Baptist and Methodist
Southeast					
Virginia	496,371	243,702	31.10	15.27	46.37
North Carolina	549,992	360,628	30.25	19.83	50.08
South Carolina	415,530	207,851	38.54	19.27	57.81
Georgia	731,886	320,058	38.27	16.73	55.00
Florida	184,147	124,944	21.34	14.48	35.82
Kentucky	372,800	131,810	21.91	7.74	29.65
Tennessee	386,571	224,019	23.05	13.36	36.41
Alabama	579,250	291,893	35.67	17.97	53.64
Mississippi	413,123	175,637	33.13	14.08	47.21
Arkansas	219,280	155,737	18.46	13.11	31.57
Louisiana	228,897	72,766	17.40	5.53	22.93
Southwest					
Oklahoma	163,291	81,906	9.90	5.54	15.44
Texas	633,622	385,674	16.08	10.73	26.81
New Mexico	9,265	8,011	3.27	3.13	6.40
Arizona	1,841	5,266	.69	1.99	2.68

Baptists and Methodists in Adult Negro Population, 1926

STATE AND REGION	Total Adult Negro Methodists: A.M.E., C.M.E., and A.M.E.Z.	Per Cent Methodists in Total Adult Negro Population	Per Cent Baptists in Total Adult Negro Population	Combined Per Cent of Methodists and Baptists in Total Adult Negro Population
Southeast				
Virginia	30,788	6.96	65.45	72.4
North Carolina	138,445	26.11	35.83	61.9
South Carolina	89,334	17.53	41.85	59.4
Georgia	101,203	13.87	47.32	61.2
Florida	59,580	21.52	32.14	53.7
Kentucky	22,976	15.21	51.71	66.9
Tennessee	54,423	17.62	42.20	59.8
Alabama	118,911	20.02	54.57	74.6
Mississippi	58,167	9.11	33.84	43.0
Arkansas	44,903	14.48	42.22	56.7
Louisiana	23,082	4.66	24.51	29.2
Southwest				
Oklahoma	15,807	14.70	39.94	54.6
Texas	52,539	9.55	38.37	47.9
New Mexico	50	1.98	15.34	17.3
Arizona	590	9.09	10.03	19.1

our kind of politics is Anglo-Saxon, why, then, why hasn't the church absolutely got to protect its own from infidels, rascals, and nigger-lovers?"

This regional politics as a culture may be tested out in relation to the second of the two situations to which we have ascribed more power than education, namely, the basic factors in the elementary agricultural economy of the Southeast. From the millions of small farmers come the support of the politician; in his poverty, ignorance, and exploitation may be found much of the basis for the demagogic power in the region. Here is fertile soil for anything. On the other hand, the old order of plantation democracy which prevents the reconstruction of the economics of the region multiplies opportunities for political demagoguery at the same time that it holds back the prosperity of the small farmer who cannot support the institutions of culture even if he were not misguided by the politicians of the lower order. Evidence of this is abundant in the biographies of the South's politicians, in the catalogue of its legislators and officials, in the measured appropriations for education, and in the discriminations against the Negro. Practical phases of this problem are presented in connection with the discussions of regional planning—the implications of which are that the Southeast cannot be capable of educational and cultural development until it has reconstructed its bottom level of agrarian culture and its top level of educational and scientific leadership, neither one of which, however, can move without the other.

Turning next to religious culture, there is again perhaps need for little further appraisal than has already been given it in pages 141 to 149 and in the statistical tables that are available. The evidence indicates a greater change going on in the church's membership and influence than is found in politics, education, and in general cultural attitudes. It still remains, however, that the region reflects a greater influence of the church than other regions; a greater place for religion in the ideology of the people; a greater influence of ministers; a greater protestantism, especially of Baptists and Methodists; a greater influence in education and politics and race. From the viewpoint of regional analysis and planning, however, the church and religion assume more nearly the rôle of natural cultural evolution, the modifications of which are brought about indirectly through the incidence of other agencies and influences. The church has done little with reference to the tenant and the laborer in the way of programs; the tenant and the laborer have played a small part in the life of the church whose fortunes will fluctuate with the prevailing culture of the region. With all its mighty influence the power of the church has been in its ideologies and conditioning attitudes and not in its program.

One significant measure of changing culture may be found in the recent

Net Paid Daily Circulation Newspapers Per 1,000 Inhabitants, 1930

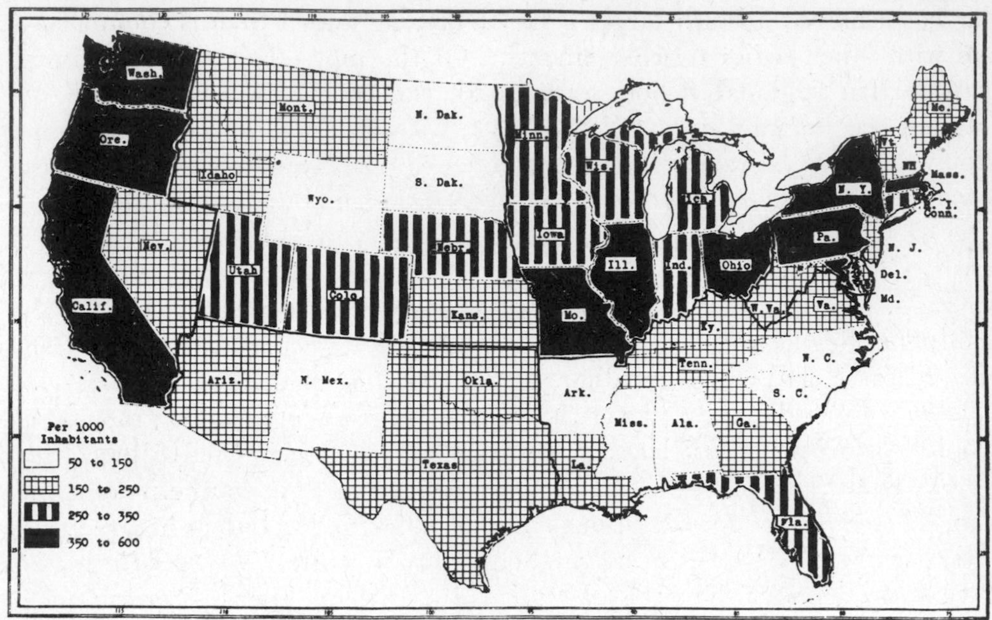

Inhabitants Per Newspaper and Magazine

STATE	Inhabitants Per Newspaper and Magazine			
	Daily Newspapers 1925	Literary Magazine 1924	Women's Magazine 1924	47 Leading Magazines 1924
Southeast				
Virginia	7.68	49.21	13.49	6.52
North Carolina	9.74	72.19	18.06	8.77
South Carolina	12.44	67.28	22.83	10.81
Georgia	8.43	98.12	21.64	10.28
Florida	4.82	30.71	7.97	3.43
Kentucky	6.63	68.85	14.41	7.68
Tennessee	5.05	70.23	15.88	7.89
Alabama	9.12	74.20	22.01	10.76
Mississippi	18.11	107.75	24.89	12.49
Arkansas	12.29	88.05	18.01	9.07
Louisiana	6.71	58.73	18.44	7.94
Southwest				
Oklahoma	5.56	57.38	11.17	5.58
Texas	5.32	54.29	11.80	5.82
New Mexico	14.30	31.14	14.32	6.18
Arizona	5.19	31.69	9.93	3.95
Northwest				
Maine	4.96	26.69	6.39	3.31
New Hampshire	7.35	24.23	5.46	2.96
Vermont	6.13	28.35	5.94	3.14
Massachusetts	1.77	24.86	6.38	3.02
Rhode Island	2.91	31.09	7.60	3.70
Connecticut	3.30	24.85	6.35	3.07
New York	1.79	31.87	7.97	3.51
New Jersey	4.70	29.94	7.21	3.54
Delaware	4.99	35.77	8.18	4.16
Pennsylvania	2.78	33.48	7.85	3.87
Maryland	2.73	36.95	9.64	4.65
West Virginia	7.00	48.96	9.86	5.08
Middle States				
Ohio	2.42	28.15	6.26	3.09
Indiana	3.16	34.05	7.08	3.70
Illinois	2.43	35.23	7.78	3.61
Michigan	3.04	30.66	6.31	3.07
Wisconsin	4.47	34.27	8.03	4.03
Minnesota	3.45	32.87	7.23	3.60
Iowa	3.77	34.17	6.19	3.32
Missouri	2.05	44.46	8.21	4.20
Northeast				
North Dakota	11.92	56.01	9.05	4.80
South Dakota	7.37	46.76	7.81	3.94
Nebraska	3.35	34.00	6.53	3.45
Kansas	4.88	39.98	7.41	4.01
Montana	5.91	31.12	7.40	3.37
Idaho	8.01	30.05	8.20	3.65
Wyoming	7.54	22.31	5.69	2.42
Colorado	3.06	22.65	6.52	2.92
Utah	4.22	30.65	9.65	4.03
Far West				
Nevada	5.52	20.98	6.83	2.79
Washington	2.59	20.16	5.37	2.40
Oregon	2.23	20.33	4.67	2.17
California	1.68	14.30	4.60	1.84
United States	3.20	35.09	8.31	3.97

literature of the region, which has reflected great vitality. Fiction in particular has achieved a much larger ratio of literary award than is commensurate with other regional achievements. Of the more than 1,000 volumes of American regional fiction since 1920, the most distinctive group of volumes was portraiture of the Southeast, with the most distinguished contributions from southern authors. The comparison of regions shows: *Northeastern Region,* no less than 257 books classified under the interesting titles of frontier and pioneer, farm life, mountain life, city life, New York artists, Greenwich Village, New York theatrical and night club life, New England town life, Northeastern States town life, industrial life, the immigrant, the Negro, religious groups, college and university life, Cape Cod life, seacoast and fishing villages, Pennsylvania Dutch. *Southeastern Region:* 186, under the titles of the Negro, Negro-white conflict, mountain people, town life, industrial scene—the people and their life, college life, the Old South, the New South, southern aristocracy, the southern common man. *The Southwestern Region:* 47, under the titles of Indian life, pioneer days, life in the Southwest, race relations, industrial life. *The Middle States Region:* 122, under the titles of Indian life, the mountains, Ozarks, rural life, town life, city life, industrial life, college life, religious groups, family-life—conflict of generations. *Northwestern Region:* 73, under the titles of Indian life, pioneer days, the farms, ranches, town and city life, industrial life, the Negro and the immigrant. *Far West Region:* 107, under the titles of Indian life, pioneer days, mountain life, rural life, industrial life, college life, family life and romance, Reno, Hollywood.

The significance of the new realism in the Southeast is found partly in the cordial reception which much of this literature received in the South, as well as through awards—the Pulitzer prizes, the Book-of-the-Month and Literary Guild selections, and in the front page reviews in *The Saturday Review of Literature* and the literary supplements of the *New York Times* and *Herald Tribune.* While something of the old romanticism was revived, the mode was predominantly that of a realistic and critical review of the life and times of the southern people. This is indicated in the classification of the principal values into some six or eight groups as already listed, with a substantial representation in each group. The majority of authors, however, receiving their support from publishers outside the region and themselves residing elsewhere, constitute a sort of independent, interregional influence in the modifying of the older culture. To this body of native literature was added also many volumes representing the work of authors who utilized the southern scene for their medium of regional criticism and characterization. But in all this new literature there was vitality and promise; an ever increasing evidence of regional ma-

Distribution by States of Dramatic Activities in the United States

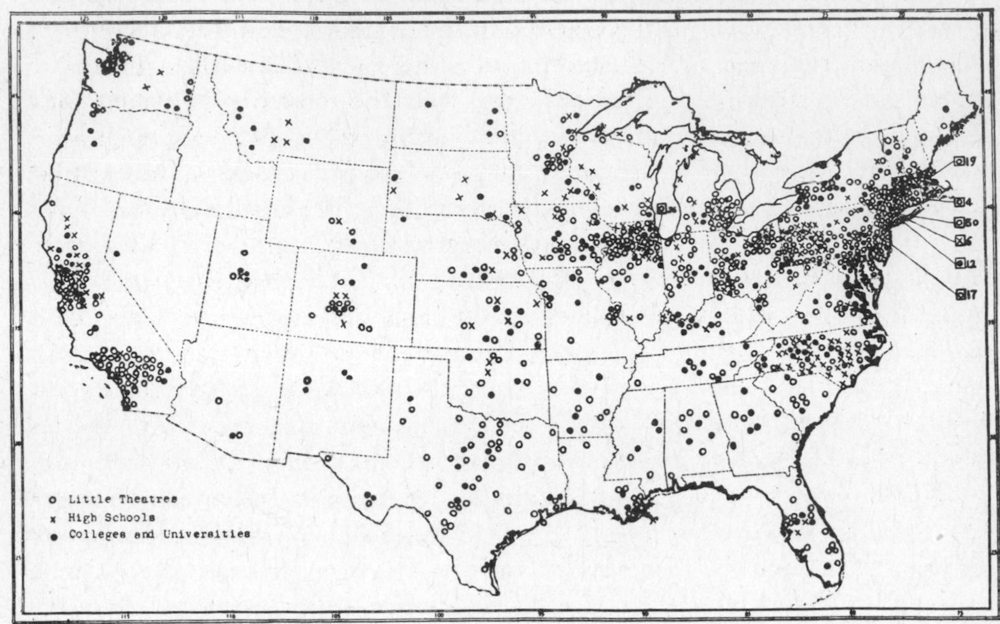

Distribution by States of Dramatic Activities in the United States

Regions	Little Theatres	High Schools	Colleges and Universities
Southeast	81	34	55
Virginia	8	1	6
North Carolina	14	29	15
South Carolina	7	..	2
Georgia	5	..	4
Florida	13	3	4
Kentucky	4	1	6
Tennessee	7	..	5
Alabama	6	..	3
Mississippi	2	..	3
Arkansas	6	..	4
Louisiana	9	.	3
Southwest	48	2	19
Oklahoma	6	2	3
Texas	39	.	12
New Mexico	1	..	3
Arizona	2	..	1
Northeast	236	43	69
Maine	2	..	1
New Hampshire	3	1	1
Vermont	3	2	1
Massachusetts	28	6	9
Rhode Island	4	..	2
Connecticut	12	..	3
New York	90	9	27
New Jersey	31	2	1
Delaware	3	..	..
Pennsylvania	48	22	16
Maryland	6	..	4
West Virginia	6	1	4
Middle States	186	67	58
Ohio	37	11	11
Indiana	16	6	5
Illinois	60	22	14
Michigan	22	11	3
Wisconsin	5	6	3
Minnesota	13	6	8
Iowa	23	5	10
Missouri	10	..	4
Northwest	25	18	32
North Dakota	1	..	4
South Dakota	..	4	4
Nebraska	5	2	5
Kansas	5	4	6
Montana	..	3	5
Idaho	..	..	..
Wyoming	2	1	1
Colorado	10	3	4
Utah	2	1	3
Far West	71	23	26
Nevada	..	..	1
Washington	7	3	5
Oregon	3	..	3
California	61	20	17
United States	647	187	259

turity protesting against the older decadence and the current immaturity.

Indeed, whatever else may be deduced from the vast array of evidence, the general culture of the region, including the people, their traditions, and their behavior reflected great vitality of many sorts. There was rugged and rural vitality of the pioneer; there was fertility, vitality of reproductive stocks; there were intensity, emotional drives, loyalties, patterns of struggle and conflict; there was vitality in the stolid survival values of the people, in their humor and recreation, in their stubborn bantering threats to outsiders, and in other defense mechanisms. So much for the White South. For the Negro again there was vitality multiplied both in his biological and his cultural status. Indeed, many measures of regional homogeneity appear in these indices of native vitality of the people and their culture. Lewis Mumford has emphasized the spiritual vitality of a "soundly bottomed regionalism" which "can achieve cosmopolitan breadth without fear of losing its integrity or virtue: it is only a sick and puling regionalism that must continually gaze with enamored eyes upon its own face, praising its warts and pimples as beauty marks. For a genuine regional tradition lives by two principles. One is, *cultivate whatever you have,* no matter how poor it is; *it is at least your own.* The other is, *seek elsewhere for what you do not possess:* absorb whatever is good wherever you may find it; *make it your own.*"

The great preponderance of evidence indicates the importance of emphasizing and appraising the nature and the degree of the immaturity of the southern culture. This is not only evidenced in the multiple measures of time lag and deficiency, of pioneer retardation and fringe, in the crudeness of material and spiritual culture, but in the major aspects of all culture, from new industry to old mountain Scotch-Irish unchanging stocks. It is manifest in lack of experience, of understanding of standards in education, politics, art, literature, in business and social clubs, in self-satisfied assumptions of superiority, in sectional isolation, in the whole Negro population, and in state pride. Evidence indicates that the great body of culture and the greater power of the people arises out of the new vital South and not from what might have become an old decadent culture fabricated of backward-looking folk in stratified institutions. This promise of vitality and maturity, which is the critical index of the future, is further evident in the states and subregions, which constitute the subject of the next chapter.

To harness this vitality and to develop this immaturity is a part of the great regional task. For here is the exuberant vigor of Emerson's "powerful uneducated man." Here is the power of a Huey Long speaking in the United States Senate after this manner: "I am not undertaking to answer the charge that I am ignorant. It is true. I am an ignorant man. I have had no college education. I have not even had a high school education. But the thing that takes me far in politics is that I do not have to color what comes into my mind and into my heart. I say it unvarnished. I say it without veneer. I have not the learning to do otherwise, and therefore my ignorance is often not detected. I know the hearts of the people because I have not colored my own. I know when I am right in my own conscience. I do not talk one way in the cloakroom and another way out here. I do not talk one way back there in the hills of Louisiana and another way here in the Senate. I have one language. Ignorant as it is, it is the universal language within the sphere in which I operate. Its simplicity gains pardon for my lack of letters and education." This is the voice of the one and the many. It is the voice of the people of, for, and by the States, to which we turn now in the next chapter.

CHAPTER X

STATES AND REGIONS

THE SIGNIFICANCE of the states in regional appraisal and planning is fourfold. First, it is not possible to understand the Southeast without sensing the peculiar place which the states hold in its history and culture. In the second place, state differences indicate the complexity of the regional culture and problem and illustrate the great subregional variety of the Southeast. In the third place, the persistence and vividness of the states accentuate the need for subregional functional groupings which cut across state boundaries and also for subregions within the states where counties which vary from type cluster in sufficiently large numbers to constitute special areas of homogeneity. And, finally, the states of the entire nation serve this same threefold function for the whole national culture and subregions as the Southeastern States do for that region, and they vivify the current problem of attaining equilibrium between federal and state authority. The close interrelationship among all these aspects together with the general framework of the Southern Regional Study emphasizes both the functional and descriptive nature of the treatment of the whole important question of states and regions.

The states we have with us always. They are the warp and woof of the federal fabric. They are the multiples of a cumulative nation. They are members of the families of historical sections and of current emerging regions. They are articulate individualists, jealous of their rights, prideful of their heritage, conscious of their autonomy. While this is especially true of the Southeast, it is likewise generally true of the nation. Yet the Federation of States, with its inevitable increasing range and power in an expanding and complex urban industrial America, we have equally and increasingly with us, constantly revivifying the problem of balance between central and local control in democratic society. It must be clear that the old state sufficiency and states' rights can no longer be effective; no more can the complete dominance of the central power. Hence, logically comes this buffer of regional arrangements to seek equilibrium between centralization of power and the doctrine and practice of states' rights, both of which still retain great vitality in the American order.

If to the current national situation which also harks back to the unquestioned dominance of the states in the pre-constitutional days of the republic, we add the southern historical state loyalties and states' rights pattern, it is easy to understand both the theoretical and practical significance of the state in the South in any realistic inventory of our regional status and problems. Dilemmas, however, are equally as realistic and as easy to understand. The states, too small, too historically incidental, too artificially set apart, manifestly are inadequate units for measurement or administration. Yet historically, legally, constitutionally, statistically, they are organic divisions which it is not possible to ignore as fundamental units of both appraisal and administration.

The states, then, represent one horn of the national dilemma. The other extreme is the federal centralization of control, which is equally as realistic a trend as the states are historical fact. Not only, however, is the theory of the state and local control a part of the American system, but it inheres in the social objectives of democracy to develop, conserve, and give representation to each demotic unit of culture. It is a part of the doctrine of equality of opportunity which applies to local group units as well as to individuals. Thus, the revivification of states' rights and sectionalism is a logical outcome of the struggle to redefine this equilibrium between individuation and socialization. But it is more than that in that it challenges regional planning to the very practical task of achieving a more perfect union and reintegration of all parts of the nation without the old sectional conflict. The task is especially important in the light of the unevenness of our national development and of the opportunity to equalize more nearly wealth and standards of well-being in the different parts of the United States. Here, as elsewhere, the Southeast affords a vivid example of both problem and prospect.

Recognizing the national culture and unity as the main motivation and criterion of American culture, we have nevertheless pointed out that, due to the bigness of the nation and its cultural backgrounds and motivations, as well as to technological considerations, the regional approach and analysis are fundamental to any successful permanent social planning program or procedure in the United States. At the same time we have recognized the difficulty of attaining satisfactory delimitations of areas which will serve both for purposes of general analysis and special functional administration. We have recognized the chaotic situation in which the nation finds itself faced with a hundred different allocations of its major regions, for the most part so designated incidentally or for special convenience. Our conclusion then was that the two essential next steps are, first, to agree upon a small number of major regions in which measures of homogeneity and functional character approximate most nearly the desired purposes; and, second, to provide for whatever subregional divisions of these major regions may be necessary for specialized purposes. If, for instance, it may appear that a larger number of major regions is needed than the six utilized in the Southern Regional Study, the answer is that, pending the nearer approximation of such divisions, it is assumed that whatever subregional reclassifications are necessary will be utilized, not only for the specialized purposes in hand, but as procedures in determining the best number and area for the all-purpose region. Or if the Far West, as is claimed, reflects an unusually great range of subareas of heterogeneity, it is no more marked than are the many subregions of the Southeast. Thus, we have pointed out that just as it is not possible to understand and plan for the aggregate nation without the aid of regional analysis, so each of the major regions is of such great expanse and diversity that its understanding and planning can be successfully achieved only through the subregional or functional analysis. Hence, the special summary in "Subregions of the Southeast," in Sections 213-216, pages 153-163.

This subregional appraisal, however, is also vitally related and indispensable to the adjustment of the states in their relative places in administration and analysis. That is, most of the specialized geographic, cultural, economic, political tasks involve the cutting across state lines to achieve a broader subregional homogeneity than is found in a single state. And within the separate states, such as California or Florida, subregional divisions are essential to realistic planning. This may be illustrated again by the Illinois *Planning Primer* which points out that "Our State is, in a sense, a pattern of *regions* of one kind or another; trade regions, drainage basins, or other configurations conditioned by the various existing physical, economic, and social unities. These regions are reflected in the overlapping of common problems, the intelligent and economical solution of which lie outside the reach of the separate municipalities or political units. The more unified and coördinated affairs may be within the boundaries of a region, the more effective the regional life. Every municipal or rural plan, large or small, needs to be viewed as part of or as a supplement to the larger regional plan. Coördinated, adjusted, and harmonious development within the bounds of any region can be accomplished only by cooperative action and by planning with a broad view to the needs of the region as a whole in mind."

This viewpoint of the importance of subregions, in relation to the states, may be examined a little further. The National Resources Committee, for instance, has expressed the judgment that "It is obvious that national planning regions will largely ignore state boundaries, since such lines rarely enter into the factors for which planning must be done. Indeed an area over which a major development project has to be planned will probably never coincide with a state or group of states." This evidently refers primarily to planning for physical development. On the other hand, the major emphasis of later reports stress state planning boards as the key to most effective planning, which necessarily recognizes states as basic units. There is likewise in another discussion of the significance of state boundaries the following verdict: "Since planning is conceived of as a long-time program involving the whole economic and social structure . . . the present administrative units such as states, counties, and perhaps townships, will have to be given due considerations. Federal and state constitutions, which defend state rights so jealously, will serve as barriers to the division of the nation into broad natural-economic regions such as the Middle West, the Palouse Wheat Country, or the Industrial Piedmont." While the extreme premises of some of the political scientists and regionalists, that the states must more and more disappear from the picture, seem quite outside the realm of immediate possibility, the objectives sought are important; but they can be attained, if at all, only through effective functional subdivisions of the regions, in which for these purposes state boundaries will be only incidental.

Another viewpoint emphasizing the subregional approach is that of Raymond D. Thomas, who, as chairman of the Southern Regional Committee, wrote: "Your suggestion that county indices be used for experimenting with methods of determining a rational regional division of the United States it seems to me is helpful. In many respects, as you quite well know, state boundaries do not mean much in useful social science research. Our states are historical accidents. I like to think of the possibility that we may move during the next hundred years far toward the actuality of regional legislation. The talk of an inter-state compact for legislation relating to petroleum resources in the Southwest is a faint evidence, it seems to me, of a possible trend in the future. Your 'county indices' divisional map, I think, in certain particulars is to be preferred to the 'state line' map. However, each of the divisions (and I am thinking particularly of the Southeast) includes a vast territory. So large is the area and so varied are the demographic, economic, and historical (institutions, traditions, thought patterns, etc.) characteristics that I am inclined to question the usefulness of a division of the country into six regions. The larger the area the more difficult is the problem of discovering regional homogeneity. More and more I am leaning toward the smaller region, both for purposes of useful research and for possibilities of regional action—planning legislation, institutional articulation, etc. It may be that in the social sciences our research should be concerned more than it has in the past with smaller units or areas."

Strangely enough, this persistence of the states accentuates the importance of subregions both within the larger national regions and within the states themselves. For whatever may be the merits of the claims for ignoring state lines, the realities of the situation are such that the states are as yet the most vivid and vital units in any regional approach. It is not only that statistical indices are based upon them, or that legal rights and privileges are inseparably bound up with the states, but the historical and cultural influences are still dominant. There is no inherent conflict in the two positions; one advocates certain all purpose major divisions of the nation, fabricated each of a certain number of states, while the other insists upon greater functional homogeneity than the states afford. Both constitute the minimum essentials necessary to meet the present reality.

While this is peculiarly true of the Southeast, it is important here as elsewhere to present the Southeast in comparison with the whole nation. When so presented, there emerges a comprehension of the real America of states and regions which it is not possible to attain in any other way. One approach to this cultural place of the states in the nation is through the eyes of literary folk as already mentioned in regional fiction. William Allen White says of American literature that it must necessarily be regional literature, with much of its best expression centering upon state scenes and portraiture. A host of writers and editors devote their best efforts to the portraiture of the states and provinces in periodical literature. During the 1930's more than a thousand such writers, young and old, were personifying the several states and regions in as many prize-seeking articles portraying the nation. Indeed, the case was fairly well stated that, for the most part, America's vitality, its humor and pathos, its immaturity and youth are abundantly expressed in the character of the states.

Here is portraiture of incredibly interesting and varied, of bright and stupid, folks: Yellow-Hammers of the Cotton State of Alabama; Apaches of the Sunset State of Arizona; Travellers from the Bear State of Arkansas; Gold Hunters from Golden California; Rovers from Centennial Colorado; Wooden Nutmegs from Connecticut; Blue Hens from Diamond Delaware; Sand Crackers from Flowering Florida; Crackers again from the Empire State of the Georgia South; Suckers from Prairie Illinois; Hoosiers from Indiana; Hawkeyes from Iowa; Jayhawkers from Sunflower and Squatter Kansas. Over there are the pictures of Corncrackers from Blue Grass Kentucky; Creoles from Pelican Louisiana; Foxes from Pine Tree Maine; Old-Liners from Maryland; Bay Staters from Massachusetts; Wolverenes from Michigan; Gophers from Minnesota; Tadpoles

Romance and History Abound in the Common Names of the States

Adapted from George E. Shankle, *State Names, Flags, Seals, Songs, Birds, Flowers and Other Symbols*

STATE AND REGION	1	2	3	4	5	6
Southeast						
Virginia	Ancient Dominion	Mother of Presidents	Mother of States	Mother of Statesmen	Cavalier State	Old Dominion
North Carolina	Land of the Sky	Old North State	Tarheel State	Rip Van Winkle State	Turpentine State	
South Carolina	Iodine State	Palmetto State	Rice State	Sand-lapper State	Swamp State	
Georgia	Buzzard State	Cracker State	Goober State	Empire State of the South	The Yankee Land of the South	
Florida	Alligator State (7) Gulf State	Everglade State	Flower State	Land of Flowers	Orange State	Peninsula State
Kentucky	Blue Grass State	Corn-cracker State	Dark and Bloody Ground State	Hemp State	Tobacco State	
Tennessee	Big Ben State	Lion's Den State	Hog and Hominy State	Mother of Southwestern Statesmen	Volunteer State	
Alabama	Cotton Plantation State	Cotton State	Lizard State	Yellowhammer State		
Mississippi	Bayou State	Border-eagle State	Eagle State	Ground-hog State	Magnolia State	Mud-wad-dler's State
Arkansas	Bear State	Bowie State	Hot Water State	Toothpick State	Wonder State	
Louisiana	Creole State	Pelican State	Sugar State			
Southwest						
Oklahoma	Boomers Paradise	Sooner State				
Texas	Lone Star State	Banner State	Beef State	Blizzard State	Jumbo State	
New Mexico	Cactus State (7) Sunshine State	Land of Cactus (8) Spanish State	Land of the Delight-makers	Land of Heart's Desire	Land of Opportunity	Land of Sunshine
Arizona	Apache State (7) Sunset Land	Aztec State (8) Valentine State	Baby State	Italy of America	Sand Hill State	Sunset State
Northeast						
Maine	Border State	Lumber State	Old Dirigo State	Pine Tree State	Polar Star State	Switzerland of America
New Hampshire	Granite State	Mother of Rivers	White Mountain State	Switzerland of America		
Vermont	Green Mountain State					
Massachusetts	Baked Bean State	Old Colony State	Old Bay State	Bay State	Puritan State	
Rhode Island	Plantation State	Little Rhody				
Connecticut	Nutmeg State	Constitution State	Blue Law State	Brownstone State	Freestone State	Land of Steady Habits
New York	Empire State	Excelsior State	Knickerbocker State			
New Jersey	Camden and Amboy State (7) New Spain	Clam State (8) State of Spain	Foreigner State (9) Switzerland of America	Garden State	Jersey Blue State	Mosquito State

from Mississippi; and "show me" from Missouri. And again, mountain treasures of Montana; silver hordes of Nevada; grey granite of New Hampshire; green gardens of New Jersey; dry sunshine of New Mexico; rich turpentine of North Carolina. There are other symbolic pictures again: Empire New York, Keystone Pennsylvania, Little Rhody Rhode Island, Volunteer Tennessee, Lone Star Texas, Salt Lake Utah, Green Mountain Vermont, Evergreen Washington, Panhandle West Virginia, and Grand Old Dominion Virginia. Yet more: Tarheels and Beagles, Clamdiggers and Badgers, Beefhounds and Butternuts, Leatherheads and Gunflints, Knickerbockers and Tuckahoes, Buckeyes and Webfeet, Clam Catchers and Sagebushers, Cornhuskers and Jersey Blues. And always banter and rivalry, firsts and lasts.

The sun shines brightest
Songbirds are sweetest,
The mountains tower proudest
Thunder peals the loudest
The landscape is the grandest
And politics the damnednest,
in Kentucky.

The "South" commonly characterized as the land of "Southern Cooking," with a Keyserling sometime accounting Virginia and Louisiana as the only civilized states, measured by tests of prandial conviviality, is also usually caricatured for fatback and greens. This and more is appropriate; yet, it is important to recall for other states as well the inseparable part of the folkways of the people which food and cooking and manners play: muffins, lobster and chowder from Maine; red snapper from Florida; terrapin, shrimp, hominy and cornsticks from Georgia; chicken from Maryland but also from Maine; from Vermont, roast turkey, maple sugar and apple jelly, doughnuts and mince pie, fish balls and baked beans. And there is New Hampshire's bay state lobster, rolls and crullers; Long Island's duck and South County sausage, frogs' legs and clams, fried smelts and cherry pie; and Keystoners' scrapple, gumbo, and pepper pot.

Still more, lighter folkways of food transcending stateways of politics: West Virginia for squabs, Virginia for ham, waffles, and spoon bread; Alabama for pickles, hot Scotch and crabs; Tennessee for possum; Mississippi for pigs; Kentucky for mint julep; Louisiana for black coffee and the high art of cooking. Arkansas and Missouri, Ohio and Illinois, Indiana and Michigan, Wisconsin and Wyoming—bean and cabbage soup, milk sweet sherbet, blackberry roll, beefsteak planked, beefsteak smothered, beefsteak Spanish, jerked beef and flap jacks. On to Kansas and Nebraska,

The Names of the States, Continued

State and Region	1	2	3	4	5	6
Delaware	Blue Hen's Chickens State	Blue Hen State	Diamond State	Uncle Sam's Pocket Handkerchief	New Sweden	
Pennsylvania	Coal State	Steel State	Oil State	Quaker State	Keystone State	
Maryland	Cockade State	Monumental State	Old Line State	Oyster State	Queen State	
West Virginia	Mountain State	Panhandle State	Panhandle of West Virginia	Switzerland of America		
Middle States						
Ohio	Buckeye State	Modern Mother of Presidents	Yankee State			
Indiana	Hoosier State	Hoosierdom				
Illinois	Corn State	Egypt	Prairie State	Garden of the West	Sucker State	
Michigan	Auto State	Lady of the Lakes	Lake State	Wolverine State		
Wisconsin	Badger State	Copper State				
Minnesota	Bread and Butter State	Gopher State	Lake State	New England of the West	North Star State	Wheat State
Iowa	Hawkeye State	Land of the Rolling Prairie				
Missouri	Bullion State (7) Show Me State	Iron Mountain State	Lead State	Ozark State	Pennsylvania of the West	Puke State
Northwest						
North Dakota	Flickertail State	Great Central State	Sioux State	Land of the Dakotas		
South Dakota	Artesian State	Blizzard State	Coyote State	Land of Plenty	Sunshine State	
Nebraska	Antelope State	Black Water State	Bug-eating State	Tree Planters State	Corn Huskers State	
Kansas	Central State (7) Sunflower State	Cyclone State (8) Squatter State	Garden State	Garden of the West	Grasshopper State	Jayhawker State
Montana	Bonanza State	Stubtoe State	Treasure State			
Idaho	Gem State	Gem of the Mountains	Little Ida			
Wyoming	Equality State	Sagebrush State				
Colorado	Buffalo Plains State	Centennial State	Lead State	Silver State	Switzerland of America	
Utah	Bee Hive State	Desert State	Land of Mormons	Land of Saints	Mormon State	Salt Lake State
Far West						
Nevada	Battle-born State	Mining State	Sage State	Sage-brush State	Sage-hen State	Silver State
Washington	Chinook State	Evergreen State				
Oregon	Beaver State	Hard-case State	Land of Hard-cases	Sunset State	Web-foot State	
California	El Dorado State	Golden State	Grape State	Land of Gold	Eureka State	

hog and hominy, pork chops with mustard. On to Colorado, wild life and zest, roast grouse and steak, venison with Apache bread. South Dakota hominy, North Dakota rye bread; rabbit from Montana, lamb from Idaho. Wine from grapes in California; wine of oranges in Louisiana and Florida. From the new Southwest, these and more: Arizona frijoles, Texas fritters, chile con carne, chillis retenas, enchilladas, tortillas.

If it be argued that these folkways of the states are unimportant except as general portraiture, several things can be said. First, such portraiture is of the utmost importance in the understanding of a culture; second, it is only necessary to explore the place of consumers' power and habit in the general economy of the state and region and to appraise the peculiar influence of diet and home hygiene upon the creative effort and work of a people. In the third place, picture the kaleidoscopic parade of festivals and carnivals, king and queen crowned youth celebrating the bounties of that particular earth bounded by state lines: apple and tobacco festivals from Virginia; Alabama deep sea fishing rodeo; strawberry festivals from Tennessee and Arkansas; peach coronations from North Carolina and Georgia; tobacco crowns from the same; and other states their quota with a possible catalogue of a hundred-fold.

To sense something of state distinctiveness, one need only compare Louisiana and Iowa, Georgia and Connecticut, Virginia and Illinois, Florida and California, Mississippi and Kansas, Alabama and Pennsylvania. Or New Orleans and Los Angeles, Charlottesville and Emporia, Savannah and Bridgeport, Chapel Hill and Hanover. Within the great range and variety in the Southeastern States may be found two contrasting pictures. The one portrays the excellence of southern cooking with its contributions to the art of living; the other the subsistence diet of the masses of marginal folk, commonly ascribed as a major factor in deficiencies of vitality and health. The one reflects superlatives in both quality and quantity; the other features woeful deficiencies in quantity and kind, such that to some biologists diet appears to be a coördinate factor with heredity in the conditioning of these marginal folk. These factors also are not unrelated to many of the general cultural problems of health, politics, religion, social relations, and leadership which lie at the heart of practical planning programs.

This catalogue of state idiosyncrasies could be extended at will, but perhaps enough of the general picture of the states has been suggested to indicate their importance and vitality in the American scene and to call attention to the fact that state loyalties, states' rights, state character are limited to no region. Rather they are adopted: Carolinas' rhododendron and dogwood; Virginia, Arkansas, and North Carolina's folk festivals;

The State Mottoes and Names

Adapted from George E. Shankle, *State Names, Flags, Seals, Songs, Birds, Flowers, and Other Symbols*

STATE AND REGION	Official Motto	Origin of State Name
Southeast		
Virginia	*Sic Semper Tyrannis. Thus ever to tyrants*	Royalty
North Carolina	*Esse Quam Videri. To be rather than to seem*	Royalty
South Carolina	*Animis Opibusque Parati. Ready in soul and resource*	Royalty
Georgia	*Wisdom, Justice, and Moderation*	Royalty
Florida	*In God We Trust*	Spanish
Kentucky	*United We Stand, Divided We Fall*	Indian
Tennessee	*Agriculture and Commerce*	Indian
Alabama	*Here We Rest*	Indian
Mississippi	*Virtute Et Armis. By valor and arms*	Indian
Arkansas	*Regnat Populus. The people rule*	Indian
Louisiana	*Union, Justice and Confidence*	Royalty
Southwest		
Oklahoma	*Labor Omnia Vincit. Labor conquers all things*	Indian
Texas	*Friendship*	Indian
New Mexico	*Crescit Eundo. It grows as it goes*	Indian
Arizona	*Ditat Deus. God enriches*	Indian
Northeast		
Maine	*Dirigo. I direct* or *I guide*	French
New Hampshire	No official motto	Locality
Vermont	*Freedom and Unity*	French
Massachusetts	*Ense Petit Placidam Sub Libertate Quietem. With the sword she seeks peace under liberty*	Indian
Rhode Island	*Hope*	Dutch
Connecticut	*Qui Transtulit Sustinet. He who transplanted continues to sustain*	Indian
New York	*Excelsior. Higher*	Personage
New Jersey	*Liberty and Prosperity*	Locality
Delaware	*Liberty and Independence*	Personage
Pennsylvania	*Virtue, Liberty, and Independence*	Personage
Maryland	*Scuto Bonae Voluntatis Tuae Coronasti Nos. With the shield of thy good-will thou has covered us*	Royalty
West Virginia	*Montani Semper Liberi. Mountaineers are always freemen*	Royalty
Middle States		
Ohio	*Imperium In Imperio. An empire within an empire*	Indian
Indiana	No official motto	Indian
Illinois	*State Sovereignty—National Union*	Indian
Michigan	*Si Quaeris Peninsulam Amoenam Circumspice. If you seek a pleasant peninsula, look around you*	Indian
Wisconsin	*Forward*	Indian
Minnesota	*L'Etoile du Nord. The star of the north*	Indian
Iowa	*Our Liberties We Prize and Our Rights We Will Maintain*	Indian
Missouri	*Salus Populi Suprema Lex Esto. Let the welfare of the people be the supreme law*	Indian
Northwest		
North Dakota	*Liberty and Union, Now and Forever, One and Inseparable*	Indian
South Dakota	*Under God the People Rule*	Indian
Nebraska	*Equality before the Law*	Indian
Kansas	*Ad Astra Per Aspera. To the stars through difficulties*	Indian
Montana	*Oro Y Plata. Gold and Silver*	Latin
Idaho	*Esto Perpetua. Mayest thou endure forever!*	Indian
Wyoming	*Equal Rights*	Indian
Colorado	*Nil Sine Numine. Union and Constit*	Spanish
Utah	Industry	Indian
Far West		
Nevada	*All for Our Country*	Spanish
Washington	*Alki. By and bye*	Personage
Oregon	*The Union*	Indian
California	*Eureka. I have found it*	Spanish

Louisiana, Mississippi, and Alabama's "Mardi Gras." More particularly with reference to the South, it seems likely that what the Southeast reflects is the stratification of early and recent loyalties, local pride and patriotism, together with a more provincial experience, than certain of the other regions. The state consciousness is thus magnified into a proportionately greater place in the total culture rather than constituting a different pattern. Yet as a part of the picture there is realism enough to demand full appraisal in any general estimate, or, what is still more important, in any adequate picture of differentials.

States, like subregions, are measures of heterogeneity as well as homogeneity. "Many states, many souths" was an early premise of regional study. This is reflected in the conclusion that Florida and Arkansas are likely to be more different, the one from the other, than Virginia from Maryland or Pennsylvania; Mississippi more different from North Carolina than Carolina is from Ohio. Even within the frame of homogeneity of the Southeastern States, each is set apart. In actual fact as well as in common reputation among the southern states there is distinctiveness in Mississippi, Georgia, and South Carolina, and, more recently, Alabama, in their folkways of lynching and mob action. The statistics tell the tale and the common ideology is apparent. Says a North Carolinian: "I don't know but what those Georgians and Mississippians have the right way to treat the 'Nigger'." So, too, there can be no doubt that Vardaman and Heflin, Watson and Blease gave folk-character and action to their states as well as being conditioned by them for their particular careers. So again, individualistic—"most American of all states" North Carolina stands in easy contrast to its bounded South Carolina and Virginia; no longer the "valley of humility between two mountains of conceit," yet nevertheless Mecklenburgers still, industrial-ruralists, and minded to blaze their own trail. Its tobacco culture, its peach orchards, its race relations, its politics are essentially different from much of Georgia's similar activities. And Virginia stands still apart from all the other states, pridefully southern, yet moving further and further away from the Southeastern fringe every year in many of its economic, political, and general cultural aspects.

One of the best ways to sample the local color and differences of the states is to glimpse the leaders of the people. More realistic than folkways the leaders of the people are of, by, and for the states. Even in the gallery of national figures, the states are still marked: Virginia and Ohio, mothers of presidents, Virginia of eight, Ohio of seven; New York four, North Carolina three, two each for Vermont and Massachusetts, one alone each for New Hampshire, Pennsylvania, Kentucky, New Jersey, Iowa.

Per Cent of Total State and Local Tax Revenue Required to Support Education at a Cost Per Unit of Educational Need Equal to that for the Country as a Whole, 1922-1932

Adapted from Leslie L. Chism's "Can the States Support an Average Program of Education: A Study in Federal Relations." *School and Society*, Vol. 42, p. 752

State and Region	Per Cent of Tax Revenue Required According to Various Measures of Educational Need		
	Average Daily Attendance	Population Aged 5-17	Units of Need
Southeast			
Virginia	47.68	52.64	45.68
North Carolina	73.69	74.83	68.84
South Carolina	82.33	95.23	76.84
Georgia	73.69	87.30	70.30
Florida	42.84	38.80	39.49
Kentucky	63.87	73.26	60.44
Tennessee	58.54	61.62	55.38
Alabama	82.97	99.77	78.05
Mississippi	105.38	104.75	99.13
Arkansas	74.21	83.14	70.30
Louisiana	51.91	63.11	48.59
Southwest			
Oklahoma	56.96	58.20	59.36
Texas	49.71	50.61	56.00
New Mexico	45.82	53.72	53.01
Arizona	27.88	31.55	31.87
Northeast			
Maine	32.83	30.81	32.18
New Hampshire	23.52	25.87	22.28
Vermont	35.36	35.75	36.31
Massachusetts	22.47	22.38	21.27
Rhode Island	23.06	25.55	21.00
Connecticut	22.61	22.01	21.32
New York	18.88	19.01	18.53
New Jersey	23.73	23.54	21.18
Delaware	25.03	27.00	24.30
Pennsylvania	26.68	27.93	24.42
Maryland	26.95	31.18	26.02
West Virginia	35.48	35.75	32.82
Middle States			
Ohio	27.37	25.49	26.86
Indiana	33.45	28.86	33.72
Illinois	24.28	24.14	24.12
Michigan	29.77	28.54	28.98
Wisconsin	30.99	31.55	32.08
Minnesota	28.41	27.28	30.13
Iowa	24.12	21.47	26.50
Missouri	30.72	29.93	32.18
Northwest			
North Dakota	35.13	34.23	42.91
South Dakota	26.28	24.53	32.08
Nebraska	27.16	24.14	32.71
Kansas	30.72	26.86	36.58
Montana	27.23	28.54	31.57
Idaho	41.00	39.23	45.68
Wyoming	31.93	28.62	37.69
Colorado	31.36	29.34	36.44
Utah	44.28	38.37	46.54
Far West			
Nevada	13.76	11.49	16.14
Washington	25.52	22.38	27.61
Oregon	25.52	21.51	30.13
California	23.90	18.38	25.75
United States	31.27	31.27	31.27

What is the measure of state differentials as indicated by at least six of the Southeastern States which would be required to spend more than two-thirds of their tax moneys for education in order to meet the national standards?

Roll call of cabinet members, two hundred strong: New York fifty, Massachusetts thirty-five, Virginia eighteen, Maryland seventeen, Kentucky sixteen, Pennsylvania sixteen, Ohio fourteen, Iowa eleven, Georgia eight, Delaware and South Carolina five each; North Carolina and New Hampshire, four each, Louisiana three, Vermont two. And other pictures of the states and their leaders too numerous to record, some were "Who's Who," some were demagogues, many were giants of the business world, others were prominent in education, religion, journalism.

So, too, the states are known by their governors and United States senators, representatives of the top ring of state politics within the Southeast. The roll call of governors during the first third of the century reflects no roster of national names, save those of the "spellbinders," yet ranks well up alongside the governors of most of the other regions. Demagogues as well as statesmen fulfill the peculiar democratic missions most appropriate to their respective states. No one can picture Mississippi, Louisiana, South Carolina without their fiery senatorial representatives. And the governor's office is the stepping stone to higher politics. Here is the record in number of governors: Virginia had nine, North Carolina eight, South Carolina eight, Georgia eleven, Florida eight, Alabama eight, Mississippi eight, Louisiana eight, Arkansas ten, Tennessee ten, Kentucky seven. From among these were recruited most of the great team of southern senatorial demagogues who have, more than any other influence, given character and caricature to southern politics in the eyes of the rest of the nation and of the world. Jeff Davis came early at the turn of the century from Arkansas; James K. Vardaman came from Mississippi just a little later; Cole Blease from South Carolina still a little later; still later Theo G. Bilbo followed from Mississippi; and Huey Long from Louisiana. The earlier vintages of Tom Watson of Georgia and Tom Heflin of Alabama did not come to the Senate by way of the governor's office.

Roll call of governors from 1900 to 1930 or overlapping years thereabout, check list for the cultural biography of a people: *Alabama:* Sandford, Jelks, Comer, O'Neal, Henderson, Kilby, Brandon, Graves; *Arkansas:* Davis, Pindall, Donaghey, Robinson, Hays, Brough, McRae, Terrell, Martineau, Parnell; *Louisiana:* Heard, Blanchard, Sanders, Hall, Pleasant, Parker, Fuqua, Long; *Mississippi:* Longino, Vardaman, Noel, Brewer, Bilbo, Russell, Whitfield; *North Carolina:* Aycock, Glenn, Kitchin, Craig, Bickett, Morrison, McLean, Gardner; *South Carolina:* McSweeny, Heyward, Ansel, Blease, Manning, Cooper, McLeod, Richards; *Tennessee:* McMillan, Fraser, Cox, Patterson, Hooper, Rye, Roberts, Taylor, Peay, Horton; *Florida:* Jennings, Broward, Gilchrist, Trammell, Catts, Hardee, Martin, Carlton; *Georgia:* Chandler, Terrell, Smith, Brown, Slaton, Har-

Composition of Southeastern States' Legislative Representatives

Adapted from a special inquiry made by W. C. Jackson for the Southern Regional Study

DISTRIBUTION	Virginia	North Carolina	South Carolina	Georgia	Florida	Kentucky	Tennessee	Alabama	Mississippi	Arkansas	Louisiana
Number of Members	100	120	124	205	95	100	100	106	140	100	100
Democrats	90	112	124	193	94	74	83	80		100	100
Republicans	4	8		11	1	26	17	2			
Independents	1			1				2			
Women	1	1		2					3	1	
Average Age		42.27				51.3	45	4[illegible].1	43.4	45.13	
Youngest		24				26	24	25	23	22	
Oldest		76				82	74	82	82	71	
Under 30 Years		7				7	17	6	34	12	
Born in State	88	111	115	190	48	97	87	80	123	76	86
Born in:											
Virginia		1	1	3	4				1		
North Carolina	2		6	3	2		1				
South Carolina		2		3	2				2		
Georgia	1	1	1		18		2	4		1	
Florida				2					1		
Kentucky					2		1		2		
Tennessee		1		1	1			1	2	3	3
Alabama			1	2	5					1	1
Mississippi					1		5	2		6	4
Arkansas							2		1		1
Louisiana		1			1				2		
Born Out of South		2		1	7	3	2		3	12	5
Born Abroad	1	1			4			1		1	2
Rural Residence	58	70	74	119	49		50	58	101	55	50
Urban under 40,000	25	38	40	70	38		26	32	37	42	28
Urban over 40,000	17	12	10	16	8		21	14	2	3	22
Military Service	22	23	16	27	24	8		13	14		
Secret Orders		65				41		70	130		
College Training	66	76	65	103	53	17		47			
Previous Service:											
in House	62	59	49	50	31	36		36	29		
in Senate		10	2	7		1			2		
in Both	1	8	2	18	3	3			4		
in Congress		1									
as Lieutenant Governor		1									
as Speaker		1									
Previous Office Holder	33	25	42		48	36		38			
Religion:											
Methodist	28	29		69	37	17	24	40	39	36	
Baptist	25	35		80	19	26	25	21	55	21	
Episcopalian	18	10		2	7		1	1	6	3	
Presbyterian	13	21		13	5	10	14	7	25	10	
Christian	5			3	3	15	14		1	5	
Catholic	1				1	5	3	1	2	2	
Church of Brethren	1										
Methodist Protestant		2									
Primitive Baptist		3		5	2	1	2	1	1		
Disciple		1									
Lutheran		3		2			1			1	
Friend		1									
Church of God		1									
Jew		1			3	1	2			1	
Disciple of Christ				1		1				1	
Congregational					1	1		1			
Latter Day Saint					1						
Church of Christ						2	3	1		5	
United Brethren							3				
Evangelical						1					
Campbellite						1					
Universalist								1			
Protestant									1	5	
Holiness										1	
Unitarian										1	
Not Given	4	13					11	10	10	8	
Lawyers	47	46	34	64	42	17	28	41	42	31	31
Professions other than Law	7	8	14	17	10	17	12	8	18	16	9
Farming and Planting	18	31	43	41	17	24	35	17	36	23	20
Business	19	28	25	36	23	31	19	16	31	20	27
Labor	1		7		2	2	2	1	3	3	11
Miscellaneous	3	4		5	1	2	4	1	7	1	1

Blank spaces indicate no data. Due to the fact that data were not available on all individuals the classifications do not always add to the totals.

ris, Dorsey, Hardwick, Walker, Hardeman; *Kentucky:* Beckham, Wilson, McCreary, Stanley, Morrow, Fields, Sampson; *Virginia:* Tyler, Montague, Swanson, Mann, Stuart, Davis, Trinkle, Byrd.

Roll call of United States senators from 1900 to the "New Deal" Democracy: *Alabama:* Bankhead, Underwood, Heflin, Black; *Arkansas:* Davis, Clarke, Robinson, Caraway; *Louisiana:* Ransdell, Broussard; *Mississippi:* Williams, Harrison, Stephens; *North Carolina:* Simmons, Overman; *South Carolina:* Smith, Dial, Blease, Tillman; *Tennessee:* McKellar, Tyson, Carmack; *Florida:* Taliaferro, Fletcher, Trammell; *Georgia:* Bacon, Harris, George, Watson; *Kentucky:* Paynter, Bradley, Sackett; *Virginia:* Riddlebarger, Martin, Swanson, Glass.

Yet perhaps members of state legislatures are, after all, most characteristic of the several states. Too numerous over the years to name and characterize, it is possible, however, to note their general qualifications and occupations as indices of working local "democracy." Here, again, the states vary greatly, although showing general homogeneity in religious affiliations, occupations, education. Of the 1800 members of the state legislatures in the Southeastern States, 95 per cent were Democrats. Over half were from rural homes, and only one in nine came from cities. Nearly 90 per cent were church members, of whom two-thirds were Methodists and Baptists. More than 300 different occupational combinations were represented in the Southeastern States.

Perhaps the greatest contrasts in states were between Mississippi and Florida. In Mississippi all of the legislators were natives of the state or of the South and represented the largest number of occupational combinations, more than a hundred. Thus samplings to balance the lawyer's portion: farmer and planter, evangelist and preacher, carpenter and editor, sheriff and jailer, football coach and barber, and others of, for, and by the people. Florida, on the contrary, recorded a dozen or more of its members born outside the South and nearly half outside the state. It was represented by no more than ten or twelve occupations. The lawyers, however, represented the largest number in each of the state legislatures. Thus, there were in the House of Representatives, 47 for Virginia, 46 for North Carolina, 34 for South Carolina, 64 for Georgia, 42 for Florida, 17 for Kentucky, 28 for Tennessee, 41 for Alabama, 42 for Mississippi, 31 for Arkansas, 31 for Louisiana. The combination of farming and planting showed considerable variation, with South Carolina having 43 such members, Georgia 41, Tennessee 35, Mississippi 36, North Carolina 31. None of the others had as many as 25. North Carolina, Georgia, and Louisiana had a larger percentage of business men in the legislature than the others. Georgia, Kentucky, Mississippi, and Arkansas had a relatively large number of pro-

States of the Southeast and Their Leaders

The story of the states is the story of their leaders. Compare Virginia's 602 leaders deemed worthy of biographical sketches in the first seventeen volumes of the *American Dictionary of Biography*, with other states: Arkansas, 1; Florida, 13; Mississippi, 39; Alabama, 48; Louisiana, 65; Tennessee, 112; Georgia, 155; North Carolina, 208; Kentucky, 238; South Carolina, 258; Virginia 602.

ARKANSAS
Jeff Davis, 1862-1913

FLORIDA: 13
Isaac Wheeler Avery, 1837-1897
Elizabeth Whitfield Croom Bellamy, 1837-1900
William Dunnington Bloxham, 1835-1911
John Mercer Brooke, 1826-1906
Napoleon Bonaparte Broward, 1857-1910
Mary Edwards Bryan, 1842-1913
Edmund Jackson Davis, 1827-1883
William Drayton, 1776-1846
John Murray Forbes, 1771-1831
Edmund Kirby-Smith, 1824-1893
Abram Newkirk Littlejohn, 1824-1901
John Baillie McIntosh, 1829-1888
George Pettus Raney, 1845-1911

MISSISSIPPI: 39
William Taylor Sullivan Barry, 1821-1868
Burrell Bunn Battle, 1838-1917
Richard Henry Boyd, 1843-1922
Gerard Chittocque Brandon, 1788-1850
George Earl Chamberlain, 1854-1928
John Francis Hamtramck Claiborne, 1807-1884
James Paul Clarke, 1854-1916
Joseph Robert Davis, 1825-1896
Varina Howell Davis, 1826-1906
Jacob McGavock Dickinson, 1851-1928
Sarah Anne Ellis Dorsey, 1829-1879
Charles Betts Galloway, 1849-1909
James Gordon, 1833-1912
Wiley Pope Harris, 1818-1891
James Albert Harrison, 1848-1911
Charles Bowen Howry, 1844-1928
Henry Hughes, died 1862
Benjamin Grubb Humphreys, 1808-1882
Prentiss Ingraham, 1843-1904
Rosa Griffith Vertner Johnson Jeffrey, 1828-1894
John Lane, 1789-1855
Greenwood Leflore, 1800-1865
Manuel Lisa, 1772-1820
George Washington Littlefield, 1842-1920
Katherine Sherwood Bonner MacDowell, 1849-1883
Anselm Joseph McLaurin, 1848-1909
Walter Malone, 1866-1915
Vannoy Hartrog Manning, 1861-1932
Edward Mayes, 1846-1917
Hernando De Soto Money, 1839-1912
Edgar Young Mullins, 1860-1928
Francis Griffith Newlands, 1848-1917
Eliza Jane Poitevent Holbrook Nicholson, 1849-1896
James Phelan, 1856-1891
Peter Perkins Pitchlynn, 1806-1881
Pushmataha, 1765-1824
Arthur Putnam, 1873-1930
Charles William Read, 1840-1890
Irwin Russell, 1853-1879

ALABAMA: 48
John Hollis Bankhead, 1842-1920
David Bell Birney, 1825-1864
William Birney, 1819-1907
Nathan Bozeman, 1825-1905
Robert Coman Brickell, 1824-1900
Frederic Arthur Bridgman, 1847-1927
William Garratt Brown, 1868-1913
Rufus Clarence Burleson, 1823-1901
John Lafayette Camp, 1828-1891
Clement Claiborne Clay, 1816-1882
Jeremiah Clemens, 1814-1865
Braxton Bragg Comer, 1848-1927
Charles Allen Culberson, 1855-1925
Mary Evelyn Moore Davis, 1852-1909
Henry Fairchild DeBardleben, 1840-1910
Elbert Hartwell English, 1816-1884
John Walker Fearn, 1832-1899
Morgan Cassius Fitzpatrick, 1868-1908
Robert Burwell Fulton, 1849-1919
Reuben Reid Gaines, 1836-1914
William Crawford Gorgas, 1854-1920
James Benton Grant, 1848-1911
John Gregg, 1828-1864
Andrew Jackson Hamilton, 1815-1875
John Hancock, 1824-1893
William Proctor Gould Harding, 1864-1930
William Harris Hardy, 1837-1917
Robert Kennon Hargrove, 1829-1905
Ethan Allen Hitchcock, 1835-1909
Henry Hitchcock, 1829-1902
Samuel Porter Jones, 1847-1906
Reuben Francis Kolb, 1839-1918
James William Lambeth, 1830-1892
Emanuel King Love, 1850-1900
Claudius Henry Mastin, 1826-1898
John Trotwood Moore, 1858-1929
John Hunt Morgan, 1825-1864
Samuel Noble, 1834-1888
William Calvin Dates, 1835-1910
Edward Asbury O'Neal, 1818-1890
Albert Richard Parsons, 1848-1887
John Pelham, 1838-1863
Edmund Winston Pettus, 1821-1907
Benjamin Franklin Riley, 1849-1925
Philip Dale Roddey, 1820-1897
William Wallace Screws, 1839-1913
James Withers Sloss, 1820-1890
Eugene Allen Smith, 1841-1927

LOUISIANA: 65
Valcour Aime, 1798-1867
Pierre Gustave Toutant Beauregard, 1818-1893
William James Behan, 1840-1928
Edouard Edmond Bermudez, 1832-1892
Newton Crain Blanchard, 1849-1922
Jean Etienne Boré, 1741-1820
Dominique Bouligny, 1771-1833
Marie Marguerite Bouvet, 1865-1915
Joseph Arsenne Breaux, 1838-1926
George Washington Cable, 1844-1925
Donelson Caffery, 1835-1906
Louis Placide Canonge, 1822-1893
Thomas Wharton Collins, 1812-1879
Pierce Francis Connelly, 1841, born
Francois Charles Delery, 1815-1880
Alexander Dimitry, 1805-1883
Paul Belloni Du Chaillu, 1835-1903
Charles Oscar Dugué, 1821-1872
Susan Blanchard Elder, 1835-1923
George Eustis, 1828-1872
James Biddle Eustis, 1834-1899
Jean Charles Faget, 1818-1884
Edgar Howard Farrar, 1849-1922
Edwin Whitfield Fay, 1865-1920
Alcée Fortier, 1856-1914
Murphy James Foster, 1849-1921
Charles Etienne Arthur Gayarré, 1805-1895
Bancroft Gherardi, 1832-1903
Louis Moreau Gottschalk, 1829-1869
Luther Egbert Hall, 1869-1921
Benjamin Morgan Harrod, 1837-1912
Louis Hébert, 1820-1901
Paul Octave Hébert, 1818-1880
Carleton Hunt, 1836-1921
Gaillard Hunt, 1862-1924
Louis Janin, 1837-1914
Margaret Thomson Janvier, 1844-1913
Duncan Farrar Kenner, 1813-1887
Robert Kennicott, 1835-1866
Grace Elizabeth King, 1851-1932
Thomy Lafon, 1810-1893
Alexandre Latil, 1816-1851
Miriam Florence Folline Leslie, 1836-1914
John Theodore Ludeling, 1827-1891
Samuel Douglas McEnery, 1837-1910
Bernard Marigny, 1785-1868
James Brander Matthews, 1852-1929
Adah Isaacs Menken, 1835?-1868
Charles Alfred Mercier, 1816-1894
James Morris Morgan, 1845-1928
Philip Hicky Morgan, 1825-1900
Paul Charles Morphy, 1837-1884
Alexander Mouton, 1804-1885
Francis Redding Tillow Nicholls, 1834-1912
Howard Osgood, 1831-1911
Thomas Harman Patterson, 1820-1889
Octave Pavy, 1844-1884
Olivier Otis Provosty, 1852-1924
Henry Hobson Richardson, 1838-1886
André Bienvenu Roman, 1795-1866
Francois Cominique Rouquette, 1810-1890
Victor Séjour, 1817-1874
Marcus Smith, 1829-1874
Edward Hugh Sothern, 1859-1933
Edmond Souchon, 1841-1924

fessions other than law. With reference to party politics, South Carolina, Mississippi, Arkansas, and Louisiana apparently were solidly Democratic. The largest ratio of those born in the state in which they served was found in Kentucky with about 97 per cent, Tennessee with 87 per cent, and North Carolina and South Carolina about 90 per cent each. Here, as in many other fields, Georgia contributed the largest number to the other states, with about 30 representatives, giving its largest single state quota, 18 or about one-fifth of the total to Florida. The states with the largest number of rural representatives were North Carolina, South Carolina, and Mississippi. Virginia and North Carolina apparently had the largest number of college trained members; approximately two-thirds of the total had some college training, while the ratio for South Carolina, Florida, and Alabama was about 50 per cent. Kentucky apparently had the lowest ratio with less than half.

Another way of characterizing the states has been the attempt to appraise a score of "leading" people in each state. About the crest of the 1920's a roll call of such leaders was made up from a list of twenty or thirty, voted by a selected list of professional folk as being the most influential leaders in that state during the first part of the century and up to about 1925 or 1926. Here again the states show considerable homogeneity of culture. One characteristic is clear in all the states, and that is that a large number of leaders so voted in the state were recorded from the ranks of colleges and universities. In every state the presidents of the leading universities were so listed, in addition to some members of the faculties and the heads of the state public school systems.

This preliminary check list for further study shows the following variations: in Virginia more than one-third of these reputed leaders were connected with educational institutions. In addition, there were two bishops, two bankers, two lawyers, two economists, two editors, the president of the Southern Railway. Of college representatives, the North Carolina list showed nine, South Carolina three, Georgia three, Alabama ten, Mississippi five, Louisiana six, Tennessee seven, Kentucky five, Florida three. The Alabama list was large because of four Negro representatives, including both Booker T. Washington and Robert Russa Moton of Tuskegee. Like Virginia, the other states also, with the exception of Mississippi, each voted its editor or journalist a place: North Carolina four, South Carolina three, Georgia four, Alabama one, Louisiana two, Tennessee six, Kentucky three, and Florida one. Of the representatives of the church, the average was, as in the case of Virginia, about two, with Alabama and Tennessee each voting for three. Officials and representatives of formal politics were represented by three in North Carolina, three in Georgia,

States of the Southeast and Their Leaders

Compare Virginia's 602 leaders which reflect a heritage of time and names distinctive from the other states. Thus there are 13 Randolphs and 13 Lees; 8 Masons and 7 Cabells; and in addition to the 10 Smiths and 7 Joneses there are as many as five each of the Carters, the Lewises, the McCormicks, the Marshalls, the Pages, the Pendletons, the Prices, the Robertsons, the Scotts. Few other states show more than 2 or 3 each of the same name.

NORTH CAROLINA: 208

William Allen, 1784-1868
Elias Milton Ammons, 1860-1925
Alexander Boyd Andrews, 1841-1915
Alfred W. Arrington, 1810-1867
John Ashe, 1720-1781
John Baptista Ashe, 1748-1802
Samuel Ashe, 1725-1813
Thomas Samuel Ashe, 1812-1887
William Shepperd Ashe, 1814-1862
Henry Atkinson, 1782-1842
William Waigstill Avery, 1816-1864
Charles Brantley Aycock, 1859-1912
George Edmund Badger, 1795-1866
Laurence Simmons Baker, 1830-1907
Robert Woodward Barnwell, 1801-1882
Daniel Moreau Barringer, 1806-1873
Rufus Barringer, 1821-1895
John Spencer Bassett, 1867-1928
Kemp Plummer Battle, 1831-1919
William Horn Battle, 1802-1879
Elisha Baxter, 1827-1899
Frederick Beasley, 1777-1845
Henry Haywood Bell, 1808-1868
Thomas Hart Benton, 1782-1858
Thomas Walter Bickett, 1869-1921
Asa Biggs, 1811-1878
William Bingham, 1835-1873
Lillie Devereux Blake, 1835-1913
Nelson Gales Blalock, 1836-1913
Timothy Bloodworth, 1736-1814
Thomas Blount, 1759-1812
William Blount, 1749-1800
Willie Blount, 1768-1835
Victor Blue, 1865-1928
John Henry Boner, 1845-1903
Braxton Bragg, 1817-1876
Thomas Bragg, 1810-1872
John Branch, 1782-1863
Lawrence O'Bryan Branch, 1820-1862
Robert Rufus Bridgers, 1819-1888
George Washington Brooks, 1821-1882
Bedford Brown, 1792-1870
Henry Andrea Burgevine, 1836-1865
Edward Burleson, 1798-1851
Otway Burns, 1775?-1850
Hutchins Gordon Burton, 1774-1836
William Preston Bynum, 1820-1909
Charles Caldwell, 1772-1853
Churchill Caldom Cambreleng, 1786-1862
Joseph Gurney Cannon, 1836-1926
Newton Cannon, 1781-1841
Elias Carr, 1839-1900
John Clark, 1766-1832
Walter Clark, 1846-1924
Francis Devereux Clarke, 1849-1913
Mary Bayard Devereux Clarke, 1827-1886
John Henry Clewell, 1855-1922
Thomas Lanier Clingman, 1812-1897
Charles Fisher Coffin, 1823-1916
Levi Coffin, 1789-1877
Henry Groves Connor, 1852-1924
William Ruffin Cox, 1832-1919
Braxton Craven, 1822-1882
John Augustin Daly, 1838-1899
Edmund Strother Dargan, 1805-1879
George Davis, 1820-1896
Henry Churchill De Mille, 1853-1893
Moses John De Rosset, 1838-1881
Robert Paine Dick, 1823-1898
James Cochran Dobbin, 1814-1857
Robert Donnell, 1784-1855
Edward Bishop Dudley, 1789-1855
Benjamin Newton Duke, 1855-1929
James Buchanan Duke, 1856-1925
John Henry Eaton, 1790-1856
Weldon Nathaniel Edwards, 1788-1873
Aaron Marshall Elliot, 1844-1910
John Willis Ellis, 1820-1861
James Bradley Finley, 1781-1856
Oscar Penn Fitzgerald, 1829-1911
William Henry Forney, 1823-1894
Francis Fries, 1812-1863
Thomas Charles Fuller, 1832-1901
George Strother Gaines, 1784-1873
William Gaston, 1778-1844
Richard Jordan Gatling, 1818-1903
John Adams Gilmer, 1805-1868
Daniel Reaves Goodloe, 1814-1902
Robert Simonton Gould, 1826-1904
Daniel Chevilette Govan, 1829-1911
Edward Kidder Graham, 1876-1918
William Alexander Graham, 1804-1875
George Alexander Gray, 1851-1912
Edward Joseph Hale, 1839-1922
Cornelius Harnett, 1723?-1781
John Harrell, 1806-1876
Benjamin Hawkins, 1754-1818
Francis Lister Hawks, 1798-1866
Joseph Roswell Hawley, 1826-1905
John Haywood, 1762-1826
Hinton Rowan Helper, 1829-1909
Archibald Henderson, 1768-1822
James Pinckney Henderson, 1808-1858
Leonard Henderson, 1772-1833
Paul Henkel, 1754-1825
Robert Andrews Hill, 1811-1900
Henry Washington Hilliard, 1808-1892
James Hogun, died 1781
William Woods Holden, 1818-1892
Theophilus Hunter Holmes, 1804-1880
Edwin Michael Holt, 1807-1884
Johnson Jones Hooper, 1815-1862
Robert Howe, 1732-1786
Robert Boyté Crawford Howell, 1801-1868
Nathan Hunt, 1758-1853
Thomas Jordan Jarvis, 1836-1915
Andrew Johnson, 1808-1875
William Ransom Johnson, 1782-1849
Joseph Forney Johnston, 1843-1913
Alexander Jones, 1802-1863
Allen Jones, 1739-1807
Willie Jones, 1741-1801
Washington Caruthers Kerr, 1827-1885
William Rufus Devane King, 1786-1853
Claude Kitchin, 1869-1923
William Walton Kitchin, 1866-1924
Augustus Koopman, 1869-1914
Joseph Lane, 1801-1881
James Franklin Doughty Lanier, 1800-1881
Sallie Chapman Gordon Law, 1805-1894
Exum Percival Lewis, 1863-1926
William Gaston Lewis, 1835-1901
James Long, 1793-1822
William Wing Loring, 1818-1886
Henderson Luelling, 1809-1878
Francis Strother Lyon, 1800-1882
Daniel McGilvary, 1828-1911
Charles Duncan McIver, 1860-1906
James Iver McKay, 1792-1853
William Gibbs McNeill, 1801-1853
Nathaniel Macon, 1758-1837
Duncan Kirkland McRae, 1820-1888
Dolly Payne Madison, 1768-1849
Willie Person Mangum, 1792-1861
Basil Manly, 1798-1868
Thomas Courtland Manning, 1825-1887
James Green Martin, 1819-1878
Jesse Mercer, 1769-1841
Augustus Summerfield Merrimon, 1830-1892
Alfred Moore, 1755-1810
Bartholomew Figures Moore, 1801-1878
Gabriel Moore, 1785?-1845?
James Moore, 1737-1777
Maurice Moore, 1735-1777
Thomas Overton Moore, 1804-1876
Alfred Mordecai, 1804-1887
Archibald De Bow Murphy, 1777?-1832
Frederick Nash, 1781-1858
Timothy Nicholson, 1828-1924
Charles Osborn, 1775-1850
James Walker Osborne, 1859-1919
Lee Slater Overman, 1854-1930
Walter Hines Page, 1855-1918
Robert Paine, 1799-1882
Richmond Mumford Pearson, 1805-1878
William Dorsey Pender, 1834-1863
James Johnston Pettigrew, 1828-1863
Israel Pickens, 1780-1827
Albert James Pickett, 1810-1858
James Knox Polk, 1795-1849
Leonidas Polk, 1806-1864
Leonidas Lafayette Polk, 1837-1892
Lucius Eugene Polk, 1833-1892
William Polk, 1758-1834
John Pool, 1826-1884
William Sydney Porter, 1862-1910
Robert Potter, 1800-1842
Thomas Frederick Price, 1860-1919
David Purviance, 1766-1847
Gabriel James Rains, 1803-1881
George Washington Rains, 1817-1898
Stephen Dodson Ramseur, 1837-1864
Matt Whitaker Ransom, 1826-1904
Kenneth Rayner, 1810-1884
Edwin Godwin Reade, 1812-1894
William Cornelius Reichel, 1824-1876
David Settle Reid, 1813-1891
Hiram Rhoades Revels, 1822-1901
Martin Ross, 1762-1827
James Finch Royster, 1880-1930
Romulus Mitchell Saunders, 1791-1867
William Laurence Saunders, 1835-1891
Lemuel Sawyer, 1777-1852
Emil Alexander de Schweinitz, 1866-1904
Thomas Fielding Scott, 1807-1867
Isaiah Sellers, 1802-1864
Thomas Settle, 1831-1888
Harry Skinner, 1855-1929
Thomas Harvey Skinner, 1791-1871
Charles Alphonso Smith, 1864-1924
Hoke Smith, 1855-1931
Robert Hardy Smith, 1813-1878
William Smith, 1762-1840
William Nathan Harrell Smith, 1812-1889
Richard Dobbs Spaight, 1758-1802
Edward Stanly, 1810-1872
John Steele, 1764-1815

three in Mississippi, with all the others having a smaller number. Only four states voted for women, with North Carolina and Mississippi three each, Georgia two, and Florida one. No state other than Alabama considered any of its major personage to be Negroes. North Carolina and Georgia voted the largest number of industrialists and business men, with Alabama, Louisiana, and Florida following four, five, and six respectively.

The names of these leaders, while ranking well up in the states' honor rolls, were not ordinarily accorded any permanent place in the nation. Of particular regional reputation were four of the bishops recorded: Candler of Georgia, Cannon of Virginia, Bratton of Mississippi, Gailor of Tennessee. Of a total number of 192 leaders for which the facts are available, less than ten were born outside the Southeastern States, among whom were Harry Woodburn Chase, president of the University of North Carolina at the time, born in Massachusetts, and Bradford Knapp of Alabama Polytechnic Institute, born in Iowa. The contribution of the several states to this list was in the following order: Virginia about 25, North Carolina 37, South Carolina 15, Georgia 32, Florida 4, Kentucky 10, Tennessee 19, Alabama 15, Mississippi 16, Arkansas 2, Louisiana 4.

One of the most interesting variations in the folk culture of the states is that found in the listing of distinguished women of the South in a Blue Book, prepared by Mrs. Bryan Wells Collier in *Representative Women of the South*. This list records 131 of a total of 323 native southerners as born in Georgia. North Carolina followed with 41, Virginia with 34, Alabama with 24, South Carolina with 24, Kentucky with 19, Tennessee with 16, Mississippi with 14, Arkansas with nine, Florida with six, and Louisiana with five. Of these 323, 291 were still living in the Southeast, thirteen were living in the Northeast, nine in the Southwest, two in the Middle States, two in the Far West, one in the Northwest, and one, Virginia's Lady Astor, in Europe. This roll call manifestly is the pattern of the Daughters of the Confederacy and of dominant Georgia leadership, in which Georgia has almost set itself a culture pattern of its own.

While these catalogues of state leadership represent only a popular professional verdict, they are significant parts of the total regional culture. As such they repay further study and elaboration. They explain part of the South's difficulties, work, loyalties, religion, politics, schools, localisms. Alongside these and as a background should be presented, however, the earlier records of leadership, in which resident sons of the Southeast filled 14 of the first 17 presidential administrations up to 1850 and in which for sixty years the chief justice of the United States was from the Southeast. Of personalities in politics deemed worthy of permanent

Samplings from Hundreds of State "Firsts" Published in Miss Rutherford's *Scrap Book*

VIRGINIA

First legislative assembly in America
First Negroes landed in America
First theatre in America
First newspaper south of Potomac
First charter granted in America
First permanent English colony
First religious service held in the first permanent English colony
First church built by English people
First trial by jury
First glass factory
First Thanksgiving Day
First child born in the first permanent colony
First to attempt education of the Indians
First to undertake the establishment of a free school
First to sound the note of local self-government
First Negroes brought to an American colony
First charter for free government
First general law in regard to roads
First colony to declare for freedom of trade
First custom house in the New World
First hospital in America
First colony to call for a general congress
First state constitution adopted in America
First President of the United States
First professor of law in the United States
First state university to establish the honor system
First State Farmers' Organization

NORTH CAROLINA

First and oldest white settlement that has been continuous in America
First child of Anglo-Saxon blood born in America
First open resistance to the British Crown
The deciding battle of the Revolutionary War
Oldest state institution of learning
The oldest school for women
Largest drug depository in the world
Largest granite quarry
Greatest peach orchard
Biggest cabbage center
Largest denims company
Largest towel manufactory
Largest gingham manufactory
Largest knit underwear factory
Largest tobacco factory
Largest single knit hosiery mill
Largest double cane bottom chair factory
Largest tobacco market in the world
Largest beds of building sand
Largest paper pulp manufactory
More medicinal herbs than all the balance of the world combined
Every known precious stone
Largest and heaviest piece of virgin gold ever dug from the earth
Largest and finest single piece of mica ever found
Highest birth rate of any state in the Union
Most famous circus clown the world has ever known

SOUTH CAROLINA

First colony to confer titles of nobility
First Negro school in America
First musical society in America
First decisive victory of the revolution
First inoculation in this country for smallpox
First native American to receive the degree of doctor of medicine
First manual labor school established in America
First indigo grown in America
First rice grown in South Carolina before 1671
First state to establish phosphate industries
First state to plant sea island or long staple cotton
First state to attempt to raise tea .
First monument in America to the slaves of the old South
First edifice in America built for the sole use of a library
First state actually to secede from the Union
First high school in America to introduce a military feature
First botanical garden established in the United States
First colony to establish an independent form of government
First state to erect a statue to an Indian
First public library in the United States

GEORGIA

First colony settled in an unselfish spirit
First and only colony aided financially by the English Parliament
First to rule slavery from the colony
First to legislate against the slave trade
First to trail the Spanish flag
First to have a commissioned ship
First to send a schooner against the British
First to send powder to Bunker Hill
Only colony to have a queen, an Emperor and an Empress
Only colony made free, sovereign and independent before the Declaration of Independence
Only colony that ever became a Military Colony
Only colony that had no tomahawking by the Indians
First of the Southern colonies to sign the U. S. Constitution
First State to defy a President of the United States for interference with her State rights
241 revolutionary heroes lie buried on her soil
According to population, Georgia sent more troops in Spanish-American War
First to plant the flag at Manila
First to legislate to make President Davis' birthday a legal holiday

FLORIDA

First church bell in the United States
First church in the United States
Oldest city in the United States, in St. Augustine
Largest phosphate beds
First National Good Roads Conference
Largest grass fibre and pulp mills
Largest kaolin plant
Most beautiful orange groves and waterways
Largest export of sponges
First in art of manufacturing ice
First state in grapefruit

(Continued on page 551)

biography by an earlier committee of the American Dictionary of Biography, 27 of the 43 Americans important in domestic affairs before the Civil War were southern. Of these, *South Carolina* furnished John C. Calhoun, Robert Y. Hayne, William Lowndes, and Robert B. Rhett. *Georgia* furnished Howell Cobb, Alexander Stephens, Robert Toombs, and William Lowndes Yancey. *Kentucky* furnished Montgomery Blair, Robert Bland, and Jefferson Davis. Of figures important in foreign affairs, *South Carolina* furnished Henry Laurens, Henry Middleton, the two Charles Pinckneys and Thomas Pinckney, and Joel Poinsett. *North Carolina* furnished Walter Hines Page. Of the figures important for the development of political theory, *South Carolina* furnished John C. Calhoun, James Henry Hammond, Hugh Legaré, and Robert B. Rhett. *Kentucky* furnished James Birney. *North Carolina* furnished Hinton Helper and Andrew Johnson. *Georgia* furnished Alexander Stephens and William Lowndes Yancey. Since the Civil War, born in the south and listed by the *American Dictionary of Biography* as important figures in domestic affairs exclusive of Woodrow Wilson, only Joe Cannon born in North Carolina, Champ Clark born in Kentucky, and Thomas E. Watson born in Georgia are recorded.

There is, of course, a special story for Virginia in which, as we have pointed out, may be recapitulated much of the Old South's contribution to earlier Americanism, so much so that one has attempted a Plutarch's lives of the Old Dominion. Here is her special record. She was the "Mother" of eight presidents, grandmother of a ninth,—George Washington, Thomas Jefferson, James Madison, James Monroe, William Henry Harrison, John Tyler, Zachary Taylor, Woodrow Wilson, and Benjamin Harrison. And of sundry vice-presidents, secretaries of state, other cabinet members, representatives in foreign courts, law makers, judges and generals, a galaxy presenting rare portraiture in the national picture! Patrick Henry, Henry Clay, John Marshall, Robert E. Lee and the other Lees, Stonewall Jackson, Joseph E. Johnson, and the others: Powhatan, John Smith, Pocahontas, Sir Thomas Dale, Sir George Yeardley, Sir William Berkeley, Francis Nicholson, Alexander Spotswood, Nathaniel Bacon, William Byrd, George Washington, Thomas Jefferson, George Mason, George Rogers Clarke, Daniel Morgan, John Sevier, Captain Lewis, James Madison, James Monroe, John Randolph, Sam Houston, John Tyler, Winfield Scott, Edgar Allan Poe, Matthew Fontaine Maury, J. E. B. Stuart, Woodrow Wilson, and Walter Reed, the conqueror of yellow fever. There was a single county that could produce two presidents and the nation's most eminent chief justice. There was a family that had furnished "to Virginia one governor, four members of the Council of State, and twelve

SAMPLINGS FROM HUNDREDS OF STATE "FIRSTS," Continued

FLORIDA *(Continued)*

First book translated from Indian into the English language
Leads all states in diversity of food products
Has 20,000,000 citrus trees
Excels in number of growing days
First in production of phosphate, naval stores, Fuller's earth
First in fishing industry
First in surface water
First in length of coastline
First in area of standing timber
First in winter-grown truck crops
First in annual rainfall
First in cocoanuts, bananas, camphor, sisal and sponges
First in muck soil
First in drainage of rich lands
First in variety of hay crops
First in equable climate

ALABAMA

First capital of the Southern Confederacy
First Negro slaves in America
First to introduce the Indian alphabet
First and only Indian to have his statue placed in the national Hall of Fame
First and only American to hold four military commissions at one time
First in America to introduce the culture of grapes and olives
First suffragette rally in America
First race track built in America
First submarine torpedo boat
First to establish a Department of Archives and History
First to determine atomic weights in America
First to scale the ramparts of Monterey during the Mexican War
First General Grand High Priest of the Royal Arch Masons of the United States
First post-graduate medical school in the United States
First to perform a successful operation on the heart
First to have an X-Ray apparatus
First to build an electric railway system

MISSISSIPPI

First native southern writer to give the Negro dialect in poetry
First to have a noted Indian chief become a prominent and distinguished citizen
First to raise the American flag over the captured capital of Mexico
First cotton plant ever mentioned was growing in a garden near the present site of Natchez
First to receive acknowledgment of a shipment of cotton
First to introduce cotton seed into this country
First to have an iron screw press for cotton
First to suggest the idea of extracting oil from cotton seed as a valuable article of commerce
First to make indigo culture a staple agricultural product
First to charter an institution of learning for the higher education of young women
First to have a military institution
First to establish an agricultural and mechanical college for Negro students
First to establish a "Literary Fund" for the free education of poor children
First to pass a law for a uniform system of public schools
First in number of newspapers published at an early date
Thirty newspapers printed in Mississippi as early as 1837
First to introduce coeducation in State University in Southern States
First to advance the use of southern textbooks
First to write a school history of the Ku Klux Klan
First to have a great highway built through the State by the War Department
First to establish State farms to be worked by convicts under State supervision
First to provide for the abolition of iniquitous system of leasing convicts
First to institute quarantine against places infected with yellow fever
First to establish an institution for the blind, for the deaf and dumb
First to organize a State Bar Association
First to have a Hall of Fame
First to solve the problem of white supremacy law
First to have a levee system
First to abolish imprisonment for debt
First to remove the common law disabilities of married women
First to collect and classify its archives
First to establish a manufacturing establishment after the War Between the States

And, finally, listen to *Arkansas*, in a characteristic boast of self-supremacy often echoed by many states. "If Arkansas were walled and cut off from all communication with the outside world," so the claim runs, "she could in a greater degree than any other state supply herself from her own resources with everything that grows, is dug from the earth, gathered in the air, or caught in the waters."

members of the House of Burgesses; to the colony of Maryland two Councillors and three members of the Assembly; to the American Revolution four members of the Convention of 1776 . . . two signers of the Declaration of Independence and their three other eminent brothers and the foremost cavalry officer of the Revolutionary War. To the Civil Service of the United States the family has furnished one attorney general and several members of Congress, and to the State of Virginia, two governors, to the State of Maryland, one governor, and to the Confederate States, the great commander of its armies, three major generals, and one brigadier general. . . ."

This old record of the eminence of leaders in Virginia and to a lesser extent in some of the other Southeastern States is of more than passing or historical interest. It is a part of the explanation of much of the present culture complex of the region. On the background of the old culture, which is no longer now the dominant culture, and in a transitional stage when the new young immature culture is struggling to find itself, there is still much of the defense mechanism, articulate in references to what was in the past. Indeed this veneration of the past is commonly assumed to be a prevailing mental attitude in the South. The feeling and the assumption that the South has been "first" in so many things and has reflected "the biggest, the greatest" in others is still constantly pressing itself forward. It is natural that a region which, in spite of its distinctive contribution, is constantly being criticized, caricatured, and patronized, should point with pride to its merits whenever and however attained.

This cataloguing of "firsts," quite a dominant motivation during most of the first third of the twentieth century, has perhaps been overlooked recently, although there is evidence of its revivification. In its quantitative aspects and its motivation it was more than a passing fad. It was a conditioning force. We have, therefore, presented samplings from the hundreds of "firsts," which were passed on in the folkways or in press and platform as they were initiated and catalogued in Miss Mildred Rutherford's *Scrap Book,* which circulated at its zenith through the medium of the Daughters of the Confederacy during the second decade of the twentieth century. At the risk of monotony and over-emphasis and as uncritical catalogues, condensed from hundreds of pages, we present a few reputed "firsts," usually contributed to the *Scrap Book* by the state historian general.

This singing of state praises in kaleidoscopic notes of reputed "firsts" reflects important folkways of loyalty and state patriotism at the same time that it calls attention to distinctive historical backgrounds and traits of the states. As such, the record is relevant to the picture. So, too, such a catalogue stands in lighter relief to the monotonous citation of "lowests"

PRISONERS IN STATE AND FEDERAL PRISONS PER 100,000 POPULATION, 1929

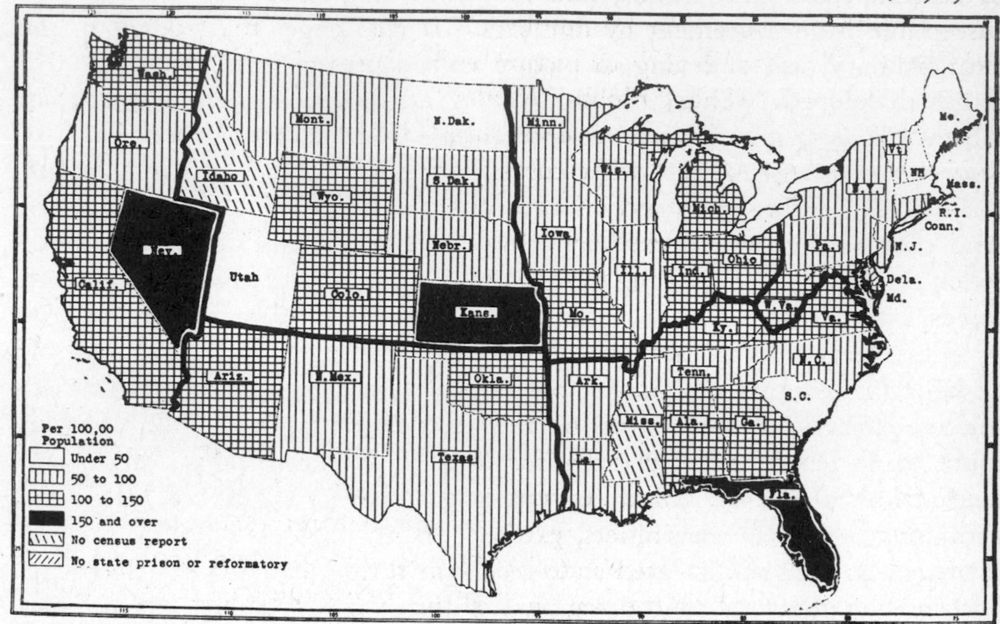

PRISONERS RECEIVED BY FEDERAL PRISONS AND REFORMATORIES PER 100,000 POPULATION, 1929

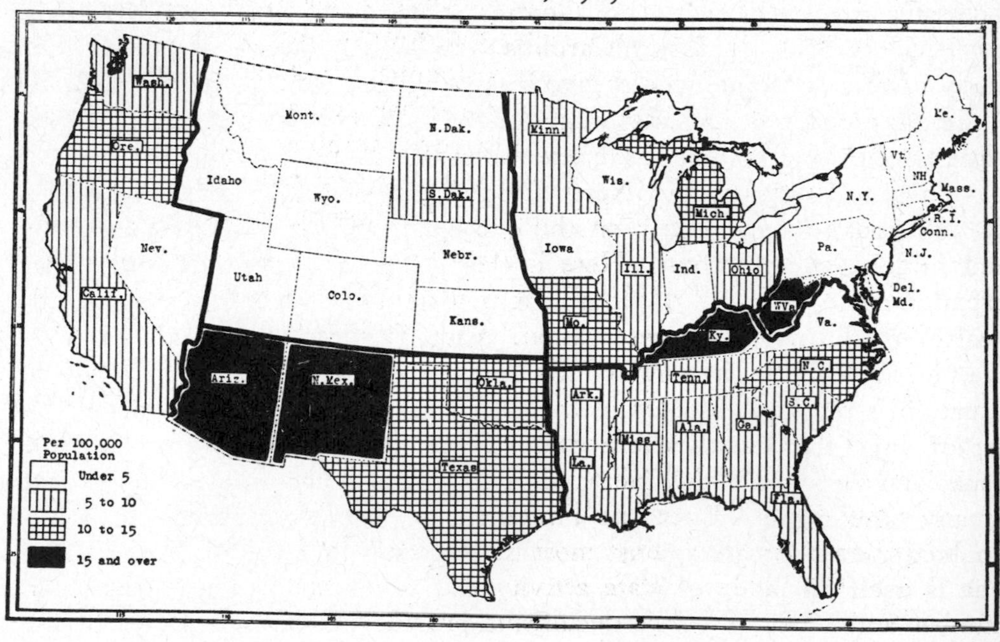

and "lasts" and "worsts" which appear throughout the regional inventory of current status and trends, and serves to emphasize many things not susceptible to measurement by numbers. It challenges the student to the extraordinary task of trying to picture each southern state as it is and as it has developed. Thus, Hobbs' *North Carolina: Economic and Social*, Allred's *Tennessee: Economic and Social*, Maclachlan's *Mississippi: A Study of Potentiality*, and other current statistical studies supplement historical treatises of reconstruction and other incidence of the several states. And they vivify the extraordinary fugitive literature of the states, seven to ten thousand titles standing to the credit of the Southeastern States themselves.

This record of publications of, for, by, and about the states is itself an object lesson in descriptive portraiture and subjective appraisal. A relatively cursory examination of the state bibliographies yields a total count of no less than 7,293 titles for the Southeastern States. Of magazine articles there are 3,892; of public documents, 2,139; of books and pamphlets, 819. Of pamphlets, extracts, and folders no man has counted them nor has anyone isolated state scenes in fiction and general literature. Such as were counted in the regional study, North Carolina and Florida have been most publicized, with North Carolina far in the lead and only approximated by Texas in the Southwest. Of the titles listed, the Southeastern States rank: North Carolina, 2,209; Florida, 789; Virginia, 713; Louisiana, 594; Alabama, 541; Georgia, 540; Kentucky, 533; Tennessee, 417; Mississippi, 332; South Carolina, 326; and Arkansas, 299. A closer study of this catalogue would give a fair portraiture of state differentials. A simple annotation indicates many of the distinctive movements, personalities, events, motivation in the several states.

Thus, to illustrate with North Carolina, her list is greatly augmented by 588 "public documents," on the one hand, and 443 special pamphlets and folders, on the other. Here is clear index of a period of industrial expansion and of rapid development in the public services of education, health, public welfare, conservation, roads, roughly during the 1920's, the period of special inquiry for the Southern Regional Study. This same situation is manifest further in the 882 magazine articles, the largest by far of any other Southeastern State, Florida being next with 584. Of books and pamphlets also North Carolina's 296 is more than double that of any other state. Even the limitations of source materials which undoubtedly discriminate against most of the states in favor of North Carolina is itself an index of state activity and promotion. The variation in number and kinds of public documents provides an unusual study of the people, their folkways, and institutions. The ranking of states in the

States and Their Principal Mineral Products in 1927*

Adapted from Isaac Lippincott, *Economic Development of the United States*, p. 320

STATE AND REGION	Percentage of Total Value for United States	Principal Mineral Products in Order of Value
Southeast		
Virginia	.84	Coal, cement, clay products, stone.
North Carolina	.24	Stone, clay products, sand and gravel, copper.
South Carolina	.09	Stone, clay products, sand and gravel, barite.
Georgia	.34	Stone, clay products, cement, fuller's earth.
Florida	.37	Phosphate rock, stone, fuller's earth, sand and gravel.
Kentucky	3.11	Coal, petroleum, clay products, natural gas.
Tennessee	.77	Coal, cement, stone, clay products.
Alabama	1.60	Coal, iron ore, cement, clay products.
Mississippi	.05	Sand and gravel, clay products, natural gas, stone.
Arkansas	1.21	Petroleum, coal, natural gas, natural gasoline.
Louisiana	1.05	Petroleum, natural gas, natural gasoline, salt.
Southwest		
Oklahoma	10.70	Petroleum, natural gas, natural gasoline, zinc.
Texas	7.64	Petroleum, natural gas, sulphur, natural gasoline.
New Mexico	.58	Copper, coal, zinc, petroleum.
Arizona	2.05	Copper, gold, silver, lead.
Northeast		
Maine	.11	Stone, lime, clay products, slate.
New Hampshire	.07	Stone, clay products, sand and gravel, feldspar.
Vermont	.30	Stone, slate, lime, talc.
Massachusetts	.33	Stone, clay products, sand and gravel, lime.
Rhode Island	.03	Stone, sand and gravel, clay products, lime.
Connecticut	.15	Stone, clay products, lime, sand and gravel.
New York	2.29	Clay products, stone, cement, gypsum.
New Jersey	1.49	Clay products, zinc, cement, stone.
Delaware	.01	Clay products, stone, sand and gravel, green sand marl.
Pennsylvania	19.11	Coal, cement, clay products, natural gas.
Maryland	.42	Coal, clay products, cement, sand and gravel.
West Virginia	7.48	Coal, natural gas, petroleum, clay products.
Middle States		
Ohio	4.63	Clay products, coal, natural gas, stone.
Indiana	2.19	Coal, stone, cement, clay products.
Illinois	3.68	Coal, clay products, petroleum, cement.
Michigan	2.53	Iron ore, copper, cement, sand and gravel.
Wisconsin	.44	Stone, zinc, sand and gravel, iron ore.
Minnesota	2.10	Iron ore, stone, cement, clay products.
Iowa	.68	Coal, cement, gypsum, clay products.
Missouri	1.55	Lead, clay products, cement, coal.
Northwest		
North Dakota	.06	Coal, sand and gravel, clay products, natural gas.
South Dakota	.17	Gold, cement, stone, sand and gravel.
Nebraska	.07	Sand and gravel, cement, clay products, stone.
Kansas	2.46	Petroleum, zinc, natural gas, cement.
Montana	1.39	Copper, zinc, coal, petroleum.
Idaho	.60	Lead, silver, zinc, stone.
Wyoming	1.15	Petroleum, coal, natural gas, natural gasoline.
Colorado	1.20	Coal, gold, zinc, lead.
Utah	1.84	Copper, lead, coal, silver.
Far West		
Nevada	.55	Copper, gold, silver, gypsum.
Washington	.45	Coal, cement, clay products, sand and gravel.
Oregon	.14	Cement, stone, sand and gravel, clay products.
California	9.37	Petroleum, natural gasoline, natural gas, cement.

*In this table iron ore, not pig iron, is taken as the basis of iron valuation, and in the case of other metals mine production (recoverable content of metals) is the basis.

number of public documents shows considerable variation from that of the totals or from the records of magazine articles. Thus, next to North Carolina in public documents, is Virginia, while Florida, second in totals, is at the bottom. Other states in order, after North Carolina are: Virginia, Louisiana, Alabama, Mississippi, Kentucky, Georgia, Arkansas, South Carolina, Florida, and Tennessee. Mississippi's large quota reflects an agricultural extension service partly responsible for its great spurt in dairying and livestock farming.

The detailed study of each state in each of the classifications nets a mine of description, a separate story in itself. For the present purpose illustration of a single group must suffice. The best illustration is found in the list of public documents of, for, and by North Carolina; even this list, abbreviated to the simplest terms, tabulates ten or fifteen pages. Thus, the largest numbers of documents are found in the fields of education with 89; agriculture and rural North Carolina with 69; government with 53; natural resources with 58; public welfare and public health with 47. Other groupings deal with industry and business, transportation, celebrations, general and miscellaneous. The educational documents cover adult education, libraries, colleges, public schools. The 71 titles on public schools include documents on elementary and grammar schools, funds and finances, high schools, laws and regulations, schoolhouse plans, state system and reports, teachers. Each of these in turn includes various subdivisions. The documents on rural life and agriculture reflect the agricultural extension program of the State Department of Agriculture and the State College and range from home and hygiene to soil and marketing. Of the 53 titles on governmental affairs, 22 deal with taxation, and an additional nine with general budgets and finances. Of the 58 on natural resources, 24 deal with forestry, 12 with minerals, 11 with water power. Others deal with birds, sea foods, flora. The 25 health reports do not include the monthly bulletins and other materials and deal largely with specific diseases and with maternity and health work. In these and other divisions there is, of course, overlapping; for instance, most of the documents on labor and industry have to do with such topics as child labor, compensation, insurance, and the like, many of which might be listed as public welfare.

Variation which is due to particular types of personalities and incidence may be illustrated in the general literature of the states for the decade of the 1920's. The presence of a particular author or authors or the incidental sponsorship of a major publisher may be responsible for a great deal of state characterization or reputation. For the ten year period 45 publishers produced more than 300 books by 150 authors native to the Southeast,

Patients in Hospitals for Mental Disease Per 100,000 Population, 1929

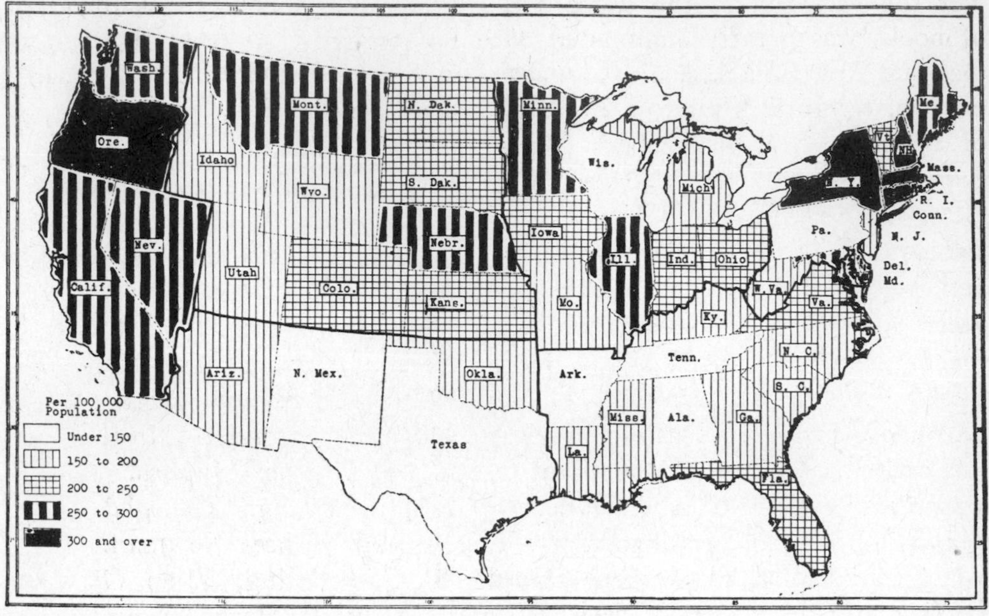

Mentally Diseased, Feeble-Minded and Epileptics in State Institutions, 1932

STATE AND REGION	Mentally Diseased	Feeble-Minded and Epileptics	Total	STATE AND REGION	Mentally Diseased	Feeble-Minded and Epileptics	Total
Southeast	*50,094*	*4,771*	*54,865*	*Middle States*	*80,733*	*28,242*	*108,975*
Virginia	5,955	939	6,894	Ohio	16,358	7,126	23,484
North Carolina	5,648	640	6,288	Indiana	7,367	2,081	9,448
South Carolina	3,344	510	3,854	Illinois	23,559	5,899	29,458
Georgia	5,671	249	5,920	Michigan	9,697	4,369	14,066
Florida	3,723	468	4,191	Wisconsin	2,389	2,121	4,510
Kentucky	5,789	......	5,789	Minnesota	8,467	2,786	11,253
Tennessee	4,462	595	5,057	Iowa	6,132	2,793	8,925
Alabama	4,173	532	4,705	Missouri	6,764	1,067	7,831
Mississippi	3,404	271	3,675				
Arkansas	3,393	......	3,393	*Northwest*	*17,826*	*5,734*	*23,560*
Louisiana	4,532	567	5,099	North Dakota	1,635	698	2,333
				South Dakota	1,572	591	2,163
Southwest	*14,462*	*2,931*	*17,393*	Nebraska	3,655	1,111	4,766
Oklahoma	3,011	785	3,796	Kansas	4,260	1,739	5,999
Texas	9,918	2,091	12,009	Montana	1,703	387	2,090
New Mexico	667	55	722	Idaho	794	472	1,266
Arizona	866	......	866	Wyoming	457	269	726
				Colorado	2,829	467	3,296
Northeast	*118,316*	*34,477*	*152,793*	Utah	921	......	921
Maine	2,198	788	2,986				
New Hampshire	1,812	547	2,359	*Far West*	*23,727*	*5,024*	*28,751*
Vermont	947	283	1,230	Nevada	301	......	301
Massachusetts	20,192	6,362	26,554	Washington	3,356	1,386	4,742
Rhode Island	2,162	596	2,758	Oregon	3,262	827	4,089
Connecticut	5,698	1,043	6,741	California	16,808	2,811	19,619
New York	54,763	13,369	68,132				
New Jersey	7,777	4,063	11,840	United States*	305,158	81,179	386,337
Delaware	811	244	1,055				
Pennsylvania	14,152	5,278	19,430				
Maryland	5,018	1,053	6,071				
West Virginia	2,786	851	3,637				

practically every major publisher in the United States being represented. Yet the variation in the states was considerable. Thus, Alabama's list of books was greatly augmented with no less than 20 from the pen of Octavus Roy Cohen, while Clement Wood was responsible for a dozen. So, too, Kentucky's total of 43 volumes was more than half from the pen of Irwin Cobb and Elizabeth Madox Roberts. Virginia's list was more than half due to James Branch Cabell's 15, Willa Cather's and Ellen Glasgow's seven each. From a list of 148 authors and 321 volumes, the states rank as follows. In number of authors North Carolina, 32; Georgia and South Carolina with 19 each, Tennessee with 16; Mississippi and Virginia with 15 each, Alabama and Kentucky with 11 each. Of authors in the national spotlight, Virginia, Kentucky, and Alabama have been mentioned. Tennessee furnished T. S. Stribling and Evelyn Scott. South Carolina contributed DuBose Heyward and Julia Peterkin. North Carolina contributed James Boyd, Paul Green, and Hatcher Hughes. Mississippi contributed William Faulkner and Stark Young. Georgia's quota included Lawrence Stallings, Corra Harris, and Frances Newman. Since 1930, in addition to previous records, T. S. Stribling, Ellen Glasgow, DuBose Heyward, Paul Green, William Faulkner, Stark Young, James Boyd, Thomas Wolfe, and some others have added especially to the lists. The leading national publishers of these books were Doubleday, Doran with more than double the number of any other publisher, and others in order: Century; Scribner's; Lothrop, Lee and Shepard; Alfred Knopf; Dodd, Mead; Houghton Mifflin; Appleton; Macmillan; Harcourt, Brace; Stokes; Holt; Little, Brown; Bobbs-Merrill; Harper.

The story of state character and differences can be continued as far as occasion justifies. Variations within the Southeastern States reflect some such similar diversity to that in which the Southeastern States are compared with other regions, but with varying degrees. Here, again, the states may reflect homogeneity or heterogeneity in proportion to the nature of the data examined or the purpose in view. This reflects again the need for subregional classifications, some within the states and others across state boundaries, at the same time that it reëmphasizes the stubborn part which the states play in any programs of planning. And it reëmphasizes the fact that it is not possible to know "the South" without knowing the states as such; and again that much of the homogeneity of the South is fabricated of many units which constitute patterns of heterogeneity. For the most part further differences between and among the states may be discerned from the statistical arrays which have been utilized to measure regional differences. The rankings are then computed from one to eleven; firsts and lasts become first and eleven in the regional classification. Per-

The People of Mississippi

TOTAL POPULATION PER SQUARE MILE, 1930

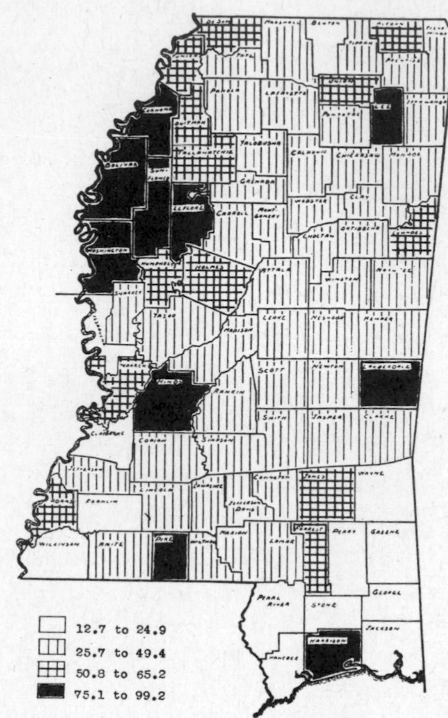

NUMBER OF PERSONS PER FAMILY, 1930

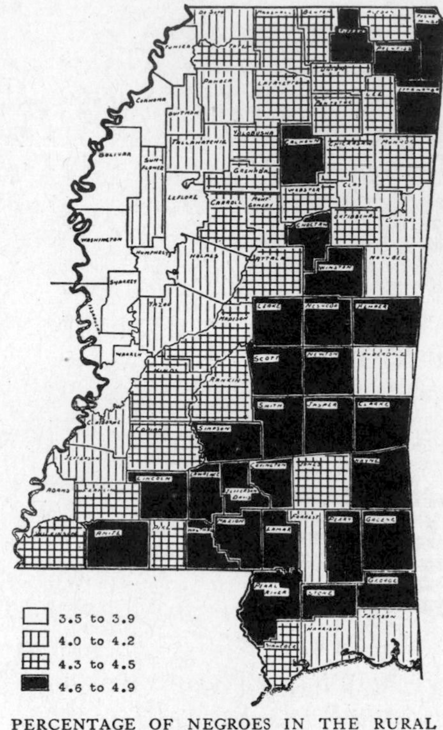

RATE OF NATURAL INCREASE OF THE WHOLE POPULATION, 1929 AND 1930 (AVERAGED)

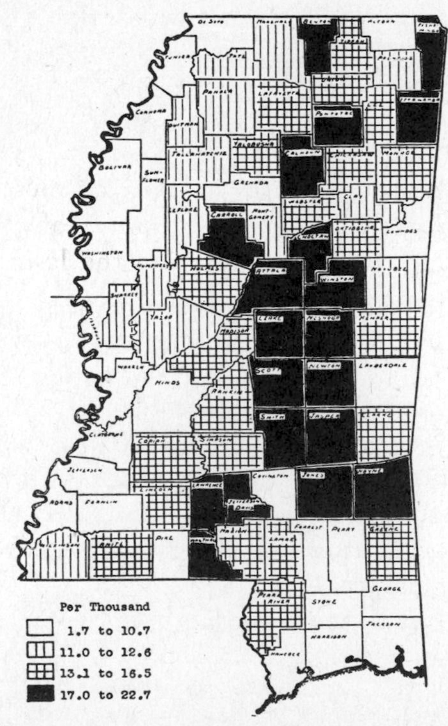

PERCENTAGE OF NEGROES IN THE RURAL FARM POPULATION, 1930

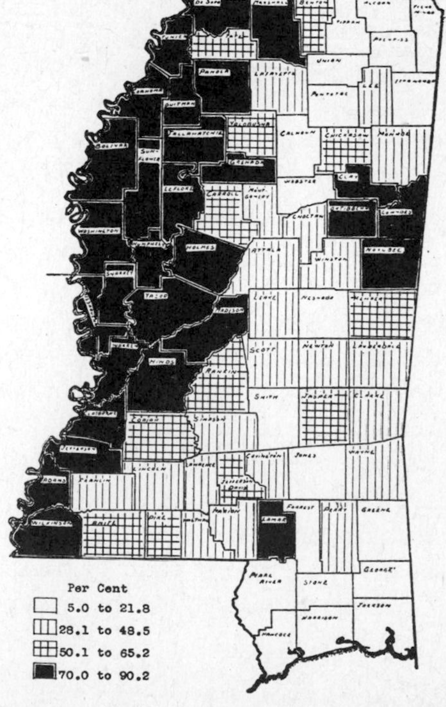

haps it is well, however, to offer samplings for illustration and to present the totals in certain composite tabular exhibits. Some of these are presented in this chapter; others in Chaper II.

There are certain general popular impressions of the several states. Many of these popular appraisals are justified; some are not. These contradictions again illustrate the patterns of heterogeneity within the larger homogeneity. Thus North Carolina is "the industrial state." This is reflected in statistics of increase in textile, furniture, and tobacco manufacture, in the increase of population, especially in centers such as Guilford, Durham, and Mecklenburg counties, where the increase for 1920-1930 averaged more than 60 per cent. Yet the state is preëminently rural in the sense that its people, its income, its institutions are still predominantly agrarian. Gaston County with its 100 mill villages is preëminently a rural county. Louisiana varies from type in that its Catholic religion distinguishes it from the other states, which are predominantly Methodist and Baptist. Yet the Louisiana legislature reflects little effect in its membership. Mississippi is "the plantation state" due to tenant subdivisions, yet has the smallest average size farms, 53 acres, of all the states. It is the only state with over half of its population Negro, yet Georgia has four times as many counties with over 90 per cent of all Negro farms being operated by tenants as does Mississippi. Kentucky had 74 of its counties decrease in population, yet Harlan increased 104 per cent. The state of "My Old Kentucky Home" has 60 counties with less than five per cent of its population Negro and 22 with less than one per cent. Alabama is reputed to be the most inhospitable to outside agitators, yet her state university enrolls a larger proportion of its students from outside the region than any other institution. Georgia is reputed the most "democratic" state of the solid South, in which is the little white house of President Roosevelt, yet its governor is among the bitterest opponents of the New Deal. Reputed to be the most "cracker" state, it has Atlanta the most "yankee" of the southern cities. Florida has the highest per capita wealth and the largest proportion of citizens and legislators born outside the state, yet has the most stringent legislation requiring all teachers to be citizens of the state. South Carolina's Charleston personifies the old South's aristocracy and grandeur, yet its Cole Blease was for a long time its most articulate representative to the outer world. Virginia is commonly considered the most "southern" of all the states, yet ranks with the Northeast in nearly half of the indices of measurement used in the study. Tennessee has provided the finest examples of the country gentleman's pattern of livestock farms, yet boasts the greatest ratio of mountain yeomanry.

It is also possible to group the several states within the Southeast

THE PROSPECTIVE POPULATION PICTURE FOR 1960

Adapted from Thompson and Whelpton's *Estimates of Future Population of States*

STATE AND REGION	Population, 1930	Population with Migration, 1960	Population without Migration, 1960
Southeast	*25,550,000*	*29,066,000*	*35,168,000*
Virginia	2,422,000	2,577,000	3,166,000
North Carolina	3,170,000	4,226,000	4,740,000
South Carolina	1,739,000	1,856,000	2,535,000
Georgia	2,908,000	2,898,000	4,048,000
Florida	1,468,000	1,997,000	1,640,000
Kentucky	2,614,000	2,943,000	3,631,000
Tennessee	2,617,000	2,892,000	3,497,000
Alabama	2,646,000	2,982,000	3,743,000
Mississippi	2,010,000	2,298,000	2,797,000
Arkansas	1,854,000	1,928,000	2,575,000
Louisiana	2,102,000	2,469,000	2,796,000
Southwest	*9,079,600*	*11,330,700*	*12,201,800*
Oklahoma	2,396,000	2,902,000	3,456,000
Texas	5,825,000	7,255,000	7,519,000
New Mexico	423,000	539,000	640,000
Arizona	435,600	634,700	586,800
Northeast	*38,026,000*	*43,130,000*	*40,790,000*
Maine	797,000	856,000	948,000
New Hampshire	465,000	487,000	496,000
Vermont	360,000	367,000	410,000
Massachusetts	4,250,000	4,613,000	4,391,000
Rhode Island	688,000	776,000	731,000
Connecticut	1,607,000	1,843,000	1,713,000
New York	12,588,000	14,548,000	12,617,000
New Jersey	4,041,000	4,930,000	4,204,000
Delaware	238,000	254,000	254,000
Pennsylvania	9,631,000	10,410,000	10,808,000
Maryland	1,632,000	1,825,000	1,768,000
West Virginia	1,729,000	2,221,000	2,450,000
Middle States	*33,961,000*	*38,325,000*	*37,502,000*
Ohio	6,647,000	7,548,000	7,096,000
Indiana	3,238,000	3,564,000	3,536,000
Illinois	7,631,000	8,544,000	7,838,000
Michigan	4,842,000	6,502,000	5,638,000
Wisconsin	2,939,000	3,312,000	3,538,000
Minnesota	2,564,000	2,690,000	3,019,000
Iowa	2,471,000	2,484,000	2,883,000
Missouri	3,629,000	3,681,000	3,954,000
Northwest	*7,385,600*	*7,929,400*	*9,253,300*
North Dakota	681,000	728,000	985,000
South Dakota	693,000	772,000	930,000
Nebraska	1,378,000	1,436,000	1,659,000
Kansas	1,881,000	1,979,000	2,228,000
Montana	538,000	503,000	650,000
Idaho	445,000	466,000	602,000
Wyoming	225,600	274,400	284,300
Colorado	1,036,000	1,117,000	1,184,000
Utah	508,000	654,000	731,000
Far West	*8,285,100*	*10,824,600*	*8,147,500*
Nevada	91,100	97,600	93,500
Washington	1,563,000	1,708,000	1,590,000
Oregon	954,000	1,075,000	949,000
California	5,677,000	7,944,000	5,515,000
United States*	122,775,000	141,124,000	143,502,000
Per Cent Southeast is of the Total	20.8	20.6	24.5

*Includes District of Columbia not in the above classification. The omission of hundreds and thousands, of course, also explains failure of totals to tally.

according to their respective rankings. Measured by the usual indices, Florida and Virginia tend to rank at the top in their modal averages. Mississippi and South Carolina tend to rank at the bottom. Again, North Carolina and Louisiana tend to rank high in the upper half, while Tennessee and Kentucky tend to rank just above the median. Alabama tends to rank just below the median, with Georgia and Arkansas well down in the lower half. These rankings are based upon 130 indices selected to represent all aspects of culture from land use and values to educational institutions. Florida ranks at the top of the firsts with 58 and Virginia next with 25. Mississippi is lowest with 43 and South Carolina follows with 20, while Georgia and Arkansas are not far behind with 17 "last" rankings each. North Carolina has 26 and 16 thirds, while Louisiana has 14 seconds, 21 thirds, 20 fourths and 16 fifths. Tennessee has 27 fourths, 19 each of fifths and sevenths, and 13 sixths. Kentucky has 24 thirds, 15 fourths and eighths and 13 sixths. Alabama has 23 tenths, 20 eighths and ninths, 17 sevenths, and 14 sixths. Or to group the states into two categories, the following states register a majority above the sixth ranking: Virginia, North Carolina, Florida, Kentucky, Tennessee, and Louisiana. Below this are South Carolina, Georgia, Alabama, Mississippi, and Arkansas. Louisiana, exclusive of New Orleans, belongs to this group, thus completing a belt of a mid-lower South of greater homogeneity than the whole Southeast.

The variations in the population of the several states is also of great importance both for understanding the South and for planning next steps. Many of the variations seem so contradictory as to "make little sense." There is, however, first of all great homogeneity in the ratio of white population native born. There is also great homogeneity in the ratio of people under 19 years of age, every state having more than 40 per cent with the lowest range of 42.6 for Florida and the highest 50.6 for South Carolina. North Carolina, Alabama, Mississippi, and Georgia, however, follow closely with an average of about 47 per cent. Here also variation among the counties is relatively small. In Negro population Kentucky and Tennessee are variates from type, while Virginia and North Carolina reflect what appears to be a culture in flux with reference to the adjustment of races. Virginia, Kentucky, and Florida stand somewhat apart in their smaller ratio of farm tenancy. In increase of population Florida and North Carolina not only outranked other Southeastern States, but most of the states of the nation, in contrast to Georgia's increase of less than one half of one per cent and South Carolina's less than four per cent. Georgia's census showed 110 counties decreasing in population as compared to five for North Carolina. The ranking of the states in total increase shows

PERCENTAGE OF FOREIGN BORN IN THE TOTAL WHITE POPULATION, 1930

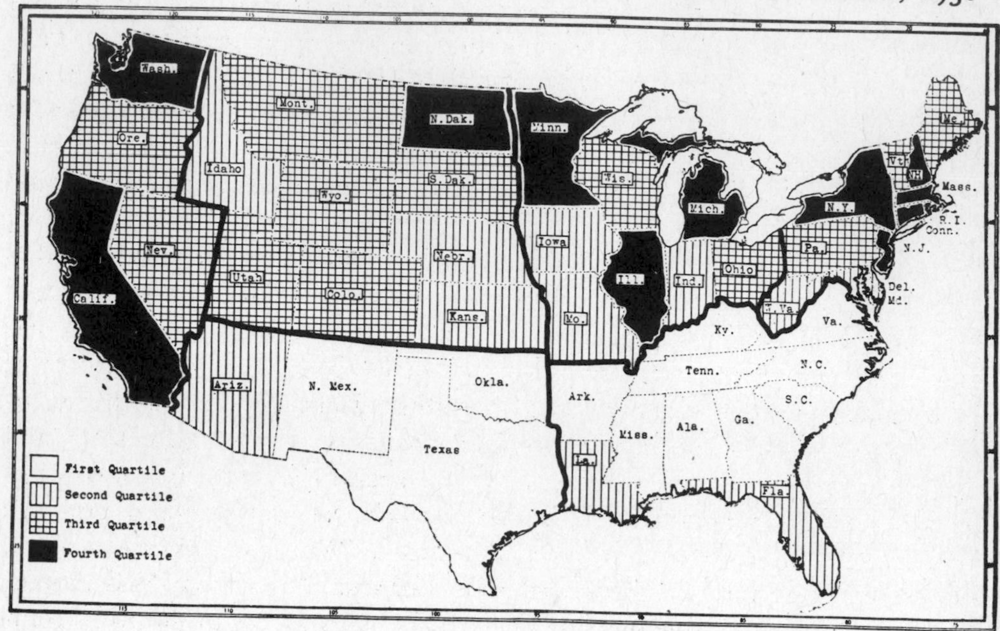

PER CENT INCREASE IN TOTAL POPULATION, 1920-1930

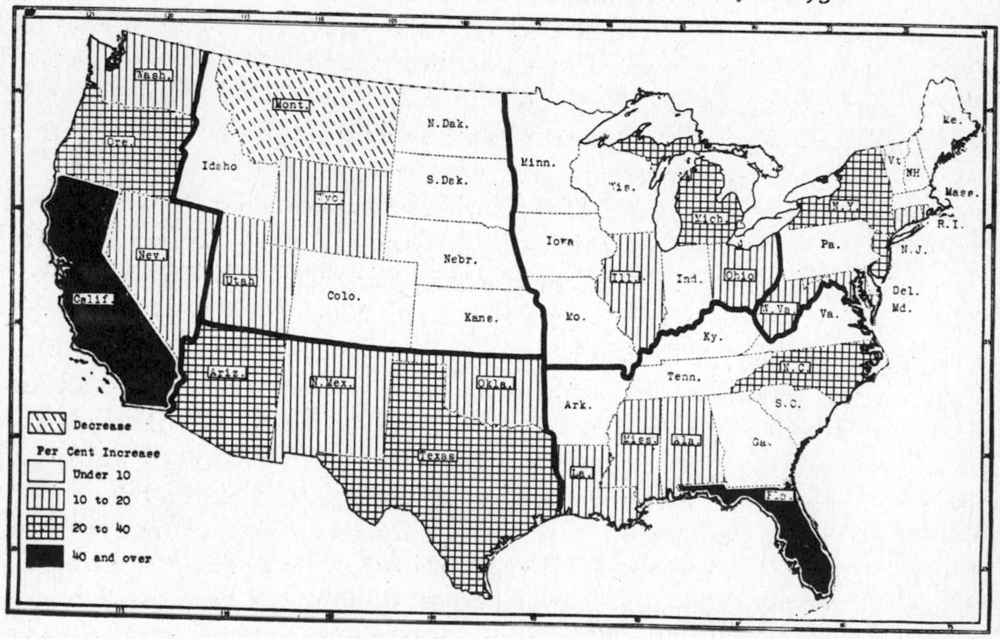

Florida with 42.6 per cent increase; North Carolina with 23.9; Louisiana, 16.9; Alabama, 12.7; Mississippi, 12.2; Tennessee, 11.9; Kentucky, 8.2; Virginia, 4.9; South Carolina, 3.3; Georgia, .04.

With reference to the composition and equipment of the population there is not only great variation among the states, but within the states much greater diversity among the counties. In illiteracy, for instance, Mississippi's low rate of 2.7 for its white population stands in surprising contrast to Louisiana's 7.8 or North Carolina's 5.7. Likewise, Mississippi's Negro illiteracy is 23.2 per cent, as contrasted with Tennessee's 36.5 and Alabama's and South Carolina's 26 per cent. Again Arkansas' white rate of 3.5 and Negro rate of 16.1 rank below Virginia's 4.8 and 19.2. Similarly, Georgia shows a relatively lower rate for both whites and Negroes, with the former 3.4 per cent and the latter 19.9. Yet in farm tenancy Mississippi, Arkansas, Louisiana, and Georgia rank at the top, each with more than four-fifths of its Negro and more than half of its white farmers tenants. Virginia's tenancy rate for both whites and Negroes, 25.1 and 38.2 ranks below Florida's 31.7 and 48.7.

When we come to examine distributions by counties the significance and complexity of the states appear and accentuate the need for appropriate subregional divisions within and across the states. This theme has already been presented in our summary of subregions, in sections 203-217, pages 153-163 and will be emphasized again in later pages. It is important here, however, to note some of the extreme county variations as examples illustrating the problem. For instance, in illiteracy the counties vary from practically no illiteracy among the whites to 17 per cent. Strangely enough, Virginia which shows a half dozen counties with less than one per cent illiterates has the highest counties recorded. Here, again, Mississippi and Georgia are the only states having a half dozen counties with less than one per cent illiterates, except Virginia and Florida, the latter having 18 such counties. Counties vary greatly also in Negro illiteracy, Florida ranging from 3.1 per cent to 45 per cent; Georgia from 6.2 to 41, and Louisiana still greater with 10.4 to 61.7. Similarly, there is the greatest of variation among the counties in the proportion of Negro population to the total. Thus, Kentucky has 22 counties with less than one per cent Negro, Arkansas has 16, Tennessee has seven, Georgia has four, Virginia and North Carolina have two each, while Alabama has one. On the other hand, Virginia's highest county has 77 per cent of its population Negro, Tennessee's 73, Arkansas' 79, Georgia's 77.9, and North Carolina's 63.5. In Mississippi and Alabama the highest counties are 85.8. A similar variation in the ratio of total land area in farms shows North Carolina with a county with 90 per cent and another with 1.2; Georgia 100 and 11; Ten-

Distilleries and Stills Seized per 100,000 Population, Year Ending June 30, 1930

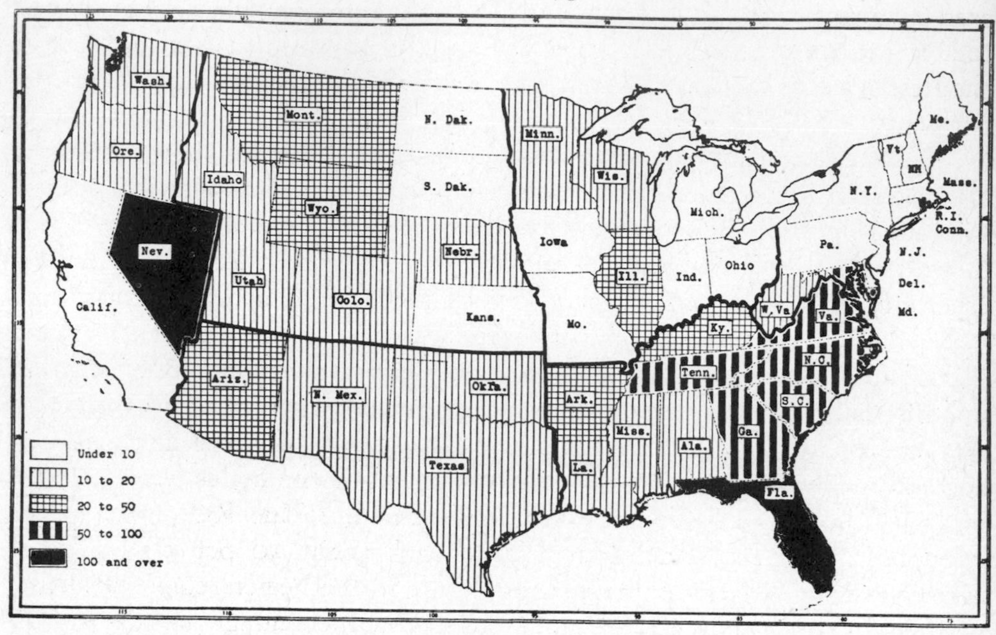

Suicides Per 100,000 Population, 1929

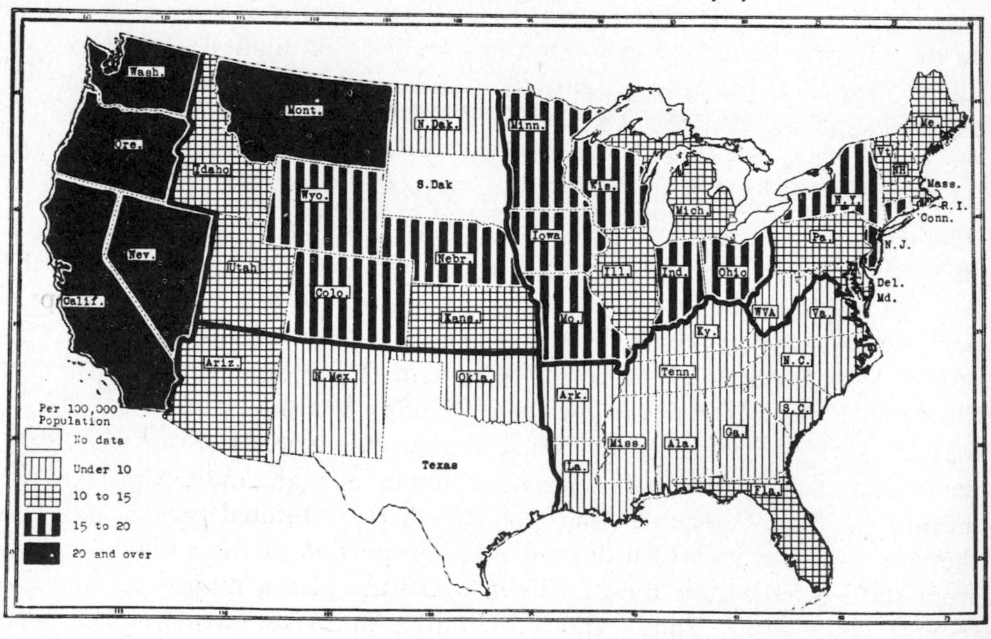

nessee, 100 and 17; Louisiana, 82 and 1.8; Kentucky with 100 and 19. Kentucky, Tennessee, and Virginia have the largest proportion of land area in farms with 77.5, 67.5, and 64.7 respectively, while their lowest county ratings are 19, 17, and 8.3 respectively. Florida's total ratio is smallest with only 14.3 per cent, the county range being from 54 to 0.2 per cent.

Woofter's study of some of these submarginal counties shows that they are generally characterized by stationary populations, predominantly rural, the rate of increase being uniformly slower than the average for the region in which they are located, and the old cotton regions decreasing rapidly, especially in Negro population. Consequently, the urban population is very small in all submarginal counties, the few towns ranging between 2,500 and 5,000 being county sites whose other functions are dependent upon agriculture. The study shows the predominance of agriculture further emphasized by the occupational distribution of those ten years of age and over. In 1930 from 60 to 75 per cent of the males were engaged in agriculture in the old cotton regions and in the Blue Ridge and Ozark Mountains. In the Cumberland Mountains about 50 per cent were in agriculture and 22 per cent in mining, while in the newer regions about 50 per cent were in agriculture and a substantial percentage in the lumber industry.

Another important factor which shows multiple handicaps is that the outward movement of young adults from these counties leaves an unusually large proportion of educable children in the population. Thus, with smaller wealth these counties are left with larger educational burdens. The per capita educational expenditures in the submarginal counties run below the state average uniformly except for the whites in the Black Belt. In this case, as in other special subregions, may be illustrated the problems of equalization, not only between counties but between whites and Negroes. In these submarginal counties, the large white per capita is caused by the fact that the small number of educable white children receive a disproportionately large share of the school funds. The real educational condition of these counties is measured by the small per capita expenditure for the great mass of Negroes in the area. County variations and their dilemmas are further illustrated by the facts that the expenditure on education per dollar of wealth in such variant counties is high, indicating that for meagre facilities these areas have to stretch their limited means and that they are the counties which draw a large proportion of their school money from state equalization funds. They constitute also a major premise for federal equalization funds and coöperative interstate arrangements and planning.

Church Denominations and Membership in the Appalachian Region, 1931

Adapted from *Economic and Social Problems and Conditions of the Southern Appalachians*

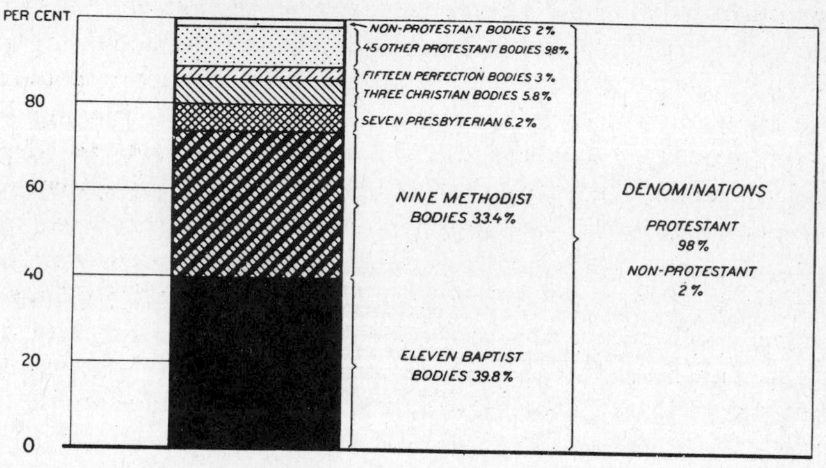

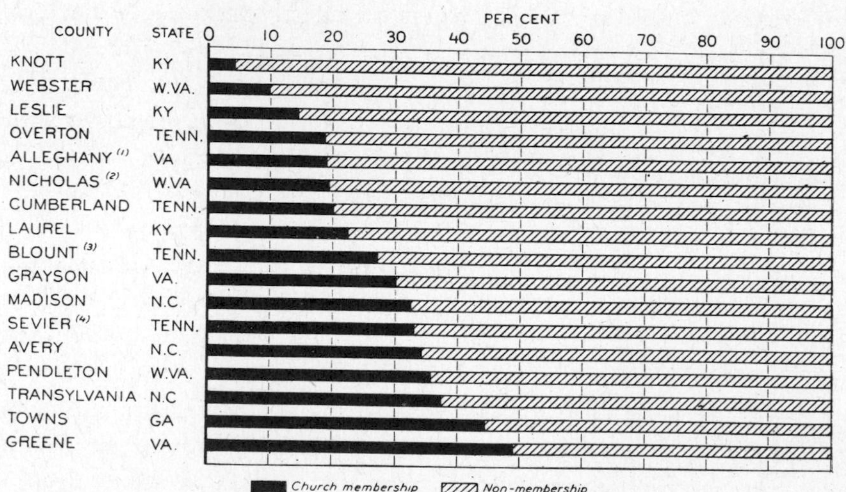

(1) EXCLUSIVE OF CLIFTON FORGE AND COVINGTON (2) EXCLUSIVE OF RICHWOOD (3) EXCLUSIVE OF MARYVILLE WITH ALCOA (4) EXCLUSIVE OF THE VALLEY SECTION

Thus it is seen that state averages mean little when they are composed of from four to five varying groups of counties. Woofter points out in his special studies of subregions that "physiography has had much to do with regional differentiations, but physiographic peculiarities alone are not always sufficient to determine the boundaries. Soil and topography do not always coincide with belts of rainfall and temperature and all of these are often cross-sectioned by industrial belts or population classes. Therefore, while physical differences are the dominant factor underlying the subregional divisions of the South, other factors have been given weight in the final determination of the boundaries of these areas.

He continues "The task of demarking and describing areas could of course be carried down to a very fine point, to such an extent that several hundred slightly differing localities could be distinguished. This, however, would eventually lead to the confusion of incidental with essential social differences. It was, therefore, decided in this project to recognize only such subregions as would be large enough to constitute important socio-economic entities and at the same time exhibit sufficiently different social characteristics from their neighboring regions to warrant the distinction between them.

"In general the geological belts of the South extend North and South, while the climate zones extend East and West. The Coast plains parallel the Atlantic, bending westward along the Gulf. Above these the Piedmont, the Appalachian ranges, the valley, and the Mississippi Bluffs and Delta all run from North to South, but the temperature zones extend from East to West and rainfall belts cross-section these. These blends of soil and climate have dictated certain crop practices, which in time, have formed the habits of the people. The combinations of these have determined the extent of some of the subregions. By this process twenty-seven subregions were delineated. As has been said, they are usually locally recognized as different from each other and they show up markedly different in regional, social, and economic averages."

Woofter believes further that "In many investigations the regional approach will prove more profitable than the use of states as units. This is especially true of institutional or agricultural planning. In fact it has for many years been the practice of State Agricultural Experiment Stations and farm demonstration forces to shape their programs according to subregions of their state rather than uniformly for the whole state. The chief contribution of this study is to show how these regions extend across state lines, and to summarize the general characteristics. A striking instance of the significance of the regions stands out in the industrial index. Much has been said of the industrialization of the South, but when the distribution

The Tobacco South

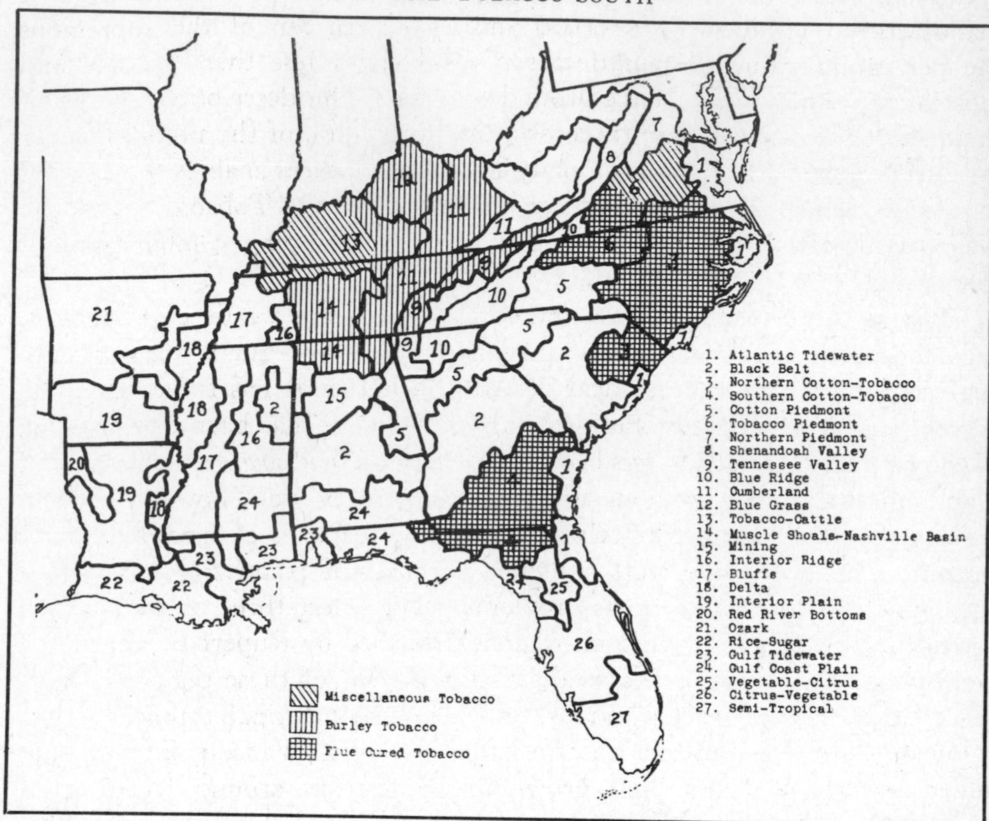

Tobacco Produced in the United States

STATE AND REGION	1000 Pounds
Southeast	*1,353,122*
Virginia	112,867
North Carolina	514,159
South Carolina	85,251
Georgia	84,616
Florida	8,995
Kentucky	423,900
Tennessee	123,334
Alabama	....
Mississippi	....
Arkansas	....
Louisiana	....

STATE AND REGION	1000 Pounds
Northeast	*121,428*
Maine	....
New Hampshire	....
Vermont	....
Massachusetts	11,270
Connecticut	30,067
Rhode Island	....
New York	1,012
New Jersey	....
Delaware	49,858
Pennsylvania	....
Maryland	24,305
West Virginia	4,916

STATE AND REGION	1000 Pounds
Middle States	*119,617*
Ohio	46,757
Indiana	14,863
Illinois	....
Michigan	....
Wisconsin	49,405
Minnesota	2,287
Iowa	....
Missouri	6,305

of industry is examined, only five of the twenty-seven subregions seem greatly affected, i.e., these are the only ones with a per capita value of manufactured products of $100.00 and over. In ten of the subregions the per capita value of manufactured products is less than $30.00, and most of the other twelve have around $50.00. The description of five of these subregions constitutes, therefore, the description of the predominately industrial South. The regional analysis of other indices enables the student to clearly picture the cotton and non-cotton South, the Tobacco South, the Negro South, the Tenant South, and many overlapping combinations of subregions."

Just as the states provide a theme for a separate treatise, so the subregions constitute an unusually promising field for further study and analysis. Although a great deal of valuable material has come from the present study, it must be clear that only a beginning has been made. One of the results of the study has been the clearly defined area of research and planning which the subregions afford. It is perhaps well, however, before leaving the subject to illustrate with still one other type of specialized subregion which may serve well both the purposes of picturizing the region and of delimiting certain of its problems. We select three or four of the agricultural-resources-production regions described by Rupert B. Vance and exclusive of the cotton belts already discussed. One of these regions is composed of a series of trucking areas, of which two principal types have developed. One is the interior and the other is coastal. Vance points out that inland market gardening has grown up in districts around larger cities where products hit the peak of production rather than the peak of prices. The coastal strip reaches in a connected series of zones along the Gulf from the Rio Grande Valley to Florida and from Florida to the Eastern Shores of Virginia and Maryland. The earliest crops of vegetables, reaching the market at the peak of prices, are grown in light, porous sandy soils of the coast, warm and well-drained. Such soils are relatively infertile; they furnish only "sunshine, shower, and support—the plant is fed fertilizer with a precision based on scientific knowledge." Each southern locality can count in normal seasons on from two to three weeks' advantage in crop maturity over the next area to the north. Higher prices offset higher transportation costs and the trucking season swings up the Atlantic coast in an ever-decreasing length of haul to urban markets.

Specialized areas, as Vance shows, participate in the swing of the trucking season up the coast. Thus the district around Hastings, Florida, is devoted to Irish potatoes, three-fourths of which are shipped before the end of May. Plant City, near Tampa, is noted for strawberries while around Sanford, Florida, lies the celery delta, a triangular area of 30,000 acres, drained by tiles, irrigated by artesian wells, heavily fertilized and intensively cultivated. Virginia Eastern Shores go in for spinach and kale. After an area specializes, be it in early cantaloupes, onions, lettuce, or cabbage, the growers come to hand down the knowledge of the particular culture, labor is skilled in its details, the stores handle packing and crating supplies, everybody possesses at least an elementary knowledge of packing and grading, and finally producers' coöperatives are formed to stabilize and perpetuate the culture.

A second specialized area is what Vance calls the rice zones and the sugar bowl, which comprises a strip of coastal prairies, 25 to 50 miles wide stretching for 250 miles through southwest Louisiana and southeast Texas, in which are found some 675,000 acres planted of rice. Together with 172,000 more acres in Arkansas in level prairie between Crowley's Ridge and the Mississippi this area replaced the tidewater Carolinas as the American rice belt. In 1930 these areas produced over 34 million bushels. A fortunate complex of geographic factors underlies this development. The prairies are far enough from the coast to be comparatively free from disastrous wind storms and the ravages of birds. They are near enough to partake of the coastal rainfall of from 40 to 45 inches annually, half of which precipitated during the growing season reduces the need of irrigation. A subsoil of clay forming a hard pan makes of the rice fields a well-nigh perfect basin through which little water penetrates. No water is wasted, and when drained the fields soon dry sufficiently to receive heavy machinery. Level topography not only allows machine cultivation but conditions equitable maturing of the grain, a result which could not be attained were the water of unequal depths. The use of machinery and superior organization enables one man to cultivate about a hundred times as much land and produce from 60 to 70 times as much rice as an oriental farmer. Thus while rice occupied in 1919 only six per cent of the land area in this subregion, it produced some 75 per cent of the value of total crops. The future of rice farming in this area finds its limits in the demands and food habits of the people. It can supply America's demands and export some 12 million bushels. The balance of this area, easily adaptable to rice culture, should not be brought into cultivation unless market prices justify such a step. Rice is notable as one southern crop which has escaped the dominion of hard tasks and field labor of women and children, by efficient machine cultivation.

A third of the Vance series of areas which constitute subregional divisions is that of the tobacco belts, in which nearly 90 per cent of the country's tobacco acreage is found in five southern states. Soil types delimit the three major zones of tobacco culture in the South. With changes in soils the tobacco plant proceeds to develop variations in size, structure, delicacy of fibre, fragrance, color, porosity, and secretion of resinous substances. Pale sandy soils grow a yellow leaf; chocolate or reddish clay soils furnish the heavy dark export tobacco; while the gray limestone soils of Kentucky produce white burley. Varying methods of curing further differentiate the types grown in each region.

Northern counties of Tennessee and western counties of Kentucky devote almost 200,000 acres to a dark fire-cured tobacco much prized by European smokers. Only 400,000 acres mainly in the Kentucky Bluegrass grow white burley, a light air-cured leaf suitable for chewing tobacco. Latest and most important, the bright belt of the Southeast devotes 1,150,000 acres to the light flue-cured tobaccos suitable for cigarettes. Here are found four sub-zones. The old belt located in the Piedmont came into prominence in 1852 when two farmer boys of Caswell County, North Carolina, discovered the capacity of sandy ridges along the central Carolina-Virginia borders to grow a light yellow leaf for finer cigarettes. The old belt now cultivates some 425,000 acres. After 1880 this culture spread eastward to the cotton plantation area of coastal North Carolina, later to a similar area in South Carolina. The Eastern North Carolina belt plants some 400,000 acres to the weed, the central Carolinas half as much. Georgia-Florida, latest addition to southern cigarette zones, plants some 130,000 acres.

A fourth region, once the most important of all except the cotton belts with which it is partly identical, is the "Piney Woods," again coming to the forefront in new industries of pulp and reforestation. This is the last of Vance's dozen regions used to illustrate our case. The Piney Woods furnish a distinctive region, far-reaching in the adjustments its native forests have occasioned. The virgin pineries accounted for some 125 of the 298 million acres of virgin forests stretching through eleven southern states from Virginia to Texas. The area's river bottoms are given over to mixed cypress, tupelo and gum, its Appalachian highlands to hardwoods, its uplands to oak and short-leaf pine, its flatwoods to slash, loblolly and long-leaf. Together these pines "formed one of the richest reservoirs of soft-woods on the earth's surface." On the major region of long-leaf pine human settlement has advanced in a series of frontiers. First came the pioneer who, in the task of clearing new ground for cultivation, triumphantly consigned pine timber to the flames of frontier log rollings. Up until about 1880 more trees were cut in the United States for the sake of clearing land than for lumber. Early in the Piney Woods developed the naval stores industry along with the extraction of resin and turpentine. Lumbering marked the third stage of exploitation in the pines, a stage that was often speeded up by the necessity of salvaging trees before they decayed from the effects of excessive turpentining. The last stage finds the South confronted with a surfeit of cut-over lands, whose absorption into grazing, agriculture, or reforestation all seem problematic. Of the 125 million acres in virgin pine, 100 million have been cut-over, ten and a half million absorbed into agriculture, and 33 million remain without new growth. The exploitation of the Piney Woods began at the northern tier of states with North Carolina which once deserved its title of Tar Heel state and swept southward until the yellow pine and naval stores industries are making their last stand in Georgia, Florida, and Mississippi. What the next steps will bring forth will depend upon the effectiveness of the new regional planning.

Returning now to our earlier discussion of the functional approach through subregions, we note that, as observed by the National Resources Committee, there are already five types of regional units designed to handle the problems of decentralized planning, for which the powers of individual states are inadequate. These include: the Regional Planning organizations formed in New England and the Pacific Northwest; the interstate metropolitan organizations of which those at St. Louis, Philadelphia, Chicago, Washington, and New York are examples; the Tennessee Valley Authority; the interstate compact such as exists between the states which use the waters of the Colorado River; the interstate coöperative organizations of state officials exemplified by the Council of State Governments.

Both the New England Planning Commission and the Pacific Northwest Planning Commission although established less than two years, have already made definite progress toward coördinated planning in the regions involved. Through their efforts, so the Committee reports, Federal agencies have been brought more closely together, coöperation between states is more pronounced, federal and state programs are being facilitated, and greater opportunity is afforded non-governmental organizations to work with government agencies. The Pacific Northwest Planning Commission includes representation from the Planning Boards of Washington, Montana, Oregon, and Wyoming, the district office of the National Resources Committee, and 266 local planning bodies. It also has the support of educational, business, transportation, and civic groups. The New England Planning Commission has representatives from the Planning Boards of Maine, Massachusetts, New Hampshire, Vermont, Connecticut, and Rhode Island. Working with the Commission is an advisory committee of 535 New England citizens interested in planning. Of this number 50 are government officials, 131 represent Chambers of Commerce, 72 represent planning boards, 114 are officers of unofficial organizations, 51 are mayors, and the remainder private individuals. The further significance of this to regional planning is indicated in the next chapter.

CHAPTER XI

TOWARDS REGIONAL PLANNING

We return now to our original premise that fundamental questions concerning the region are valid only in proportion as they can be answered in terms of realistic inventory of fact and of the actualities of what is to be done. It was pointed out that the time has come to follow up the earlier broadsides and critical appraisals of southern culture with more nearly approaching functional analysis and working specifications. Basic to such an objective, we have pointed out, in addition to sensing the immensity and time quality of cultural reconstruction and the exceedingly complex nature of the regional culture involved, are the motivation and capacity to focus upon a relatively small number of elemental factors toward which practical study and planning may be directed.

Yet the objections to any attempt to focus the findings of the Southern Regional Study upon regional planning are numerous and for the most part apparent. Some of these are apparent in the brief syllabus and summary "Towards Social Planning," already presented in Sections 253-272, on pages 187-205. Such difficulties were also implied in the cautious statement of a planning objective, set forth in the preliminary work memorandum for the study in 1931 in which it was pointed out that it might be "at least an approach to social planning. It may be an introduction to a program of regional planning." The objections to planning are inherent in the difficulties of actual achievement in the face of public skepticism and opposition as well as in the limitations of present-day planning. It is quite clear that the people are not ready for social planning, that facts and specifications are not yet available, that immaturity marks the great body of plans and proposals, and that administrative difficulties seem well nigh insurmountable. The public is accustomed to be not only skeptical but genuinely afraid of all this planning talk, and for several reasons. One is that the public confuses orderly, progressive and flexible social planning with "economic planning," "planned economy," "national planning." Another is that the people are always skeptical of too much theorizing and experimentation. The public pokes abundant fun at the experts and the specialists. And social planning must be done by specialists and experts. The public, further, is inclined to take social planning talk as either mere jargon or more utopian idealism which will amount to little. Or if not this, if it is to be successful, it is conceived of as something quite radical, un-American, taking away American liberties, contrary to the Constitution. In so far as the public is willing to accept the planning hypothesis, there are fears of the dangers of artificial society and supertechnology superimposed upon the people by immature administrators through bureaucratic organization and through experimentation not sufficiently matured and balanced with actualities. Of special importance is the fear of the states and of the regions that their autonomy will be endangered and that regional advantages and resources will be ignored in favor of sectional priorities in economics and politics. And, of course, social planning is the most difficult and the least emotional and sentimental way, requiring time, skill, technical training, extraordinary ability, patience, courage.

Since our earlier premise of 1931, events have moved rapidly; both concepts and action in the field of social planning have been multiplied and accelerated; regionalism has developed much more rapidly and realistically than was generally expected at the time. There is, therefore, added obligation and opportunity to explore the possibilities of utilizing this regional analysis in terms of regional and national social planning. By the same token and because of much promiscuous experimentation at Washington which has been designated "planning," more of the difficulties have become apparent than were manifest before so much discussion had focused attention upon planning and regionalism.

Evidences of this increasing emphasis upon social planning need be enumerated here only as they bear upon the present work. There is increasing evidence to justify the conclusion that America, in competition with other sovereign forms of social control, must work out its enduring balance between individualization and socialization through a planned and orderly transitional democracy. In this process regional balance is a key problem: balance between the people and their resources; between agriculture and industry; balance of population itself in the attempt to adjust the people to the regional pattern. This is normal dilemma accentuated by emergency developments. More than a thousand titles stand as the visible measures of the widespread discussion of this dilemma during the last few years. Many organizations, national and local, have grown out of the realistic needs everywhere so apparent. Whether these and others will make valid contributions remains to be seen. Typical is the American Society of Planning Officials, which has been recently organized and has instituted a regular service "to promote efficiency in land and community planning." Another is the National Economic and Social Planning Association, which, through its *Plan Age* and other means, undertakes to study "methods for the full utilization of the productive resources of the United States to give the American people the highest possible material and cultural standard of living." The purposes of the Association are further to "maintain contacts between persons interested in economic and social planning; to stimulate the formation of groups in various sections of the United States for discussion and for possible practical action; and to carry on systematic educational work."

Again, numerous experiments and explorations have been made in the field of action. State planning boards have been set up in all of the states except two, enlisting the interest of a personnel of more than 700 individuals participating in the work of state planning boards. Enabling legislation has been passed in many of the states. At least two regional planning boards have been organized. The National Planning Board was organized and later became the National Resources Board, which still later was changed to the National Resources Committee. From this Board and Committee have come a number of excellent reports on social planning and a great body of mimeographed materials projected for promotion, publicity, and organization. From the Mississippi Valley Committee of the Public Works Administration has come an extraordinary volume dealing primarily with the physical aspects of the Mississippi Valley. The Tennessee Valley Authority has appeared continuously as an example of exploration in national-regional and subregional planning. Other examples of the planning approach may be found in the Rural Electrification Administration, the Agricultural Adjustment Administration, and some other New Deal organizations and experiments in which inhere the beginnings of realistic planning. These and others, together with numerous conferences, large and small, have tended to establish a planning premise in the United States as a framework for both "scientific" and "practical" programs.

Allowing for many false starts, for the too free use and abuse of the term, and for all the limitations and difficulties inherent, the conclusion still seems justified that in the next period of development in American culture there will be an increasing emphasis, in both social study and social action, upon the concept and techniques of social planning. Such social planning, however, attempts no utopian tasks superimposed through dictation. It is important, therefore, to project the social planning concept and technique not only upon the very realistic foundations of the present emergency but upon the framework of American institutions. American social planning, while specifying an ordered society with more and more directed processes, nevertheless calls for coöperative and coördinated design of, for, and by all institutions and all regions rather than by government alone through centralized autocracy. It is an extension and transubstantiation of the first great American experiment in social planning, namely, the Constitution of the United States. Such planning will comprehend a working equilibrium in the whole culture process and function, featuring a series of priority schedules, in contradistinction to a mere social *plan* or to a planned economic order constituted as a single project in which inheres the sovereign power to execute. It will utilize the full capacity of a social engineering competent to build not only new structures for the nation but to carry in the meantime the traffic of all the institutions in a transitional society and within these institutions to permit of orientation, spontaneity, flexibility.

The assumption seems further justified that social planning has already gone beyond the discussion stage and is becoming a part of the fabric of the new culture. Uncontrolled and undesigned the planning movement itself might well nigh defeat its own objectives and retard the nation. It follows, therefore, if permanence and stability are to be attained, that there is need for the long-time view based upon the actualities of both cultural development and scientific principles and upon practical, workable techniques growing out of factual inventories. Inherent also in the present stage of planning are not only design but motivation. Thus, the subject of social planning must be given the most careful consideration possible from both the popular viewpoint of public interest and interpretation and from the scientific viewpoint of social study and social action. On the one hand, there can be no success without an extraordinary effort in adult education, carrying to the people the power of both fact and thinking. There is need for a powerful regional motivation and also a spontaneous folk movement. And, again, here is supreme test for all the techniques and mastery of social science. The first stages are, therefore, frankly "scientific," "theoretical," and promotional. These, however, constitute the first essentials for all practical working programs.

There appears to be ample evidence also for another premise, namely, that due to the bigness of the nation and to its cultural backgrounds and motivations, as well as to technological considerations, the regional approach and analysis are fundamental to any successful permanent social planning program or procedure in the United States. This evidence like that in relation to planning is of many sorts. There is, first of all, a large body of literature and hundreds of regional and subregional classifications of the nation and the states looking toward a more accurate understanding of facts and the more effective administration of programs. To cite one example, there has come from a special Committee on Regional Study, set up by the National Resources Committee, a series of reports on "Regional

Factors in National Planning and Development." In these reports, in addition to certain summaries of what has been written have been emphasized to a considerable extent the recent developments and prospects not only in the general objectives and concepts of regionalism, but many special factors. Among these are regional factors as revealed in state relations, as revealed by federal departmental experience, by federally created regional authorities, provisions for organizations, interstate compacts, better delineation of regions, and others.

In addition to points of emphasis already presented in Chapter I, Sections 203-228, pages 153-173, and throughout Chapter III, perhaps a single conclusion from the Committee's report will be adequate to reëmphasize the regional emphasis. "We reiterate," the Committee continues, "that regional science reveals clearly that certain geographic principles, involving the interrelationship of economic, social, political, and environmental factors, are the fundamental elements of regionalism. These, therefore, should be the basic criteria underlying any regional devices which may be proposed and set up for planning and planned development. The Committee wishes to point out that there is a growing need for emphasis upon the regional point of view in both research and public administration. Adequate planning for the next period in American development must be based upon an appreciation of tremendous regional differences in the nation. The careful delineation of the basic regions of the United States becomes, therefore, an important matter."

From the vantage point of the present work, certain other general considerations underlie both the "theoretical" and "scientific" framework of regional planning and actual beginnings in the way of comprehensive and definite action. One such point of emphasis is the whole body of attitudes, beliefs, and practices in the southern regions toward the general concept of a planned society and toward the many issues and specific problems involved. These attitudes and their resulting conditioning of both the southern regions and of the nation at large are basic to both the nature and strategy of social action. Thus, to cite an illustration, certain spokesmen for the great Texas part of the Southwestern Region affirm that, "in spite of all the oracular decrees of the economic planners, the path of Texas lies forward. . . . Plain common sense, it seems to us negatives the idea that Texas or any other similar region in the United States can be disciplined or controlled by any central authority . . . in such a way as to prevent development and progress. The momentum of past development and progress is too strong, and the room for expansion too great, for anything of the kind to be done successfully. We are inclined to believe that this very circumstance precludes the success of any such national plan as some gentlemen talk so glibly about. But whether this be true or not, certain it is that Texas will remain 'free territory,' so to speak, no matter what happens to the country taken as a whole."

Attitudes are further involved in fundamental issues of wage differentials between North and South and in the South between white and Negro, which affect the whole planning structure for production and consumption and for living standards and purchasing power. Involved also are other factors, such as the will and capacity to provide the tools of science and training for skilled workers. So, too, are involved attitudes and practices toward other race differentials; the conflict between urban and rural life; the attitude toward cultural adequacy and the support of institutions.

Moreover, the attitudes and practices of other regions and of the federal government are also basic to successful planning. The task of coöperative effort and control is not just one of temporary relief for a region through some grand philanthropy or subsidy or of arbitrary apportionment of prorata allotments, nor is it to be attained merely through yielding to political pressure. Nor is successful planning or reconstruction to be achieved on any basic concept which envisages the regions as mere units of contest and conflict and drain, or as sections upon which may be foisted immature experiments or inferior goods or adventurous misfits from the metropolis. Rather are they to be integrated as great regional provinces, so necessary to the adequacy of a great nation, to be built up for the normal expansion of population and trade. Nor is it possible to effect an integrated plan for national development through the present phenomenal ignorance, one region of another, the nation of all. Furthermore, regional participation in reconstructed plans for controlled organization and production should not be expected if the national mind reflects such mass immaturity as has been manifest in intolerant reform propaganda, in the extraordinary results which were expected from such independent movements as humanism, technocracy, self-contained America, or in the narrow regimentation of people to artificial standards, or in many of the immature New Deal plans which ignored regional reality.

A part of the dilemma of attitudes is the determining of policy with reference to regional and sectional participation in national affairs and the extent to which regions propose to be self-contained and sectionally minded. In the case of the southern regions it is imperative that a decision be made at the outset as to whether the regions can or should develop without outside aid. The conclusions of this study indicate that it is not possible for the South to so master its situation as to transvaluate its deficiency into adequacy without a great deal of outside coöperative assistance in men and money and technics, from federal aid, from business enterprise, from endowed agencies. The Texas declaration of "free territory" for independent action was predicated upon the assumption of returning prosperity which, admittedly due to cotton and petroleum prices, however, had followed in the wake of federal participation to the amount of more than one hundred million dollars. The State's quota of more than forty-five million dollars from land rentals was more than half of all that was paid to all the other states. The State had received more than three million dollars in loans for seed, feed, drought recovery; many millions of dollars for public relief in a short period in which the State itself made a negligible matching of funds. The Southeast and the Southwest had received two-thirds of the total funds for crop losses and 85 per cent of all the land rental moneys for the whole nation; millions of dollars in CWA, PWA, FERA and WPA; other millions of dollars on the TVA project.

Likewise, in the past the national philanthropic foundations have made special case of the region. The Carnegie Corporation has expended more than half of its total in the South. The Rosenwald Fund has made the South its special field in the development of Negro schools. The Rockefeller groups have spent more than a hundred million dollars; while the earlier Peabody funds had greatly enriched the teacher-training facilities of the entire region. The aggregate of additional private philanthropy had been enormous, while the total of federal funds in land grant institutions, public health and sanitation, public highways, public works and the other supplementary services has aggregated staggering amounts. The importance of interregional-national coöperation may be indicated by certain questions. First, what would be the dilemma of the southern regions if they could not borrow public and private funds from the East? Second, is it possible for a region which has no universities of the first rank to build up its institutions in any reasonably short time without outside help? On the other hand, is it possible to have social adequacy without the support and leadership inherent in universities? If the South proposes to develop without outside help, how can it be done? If, on the other hand, it must have supplementary aid, must there not be some sort of coöperation and designed order in which the South must do its part, through which progress can be made?

Other general basic factors may be emphasized through a series of premises which have to do with the actual inventory and planning in the major fundamentals of regional culture. The first is that of planning for the reorganization and development of the agricultural South through practical programs of optimum production of the main commodities worked out in relation to industrial development and foreign trade. Planning for industry and its balance with agriculture constitutes a second premise upon which regional development will depend. The third major grouping of problems centers around politics and government. These include the powerful political culture of the "Solid South," as well as legislation for security and public welfare and fiscal policies and reorganization of government through the new alignment of public administration and economic reconstruction. The fourth grouping of problems centers around the supreme task of planning for a very genuine development of institutions of higher learning, for programs of research, of science and technical arts, and for interregional cultural expansion. Although effective planning programs are needed for each of these clusters of problems, the conclusion seems justified that the first obligations are toward the first and fourth, as being minimum next steps for planning, on the one hand, in the lower but basic level of agricultural economics and, on the other, the higher and equally basic level of education, research, science, technics, and leadership. The evidence seems overwhelming that there can be no adequate culture in the South without the reconstruction of its agriculture and that, if the regions would support adequately the institutions and tools of science and learning, the future of its economics and government would be safe. This assumes a trained leadership and research programs adequate to evolve policies for such fundamentals as population and social-industrial relationships.

We have pointed out again and again that planning for a reconstructed agriculture in the Southeast will require rare strategy, skill, boldness. It is essentially a problem of ascertaining and achieving a program of optimum production. It is more than land utilization. It is more than controlled production and increased prices in cotton and tobacco. There is the dilemma of an agriculture devoted to the production of export crops, with exports on the decrease. This commercial farming policy is in an area preëminently well adapted to food crops and diversified farming and with nearly half of its people living below any reasonable standard of culture and abundance. There is the phenomenon of annual increment in deficiency from land waste and of increase in tenant dependency, and consequently decrease in the value and income-capacity of southern farms. There is the spectacle of the Southwest increasing its capacity and its actual production, at lower costs, of the cash crops for export with every indication that its capacity will soon be equal to the world's supply of cotton. The Southeast must plan readjustments in the light of this sort of competition.

It seems likely that the main problems for immediate adjustment will include the following: some readjustment at once that will reconstruct the present tenant system; new provisions for an adequate credit system; some readjustment and redistribution of the present crop land uses, with some new crops and a very large increase in ratio of food and feed crops; some immediate methods of raising the standard of consumption of commodities by the southern people, both in the rural areas and in the cities; some arrangement whereby interregional exchange and trade may be promoted; an economy which will enable the farmer to spend his cash money for needed goods rather than for commercial fertilizer and food and feed crops supplies; some way to increase the technical facilities whereby the production and processing of commodities may be more effective; some practical way of adding to the technical comforts and conveniences of farm and home life; some method for the redistribution of submarginal lands and people within the present subregional area rather than wholesale retirement of lands and shifting of people; some increasingly effective arrangements for the increase of agricultural exports. If the southern regions could devote a fourth of the technology and work to their agricultural problems that has been developed in the far western regions, they would become literally garden spots of the world. Yet this can be done only through a well motivated coördinated planning program.

That these problems, in addition to their average application to any agricultural region, are affected by regional differentials calls for exceptional planning strategy. The kind of people and their experience and training and backgrounds must be taken into consideration before specifications for particular crops and land uses and credit and consumption habits can be determined. The mastery of climate and of the home hygiene and diet regimen is of first importance. Thus there will be needed a twofold planning approach. One will be a planning strategy such as becomes necessary for the reconstruction of the whole system of commercial agriculture, of markets, production, and the like. The other will be a specialized planning strategy directed toward the complete reconstruction of the system which at present crushes the tenant and the small farmer, now bordering near peasantry or a submarginal level.

For this planning there will be needed federal, state, and local public and semi-public aid directed toward the actual working out of specific next steps. In addition to a federal reserve or revolving fund, the samplings of the necessary semi-public and community projects would include the following: the pooling of rural labor available for carrying forward projects of rural rehabilitation especially where farm mechanics and organization are involved; the pooling in county and/or community of heavier machinery for harvesting, threshing, storing and processing farm products; special smaller new industries relating to the breeding, distribution, and planting of lespedeza, legumes, smaller winter grains, special industries relating to fence posts, fencing and building of farm buildings such as tool and hay sheds, storage houses; special county unit plans for utilizing and developing forest and grass lands, for clearing rich bottom waste lands and for squaring off farm fields to the end that thousands of waste "patches" are eliminated; and other practical ways of providing the smaller farmer or tenant with the minimum technological ways of realizing on his meager beginnings; coöperative arrangements with purebred livestock breed clubs, state clubs, county and community organizations, and all federal, state, and county farm and home agents.

In somewhat the same way, planning strategy for regional industry would be of two sorts. One is that which undertakes to work out satisfactory adjustments and expansion of the general field of industry, including large and small industries, special new industries, home and foreign markets, regional differentials, labor organization and supply, freight rates and interregional exchange, technological aspects of production, distribution, and financing. We have pointed out essential criteria for the planning of new industries and for the utilization of regional materials in the best perspective to inter-regional exchange. It is assumed, also, that planning for an increased industrial South is not itself a special project in which will inhere the necessary specifications. On the other hand, the second sort of planning will integrate the whole industrial region with the agricultural reorganization, including special planning for decentralized industry, for village and community industries, for a large number of new smaller industries, and for at least two six-year periods of semi-civil or public works programs looking toward the rehabilitation of farms and farm houses, of reforestation and erosion work, of housing deficiencies, and especially for equalizing work and facilities for Negroes in schools, health, sanitation, and the like. Citing a type of new industry, for instance, it must be clear that a region incomparably adapted to the production of raw materials necessary for cheese production and now affording less than three per cent of the cheese processing plants in the country, offers an excellent field for planning new opportunities.

Planning strategy with reference to politics, government, and public administration, again, is a complex problem. Basic to all considerations will be the economic backgrounds, such as have already been characterized as in many cases incapable of supporting the usual services of modern government. This again involves the question of federal coöperation and federal support and the whole attitude of the southern regions with reference to sectionalism and political representation. It involves again the problem of fundamental deficiencies for the time being—apparently insolvable difficulties—with reference to the Negro's part in government and social control. Here the strategy of planning is of the greatest significance in that it may make the incidence through which folkways may be changed and fairer practices inaugurated. Certain technical procedures, such as might be available in the TVA areas, for example, might initiate new practices which, being logical and an essential part of the development, would inaugurate fairer practices for the whole region. From these formal "stateways" could be developed far-reaching measures, which apparently cannot be set up as effectively in any other way. Other special aspects of the problem which relate particularly to the cultural foundation of the region involve the task of influencing southern politics to concern itself more with principles of economy and efficiency than with personal and party issues. Modification of the political culture of the region, probably the most powerful single factor, through gradual workable methods, therefore, lies at the base of any planning approach. In addition to these general aspects of the problem, it is understood that the usual technical problems of public administration, consolidation of local units of government, reorganization of state governments, new legislation, social security, and other special phases are particularly in need of special efforts.

The assumption underlying the premise that the supreme need for planning is in the field of higher education, science, and other cultural institutions is that any region which has the will and capacity to support educational and scientific institutions of the highest order, because of this desire and capacity and because of what the institutions achieve in leadership and technology in economic and political direction, in upraising of standards and in social guidance, will automatically develop increasingly an adequate culture. The contrary assumption seems equally clear: that it is not possible to develop the highest culture without the highest types of technical and cultural tools. A planning strategy, therefore, is doubly necessary in proportion as there may be lacking either the motivation or the capacity for such institutions. That these are lacking is indicated by the fact that the Southeast, which might reasonably score 600 points in a given measure of its universities, scores only 30. Yet, how great is the problem of a region which assigns the largest ratio of any region of its total wealth to school property yet registers the lowest rating in nearly all of its educational achievements? Or what is the problem of strain and cultural revolution going on in the southeastern universities, whose ratio of out-of-the-region students, from North, East, West, is greater than that of similar insitutions in any other region? Or what is the measure of drain and waste in the multiplicity of institutions and the duplication of the functions? Or again can any one or two or three institutions lead the way for the region unless they have also a constituency and an administrative fellowship from other institutions? Can the boards and administrative officers of universities now far below the level which they desire venture upon bold strategy for growth without the united support and fellowship of others? Is it, therefore, practicable to provide such support and strategy through a planning group and through a reserve fund to be provided from federal equalization funds, endowed agencies, state appropriations, private groups and individuals, to be made available under such definite and mutually satisfactory terms as will transvaluate the whole system in a relatively short time?

If we assume the twofold irreducible minimum, namely, working from the lowest economic level, without which education, science, and leadership have no firm basis upon which to build, and from the upper brackets of science, educational institutions, and leadership, without which adequate modification of the lower level and the total culture cannot be attained; and if we assume that leadership, planning, and action must begin from the upper brackets of educational leadership, there appear to be three main approaches. The *first* of these is through the strengthening of a limited number of *regional institutional centers* in which would be concentrated a greater degree of research, technological arts, and training for public service. The second approach would be through a comprehensive *functional framework* of inquiry and action, in which the major problems and the areas of deficiency would be attacked through special but well integrated programs of work. The third would be through well designed, *experimental units of work.* In each of these approaches to provide modification of culture, namely the institutional, the functional, and the experimental, the irreducible minimum is a realistic, bold program of appraisal and action, in which results are to be attained through specific, actual, working, technical units of work rather than merely through mass ideology, mass attack, or general education and propaganda.

Each of these approaches is susceptible to such elaboration and development as will be commensurate with the resources and capacities of the region. *First,* with reference to the *institutional approach,* we have already emphasized the necessity of institutions of the highest order and of science and skills if the region is to realize anything like its maximum opportunities. With such institutions, science, and technology, it can go forward; without them it cannot. On the other hand, it has been difficult to establish, endow, and develop institutions of the highest ranking due to limitation of funds, to lack of university-mindedness, to lack of coöperation, to inter-institutional and inter-state jealousies, as well as to lack of funds from outside the region in sufficiently large amounts as to insure initial caliber and standards adequate to attract continuing funds and support, both within and without the region.

These difficulties, however, but accentuate the importance of such a concentration to the South. The framework of such regional concentration of institutions of higher learning and of research centers will comprehend a number of special features in addition to standard specifications which would inhere in any university program. The number and location of the regional centers must be worked out alongside a realistic appraisal of possibilities not only for the present but for continuing support. Such regional centers must provide for agricultural and technical research and for technical and professional training, as well as for the more formal university training and departmental researches. To illustrate, of special importance in order to insure the national-regional quality of these universities would be exchange professors; such exchange arrangement should provide for not only exchange of professors between southern and eastern and western institutions, but also inter-institutional exchange within the Southeast itself. Such exchanges would range from a quarter or semester to a year and would be negotiated not only between the larger universities, but also between the smaller colleges and teacher training schools and the larger institutions. In each instance it would be necessary to meet the differentials between salaries in the larger and smaller institutions in the region and between eastern and western and southern institutions. Similar arrangements would be provided for exchange fellowships between northern and eastern and southern institutions, while field work and research projects within the southern region should be worked out with suitable arrangements to coöperate with various institutions and subregions of the Southeast.

Since research constitutes one of the major needs of the region and is a vital element in any planning program, it is of the utmost importance that a larger coördinated plan of research should be an integral part of any program. The task is to join reality and research. Manifestly, there would be areas of research which would justify definite priority schedules, such as the study of marginal and submarginal groups, the quality and movement of population, racial and regional differentials, factors of climate and diet in relation to work and creative effort, agricultural and technical research, and sound theory and practice in programs of optimum production and consumption programs. Thus, hand in hand must be planned the development of natural resources, industry, agriculture, with the commensurate development of the people, trained and equipped with skills necessary to meet the needs of a changing competitive culture.

Research projects within these areas, however, will not be restricted to the face problems of housing or electrification or erosion or submarginal lands, but to a wide range of inquiries with reference to the capacities of the people themselves, to differentials between different groups of tenants, of white and Negro, of southeastern and southwestern groups; to the range of new and increased old occupations needed to meet the needs of the new economy; to the measuring of cultural conditioning of tenant folk as contrasted with innate capacity. Similarly, research into the uses and capacity of land will contemplate measures of capacity for reintegration into the new economy, for adding value to land and farms, and to specialized relocation of families rather than wholesale redistribution. These are representative of the fruitful areas to which should be added comparative studies of the relative value to the region of the 3,000 million dollars, representing the maximization of the engineers' plans for flood control alone in the Southeast as compared to the much smaller amounts of 100 or 200 million dollars for attacking the tenant problem at the bottom. It would be difficult, also, to find a more significant and neglected field of research than that of rural housing, rural standards of diet, and home hygiene. So, too, multiple projects of research within the areas opened up by new electrification, including the new housing, the new possibilities of cooling techniques for the wide application to southern homes and offices.

One or two other indices are important in the selection of research areas. One such index would be determined by the viewpoints or motivation with which specialized research might be undertaken. For instance, one whole group of projects might be undertaken from the viewpoint of the tenant himself and his family. That is, these inquiries would focus upon human factors, seeking data on what is to become of the tenant farmer in the new arrangements. Another viewpoint would focus upon the land, its use, its abuse, its redistribution and conservation, with a view to the ultimate fortunes of the region. Still another viewpoint for research would focus upon the whole cotton economy itself rather than upon the workers or the land. A number of other projects would be selected with a view to their interregional relationships as between the Southeast and the Southwest or the Southeast and the Middle States, while still others would be chosen to experiment and demonstrate techniques and procedures of cooperation between the physical sciences and the social sciences. And finally projects would be chosen in proportion as they were susceptible of practical research commensurate with the personnel, resources, and facilities available for the purpose.

In so far as it is practicable to envisage a broad area of research, projected with a view to utilizing continuous but flexible techniques susceptible of workable units or smaller areas integrated into the whole fabric, it would seem profitable to formulate a region-wide plan for research in optimum programs. This would involve, first of all, studies of population in the

South, in which comparatively little has ever been attempted. This again involves not only the optimum population, but the kind of people, the rate of increase, problems of population limitation, migration and distribution. It involves new techniques and procedures for more dependable measures of what constitutes marginal and submarginal people, new indices of man-land ratios, worked out in accordance with the nature of the land and of men and of crops. Such a program would feature especially new techniques and ways of studying consumption and standards of living, emphasizing original data and projects approximating the experimental method of research in basic consumer's capacity for food, clothing, housing, producer's goods. The project would inquire not only into optima of population and of consumption, but particularly also into the optimum uses of amounts of land and cultivation alongside projects inquiring into optimum production within the region, as well as interregional optima.

Here, again, the projects would call for new techniques and measures for determining the nature and disposition to be made of marginal and submarginal lands, avoiding many of the paradoxes, overlappings, duplications, and waste of much research and action in this field. The areas for the study of optimum programs of production have already been indicated, but so far no one has succeeded in formulating an adequate program with dependable methods and resources, which would include researches in the areas of major agricultural commodities, of farming in relation to decentralized industry, of workowner farms, of self-sufficiency support. No adequate studies have been made of the capacities of the people, both for achievement in their present situation and for improvement. No adequate studies have been made of regional differentials, or race differentials, or of differentials within and among different groups of people and occupations, or of commercial situations, such as freight rates. There is also needed a great deal more research into the theoretical aspects of optimum concepts and programs. There is needed, furthermore, dynamic research into the theoretical and practical aspects of regionalism and social planning. Within this broad frame of study would be an almost unlimited number of smaller areas for subregional analysis, for the analysis of elemental deficiencies, of submarginality, and particularly of factors of climate, and of diet.

The *second* type of general educational approach to planning listed is through an *adequate functional* framework well adapted to the region. Such functional approach naturally will involve institutions and institutional centers and will focus upon many of those elemental factors, already emphasized, towards which practical study and planning may be directed. Here, as in the case of the research program, certain areas and fields appear to be susceptible to special priority schedules. In general, these areas of emphasis will be determined not only in relation to the principal regional problems but also in relation to those areas of action in which the federal government is functioning, in which state and local governments and institutions are functioning, and in which private organizations and endowed institutions are or may be at work. Points of emphasis, programs, and procedures, and priority schedules themselves will be determined and interrelated with each of these factors in mind. Among the special areas, for instance, in which the federal government is working, are soil erosion, rural resettlement, rural electrification, water resources and pollution, experimental and demonstration home and farm work, and agricultural research. Within this framework of activity the planning approach will provide for better coördination and integration among various institutions; between the white land grant colleges and the Negro land grant colleges; between institutions of higher learning for whites and Negroes; for coöperative programs of both research and actual work between Negroes and whites; closer coöperation between the home and farm demonstration agents and public welfare and social work agencies; and between and among state planning boards and state and federal departments and activities. Other important areas would include adult education programs, providing especially for instruction and organization in politics and public relations, and in the field of social science and social problems; increased and more effective training of personnel for public service and special programs in public administration, public health, public welfare; special programs of teacher training, and especially in the training of faculties in teacher-training institutions; special programs for the strengthening of state departments of education and for coördinating these with state educational institutions; continued enlargement and support of libraries and library work.

The *third* approach to regional planning, namely *the experimental*, will, of course, overlap and utilize the other two approaches in so far as they have become effective. Some experiments will fall within the areas and programs already specified. More particularly, however, the experimental approach offers great promise in such programs as subregional planning, in which a relatively small number of units of activity within a relatively small subregion of the highest attainable degrees of homogeneity for the purposes in mind are utilized to test out in the reality of everyday practice the recommendations that have come from recent years of study and research. Thus, to illustrate, it would be possible to select a limited number of contiguous counties, constituting, let us say, a small belt of the Cotton Piedmont, in which a very large number of problems are available for the application of a relatively large number of planning activities. In such a region, for instance, may be found such problems as erosion, tenancy, Negro-white relationships, rural housing, forestry, water uses and control, small industries, part-time industries, the textile industry, community organization combining the tenant and mill village worker, town and village, public health and relief, illiteracy and education. Under the present system of state, federal, and local government it is possible to test out the results of study, research, and planning programs in such an area only through well planned coöperative experiments. Other smaller areas abound in such numbers and geographic location as to make the limit of experimentation bounded only by resources and mutually acceptable arrangements. Such areas might be found in the Mountain-Piedmont, in subregions of the Tennessee Valley, in the Flat Woods of Mississippi, in the Piney Woods of Alabama and Georgia, in "rural" counties in which there is a preeminence of small textile industries, or in such vital regions as the Birmingham steel area.

Other types of experimental approach may center upon the problem rather than the area, such as, for instance, the problem of farm tenancy. In such an experimental approach there is again a wide range of choices. Isolated experiments may be made with isolated tenants, in which special coöperative arrangements with landowners may be effected to test proposed plans for reconstruction. Other experiments would focus upon a relatively large group of tenants, experimenting in community arrangements where there is a large measure of homogeneity within specified areas. Still other experiments would focus especially upon the Negro tenant. In all of these, again, the experiments might vary; one to explore methods of encouraging home ownership; another to explore special types of diversification of farming; still another to explore special crop farming and still another to explore the methods of increasing home consumption and of readjusting trade and credit. Or again the experiments might focus upon the people instead of the type of farming or land or economic arrangements. In such experiments education, health, diet, recreation, and general cultural opportunities might be the focus around which rural electrification, farm arrangements, coöperatives, and community organization would center.

Other illustrations might be multiplied in the several aspects of regional life. In education, special experiments in teacher training institutions, in curricula in the social sciences, in adult education, in the consolidation of smaller institutions, and in special activities in the various high schools and junior colleges would provide a wide range of opportunities. Representative of these might be experiments in municipal support of higher education, in coöperation among southern institutions, and especially in a number of smaller colleges in which values and objectives might be tested.

Common objections to the attempt to present a planning program are that what seems timely today may appear outmoded tomorrow; that detailed specifications seem out of place in any such general framework as would be comprehensive; and that such a general presentation in turn appears abstract, visionary, theoretical, presumptuous. Yet it is necessary, both in the range and content of planning programs and in the methods and means of approach, to indicate a theoretical framework which permits of such universal application and flexibility as to constitute a sound working basis. Thus, if we accept the foregoing types of approach, it is possible to indicate four major basic requirements both sufficiently general and specific as to indicate next steps.

The first is a more effective strategy and maturer program of federal-state equalization and reintegration. This implies not only technical organization and arrangements through which equalization funds may be administered, but a more realistic concept and practice of regionalism in contradistinction to the narrow provincial assumptions that have too often confused regionalism with localism and sectionalism. Such a strategy and philosophy involve more than mere equalization of funds; they involve personnel and interregional contacts looking toward the equalizing of economic opportunity, social experience, and cultural relationships, such as is fundamental to the readjustment of American ideals and practices in local, state, and federal relationships. Here appear to be involved the special phases of cultural attitudes already implied. Necessary on the part of the South are a more realistic facing of facts, a realization of the critical nature of its dilemmas, a greater unity of effort and reduction of internal jealousies and rivalries, and an intelligent willingness to pay the price. On the part of the nation at large there appear to be needed especially a clearer recognition of the natural, logical, evolutionary nature of the South's culture, a better understanding of the size and importance of the problem of regional reintegration in the nation, and a maturer design and wiser counsel in regional matters such as will be commensurate with the needs and opportunity, and more actual participation by representatives of other regions in southern programs. Over and above all of these, it is understood, of course, it will be necessary to have adequate organization and techniques for the analysis and administration of regional programs.

The second major essential follows naturally the first. This is the need for adequate national-regional and regional-national advisory planning councils. This assumes, of course, the broad framework of social planning in which all institutions and regions may be represented in the democratic process and in which provisions are made for referenda to the people. On the assumption of a national planning council so constituted as an official function of the federal government and on the assumption of continuing state planning boards, the minimum essential would be the regional planning board or advisory council. The first essential here is some sort of uniformity and agreement in the delimitation of major regions as opposed to the present conflicting and multiple regional administrative divisions. It must be clear that if some sort of planning procedure is assumed for the main currents of national life, regional divisions and arrangements cannot be left to the incidence of individual preferences and temporary convenience. Regional divisions having been determined, the regional advisory planning board would follow logically, on the one hand, as a regional representation of the national planning council and, on the other, as a coöperating representative agency for the state planning boards. On the hypothesis of the continuing Tennessee Valley Authority, ex-officio direction of such a regional planning board for the Southeast would fall logically to a member of the TVA with each of the eleven Southeastern States represented by an ex-officio member of the state planning boards. In addition to these there is need for certain national-regional advisory councils in which private agencies and institutions can formulate programs, promote research and experimentation, and contribute to a continuing reintegration of the region in the national culture.

Perhaps little need be said about the third major essential for this regional planning approach except that funds for the specific purposes in hand must be adequate and available for definite periods of time and for specified priority schedules. On the part of the Federal Government, funds specially appropriated and earmarked for regional purposes and for interstate coöperative programs would be effective. There would be many variations in the nature and purpose of such funds, the presumption being that they would be determined by the combined counsel of the groups and boards already designated. On the part of private agencies a reserve fund, adequate and properly earmarked and allocated to such regional priority schedules over a sufficiently long period of time, would be most effective. Here, again, the assumption would be for a clear-cut and bold strategy in which the endowing individuals and foundations would employ the same coöperative measures as are recommended for governmental agencies, and that their conclusions would be reached after careful examination of broad factual evidence and in conference with such advisory boards as were available. On the part of state and local agencies and institutions, the assumption would be for a fair measure of coöperative effort, for a fair share of equalizing funds, and for the same coöperative strategy as is assumed for the national and regional groups. It must be clear that both in theory and practice, the federal, the regional, the state, and the local interests and agencies are mutually interdependent in matters of finance as well as in counsel and action.

The fourth requirement for the type of regional approach suggested here is for such definite time periods as will provide for a relatively long-time program with, however, priority schedules which will be well adapted to the necessary sub-units which in turn will be susceptible to completion in shorter periods of time. The maximum-minimum number of years for the major strategy should be large enough to insure adequate technical organization and personnel and to guarantee a fair testing of experimental programs; yet the period should be short enough to insure continuity, definiteness, and measurability. The mere statement of the need for the "longtime view" or for a "longtime plan" is not only not enough but might easily defeat the immediate practical ends of planning through abstraction and postponement. On the other hand, to expect definite results or the modification of culture in such short periods as three or five years is to expect the impossible. It is not possible in most instances to create and stabilize the incidence of change in so short a period. So, too, the six-year division will meet many objections to the five-year period which is too short and the ten-year period which is too long for certain specific appropriations. Again, the optimum time limits must be determined variously by the nature and motivation of the planning programs contemplated, by the nature of the region or regions involved, and by the nature and amount of organizations and finances in prospect.

With all these factors in mind we have estimated the minimum period for setting up such adequate priority schedules and for envisaging the whole regional development in relation to the national culture, and for the special objectives set forth for the Southeast to be twelve years. The special priority schedules would be geared together with the entire program yet timed to two six-year periods, and to whatever combinations of one, two, or three three-year periods or of as many two-year periods as might be most effective. For practical and administrative purposes these periods would conform to natural economic, political, and educational arrangements. In addition, such a period of time would appear to constitute a fair measure of the region's capacity for production and consumption of commodities commensurate with its possibilities of equalizing its achievements more nearly with its resources. Such a period, moreover, would culminate around the mid-century as a major motivating milepost. Enough of the applications of such a schedule have been enumerated in section 273, pages 203-204, to indicate their essential practicability as opposed to mere arbitrary estimates.

Finally, it is important to emphasize again the nature and practice of regional planning by pointing to the difference between the slow moving process of mass education and the accelerated definite planning programs in which specified results are to be attained in specified areas through specific, technical tools and units of work. We may illustrate in the case of certain programs for agricultural and rural reconstruction in the Southeast, where there is ample factual evidence to show the practical and realistic features of the sort of planning which emerges from the present study. We select, for example, diversification of crops and livestock farming, soil erosion work, and rural electrification. For many years the land grant colleges and their extension divisions have promoted these and other improved methods and practices through general education, through classroom, and through extension demonstration. The results have been notable in the upraising of standards. Yet the quantitative results have been proportionately extraordinarily small as compared to the need and the total possibilities. And in the decade from 1919-1929 livestock actually decreased in practically all of the Southeastern States.

Then came that particular part of the Agricultural Adjustment Administration which provided specific ways in which the farmer could profitably retire parts of his land from cotton culture in return for which he could grow feed crops to be utilized on his own farm. Two things have happened. One is that every state has increased its livestock and feed crops from 1930 to 1935, and large numbers of the farmers are so pleased with the change that they propose to continue such diversification. If we can assume the figures from the farm census, showing increases from 1930 to 1935, are actual measures of the effectiveness of technical planning, the results are convincing. In increase of all cattle and all hay and sorghum for forage the cotton states range from 25 to more than 40 per cent. Thus, South Carolina increased its acres in hay from 217,441 to 668,426 and its tons of hay from 168,456 to 420,431. Its cattle increase was from 235,163 in 1930 to 385,179 in 1935. Alabama increased its acreage of hay from 464,696 to 906,286 and its tonnage from 364,853 to 657,603. The increase for its cattle was from 681,298 to 1,125,208. North Carolina's increase for hay acreage was from 552,976 to 1,009,344 and its cattle from 467,012 to 684,266. Louisiana's increase in hay acreage was from 163,668 to 351,876 and its cattle from 618,503 to 1,081,697. On the contrary, Tennessee, Kentucky, and Virginia, where no program was in force, show very little increase. Manifestly, the permanent results will depend upon a longer time continuance of these practices which in turn will depend upon similar technical ways for balancing production and consumption through home consumption and adjusted markets. A similar measure of soil erosion transformation work is found in the actual number of counties which utilize soil erosion technical units in the remaking of millions of farm acres and the prospect of many counties in which the trend is toward the ultimate terracing of nearly all farms in the county. Rural electrification, too, is progressing through actual units of construction provided through definite specifications and arrangements which insure great extension into many new areas. Thus, the increase in land values, the increase in income and subsistence production, hand in hand with the increase of the attractiveness and profitableness of farm life, are attained as visible ends of technical planning for the same ends for which the general education programs can only set the ideals. Similar achievements are desirable in forestry, in flood control, in coöperative arrangements, in home ownership, and in the higher brackets of education and community organization.

Yet it must be clear that technical provision for isolated or separate aspects of farm and community improvement does not constitute planning in the more permanent and stable programs of local, state, and regional culture. The farmer who is urged in the morning to sign up to sell his crops through the coöperatives and in the afternoon to sign up for rural electrification in order to have his home refrigeration of meats and dairy products, his home manufacturing of feeds and mixing of fertilizers, is in a real quandary. The same is true of uncoördinated efforts of many kinds not only in rural life and agriculture, but in industry, public health, public welfare, adult education, youth administration. The essence of design and planning is that it coördinates and plans for the long-time stable and continuing achievements. The planning approach recognizes the difficulties in the way of many groups and agencies and individuals working at cross purposes. It recognizes the futility of mere ideological concepts and emotional professions. It acknowledges the failures of cooperative groups, of business and trade associations, of state development associations, of educational and sociological and economic associations and councils. Their failure was not in motivation or objectives, but in the lack of integration, social discipline, comprehensive design, factual substance, and administrative effectiveness. The planning approach provides for new ways for the "better ordering" of the total economic and social culture.

It must be clear, therefore, that the first essential is frankly a "scientific" and "theoretical" framework from which can emerge both the larger long-time programs and the more detailed short-time units, geared together to match flexibility with necessity, control with the democratic process, and federal-regional forces with state and local autonomy. Yet such "theory" is of the very essence of the ultimate "practical" program, because it is the minimum essential for permanent and stable results. Thus, it is in no sense the function of a regional study to undertake a planning program or programs, nor to set up detailed specifications, which are themselves inherent in the practical planning programs ultimately determined upon. Such a study can provide ample factual basis; it can furnish tools of information; it can set the motivation; it can point to general ways and means; and can show next steps. It can go further and provide the basis and motivation for the coöperation of, by, and between federal, regional, and state governmental agencies, on the one hand, and of private or business agencies and groups within the states and counties, on the other. And it can focus continuously on the fundamental organic relationships which exist between the state and local units and the national culture.

This, then, is the relation of regional planning to the twofold objective of the present work. In terms of facts and appraisal, is the inventory, on the one hand, of the region's superabundance of natural wealth and its technological mastery, or capacity for mastery in human use ends and in resulting wealth; and, on the other, of its superabundance of human wealth, with its pathological hazards, together with social achievement or capacity for social achievement for a richer culture and social well-being. On the purposive or planning side are the objectives of a greater immediate realization of the inherent capacities of the southern regions through the bridging of this chasm between the superabundance of researches and their development and use and an increasingly more vital reintegration of the regional culture in the national picture.

Here, however, is a sort of minimum framework of a task for which apparently neither the South nor the nation is quite ready. This is not different from many of the other problems of the nation which demand more mature planning than has yet been achieved. It does not seem likely, therefore, that either the South or the nation will be sufficiently motivated to undertake a program of the first order until they can sense the extraordinary chasm between the two extremes of "what will happen or is likely to happen" under the respective economies of design and of drift. This again is a logical, realistic dilemma. On the one hand, the extraordinary possibilities of developed resources and institutions offer rare promise; on the other, there may be pathology in prospect in all the realms of economic, social, moral, aesthetic life of the people, and consequently drain of both the region and the nation. Repeat again, the task is one not only for regional mastery but for national participation. It is a test of reintegration and equalization in the democratic process. In so far as the task is one of planning, it is a test of social science and social technology, working with physical science and mechanical technology; of social inventions meeting the crises incident to mechanical inventions; of the old order of states and sections providing necessary arrangements incident to the changing regions and federal complexity. Whether we look at it from the "theoretical" viewpoint of the architecture of a regional civilization or from the "practical" viewpoint of economic survival, or of the general welfare, or the "American dream" of wealth and weal, it is a task in which we must bridge the chasm between research and reality; in which scholarship and statesmanship, reputed symbols of the Jeffersonian ideal, must join hands.

But always we return to the twofold dilemma—the one of difficulties and limitations, the other of translating sound theory into workable practice. The premise upon which we base our flexible planning programs, providing for priority schedules of action to conform to sound theory and practical reality, is that progress consists of step by step attainments in which gains are measured in terms of units of actual work and experimentation and in which research and factual analysis are joined with public administration and folk motivation. This is the only basis upon which mastery may be expected over such limitations as are inherent in the southern regions: financial deficiencies within and control from without; powerful regional differentials in the heritage of training and equipment; competitive institutions of the different races; freight rates and cumulative handicaps of domestic and foreign trade; submarginal lands and marginal folk; and the complex problems of population growth, development, and distribution. Only in this way, too, may be expected substantial gains in the transitional periods between first steps and subsequent larger undertakings, which in turn depend upon an effective framework and execution of specified priority schedules adequate to comprehend the necessary objectives.

The practical arrangements necessary for reasonable success we repeat, would appear to conform to the elemental factors already specified for the new and more vital national policy of reintegration; namely, the federal, the regional, and the state forces. That is, in addition to the many specifications indicated and implied in our regional analysis and design and in the need for a powerful motivation, the presumption is for authentic, able, and articulate advisory groups—federal, regional, and state planning boards whose selection, qualifications, and duties will be commensurate with both the needs and the spirit of the American domain and institutions. The practical test of all this will be in its application to such special states and regions as are comprehended in the Southeast.

The functions of the state planning board may be appraised from two viewpoints. The first is in relation to its work within the state itself. The second relates to its opportunities and obligations within the broader field of federal, regional, and state planning policies and techniques. Within the state itself, again, the board has two major functions. One is that of motivation in which it can point the way, raise standards, make the state "planning conscious," and set up framework through which by adult education, by publicity and promotion, and by actual experimentation it can exert important functions of leadership. The second function within the state is for actual planning programs, for research into the basic problem areas, for experimentation in units of the planning framework, such as the conservation and development of resources and the promotion of social well-being, and for advice to the Governor and other public officials.

In its relation to the broader national policies and techniques of planning the state planning board again has a twofold function. One is the very definite function of promoting a more mature plan of federal-state equalization and reintegration programs in relation to state and federal coöperation. The other is the integration of regional planning programs within and among neighboring states. All of this is particularly fundamental at the present time when the nation is attempting to work out its equilibrium between federal and state functions and between various administration groups and their local participation in the democratic process. Within the Southeast, it would be difficult to formulate a more important task than for these states to become more articulate in more coöperative arrangements with the resulting less rivalry and conflict.

The functions of the regional planning group follow logically: first to integrate state planning and second to serve as buffer between local and federal areas of control and direction; and conversely to make the federal programs and policies more unified and articulate. These functions comprehend also the task of perfecting such multifactor regional divisions of the nation as will meet the needs of the next immediate period of American development. The National Resources Committee has stated well the ends in view for such regional divisions. They would "it is hoped: (a) decentralize the present Federal assumption of planning from the National Capital; (b) give additional support and redirection to the energies now going into State planning; and (c) bring nearer to the common citizen the relevant aspects of national planning. Moreover it is hoped that such a real arrangement will utilize that general sectional loyalty and consciousness which now exists by turning it directly into planning activity rather than allowing it to be diluted or lost in a general national current. In the latter, there is all too much chance of such valuable motivations developing into violent back-eddies and swirls of Federal distrust or jealousy rather than reinforcing the main current."

We must repeat here the conclusion that while it is not possible to set up the perfect regional division of the nation, the sixfold arrangement used in the present volume is based upon a very large number of practical considerations as well as technical indices. The divisions are preëminently "practical" to the extent that they serve as the basis for further analysis and continuing attempts to arrive at the best regional arrangements; to the extent that they may be "useful" in next steps; and to the extent that they have served their main purpose, namely, to give the best regional picture possible. We must emphasize again not only the significance of states in the present order of development, but the absolute necessity, for the present, of utilizing them in all major groupings for planning and for interstate compacts. Thus, although critics of the "group-of-states" delineation of regions rightly point to the fact that such regions are largely in the nature of loose combinations of states and that exact delineation of regional bounds is not possible, the facts are that the supreme practical test of any regional arrangement must be in its acceptance and utilization by the states.

When it comes to specifications for the third practical requirement it is not within the bounds of this volume to discuss the nature, functions, and constitution of the proposed National Planning Board except to point out its integral place in any such regional planning approach as has been indicated for the southern regions. As such an integral unit, practically constituted for stability and continuity of tenure, it follows that the effectiveness of state and regional programs will vary directly with the successful functioning of the National Board, duly authorized by Congress and so constituted as to represent not only the people but to make available for the whole people a continuous expert inventory of the needs and trend of the nation; and not only to act as buffer and balance between nation and regions but also as joint servant of the administrative, legislative, and judicial branches of the government. The extremely practical implications of such a board may be seen from the many and varied considerations in the foregoing pages; or from an examination of the dilemmas due to the present complicated federal-regional arrangements; or again from the almost universal recognition for the need of some such body as a stabilizing tool for the many conflicting bodies, agencies, and "isms."

After all, however, so far as the conclusions drawn from the Southern Regional Study are concerned, the supreme test of practicality must be twofold. One is the test of stability and permanence; the other is in terms of what can be done, how much can be done, how well and how enduringly it can be achieved, when and how next steps can be taken. In fine, the test must be measured by the needs which must be met in order to insure the success of these new and essential difficult policies and procedures. In still other words, practicality is the master which must determine practicability, even as necessity drives the region to new discovery and technical mastery over its whole physical and cultural domain. Keeping in mind the general objectives which we have set up and the detailed procedures which we have enumerated, the first step in practicality is, after all, the beginning. And of the beginning, a first essential is frank recognition of the need for a redirected economy. And in this facing of facts, another essential is the recognition that planning does not consist of utopian reconstruction, but in the achievement of optimum programs of production, of balanced agriculture, of equilibrium between agriculture and industry, of institutional development, and of population development and distribution. More "next steps" follow logically: the selection of areas of planning; the assembling of the necessary facts for each field; the practical coöperation between research and education groups and those who determine public policy; coöperation between the necessary agencies, local, state, regional, federal; full recognition of the difficulties involved, of the failures in the past, of limitations of present personnel; and then the ignoring of these obstacles, except as they must be overcome by definite priority schedules of plan and work.

It must be clear, therefore, why the combined interrelated forces of state, regional, and national agencies are predicated as the minimum practical requirements for the Southeast which must somehow combine a new motivation and realistic design with adequate stabilizing and permanently reinforced agencies of action. The earlier premise of regional-national coöperation as the minimum essential for bridging the extraordinary chasm between the region's possibilities and its actualities thus reappears as the practical test of the region's capacity for development. The urgency of the situation justifies the conclusion that this test of American Regionalism should be made before the turn of the mid-century.

PART III

BIBLIOGRAPHY AND SOURCE MATERIALS

The arrangement of bibliography and source materials for inclusion in the present volume follows the general framework of the study. That is, although the books and articles are listed in the usual alphabetical way, the subject matter corresponds to a multiple functional grouping, in each of which a small number of volumes only is selected. The functional arrangement provides for groups of references in the following general fields: geographic factors and physical environment; historical factors and cultural environment; regional factors and regional development; American regionalism; special southern regional problems; social and regional planning; and literature dealing with recent economic and social problems and tension.

This arrangement still leaves out a very large body of source material and literature included in the following: the United States Census and its related publications; special United States government publications, such as those dealing with broader aspects of forestry, railroads, commerce, airways; more specialized United States publications in the several bureaus, such as the Children's Bureau, Bureau of Agricultural Economics; emergency publications, such as those dealing with NRA codes and FERA research. In this general grouping of government publications a few are listed as illustrative, such as the publications of the National Resources Committee, the Mississippi Valley Committee, and special committees presenting programs for American forestry.

Another grouping, manifestly too extensive for listing, is found in official and special publications of state governments and state institutions and about state affairs within the Southeastern Region, of which the list to date numbers some 12,000. These range all the way from population studies to soil conservation, from the woman on the farm to the new lespedeza sericia. A special catalogue of research studies in a single state college of agriculture, North Carolina, for instance, revealed more than two thousand titles within the last two or three decades. In the same way hundreds of publications dealing with public health, public welfare, public education, and conservation of resources have been issued from most of the states. In somewhat the same way a catalogue of several thousand titles of articles, bulletins, and monographs dealing with the character and resources of the several states and their people reveals an extraordinarily rich source of material for exhaustive study. So, too, in state histories an authentic list of a hundred volumes might well be listed, while a recent *Bibliography of Virginia History Since 1865* alone contains 6,242 titles published in 900 pages.

Another group of volumes of great comparative value is found in what is sometimes called social fiction, dealing with the regional character of the Southeast during the last two decades. More than two hundred such volumes of major importance constitute an interesting bibliography in the portraiture of a region. Illustrative of these are the volumes of Glasgow, Stribling, Faulkner, and Young, as well as the drama represented by Green, Stallings, and Hughes.

Manifestly, it is not within the bounds of such regional picturization as is encompassed in the present volume to comprehend such a bibliography, except to point to its existence. Manifestly, also, it is fundamental for the reader and for the continuing student of the South and American regionalism to have a nucleus for quick reference and as a basis for developing specialized bibliographies of the source materials utilized in the present book. For the rest, there are special bibliographies available. L. R. Wilson's new volume on *County Library Service in the South* has an excellent bibliography on libraries. Benjamin B. Kendrick's *The South Looks at Its Past,* published as a unit in the Southern Regional Study, has a special bibliography dealing with historical aspects. Rupert B. Vance's *Human Geography of the South* includes a special bibliography. Evelyn C. and Lee M. Brooks' *A Decade of "Planning" Literature,* was prepared for the Southern Regional Study and reprinted from *Social Forces.* Howard W. Odum's *American Epoch* includes a bibliography from pages 344-366. Monroe N. Work's special Negro bibliography and Carter Woodson's publications from the Association for the Study of Negro Life and History are sources for specialized study of the Negro. The North Carolina Social Study Series includes some forty volumes. The University of Virginia Institute for Research in the Social Sciences has published a special series of state studies. The Louisiana State University Press lists a number of special state and regional studies. The state planning boards in some of the states are producing important source materials.

So also *Social Forces* has published within the last decade more than a hundred articles dealing with regional appraisal. The other southern magazines making valuable contributions to regional literature include *The South Atlantic Quarterly, The Virginia Quarterly Review,* the *Southwest Review,* the *Proceedings* of the Southern Economic and Political Science Associations. Another special source of valuable materials is found in the large list of doctoral dissertations in economics, history, government, and sociology pursued in the larger universities of the nation. Since 1900, for instance, there have been more than one hundred such doctoral dissertations undertaken in the field of economics alone, with a list approximating the same range and scope in history and government and a lesser list in sociology and social work. These studies run almost the whole gamut of southern culture, from the consolidation of the petroleum industry to tobacco workers. Likewise, there is an unusually large number of unpublished master's theses in the southern universities. The Southern Regional Study has also prepared bibliographies on mountain folk, county organization, population problems and policies, submarginality, and others in lesser degree, some of which are annotated for further study.

It will be understood, therefore, that even in the selected list many titles are omitted which might well be included. The original bibliography on geographic factors and regionalism, for instance, includes many titles dealing with special European and other national aspects of regionalism. A few only have been included as specially significant to American regionalism. On the other hand it might appear possible to exclude a number of special titles which have been listed because of their particular interest or application to the present study.

BOOKS

Abernethy, T. P. *From Frontier to Plantation in Tennessee; A Study in Frontier Democracy*. Chapel Hill: University of North Carolina Press, 1932.

Adams, J. T., Graves, H. S., *et al.* *New England's Prospect: 1933*. New York: American Geographical Society, 1933.

Adams, Thomas, *et al.* *Population, Land Values and Government*. New York: Regional Plan of New York and Its Environs, 1929.

American Geographical Society. *Pioneer Settlement, Coöperative Studies by Twenty-six Authors*. New York: American Geographical Society, 1932.

Anderson, William. *The Units of Government in the United States*. Chicago: Public Administration Service, 1934.

Ball, W. W. *The State that Forgot; South Carolina's Surrender to Democracy*. Indianapolis: Bobbs-Merrill, 1932.

Banbury and District Joint Regional Planning Commission. *The Regional Planning of Banbury and District: An Explanatory Memorandum*. Banbury, Eng.: Town Hall, T. F. Thompson, 1933.

Barnes, Joseph (ed.). *Empire in the East*. Garden City: Doubleday, Doran and Company, 1934.

Beck, P. G., and Forster, M. C. *Six Rural Problem Areas: Relief-Resources-Rehabilitation*. Division of Research, Statistics and Finance of Federal Emergency Relief Administration. Washington, 1935.

Benedict, Ruth. *Patterns of Culture*. Boston: Houghton Mifflin, 1934.

Bennett, H. H. *The Soils and Agriculture of the Southern States*. New York: Macmillan, 1921.

Berle, A. A., and Means, G. C. *The Modern Corporation and Private Property.* New York: Macmillan, 1934.

Bizzell, W. B. *Farm Tenancy in the United States.* New York: Macmillan, 1921.

Boas, Franz. *Anthropology and Modern Life.* New York: W. W. Norton and Co., 1928.

Bond, B. W., Jr. *The Civilization of the Old Northwest: A Study of Political, Social, and Economic Development, 1788-1812.* New York: Macmillan, 1934.

Bond, H. M. *The Education of the Negro in the American Social Order.* New York: Prentice-Hall, 1934.

Bowen, Ezra. *An Hypothesis of Population Growth.* New York: Columbia University Press, 1931.

Bowman, Isaiah. *Geography in Relation to the Social Sciences.* New York: Charles Scribner's Sons, 1934.

——— *The Pioneer Fringe.* New York: American Geographical Society Research Series No. 13, 1931.

Branch, E. D. *Westward; The Romance of the American Frontier.* New York: D. Appleton and Co., 1930.

Brearley, H. C. *Homicide in the United States.* Chapel Hill: University of North Carolina Press, 1932.

Brunhes, Jean. *Human Geography.* Translated by Le Compto. Edited by Bowman and Dodge. Chicago: Rand, McNally and Co., 1920.

Brunner, E. de S. *Church Life in the Rural South.* New York: Doran, 1923.

Bryan, P. W. *Man's Adaptation of Nature, Studies of the Cultural Landscape.* New York: Henry Holt, 1933.

Buckle, H. T. *History of Civilization in England.* New York: D. Appleton, 1858-61. 2 vols.

Campbell, J. C. *The Southern Highlander and His Home Land.* New York: Russell Sage Foundation, 1921.

Cole, G. D. H. *Economic Planning.* New York: Alfred A. Knopf, 1935.

Couch, W. T. (ed.) *Culture in the South.* Chapel Hill: University of North Carolina Press, 1934.

Crane, V. W. *The Southern Frontier, 1670-1732.* Durham, N. C.: Duke University Press, 1928.

Crowther, Samuel. *America Self-Contained.* Garden City: Doubleday, Doran, 1933.

Denison, J. H. *Emotional Currents in American History.* New York: Scribner, 1932.

Dixon, R. B. *The Building of Cultures.* New York: Scribner, 1928.

Doane, R. R. *The Measurement of American Wealth.* New York: Harper, 1933.

Dodd, W. E. *The Cotton Kingdom.* New Haven: Yale University Press, 1921.

Dublin, L. I. (ed.) *Population Problems in the United States and Canada.* Boston: Houghton Mifflin, 1926.

Elton, C. S. *The Ecology of Animals.* London: Methuen and Co. ltd., 1933.

Embree, E. R., Alexander, W. W., and Johnson, C. S. *The Collapse of Cotton Tenancy.* Chapel Hill: University of North Carolina Press, 1935.

Engeln, O. D. *Inheriting the Earth; or, the Geographical Factor in National Development.* New York: Macmillan, 1922.

Fawcett, C. B. *A Political Geography of the British Empire.* Boston: Ginn and Company, 1933.

Finch, V. C., and Baker, O. E. *Geography of the World's Agriculture.* Washington, D. C.: United States Department of Agriculture, 1917. (Gov't Printing Office).

Fleure, H. J. *The Geographical Background of Modern Problems.* New York: Longmans, Green, 1932.

Fox, D. R. (ed.) *Sources of Culture in the Middle West.* New York: D. Appleton-Century Company, 1934.

Frayser, M. E. *A Study of Expenditures for Family Living by 46 South Carolina Rural Families.* (Bulletin 299). Clemson College: S. C. Agricultural Experiment Station, September, 1934.

Frederick, J. H. *The Development of American Commerce.* New York: Appleton, 1932.

Galpin, C. J., and Manny, T. B. *Interstate Migrations among the Native White Population as Indicated by Differences between State of Birth and State of Residence.* Washington, D. C.: Bureau of Agricultural Economics, U. S. Department of Agriculture, October, 1934.

Garside, A. H. *Cotton Goes to Market.* New York: Frederick A. Stokes, 1935.

Garver, F. B., *et al.* *The Location of Manufactures in the United States, 1899-1929* (Employment Stabilization Research Institute, Vol. II. No. 6). Minneapolis: University of Minnesota Press, 1934.

Gee, Wilson. *Research Barriers in the South.* New York: Century, 1932.

Giddings, F. H. *Civilization and Society.* Arranged and edited by Howard W. Odum. New York: Holt, 1932.

Goodrich, C. L., Allin, B. W., and Hayes, Marion. *Migration and Planes of Living, 1920-1934.* Philadelphia: University of Pennsylvania Press, 1935.

Gosnell, C. B. (director). *Political and Economic Problems of the South.* Bulletin of Emory University. Institute of Citizenship. Emory University (July, 1935).

Gray, L. C. *History of Agriculture in the Southern United States to 1860.* 2 vols. Washington: The Carnegie Institution of Washington, 1933.

Gray, L. C., *et al.* *Economic and Social Problems and Conditions of the Southern Appalachians* (Miscellaneous Publication No. 205, U. S. Department of Agriculture). Washington, D. C.: U. S. Government Printing Office.

Gregg, Josiah. *The Commerce of the Prairies.* Chicago: R. R. Donnelley and Sons, 1926.

Gruening, E. *These United States.* 2 Vols. New York: Boni and Liveright, 1923.

Hale, W. J. *The Farm Chemurgic; Farmward the Star of Destiny Lights Our Way.* Boston: The Stratford Company, 1934.

Hart, J. K. *Education for an Age of Power; The TVA Poses a Problem.* New York: Harper, 1935.

Heer, Clarence. *Income and Wages in the South.* Chapel Hill, N. C.: University of North Carolina Press, 1930.

Herring, H. L. *Welfare Work in Mill Villages: The Store of Extra-Mill Activities in North Carolina.* Chapel Hill: University of North Carolina Press, 1929.

Hobbs, S. H. *North Carolina Economic and Social.* Chapel Hill: University of North Carolina Press, 1930.

Hobhouse, L. T., Wheeler, G. C., and Ginsberg, M. *The Material Culture and Social Institutions of the Simpler Peoples.* London: Chapman and Hall, 1915.

Holland, W. L. (ed.). *Commodity Control in the Pacific Area: A Symposium on Recent Experience.* Stanford University, California: Stanford University Press, 1935.

Hooker, Elizabeth. *Religion in the Highlands.* Native Churches and Missionary Enterprises in the Southern Appalachian Areas. New York: Home Missions Council, 1933.

Hulbert, A. B. *Frontiers, the Genius of American Nationality.* Boston: Little, Brown, 1929.

——— *Soil. Its Influence on the History of the United States.* New Haven: Yale University Press, 1930.

Huntington, C. C., and Carlson, F. A. *Environmental Basis of Social Geography.* New York: Prentice-Hall, 1929.

Huntington, Ellsworth. *Civilization and Climate.* New Haven: Yale University Press, 1915.

Huntington, Ellsworth, and Cushing, S. W. *Principles of Human Geography.* New York: John Wiley and Sons, 1934.

Huntington, Ellsworth, Williams, F. E., and von Valkenburg, Samuel. *Economic and Social Geography.* New York: John Wiley and Sons, 1933.

Innis, H. A., and Plumptre, A. F. W. (eds.). *The Canadian Economy and Its Problems.* Toronto: Canadian Institute of International Affairs, 1934.

Jenkins, W. S. *Pro-Slavery Thought in the Old South.* Chapel Hill: University of North Carolina Press, 1935.

Jillson, W. R. *The Big Sandy Valley, A Regional History Prior to the Year 1850.* Louisville: J. P. Morton, 1923.

Johnson, C. S. *The Economic Status of Negroes.* Nashville: Fisk University Press, 1933.

——— *Shadow of the Plantation.* Chicago: University of Chicago Press, 1934.

Johnson, G. B. *Folk Culture on St. Helena Island, South Carolina.* Chapel Hill: University of North Carolina Press, 1930.

Kendrew, W. G. *Climate, A Treatise on the Principles of Weather and Climate.* Oxford: Clarendon Press, 1930.

Kirkland, E. C. *A History of American Economic Life.* New York: F. S. Crofts, 1932.

Kiser, C. V. *Sea Island to City; A Study of St. Helena Islanders in Harlem and Other Urban Centers.* New York: Columbia University Press, 1932.

Lasker, Bruno, and Holland, W. L. (eds.) *Problems of the Pacific, 1933.* Chicago: The University of Chicago Press, 1934.

League for Social Reconstruction (Research Committee). *Social Planning for Canada.* Toronto: Thomas Nelson and Sons, 1935.

Leven, Maurice, Moulton, H. G., and Warburton, Clark. *America's Capacity to Consume.* Washington, D. C.: The Brookings Institution, 1934.

Leyburn, J. G. *Frontier Folkways.* New Haven: Yale University Press, 1935.

Lippincott, Isaac. *Economic Development of the United States.* Third Edition, Revised and Enlarged. New York: Appleton, 1933.

Lorimer, Frank, and Osborn, Frederick. *Dynamics of Population; Social and Biological Significance of Changing Birth Rates in the United States.* New York: Macmillan, 1934.

Lowie, R. H. *Culture and Ethnology.* New York: P. Smith, 1929.

MacKaye, Benton. *The New Exploration; A Philosophy of Regional Planning.* New York: Harcourt, Brace, 1928.

Mackintosh, W. A., and Joerg, W. L. G. *Canadian Frontiers of Settlement.* Toronto, Canada: Macmillan Company of Canada Limited, 1934.

Marburt, C. F., *et al. Soils of the United States.* Bulletin 96, Bureau of Soils. Washington: U. S. Govt. Print. Office, 1913.

McAdie, A. G. *Man and Weather.* Cambridge: Harvard University Press, 1926.

McCuistion, Fred. *Higher Education of Negroes.* Nashville, Tennessee, 1933.

McDonald, Lois. *Southern Mill Hills.* New York: A. L. Hillman, 1928.

McKenzie, R. D. *The Metropolitan Community.* New York: McGraw-Hill Book Company, 1933.

McLean, W. H. *Regional and Town Planning, in Principle and Practice.* London: Crosby, Lockwood and Sons, 1930.

McNeely, J. H. *Faculty Inbreeding in Land-Grant Colleges and Universities* (Office of Education) Washington: Govt. Print. Office, 1932.

Miller, G. J., and Perkins, A. E. *Geography of North America.* New York: John Wiley and Sons, 1928.

Mills, F. C. *Economic Tendencies in the United States.* New York: J. J. Little & Ives, 1932.

Mims, Edwin. *The Advancing South.* Garden City: Doubleday, Page & Co., 1926.

Mississippi Valley Committee. *Report of the Mississippi Valley Committee of Public Works Administration.* Washington: Supt. of Doc., October, 1934.

Mitchell, Broadus. *Rise of the Cotton Mills in the South.* Baltimore: Johns Hopkins Univ., 1921.

——— *William Gregg: Factory Master of the Old South.* Chapel Hill: University of North Carolina Press, 1928.

Mitchell, G. S. *Textile Unionism and the South.* Chapel Hill: University of North Carolina Press, 1931.

Molyneaux, Peter. *What Economic Nationalism Means to the South.* Foreign Policy Association and World Peace Foundation, 1934 (World Affairs Pamphlets No. 4).

Montgomery, R. H. *The Coöperative Pattern in Cotton.* New York: Macmillan, 1929.

Moser, Charles K. *The Cotton Textile Industry of Far Eastern Countries.* Boston: Pepperell Manufacturing Co., 1930.

Mukerjee, Radhakamal. *Regional Sociology.* New York: Century, 1926.

Murchison, C. T. *King Cotton Is Sick.* Chapel Hill: University of North Carolina Press, 1930.

Myres, S. D., Jr. (ed.) *The Cotton Crisis.* Proceedings of Second Conference of Institute of Public Affairs. Dallas: Southern Methodist University, 1935.

National Resources Board Report. Part I—Findings and Plans; Part II—Land; Part III—Water; Part IV—Minerals; Part V—Surveys and Maps. Washington: Supt. of Doc., December, 1934.

National Resources Committee. *Inventory of the Water Resources of the United States.* Washington, D. C.: N. R. C., 1935.

——— *Economics of Planning Public Works.* Washington: Supt. of Doc., 1935.

——— *State Planning in the United States.* 1936.

——— *Land Planning in the United States.* 1936.

——— *Regional Factor in National Planning and Development.* 1936.

Nourse, E. G., and Associates. *America's Capacity to Produce.* Washington: Brookings Institution, 1934.

Odum, H. W. *An American Epoch; Southern Portraiture in the National Picture.* New York: Holt, 1930.

——— *The Regional Approach to National Social Planning.* New York: Foreign Policy Association and Chapel Hill: University of North Carolina Press, 1935.

Odum, H. W. (ed.) *Southern Pioneers in Social Interpretation.* Chapel Hill: University of North Carolina Press, 1925.

Ogilvie, A. G. (ed.) *Great Britain; Essays in Regional Geography.* New York: Macmillan, 1930.

Ormsby, Hilda. *France; A Regional and Economic Geography.* London: Methuen, 1931. (Also New York: Dutton, 1931).

Owsley, F. L. *King Cotton Diplomacy.* Chicago: University of Chicago Press, 1931.

Pack, A. N. *Forestry; An Economic Challenge.* New York: Macmillan, 1933.

Pate, I. C. (ed.) *Studies in Regional Consciousness and Environment.* London: Oxford University Press, 1930.

Paullin, C. O. *Atlas of the Historical Geography of the United States.* (Edited by J. K. Wright). Carnegie Institution of Washington and the American Geographical Society of New York, 1932.

Pearse, A. S. *Animal Ecology.* New York: McGraw-Hill, 1926.

Poggi, E. M. *Prairie Province of Illinois; A Study of Human Adjustment to the National Environment.* Urbana: University of Illinois Press, 1931.

Pomfret, J. E. *The Geographic Pattern of Mankind.* New York: D. Appleton-Century Company, 1935.

Potwin, Marjorie. *Cotton Mill People of the Piedmont; A Study in Social Change.* New York: Columbia University Press, 1927.

Raper, Arthur. *The Tragedy of Lynching.* Chapel Hill: University of North Carolina Press, 1933.

Recent Economic Changes in the United States. Report of the Committee on Recent Economic Changes of the President's Conference on Unemployment. New York: McGraw-Hill, 1929.

Recent Social Trends in the United States. Report of the President's Research Committee on Social Trends. New York: McGraw-Hill, 1933.

Redcay, E. E. *County Training Schools and Public Secondary Education for Negroes in the South.* Washington: The John F. Slater Fund, 1935.

Rhyne, J. J. *Some Southern Cotton Mill Workers and Their Villages.* Chapel Hill: University of North Carolina Press, 1930.

Richardson, R. N., and Rister, C. C. *The Greater Southwest.* Glendale, California: The Arthur H. Clark Co., 1934.

Riegel, R. E. *America Moves West.* New York: Holt, 1930.

Robertson, J. Mackinnon. *Buckle and His Critics.* London: Swan Sonnenschein, 1895.

——— *Evolution of States.* London: Watts, 1912.

Robertson, W. J. *The Changing South.* New York: Boni and Liveright, 1927.

Ross, E. A. *Roads to Social Peace.* Chapel Hill: University of North Carolina Press, 1924.

Sauer, C. O. *The Geography of the Ozark Highland of Missouri.* Chicago: University of Chicago Press, 1920.

Schimper, A. F. W. *Plant-Geography Upon a Physiological Basis.* (Translated by Fisher). Oxford: Clarendon Press, 1903.

Schoffelmayer, V. H. *Texas at the Crossroads.* Dallas: A. H. Belo Corporation, 1935.

Semple, Ellen. *The Geography of the Mediterranean Region; Its Relation to Ancient History.* New York: Holt, 1931.

Shankle, G. E. *State Names, Flags, Seals, Songs, Birds, Flowers, and Other Symbols.* New York: H. W. Wilson, 1934.

Simkins, F. B. *Tillman Movement in South Carolina.* Durham, N. C.: Duke University Press, 1926.

Skaggs, W. H. *Southern Oligarchy.* New York: Devin-Adair, 1924.

Smith, J. R. *American Lands and Peoples.* Chicago: John C. Winston, 1932. (Also a 1934 edition).

——— *Industrial and Commercial Geography.* New York: Holt, 1930.

Smith, R. G. "The Culture Area Concept." *Fugitive Papers.* New York: Columbia University Press, 1930.

Stahl, J. M. *Growing with the West; the Story of a Busy Quiet Life.* New York: Longmans, Green, 1930.

Sumner, W. G. *Folkways.* Boston: Ginn, 1907.

Tannenbaum, Frank. *Darker Phases of the South.* New York: G. P. Putnam and Sons, 1924.

Taylor, Paul S. *Mexican Labor in the United States.* Migration Statistics. Berkeley, California: University of California Press, 1929.

Thomas, Franklin. *The Environmental Basis of Society.* New York: Century, 1925.

Thompson, W. S., and Whelpton, P. K. *Population Trends in the United States.* New York: McGraw-Hill, 1933.

Turner, F. J. *The Significance of Sections in American History.* New York: Holt, 1932.

United States Department of Agriculture. *Achieving a Balanced Agriculture.* Washington: Government Printing Office (August, 1934).

United States Forest Service. *The Forest Situation in the United States.* A Special Report to the Timber Conservation Board. (January 30, 1932).

Vance, R. B. *Human Factors in Cotton Culture.* Chapel Hill: University of North Carolina Press, 1929.

——— *Human Geography of the South.* Chapel Hill: University of North Carolina Press, 1932.

——— *Regional Reconstruction; A Way Out for the South.* New York: Foreign Policy Association and Chapel Hill: University of North Carolina Press, 1935.

Vidal De la Blache, Paul. *Principles of Human Geography.* Translated by Bingham. New York: Holt, 1926.

Ward, R. De. C. *Climates of the United States.* New York: Ginn, 1925.

Weaver, J. E., and Clements, F. E. *Plant Ecology.* New York: McGraw-Hill, 1929.

Webb, W. P. *The Great Plains.* Boston: Ginn, 1931.

Whitbeck, R. H., and Thomas, O. J. *The Geographic Factor; Its Rôle in Life and Civilization.* New York: Century, 1932.

Whitney, Milton. *Soils and Civilization.* London: D. Van Nostrand, 1925. (Also New York: D. Van Nostrand, 1925).

——— *Soils of the United States.* United States Bureau of Soils, Bulletin No. 55.

Willey, Malcolm. *The Country Newspaper.* Chapel Hill: University of North Carolina Press, 1926.

Wilson, L. R., and Wight, E. A. *County Library Service in the South.* Chicago: University of Chicago Press, 1935.

Winston, Sanford. *Illiteracy in the United States.* Chapel Hill: University of North Carolina Press, 1930.

Wissler, Clark. *An Introduction to Social Anthropology.* New York: Holt, 1929.

Wolfanger, L. A. *The Major Soil Divisions of the United States.* New York: John Wiley and Sons, 1930.

Woods, E. A., and Metzger, C. B. *America's Human Wealth; The Money Value of Human Life.* New York: F. S. Crofts, 1927.

Woofter, T. J., Jr. *The Plight of Cigarette Tobacco.* Chapel Hill: University of North Carolina Press, 1931.

Zimmermann, E. W. *World Resources and Industries.* New York: Harper, 1933.

ARTICLES

American Civic Association. "Regional Planning in the United States." Ser. 4, (April, 1929).

Andrews, J. B. "Workmen's Compensation Legislation in the South." *The Annals of the American Academy of Political and Social Science*, 153, pp. 188-192 (January, 1931).

Aronovici, C. "Let the Cities Perish." *Survey*, 68, pp. 437-440 (October 1, 1932).

——— "Regional Planning Versus Metropolitanism." *Scholastic*, 24, pp. 11-13 (March 17, 1934).

Ascher, C. S. "Public Tools for Regional Planning." *Survey*, 68, pp. 472-473 (October 1, 1932).

——— "Regionalism Charting the Future." *Survey*, 66, pp. 460-461 (August 15, 1931).

Baker, D. M. "Community Planning with Uncle Sam: the Southwest Gets Ready for Regional Planning and to Make a Part of the Big National Plan." *Southern California Business*, pp. 10-11 (February, 1934).

Baker, J. E. "Regionalism in the Middle West." *American Review*, IV, 603-614 (March, 1935).

Baker, O. E. "Agricultural Regions of North America." *Economic Geography*, 2, pp. 50-86 (January, 1927); 3, pp. 309-339 (July, 1927).

Barrows, E. M. "United Regions of America, A New American Nation." *New Outlook*, 161, pp. 17-21 (May, 1933).

Beard, C. A. "Some Aspects of Regional Planning." *American Political Science Review*, 20, pp. 273-283 (May, 1926).

——— "Some Regional Realities." *Survey*, 56, pp. 85-87 (April 15, 1926).

Bossard, J. H. S. "Sociological Fashions and Societal Planning." *Social Forces*, 14, pp. 186-193 (December, 1935).

Botkin, B. A. "We Talk About Regionalism—North, East, South and West." *Frontier* (May, 1933).

Brearley, H. C. "Homicide in South Carolina, A Regional Study." *Social Forces*, 8, pp. 218-221 (December, 1929).

Brocard, Lucien. "Regional Economy and Economic Regionalism." Translated by F. Cyril James from an article appearing in *Revue Economique Internationale* (November, 1931) and reprinted in translation in *Annals of the American Academy of Political and Social Science* 162, pp. 81-92 (July 1932).

Brooks, E. C., and L. M. "A Decade of 'Planning' Literature." *Social Forces*, 12, pp. 427-59 (March, 1934).

——— "Five Years of 'Planning' Literature." *Social Forces*, 11, pp. 430-65 (March, 1933).

Brown, E. F. "The Tennessee Valley Idea." *Current History*, 40, pp. 410-417 (July, 1934).

Bruère, R. W. "Giant Power, Region Builder." *Survey*, 54, pp. 161-164 (May 1, 1925).

Bruton, P. W. "Cotton Acreage Reduction and the Tenant Farmer." *Law and Contemporary Problems*, 1, pp. 275-291 (June, 1934).

Burns, Aubrey. "Regional Culture in California." *Southwest Review*, XVII, 373-394 (July, 1932).

Buttenheim, H. S. "Trends in Present-day City and Regional Planning in the United States." *City Planning*, 10, pp. 62-77 (April, 1934).

Carson, W. J. "Banking in the South: Its Relation to Agricultural and Industrial Development." *The Annals of the American Academy of Political and Social Science*, 153, pp. 210-223 (January, 1931).

Clark, H. F. "Planning in America." *National Education Association Journal*, 21, pp. 85-87 (March, 1932).

Cole, W. E. "Personality and Cultural Research in the Tennessee Valley." *Social Forces*, 13, pp. 521-527 (May, 1935).

Comey, A. C. "What Is National Planning?" *City Planning*, 9, pp. 164-167 (October, 1933).

Crane, Jacob. "Large Scale Regional Planning. The Unit: Watershed or States." *The American City*, 49, pp. 60-61 (January, 1934).

Davidson, Donald. "Dilemma of the Southern Liberals." *The American Mercury*, 31, pp. 227-235 (February, 1934).

——— "Regionalism and Education." *American Review*, 4, pp. 310-325 (January, 1935).

——— "Regionalism and Nationalism in American Literature." *American Review*, 5, pp. 48-61 (April, 1935).

——— "Sectionalism in the United States." *Hound and Horn*, 6, pp. 561-589 (July-September, 1933).

——— "Where Regionalism and Sectionalism Meet." *Social Forces*, 13, pp. 23-31 (October, 1934).

Eckel, E. C. "The Iron and Steel Industry of the South." *The Annals of the American Academy of Political and Social Science*, 153, pp. 54-62 (January, 1931).

Eliot, C. W., 2d. "National Planning." *City Planning*, 10, pp. 103-111 (July, 1934).

Elmer, M. C. "Century-Old Ecological Studies in France." *American Journal of Sociology*, 39, pp. 63-70 (July, 1933).

Evans, M. G. "Southern Labor Supply and Working Conditions in Industry." *The Annals of the American Academy of Political and Social Science*, 153, pp. 156-162 (January, 1931).

Fairchild, H. P. "Optimum Population." *Proceedings of the Sixth International Neo-Malthusian and Birth Control Conference*, II, pp. 31-36 (1926).

———— "Optimum Population." *Proceedings of the World-Population Conference*, pp. 72-85 (1927).

Fenneman, N. M. "Physiographic Divisions of the United States." *Annals of the Association of American Geographers*, XVIII, 261-353 (December, 1928).

Fletcher, J. G. "Is This the Voice of the South?" *The Nation*, 137, pp. 734-735 (December 27, 1933).

Frazier, E. F. "Folk Culture in the Making." *Southern Workman*, 57, pp. 195-199 (June, 1928).

Gee, Wilson. "Rural Population Research in Relation to Land Utilization." *Social Forces*, 12, pp. 355-359 (March, 1934).

Giddings, F. H. "Inhabitants and Societies." *Social Forces*, X, 157-164 (December, 1931).

Gras, N. S. B. "Regionalism and Nationalism." *Foreign Affairs*, VII, 459 (April, 1929).

Hanna, John. "Agricultural Coöperation in Tobacco." *Law and Contemporary Problems*, 1, 292-324 (June, 1934).

Harrison, S. M. "Some Forerunner of Regional Research." *Publication of the American Sociological Society*, XXIX, 31-84 (August, 1935).

Heath, M. S. "The Prospect for Optimum Regional Production in the Southern Regions." *Social Forces*, 13, pp. 31-36 (October, 1934).

Herring, H. L. "Early Industrial Development in the South." *The Annals of the American Academy of Political and Social Science*, 153, pp. 1-10 (January, 1931).

Hill, T. A. "Negroes in Southern Industry." *The Annals of the American Academy of Political and Social Science*, 153, pp. 170-181 (January, 1931).

Hinchman, W. S. "States Rights and Section Wrongs." *Forum*, 80, pp. 286-289 (August, 1928).

Hitchcock, L. B. "Chemical Resources and Industries of the South." *The Annals of the American Academy of Political and Social Science*, 153, pp. 76-83 (January, 1931).

Hypes, J. L. "Geography, A Social Determinant." *Journal of Rural Education*, 4, pp. 193-204 (January, 1925).

Ickes, H. L. "Saving the Good Earth; The Mississippi Valley Committee and Its Plan." *Survey Graphic*, 23, pp. 52-59 (February, 1934).

Kendrick, B. B. "Research by Southern Social Science Teachers." *Social Forces*, IX, 362-369 (March, 1931).

———— "A Southern Confederation of Learning." *Southwest Review*, XIX, 182-195 (January, 1934).

Kent, F. R. "Sectionalism in America." *Spectator*, 135, pp. 296-297 (August 22, 1925).

Kern, P. J. "The Bankhead Experiment." *Law and Contemporary Problems*, 362-372 (June, 1934).

Kiessling, O. E. "Coal Mining in the South." *The Annals of the American Academy of Political and Social Science*, 153, pp. 84-93 (January, 1931).

Kirke, Edmund. "The Southern Gateway of the Alleghanies." *Harpers Magazine*, 74, pp. 659-676 (April, 1887).

Knappen, T. M. "The Nation's Social Experiment in Tennessee Valley: Power Regulation and Social Reconstruction Combined in a Gigantic Venture." *Magazine of Wall Street*, 53, pp. 338-40 (January 20, 1934).

Kroeber, A. L. "American Culture and the Northwest Coast." *American Anthropologist*, 25, pp. 1-20 (January, 1923).

Krout, M. H. "Race and Culture; A Study in Mobility, Segregation, and Selection." *American Journal of Sociology*, 37, pp. 175-189 (September, 1931).

Landon, C. E. "Tobacco Manufacturing in the South." *The Annals of the American Academy of Political and Social Science*, 153, pp. 43-53 (January, 1931).

Lewis, B. G. "Regionalism: A Plan of Uniting the States More Effectively." *Forum*, 89, pp. 136-141 (March, 1933).

Lorwin, L. L. "Planning in a Democracy." *Publication of the American Sociological Society*, XXIX, 41-48 (August, 1935).

Macfadyen, Dugald. "Sociological Effects of Garden Cities." *Social Forces*, 14, pp. 250-256 (December, 1935).

Mackaye, Benton. "Regional Planning." *Sociological Review*, 20, pp. 293-299 (October, 1928).

——— "Tennessee, Seed of a National Plan." *Survey Graphic*, 22, pp. 251-254 (May, 1933).

Mackmurdo, A. H. "Regional Social Unit." *Sociological Review*, 24, pp. 14-23 (January, 1932).

Macleod, Norman. "Notes on Regionalism." *Sewanee Review*, 39, pp. 456-459 (October, 1931).

Maggs, D. B. "Congressional Power to Control Cotton and Tobacco Production." *Law and Contemporary Problems*, 1, pp. 376-389 (June, 1934).

Marett, R. R. "Jersey: Suggestions Towards a Civic and Regional Survey." *Sociological Review*, 24, pp. 233-247 (April, 1932).

McKenzie, R. D. "The Ecological Approach to the Study of the Human Community." *American Journal of Sociology*, 30, pp. 287-301 (November, 1924).

——— "The Scope of Human Ecology." *Papers and Proceedings of American Sociological Society*, 20, pp. 141-154 (July, 1926).

Mitchell, Broadus. "Growth of Manufactures in the South." *The Annals of the American Academy of Political and Social Science*, 153, pp. 21-29 (January, 1931).

Mitchell, G. S. "Organization of Labor in the South." *The Annals of the American Academy of Political and Social Science*, 153, pp. 182-187 (January, 1931).

Mukerjee, Radhakamal. "Concepts of Distribution and Succession in Social Ecology." *Social Forces*, 11, pp. 1-7 (October, 1932).

——— "The Ecological Outlook in Sociology." *American Journal of Sociology*, 38, pp. 349-355 (November, 1932).

——— "Ecological Un-balance of Man." *Sociological Review*, 25, pp. 233-243 (October, 1933).

——— "Regional Balance of Man." *American Journal of Sociology*, 36, pp. 455-460 (November, 1930).

Mumford, Lewis. "Regionalism and Irregionalism." *Sociological Review*, 19, pp. 277-288; 20, pp. 18-33, 131-141 (October, 1927-April, 1928).

——— "Regions, to Live In." *Survey*, 54, pp. 151-152 (May, 1925).

——— "The Theory and Practice of Regionalism." *Sociological Review*, 20, pp. 18-33, pp. 131-141 (January-April, 1928).

Murchison, C. T. "Nationalism and the South." *The Virginia Quarterly Review*, 10, pp. 1-15 (January, 1934).

——— "Southern Textile Manufacturing." *The Annals of the American Academy of Political and Social Science*, 153, pp. 30-42 (January, 1931).

Odum, H. W. "The Case for Regional-National Social Planning." *Social Forces*, 13, pp. 6-23 (October, 1934).

——— "Folk and Regional Conflict as a Field of Sociological Study." *Publications of the American Sociological Society*, 25, pp. 1-17 (May, 1931).

——— "Notes on the Study of Regional and Folk Society." *Social Forces*, 10, pp. 164-175 (December, 1931).

——— "Regionalism versus Sectionalism in the South's Place in the National Economy." *Social Forces*, 12, pp. 338-354 (March, 1934).

Ogburn, W. F. "Does It Cost Less to Live in the South." *Social Forces*, 14, pp. 211-214 (December, 1935).

Osborn, Frederick. "Characteristics and Differential Fertility of American Population Groups." *Social Forces*, 12, pp. 8-16 (October, 1933).

Otey, E. L. "Women and Children in Southern Industry." *The Annals of the American Academy of Political and Social Science*, 153, pp. 163-169 (January, 1931).

Owsley, F. L. "Pillars of Agrarianism." *The American Review*, IV, 529-547 (March, 1935).

Parsons, P. A. "The Northwest Regional Planning Conference." *Commonwealth Review*, 16, pp. 1-6 (March, 1934).

Pipkin, C. W. "Legislation and Social-Economic Planning." *Southwest Review*, XVIII, 207-224 (April, 1933).

——— "The Southern Philosophy of States' Rights." *Southwest Review*, XIX, 175-182 (Winter, 1934).

Powell, J. W. "Physiographic Regions of the United States." *National Geographic Monographs*, Vol. 1, pp. 65-100 (1895).

Pratt, J. H. "The Lumber and Forest-Products Industry of the South." *The Annals of the American Academy of Political and Social Science*, 153, pp. 63-75 (January, 1931).

Pritchett, C. H. "Regional Authorities through Interstate Compacts." *Social Forces*, 14, pp. 200-210 (December, 1935).

Radcliffe, G. L. "Some Governmental Aspects of Regional Planning." American Philosophical Society *Proceedings*, 74, No. 1, pp. 1-13 (1934).

Ransom, J. C. "The Aesthetic of Regionalism." *The American Review*, II, 290-310 (January, 1934).

Redfield, Robert. "The Regional Aspect of Culture." *Publications of the American Sociological Society*, XXIV, 33-41 (May, 1930).

Reed, T. H. "Region, a New Governmental Unit." *National Municipal Review*, 14, pp. 417-423 (July, 1925).

Reeves, F. W. "Rural Educational Problems in Relation to New Trends in Population Distribution." *Social Forces*, 14, pp. 7-16 (October, 1935).

——— "The Social Development Program of the Tennessee Valley Authority." *The Social Service Review*, 8, pp. 445-457 (September, 1934).

Renner, G. T. "NRC—The National Planning Agency." *Social Forces*, 14, pp. 300-302 (December, 1935).

Roach, H. G. "Sectionalism in Congress, 1870-1890." *The American Political Science Review*, 19, pp. 500-526 (August, 1925).

Robinson, E. E. "Recent Manifestations of Sectionalism." *The American Journal of Sociology*. 19, pp. 446-467 (January, 1914).

Ross, E. A. "Sectionalism and Its Avoidance." *Social Forces*, 2, pp. 484-487 (May, 1924).

Sauer, C. O. "The Morphology of Landscape." *University of California Publications in Geography*, 2, No. 2 (1925).

Saville, Thorndike. "The Power Situation in the Southern Power Province." *The Annals of the American Academy of Political and Social Science*, 153, pp. 94-123 (January, 1931).

Survey Graphic, Regionalism Number, May, 1925. A Symposium on Regional Planning.

Tate, Allen. "Regionalism and Sectionalism." *The New Republic*, 69, pp. 158-161 (December 23, 1931).

Taylor, P. S. "Opportunities for Research in the Far West." *Publication of the American Sociological Society*, XXIX, pp. 102-106 (August, 1935).

Townroe, B. S. "Twelve Planning Regions Established." *The American City*, 49, p. 81 (April, 1934).

Tugwell, R. G. "National Significance of Recent Trends in Farm Population." *Social Forces*, 14, pp. 1-7 (October, 1935).

Tylor, W. R. "Socio-Economic Aspects of Territorial Planning with Special Reference to the Mississippi Valley Plan." *Social Forces*, 14, pp. 193-200 (December, 1935).

Upshaw, Lois. "Southwest Ego." (Letter). *Southwest Review*, 17, p. 245 (January, 1932).

Vance, R. B. "Concept of the Region." *Social Forces*, 8, pp. 208-218 (December, 1929).

———— "Cotton Culture and Social Life and Institutions of the South." *Publications of American Sociological Society*, 23, pp. 51-59, 1929.

———— "Human Factors in the South's Agricultural Readjustment." *Law and Contemporary Problems*, 1, pp. 259-274 (June, 1934).

———— "Implications of the Concepts 'Region' and 'Regional Planning'." *Publication of the American Sociological Society*, XXIX, 85-93 (August, 1935).

———— "Planning the Southern Economy." *Southwest Review*, XX, pp, 111-123 (January, 1935).

———— "What of Submarginal Areas in Regional Planning?" *Social Forces*, 12, pp. 315-329 (March, 1934).

Viles, Jonas. "Sections and Sectionalism in a Border State." *Mississippi Valley Historical Review*, 21, pp. 3-22 (June, 1934).

Whitaker, J. R. "Regional Interdependence." *Journal of Geography*, 31, pp. 164-165 (April, 1932).

Whitten, Robert. "Some Regional Planning Principles." *American Civic Annual*, 1932.

Wirth, Louis. "The Prospects of Regional Research in Relation to Social Planning." *Publications of the American Sociological Society*, XXIX, 107-114 (August, 1935).

Wolfe, A. B. "On the Criterion of Optimum Population." *The American Journal of Sociology*, 39, pp. 585-99 (March, 1934).

Woofter, T. J., Jr. "Southern Population and Social Planning." *Social Forces*, 14, pp. 16-22 (October, 1935).

——— "The Subregions of the Southeast." *Social Forces*, 13, pp. 43-50 (October, 1934).

——— "The Tennessee Basin." *The American Journal of Sociology*, 39, pp. 809-817 (May, 1934).

——— "Tennessee Valley Regional Plan." *Social Forces*, 12, pp. 329-338 (March, 1934).

Woofter, T. J., Jr., and Webb, Edith. "A Reclassification of Urban-Rural Population." *Social Forces*, XI, 348-351 (March, 1933).

Zimmermann, E. W. "Resources of the South." *The South Atlantic Quarterly*, 32, pp. 213-226 (July, 1933).

ACKNOWLEDGMENTS AND GENERAL PLAN OF THE SOUTHERN REGIONAL STUDY

During the late autumn of 1931 a special grant was made by the General Education Board to the Social Science Research Council for a southern regional study. The grant was to terminate at the end of two years, with a possible extension for a third year, the funds to be administered by the Council. The study was formally completed with the termination of the grant on December 31, 1934, with the subsequent completion of the work as indicated elsewhere. While a special report of procedures and methods will afford excellent opportunity to discuss other aspects of the study, a brief statement of the general plan and objectives is important here.

For a number of years the Council had been appointing annually a Southern Regional Committee as an experimental approach to research and the promotion of the social sciences in the South. The Committee for 1931-1932 consisted of Benjamin B. Kendrick, chairman, Woman's College, University of North Carolina; Wilson Gee, University of Virginia; Walter J. Matherly, University of Florida; George Fort Milton, *Chattanooga News;* Charles W. Pipkin, Louisiana State University; George W. Stocking, University of Texas; Raymond D. Thomas, Oklahoma A. & M. College. To this Committee the Council assigned the special sponsorship of the proposed Southern Regional Study. It was agreed that the author of the present volume, a former chairman of the Committee, but no longer a member, should undertake the study. In conference and collaboration with members of the Committee and the Special Advisory Work Committee, he, therefore, prepared a work memorandum outlining the general objectives and scope of the study, submitting as part of the set-up an Advisory Work Committee composed of Clarence Heer, Harriet L. Herring, S. H. Hobbs, Jr., Katharine Jocher, Rupert B. Vance, and T. J. Woofter, Jr.

The preliminary *Work Memorandum* submitted to the Social Science Research Council for general approval was dated April 18, 1932 and entitled *A Southern Regional Study: Emphasizing Among Other Features, Especially the South's Capacity for Educational and Social Development.* Part I, giving the general nature and objectives of the study is reproduced here as part of the methodology and with a view to indicating changes that appeared necessary as the study proceeded. The full report of the plan and procedures, however, will constitute a separate story.

I

"As characterizing its objectives and methods, the study will be (1) *descriptive and explanatory*, (2) *comparative*, (3) *purposive*.

"1. It will aim to be descriptive and explanatory in the scientific sense of gathering and presenting the facts and of interpreting them by means of all methods available for the limits and purposes of this study. It will present statistics but it will also utilize culture charts or composite social base maps, or whatever other technical devices may guarantee an appropriate, emerging regional portraiture. There will be samplings and aggregrates of materials in due relation to control classifications in two greater basic groupings, which will comprehend the usual "social, economic, educational" survey, but with special adaptations and added features.

"a. Physical geography and natural resources, together with the visible and measurable ends of industrial and scientific activity in their utilization.

"b. Population and cultural resources, together with the visualized ends of social (economic, political, educational, 'social') activity towards organization and achievement in their development.

"In these groupings, with their manifold subdivisions, the amount of material necessary for successful results will be enormous but the opportunity, due to regional and subregional delimitations, to the methods used for classifying secondary source materials, and to data already available will also be very great. It follows naturally that there will be a premium on industry, thoroughness, concentration, and inventiveness.

"2. The study will be *comparative*, but more for the purpose of description and interpretation than for the implications of final evaluation or uniformly desirable change toward the levelling or standardizing of activities and cultures. That is, the study will attempt to present, *first*, the picture of the Southern region as it is and how it came to be as it is, and, *secondly*, to present this picture in comparisons with other regions in the United States as well as to emphasize the subregional comparisons within the larger Southern area. Such comparison will be a way of measuring the region in general known terms and of interpreting it to other regions as well as to the South itself, but it will also afford opportunity for the possible discovery of new truths through the study of differences and resemblances; and for possible pioneering in new ways of doing things as well as old ways of following beaten paths. Presumably, a chief merit of the Southern region and its subregions, for the purpose of such a study, is that they offer a rare combination of situations and facilities for effective regional research and planning.

"Partial and varying comparisons will be made among six different regions as shown in [an accompanying map]: the Southeast, the Southwest, the Northeast, Middle-America, the Middle West, and the Far West. And within the Southern Region, the comparisons will be not only between the two great areas, Southeast and Southwest, but various state-by-state and subregional classifications. To illustrate one significant hypothesis, it seems quite likely that emerging from this study will be adequate evidence that there is no longer a "South" or "Southern" region, in the sense that it has been used or is now used. On the contrary, the southern part of the nation extends in one sweeping expanse from Georgia and Florida across New Mexico and Arizona to Southern California. However, the new regional culture of the Southwest has so completely emerged as to set it off distinctly from the "Old South" or "the South" of popular impression.

"3. The study will be *purposive* in that its objectives will be definitely pointed up toward several ends. One is that there must be a general *emerging picture* and a series of pictures rather than merely masses of statistical and historical data or a series of contributed papers or studies. These pictures ought to be more vivid and authentic than has yet been presented of this region. This objective will be in some contrast to the usual formal survey or exhaustive research into minute details. It will also be in some contrast to the type of coöperative, collaborated study now being published by the American Geographic Society under the title of *New England's Prospect*, 1932, in which more than a score of distinguished authorities contribute chapters.

"A second objective will be the practical one of appraising the South's *capacity for educational and social development*. There will be varied aspects of this objective, one of which will be special emphasis upon *institutions of higher learning*. The appraisal will apply to the capacity of the South to develop its resources and to utilize better its available public income as well as its capacity to raise and absorb funds from special private endowment and from outside areas.

"A third objective will be at least an approach to social planning. It may be an *introduction to a program of regional planning*, the extent and nature of which will be determined by the results of the study, by the resources and facilities at hand when the present study is finished, and by the practicability of such a regional planning study and program as may be projected.

"A fourth objective is frankly *theoretical* and there are several aspects of this. One is to explore the best methods of *making an effective regional study*. What are the standard basic categories under which information should be sought not only for this study, but for similar studies? Or for continuous permanent recording of information about every region? Can this study make some contribution in this direction at the same time that it gains its own ends?

"Another theoretical aspect is found in the presentation of this picture of the Southern Region as a unit in the scientific *study of modern contemporary society* in the United States. It would be a unit in *America: States and Regions,* with the implication that the present study would be adapted and that the other four regions would be added in such further details and emphasis as would be required to present the larger picture. It would be a study not only of the South but of the South's growing part in the national development.

"Still another theoretical objective is found in the effort to carry a little further the study of *regional and folk society* as an important approach to the study of all society, especially of social transition and change."

The plan and procedure which have been followed in the Southern Regional Study have conformed in the main to the original outline and objectives. A number of variations, however, were necessary. First, there has been less emphasis upon the institutions of higher learning for two or three reasons. One was that through the Council a special grant was made available for a study by Professor Wilson Gee which was later published in an excellent volume, *Research Barriers in the South.* This was a study of southern colleges and universities compared with universities and colleges of other regions in relation to the faculty, their equipment, their assignments, their migration to and from the South, and other important factors.

Another larger grant was made to the Committee in order that the Chairman, Professor Benjamin B. Kendrick, might visit a number of southern universities, confer upon the curriculum and discuss problems and policies of administration and coöperation in the teaching of the social sciences. The major emphasis here in contradistinction to the Council's and the Committee's earlier work was on teaching rather than research and on undergraduate courses more than graduate. As the program related to the graduate level Professor Kendrick's recommendations were published in the *Southwest Review* for January, 1934, under the title of "A Southern Confederation of Learning" and subsequently revised and reprinted for distribution. Special visits were made by Professor Kendrick to the University of North Carolina, to Emory University, to Vanderbilt University, to Louisiana State University. At the Florida meeting of the Southern Regional Committee in 1933, general approval was voted to the plan of the Southern Confederation of Learning. Due to great differences of opinion on the advisability and practicability of the plan, however, it was never developed or presented to the several universities.

Another change in procedure was the separate publication of the volume, *The South Looks at Its Past* by Benjamin B. Kendrick and A. M. Arnett. In the original work memorandum submitted to the Council on April 18, 1932, the very excellent statement of the historical background of the study, prepared by Professor Kendrick, was incorporated as an integral part of the plan of presentation. Subsequently, due to the priority of Professor Kendrick's other activities as mentioned above this could not be completed in time to be incorporated into the basic study. Professor Kendrick's and Professor Arnett's preference to have it published separately was entirely appropriate. The volume, published prior to the appearance of the main study, embodies not only the historical approach suggested in the original work memorandum, but also something of the theories of regionalism set forth in the series of articles enumerated in Chapter III, page 261.

In the original plan it was expected that the main volume of findings of the Southern Regional Study would give a picturization of both the Southeast and the Southwest. To this end a special allocation of this field was made to Professor Raymond D. Thomas of Oklahoma Agricultural and Mechanical College, and through conferences with him other assignments were made to Professor J. J. Rhyne and Clyde Russell Rhyne of the University of Oklahoma. From these assignments came an extraordinarily large and valuable mass of materials. It became increasingly evident, however, that it would not be possible to include the study of the two regions in the same volume, such was the mass of material, the great differentials in the two regions, and the technical difficulties of doing justice to either or to both regions. It was, therefore, decided to focus upon the Southeastern Region with the hope that a similar presentation might be made of the Southwest with such variations and improvements as experience justified. The brief summary of Dr. Thomas' study in the present volume is not a fair index of his total work, while the valuable typed monograph of Dr. and Mrs. Rhyne on *The Social Population of the Southwest* has been utilized scarcely at all.

In the late Spring of 1933 a supplementary grant was made for the purpose of utilizing the Tennessee Valley as a subregion for an exploratory study. A special committee, of which Mr. George Fort Milton was chairman, was appointed, and Dr. T. J. Woofter, Jr., was assigned this part of the study with headquarters at the University of Tennessee, at Knoxville. The report of this study, which was largely exploratory and technical, is not included in the present volume except as it enables us to present the Tennessee Valley subregion as a sort of epitome of regional areas, regional study, and regional planning. This part of the study requires a separate report.

A special Conference was held at Chapel Hill in the Spring of 1933, in conjunction with the Committee's meeting, to explore the practicability of specializing upon optimum programs of production as related to regional development. The two day Conference resulted in a number of contributions which, in addition to those already published, appear to be of value to future plans. Neither the Committee nor the Council appeared convinced of the feasibility of the project. Consequently the study is limited to those aspects of regional optima which underlie agricultural reconstruction and equilibrium between cotton economy and a better balanced agriculture.

The other variation, namely, the postponement of the completion and publication of the study, has been mentioned in the preface. The original grant provided for a two year period, with a year's extension if needed, in which to complete the study. The formal study was completed within the third year, the arrangement with the Council was duly terminated, but the final completion and presentation were postponed in order to insure a more comprehensive picture, to obtain first-hand observations in the Southwest, the Far West, and the Northwest for comparative purposes, to check results of the study with many New Deal researches and publications which had appeared since the study was started, so that the enduring record might be as authentic as possible.

It is not possible in such a study to give full expression and appreciation for all assistance that has been rendered through conferences, criticisms, as well as actual work. In addition to the acknowledgments given in the Introductory Note, special assistance rendered by the several collaborators in the Southern Regional Study may be indicated in the list of acknowledgments given below. During the period of the study all members of the Work Committee were in residence at Chapel Hill except that Professor Heer was on leave parts of two years and Professor Woofter and Miss Herring were busy with a number of special assignments. Some of the data gathered by them have been published as indicated in the bibliography. It is hoped that more of the large amounts of materials may be utilized by them and others as opportunity offers. Needless to say, it is not possible to acknowledge fully the generosity of their time and the value of their counsel on many occasions.

It seemed best to have the text of the present volume written by one author. This the Director of the Study has done except in those cases where text matter is quoted or designated as substantially adapted from the work of the collaborator. Pages so adapted from *work memoranda* prepared by collaborators are indicated in the text; contributions which have been bound together as *work memoranda* on file are indicated by asterisks. The list of collaborators with the special subject matter follows in alphabetical order.

Columbus Andrews, studies of county administration* and natural resources; A. M. Arnett, collaborator with Benjamin B. Kendrick in *The South Looks at Its Past;* Elma Ashton, studies of woman's education in the South; John Beecher, discussion of the Birmingham steel area; Gordon Blackwell, comparative studies in regional public welfare* and public relief;* Axel Brett, Tennessee Valley Studies; Evelyn C. Brooks, bibliographies on planning and regionalism;* Lee M. Brooks, bibliographies on regional and social planning;* Coit Coker, studies on wild life and game preserves; William E. Cole, special studies of social organization and public welfare in the Tennessee Valley;* Marius Farioletti, Tennessee Valley Studies; Robert Gee, special designing of maps; Margaret Jarmon Hagood, consolidating indices and making index; P. M. Hamer, studies in the Tennessee Valley; T. P. Harrison, studies in dramatic activities; Elizabeth Head, studies in church and religious life;* Clarence Heer, statistics of wealth and public finance; Harriet L. Herring, studies of manufacturing industries, standards of living,* state in depression;* S. H. Hobbs, Jr., state classifications, new industries,* general resources; T. L. Howard, studies of county government in the Tennessee Valley; William L. Hunt, studies of regional horticulture and gardening; W. C. Jackson, studies of southern legislatures;* Katharine Jocher, regional participation and administrative activities, arrangement and checking of charts, maps, graphs, and tables; Guy B. Johnson, special studies of Negro participation; E. W. Knight, studies of southern education in the depression;* Dan M. Lacy, studies in transportation and railroad development; Emily White Maclachlan, studies in standards of living, home hygiene and diet;* John Maclachlan, studies of southern dairying,* fertilizer economy,* farm tenancy,* submarginality; Walter J. Matherly, studies in commercial education in the South,* to be published as indicated in the Introductory Note; Helen Irene McCobb, studies in regional literature and folkways;* Martha McKee, studies in agricultural commodities and optimum production;* Harold D. Meyer, studies in regional recreation, parks and playgrounds;* Bernice M. Moore, bibliographies on regionalism;* Eugene Odum, studies in natural life and game preserves; W. F. Prouty, studies in natural resources and water power; Clyde Russell Rhyne, studies in population and social problems of the Southwest;* Jefferson Jennings Rhyne, studies in population and social problems of the Southwest;* Mildred Rubin, assembling indices; Lyda Gordon Shivers, studies in public welfare and social work;* G. Wallace Smith, drafting of maps; Elizabeth L. Speer, standard of living studies in the Tennessee Valley; Stanley Stevens, studies in problems of climate; Catherine Stewart, Tennessee Valley Studies; A. Monroe Stowe, studies of women's colleges in Virginia and North Carolina; M. D.

Taylor, studies of marketing areas in the Tennessee Valley;* Raymond D. Thomas, economic inventory of the Southwest;* G. L. Tillery, studies in freight rates;* Rupert B. Vance, critical studies of agriculture, tenancy, subregions, planning, submarginality; Paul W. Wager, studies in forestry resources;* Charles P. White, Tennessee Valley Studies; Edith Webb Williams, studies in farm production and land use, state bibliographies; T. J. Woofter, Jr., studies of submarginality,* subregional classifications,* population, in addition to Tennessee Valley area listed below; Waller Wynne, special statistical studies and map drafting; N. C. Young, studies in institutional care of children.

Raymond D. Thomas of the University of Oklahoma was in charge of the economic inventory of the Southwest. T. J. Woofter, Jr., in addition to the studies in population and subregions already mentioned, was in charge of the Tennessee Valley unit of the study, full report of which is yet to be presented.

In addition to Belle Mooring, secretary for the Study, Treva Williams Bevacqua carried a major portion of the secretarial and clerical details. Credit is likewise due for statistical, secretarial, and clerical assistance to the following: Jessie Alverson, W. C. Baker, Mrs. Vergie L. Bean, Mrs. Gerald L. Bell, Mrs. John D. Black, Ellen B. Burrill, A. O. Carraway, H. W. Chandler, Clifford Cruze, Charles Dreblow, Juanita Duncan, Leo E. Eberwein, Lucy Evans, Ola Maie Suttenfield Foushee, Mrs. C. R. Goering, J. Otis Gossett, Edith Harbour, Clarence Henderson, Naomi Hocutt, Margaret Howard, Mrs. B. B. Kendrick, Jr., D. Kiefer, Evelyn J. Lewis, Billy Linthicum, Annie Lee McCauley, Harold McElroy, Bernice M. Moore, Nettie Rollins, Martha Royster, Walter Schierloh, Mrs. Evelyn Ward, Corinne M. Womack, Robert N. Woodworth, M. G. Zervigon.

LIST OF MAPS

LIST OF CHARTS AND TABLES

PAGE

SUBJECT INDEX OF MAPS, CHARTS, AND TABLES

See also Page Index of Maps, Charts, and Tables, and the General Index to the Text

GENERAL INDEX OF TEXT

Exclusive of persons, publications, localities, states. For index of subject matter in maps, charts, tables, see pp. 648-649.